Nineteenth-Century Literature Criticism

Guide to Gale Literary Criticism Series

For criticism on	Consult these Gale series
Authors now living or who died after December 31, 1959	*CONTEMPORARY LITERARY CRITICISM (CLC)*
Authors who died between 1900 and 1959	*TWENTIETH-CENTURY LITERARY CRITICISM (TCLC)*
Authors who died between 1800 and 1899	*NINETEENTH-CENTURY LITERATURE CRITICISM (NCLC)*
Authors who died between 1400 and 1799	*LITERATURE CRITICISM FROM 1400 TO 1800 (LC)* *SHAKESPEAREAN CRITICISM (SC)*
Authors who died before 1400	*CLASSICAL AND MEDIEVAL LITERATURE CRITICISM (CMLC)*
Black writers of the past two hundred years	*BLACK LITERATURE CRITICISM (BLC)*
Authors of books for children and young adults	*CHILDREN'S LITERATURE REVIEW (CLR)*
Dramatists	*DRAMA CRITICISM (DC)*
Hispanic writers of the late nineteenth and twentieth centuries	*HISPANIC LITERATURE CRITICISM (HLC)*
Native North American writers and orators of the eighteenth, nineteenth, and twentieth centuries	*NATIVE NORTH AMERICAN LITERATURE (NNAL)*
Poets	*POETRY CRITICISM (PC)*
Short story writers	*SHORT STORY CRITICISM (SSC)*
Major authors from the Renaissance to the present	*WORLD LITERATURE CRITICISM, 1500 TO THE PRESENT (WLC)*

ISSN 0732-1864

Volume 48

Nineteenth-Century Literature Criticism

Criticism of the
Works of Novelists, Poets, Playwrights,
Short Story Writers, Philosophers, and Other
Creative Writers Who Died between 1800
and 1899, from the First Published Critical
Appraisals to Current Evaluations

Marie Lazzari
Editor

Catherine C. Dominic
Jelena O. Krstović
Associate Editors

72053

Gale Research Inc.

An International Thomson Publishing Company

I(T)P

NEW YORK • LONDON • BONN • BOSTON • DETROIT • MADRID
MELBOURNE • MEXICO CITY • PARIS • SINGAPORE • TOKYO
TORONTO • WASHINGTON • ALBANY NY • BELMONT CA • CINCINNATI OH

STAFF

Marie Lazzari, *Editor*

Catherine C. Dominic, Jelena O. Krstović, *Associate Editors*

Matthew C. Altman, Dana Ramel Barnes, Mary L. Onorato, *Assistant Editors*

Marlene H. Lasky, *Permissions Manager*
Margaret A. Chamberlain, Linda M. Pugliese, *Permissions Specialists*
Susan Brohman, Diane Cooper, Maria L. Franklin, Arlene Johnson,
Josephine M. Keene, Michele Lonoconus, Maureen Puhl, Shalice Shah,
Kimberly F. Smilay, Barbara A. Wallace, *Permissions Associates*
Edna Hedblad, Tyra A. Phillips, *Permissions Assistants*

Victoria B. Cariappa, *Research Manager*
Barbara McNeil, *Research Specialist*
Frank Vincent Castronova, Eva M. Felts, Mary Beth McElmeel, Donna Melnychenko,
Tamara C. Nott, Tracie A. Richardson, Norma Sawaya, *Research Associates*
Alicia Noel Biggers, Maria E. Bryson, Julia C. Daniel, Shirley Gates,
Michele P. Pica, Amy Terese Steel, Amy Beth Wieczorek, *Research Assistants*

Mary Beth Trimper, *Production Director*
Mary Kelley, *Production Associate*

Barbara J. Yarrow, *Graphic Services Supervisor*
Sherrell Hobbs, *Macintosh Artist*
Willie F. Mathis, *Camera Operator*
Pamela A. Hayes, *Photography Coordinator*

∞™ This book is printed on acid-free paper that meets the minimum requirements of American National Standard for Information Sciences—Permanence Paper for Printed Library Materials, ANSI Z39.48-1984.

Library of Congress Catalog Card Number 84-643008
ISBN 0-8103-8939-8
ISSN 0732-1864
Printed in the United States of America

I(T)P™   Gale Research Inc., an International Thomson Publishing Company.
ITP logo is a trademark under license.

10 9 8 7 6 5 4 3 2 1

Contents

Preface vii

Acknowledgments xi

Women's Diaries

Preface

Since its inception in 1981, *Nineteenth-Century Literature Criticism* has been a valuable resource for students and librarians seeking critical commentary on writers of this transitional period in world history. Designated an "Outstanding Reference Source" by the American Library Association with the publication of its first volume, *NCLC* has since been purchased by over 6,000 school, public, and university libraries. The series has covered more than 300 authors representing 26 nationalities and over 15,000 titles. No other reference source has surveyed the critical reaction to nineteenth-century authors and literature as thoroughly as *NCLC*.

Scope of the Series

NCLC is designed to introduce students and advanced readers to the authors of the nineteenth century, and to the most significant interpretations of these authors' works. The great poets, novelists, short story writers, playwrights, and philosophers of this period are frequently studied in high school and college literature courses. By organizing and reprinting commentary written on these authors, *NCLC* helps students develop valuable insight into literary history, promotes a better understanding of the texts, and sparks ideas for papers and assignments. Each entry in *NCLC* presents a comprehensive survey of an author's career or an individual work of literature and provides the user with a multiplicity of interpretations and assessments. Such variety allows students to pursue their own interests; furthermore, it fosters an awareness that literature is dynamic and responsive to many different opinions.

Every fourth volume of *NCLC* is devoted to literary topics that cannot be covered under the author approach used in the rest of the series. Such topics include literary movements, prominent themes in nineteenth-century literature, literary reaction to political and historical events, significant eras in literary history, prominent literary anniversaries, and the literatures of cultures that are often overlooked by English-speaking readers.

NCLC continues the survey of criticism of world literature begun by Gale's *Contemporary Literary Criticism (CLC)* and *Twentieth-Century Literary Criticism (TCLC)*, both of which excerpt and reprint commentary on authors of the twentieth century. For additional information about *TCLC*, *CLC*, and Gale's other criticism series, users should consult the Guide to Gale Literary Criticism Series preceding the title page in this volume.

Coverage

Each volume of *NCLC* is carefully compiled to present:

- criticism of authors, or literary topics, representing a variety of genres and nationalities
- both major and lesser-known writers and literary works of the period
- 7-10 authors or 4-6 topics per volume
- individual entries that survey critical response to an author's work or a topic in literary history, including early criticism to reflect initial reactions, later criticism to represent any rise or decline in reputation, and current retrospective analyses.

Organization

An author entry consists of the following elements: author heading, biographical and critical introduction, list of principal works, excerpts of criticism (each preceded by an annotation and followed by a bibliographic citation), and a bibliography of further reading.

- The **Author Heading** consists of the name under which the author most commonly wrote, followed by birth and death dates. If an author wrote consistently under a pseudonym, the pseudonym will be listed in the author heading and the real name given in parentheses on the first line of the biographical and critical introduction. Also located at the beginning of the introduction to the author entry are any name variations under which an author wrote, including transliterated forms for an author whose language uses a nonroman alphabet.

- The **Biographical and Critical Introduction** outlines the author's life and career, as well as the critical issues surrounding his or her work. References are provided to past volumes of *NCLC* in which further information about the author may be found.

- Most *NCLC* entries include a **Portrait** of the author. Many entries also contain reproductions of materials pertinent to an author's career, including manuscript pages, title pages, dust jackets, letters, and drawings, as well as photographs of important people, places, and events in an author's life.

- The list of **Principal Works** is chronological by date of first publication and identifies the genre of each work. In the case of foreign authors with both foreign-language publications and English translations, the English-language version is given in brackets. Unless otherwise indicated, dramas are dated by first performance, not first publication.

- **Criticism** in each author entry is arranged chronologically to provide a perspective on changes in critical evaluation over the years. All titles of works by the author featured in the entry are printed in boldface type to enable the user to easily locate discussion of particular works. Also for purposes of easier identification, the critic's name and the publication date of the essay are given at the beginning of each piece of criticism. Unsigned criticism is preceded by the title of the journal in which it appeared. Publication information (such as publisher names and book prices) and parenthetical numerical references (such as footnotes or page and line references to specific editions of works) have been deleted at the editors' discretion to provide smoother reading of the text.

- Critical excerpts are prefaced by **Annotations** providing the reader with information about both the critic and the criticism that follows. Included are the critic's reputation, individual approach to literary criticism, and particular expertise in an author's works. Also noted are the relative importance of a work of criticism, the scope of the excerpt, and the growth of critical controversy or changes in critical trends regarding an author. In some cases, these annotations cross-reference excerpts by critics who discuss each other's commentary.

- A complete **Bibliographic Citation** designed to facilitate location of the original essay or book follows each piece of criticism.

- An annotated list of **Further Reading** appearing at the end of each entry suggests secondary sources on the author. In some cases it includes essays for which the editors could not obtain reprint rights.

Cumulative Indexes

- Each volume of *NCLC* contains a cumulative **Author Index** listing all authors who have appeared in Gale's Literary Criticism Series, along with cross-references to such biographical series as *Contemporary Authors* and *Dictionary of Literary Biography*. Useful for locating authors within the various series, this index is particularly valuable for those authors who are identified with a certain period but who, because of their death dates, are placed in another, or for those authors whose careers span two periods. For example, Fyodor Dostoevsky is found in *NCLC,* yet Leo Tolstoy, another major nineteenth-century Russian novelist, is found in *TCLC* because he died after 1899.

- Each *NCLC* volume includes a cumulative **Nationality Index** which lists all authors who have appeared in *NCLC,* arranged alphabetically under their respective nationalities, as well as Topics volume entries devoted to particular national literatures.

- Each new volume in Gale's Literary Criticism Series includes a cumulative **Topic Index,** which lists all literary topics treated in *NCLC, TCLC, LC 1400-1800,* and the *CLC* Yearbook.

- Each new volume of *NCLC,* with the exception of the Topics volumes, contains a **Title Index** listing the titles of all literary works discussed in the volume. In response to numerous suggestions from librarians, Gale has also produced a **Special Paperbound Edition** of the *NCLC* title index. This annual cumulation lists all titles discussed in the series since its inception and is issued with the first volume of *NCLC* published each year. Additional copies of the index are available on request. Librarians and patrons have welcomed this separate index: it saves shelf space, is easy to use, and is recyclable upon receipt of the following year's cumulation. Titles discussed in the Topics volume entries are not included in the *NCLC* cumulative index.

Citing *Nineteenth-Century Literature Criticism*

When writing papers, students who quote directly from any volume in Gale's Literary Criticism Series may use the following general forms to footnote reprinted criticism. The first example pertains to material drawn from periodicals, the second to material reprinted from books:

[1]T.S. Eliot, "John Donne," *The Nation and Athenaeum*, 33 (9 June 1923), 321-32; excerpted and reprinted in *Literature Criticism from 1400-1800,* Vol. 10, ed. James E. Person, Jr. (Detroit: Gale Research, 1989), pp. 28-9.

[2]Clara G. Stillman, *Samuel Butler: A Mid-Victorian Modern* (Viking Press, 1932); excerpted and reprinted in *Twentieth-Century Literary Criticism,* Vol. 33, ed. Paula Kepos (Detroit: Gale Research, 1989), pp. 43-5.

Suggestions Are Welcome

In response to suggestions, several features have been added to *NCLC* since the series began, including annotations to excerpted criticism, a cumulative index to authors in all Gale literary criticism series, entries devoted to criticism on a single work by a major author, more illustrations, and a title index listing all literary works discussed in the series.

Readers who wish to suggest authors or topics to appear in future volumes, or who have other suggestions, are cordially invited to write the editors.

Acknowledgments

The editors wish to thank the copyright holders of the excerpted criticism included in this volume and the permissions managers of many book and magazine publishing companies for assisting us in securing reprint rights. We are also grateful to the staffs of the Detroit Public Library, the Library of Congress, the University of Detroit Mercy Library, Wayne State University Purdy/Kresge Library Complex, and the University of Michigan Libraries for making their resources available to us. Following is a list of the copyright holders who have granted us permission to reprint material in this volume of *NCLC*. Every effort has been made to trace copyright, but if omissions have been made, please let us know.

COPYRIGHTED EXCERPTS IN *NCLC*, VOLUME 48, WERE REPRINTED FROM THE FOLLOWING PERIODICALS:

Biography: An Interdisciplinary Quarterly, v. 10, Spring, 1987 for "From Faceless Chronicler to Self-Creator: The Diary of Louisa Galton, 1830-1896" by Cynthia Huff. © 1987 by the Biographical Research Center. All rights reserved. Reprinted by permission of the publisher and the author.—*Early American Literature,* v. XXI, Fall, 1986 for "Joel Barlow's Dialectic of Progress" by Gregg Camfield; v. XXV, 1990 for "Joel Barlow and 'The Anarchiad'" by William C. Dowling. Copyrighted, 1986, 1990 by the University of Massachusetts. Reprinted by permission of the publisher and the author.—*The New Criterion,* v. II, June, 1984 for "Piece Work: Writing the Essay" by Joseph Epstein. Copyright © 1984 by The Foundation for Cultural Review. Reprinted by permission of the author.—*The New York Times Book Review,* July 1, 1923. Copyright 1923 by The New York Times Company. Reprinted by permission of the publisher.—*The Saturday Review of Literature,* v. XXXIV, March 10, 1951. Copyright 1951, renewed 1979 *Saturday Review* magazine. Reprinted by permission of the publisher.—*The Virginia Quarterly Review,* v. 24, Autumn, 1948. Copyright, 1948, renewed 1976, by *The Virginia Quarterly Review,* The University of Virginia. Reprinted by permission of the publisher.—*Women's Studies: An Interdisciplinary Journal,* v. 14, 1987. © Gordon and Breach Science Publishers. Reprinted by permission of the publisher.

COPYRIGHTED EXCERPTS IN *NCLC*, VOLUME 48, WERE REPRINTED FROM THE FOLLOWING BOOKS:

Adorno, Theodor W. From *Notes to Literature, Vol. 1*. Edited by Rolf Tiedemann. Translated by Sherry Weber Nicholson. Columbia University Press, 1991. Copyright © 1991 Columbia University Press, New York. All rights reserved. Reprinted with the permission of the publisher.—Aldridge, A. Owen. From *Early American Literature: A Comparatist Approach*. Princeton University Press, 1982. Copyright © 1982 by Princeton University Press. All rights reserved. Reprinted by permission of the publisher.—Atkins, G. Douglas. From *Estranging the Familiar: Toward a Revitalized Critical Writing*. The University of Georgia Press, 1992. © 1992 by the University of Georgia Press. All rights reserved. Reprinted by permission of the publisher.—Beauchamp, Virginia Walcott. From an introduction to *A Private War: Letters and Diaries of Madge Preston, 1862-1867*. Rutgers University Press, 1987. Copyright © 1987 by Rutgers, The State University. All rights reserved. Reprinted by permission of Rutgers, The State University.—Blauvelt, Martha Tomhave. From "'This Altogather Precious tho Wholy Worthless Book': The Diary of Mary Guion, 1800-1852," in *Anxious Power: Reading, Writing, and Ambivalence in Narrative by Women*. Edited by Carol J. Singley and Susan Elizabeth Sweeney. State University of New York, 1993. © 1993 State University of New York. All rights reserved. Reprinted by permission of the publisher.—Bunkers, Suzanne L. From "Midwestern Diaries and Journals: What Women Were (Not) Saying in the Late 1800s," in *Studies in Autobiography*. Edited by James Olney. Oxford University Press, 1988. Copyright © 1988 by Oxford University Press, Inc. All rights reserved. Reprinted by permission of the publisher.—Coles, Robert. From "Psychoanalytical Observations on Elizabeth Barrett Barrett's Diary," in *Diary by E.B.B.: The Unpublished Diary of Elizabeth Barrett Barrett, 1831-1832*. Edited by Phillip Kelley and Ronald Hudson. Ohio University Press, 1969. Copyright

The Connecticut Wits

INTRODUCTION

The Connecticut Wits, also referred to as the Hartford Wits and the Friendly Club, were a group of colonial American intellectuals living in and around Hartford, Connecticut, who met regularly during the 1780s and 1790s to discuss politics, literature, and their own writings. The membership of the club fluctuated over the years, but the best-known Wits included John Trumbull, Timothy Dwight, Joel Barlow, David Humphries, Theodore Dwight, Richard Alsop, Elihu Hubbard Smith, Mason Cogswell, and Lemuel Hopkins. Although they were engaged in different professions—farming, business, the law, medicine, education, the ministry—they were united by their affiliation with Yale College, Calvinist faith, conservative political views, and their strong interest in the creation of a national literature.

The group members' similarity in political outlook and literary taste is evident from their three anonymously published collaborative publications, satires written in a neoclassical style influenced by the works of Samuel Butler, Alexander Pope, Oliver Goldsmith, and Charles Churchill. Writing in the postrevolutionary period, the Wits desired to celebrate American independence from England in their works, yet they were troubled by the political instability and the turbulent economic climate that prevailed in the new republic. Their first joint effort, *The Anarchiad: A Poem on the Restoration of Chaos and Substantial Night*, published in the *New Haven Gazette* from October 1786 to September 1787, is a collection of scathing satirical essays criticizing individual greed, political rebellion, and the reluctance of some states to ratify the Constitution. Members of the society also advocated a strong central government to bring nascent disagreements and unscrupulous business practices under control, and they reacted vehemently against Thomas Jefferson's liberal, democratic ideals then gaining popularity. The Wits burlesqued the views of Jefferson and his supporters in *The Echo*, a collection of verse published between 1791 and 1805. Many numbers of *The Echo* appeared individually in the *American Mercury* and were so popular that they were reprinted as pamphlets and broadsides before being published in book form. *The Political Greenhouse*, the work of Richard Alsop, Lemuel Hopkins, and Theodore Dwight, is a verse satire written from the federalist perspective describing events taking place in 1798. First appearing in the *Connecticut Courant*, it was reprinted in book form in 1799.

Aside from participation in the group's projects, three of the Connecticut Wits distinguished themselves in individual literary careers. Trumbull's two best-known works, *The Progress of Dulness* and *M'Fingal*, written in 1772-73 and 1782 respectively, are political satires that enjoyed enormous popularity in their time. Modeled on Butler's *Hudibras*, *The Progress of Dulness* narrates the events in the career of a farmer's son, named Tom Brainless, who ineptly makes his way through school, society, and, eventually, the ministry. Composed in a similar but more pointed vein, *M'Fingal* ridicules the Tory and Loyalist causes as it glorifies American independence; a mock epic, the poem deals with a Tory colonial official who is tarred and feathered by the townspeople of whom he is supposedly in charge. Following in the patriotic mode of Trumbull's works, Barlow in the *The Columbiad* (1807) looks back to the time of Christopher Columbus and weaves a mythological version of America's past. The premise of the poem is that Columbus, imprisoned by Spain's King Ferdinand, has a vision which encompasses the past, the present, and the future, and which foretells the discovery of America as well as explains the ramifications of that discovery for all humankind. Considered a highly ambitious undertaking, the epic was originally published in 1787 as *The Vision of Columbus*; Barlow expanded and extensively revised this early version in writing *The Columbiad*, but critics have generally preferred the first work because of its simpler style and less pompous treatment of the subject matter. The work that most endeared Barlow to his American readers, however, was a poem entitled *The Hasty Pudding*. Written during his travels in England in 1793 and published in 1796, it enthusiastically praises the farming life and the agrarian ideal. In a similar vein, Dwight's *Greenfield Hill*, published in 1794 and written in heroic couplets imitative of John Denham and James Thomson, celebrates American rural life as a source of poetic inspiration. Dwight's most noted work, *The Conquest of Canaan*, published in 1785, is considered by many commentators the first American religious epic. In it, he extols American values by way of biblical analogy with the *Book of Joshua*, retold in 10,000 lines of heroic couplets.

Criticism about the Connecticut Wits has focused on their historical significance as the first American school of poets and on their writings considered in the context of the conservative response during the postrevolutionary period in America. Their works have been studied as a kind of barometer to the changing values of the young American nation as it slowly shifted away from federalism and toward democracy. Some scholars have noted an inconsistency in the Wits's writings, pointing out that while they were earnest proponents of American literary, intellectual, and political independence from Europe, their works reveal a troubling tendency to imitate European forms and style. More recently, commentators have explored the ideas of the major Wits in terms of their relationship to the values of the enlightenment, humanism, and radical political and philosophical thought in Europe. In summarizing the importance of the Wits in American literature, Leon Howard has written that "the greatest value of [their] writings,... both in verse and in prose, lies in the illumination they cast upon an age which was to have, socially and aesthetically, an extraordinary influence upon the future. Their story shares how men of different temperaments found sustenance for their dispositions in a limited provincial environment and...prepared the way for a new literature and formed a new national character."

REPRESENTATIVE WORKS

Richard Alsop
    The Charms of Fancy 1856
    The Anarchiad: A Poem on the Restoration of Chaos
       and Substantial Night 1786-87
Joel Barlow
    The Vision of Columbus 1787
    The Hasty Pudding 1796
    The Columbiad 1807
Timothy Dwight
    The Conquest of Canaan 1785
    The Triumph of Infidelity 1788
    Greenfield Hill 1794
    Travels in New England and New York 1821-22
    The Echo 1791-1805
Lemuel Hopkins
    The Guillotina, or a Democratic Dirge 1796
David Humphries
    A Poem on the Happiness of America 1780
    A Poem on the Industry of the United States of America
       1783
    The Political Greenhouse 1799
Elihu Hubbard Smith
    American Poems (editor) 1793
John Trumbull
    The Progress of Dulness 1772-73
    M'Fingal 1782

GENERAL OVERVIEWS

Annie Russell Marble

SOURCE: "A Group of Hartford Wits," in *Heralds of American Literature*, The University of Chicago Press, 1907, pp. 149-89.

[*In the essay below, Marble surveys the major figures and literary output of the Connecticut Wits.*]

Classification is a common substitute for literary criticism. Often a relative convenience, it has sometimes only obscured the distinct traits of an author. Occasionally an individual daunts the cataloguer and stands in comparative isolation—like Dante, Carlyle, Thoreau, or Tolstoy. Classification is often based upon the governing motif of the writers—as the "Transcendentalists," the "Pre-Raphaelites," and the "Decadents." The more common allotment is by eras and localities; the "Augustan age," the

"Elizabeth dramatists," the "Victorian novelists," are phrases as familiar as the "Oxford Movement," the "Lake Poets," the "Knickerbocker Group," or the "Hartford Wits."

After the middle of the eighteenth century the center of literary activity in America was transferred from the vicinity of Boston, where it had been for many years inspired by Harvard College, to the environment of the younger colleges, Nassau Hall, or the College of New Jersey, which later became Princeton, and the College of Philadelphia, which formed the nucleus of the University of Pennsylvania. Graduates of these institutions became progressive leaders in political and literary zeal. At Yale College, also, victory for modern educational methods had been gained, at about the same time that the first notes were sounded against British tyranny and in behalf of independence. John Trumbull was the leader among the Connecticut reformers and satirists, but his life reflected his association with a few companions, often called the "Hartford Wits." While the burlesques and satires that gave fame to Trumbull were written during the early years of the war, many of his later efforts in satire and reform were in collaboration with some patriot-comrades who realized the dangers which imperiled the new nation.

Although independence had been won, anarchy was menacing; government, finance, and commerce were unstable. Such affairs formed subjects for grave discussion, varied by witty verse, at the gatherings of a "Friendly Club" in Hartford. Among the nine names mentioned of those who formed the original membership of this club, there is a major and a minor list: familiar to our ears are the names of John Trumbull, Timothy Dwight, Joel Barlow, and David Humphreys; seldom recalled are their associates, Theodore Dwight, Richard Alsop, and the three physicians, Elihu Smith, Mason Cogswell, and Lemuel Hopkins. Other men, possibly allied with this coterie, were Congressman Uriah Tracey, Judge Tappan Reeve, and Zephaniah Smith. The series of publications assigned to this first group of wits dated from 1785 to 1807.

Seventy-five years seems to us an incredibly long period to elapse between the appearance of some literary work in a journal and its first publication in book-form. On the title-page of *The Anarchiad*, dated 1861, is this editor's note, "Now first published in book form." Research shows that the twelve satiric papers constituting *The Anarchiad* were printed first in the *New Haven Gazette*, beginning October 26, 1786, and continuing, at intervals, until September 13, 1787. They were copied in Federalist journals throughout many of the states of the Union. In this first, belated edition of *The Anarchiad*, its editor, Luther G. Riggs, expresses an assurance "that he is in performance of a duty—that he becomes, as it were, an instrument of justice, a justice delayed for more than half a century, to the genius and loyalty of its authors, who were among the noblest and most talented sons of the Revolution." We would exchange his term "genius" for "wit," but we cannot question the quality of patriotism and the influence of these satires in subduing threatened anarchy, and in arousing higher ideals during the crucial years after the war, while feeling was strong regarding the Constitution and the basis of political and financial security.

The name, borrowed from Miltonic Anarch, suggested the purpose, which was further explained in the sub-title, *A Poem on the Restoration of Chaos and Substantial Night.* The wits wished to show, with forceful satire, the warfare waged against the stability of the new nation by the promoters of local rebellion, paper money, and selfish greed. Although the papers were sent unsigned to the newspaper, and the various portions have never been perfectly identified, the series was undoubtedly the work of four men who had shown earlier evidence of their patriotism either by service in the army or by their writings—John Trumbull, David Humphreys, Joel Barlow, and Dr. Lemuel Hopkins.

To Colonel Humphreys belonged the credit for suggesting this unique literary plan. While abroad, serving on the commission for treaties with foreign powers, he had shared in the popular curiosity over an anonymous English satire, *The Rolliad.* Returning to America, he saw with dismay the signs of insurrection in Shay's Rebellion and other dangers. He suggested the use of satire in verse, akin to the form of *The Rolliad* and Pope's *The Dunciad,* to arouse public curiosity and also to teach lessons of patriotism.

The prose "Introduction" to the first paper mystified the readers and entertained them. It is an interesting commentary upon the credulity and emotional ferment of the period. The supposed archaeologist thus addressed the publishers of the *New Haven Gazette:*

> I have the felicity to belong to a society of critics and antiquarians, who have made it their business and delight for some years past, to investigate the ancient as well as natural history of America. The success of their researches in such an unlimited field, pregnant with such wonderful and inexhaustible materials, has been equal to their most sanguine expectations. One of our worthy associates has favored the public with a minute and accurate description of the monstrous, new-invented animal which had, till its elaborate lucubration, escaped the notice of every zoologist. . . . Others have spared no pains to feast the public curiosity with an ample supply of great bones from the Wabash, and, at the same time, to quench the thirst for novelty from the burning spring on the Ohio.
>
> It has happily fallen to my lot to communicate through the medium of your paper, a recent discovery still more valuable to the republic of letters. I need scarcely premise that the ruins of fortifications yet visible, and other vestiges of art, in the west country, had sufficiently demonstrated that this delightful region had once been occupied by a civilized people. Had not this hypothesis been previously established, the fact I am about to relate would have placed it beyond the possibility of doubt. For upon digging into the ruins of one of the most considerable of these fortifications, the labourers were surprised to find a casement, a magazine, and a cistern almost entire. Pursuing their subterranean prog-

> ress, near the north-east corner of the bastion, they found a great number of utensils, more curious and elegant than those of Palmyra and Herculaneum. But what rendered their good fortune complete, was the discovery of a great number of papers, manuscripts, etc., whose preservation, through such a lapse of years, amid such marks of hostility and devastation, must be deemed marvellous indeed, perhaps little short of miraculous. This affords a reflection, that such extraordinary circumstances could scarcely have taken place to answer only vulgar purposes.
>
> Happening myself to come upon the spot, immediately after this treasure had been discovered, I was permitted to take possession of it, in the name and for the use of our society. Amongst these relics of antiquity, I was rejoiced to find a folio manuscript which appeared to contain an epic poem, complete; and, as I am passionately fond of poetry, ancient as well modern, I set myself instantly to cleanse it from the extraneous concretions with which it was in some parts enveloped, defaced and rendered illegible. By means of a chemic preparation, which is made use of for restoring oil paintings, I soon accomplished the desirable object. It was then I found it was called *The Anarchiad, A Poem on the Restoration of Chaos and Substantial Night,* in twenty-four books.

While public curiosity was thus assailed, the second, and ulterior, motive of patriotism was emphasized by some interwoven verses. Choosing Shay's Rebellion as a pivotal example of anarchy, the vision of its "mob-compelling," destructive course was outlined by the supposed prophet:

> Thy constitution, Chaos, is restor'd,
> Law sinks before thy uncreating word;
> Thy hand unbars th' unfathomed gulf of fate,
> And deep in darkness whelms the new-born
>   state.

In addition to the insurrections against martial laws and state organizations, there was another lurking evil, especially in New England—the futile paper money, and the consequent depreciation and instability of all industries. Rhode Island was suffering much from this cause, and seemed to be in the power of wary, selfish schemers. In the second and third numbers of "American Antiquities," as the *Anarchiad* series was called, mock-heroics in verse were mingled with serious advice, in prose, from Connecticut to her oppressed neighbor state. With direct truth it was asserted:

> For it will scarcely be denied in any part of the United States, that paper money, in an unfunded and depreciating condition, is happily calculated to introduce the long-expected scenes of misrule, dishonesty, and perdition.

The fourth and fifth papers in the series appealed for a revival of national pride and progress. Hesper, the promise of Dawn, confronts Anarch, god of Night, and by the contention seeks to arouse loyalty among the people:

> Teach ere too late, their blood-bought rights to
>   prize,

Bid other Greenes and Washingtons arise!
Teach those who suffer'd for their country's
    good,
Who strove for freedom and who toil'd in blood,
Once more in arms to make the glorious stand;
And bravely die or save their natal land!

In the fifth article of the series was an ode, "Genius of America"—a favorite title of the day. In offering it, the authors expressed a hope that, "should the taste of their countrymen in general be uncorrupted, as they flatter themselves it is, they expect this song will be introduced into most of the polite circles of the United States." The author of this ode was Humphreys; for it was included later among his poems. He must have rejoiced—for he sought appreciation—when the song was "introduced" and reprinted. Sung to the tune of "The watery god, great Neptune, lay," it won much popularity; but in thought and meter it ranks among the most inferior portions of *The Anarchiad*. A single stanza will indicate both form and theme—the dangers which threatened to destroy America's glory:

Shall steed to steed, and man to man,
With discord thundering in the van,
    Again destroy the bliss!
Enough my mystic words reveal;
The rest the shades of night conceal,
    In fate's profound abyss!

The dialogue between Anarch and his pupil Wrongheads, in the sixth and seventh portions, extorted a confession from the demagogue that his aim was selfish greed, and the enemies whom he most feared were the friends of law, justice, and education.

One of the objects of special censure by the Democrats, who feared the tendencies toward monarchy and militarism, was the Society of the Cincinnat. In eastern Connecticut there lived William Williams, a prominent lawyer, who had ventured to question the wisdom of continuing the Cincinnati as a banded society. Williams was a fine scholar, and had proved himself a staunch patriot during the war, by giving lavishly of his money and service in town offices. Later he became judge of Windham County, and married the daughter of Governor Trumbull. His criticisms of the Cincinnati, however, had aroused Barlow and Humphreys, who were prominent among its members and orators, and they found an opportunity to retaliate. In April, denial that "America had produced a Man of Genius in one single Art or one single Science" seemed anathema to these versifiers, who considered each other men of genius. They poured forth their wrath also against fictitious narratives about America by foreign writers, especially the false and maligning stories of Washington's *amours,* as told by D'Auberteul. Perhaps it was Humphreys who hurled that last shaft of invective, to redeem the honor of his commander:

In wit's light robe shall gaudy fiction shine,
And all be lies, as in a work of thine.

The Anarchiad was essentially a literary curiosity, although it had immediate influence upon the policies of Connecticut and more distant states. It is uneven in merit, and often anticlimactic. Probably it was written without any perfected plan, or expectation of publication in sequential form; later numbers were intended by the authors, if circumstances should call them forth. The series corresponded to the more didactic and aggressive columns of arguments in behalf of federalism which were contributed at the same time to newspapers in Massachusetts, New York, Pennsylvania, and other states where there was contest over the adoption of the new Constitution, in place of the old Articles of Confederation.

The Echo was, in a way, a continuation of these satiric papers, although the members of the Hartford coterie had changed somewhat, and the subjects chosen for ridicule or remonstrance were more varied. *The Echo* had less significance in the politico-literary history of the age, yet here were satires of strong feeling directed against political evils, and lampoons upon democratic publications. A secondary motive of the writers was to caricature the excesses of literary style found in many publications of the time. Of the group who had written *The Anarchiad* in collaboration, Humphreys and Barlow were abroad when *The Echo* series appeared, and Trumbull's part has been questioned. Dr. Lemuel Hopkins, alone of the earlier coterie, was assuredly a contributor to the later series. Associated with him were Theodore Dwight, Richard Alsop, Dr. Elihu Smith, and Dr. Mason Cogswell.

That Trumbull had a vital interest in these papers written by his friends, and was informed regarding many matters there suggested, is shown by a copy of *The Echo* which belonged to him and bears his name, to be found now at the Connecticut Historical Society. His notes, in ink, assist one in deciding the authorship of certain portions. In the preface to the collected papers the explanation was given that the idea of these word-cartoons came

of a moment of literary sportiveness at a time when pedantry, affectation and bombast pervaded most of the pieces published in the gazettes, . . . thus to check the progress of false taste in American literature, the authors conceived that ridicule would prove a powerful corrective, and that the mode employed in *The Echo* was the best suited to this purpose.

The political evils were also emphasized and the plan of the authors to scathe and correct

that hideous morality of revolutionary madness, which levelled the boundaries of virtue and vice, . . . that destructive torrent which threatened to overwhelm everything good and estimable in private life, everything venerable and excellent in political society.

The first "Echo" appeared August 8, 1791, in the *American Mercury*—a weekly newspaper started in 1784 by Joel Barlow and Elisha Babcock. It was a parody upon a florid report in a Boston newspaper. The latter, in recording a thunderstorm, had used such language as this: "uncorking the bottles of Heaven, revealing livid flame, disploding thunders, amid the brilliance of this irradiated arch!" The wits thus parodied the prose:

Even the last drop of hope, which dripping skies,
Gave for a moment to our straining eyes,

Like *Boston Rum,* from heaven's *junk bottles*
  broke,
Lost all the corks and vanished into
  smoke. . . .

The sons of Boston, the elect of Heaven,
Presented Mercy's Angel, smiling fair,
Irradiate splendors frizzled in his hair,
Uncorking demi-johns, and pouring down
Heaven's liquid blessings on the gaping town.

The ornate phrases of Hugh Henry Brackenridge and Governor John Hancock, John Adams, striving to please both aristocrats and democrats, certain demagogues of Jacobin type, a Philadelphia "Mirabeau" who ventured to attack the politics and literary abilities of the Hartford group—such were some of the individuals singled out for special ridicule by the authors of *The Echo.* Many of the numbers appeared first in the *American Mercury,* and were reprinted in other newspapers, from 1791 to 1800. In the years that intervened before they were collected and published in book-form, in 1807, some of them appeared as broadsides or pamphlets, generally soon after they were written. Often the papers were intended as New Year's verses.

One of the most representative of the satires, which won popular reading among the Federalists and was printed in pamphlet form, was by Dr. Hopkins, *The Democratiad: A Poem in Retaliation, for the Philadelphia Jockey Club. By a Gentleman of Connecticut. 1795.* This passed into at least two editions; it is No. XVIII in *The Echo.* The Philadelphia Jockey Club, the publication which had roused the wrath of the Wits, gave the example of the Hartford writers and William Cobbett, or "Peter Porcupine," whom they echoed, as an excuse for its attacks upon individuals of prominence among Federalists. Thus, the Philadelphia satirists declared their course of personal attack was "authorized by the precedent of the infamous PETER PORCUPINE and the literary out-law Snub, whose political squabbles have involved the characters of many respectables." In his answering satire, Hopkins attacked the Democrats and Jacobins, leveling his shafts of abuse especially against Benjamin Franklin Bache, the editor of the *Aurora,* and a grandson of Franklin:

Thou great descendant of that wondrous man,
Whose genius wild through all creation ran—
That man who walk'd the world of science o'er,
From ink and types to where the thunders
  roar,—
To thee, friend Bache, these lines I now address,
Prepar'd on purpose for thy hallow'd press,
I've pick'd thee out because I highly prize,
Thy grandsire's memory and thy knack at lies.

After further invective against the leaders of the Jacobinical faction, the author said in apostrophe to Washington:

ILLUSTRIOUS MAN! thy indignation shew,
And plunge them headlong where they ought to
  go,
Then turn thine eye, this mighty realm survey,
See Federal Virtue bless thy glorious sway.

The next year Dr. Hopkins was again chosen to write the New Year's verses in *The Echo* series,—"The Guillotina;

or, A Democratic Dirge: A Poem. By the Author of Democratiad." They first appeared in the *Connecticut Courant,* January 1, 1796, and were afterward published as a pamphlet, possibly also as a broadside. The bald witticisms are recognized as those of Hopkins, as in the stanza:

Come sing again! since Ninety-Five,
Has left some *Antis* still alive,
Some Jacobins as pert as ever,
Tho' much was hoped from Yellow-fever.

"The Political Green-House for 1798" was another widely quoted composition by this group. According to the record by Trumbull, in his copy of *The Echo,* this was written by Lemuel Hopkins, Richard Alsop, and Theodore Dwight. With earnest patriotism and wit blended, the verses began:

Oft has the NEW YEAR'S Muse essay'd,
To quit the annual rhyming trade,
Oft has she hop'd the period nigh,
When fools would cease, and knaves would die,
But each succeeding year has tax'd her
With "more last words of Mr. Baxter."
And most of all has Ninety-Eight
Outstripp'd the years of former date,
And while a Jacobin remains,
While Frenchmen live and Faction reigns,
Her voice, array'd in awful rhyme,
Shall thunder down the steep of Time.

With unexpected details, the authors of this New Year's message gave specific directions how to avoid contagion from yellow fever, which was the scourge of that year in New York. There was a reason for these references, since one of the wits had fallen victim to the fever and died, Dr. Elihu Smith. He made the first large compilation of American poetry during the summer of 1793, while he was resting at his home in Litchfield, Connecticut. He thus preserved many scattered verses by his friends and other writers, which would otherwise have remained unknown. Although associated somewhat with the Hartford Wits, he was more closely linked with the early writers of fiction and drama in New York. . . . According to a note by Trumbull, Dr. Smith was the author of one paper in *The Echo* series, "Extracts from Democracy by Aquiline Nimblechops." He probably assisted in collaborating others.

Burlesque and satire characterize the pages of *The Echo,* but there are also lines of earnestness, as these in "The Guillotina":

Spread knowledge then; *this only Hope*
Can make each eye a *telescope,*
Frame it by microscopic art;
To scan the hypocritic heart.

One poem, assuredly assigned as the composition of Theodore Dwight, was a feigned rejoicing at the election of Jefferson. It was entitled "The Triumph of Democracy," and revealed the feeling of bitterness on the part of the Federalists against Jefferson, with scornful innuendo against Aaron Burr, in the closing lines:

Let every voice with triumph sing—
JEFFERSON is chosen king!
Ring every bell in every steeple,
T' announce the "Monarch of the People!"

Stop,—ere your civic feasts begin,
Wait till the votes are all come in;
Perchance, amid this mighty stir,
Your Monarch may be Col. BURR!
Who, if he mounts the sovereign seat,
Like BONAPARTE will *make you sweat,*
Your Idol then must quaking dwell,
Mid Mammoth's bones at *Monticelle,*
His country's barque from anchors free,
On *"Liberty's tempestuous sea,"*
While all the Democrats will sing—
THE DEVIL TAKE THE PEOPLE'S KING!

While we acknowledge only occasional literary merit in the work of the Hartford Wits—and a large part of it has political rather than literary interest—it must be confessed by one who examines their writings in detail that they reflect strong, unique personalities. They have received far less attention than their predecessors in political and social progress, yet they bore a part in the development of an upright and sane Americanism. If Trumbull was considered the leader, as we have said, he had companions in fame, among his contemporaries,—Timothy Dwight, Joel Barlow, and David Humphreys. These Connecticut men formed a mutual-admiration society seldom equaled in extravagant tribute, which reads like a farce today. Thus Alsop praised

> Majestic Dwight, sublime in epic strain,
> Paints the fierce horrors of the crimson plain,
> And in Virgilian Barlow's tuneful lines
> With added splendour great Columbus shines.

In the eighth book of *The Columbiad,* Joel Barlow became effusive over the poetic gifts of the Connecticut poets, especially Trumbull, Timothy Dwight, and Humphreys:

> See TRUMBULL lead the train. His skilful hand
> Hurls the keen darts of satire round the land.
> Pride, knavery, dulness feel his mortal stings,
> And listening virtue triumphs while he sings.
> Britain's foil'd sons, victorious now no more,
> In guilt retiring from the wasted shore,
> Strive their curst cruelties to hide in vain,
> The world resounds them in his deathless
>   strain. . . .
>
> See HUMPHREYS glorious from the field retire,
> Sheathe the glad sword and string the soothing
>   lyre;
> His country's wrongs, her duties, dangers,
>   praise,
> Fire his full soul and animate his lays:
> Wisdom and War with equal joy shall own
> So fond a votary and so brave a son. . . .
>
> For DWIGHT's high harp the epic Muse sublime,
> Hails her new empire in the western clime.

The lines just quoted will suffice to indicate the exuberance of phrases, and the triteness of thought, which seem to have been the chief characteristics of the once famous Joel Barlow. Of all the Hartford group he was the most prominent in the earlier years. He was a chaplain in the war, was agent in Paris of the Scioto Land Company of Ohio, and served abroad on commissions for treaties with the Barbary tribes and other peoples. In spite of the popular verdict of his own day upon his voluminous *Vision of Columbus,*

"Conspiracy of Kings," and *The Columbiad,* he will be remembered, if at all, by the simple rhyme of *Hasty-Pudding,* written during an hour of loneliness on foreign soil.

Barlow's published writings of varied sorts—poetry, addresses, "Advice"—are found at many libraries, and his life has been more often studied than that of contemporary writers and friends. In the Pequot Library at Southport, Connecticut, is a rare collection of manuscript letters, written by Barlow, only a few of which have been printed. The letters to his wife, which form the large part, are interesting revelations of the personality of this man who promised so much and achieved so little, in diplomacy, business, and literature. In the letters to his wife from Paris, in 1789, he describes the Revolution as he has witnessed it, and feels that it is "no small satisfaction to have seen two complete revolutions in favor of Liberty." With frequent apologies for remaining abroad, he explains that his "affairs are still in a degree of uncertainty." The chief faults which his friends deplored were vacillation and a proneness to speculate with money, both his own and that of others. Manuscript poems in embryo, especially inspired by his acquaintance in Paris with Robert Fulton, are found among these letters.

After Barlow's return to America, and the publication of his long poems, he expected wide recognition among his countrymen; but he was embittered by indifference on some sides, and criticisms from other sources upon his political vacillation and seeming infidelity. Two of his letters, unpublished and here given by permission, indicate his sensitiveness, and they also show his foresight regarding national evils. The first was addressed to Gideon Granger, postmaster-general, and urged the appointment of a friend to office, emphasizing his scholarship and mental abilities:

> It is really discouraging to all liberal pursuits, & proves that the government is accessory to the great national sin of the country, which I fear will overturn its liberties,—I mean the inordinate & universal pursuit of wealth as a means of distinction.
>
> For example, if I find that writing the *Columbiad,* with all its moral qualities, literature, & science which that work supposes, will not place me on a footing with John Tayloe, who is rich, why then (God damn you) I'll be rich too. I'll dispise my literary labors (which tend to build up our system of free government) & I'll boast of my bank shares (which tend to pull it down) because *these* & not *those,* procure me the distinction which we all desire.
>
> I will teach my nephews by precept & all the rising generation by example that merit consists in oppressing mankind & not in serving them.

Another significant letter was written by Barlow to Jonathan Law, a prominent citizen of Hartford, with political influence in answer to charges brought against the would-be poet "by the malicious hypocrisy of such men as Dwight, & Parke & Coleman":

> I know as well as they do that all they say against me is false. All they mean or ever did mean by

calling me an antichristian is that I am a republican. This latter appellation they don't like to quarrel with openly, & for that reason they disguise it under the other. . . . But I shall probably never condescend to give my calumniators any sort of answer. I ask nothing from them, not even to let me alone. Poor fellows, they must live. Parke says individuals & nations have a right to get their bread in any manner they can. And these men slander me to get their bread.

I remember to have seen a song in praise of the guillotine in one of Cobbett's pamphlets about a dozen years ago, which he said was written by me. It might have served the purpose of the faction at the time to lay it to me; whatever might be their motive it was a forgery.

Timothy Dwight was deeply interested in the publications of this band of Hartford wits, but he did not contribute directly to their writings. He was included in their effusive praises of each other, and his ambitious *Conquest of Canaan* and *Greenfield Hill* were considered works of lasting renown. These voluminous poems are seldom read today, but the reposeful, hymnal lines by Dr. Dwight, and his strong influence upon young men in behalf of better citizenship, have won for him a revered name in American history. He was an ardent patriot and a great admirer of Washington. A letter to Oliver Wolcott, Jr., written after Dwight's visit to Philadelphia, in 1793, denounced Freneau and his paper for its attacks upon Washington. It was evident that Dwight considered Freneau's *Gazette* as a Jeffersonian organ:

The late very impertinent and shameless attacks on the first Magistrate are viewed with a general and marked indignation. *Freneau* your printer, Linguist, &c., is regarded here as a mere incendiary, or rather as a despicable tool of bigger incendiaries; and his paper as a public nuisance.

A few miles from New Haven is the hill-town of Derby. Here is an active chapter of the Daughters of the American Revolution—the Sarah Riggs Humphreys chapter—that has preserved many relics which pertain to the life-history of David Humphreys. As a young captain in the army under Colonel Meigs, and later as aide-de-camp to Generals Putnam, Greene, and Washington, Humphreys showed his alertness of mind, his courage, and his zeal for American progress. After the war he was with Jefferson, for a time, at Paris on the commission for treaties with foreign powers, and also served as diplomat at Lisbon and at Madrid. With these manlier traits he blended gallantry and cleverness, which made him a social favorite in foreign circles of society, but which called forth censure from some court-despising Americans. After he had returned to America, he was invited to visit at Mount Vernon, and Washington offered him aid in pursuing a literary plan which he had mentioned in his letters, namely, to write a history of the Revolution. At first thought, it may seem unfortunate that this plan was abandoned by Humphreys because of its magnitude. His tastes and effusive style, however, would not have produced a history of permanent value. His biographic essays on Israel Putnam were subjected to severe censure, but they gave the materials for later historians to utilize with better results.

In letters and poetic ventures, Humphreys left a vivid impression of Washington's life at Mount Vernon, in the years between the close of the war and his presidency. He pictured him as supervising his eight hundred acres of wheat and seven hundred acres of corn, and giving his personal attention to the task of navigating the Potomac, and extending the settlement of the western boundaries of the country. Humphreys was very proud of his friendship with Washington, and often referred to the latter with deep admiration, marred sometimes by such lines of egotism as in this stanza:

Let others sing his deeds in arms,
A nation saved and conquest's charms
        Posterity shall hear.
'Twas mine, return'd from Europe's courts,
To share his thoughts, partake his sports,
        And soothe his partial ear.

This soldier-versifier was vain and aspiring to literary fame, but he showed sturdier qualities when occasion called them forth. He took command of a band of men to guard the arsenal at Springfield, when it was threatened in Shay's Rebellion; he served in the state assembly during the years when he was collaborating with his friends in the series of papers of *The Anarchiad*. His "Poem Addressed to the Armies of the United States of America," first published in 1780, was reprinted in Paris six years later; this sign of appreciation gave him much delight. While abroad he lived in a style which attracted attention for its luxury, but which he seemed to defend in a manuscript letter to Timothy Pickering, which I am permitted to print here. It was written soon after his appointment as minister at Madrid; he explained the necessary expenses involved in moving his effects from Lisbon to Madrid:

I do not wish to make any unnecessary display, foreign to the dignified simplicity so becoming, in every character, but more particularly in that of a Republican Miniter; or to live in any respect in an ostentatious manner; but I desire to be able to live in a decent style (as other ministers are accustomed to do) without being under the necessity of incurring debts. . . . I hope & believe I shall never affect a style of hauteur; and whenever I cannot live abroad without embarrassment or meanness, I shall think it time to retire from public life—for sometimes the embarrassed conduct of a Diplomatic Agent extends beyond his individual Character and leaves an unfavorable impression of the Character of his Nation on the Minds of foreigners. . . . The transportation of my Carriages (of which I shall be obliged to carry four) Baggage, and necessaries will certainly, in the augmented price of forage, etc. cost me a good sum of money—for besides taking with me my own horses, I must order six or seven Mules to be sent from Madrid, and moreover employ a considerable number of common Carriers.

In spite of such indications of coxcombry in Humphreys, shown also in his delight to introduce foreign forms into the President's levees in New York, he was a true patriot in his impulses and aims. At forty-five, while abroad, he married the daughter of an English banker, but he was unwilling to live abroad, after his diplomatic missions were ended. As he had shared in gaining the liberty of America, so he wished to help in fostering her industries and arts. While at Lisbon he had written "A Poem on Industry," which ranked with his poem to the armies in its patriotism, as well as its verbosity; Humphreys could not write in simple English. The poem, however, and his practical success in manufacturing homespun cloths, entitle him to credit for noble motives. He brought with him from Spain, in 1802, one hundred and fifty merino sheep, as a nucleus for his enterprise. Near his Derby home he established a number of mills which made the settlement, at first called Chusetown and later Humphreysville, a flourishing village. The fulling-mill, cotton-mill, and paper-mill were opened in turn, and employment was given to scores of artisans. He brought several boys from the New York almshouses as apprentices. From England came masterworkmen to superintend the manufacture of cloth, which was worn by Jefferson and other statesmen, and which encouraged the growth of American industries.

Humphreys was not alone a patriotic manufacturer, but he was also a pioneer social settler. In his village he sought to produce fine manhood as well as fine cloth. He furnished a library and recreation-room for his operatives, led his boys in military drills, took part with them in games; and coached them in rehearsals of various plays and "pieces" of his own composition. One of these, *The Yankey in England,* was acted in 1815, and printed. In studying the life of Humphreys, we always find many evidences of his besetting sin, literary vanity. He won respect as a soldier and a promoter of industry, but he sought for rank in letters. This he obtained among his friends, and often he was highly praised in journals of the day. He cultivated his inferior talents too ardently, forgetting the moral in "The Monkey Fable," probably finished by Trumbull:

> Who cannot write, yet handle pens,
> Are apt to hurt themselves and friends.

In contrast with the admiration which Humphreys craved, and often gained in America, was the frank disgust of Southey. He had met Humphreys at Lisbon, and wrote later to a friend:

> Timothy Dwight, an American, published in 1785 an heroic poem on the Conquest of Canaan. I had heard of it, and long wished to read it, in vain; but now the American Minister (a good-natured man, whose poetry is worse than anything except his criticism) has lent me the book. There certainly is some merit in the poem: but when Col. Humphreys speaks of it, he will not allow me to put in a word in defense of John Milton.

His writings were prefaced by long notes of explanation and tribute.

The poems which are least effusive and offensive in form, among those included in his *Miscellaneous Works,* were the odes descriptive of the burning of Fairfield by the British, in 1779, and that on the "Happiness of America." The stanza in the latter which portrays the interior scene of a humble American home in winter may be fittingly recalled:

> The cattle fed—the fuel pil'd within—
> At setting day the blissful hours begin;
> 'Tis then, sole owner of his little cot;
> The farmer feels his independent lot;
> Hears with the crackling blaze that lights the wall,
> The voice of gladness and of nature call;
> Beholds his children play, their mother smile,
> And tastes with them the fruit of summer's toil.

During the War of 1812, Humphreys was general of a company of war veterans for home protection, and he wrote, with rejoicing, of his country's victories on the sea. His monument, erected soon after his death in 1818, stands near the entrance to the old cemetery at New Haven, close to Yale University buildings. Its verbose Latin epitaph was written by his friend John Trumbull.

Associated with the men of greater renown in their own day—Timothy Dwight, Trumbull, Barlow, and Humphreys—were three collaborators of less familiar but influential lives—Theodore Dwight, Richard Alsop, and Dr. Lemuel Hopkins. Theodore Dwight, the elder, and brother of Timothy, was a lawyer, and was editor of the *Connecticut Mirror* from 1809 until 1815. For two years previously, 1806-7, he was a member of Congress. The latter part of his life was passed in New York, where he conducted the *New York Daily Advertiser* from 1817 to 1835. He wrote a partisan study of Jefferson's character, a fervent hymn on Washington, some strong orations and an etymological dictionary. To him we owe the preservation of the long poem by Richard Alsop, *The Charms of Fancy,* and many interesting revelations of the poet, who was not alone Dwight's friend, but also his brother-in-law.

Alsop was probably the editor of the papers known as *The Echo,* when they were first printed. A letter, in manuscript, from him to Dr. Mason Cogswell is in the copy of *The Echo* owned by John Trumbull, now at the Connecticut Historical Society. Alsop mentioned some errata and continued, regarding the tone of the papers:

> I should be very sorry to have The Echo considered as a party production, as it must considerably lessen its reputation, & any alterations which will take off from that appearance without injury to the object in view, in my opinion will be best.

Born in Middletown, Connecticut, Alsop prepared for college, but continued his studies at home, becoming a fine translator of Runic poetry, Homer, Ossian, and Molina's *History of Chili.* For a time he had a bookstore in Hartford, where he lived with his sister. In an address, *To the Freemen of Connecticut,* (which is classified as his by an ink ascription in a copy at the Massachusetts Historical Society, dated Middletown, September 12, 1803,) he expressed confidence that God would protect "the Vine of this state" against "the rude shocks of democratic violence, nor will He suffer its ripened clusters to be trampled in the dust."

In William Dunlap's manuscript journal, 1797, he mentions a visit to Alsop at Middletown, "to shoot ducks;" later he accompanied Alsop "in a chaise to Hartford where lived, at that time, Miss Fanny Alsop."

In the "Memoir" of Alsop which prefaced his visionary

poem, *The Charms of Fancy,* we learn of his scholarship and scientific interests which blended with his poetic tastes. His sister said: "He seemed to know every variety of birds, and I might almost say, every feather." In boxes of his own design he kept his natural-history specimens—a large collection. His long, ambitious poem on fancy, and its inspiration for poet, painter, and musician, has a few fine lines, and reveals his wide reading and patriotic zeal for America's progress in the arts. The poem by Alsop which seems to me the most worthy, however, was not printed in permanent form, except in collections of poetry, but it suggests, as a forerunner, Bryant's "To a Waterfowl." Alsop's poem was entitled "Verses to a Shearwater on the Morning after a Storm at Sea":

> . . . On the fiery tossing wave,
>   Calmly cradled dost thou sleep,
> When the midnight tempests rave,
>   Lonely wanderer of the deep! . . .
>
> Far from earth's remotest trace,
>   What impels thee thus to roam?
> What hast thou to mark the place,
>   When thou seek'st thy distant home?
>
> Without star or magnet's aid,
>   Thou thy faithful course dost keep;
> Sportive still, still undismay'd,
>   Lonely wanderer of the deep!

Alsop spent the last years of his life in the vicinity of New York. He died at Flatbush in 1815. In his lifetime he was generally known as author of one of the most widely quoted elegies on Washington, and was honored for his translations from the *Eddas,* and from Spanish and Italian.

The sharpest wit among the Hartford writers was Lemuel Hopkins. He used travesties and imagery which defied all poetic standards. As a physician he ranked among the progressive leaders of his day; in his memory the Hopkins Medical Society was formed in 1826. Born at Hopkins Hill, in Waterbury, in 1750, he served as a soldier for a time, but lost no opportunity to study for the profession of medicine, which he had chosen in youth as a goal. After gaining some experience with two noted men of his day and state—Dr. Seth Bird, of Litchfield, and Dr. Jared Potter, of Wallingford—he settled in Hartford, in 1784, where he remained until his death sixteen years later. By success in his profession, and by his courageous advocacy of inoculation for small-pox, use of anaesthetics, and radical remedies for yellow fever, he gained repute outside his state and was often called into consultation. Yale conferred an honorary degree upon him.

Many traditions and local stories cluster about his personality. He was nervous, brusque, with keen eyes, and a peculiar, awkward gait. One story illustrates his brusqueness combined with faithfulness. On a stormy night he rode four miles to assure himself that a certain remedy was accomplishing the desired results. Arriving at the house, he entered, made a silent examination, refused to speak to any of the inmates, and rode away. He was a dreaded enemy of impostors and quacks. Another anecdote indicates this trait. With Dr. Cogswell, he was attending a patient who was dying of tubercular disease. The sister of the sick girl unreasonably besought the doctors to use some

"fever powders," which she had bought from a peripatetic quack. Dr. Hopkins asked her to bring the powders, announced that one and a half was recorded as the largest dose which it was safe to take, calmly mixed twelve of the powders in molasses, and swallowed them, remarking to his colleague: "Cogswell, I am going to Coventry today. If I die from this, you must write on my tombstone: 'Here lies Hopkins, killed by Grimes'." In indignation against a "cancer doctor" who had troubled the neighborhood, he wrote the rugged verse, "On a Patient Killed by a Cancer Quack":

> Here lies a fool, flat on his back,
> The victim of a cancer quack;
> Who lost his money and his life,
> By plaister, caustic and by knife.

More dignified were the ironical stanzas, "The Hypocrite's Hope":

> He tones like Pharisee sublime,
>   Two lengthy prayers a day,
> The same that he from early prime,
>   Has heard his father say. . . .
>
> Good works he careth nought about,
>   But faith alone will seek,
> While Sunday's pieties blot out,
>   The knaveries of the week.

A few letters from Dr. Lemuel Hopkins to his friend Oliver Wolcott, Jr., are in manuscript at the Connecticut Historical Society; I have been given the privilege of quoting from them. One written in October, 1783, reveals Hopkins' wit and his interest in political affairs:

> I thank you for your inteligence & thoughts on politicks; but have not time to tell you my own. But I lament with you the ill aspect of our affairs, and am afraid to think much of the next scene for of late, when I have indulg'd such thoughts, the Ghost of a certain text has grinn'd *horrible* at me *a ghastly smile,*—'tis this—"Wo unto thee oh land when thy king is a fool."

In a letter from Hartford, after his removal there from Litchfield, he refers to the *American Antiquities (The Anarchiad)* as having "given a considerable check to a certain kind of popular intrigue in this state."

During the prevalence of small-pox in the summer of 1793, he wrote to Mr. Wolcott regarding inoculation, which he practiced freely:

> This business is much like that of the Treasury Department in regard to existing jealousies, raising party spirit &c., yet, from certain causes, my particular mode of conducting it, in case of any suspicion of wrong measures, does not admit of so unanswerable a justification.

There are some philosophic sentences in the same letter regarding the influences of city and village life, which are interesting today:

> The more a man is among all sorts of people, the more fully will he learn the unmeasured difference there is between the sentiments of newspapers, replete with local politics, and the opinions of an enlighten'd people in the peaceable and

successful pursuit of wealth & happiness.—I find more & more that a busy set of wrongheads can at pleasure stir up, for a time, any sentiments they please in cities—and that there is a great aptitude in most men to consider *cities* as *worlds,* or at least as the manufactories of sentiments for whole countries—and much of this may be true in the old world; but in N. England the contrary is, and ever will be true, as long as our schools, presses & Town-corporations last.

With his shrewd insight into the diseases of individuals and of the nation, with his urgent desire for progress through education, Dr. Hopkins was a good type of his time, and especially of this group of Connecticut writers. They were earnest, as well as witty; they sought to use their talents for the advance of industry and political sanity. Their writings mirrored many of the aspirations and fears of the period which followed the war and was concerned with the establishment of stable government.

Henry A. Beers

SOURCE: "The Connecticut Wits," *The Yale Review,* Vol. XI, No. 2, January, 1913, pp. 242-56.

[*Beers is an American historian, researcher, and critic. Here, he offers a mixed assessment of the works of the Con-*

THE ANARCHIAD:

A New England Poem.

WRITTEN IN CONCERT BY

DAVID HUMPHREYS, JOEL BARLOW, JOHN TRUMBULL, AND DR. LEMUEL HOPKINS.

Now first published in book form.

EDITED, WITH NOTES AND APPENDICES,

BY LUTHER G. RIGGS.

New Haven:
PUBLISHED BY THOMAS H. PEASE,
828 CHAPEL STREET.

1861.

Title page of The Anarchiad, *1861.*

---

necticut Wits, acknowledging that their "patriotic enterprise of creating a national literature by tour de force *was undertaken when Minerva was unwilling"—that is, under inauspicious circumstances.*]

In the days when Connecticut counted in the national councils; when it had *men* in the patriot armies, in Washington's Cabinet, in the Senate of the United States—men like Israel Putnam, Roger Sherman, Oliver Wolcott, Oliver Ellsworth,—in those same days there was a premature but interesting literary movement in our little commonwealth. A band of young graduates of Yale, some of them tutors in the college, or in residence for their Master's degree, formed themselves into a school for the cultivation of letters. I speak advisedly in calling them a school: they were a group of personal friends, united in sympathy by similar tastes and principles; and they had in common certain definite, coherent, and conscious aims. These were, first, to liberalize and modernize the rigidly scholastic curriculum of the college by the introduction of more elegant studies: the *belles lettres,* the *literæ humaniores.* Such was the plea of John Trumbull in his Master's oration, "An Essay on the Use and Advantages of the Fine Arts," delivered at Commencement, 1770; and in his satire, *The Progress of Dulness,* he had his hit at the dry and dead routine of college learning. Secondly, these young men resolved to supply the new republic with a body of poetry on a scale commensurate with the bigness of American scenery and the vast destinies of the nation: epics resonant as Niagara, and pindaric odes lofty as our native mountains. And finally, when, at the close of the Revolutionary War, the members of the group found themselves reunited for a few years at Hartford, they set themselves to combat, with the weapon of satire, the influences towards lawlessness and separatism which were delaying the adoption of the Constitution.

My earliest knowledge of this literary coterie was derived from an article in *The Atlantic Monthly* for February, 1865, "The Pleiades of Connecticut." The "Pleiades," to wit, were John Trumbull, Timothy Dwight, David Humphreys, Lemuel Hopkins, Richard Alsop, and Theodore Dwight. The tone of the article was ironic. "Connecticut is pleasant," it said, "with wooded hills and a beautiful river; plenteous with tobacco and cheese; fruitful of merchants, missionaries, peddlers, and single women,—but there are no poets known to exist there . . . the brisk little democratic state has turned its brains upon its machinery . . . the enterprising natives can turn out any article on which a profit can be made—except poetry."

Massachusetts has always been somewhat condescending towards Connecticut's literary pretensions. Yet all through that very volume of the *Atlantic,* from which I quote, run Mrs. Stowe's "Chimney Corner" papers and Donald Mitchell's novel, *Doctor Johns;* with here and there a story by Rose Terry and a poem by Henry Brownell. Nay, in an article entitled "Our Battle Laureate," in the May number of the magazine, the "Autocrat" himself, who would always have his fling at Connecticut theology and Connecticut spelling and pronunciation ("Webster's provincials," forsooth! though *pater ipse,* the Rev. Abiel, had been a Connecticut orthodox parson, a Yale graduate, and a son-in-law of President Stiles),—the "Autocrat," I say, takes off his hat to my old East Hartford neighbor, Henry Howard Brownell.

He begins by citing the paper which I have been citing: "How came the Muses to settle in Connecticut? . . . But the seed of the Muses has run out. No more Pleiades in Hartford . . ."; and answers that, if the author of the article asks Nathaniel's question, putting Hartford for Nazareth, he can refer him to Brownell's "Lyrics of a Day." "If Drayton had fought at Agincourt, if Campbell had held a sabre at Hohenlinden, if Scott had been in the saddle with Marmion, if Tennyson had charged with the six hundred at Balaclava, each of these poets might possibly have pictured what he said as faithfully and as fearfully as Mr. Brownell has painted the sea fights in which he took part as a combatant."

Many years later, when preparing a chapter on the literature of the county for the *Memorial History of Hartford,* I came to close quarters with the sweet influence of the Pleiades. I am one of the few men—perhaps I am the only man—now living who have read the whole of Joel Barlow's *Columbiad.* "Is old Joel Barlow yet alive?" asks Hawthorne's crazy correspondent. "Unconscionable man! . . . And *does* he meditate an epic on the war between Mexico and Texas, with machinery contrived on the principle of the steam engine?" I also "perused" (good old verb—the right word for the deed!) Dwight's *Greenfield Hill*—a meritorious action,—but I cannot pretend to have read his *Conquest of Canaän* (the diæresis is his, not mine), an epic in eleven books and in heroic couplets. I dipped into it only far enough to note that the poet had contrived to introduce a history of our Revolutionary War, by way of episode, among the wars of Israel.

It must be acknowledged that this patriotic enterprise of creating a national literature by *tour de force,* was undertaken when Minerva was unwilling. These were able and eminent men: scholars, diplomatists, legislators. Among their number were a judge of the Connecticut Supreme Court, a college president, foreign ministers and ambassadors, a distinguished physician, an officer of the Revolutionary army, intimate friends of Washington and Jefferson. But, as poetry, a few little pieces of the New Jersey poet, Philip Freneau,—"The Indian Student," "The Indian Burying Ground," "To a Honey Bee," "The Wild Honeysuckle," and "The Battle of Eutaw Springs,"—are worth all the epic and pindaric strains of the Connecticut bards. Yet "still the shore a brave attempt resounds." For they had few misgivings and a truly missionary zeal. They formed the first Mutual Admiration Society in our literary annals.

> Here gallant Humphreys charm'd the list'ning
>   throng:
> Sweetly he sang, amid the clang of arms,
> His numbers smooth, replete with winning
>   charms;
> In him there shone a great and godlike mind,
> The poet's wreath around the laurel twined.

This was while Colonel Humphreys was in the army—one of Washington's aides. But when he resigned his commission,—hark! 'tis Barlow sings:—

> See Humphreys glorious from the field retire,
> Sheathe the glad sword and string the sounding
>   lyre,
> O'er fallen friends, with all the strength of woe,
> His heartfelt sighs in moving numbers flow,
> His country's wrongs, her duties, dangers,
>   praise,
> Fire his full soul, and animate his lays.

Humphreys, in turn, in his poem "On the Future Glory of the United States of America," calls upon his learned friends to string *their* lyres and rouse their countrymen against the Barbary corsairs who were holding American seamen in captivity:—

> Why sleep'st thou, Barlow, child of genius? Why
> See'st thou, blest Dwight, our land in sadness
>   lie?
> And where is Trumbull, earliest boast of fame?
> 'Tis yours, ye bards, to wake the smothered
>   flame.
> To you, my dearest friends, the task belongs
> To rouse your country with heroic songs.

Yes, to be sure, where *is* Trumbull, earliest boast of fame? He came from Watertown (now a seat of learning), a cousin of Governor Trumbull—"Brother Jonathan"—and a second cousin of Colonel John Trumbull, the historical painter, whose battle pieces repose in the Yale Art Gallery. Cleverness runs in the Trumbull blood. There was, for example, J. Hammond Trumbull (abbreviated by lisping infancy to "J. Hambull") in the last generation, a great sagamore—O a very big Indian,—reputed the only man in the country who could read Eliot's Algonquin Bible. I make no mention of later Trumbulls known in letters and art. But as for our worthy, John Trumbull, the poet, it is well known and has been often told how he passed the college entrance examination at the age of seven, but forebore to matriculate till a more reasonable season, graduating in 1767 and serving two years as a tutor along with his friend Dwight; afterwards studying law at Boston in the office of John Adams, practising at New Haven and Hartford, filling legislative and judicial positions, and dying at Detroit in 1831.

Trumbull was the satirist of the group. As a young man at Yale, he amused his leisure by contributing to the newspapers essays in the manner of *The Spectator* (*The Meddler, The Correspondent,* and the like); and verse satires after the fashion of Prior and Pope. There is nothing very new about the Jack Dapperwits, Dick Hairbrains, Tom Brainlesses, Miss Harriet Simpers, and Isabella Sprightlys of these compositions. The very names will recall to the experienced reader the stock figures of the countless Addisonian imitations which sickled o'er the minor literature of the eighteenth century. But Trumbull's masterpiece was *M'Fingal,* a Hudibrastic satire on the Tories, printed in part at Philadelphia in 1776, and in complete shape at Hartford in 1782, "by Hudson and Goodwin near the Great Bridge." *M'Fingal* was the most popular poem of the Revolution. It went through more than thirty editions in America and England. In 1864 it was edited with elaborate historical notes by Benson J. Lossing, author of *The Field Book of the Revolution.* A reprint is mentioned as late as 1881. An edition, in two volumes, of Trumbull's poetical works was issued in 1820.

Timothy Dwight pronounced *M'Fingal* superior to *Hudibras*. The Marquis de Chastellux, who had fought with Lafayette for the independence of the colonies; who had been amused when at Windham, says my authority, by Governor Jonathan Trumbull's "pompous manner in transacting the most trifling public business"; and who translated into French Colonel Humphreys's poetical "Address to the Armies of the United States of America,"—Chastellux wrote to Trumbull *à propos* of his burlesque: "I believe that you have rifled every flower which that kind of poetry could offer. . . . I prefer it to every work of the kind,—even *Hudibras*." And Moses Coit Tyler, whose four large volumes on our colonial and revolutionary literature are, for the most part, a much ado about nothing, waxes dithyrambic on this theme. He speaks, for example, of "the vast and prolonged impression it has made upon the American people." But surely all this is very uncritical. All that is really alive of *M'Fingal* are a few smart couplets usually attributed to *Hudibras*, such as—

> No man e'er felt the halter draw
> With good opinion of the law.

M'Fingal is one of the most successful of the innumerable imitations of *Hudibras*; still it is an imitation, and, as such, inferior to its original. But apart from that, Trumbull was far from having Butler's astonishing resources of wit and learning, tedious as they often are from their mere excess. Nor is the Yankee sharpness of *M'Fingal* so potent a spirit as the harsh, bitter contempt of Butler, almost as inventive of insult as the *sæva indignatio* of Swift. Yet *M'Fingal* still keeps a measure of historical importance, reflecting, in its cracked and distorted mirror of caricature, the features of a stormy time: the turbulent town meetings, the liberty poles and bonfires of the patriots; with the tar-and-feathering of Tories, and their stolen gatherings in cellars or other holes and corners.

After peace was declared, a number of these young writers came together again in Hartford, where they formed a sort of literary club with weekly meetings—"The Hartford Wits," who for a few years made the little provincial capital the intellectual metropolis of the country. Trumbull had settled at Hartford in the practice of the law in 1781. Joel Barlow, who had hastily qualified for a chaplaincy in a Massachusetts brigade by a six weeks' course of theology, and had served more or less sporadically through the war, came to Hartford in the year following and started a newspaper. David Humphreys, Yale 1771, illustrious founder of the Brothers in Unity Society, and importer of merino sheep, had enlisted in 1776 in a Connecticut militia regiment then on duty in New York. He had been on the staff of General Putnam, whose life he afterwards wrote; had been Washington's aide and a frequent inmate at Mount Vernon from 1780 to 1783; then abroad (1784-1786), as secretary to the commission for making commercial treaties with the nations of Europe. (The commissioners were Franklin, Adams, and Jefferson.) On returning to his native Derby in 1786, he had been sent to the legislature at Hartford, and now found himself associated with

Trumbull, who had entered upon his Yale tutorship in 1771, the year of Humphreys's graduation; and with Barlow, who had taken his B.A. degree in 1778. These three Pleiades drew to themselves other stars of lesser magnitude, the most remarkable of whom was Dr. Lemuel Hopkins, a native of Waterbury, but since 1784 a practising physician at Hartford and one of the founders of the Connecticut Medical Society. Hopkins was an eccentric humorist, and is oddly described by Samuel Goodrich—"Peter Parley"—as "long and lank, walking with spreading arms and straddling legs." "His nose was long, lean, and flexible," adds Goodrich,—a description which suggests rather the proboscis of the elephant, or at least of the tapir, than a feature of the human countenance.

Other lights in this constellation were Richard Alsop, from Middletown, who was now keeping a book store at Hartford, and Theodore Dwight, brother to Timothy and brother-in-law to Alsop, and later the secretary and historian of the famous Hartford Convention of 1814, which came near to carrying New England into secession. We might reckon as an eighth Pleiad, Dr. Elihu H. Smith, then residing at Wetherfield, who published in 1793 our first poetic miscellany, printed—of all places in the world—at Litchfield, "mine own romantic town": seat of the earliest American law school, and emitter of this earliest American anthology. If you should happen to find in your garret a dusty copy of this collection, *American Poems, Original and Selected*, by Elihu H. Smith, hold on to it. It is worth money, and will be worth more.

The Hartford Wits contributed to local papers, such as the *New Haven Gazette* and the *Connecticut Courant*, a series of political lampoons: *The Anarchiad*, *The Echo*, and *The Political Greenhouse*, a sort of Yankee *Dunciad*, *Rolliad*, and *Anti-Jacobin*. They were staunch Federalists, friends of a close union and a strong central government; and used their pens in support of the administrations of Washington and Adams, and to ridicule Jefferson and the Democrats. It was a time of great confusion and unrest: of Shay's Rebellion in Massachusetts, and the irredeemable paper currency in Rhode Island. In Connecticut, Democratic mobs were protesting against the vote of five years' pay to the officers of the disbanded army. *The Echo* and *The Political Greenhouse* were published in book form in 1807; *The Anarchiad* not till 1861, by Thomas H. Pease, New Haven, with notes and introduction by Luther G. Riggs. I am not going to quote these satires. They amused their own generation and doubtless did good. *The Echo* had the honor of being quoted in Congress by an angry Virginian, to prove that Connecticut was trying to draw the country into a war with France. It caught up cleverly the humors of the day, now travestying a speech of Jefferson, now turning into burlesque a Boston town meeting. A local flavor is given by allusions to Connecticut traditions: Captain Kidd, the Blue Laws, the Windham Frogs, the Hebron pump, the Wethersfield onion gardens. But the sparkle has gone out of it. There is a perishable element in political satire. I find it difficult to interest young people nowadays even in the *Biglow Papers*, which are so much superior, in every way, to *M'Fingal* or *The Anarchiad*.

Timothy Dwight would probably have rested his title to

literary fame on his five volumes of theology and the eleven books of his *Conquest of Canaän.* But the epic is unread and unreadable, while theological systems need constant restatement in an age of changing beliefs. There is one excellent hymn by Dwight in the collections,—"I love thy kingdom, Lord." His war song, "Columbia, Columbia, in glory arise," was once admired, but has faded. I have found it possible to take a mild interest in the long poem, *Greenfield Hill,* a partly idyllic and partly moral didactic piece, emanating from the country parish, three miles from the Sound, in the town of Fairfield, where Dwight was pastor from 1783 to 1795. The poem has one peculiar feature: each of its seven parts was to have imitated the manner of some one British poet. Part One is in the blank verse and the style of Thomson's *Seasons;* Part Two in the heroic couplets and the diction of Goldsmith's *Traveller* and *Deserted Village.* For lack of time this design was not systematically carried out, but the reader is reminded now of Prior, then of Cowper, and again of Crabbe. The nature descriptions and the pictures of rural life are not untruthful, though somewhat tame and conventional. The praise of modest competence is sung, and the wholesome simplicity of American life, under the equal distribution of wealth, as contrasted with the luxury and corruption of European cities. Social questions are discussed, such as, "the state of negro slavery in Connecticut"; and "what is not, and what is, a social female visit." Narrative episodes give variety to the descriptive and reflective portions: the burning of Fairfield in 1779 by the British under Governor Tryon; the destruction of the remnants of the Pequod Indians in a swamp three miles west of the town. It is distressing to have the Yankee farmer called "the swain," and his wife and daughter "the fair," in regular eighteenth century style; and Long Island, which is always in sight and frequently apostrophized, personified as "Longa."

> Then on the borders of this sapphire plain
> Shall   growing   beauties   grace   my   fair
>   domain . . .
> Gay groves exult: Chinesian gardens glow,
> And bright reflections paint the wave below.

The poet celebrates Connecticut artists and inventors:—

> Such forms, such deeds on Rafael's tablets shine,
> And such, O Trumbull, glow alike on thine.

David Bushnell of Saybrook had invented a submarine torpedo boat, nicknamed "the American Turtle," with which he undertook to blow up Lord Admiral Howe's gunship in New York harbor. Humphreys gives an account of the failure of this enterprise in his *Life of Putnam.* It was some of Bushnell's machines, set afloat on the Delaware, among the British shipping, that occasioned the panic celebrated in Hopkinson's satirical balled, *The Battle of the Kegs,* which we used to declaim at school. "See," exclaims Dwight,

> See Bushnell's strong creative genius, fraught
> With all th' assembled powers of skillful
>   thought,
> His mystic vessel plunge beneath the waves
> And glide through dark retreats and coral caves!

Dr. Holmes, who knew more about Yale poets than they know about each other, has rescued one line from *Green-*

field Hill. "The last we see of snow," he writes, in his paper on *The Seasons,* "is, in the language of a native poet,

> The lingering drift behind the shady wall.

This is from a bard more celebrated once than now, Timothy Dwight, the same from whom we borrowed the piece we used to speak, beginning (as we said it),

> Columby, Columby, to glory arise!

The line with the drift in it has stuck in my memory like a feather in an old nest, and is all that remains to me of his *Greenfield Hill.*"

As President of Yale College from 1795 to 1817, Dr. Dwight, by his sermons, addresses, and miscellaneous writings, his personal influence with young men, and his public spirit, was a great force in the community. I have an idea that his *Travels in New England and New York,* posthumously published in 1821-1822, in four volumes, will survive all his other writings. I can recommend Dwight's *Travels* as a really entertaining book, and full of solid observation.

Of all the wooden poetry of these Connecticut bards, David Humphreys's seems to me the woodenest,—big patriotic verse essays on the model of the *Essay on Man:* "Address to the Armies of the United States"; "On the Happiness of America"; "On the Future Glory of the United States"; "On the Love of Country"; "On the Death of George Washington," etc. Yet Humphreys was a most important figure. He was plenipotentiary to Portugal and Spain, and a trusted friend of Washington, from whom, perhaps, he caught that stately deportment which is said to have characterized him. He imported a hundred merino sheep from Spain, landing them from shipboard at his native Derby, then a port of entry on the lordly Housatonic. He wrote a dissertation on merino sheep, and also celebrated the exploit in song. The Massachusetts Agricultural Society gave him a gold medal for his services in improving the native breed. But if these sheep are even remotely responsible for Schedule K, it might be wished that they had remained in Spain, or had been as the flocks of Bo-Peep. Colonel Humphreys died at New Haven in 1818. The college owns his portrait by Stuart, and his monument in Grove Street cemetery is dignified by a Latin inscription reciting his titles and achievements, and telling how, like a second Jason, he brought the *auream vellerem* from Europe to Connecticut. Colonel Humphreys's works were handsomely published at New York in 1804, with a list of subscribers headed by their Catholic Majesties, the King and Queen of Spain, and followed by Thomas Jefferson, John Adams, and numerous dukes and chevaliers. Among the humbler subscribers I am gratified to observe the names of Nathan Beers, merchant, New Haven; and Isaac Beers & Co., booksellers, New Haven (six copies),—no ancestors but conjecturally remote collateral relatives of the undersigned.

I cannot undertake to quote from Humphreys's poems. The patriotic feeling that prompted them was genuine; the descriptions of campaigns in which he himself had borne a part have a certain value; but the poetry as such, though by no means contemptible, is quite uninspired. Homer's catalogue of ships is a hackneyed example of the way in which a great poet can make bare names poetical. Humphreys had a harder job, and passages of his battle pieces read like pages from a city directory.

> As fly autumnal leaves athwart some dale,
> Borne on the pinions of the sounding gale,
> Or glides the gossamer o'er rustling reeds,
> Bland's, Sheldon's, Moylan's, Baylor's battle
>   steeds
> So skimmed the plain. . . .
> Then Huger, Maxwell, Mifflin, Marshall, Read,
> Hastened from states remote to seize the
>   meed; . . .
> While Smallwood, Parsons, Shepherd, Irvine,
>   Hand,
> Guest, Weedon, Muhlenberg, leads each his
>   band.

Does the modern reader recognize a forefather among these heroic patronymics? Just as good men as fought at Marathon or Agincourt. Nor can it be said of any one of them *quia caret vate sacro.*

But the loudest blast upon the trump of fame was blown by Joel Barlow. It was agreed that in him America had produced a supreme poet. Born at Redding—where Mark Twain died . . . ,—the son of a farmer, Barlow was graduated at Yale in 1778—just a hundred years before President Taft. He married the daughter of a Guilford blacksmith, who had moved to New Haven to educate his sons; one of whom, Abraham Baldwin, afterwards went to Georgia, grew up with the country, and became United States Senator.

After the failure of his Hartford journal, Barlow went to France, in 1778, as agent of the Scioto Land Company, which turned out to be a swindling concern. He now "embraced French principles," that is, became a Jacobin and freethinker, to the scandal of his old Federalist friends. He wrote a song to the guillotine and sang it at festal gatherings in London. He issued other revolutionary literature, in particular an *Advice to the Privileged Orders,* suppressed by the British government; whereupon Barlow, threatened with arrest, went back to France. The Convention made him a French citizen; he speculated luckily in the securities of the republic, which rose rapidly with the victories of its armies. He lived in much splendor in Paris, where Robert Fulton, inventor of steamboats, made his home with him for seven years. In 1795, he was appointed United States consul to Algiers, resided there two years, and succeeded in negotiating the release of the American captives who had been seized by Algerine pirates. After seventeen years' absence, he returned to America, and built a handsome country house on Rock Creek, Washington, which he named characteristically "Kalorama." He had become estranged from orthodox New England, and lived on intimate terms with Jefferson, and the Democratic leaders, French sympathizers, and philosophical deists.

In 1811 President Madison sent him as minister plenipotentiary to France, to remonstrate with the emperor on the subject of the Berlin and Milan decrees, which were injuring American commerce. He was summoned to Wilna, Napoleon's headquarters in his Russian campaign, where he was promised a personal interview. But the retreat from Moscow had begun. Fatigue and exposure brought on an illness from which Barlow died in a small Polish village near Cracow. An elaborate biography, *The Life and Letters of Joel Barlow,* by Charles Burr Todd, was published by G. P. Putnam's Sons in 1886.

Barlow's most ambitious undertaking was the *Columbiad,* originally printed at Hartford in 1787 as *The Vision of Columbus,* and then reissued in its expanded form at Philadelphia in 1807: a sumptuous quarto with plates by the best English and French engravers from designs by Robert Fulton, altogether the finest specimen of book-making that had then appeared in America. The *Columbiad*'s greatness was in inverse proportion to its bigness. Grandiosity was its author's besetting sin, and the plan of the poem is absurdly grandiose. It tells how Hesper appeared to Columbus in prison and led him to a hill of vision whence he viewed the American continents spread out before him, and the panorama of their whole future history unrolled. Among other things he saw the Connecticut river—

> Thy stream, my Hartford, through its misty
>   robe,
> Played in the sunbeams, belting far the globe.
> No watery glades through richer vallies shine,
> Nor drinks the sea a lovelier wave than thine.

It is odd to come upon familiar place-names swoln to epic pomp. There is Danbury, for example, which one associates with the manufacture of hats and a somewhat rowdy annual fair. In speaking of the towns set on fire by the British, the poet thus exalteth Danbury, whose flames were visible from native Redding:—

> Norwalk expands the blaze; o'er Redding hills
> High flaming Danbury the welkin fills.
> Esopus burns, New York's deliteful fanes
> And sea-nursed Norfolk light the neighboring
>   plains.

But Barlow's best poem was *Hasty Pudding,* a mock-heroic after the fashion of Philips's *Cider,* and not, I think, inferior to that. One couplet, in particular, has prevailed against the tooth of time:—

> E'en in thy native regions how I blush
> To hear the Pennsylvanians call thee mush!

This poem was written in 1792 in Savoy, whither Barlow had gone to stand as deputy to the National Convention. In a little inn at Chambéry, a bowl of *polenta,* or Indian meal pudding, was set before him, and the familiar dish made him homesick for Connecticut. You remember how Dr. Holmes describes the dinners of the young American medical students in Paris at the *Trois Frères*; and how one of them would sit tinkling the ice in his wine glass, "saying that he was hearing the cowbells as he used to hear them, when the deep-breathing kine came home at twilight from the huckleberry pasture in the old home a thousand leagues towards the sunset."

Vernon Louis Parrington

SOURCE: An introduction to *The Connecticut Wits,* ed-

Title page of The Echo, *1807.*

ited by Vernon Louis Parrington, Harcourt Brace Jovanovich, 1926, pp. ix-xlvi.

[*Parrington was an American historian, critic, and educator who contributed regularly to such prestigious reference works as* Encyclopaedia Britannica *and* The Cambridge History of American Literature. *He was awarded a Pulitzer Prize for the first two volumes of his influential* Main Currents in American Thought *(1927); the third volume remained unfinished at the time of his death. In this series, Parrington composed, according to Michael O'Brien, "not a study of American literature so much as of American political thought refracted through literature." While his efforts are still widely admired today, many critics contend that his unabashedly liberal bias, and his summary judgments of Edgar Allan Poe, Nathaniel Hawthorne, Henry James, and others, compromised his work. In the following introduction to his* The Connecticut Wits *(1926), Parrington assesses the contribution of the Wits, noting that, "though they fell short of their ambitious goal, their works remain extraordinarily interesting documents of a critical period."*]

For a good many years now the members of the literary coterie that forgathered in Hartford in the closing years of the eighteenth century, and proffered their wit and wisdom to all New England, have enjoyed such shadowy fame as comes from the reprinting of their names in successive school histories of our literature. Their several individualities have long since gone the way of mortality, but their composite reputation has been happily preserved by the salt of a phrase. Under the quaint title of the Connecticut or the Hartford Wits—a title which, to borrow Whitman's Gallicism, has proved to be their *carte de visite* to posterity—they are annually recalled by a considerable number of undergraduates on the eve of an examination; but what sort of men they were, and what they severally and jointly contributed to a little world sadly wanting sweetness and light, are questions about which no undergraduate ever concerns himself. Their works lie buried in old libraries with the dust of years upon them; their descriptive title alone dwells among the living. To rescue them if possible from the obscuring shadow of their collective reputation, to permit them once more to speak for themselves in their eighteenth century vernacular, is the purpose of this partial reprinting of their works. The record as they left it, very likely will not appeal to the taste of a far different age. We shall probably find their verse stilted and barren, and their robust prejudices hopelessly old-fashioned; but stilted and barren though their couplets may be, and extraordinary though their dogmatisms may seem to us, they throw a clear light on provincial New England in the acrid years of the seventeen-nineties, when America was angrily debating what path to follow in order to arrive at its predestined objective. The Hartford Wits may not deserve the high title of poets; they were smaller men than they esteemed each other and their generation rated them; but though they fell short of their ambitious goal, their works remain extraordinarily interesting documents of a critical period.

The title of the group sufficiently reveals their intellectual antecedents. That they alone amongst our early dabblers in verse succeeded in preëmpting the excellent name of Wits, suggests how late the spirit of eighteenth century English culture came to expression in America, and also how inadequately. That they were not alone in their efforts to shape American letters after the Augustan pattern, every student of our early verse knows. Others before them aspired to be Wits, and others after them. From Mather Byles to Robert Treat Paine the refinement of Pope and the trenchant severity of Churchill had been the admiration of American poetasters; but they alone achieved a measurable degree of success in domesticating the Wit ideals, and by their persistent labors in the field of satire they created for the first time in America what may be called a school of poetry. By the end of the century their reputation had spread well beyond the confines of New England, and when an ambitious collection of native verse was issued in New York in 1794, under the title of *The Columbian Muse,* the editor felt constrained to give up considerably more than half the total space to their work. Only Philadelphia could hope to enter into poetic rivalry with the Connecticut group. In the social and literary capital of America poetry was sedulously cultivated. Francis Hopkinson, an amiable dabbler in polite arts, had contributed a number of sprightly *jeux d'esprit;* young William Cliffton was preparing to dedicate his short life to verse; and Peter Porcupine—the brutally caustic William Cobbett—was achieving a lively notoriety as a purveyor of virulent couplets. But the culture of Philadelphia was smutched by the strife of partisan rivals. Young enthusiasts for the rights of man gathered there—Philip Freneau from New Jersey, and idealists from overseas—to throw their literary brickbats at the spokesmen of conservatism. There was wanting the solidarity of polite opinion that gave a sanction of authority to upper-class Yankee views, and no school of poetry arose to enshrine in clever couplets the culture of a homogeneous society.

This is what lends its chief significance to the work of the Hartford group. They embodied a conception of life and society that had taken form during nearly two hundred years of provincial experience; and they phrased that conception at the moment when vast changes were impending and the traditional New England was on the point of being caught in the grasp of forces that were to destroy what was most native in her life. The "Wits" were the last representatives of a literary mode that had slowly percolated through the crust of Puritan provincialism and imparted a certain sprightliness to a dour temper. They were the literary old guard of eighteenth century Toryism, the expiring gasp of a rationalistic age, given to criticism, suspicious of all emotion, contemptuous of idealistic programs. But though they aspired to follow the latest London modes, they could not wholly lay aside congenital prejudices, and they unconsciously gave to the imported fashion a homely domestic cut. If they were Wits they were Yankee Wits, and their manners were formed in Connecticut rather than at St. James's, at Yale College rather than Brooks Club. They aspired to unite culture with godliness, and this Puritan predilection for righteousness adds a characteristic native savor to their wit.

Although their writing was done at a time when the romantic revolution, soon to set all western civilization in ferment, was well under way in France, and had already entered America, there is in them no suggestion of sympathy for the new ideas. As good Calvinists and honest men they would hold no commerce with "French infidel philosophy." They stood stoutly by the customary and familiar. The age was visibly falling to decay before their eyes, yet they set themselves with the fury of dogmatic conviction to new-prop an order that had contented their fathers. They were the self-satisfied embodiment of the outworn. The nineteenth century was knocking at their door, but they would not open to it. And as they saw that century coming in the guise of revolution, exciting to unheard-of innovations in the fields of politics and economics and religion and letters; as they observed it sweeping triumphantly through Virginia, turmoiling the pugnacious society of Philadelphia, expressing itself in the rebellious work of Philip Freneau and Tom Paine and Matthew Carey, in Jacobin Clubs and Jeffersonian democracy, they set themselves seriously to the work of barring its progress in their own little world. They conveniently associated the economic unrest of post-war days—that gave birth to a strange progeny in Rhode Island and New Hampshire and Massachusetts—with the contamination of French atheism, charged all unrest to the account of democracy, and hastened to put it down in the name of law and righteous-

ness. They hated new ways with the virtuous hatred of the well-to-do, and piously dreamed of a future America as like the past as one generation of oysters is like another.

I

There is a certain historical fitness in the fact that the Wits should have arisen in Connecticut and been the intellectual and spiritual children of Yale. For generations the snug little commonwealth had been the home of a tenacious conservatism, that clung to old ways and guarded the institutions of the fathers with pious zeal. In no other New England state did the ruling hierarchy maintain so glacial a grip on society. The Revolution of '76 had only ruffled the surface of Connecticut life; it left the social structure quite unchanged. The church retained its unquestioned control of the machinery of the commonwealth; and the church was dominated by a clerical aristocracy, hand in glove with a mercantile aristocracy. The Connecticut yeomanry was extraordinarily docile, content to follow its traditional leaders with implicit faith in their godliness. Those leaders would have been scarcely human if they had not come to regard authority as an inalienable prerogative of their caste, and office-holding as a natural right. To seek to turn a gentleman out of a place to which he had once been chosen, was reckoned by them wickedly Jacobinical. A small interlocking directorate controlled religion, business, and politics. Church, state, and trade were managed by the same little group to the common end of keeping all poachers off their preserves. If politics centered about the church it was because the church was the particular guardian of politics. In self-defense "her preachers were politicians and her politicians preachers," to quote a recent historian [Purcell, *Connecticut in Transition*]. So narrowly oligarchical was the domination of this clerical-mercantile group of politicians, that a contemporary Republican described Connecticut as an "elective despotism or rather elective aristocracy"—a domination that was never seriously threatened till the revolution of 1818 finally unseated the old order. Other commonwealths might yield to the blandishments of the Jacobins, but so long as Timothy Dwight and Governor Trumbull lived Connecticut would keep to her ancient ways.

It was her aloofness more than anything else that held the little commonwealth back from the plunge into the maelstrom of nineteenth century change. Few immigrants came bringing different ideals; the yeomanry followed a familiar round of life; currents of thought that were stirring the pulpits of eastern Massachusetts—suggestions of Arianism that was to be the forerunner of a Unitarian movement destined to create a schism in the traditional church order—did not reach so far as New Haven, and the intellectual life of Connecticut was undisturbed by the inchoate liberalisms of pre-Revolutionary days. Year after year her brightest young men went up to Yale to be trained in the orthodox Calvinism, and departed thence to re-thresh the old straw in every steepled meeting-house in the commonwealth. Yale College was a very citadel of political and theological orthodoxy. It had been founded by devout Calvinists to offset the supposed defection of Harvard, and in the intervening years it had stood loyally to its purpose. No doubt Yale undergraduates were not always models of Calvinistic propriety—as Trumbull plainly suggests in *The Progress of Dulness;* certainly during the early days of the French Revolution many of them were polluted by French atheism; but with the coming of Timothy Dwight to the presidency, all such uncleanness was swept away, and Yale dutifully turned to the pious work of preserving the commonwealth from all democratic innovation. The clergy who gathered for Commencement welcomed the young recruits to their ranks, impressing upon them the sacredness of the existing order with which their lives were to be linked, and dilating upon the social responsibility devolving on the holder of a Yale degree. If every Yale graduate were not a sound Calvinist and a sound Federalist it was no fault of a school that removed an instructor for espousing the Republican faith.

The daily round of life in Connecticut centered in the church to a degree that a later generation has difficulty in comprehending. Society was strait-laced in rigid dogma, and because that dogma was built about the core of total depravity, it imparted a peculiarly unfortunate bias to everyday thought. It is unnecessary here to discuss the familiar five points of Calvinism, but the intimate relations between those doctrines and the social and political faith of Connecticut require a measure of consideration. The Wits were stanch old-school Calvinists, and the robust prejudices that impart to their pronouncement a more than Johnsonian dogmatism, were the sour fruit of their religious faith. It is too often overlooked that historically and practically the doctrine of total depravity, in its larger implications, was quite as much social and political as theological; that it emerged originally as a by-product of social caste and carries in its face the mark of aristocracy; and that it has everywhere been pressed into the service of social inequality. Endowed with high theological sanction, pronounced by the church to be the inscrutable decree of God, it is perhaps the most pernicious doctrine that western civilization has ever given birth to. But pernicious as it is, carrying over into eternity the caste divisions of temporal orders, it has proved too convenient a doctrine to be lightly surrendered by those who find it useful. It wove itself through the entire fabric of social thought in old Connecticut. It provided an authoritative foundation for Connecticut Federalism. In the eyes of men like Timothy Dwight it sufficed to disprove the validity of all democratic aspiration. If the mass of men were outcasts from God—as the doctrine assumed—if they had no title or interest in the prerogatives of the elect, it was a presumption little short of blasphemous to assert that they were competent to manage the temporal affairs of society. Surely it was never intended by the divine wisdom that the sons of Adam should rule the children of God, that the powers of darkness should legislate for the lovers of light. In the background of Calvinistic thought the assumption persisted that the Saints are God's delegated policemen on whom devolves the responsibility of keeping order amongst the sinners. The politician seeking the votes of sinners would not, of course, put it so bluntly; but the doctrine was there implicitly, providing a high sanction for the major premises of New England Federalism. It was this translation into political terms of a decadent dogma that the democratic doctrine of natural rights ran full against in its slow progress through New England. It colored the thinking of

the upper class, provided a useful sanction for their strict censorship of society, authorized their rigid monopoly of all political power. It is not easy to understand high Federalists like Jedidiah Morse, who taught the youth of New England in his *Geography* that the clergy was an autocratic balance against democracy, unless they are set against the background of such obsolete dogma.

A special and particular justification of the doctrine, in the opinion of New England conservatives, was provided in the disturbant spread of populistic heresies. The years following the peace of 'eighty-three were an unhappy period for a New England sadly confused by its Shays' Rebellion and its New Hampshire and Rhode Island agrarianism. A motley brood of war chickens were coming home to roost, and there was much unseemly clamor in the New England farmyard. Respectable fowls of the old breed resented the scrambling of newcomers for the best perches, and the nondescript loudly demanded what liberty meant if they were still to have no place to roost. In the opinion of honest gentlemen government was becoming mob-ridden and populistic legislatures were officially profaning the sacred principle that the political state should function in the interests of the well-to-do. Naturally they began to inquire into the causes of such untoward happenings, and took counsel with each other how best to prevent any such in the future. It was quickly agreed that democracy was the mother of the mischief abroad in the land, and that if the ancient virtues of New England were not to go down before the mob, gentlemen must reassert the authority of their traditional stewardship. On them rested the responsibility of saving society from anarchy.

It was from the passions let loose by the profound social readjustments then going forward, that New England Federalism was born, of which the Connecticut Wits were such stalwart exemplars. It was the political philosophy of the Puritan-Yankee, and its principles were derived from the dogmas of Calvinism and the needs of mercantilism. In its beginnings it was a reaction from agrarianism. It had first taken coherence from the menace of Shays' Rebellion, but it was enormously strengthened by the later spread of French Revolutionary doctrines. The appearance of Jacobinism in America put all respectable New England in a panic, and the virulence of dislike increased with the rise of the Democratic Societies. The doctrine of equalitarianism was a stench in the nostrils of all who loved the aristocratic ways of an earlier America, and they watched with growing concern the flocking to New England of old-world enthusiasts for liberty who threw in their lot with the disaffected amongst the native yeomanry. The Irish seem to have been the most offensive equalitarians. A New England gentleman, traveling in Pennsylvania in the 'nineties, wrote home: "I have seen many, very many, Irishmen, and with a few exceptions, they are . . . the most God-provoking Democrats on this side of Hell." And in 1798 Harrison Gray Otis, the Federalist boss, wrote: "If some means are not adopted to prevent the indiscriminate admission of wild Irishmen & others to the right of suffrage, there will soon be an end to liberty & property." To prevent, if possible, such an unhappy outcome, the upper classes of New England fell to drilling and organizing all the elements of conservatism for the purpose of a common defense. They wrote and spoke and preached, till the mind of respectable New England was saturated with prejudice. It was a golden age of propaganda. The democratic principle was converted into a bogy to frighten the simple. Such a hideous misshapen imp of darkness, such a vile hag of anarchy had never before been painted for the imagination of honest Yankees to shudder at; and if democracy seemed to them a wild and fearsome thing making ready to destroy their ancient social order, they only believed what the minister preached on the sabbath and the squire asserted on week-days. What headway could the plebeian democrat, very likely in debt, hope to make against the organized respectability of society! He was overwhelmed by a combined *odium theologicum et politicum.*

II

This well-bred composite of old prejudice and present interest, this close alliance of Calvinistic dogma and mercantile profits, provides the background against which the Connecticut Wits must be placed. They were stalwart Federalists of the common New England school, and of this dignified Federalism John Adams was the philosopher, Fisher Ames the orator and pamphleteer, and Timothy Pickering the practical politician. Meticulous in dress, careful to appear well in public, professing to be the special custodian of every public and private virtue, it presented to a credulous constituency the similitude of an angel of light warring against the ancient powers of darkness. It was as the sword of Gideon to smite the Philistines. But for the comprehension of a more sophisticated generation it may be designated as the tie-wig school of American politics. The phrase sufficiently suggests its aristocratic antecedents. It was the party of the gentry. It was the last marshaling of the eighteenth century against the gathering forces of revolution, a stubborn attempt to bind changing conditions upon an earlier experience, a final effort to retain minority control of a society fast slipping from its grasp. Its affections were engaged to the past, to those static times when successive generations followed in the footsteps of the fathers, content to preserve what had hitherto existed. Aristocratic in taste, it was mercantile in its economic interests. Taking form before the rise of Lowell, industrialism changed the dominant economic interest of New England, it approved the dignified ways of legitimate trade, and disapproved the rising spirit of speculation.

The philosophy of this old-fashioned Federalism is an open book to whoever will take the trouble to turn a few pages of the yellow tracts. In part it derived from certain principles of Locke; in its major premises it was akin to English Whiggery; but its particular form was shaped by the traditional spirit of New England. As amplified in the solid works of John Adams it rested on a few broad principles, which, in his opinion, were as demonstrable as any theorem in Euclid. As a sound eighteenth century realist he discovered the basis of all politics in economics. Natural endowment, he was fond of pointing out, divides men into classes. Since every civilization rests upon exploitation, the strong and capable will rise to power on the backs of the weak, and those who have gained control of the eco-

nomics of society will in the very nature of things rule society. The principle of aristocracy, hence, is implanted in the constitution of man, and to assume the principle of equality is to fly in the face of nature. From this universal fact of natural social classes arises the perennial problem of government, which is to secure order and justice in a society where few are friendly to their sway. In every society a potential class war for ever impends, and when customary restraints are loosed it breaks forth to find issue either in the anarchy of the mass or in the tyranny of the despot. Thus far Adams was translating Calvinistic dogma into political terms; under the mask of natural aristocracy and the incompetency of democracy, reappear the familiar doctrines of total depravity and the remnant of the Saints. But he was far too thoughtful a student of history and too sincerely concerned for political justice, to deduce from his premises conclusions wholly congenial to New England Federalism. He refused to narrow his philosophy to serve the ends of a particular class. That work fell to the ready hands of Fisher Ames, the idol of respectable New England, the complete embodiment of the prejudices of the tie-wig school. What particular twist Fisher Ames gave to the current philosophy, and from what sources he drew those asperities of conviction that edged his political views, are peculiarly suggestive to one who would understand the acrid dogmatisms of Theodore and Timothy Dwight or the acerbities of Dr. Lemuel Hopkins.

A caustic little gentleman suffering from an aggravated case of the political spleen, was this orator and pamphleteer who won such great renown among his fellow Yankees. Vivacious and intolerant, he nodded his tie-wig dogmatically and pronounced his opinions oracularly. A confirmed realist, he walked the streets of Boston a visible embodiment of a century that was passing. He relished his ample store of prejudices and prided himself on the skill with which he set them forth. If he was not the repository of all political wisdom that he believed himself to be, he could at least give a reason for the faith that was in him. His political philosophy, the sufficiency of which he never doubted, was an amalgam of Puritanism and economics, an ethical adaptation of the stake-in-society principle that conferred a special sanction on the rule of the squirarchy. In the primitive Calvinist-Yankee world, it must be remembered, such political theory as developed was shaped by the theocratic conception of stewardship, by which was meant an authoritative leadership reposing in the best and the wisest, serving the divine purpose and subject to the will of God as revealed in the Bible. Minister and magistrate, in consequence, professed to justify their acts, not by expediency or temporal interest, but by absolute ethical standards. The will of God was acknowledged to be the single source of law. Of that perfect law the minister was the expositor and the magistrate the executive. In the theocracy there was no place for the conception of democracy; the will of the majority was unrecognized; government was simplified to the narrow routine of adjudicating causes in accordance with the divine decrees. But unhappily the business of stewardship proved to be as tempting there as elsewhere. The interests of the steward too often confused themselves with God's, and as the Saints prospered they more and more confounded ethical and economic values, until the primitive doctrine of the stewardship slid over into the later doctrine of the stake-in-society. The sacred rights of property came to be the final objective of law and order, and government was looked upon as an agency to serve the interests of the dominant class.

Of this school of Puritan-Yankee theory Fisher Ames was a convinced disciple. Instinctively aristocratic, a lawyer with a narrow legalistic mind, he interpreted justice in terms of the common law of contract, and stewardship as the prerogative of the well-to-do to police society. The political state he regarded as the particular guardian of vested interests. "But the essence, and almost the quintessence, of good government is," he argued, "to protect property and its rights. When these are protected, there is scarcely any booty left for oppression to seize; the objects and motives to usurpation and tyranny are removed. By securing property, life and liberty can scarcely fail of being secured; where property is safe by rules and principles, there is liberty." In every society, he believed, the persistent enemy of property are the propertyless. The major business of government becomes, therefore, the problem of keeping in due subjection to law and order the dangerous mass of the poor and vicious. That the poor in the main are vicious, and the vicious poor, he accepted as social axioms. Hence followed two major principles that he regarded as fundamental in any rational political theory: that government must be energetic to inspire fear in its subjects; that it must be strong to hold in subjection the unruly. The principle of coercive sovereignty he advocated as vehemently as Hamilton. In the doctrine of good will he put no faith. "Government does not subsist by making proselytes to sound reason, or by compromise and arbitration with its members; but by the power of the community compelling the obedience of individuals. If that is not done, who will seek its protection, or fear its vengeance?"

Since in every society it is the improvident mass that is dangerous to the established order, the folly of the democratic principle seemed to him too patent to be worthy of serious consideration. All about him he discovered a selfish and licentious multitude unfriendly to justice, to that sober restraint and respect for rights necessary to a well-ordered society. To permit sovereign power to fall into such hands was to invite anarchy. The mortal disease of all democracies he discovered in their immorality. That the wicked will rule wickedly, seemed to him as plain as way to parish church. A democracy, he used to assert, sooner or later will make every people "thoroughly licentious and corrupt." "The known propensity of a democracy is to licentiousness, which the ambitious call, and the ignorant believe to be liberty." "There is universally a presumption in democracy that promises everything; and at the same time an imbecility that can accomplish nothing, not even preserve itself." The sole security of society he discovered in the wisdom and firmness of the minority; and that minority, in the nature of things, must be the minority of the wealthy. The rich alone may permit themselves the luxury of disinterestedness. The propertied classes alone enjoy the leisure that is prerequisite to culture. Weighted with responsibility, they alone may be trusted to act as just stewards of society. To preserve New England, gravely threatened by demagogues like Daniel Shays—"bankrupts and sots, who have gambled or slept

away their estates"—to prevent the devastating incursions of democracy, to assure the wise rule of a responsible minority, became therefore the master passion of Fisher Ames's life, to which he devoted himself with ever diminishing faith in the honesty of his fellow men. With all the intensity of his nature he hated Jefferson and Madison, "those apostles of the race-track and the cock-pit," and the French romantic philosophy they did so much to spread. But though black pessimism grew upon him in his later years, he discovered certain crumbs of comfort in his own virtue and the virtue of that Federalistic remnant that might even yet save Israel from the democratic despoilers. An unreconstructed Tory of a passing age, he was the most distinguished representative of the tie-wig school of political realism.

III

Of this virtuous remnant the Connecticut Wits were self-confessed exemplars. They were apostles of culture and patriotism to a people in grave danger of being seduced by strange gods. As they looked affectionately upon the pleasant little commonwealth of Connecticut, they feared for the future of this "model of free states." Agrarian dangers threatened from beyond the borders, and within matters were not going well. Her best sons were being drained off by the western frontier; her stagnant agriculture was proving inadequate to the economic needs of the people; a new capitalism was emerging with the development of banking and insurance; shipping and industrialism were making headway, and the towns were growing at the expense of the country. In short Connecticut was at the beginning of profound economic changes that in the next generation were to produce a political revolution. As the members of the little group contemplated these impending changes they were filled with concern. Their loyalties and their interests alike held them to the old order, so far as Connecticut was concerned, but their patriotism went out to the new venture in nationalism. Narrowly provincial in their local affections, they loved to envisage a glorious future for the emancipated states. A fervid patriotism runs through much of their work. The tremendous stir that came with the close of the Revolutionary War touched all the fields of polite culture, and summoned the Wits to activity. The duty of nationalism had been suddenly laid upon the conscience of thoughtful men. It was time for a free people to rid themselves of their colonial subservience to old-world culture. All things were being new-made, why not letters? To throw off the incubus of the past, and create a national literature, dedicated to the new America that was rising, seemed to many a patriotic duty. In this pressing work men wholly diverse in political sympathies joined heartily. The arch conservative, Noah Webster, devoted his life to differentiating the language of independent America from that of monarchical England; and Philip Freneau paused in his labors of berating the Federalists, to lament the intellectual subservience of America to old-world scholarship, as evidenced by its proneness to import British school-masters. The result was a premature attempt to write a declaration of intellectual independence, the youthful beginning of a long endeavor that needed more than a hundred years to accomplish.

Yet by a curious turn of the tide the work of emancipation was stopped almost before it was well begun. The extraordinary rise of French liberalism, with the resultant breakup of old orders, produced a panic amongst the cultivated classes of New England, and the imperialistic career of Napoleon threw them back into the arms of England. The earlier patriotism of revolution that was eager to make over all things, gave way to the patriotism of conservatism that desired nothing changed. The term "innovation" came to assume a sinister meaning in respectable ears. "A change, though for the better, is always to be deplored by the generation in which it is effected," asserted Fisher Ames. "Much is lost and more is hazarded." The disintegrating triumphs of political romanticism brought under a cloud the ideals of literary romanticism, and with the resurgence of the conservative spirit literature turned back to earlier models, with the consequent strengthening of the decadent Wit ideal. The romantic school discovered no followers in New England till the War of 1812 dissipated the dun twilight of the old and brought a new century to Boston. Between the years 1807 and 1812, marked by Bryant's *The Embargo* and *Lines to a Waterfowl,* occurred the great transition from the old century to the new, from the Wit ideal to the romantic.

The beginnings of the literary movement that produced the work of the Connecticut group, perhaps are to be found in the quickening interest in polite letters at Yale College in the late 'sixties. When Trumbull and Dwight became tutors there, they joined in the attempt then under way to revive a dead curriculum by the introduction of contemporary English literature, and they exemplified their creative interest by producing original work, Trumbull contributing *The Progress of Dulness* and Dwight *The Conquest of Canaan.* The literary fashion thus introduced was late Augustan, dominated by Goldsmith and Churchill, but supplemented by Pope and Thomson of an earlier generation. The work was consciously imitative. The immediate influence of Goldsmith and Denham on Dwight's *Greenfield Hill* is so evident as scarcely to need comment; *The Deserted Village* and *Cooper's Hill* suggested the theme and indicated the method of treatment. When they essayed greater originality, as became free poets of a republic, their work was likely to issue in a dubious exploitation of biblical themes or in an exuberant patriotism. *The Conquest of Canaan* and *The Vision of Columbus* are representative of the impulses that swayed the minds of the young Wits before the rise of domestic revolution threatened the permanence of the traditional Connecticut order.

But only a portion of the work of the "Wits," after all, was primarily literary. The times soon became too exigent for belletristic philandering, and with the demands of partisanship laid upon them they dedicated their pens to successive causes. The war first summoned them, then the contest with populism, then the cause of the federal union, and finally the acrimonious struggle against French romantic philosophies and the party of Jefferson. Their verse became increasingly militant, and the note of satire rose above the occasional bucolic strains. For the serious business of poetic warfare they sought inspiration from Churchill and the contemporary English satirists. The long party struggle between Whig and Tory in England, and the later contest between Toryism and Jacobinism, produced an abundant crop of scurrilous satire that debased the tone of English letters for half a century. Pope's mean and vindictive *Dunciad* and Butler's *Hudibras*—jaunty octosyllabics providing a brisk variation from the barbed pentameters—had shown that satire could be as useful to a gentleman as the small sword, and the literary dueling of rival partisans went on briskly. In this warfare of the English poetasters the American Wits found their weapons provided for them, and they hastened to follow the overseas example. They seized eagerly upon such works as the *Rolliad,* a contemporary English satire written by bright young politicians in defense of Fox and Sheridan, as suggestive models. They sharpened their quills to a needle point, dipped them in bitter ink, and pricked their opponents as mercilessly as English gentlemen were doing. It is not pleasant writing, much of it is ill done, it runs the scale from crude burlesque to downright blackguardry; but it suggests, as the soberer prose of the times does not, the raw nerves of a generation trying to stave off a rout. To ignore such a work as *The Anarchiad,* on the ground that it is very bad poetry, is to miss what is perhaps the most significant phase of their contribution to a generation perplexed by rival counselors.

The membership of the group was a bit elastic, additions and withdrawals changing the personnel as the years passed. The more important members were John Trumbull, Timothy Dwight, Joel Barlow, Lemuel Hopkins, David Humphreys, Richard Alsop, and Theodore Dwight. To these are frequently added the names of Dr. Elihu Hubbard Smith and Dr. Mason F. Cogswell, who were rather friends than active collaborators. Of the entire group Trumbull was perhaps the most gifted, Barlow the most original, and Timothy Dwight the most prolific. None to be sure loved the pruning knife, and none stinted the ready flow of his verse; yet the indefatigable Timothy managed to outrun the rest. They were all pretty much of an age. The oldest were Trumbull and Dr. Hopkins, both born in 1750; Timothy Dwight and Colonel Humphreys were two years younger; Barlow was born in 1754, Alsop in 1761, and Theodore Dwight, the baby of the group, was born in 1764 and survived till 1846. Collectively they were fairly representative of the oligarchical upper class of the provincial Connecticut society. Timothy Dwight, grandson of Jonathan Edwards, was a minister and president of Yale; Hopkins, Smith, and Cogswell were physicians of high standing, Trumbull and Theodore Dwight were lawyers, Barlow and Humphreys found their way into the diplomatic field, and Alsop was a merchant. They were all comfortably well off and several were wealthy. Alsop was one of the few millionaires of the time; Barlow acquired a fortune in France; and Humphreys late in life established a textile industry incorporated for half a million.

Although their literary work reveals little individual differentiation, they were men of notable ability and striking individuality, who would have made themselves felt in any community. The lesser members were quite as interesting as the major. The caustic tongue of Hopkins and the genial ways of Alsop were as individual as the distinguished manners of Colonel Humphreys, or the brilliant acerbity of Theodore Dwight. Perhaps the most attractive of the entire group was David Humphreys, son of a clergyman of Derby, Connecticut, and personal aide to Washington, whose Yankee provincialisms were worn away by much travel and familiar intercourse with distinguished men in Europe and America. That he was an unusually likable man, as well as capable, is suggested by his extraordinary advancement and the warm affection felt for him by those high in position, as well as by the plump face and easy tie-wig that appear in his portrait. Upwards of fourteen years he spent abroad. His friendships were many and his polished manners seem to have won all hearts. His love of country was great and constant, and his disinterested endeavors to further the well-being of America were widely recognized. He entered Yale in 1767, where he fell in with Trumbull and Dwight. In 1775 at the age of twenty-three he joined the army with the rank of captain. Three years later he was assigned to the staff of General Putnam with the rank of major, and in 1780 he joined Washington's staff with the rank of colonel. He is said to have distinguished himself at the siege of Yorktown and was voted a sword by Congress for gallantry; but as such rewards were commonly political, the distinction must not be taken too seriously. After the peace he went to Paris as Secretary to the Legation under Franklin and Adams, but returned to Hartford on the eve of the outbreak of Shays' Rebellion. He was appointed to the command of a regiment of Western Reserves—raised under authority of Congress to put down domestic disturbances; but on the suppression of the revolt he went to Mount Vernon and remained there for upwards of a year, acting as Washington's aide on the trip to New York where the new President took the oath of office. From 1791 to 1802 he was minister to Lisbon and Madrid, where through the skillful agency of Barlow he secured a treaty with the Barbary states for the release of American captives. In 1795 he married an Englishwoman of considerable fortune. He was elected a fellow of the Royal Society of London, was on intimate terms with the Duc de La Rochefoucauld-Liancourt in France, and when he returned to America soon after the accession of Jefferson, he was one of the distinguished men of his generation of Americans.

The Connecticut to which he returned in 1802 was in the midst of a far-reaching revolution that was silently transforming the traditional order of life. Banking, insurance, and shipping were going forward amazingly, but agriculture was stagnant, the domestic economy prevailed on the farms, there was no important staple for export, and industrialism was in its infancy. It was to a situation becoming acute that Humphreys brought his old-world observations, and the solution on which he settled assumed the double form of improving agricultural methods and encouraging the production of a staple for manufacturing purposes. While at Madrid he had interested himself in the quality of wool grown by the Merino sheep. The Spanish jealously guarded their flocks against export, but on his quitting his post he was permitted, in lieu of the usual gift to departing ministers, to ship one hundred head to his estate in Connecticut. He at once engaged in the business of breeding, and set on foot a movement to educate the Connecticut farmers in wool growing. He established looms to weave a fine woolen cloth, and when Madison took the

oath of office in 1809 he was dressed in a suit of domestic goods, the coat of which was provided by Colonel Humphreys. Entering upon the work as an experiment, he expanded the industry till in 1810 the Humphreysville Manufacturing Company was chartered, with a capital stock of $500,000. But his major interest, as was natural to an eighteenth century squire, lay in agriculture. He turned his farm into an experiment station and in 1817 he founded the Connecticut Agricultural Society.

To further the cause in which he was embarked Humphreys frequently impressed his pen into service. While in Europe he had often meditated on the beneficent effects of sober habits of industry, and in particular how such industry must assure an expanding well-being in America with its vast potential resources. To inculcate this spirit he had written several didactic poems—*On the Happiness of America,* and *On the Future Glory of the United States of America*; but the completest expression of the ideal to which his later years were devoted is given in a poem *On the Industry of the United States of America,* which provides an excellent summary of his social and economic views. As literature it is scarcely notable, but as a document of the times it deserves recalling. An honest and capable man was Colonel David Humphreys—what we should call today a public-spirited citizen, devoted to republican freedom and concerned for the well-being of his fellow Americans. Although he was one of the first Yankee industrialists to popularize the philosophy of industrialism, he remained at heart a son of that older world that honored agriculture above all other callings.

Dr. Lemuel Hopkins, son of a Waterbury farmer, was the most picturesque member of the group, the most characteristically Yankee. Brought up at the plow tail, he received nevertheless an excellent education, and because of a hereditary predisposition to consumption turned to the medical profession. After serving his apprenticeship with a physician at Wallingford he entered upon his practice at Litchfield in 1776. During the Revolution he served for a short time as a volunteer, but soon returned to his lancet and medicine case. In 1784 he removed to Hartford to spend the remainder of his life there as physician and man of letters. In person he was tall, lean, stooping, rawboned, with coarse features and large brilliant eyes. His uncouth appearance and eccentricity of manner made him a striking figure, and his caustic wit made him a redoubtable antagonist. His memory was a marvel to his friends. "He could quote verbatim," writes Kettell, "every writer, medical and literary, that he had ever read." As a physician he stood at the head of the Connecticut profession, both in reputation and in skill. He was one of the founders of the Medical Society of Connecticut, and as a frequent contributor to medical literature he exerted a wide influence on the current practice.

The eccentric Doctor seems to have been as honest as he was outspoken. He was uncompromising in his warfare on all quacks, both medical and political. For a time as a young man he was a disciple of French infidel philosophy, but he cured his mental indisposition by a severe biblical regimen, and having restored himself to the robust health of Calvinistic Christianity, he devoted himself to the work of curing others. He became in consequence a specialist in the treatment of the *Bacillus gallicus*. Kettell is authority for a story that reminds one of his *Epitaph on a Patient Killed by a Cancer Quack*. Calling one day with Dr. Cogswell on a patient in the last stages of consumption, he was shown a packet of "fever powders" reputed to be of marvelous curative potency, got from a well known local quack. "How administered?" the Doctor asked the nurse. "In molasses," she replied. Some molasses was brought and Hopkins took an entire paper of the powders, stirred it in a cup, and disregarding the protestations of the nurse, drank off the whole. Turning to Cogswell, he remarked: "I am going to Coventry today. If I die from this, write on my tombstone—'Here lies Hopkins killed by Grimes.'" A man who was willing to take a chance in order to demonstrate the quackery of a peripatetic dispenser of miraculous powders would have scant respect for any sort of humbug. For all political nostrums not listed in the Federalistic materia medica, he exhibited the same brusque contempt. He would temporize with what he regarded as quackery in government no more than in medicine, and when the Rhode Island legislature passed its paper money act in 1785, and six months later Shays' Rebellion broke out, and mobs were besieging the legislature of New Hampshire, he proposed to speak plainly to the good people of Connecticut on the follies of popular delusions. This would seem to have been the origin of *The Anarchiad*, the most celebrated political satire of the times. It sprang from the indignation of Dr. Hopkins, when, to quote from the poem,

> In visions fair, the scenes of fate unroll,
> And Massachusetts opens on my soul.
> There Chaos, Anarch old, asserts his sway,
> And mobs in myriads blacken all the way.

That Hopkins was chiefly responsible for *The Anarchiad* may be regarded as fairly certain, and that he contributed its most caustic portions may be accepted likewise. Kettell specifically attributed to him the portion entitled "A Plea for Union and the Constitution." The sardonic temper of the Doctor fitted him for virulent satire, and in this bitterest of the productions of the Wits the reins were on the neck of his muse. Some hand he had also in the writing of *The Echo*, but his chief contributions are believed to have taken the form of suggestions which Alsop put into verse. Other works in which he is supposed to have had a share were: *The Political Greenhouse*, done in collaboration with Alsop and Theodore Dwight—Hopkins' contributions being the passages on Tom Thumb and the arrival of Genet; *The Democratiad*, a personal and political satire written for the Philadelphia Jockey Club; and *The Guillotina, or a Democratic Dirge*, written for the *Hartford Courant* as a New Year's offering and printed January 1, 1796. Three other satires attributed to him are: *The Hypocrite's Hope, The Epitaph on a Patient Killed by a Cancer Quack*, and *Verses on General Ethan Allen*. That he had a knack at trenchant satire is sufficiently evident; and that he loved to impale a pretender with a poisoned epithet—that he could not resist the temptation to stick a pin in any bladder he met with, would argue that Dr. Lemuel Hopkins was a man who loved to speak his mind.

To recover the authentic lineaments of Richard Alsop

from the faded records, is no easy task. The years have almost wholly obscured a fame that in his lifetime was as bright as a May day, with the poetic fields all abloom. A pleasant-mannered, agreeable gentleman, he seems to have been; with the exception of Trumbull perhaps the wittiest if not the cleverest of the group. He was born in Middletown, where his father, a prosperous merchant in New York, and for five years a member of the Continental Congress, had been born before him, and whither the latter removed upon the occupation of New York City by the British forces. He attended Yale for a time but did not take his degree, having been withdrawn by his father to be bred up in the mercantile business. This was the golden age of Connecticut shipping, and his ventures proved unusually successful. From the coastwise and West Indian traffic he amassed a great fortune. All his life he seems to have been a bookish man. To an excellent knowledge of the classics he added a generous acquaintance with English literature, and he even carried his studies into continental fields, French, Italian and Spanish, extending them so far as to embrace the Scandinavian literatures. A pronounced leaning towards the new gothic spirit that was undermining the Wit ideal in England, is revealed in his translations from *Ossian* and his fondness for the *Eddas*. Pale and exotic as such work might be, it sets him apart from the other members of the group, allying him with certain of the minor Philadelphia poets who followed the gothic fashion more closely. His genial temperament made him a general favorite, and his ample means afforded him abundant leisure. He was warm-hearted, simple and unaffected in manners. His lively imagination and playful humor made him an excellent companion; and his inexhaustible enthusiasm for poetic composition thrust him into every undertaking of the group. The collective reputation of the Wits seems to have owed much to the pen of Alsop. He died at Flatbush, Long Island, in 1815.

His writings have never been collected and much remains unprinted. He was distinctly an amateur in letters and turned to whatever theme caught his fancy. He was an incorrigible imitator of late eighteenth century English modes, and his most ambitious poem, *The Charm of Fancy*—a philosophical work in four cantos, only a fragment of which has been printed—is an echo of Akenside's *Pleasures of the Imagination*. Other ambitious attempts were a versification of Ossian, Habakkuk, and *The Twilight of the Gods*. Like every other poetaster of the times he lamented the death of the first President, his contribution taking the form of a *Monody on the Death of George Washington*. Later he translated from the Italian *The Natural and Civil History of Chili*, and just before his death he edited *The Captivity and Adventures of J. R. Jewett Among the Savages of Nootka Sound*. His most interesting work lay in the field of satire. In collaboration with Theodore Dwight he conceived *The Echo* and wrote considerable portions, in particular Number IX, Governor Hancock's Message on Stage Plays, and Number XX, Jefferson's Inaugural. The playful note of *The Echo*, that sets it sharply apart from the bitter *Anarchiad*, was attributed at the time to Alsop, and the genial burlesques of current provincialisms remain his most important contribution to the verse of New England. It was started to amuse the members of a club at Middletown, and was printed in the

American Mercury. Cogswell, Smith, and Hopkins had a hand in its composition, but to Alsop and Dwight belongs the major credit.

In his own time Theodore Dwight, lawyer, editor, politician, and poetaster, was one of the most noted of the Wits; but the years have proved ungrateful, and his personality has become as dim as Alsop's. More deeply immersed in practical politics than any other member of the group, he was perhaps the most vehemently Federalistic—if shades may be discerned where all were dipped in the same strong dye. He was born at Northampton, Massachusetts, and took his degree at Yale. A cousin of Timothy Dwight, he studied law in the office of another kinsman, Judge Pierrepont Edwards, an eminent lawyer, high in the ruling aristocracy of Connecticut. From his tutor he seems to have learned little of that political liberalism that afterwards made Edwards the leader of the Connecticut Jeffersonians. He practiced his profession for a time at Hartford, later removing to New York to become a partner in the office of his cousin Aaron Burr; but dissenting from Burr's political opinions, he returned to Hartford. He served in Congress for a year, where he ventured into combat with John Randolph of Roanoke. In after years he devoted much time to newspaper work. In 1810 he founded *The Connecticut Mirror,* later removed to Albany to edit *The Daily Advertiser,* and in 1829 he went to New York City as editor of *The Daily Advertiser* of that place.

Better perhaps than any other member of the group he reveals the close interrelation in Connecticut of religion, politics, and business. He was a director of the Connecticut Bible Society—a religious political organization, the lay trustees of which, according to Purcell, were "Federalist bosses," and which was generally accounted by the opposition as being under clerical control. With his cousin Timothy he was a director of the Eagle Bank, a strong Federalist institution, and was bitterly opposed to the chartering of rival Republican banks. When the Phoenix Bank, a Republican-Episcopalian institution, applied to the legislature for a charter, he denounced it as "the child of intrigue and the mother of Discord." The new banking power was too useful to the ruling Congregational-Federalist party, to be suffered to pass into the hands of the disaffected. Politically Dwight seems to have been under the influence of Fisher Ames, Timothy Pickering, and Harrison Gray Otis. He served as secretary to the Hartford Convention, and later as its historian, publishing its *Journal* in 1833 with a defense of the movement. He was appealed to by Ames to introduce *The Boston Palladium*—the organ of high Federalism in Massachusetts—amongst "the clergy and good men" of Connecticut. He defended the preaching of politics in the pulpit as an excellent means of thwarting the democratic partisans who were seeking to "discredit the ministry, decry religion, and destroy public worship." Democracy was anathema to him, and he agreed with Otis that something must be done to stem the tide of old-world democrats who threatened to submerge the familiar landmarks of New England. Commenting on the spread of republicanism, he attributed to it the decay of religion and morality, and the impending break-up of family ties, exclaiming with somewhat extreme vivacity: "The outlaws of Europe, the fugi-

tives from the pillory, and the gallows, have undertaken to assist our own abandoned citizens, in the pleasing work of destroying Connecticut . . . Can imagination paint anything more dreadful on this side of hell?"

Dwight is reputed to have been a brilliant debater, and his political writings are crisp and vigorous. His chief contributions to the work of the Wits are to be found in *The Echo* and *The Political Greenhouse.* The more biting pieces in the former are generally attributed to him. In the use of Hudibrastic verse he was probably the cleverest of the group if we except Trumbull; his sharp and bitter nature seeming to enjoy inflicting pin-pricks on his enemies. Of high personal integrity he permitted himself an occasional indulgence in humanitarianism, and like his cousin Timothy he was an outspoken opponent of slavery. Yet after all Theodore Dwight was not an important man in spite of his heritage of Edwards blood. The liberalism of his grandfather seems not to have descended to him, for he lived and died an acidulous upholder of the old order, the last of the tie-wig school of Federalists.

IV

Remain for brief comment the three members of the group whose reputations still exhibit some evidences of vitality. . . . The lesser men have survived collectively, in those collaborations that comment pungently on the ways of the hour. Suggestive as such comments are to the historian, they do not rank high in a history of American *belles-lettres,* and the several individualities of the contributors are so merged that the critic finds difficulty in separating the whole into its parts. But Trumbull, Dwight, and Barlow may be accounted authentic men of letters, whose work is individual enough to be of some little importance in the development of our early literature. The striking variation of the Yankee character, as revealed in the scholarly Trumbull, the vigorously dogmatic Dwight, and the rebelliously energetic Barlow, is an interesting commentary on the fertility of that old New England in breeding men of diverse capacities.

There was the best of Yankee blood in the veins of John Trumbull. Among his kinsmen were the Reverend Benjamin Trumbull, historian of Connecticut, Governor Jonathan Trumbull—Washington's Brother Jonathan—and John Trumbull the painter. On his mother's side he was descended from the vigorous Solomon Stoddard, grandfather of Jonathan Edwards. His father was a scholarly minister, long a trustee of Yale College, at which school the son spent seven years as undergraduate and tutor. He was a precocious youth with a strong love of polite letters, and a praiseworthy desire to achieve literary distinction. Greek and Latin were the toys of his childhood and when he was seven years of age he passed the entrance examination to college. During the period of his tutorship he joined with Dwight and Joseph Howe in the work of overhauling the curriculum, supplementing Lilly's Grammar and Calvin with Pope and Churchill. Like other aspiring youths of the time he dabbled with Spectator papers, practiced his couplets, and eventually produced *The Progress of Dulness,* the cleverest bit of academic verse till then produced in America. At heart Trumbull was thoroughly academic, and nothing would have suited his temperament better than the life of a Yale professor; but the prospects seeming unfavorable, he began to mingle Blackstone with the poets in preparation for his future profession.

He was thus engaged during the middle years of the long dispute with England, the bitter wranglings of which seem not to have penetrated his quiet retreat. But in 1773 he resigned his tutorship to prepare himself further in the law. Removing to Boston he entered the office of John Adams, then rising to prominence as a spokesman of the popular party; and he took lodgings in the house of Caleb Cushing, Speaker of the Massachusetts Assembly. Placed thus at the storm center of provincial politics, he was soon infected with the common dissatisfaction with ministerial policies, and joined himself to the patriotic party. When Adams went to Philadelphia to sit in the Congress, Trumbull withdrew to Hartford, where he established himself. Before quitting Boston he published an *Elegy on the Times,* a political tract that seemed to Adams so useful to the cause that he marked the young poet for future service, and the year following he encouraged the writing of *M'Fingal,* the first part of which appeared in 1775. So great was the prestige that followed its appearance that Trumbull tinkered with it during the next seven years, publishing it finally in its completed form in 1782. The law seems to have been a jealous mistress then as now, and his dreams of further literary work were inadequately realized. He is believed to have had a hand in *The Anarchiad,* and he wrote some minor poems; but he soon drifted into politics, went on the bench, finally removed to Detroit in 1825, and died there at the home of his daughter in 1831, at the age of eighty-one. He had outlived his revolutionary generation, long outlived his literary ambitions, and was pretty much forgotten before he died. His collected works, published in 1820, proved a losing venture for the printer. America was turning romantic and few, it seems, cared to invest in two volumes of echoes.

Trumbull's reputation rests almost exclusively on *M'Fingal.* It was immensely popular in its time. More than thirty pirated editions were issued. It was broadcast by "newspapers, hawkers, pedlars, and petty chapmen," and it served its partisan purpose. The author was complimented by the Marquis de Chastellux on fulfilling all the conditions of burlesque poetry as approved since the days of Homer; but in spite of the indisputable cleverness of some of the lines, it is not a great work. In its final form it is spun out to extreme length, and pretty much swamped by the elaborate machinery on which the author visibly prided himself. Even in the thick of attack Trumbull did not forget his reading, but explains his allusions with meticulous care. He seems, indeed, rather more concerned about the laws of the mock epic than the threatened rights of America. The Scotch Tory hero is a figure so unlike the real Tory—the Olivers and Leonards and Hutchinsons, with their love of power and dignified display—that the caricature loses in effectiveness. Trumbull's patriotism was well bred and unmarked by fierce partisanship. His refined tastes ill fitted him for the turmoil of revolution. The ways of the radical were not lovely in his eyes; the Sons of Liberty with their tar and feather beds were too frequently rough fellows, and although they provided comic material to offset the blunderings of the Squire, they no

doubt seemed to him little better than tools of demagogues. Very often this tousle-headed democracy behaved like a mob, and Trumbull in his tie-wig did not approve of mobs.

The more thoughtfully one reads *M'Fingal,* throwing upon it the light of the total career of its author, the more clearly one perceives that John Trumbull was not a rebellious soul, the stuff out of which revolutionaries are made. In the year 1773, while projecting some fresh adventures in the Spectator vein, "he congratulated himself on the fact 'that the ferment of politics' was, as he supposed, 'pretty much subsided,' and that at last the country was to enjoy a 'mild interval from the struggles of patriotism and self-interest, from noise and confusion, Wilkes and liberty.' " He had then no wish for embroilment in civil war. All his life he seems to have suffered from ill health, which probably sapped his militancy and lessened his pugnacity. From this settled mood came a certain detachment that suffered his partisanship to remain cooler than the passions of the time commonly allowed. He could permit himself the luxury of a laugh at the current absurdities; and it is this light-heartedness that made *M'Fingal* so immediately effective. The rollicking burlesque of the Tory argument, the telling *reductio ad absurdum* of their logic, must have tickled the ears of every Whig and provoked many a laugh in obscure chimney-seats. Laughter is the keenest of weapons, and Trumbull's gayety must have opened weak points in the Tory armor that were proof against Freneau's animosity. It was a rare note in those acrimonious times that produced the bitter invective of Jonathan Odell, and one likes Trumbull the better for minding his manners and engaging in the duel like a gentleman. After all this son of Yale had certain characteristics of the intellectual, and if his environment had been more favorable and the law had not claimed him, if he had enjoyed the ample leisure of Alsop, very likely he would have given a better account of the talents that were certainly his. He wrote with ease if not with finish, and he possessed the requisite qualities of a man of letters. A lovable man he seems to have been, but somewhat easy-going and indolent, too easily turned from his purpose; and in consequence his later life failed to realize the expectations of his early years.

Easy-going and lovable are certainly the last adjectives one would think of applying to the massive character of Timothy Dwight—a man armed at all points and walking amongst his fellows with magnificent confidence in his powers, a scholar who put his scythe in every field of knowledge and with flail and bellows separated the clean wheat from the tares, a mighty dialectician who annihilated Hume and Shaftesbury and Voltaire before breakfast and like Hotspur could say, "Fie upon this quiet life, I want work!" A tremendous figure indeed, a great preacher, an authoritative theologian, a distinguished educator— "every inch a college president"—a helpful counselor on any knotty point be it in law or politics or finance or literature or agriculture, a born leader of men, and by way of recreation an inditer of Hebraic epics and huge didactic poems and ample Connecticut pastorals, a confirmed traveler observing the ways of New England and adjoining states and preserving his observations in solid volumes for the enlightenment of others—here was a man to compel the admiration of his fellows and put his stamp upon his age. So vast was the reputation of Timothy Dwight and so many-sided, that after all these years one hesitates to question the superiority of his qualities or insinuate a doubt as to the fineness of this nugget of New England gold.

And yet the more curiously one considers the laborious life of the great President of Yale, the more insistent become one's doubts. It would seem that he impressed his fellow citizens by the completeness with which he measured up to every Connecticut ideal. He was a walking repository of the venerable *status quo*. His commanding presence and authoritative manner, his sonorous eloquence, his forwardness in defense of what few doubted, his vehement threshing of straw long since reduced to chaff, his prodigious labors, his abundant printing, seemed to his open-mouthed contemporaries the authentic seal of greatness. In his presence none had the temerity to deny it. Yet oddly enough that greatness has not survived the ravages of time. It has bated and dwindled sadly. Even Moses Coit Tyler, kindliest and most generous of critics, cannot take the great Timothy quite seriously. The figure would seem to have been blown to excessive dimensions by his admirers. He was certainly not so great as they esteemed him. He was very much smaller indeed, almost amusingly so. Scrutinize this father in Israel closely, remove from the scale the heavy weight of contemporary eulogy, and it appears that Timothy Dwight was not a real prophet, not an authentic voice at all, but only a sonorous echo; extraordinarily lifelike, to be sure, but only an echo. There was no sap of originality in him, no creative energy, but instead the sound of voices long silent, the chatter of a theology long since disintegrating, the authority of a hierarchy already falling into decay, the tongue in short of a dead past.

The intellectual inquisitiveness that gave birth to disintegrating tendencies in the mind of his grandfather Jonathan Edwards, and that made him such a revolutionary force in his time, was wholly lacking in the grandson. Timothy Dwight refused to follow the questioning intellect into unsurveyed fields. He would not meddle with change. His mind was closed as tight as his study windows in January. He read widely in the literature of rationalism, but he read only to refute. Now and then to be sure, certain liberal promptings visited him: he spoke out against slavery; he encouraged the higher education of women. But from such temptations to become a living voice he turned away to follow the main-traveled road of Connecticut prejudice. His eyes were fixed lovingly upon the past, and his fondest dreams for New England hovered about the ideal of a godly church-state which John Cotton had labored to establish and Increase Mather to preserve. Those capable theocrats of earlier days were his spiritual brothers. Two men could scarcely be more like than Timothy Dwight and Increase Mather; their careers ran in parallel lines; each of them was the unmitered pope of his generation, and each owed his extraordinary influence to the same sterling qualities. As ecclesiastical politicians they drew no line between religious and secular affairs, but were prompt with a hand in every affair of the commonwealth. They

Richard Alsop

spoke and wrote with unquestioned authority. They regarded the minister as the responsible leader of society who must not suffer his flock to be led astray. The church was the guardian of morality and the state was its secular arm. The true faith must not be put in jeopardy by unfaith. To Timothy Dwight infidelity and republicanism went hand in hand, and to suffer the commonwealth to fall into the power of the godless meant an end to all religion and morality. To uphold the established order was for him, therefore, the first of Christian duties. A stalwart Federalist, he was a good hater of all Jacobins and a stout defender of the law and order for which he drew the plans and specifications. It was sometimes hinted that he was too much an aristocrat to feel the warmest sympathy for the unprosperous, and there seem to have been grounds for the suspicion. The unprosperous were likely to be republicans, and as he watched them being drawn off to the western frontier, he rejoiced that their voting power was no longer to be feared. Such restless spirits, he pointed out, "are impatient of the restraints of law, religion, and morality; grumble about the taxes, by which Rulers, Ministers, and Schoolmasters are supported . . . We have many troubles even now; but we should have more, if this body of foresters had remained at home." If the disaffected did not like the way the Congregational-Federalist party managed the good state of Connecticut, it were a godsend if they should remove beyond its boundaries.

But it is with the literary work of Timothy Dwight that

we are more immediately concerned, and in all his abundant output, totaling fourteen volumes and perhaps as much more in manuscript, the same solid qualities are revealed. It is the occasional work of a man wanting humor, wit, playfulness, artistry, grace, lacking subtlety and suggestiveness, but with a shrewd common sense, a great vigor, and a certain grandiose imagination. A sonorous declaimer, he dearly loved combat and the shock of marshaled argument. He was always inviting majestic effects. In *The Conquest of Canaan* he described so many thunderstorms that Trumbull suggested he ought to furnish a lightning-rod with the poem. Such a man could not move easily in narrow spaces. An epic was none too slight to contain his swelling fancies or satisfy his rhetoric; he walks with huge strides; he is prodigal of images; one canto finished, other cantos clamor to emerge upon the page. His ready versification, one often feels, runs like a water pipe with the faucet off. There is never a pause to pick or choose; his words flow in an unbroken stream from his inkwell. Yet even in his amazing copiousness there is vigor; a well-stocked mind is pouring out the gatherings of years. When he pauses to give advice—as he was fond of doing—his abundant sense is worth listening to. The homely wisdom of his talk to the farmers in the sixth part of *Greenfield Hill* is not unlike Franklin. As a satirist he belongs to the Churchill school; he is downright, abusive, often violent, quite lacking the lightness of touch and easy gayety that run so pleasantly through *M'Fingal*. His *Triumph of Infidelity* is good old-fashioned pulpit-thumping. The spirit of toleration was withheld from him by his fairy godmother, and he knows no other way of dealing with those who persist in disagreement after their mistakes have been pointed out, than the cudgel. In this tremendous poem he lays about him vigorously. On Hume and Voltaire and Priestley, and all the host of their followers, his blows fall smartly. Bloody crowns ought to be plentiful, but—though the Doctor does not seem to know it—most of the blows fall on straw men and none proves to be mortal. On the whole one prefers him in the pastoral mood when he lays aside his ministerial gown, and *Greenfield Hill*, apart from *Travels in New England and New York*, justly remains his most attractive work. But even that is sadly in need of winnowing. A great college president Timothy Dwight is conceded to have been; he was worshiped by his admirers only this side idolatry; but a great thinker, a steadfast friend of truth in whatever garb it might appear, a generous kindly soul loving even publicans and sinners, regardful of others and forgetful of self, he assuredly was not. That he could ever have been looked upon as a great poet, is a fact to be wondered at.

That he should have long associated with the Hartford Wits and collaborated with them in defense of Connecticut Federalism, must have seemed to Joel Barlow in after years the choicest bit of comedy in his varied career. His subsequent adventures led him far from the strait path of Yale orthodoxy. In those ripe later years life had pretty well emptied him of all dogmatisms and taught him the virtue of catholic sympathies. He had become acquainted with diverse philosophies and had observed the ways of alien societies, and from such contacts the horizons of his mind had broadened and his character mellowed. It was a long road that he traveled from New Haven to his Washington *salon*. Born a Connecticut Yankee, he accepted in his youth all the Connecticut conventions, and graduated from Yale with as complete an assortment of respectable opinions as his classmate Noah Webster. An energetic capable fellow, he wanted to get on in life. He wanted to be rich and famous, and he tried many roads that promised to lead to that desirable goal—law, politics, journalism, poetry, psalmody, speculation. Wanting a job he volunteered soon after graduation as chaplain in the army. He had not prepared for the ministry and while preaching somewhat indifferently to ragged soldiers he dreamed of poetic fame, and devoted more time to his couplets than to pious meditation. His abilities discovering no more congenial field for their exercise than writing poetry, he was pretty much at a stand till chance sent him abroad as agent for one of the speculative land-companies that were rising like mushrooms in America. There he found his opportunity. In France, where he established his headquarters, he entered a world of thought vastly different from that of prim little Hartford. It was an extraordinarily stimulating experience into which he threw himself with zest. Eighteen years, from 1787 to 1805, he spent abroad on that first trip, and those years changed the provincial Yankee into one of the most cosmopolitan Americans of his generation. From a member of the Hartford Wits, ardent in defense of the traditional Connecticut order, he had become a citizen of the world, outspoken in defense of the rights of man.

It was this later Barlow, completely new-outfitted by French romantic tailors, that after years remember and that early friends could not forgive. In adopting the Jacobin mode and setting himself to the serious business of thinking, he invited the severe criticism of his former associates; yet nothing in his life was more creditable or marks him more definitely as an open-minded, intelligent man. He was as receptive to new ideas as Timothy Dwight was impervious. He plunged boldly into the maelstrom of speculation then boiling in Europe. He moved in the society of the intellectuals, inquired into the latest political and social theories, turned humanitarian, re-examined his Calvinistic theology in the light of current deism, and became one of the free democratic thinkers swarming in every European capital. He was equally at home in London and Paris, passing long periods of time in both cities. An active member of the Constitutional Society of London, he was intimate with Joseph Priestley, Horne Tooke, and Tom Paine, sympathized with every liberal movement and offered his pen to the cause of a freer England. His *Advice to the Privileged Orders* was eulogized by Fox on the floor of Commons, and the Pitt ministry was moved to suppress the work and proscribe the author. Thereupon Barlow went into hiding. There seems to have been considerable provocation for the government's action. "It is safe to say," remarks his biographer, "that no political work of the day created so wide an interest or was so extensively read." With Paine and Barlow both loose in England there was need of the government looking to its fences. In 1793 he was made a citizen of France. His French career was not unlike Paine's, whom he resembled in many ways. He had much of the latter's genius for publicity and skill in propaganda, and his career was a great stimulus to radicals at home. He risked his life to serve the

American prisoners in Africa and by his skill and address eventually freed them. In the meantime he had not neglected his private affairs. He made a fortune in the French funds, which he increased by able merchandising. He had come to his goal by distant roads, and on his return to America in 1805 he took up his abode at Washington, creating a delightful country seat on the outskirts of the capital where he maintained a *salon* for American liberals. Unlike Colonel Humphreys he felt no inclinations toward Connecticut; the old ties were broken past mending; the French Jacobin could not fit into the grooves of Hartford Federalism. Six years later he was impressed a second time into the diplomatic service, was sent to France on a difficult mission, followed Napoleon, then on the Russian campaign, was caught in the break-up of the grand army, suffered exposure, contracted pneumonia, and died in a village near Cracow in Poland—a fate which honest Federalists regarded as amply merited by his vicious principles.

The later reputation of Barlow has been far less than his services warranted or his solid merits deserved. His admirable prose writings have been forgotten and the *Columbiad* returns always to plague him. The common detraction of all Jacobins and republicans fell heavily on so conspicuous a head. "It is simply impossible," says his biographer, "for the historian of Federal proclivities and environment, to do justice to the great leaders of Republicanism in America." Barlow paid a heavy price for his intellectual independence. Thus John Adams, who had suffered many a sharp thrust from him, wrote to Washington, "Tom Paine is not a more worthless fellow." Of the Yale dislike Barlow was well aware, for he once confessed that he would have presented the school with some needed chemical apparatus but he "supposed that, coming from him, the college authorities would make a bonfire of them in the college yard." Yet it is hard for a later generation to discover wherein lay the viciousness of his principles. A warm-hearted humanitarian, he was concerned always for the common well-being. The two major passions of his life were freedom and education. During the last years at Washington he was ardently promoting a plan for a great national university at the seat of government, and had he lived ten years longer his wide influence would probably have accomplished it. His sins would seem to have been no other than an open break with the Calvinism and Federalism of the Connecticut oligarchy—somewhat slender grounds on which to pillory him as an infidel and a scalawag.

The social foundation of Barlow's political philosophy is lucidly presented in the *Advice to the Privileged Orders,* partly reprinted in this edition; a work that deserves a place beside Paine's *Rights of Man* as a great document of the times. It does too much credit to American letters to be suffered to lie buried with a dead partisanship. It is warm with the humanitarian enthusiasm that was a common heritage from the Physiocratic school of social thinkers. Two suggestive ideas lie at the base of his thinking: the doctrine of the *res publica,* and the doctrine of social responsibility for individual well-being. The former, given wide currency by the *Rights of Man,* resulted from the imposition of social conscience on abstract political theory,

out of which was derived a new conception of the duty and function of the political state—that the state must become an agent of the whole rather than the tool of a class, and that its true concern is the *public thing,* safeguarding the social heritage as a common asset to succeeding generations; the latter is a more specific inquiry into the relation of the political state to the individual citizen. . . .

Leon Howard on the contribution of the Connecticut Wits:

[The] greatest value of the writings by the Connecticut Wits, both in verse and in prose, lies in the illumination they cast upon an age which was to have, socially and aesthetically, an extraordinary influence upon the future. Their story shows how men of different temperaments found sustenance for their dispositions in a limited provincial environment and, broadening their fields of activity with those of their country, absorbed the many cultural influences that prepared the way for a new literature and formed a new national character. Few groups of writers, in any country, have started from a common point of departure and left such comprehensive records of so many interests and such varied activities. Their intellectual horizons were as broad as those of any other Americans in their generation; and there was hardly a profession that one of them did not follow, hardly a place in the Western World that one of them did not visit. . . . They made laws, preached sermons, fought battles, treated illness, taught school, pleaded cases, passed judgments, negotiated treaties, manufactured goods, farmed land, bred livestock, speculated in real estate, promoted colonization, edited periodicals, founded missionary societies, kept shop, and directed banks. They ranged from Africa to Russia, from Virginia to the Vermont and Michigan frontiers. Their experiences were, in epitome, those of the new American people; and most of their experiences were reflected, in one way or another, in their writings.

Leon Howard, The Connecticut Wits, *The University of Chicago Press, 1943.*

Leon Howard

SOURCE: "The Wicked Wits," in *The Connecticut Wits,* The University of Chicago Press, 1943, pp. 169-205.

[*Howard was an American critic who published widely on American and English literature. His* The Connecticut Wits *(1943) is considered an authoritative guide to the subject of the Wits, their time period, and their writings. In the following excerpt from that work, Howard explores the early satirical writings of the Wits and concludes that their involvement in bitter public debate in periodicals took them away from more important literary work.*]

I

During the years that followed the Revolution the United States faced the problem of restoring trade and commerce with neither the advantages nor the disadvantages of membership in the British Empire. Massachusetts, Rhode Island, and, to a considerable extent, New York were looking across the ocean for prosperity; but Connecticut, although lacking a good seaport, had an excellent river highway to the interior, and the town of Hartford, on the edge of the upper valley, soon became the flourishing commercial center of the state. Trumbull had moved there as early as 1780, Barlow had taken a house in his neighborhood during the winter of 1782-83, and Lemuel Hopkins and his wife had arrived in 1784, making their residence with the Barlows until they were able to set up their own establishment. By the autumn of 1786 all three poets were substantial citizens. Trumbull was a successful, well-established lawyer with good connections and some prospects, if health and energy permitted, of a political future. Barlow, less successfully established in a profession, nevertheless was also a member of the Common Council and a person of some importance in the town. Hopkins had built up a professional reputation that made him so nearly Connecticut's leading physician that he had been specially called from Hartford to attend the aged and beloved Governor Jonathan Trumbull in his last illness. They had known one another for a long time; Hopkins had probably been one of the contributors to "The Correspondent," and they had all collaborated after a fashion upon Barlow's edition of Dr. Watts's *Psalms.* But their literary productivity had become very casual. One had been fairly well disillusioned concerning the prospect of achieving fame and fortune through literature; another was still waiting to test the results of his efforts; and the third, Hopkins, had never been stirred by any great literary ambition.

Hopkins, as a matter of fact, lacked the first requisite to practical literary ambition, for he was wholly skeptical concerning the patriotic optimism which most American poets seemed to accept as a necessary ingredient in successful composition. "My best compliments to Trumbull and Barlow," he had written Oliver Wolcott shortly before he moved to Hartford:

> Tell them that I am glad we have some poets who have not liv'd long enough to see all the variety of folly and perversness the humane is capable of: for I hope posterity will judge of a century or two to come by their poetic prophecies provided no historian should think it worth his while to write a word about it.

Yet he was an exceptionally generous man, tolerant of his friends' faults; and, if he had a brusque, eccentric manner to match his ungainly figure and bright staring eyes, his sharp tongue could lay bare pretensions with an efficiency that even Trumbull had to admire. He had not attended Yale, but his professional achievements and his knowledge of the classics had been recognized by an honorary Master's degree in 1784. And he had demonstrated his individual talent for versification in the *Connecticut Courant* for November 7, 1785, by "A new and certain CURE for CANCERS! In an EPITAPH on a Patient Who Died of a Pimple in the Hands of an Infallible Doctor." From its beginning—

> Here lies a fool flat on his back,
> The victim of a Cancer Quack—

to its moralizing conclusion—

> Go, readers, gentle, eke and simple,
> If you have wart, or corn, or pimple;
> To quack infallible apply;
> Here's room enough for you to lie.
> His skill triumphant still prevails,
> For *Death's* a cure that never fails—

the poem announced, in almost every line, the appearance of a new writer whose rough, nervous wit was as stimulating in its matter-of-fact purpose as it was unpretentious of the "higher" literary aims of more ambitious men.

Such wit on the subject of medical quacks had aroused a host of vehement "enemies" when Trumbull tried it before the Revolution, but in the Hartford of 1785 it was almost completely lost amid the post-war concern for more gross and violent stimulants. The town may have been small enough to have a characteristic smell of new lumber, molasses, and old Jamaica, but it was frequented by men who had moved far abroad and were alert to everything that was happening in the new country which had just burst its colonial bounds. Colonel Jeremiah Wadsworth—the "certain Jere" who had assisted the devil to inspire David Humphreys in New Haven nearly seven years before—was perhaps the leading host in the town; and, although he was still appreciative of literature, he was more concerned with the possibilities of making a fortune. The breadth of his interests, which ranged from poetry to politics, from land speculation to manufacturing, was the measure of Hartford. Some of its inhabitants and their numerous visitors occasionally got together in the evening to discuss philosophical and literary subjects, but they spent so much of their time talking of more "practical" matters that stronger-minded poets than the Connecticut Wits would have found their attention diverted from abstractions to immediate concerns.

Two topics of immediate concern played an important part in the origin of a new, co-operative literary venture by Trumbull, Barlow, Hopkins, and their regular visitor, David Humphreys: the disposal of the public lands and the growing influence of the debtor classes upon the government of neighboring states. The first, in all its complicated ramifications, provided the original motive for the satiric enterprise which formally introduced the Connecticut poets to the world as "wits"; the second provided a secondary motive and an excuse for their activities. As their work became more self-consciously literary and their wit began to form a burlesque epic, they found additional, more patriotic excuses for writing; but the beginning was neither patriotic nor entirely excusable.

II

The first of the land controversies which involved the Hartford poets and had some effect upon their writing grew out of the conflicting claims of Connecticut and Pennsylvania to the territory including the Wyoming Valley. This section of what is now Pennsylvania had been developed by the Susquehanna Company of New England interests and settled largely by Connecticut families. Doubtful titles, however, had caused a good deal of trouble. In 1782 a court of arbitration meeting in Trenton had awarded the section to Pennsylvania without settling the matter permanently, for the court's decision led to the "Pennymite and Yankee war" in 1784, when state authorities tried to enforce the award; and subsequent appeals to Congress to review the decision met with no response. The Susquehanna Company, meeting in Hartford in July, 1785, had voted to support its claims before Congress and, in the meantime, to offer inducements to "able-bodied and effective" men who would settle in the territory and protect the company's interests by force of arms. The company also induced Colonel Ethan Allen to interest himself in the business, apparently with some notion that if events justified it he might play the same role in the amputation of Wyoming Valley from Pennsylvania that he had played in removing Vermont from New York. Allen, after seeing his *Reason: The Only Oracle of Man* through the press, visited the settlers in April, 1786, paraded in full regimentals for the encouragement of the Yankees, promised to bring in a lot of Green Mountain Boys, and put the Pennsylvanians in a high state of excitement. On May 17 he was in Hartford to attend another meeting of the company and apparently to encourage its defiance of court, Congress, and the state of Pennsylvania; for in December, 1786, the organization of proprietors met and threw its full weight into an effort to protect its interests—an effort which, incidentally, turned out to be in vain.

The affair must have caused a large amount of talk in Hartford during the summer of 1786, when the numerous citizens interested were throwing straws in the political wind and planning the course of action they would adopt in the December meeting. In any case it affected the local poets in two ways. First, it roused Dr. Lemuel Hopkins to an outburst of disapproval. The Green Mountain colonel's book offended every standard of sense, orthodoxy, and rhetoric to which he subscribed; and the demagogy represented by Allen was more than could be stomached by a man who had seen the public incited before and had observed that, on such occasions, a certain text "grin'd horrible a ghastly smile" at him: "wo unto thee, oh land, when thy king is a fool." Accordingly, he burst forth in the *American Mercury* for July 27 with a satiric denunciation of "the seer of Antichrist," who a few months before had descended

> To feed new mobs with Hell-born manna
> In Gentile lands of Susquehanna,

with "one hand. . . . clench'd to batter noses, While t'other scrawls 'gainst Paul and Moses." Individual and independent though Hopkins was, however, he could hardly have realized the complexities of the Susquehanna affair. For the event which provoked his denunciation involved at least one of his fellow-poets in land speculation and eventually led to Hopkins' own service as a literary cat's-paw for some of the very people who had sent Allen into Pennsylvania.

This second, indirect effect of the Susquehanna affair upon the activity of the poets was accomplished through the medium of Joel Barlow, who was interested in the affairs of the company and who served as secretary pro tem at the December meeting and afterward as one of the board of commissioners appointed to investigate the company's

chances and act accordingly. The federal Congress had already attempted to compromise with Connecticut's land claims by guaranteeing the state's title to the Western Reserve; and, as a consequence, many of the speculators—including Barlow—turned their attention to the possibilities of opening the country on the banks of Lake Erie. Plans for the disposal of the Western Reserve were still undetermined; but it was generally understood that, whereas the United States was expecting to sell its western lands at the basic price of one dollar an acre, Connecticut was to undertake a quicker disposal at half that price. Details, however, remained to be settled, and in the summer of 1786 two schemes were under discussion. The first called for the sale of unlocated lands, with both state and Continental securities accepted at par in payment. The second proposed that the sale be made by townships, with the acceptance of Connecticut paper alone at par. The difference between the two plans was momentous. One encouraged a rapid sale and favored the large companies which could survey and locate the most desirable holdings; it also meant that the state would be paid in Continental obligations, which it could use to pay off a share of the national indebtedness that admittedly could not be paid by the current methods of taxation. The other looked toward the retirement of the state debt and the ignoring of national obligations. The second plan also meant a positive first step toward disunion, although the fact may not have been at first widely appreciated.

The particular difference between the two proposals which excited the citizens of Connecticut, however, was less momentous. The first favored the officers and men of the Revolutionary army who held commutation certificates—the most depreciated form of Continental securities—and who might be expected to profit more than the holders of Connecticut paper by the acceptance of their securities at face value. The second gave the advantage to the state militia and in effect excluded the members of the Continental Army from participation in the speculative profits of their patriotism. Since Connecticut had paid its own militia longer than any of the other warring colonies, the amount of state paper in circulation was large, and the division of economic interests within the state was correspondingly acute. Yet it cannot be really determined to what extent differences of opinion concerning the disposal of the Ohio lands were affected by financial self-interest and to what extent they were caused by an appreciation of the larger implications of the two plans. The men who had acquired a more or less national point of view through associations in the Continental service stood to make a profit through the sort of land sale that would promote national unity, whereas the neighborhood-minded militia would find it profitable to repudiate national obligations. Patriotic vision, temperamental disposition, and economic self-interest were inextricably confused from the very beginning to such an extent that even the people concerned could not have given an accurate account of their primary motives. The dissension did not continue long enough to become really serious, for it was relieved, on the one hand, by the tendency of the Connecticut legislature toward the satisfaction of state interests and, on the other, by the formation of the Ohio Company with good prospects for obtaining fifty-cent land from Congress. But in the meantime the land-conscious citizens were divided into two camps that eyed each other with mutual suspicion; and differences growing out of a temporary condition were to be sustained on other grounds.

Such was the situation during the summer when notices appeared in the Connecticut newspapers requesting a full attendance of the Society of the Cincinnati at the regular September meeting. The organization was composed of officers in the regular army of the Revolution; its members held quantities of commutation certificates; and a decision had been reached, in the first triennial meeting in 1784, that the state chapters would act together in exerting pressure upon Congress for an early grant of western lands. The Cincinnati were suspected because of their unity of interests and also because their original provision for a hereditary membership was taken by many people as an indication that they were trying to establish an order of nobility. Accordingly, the hint of an important meeting at this particular moment aroused suspicion among some of the land-conscious officers and men of the militia, as well as among citizens who had no military connection. Judge William Williams of Lebanon, the serious-minded, public-spirited son-in-law of the late Governor Trumbull, brooded over the situation and prepared an address in which he outlined the two plans for disposing of the lands and strongly supported the second. He sent a copy to Joseph Hopkins, of Waterbury, inclosed in a private letter that hinted at his fears of the Cincinnati and suggested the publication of the address before the regular county meetings of Freemen, which were scheduled for the same day as the meeting of the Society. The letter, however, was opened in transit, copied, and withheld from Hopkins until a few days before the scheduled meeting.

Judge Williams, who was in the embarrassing position of trying to prevent the uncertain actions of an organization in which his brother-in-law, Colonel John Trumbull, the painter, was secretary and an active member, had begged that his name be kept "impenetrably concealed"; but on October 9 the letter was published in the *Connecticut Courant,* in Hartford, followed by a burlesque version in octo-syllabic couplets signed "William Wimble," in a thin disguise of the real author's name. The parody represented the letter-writer as comically self-important, mildly peccant, and suspicious of others from a consciousness of his own political chicanery. It also cast similar aspersions upon the recipient, whose identity was revealed by an allusion to the "copper-coining mint" that Joseph Hopkins had been operating in Waterbury up to the preceding June. The poem seems to have had no important purpose. Though it would inevitably sting so self-conscious a man as Williams and embarrass him in his personal relationships, it was probably no more than a slightly malicious warning for him to mind his own business—for he had guessed completely wrong concerning the reason for the special call to the Cincinnati. As a literary exercise it was clever and smooth, but notable primarily for its success in rhyming "to the rabble" and "impenetrable" and so copying, if not really rivaling, the "innumerable" and "consume-a-Rabble" standard of multiple rhyme which Swift had set for the octosyllabic couplet.

The *New Haven Gazette and the Connecticut Magazine* immediately copied the letter and the parody, and, as innocuous as the latter was, it seems to have put ideas in the head of Josiah Meigs, the editor, who had been running a series of "Observations on the Present Situation and Future Prospects of This and the United States" under the signature of "Lycurgus." The series of ironical essays had pointed out the dangers of a federal government that had no power, made use of "Anarchus" in a pretended attack upon Washington and the late Governor Trumbull, and expressed an ironic preference for a poverty-stricken country over a prosperous one. The stand taken by Williams with regard to the Western Reserve was clearly opposed to the Federalist position supported by Meigs, and the *Gazette* quickly set out to destroy the political reputations of both Williams and the sympathetic Hopkins, who was nicknamed "Joseph Copper" in an effort to associate him with the idea of a depreciating currency—for Hopkins' coins had already begun to be held at less than face value. Accordingly, the next issue of the paper carried an alleged "answer" to Williams' letter, supposedly by Hopkins, and another burlesque in octosyllabics. The parody of the second letter—which Williams insisted was itself a forgery—was both less clever and more vicious than the poem of the previous week. It represented the author as a politician and a rogue whose cynical philosophy might be expressed briefly:

> However the public's torn and tatter'd,
> The people must be coax'd and flatter'd—
> Their interest, sir, and ours, require it—
> We'll ride this hobby till we tire it:
> You know I've labor'd in this vineyard,
> And led our chosen like a swine herd.

His confidant, by implication, was no better; and it was hinted that he would not be returned to the assembly after the spring session. The new poem had the air of a premeditated, purposeful attack; and, although lower in quality than the first, it contained one insidious phrase in "Copper's" defiance of "all the wicked wits" who had attacked him.

The first poem, which had given Williams the name "William Wimble," had done so with the purpose of associating him with the Will Wimble of the *Spectator* and so branding him as a trifler. The second, in making him—with Hopkins—a type of demagogue, was attacking him by associating his political activity with the mob rule that was beginning to fill the newspapers with dispatches from Massachusetts. For several years there had been sporadic outbursts of mob activity in the rural sections of New England, where the farmers were suffering from a post-war depression and the lack of currency; and by the late summer of 1786 the situation had grown critical. The state legislature of Massachusetts had adjourned without providing a hoped-for relief, with the result that popular conventions had been held in the western part of the state to demand unsecured paper currency and the restraint of legal actions against the debtors. As the autumn sessions of the courts of common pleas approached, with the usual crowded calendars of suits and the prospect of numerous imprisonments for debt, the people who had previously been excited by the Rev. Samuel Ely, of Hampshire County, rose as mobs and, on August 29, prevented the sitting of the court at Northampton. A week later the courts at Worcester were also closed by a mob. On September 12, Job Shattuck led another outbreak that closed the scheduled session of the court at Concord. Luke Day and Daniel Shays were the leaders of the western uprisings, and late in September they led their followers on Springfield in an effort to close the supreme judicial court from which they might receive indictments for their earlier activities. The militia was ordered out, and the court sat for three days but was forced to adjourn on September 28 without having transacted any business. By this time reports of the uprising were beginning to pour into the Connecticut newspapers, emphasizing the fears caused by earlier reports of the New Hampshire outbreak under Moses French; and when the "Joseph Copper" letter was published on October 23 the implication of demagogy and of an association with depreciating currency was a serious political charge

In the meantime, while the first news of the Massachusetts insurrections was appearing in the papers, Humphreys was in Hartford on a visit, between the September meeting of the Cincinnati and the October meeting of the general assembly, both of which he attended in New Haven. He was already viewing the situation with alarm in his "Mount Vernon: An Ode," which he published in the *Courant* for October 9, and he doubtless found his sentiments shared by most of his friends and associates. Dr. Hopkins had forcefully expressed his opinion of men whose fists were "clench'd to batter noses"; and a rising young lawyer like Barlow, no matter how he may have felt about Colonel Allen's activities in Pennsylvania, must have looked askance at the closing of courts so near by and the mobs' violent objections to the legal profession. At this time Barlow's efforts were frankly devoted to attaining "an interest," and he had not yet firmly established his humanitarian convictions. Accordingly, though he had opposed imprisonment for debt in his dissertation submitted for admission to the bar, he probably convinced himself that the law should be obeyed until it was changed— especially when he realized that his classmates, Noah Webster, Oliver Wolcott, Jr., and Josiah Meigs, and such prized friends as Dr. Hopkins, Trumbull, Humphreys, and Colonel Wadsworth were strongly of that opinion. There had never been any doubt concerning Trumbull's feeling about the checked-shirt-and-leather-apron men, even when he had been a patriotic poet writing about patriotic mobs, and *M'Fingal* had already been quoted in a Massachusetts newspaper against the insurrectionists.

It may have been while Humphreys was in Hartford that he discussed with his friends the possibility of some continuous satire directed against the conditions that threatened the American experiment in republican government. Colonel Wadsworth had been in England while a group of poets were causing much excitement with "The Rolliad" in the *Morning Herald* for 1784; and Humphreys had visited London while the same satire was still popular in book form and while sequels to it, by the same group of wits, were appearing periodically. Other members of the group may also have seen the publications, which professed to be criticisms of an ancient epic that foretold con-

temporary political developments, and Trumbull had already used the device of an ancient prophetic manuscript for purposes of satire in "The Correspondent." Dr. Hopkins had expressed, three years before, a sardonic conviction that the optimistic glimpses into the future presented by his friends in their commencement poems were altogether at variance with the real prospects; and he was doubtless ready to help them correct their youthful mistakes. Thus the minds of a group of accomplished versifiers were prepared for the idea of a satire based upon the "discovery" of an ancient prophetic manuscript; and, if Noah Webster had been riding his hobbyhorse of antique fortifications on the banks of the Muskingum during his June visits to Hartford, the location of the discovery had already been fixed in the Ohio country, in which some members of the group were actively interested at the time.

No single person need necessarily have been responsible, but somehow out of this ferment there arose a scheme for a series of satiric papers on American antiquities—critical observations on the *Anarchiad: A Poem on the Restoration of Chaos and Substantial Night,* with extensive quotations from its twenty-four books. There was no novelty to Trumbull, Humphreys, and Barlow in the situation of "the prophetic bard," who seemed "to have taken for the point of vision one of the lofty mountains of America, and to have caused, by his magic invocations, the years of futurity to pass before him." But there was novelty in a vision of the rising glory of America that began "with unfolding the beautifying scenes when those plagues to society, law and justice, shall be done away with; when every one shall be independent of his neighbor; and when every rogue shall literally do what is right in his own eyes." The poets, who were still comparatively young men, were not profoundly disturbed; but the facile optimism of their earlier years had been displaced either by disillusionment or by less passive ideas of progress, and they began to affect pessimism in a literary effort to counteract the influences leading toward a social revolution unanticipated during the civil war against England.

If Humphreys took a fully matured proposal for the *American Antiquities* to New Haven when he and Wadsworth left to attend the general assembly, Josiah Meigs undoubtedly gave him enthusiastic encouragement; for the Lycurgus papers had been exhausted the preceding April and he had found no similar series that would take their place as featured satires directed against federal impotency, extreme democracy, state debt, and paper money. The first number appeared in the *New Haven Gazette* for October 26. It outlined the plan for the series by describing the supposed discovery and gave a brief sample of the *Anarchiad* in the form of heroic couplets presenting a vision of Massachusetts. The mobs of Day, Shays, and Shattuck had risen, the court had fallen as the frightened official ran to cover, and the constitution of Chaos had been restored as the "newborn state" was overwhelmed in the gulf of darkness. A week later the second number appeared with "a fragment of the speech which the old Anarch makes to Beelzebub, for the purpose of persuading him to come over and help his faithful friends in our Macedonia, since his affairs were in so thriving a posture in Massachusetts and Rhode Island." Like the Joseph Copper letter in the

Courant, this was marked by bitter personal satire, with more than a dozen offensive allusions to individuals in less than twice as many couplets. Williams and Hopkins appeared again as "Wimble" and "Copper"; General James Wadsworth, of Durham, the state's leading advocate of a loose confederacy, was introduced under the name of "Wronghead"; Samuel Ely was referred to as "Froth, the sep'rate," glowing "with pop'lar rage"; Thomas Goodman, of New Hartford, was mentioned with him as a type of dotard from the lawless north; old Dr. Benjamin Gale, of Killingworth, received a sneering allusion; and a number of others were mentioned under aliases that can perhaps no longer be penetrated. They were all fairly prominent citizens of Connecticut—with the exception, perhaps, of Leonard Chester, who was satirized as "Laz'rus"—and all were identified as "Anarchists" by their opposition to the requisitions of Congress for the settlement of the national debt.

It was nearly two months before another number of *American Antiquities* appeared, but this issue had made it clear that a coordinated political attack was being organized by a group of men who made high-spirited references to themselves as "the wicked wits." Growing out of such a complexity of motives, the satires cannot be unmistakably attributed to particular authors. Unsympathetic contemporary opinion, as expressed by an anonymous poet in the *Courant* for November 20, held that it was "*Hudy's* great rival" (John Trumbull) who was "thrumming his lute." Humphreys wrote Washington, on November 16, that he, Trumbull, and Barlow were the authors of the papers. And a persistent tradition, beginning soon after the last of the group died, has insisted that Lemuel Hopkins was a prime mover in the business. Judge Williams, who was deeply hurt by the whole affair, publicly expressed the conviction, in October, that the Cincinnati were back of the attack upon him and that General Samuel H. Parsons, president of the Connecticut Society, had taken the lead in "employing a poet" to burlesque a letter dishonorably obtained. Parsons immediately denied the accusation with an irate honesty which the Wits soon indorsed by promoting and ridiculing a public quarrel between the two men. The Cincinnati were perhaps unofficially back of the William Wimble burlesque. They had been unjustly accused of scheming for preferential treatment in the Western Reserve (their special request for a full attendance having been made for entirely different reasons), and they had been subjected to so much criticism that they were highly sensitive; but the most likely instigator was Colonel Jeremiah Wadsworth, vice-president of the Society, who was intimate with the entire body of Hartford versifiers. The poet was probably Trumbull. He was Wadsworth's close friend and a sort of unofficial adviser to the inner circles of the Cincinnati, and the original poem has all the stylistic marks of such burlesques as his "Epithalamium" and *M'Fingal*. Trumbull could hardly have written the Joseph Copper burlesque, however, unless he had suddenly lost the smoothness and facility that had characterized his use of the octosyllabic couplet during the previous seventeen years. Barlow, who was soon to become a shareholder in the Ohio Company and so had financial interests at stake, may have done it, either of his own accord or at the instigation of Meigs. The first number of *American Antiquities*

was undoubtedly planned and probably written in conference by the authors mentioned by Humphreys—himself, Trumbull, and Barlow. The second could not have been prepared under such circumstances because the authors were separated by half the state. They may have followed the procedure adopted for the later *Echo* of sending the manuscripts around, when the authors were separated, for emendations and additions. The first paragraph of the prose criticism and some parts of the verse reveal a quality of phrasing that was characteristic of Hopkins alone among the members of the group, and the probability is that it was begun by Barlow and Hopkins working in collaboration, passed through Trumbull's hands, and was sent to Humphreys for final improvements and publication. Humphreys, who had spent only a few days in Hartford since Hopkins had moved there, could have had only a bare acquaintance with him and probably was unconscious of the physician's contribution. The intimacy of Trumbull, Barlow, and Hopkins was such that the latter was sure to have had a part in any literary activity that interested the other two and fitted his satiric temper; but the informal collaboration of a "friendly club" including Humphreys was physically impossible. In any event the activities of the wits became so complex that even their best friends were soon uncertain about what was going on; and, though Humphreys remained, perhaps, the guiding spirit of the *American Antiquities*, his associates became engaged in a high-spirited quizzing too subtle for his participation and too much like lèse majesté for his approval.

This new development at first had no serious political purpose and apparently was the result of the temptation provided by an exchange of public letters between Williams and General Parsons. Late in October Williams had sent a brief note to the *Connecticut Journal and New-Haven Post-Boy* explaining the circumstances of the earlier letter, accusing General Parsons of being responsible for the burlesque, and insisting that the alleged reply from Hopkins had been a forgery. The *Gazette* reprinted this communication on November 2 with an aggressive reply from Parsons, in which he denied his responsibility for any of the actions of which he was accused. A week later, David Smith, one of the carriers of the letter, who had been charged with providing the Cincinnati with a copy, wrote in his own defense; and the same issue of the *Gazette* carried corrections by Williams designed to place the true contents of his first letter before the public. The tone of Parsons' letter and the agitation of Williams were an open invitation to the Wits, who undoubtedly were aware of the General's innocence; and they published, on the first page of the *Gazette* for November 23, another octosyllabic burlesque signed "Trustless Fox," with a postscript to the effect that it might have been signed "great General P—rs—ns" were the other name not more suited to his "unbooted" character. The same issue also contained an ironic prose defense of Williams, signed "Benevolence, Jr.," which professed to support him against "the *wicked wits* and snarling critics" who had inconsistently tried to represent him as both a knave and a fool. The tenor of the "defense" was to show that Williams was the latter, though the author refused to venture his own opinion of the appropriateness of the nickname; and it concluded on a note of sympathy "that an honest man should be a little disturbed, when so many wicked and malicious heads should be jumbled in HOTCHPOT to deprive him of his good character and office."

Benevolence, Jr., closed with a political hint which was fully developed when the Wits returned to the attack in the *Gazette* for December 14 in an ironically fatherly letter by "Benevolence, Sr." The supposition that Williams would lose his place in the next election was emphasized; and the author advanced the opinion, with ironic regretfulness, that "nothing could have been more opportunely, more happily, and more effectually calculated, than your essay, to fix indelibly the nickname 'William Wimble' upon Mr. Williams, and to exclude him from a seat in the upper house." Every implication contained in the letter by Benevolence, Jr., was made clear by the supposed father's attempt to warn him against "the *wicked* wits who are already sufficiently formidable to some of the grave pillars of our state." The letter concluded with a veiled hint that Benevolence, Jr., was the disliked "Laz'rus" of the *Anarchiad* and so gave a starting-point for "Anonimous," who contributed another letter, in the December 21 issue of the *Gazette,* addressed to Benevolence, Jr., or "Grey Goose the Younger." This letter developed the theme that "as Don Quixote had his *Sancho Panca,* Hudibras his Ralpho and M'Fingal his Constable, so hath William Wimble been accompanied to combat by his trusty squire Benevolence Jun." Anonimous was somewhat ironic about General Parsons; but his main effort was directed toward representing Williams as both a fool and a knave, for he not only associated him with the burlesque heroes of literature but accused him, in a bit of verse later included in the eighth number of *American Antiquities,* of leaguing with Joe Copper for the purpose of buying votes.

While the wicked Wits were carrying on at Hartford—probably under the direction of Trumbull, who had been well trained in this sort of darting, ingenious attack—Humphreys was active in other things. He had been appointed by the assembly on October 20 to raise a regiment of Connecticut militia for defense against a possible Indian uprising along the border, and he was busy making plans for recruiting and carrying out his legislative duties. He also took occasion to place his name before the public in a literary way. He arranged the series of documents which he published with an introduction, in the *Gazette* for November 16, as "The Conduct of General Washington, Respecting the Confinement of Capt. Asgill, Placed in Its True Point of Light"; and he also reprinted in the same issue his "Mount Vernon: An Ode," which had been originally published in the *Courant* five weeks before. Although the ode was pessimistic about existing conditions, it concluded with an optimistic belief that Providence would not leave "imperfectly achiev'd" the task begun in America. The *Gazette* for November 9 and December 7 also carried extracts from *A Poem on the Happiness of America.* The latter selection was accompanied by an introductory note in which the editors explained that it was printed in an effort "to put their Readers in better temper with respect to themselves, their neighbours, the community at large, and their fellow creatures in general"; and the reprinting of these pieces—which was almost certainly done with Humphreys' approval—would seem to indicate

that the poet might be using his old optimism to cover his retreat from satiric activity. The concluding sentence of the editor's note approved the activities of the Wits, however, in a declaration that it was an effort "not less worthy of patriotic genius" to demonstrate to one's fellow-citizens "that the perverse disposition which induces them to spurn at greater privileges and blessings than are bestowed on any other nation, is madness to themselves, injustice to posterity, and the blackest ingratitude to heaven." Meigs had no intention of talking his prize satirist out of making new contributions.

Humphreys himself, as he indicated in his letters to Washington, was too firmly convinced that the antifederal and paper-money men were all demagogues and evil characters to give up his role as savior of his country. By the latter part of December he had rounded up the wicked Wits of Hartford and brought them back into the marked-out path of *American Antiquities.* The third number appeared in the *Gazette* for December 28, fulfilling the promise made in each of the earlier issues to present a selection from the epic episode dealing with Rhode Island. The paper-money party had come into power in that state during the spring elections, choosing John Collins as governor and Daniel Owen as lieutenant-governor, and their large issue of paper had immediately been subject to an enormous depreciation. An enforcing act had been passed requiring that the new currency be accepted at face value and providing that debts might be paid—if the creditor refused the legal tender—by depositing the requisite amount with the local court and advertising the fact in the newspapers. The neighboring states were full of such stories as that of the Connecticut man who inadvertently drove a load of wood over the Rhode Island line and was forced to sell it for worthless paper. The enforcing act had already been brought before the state court, and, though it had been vigorously supported by Henry Goodwin, a Newport attorney, it had been declared unconstitutional in September. But in spite of this legal doubt cast on the efficacy of paper money in Rhode Island and the fact that a paper-money proposal had already been easily defeated in the Connecticut legislature, the satirists launched a bitter personal attack upon Collins, Owen, and Goodwin (who was charged with writing the governor's speeches) and upon the Sodom-like "Island" of unrighteous rogues. "For it will scarcely be denied, in any part of the United States," they explained, "that paper money, in an unfunded and depreciating condition, is happily calculated to introduce the long expected scenes of misrule, dishonesty, and perdition."

When the time came around for the annual New Year's verses for the carriers of the Hartford papers, the local Wits took a holiday from the purposeful satire which Humphreys was fathering. Their masterpiece was the two-poem broadside for the *Connecticut Courant.* The first poem was a burlesque "Eclogue," consisting mostly of a dialogue between Ira Jones and Tertius Dunning, carriers of the *Courant* and the *Mercury.* The two boys professed to have received their respective verses from "a Bard sublime," who was given to rhymed compliments and from "the wittiest Bard in Town"; Tertius claimed only that he sang the news dealt out to man by Jove's own Mercury, and Ira that he was inspired by "the Politics of these intriguing Days." Both took liberties with the Connecticut poets. Tertius begged:

> Inspire me, Phoebus! in my Wimble's praise,
> With Humphreys' strains, and Barlow's moving
>   lays;
> No more his Plots reveal'd should he deplore,
> And wicked Wits should versify no more;

while Ira wished:

> Oh, in our Poet's Corner could I write
> As Trumbull witty, and sublime as Dwight;
> Copper should brighten in the polish'd strain,
> And trustless Foxes seek their Holes again.

They glanced at the Rhode Island paper money, the New York impost, and the Massachusetts mobs; and, when they were stopped by the printer, they had begun to query each other about the authors of the *Anarchiad* and about how a republican government might exist without power. The poem was a good-humored piece of nonsense and was immediately ridiculed in the accompanying "The News-Boy's Apology for the Foregoing Verses. Written by Himself." In the "Apology" Ira complained that he had given one of the poets five shillings for the "confounded Eclogue" and had been able to get neither his money back nor another poem. He had protested that he had never talked in such a way to Tertius and, that point of view having made no impression on the poet, had objected to the political allusions:

> So I told him flat and plain I thought 'twas quite
>   improper,
> To say any thing in New-Year's Verses about
>   Wimble and Joe Copper;
> And besides it was not politic, for all these Jokes
>   so tickle us,
> It made them Folks important instead of being
>   ridiculous,
> And when you keep pelting at 'em, and trying
>   to be so witty,
> Their Friends will stick to 'em like sheep-ticks
>   and vote for 'em out of pity.
> And I told him as to Shaise and all his Fraterni-
>   ty,
> I didn't care if they got in a Snow-Drift and
>   stay'd there to all Eternity.
> And as to Paper Money, now Cash they say so
>   scarce is,
> I don't care a farthing about it, if they won't ten-
>   der it to me for my Verses.
> For my Master-Printers and I, satisfied with our
>   Conditions,
> Don't mean to torment ourselves by turning
>   great Politicians,
> We are all true-born Yankies, to our Country
>   firm and hearty,
> And join of your Factions, but print for every
>   Party.

That argument did not work, either, and though Ira concluded by talking "to him out of the Decalogue" the only satisfaction he could get was that the poet had the money and he "must take the Eclogue." Accordingly, he could only apologize and suggest that he be paid double because of all his difficulties.

The comic "Eclogue" and the "Apology" (which was modeled after Swift's poetic representation of Mrs. Harris' petition "To Their Excellencies the Lord Justices of Ireland") were reprinted in the *Gazette* for January 11; and two weeks later the same paper published the New Year's verses from the *Mercury*, introduced by a note from the *Massachusetts Centinel*, which claimed that "Pegassus is not perhaps back'd by better Horseman from any part of the Union, than he is by those from the State of Connecticut." The "poetic Horsemanship" used to illustrate the claim consisted of octosyllabics based on the conceit of a chain of being extending from Jove's great toe to the earth; but, in spite of the insistence attributed to the carrier in the "Eclogue" that he sang only the news, the poem contained a light political satire more pointed than anything found in earlier *Mercury* verses for the New Year. In the meantime, other self-elected "wits" were trying to join in the chorus of verse. The *Gazette* for January 18 contained an announcement that the editors had recently "received a piece entitled American Antiquities No. 3" but that it was "evidently a spurious production" and so had not been printed, because "when any one assumes to write under a particular title, we think he ought not to be interfered with." Some verse "Advice to the Wits and Poets" adapted to "the Latitude and Longitude of Connecticut" appeared a week later, urging the Wits to let Wimble, Wronghead, and Copper alone and direct their attentions toward "the Spectator" who had undertaken to defend the actions of the legislature against the sensitive federalism of "Cato." A professed admirer of the *American Antiquities* offered "The Soliloquy of the Spectator" in satiric blank verse, for February 1, from a manuscript of tragedies recently discovered in Kentucky. A "Female Patriot" took her pen in hand two weeks later to speak while Anarch slept. The *Courant*, also, accepted contributions from outside the circle of "wicked wits"; and even the issue of February 26, which omitted all advertisements because the paper was so full of insurrection news, found room for "A Song" beginning "Come, come my bold boxers, 'tis Liberty calls," satirizing the "Tag, Rag, and Bobtail" mobs.

The inner circle of Wits, however, kept to their regular plan and on January 11 published their most ambitious selection from the *Anarchiad* in the form of preliminary speeches by Anarch and Hesper before their epic battle. Anarch contrasted the gold-respecting, patriotic British to the paper-money hypocrites in America; found evidence of his existing reign in the boldness of Shays and the insurrectionists, the Barbary corsairs, and the border Indians; and saw the "ghost of empire" stalking "without a head" in America. He also found encouragement in the retirement of Washington and the recent death of Greene, though he professed to fear that the time would come when there would be a reaction from mobs to monarchy. Hesper, in his turn, attacked Aedanus Burke for his pamphlet against the Cincinnati, prophesied a bad end for Shays, and called on new Greenes and Washingtons to rise. The selection broke off as they rushed to combat, but the paper closed with a note of optimism in a "conjecture that the combat ended with some disadvantage to old Anarch." There was, in fact, reason for the optimism, for the newspapers had already reported the successful outcome of Colonel Hichborn's campaign against the Middlesex mob and the capture of Shattuck, Parker, and Page; and the suppression of the insurrection in Vermont had been announced. When Humphreys' "The Genius of America: A Song" appeared as a supplementary manuscript to the *Anarchiad* for the fifth number of *American Antiquities,* on January 25, 1787, the author could only call for peace without venturing a prophecy of the outcome, which he still felt to be concealed in "shades of night." Yet on that very day General Lincoln met and permanently dispersed Shays' mob, bringing the insurrection to an end as far as the Wits were concerned, except for an aftermath of dispatches and the February tour of Humphreys' Connecticut regiments through the scenes of January excitement.

By February the Wits were convinced of the necessity of a formal attempt at a stronger federal union; and, with the dying-out of the excitement over regulators in the west and paper money in the east, they were free from emotional compulsion to slash out at their neighbors and so could direct their satire toward some constructive end. Their first campaign was to destroy the political influence of General James Wadsworth, leader of the anti-Federalist forces in the Upper House, whom they had already introduced into their papers as "Wronghead." On February 22 they presented his soliloquy, representing him as railing against Congress, courts, legal powers, trade, great men, and lawyers in *"cant pretense of Liberty"*; enjoying the salaries of his many offices; selfishly scheming for the destruction of the Union in order to preserve his own position; and fearing the military forces authorized to "awe each mob, and execute the laws." Anarch, invoked by his fears, warned him that the greatest threat against him came not from force but from the free appeal to reason and that his plans would never succeed until reading and writing were practically eliminated, the press restrained, and the Wits hanged. On March 15 they returned to the attack even more directly and unmistakably. Wadsworth was presiding justice of the New Haven County Court of Common Pleas, a delegate to the Continental Congress, member of the Executive Council of Connecticut, comptroller of the state, and registrar or town clerk of Durham, as well as a former major general of the militia. They taunted him with being a "milleped of office" drawing a salary for every position, accused him of cowardice at the time of Tryon's first invasion of the state, denounced him for opposing the requisitions of Congress and the state and impost taxes recommended by the federal body, charged him with trying to protect the state from commerce by isolating it from the others, and laughed at him for joining with Wimble to save the people from the fancied machinations of the Cincinnati. And in conclusion they wished that he might "in *brighter* reations *burn*" as a *"glowing* seraph" after death.

The Wits were also after their original butt, Judge Williams. While in Hartford during February, recruiting his regiment of militia for service on the border, Humphreys took time to write a fable on "The Monkey Who Shaved Himself and His Friends," which was "Addressed to the Hon. William Wimble" and published in the *Courant* for February 26. According to the story, the monkey (who represented Williams) was wonderful at imitating his mas-

ter, a York barber (presumably Governor George Clinton, against whom Federalist activity was being organized); and, after frightening his friends by his efforts to shave them, he lathered himself and—in a couplet contributed by Trumbull:

> Drew razor swift as he could pull it,
> And cut, from ear to ear, his gullet.

The renewal of the attack on Williams was stimulated by a continuation of his quarrel with General Parsons, with whom Humphreys was closely associated as an active member of the Cincinnati. During the unusually cold month of December, Williams had adjourned the Windham County Court and had immediately been charged with being under the influence of the Massachusetts mobs. He had defended himself in the *New London Gazette* by a letter which was reprinted in the *Courant* for January 1. Parsons had published satiric comments on his defense three weeks later, and on February 19 Williams lost patience and responded with a severe personal attack upon Parsons. Humphreys' poem was designed to suppress Williams by making him lose confidence in his literary ability, and the "Moral" of his fable was specific:

> Who cannot write, yet handle pens,
> Are apt to hurt themselves and friends.
> Though others use them well, yet fools
> Should never meddle with edge tools.

As the spring elections approached, however, it became apparent that Williams had hurt himself little, if at all, by his communications to the papers, and there were whispers of plans to make him lieutenant-governor instead of Oliver Wolcott. The Wits, accordingly, set out to hang him, bury him, and pronounce "An Elegy on a Patriot" over his grave. The ballad elegy, which was supposedly taken from an ancient Ohio newspaper, appeared as the eighth number of *American Antiquities* on March 22; and on April 3, General Parsons published in the *Courant* a bad-humored prose attack on Williams. But neither served its purpose. In the May elections Williams received the third highest vote for membership on the governor's council; and within a year, as a member of the convention for considering the new federal constitution, he surprised his enemies by voting for its ratification. Hopkins, also included in the attack, was re-elected to office and eventually gave his approval to the plan of union. And James Hillhouse, who was satirized as the "Sachem of Muskingum," was chosen delegate to the Continental Congress, though he refused to attend. Humphreys had sent some of the *American Antiquities* to Washington with the comment that "pointed ridicule is found to be of more efficacy than serious argumentation"; and he informed his chief, in a letter of March 24, that the Connecticut assembly was under the influence of a few "miserable, narrow minded and. . . wicked Politicians." But he was wrong in each observation. The Wits accomplished no measurable results by their satire; and in several cases they failed to estimate correctly the men they were opposing, with the result that they spent a good part of their energy denouncing enemies who existed solely in their imagination.

It may be that most of them had no really serious political purpose anyway; for, instead of pushing their attacks upon

Connecticut politicians up to the eve of the May elections, they turned their eyes to New York. Stephen Mix Mitchell, a delegate to the federal Congress, had written Jeremiah Wadsworth in January that "the Anarchiad, book 23d is read here, with much pleasure and obtains applause"; he had added that it was "judged to be a meritorious performance." The authors, who were having the satisfaction of finding the papers generally "reprinted in more papers and read with greater avidity than any other performances," were particularly pleased with their new audience. Accordingly, they prepared another selection from the twenty-third book for the benefit of their New York admirers and published it on April 5. Representing the soliloquy of Anarch after having been vanquished by Hesper, and the consolations of his mother Night, this ninth number emphasized New York's rejection of Congress' request for a federal impost and satirized the antifederal leaders in that state. Governor Clinton was attacked as an "illustrious changeling," who had begun to "court the low crowd"; Samuel Jones was satirized for his personal appearance, for his legal activities within the British lines during the Revolution, and for his antifederal leadership in the state legislature; and another of Clinton's followers was represented as "blind Belisarius," full of fantastic fears of congressional power. All these satiric portraits were personal and offensive, though the characters were perhaps sufficiently concealed to be recognized only by the initiate. But the Wits were most brutal and clearly outspoken in their attack upon Abraham Yates, author of some of the "Rough-Hewer" essays and New York delegate to the Congress, who was considered by some members the man of least understanding in the federal body because of his constant and undeviating opposition to anything that looked toward a closer union. This selection of the *Anarchiad* was undoubtedly composed for the amusement of those members of Congress who were already fixed in their political beliefs rather than for the purpose of influencing the public. But young Alexander Hamilton was credited by name with a brilliant speech in the New York legislature favoring the impost; and his failure to carry his point was explained by satiric reference to the "band of mutes," who, according to a New York wit, had strangled the measure by voting against it without making any attempt to answer Hamilton. The theme of the entire piece was that, though Anarch had been vanquished by Hesper, mother Night still had dreams of establishing her realm with the assistance of the new leaders that were springing up in New York.

The tenth number of *American Antiquities,* published on May 24, was not satiric at all. The constitutional convention had just begun its meetings in Philadelphia, and Hesper, in the concluding book of the *Anarchiad,* was represented as addressing the assembled sages in the interest of union. The heroes who had fallen on the battlefields of the Revolution were celebrated, the dangers of faction and of irresponsible rule were pointed out, and the patriotism of the federal leaders was praised. Anti-Federalists were warned that disorder would inevitably lead to monarchy; and the point was made that a loose confederation of states, forming a restless government by factious crowds, going from one extreme to another, would be just as bad. The sons of freedom who had settled in America, however-

er, did not have to choose necessarily between license and despotism. They had resigned enough of their power and natural rights to form social leagues, and from ancient habit they obeyed the local powers. But their establishments had not taught them reverence for a general government, nor had it given them an interest in the federal welfare. The point at issue, therefore, was not the fundamental principle of union but the practical expedients of standing against foreign foes, regulating finance, and controlling trade. Yet action was necessary, for the country had reached the point where it would have to take seriously the warning "Ye Live United, or Divided Die!"

The concluding numbers of the *American Antiquities* made an anticlimax. Publishing their observations on August 16 and September 13, while the constitutional convention was meeting in Philadelphia, the Wits had nothing further to say in the interest of union and no ideas to contribute toward the solution of practical problems. Instead, they went back to the seventeenth book of the *Anarchiad* in order to represent "the land of annihilation" and "the region of pre-existent spirits," in which the politicians satirized in the earlier numbers and the writers critical of America and American institutions passed in review. The Abbé Raynal, the Count de Buffon, and the Abbé de Pau were denounced for their derogatory comments on American genius and the American climate and soil; Dr. Robertson was satirized for echoing their opinions; and Robert Morris was intemperately condemned as a worshiper of Mammon because he had publicly indorsed Raynal's statement concerning the absence of literary genius in America. Aedanus Burke was again attacked for his pamphlet against the Cincinnati, Demeunier for borrowing an account from him for the *Encyclopédie méthodique,* and Mirabeau and Linguet for their writings against the society. Significantly, however, Jefferson was not mentioned. Humphreys thought and had informed Washington that the foreign minister and not Burke was the source of the article against the Cincinnati in the *Encyclopédie,* but it may have been that he felt it wise to refrain from satirizing a man from whom he might expect further employment in a public capacity. The last group to pass in satiric review were the imaginative writers on American history and politics—the Abbé Mably, Target, D'Auberteul, and even the Rev. Samuel Peters, "the fag-end man of M'Fingal," who had published his libelous history of Connecticut from the safety of London five years before. Such satire at that time, however, was rather pointless, and the Wits seem to have engaged in it only because they hated to give up a series of literary productions that had been so spontaneously popular. It was not until February 21, 1788, that they brought the series to a definite close, allowing Anarch to bury all his followers and issue an "Edict of Penance."

When the Philadelphia convention presented a definite plan of union in the form of a constitution, the Wits had nothing to say. As a group they kept completely silent during the controversy over its adoption. The New Year's verse of the Hartford *Courant* for 1788 dealt with "The Forc'd Alliance" in the form of "A Dialogue" between two patriots, Wronghead (General James Wadsworth) and Lamb (John Lamb, collector of customs at New

York), in which the Constitution was discussed. The author—probably Lemuel Hopkins—considered the approval a foregone conclusion and had Wronghead regret that Connecticut could not be surrounded by a wall of brass which would protect the blue laws, the rude living conditions, and the "equal poverty" of the old days of dependence upon the "hard-bound soil." Lamb, for his part, praised the imperial position of New York, with a state impost forcing tribute from the sister-states; expressed confidence in the efforts of Clinton, Jones, and Yates to protect the state against outside influences; and found encouragement in the "trite objections" to the Constitution made by Gerry, Mason, Lee, and other "scribblers." Thus opposition to the new plan of union was branded as the result of ignorant conservatism and contemptible self-interest; but there was no concerted action even to influence the Connecticut convention which was to meet in January. Humphreys, whose ambition had probably kept the Wits together as a more or less unified group, had gone to spend the winter with Washington at Mount Vernon; and even before he left he had turned his mind to the idea of gaining fame through the medium of the drama. The literary possibilities of the *Anarchiad* had been exhausted just as it had begun to have some large political significance.

The Wits themselves had applied the term "hotchpot" to their activities, and they perhaps could have selected no better. The motives that lay back of their writings were certainly complex and varied. Barlow and possibly Trumbull had some speculative interest in the disposal of western lands; and Humphreys, as a former army officer, may also have retained commutation certificates that gave him some concern in the matter. Trumbull and Hopkins both had a deeply rooted antagonism to mobs and the irrational activities of the crowd. Humphreys and Barlow were members of the Society of Cincinnati, Trumbull had been closely associated with the organization since its first general meeting, and all were sensitive to the criticism—much of it unfair—to which the Society had been subjected. Trumbull and Barlow were lawyers at a time when the people were closing courts, disrupting legal procedure, and promising violence to lawyers; and naturally they saw their livelihood threatened. None of them owned any considerable amount of real property, the economic welfare of those who resided in Hartford was dependent upon the growth of manufacturing and trade, and all were peculiarly vulnerable to the dangers of paper money. They were men of better education, wider experience, and broader vision than the average citizen; and their friends—particularly Humphreys'—were men whose horizons extended far beyond Connecticut. In addition, Hopkins and Trumbull were high-spirited men with a peculiar talent for satiric writing and an unquestioning belief that the rod was proper to a fool's back; Humphreys had a solemn conviction that he should benefit his country with his pen as well as with his sword; and Barlow was sufficiently adjustable, high-spirited, and ambitious to keep on good terms with them all. Living in a land of steady habits from which the wilder spirits had already emigrated, a state which had remained unaffected by the new fashions for constitutions and so had kept the lower classes safely disenfranchised, the Wits had to look beyond their borders for political

bugbears or else create them out of their own imaginations. Accordingly, they had never been welded into a close group by the heat of any real passion of fear or belief. They were held together by literary success and the accidental similarity of their wayward impulses; and, when they lost the stimulation of their first objects of satire and worked their literary design up to a climax, the political job which remained to be done had no great appeal for them, even though they had finally achieved some unity of belief and purpose.

The superiority of their literary ambitions over their political inspiration was revealed by the growing plan of their burlesque in comparison with the continued "hotchpot" of their satire. The design of the *American Antiquities* was suggested by the *Rolliad* papers; but the poets attempted humorous effects by calling to their readers' minds, by allusion and parody, more familiar poetry than that written by the *Rolliad* group. At first, though the authors suggested that they might show, in a future essay, that Homer, Virgil, and Milton had borrowed "many of their capital beauties" from the *Anarchiad,* they contented themselves entirely with a parody of Pope. The subtitle describing their work as "A Poem on the Restoration of Chaos and Substantial Night" was, of course, suggested by the *Dunciad;* and a considerable section of the first two numbers was nothing more than a re-wording of the vision in the third book of Pope's poem. The picture of Rhode Island in the third number probably owed something to the English poet's representation of England in the same vision, but the borrowing was less definite; and in the fourth number the *Essay on Man* was also called upon for a contribution. In addition, Humphreys had paid his own *Poem on the Happiness of America* the tribute of parody in the second number. It was not until the poets had reached Number VI that they began to give their selections a definite place in the epic from which they were supposedly quoting (though they had previously used the Homeric and Miltonic councils of war and lists of heroes); but with the citation of particular books they also began to take on a more positive epic manner, and the "dark world" invoked by Wronghead was that revealed by Sin when she opened Hell-gate in the second book of *Paradise Lost.* The next selection returned to the heroic games of an earlier part of the imaginary epic, and again the poets drew on the *Dunciad* for the opening lines. The soliloquy and consolation of Anarch after having been vanquished by Hesper—a conventional bit of epic action—was based upon Milton; and the advice of Hesper to the assembled sages, supposedly taken from the concluding book of the *Anarchiad,* was structurally characteristic of the moral epic from *Paradise Lost* to *The Vision of Columbus.* When the poets tried to carry on their work after the climax of Hesper's address, they leaned heavily on literary precedent for their representation of the lower world, citing in their critical notes Homer, Virgil, Milton, "the Gothic bards," Tasso, Ossian, and Dante; and the poem concluded with an imitation of Pope's versification, in the *Messiah,* of the prophetic passages of Isaiah. Throughout there was a good deal of additional literary allusiveness (including one couplet borrowed from Churchill's *Rosciad*), echoes of Virgil, Homer, and even *The Conquest of Canäan.* Barlow and Humphreys frequently imitated their own serious works, perhaps both consciously and inadvertently; the selections contained a number of allusions to and verbal echoes of *M'Fingal;* and on one occasion, in the fourth number, Hopkins used phrases and ideas that he later developed into an independent poem. In general, the history of the *Anarchiad* was like that of *M'Fingal;* it began as a rather haphazard political satire, containing a large element of simple parody, and it grew into a literary burlesque to which the satire was subordinate, at least in the minds of the authors. As in the case of *M'Fingal,* too, the tradition of its political effectiveness seems to be mostly a myth.

The significance of the *American Antiquities* series lies in the fact that it illustrates how easily even such serious poets as Barlow and Humphreys could be diverted from their chosen "road to fame" into a superficial "hotchpot" of satire and how trivial and literary their interests remained in the face of momentous political changes. All four of the authors were comparatively young men, and men of some vision; naturally they were inclined to be impatient with such older conservatives as William Williams and James Wadsworth and to be sympathetic toward the experimental proposal for a closer union under a strong general government. Yet they were led by the example of the *Dunciad* to waste their energies with ineffectual attacks upon harmless individuals, condemning mobs and paper-money movements on grounds already discounted by the participants, and, in general, climbing on the bandwagon of public opinion instead of trying to lead it. As the issue of federalism gradually became clarified for them, they did take sides and try to be of some practical political use; but when the issue became acute they quit writing. It was not because they failed to appreciate the situation: Barlow, in a Fourth of July address before the Society of Cincinnati in 1787, devoted a large part of his speech to the constitutional convention and concluded:

> Every possible encouragement for great and generous exertions, is now presented before us. Under the idea of a permanent and happy government, every point of view, in which the future situation of America can be placed, fills the mind with a peculiar dignity, and opens an unbounded field of thought. The natural resources of the country are inconceivably various and great; the enterprising genius of the people promises a most rapid improvement in all the arts that embelish human nature; the blessings of a rational government will invite emigrations from the rest of the world, and fill the empire with the worthiest and happiest of mankind; while the example of political wisdom and felicity here to be displayed will excite emulation through the kingdoms of the earth, and meliorate the conditions of the human race.

This sort of oratorical optimism and broad point of view—like the cheerful belief expressed in the same address that "the majority of a great people, on a subject which they understand, will never act wrong"—was much more characteristic of Barlow and of Humphreys than the irresponsible wit of the *American Antiquities.* But these two poets, who might have been expected to guide the series safely past trivialities, were hagridden by self-consciousness and

awareness of precedents; and they seem never to have realized that a writer might adopt a literary form and then so completely lose himself in it that he could devote his entire energies to some serious purpose. As concerned as they were with literature, they were in an environment in which spontaneous energy expressed itself in other ways, and they never escaped from a basic assumption that poetry was not quite real—that polite literature, like polite behavior, was a cultivated affectation.

III

For two of the wicked Wits the Hartford episode was a halfway point in careers that were to take new directions toward more varied activities in a wider world. For the other two it was a dead end. Lemuel Hopkins, to whom verse was never more than a social activity or a relief from occasional irritation, continued to write in the peculiarly caustic vein that makes his work the most distinctive of the group. A new body of wits grew up: Theodore Dwight, the younger brother of Timothy, who was later to become a distinguished newspaper editor; Richard Alsop, a remarkably well-read young man from Middletown, who was talented enough to become a fine poet had he been willing to devote himself wholeheartedly to the art; Elihu H. Smith, a young physician from Litchfield with unusual literary ambitions, who was to die of yellow fever before he fully revealed his independence of mind; Mason W. Cogswell, another young physician, who was too modest

John Trumbull

about his literary ability to co-operate fully with the others, although he wrote copiously in secret; and Nathaniel Dwight, another of Timothy's younger brothers, who occasionally contributed bits to the collaborated efforts of the others. Hopkins joined them and guided their efforts. They began *The Echo,* which reversed the line of development of the *American Antiquities* by starting as literary burlesque in the *American Mercury* for August 8, 1791, turning to political and personal satire, and finally going to pieces in a "hotchpot" of New Year's verse and individual satires. The *Courant* offered a rival burlesque, "The Versifier" (probably by Cogswell), for a short while in 1793; but when *The Echo* became politically embarrassing to the democratic *Mercury,* the Federalist *Courant* took it over and perhaps made Elisha Babcock regret that he had ever encouraged such irritating young men.

Hopkins, who was always loyal to his friends no matter how he may have reprobated their opinions, spent some years in indifference but apparently wrote the New Year's verses for the *Mercury* in 1793 and 1794. As he became aroused by French machinations and the activities of southern politicians, however, he came to feel more at home in the *Courant,* into which he moved in January, 1795, followed by *The Echo* upon its next appearance in August. There he began, in 1796, "The Guillotina," an annual post-boy's satire as sharp as its name, which he continued until his death. His most important single work, however, was an attack upon medical quackery, aroused by the "metallic points to relieve pain," patented by Dr. Elisha Perkins in February, 1796. These "tractors," designed to cure disease by the "electrical fluid" of galvanism, marked the high point of charlatanism in Connecticut medical history; and, when a pamphlet of enthusiastic testimonials appeared in October, 1796, Hopkins responded with a long satiric "Patent Address" in the *Courant* for November 7. Full of medical terminology but as biting as anything Hopkins had ever written, it probably had a good deal to do with encouraging the members of the state medical society to expel Perkins at their next spring meeting. Hopkins himself, during this time, was acquiring distinction as a physician and teacher of medicine and laying the foundation for lasting fame as a rival of Benjamin Rush in his treatments of consumption. His sudden death of pneumonia, on April 14, 1801, brought a close to the career of one of the few literary men of the time whose reputation for good sense and forthrightness was such that it could earn from an editor of opposite political views one simple comment: "He was an honest man."

Trumbull was less active in literature than Hopkins. Although he retained his sardonic attitude toward the world, even describing Washington as "all-fragrant with the odour of incense" during the first year of his presidency, he kept such comments for the ears and eyes of his friends and restrained himself in public. Political ambitions may have influenced his discretion, for after serving as one of the city fathers of Hartford he was appointed county attorney in 1789 and elected to the state legislature in 1792. But he probably shared Hopkins' indifference to politics during the first term of Washington's administration and found little in the affairs of the nation that could whip his indolent spirit into expression. In any case the state of his

health induced more melancholia than satire. Hopkins was worried about both the health and the spirits of his friend during the summer of 1792 but reported that he was "much better" the following year. Trumbull himself showed sufficient signs of recovery in May, 1793, to compose a virulent attack in verse upon Pierrepont Edwards, which he perhaps recognized as the most vicious poem he had ever written and, consequently, did not publish. He was one of the managers of the lottery authorized for building the Hartford courthouse, in 1794, but he had to spend so much of his time traveling to various watering places for his health that he was despondent about his political prospects. Eventually, however, he recovered and in 1800 again went to the state legislature, from which he was elevated a year later into a judgeship on the superior bench. From that time on he "declined," as he said, "any interference in the politics of the state, and applied himself exclusively to the duties of his office—being of the opinion, that the character of a partizan and political writer was inconsistent with the station of a judge and destructive of the confidence of suitors in the impartiality of judiciary decisions." He was also made judge of the Supreme Court of Errors in 1808 and retained both offices until the spring of 1819, when the democrats finished taking over the state.

Unless Trumbull's character had changed greatly during these years, he must have had some difficulty in keeping his hand from the pen. His literary reputation had flourished during the nineties, when the Federalists found so many of the sentiments of M'Fingal useful to their own purposes; but the democrats had taken advantage of the situation by attributing to the author some of the most objectionable opinions of the Tory spokesman. Leonard Chester, in particular, took a belated revenge at his appearance in the *Anarchiad* by giving a cruel portrayal of Trumbull in *Federalism Triumphant in the Steady Habits of Connecticut Alone,* a political farce widely circulated by the democrats in 1802. In addition to representing Trumbull as M'Fingal himself in his more objectionable moments, Chester told a libelous story of an ingenious Federalist scheme to get the author into the legislature and thence on the bench: "Thode" Dwight had been sent around the country saying that Trumbull "had been in a state of intoxication for years" and was utterly worthless—which made the republicans heatedly insist that Trumbull's opinion drunk was better than Dwight's sober and so elect him. There was probably just enough truth in the suggestion of the poet's interest in the bottle to drive Trumbull to a fury. How the former "Correspondent" and author of the second part of *The Progress of Dulness* managed to remain quiet is a mystery, but he apparently stayed out of the Connecticut controversy although he made occasional surreptitious contributions to the *New-England Palladium* in Boston. The only literary work attributed to him during his years on the bench was a short *Biographical Sketch of Governor Trumbull,* published in 1809.

Yet Trumbull retained his interest in literature. He kept an approving eye upon the satires of *The Echo* poets and may have made occasional contributions to them. When the collection was published as a volume in 1807 he was able to annotate his copy and note the authorship of many individual pieces. He also kept up with the new poets of his time, making notes for critical essays or expressing opinions concerning modern literature in letters to his friends. He had always been interested in the art of poetry and particularly enthusiastic about the metrical variety Pope achieved within the bounds of the heroic couplet; and in a discussion of prosody for the second part of Noah Webster's *Grammatical Institute of the English Language* he had attempted to point out the possibilities of that measure. The new writers who seemed to depend upon novelty rather than craftsmanship for their effects had no charm for him. They were "discordant" and "unnatural," given to "confusion," "rant," and "eccentricity." He had no use for the "lullaby of *Wordsworth's* lyrical ballads" and none for Crabbe's *The Borough* or for Southey's *Thalaba* or *The Curse of Kehama*. As one who had been early taught by Lord Kames to prize the complete visual image, he saw Crabbe and Wordsworth "bathing in the muddy bottom of the streams of Helicon" and certainly would have found nothing more than pure confusion in the association of ideas that led away from the actual scene in "Tintern Abbey." Coleridge (and perhaps Southey as well) wrote "as though a poetical Bedlam was about to be erected on the summit of Parnassus." Thomas Moore, with a "poetic fire" that was "mostly phosphoric," delighted in "gaudy" images, painting similes when he should have been describing the object. Byron also failed to excel in description, specializing in passion and feeling "of the *worst* sort." As a moralist, Trumbull saw no excuse, in 1820, for "the voluptous licentiousness of T. Moore, the profligate buffonery of Peter Pindar, or the unprincipled spleen and misanthropy of Lord Byron." As an artist, he found fault, in 1814, with all blank verse—even that of the previously admired Milton. He did not approve, on any score, German ballads or Scottish imitations of them. Not one of the Connecticut Wits, as time went on, grew further out of touch with his age.

But Trumbull could not realize it. The substance of his irritability had produced a few poetic pearls, but most of it ultimately went into the shell that he built around himself for protection against the world. His friend Samuel G. Goodrich published his *Poetical Works* in two well-printed volumes in 1820 and lost a thousand dollars on the venture. The thousand dollars went to the poet as advance royalty, but he never fully believed that the sale of his works could barely pay the cost of printing and was never quite convinced that he had not been mistreated. He remained in Hartford until 1825, composing rather surprisingly mild and cheerful New Year's verse for the *Courant* in 1824, then joined his daughter in Detroit, where he lived the last six years of his life, dying on May 11, 1831, the longest lived of all the Wits, although he had been the first to give up the struggle for literary distinction.

MAJOR WORKS

Benjamin Franklin V

SOURCE: An introduction to *The Prose of the Minor Connecticut Wits, Vol. I,* by Theodore Dwight, edited by

Benjamin Franklin V, Scholars' Facsimiles & Reprints, 1974, pp. iii-xv.

[Franklin is an American educator, editor, and critic. Below, he comments on the breadth and variety of prose pieces composed by the major and minor Connecticut Wits.]

It is the custom for each new appreciator of the Connecticut Wits to acknowledge that group's important place in the history of American letters and then lament that their books, some of which were among the most ambitious of their day, rest neglected on library shelves with two centuries of accumulated dust as coverlets. In the middle years of this century the Wits have been ignored because of the dominance of the useful but limited new criticism, because of a widely held but generally unchallenged belief that little of literary merit was written in this country before 1800, and because, frankly, their works do not constitute great literature. In the past decade, however, there has been a revival of interest in the Wits . . . , and the reasons for it are not difficult to discern. The Wits did not approach the genius of their mentor Pope in poetry and they did not possess the skills of Addison or Steele in their prose, but they were able and energetic literary craftsmen who fashioned the events of their day into productions that were on occasion very well received (e.g., *M'Fingal*), who defended America against foreign writers who branded it neither fit subject for nor adequate inspirer of artistic expression (e.g., *Greenfield Hill*), and who were not reluctant to attempt an occasional epic (e.g., *The Conquest of Canäan*). Their ambitions, accomplishments, and the esteem in which they were held helped make them, quite simply, the most formidable American authors in the last quarter of the eighteenth century.

. . . Membership in the group was unofficial, but the nine men whose names are most often associated with it fall conveniently into a Major and a Minor group, with the division being made in large part on the quantity and quality of literary output and the ages of the individuals. Joel Barlow (1754-1812), Timothy Dwight (1752-1817), David Humphreys (1752-1818), and John Trumbull (1750-1831) constitute the Majors, and Richard Alsop (1761-1815), Mason Fitch Cogswell (1761-1830), Theodore Dwight (1764-1846), Lemuel Hopkins (1750-1801), and Elihu Hubbard Smith (1771-1798) comprise the Minors. The Majors, with the exception of Humphreys, may be read today with some degree of pleasure, but so may the Minors, even though as a group they are considerably less heralded than the Majors. . . .

The light in which most of the Minor Wits' prose must be read is that of the politics of their day, and in their prose one may trace the decline of the Federalism that they embraced with such vigor. Especially instructive are Theodore Dwight's heretofore neglected pamphlets that were written between 1792 and 1810, years during which the Federalists lost their popular support and became, in large part, a party of memory.

Dwight's address to the Society of the Cincinnati in Hartford on 4 July 1792 reflects the thoughts of a man whose beliefs had been borne out by recent history. At that time the Constitution was five years old, the Bill of Rights and the Bank of the United States were but one, Washington was still in his first term in office, and the future looked bright for America. So in 1792, and especially on the anniversary of America's independence, Dwight could speak of the antebellum England as the "most haughty nation on earth" and could not only applaud without reservation America's revolution but could, in full confidence, call for the freedom of all oppressed people, be they French, Swedish, Russian, German, Negro, or female. After quoting from the book of Isaiah, Dwight concludes his address with these words: "The perdition in scripture of a season of universal freedom, and tranquility, is rapidly fulfilling; a spirit of toleration pervades all nations; and the religion of EMANUAL is extending its influence over the the [*sic*] regions of bigotry, persecution, and idolatry."

Two years later Dwight delivered an oration in which he continued to call for the freedom of all people, but his specific interest this time was the Negroes in Connecticut and the country at large who were being denied their basic human rights. (It is a mistake to consider the politically conservative Federalists backward in all matters. Both Dwight and Smith wrote eloquently for the manumission of slaves, and Smith was apparently a supporter of women's rights.) Dwight here announces that he is more concerned with justice for Negroes than he is with peace for Americans, and he writes convincingly that the only strong argument for the retention of slavery is interest, and "when it shall cease to be for the interest of mankind, to torture their fellow creatures in this wicked commerce, not one solitary individual will be found trafficking in human flesh." Dwight holds as an example to American slave owners the French Revolution and the revolt of the slaves against the government in St. Domingo in August 1791. He goes on to damn for the first time the excesses of the French Revolution, but his larger concern remains that all oppressed people should and shall be free.

His compassion is nowhere present in the oration of 4 July 1798. Gone is his advocacy of universal brotherhood, gone is his belief that America is a united country, and gone is his willingness to accept political idiosyncrasies. Dwight, a rabid Federalist, is here concerned with foreign and domestic influences that he thought threatened America's still fledgling government, and he calls on all citizens to be influenced neither by the example of the French government nor by its apostle in this country, Thomas Jefferson. Dwight breaks from the usual practice of eulogizing liberty on the fourth of July as he announces his topic: "THAT THE UNITED STATES ARE IN DANGER OF BEING ROBBED OF THEIR INDEPENDENCE, BY THE FRAUD AND VIOLENCE OF THE FRENCH REPUBLIC" and "that there has been for many years, a steady effort on the part of France, to destroy the Independence of this country." He disposes of the argument that we are still indebted to the French for their assistance during our war with England, and then takes the offensive throughout the rest of his address by reconstructing the case against Citizen Genêt and the French ambassadors who followed him. It is understandable to Dwight why Americans would sympathize with the new French government; after all, we are a people who love liberty and naturally side with revolution against tyranny. Yet, grievous excesses did occur after the revolu-

tion in France, and Dwight proposes several ways to keep similar excesses from visiting our shores: by being aware of individuals such as Jefferson "who wish to barter our freedom"; by keeping foreigners, and especially the Irish, out of elective office; and by a general resolve amongst our citizenry "to defend our Constitution, and Country, against every foreign encroachment; and especially against the encroachment of France."

The worst fears of Dwight and the Federalists came true when Jefferson became President in 1801, and it was in part in response to that election (and to the greater issue of a growing constituency for the Republicans) that Dwight delivered his oration on 7 July of that year, again ostensibly to celebrate the anniversary of America's independence, but in fact to place all evil on the Republicans and to claim virtue and godliness as the private possessions of the Federalists. He warns that the Jacobins (as the Federalists repeatedly called Jefferson's party's members) will not only destroy the national and state governments, but they will also bring about irreligion, immorality, and chaos. In all of this Dwight embraces religion, family, and general morality and thinks "how glorious it will be for Connecticut to stand firmly amidst the convulsions, and downfall of the nations of the world." He is obviously on the defensive, but even though his *ad hominem* arguments seem ludicrous after two centuries, they were strongly felt by him and his party after the government of Washington and Adams fell into the hands of the hated Jefferson.

Dwight's *Remarks on the Documents Accompanying the Late Message of President Madison* was first published in three consecutive numbers of his own *Connecticut Courant* (18 and 25 December 1809; 1 January 1810) in response to the documents published after Madison's message of 27 November in which he announced that he was dismissing the British Minister Francis James Jackson because he had insulted the American government. The accompanying documents were the correspondence between Jackson and the American Secretary of State Robert Smith which were made public in December to show that, in Madison's words, "forgetting the respect due to all governments, [Jackson] *did not refrain from imputations on this, which required that no further communications should be received from him.*" Dwight agrees that if our government had indeed been insulted by Jackson then Madison's seemingly precipitate action would therefore be justified, but what he attempts in this pamphlet is a close analysis of the Jackson-Smith correspondence to discern for himself whether or not Madison acted correctly. His bias is of course anti-Madison and pro-England so it is not surprising that he concludes that the President acted not only incorrectly but also foolishly since to dismiss the English Minister might well lead to war with England that would force America into the supportive yet dangerous arms of France. Such a dependence on France is what the Federalists believed the Republicans wanted, and "it is . . . much to be feared, that the instructions of the master have not been lost on the pupil—that the precepts and example of Mr. Jefferson, while President, sunk too deeply into the mind of Mr. Madison, while Secretary of State."

As Federalism became less popular with the electorate

and as the party's powers therefore waned after Jefferson's election in 1800, Dwight's publications became more lengthy and detailed in their attacks on the Republicans and their policies. His six short pieces grew from eighteen to forty-eight pages between 1792 and 1810, but his next three efforts, in 1816, 1833, and 1839, were more ambitious undertakings that demanded the hard covers of books to contain his thoughts. In all three works he relies heavily on logic, documents, and history to support his continued assault, but his obviously hostile attitude toward events and personalities well in the past undercut much of the force of his arguments.

The first of these, written as Federalism continued to flourish only in Connecticut, was *An Answer to Certain Parts of a Work Published by Mathew Carey, Entitled "The Olive Branch,"* or *"Faults on Both Sides,"* published anonymously by "A Federalist" in 1816. *The Olive Branch* appeared in 1814 and was a call for the reconciliation of factions after the War of 1812. In his answer to the seventh edition of Carey's book Dwight congratulates the author for condescending to admit that the Republicans had erred in the past, but he upbraids him sarcastically and unmercifully for stating what the Federalists had always known—that the Republicans had opposed Federalist programs and ideas (viz., Jay's Treaty, the Alien and Sedition Acts, and a navy) not because they lacked merit but because they were endorsed by the Federalists. Dwight says that just to admit those errors after a number of years is insufficient, that the Republicans should be made to pay dearly for their spiteful behavior.

But while he faintly praises Carey for admitting Republican errors, he damns him for finding any fault with the Federalists. He defends his party against the charge that it caused the War of 1812 and then failed to support it, and he in turn places the full blame for that war directly on Madison. Dwight restates his 1810 argument on the Madison-Smith-Jackson matter and concludes that the war, finally, was fought over the problem of impressment. The book ends with a defense of the Hartford Convention and with a dismissal of Carey's book as worthless.

As executive officer, Dwight was the only nonmember present at the Hartford Convention in 1814-15, and in *The History of the Hartford Convention* (1833) he summarizes his position in the following manner: the executive officer "was the only disinterested witness of what was transacted by the convention. He was present throughout every sitting, witnessed every debate, heard every speech, was acquainted with every motion and every proposition, and carefully noted the result of every vote on every question. He, therefore, of necessity was, ever has been, and still is, the only person, except the members, who had the opportunity to know, from personal observation, every thing that occured. His testimony, therefore, must be admitted and received, unless he can be discredited, his testimony invalidated, or its force entirely destroyed." Dwight's purpose in writing this book was to defend the Convention against ignorant criticism, but his credentials hardly need have been presented since what he wrote is not an history of the Convention at all; rather, it is a lengthy and detailed attack on Jefferson, Madison, and the Republican's rea-

sons for entering and continuing the War of 1812. He reiterates the arguments and observations he made in his earlier publications (the Republicans were pro-French and anti-British; Jefferson opposed funding, banks, Hamilton, and the Jay Treaty; the difficulty between Madison and Francis James Jackson; Jefferson's Mazzei Letter; and so on), rehashes the reasons for the war, and again concludes that the only legitimate reason for the war was the easily resolved problem of impressment. The Federalists were convinced that the war was permitted to continue after all issues had been resolved solely to humiliate Great Britain.

What passes for the history of the Hartford Convention in roughly the last fifth of the book is more a presentation of documents than an actual history. There were twenty-six delegates (including Harrison Gray Otis and Roger Sherman) from five New England states, and they considered revising the Constitution so it would permit the states to have more rights. (They did not, as is commonly asserted, propose seceding from the Union.) But however noble the aims of those men were, their efforts were entirely without effect because the conclusion of the war was announced shortly after they adjourned. With the end of the war sectionalism and party factionalism all but died in New England, even though there was a hard core of Federalists who would never forgive nor forget the chicanery of Jefferson, Madison, and their followers, as is illustrated by Dwight's *History*.

Dwight's final book was *The Character of Thomas Jefferson, as Exhibited in His Own Writings* (1839), a volume in which he attacks for the last time the man whose ideas he found consistently unacceptable since his 1798 pamphlet. But while he was aware that "the federalists, as a political party, have long ceased to act, or even exist," and that the election of 1800 signalled their demise, his purpose in writing this book was to show to a younger generation of Americans the principles on which the Republic was founded and how Jefferson himself deviated from them. In order to do this, he quotes extensively from Jefferson's own published correspondence so that the portrait that emerges of our third President "is drawn by himself, and therefore must be a likeness." One may of course question the verisimilitude of Jefferson's portrait, but the most striking picture in the book is the one of the author himself.

It is clear from reading his published prose that Dwight was a citizen who dutifully concerned himself with the issues facing his state and nation and had the ability to put his impressions of those issues in writing and into print. But while his earliest publications extol the virtues of all men, with the excesses of the French Revolution and then the election of Jefferson he became dedicated to a defense of Federalism and of the old ways. As the eighteenth century grew into the nineteenth and as it in turn progressed, as the country expanded westward and as the population began to swell (from about 4 million in 1790 to more than 17 million in 1840), Dwight was not able to enlarge his own political and social vision and grow apace. Instead, if anything his vision narrowed until it became fixed finally not on what he took to be the foibles of the early Republicans, but specifically on the one man he saw as responsible for the ruin of the pure American government that was best embodied in Washington. By 1839 Jefferson had been out of office for thirty years and dead for thirteen; Madison and Monroe had each served two terms, John Quincy Adams one, Jackson two, and Van Buren was in the midst of his one term; American literature, which had offered little of unqualified merit at the time of Dwight's 1792 pamphlet, had by 1839 produced the complete works of Charles Brockden Brown, most of the major productions of Irving and Cooper, Bryant's best poems, substantial work by Poe, Hawthorne, Simms, Emerson, and Longfellow, and the rough humor of the old Southwest was being read in the *Spirit of the Times;* literary romanticism was being established in this country, and transcendentalism had begun to flourish practically next door to Dwight—during the years between his first and last published efforts, then, Dwight became a grouch, a sore loser who was unable to forget and move past a defeat incurred as the new century began. His book on Jefferson is a sad portrait of an anachronistic figure trying for the last time to recapture the past by vilifying the memory of his detested political foe.

Richard Alsop, who was, in verse, the most politically assertive of the Minor Wits, wrote but one political tract in prose, and it was inspired by a pamphlet war during the 1803 campaign to elect twenty nominees to the Connecticut State Legislature. In that year the Federalists were of course struggling to maintain what favor they held with the electorate, and, in hopes of assuring the election of their own men to the General Assembly on 19 September, they published an essay entitled "An Address to the Freemen of Connecticut" in the *Connecticut Courant* on 8 June. In that piece they pointed out that Connecticut government under the Federalists had been good for all people in the past, so there was no need to change to a government of "visionary theories, or the mad projects of designing men . . . ," especially when the Republican national government was attempting "to subvert the system of our State government. . . . " The piece concludes with a list of the names of twenty Federalists to be supported.

They evidently issued their appeal too early, however, because the Republicans had time to publish a rebuttal in the form of a pamphlet, *Republican Address to the Free Men of Connecticut,* dated 30 August 1803. Here the General Committee of the Republicans attacks the Federalists for their blind acceptance of the *status quo,* for their dedication to a master/slave society, and for their monarchical leanings, and it concludes that a state government under the Federalists would set Connecticut "in hostile array" against the national government. Therefore, the freemen of Connecticut should vote for the twenty Republicans whose names appear at the end of their pamphlet. This tract apparently was persuasive because the Federalists felt the need to reprint their essay in the *Connecticut Courant* for 7 September, twelve days before the election, and to publish it as a pamphlet.

The Federalists issued two other pamphlets which attacked the Republican piece and defended the integrity of their own, and one of them was Alsop's *To the Freemen of the State of Connecticut.* What Alsop wrote, then, was

a Federalist response to the Republican response to the Federalists, and in it he questions the candor of the Republicans, defends his own party against the charge of monarchism, and concludes that God will protect the Federalists "against the rude shocks of democratic violence. . . . " He is defensive throughout and evinces none of the biting satire that is found in his poetic contributions to the individual numbers of *The Echo* that first appeared in the 1790s. There is a sense of doom in this pamphlet, an underlying acknowledgment that the freemen of Connecticut were at that moment slipping even further than before out of the political camp of the Federalists. That the Federalists won that particular election was only a short-lived comfort for them as the Republicans thereafter did continue to gain more support from the electorate, but as his party dwindled Alsop did not attempt to resurrect it and live in the past.

But, when he chose in 1808 to translate Étienne Gosse's *The Lovers of La Vendee, or Revolutionary Tyranny,* which was originally published in four volumes in France in 1799, he was making available for the first and only time to American readers this novel about the horrors of the civil war that was fought in the maritime department of Vendée, France, between the peasants of that area and the republicans. The melodramatic story of Emily Dorman, her father, and her seemingly immortal lover Darcourt is engaging enough, but Alsop was taken with the novel not because of its art but because "it exhibits but too true a picture of the state of La Vendée and the sufferings of the unfortunate inhabitants, during the civil war provoked by the cruelties of the Revolutionary Government." He thought his effort would be well rewarded if it would "impress on one of his countrymen a deeper conviction of [civil war's] baleful effects. . . . " So while less consistent and less vociferous than Dwight in his damnation of the excesses of the French Revolution, Alsop was nonetheless fretful, as Jefferson's second term was about to end, that the American Jacobins might cause in this country a destruction such as that their French counterparts caused in La Vendée.

The most popular piece of prose by any of the Minor Wits was Alsop's *A Narrative of the Adventures and Sufferings, of John R. Jewitt* (1815), a book that has gone through about twenty editions and which is not included in this volume because it has been published in facsimile elsewhere. (Also not included is Alsop's translation of Abbe Don J. Ignatius Molina's *The Geographical, Natural and Civil History of Chili,* 1808.) Jewitt was an Englishman who was, in 1802 at age nineteen, the armorer on the *Boston* that was bound for the American northwest. When the ship stopped at Nootka Sound in Vancouver, twenty-five of the twenty-seven men on board, including the captain, John Salter, were decapitated by the natives who were led by their chief Maquina. Jewitt and the sailmaker John Thompson were able to avoid the mob's wrath, and they lived with the Indians for twenty-eight months, from March 1803 to July 1805. Jewitt and Thompson were rescued by Capt. Samuel Hill and the *Lydia* as it was sailing for the Orient, and they finally arrived in Boston in 1807, the year Jewitt published his diary as *A Journal, Kept at Nootka Sound. . . .*

In 1813 Jewitt and his wife of four years moved to Middletown, Connecticut, where he became friendly with Alsop to whom he recounted his exploits. Alsop took the original *Journal,* embellished it with the details Jewitt added orally, and had this enlarged edition published as the *Narrative* in 1815, the year of his own death. Jewitt's *Journal,* as published in 1807, contains forty-eight pages of entries such as this one: "*March* 1. (Wednesday.) Clear weather. Saw twelve whales out in the offing." Alsop's edition of over two hundred pages clothes the skeletal nature of the original, but it does more than just elaborate on the specific events that are detailed there. The earlier document begins with Jewitt's arrival and ends abruptly with his departure from Nootka Sound, but the 1815 account begins with the young Jewitt in England where the captain and certain crewmen of the *Boston* visit his father, and when the reader soon sees the heads of Capt. Salter and William Ingraham among those aligned on the *Boston*'s deck, there is a feeling of loss that is not gained from a reading of the 1807 edition. The most striking difference between the two, however, is the amount of space Alsop gives to the customs and habits of Maquina's people. We learn that they were poor hunters but excellent fishermen, that their music was soft and harmonic and was often accompanied by a drum, that they had difficulty felling the trees that would become their canoes, and that the other tribes in the area were actual and not merely abstractions.

The great temptation with this book is to compare it to the early works of Herman Melville, and especially to his first novel, *Typee.* In each of the works the narrator suffers an injury that does not heal immediately, has as a companion a crewman from his ship, is held in benign slavery by the natives, and is both pleased and saddened to leave the people who cared for him throughout his captivity. But while these parallels do in fact exist they are only superficial, and Alsop's tale of Jewitt's sufferings offers considerably less artistry than does Melville's story of Tommo. . . .

Alsop published little prose, but that that he did reveals a man who expressed his political views more obliquely and subtly than Dwight, who understood the craft of fiction although he created none himself, and who was competent with languages, as his translations from the Spanish and French attest. . . .

Elihu Hubbard Smith was the last of all the Wits to be born and the first to die, but in his short life he became a doctor (he died from the yellow fever that he was helping others overcome), published several letters to Dr. William Buel on the 1795 fever epidemic in New York, and helped edit *The Medical Repository* (1797-98). He also wrote poems, an opera (*Edwin and Angelina*) in 1797, and edited his best known work, *American Poems, Selected and Original* (1793), the first anthology of American poetry. Smith wrote little prose, but what he did write is significant and reveals his quality of mind.

His 1798 *Discourse* on the manumission of slaves is a brief recounting of the history of slavery and a statement on the basic dignity of all men. After asserting that "the history of man is the history of slavery," he goes on to trace that history to the time of the wrathful John Woolman and the more subdued Anthony Benezet, Quakers who sounded the call in this country for the freedom of all slaves. Smith's target is the slave owners who tried to defend themselves on the grounds of justice (they owned slaves and were therefore entitled to them), on the grounds of humanity (they improved the plight of the unfortunate Africans), on the grounds of policy (other nations do not frown upon slavery), on the grounds that "it is for *individual interest,* and thus for *national benefit,* that slavery be permitted," and finally on the grounds that even if slavery is undesirable they can do nothing to correct it because the institution began with their fathers' fathers, and to do away with it would be to destroy the social fabric. Smith finds all of these arguments fallacious and inhumane and concludes that if Negroes are on occasion less than totally satisfactory as human beings, it is not their fault since any people would be corrupted if they were constantly exposed to debauchery, drunkenness, and other such behavior as exhibited by their masters. Despite their ill treatment, however, the Negroes "exhibit many examples of humble, but of cheering virtue." Such a statement today sounds dated, but his *Discourse* is evidence that Smith was a man who was genuinely concerned about the plight of slaves and was a man who could and did speak eloquently in their behalf. (His humanitarian leanings are also evident in his willingness to write an advertisement for Charles Brockden Brown's *Alcuin, A Dialogue* that was published anonymously in New York in 1798. *Alcuin* is an early radical argument for women's rights, and Smith evidently shared that attitude with his friend Brown. He also wrote, with Samuel L. Mitchill and Edward Miller, *Address, &c* [1796] in which the three doctors argue against the absurd medical practices of the past and announce that their *Medical Repository* will be an attempt to produce facts which "are the only rational basis of theory.")

Perhaps the most interesting of all of Smith's publications is the series of six short pieces he wrote for *The Monthly Magazine* in London in 1798, half of which were published after his death in September of that year. Here he gives biographical and critical sketches of five of the Wits—Timothy Dwight (July, pp. 1-3), John Trumbull (August, pp. 81-82), David Humphreys (September, pp. 167-68), Joel Barlow (October, pp. 250-51), and Lemuel Hopkins (November, pp. 343-44)—in addition to a defense of the collaborative *Anarchiad* in which he permits excerpts from that satiric poem to speak for themselves (December, pp. 418-19).

Smith wrote these pieces because he had noticed a factual error in an advertisement for one of Timothy Dwight's books in *The Monthly Magazine* and because he therefore wanted to offer an accurate account of "the progress of the fine arts" in America. Marcia Bailey, in *A Lesser Hartford Wit, Dr. Elihu Hubbard Smith,* makes the case that Smith was, with these sketches, among the first to offer biographical information about the most important men of letters in this country at that time, that he was among the first Americans to defend the talents of American artists in British publications, and that he, the first anthologist of American poetry, was America's "first literary spokesman abroad." While such claims may in fact be accurate, they suffer from too great an effort to make Smith's contributions more significant than they are. Much more to his credit is the quality of these sketches that were written at a time when Americans tended to apotheosize most things indigenous to their country. Smith knew these five men intimately, so one would expect him to laud their literary productions without reservation, especially when writing to a foreign audience. Instead of doing that he offers a balanced and intelligent criticism of their work that is as accurate today as it was then. Timothy Dwight was his mentor and was one of the most formidable men of his time, yet Smith laments that his elder's poetic powers have produced works which no longer appeal to the modern reader and therefore will not "promote the welfare of mankind, in any remarkable degree." Similarly, he finds Humphreys an ordinary poet who possesses no great originality or enthusiasm, asserts that Hopkins is "more remarkable for invention than for execution," and avers that Barlow's *Vision of Columbus* lacks "bold and original flights of genius" and that "some of its most interesting passages are close copies of correspondent descriptions in the Incas of Marmontel." All is far from negative in these comments as Smith is arguing for the validity of America's literature, but this kind of integrity from a friend of those he is recommending is refreshing.

While these pieces were first published in England, they were noticed in this country as well. Joseph Dennie, who was a friend of Smith's and who was to gain fame as editor of *The Port Folio* in Philadelphia, was editor of the *Farmers' Museum, or Lay Preacher's Gazette* in Walpole, New Hampshire, a newspaper in which he published the five biographical sketches in the numbers of 1, 15, and 29 April; 2 and 23 September 1799. To several of them Dennie added his own comments in which he condemns America for forcing Smith to send his productions to foreign publications and for offering in our own press "meargre memories of a bloated 'General,' the adventures of a cattle convict, and the 'experiences and awakenings' of a baptist preacher" to inquisitive foreigners as examples of illustrious Americans. (Dennie thought so highly of the sketches that he reissued them in *The Spirit of the Farmers' Museum, and Lay Preacher's Gazette,* an anthology he edited in 1801.) Dennie's railing at his countrymen and journalists did not go unheeded as *The Monthly Magazine and American Review,* edited in New York by C. B. Brown, printed the five sketches in May, August, and September-December 1799, and June 1800. Within three years, then, these short yet significant pieces were published four times and therefore rank behind Alsop's story of Jewitt as the most popular prose pieces by the Minor Wits.

Smith was the most liberal, least political, and least doctrinaire of the Minor Wits, and, even though he died before he was thirty, he is the most interesting of the group. Hitherto unavailable but valuable Smith material has recently appeared in James E. Cronin's edition of *The Diary of Elihu Hubbard Smith (1771-1798)* (1973).

The Minor Wits were neither extremely talented nor popular writers of prose, and to see them at their artistic best one must examine their poems. But their prose, and especially that of Dwight, offers the view of bright men as they responded to the deterioration of their revered Federalist

party. It is nonetheless too simple to brand them as only political conservatives who became anachronistic as a new century began: they were men who cared deeply for their country, who had a belief in the basic dignity and worth of all men, who were generally humane, and who were men of varied if modest literary talents. . . .

Benjamin Franklin V

SOURCE: An introduction to *The Poetry of the Minor Connecticut Wits,* edited by Benjamin Franklin V, Scholars' Facsimiles & Reprints, 1970, pp. xi-xxii.

[*In the following excerpt from a 1967 introduction, Franklin presents a brief overview of the poetry of the lesser-known Connecticut Wits.*]

John Trumbull, Timothy Dwight, David Humphreys, and Joel Barlow dominated the American literary scene in the last two decades of the eighteenth and the first decade of the nineteenth century. These poets, all born between 1750 and 1754 and all graduates of Yale College, wrote poetry that for the most part praised the history and the society of our new nation. All but Barlow were politically, social-

"You'll rue this inauspicious morn / And curse the day you e're were born": an illustration from Trumbull's McFingal.

ly, and religiously conservative and were the first Americans to speak out against the freethinking and, as they saw them, ignorant masses. Contemporary to and closely associated with these poets was another literary coterie that included Richard Alsop (1761-1815), Mason Fitch Cogswell (1761-1830), Theodore Dwight (1764-1846), Lemuel Hopkins (1750-1801), and Elihu Hubbard Smith (1771-1798). These nine men have been known collectively as the Connecticut, or Hartford, Wits, but in 1907 Annie Russell Marble correctly divided them into a "major" (the former) and a "minor" (the latter) group (*Heralds of American Literature,* 1907). With the exception of the Deist Smith, the Minor Wits held the same cultural beliefs as the major group, the average age of the Minors was ten years younger than the Majors, and Cogswell (in 1780) and Smith (in 1786) earned degrees at Yale while Alsop, Theodore Dwight (both in 1798), and Hopkins (in 1784) were awarded honorary degrees there. The most noticeable distinction between the two groups is the amount of poetry they produced. The Major Wits were prolific to the extent of tedium, while, the Minor Wits do not equal in quantity the collected poems of a Barlow or a Timothy Dwight.

At the time the English literati were aware of the newnesses of the *Lyrical Ballads,* the Minor Wits, as did all Federalist poets, emulated the poetics of the English neoclassicists in general and of Pope in particular. The logical patterns of parallel and contrast, the metaphoric meanings, puns, diction, and heroic couplets—all derived from Pope and the Augustans—may be seen in the poetry of the Minor Wits. Gordon E. Bigelow has noticed that the American poets writing around 1800, not unlike the Augustans, "looked upon these 'ornaments,' as the 'enamel,' 'painting,' or 'colors' which a poet could apply, as it were, from the outside, which could be manipulated or revised according to rules which had no reference to the inner intent of the particular poem" (*Rhetoric and American Poetry of the Early National Period,* 1960). Although not every poem by the Minor Wits contains all of these devices, almost all of their poems include some of them.

The eighteen numbers of "The Echo" which were collected in *The Echo; With Other Poems* are the basis for whatever fame or notoriety the Minor Wits today possess. It is generally agreed that Alsop edited these parodies, burlesques, satires, and lampoons, but Cogswell, Dwight, Hopkins, and Smith either co-authored various numbers with Alsop or wrote some individually. The individual "Echoes" attack the elderly Samuel Adams, the philosophy of H. H. Brackenridge, speeches by John Hancock, the general behavior of the Jacobins or Democrats, the French Revolution, and the archenemy of the Federalists, Thomas Jefferson. The Federalist *Echo,* then, ridicules in heroic couplets the principles of the Democrats. Alsop and the other Minor Wits,

> using every tactic of the smear and the big lie, . . . branded the republican Tammany sometimes as 'Jacobin,' a term equivalent to the modern 'Red' or 'Commie,' and hurled personal abuse at men of their own kind . . . whose espousal of republican principles made them traitors to their class. They stirred up class prej-

udice against 'high-flying mushrooms,'—against newly-made citizens of Irish birth in particular—and against native born 'people's friends' like John Hancock of Massachusetts, who not only fraternized with foreigners but treated 'Negroes to a royal dance' (Mary Dexter Bates, "Columbia's Bards: a Study of American Verse from 1783 through 1799," Unpub. diss., [Brown Univ., 1954]).

The spirit of *The Echo* is accurately captured in the plates by the miniature painter Elkanah Tisdale. . . . Tisdale, who allegedly wrote and illustrated the political satire entitled *The Gerry Mander* (Salem, 1812), was also responsible for the plates in Trumbull's *M'Fingal.* It appears that since Tisdale did the plates in both *The Echo* and *M'Fingal,* two of the most important volumes in our early National period, he possessed at least the spirit of the Wits. Scholarship into the *ethos* of Tisdale the man and the artist might well be a fruitful venture.

In another joint effort Alsop teamed with Dwight and Hopkins to write *The Political Green-House, for the year 1798.* This political satire was patterned after the new year's verses of the day; like *The Echo,* it denounces Jefferson, the Democrats, and the Jacobins. It vividly limns post-Revolutionary France as a wasteland, and it praises the state of Vermont for purging its government of Jacobins. This poem praises Benjamin Rush, but it lampoons the Major Wit Joel Barlow, the conservative turned Democrat.

The remainder of Alsop's poetry is non-political. His most ambitious effort was *The Charms of Fancy,* a work written in 1788 but not published until 1856. If this is Alsop's most ambitious poem, it is not his most successful. The notes are ponderous, the diction is stilted, and "in all its 2300 lines of heroic couplets [it] contains not a fresh image or an original idea" (William P. Trent, *et al.,* ed., *Cambridge History of American Literature,* 1917).

Alsop's two best poems are two of his shortest. In "Verses to the Shearwater—On the Morning After a Storm at Sea" (or "Ode to the Sheer Water"), the poet effectively captures the sailor's thoughts after an uneasy night, and he neatly juxtaposes the tumult of the waves and the civilization of the sailor with the simple existence of the bird. "Song from the Italian" may well not be a translation at all since there is nowhere a reference to a specific Italian verse. This *carpe diem* poem, while not possessing the urgency of Marvel's "To His Coy Mistress," is nonetheless a delightful attempt by the speaker to seduce, by means of logic, the "fair Iola." It may be true that "as a poet Alsop was often elegant, but his verse was generally without energy" (Rufus W. Griswold, *The Poets and Poetry of America,* 1842); still, these two short poems indicate that on occasion Alsop's "powers were certainly above the ordinary level of our native authors" (Samuel Kettell, *Specimens of American Poetry,* 1829).

Alsop, proficient in several languages, translated a number of poems into English, especially from the Italian. His longest translation is *The Enchanted Lake of the Fairy Morgana,* a translation of the second book of the comic Italian poet Francisco Berni's *Orlando Inamorato.* Alsop is here "unhampered by that self-consciousness and stiffness of expression which are the most common faults of the inexperienced translator" (William B. Otis, *American Verse 1625-1807,* 1909), and the poem is enhanced by the poet's own corrections and notes.

Elihu Hubbard Smith, editor of *American Poems, Selected and Original,* the first anthology of American poetry, produced little poetry himself. Smith's version of Goldsmith's ballad "Edwin and Angelina," the opera *'Edwin and Angelina, or the Banditti, an Opera in Three Acts,* contains the abundance of romanticism that was characteristic of the late eighteenth century. It was performed only once on the New York stage. This first American drama of outlaws probably influenced Dunlap to write the second outlaw drama, *The Man of Fortitude* (Marcia E. Bailey, *A Lesser Hartford Wit, Dr. Elihu Hubbard Smith 1771-1798,* 1928).

In "Occasional Address" Smith apotheosizes the theater. He traces the history of the theater from the mystery plays to the English actor Barton Booth (d. 1733), and he believes that a play should delight,

> But greater still, and far more nice the art,
> To fix the impressive moral in the heart.

Smith also begs his audience to be patient and not to chide actors or dramatists who do not compare favorably with Shakespeare, Dryden, or Colley Cibber. Although it contains an abundance of names and allusions and although it is at best a minor occasional piece, this poem appears to be ideally suited for the theater audience to which it was presented by the actor John Hodgkinson.

Smith also wrote twenty-one of the thirty-five poems in the Ella- Birtha-Henry correspondence. Smith, who signed his name "Ella" in a 1791 letter to Cogswell, was "Ella," Joseph Bringhurst, Jr., was probably "Birtha," and Mason Fitch Cogswell was "Henry." These poems were published in the *Gazette of the United States* (Philadelphia) from February to August, 1791.

During the eighteenth century the sonnet became an ignored poetic form. Five of Smith's sonnets were written in 1788 and are characterized by the "overstrained sensibility of his period, by the usual colorless personifications, and by an amount of inversion and ineptness in adjusting his structure and rhymes to the Italian sonnet scheme which are in striking contrast to his later fluency, and are doubtless due to the immaturity of the writer" (Bailey). Smith's mature poetry, while infested with unimaginative diction, possesses a sincerity, especially in "Ode Written on Leaving the Place of My Nativity," that makes his poetry more readable than that of many of his contemporaries.

There has been little written about the poet Theodore Dwight, the younger brother of Timothy. It is known that, next to Alsop, Dwight wrote most of *The Echo,* that his effort in *The Political Green-House* was equal to that of Alsop and Hopkins, and that he wrote the "Triumph of Democracy, A Poem" and "Sketches of the Times, For the Year 1807" which are included in *The Echo* volume. However, only a few other of his poems are extant. Jared

P. Kirtland's notes to "Jefferson and Liberty" . . . attribute "Moll Carey" to Dwight. Dwight wrote "Moll Carey" to satirize the Democrats' singing of "Jefferson and Liberty" in which they commemorated Jefferson's election to the Presidency. Dwight is biting, sarcastic, and unfair throughout the poem, and his are the most caustic comments made toward the Democrats by the Minor Wits.

In "Lines Addressed to a Mother" Dwight sensitively captures a mother's feelings for her child, and in "Lines on the Death of Washington" he skillfully avoids the temptation to which Alsop succumbed in his poem on the same subject. Alsop was unable to limit his poem; it is weakened by the long and superfluous summary of a life that was well known to all Americans. Dwight's eulogy is straightforward and concise, and it is only when he ranks the dead hero above all the ancient sages and refers to our "widow'd country" that his emotion becomes overly patronizing. . . .

Lemuel Hopkins composed "Echo XVIII"—which was published separately as *The Democratiad,*—and *The Guillotina,* both of which comment on repercussions from the Jay Treaty. He also was co-author of *The Political Green-House* and was, with Humphreys, Trumbull, and Barlow, one of the authors of *The Anarchiad.* . . .

Hopkins is perhaps best known for his three shortest poems. When he wrote "Epitaph on a Patient killed by a Cancer Quack" in 1785, the medical profession was in its infancy and was in danger of becoming overwhelmed by folk remedies and superstition. In medicine there were many able and outstanding doctors, but there was also an abundance of quacks (Richard H. Shryock, *Medicine and Society in America, 1600-1860,* 1962). It was those quacks that the poet-physician Hopkins satirizes in his masterfully crafted poem. Leon Howard has noticed that in this poem Hopkins "announced in almost every line, the appearance of a new writer whose rough, nervous wit was as stimulating in its matter-of-fact purpose as it was unpretentious of the 'higher' literary aims of more ambitious men" (*The Connecticut Wits,* 1943). Both "The Hypocrite's Hope" and "On General Ethan Allen" are similar harsh attacks on hypocrisy and Deism, or, as Hopkins saw it, atheism. Hopkins aided Barlow in versifying Dr. Watts's Psalms in 1785. Despite a considerable controversy over who versified the individual Psalms, it is generally agreed that Hopkins did Psalm LXXXVIII.

Hopkins had no literary ambitions, but his caustic writing makes him the most easily identifiable of the Minor Wits. He possessed a good power of description, a keen sense of satire, and an original and pungent humor. Stanley T. Williams has observed that "Hopkins' verses indicate the inclination among the Wits, not merely toward the grandiose aims of Humphreys, Barlow, and Dwight, but toward poetry as a kindly, witty instrument for daily incidents and human foibles" (*The Literature of Connecticut,* 1936). Hopkins did indeed comment on "daily incidents and foibles" in poetry that was far from kindly. This poet's lampoons are among the most vicious poems written by the Minor Wits.

Mason Fitch Cogswell is the most perplexing of the Minor Wits. His name is continuously mentioned as a member of the coterie; yet with the exception of a few unenumerated lines in the "Henrico Echo" ("Echo X") and the "Henry" poems, we possess none of his poetry. Kettell records that Cogswell was present at William Brown's office in Hartford with Alsop, Theodore Dwight, and "a few others" when the idea for *The Echo* was conceived (*Specimens of American Poetry, II*); Francis Parsons claims, without foundation, that Cogswell was "one of the chief contributors to 'The Echo'" (*The Friendly Club, And Other Portraits,* 1922); and Leon Howard, also without foundation, contends that Cogswell "was too modest about his literary ability to cooperate fully with the others, although he wrote copiously in secret" (*The Connecticut Wits*). Aside from a 1793 letter from Alsop to Cogswell which proves that Cogswell helped compose *The Echo,* conclusive evidence that Cogswell wrote poetry is found in a letter from Smith to Cogswell in March, 1791: "I have written to Theodore [Dwight] on the subject of a poetical correspondence and I hope you will be persuaded to cast in your contributions, even if it be like the poor widow's mite. I have begun and done something in the business and am prepared to carry it on somewhat further. To receive assurance of support from you will encourage me to act with the more vigour and attention. You have already many small pieces in your hands and it requires neither much time or much severity of application to produce others" (Quoted from Bailey). The "poetical correspondence" is the Ella-Birtha-Henry correspondence. This letter leaves no doubt that Cogswell was "Henry": he was aware of the correspondence, Smith asked him to enter into the correspondence which was already begun, and Henry did not contribute a poem until two months after the correspondence began in February, 1791.

Grace Cogswell Root, a descendent of Cogswell, grants that Trumbull, the two Dwights, Humphreys, Hopkins, Alsop, and Smith were "part of M.F.C.'s background, and occasionally of his foreground, in Hartford," but she doubts that the belief "that he was an official member of 'the Hartford Wits' has any corroborating testimony" (*Father and Daughter, A Collection of Cogswell Family Letters and Diaries, 1772-1830,* 1924). It must be recalled that membership in this coterie was not "official"; Cogswell's literary status, while still undefined, rests somewhere between the claims of Parsons and Root. Cogswell was probably not a major contributor to *The Echo,* and he was probably the least prolific of the Minor Wits. Nonetheless, there is no discussion of the Minor Wits that fails to include Cogswell as at least a confidant to the others of that group. Even if he was not an "official member" of the Minor Wits, Cogswell, like Tisdale, embodied the spirit of that group . . . .

Luther G. Riggs

SOURCE: A preface to *The Anarchiad* by David Humphries and others, edited by Luther G. Riggs, 1861. Reprint by Scholars' Facsimiles & Reprints, 1967, pp. iv-viii.

Patterson on Trumbull's *M'Fingal:*

A careful reading of the poem will surely not reveal to the present day reader any lines conspicuously touching the heights sublime and candor will forbid his accepting an overstatement of its merits. Nevertheless, one can hardly peruse those . . . cantos of John Trumbull with their at times sparkling and not too bitter humor, their rugged characterization of men and events, their turgid raillery, without experiencing through the mere reading something of that feeling which doubtless in the day of its appearing caused men to be touched and moved by its vigor of word and phrase, its extravagant speechifying, its very "spread eagleism," a quality, indeed, in our literary work as a nation which lingered on even to, if not beyond, the mid-years of the following century. At all events, *M'Fingal* was most popular, if we may judge by the fact, as one investigator does, "that there were more than thirty pirated impressions of the poem in pamphlet and other forms" appearing in its time.

Samuel White Patterson, The Spirit of the American Revolution, *R. G. Badger, 1915.*

[*In the following excerpt from his preface to his 1861 edition of* The Anarchiad, *Riggs comments on its historical context and significance.*]

In presenting *The Anarchiad* to the public, now for the first time in book form, the editor feels that he is in the performance of a duty—that he becomes, as it were, an instrument of justice—a justice delayed for more than half a century, to the genius and loyalty of its authors, who were among the noblest and most talented sons of the American Revolution.

Why a work possessing the merits of *The Anarchiad* has not, ere this, been called up from its oblivious sleep to take its appropriate place among the honored volumes in the homes of the people—by what strange oversight it has not before been brought to public view, and placed within the reach of all, we will not attempt to say.

In 1786, Hartford was the residence of a number of the most celebrated poets of the eighteenth century—among whom, were DAVID HUMPHREYS, JOEL BARLOW, JOHN TRUMBULL, and Dr. LEMUEL HOPKINS;—and the veins of satire which were given forth in many of their literary productions, gained for them the appellation of *"the Hartford wits."* . . .

The Anarchiad is universally conceded to have been written in concert by Humphreys, Barlow, Trumbull, and Hopkins; but what particular installment or numbers was written by either, has never been definitely ascertained. The fact that the papers were anonymously communicated to the publishers at New Haven, and that the authorship of any given portion of the work was never divulged by the members of this literary club, renders it almost impossible to fix upon any particular paper, or portion of a paper, and arrive at a certain knowledge in relation to its writer.

The Anarchiad is a mock-critical account of a pretended

ancient epic poem, which a member of a society of critics and antiquarians had accidentally found among some recently discovered ruins, imbedded with "utensils more curious and elegant than those of Palmyra or Herculaneum," and whose preservation, through such a long lapse of years, and amid marks of hostility and devastation, was indeed little short of miraculous. The author assumes to have taken possession of this poem in the name and for the use of the society of which he was a component part. Being passionately fond of poetry, he immediately set about cleansing it from the extraneous concretions in which it was enveloped; and by means of a chemic preparation made use of in restoring oil paintings, he soon succeeded in rendering it tolerably legible. It was then that he ascertained the production to be styled *The Anarchiad: A Poem on the Restoration of Chaos and Substantial Night.*

When this fabulous announcement was first made in the print of the *Gazette,* it was received with a remarkable degree of credulity by many readers. The plan was well conceived, and the details relating to it were narrated in a plausible manner; and, upon the whole, it was not half as absurd as the celebrated "moon hoax" perpetrated by the New York *Sun* newspaper, many years afterwards, and readily believed by multitudes in all parts of the country. Besides, public attention, but a few months previous to the announcement of the exhuming of *The Anarchiad,* had been somewhat aroused by the discovery of several ruined Indian fortifications, with their singular relics: the story of the early emigration of a band of Britons and Welch to this country, and of an existing tribe of their descendants, in the interior of the continent, had also quite recently been revived and circulated.

The Anarchiad is pre-eminently a NEW ENGLAND POEM. Its publication, at a time when New England was convulsed by the evils growing out of the war of our Revolution, and when insurrectionary mobs had arisen in various parts of the land, and fears were entertained of their proceedings being imitated in others—at such a time, this fearless satire, being scattered broadcast into the homes of the people, through the columns of the weekly press, is supposed to have exerted great and beneficial influence upon the public mind, and to have tended in no small degree to check the leaders of insubordination and infidel philosophy.

But when we say that it is a New England Poem, treating mainly of affairs in that part of the Union, as they existed at the time when it was written, we say, also, that it is no less a NATIONAL POEM, battling nobly for the right universal, for the majesty of law, and for the federal government. Many passages in it seem peculiarly adapted to the exigencies of the present time; and the wholesome sentiments which everywhere pervade its pages can hardly fail of being as heartily endorsed by every lover of his country, and every loyal citizen, as they will unquestionably be regarded with feelings of the most bitter execration by every traitorous and degenerate son of this brightest and fairest of lands. But these soul-inspiring sentiments are too numerous for us to particularize. The reader will find them in plenteous profusion as he reviews its pages. . . .

William C. Dowling

SOURCE: "Joel Barlow and *The Anarchiad,*" *Early American Literature,* Vol. XXV, No. 1, 1990, pp. 18-33.

[*Dowling considers the "puzzle" of Barlow's role in the making of* The Anarchiad, *concluding that his participation must have been the result of "a certain limited and privileged moment in which men employing separate mental worlds could suppose themselves to be making identical sense out of issues identically urgent to them and their fellow citizens."*]

There are two puzzles associated with Joel Barlow's role in relation to *The Anarchiad,* the fragmentary mock-epic composed by a group of Hartford literati between October 1786 and September 1787 in hopes of influencing the momentous debate that would ultimately engender the United States Constitution. These may be called the compositional and the ideological, the first being simply the question of which numbers of *The Anarchiad,* or which parts of which numbers, were actually written by Barlow. It remains a puzzle because, although the external evidence for Barlow's participation is wholly persuasive—shortly after the appearance of the first number, David Humphreys wrote a letter to Washington naming himself, John Trumbull, and Barlow as collaborators in the project—most modern commentators have taken the matter of individual contributions to be something of a permanent mystery; "which portions were written by which authors," says Arthur L. Ford in a recent discussion of Barlow and *The Anarchiad,* "is impossible to determine" [*Joel Barlow,* 1971].

The ideological puzzle posed by Barlow's role in *The Anarchiad,* on the other hand, concerns that dramatic alteration in intellectual and political convictions sometimes spoken of as his "conversion"—from (on the usual account) the Calvinist orthodoxy of his Connecticut upbringing to the sort of skeptical Deism associated with Paine's *Age of Reason,* from the moderate or conservative republicanism of his friends Dwight and Humphreys to the more radical egalitarianism associated with the French Revolution, and from a cyclical theory of civilization inherited from Graeco-Roman historiography to the progressive theory of history unfolded in works like Condorcet's *L'Equisse d'un tableau historique des progrès de l'esprit humain.* For at the moment in which we have always supposed him to have been at work on his contributions to *The Anarchiad,* Barlow was already poised on the very threshold of his ideological conversion; he would set sail for England in a matter of months after *The Anarchiad* had been brought to completion, and the next voice the world would hear would be that of the radical Barlow who speaks so thunderously in *Advice to the Privileged Orders, A Letter to the National Convention,* and *The Conspiracy of Kings.*

The special problem posed by *The Anarchiad* is thus the way it complicates the account usually given of Barlow's ideological conversion, which has been told, generally speaking, as the story of his abandonment of a settled and traditional Connecticut Federalism in favor of more democratic or progressive ideals. For the great point about Federalism in this context is that it was neither settled nor traditional, that it was born as an ideology at the same time and out of precisely the same turbulent circumstances as *The Anarchiad* itself: Shays's Rebellion, the paper-money crisis in Rhode Island and elsewhere, and the mounting demands of a radical egalitarianism that directly anticipated the Jacobin radicalism of the French Revolution. A particular value of *The Anarchiad* now, as Robert D. Arner has recently demonstrated [in *American Literature, 1764-1789*, ed. by Everett Emerson, 1977] is just that it so vividly allows us to recover a sense of Federalism as an ideology born in crisis:

> For see! proud Faction waves her flaming brand,
> And discord riots o'er the ungrateful land;
> Lo! to the north, a wild, adventurous crew,
> In desperate mobs, the savage state renew;
> Each felon chief his maddening thousands draws,
> And claims bold license from the bond of laws.
>
> (57)

This is from *The Anarchiad* no. 10, the installment of the poem published on the eve of the Philadelphia Convention and portraying in urgent terms postrevolutionary America as it appeared to those who were even now emerging as Federalists, spokesmen for a limited or tempered revolution that would preserve the rights won by Americans while forestalling a dissolution into anarchy and bloodshed. It was, as David Humphreys would say with an air of profound relief in 1789, shortly after the adoption of the new federal Constitution, the very "hour of humiliation" in which America discovered she had no government at all, in which men had begun seriously to dread "that the prospect of national happiness, which invigorated our arms and cheered our hearts through the perilous struggle for independence, must vanish for ever from our view: and that the hope of establishing the empire of reason, justice, philosophy, and religion . . . would be considered but the illusion of a heated imagination." For what could be more humiliating to those who had fought for American independence, asked Humphreys rhetorically, "than to perceive our countrymen ready to rush headlong on their ruin—ready to destroy the asylum which was just offered for suffering humanity—ready to verify the predictions of our foes, that our independence would prove a curse to its votaries?"

The America of *Anarchiad* no. 10, in short, is a polity poised on the very brink of the sort of collapse into anarchy and terror that within a few short years would so disillusion most early sympathizers with the French Revolution, the bloodshed and mob violence and reckless demagoguery that would call forth Burke's bitter polemic in the *Reflections on the Revolution in France*. The very essence of Federalism as an ethic of balance and restraint forged in a prolonged moment of national crisis is caught in no. 10's dark vision of uncontrolled democracy as a state of affairs always veering uncontrollably towards mere anarchy:

> Nor less abhor'd, the certain woe that waits
> The giddy rage of democratic States,
> Whose pop'lar breath, high-blown in restless tide,
> No laws can temper, and no reason guide:

> An equal sway, their mind indignant spurns,
> To wanton change, the bliss of freedom turns;
> Led by wild demagogues, the factious crowd,
> Mean, fierce, imperious, insolent and loud,
> Nor fame, nor wealth, nor power, nor system draws.
>
> (61)

When events in France do take their bloody turn towards regicide and Terror, by the same token, it will seem to many of Federalist temperament, looking back on these perilous months in 1786-1787, that America in her hour of postrevolutionary crisis had escaped a similar fate by only the narrowest of margins. This is what lends a special urgency, for instance, to David Humphreys's angry sonnet "On the Murders Committed by the Jacobin Faction in the Early Period of the French Revolution," and in particular to his heated denial that the American and French Revolutions embody an identical set of republican principles: "Those blood-stain'd Jacobins in turn shall fall,/Murd'rers of millions under freedom's name!/But not the blood that delug'd frantic Gaul,/In calm Columbia quenches reason's flame,/Or blots with bloody slur our fair Republic's fame" (237). The republic whose fair name Humphreys is defending at such moments, the "empire of reason, justice, philosophy, and religion" of which he had spoken in his 1789 oration, is precisely the vision of the republic urged in satiric terms throughout *The Anarchiad*, its always-implied alternative to the gloomy picture of an America ruled by "desperate mobs" and "wild demagogues."

Yet the reason Humphreys feels so strongly compelled to dissociate the American Revolution from the events running their fateful course in France is precisely that certain ideologues, not only among the French radicals but among his own countrymen, had proclaimed the two revolutions to be, in essence, the same revolution. There is, even at this distance, a certain poignancy in our awareness that chief among these was Barlow, Humphreys's old friend from Hartford days and his collaborator on *The Anarchiad*. In point of fact, of course, Barlow would stop short of attempting to justify either the execution of Louis XVI or the Reign of Terror—would, in fact, feel himself to be in some danger from the Revolutionary Tribunal during a period when so staunch a republican as Paine could be arrested and imprisoned—but the Barlow whose voice was heard at home was nonetheless the uncompromising radical of *Advice to the Privileged Orders*, calling for death to tyrants everywhere and thus associated in the public mind with the worst subsequent excesses of the French Revolution.

Although Barlow's voice in *Advice to the Privileged Orders* and *Letter to the National Convention* is less the voice of an American citizen merely than of a member of what in *The Columbiad* he will call "the commonwealth of man," its authority always derives from his own firsthand familiarity with the great American experiment in republican government, that successful revolution against tyranny that so many French revolutionists took as their model in the heady period of constitution-making that preceded the Reign of Terror. This is especially true of Barlow's most radical utterance during this same period, *The Conspiracy of Kings,* a poem addressed, as its title page announces, "to the inhabitants of Europe, from another quarter of the world" (1: 67). The voice of the speaker in *The Conspiracy of Kings* is specifically the voice of the New World, radiant with its own millenarian promise, congratulating the Old on its slightly tardier approach to earthly glory:

> From Orders, Slaves and Kings,
> To thee, O MAN, my heart rebounding springs.
> Behold th' ascending bliss that waits your
>   call, . . .
> From shade to light, from grief to glory rise.
> Freedom at last, with Reason in her train,
> Extends o'er earth everlasting reign;
> See Gallia's sons, so late the tyrants' sport,
> Machines in war and sychophants at court,
> Start into men, expand their well-taught mind,
> Lords of themselves and leaders of mankind.
>
>   (1:82)

This is the Barlow who denounces Burke as a "degenerate slave" for having presumed to doubt the wisdom and motivation of the French revolutionists, and whose own vision of history is that of a dark conspiracy among the privileged few to maintain themselves in power and obscene opulence while millions starve. It is the Barlow, in short, whose name will almost from this moment be anathema to the New Haven and Hartford friends in whose company he had come intellectually of age. The seriousness of the rupture would become outwardly apparent only in 1804, when on returning to the United States Barlow would choose as his place of residence the new national capital, with Jefferson in the White House, rather than his own state of Connecticut, but it is to all intents and purposes complete now, as Barlow rapturously celebrates the fall of the Bastille and the Declaration of the Rights of Man and the rise of France "from shade to light, from grief to glory." The distance between Barlow and such men as Timothy Dwight and David Humphreys at this moment might be very precisely measured, we would normally be entitled to suppose, as the ideological distance separating *The Conspiracy of Kings* from *The Anarchiad.*

Yet we are not entitled to suppose this, for what a careful comparative reading of *The Anarchiad* and *The Conspiracy of Kings* discloses is that, as W.B. Otis noticed almost parenthetically at the beginning of our own century [in *American Verse, 1625-1807,* 1909], none other than Joel Barlow is the author of *Anarchiad* no. 10, precisely that blistering attack on the "giddy rage" of popular insurrection that virtually epitomizes the Federalist reaction to radical republicanism and unbridled democracy. This is the context in which what I have called the compositional and ideological puzzles posed by *The Anarchiad* collapse suddenly and rather dramatically into a single larger puzzle, for the evidence that Barlow wrote *Anarchiad* no. 10 is certain lines then taken over almost without alteration into *The Conspiracy of Kings.* There is, to be sure, a shift in context. In *The Anarchiad,* Barlow is warning his American readers about the state of tyranny that must inevitably ensue if the downward spin into anarchy is not halted forthwith:

> Go, view the lands to lawless power a prey,
> Where tyrants govern with unbounded
>   sway; . . .
> High on the moving throne, and near the van,
> The tyrant rides, the chosen scourge of man:
> Clarions, and flutes, and drums, his way pre-
>   pare,
> And shouting millions rend the conscious air—
> Millions, whose ceaseless toils the pomp sustain,
> Whose hour of stupid joy repays an age of pain.
>
>   (59-60)

In *The Conspiracy of Kings,* on the other hand, Barlow is speaking in the conventionally outraged tones of European radicalism about the weight of feudal institutions on masses so oppressed that they do not recognize their own misery:

> The gazing crowd, of glittering State afraid,
> Adore the Power their coward meanness
>   made; . . .
> High on a moving throne, and near the van,
> The tyrant rides, the chosen scourge of man;
> Clarions and flutes and drums his way prepare,
> And shouting millions rend the troubled air;
> Millions, whose ceaseless toils the pomp sustain;
> Whose hour of stupid joy repays an age of pain.
>
>   (1:82)

Nonetheless, the two passages are not only nearly identical but have their origin in an identical sense of moral outrage, which is why the glimpse they provide of Barlow's deepest ideological convictions strongly suggests that the story of his "conversion" demands to be told in somewhat altered terms. For what becomes obvious is that the notion of a sudden or abrupt personal transformation, a Barlow who at home encounters Shays's Rebellion as a staunch Federalist and then surfaces in Paris a few years later cheering on the *sans-culottes,* has never been more than a convenient myth. It is, to be sure, a myth containing an element of truth, for what remains true is that Dwight and Humphreys and Trumbull mistook Barlow for a kindred spirit right up to his departure for England in 1788— Humphreys, in particular, would never have agreed to literary collaboration with the Barlow who wrote *The Conspiracy of Kings*—but it also ignores the insistent evidence that Barlow's conversion to radical principles had taken place much earlier and had been much more gradual than we have supposed. The great question about Barlow's political convictions thus concerns not some sudden shift to an unforeseen radicalism, but the nature of a radicalism that could for so long go unremarked by friends who were to emerge as major voices of New England Federalism.

This is the feature of Barlow's ideological situation that instructs us to look for a system of symbols or concepts ambiguous enough to permit him openly to express his most radical sentiments even while being read by Dwight and Humphreys as a writer loyal to their own Federalist convictions. For it is the essence of the puzzle here that Barlow made absolutely no attempt to disguise his growing allegiance to an emergent set of radical ideals as yet unglimpsed by his Connecticut contemporaries. Had he simply talked one way among his friends and thought another way in private the problem of his political convictions, and these as they governed his poetic expression from the early *Prospect of Peace* to *The Columbiad,* would cease to be problematical. The problem arises precisely because, in both *The Vision of Columbus* and his contributions to *The Anarchiad,* Barlow was, if one but knew how to read, publishing his most radical notions for all to see. This is the moral of those lines and verses that could be carried forward with little or no alteration from *The Anarchiad* to *The Conspiracy of Kings.*

The shared system of symbols or concepts that permitted Barlow and his circle to imagine themselves as dwelling in a state of ideological consensus, providing what Frederic Jameson calls [in *The Political Unconscious,* 1981] "the general unity of a shared code," comes into view most readily, I think, when we look back at that period of illusory consensus in light of the rupture that eventually took place. For this was a rupture not just between Barlow on the one side and Dwight and Humphreys on the other, but, as John Griffiths has persuasively argued [in *Early American Literature* 10 (1975-76)], between two visions or theories of history: the "progressive linearism," as P. A. Sorokin calls it [in *Social and Cultural Dynamics,* 1937], associated with Condorcet or Paine or Barlow's own *Columbiad,* and the cyclical theory, inherited from Herodotus and Aristotle and Polybius, that was a central feature of civic humanism or classical republicanism as it has recently been so brilliantly analyzed in the work of J. G. A. Pocock and others. This was the theory that Dwight, in particular, had taken over from literary Augustanism—his eager reading of Pope and Thomson and other Opposition poets in his undergraduate days at Yale—and had reinterpreted to fit harmoniously with the orthodox Calvinism of his own Northampton upbringing. The monument of his synthesizing energies is his poem *Greenfield Hill.*

So greatly does Dwight succeed in expressing a cyclical vision of history in Calvinist vocabulary, in fact, that there has always been a temptation to represent his ideological breach with Barlow exclusively in terms of competing millenarian visions. Dwight on this account is the orthodox Puritan poet and clergyman who insists on an orthodox view of the millennium as an earthly prelude to actual Apocalypse, the Day of Doom and the immolation of created nature in fire and ruin, while Barlow in his later years has become the secular millenarian, looking forward not to some airy Jerusalem in the clouds but to an earthly millennium of social and political equality brought about by the ineluctable forces of a progressive history. Such works as *Advice to the Privileged Orders* and *The Columbiad* would by this token be anticipations of Hegel's grand project of relocating the telos of divine Providence within a History dialectically conceived, or, more pertinently for the idea of a "radical" Barlow, the salvational story that Marx, under Hegel's inspiration, would present in *Das Kapital* and elsewhere as a scientific theory of history.

This picture of Barlow, which has been the basis of some of the best work done on him as a writer, contains a great deal of truth. This was the Barlow some years ago of Tuveson's *Redeemer Nation,* for instance, and it is today the Barlow, to one or another extent, of Mason Lowance and Cecelia Tichi and Ruth Bloch. Should we emphasize the

writer whose secular millenarianism constantly felt the backward pull of an earlier Calvinism, on the other hand, we have the conflicted and very often contradictory Barlow of Leon Howard [in *The Connecticut Wits,* 1943] and, more recently, Emory Elliott [in *Revolutionary Writers, 1725-1810,* 1982], trying in works like *The Vision of Columbus* to fight his way free of an inherited system of theological and moral values into the emancipatory space portended by a progressive vision of history. There is a great deal of truth in this picture as well, and as Leon Howard demonstrated more than thirty years ago in an argument that still exerts its force (see "An Age of Contradiction"), it is simultaneously a truth about the situation of the writer in the early American republic. The code shared by Barlow and such men as Dwight and Humphreys would on this account be an orthodox or Puritan millenarianism taken by him, under the influence of writers like Paine and Richard Price, in a wholly unorthodox direction.

The great problem with so otherwise attractive an hypothesis is that it leaves altogether out of account that cyclical theory of history that Griffiths sees as being the major point of ideological contention between Dwight and Barlow. For the cyclical theory is crucial in this context, quite apart from the question of Barlow's breach with his friends, as a major part of the explanation of how men as conservative in temperament and values as Dwight and Humphreys became wholehearted supporters of the American Revolution. In the immediate background here, in short, lies not simply the cyclical theory of history but the ideological paradigm of civic humanism of which it was a central element, and in particular the local version of civic humanism called Country ideology which scholars like Pocock and Bailyn and Gordon Wood have shown to be one of the ideological wellsprings of the revolution in the American colonies. It is Barlow's use of the language of civic humanism, I want to argue, always taken by Dwight and Humphreys to imply a cyclical vision of history identical to their own, that would mask Barlow's growing progressivism right through the period of *The Anarchiad,* thus allowing Barlow, guiltless of prevarication or duplicity, to sail for England unrevealed as a radical.

This is the context in which Barlow's incorporation of verses from *The Anarchiad* into *The Conspiracy of Kings* amounts to an ideological unveiling, a public announcement that the classical-republican or civic-humanist ideals he once shared with his Connecticut circle have undergone a transmutation into radical republicanism of the sort associated with Price or Priestly or the later Tom Paine. For to read Barlow's portrayal of the tyrant as "the scourge of man" as it occurs in *The Conspiracy of Kings,* his angry description of societies where the "ceaseless toil" of oppressed millions sustains the pomp of a privileged few, is immediately to recognize that we are in the near vicinity of a radical manifesto like Paine's *The Rights of Man.* Yet when the identical lines are transposed back into their original context in *Anarchiad* no. 10, the effect is one almost of perceptual illusion, for now Barlow is just as recognizably speaking a language perfectly in accord with the Federalist vision of Dwight and Humphreys. Here, for instance, is Dwight in *Greenfield Hill,* describing European society as a sphere where the rich are born to "foul oppression," where tyrants and aristocrats riot on wealth wrung "from plunder'd throngs," and where ordinary subjects die by the millions in mere power struggles among sovereigns (by "crimes of balanced sway" Dwight here means "wars wrongfully fought to preserve the illusory ideal of a 'balance of power' "):

> See, far remote, the crimes of balanced sway!
> Where courts contract the debt, and subject pay;
> The black intrigue, the crush of self-defence,
> Th' enlistment dire, foul press, and tax immense,
> Navies, and hosts, that gorge Potosi whole;
> Bribes, places, pensions, and the auction'd soul:
> Ills, that, each hour, invoke the wrath of God,
> And bid the world's wide surface smoke with
>   blood,
> Waste human good, in slavery nations bind,
> And speed untimely death to half mankind.

(510; VII, 95-105)

In retrospect, of course, we are able to see that Dwight's language here includes elements almost never found in Barlow's poetry, even in such early effusions as *The Prospect of Peace* and the Yale Commencement poem of 1781. This is the language of corruption and civic degeneration taken over directly from the Opposition poetry of Augustan England, the terms—"Bribes, places, pensions, and the auction'd soul"—of the unremitting struggle fought by Pope, Swift, Bolingbroke, Thomson, and scores of lesser poets and polemicists against Walpole and the Robinocracy, demonic representatives of a modernity in which stockjobbers and finance managers were engrossing to themselves the power earlier reserved to the landed classes, and in which the values of traditional society were being irresistibly eroded by the impersonal forces of a new money or market economy. It is the language, in short, of literary Augustanism and Country ideology as these would sustain, in the poetry of Dwight and Humphreys, a vision of America as the early Roman republic providentially reborn as the young United States, a revolution in the cycles of history that, at a time when Europe has grown old and irredeemably corrupt, has on American soil re-created the state of virtuous simplicity and hardy patriotism celebrated in Livy's history or Virgil's *Georgics*.

This imagined world would during the next thirty or forty years of American history give way ideologically to the earthly millennium envisioned in the progressive theory of the later Barlow—thus leaving writers like Dwight and Humphreys, not coincidentally, the speakers of a lost poetic and mythological language—but at the moment of *The Anarchiad* it is particularly easy to see the manner in which two alternative schemes of historical change and civic virtue for a time converged and overlapped, with the cyclical and progressive theories of history, the older classical-republican and the newer radical-republican visions of human society, seeming for a time to be mutually intelligible and even mutually affirming. This is the moment of ideological convergence in which Dwight or Humphreys could pick up *Anarchiad* no. 10 and, reading there a denunciation of corrupt European states that echoed a score of similar passages in their own poetry, could see in Barlow's denunciations of tyranny nothing more than a mirror of their own deeply held Federalist convictions.

A last complication arises from Barlow's authorship of *Anarchiad* no. 10, however, one having to do with the degree to which, even as he is about to break free of that illusory consensus he shared with Dwight and Humphreys and Trumbull, he is still speaking the language of civic humanism and cyclical history that he himself had learned from literary Augustanism and the tradition of Graeco-Roman historiography from which it drew its sustaining myths. This is the significance, for instance, of Barlow's sincere and angry denunciation, at the time of Shays's Rebellion and the paper-money crisis, of "the giddy rage of democratic States," which directly follows a blistering attack on monarchical government ("Hereditary kings, by right divine") and government by oligarchy (where "each aristocrat affects a throne"). This is the theme, tracing back through Florentine political theory to Polybius and Aristotle's *Politics*, of states that retain their civic virtue by ensuring a perpetual balance among the powers of the one, the few, and the many, thus preventing a degeneration into tyranny, oligarchy, or democracy in their unmixed, and therefore highly unstable, states.

In the immediate background of Barlow's denunciation of the Shays rebels as a desperate mob caught up in giddy rage, then, there lies a wisdom going back to Plato and Aristotle concerning the inevitability that states degenerating into anarchy will pass into the control of a single strong ruler able to control lawlessness and restore order by force. It is the same wisdom, ironically enough, that will lie behind Burke's uncanny "prediction" of the rise of Napoleon in *Reflections on the Revolution in France*, and it permits us to see the sense in which, even during the great ideological fissuring that occurs in the last decade of the eighteenth century in both England and America, all parties to that increasingly bitter dispute were yet speaking a common language. For the Barlow who in *The Conspiracy of Kings* will denounce Burke as a "degenerate slave," and who will attack him as well in *Advice to the Privileged Orders*, is here in *The Anarchiad* still drawing confidently on a Polybian theory of the mixed or balanced state taken by both him and Burke from the civic humanist tradition that will, during these same years, also sustain the Federalist vision of Dwight and Humphreys.

The great monument of Polybian theory in American history is, of course, the federal Constitution, miraculous as a compromise not least because it was able one last time to reactivate the improbable ideological consensus that had carried a wildly disparate group of leading spirits, solid personages like John Adams and Timothy Dwight as well as fiery souls like Samuel Adams or Patrick Henry, through the War of Independence in unanimous opposition to British tyranny. If the episode of Barlow's contributions to *The Anarchiad* suggests anything, it is that this consensus as well was the unintended consequence of ideological convergence, a certain limited and privileged moment in which men employing separate political vocabularies and inhabiting separate mental worlds could suppose themselves to be making identical sense out of issues identically urgent to them and their fellow citizens. So far as the tenth number of *The Anarchiad* contributed to that last reactivation of consensus, and thus to the making of the Constitution, it was Joel Barlow's valedictory gift to the Connecticut friends whose values, at bottom, he had never really shared.

William Bradley Otis

SOURCE: "Political and Satirical Verse," in *American Verse 1625-1807,* Moffat, Yard and Company, 1909, pp. 88-171.

[In the excerpt below, Otis considers Trumbull's M'Fingal *and Barlow's* Columbiad *as two of the most important literary productions of the Connecticut Wits.]*

The most popular and by far the best of the Revolutionary satires, both in plan and execution, is the *McFingal* of John Trumbull. It is a mock-heroic modelled upon *Hudibras,* and is scarcely inferior to Butler's masterpiece in the sparkling quality of its wit. *McFingal* was written at the urgent request of members of the American Congress, who believed that Trumbull could aid the cause of Independence by writing a poem which should weaken the Tory cause by turning it to ridicule. The first two cantos were published in Philadelphia in 1775, when the author was but twenty-five years of age. The poem was not completed until 1782, and was published that year in its final form at Hartford. McFingal is represented as a blustering, self-assured Tory squire. He lives in a village near Boston, is a justice of the peace, and in Town Meeting makes long speeches against the Whigs. His over-emphasis of attack reacts upon and injures his own cause:

Joel Barlow

Thus stored with intellectual riches,
Skill'd was our Squire in making speeches;
Where strength of brains united centers
With strength of lungs surpassing Stentor's.
But as some muskets so contrive it,
As oft to miss the mark they drive at,
And though well aim'd at duck or plover,
Bear wide, and kick their owners over;
So fared our Squire, whose reasoning toil
Would often on himself recoil,
And so much injured more his side,
The stronger arguments he applied.

McFingal is "the vilest Tory in the town," and he finally makes himself so obnoxious that he is tarred, feathered, and ridden around town followed by a hooting mob. All besmeared with tar he returns home, summons his Tory companions to a secret meeting in his cellar, and relates to them a "vision" which has suddenly come to him since the tarring. He announces that his prophetic sense of "second sight" has made it clear that the American cause will win, that the colonists will be free and independent, and that a great and flourishing nation will arise. He advises his fellow Tories to waste no time in joining the Whigs. Just at this moment a panic is created among those assembled in the cellar by a report that the Whigs have returned with a mob upon hearing that a Tory meeting is in secret session. The lights are extinguished and McFingal, escaping through a window, flees to Boston. Thus the poem ends.

McFingal was written for a special purpose at a special time, and was written for the masses. No doubt the Yale tutor would have preferred a more elevated style, but it was necessary to appeal to the people in a familiar, and even in a coarse, manner. What Trumbull considered the higher art was sacrificed for love of country. The author had a keen sense of the ridiculous, and he embodied it in crisp, snappy couplets. He was thoroughly familiar with the public men and events of the day, and there were very few Tories of prominence who escaped the trenchant quality of his wit. *McFingal* went through more than thirty editions, and the influence of the poem in aiding and encouraging the spirit of independence can hardly be overestimated. . . .

As a statesman, a financier, a man of affairs, [Joel] Barlow was a person of brilliant and exceptional ability. As a poet, too, he had powers which, with proper pruning and training, might have resulted in productions of permanent beauty. That this army chaplain, honorary citizen of the French Republic, spectacular financier and negotiator of national treaties, had a magnificent and poetic vision there can be no question. Had he not attempted to soar so high, in flights which his talents could not sustain; had he been content to give us his spontaneous self as in *The Hasty Pudding,* and to class himself with lesser bards than Homer and Virgil, much could have been forgiven. This man of the world who, in his relations with princes and kings, displayed remarkable wisdom and tact, at one period in his life lost the sense of true proportion, and wrote *The Columbiad. The Vision of Columbus,* upon which the larger poem is based, was published, in modest form, in 1787, and received favorable notice in America, France, and England. Although too long it was exactly what the title indicated,—a vision. The talents which it displayed were sufficient to bring its author at once prominently before the public as a leading American man of letters. Stimulated by this success into an incomprehensible and inordinate vanity, Barlow at once began preparations for the enlargement of his poem into the epic form. *The Columbiad* was published in Philadelphia in 1807, in quarto, dedicated to the author's intimate friend, Robert Fulton, and embellished with twelve engravings from designs by Smirke, executed by the best London engravers. The edition was so large and costly that only men of means could afford a copy. There was something in the overgrown size of the book so in accord with the inflated plan of the poem that critics were not slow in appropriating the idea. *The Columbiad* was as generally condemned as *The Vision* had been applauded. The principal idea of the poet is simple enough. Columbus, lying in chains in a dungeon of King Ferdinand's palace in Valladolid, is bemoaning his fate when suddenly

> O'er all the dungeon, where black arches bend,
> The roofs unfold, and streams of light descend.

This supernatural manifestation is the prelude to the entrance of Hesper, brother of Atlas, "the guardian Genius of the Western Continent," who proceeds to lead Columbus forth to the Mount of Vision "which rises o'er the western coast of Spain." From this tremendous height, and with the aid of miraculous vision granted by Hesper, Columbus scans the world of the past, present, and future, and is recompensed for his misery in the knowledge that his great discovery is destined to work through untold ages for the amelioration of mankind. Over seven thousand lines are required to portray and interpret the glorious destiny which is to be America's. After a description of the physical characteristics of the new continent, and a discussion of the origin of tribes and nations, the poet digresses into a long history of Peru. Having next explained the beneficent influence upon Europe of Columbus's discovery, Hesper turns again to America. Here the formation of the colonies, the French and Indian and Revolutionary wars, are each in turn exhausted for material to feed the appetite of this insatiate epic.

The national freedom in which the Revolution resulted serves as a basis of attack upon African slavery in America. Why deny to the negro that personal liberty for which the colonists themselves have just shed so much blood? This portion of the poem is one of the most commendable, and in places rises to high poetic majesty. The last two books concern themselves with a philosophic disquisition on the general nature of progress and enlightenment, in which republicanism is the most efficacious factor, and the poem closes with an optimistic look into the future, to the time when wars shall cease and when all mankind will be united in political unity and brotherly love. Even as a "vision" such a poem must have appeared grandiose in the hands of any but a poet of the first rank, and not even genius could have moulded it into epic form. It lacks the carrying power of epic narrative, and is destitute of the first of all considerations, epic unity. The digressions are too many and lengthy, and are too loosely hung upon the framework of the central idea. In reading the poem one is impressed with the lack of compactness, of consistency,

of purpose, of goal. The mind of the poet is "uneasily swelling" [Moses Coit Tyler, *Three Men of Letters*] with some great conception of which he is not master. The imagery, for the most part, is laborious and vague, and the vocabulary extravagant. When *The Columbiad* was issued, twenty years had passed since the publications of *The Vision of Columbus*. In the meantime America had been developing a taste for letters and had made some advance in the field of literary criticism. Moreover, these twenty years had seen tremendous strides in the growth of Romanticism, and *The Columbiad,* with its heroic verse, came, a belated traveller, to find the school of Pope in eclipse, and Wordsworth, Scott, and Coleridge the new captains of literary progress.

But while *The Columbiad* failed as a work of art, it will live in literary history, partly because of the titanic nature of the failure itself, but more especially because of the impulse which gave it birth. Barlow, as all the "Hartford Wits," was filled with a genuine and overflowing love of country, not a provincial passion, but one, as we have seen, broad enough to include in vision the whole of mankind. He was a thorough republican, and hoped and believed that the nations of the world would all eventually adopt that form of government. Moreover, the ethical purpose of the poem is evident in all parts of the work. "My object," he says, "is altogether of a moral and political nature. I wish to encourage and strengthen, in the rising generation, a sense of the importance of republican institutions, as being the great foundation of public and private happiness, the necessary aliment of future and permanent meliorations in the condition of human nature." And in a letter [dated 1809] to his friend Henri Gregoire, formerly Bishop of Blois, in reply to the latter's assertion that *The Columbiad* was detrimental to religion, Barlow says:

> On the contrary, I believe, and you have compelled me on this occasion to express my belief, that the Columbiad, taken in all its parts of text and notes and preface, is more favorable to sound and rigid morals, more friendly to virtue, more clear and unequivocal in pointing out the road to national dignity and individual happiness, more energetic in its denunciations of tyranny and oppression in every shape, injustice and wickedness in all their forms, and consequently more consonant to what you acknowledge to be the spirit of the gospel, than all the writings of all that list of Christian authors of the three last ages whom you have cited as the glory of Christendom, and strung them on the alphabet, from Addison to Winkelman. Understand me right, my just and generous friend; I judge not my poem as a work of genius. I cannot judge it nor class it nor compare it in that respect, because it is my own. But I *know* it is a moral work; I *can* judge and *dare* pronounce upon its tendency, its beneficial effect upon every candid mind, and I am confident you will yet join me in opinion.

This frank statement forced from the author in self-defense may be accepted as essentially true. As an opponent of war, of slavery, of every kind of moral and political evil, as an upholder of personal and institutional virtue, Joel Barlow's *Columbiad* was in spirit distinctly ethical.

And in this it was distinctly American and a legitimate descendant of the earlier Puritan literature. *The Columbiad,* then, while a failure as a work of art, deserves recognition in the history of American literature because it typified three of the most important national characteristics of the time,—love of country, enthusiasm for republican principles, and emphasis upon the ethical in its application to national life. . . .

William Bradley Otis on Barlow's *Hasty Pudding*:

There is, to be sure, in the crack of the corncobs more than a faint suggestion of the crack of Pope's "whalebones," but even so the truth of the colonial picture is in no way marred. In this poem Barlow has given evidence of what he might have done had he been impelled by less Homeric visions, and it is difficult to realize that *The Hasty Pudding* and *The Columbiad* are by one and the same hand. The author will probably live longer for having produced in a few hours this short and spontaneous, but simple and true, poem than for having composed during many of the best years of his life, the ambitious, formal, inflated, and overelaborate epic which he was pleased to call **The Columbiad.**

William Bradley Otis, American Verse 1625-1807: A History, Moffat, Yard & Co., 1909.

Karl P. Harrington (essay date 1939)

SOURCE: "Alsop's Satirical Writings," in *Richard Alsop: "A Hartford Wit,"* 1939. Reprint by Wesleyan University Press, 1969, pp. 48-74.

[*Here, Harrington explores Alsop's contributions to the satirical* Echo, *praising his "keen sense of humor and ability to express the intended lesson in such mock-heroic style as appeals at once to the risibilities of the reader."*]

Alsop is said to have almost "lisped in numbers" and to have contributed to such papers as the *Middlesex Gazette* at a very early age. It was during his youth and young manhood that he completed the remarkable *Charms of Fancy,* unpublished till long after his death, but he first achieved fame from his satirical poetry.

Satirical writings, mostly political in character, were notably common in America in the latter part of the 18th century. The intensely partisan feelings aroused by the controversies connected with the transition from the more loose earlier federation of states to a more closely knit United States of America under the proposed new constitution were largely responsible for the amount and the quality of these publications. Connecticut was one of the most prominent battlegrounds of discussion of the questions involved, and the literature arising from these ardent differences of opinion is correspondingly intense. . . .

It was on August 8, 1791, that Alsop, with the collaboration of his brother-in-law Theodore Dwight (brother of Timothy Dwight, president of Yale College, and grandson

of Jonathan Edwards), published the first satirical poem called *The Echo* in the *American Mercury* at Hartford. This was followed at intervals during the next dozen or fifteen years by other verses under the same title. In 1807 these, with some additions and subtractions, were published in book form under the same title. Probably most of the twenty numbers of *The Echo* were written by Alsop and Dwight, and, it may not be amiss to conclude, the major part by Alsop.

As in the Ciceronian Age Catullus and his boon companion Licinius Calvus amused themselves by vying in the composition of hilarious and perhaps audacious verses, so Alsop and Dwight in Middletown (not Hartford), started this series of burlesques in an idle "moment of literary sportiveness" when they were suddenly inspired by the absurd "pedantry, affectation and bombast" which characterized the gazettes of the day. It was a florid description of a local thunderstorm printed in a Boston paper of July 14, 1791, which gave them the cue for their initial bit of mockery, written without any thought of publication; and their idea was that of literary criticism of the pompous style of the original prose which contained such passages as these:

> The clouds soon dissipated and the appearance of the azure vault left trivial hopes of further needful supplies from the uncorked bottles of Heaven. In a few moments the horizon was again over-shadowed and an almost impenetrable gloom mantled the face of the skies . . . . The majestic roll of disploded thunders now bursting with a sudden crash and now casting the rumbling echo of their sounds in other lands added indescribable grandeur to the sublime scene. The windows of the upper regions appeared as thrown wide open and the trembling cataract poured impetuous down.

A closing paragraph stated that a barn belonging to a Mr. Wythe was burned.

The amused *Echo* of all this eloquence ran thus:

> Those mighty tales which great events rehearse
> To fame we consecrate in deathless verse.
>
> On Tuesday last great Sol, with piercing eye,
> Pursued his journey thro' the vaulted sky,
> And in his car effulgent roll'd his way
> Four hours beyond the burning zone of day;
> When lo! a cloud o'ershadowing all the plain,
> From countless pores perspir'd a *liquid* rain,
> While from its cracks the lightnings made a peep,
> And chit-chat thunders rock'd our fears asleep.
> But soon the vapoury fog dispers'd in air,
> And left the azure blue-eyed concave bare:
> Even the last drop of hope, which dripping skies
> Gave for a moment to our straining eyes,
> Like *Boston Rum,* from heaven's *junk bottles* broke,
> Lost all the corks, and vanish'd into smoke.
>
> But swift from worlds unknown, a fresh supply
> Of vapour dimm'd the great horizon's eye;
> The crazy clouds, by shifting zephyrs driven

Wafted their courses through the high-arch'd
    heaven,
Till pil'd aloft in one stupendous heap,
The seen and unseen worlds grew dark, and na-
    ture
    'gan to weep.
Attendant lightnings stream'd their tails afar,
And social thunders wak'd ethereal war,
From dark deep pockets brought their treasur'd
    store,
Embattled elements increas'd the roar—
Red crinkling fires expended all their force,
And tumbling rumblings steer'd their headlong
    course,
Those guarded frames by thunder poles secur'd,
Tho' wrapp'd in sheets of flame, those sheets
    endur'd,
O'er their broad roofs the fiery torrents roll'd,
And every shingle seem'd of burning gold.
Majestic thunders, with disploding roar,
And sudden crashing, bounc'd along the shore,
Till, lost in other lands, the whispering sound
Fled from our ears and fainted on the ground.
Rain's house on high its window sashes op'd,
And out the cataract impetuous hopp'd,
While the grand scene by far more grand ap-
    pear'd
With lightnings never seen and thunders never
    heard.
More salutary showers have not been known,
To wash Dame Nature's dirty homespun
    gown—
For several weeks the good old Joan's been seen,
With filth bespatter'd like a lazy quean.
The husbandman fast travelling to despair,
Laid down his hoe and took his rocking chair,
While his fat wife the well and cistern dried,
Her mop grown useless hung it up and cry'd.

Two rain-bows fair that Iris brought along,
Pick'd from the choicest of her colour'd throng;
The first-born deck'd in pristine hues of light,
In all its native glories glowing bright,
The next adorn'd with less refulgent rays,
But borrowing lustre from its brother's blaze;
Shone a bright reflex of those colours gay
That deck'd with light creation's primal day,
When infant Nature lisp'd her earliest notes,
And *younker Adam* crept in petticoats:
And to the people to reflection given,
"The sons of Boston, the elect of heaven",
Presented Mercy's Angel smiling fair,
Irradiate splendours frizzled in his hair,
Uncorking demi-johns, and pouring down
Heaven's liquid blessings on the gaping town.

N. B.   At Cambridge town, the self-same day,
A barn was burnt well-fill'd with hay.
Some say the light'ning turn'd it red,
Some say the thunder struck it dead,
Some say it made the cattle stare,
And some it kill'd an aged mare;
But we expect the truth to learn,
From Mr. Wythe, who own'd the barn.

A footnote at the end declares that "the design of these verses is to respond to the public ear, from time to time, as they occur, those news-paper performances which may justly claim superior merit, that the fugitive efforts of the

American genius may be preserved 'Till moons shall wax, and wane no more'."

The success of this literary satire when published encouraged further attempts; but the objects of the author's telling shafts soon changed. Instead of a criticism of bad taste, *The Echo* became an attack on certain political tendencies of the times, the "hideous morality of revolutionary madness". A paragraph in the preface explains the shift:

> Disgusted with the cruelties exhibited by the French Revolution at a very early stage of its progress, and viewing it as a consuming fire which in the course of its conflagration threatened to destroy whatever was most valuable in society, the authors wished to contribute their efforts in stemming the trend of Jacobinism in America and resolved to render *The Echo* subservient to that purpose. They therefore proceeded to attack as proper objects of satire those tenets as absurd in politics as pernicious in morals, the visionary scheme of equality, and the baleful doctrine that sanctions the pursuit of a good end by the most flagitious means.

In some cases, to be sure, the theme of an issue of *The Echo* was non-political, as in No. 6, where the author ironically rises to the defense of the Newtonian philosophy in a manner that would have startled Lucretius. . . .

No. 9 ridicules a couple of speeches by Governor John Hancock, of Massachusetts, for his extreme jealousy of the laws and the state rights of that proud Commonwealth. The first protested against infraction "by aliens and foreigners" of the laws against "stage-plays, interludes, and theatrical entertainment". *The Echo* does not hesitate to poke fun at the famous governor and the pride of Massachusetts as well as at the act in question. . . .

It was toward Virginia next that Alsop's hottest bolts were turned. A letter in the *Virginia Gazette* of Dec. 6, 1792, after the Electors of that state had voted for George Clinton for the vice-presidency in 1792, raised a protest against the abuse thrown upon them, in which they were called "Jacobins", and proceeded to magnify the achievements of said Jacobins in fulsome praise. "Are they not", the protestant proceeded, "the authors of the greatest and most glorious revolution of which the annals of history can boast? Have they not loosed the shackles of slavery from thirty millions of people? Have they not fanned the sacred blaze of liberty in every region of the earth? Have they not dethroned tyranny, monarchy, aristocracy, priest-craft and all their satellites?" This election too, the writer indicated, was a condemnation of the previous vice-president, John Adams, the most prominent New Englander in the national government in its earlier years.

Alsop, speaking of course in the name of a Virginian, makes various telling thrusts at Virginia and the political quarrels of the day, setting forth the idea that the Democratic part of the Old Dominion is composed of descendants of Pokahontas. He assumes her as "Virginia's tutelary saint", and holds that the electors were full of whiskey when they voted for Clinton:

> Wak'd by his speech Virginia's sons arise,
> His grateful liquor sparkling in their eyes;

And her Electors, with consenting voice,
Have made George Clinton their united choice.

Reference is made to "the celebrated Equality Ball given to the negroes of Boston by Governor Hancock":

While joyous sing the people's friends and
  prance,
And treat the Negroes to a royal dance,
And loud to Anarchy their voices raise
In hallelujahs and in hymns of praise,
To the sweet Tune of *Freedom born anew*;
That Tune so charming and so novel too,
That Tune by tinkers sung, by cobblers loved,
Which to the Cow of old so fatal proved,
That from this world with joy she took her
  flight,
And bade her ancient friends a long Good
  Night.

In the *History Magazine* is the following paragraph:

No one in Boston was stronger in the affection
of his servants than Mr. Hancock, and the fame
of African Cato of the Hancock House, the skillful flute player, postilion and waiter, will ever be
remembered. On one occasion the governor, it
is related, indulged his servants in 1792 with the
privilege of a great entertainment in his festive
hall at his expense, composed of colored people,
which was amusingly parodied by a political opponent, Richard Alsop, in the New Years address of the Hartford *American Mercury* of
1793.

The newspaper letter that inspired this diatribe had been signed with the pseudonym "Henrico". This appears four times in a refrain of varying forms, thus:

Rejoice! ye Pokahontian Tribes rejoice!
In loud *Te Deums* raise your clam'rous voice!
Proclaim from Anarchy what blessings spring!
"Shall CLINTON reign, and HENRICO not sing?"

Rejoice! ye anti-Fed'ral clan rejoice!
'Gainst *Bank* and Funding-system raise your
  voice!
Declare from *Ruin'd Faith* what honors spring!
"Shall CLINTON reign, and HENRICO not sing?"

Rejoice! ye pious Jacobins, rejoice!
Ye graceful Fish-women strain high your voice!
Proclaim from bloody heads what transports
  spring!
"Shall CLINTON reign, and HENRICO not sing?"

Rejoice! ye noble Levellers rejoice!
Ye democratic Tribes exalt your voice!
Declare what joys from prostrate morals spring!
"Shall CLINTON reign, and HENRICO not sing?"

The prophecy that, "Adams must fall and Clinton shall prevail," recurs from time to time, and many indications of growing sectional bitterness appear. The extremes of the French revolutionists are illustrated in many ways. . . .

That men in public life were never immune from the suspicion of graft and various other possible immoralities is evident. No. 11 of *The Echo* is based on an attack of this kind at the beginning of the administration of George Washing-

ton, and foreshadows the modern very common senatorial investigation. Alsop eggs on the eager scandal-mongers thus:

Pray sir go on—complete the work begun,
State facts, produce your vouchers one by one;
On whom soe'er your wise suspicions light,
Call forth the villains, be they wrong or right—
Yoke up your *"minute men"*, hitch fast a chain,
Grease Faction's wheels, and drag them o'er the
  plain;
Load the old cart with every crippled dog,
Each speculating money-asking rogue;
No matter who, nor what—if once they're taken
We'll smoke the rascals into human bacon. . . .

  No guilty soul is to escape:
"Vice-Presidents, and Registers, Inspectors,
Old Gifford Dallies, Senators, Collectors,
Comptrollers,   State-Comptrollers,   Office-
  Writers,
Drummers and Fifers, Minters, and Auditors,
Accountants, Representatives, and Runners,
Clerks, Colonels, Treasurers, Quartermasters,
  Gunners,
Postmasters, Supervisors, Secretaries,
Chaplains, Philosophers, and Antiquaries,
Whate'er their shape, importance, state or name,
How great soe'er their wealth, or small their
  fame,
Pluck off the mask, the face infernal shew,
And hold the monsters up to public view.

A notorious scandal related in Holy Writ is used for comparison:

Astonish'd Jebus saw her race expire,
Her town in ruins, and her fields on fire,
Merely because, inspir'd by love and wine,
The sons of Belial kiss'd a concubine.
What strange ideas govern'd in those days,
When things so slight so fierce a strife could
  raise,
How much improv'd the morals of our time
When kissing concubines is held no crime.

But the next comparison places the slummer in his true light, and leaves him little satisfaction in the job he has undertaken after he realizes how he appears to his fellow citizens:

When lazy Sol at both ends clips the day,
And chill November calls out beasts of prey,
Like you, great Sir, well charged with awful
  spunk,
From his deep burrow struts the stately skunk;
While men and beasts with upturn'd noses fly,
As the pied Warrior rears his tail on high.

The scathing sarcasm of *The Echo* is again in No. 12 flung in the face of those who supported the horrors of the French Revolution as deserved by the French King and his supporters:

Have they not prov'd mid every trying scene,
Their love most strong for Louis and his Queen?
First, in forgetting what a brood of kings,
Old Despotism had fledg'd beneath her wings;
Then in depriving him of legal sway,
Lest he should take *French leave* and scud away;

Next in confining him with so much care,
From the rude peltings of external air;
And lastly, what I deem by far the best,
Of love and loyalty the happy test,
In cutting off his head, to save his life
From scenes of woe, of horror, and of strife;
And thus by *certain means,* to keep away
Old age, that mournful period of decay.

He rings the charges on "Egalité", slogan of the Revolutionists and also nickname of the monstrous Duke of Orleans, Louis Philippe Joseph, unspeakable in his scandalous life:

Then since base acts a saving grace confer,
Those who adopt such means can never err—
Such means, O France! thy great redeemers use,
Such good Egalité with zeal pursues.
Hail chief! renown'd for deeds of blackest
      shame,
D'Orleans, Egalité whate'er thy name,
Whose head and heart with equal lustre shine,
And in thyself both fool and villain join! . . .

O cursed thirst of absolute controul,
The youngest offspring of Hell's fiery hole!
Sworn friend to tyrants, emperors, and kings,
Thy smiles coquettish are most dangerous
      things.
By thee betray'd we lose the narrow way,
From virtue swerve, and far from duty stray,
And like Dupont, the pious, brave, and good,
Hurl bold defiance to the arm of God,
His altars raze, his holy temples burn!
And hold Religion up to public scorn.
For nought the sacred Majesty can please,
But what conduces to his creatures' ease;
And France has proved that what mankind
      abhor,
Fire, murder, rapine, Jacobins and war,
Are far more useful, than that truth and peace,
Should bid the jarring world from slaughter
      cease.

These echoes of publications at length began to draw the fire of those who disapproved of the federalist publications in New England, especially in Hartford. To them the satirists next turned, echoing a letter signed "Mirabeau", published in Philadelphia. But after writing a broadside based on this letter, they recalled it, and only small parts of it appear in the book as samples of the style which was used. . . .

A thunderstorm described in the *Norwich Packet* gave opportunity for *The Echo* (No. XIV) to outdo itself in figurative extravaganzas. . . .

The next two numbers of *The Echo* are variations on the familiar general theme of Jacobinism, in which bitter satire is directed against some of the individuals prominent among the champions of the French. No. 17 turns to Connecticut State politics, with references to the legislature, to the band of reformers called the *"Stelligeri",* and perhaps to local politics in the couplet:

Lot, with *two daughters,* shunn'd *alone* the
      shower,
By fleeing early to the town of Zoar.

At any rate it was a familiar quotation in Middletown after Lot Van Sands moved to "Zoar", that "Lot fled to Zoar".

The succeeding numbers deal with the proposed new treaty with Great Britain and some objections to the Senate's secrecy in discussing it, and with certain familiar domestic political problems, such as the illiteracy of congressmen, "imperialism" and the Louisiana Purchase, the political prominence of the Irish in America, and the Freedom of the Press. . . .

The merit of the satirical compositions which make up *The Echo* lies chiefly in their keen sense of humor and ability to express the intended lesson in such mock-heroic style as appeals at once to the risibilities of the reader. With the rough-and-ready hits and the colloquial language of the day are combined, with telling effect, scriptural and classical allusions and mythology. The easy and familiar verse form is handled with confident abandon. The message of this verse had an immediate and direct appeal and the authors were sure of it. . . .

Mason I. Lowance, Jr.

SOURCE: "Joel Barlow and the Rising Glory of America," in *The Language of Canaan: Metaphor and Symbol in New England from the Puritans to the Transcendental-*

"Poise with one hand your bowl": an illustration from Barlow's Hasty Pudding.

ists, Cambridge, Mass.: Harvard University Press, 1980, pp. 208-46.

[*Lowance is an American critic and educator who has written extensively on early American literature. In the following excerpt, he discusses how Barlow adapted the traditional language of religious millenialism in writing the* Columbiad, *his epic about "America's technological and political future."*]

The problem of language and its relation to genre or form was resolved in Puritan New England by writers and preachers whose rhetorical responses to political, social, and spiritual conditions were governed by biblical precedent. For example, just as the theocracy of early Massachusetts Bay Colony had been established following the model of the Old Testament theocracy and was originally sanctioned by God's law, the historians and ministers of early New England attempted to model their rhetorical styles according to the language of Canaan by which the writer, with God's grace, might raise words up into life, giving the colonies a specific, ordered relationship to the prophetic writings of Scripture. As a part of the process of fulfillment in divine history, the Puritans were certain that the biblical models would give their literature the didactic purpose that guided the originals. Thus William Bradford's *Of Plimouth Plantation* is an attempt to write providential history from the perspective of a leading participant, and Edward Johnson's *The Wonder Working Providence of Sion's Saviour in New England* is a metaphorical accounting of the New England experience that has the structure and form of myth. Cotton Mather's *Magnalia Christi Americana* "dissolves history into biography," as Peter Gay reminds us, and brings together the classical and Judeo-Christian historical method in an attempt to create an authentic epic of New England.

For the writers of the late eighteenth century, particularly . . . the poets of the American Revolution, the task of finding the appropriate form to express a conflation of biblical and classical theme was much more complex. The dominant genres were neoclassical, and the influence of English writers like Alexander Pope and the Christian humanist John Milton was strong. If Milton had found a satisfactory form in the epic-dramatic structure of *Paradise Lost* to "justify the ways of God to men," the poets of the revolutionary era were faced with the problem of reconciling a secular, enlightened, and progressive view of America's future with more traditional and theological positions, expressed in the figures, symbols, and forms of biblical language, that prophetic language of Canaan which had given America's writers spiritual conviction from John Winthrop to Timothy Dwight. The transition to a secular version of this richly metaphorical, highly figural biblical language was not achieved at once, nor were writers consciously scheming to utilize the rhetorical framework of the past in order to generate enthusiasm among their contemporary readers. Rather, the expectations of America's national future seemed to respond well to the rhetorical strategies of earlier models, and it was natural that the millennial enthusiasm so prominent in the writings of Jonathan Edwards and the New Light movement should reappear in the progressive, optimistic neo-

classical epics of Joel Barlow and the early federalist and republican poets. Millenialism, indeed, may be found in the expansionist poetry of Walt Whitman, who could hardly be linked to William Bradford or Cotton Mather in any way other than that they all shared a common expectation of America's fulfillment of the idealistic prophecies of Isaiah and Revelation.

Thus the problem became one of emphasis and imagery. For Bradford, Mather, and Edwards, the real possibility that a religious millennium might be realized in North America energized fantastic visions of the future glory of New England. But Dwight, Barlow, and Freneau anchored their beliefs in the progressive optimism of federalist or republican expectations, while utilizing the Scripture rhetoric they had inherited from the early settlers through Jonathan Edwards and the New Lights.

The crux of the problem became the composition of an epic poem to celebrate the rising glory of America, and a full-fledged genre of epic writing resulted from the numerous attempts made between 1760 and 1807, when Joel Barlow's *Columbiad* consummated all previous efforts. It was not simply a matter of establishing a form, which, after all, was provided by the ancient writers—both biblical and classical—who had already developed literary structures that would bring together the elements of psychology, history, religion, and human drama to represent the values and attitudes of a culture. The Puritans were certainly aware of these precedents, and Cotton Mather argued, as we have seen, the necessity of utilizing biblical biographical models in writing the history of New England. Epic and history were inseparable, but the rhetorical patterns of epic writing had to be adapted from scriptural and figural usage to herald the evolving emphasis on America's secular glory.

It is therefore no creative or artistic flaw that caused Joel Barlow to experiment with a proper epic language and an appropriate form. Like his predecessors among the Puritans, and like Walt Whitman whose epic grandeur is resonant in every line of his newly liberated "free verse" form, Joel Barlow was accommodating the language of Canaan to its new theme—the glory of America's technological and political future. To distinguish this from the earlier prospects for America's spiritual fulfillment of Scripture prophecy, and to express the result in language consonant with America's epic greatness, became the focus of Barlow's career. . . .

The writing of *The Columbiad* and its publication on Christmas Eve, 1807, may have been the grandest extravagance in American literary history. It is well known that Barlow revised the early drafts numerous times, incorporating whole sections of *The Vision of Columbus* and reworking his theme to fit the new epic format. But the book's production and design also consumed the poet. He personally selected the fine paper on which it was printed, contributed one thousand dollars (and solicited another five thousand from the inventor Robert Fulton) to commission paintings by Robert Smirke which would decorate the book as engravings. As though its form celebrated the content in the way that the content celebrated America, the book was a magnificent product in every way. "Even the caustic Francis Jeffrey in the *Edinburgh Review* said he never had seen a more attractive book published in England. He conceded: 'The infant republic has already attained to the very summit of perfection in the mechanical art of bookmaking.'" But in order to complete the epic poem—an achievement which had eluded Barlow as he struggled with other forms to celebrate America's promise—he was forced to refuse other commissions that would have probably given him a more exalted place in the evolution of national literature in the United States.

> Barlow squandered his months in fanning the thin, feeble coals of poetic fire when he might have been writing the history of the United States. In so doing, he missed a chance that comes to very few men. Jefferson and Madison were urging him to write the history and were offering the resources of the government archives and their own files. They were also ready with their memories and interpretations of men and events. In July, 1806, the President, sent Barlow four boxes of papers and pamphlets for use in the history, but always there was another more pressing project, and at this moment it was *The Columbiad.* [James Woodress, *A Yankee's Odyssey: The Life of Joel Barlow,* 1958]

Moreover, the poem was not received as an outstanding achievement, although the author had made unusual sacrifices to complete his life's ambition of establishing the epic grandeur of the new nation. In the *Edinburgh Review,* Francis Jeffrey, who had praised the technical aspects of the book's production, had this to say:

> As a great national poem, it has enormous—inexpiable—and, in some respects, intolerable faults. But the author's talents are evidently respectable: and severely as we have been obliged to speak of his taste and his diction in a great part of the volume, we have no hesitation in saying that we consider him a giant, in comparison with many of the puling and paltry rhymsters, who disgrace our English literature by their occasional success. As an Epic poet, we do think his case is desperate; but as a philosophical and moral poet, we think he has talents of no ordinary value; and, if he would pay some attention to purity of style, and simplicity of composition, and cherish in himself a certain fastidiousness of taste,—which is not yet to be found, we are afraid, even among the better educated Americans,—we have no doubt that he might produce something which English poets would envy, and English critics applaud.

Barlow's critics—contemporary and modern—are all aware that *The Columbiad* was no mere rewriting of the narrative vision composed in 1787. "*The Columbiad* [is] more than a revision of *The Vision of Columbus,*" writes William Andrews. "Underlying the second poem is an increased optimism about the capacity of society to improve itself and move of its own accord toward perfection . . . *The Columbiad* articulates a vision of universal peace and happiness which replaced the strictly nationalistic one founded on the application of the *translatio* exclusively to America." And Leon Howard, who has given Joel Barlow special tribute for his contributions to the development of

an American national literature, sees in *The Columbiad* an expression of Barlow's sense of national optimism at the turn of the century: "The system of philosophy Barlow adopted for *The Columbiad* was that used in his more speculative, less practical political writings. It was, of course, optimistically progressive; and, as in *The Vision of Columbus,* the progress was in accord with a predetermined plan. In the latter poem, however, the plan was Nature's rather than God's" [Leon Howard, *The Connecticut Wits,* 1943]. This alteration was significant; by moving away from the divine drama that had provided a structure for the millennial and figural writings of prerevolutionary America, Barlow was obligated to find new ways to use the language of Canaan, which he had employed in the earlier poem, to celebrate the progressive, secular evolution of America's national destiny.

The external differences between the two poems are simple: the historical introduction was retained, but Barlow added a lengthy philosophical preface in which he explained that "*The Columbiad* is a patriotic poem; the subject is national and historical" but that his "object is altogether of a moral and political nature. I wish to encourage, and strengthen, in the rising generation, a sense of the importance of republican institutions; as being the great foundation of public and private happiness, the necessary aliment of future and permanent meliorations in the condition of human nature." This grand design was accomplished by expanding the original eight books to nine, even though Barlow did not alter much of the original plan in the first five books, where both poems describe parts of America and trace the development of western civilization from its beginnings in the Inca empire. But Books VI, VII, and VIII are changed significantly; the treatment of the American Revolution, confined to Books VI and VII in the *Vision,* fills all three in *The Columbiad,* thus necessitating the addition of a final, or ninth and concluding book.

In assessing the changes Barlow made in the text of the *Vision* when he began to compose *The Columbiad,* it is useful to compare selected passages from the two prominent editions of the *Vision,* the 1787 Hartford and the 1793 Paris, with the 1807 Philadelphia printing of *The Columbiad.* Some of the shifts are subtle, others blatant and obvious; nearly all are substantive. Clearly, an extensive textual analysis is beyond the scope of this study; however, a few relevant passages reveal clearly Barlow's later emphasis on a more rational development than *The Prospect of Peace* and the *Vision* had displayed, and the later stanzas show a renewed emphasis on learning as a resolution of those human problems that millennial paradise was originally designed to redress. Barlow's progressive vision is clearly postmillennial in that he asserts the perfectibility of society through projects of self-improvement such as universal education. In the final book of the 1787 *Vision,* for example, Columbus sees a perspective of the apocalypse and commencement of the millennial period:

> Now, fair beneath his view, the important age
> Leads the bold actors on a broader stage;
> When, clothed majestic in the robes of state,
> Moved by one voice, in general council meet
> The father of all empires: 'twas the place,
> Near the first footsteps of the human race;

Where wretched men, first wandering from their
    God,
Began their feuds and led their tribes abroad.

The language of Canaan so prominent here, invoking the original sin through which mankind has historically departed from God's predetermined plan, is dropped completely in the final book of *The Columbiad,* where the passage reappears in modified form to reflect a more rational explanation for social problems based on an understanding of primitive social organization:

Fill'd with unfolding fate, the vision'd age
Now leads its actors on a broader stage;
When clothed majestic in the robes of state,
Moved by one voice, in general congress meet,
The legates of all empires. 'Twas the place
Where man first sought to socialize his race;
Ere yet beguiled, the dark delirious hordes
Began to fight for altars and for lords;
Nile washes still the soil and feels once more
The works of wisdom press his peopled shore.

Similarly, Barlow shifts the imagery and meaning of comparable passages by altering several important words from 1787 to 1793 to 1807. In Book VIII of the *Vision* (which becomes Book IX in the expanded version of *The Columbiad*) we find:

To whom the Angelic Power; to thee 'tis given,
To hold high converse, and enquire of heaven,
To mark uncircled ages and to trace
The unfolding truths that wait thy kindred race.
Know then, the counsels of th' unchanging
    Mind,
Thro' nature's range, progressive paths design'd,
Unfinish'd works th' harmonious system grace,
Thro' all duration and around all space;
Thus beauty, wisdom, power, their prats unroll,
Till full perfection joins the accordant whole.

The fusion of progressive improvement and revealed religion is even more explicit in the 1793 version, but both retain the "Angelic power" through whom the vision is accomplished, and the harmonious perfection achieved remains the product of a divine power, either "th' unchanging Mind" (1787) or "the Maker's mind" (1793). The concluding line of the stanza in the 1793 version, cited below, makes clear Barlow's continued emphasis on a reconciliation between faith and progress:

To whom th' Angelic Power:—To thee 'tis given
To hold high converse and enquire of Heaven,
To make untravers'd ages, and to trace
The promis'd truths that wait thy kindred race.
Know then, the counsels of the Maker's mind,
Thro' nature's range, progressive paths design'd.
Progressive works at every step we trace,
Thro' all duration and around all space;
Till power and wisdom all their parts combine,
And full perfection speak the work divine.

The Columbiad, however, represents a shift away from this attempted reconciliation toward an Enlightenment interpretation of nature's progressive course that is clearly guided more by truth and wisdom than by God's grace:

To whom the guardian Power: To thee is given
To hold high converse and enquire of heaven,

To mark untraversed ages, and to trace
What'er improves and what impedes thy race.
Know then, progressive are the paths we go
In worlds above thee, as in thine below.
Nature herself (whose grasp of time and place
Deals out duration and impalms all space)
Moves in progressive march; but where to tend,
What course to compass, how the march must
    end,
Her sons decide not; yet her works we greet
Imperfect in their parts, but in their whole com-
    plete.

The slight changes in syntax and the substantive alterations in nominative form are significant. "Angelic" becomes "guardian," "(a)wait" becomes "improves" and the "progressive march" becomes a secular, natural phenomenon that is independent of divinity and does not rely on the "Maker's mind" to provide harmonious design or completion. It is the piecing together of the puzzle that renders the whole, and it is man's reason that enables individuals and civilizations to develop toward this goal of harmonious perfection. Indeed, in his notes for *The Columbiad,* Barlow cites the advancement of learning and the progressive evolution of technology as hallmarks of societal improvement:

I conceive it no objection to this theory that the
progress has hitherto been slow; when we consider the magnitude of the object, the obstruc-
tions that were to be removed, and the length of
time taken to accomplish it. The future progress
will probably be more rapid than the past. Since
the invention of printing, the application of the
properties of the magnet, and the knowledge of
the structure of the solar system, it is difficult to
conceive of a cause that can produce a new state
of barbarism; unless it be some great convulsion
in the physical world, so extensive as to change
the face of the earth or a considerable part of it.

Ultimately, it is the spirit of commerce that complements science as the generator of millennial prosperity and progress; the cycles of spiritual regeneration and progress that were so apparent in the historical patterns of biblical dispensation have been replaced by a new force—the advancement of society through education and politics and the progressive improvement of the world through commercial intercourse. If for Edwards, the mariner's compass had been invented to facilitate the spreading of the Gospel, for Barlow the mariner's compass enabled nations to conduct commercial affairs more expeditiously and efficiently.

The spirit of commerce is happily calculated to
open an amicable intercourse between all countries, to soften the horrors of war, to enlarge the
field of science, and to assimilate the manners,
feelings, and languages of all nations. This leading principle, in its remoter consequences, will
produce advantages in favor of free government,
give patriotism the character of philanthropy,
induce all men to regard each other as brethren
and friends, and teach them the benefits of peace
and harmony among nations.

In spite of these pressures on the language to accommodate a new system of belief and new forms of expression, the language of Canaan continued to be a vehicle for carrying the progressive, millennial vision of future times. If it was now endowed with new value and meaning, and if the old figures were now used to render new meanings, the forms themselves were firmly held as metaphorical structures through which the new values were expressed. Barlow continued to utilize biblical figures in his *Vision of Columbus* but he was clearly moving away from the typological value these figures had carried in the contemporary writing, of the New Light movement. A brief examination of Barlow's specific program for societal improvement will make this clear.

Like Jonathan Edwards, Barlow envisioned a perfect society wrought from history in cycles of dispensation; however, this postmillennial, progressive vision was expressed in the language of scriptural prophecy but realized through the agency of scientific improvement and commercial expansion. It is an indication of the power of the biblical language to hold on during a time of transformation that in the notes to *The Vision of Columbus,* Barlow provides a prose gloss for his view that progress would come through scientific advancement rather than through spiritual regeneration, though the language of the poem clearly exemplifies biblical analogies and is resonant with figures drawn from the types and figures:

> It has long been the opinion of the Author, that such a state of peace and happiness as is foretold in scripture and commonly called the millennial period, may be rationally expected to be introduced without a miracle. *Nec deus intersit nisi dignus vindice modus,* is a maxim, as useful to a Christian Philosopher as to a Heathen Poet. Although, from the history of mankind, it appears, that the progressive improvement has been slow and often interrupted, yet it gives pleasure to observe the causes of these interruptions, and to discern the end they were designed in the course of Providence to answer, in accelerating the same events, which they seemed for awhile to retard.

Barlow excised this passage from his notes to *The Columbiad,* further indicating his focus on a technological scheme of progress that had no corollary in Scripture prophecy. And he attributes, in the notes to Book IX of *The Columbiad* (1807), the happiness of society to the expansion and growth of commerce and to the progress of science rather than any further stage of divine dispensation. "The spirit of commerce is happily calculated by the Author of Wisdom to open an amicable intercourse between all countries," Barlow argued, echoing some of the sentiments Jonathan Edwards had announced in the *Miscellanies* as he attempted a reconciliation between the dispensations of the "Divine Author" and the inevitable cycles of historical progress. But Barlow's emphasis is clearly secular; he argues that commerce will "soften the horrors of war, enlarge the field of science and speculation, and assimilate the manners, feelings, and languages of all nations." And the secular emphasis is transformed immediately into political and social patriotism, exhibited throughout in Barlow's republican enthusiasm through which both commerce and agriculture became allies in the progressive realization of a perfect society.

> This leading principle, and its remoter consequences, will produce a thousand advantages in favor of government and legislation, give Patriotism the air of Philanthropy, induce all men to regard each other as brethren and friends, eradicate all kinds of literary, religious, and political superstition, prepare the minds of all mankind for the *rational reception of moral and religious truth* [italics mine] and finally evince that such a system of Providence, as appears in the unfolding of these events, is the best possible system to produce the happiness of men.

The progressive cycles of history are clearly designed to culminate in a perfect ordering of society which is enlightened, harmonious, and future. But the language of Barlow's earlier poem reflects the strong influence of biblical imagery in the realization of this vision, so that we may also contrast passages that have no specific parallels in the companion poem but which reflect, nevertheless, dramatic changes of emphasis. For example, in the *Vision,* Barlow discusses the source of the system in the full flower of Canaan's metaphors, a section which he dropped altogether from *The Columbiad:*

> Progressive thus, from that great source above,
> Flows the fair fountain of redeeming love.
> Dark harbingers of hope, at first bestow'd,
> Taught early faith to feel her path to God;
> Down the prophetic, brightening train of years,
> Consenting voices rose of different seers,
> In *shadowy types* display'd the accomplish'd plan,
> When filial Godhead should assume the man,
> When the pure Church should stretch her arms abroad,
> Fair as a bride and liberal as her God;
> Till warm benevolence and truth refined,
> Pervade the world and harmonize mankind.

The scriptural language and patterns of typological prophecy and fulfillment are clear; Barlow intends not only a vision of progress but one that is at least partially derived from the historical authority of divine dispensation. But it is equally clear that he anticipates the wholly secular version of progress offered by *The Columbiad,* because the lines above are followed by these:

> And thus fair Science, of celestial birth,
> With times long circuit, treads the gladsome earth;
> By gradual steps to mark the extended road,
> That leads mankind to reason and to God.

It is important that the passage had been deleted entirely from the 1793 edition, and it is omitted in *The Columbiad.* The strong biblical references and the prophetic force of the language were not appropriate to Barlow's more enlightened and rational purpose. Instead, the imperial course is guided by science and reason, so that in the Paris edition of the *Vision* we find the following stanza in place of the "shadowy types" cited above:

> 'Tis thus meek Science, from creation's birth,
> With time's long circuit treads the darksome earth,
> Leads in progressive march th' enquiring mind,
> To curb its passions and its bliss to find,

To guide the reas'ning power, and smoothe the
        road,
That leads mankind to nature and to God.

Thus religion—in this case specifically the spiritual dispensations understood by the Judeo-Christian work of re-
demptive history—is subordinated to "rational reception
of moral and religious truth"; piety is supplanted by mor-
alism, "that only criterion of truth that we are able to obtain." Barlow laments the slow progress of the past unfolding of God's plan and seems to explain it by showing
how rational science was not until recently available to assist the divine author: "It is possible that some considerable revolutions are yet to happen, before the progress will
be entirely free from embarassments. But the general system appears so *rational and complete,* that it furnishes a
new source of satisfaction, in contemplating the apparent
dispensations of Heaven." But Barlow adheres to the historical scheme of cyclical dispensation when he prophesies
that progress will be attained through a movement toward
universal harmony and perfection:

> It seems necessary that the arrangement of
> events in civilizing the world should be in the
> following order: *first,* all parts of it must be con-
> siderably peopled; *second,* the different nations
> must be known to each other; *third,* their wants
> must be increased, in order to inspire a want for
> commerce. The first of these objects was not
> probably accomplished till a late period. The
> second for three centuries past has been greatly
> accelerated. The third is a necessary conse-
> quence of the two former.

It is significant that rational perception, as contrasted with
spiritual revelation, has become the vehicle of epistemology, the means through which individuals are to know and
to understand truth. Of course, Jonathan Edwards had already done much to reconcile Lockean epistemology with
divine revelation, . . . but Barlow is here shifting the emphasis away from Scripture altogether, citing the physical
world and its condition as the standard for measuring stability and change in the cycles of revolution. It is equally
significant that Barlow retained much material from these
notes in the ninth book of *The Vision of Columbus* in his
revision of the notes to *The Columbiad,* Book X. In short,
the prophetic books of both the *Vision* and *The Columbiad*
are reflections of the changes in language that had taken
place even as Barlow composed the earlier poem. Although biblical images are used in the *Vision* to suggest
progressive evolution and development, by 1806 much of
this had been stripped away. Leon Howard said [in *Connecticut Wits*], "Barlow no longer felt that man's hope depended upon some internal sense: it depended, instead,
upon the overthrow of error by scientific investigation and
the formation of new, more trustworthy habits of thinking." The poet himself had warned in the Preface, "There
are two distinct objects to be kept in view in the conduct
of a narrative poem: the *poetical* object and the *moral* object. The poetical is the fictitious design of the action; the
moral is the real design of the poem." The traditional imagery of *The Vision of Columbus,* the "poetical" design or
"fictitious" design of the earlier poem, has been supplanted by a more wholly neoclassical design, an epic structure
rather than a narrative vision, and the poem's content—

what he chooses to call the "moral design"—is clearly
more philosophical and political than it had been in the
earlier prototype.

> This brave new world which Columbus was al-
> lowed to see was, physically, very much like the
> one he had seen in the earlier poem. Intellectual-
> ly, however, it was different. Barlow had become
> more clearly utilitarian in his social philosophy
> and more completely a rationalist in morals. He
> placed more emphasis upon "interest" as a force
> for uniting the world and less upon "sympathy"
> and "friendship." And he expressed greater con-
> fidence in the ability of men's minds to expand
> beyond "local" limits and consider the "strength
> and happiness of all humankind." Instead of
> "blest Religion" leading the "raptured mind,"
> he saw a rational "Moral Science" conducting
> the inquisitive, "lively" mind toward its proper
> goals. [Howard]

Similarly, Barlow's image patterns shifted away from a
spiritual use of the language of Canaan toward a secular
meaning and a secular employment of those types and figures which had earlier, in other contexts, exhibited altogether different interpretations and meanings. The transformation was complete; America's future promise was
often sung in the prophetic images of biblical verse; but no
longer did the metaphors carry the freight of biblical
meaning or scriptural typology and prophecy. If the parliament of man in Book X of *The Columbiad* resembles the
commencement of millennial harmony and peace, it no
longer signifies a spiritual millennium which must be
wrought by the author of history. Rather, the figures provide Barlow's readers with a comforting, traditional system for understanding the greatness of America and the
brightness of her future, without the added expectation
that God's millennial paradise will be realized, either spiritually or literally, in this "American quarter of the
globe."

The continuity of Puritan imagery was not lost, however,
in the transformation of the early American dream into
federalist and republican visions of American glory. Concurrent with the development of the rising glory genre of
poetry and the political transitions that marked the era of
the American Revolution was the gradual influence of
Jonathan Edwards and the New Light epistemology on
late eighteenth-century American thinking. Edwards successfully wrought a new epistemology out of a new understanding of nature provided by scientific advances without
violating the integrity of Scripture or his belief in a millennial future. It was Edwards, rather than Barlow, who survived the industrial revolution in America, though Barlow's epic verses are echoed in Whitman's epic *Song of
Myself.* The secular promise of America was indeed derived from the spiritual and eschatological visions of the
Puritans, and Edwards' "new sense of things" would provide the transcendental thinkers with a prophetic vision
of the future that was rooted in the epistemology of New
England's Puritan past. The secular and spiritual progressivists thus continued to parallel each other, and the heralds of America's scientific and technological progress—
men like Jedediah Morse, Noah Webster, and Edward Everett, had antiphonal voices to those of Emerson, Tho-

reau, and Whitman, who, following Edwards' earlier example, developed a language grounded in the language of
Canaan so prominent in America's first two centuries.
Meanwhile, the prophets of technological progress explored America's future promise with a new vocabulary,
too—one evolved from neoclassical and enlightenment
rhetoric of the eighteenth century, which either transformed the images and figures of biblical rhetoric into a
secular and progressive myth, or abandoned the Scripture
figures altogether. Barlow himself wrote,

> Our language is constantly and rapidly improv-
> ing. The unexampled progress of the sciences
> and arts for the last thirty years has enriched it
> with a great number of new words, which are
> now become as necessary to the writer as the an-
> cient mother tongue. The same progress which
> leads to further extensions of ideas will still ex-
> tend the vocabulary; and our neology must and
> will keep pace with the advancement of our
> knowledge.

For Barlow and the technological progressivists, the language of Canaan was now a system of metaphors for analogical use only, lacking the deep conviction and prophetic
meaning that governed its use during the seventeenth and
eighteenth centuries in New England. The alternative and
parallel strain, from the early Puritan settlers through
Jonathan Edwards to Ralph Waldo Emerson and the transcendentalists, extended this rich language into the nineteenth century and provided Walt Whitman with a prophetic vocabulary that would soon sing America's continental expansion and imperial design.

An excerpt from the Preface to *The Columbiad*

My object is altogether of a moral and political nature.
I wish to encourage and strengthen, in the rising generation, a sense of the importance of republican institutions;
as being the great foundation of public and private happiness, the necessary aliment of future and permanent
meliorations in the condition of human nature.

This is the moment in America to give such a direction
too poetry, painting and the other fine arts, that true and
useful ideas of glory may be implanted in the minds of
men here, to take place of the false and destructive ones
that have degraded the species in other countries; impressions which have become so wrought into their most
sacred institutions, that it is there thought impious to detect them and dangerous to root them out, tho acknowledged to be false. Wo be to the republican principle and
to all the institutions it supports, when once the pernicious doctrine of the holiness of error shall creep into the
creed of our schools and distort the intellect of our citizens.

Joel Barlow, The Works of Joel Barlow, Volume II:
Poetry, *Scholars' Facsimiles & Reprints, 1990.*

William C. Dowling (essay date 1990)

SOURCE: "Connecticut Georgic," in *Poetry and Ideology
in Revolutionary Connecticut,* The University of Georgia
Press, 1990, pp. 63-94.

[*In the following excerpt, Dowling analyses Dwight's*
Greenfield Hill *as a poem about American independence—
moral and political—and the dangers of losing it.*]

Perhaps nothing so vividly reveals the degree to which the
American Revolution had been based on an imaginary or
illusory consensus, or the degree to which the illusion had
been sustained by Country ideology as a mainly negative
or demystifying strategy without concrete content of its
own, as the speeches made by Patrick Henry against the
United States Constitution. For when the Revolution is
over and the time has arrived to declare what positive vision of the new republic has animated their struggle, its
leading spirits discover again and again that the vision to
which they have appealed has all along meant different
things to different people. Thus it is that Patrick Henry in
thundering against the new Constitution speaks what is
recognizably the language of Country ideology, invoking
the notion of a peaceful agrarian society of independent
freeholders, but also, just as recognizably, the language of
what Timothy Dwight and his fellows would have seen as
false georgic: "Go to the poor man, ask him what he does;
he will inform you, that he enjoys the fruits of his labor,
under his own fig-tree, with his wife and children around
him, in peace and security. . . you will find no alarms and
disturbances: Why then tell us of dangers to terrify us into
an adoption of this new government?"

The evolution of georgic in this pastoral or Arcadian mode
into a separate ideology would then involve, as Pocock has
shown, the identification of land itself with civic virtue, a
sort of grand inversion of neo-Harringtonian metaphysics
in which, if the landed gentry are repositories of the virtue
of a nation, a nation in which everyone is landed gentry
becomes collectively virtuous. Something like this idea, at
any rate, is at the heart of Jeffersonian agrarianism, as in
Jefferson's well-known letter to John Adams of 28 October 1813:

> Before the establishment of the American States,
> nothing was known to history but the man of the
> old world, crowded within limits either small or
> overcharged, and steeped in the vices which that
> situation generates. A government adapted to
> such men would be one thing; but a very differ-
> ent one, than for the man of these States. Here
> every one . . . by his property, or by his satisfac-
> tory situation, is interested in the support of law
> and order. And such men may safely and advan-
> tageously reserve to themselves a wholesome
> control over their public affairs, and a degree of
> freedom, which, in the hands of the *canaille* of
> the cities of Europe, would be instantly pervert-
> ed to the demolition and destruction of every-
> thing public and private.

Yet the reason Jeffersonian agrarianism would seem to
Dwight and Humphreys to represent a mode of false georgic had less to do with its equation of land and virtue than
with the way that equation was invisibly sustained by a

deeper system of beliefs, notably Deism and Pelagianism in religion and, at the level of history, belief in a progressive and linear rather than a cyclical order of human cultural development. This is the context in which Connecticut georgic will assert that classical republicanism becomes a meaningless parody of itself at the instant it is divorced from certain opposing assumptions about the world, the most important of which are the cyclical theory of history, whose point in Augustan thinking is always to insist on the meaning of history as something lying outside the historical process; an Augustinian vision of mortal existence as a tragic state of alienation from the divine, whose point is to insist on corruption as a product of human moral nature rather than external circumstance; and the moral truth of Christianity, whose point is to put the human and suffering Christ at the center of theological understanding, in contrast to the remote and abstract Creator of eighteenth-century Deism.

In the immediate background of Connecticut georgic, then, lies a momentous ideological struggle over the true meaning of classical republicanism, giving us Dwight and Humphreys as the voices of a literary and cultural Augustanism that, for all its earlier importance in bringing about the revolution in the American colonies, would with their own last poems be all but extinguished as a living strain in American thought. The last poignant testimony to this Augustanism, by the same token, would be the decision of Dwight and Humphreys to wage the ideological struggle through poetry, thus improbably sustaining into the waning years of the eighteenth century the great tradition of poetry-as-intervention looking back through Pope and Dryden to Virgil and Horace in the age of Caesar Augustus. In a poem like Dwight's *Greenfield Hill* we thus have a last reminder of the role played by Augustan poetry—Pope's Horatian satires and Swift's anti-Walpole verses and Thomson's *Liberty*—in preparing the way for American independence, as well as the more obvious and urgent message that this independence, though now secured politically, may yet be morally lost.

Yet the decision to wage through poetry the struggle in favor of a specific moral vision of the new American republic was in no sense merely valedictory, a last ceremonial gesture toward the literary tradition in which the Connecticut poets had their common roots. For what Dwight and Humphreys, especially, recognized was that the image of the ideal republic as it had developed inside poetry through the long centuries between Virgil and Pope had itself taken on some of the weight of human existence concretely lived, and that this suggestion of the actual, in a climate increasingly dominated by the abstract or generalizing tendencies of utopian political thought, possessed in itself a certain ideological value. In one important strategic sense the claim of Connecticut georgic will be that it has absolutely nothing new to say, which is why, reading the poetry of Augustan England after having read Dwight and Humphreys, one so often has the uncanny impression of having stumbled in advance upon Connecticut georgic. Thus, for instance, the hymn to the moral independence of the freeman in Thomson's *Liberty*. "Hail, INDEPENDENCE . . . ," sings the goddess Liberty,

By rills from thee deduc'd, irriguous, fed,
The private field looks gay, with nature's wealth
Abundant flows, and blooms with each delight
That nature craves. Its happy master there,
The ONLY FREE-MAN, walks his pleasing round:
Sweet-featur'd peace attending; fearless Truth;
Firm Resolution; Goodness, blessing all
That can rejoice; Contentment, surest
    friend. . . .

Meantime true-judging moderate desires,
Economy and taste, combin'd, direct
His clear affairs, and from debauching fiends
Secure his little kingdom.

                                            (5.132-47)

This is the state of moral independence that Connecticut georgic will always portray as the indispensable basis of political independence, the ground of moderation and honorable toil that may preserve the new republic in civic virtue while other societies succumb to luxury and corruption. Though Dwight's own ultimate expression of this theme will come in *Greenfield Hill,* the moral imperative he associates with the classical republican vision is already visible years before . . . in *The Conquest of Canaan,* the more central theme of which is the Judaeo-Christian tradition as the wider context within which civic humanism or classical republicanism take on their genuine meaning. Thus it is, for instance, that Joshua calling the Israelites to battle will speak the language of what is recognizably civic humanist morality, employing a vocabulary that would have been instantly identifiable to anyone familiar with Opposition thought in England, and that the militiamen of the American colonies, summoned into the field by the same rhetoric of virtue and corruption, would have just as instantly taken as applying to themselves: "Plain, generous manners vigorous limbs confess," says Joshua, gazing out over the assembled Israelite army, "And vigorous minds to freedom ardent press; / In danger's path our eyes serenely smile, / And well-strung sinews hail accustom'd toil" (1.729-32).

Such moments in *The Conquest of Canaan* give us the essential context within which we are to interpret the mature georgic vision of *Greenfield Hill,* in whose verses overtly theological preoccupations will have dropped into the background in favor of a more universalized Augustanism suited to the ideological reality of the postrevolutionary moment, a new United States of America heterogeneous in its creeds and local ideologies and sharing as a common tradition only the revolutionary mythos of the immediate national past. Yet what gives *The Conquest of Canaan* this privileged status is precisely that the georgic vision of *Greenfield Hill* is already carried within it, such that one is always aware of the vital relation between an Augustinian view of human moral nature and the implications of georgic as understood by the later Dwight and Humphreys. When Joshua in book 10 is taken by the angel to a high place and granted a vision of Canaan as the goal toward which he is leading his people, what he sees is, in effect, Connecticut, the first book of *Greenfield Hill* in embryo:

At once a spacious land is seen,

Bright with young cornfields, and with pastures
green;
Fair shine the rivers; fair the plains extend;
The tall woods wave, and towering hills ascend;
Ten thousand flocks around them spread,
Sport o'er the lawns, and crop the verdant blade;
Bless'd swains with music charm their useful
toil,
The cheerful plowmen turn the sable
soil. . . .

(19-26)

If this is Canaan as Connecticut, however, it is also Canaan as the idealized England we come across in Dyer's *The Fleece* or Thomson's *Liberty or The Seasons,* reminding us, as Dwight even in his most pronouncedly theological moments means to remind us, that he is drawing constantly on the civic mythology of the Augustan or classical republican tradition. For Dwight's great project of working out in poetry a synthesis of the traditions of civic humanism and Puritan or covenant theology will always involve a convergence, at essential moments, of the two systems of thought, suggesting without directly asserting that each represents simply a different angle of vision on an identical moral reality. Thus it is, for instance, that we not only find the language of civic humanism employed throughout *The Conquest of Canaan,* but that we also find the Puritan millenarianism that Ursula Brumm and others have taught us to emphasize in Dwight's biblical epic still powerfully present in *Greenfield Hill:* "till millennial suns / Call forth returning Eden," says Dwight in book 1, looking out at a Long Island Sound newly peaceful after the alarms of the Revolution, "arts of peace / Shall triumph here. Speed, oh speed, ye days / Of bliss divine! when all-involving Heaven, / The mystery finish'd, come the second birth / Of this sin-ruin'd, this apostate world, / . . . All climes shall clothe again with life, and joy, / With peace, and purity" (412-20).

Yet this same millenarian strain in Dwight's poetry, extending to the new American republic his grandfather Edwards's hope that New England was to witness the actual beginning of the thousand-year reign of earthly peace preceding the Apocalypse, operates simultaneously to diminish the importance of the earthly millennium, to remind us that the "true Canaan," as Dwight once calls it, is the home with God won through salvation, a world of "life, and joy" and "peace, and purity" compared with which the deepest joys of mortal existence are but dim shadows of the glory to come. This is why, in *The Conquest of Canaan,* the description of Apocalypse—"Clouds of dark blood shall blot the sun's broad light, / Spread round th' immense, and shroud the world in night, / . . . Storms rock the skies; afflicted ocean roar, / And sanguine billows dye the shuddering shore" (10.751-56)—constitutes, as much as a millenarian prediction, a warning against any misguided millennialism. The ways of God are mysterious, and one can only guess when the millennium may arrive; until then one's business is to navigate one's way through what Dwight calls a sin-ruined, apostate world.

In always insisting on this point, Dwight will simply be raising to explicitness that Augustinian view of human moral nature always implicit in Augustan writing, where

it exists not as a matter of doctrine but as a way of comprehending the moral reality permanently inhabited by men and women. For in Augustan England, the common perception that could hold together in the same circle a Deist like Bolingbroke and a Roman Catholic like Pope and an Anglican like Swift was not some formal assent to a doctrine of Original Sin but a deep conviction that what Original Sin and the myth of the Fall are about—the reality of a moral nature that causes us to fall constantly into weakness and error even when we try most single-mindedly to rise above them—is a truth in every age and every clime, a moral reality common to ancient Greeks and Romans and modern Englishmen and the far-flung inhabitants of Britain's American colonies. To pretend otherwise, to assert with Shaftesbury or other eighteenth-century Pelagians that man is possessed of a moral nature innately innocent or good, is wittingly or unwittingly to tell a great lie about the world.

To call this perspective Augustinian, as Fussell and other students of Augustan writing have been disposed to do, is simply to remind ourselves that Saint Augustine, drawing through Plotinus on a Platonic philosophical tradition saying virtually the same thing in non- or pre-Christian terms, had given it permanent expression in the image of mortal life as a tragic state of exile or alienation from the divine. "My soul," cries Augustine in the *Confessions,* " . . . do not let the din of your folly deafen the ears of your heart. For the Word himself calls you to return. . . . In the land of death you try to find a happy life: it is not there" (81-82). "Thou art the source and center of all minds," says Cowper in *The Task,* his elegiac Augustanism as always putting him closer to Dwight than any other English poet of the time, "Their only point of rest, eternal Word! / From thee departing, they are lost, and rove / At random, without honor, hope, or peace" (5.596-99). The exile in which Cowper's souls wander without hope or peace—Augustine's land of death and Dwight's sin-ruined, apostate world—is a reality known on virtually the same terms by Socrates and Plotinus and Dryden and Samuel Johnson, and the great point of Connecticut georgic will always be that it has not somehow miraculously vanished with America's political independence from Britain.

This is the great point as well of all those extended moments in *The Conquest of Canaan,* no doubt tedious even to eighteenth-century readers unaware of the momentousness of the issues being fought out, in which the epic narrative is suspended to permit a glimpse of an older story, the myth of the Fall of Man and earthly existence as exile. Thus we have, for instance, Mina recounting to the Gibeonites the story of Adam's disobedience and its consequences for humankind—"The sacred stamp the mind forever lost, / . . . Else had our life roll'd on, from sorrow clear, / A semblance bright of heaven's eternal year" (2.429-32)—or her image of death as a voyage out of this world into a realm of eternal peace: "Then shall we see diviner winds arise, / The main grow calm . . . : / With joy, our spirits leave the fading shore, / And hear the lessening storms at distance roar" (2.226-34). It is the point, too, of Irad's theodicy in book 5, in which Dwight will counter the physicotheological rapture of a hundred eighteenth-century poems that, under the equal influence of Newtonian celestial mechanics and Shaftesburian ethical theory, deduce from the starry canopy the existence of an indiscriminately benevolent Creator. Dwight's response, suggesting a wide and sympathic reading of eighteenth-century poetry as well as a notable generosity of spirit, is to grant physicotheology its own large measure of truth but then to insist as well on the conditional nature of that truth:

> These splendid scenes surprise thy curious
>   mind;
> For worms too noble, or too kind, they shine,
> The works of wisdom, power, and love, divine.
> From morn's gay bounds, to skirts of distant
>   even,
> They teach the hand, and spread the name of
>   Heaven;
> In beauty, grandeur, make JEHOVAH known,
> But mark, with faded charms, a world undone.
> Yet these, could man the common bliss pursue,
> Would gentle peace, and smiling joy, renew,
> Light, with soft-beaming hope, the cheerful day,
> And drive grim war, and cankering hate, away.

(5.107-17)

Yet the point of Irad's theodicy is not simply to provide a counterstatement in poetry to such eighteenth-century poems as John Gilbert Cooper's *The Power of Harmony* or Akenside's *The Pleasures of Imagination,* but to suggest at the same time a virtual theology of the *ricorso* envisioned in classical republican theory. For the world of gentle peace and smiling joy imagined by Irad at this moment is none other than the returning Eden of biblical prophecy, and Dwight's point throughout *Greenfield Hill* will be that the virtuous early republic of civic humanism is simply this same world in a different guise. Thus Humphreys, for instance, will utter in his *Poem on the Happiness of America* the conventional thought that the new United States, as a restoration of the virtuous republic, represents on the cultural level the *aurea mediocritas,* or golden mean, of Aristotelian ethics: "Here exists, once more, th' Arcadian scene, / Those simple manners, and that golden mean: / Here holds society its middle stage, / Between too rude and too refin'd an age" (422-25). This will be the civic ideal central to Dwight's thought as well, but always with the proviso that the ancient philosophers, without being in a position to realize it, had uncovered a divinely sanctioned principle: the golden mean works, so to speak, because it was ordained by God as part of natural law. When one has seen this, what one sees is not some nebulous American virtue or innocence but, in all its splendid particularity, Connecticut:

> But chief, Connecticut! on thy fair breast
> These splendors glow. A rich improvement
>   smiles
> Around thy lovely borders; in thy fields
> And all that in thy fields delighted dwell.
> Here that pure, golden mean, so oft of yore
> By sages wish'd, and prais'd, by Agur's voice
> Implor'd, while God th' approving sanction
>   gave
> Of wisdom infinite; that golden mean,
> Shines unalloy'd; and here the extended good,

> The mean alone secures, is ceaseless found.

(1.215-24)

To see that the vision of classical republican thought is reabsorbed at such moments into an older paradigm of divinely ordained natural law is in one sense to see Connecticut as it has always been assumed to exist for Dwight in *Greenfield Hill* and elsewhere, as a symbol of the godly Puritan state that has improbably managed to survive into the postrevolutionary period, and which therefore offers the new United States a model, only slightly secularized, of an older New England theocratic ideal. This is, in short, the Connecticut of the Fundamental Orders as it lingers in living memory, the state of society a Congregational clergyman like Samuel Woodbridge had in mind when in 1724 he preached to the Connecticut General Assembly a sermon, *Obedience to the Divine Law, Urged on All Orders of Men,* reminding it that the "exercise of government" was instituted solely that "subjects may lead a peaceable and quiet life in all godliness and honesty". It is Connecticut precisely as an embodiment of peaceable godliness, we have always been inclined to suppose, that leads Dwight so constantly to speak of its way of life as providing "the solid foundations, which appear to be laid for the future greatness and prosperity of the American republic" (372).

Yet Connecticut as symbol in *Greenfield Hill,* or in the long excursus Humphreys would add to the 1804 version of *Poem on the Industry of the United States*—"Hail favor'd state! Connecticut!"—assumes not some undisturbed ideal of godliness in an otherwise unregenerate world but a story of disintegration or decline in which the stable and harmonious Connecticut society of the Fundamental Orders is itself subjected to the stresses and strains of an emergent modernity. This is not the standard story of second- and third-generation Puritan declension told a generation ago by Perry Miller, nor yet the revisionary stories more recently told by Bercovitch and other students of New England thought as a corrective to Miller, but one having to do with population pressures and markets and currency speculation: a story, in short, in which there may be glimpsed certain overwhelming parallels between eighteenth-century Connecticut and the England of Pope and Swift and Bolingbroke, the society and the moral climate of Walpole and the Robinocracy, the South Sea Bubble and Change Alley and the national debt.

The story as it stands as a background to the poetry of Dwight and Humphreys, and with certain adjustments of emphasis to that of Trumbull and Barlow as well, has been splendidly traced by Richard Bushman in *From Puritan to Yankee,* where, for all Bushman's careful and detailed marshalling of demographic and economic statistics, its essentially mythic outlines may nonetheless be glimpsed. Yet, precisely as in England during roughly the same period, this is myth in which the unleashed forces of an emergent capitalism themselves acquire a mythic or demonic role, with the growth of a new class of small traders and speculators unsettling the traditional Puritan order of the seventeenth century, and with James Fitch and the "native right" men, in whose hands the land of western Connecticut would be transformed into a new form of speculative wealth, playing in local terms the role of Walpole and the Robinocracy. It was the schemes of the "native right" faction, the Upper House of the Connecticut Assembly would declare during its endless troubles with Fitch, giving vent to an anger that would have been immediately recognizable to any reader of Pope's satires or Bolingbroke's *Craftsman,* that had been "the principle bane and ruin of our ancient order and peace".

In the same way, there will lie in the immediate background of Connecticut georgic not simply a widespread cultural perception of traditional society as being somehow destabilized or radically altered by underlying economic forces but a determined attempt to grasp the meaning of the transformation within existing categories of thought. In Augustan England, as we have seen, this gives us the universal attempt to grasp the disintegrative energies of an emergent capitalism within the classical category of Luxury, itself then buttressed by the cyclical theory of history and an admonitory story of civilizations ruined from within by corruption and material excess. In Connecticut the categories within which change is grasped tend to be, as we might expect, theological. There has been a great cry in the land about oppression and hard usage, Jonathan Marsh would say in 1721, which in the new speculative climate men are given to attributing to "the want of a medium of trade." But lack of currency or credit is hardly their problem. The issue is moral and religious: "The concern is not as heretofore to accommodate themselves as to the worship of God, . . . but where they can get most land, and be under best advantages to get money." Men have grown more serious, in short, about getting "land and money and stock, than they be about getting religion revived, and securing the salvation of their souls".

This is the background against which Timothy Dwight and his undergraduate circle at Yale, reading the poets of Augustan England in the midst of an ideological crisis that would shortly lead to America's declaration of independence from a Britain grown irredeemably corrupt, would learn to recognize an essential equivalence between the languages of classical republicanism and covenant theology, would find in Country ideology as it informs the poetry of Pope and Thomson or the brilliant polemic of Bolingbroke a civic mythology bringing their own remote Connecticut society into sudden revelatory alignment with the history of Europe and the ancient civilizations of Greece and Rome, and would then find in the Puritan theology and millenarian traditions of their own New England upbringing a framework of ultimate explanation within which classical republican theory is seen to borrow its validity from divine law. This is the context in which the georgic mode developed by Dwight and Humphreys will portray Connecticut society not as some forgotten outpost of New England theocracy improbably lingering on into the modern world, but precisely as a vision of *ricorso,* what the classical republican would call a return to moral origins or first principles and what we have heard a member of Connecticut society, troubled by an identical modernity, call "our ancient order and peace."

In *The Conquest of Canaan* and *Greenfield Hill,* then, Dwight will be not so much working out a synthesis of classical republicanism and covenant theology as dwelling on an essential convergence he perceives already to exist, and this will be true as well of Humphreys, especially in the later poetry where Connecticut society comes to assume for him much the same symbolic value it has for Dwight. This is where georgic, as a poetic mode already in a manner associated with classical republican notions of the virtuous republic but also stressing a generalized piety or religious sense as the indispensable ground of civic virtue, will become the grand medium of a synthesizing vision, a way of compellingly suggesting to the new United States that there exists even now in Connecticut, partly at the level of everyday actuality and partly as a living ethical memory, the basis of its virtue as a nation. When it considers the "enterprise, industry, economy, morals, and happiness, of New England," says Dwight in one of those endnotes to *Greenfield Hill* offered as a supplementary prose treatise on georgic principles, especially Connecticut, the patriotic mind can only rejoice at the thought that "the manners of New England appear to be rapidly spreading throughout the American republic" (530). The name of the same hope expressed as poetry is *Greenfield Hill* itself.

The immediate means through which *Greenfield Hill* translates the older language of covenant theology into the now more universal idiom of classical republicanism is the image of Connecticut as a society sustained in georgic virtue by the rigor of its physical circumstances: "Cold is thy clime, but every western blast / Brings health, and life, and vigor on his wings; / . . . and firms the soul / With strength and hardihood" (1.92-95). This is the myth of northern liberty and hardy virtue being taken over directly from Country ideology—in short, Switzerland as seen in Thomson's *Liberty* or Goldsmith's *The Traveller,* Lapland as we have heard Thomson describe it in *The Seasons,* georgic societies always seen in moral contrast to that state of southern sloth and servitude introduced into Augustan poetry in Addison's *Letter from Italy.* The moribund civilizations of the Mediterranean make their appearance as well in Dwight's description of Connecticut climate and geography—they are, in the standard language of Country ideology, the "lazy plains, dissolv'd in putrid sloth" (1.107) mentioned in the same passage—but now as the most distant of ideological echoes, simple assurance that the seat of georgic virtue has migrated transatlantically to New England: "Thy rough soil / Tempts hardy labor, with his sturdy team, / To turn, with sinewy hand, the stony glebe / And call forth every comfort from the mould, / . . . Thy houses, barns, / Thy granaries, and thy cellars, hence are stored / With all the sweets of life" (1.107-14).

This image of Connecticut society, translated at a higher level of generality into moral terms, will become the basis of Connecticut georgic as a model for the new American republic. The translation occurs, first, as a notion of rigorous or demanding physical circumstances internalized as a mode of being in the world, the Connecticut freeholder as Virgilian swain: "His lot, that wealth, and power, and pride forbids, / Forbids him to become the tool of fraud, / Injustice, misery, ruin; saves his soul / From all the needless labors, griefs, and cares, / That avarice, and ambition, agonize" (1.462-66). To see that such a state of georgic virtue may become general throughout the United States—this will be the counterstatement of Dwight and Humphreys to what they would have seen as the vacuous optimism of Jeffersonian agrarianism—is then to see that the great *O fortunatos nimium* passage of Virgilian tradition has, in the wake of the American Revolution, taken on a triumphantly new meaning. The Virgilian swain is contentedly at work in his fields and vineyards, as he has been for eighteen centuries, but now the clients at the gate are separated from him by three thousand miles of ocean:

> Ah! knew he but his happiness, of men
> Not the least happy he, who, free from broils,
> And base ambition, vain and bust'ling pomp,
> Amid a friendly cure, and competence,
> Tastes the pure pleasures of parochial life.
> What though no crowd of clients, at his gate,
> To falsehood, and injustice, bribe his tongue,
> And flatter into guilt; . . .
>
> What though no swarms, around his sumptuous
>   board,
> Of soothing flatterers, humming in the shine
> Of opulence, and honey from its flowers,
> Devouring, 'till their time arrives to sting,
> Inflate his mind. . . .

(1.430-52)

Yet we mistake utterly the meaning of Connecticut georgic unless we recognize that this Virgilian vision, even as it is offered as a model to the new nation, is a threatened or imperiled vision, and that the threats to it, when enumerated, add up to a somber insistence that the American republic, for all its millennial promise, yet inhabits a fallen reality, an Augustinian world outside the Garden of Eden. This will become the thrust of New England Federalism against Jeffersonian republicanism, and it gives us the important sense in which Connecticut georgic represents a continuation of the Augustan enterprise in an ideological climate increasingly dominated by "easier" visions of American innocence or virtue, an attempt generously to grant all that is to be granted to Jeffersonian optimism— the equation of land with virtue, so long as this is understood in a context of georgic piety, America as returning Eden or millennial New Earth, so long as this is understood in orthodox theological terms—while resisting to the uncompromising end its underlying Pelagianism, that new belief, deriving ultimately from Shaftesburian ethical theory and Latitudinarian theology in England, in what Humphreys once testily called "the vaunted perfectibility of human nature" (363).

The first great threat to georgic or Virgilian innocence in the new republic is history itself, which in *Greenfield Hill,* as John Griffith has seen, remains remorselessly cyclical, a kind of impersonal fate or doom lying just outside the sunlit borders of any premature celebration of American virtue, reminding the thoughtful student of history and human nature that the revolving course of mighty time, to borrow Dyer's phrase once more, makes no more exemptions for civilizations than does death for individuals. Thus, for instance, Dwight's meditation on the departure of glory from England, in which we are taken in thought some centuries forward to see the "queen of nations" become a wasteland—"In dust, thy temples, towers, and

towns decay; / The forest howl, where London's turrets burn; / And all thy garlands deck thy sad, funereal urn" (4.61-63)—must be read not simply as another declaration of *translatio* and America's rising glory, though on one level it is that as well, but also as the soberest of warnings about a heedless national optimism. For the rising glory theme in *Greenfield Hill* will always be counterpointed by a sense of the rise and fall of civilizations as melancholy as anything in Dyer or Thomson or Pope: "Where o'er an hundred realms, the throne uprose, / The screech-owl nests, the panther builds his home; / . . . Tall grass around the broken column waves; / And brambles climb, and lonely thistles bloom: / . . . And low resound, beneath, unnumber'd sunken graves" (4.28-36).

Yet the primary means through which *Greenfield Hill* will incorporate into its georgic vision of the American republic a monitory sense of cyclical history is its elegiac portrayal of Indian culture—the tribal or forest civilization of North American natives before the arrival of Europeans—as a vanishing reality. This is the theme of part 4 of *Greenfield Hill,* "The Destruction of the Pequods," which is both about the end of Indian civilization and about its narrator or poetic speaker as a representative American consciousness attempting to come to terms with its extinction at the hands of Europeans in general and, in particular, the colonial forefathers of those who are now the citizenry of the new United States. For Dwight is clear-eyed and uncompromising about the matter of European guilt; the Indians have been driven from their lands because of the sheer greed of the white man—because, as Dwight himself puts it, "Avarice pin'd for boundless breadth of land" (4.309)—have been condemned to disease and the "slow death" of cheap rum by traders eager to exploit them, and have in general been pushed thoughtlessly aside by an expanding European culture actually and willfully unconscious that its civilization in the New World is being built on the ruins of an innocent people.

Yet the elegiac theme of vanished or vanishing Indian civilization in *Greenfield Hill* also represents an attempt at imaginative redemption that will in a sense compensate for the melancholy fact of European guilt. For Dwight will always imagine the Europe that has extinguished Indian culture as that same corrupt Europe from which the American colonies have themselves won a moral as well as a political independence; what remains is to do what justice may be done to the remnants of the eastern tribes, and beyond that to reimagine their civilization in a way that gives it permanent status in the cultural memory of the new United States. The obstacle to doing so is that through the long centuries that European civilization has been developing an advanced intellectual and material culture, the Indians have, so to speak, remained outside history, in a timeless or steady-state existence in which cultural progress as such is simply unknown. This gives us the significance of the movement through which Dwight, echoing the graveyard speaker of Gray's *Elegy,* will reimagine Indian civilization within the categories of European historical experience, making it a story of unrecorded wars, unmedaled heroes, unwritten epics: "Even now, perhaps, on human dust I tread, / . . . Here sleeps, perchance, among the vulgar dead, / Some Chief, the lofty theme of Indian rhyme, / Who lov'd Ambition's cloudy steep to climb / . . . And soar'd Caesarean heights" (4.100-109).

As in Gray's *Elegy,* the point of such meditation is to remind us, grown too immersed in the world to remember our birth and our destiny, of the perspective that saves sanity, if not souls: the world is a passing show, the paths of glory lead but to the grave. Yet in Dwight's imagining of the vanished Indian chief as the Caesar or Alexander of a silent age, a precisely opposite movement begins to make itself felt, such that the lost Indian tribes of eastern North America begin to be swept up into that larger story of rise and fall, of Persia and Carthage and Greece and Rome, that had so come to dominate the European imagination in the years leading up to the American Revolution. The final redemption both of Indian civilization and European guilt is thus that moment of grand thematic resolution in which the vanished tribes pass into collective American memory as a permanent reminder of the cyclical history that stands as a monitory doom over states still young in virtue and heedless in their growing strength:

> In you small field, that dimly steals from sight,
> (From yon small field these meditations grow)
> Turning the sluggish soil, from morn to night,
> The plodding hind, laborious, drives his plough,
> Nor dreams, a nation sleeps, his foot below.
> There, undisturbed by the roaring wave,
> Releas'd from war, and far from deadly foe,
> Lies down, in endless rest, a nation brave,
> And trains, in tempests born, there find a quiet
> grave.
>
> (4.109-17)

At the same time, the European corruption that has reached out in the form of greed and exploitation to bring about the ruin of Indian civilization, though it has been temporarily banished from American shores by the victory over Britain, remains a threat to the new republic. Nowhere do *Greenfield Hill* and Connecticut georgic generally more clearly demonstrate their continuity with the Opposition poetry of Augustan England, and with the efflorescence of Country ideology in the colonies prior to the Revolution, than in those passages focusing on the theme of European corruption, the terminal result of which now stands revealed as a structure of exploitation that maintains a few in obscene opulence while millions exist on the brink of actual starvation: "See hounds and horses riot on the store, / By HEAVEN created for the hapless poor! / See half a realm one tyrant scarce sustain, / While meagre thousands round him glean the plain! / See, for his mistress' robe, a village sold, / Whose matrons shrink from nakedness and cold" (*Greenfield Hill,* 2.139-44). This is the controlled lamentation of Goldsmith's *Deserted Village* already tending toward the grim realism of Crabbe or the social anger of Cobbett in the next century, the georgic vision moving toward that register in which, given intolerable provocation, it will become agrarian radicalism.

Yet the strain of social anger that so often makes Dwight in *Greenfield Hill* sound uncannily like the later, "radical" Barlow is in fact monitory, a vision of European corruption meant to warn a still-virtuous American republic of the dangers involved in giving way, in this initial moment

Hesper appearing to Columbus in prison: an illustration from Barlow's Columbiad.

of national optimism, to the insidious forces of luxury and corruption. For the great point enforced by Connecticut georgic, its reason for dwelling on the theme of corruption even in the postrevolutionary period when the need for doing so would seem to have passed, is that corruption is only contingently and transiently something to be identified with European autocracies or ministerial tyranny in Britain; it is, first and foremost, something lurking in the moral constitution of humanity, and as such is present in the United States even now. Thus, for instance, Washington as he is heard in Humphreys's *Poem on the Happiness of America,* addressing before going into rural retirement both the disbanding army and the new nation, will retain the pure language of Country ideology: "Shun fell corruption's pestilential breath, / To states the cause, and harbinger of death. / Fly dissipation, in whose vortex whirl'd, / Sink the proud nations of the elder world" (35-38).

In Connecticut georgic, which in this register represents Country ideology transformed from a revolutionary doctrine into a permanent ethic of republican virtue, Europe is thus no longer merely the entangled system of governments and alliances from which America has successfully broken free, but a state of mind, a half-suppressed longing after the glitter and complexity of life in what Washington calls the elder world as seen from the simple or rustic perspective of a georgic society. The danger to the new American republic, in short, is the danger succumbed to by Demas in Dwight's *Triumph of Infidelity,* who when at home lives precisely the life portrayed in *Greenfield Hill*—"modest, decent, in life's lowly vale, / Pleas'd he walk'd on"—but who in Europe allows himself to be seduced not directly by vice or depravity but by social glamor: "Great houses, and great men, in coaches carried; / Great ladies, great Lord's wives, tho' never married; / Fine horses, and fine pictures, and fine plays, / And all the finest things of modern days. / Cameleon-like, he lost his former hue, / And, mid such great men, grew a great man too" (360).

As in his *Epistle to Colonel Humphreys,* Dwight is borrowing here the Grand Tour motif of Augustan satire, that tale of moral fecklessness in which, as in Pope's *Dunciad,* the young man goes abroad for a sojourn in societies sunk further in corruption than his own and, not through any innate viciousness but from a mere pathetic desire to shine socially, becomes as depraved as they. This is a move in which Dwight had been anticipated by his friend Trumbull in *The Progress of Dulness,* but in the postrevolutionary moment the half-laughing tone of Trumbull's satire gives way to a note of deadly seriousness, for the point now is that a mere obeisance to what both Dwight and Humphreys call fashion, the seemingly foolish and relatively harmless pursuit of a spurious cosmopolitanism, masks the direst threat to what Dwight describes as "the dignified character of free republicans" (529). For "fashion" equals "Europe," and Europe as a state of mind or moral consciousness is dangerous precisely because it disguises an inward corruption with the outward glitter of high civilization; this is the elder world as, once again, Dwight's "foul harlot, Europe"—all jewels and flashing brocade on the outside, while inside there is rottenness and dead men's bones.

That rottenness is precisely what Dwight means to expose in focusing so relentlessly on European society as a scene of inequality and exploitation, a world where rich men feed dainties to their very dogs while the poor perish for want of bread. Yet Dwight's great point about such a world—it is a thought that goes back to the Stoics—is that in it the rich and powerful are ultimately as degraded by their situation as the poor and powerless, which is why, throughout modern Europe, "foul luxury taints the putrid mind, / And slavery there imbrutes the reasoning kind" (2.151-52). This is the fallen and unlovely social reality to which the vision of Connecticut georgic is meant, with urgent seriousness, to suggest a permanent alternative, with the relative equality of material conditions—what Dwight calls the ideal of competence: a society in which everyone has a sufficiency and no one is very rich or poor—providing a perpetual source of civic virtue, which in turn preserves the society in its state of georgic happiness; here, the poetic speaker of part 3 of *Greenfield Hill* will say, "Whate'er adorns the reasoning name, / Or emulates an angel's fame, / The just, the good, the humble thrive, / And *in this sweet republic live*" (393-96).

Within the American republic as a whole, the rottenness that "imbrutes the reasoning kind" is Negro or chattel slavery, which Dwight by careful indirection exposes both as the basis of false georgic of Patrick Henry's sort and as the paradox at the heart of Jeffersonian progressivism. For it is not simply that the South, where a privileged few live in opulence on the anonymous toil of driven millions, corresponds in obvious terms to the state of European corruption so scathingly portrayed in *Greenfield Hill*—Dwight's image of the "foul harlot, Europe" is always to this extent a coded description of the slaveowning South—but that so monstrous a social fact then also vitiates any ideological claims that might be made by a Patrick Henry or a Richard Henry Lee or a Thomas Jefferson about the nature of the virtuous republic. This is the context in which Patrick Henry's "georgic" exposes itself as an idyll silently assuming the ownership of human beings as property, and the Jeffersonian ethic of states' rights and individual liberties as, implicitly, a doctrine meant to guard a slaveowning minority from interference by a United States government to whom the thought of property in human beings might very well become intolerable. "How is it," Dr. Johnson had asked at the end of *Taxation No Tyranny,* "that we hear the loudest *yelps* for liberty among the drivers of negroes?" (*Life,* 3.201:n. 1). This is very close to the judgment rendered by *Greenfield Hill.*

Yet that judgment is never rendered in direct terms, for the simple reason that Dwight represents a New England consciousness continuing desperately to hope that the South, having in a sudden paroxysm of horror seen the intolerability of its ways, will yet in a single stroke renounce slavery and redeem the virtue of the new American republic. Thus it is that *Greenfield Hill* gives us a moving portrayal of Negro children suddenly gone spiritless when they realize they are not free, and Negro adults whose moral nature is being debased by slavery, and yet all this occurs not in South Carolina or Virginia but on Dwight's own native ground in Connecticut, where the anomalous sight of a Negro farm laborer prompts his musings on slavery as an institution. Thus too the angry protoabolitionist picture of the slaveowner's cruelty—whips, thongs, the screams of innocent victims—takes as its setting the West Indies. By the time Dwight's anger mounts to a crescendo in his denunciation of slavery as the moral gangrene of the new republic, the great unmentioned fact—the silence that shrieks with an implication inescapable to those reading the poem in Savannah or Charleston or Charlottesville—is the existence of the slave states: "Thou spot of hell, deep smirch'd on human kind, / The uncur'd gangrene of the reasoning mind; / Alike in church, in state, and household all, / Supreme memorial of the world's dread fall; / O slavery!" (2.255-59)

The direct means through which slavery curses any society harboring it as an institution is by undermining work or physical labor as the basis of civic virtue, the Hesiodic principle of *ponos* that Thomson has in mind when he speaks of the husbandman's hard, laborious life, or, elsewhere, using the term always favored by Dwight and Humphreys, of "industry": "rough Power! / Whom Labor still attends, and sweat, and pain; / Yet the kind source of every gentle art, / And all the soft civility of life: / Raiser of human kind!" (*Autumn,* 43-47). The importance of industry or work, says Humphreys in the preface to his *Poem on the Industry of the United States,* catching in a phrase the entire metaphysics of the georgic vision of society, is that it "furnishes a kind of moral force for overcoming the sluggishness of matter, which constantly inclines to repose" (94). This is physical labor, in short, of which the highest ethical type and the ground of all else is agricultural work, as an activity situating a society at that intersection of the human and divine worlds from which civic happiness flows as from a perpetual source. A slaveowning society is built on rotten foundations not least because it is out of touch with industry as a source of civic virtue, giving us the sense in which Connecticut georgic embodies the antithesis of such a society:

> Thus warm'd with industry, behold my swains!
> Guide the smooth plough, and dress the grateful
>   plains;
> From earth's rich bosom, bid all products rise,
> The bless'd creation of indulgent skies;
> The grass-grown hills with herds unnumber'd
>   crown,
> And bid the fleecy nations fill the down; . . .
>
> Or ocean's chambers, with bold hand, explore,
> And waft his endless treasures to the shore!
>   (*Greenfield Hill*, 7.233-44)

By the same token, as Dwight's unperturbed mention of grazing sheep and seagoing vessels may suggest, the power of georgic labor to sanctify the modes of economic activity deriving from it means that an agricultural society need not, to remain virtuous, remain either rustic or wholly agrarian. At the heart of Connecticut georgic we thus discover an ideal of Augustan commerce going back through Pope's *Windsor-Forest* to Denham's *Coopers Hill*, one always presenting itself as the antithesis of a "Whig" conception of commerce as involving credit and speculation and, as in Defoe's paens to the new economic order, the emergence of a distinct and powerful merchant or trading class. "Ye generous Britons," cries Thomson in *Spring*, catching perfectly the notion of a commerce sanctified by its basis in georgic virtue, "venerate the plow!" for then, "as the sea / . . . from a thousand shores / Wafts all the pomp of life into your ports; / So with superior boon may your rich soil, / Exuberant, Nature's better blessings pour / O'er every land" (67-76). This is commerce as in *Windsor-Forest*, an alternative to war, a benign competition through which each nation relieves the wants of others with its own superfluities, thus at once raising its own level of prosperity and doing a material kindness to populations whom it might once have met only on the field of battle.

When Humphreys speaks in his *Considerations on the Public Defence* of the United States as becoming "a commercial, a rich, and a powerful people" (340), it is thus the notion of Augustan commerce he has in mind, that larger vision of society as "a reciprocation of wants and aids" which, as he elsewhere puts it, "rivets man to his fellows": "What isolated person can perform for himself every act which his helpless and feeble state requires? By a combination of well-directed efforts, what miracles of improvement, what prodigies in refinement, may be effected!" (93). The great paean to Augustan commerce in eighteenth-century poetry is Dyer's *The Fleece*, in which the close relationship between the georgic life of the countryside and the farthest reaches of commercial empire is the actual subject of the poem—"What bales, what wealth, what industry, what fleets! / Lo, from the simple fleece how much

proceeds!" (304)—and in which the commanding image is that of sails above the trees, trading vessels in inland waterways bearing wool and agricultural products to the coast: "E'en now behold, / Adown a thousand floods, the burthen'd barks, / With white sails glistening, through the gloomy woods / Haste to their harbors" (304). Dwight will take the image over in *Greenfield Hill* as the very emblem of Connecticut georgic; "Rough is thy surface," he says in apostrophe to his native state,

>   but each landscape bright,
> With all of beauty, all of grandeur dress'd,
> Of mountains, hills, and sweetly winding vales,
> Of forests, groves, and lawns, and meadows
>   green, . . .
>
>   Springs bubbling round the
>   year,
> Gay-wand'ring brooks, wells at the surface full,
> Yield life, and health, and joy, to every house,
> And every vivid field. Rivers, with foamy course,
> Pour o'er the ragged cliff the white cascade,
> And roll unnumber'd mills; or, like the Nile,
> Fatten the bounteous interval; or bear
> The sails of commerce through the laughing
>   groves.
>   (1.121-34)

With this expanded georgic vision, *Greenfield Hill,* which has always been understood as a poetic answer to Goldsmith's *Deserted Village,* becomes as well an answer to the entire mode of elegiac Augustanism of which Goldsmith's poem is merely a prominent example. For while *The Deserted Village* mourns a world in which organic or traditional society has been fatally undermined by an emergent capitalism, locally represented by that usurping oligarchy of titled upstarts who, as absentee landlords, are driving the villagers from the land, and while *Greenfield Hill* directly opposes to that melancholy picture the image of flourishing Connecticut villages still happily untouched by luxury and corruption—"No griping landlord here alarms the door, / To halve, for rent, the poor man's little store. . . . / Nor in one palace sinks a hundred cots; / Nor in one manor drowns a thousand lots" (2.81-88)—the deeper implication is that elegiac Augustanism represents a misdiagnosis of history, a premature and misplaced despair about the power of georgic virtue, given circumstances beyond the reach of local corruption or decline, to sustain a society in peace and prosperity. The lament for traditional society heard in *The Deserted Village* or *The Task* represents a true enough judgment about English society but a mistaken judgment about Augustan values.

The essence of Connecticut georgic thus becomes its vision not simply of a society preserved in virtue by piety and toil, the Virgilian vision returned from exile in the lowly vale of everyday life on Connecticut homesteads, but its sense of that society as a permanent or self-perpetuating state of affairs. This is the point of Dwight's unremitting insistence on the moral equipoise he calls moderation and the economic equilibrium he calls competence, that golden mean of personal wealth in which no man is very rich and none is very poor, giving rise to a society in which class antagonisms are drained off before they accumulate and every citizen is disposed to consider him- or herself as involved in a common and worthy enterprise. The self-perpetuating nature of the Connecticut social system thus derives from an arrangement where, as Dwight says, "all to comfort, none to danger, rise; / Where pride finds few, but nature all supplies. . . . / Here every class (if classes those we call, / Where one extended class embraces all, / All mingling, as the rainbow's beauty blends, / Unknown where every hue begins or ends) / Each following, each, with uninvidious strife, / Wears every feature of improving life" (2.167-76).

This is Connecticut georgic as the dream of a world outside history and ideology, a society not subject to the revolutions of historical change because spared the temptations and derangements of material inequality, and free of ideology because harboring no group or class needing to represent its own interests, by whatever subterfuge, as the values of the community as a whole. In both Dwight and Humphreys, the chosen image of this timeless world is the homestead in winter, a moment when, snow and storm having suspended communications within the larger society, the homestead turns inward upon itself as a miniature and self-contained community. This is the time, in *Greenfield Hill,* when family and neighbors gather around "the nutwood fire," and, in Humphreys's *Poem on the Happiness of America,* when the tiny community rejoices in its self-sufficiency: "Their gran'ries fill'd—the task of culture past—/ Warm at their fire, they hear the howling blast. / While patt'ring rain and snow, or driving sleet, / Rave idly loud, and at their windows beat: / Safe from its rage, regardless of its roar, / In vain the tempest rattles at the door" (187-92).

The tempest raging outside the door is the wind and sleet of a Connecticut winter, of course, but in a certain sense it is also the roar of history itself, a world caught up in change and struggle as distantly heard from within a peaceful scene that in its essentials is identical with the rustic homestead of Virgil's *Georgics* a thousand and more years before. For the ultimate meaning of georgic always has to do with this contrast between timelessness and temporal flux, with "history" as the name of a derangement that occurs only when the georgic world has lost the inner equilibrium that sustains it in piety and peace. In Humphreys's poem this then gives us the extraordinary moment in which the American Revolution itself becomes before our eyes a fireside tale told in winter by one of its veterans, an "old warrior, grown a village sage," in which the roar of history is reduced to a sound effect inside a story meant to widen the eyes of listening children: "Then ensigns wave, and signal flags unfurl'd, / Bid one great soul pervade a moving world; / Then martial music's all-inspiring breath, / With dulcet symphonies, leads on to death: . . . / While furious coursers, snorting foam and gore, / Bear wild their riders o'er the carnag'd plain, / And, falling, roll them headlong on the slain" (*A Poem on the Happiness of America,* 242-66).

This is a society sustained not only by a sense of its own heroic past but, in a grand reversal of cyclical theory, by the idea of its climactic struggle as an escape from rather than an entry into history as such. For the tragedy of the free states of the past had always been that the victory signaling their supremacy as states had marked the beginning of their decline as cultures. Greece had fought magnificently to defeat the designs of Persian tyranny only then to disintegrate in the bloody internecine broils of the Peloponnesian War; Rome had defeated Carthage only to see its free republic dissolve in civil war and end in arbitrary rule. The vision of Connecticut georgic, for which Greece and Rome remain the great parables of historical process, thus comes to rest on the contrary notion of the American Revolution as a break with change and mutability, a release from temporal cyclicity into a timeless world of georgic peace in which modernity itself, now safely reimagined as a Europe caught up in the turbulence of its own cultural disintegration, becomes little more than a receding memory. This is the theme of part 7 of *Greenfield Hill,* "The Vision."

This last section of Dwight's last poem has always been read in terms of a Puritan millenarianism resulting from his Northampton upbringing, that hope of Jonathan Edwards and the more fervent among his flock that the actual millennium, the thousand-year reign of peace and earthly glory prophesied in the New Testament, was taking place in eighteenth-century America. Nor is this finally mistaken, so far as that convergence of Puritan theology and classical republicanism first dramatized as a theme by Dwight in *The Conquest of Canaan* is given ultimate expression in the concluding section of *Greenfield Hill.* Yet "The Vision" is nonetheless an Augustan valediction, Dwight's conscious farewell to the poetic tradition of Dryden and Pope and Thomson, and his announcement in the symbolic language of that tradition that in postrevolutionary America the lost republic of Augustan poetry and classical republican theory either is or is not about to take on existence in the world. For "The Vision" is on one level the expression of a hope, but beyond that it is a declaration that the story that had begun with the vanishing of the Roman republic into the verse of Virgil and Horace eighteen centuries before is to have its ending, for better or worse, in the new United States.

The symbolic means through which Dwight makes this announcement is an invocation of the classical genius loci tradition as already given prophetic overtones in the Opposition poetry of Augustan England. For the vision of part 7 of *Greenfield Hill* is not Dwight's vision but that of the Genius of the Sound, a Neptune figure who rises, half-hidden in an amber cloud, from the waters separating the Connecticut shore from Long Island across the way, the immediate poetic descendant of that Genius of the Thames who speaks his prophetic vision in Pope's *Windsor-Forest* and, more proximately, the Genius of the Deep who rises up as a tremendous figure in Thomson's *Liberty:* "Around him clouds, in mingled tempest, hung; / . . . And ready thunder redden'd in his hand, / . . . Where-e'er he look'd, the trembling waves recoil'd" (4.398-401). The prophecy uttered by Thomson's sea deity is, as such language may suggest, bellicose and unabashedly imperial, a visionary tale of naval intrepidity forecasting Britain's role as mistress of the oceans. To this the vision of Dwight's Genius of the Sound constitutes the mildest and yet the firmest of rebukes, a picture of Connecticut as a flourishing georgic society with no ambitions beyond piety and peace, and then a hopeful postulation of the new American republic as a greater Connecticut:

> See the wide realm in equal shares possess'd!
> How few the rich, or poor! how many bless'd!
> O happy state! the state, by HEAVEN design'd
> To rein, protect, employ, and bless mankind;
> Where Competence, in full enjoyment, flows;
> Where man least vice, and highest virtue, knows;
> Where the mind thrives; strong nerves th' inven-
>   tion string;
> And daring Enterprise uplifts his wing;
> Where Splendor spreads, in vain, his peacock-
>   hues;
> Where vagrant Sloth, the general hiss pursues;
> Where Business reigns, the universal queen;
> Where none are slaves, or lords; but all are men:
> No nuisant drones purloin the earner's food;
> But each man's labor swells the common good.
>   (7.125-38)

Through the vision of the Genius of the Sound is also proclaimed a last triumphant convergence of covenant theology and classical republicanism, the older language of Puritan New England and the newer idiom through which, in its contemporary guise as Opposition or Country ideology, the American colonies had been brought to a united stand against British tyranny and corruption. For the idea of the new American republic as a genuinely georgic society—a greater Connecticut in which citizens dwell perpetually "in the mean, 'twixt poverty and pride" (7.546), spreading out from their eastern settlements over a trackless continent, doing away with chattel slavery and treating the Indian tribes they encounter as brothers rather than as enemies or victims—simply is the millennium under a different name, a release from history as struggle and turmoil and pain so sudden and breathtaking that, should it really occur, one would be bound to see in it the hand of God himself. Thus it is that the Genius, a minor classical deity speaking from within a neoclassical poetic tradition, falls spontaneously nonetheless into the language of Christian revelation: "Thus, thro' all climes, shall Freedom's bliss extend, / The world renew, and death, and bondage, end; / All nations quicken with th' ecstatic power, / And one redemption reach to every shore" (7.311-14).

Yet for all its blending of classical and Christian thought, *Greenfield Hill* remains an Augustan poem, and one, moreover, half conscious of its probable status as the last Augustan poem that will be written in either England or America. This is what Dwight meant to announce when, in a deliberate imitation of Pope's own youthful imitations of earlier English poets, he chose to undertake a poem in the various eighteenth-century modes, orchestrating within a single poetic composition the resonant voices of high Augustanism as heard in Dryden and Pope, the impassioned Opposition utterance of Thomson and Akenside, the mid-century movement toward melancholy nostalgia found in the Wartons or Gray or Beattie, and, finally, the elegiac Augustanism of Goldsmith's *Deserted Village* and Cowper's *Task,* from which *Greenfield Hill* as a poem and Connecticut georgic as a mode represent, in the quietest way and with the utmost respect, a grand dissent. The ultimate meaning of Connecticut georgic thus has to do both

with the American republic as in some sense a creation of Augustan poetry and with that republic, once created, as the natural end of the Augustan tradition.

The ultimate meaning of *Greenfield Hill,* by the same token, has to do with the way its concluding vision or prophecy leaves the poem suspended between opposing alternatives, either of which would imply the end of Augustanism both as a poetic mode and a cultural tradition. The first alternative gives us the context in which the prophecy offers itself as a vision meant to be absorbed into history itself, looking without anxiety toward a moment when, in comparison with the shining actuality of the new American republic, it would become merely pallid or spiritless as poetry. This is the possibility at which Humphreys is glancing in direct terms when, speaking of America's prosperity under equality of law, he observes that "with us, the successful issue has been the best panegyric on such a system" (93). In specific or local terms, the sentiment prefigures that grander sequel always posited by Connecticut georgic, a moment when poetry would cease and America itself would become the last, best poem of the Connecticut Wits: "How bless'd the sight of such a numerous train / . . . tasting every good / Of competence, of independence, peace, / And liberty unmingled; every house / On its own ground, and every happy swain / Beholding no superior, but the laws" (*Greenfield Hill,* 1.42-47).

At the same time there broods over the ending of *Greenfield Hill* the dark unspoken reality, insisted on throughout the earlier sections of the poem, of an Augustinian moral nature that does not give way easily to schemes or visions of republican virtue, a gloomy center of human existence that in its secret urgings reminds us constantly that we inhabit, even in the most propitious circumstances, a world outside the Garden. The circumstances that have made possible the hopeful prophecy of the Genius of the Sound are those that have improbably rescued postrevolutionary America from anarchy or misrule—Shays's Rebellion, the paper-money crisis in Rhode Island and elsewhere, populist revolt in the middle colonies and the South—and all but miraculously brought about a reassertion of moral order and national purpose: the Philadelphia Convention, the new Constitution, the assumption of the presidency by Washington. Yet during the period before Philadelphia another possible America had come terrifyingly into view as well: "So rag'd the storm of anarchy—the crowd / By demagogues excited, mad and loud, / their Pandemonium held—no more was seen / The calm debate—till Washington serene / From every State conven'd the chosen sires" (Humphreys, *On the Death of Washington,* 569-73).

This is the turbulence of history as such, the Augustinian reality of human pride and ambition and weakness against which Augustan poetry from the time of Virgil and Horace had always asserted its countervision of a society in which men live lives of simple virtue and honorable companionship. And there is a sense in the last poetry of Dwight and Humphreys that the episode of the Constitution and Washington's presidency may only have been a hopeful interlude after all, that with the cataclysmic event of Washington's death—"Fall'n is the mighty—Washington is dead—/ Our day to darkness turn'd—our glory fled" (*On the Death of Washington,* 17-18)—the scales of history have returned to trembling equipoise and the whole story is about to begin anew. The other possibility that would mean the end or extinction of the Augustan tradition lies here: should the new American republic now fall into the hands of those Humphreys calls "the guileful regents of the people-king," should a mindless and indiscriminate populism ever become a ruling ideology so powerful as to sweep all else away, the complex moral vision of Connecticut georgic would in an instant be rendered incomprehensible, and poems like *Greenfield Hill* left to moulder away on library shelves in some world of the future whose populace had other, unguessable tastes.

INTELLECTUAL CONTEXT

A. Owen Aldridge

SOURCE: "The Concept of Ancients and Moderns in American Poetry of the Federal Period," in *Early American Literature: A Comparatist Approach,* Princeton University Press, 1982, pp. 158-85.

[*The editor of* Comparative Literature Studies, *Aldridge is an American educator and author. Among his works on the eighteenth century are* Benjamin Franklin and His French Contemporaries *(1957) and* Man of Reason: Life of Thomas Paine *(1959). Here, he analyses "the literary traditions affirmed by [the Federal period] poets" and the ideological effects of their embracing of Augustan Age values.*]

Ordinarily the expression Augustan Age when applied to the modern world comprises English literature during the first half of the eighteenth century, but an essayist under the name of the Meddler in a Connecticut newspaper of 1791 remarked that "the Augustan age bears greater resemblance to the present, than to any intermediate period." In reference to what is now called the Federal period of American literature, the Meddler observed, "Under a similarity of circumstances, America has at length become the seat of science, and the great mirror of freedom and politics. Her Attica has produced a Homer, who leads the way; a Virgil, who was the pupil of that great master, and a Horace, who resides at the seat of Augustus." The American Homer here referred to is Timothy Dwight, author of a Biblical epic *The Conquest of Canaan* (1785); the American Virgil is Joel Barlow, author of a patriotic epic, *The Vision of Columbus* (1787); and the American Horace is Philip Freneau, author of miscellaneous lyrics and satires. These three are generally considered to be the outstanding poets of the Federal period, a roster completed with the addition of two other New England names, David Humphreys and Robert Treat Paine.

A similar description of American letters in terms of the ancients appeared in a Massachusetts poem of 1789 entitled *Anticipation of the Literary Fame of America.* The anonymous author predicted the rising in the near future of "Columbian *Livies,*" "countless *Cicero's,*" "another Plato," "another Stagyrite," "some new Euripides," "some future *Virgil,*" and "some modern Ovid." As a consequence of this emergence of counterparts of Greek and Latin authors, the anonymous poet forecast that

> The brilliant treasure of the Attick mine,
> Shall glow refulgent in our western clime.

Although Dwight, Barlow, and Freneau were the outstanding American poets of their time, they are read today less for esthetic pleasure than for the ideological and social riches they contain. Their relative lack of emotional and esthetic appeal has been attributed in large measure to the tradition of classical rhetoric to which they belong. According to one modern critic, they tended in practice to obscure the dichotomy in the adage "Poeta nascitur, orator fit," and classical forms and figures became their stock in trade. One is hard put to decide today, therefore, "whether the works of such men as Robert Treat Paine are more properly described as declamatory poems or poetic orations" [Gordon E. Bigelow, *Rhetoric and American Poetry of the Early National Period,* 1960]. Other critics have charged that most of the American poets of the Federal period slavishly imitated the neoclassical rhetoric of Pope and the Augustan English poets. Sometimes the classical and the neoclassical traditions are indistinguishable in their work, as are the images and symbols associated with one or the other style. Frequently a reference to a neoclassical author could be substituted for a classical one without changing the fundamental meaning. An example is the following line from a lyric by Freneau.

> To such wild scenes as Plato lov'd.

In a later version of the poem, Freneau simply inserted Shenstone for Plato.

It is not my purpose, however, to discuss the quality of Federal poetry or to affirm or deny the thesis that either classical or neoclassical rhetoric is responsible for its alleged deficiencies. I intend rather to investigate the literary traditions affirmed by these poets and to attempt to ascertain whether their outward subservience to classical models was accompanied by the kind of ideological commitment to the ancient world which is associated with the Augustan Age of English literature at the beginning of the eighteenth century. A definite pattern may be discerned among these poets, consisting of superficial discipleship combined with fundamental rejection. They imitated the style of the ancients and conformed to Aristotelian notions of genre, but repudiated many of the intellectual traditions associated with antiquity. This is the first principle that I hope to establish. The second is that the verse and critical writings of these poets contain close parallels with concepts in the European quarrel between the ancients and moderns.

The formal stage of this famous polemic belongs to the seventeenth and eighteenth centuries and concerns French literature primarily, but the attempt to decide the relative merits of the intellectual achievements of the ancient world and those of later ages goes back at least as far as the Renaissance. The question is one part of the idea of progress, and treatments of it exist in all Western European literatures. A parallel to one of the esthetic aspects of the question—consideration of the degree to which literary works should conform to critical standards of the past—has even been shown to exist in the thought of ancient China.

American writers in the Federal period, in common with almost all authors in Western culture after the Renaissance, drew upon both a generally accepted literary tradition from the past and a less orthodox but nonetheless familiar body of writings from their own century. Insofar as America is concerned, these connections may be represented graphically by horizontal and vertical lines, the horizontal one going back to the Greek and Latin classics, and the vertical extending across the Atlantic to the European continent. Nobody doubts the influence in eighteenth-century America of the social theories of Montesquieu, the sentimental psychology of Richardson, or the poetic structure of Pope. It seems logical to assume that many of the issues in the quarrel of the ancients and moderns should also be debated in the New World even though the French treatises of La Motte, Fontenelle, and Perrault may not have been available in American libraries. It is true that none of the poets I mention refers to the ancients-modern quarrel as such or cites its main protagonists, but the relevant passages in the works of such English combatants as Sir William Temple, Jonathan Swift, Joseph Addison, and Oliver Goldsmith were probably as well known to the American literati of the eighteenth century as they are today.

A striking illustration may be found in the critical theories of the so-called American Homer, Timothy Dwight, and the American Virgil, Joel Barlow. Both wrote prose essays attempting to dislodge Homer from his pedestal and using arguments strongly resembling those of the moderns in the French phase of the quarrel of the ancients and moderns. Dwight in a *Dissertation on the History, Eloquence, and Poetry of the Bible* (1772), published thirteen years before his *The Conquest of Canaan,* argued that the beauties of the Bible are at least equal to those of the greatest classical writers and in many passages greatly superior to them. After observing that Homer has been praised for giving life to every object which he attempts to describe, Dwight maintains that he is excelled by the Old and New Testaments. There, according to Dwight,

> objects are not barely endued with life; they breathe, they think, they speak, love, hate, fear, adore, & exercise all the most extraordinary emotions of rational beings. *Homer* or *Virgil* can make the mountains tremble, or the sea shake, at the appearance of a God; in the *Bible* the mountains melt like wax, or flee away; the Deep utters his voice, and lifts up his hands on high, at the presence of the LORD of the whole earth.

Admitting that the Scriptures would be found wanting were they to be judged by the rules associated with classical criticism, Dwight had no hesitation in disparaging these rules. Confronting an imaginary critic, Dwight replied: "When you can convince me that *Homer* and *Virgil* . . . were sent into the world to give Laws to all other authors; when you can convince me that every beauty of fine writing is to be found, in its highest perfection, in their works, I will allow the beauties of the divine writers to be faults. 'Till that can be demonstrated, I must con-

tinue to admire the most shining instances of Genius, unparallel'd in force, or sublimity". Sentiments such as this explain why Dwight selected as the subject matter of his own epic, not a secular theme such as Camoëns and Voltaire had exploited, but one based on the Old Testament account of the gory victory of Joshua over the Canaanites. In the structure of his poem, Dwight prided himself on giving unity to the entire action, but in doing so he grossly garbled the facts of his historical source. He tended as a consequence "to dilute, to render garrulous, and to cheapen, the noble reticence, the graphic simplicity, of the antique chronicle" [Moses Coit Tyler, *Three Men of Letters,* 1895]—the model that he had taken pains to exalt above the Greek and Roman epics precisely because of its noble sublimity of style. But we are not concerned with esthetic achievement, but with ideas, the reasons for Dwight's choosing biblical subject matter over pagan and historical themes. He was following not only the example of Milton, but also the arguments of a French champion of the moderns, Desmarets de Saint-Sorlin, in a prose *Discourse to Prove that Only Christian Subjects are Appropriate to Heroic Poetry* (1673). [*Discours pour prouver que les sujets chrétiens sont seuls propres à la poésie héroïque*].

Joel Barlow also adopted the form of the classical epic while rejecting the authority of Homer and Virgil, but his objections to the ancient poets were based not on subject matter, but on political ideology. Barlow published his *Vision of Columbus* in 1787 and twenty years later brought out a revised and greatly expanded version under the more Virgilian title of *The Columbiad.* In the preface to the latter, Barlow drew a distinction between the poetical object of an epic and its moral object, the first representing the fictitious design of the action; the latter, the real design or ideological purpose. Since the poetical object of the *Iliad,* which is to portray the anger of Achilles, excites a high degree of interest, it is extremely important, according to Barlow, that the real design should be beneficial to society. In reality, however, the real design has just the reverse effect. "Its obvious tendency was to inflame the minds of young readers with an enthusiastic ardor for military fame; to inculcate the pernicious doctrine of the divine right of kings; to teach both prince and people that military plunder was the most honorable mode of acquiring property; and that conquest, violence and war were the best employment of nations, the most glorious prerogative of bodily strength and of cultivated mind". Barlow found the moral tendency of the *Aeneid* to be "nearly as pernicious." Virgil's real design, in Barlow's opinion, "was to increase the veneration of the people for a master, whoever he might be, and to encourage like Homer the great system of military depredation". The only ancient epic poet whom Barlow would accept as a republican was Lucan. The ancients in general, and the Greeks in particular, were widely appealed to throughout the eighteenth century in both Europe and America as noble examples of republican virtues. The Whig historian Catherine Macaulay, for example, attributed her liberal political philosophy to the spirit of liberty in classical literature. It is somewhat unusual to see an American poet condemning both Homer and Virgil for inculcating political sentiments which allegedly enforce subjection and constraint. In judging the ancients by modern moral and sociological standards, Barlow was following the practice of the *Discourse on Homer* [*Discours sur Homère* (1714)] of abbé La Motte, who, as a leading exponent of the moderns, insisted that criticism had the right to condemn the barbarous conditions portrayed in the *Iliad*.

One of the subsidiary questions discussed in the quarrel of ancients and moderns was that of the comparative beauty of the classical and modern languages and their relative fitness for poetry. On this question, Barlow affirmed that when writing *The Vision of Columbus* he had labored under "the error of supposing that the ancients had a poetical advantage over us in respect to the dignity of the names of the weapons used in war," but that he became convinced that the advantage is actually on the side of the moderns. "There are better sounding names and more variety in the instruments, works, strategems and other artifices employed in our war system than in theirs. In short, the modern military dictionary is more copious than the ancient, and the words at least as poetical" [p. xv]. The circumstances of battle in ancient times, Barlow admitted, gave the ancients an advantage in the description of single combats, but in "a general engagement, the shock of modern armies is, beyond comparison, more magnificent, more sonorous and more discoloring to the face of nature, than the ancient could have been; it is consequently susceptible of more pomp and variety of description".

In keeping with his dichotomy of the narrative design and the real design of an epic, Barlow indicated that the superficial object of *The Columbiad* was to survey the labors and achievements of Columbus and to portray him as "the author of the greatest benefits to the human race". The real object of the poem, however, was "to inculcate the love of rational liberty," to "discountenance the deleterious passion for violence and war," to show that all good morals as well as all good government must be founded on republican principles, and to persuade that "the theoretical question of the future advancement of human society" remains unsettled only because of the lack of experience of organized liberty in the government of nations. In other words, *The Columbiad* was designed to teach the doctrine of progress, an essential notion of the moderns. In his notes to the poem, Barlow particularly rejected the notion of a Golden Age "or the idea that men were more perfect, more moral and more happy in some early stage of their intercourse," as well as the related doctrine that the world has been perpetually degenerating or growing worse [no. 50]. Both doctrines were widely used by the ancients in their quarrel with the moderns. In another note connected with the controversy, Barlow admits that the ancients may perhaps claim to be unrivalled in some of the arts which depend upon the imagination, those such as architecture, statuary, painting, eloquence, and poetry, but he points out that these are not the arts which "tend the most to the general improvement of society" [no. 47]. In particular reference to Homer, Barlow repeated the accusation of his preface that the *Iliad* was filled with the pernicious doctrine of the divine right of kings [no. 42].

Even stronger evidence of Barlow's adherence to the moderns may be found in his earlier *Vision of Columbus* (1787), but this evidence requires interpretation. Barlow

followed as one of the models for this poem a modern rather than a classical epic—a sixteenth-century work in Spanish, *La Araucana* by Alonso de Ercilla—and he did so because of reading a description of it in an essay by Voltaire, the author of another modern epic, *La Henriade*. In order to prepare advance publicity for a London edition of *La Henriade,* Voltaire published in English an essay, *Epick Poetry of the European Nations from Homer down to Milton* (1727), a pioneer treatment of the study of literary genres. Barlow explained in the notes to his *Vision* that it was entirely due to Voltaire's essay (probably in a later French version) that his mind had been opened to "a new field of Poetry, rich with uncommon elements." In treating the preliminary section of *La Araucana,* a description of the geography, manners, and customs of Chile, Voltaire had argued that the strangeness of the American continent to European readers made the introduction of this type of material necessary, although otherwise it would have been quite out of place. This justification inspired Barlow to include geographical and sociological passages in his own epic, as well as a treatment of South America and its native population. In his notes Barlow also complained bitterly about not being able to procure a copy of either *La Araucana* or the parallel Portuguese epic, *Os Lusiadas* by Luis de Camoëns, considering the lack of materials one of the "disadvantages that an Author, in a new country, and in moderate circumstances, must have to encounter."

Besides its indebtedness to Voltaire and Ercilla, *The Vision of Columbus* is important internationally because of a dedication to Louis XVI of France, who returned the compliment by subscribing for twenty-five copies.

In a sense, Voltaire, in acquainting Barlow with Ercilla and Camoëns, was posthumously repaying a debt to Anglo-Saxon letters. The English poet William Collins told Joseph Warton that the former's uncle, Col. Martin Bladen, "had given to Voltaire, all that account of Camoëns inserted in his essay on the Epic Poets of all Nations, and that Voltaire seemed before entirely ignorant of the name and character of Camoëns" [*Works of Alexander Pope,* ed. W. L. Bowles, 1806]. Nothing is known about Voltaire's first acquaintance with Ercilla, but it may equally have been through the agency of Colonel Bladen, who had served as an officer in Spain.

On the surface there seems to be a close relationship, ideological if not historical, between the doctrine of progress and the poetic themes of *translatio studii* and *translatio empirii,* which flourished in classical times and in the Middle Ages and have been widely recognized by scholars of early American literature. The most famous English version is, of course, Bishop George Berkeley's "Verses on the Prospect of Planting Arts and Learning in America," written in 1726, but not published until 1752. Joining *translatio studii* with the imagery of the stage and the theological doctrine of the millennium, he predicted that the fifth act of the human drama would take place in the West and affirmed that "Time's noblest offspring is the last." Later in the century the theme of *translatio studii* was joined to that of the rising glory of America, but it flourished in the colonies long before either the Revolution or the publication of Berkeley's verses. A single example will suffice, one taken from a Pennsylvania almanac of 1729 and reprinted in the *Gentleman's Magazine*.

> Rome shall lament her ancient Fame declin'd
> And Philadelphia be the Athens of mankind.

. . . Superficially it would appear that the *translatio* theme represents evidence of the dedication of early American literature to its classical heritage, but analysis reveals that classical antecedents are consistently portrayed as inferior to contemporary manifestations. The *translatio* theme is one aspect of the idea of progress and as such weighs on the side of the moderns rather than the ancients. In other words, whatever salutary concept is considered as originating in Greece and Rome, it is always improved or brought to perfection in the West. Indeed, if the theme were carried to the extreme, future development could be envisaged as even transcending the European settlements of America. The same author who compared Dwight, Barlow and Freneau to their classical counterparts reminded his readers that the descendants of the barbarians who had overturned the Roman Empire had become the modern cherishers of the arts and sciences. The Americans, he observed, are the posterity of "those whom the Romans once held in as little esteem, as that in which we at present hold the [Indian] nations of the West." While considering the likelihood extremely remote, he nevertheless expressed the possibility that America, like the Roman Empire, might in the future "be again repeopled and governed by her native inhabitants" [Meddler no. II]. The only aspect of the *translatio* theme which may be effectively counted as a tribute to the ancients is that which treats political liberty as their contribution to civilization. There existed another widespread notion throughout the Enlightenment that liberty, as manifested in European thought, had not emerged from the Greeks at all, but had developed instead from the nations of northern Europe. Any motif, such as *translatio,* that would restore liberty to the ancients could in this sense legitimately be considered as supporting the prestige of the Greeks and Romans. A pseudonymous poem in the *Pennsylvania Gazette,* 30 May 1778, neatly resolved the question by assuming an autochthonous origin.

> Even Liberty herself from Heaven shall come,
> And fair America shall rival Rome.

One of the most extreme statements against the Old World came from the pen of the lexicographer Noah Webster, who instead of treating *translatio studii* in the conventional sense, suggested in the preface to his *Spelling Book* (1783) that it would be better to reject everything from the past and make a completely new beginning. In his words, "Europe is grown old in folly, corruption and tyranny—in that country laws are perverted, manners are licentious, literature is declining and human nature debased. For America in her infancy to adopt the present maxims of the Old World, would be to stamp the wrinkles of decrepit age upon the bloom of youth and to plant the seeds of decay in a vigorous constitution." In a sense, this repudiation of the past is a logical extension of Paine's metaphor in *Common Sense* that "youth is the seed time of good habits, as well as in nations as in individuals" and his amazing state-

ment "we have it in our power to begin the world over again."

In addition to abstract notions such as liberty and freedom, the idea of progress incorporated scientific discoveries and the material advances of civilization such as mechanical inventions. The printing press symbolized the combination of enlightenment and technology. As such, it represented one of the milestones in human advancement. The theme was introduced into America thirty years before the Federal period, specifically by James Sterling in a poem dedicated to Samuel Richardson, author of *Pamela,* entitled "On the Invention of Letters and the Art of Printing" (1757). The poem particularly describes the triumph in philosophical thought of the moderns over the ancients as well as the progress in science and technology, symbolized by the printing press. The same theme was developed in 1795 by Robert Treat Paine in a poem with an almost identical title, *The Invention of Letters.* The work, like Sterling's, does not concern polite or belles lettres, but the process of printing, without which, according to Paine, scarcely any scientific discoveries or political reforms would have been possible. That Paine should have written on such a theme is remarkable since he was probably the most dedicated to classical traditions of all American poets of the time. Paine was so gifted that when he was assigned a Greek oration at Harvard, instead of following the general practice of reciting a passage from Demosthenes, Isocrates, or Plutarch, he "chose to write his own in Greek, without first preparing in English" [*Works in Verse and Prose of the Late Robert Treat Paine,* 1812]. Despite his dedication to classical civilization, he clearly espoused in *The Invention of Letters* the side of the moderns in the polemic between the two factions.

> No more presume with bigot zeal to raise,
> O'er modern worth, the palm of ancient days.
> No more let Athens to the world proclaim,
> Her classick phalanx holds the field of fame.

In subsequent lines, Paine elevated Gutenberg to a position of universal eminence.

> The barbarous Rhine now blends its classick
>   name,
> With Rome's, Phoenicia's, and Achaia's fame.

The major writers in the French Enlightenment tended to recognize the preeminence of the ancients in the realm of eloquence, but otherwise considered the moderns superior. Following this tradition, David Humphreys in the "Advertisement" to a *Poem on the Death of General Washington* (1800), reflects the tendency to grant to the ancients superiority in the area of rhetoric, even though he leaves the question open without settling it unequivocally. "It is not intended to be decided here," he observes, "that the Greek and Latin poets possess no advantage over the moderns in the copiousness or melody of their languages; or that poesy in those languages does not admit of more boldness in the figures, pomp in the diction, music in the cadences, variety in the numbers, or greater facility for imitative beauty in making the sound an echo to the sense, than in most of the languages." Instead of asserting the supremacy of the moderns in such areas as science or the plastic arts, however, he turns to the examples of illustrious men and finds more inspiring ones in America, the most sublime of whom is, of course, George Washington.

In a shorter poem "On the Love of Country," Humphreys even impugns the patriotism which had throughout the century been accorded to the Romans as one of their outstanding virtues.

> Perish the Roman pride a world that braves,
> To make for one free state all nations slaves;
> Their boasted patriotism at once exprest,
> Love for themselves and hate for all the rest.

Exactly the same disparaging description of classical patriotism appears in Barlow's *Columbiad*.

> Where Grecian states in even balance hung
> And warm'd with jealous fires the patriot's
>   tongue,
> The exclusive ardor cherisht in the breast
> Love to one land and hatred to the rest.
> And where the flames of civil discord rage,
> And Roman arms with Roman arms engage,
> The mime of virtues rises still the same
> To build a Caesar's as a Pompey's name.
>   [Book X, l. 321-28]

So far as I know, this argument appeared first in Thomas Paine's *American Crisis* no. V [1778]. "The Grecians and Romans were strongly possessed of the *spirit* of liberty," Paine remarked, "but *not the principle,* for at the time that they were determined not to be slaves themselves, they employed their power to enslave the rest of mankind."

Madison in *The Federalist* [no. 14] similarly considered it to the glory of the American people that "whilst they have paid a decent regard to the opinions of former times and other nations, they have not suffered a blind veneration for antiquity, for custom, or for names, to overrule the suggestions of their own good sense." Hamilton in the ninth *Federalist* reacted with "horror and disgust" to "the history of the petty republics of Greece and Italy" because of the "distractions with which they were continually agitated" and "the rapid succession of revolutions, by which they were kept perpetually vibrating."

The pattern of superficial obeisance to the classic tradition combined with a rejection of it ideologically is highlighted in an anonymous biblical poem in the *New Haven Gazette* (21 September 1786) entitled "The Trial of Faith." The poem itself does not concern us, but its epigraph from Virgil reveals the paradoxical ambivalence toward the classics which we have been discussing.

> Sicelides Musae, paulo majora canamus!

The paraphrase of this line supplied by the author announces that "American Muses aim at higher subjects than those commonly sung in the Eastern continent."

A similar ambivalence is shown by Philip Freneau in regard to the value of studying the classical languages. He was trained at Princeton in both Latin and Greek, filled his poems with classical allusions, wrote an imitation of Horace, and embellished his works with quotations from Virgil, second in number only to those from Shakespeare. At the commencement exercises, 25 September 1771, when Freneau himself was graduated, there was featured

on the program "An English forensic dispute on this question, 'Does ancient poetry excel the modern?' " Freneau had been chosen as affirmative "respondent," but was absent from the ceremonies. His remarks were read by another student and answered by a second, who was in turn refuted by a third.

Despite this academic flourish, Freneau later unequivocally disparaged the role of ancient languages in the educational system. In a poem entitled "Expedition of Timothy Taurus, Astrologer" (1775?), he affirms:

> This age may decay, and another may rise,
> Before it is fully revealed to our eyes,
> That Latin and Hebrew, Chaldaic, and Greek,
> To the shades of oblivion must certainly sneak;
> Too much of our time is employed on such trash
> When we ought to be taught to accumulate cash.

Although these lines are intended to be humorous, they are not meant ironically. Freneau expresses an even stronger antagonism in another of his poems, "Epistle to a Student of Dead Languages."

In France, the relative merits of the classical and modern languages had been treated as part of the battle of ancients and moderns. As early as 1683, for example, François Charpentier published his treatise *On the Excellence of the French Language,* making among other points the practical one that French rather than Latin should be used for inscriptions on public monuments. An essayist in the *New Haven Gazette* (DECIUS, 2 and 16 March 1791) applied the controversy to the subjects of study at Yale University. In his opinion, the traditional curriculum was outmoded in Europe, but still entrenched in America and, therefore, all the more absurd in a new environment. His main point was not that the classical languages were objectionable in themselves, but that the candidate was required to spend two years "in getting a useless smattering of latin and greek" at the end of which he could not even translate a single page of a single book. This author considered Latin and French "desirable, and even necessary," but he felt that knowledge of our own language and literature was indispensable. The worst abuse of the system was the teaching of New Testament Greek by rote. In his words, "The time for education is short. From twelve years of age to twenty-one, is a period of nine years, and two of these should be employed, by almost every one, in obtaining professional knowledge.—Seven remain. If part of these must be spent in acquiring words, the English and French, are decidedly, the most learned ever spoken by man; nor can I make exception, even of the *Hebrew* or *Mohegan.*"

In treating essays in the *New Haven Gazette,* we have digressed from the poets of the time, but the newspaper background is relevant as exposing the climate of opinion in which these poets developed. The sentiments expressed by the *Gazette* essayist are mild, moreover, compared with those previously set forth in satirical verse by John Trumbull in *The Progress of Dulness* (1772). The latter affirms that half of classical learning merely displays the follies of former days and denies that knowledge must be conveyed to the brain in "ancient strains." At the same time he calls for criticism to accord to "ancient arts" their "real due" and "explain their faults, and beauties too." Another essay in the *New Haven Gazette,* one in the same issue with the criticism of the Yale curriculum, contrasts ancient learning with the doctrine of progress in the precise terms in which the debate had been carried on in Europe [*Meddler* no. VIII, 16 March 1791]. According to the essayist, "The sophistical reasoning of the ancient schools, served only to lead the minds of men into continued mazes of error and absurdity. . . . The improvements made in the arts and sciences, in the course of the last century, have been more rapid than they ever were at any former period; and if we were to reason from analogy, we should conclude that future improvements will be in an inverse ratio, with the time at which they are distant. . . . The moderns have a manifest superiority over the ancients, in most of the arts and sciences."

The particular American cachet which is placed upon this essay is a reference to developments in political theory, a consciousness of which grew out of the pamphleteering in the American Revolution. The essayist proceeds imperceptibly from the Baconian theme of the deficiencies of Aristotelian philosophy to the millennial one of international harmony which concludes many of the poems of the Federal period, including Dwight's "America: or, a Poem on the Settlement of the British Colonies" (1780) and Barlow's *The Columbiad.* The essayist concludes,

> We are so far enlightened in the present age, as to discard most of the fictions of the ancient schools and render the unknown abstrata [*sic*] by which Aristotle and his followers solved the knotty points of philosophy, into a mere object of ridicule. Should our successors continue to make improvements upon our knowledge, as we have upon that of our *predecessors,* they will become so thoroughly acquainted with the true nature and principles of government, as to form institutions of society, which will promote the internal prosperity of nations, and by shewing the blessings of peace, bring on a universal harmony among the different nations of the earth.

The last sentence could almost serve as a paraphrase of the concluding book of *The Columbiad,* which portrays the future progress of society in all areas including government and reveals, in the words of the "Argument," a "general Congress from all nations assembled to establish the political harmony of mankind." Thomas Paine in *Rights of Man* even used the political argument to support one of the earliest positions of the moderns in the European phase of the ancients-moderns debate, Bacon's paradox *Antiquitas saeculi juventus mundi,* "ancient times are the youth of the world." According to Paine, the only value in studying governments in ancient times is "to make a proper use of the errors or the improvements which the history of it presents. Those who lived a hundred or a thousand years ago, were then moderns as we are now." Paine in an earlier essay also touches on the millennial theme and joins it with disparagement of the ancients for their vanity and ignorance. "Improvement and the world will expire together," he remarks. "And till that period arrives, we may plunder the mine, but can never exhaust it! That *'We have found out everything,'* has been the motto of every age. Let our ideas travel a little into antiquity, and we shall find larger portions of it than now; and so unwill-

ing were our ancestors to descend from this mountain of perfection, that when any new discovery exceeded the common standard, the discoverer was believed to be in alliance with the devil" [*Writings,* 2: 1111].

One cannot solely on the evidence of the foregoing passages maintain that the European quarrel of the ancients and the moderns extended itself in a kind of *translatio studii* to the Western world, but there can be no doubt, on the other hand, that many of the same principles of that debate were seriously discussed in the Anglophone areas of America throughout the second half of the eighteenth century. Certainly the debate reached university circles in America, for John Witherspoon of Princeton in an essay "Of Eloquence" summarized the European background of the "controversy . . . upon the preference being due to ancient or modern writers." Although taking an eclectic position by recognizing good in both camps, Witherspoon seemed to join Dwight and Barlow in feeling that Homer had been overpraised. "Now the beauties of Homer we are easily capable of perceiving," he wrote, "though perhaps not his faults. The beauty of a description, the force of a similitude, we can plainly see; but whether he always adhered to truth and nature, we cannot tell, because we have no other way of knowing the manners and customs of his times but from what he has written."

Even though most of the evidence consists of parallel themes, there certainly exists a strong possibility that most of the Americans who expressed themselves in regard to the amount of subservience due to the ancients were fully aware of the ramifications of the ideas they expressed. It is hard to believe, for example, that most of them had not read Swift's *Tale of the Tub* and *Battle of the Books* in which the battle lines were clearly drawn. The poets in question were in a sense products of two cultures—the classical and the modern—and they sought to identify themselves with both.

The painter John Trumbull, who flourished during the period with which we are concerned, recalls in his *Autobiography* a discussion in his youth with his father over his desire to embrace the pictorial arts as his life's work. His father listened gravely to the aspiring painter dwelling rhapsodically upon "the honours paid to artists in the glorious days of Greece and Athens." The senior Trumbull then rejoined, "You appear to forget, sir, that *Connecticut is not Athens*". This is a cryptic remark, and, like the young Trumbull, we cannot be sure whether preference was meant to be accorded to ancient Greece or to eighteenth-century America. My discussion of the five major poets of the Federal period in American literature reveals that they shared a similar ambivalence.

By suggesting that American poets were aware of the European quarrel between ancients and moderns and that they consciously espoused the modern side, I am by no means attempting to diminish the stature of the Greek and Latin traditions in early American letters or to portray these poets as unequivocally opposed to classical learning. It could even be maintained that to engage in the debate at all on either side one had to possess both an appreciation and a knowledge of classical culture. Certainly every one of the European critics who espoused the moderns was at the same time skilled in at least the Latin language and possessed more than a rudimentary knowledge of Greek and Latin masterpieces. Boileau, for example, who cherished the ancients with an informed devotion, fought valiantly in their behalf for most of his career until eventually forced to admit with great reluctance that "the Age of Louis XIV is not only comparable but superior to the most famous ages of antiquity, even the Age of Augustus." Voltaire likewise derived more pleasure from being known as the French Sophocles than from any other of his literary distinctions; yet he insisted on the preeminence of the French stage over that of the ancients with the same vigor with which he defended Newton in the realm of science. In England, the best informed classical scholar in the controversy was Richard Bentley, the Royal librarian. It was precisely his classical learning which proved to be most damaging to the position of the British defenders of the ancients.

The classical training of the five American poets with whom I am concerned is impressive to say the least. Dwight, Barlow, and Humphreys were graduates of Yale; Freneau of Princeton, and Paine of Harvard. Even though, according to one of the adverse critics whom I cite, the teaching methods may have depended too greatly on rote learning, graduates of these institutions in the late eighteenth century must inevitably have attained both linguistic and literary competence in both Latin and Greek. Graduates in Barlow's class at Yale, for example, were at the end of their course of studies examined on Cicero and on the Greek Testament. These poets were also living in times of intense nationalism and patriotic fervor, however, times in which in any expression of the superiority of former societies would have seemed a betrayal of the ideals of the Revolution. It was acceptable for poets to praise their classical heritage, but they were careful to do so in a manner which made this heritage contributory to American glory and subservient to it. David Humphreys in a poem entitled "On the Happiness of America" written in 1780 during the midst of the Revolutionary War went so far as to portray every society previous to that of America as inferior.

> All former empires rose, the work of guilt,
> On conquest, blood or usurpation built:
> But we, taught wisdom by their woes and
>   crimes,
> Fraught with their lore, and born to better times;
> Our constitutions form'd on freedom's base,
> Which all the blessings of all lands embrace;
> Embrace humanity's extended cause,
> A world our empire, for a world our laws.

The strongest evidence of the pervasiveness of classical influences is that found in the poem "Anticipation of the Literary Fame of America," which recasts the appearance of an American masterpiece in many of the classical genres and which describes them in terms of Greek or Latin prototypes.

> Columbian *Livies* throng the historick field,
> A brighter band than ever Greece could yield.
> The morn of eloquence again shall dawn,
> And courtless *Cicero's* our courts adorn.
> Another Plato utter truths divine,

> Another Stagyrite our taste refine.
> Some new Euripides, with tragick art,
> Shall calm the passions, and shall touch the
>   heart,
> Describe with energy *Orestes'* rage,
> And prompt to virtue from the moral stage.
> Some future *Virgil* shall our wars rehearse
> In all the dignity of epic verse.
> Some modern *Ovid* paint his fair one's charms,
> Her eyes bright sparkling and her twining arms;
> The panting bosom and the ambrosial kiss,
> The dying languor and the heavenly bliss.
> In—'s bowers new porticoes shall rise,
> And fairer *Lyceums* glad our wondering eyes.
> Groves academic grace the sylvan scene,
> And Tully's Tusculum again be seen.
> The brilliant treasure of the Attick mine,
> Shall glow refulgent in our western clime,
> Till the Archangel's trump thro' ether ring,
> Till earth exulting own the eternal King,
> Till ruling planets, from their orbits hurl'd,
> Announce the dissolution of the world.

The concluding lines of this poem significantly set forth the millennial doctrine which exists also in the works of Dwight, Barlow, and most other poets of the time. Although this work must certainly be considered as important evidence of the vogue of classical models in American literature, it must not be assumed that the designation of classical prototypes is peculiarly an American phenomenon or that the practice makes American literature any more classical than others in Western Europe. Goethe, who deplored the popularity of poetic imitation in Germany, remarked in his *Autobiography* concerning the common practice: "We now possessed, if not Homers, yet Virgils and Miltons; if not a Pindar, yet a Horace; of Theocrituses there was no lack." Looking back from the perspective of the nineteenth century, Goethe realized that the period of neoclassical imitation had passed and that different standards and objectives were necessary for the literature of his age.

The same judgment may, of course, be rendered post facto against the American critics who awaited the appearance of new Virgils or new Ovids. They failed to realize that the time for neoclassical imitation had passed in America also. Not only were Latin and Greek models about to lose their vogue, but the traditional genres were giving way to new ones such as the novel, the romance, the short story, and the personal lyric. Apart from the prose of Franklin and Paine, the first works of American literature to obtain international recognition grew out of the new wave of what is now known as Romanticism. The first of the poets of this school, William Cullen Bryant, took full advantage of the classical tradition—witness, for example, the title of his best-known lyric "Thanatopsis"—but he reacted against the artificial or superficial elements of neoclassical rhetoric. He remarked in 1827, "I am aware that in modern poetry nothing is generally so nauseous and revolting as the introduction of the Pagan deities. Nothing turns us away from the perusal of a copy of verses so soon as any talk about Venus and Cupid, about Bacchus and his bowl, and about Sol and his chariot."

Two of the labels that have been used for the period under discussion—the quarter of a century from the Revolution to the end of the eighteenth century—are paradoxically conflicting, but still relatively accurate. It was a new Age of Augustus in the rhetoric and structure of its literature, based as it was upon arbitrary rules requiring adherence to a single standard of propriety and order. It was the Federal period in ideology, however, allowing for a mixture of intellectual codes in the sense that "in the shallow structures of the mind several cultural codes can operate successfully at the same time." Intellectually, the Federal period was as pluralistic as the political system of the newly organized United States of America.

The history of the debate in eighteenth-century America over the educational value of Latin and Greek has been exhaustively treated by Meyer Reinhold in two articles in the *Proceedings of the American Philosophical Society*: Vol. 112 (1968): 221-34 and Vol. 119 (1975): 108-32. In the later article, Professor Reinhold declares that it is "methodologically wrong" to view the dispute over classical languages in the schools "as a renewal of the debate between the Ancients and the Moderns in the earlier Battle of the Books in Europe, or as a contrast between conservatives and liberals". My own methodology in the preceding survey has consisted entirely in quoting American authors and suggesting parallels to notions expressed in the European debate. I am inclined to believe, however, that one could legitimately argue that the fundamental issues of the controversy were very much alive in eighteenth-century America and that the debate was continued there rather than merely renewed. The ancient side was favorably presented by John Wesley in his *Survey of the Wisdom of God in the Creation*, which contains long extracts from a work originally printed in French by John Dutens, *An Inquiry into the Origin of the Discoveries attributed to the Moderns: Wherein It is Demonstrated, That our most celebrated Philosophers have, for most part, taken what they advance from the Works of the Ancients*. The Dutens extracts were added to the second edition of Wesley's work (Bristol, 1777) and repeated in subsequent editions. It is impossible to tell how extensively this work circulated in America during the eighteenth century, but it appears to be one of those books which people read in their homes, but was not bought for libraries. It is not listed in Evans, *American Bibliography*. The Library of Congress holds the "3d American ed., rev. and enl.; with notes, by B. Mayo. New York, Pub. by N. Bangs and T. Mason, for the Methodist Episcopal Church, 1823." I do not know when the first American edition appeared. The British Museum contains only three editions, the first (Bristol 1763) [which does not have the Dutens extracts], the second (Bristol, 1777) and an unnumbered "new edition . . . adapted to the present state of science by R. Mudie. 3 vol. London, 1836."

As far as political principles are concerned, I am not aware of any serious attempt to join the debates over either classical languages in the curriculum or the preeminence of ancient or modern learning to party or social divisions. Freneau and Barlow conveyed democratic ideals whereas Dwight, Humphreys, and Robert Treat Paine revealed aristocratic sentiments. By and large, however, the democratic writers (those loyal to the administration of Thomas Jefferson in the first decade of the nineteenth century) continued to predict eventual American supremacy in the realm of literature; whereas the opponents of Jefferson (the Federalists) lamented what they considered to be the lack of distinction in American letters.

The opposition to classical languages in the academic curriculum has been partly attributed to the influx of Scottish educators such as William Smith of Pennsylvania and John Witherspoon of Princeton. Perhaps because the speech of their country had been traditionally ridiculed by the English, they placed a premium upon the strength and purity of the English language and maintained that this purity was threatened by the emphasis on Latin and Greek. Even before Smith's appearance in Philadelphia, however, Franklin had proposed that in the institution that eventually became the University of Pennsylvania "all should not be compell'd to learn *Latin, Greek,* or the modern foreign languages." He later called Latin and Greek "the quackery of literature." Benjamin Rush, although ambivalent about Scottish educators, expressed grave doubts concerning the value of classical instruction in his *Observations upon the Study of the Latin and Greek Languages* (1789).

Many in the Federal period agreed with Franklin that the classical languages were nothing but elegant and useless ornaments. Thomas Paine not only shared this opinion, but maintained in addition that organized religions had imposed the study of dead languages in order to preserve the system of Christian dogma and to prevent its falsehood from being exposed through scientific discoveries. "It became necessary to their purpose," he charged in *The Age of Reason,* "to cut learning down to a size less dangerous . . . , and this they effected by restricting the idea of learning to the dead study of dead language." This reasoning was duplicated by one of Paine's Latin American disciples, Camilo Henrìquez of Chile, in an essay "On the Influence of Enlightenment Writings on the Fate of Humanity" (1812). . . . Continuing to teach sciences in Latin, Henrìquez affirmed, is the major obstacle which can be offered not only to the diffusion of the Enlightenment, but also to its perfection. "The method of scholasticism, the system of studies of the schools, the obstacles which the popularization of useful books has encountered, have had an enormous influence in the backwardness of letters."

Carla Mulford

SOURCE: "Radicalism in Joel Barlow's *The Conspiracy of Kings* (1792)," in *Deism, Masonry, and the Enlightenment: Essays Honoring Alfred Owen Aldridge,* edited by J. A. Leo Lemay, University of Delaware Press, 1987, pp. 137-57.

[*In the following essay, Mulford discusses the themes of Barlow's* Conspiracy of Kings *in the context of his relationship to eighteenth- and nineteenth-century radical thought, particularly the notion that "the people had the power to reinvent their world."*]

In his 6 March 1792 letter to William Hayley, Joel Barlow promised, "I shall send you the little mad poem when printed." He fulfilled the promise on 5 April, enclosing with his letter copies of *The Conspiracy of Kings* for both

Timothy Dwight

Hayley and James Stanier Clarke. Humorously he cautioned, "If you can find a secret corner in your house, to hide it from the view of your visiters, it may be no injury to your reputation. but it must not be known that you have any knowledge of such a reprobate as the Author must have been." Barlow was finding himself increasingly unpopular with the British government, and for good reason, according to the conservatives. After the first part of Barlow's *Advice to the Privileged Orders* appeared in February 1792, Barlow's name was circulated with Thomas Paine's as a foremost reformer. Horne Tooke, secretary of the Society for Constitutional Information, nominated Barlow on 9 March for membership in that reform group. Printed mid-March to "a great noise," *The Conspiracy of Kings* no doubt aided Barlow's unanimous election to the Society for Constitutional Information. Barlow might have read with self-consciously jocular uneasiness Clarke's comments of 25 March: "I think I shall hear of you in the Tower before long. If so take care to procure good apartments for we will certainly come to see you often." In mid-April Barlow traveled to Holland—as much to escape the increasingly conspicuous watchfulness of the British government over his activities as for business reasons.

Yet despite Barlow's contemporary reknown (indeed his infamy, to conservatives like Edmund Burke and Timothy Dwight); despite his popularity and influence with the leading writers, political philosophers, reformers, and statesmen of his day (people like William Hayley, William Blake, William Godwin, Richard Price, Horne Tooke, Mary Wollstonecraft, Thomas Paine, Thomas Jefferson,

Constantin Volney, Brissot de Warville, Marquis de Lafayette); and despite the recent appreciations of Barlow's poetry by scholars like J. A. Leo Lemay, Robert Arner, and Robert Richardson—Joel Barlow still continues to be mentioned among the conservative federalist contemporaries from his Yale days as a "Connecticut Wit" and continues to suffer the unhappy rubric as the "poet of cornmeal mush." This condescending attitude pervades the recent biographical and critical essay on Barlow in the *Dictionary of Literary Biography*. Such condescension reveals more about critics' post-Romantic tendency to view as stultifying those poets who use neoclassic forms than it does about Barlow and his writings.

Perhaps more than any other of Barlow's poems, *The Conspiracy of Kings* reveals his belief that the poet should be not only the corrector of the old order but the seer and speaker of the new. The poem is not the stale "juvenalian" satire Cecelia Tichi calls "utterly lifeless". Rather, like *The Hasty-Pudding* (1793), it shows Barlow's adept fashioning of radical ideology in a denunciation of Burke and the conservative tendencies that could lead to more war and to anarchy. Barlow developed in the poem the kinds of paradox the radicals, especially William Blake, were using at the time. He used the notion of the *Translatio Studii* changed to *Translatio Libertatis* (from America to France to England) popular with the radical initiate. He used images and conceptions from his readings of the *encyclopedistes,* Constantin Volney, and others. Finally, he informed the poem with a poetic voice (probably adopted as a result of reading Diderot) of a creator/seer, not a juvenalian complainer.

Perhaps Barlow wished the uninitiated audience—the audience not familiar with radical ideology—to be misled into thinking *The Conspiracy of Kings* was simply the invective of a juvenalian satirist. The poet-speaker says that he will not "croak with omen'd yell" (1.25) about a future hell. And this poet-speaker says that "Indignant Man" (1.57) now "Displays the unclad skeletons of kings" (1.59). In the pamphlet edition of the *Conspiracy,* Barlow's annotation for this line reads: "Ossa vides regum vacuis exhausta medullis. Juvenal, Sat. 8." The mention of "croak[ing]" and of Juvenal's eighth satire might seem reason enough to conclude that Barlow wrote the poem as a juvenalian political satire. Indeed, Juvenal's eighth satire would have been a good satire for Barlow to have imitated in his antimonarchical satire on Burke and on the conservative politics that sought the continuation of an obsolete distinction by rank and title. Juvenal's eighth satire began with a similar message: that although we may derive rank and title from our ancestors, yet if we degenerate from the virtues by which they obtained them, we are not truly noble. It is easy to understand why scholars have assumed that Barlow's poem is just another juvenalian satire after the manner of Pope or Swift.

But Barlow's allusion to Juvenal's eighth satire is misleading. He did not have Juvenal—or the eighth satire—specifically in mind when he wrote the poem. In fact, Juvenal's line was supplied him by William Hayley late in (or after) the period of composition. In addition, Barlow (and perhaps Hayley) quoted inexactly. In his 6 March 1792 letter to Hayley, Barlow thanked Hayley for having given him the Latin line:

> I thank you, my dear friend, among all your kind attentions to me, that you was so good as to find to our good Santo padre the motto, *ossa vides regum vacuis exhausta medullis.* I shall make use of it in the little Poem, which is now with the printer, but it remains to know to what latin poet we are originally indebted for it, because I wish to make the account stand even with him as I go along, by placing it to his credit. Neither his Holiness nor myself were able to recollect the author.

As Victor C. Miller has pointed out, Juvenal's original line (Satire 8.90) reads: *Ossa vides regum vacuis exsucta medullis,* You see the very bones of kings sucked dry, with the marrow extracted. The inexactness of the quotation (i.e., "exhausta" for "exsucta") might perhaps have been intentional. But Barlow clearly did not intend his poem to be a slavish or even slightly derivative imitation of Juvenal. *The Conspiracy of Kings* is indeed a satire, but a satire of a different order.

The Conspiracy of Kings ostensibly addresses the French émigrés, largely of the nobility, who after the fall of the Bastille (14 July 1789), fled to Coblenz and there had been gathering forces under the assumed leadership of the Comte d'Artois, Louis XVI's brother. From Coblenz, the émigrés watched the uneasy agreements made between the Assembly and Louis XVI and quietly planned and worked for a restoration of the old regime in France, with or without Louis XVI as king. Barlow couples his attack against these émigrés with one against the potential royal coalition of Europe and the German states. He specifically targets Gustavus III; Catharine II of Russia; Frederick William II of Prussia; and Leopold of Austria, Marie Antoinette's brother, the persuasive force behind the coalition intended to restore power to the French monarchy. But though the speaker of the poem clearly attacks these devious, dying older orders, he more fervently abuses those English conservatives who followed Edmund Burke in supporting the sinking cause of royal servitude by attempting to get government backing for the émigrés and for a royal alliance against the French republic.

Burke's *Reflections on the Revolution in France* (1790) opened him to abuse from the radicals. His *Reflections* took as its starting point a denunciation of the dissenting minister Rev. Richard Price's "Discourse on the Love of Our Country" (preached before the Revolution Society at the Old Jewry 4 November 1789) and reached a rhetorical pitch in Burke's famous lament that "The age of chivalry is gone . . . the glory of Europe . . . extinguished forever." Radicals and moderate reformers were surprised at Burke's seeming shift away from the freedoms about which he had spoken as inalienable rights in support of the American cause against the British crown. When it became clear by July 1791 that Burke, interested in finding British government support for the French émigrés, was cooperating with Calonne, chief adviser to the Comte d'Artois, the radicals were outraged. They rallied to praise Price and the French Revolution, which they figured forth as the dawning of equal rights due men around the world.

The concept of *figuring forth* is an important one, for the referent—the historical event called the French Revolution and all the facts reported with regard to that event—is finally of less importance than the poetic language and images chosen by writers in order to persuade readers to accept or at least to entertain as acceptable those writers' political-ideological positions. One example should suffice. Burke's correspondence, before, during, and after writing his *Reflections* reveals his distrust of Marie Antoinette and her propensities for, in his words, "Court Intrigue." Yet, despite Philip Francis's urgings before publication that Burke remove the "pure foppery" about the queen, Burke held with his rhapsodic picture of the former dauphiness, the "persecuted woman" who, with "All the decent drapery of life . . . rudely torn off," "had but just enough time to fly almost naked, and through ways unknown to the murderers . . . to seek the refuge at the feet of the king and husband, not secure of his own life for a moment." Burke seems knowingly to have distorted the "facts," then, so he could create a rhapsodic and shocking lamentation that "the age of chivalry is gone"—in order to persuade his readers that an irreparable loss has been created by the revolutionaries, a loss that might take place in England if the English reformers like Richard Price are allowed to promote the revolution in France in behalf of their own interests in English constitutional reform.

The radicals were indeed seeking English constitutional reform. Conservatives held that these radicals shielded their intent for more extensive political revolution under the name of reform. Burke and other conservatives propagandized the popular conservative position that the English radicals were secret conspirators against the crown, their reform societies secret organizations preparing for the king's overthrow—as precedented, according to the conservative position, by the Gordon Riots of 1780. The conservatives further implied that the necessary corollary of such conspiracy would be tyranny, the radicals supplanting one long-standing reign they wrongly called tyranny with a tyranny more threatening because new and untried and because it emanated from the masses, not the aristocracy. Such a revolution, the conservatives held, would bring anarchy.

Barlow and other radical political philosophers flaunted such conservative propaganda by transvaluing its referents. That is, the radicals used the conservative propagandists' names to *re*name, to give different (often completely opposite) valuation to, the phenomenon discussed by the conservatives. Their message to Burke and others was twofold: that if the inevitable revolution can be seen as a conspiracy, then conservative factions were in conspiracy against it; and that the so-called tyranny of mob rule (Burke's "swinish multitude," the fear of which was associated with Burke's terror of the sublime) was no worse than the tyranny of a dead and dusty conservatism that led to suppression of the energies of free people. The anarchic forces, the radicals insisted, were those forces working against the necessary revolution for freedom.

So Barlow titled his poem *The Conspiracy of Kings* to indicate his own radical propagandist message that the conservators of the old orders were conspiring, not just against the politically radical groups, but against equality and liberty, the inalienable rights of every person. Barlow thus makes his own process of transvaluation apparent in the title. The speaker of the poem, too, makes known that the old orders have valorized events and beliefs by naming them in ways to suit their need for political and ideological power over the masses. Echoing Constantin Volney's *Ruins,* Barlow's speaker addresses the "Drones of the Church and harpies of the State,"

> Ye, who pretend to your dark host was given
> The lamp of life, the mystic keys of heaven;
> Whose impious arts with magic spells began
> When shades of ign'rance veil'd the race of man;
> Who change, from age to age the sly deceit
> As Science beams, and Virtue learns the cheat.
>
> (15-20)

The speaker makes aware his belief that officials of Church and State have been deluding the ignorant world, and as they found it necessary, have simply "change[d], from age to age the sly deceit," for their own political ends. The poet-speaker again alludes to such false valorization when he rhetorically asks:

> Where then, forsaken villains, will ye turn?
> Of France the outcast and of earth the scorn;
> What new-made charm can dissipate your fears?
> Can Burke's mad foam, or Calonne's House of
>   Peers?
>
> (96-100)

The poet-speaker insists that the émigrés and the conservatives have run out of "new-made charm[s]," that they have run out of objects that they can name in order better to institutionalize their ecclesiastical and civil hierarchies. In this new age, the émigrés and conservatives are simply "forsaken villains," forsaken largely because of the false naming and the false valorizations they sought to impose on an ignorant populace. In other words, the age of the conservatives' naming is being replaced by an egalitarian age that will rename according to the instruction of "Eternal Truth."

The Conspiracy of Kings is developed entirely as a transvaluation. The émigrés, "Drones of the Church and harpies of the State," have only been engaged in setting up "crested reptiles to a throne." By the end of the second stanza, the speaker has suggested that a transvaluation—an appropriate renaming—is necessary because of the hypocrisy of Church and State officials who have made the people fear a god in whom the officials themselves do not believe:

> Think not I come to croak with omen'd yell
> The dire damnations of your future hell,
> To bend a bigot or reform a knave,
> By op'ning all the scenes beyond the grave.
> I know your crusted souls: while one defies
> In sceptic scorn the vengeance of the skies,
> The other boasts,—"I ken thee, Power divine,
> But fear thee not; th' avenging bolt is mine."
>
> (23-30)

The implied message is that such hypocrisy has by necessity to be devalorized, for

> The hour is come, the world's unclosing eyes

> Discern with rapture where its wisdom
>   lies. . . .

> No turn, no shift, no courtly arts avail,
> Each mask is broken, all illusions fail.
>
> (159-60; 169-70)

The implication of such a transvaluation openly announced is that the old myths—particularly with regard to politics and, especially, to religion—are now known to have been lies. It is an implication common to Enlightenment philosophers, available perhaps most notably in the *Encyclopédie,* entries from which Barlow carefully translated and entered into at least one notebook.

Barlow's interest in comparative religion and mythology began as early as 1787, when he published *The Vision of Columbus.* Barlow there included a "Dissertation on the Genius and Institutions of Manco Capec" in which he asserted that "Those constitutions of government are best calculated for immediate energy and duration, which are interwoven with some religious system. The legislator, who appears in the character of an inspired person, renders his political institutions sacred, and interests the conscience as well as the judgement in support." As proof, Barlow examined the institutions of Moses, Lycurgus, Solon, Numa, Mahomet, and Peter of Russia, all of whom he unfavorably compared to the benevolent "Peruvian Lawgiver" Manco Capec. Early in his career, then, Barlow had acknowledged his belief that a religious system aided political power. The "Dissertation" shows that Barlow was conversant with Voltaire's *Philosophical Dictionary,* William Robertson's *History of America,* and Garcilaso de la Vega's *Royal Commentaries of Peru.* A note in Book 11 of the *Vision* indicates that Barlow was reading Richard Price as well. Barlow's interest in theories of political philosophy common to Enlightenment political and religious philosophers thus seem to have begun as early as 1787. He was working with many theorists, in addition to those mentioned, as he revised *The Vision* for a 1793 Paris edition.

A more immediate source for some of Barlow's comments in *The Conspiracy of Kings* about religion and its political mystique might be Constantin Volney's *The Ruins, or, Meditation on the Revolutions of Empires,* published originally in Paris in 1791. J. A. Leo Lemay has suggested that Barlow knew the works of both Volney and Charles François Dupuis, author of *Mémoire sur l'origine des constellations et sur l'explication de la fable par le moyen de l'astronomie* (Paris 1791), well enough to use them while writing *The Hasty-Pudding* in 1793. Both works argued that all cultures have based their religions on their incomplete knowledge of the natural world; Volney's *Ruins* premised upon this notion its criticism of political power based on the superstitious ignorance of the populace. Barlow published in 1802 a translation, which Jefferson had begun, of *The Ruins.* I suspect Barlow had done some careful reading of Volney—if not some translation (or reading of Jefferson's partial translation) of *The Ruins*—by February 1792, when he was writing *The Conspiracy of Kings.* Parts of his poem seem reminiscent of his translation of Volney's book: compare, for instance, lines 70-118 of *Conspiracy* with Volney's chapter 12, "Lessons of

Times Past Repeated on the Present." The working conception of both texts is that a "genius" of light and truth has arrived to tear "the strong bandage from the eyes of man" (Barlow, *Conspiracy* 1. 272), has arrived to show truth to men who "walked with a bandage on our eyes" (Volney 1802). Barlow, evidently fond of the metaphor of removing bandages from eyes, used it in Part 1 of his *Advice to the Privileged Orders,* published a month before the *Conspiracy* in February 1792. There Barlow had insisted, "The church in that country [France] was like royalty,— the prejudices in its favor were too strong to be vanquished at once. The most that could be done, was to tear the bandage from the eyes of mankind, break the charm of inequality, demolish ranks and infallibilities, and teach the people that mitres and crowns did not confer supernatural powers." Both *The Conspiracy of Kings* and *Advice to the Privileged Orders*—in addition to *The Hasty-Pudding* written a year later—are based on conceptions about Church and State available in Volney's *Ruins.* What distinguishes the *Conspiracy* from the other two works is Barlow's relentless insistence that a re-visioning based on the knowledge of the history of religion and its political manipulability is unquestionably necessary.

In *The Conspiracy of Kings* Barlow bases this re-visioning on a transvaluation of the myth of creation and divinity. The poet-speaker makes of Burke at once a kind of Miltonic Antichrist and a creator of a false myth of creation. Like Milton's story (in *Paradise Lost,* Book 6) of Christ's battling Satan, the poet-speaker announces in explanation of Burke's demise (in 1. 151, Burke is a "lost man"):

> . . . 'twas Heav'n's returning grace,
> In kind compassion to our injur'd race,
> Which stripp'd that soul, ere it should flee from
>   hence,
> Of the last garb of decency or sense,
> Left thee its own foul horrors to display,
> In all the blackness of its native day,
> To sink at last, from earth's glad surface hurl'd,
> The sordid sov'reign of the letter'd world.
>   (141-48)

Burke is Antichrist hurled from heaven as a kindness to the "injur'd race." But also, according to the "Muse indignant" (106), Burke has created his own world out of the fragments of crumbling chaos, like a would-be God. The poet-speaker's periodic construction adds emphasis to the indignation of the Muse:

> Oh Burke, degenerate slave! with grief and
>   shame
> The Muse indignant must repeat thy name.
> Strange man, declare,—since, at creation's birth,
> From crumbling Chaos sprang this heav'n and
>   earth
> Since wrecks and outcast relics still remain,
> Whirl'd ceaseless round Confusion's dreary
>   reign,
> Declare, from all these fragments, whence you
>   stole
> That genius wild, that monstrous mass of soul.
>   (105-12)

Reminiscent of Milton's chaos-hell (*Paradise Lost,* Book 2), Burke's world, made of creation's leftovers, with "ge-

nius wild" and spread in the waste of extremes, is, the poet has assured the reader, a "weak delusion" (39). Burke is not the maker: "Burke leads you wrong, the world is not his own" (40). Nor is he the proper celebrator of such a "mad-man's thread-bare theme" (41). That is, like Milton's anarchic Satan, Burke has named events improperly: the world about which Burke speaks is one of his own creation, a creation made of chaotic fragments having no basis in any real creation that is "the gift of God" known to the Muse "Eternal Truth" (1), which guides the present speaker.

Thus by contrast, "the present world . . . prompt[ing] the song" is better described (better named) by the poet-speaker who has been "len[t]" the trumpet of "Eternal Truth":

> *"For heav'n and earth,"* the voice of God or-
>   dains,
> *"Shall pass and perish, but my word remains,"*
> Th' eternal WORD, which gave, in spite of thee
>   [Burke],
> *Reason* to man, that bids the man be free.
>   (137-40)

The poet-speaker who knows God's true word of reason has "come not to croak with omen'd yell / The dire damnations of a future hell" (23-24), for this is a speaker free of the "mad-man's thread-bare theme" that would "veil the race of man" in "shades of ign'rance" (18) so as to gain political power. That is, this speaker is not like Burke a "degenerate slave" to impotent and tyrannous custom, particularly religious custom, but one who has come to tell of "nations, rising in the light of truth, / Strong with new life and pure regenerate youth" (43-44). Burke's old myth has been transformed into a groundless lie; the poet-speaker's creation message about "MAN, exalted title! first and best" (175) is not only new but engendered by God, "On God's own image by his hand imprest" (176).

The poet-speaker of Barlow's poem conflates religious history and the history of political freedom in announcing and celebrating the rise of "MAN" in France. No longer will the politics of oppression be tied to a repressive religion, the poet-speaker implies. On one level, the poet-speaker celebrates the new political and religious history by renaming the events of the Christian myth. As Paulson has suggested, the revolutionaries found the assimilation of Christian symbolism a valuable means as propaganda because "Christian symbolism was the only available form known to large numbers of the poor and illiterate." Barlow's poet-speaker announces that the change brought by the French Revolution "Make[s] patriot views and moral views the same" (260). That is, the views of State and Church will no longer be founded upon ignorance of seeming mysteries but upon reason, which will bring politics and religion in line with "Eternal Truth." According to the Bible, God's word was made flesh in Adam, thus freeing Adam from the earth. When Adam transgressed against God's word, he was punished but was redeemed by Christ. Like many of the radicals—most notably William Blake—Barlow plays on this generative/regenerative myth. This poet-speaker announces that God gave *"Reason* to man, that bids the man be free." In this transvaluation, Christ is no longer the redeemer, man's reason is:

"'twas Heav'n's returning grace,/ In kind compassion to our injur'd race" (141-42). The race, according to the poet-speaker's story, was not "injur'd" by the godhead because of a betrayal of God's word. Rather, the race was betrayed by its own ignorance into the hands of false gods like the conservative Burke. As indicated by the French Revolution, the poet-speaker's story goes, the race is regenerated: "nations [are] rising in the light of truth,/ Strong with new life and pure regenerate youth" (43-44). Grace has come to man in the form of reason, as a "trust by Heav'n's own hand consign'd, / The great concentred stake, the interest of mankind" (47-48). The poet-speaker in the *Conspiracy* has thus renamed events in the Christ myth to fit the myth of the French Revolution. Man can redeem himself, in this myth, so that he becomes at once redeemer and redeemed in the new history of Adam.

Barlow conflates this transvalued Christian myth with another myth related to freedom and associated with the death of Osiris. The "great concentred stake" is the figure Barlow uses for this conflation. As Paulson has shown, the radicals (particularly Blake) attached import to the cause of freedom by imaging their position in terms of virile masculinity on the rise, bound upward to express its freedom or ascending or descending into bowels of darkness to bring into fruition light and energy. Light, energy, and sexuality are the images associated with the myth. Barlow uses such images throughout *The Conspiracy of Kings*.

He ties the figures to the rise of a new "religion" of man, basing on his study of comparative religion the transvaluation of the Christian myth into a masculine regenerative myth. Barlow's "Genealogy of the Tree of Liberty," as he recorded it in an undated notebook (the source I use below), provides an informative context for this aspect of the poem. The "Genealogy" traces the basis of religious worship to the myth of Osiris (the sun), killed in a battle against Typhon (the power of darkness), who dismembered Osiris and threw him into the Nile. Isis (the moon), wife of Osiris, collected all Osiris's parts "except the precious fragment that was lost in the river," which "genitals . . . communicated a fecundating power to that river" and "became the source of life & vegetation to all Egypt." Barlow continues, "To commemorate at once the tragical death of Osiris and the great benefits that resulted to mankind from the posthumous power of his organs of generation a solemn feast was instituted in which the Phallus in a posture of strong erection was carried in procession. The same fable of Osiris was extended to other countries under different names with a little variation." When the fables reached Greece, the death and resurrection "were celebrated with a variety of ceremonies" in honor of "Bachus," and "the procession of the Phallus always made a conspicuous figure." The "freedom and licentiousness that reigned in these nocturnal assemblies" brought the god the name Eleutheros—"free" or "freedom," and, when carried to Rome, the god became "known by the epithet *Liber, (Free),* so that the Phallus became the emblem of *Libertas.*" Through the ages the original meaning was lost, and the English have attached to their maypole or liberty pole the simple notion of the "liberty of a frolick . . . without ever dreaming of the origin or *antetype* of this curious emblem." The pole passed to America in a more

"venerable" fashion, where "it grew to an enormous mast" and came to be "a solid emblem of *political Liberty.* From thence it has recrossed the Atlantic to extend its blessings to its native continent [where] it is now placed in the public places all over France . . . inspiring with enthusiasm the hosts of heroes who swell the triumphs of that victorious Republic."

Barlow's readings in comparative religion and philosophy had indicated to him that all religious worship is based on worship of natural phenomena having natural causes. These phenomena, not understood by the mass of men, were mythologized to create mystical meaning, which enabled those who pretended interpretive powers to have political power. Manco Capec was for Barlow the best lawgiver of former times because he used benevolent control over men, control gained because, knowing more than the savages he came to conquer, he assumed political power by implying he had mystical (religious) power. During the French Revolution, as political power was transferred from the king to the people, radicals hoped for what they figured forth as a freeing of the populace from this kind of religious superstition. Thus, revolutionaries sought to effect a shift from worship of Christian objects to a worship of liberty, figured forth for the populace as liberty poles, capped with red liberty caps. By attempting to have the people worship liberty poles, "patriot views and moral views [could become] the same," for the people would be worshipping their political freedom while engaging in a kind of religious practice in behalf of morality.

In the "great concentred stake, the interest of mankind," Barlow figured forth the phallus of the Osiris myth transformed as the stake of liberty for the masses. The "great concentred stake" was a trust "by Heav'n's own hand consigned" because (not Christ but) *"Reason,"* "Heav'n's returning grace," brought a regenerative redemption. By using a system of transvaluation, the poetic voice informing the poem insists by implication that if a religion is to exist, it should be a religion of man's worship of man's own ability, not of a substitute man (Christ) viewed as some mystical agent of redemption.

Arguing in behalf of the French Revolution and using metaphors that marked revolutionary philosophy, Barlow created a masculine and regenerative metaphor throughout the poem. The liberty pole in a state of erection is figured forth as the "great concentred stake." The men the poet speaks of have been "rous'd from sloth" (35) to use their "deep-descending steel" (37) to "teach dull nerves to feel" (37). Nations are "rising in the light of truth" (43), because "Indignant Man resumes the shaft" (57) to "Disarm the tyrant" (58). France has "rent the dark veil" (62) with the "great concentred stake" (48). In contrast with these images of virility and power are those of the conservative, dying orders. Leopold II of Austria, for instance, is "too wise to trust his sword" (84) against such powerful combatants. "Artois' sword" (101) "Burn'd with the fire of fame, but harmless burn'd / For sheath'd the sword remain'd, and in its sheath return'd" (103-4). The impotent Burke, who wields only an "infuriate quill" (129), is plunging like Phaeton a "wasting course, / The great Sublime of weakness and of force" (122-23). The forces that would oppose the French are not fiery and virile. In fact, "Dim, like the day-struck owl, [they] grope in light, / No arm for combat, no resource in flight" (163-64). They are weak against the "ascending bliss that waits [man's] call" (245), for they have "erect[ed] their thrones amid [a] sanguine flood, / And dip[ped] their purple in the nation's blood" (217-18). They are mere "unclad skeletons" (59), "Spectres of power, and serpents without stings" (60). They have only "infuriate quill[s]" to spend against "Heav'n's own bequest, the heritage of all" (249). For "Freedom at last, with Reason in her train" (249), has made "Gallia's sons" (251) "Start into men" (253).

The masculine, regenerative myth is reflected in the reference to Alcides of Greek mythology as well. In a series of rhetorical questions, the poet-speaker suggests the émigrés would be asking the impossible:

> Bid young Alcides, in his grasp who takes,
> And gripes with naked hand the twisting snakes,
> Their force exhausted, bid him prostrate fall,
> And dread their shadows trembling on the wall.
> (65-69)

The mention of Alcides, a patronymic of Heracles (Hercules), recalls the many labors of this hero known for strength, courage, endurance, good nature, compassion, appetite, and lust. In his cradle, Heracles strangled two serpents, sent against him by Hera. The young Alcides, then, has fought the "crested reptiles" of the conservatives. Indeed, according to the *Century Dictionary,* Heracles has long been seen as the borrowed Phoenician sun-god. That is, Heracles is a type of Osiris and a type of Christ. All three of them are reflected in the liberty pole that represents for the first time in history, according to revolutionary mythology, the conflation of meanings religious and political in one emblem in behalf of reason and eternal truth.

In *The Conspiracy of Kings* Barlow is using a revolutionary mythology that informs most of the writings of English supporters of the revolution, William Blake most prominently. David Erdman has indicated that Blake most likely attended some of the dinners that radical printer Joseph Johnson (Barlow's printer) offered his authors and that Blake surely knew of the Society for Constitutional Information. Erdman has shown that Blake was indebted to Barlow for aspects of the machinery and conception of *America: A Prophecy,* published in 1793. I find Blake's *America, Song of Liberty,* and *The Visions of the Daughters of Albion,* all dating to 1793, reminiscent of Barlow's *Conspiracy.* Blake's fiery Orc come to confront the hoary Urizen gives a particularized picture of Barlow's more generalized "MAN" who confronts the old conservative orders represented by the émigrés and Burke. In addition, both poets stress the image shift from *Translatio Studii* to *Translatio Libertatis.* Barlow's poet-speaker announces that the voice.

> . . . borne on western gales from that far shore
> Where Justice reigns, and tyrants tread no more,
> Th' unwonted voice, that no dissuasion awes,
> That fears no frown, and seeks no blind applause,
> Shall tell the gift that Freedom sheds abroad,

> The rights of nature and the gifts of God.
> (3-8)

Midpoem, the speaker reminds the listener:

> The hour is come, the world's unclosing eyes
> Discern with rapture where its wisdom lies;
> From western heav'ns th' inverted Orient springs,
> The morn of man, the dreadful night of kings.
> (159-62)

And in conclusion, the poet insists:

> And deign, for once, to turn a transient eye
> To that wide world that skirts the western sky;
> Hail the mild morning, where that dawn began,
> The full fruition of the hopes of man.
> (275-78)

The poet-speaker emphasizes throughout *The Conspiracy of Kings* that freedom has traveled from America to France, and it soon will arrive in England. The normal course of revolution from east to west has been inverted into a revolution west to east. Blake's *Visions of the Daughters of Albion* (1793) likewise derives from the attempt of the revolutionary principle to travel from America to Europe in a kind of *Translatio Libertatis.* In Blake's poem, freedom's procreative impulses are frustrated; in Barlow's poem, that frustration surfaces as an acid attack against Burke and the conservatives and is coupled with an insistence that the morn of man has arrived. Barlow's poem suggests the fulfillment of the procreative urge:

> O Man, my brother, how the cordial flame
> Of all endearments kindles at thy name!
> In every clime, thy visage greets my eyes,
> In every tongue thy kindred accents rise;
> The thought expanding swells my heart with glee,
> It finds a friend, and loves itself in thee.
> (181-86)

The urge for procreative love is one Blake left frustrated in *The Visions of the Daughters of Albion.* In Blake's view, regenerative freedom was not available for the England of Edmund Burke.

Barlow's view was clearly propagandist. He adopted the metaphors used by leading radicals in order to convey a political message; he adopted the language of the revolutionaries to clarify that message. Thus, all men become for the poet-speaker "my brother" (181), all mankind the "fraternal family divine" (187). The "dark deception . . . the glare of state" (205) kept the "cordial flame / Of all endearments" (181-82) from burning in ages past. The message and language are radical and revolutionary; the implication is finally what most readers—if asked for a name—would call Romantic. Now that the poet has spoken the word of God (cf. 137-40) via the muse of "Eternal Truth," now that the poet has "name[d]" (182) "Man" in his "exalted title, first and best" (177)—a cordial flame "kindles at the name" and "kindred accents rise" (184). The poet concludes not by summarizing the message past but by forcing the listener-reader—along with the émigrés (and, by implication, all conservatives)—to engage in the poetic experience, the creative act both visual and imaginative. As Stanislaus of Poland "Points the progressive march, and shapes the way, / That leads a realm from darkness into day" (273-74), so the poet points the listener-reader to "turn a transient eye / To that wide world that skirts the western sky" (275-76). Whereas the poet had himself "hail[ed] Man" (177), the listener-reader now must participate and "Hail the mild morning, where the dawn began, / The full fruition of the hopes of man" (277-78). A participation on the listener-reader's part would replicate the poet's "thought expanding" (185) into the love of freedom and his fellow man. It would fulfill in the listening-reading act the poet's "sacred cause" emblematized in the seeming paradoxical "rare union, Liberty and Laws" and spoken "to the reas'ning race" in the message "to freedom rise, / Like them [Americans] be equal, and like them be wise" (281-82). In looking to freedom's model in America, the listener-reader would be himself engaging in the idol-worship the poet celebrates.

Barlow's *Conspiracy of Kings* is not a closed expression in a discursive mode but a progressive and revolutionary message encouraging active participation both political and philosophical. Barlow's "little mad poem" is based on the same politics as his *Advice to the Privileged Orders,* but it is based on a synthetic discourse that is emblematic and suggestive rather than analytical and discursive. As early as 1752 Denis Diderot had said in his now famous passage in *Lettre sur les sourds et muets* that the primary characteristic of poetry is suggestiveness, the true poet a creator:

> *Il passe alors dans le discours du poëte un esprit qui en meut et vivifie toutes les syllabes. Qu'est-ce que cet esprit? j'en ai quelquefois senti la présence; mais tout ce que j'en sais, c'est que c'est lui qui fait que les choses sont dites et représentées tout à la fois; que dans le même temps que l'entendement les saisit, l'âme en est émue, l'imagination les voit et oreille les entend, et que le discours n'est plus seulement un enchaînement de termes énergiques qui exposent la pensée avec force et noblesse, mais que c'est encore un tissu d'hiéroglyphes entassés les uns sur les autres qui la peignent. Je pourrais dire, en ce sens, que toute poésie est emblématique.*
>
> *Mais l'intelligence de l'emblème poétique n'est pas donnée à tout le monde; il faut être presque en état de le créer pour le sentir fortement.*

Diderot here spoke of the newer poetic aesthetic of the mid-eighteenth century. By the time of the French Revolution, poets like Blake were freely experimenting with language and poetic emblems as hieroglyphs of meaning, and poet-revolutionaries like Barlow were exploring the extent to which a renaming could propagandize a political message.

Part of that revolutionary message was that the people had the power to reinvent their world—as the French were reinventing time and street designations. Paine had announced in the *Age of Reason,* part 2, "The present age will hereafter merit to be called the Age of Reason, and the present generation will appear to the future as the Adam of a new world" (1894-96). Barlow's poet-speaker insisted

To thee, O Man, my heart rebounding springs.

Behold th' ascending bliss that waits your call,
Heav'n's own bequest, the heritage of all.

According to the poetic voice, each man had the power to call anew his world to freedom and to progress toward happiness. Revealed religion, in this view, could not offer the miracle that every man might find if he would only see ("Behold") and name ("call") that force to which his "heart springs"—freedom. The message of this poet and the poem *The Conspiracy of Kings* seems an unusually appropriate antecedent to Emerson's statement that "Society everywhere is in conspiracy against the manhood of every one of its members," to Thoreau's "The mass of men lead lives of quiet desperation," to Whitman's "Song of Myself." Barlow's *Conspiracy of Kings* is not an "utterly lifeless" poem. It utters life.

Gregg Camfield

SOURCE: "Joel Barlow's Dialectic of Progress," in *Early American Literature,* Vol. XXI, No. 2, Fall, 1986, pp. 131-43.

[*Here, Camfield explores Barlow's understanding of Enlightenment and humanistic concepts as mirrored in several of his works.*]

If, as Emory Elliott suggests [in *Revolutionary Writers,* 1982], contradictions and inconsistencies make Joel Barlow's *The Vision of Columbus* interesting in spite of itself, then by the same standards Barlow's political pamphlets of the early 1790s are doubly interesting: while vibrant and powerful in their own right, they are also "full of contradictions." The contradictions in these prose works are not symptoms of his conversions or signs of his "desperate effort to make sense of his evolving world view" (Elliott) because, by 1790, Barlow had passed through the intellectual upheaval that had converted him from Calvinism to Deism and from Federalist conservatism to Jeffersonian progressivism. With the courage of his new convictions, Barlow seemed aggressively to indulge in paradox rather than to be a victim of changing opinions. On the bases of *Advice to the Privileged Orders* and *Letter to the French Convention* alone, one could call Barlow a militarist or a pacifist, a Baconian empiricist or a Cartesian systematist, a capitalist or a communist, a bourgeois elitist or a leveler, an intellectual or an anti-intellectual, and so forth. He seems to have been too articulate, too methodically rational, too well versed in Enlightenment philosophy to make such apparent mistakes out of stupidity or ignorance; he seems instead to have relished a good paradox against all the natural "laws" of Enlightenment epistemology.

Barlow's use of contradictions can be partly explained as a consequence of the developing contradictions of late eighteenth-century thought. The conflicts between Rousseau's proto-romanticism and the rationalism of the Encyclopedists, between progressive and mechanical or cyclical models of history, and between empirical and "idealistic" philosophies eventually broke the humanistic consensus of Enlightenment thought into opposing camps of rational materialists and romantics. Barlow, who, according to Griffiths was "not a profound nor even very original" thinker, certainly to some extent eclectically drew opposing ideas from his intellectual milieu without great regard for the systematic implications of his arguments. He wrote political manifestos, not philosophy, and he consequently concerned himself more with stimulating or justifying political actions than with writing "the truth."

Yet Barlow's writings do not merely mirror the strains of Enlightenment thought; they try to hold on to that deteriorating humanistic consensus. Barlow had a flexible and optimistic enough mind to find within Enlightenment tradition the tools to bridge the rifts between opposing points of view. His intriguing, though probably not completely conscious, originality lies in his leaps over conventional dilemmas using conventional thought. He tentatively advances a model of cultural relativity based on his adaptations of Enlightenment models of "human nature," and, working from this base, he flirts with a model of progress based on a dialectic between the relative truths of culture and the absolute truths of "natural law."

Barlow's conversion to Deism led him to abandon his belief in the fallen nature of man, a belief that justified authority in opposition to the wishes of the people. Instead, he adopted Locke's idea that a just government accurately represents the will of the people:

> The sure and only characteristic of a good law is, *that it be the perfect expression of the will of the nation;* its excellence is precisely in proportion to the universality and freedom of consent. And this definition remains the same, whatever be the character of the nation, or the object of the law. Every man, as an individual, has a will of his own, and a manner of expressing it. In forming these individuals into society, it is necessary to form their wills into a government; and in doing this, we have only to find the easiest and clearest mode of expressing their wills in a national manner. (*Convention*)

The "we only," as Barlow belittles this two-part problem of both forming and expressing a national will, is of course one of the central problems of Locke's political philosophy. The political empiricism Locke vaunted showed no examples of cultural unanimity and therefore no examples of an expression of such a unanimous will. Furthermore, unanimity is not the only standard of justice: a government may possibly express the unanimous but evil will of the people it represents. Locke and his followers avoided these dilemmas in part by accepting the originally Platonic idea that both evil and idiosyncratic conceptions of self-interest are merely consequences of ignorance. An educated population, they argued, cannot act wrongly or idiosyncratically because enlightened self-interest and absolute moral behavior correspond perfectly. This point, too, Barlow incorporates into his polemical version of Enlightenment philosophy:

> Place society on [a moral] footing, and there will be no aid or duty that the general interest can require from individuals, but what every individual will understand. His duties, when first proposed, will all be voluntary, and being clearly understood to be founded on the good of the whole community, he will find a greater personal

interest in the performance than he would in the violation. (*Advice*)

Education, then, is the necessary and sufficient condition for a perfect society. One need only secure perfect individuals to secure a perfect society; to secure perfect individuals, one need only enlighten them.

The progressive supposition that people are in fact able to be enlightened stemmed from Locke's model of human understanding. According to Locke, each individual has the natural capacity, by means of reliable sensory impressions, to understand the truth. Reason is allied to the senses perfectly; what one perceives, the reason merely records as ideas or combines with other ideas into complex ideas. To enlighten individuals, therefore, one need only present them with information. Their senses and reason will do the rest.

If, however, reason and perception are so accurate in discerning the truth, socially aberrant behavior and governmental oppression should never exist. Locke explains the existence of such social evils in part in his observations on language. Words, according to Locke, often do not mirror the accuracy of the senses. Since words act as symbolic intermediaries between fact and vicarious perception of fact, words must be reduced to a one-to-one correspondence with the objects and ideas they represent in order for an enlightened person to educate an unenlightened person. Because sign and referent do not always correspond, language has been debased as a tool of understanding. Error in understanding in turn facilitates social and political evils.

While Barlow does agree that corrupt language is a significant source of social evil, he does not stress language as the primary source. If reason is merely an extension of any person's natural ability to perceive the truth, then debased language alone could not account for the persistence of prejudice and ignorance. After all, each individual has access to *a priori* truths via the incorruptible senses. Barlow on the contrary accepts the primarily romantic idea that reason can be estranged from truth by the forces of a corrupt society:

> [There] is a perpetual conflict between principle and precedent,—between the manly truths of nature, which we all must feel, and the learned subtilties of statesmen, about which we have been taught to reason. (*Convention*)

At first glance, the interposition of an active agent, society, between understanding and perception more plausibly explains the existence of evil than does the interposition of a passive tool, language. The logical problem remains, nevertheless, the same. How, if effects all require sufficient cause and if natural laws are ultimate causes, could humankind diverge from its nature? How, if individuals are innately good, could society corrupt them? Either the cause-and-effect reasoning is wrong, or the definition of human nature is insufficient. Barlow, rather than rejecting traditional metaphysics, found in the writings of the French skeptic philosopher Fontenelle a definition of human nature that would allow him to preserve the absolute truths of natural law without sacrificing his belief in the ultimate good of human beings:

> When a person was repeating to Fontenelle the common adage *l'abitude est la seconde nature,* the philosopher replied, *Et faites moi la grace de mire dire, quelle est la premiere.* . . . The *habit of thinking* has so much of nature in it, is so undistinguishable from the indelible marks of the man, that it is a perfectly safe foundation for any system that we may choose to build upon it; indeed it is the *only* foundation, for it is the only point of contact by which men communicate as moral associates. As a practical position, therefore, and as relating to almost all places and almost all times, in which the experiment has yet been made, Aristotle was as right in teaching *That some are born to command, and others to be commanded,* as the national assembly was in declaring, That *men are born and always continue free and equal in respect to their rights.* The latter is as apparently false in the diet of Ratisbon, as the former is in the hall of the Jacobins.

> Abstractly considered, there can be no doubt of the unchangeable truth of the assembly's declaration; and they have taken the right method to make it a *practical* truth, by publishing it to the world for discussion. A general belief *that it is a truth,* makes it at once practical, confirms it in one nation, and extends it to others. (*Advice*)

By interpreting Fontenelle's skepticism in Enlightenment terms, Barlow appears to define the problem of evil away. By equating habit with humankind's social "nature" and absolute truth with individual human "nature," Barlow salvages the innate goodness of each person at the same time he finds a sufficient cause for the corruption of that good. He explains corrupt individuals while he absolves individuals of responsibility for corruption. He embraces a skeptical belief in social relativity without giving up a belief in absolute truth, and finally, he explains the weakness of human reason without abandoning a belief in its ultimate powers to perceive this absolute "truth."

Interestingly, though, nature becomes not a force of harmony and order but one of "perpetual conflict between principle and precedent," between sides of human nature, and ultimately between human beings who reason by "habit" or "precedent" and those who reason by "principle" or "truth." This conflict is the center of Barlow's vision of progress; he sees human progress in a gradual resolution of this conflict between the two facets of human nature.

With nature in conflict with nature, Barlow's solution to the problems of unjust government would seem to be worse than the problem, but once again, Barlow drew eclectically on his intellectual tradition for solutions. Dialectic, at least as old as the fourth century BC, had by the 1790s found two new influential proponents who applied its principles to society at large. Barlow knew of and appreciated Adam Smith's economic model in which the independent competition of self-interested individuals would yield general social good. More importantly for his political philosophy, Barlow accepted Jefferson's belief that the free competition of individual interests, even if the

individuals were to express unenlightened self-interests, would yield not only a national will, a national consensus, but also an enlightened consensus:

> They say that mankind are wicked and rapacious, and "it must be that offences will come." This reasoning applies to individuals, and to countries when governed by individuals; but not to nations deliberately speaking a national voice. I hope I shall not be understood to mean, that the nature of man is totally changed by living in a free republic. I allow that it is still *interested* men and *passionate* men, that direct the affairs of the world. But in national assemblies, passion is lost in deliberation, and interest balances interest; till the good of the whole community combines the general will. (*Advice*)

Not only do interests negate one another to yield a balance, Barlow suggests, but the process of conflict in the proper arena yields rationality rather than passion and eventually results in a higher good. Using this model of conflict to describe the entirety of human experience, Barlow reconciles his explanation of evil with his belief in the possibility of human progress. Predicated on conflict between the two sides of human nature, Barlow's writings describe human nature, human society and human history in terms of progressive, synthetic improvements engendered by the competition of opposites.

Even though the fundamental conflict is based in the individual, the battle must first play itself out on a social, and therefore historical, level. Though in the abstract Barlow considers the perfect society to be composed of the compacted wills of responsible individuals, he finds this abstract ideal impossible to implement. Such a society would depend on each individual's perception of natural truth and on the congruence between natural truth and social organization. Since individuals are, however, born into existing societies, no individual can accommodate natural truth with social needs:

> The great out-lines of morality are extremely simple and easy to be understood; they may be said to be written on the heart of a man antecedent to his associating with his fellow-creatures. As a self-dependent being he is self-instructed; and as long as he should remain a simple child of *nature,* he would receive from nature all the lessons necessary to his condition. . . .

> Though society . . . be a state to which mankind naturally recur to satisfy their wants and increase the sum of their happiness—though all its laws and regulations may be perfectly reasonable, and calculated to promote the good of the whole—yet, with regard to an individual member, his having *consented* to these laws, or even chosen to live in the society, is but a *fiction. . . .* He first opens his eyes on that state of human affairs in which the interests of his moral associates are infinitely complicated . . . that nature can give him but little assistance in finding them out. His morality itself must be arbitrary. (*Advice*)

Though the human being has two natures, the deck is clearly stacked in favor of the social. If, furthermore, society wishes to stunt the individual's ability to perceive natural truths, it need only exercise its power. Since "every society, considered in itself as a moral and physical entity has the undoubted faculty of self-preservation . . . [and] a right to use this faculty" (*Advice*), each society will inevitably try to shape individuals to fit its truths, whether these truths correspond to natural truths or not. Thus, progress toward a perfect individual and thence a perfect society, progress toward abstract, natural truth, depends more on society than on the individual.

While this approach explains how natural man can stray from his instinctive virtue, it does not explain the divergence between social morality and natural morality. Barlow attempts to avoid this issue by developing a mythological progression from one state of divergence to another without explaining the origin. He postulates four ages of European society in which four separate myths supported a social morality divergent from natural morality:

> From the time when the predatory spirit, which led the northern Barbarians to ravage the south of Europe, had subsided, and given place to its natural offspring, in the establishment of feudal monarchy, the history of this quarter of the world begins to assume a consistent shape; and it offers itself to our contemplation, as relative to the spirit of nations, under three successive aspects. These are the spirit of Hierarchy, the spirit of Chivalry, and the spirit of Commerce. Out of these different materials the genius of the government has forged instruments of oppression almost equally destructive. It has never failed to cloud the minds of the nation with some kind of superstition, conformable to the temper of the times. In one age it is the superstition of religion, in another the superstition of honour, in another the superstition of public credit. (*Advice*)

All of these "spirits" of history force society away from a "state of nature," which Barlow rather strikingly defines not as primitive simplicity of social organization, but as people living off their own industry rather than off "plunder from abroad" (*Convention*). In all cases, the oppressive elements of society and the most oppressed are perverted by living apart from a state of nature. Their lack of contact with natural needs leads to an increasingly artificial form of society. With regard to commerce in particular, the "contracted meanness" (*Advice*) of commercial exploitation in contrast to the international needs of commerce and industry provides the conflict that will end exploitative social structures altogether:

> The spirit of commerce has brought us acquainted with those people [who our kings told us were our enemies and should be killed]; we find them to be like other men, and that they are really useful to us in supplying our wants. . . . But as commerce may deal in human slaughter as well as in other things, when ever the government will offer us more money for destroying our neighbors than we can get by other business, we are ready to make enemies of our best friends, and go to war, as we go to market, on a calculation of profit.

This is the true spirit of commerce as relative to

war. But as this spirit has made us better acquainted with all foreign nations, and with ourselves, it has excited a disposition for enquiry into the moral relation of men, with a view of political happiness. The result of this enquiry is now beginning to appear. It has already convinced us that there can be no possible case in which one nation can be the *natural* enemy of another; and this leads us to discover the cause why they have been *factitious* enemies. . . . The same spirit of enquiry is now leading the people to change the form of their governments, that society may be restored to its proper foundation. (*Advice*)

Thus, according to Barlow, the spirit of exploitation, by moving away from natural economic production while remaining dependent upon it, plants the seeds of its own destruction. Economic efficiency requires commerce, but commerce tends to undermine exploitation in that it exposes the natural fallacies of cultural myths. However, the very motive for commerce, i.e., exploitation, demands a purer, more "contracted" adherence to oppressive cultural myths. The very "spirit" that exposes the oppression of natural law by social law magnifies that oppression. Together, awareness of and degree of oppression yield revolution.

In suggesting that historical events are caused neither by personal intention nor by special providence but by spirits of history, Barlow takes his most daring step out of the realm of eighteenth-century metaphysics. True, the very fact that he could title a poem *The Conspiracy of Kings* after he wrote the first part of *Advice* suggests that Barlow did not entirely abandon his enlightened faith in a "presumed identity between cause and effect, between motive and deed." As Gordon Wood points out [in "Conspiracy and the Paranoid Style," *William and Mary Quarterly* 39 (1982)], this "presumed identity," on which Enlightenment ethics were based, made "conspiratorial explanations of complex events . . . normal, necessary, and rational." Yet Barlow did not insist on explaining events as the results of simple conspiracies; because of his belief in the practical moral relativity of habit, he found no need to blame individuals for social evils. Having assigned social evils to systems, he could develop a new "identity between cause and effect" that did not really require an identity between individual "motive and deed" but was instead based on the more complex causation of historical necessity and that included the possibility that intentions could have unintended consequences.

Barlow's understanding of history and progress generally supports middle-class revolution. To his mind, the general human needs for production and commerce maintain a conflict between the class that continues to practice industry and is therefore in touch with natural morality, and those that do not. This industrious class, namely the middle class, must battle hierarchical society in order to create republican government.

> The oppressors and the oppressed, of every denomination, are, in general, just as wicked and just as absurd as the system of government requires. In mercy to them all, let the system be

changed, let society be restored, and human nature retrieved.

> Those who compose the middle classes of mankind, the classes in which the semblance of nature most resides, are called upon to perform this task. (*Advice*)

Over the course of history, Barlow postulates, the industrious middle class has grown in prominence and importance, until, under the "spirit of commerce," it has finally discovered the natural truth that all men are of right equal and free. The conflict of opposites in a social rather than an individual context led to republican revolutions in both America and France. Revolution's perfection, however, depends on the degree of corruption of society and its consequent degree of oppression.

In the American revolution, the people have not rejected all European ideas of hierarchy and oppression because the initial oppression that led to revolution was not great enough to force the creation of a perfect society:

> The Americans cannot be said as yet to have formed a national character. The political part of their revolution, aside from the military, was not of that violent and convulsive nature that shakes the whole fabric of human opinions, and enables men to decide which are to be retained as congenial to their situation, and which should be rejected as the offspring of unnatural connections. (*Advice*)

Barlow implies that the French situation will require the political and social violence that the American situation did not, precisely because the French monarchy oppressed its subjects more than the British monarchy oppressed its American subjects. Even in the extreme French case, though, the creation of a perfectly republican society will not come quickly or in a single step. All social progress requires more than simple revolution; it requires a careful, multiple-step progression from habitual delusion to a perfect understanding of all natural truths:

> On considering the subject of government, when the mind is once set loose from the shackles of royalty, it finds itself in a new world. It rises to a more extensive view of every circumstance of the social state. Human nature assumes a new and more elevated shape, and displays many moral features, which, from having been always disguised, were not known to exist. In this case, it is a long time before we acquire a habit of tracing effects to their proper causes, and of applying the easy and simple remedy to those vices of our nature which society requires us to restrain. (*Convention*)

Barlow does not suggest that he can predict the future or know all "truth" because he, too, is trapped by habits of thought. Knowing this, he remains comfortable with speculation and frequent inconsistency.

In any event, he stresses the need to develop the *habit* of understanding natural law. Revolution fulfills its very purpose when it restores human society to a natural footing, when social and natural laws no longer diverge. Barlow thought, somewhat typically for a patriotic American of his religious background, in millennial terms; he looked forward to the end of history in both temporal and teleological terms when still a Calvinist, in only teleological terms thereafter. One expects, therefore, to find Barlow predicting a bourgeois utopia at the end of what he argues in *Advice* will be worldwide republican revolution.

While for the most part Barlow does imply that revolution will end with bourgeois republicanism, he willingly allows himself another inconsistency in occasionally suggesting that revolution may not end with the victory of the middle class. In the extreme, Barlow suggests that the unfolding reconciliation of social and natural laws through progressive revolution will dethrone property as well as political hierarchy, leaving (though he does not ever use the term) a socialistic society:

> The different portions of . . . society, that call themselves nations, have generally established the principle of securing to the individuals who compose a nation, the exclusive enjoyment of the fruits of their own labour; reserving however to the governing power the right to reclaim from time to time so much of the property and labour of individuals as shall be deemed necessary for the public service. This is the general basis on which *property*, public and private, has hitherto been founded. Nations have proceeded no farther. Perhaps in a more improved state of society, the time will come, when a different system may be introduced; when it shall be found more congenial to the social nature of man to exclude the idea of separate property, and with that the numerous evils which seem to be entailed upon it. (*Advice*)

Whether or not Barlow would finally have endorsed this most radical of his own projections, his consistent insistence on the power of habitual thought allows him to indulge himself in contradictory or at least incompatible speculations.

In summary, Barlow explained the existence of evil societies without abandoning a belief in the perfectibility of humankind by postulating a fundamental antithesis between two innate facets of human character, loosely identified as the natural and the social. As this antithesis develops through history, the moral demands of societies diverge from natural morality until they force a conflict between people who perceive and abhor the divergence and those who wish to perpetuate it on account of either interest or habit. The conflict yields a progressively better understanding of natural morality and in turn allows for syntheses of social forms that are progressively more congruent with natural morality.

Since he believed that natural truths battle social truths, that deductive reasoning is not necessarily congruent with empirical reasoning, that education is both the cause of evil and the tool to rectify evil, that private property will both help to cause the demise of monarchical oppression and will in turn be the next oppression to be overthrown, and that warfare is the evil of kings but necessary to overthrow kings, Barlow is not simply or unknowingly self-contradictory in his alternations. To him, opposites must balance or consume each other in order to yield truth.

Correlatively, people who wish to perfect themselves must willingly change their minds as social change unveils new truths.

In spite of the radical tendencies of much of his thought, Barlow's philosophies do not realize those radical potentials because he chose not to abandon his faith in Enlightenment rationalism. Ironically, while he insisted that the future would uncover new truths, he did not expect it to uncover new ways of seeing the truth. He expected progress to reveal natural laws more clearly so that it would be easier to trace "effects to their proper causes" (*Convention*), and he of course expected these causes to reflect the absolute morality of natural law, not the relative morality of social habit. Only when social habit diverges from natural law, only when natural morality is habitually "disguised," is it difficult to unravel the identity between intention and effect. Thus, to Barlow, unintended consequences of intended action will only develop when habit diverges from nature.

As Gordon Wood points out, many people, shocked by the violence of the French Revolution, began to question the Enlightenment belief in human perfectibility as well as the Enlightenment belief in the identity between intention and effect. These reactions, as well as fueling a conservative backlash against belief in human perfectibility, encouraged a Romantic interest in the psychology of motivation.

In developing his model of historical progress, Barlow certainly took part in this reaction, yet armed with his confidence in rationality and human perfectibility, he would not, at least in the early 1790s, take fright at the tumult and violence of either revolution he had witnessed. Rather than worry about the possibility of good intentions leading to evil results, as did Charles Brockden Brown by decade's end, the optimistic Barlow chose to insist that good results could come from self-interested, even evil intentions. In this application of Adam Smith's economics to the entirety of human endeavor, Barlow stands at the beginning of an American tradition of institutionalized individualism, a tradition that peculiarly vaunts individual action at the same time it ignores individual psychology, that vaunts individual virtue while attributing to individual morality no large-scale consequences. These confused implications of Barlow's thought, for their very longevity in American culture, are perhaps the most interesting "contradictions" of Barlow's prose.

FURTHER READING

Arner, Robert D. "The Connecticut Wits." In *American Literature 1764-1789: The Revolutionary Years,* edited by Everett Emerson, pp. 233-52. Madison: The University of Wisconsin Press, 1977.
> Concise overview of the works of the Wits. Arner concludes that, although their literary contributions have been by and large forgotten, "Barlow's democratic idealism and the dissenting voices raised by Trumbull and

Dwight are perhaps their most important legacies to us."

Boynton, Percy. "Timothy Dwight and His Connecticut." *Modern Philology* XXXVIII, No. 2 (November 1940): 193-203.
> Discusses Dwight's impressions of the state of Connecticut.

Boys, Richard C. "The Beginnings of the American Poetical Miscellany, 1714-1800." *American Literature: A Journal of Literary History, Criticism, and Bibliography* 17, No. 2 (May 1945): 127-39.
> Survey of miscellaneous colonial American poetry that includes mention of several of the Wits.

Briggs, Peter M. "English Satire and Connecticut Wit." *American Quarterly* 37, No. 1 (1985): 13-29.
> Analyses the humor of the Wits, especially John Trumbull, noting that he and "his fellow Wits seem to mark the stretching-thin of an older English tradition of satiric humor more clearly than they signal a new beginning for American satire."

Brooks, Van Wyck. "New England." In his *The World of Washington Irving,* pp. 44-65. New York: E.P. Dutton & Co., 1944.
> Views the period in which the Wits wrote as a kind of golden age in Connecticut culture.

Cronin, James E. "Elihu Hubbard Smith and the New York Friendly Club, 1795-1798." *PMLA* LXIV, No. 3, Part I (June 1949): 471-79.
> Explores Smith's club through his comments in his diary.

Ford, Arthur L. *Joel Barlow.* New York: Twayne Publishers, 1971, 144 p.
> Detailed survey of Barlow's life and works.

Gimmestad, Victor E. *John Trumbull.* New York: Twayne Publishers, 1974, 183 p.
> Biocritical overview.

Howard, Leon. "The Late Eighteenth Century: An Age of Contradictions." In *Transitions in American Literary History,* edited by Harry Hayden Clark, pp. 51-89. 1954. Reprint. New York: Octagon Books, 1967.
> Supplies context for the period of the Wits, characterizing the era as one "in which events were moving ahead of thought and the human mind was finding it unusually difficult to keep meditatively abreast with its practical activities."

Loschky, Helen. "The *Columbiad* Tradition: Joel Barlow and Others." *Books at Brown* XXI (1966): 197-206.
> Compares Barlow's two Columbus poems with similar verse by Richard Snowden and James Lovell Moore.

Silverman, Kenneth. *Timothy Dwight.* New York: Twayne Publishers, 1969, 174 p.
> Biocritical study that traces "Dwight's views on American society and his disenchantment with America."

Woodress, James. *A Yankee's Odyssey: The Life of Joel Barlow.* Philadelphia: J. B. Lippincott Co., 1958, 347 p.
> Biography of Barlow that contains detailed discussions of his literary and other careers.

The Familiar Essay

INTRODUCTION

During a period spanning the entire nineteenth century and the early decades of the twentieth, informal and discursive prose became a popular form of instruction and entertainment in England and North America, and the familiar or personal essay emerged as a distinct genre. Best represented by the works of William Hazlitt and Charles Lamb, the familiar essay has been explored from both historical and literary perspectives. Commentators examining the development of the essay have focused on its formal characteristics, the merits of its chief contributors, and its significance in world literature. The familiar essay is characterized by its brevity and discursive style. As the genre gained critical acceptance, attempts to arrive at a more functional definition of the essay proliferated, resulting in a division of essays into such categories as instructive, aphoristic, historical, literary, and familiar. Modern critics, however, have often found these classifications inaccurate, and many commentators agree that the term "essay," used indiscriminately for centuries in reference to philosophical, religious, political, and personal compositions, almost defies definition.

Sir Francis Bacon is generally credited with introducing and popularizing the essay in the English-speaking world. Influenced by the French essays of Michel de Montaigne, who first used the term "essais" (or "attempts") to describe his prose reflections on commonplace topics and occurrences, Bacon published *Essays, Religious Meditations, Places of Persuasion and Dissuasion* in 1597. For much of the seventeenth century, essay writing reflected Bacon's aphoristic style and incorporated elements of the commonplace book, the character sketch, and the personal letter. Thus, it gradually became less abstract and more familiar, appealing to a wider audience. The inception of the periodical magazine in the eighteenth century was instrumental to the development of the familiar essay. Joseph Addison and Sir Richard Steele's *Tatler* and *Spectator*, as well as Samuel Johnson's *Rambler* and Daniel Defoe's *Weekly Review of Affairs in France*, featured prose designed to entertain and instruct the English middle class. In addition to providing guidance in matters of wardrobe and proper behavior, Addison and Steele's periodical essays discuss such popular subjects as witchcraft and duelling, and satirize the aristocracy. Immensely popular during their time, the early periodical essayists are esteemed for introducing humor and less formal diction into the English essay. In the early nineteenth century, Hazlitt commented that the essays of Addison and Steele "are more like the remarks which occur in sensible conversation and less like a lecture. Something is left to the imagination of the reader."

The periodical essay was thus modified by Hazlitt, Lamb, Leigh Hunt, Thomas De Quincey, and other writers, many of them associated with the Romantic movement, who augmented the essay's scope and length, developing a highly personal voice. These writers produced some of the most popular and skillfully rendered prose works in English literature, addressing nearly any topic that came to mind. The typical familiar essay, whatever its theme, seemed to carry the reader into a personal conversation with a writer who was "tolerant, broad-minded, highly cultivated, endowed with the most enlightened views on art, eloquent, humorous, and very human," as Orlo Williams wrote of Hazlitt, adding, "his style is smooth and brilliant, yet he has the charm of seeming intimately conversational; he can soar on the wings of eloquence, yet his common sense is unimpeachable." Hazlitt is renowned for his familiar essays, such as "On Going a Journey," "Genius and Common Sense," and "Living to Oneself." Among the English familiar essayists Lamb is widely considered preeminent. His essays "Old China," "A Dissertation upon Roast Pig," and "All Fool's Day," are considered models of the nineteenth-century essay. In Britain, the familiar essay tradition was continued through the late nineteenth century and into the twentieth by Robert Louis Stevenson, Robert Lynd, G. K. Chesterton (author of "What I Found in My Pocket," "Dogs with Bad Names," and several hundred others), and Hilaire Belloc, who published such familiar essay collections as *On Everything* (1909), *On Anything* (1910), *On Nothing* (1908), and simply *On* (1923). In the United States, prominent writers of the familiar essay included Oliver Wendell Holmes, creator of the avuncular highly opinionated speaker who holds forth in *The Autocrat of the Breakfast Table* (1858) and two other such collections, as well as Washington Irving, Nathaniel Hawthorne, Walt Whitman, and Agnes Repplier, among others.

Writing of the familiar essay became less widely practiced in the early decades of the twentieth century, though the prolific Repplier, Chesterton, Belloc, and Lynd extended the genre well into the 1930s and early 1940s. Increasingly, commentators have cited the utilitarian, fast-paced modern world, with its increasing loss of leisure time for reading and reflection, the modern reader's preference for information rather than knowledge, and the dearth of magazines inclined to provide space for familiar discourses as among the key factors contributing to the familiar essay's decline. In addition, critics have noted the perception of the familiar essay as an old-fashioned holdover from bygone days.

REPRESENTATIVE WORKS

Charles Brockden Brown

96

The Rhapsodist and Other Uncollected Writings 1943
John Brown
  Horæ Subsecivæ. 3 vols. 1858-1882
John Burroughs
  Birds and Poets, with Other Papers 1895
Samuel Taylor Coleridge
  The Friend 1818
George William Curtis
  Prue & I 1892
Charles Dickens
  The Uncommercial Traveller 1860
Ralph Waldo Emerson
  Society and Solitude 1870
Nathaniel Hawthorne
  Twice-Told Tales 1837
  Mosses from an Old Manse 1846
William Hazlitt
  Table Talk; or, Original Essays on Men and Manners.
    2 vols. 1821-22
  The Spirit of the Age 1825
  Winterslow: Essays and Characters Written There 1850
Oliver Wendell Holmes
  The Autocrat of the Breakfast-Table 1858
  The Professor at the Breakfast-Table 1860
  The Poet at the Breakfast-Table 1872
Leigh Hunt
  The Seer. 2 vols. 1840-41
  Men, Women and Books 1847
  Table Talk 1851
Washington Irving
  *Salmagundi; or, The Whim-Whams and Opinions of
    Launcelot Langstaff, Esq., and Others.* 2 vols. [with
    others] 1807-08
  The Sketch Book of Geoffrey Crayon, Gent. 1820
Charles Lamb
  *Elia: Essays Which Have Appeared under That Signa-
    ture in the "London Magazine"* 1823
  The Last Essays of Elia 1833
Andrew Lang
  Essays in Little 1891
Donald Grant Mitchell
  Reveries of a Bachelor; or, A Book of the Heart 1850
  Dream Life: A Fable of the Seasons 1852
Agnes Repplier
  Essays in Idleness 1893
  In the Dozy Hours 1894
Henry Dwight Sedgwick
  An Apology for Old Maids, and Other Essays 1916
Robert Louis Stevenson
  Virginibus Puerisque, and Other Papers 1881
  Memories and Portraits 1887
  Across the Plains 1892
William Makepeace Thackeray
  The Proser 1850
  Roundabout Papers 1863
Henry David Thoreau
  Excursions 1893
Henry T. Tuckerman
  Leaves from the Diary of a Dreamer 1853
Charles Dudley Warner
  My Summer in a Garden 1871
Walt Whitman

Speciman Days and Collect. 2 vols. 1882-83
Nathaniel P. Willis
  Pencillings by the Way 1835

DEFINITIONS AND ORIGINS

Elizabeth Drew

SOURCE: "The Essay," in *The Enjoyment of Literature,* W. W. Norton & Company, Inc., 1935, pp. 38-61.

[*In the following excerpt, Drew traces the development of the familiar essay from Montaigne and Bacon through the periodical essayists of the eighteenth century and on to the era of Robert Louis Stevenson.*]

The essay is the simplest of all forms of literature, but with it we enter that world where we shall remain throughout the rest of this book, the world of the conscious art of writing. From the lowest to the highest, from the simplest to the most complex kinds of literature, we shall find henceforth that the enjoyment of it is always twofold. There is the pleasure we receive from the conscious stimulus of certain recognizable parts of our being: to our curiosity about the stories and situations of other human beings, to our emotions, to our intellectual faculties, to our moral nature, to our senses. The pleasure of sharing the adventures of Robinson Crusoe, of meeting Elizabeth Bennet, of being stirred by Milton or enraptured by the sheer music of *The Eve of St. Agnes.* Here we know clearly what it is that pleases us; we recognize both the cause and the effect of the sense of satisfaction. But in the other kind of pleasure which literature creates, we are clearly conscious only of its effect. Form works upon the consciousness as a whole; it stimulates the consciousness as a whole; it satisfies it as a whole. If it is there, the sensitive reader recognizes it at once without analysis: the whole thing is 'right,' and the reason of its rightness is not questioned. But if perfection of form is absent, if the thing is 'wrong,' the reader is conscious that something vital is lacking. Detached faculties may still receive pleasure, human curiosity may be provoked, the mind quickened, the senses stirred, but that fusion of all faculties into one general sense of satisfaction in which the whole man is involved, is not there. Just as in a ballet the individual movements may be supple, the individual poses superb, the individual dexterity amazing, the décor perfect, but if the whole has not been bound together, fused, unified by one general spirit of rhythm, the harmony is not complete. What distinguishes the real artist from the amateur, says Goethe, is that power of execution which creates, forms and constitutes the whole.

What is an essay? It is impossible not to agree with J. B. Priestley that the simplest and safest definition of the essay is that it is the kind of composition produced by an essayist. The term is indeed so wide that it is meaningless. If we try to bring Locke's *Essay on the Human Understanding* and Lamb on "Old China" within the limits of a single definition it obviously cannot be done. The essay may be a dissertation, a piece of rhetoric, an argument, a discussion. It may deal with a religious, economic, historical, sociological, scientific or philosophical subject, or any other kind of subject. But it is clear that there is something very much narrower in definition which we really mean when we speak of the essay in any general discussion of literature. We mean a form of writing which aims definitely at certain *literary* values: that is, it aims at using language as a medium to present life in a way of its own.

> Of all forms of literature, the essay is the one which least calls for the use of long words. The principle which controls it is simply that it should give pleasure; the desire which impels us when we take it from the shelf is simply to receive pleasure. Everything in an essay must be subdued to that end. It should lay us under a spell with its first word, and we should only wake refreshed with its last. In the interval we may pass through the most varied experiences of amusement, surprise, interest, indignation . . . but we must never be roused. The essay must lap us about and draw its curtain across the world.

'So great a feat is seldom accomplished,' Virginia Woolf continues, 'though the fault may well be as much on the reader's side as on the writer's. Habit and lethargy have dulled his palate.' This may be so, and yet, if the truth must be told, the reader has a good deal of excuse, for as a student he has generally been surfeited with essays, and unless the essay is superlatively good it is the dullest form of all reading. A soliloquy is a most difficult form to sustain, and the essay is all soliloquy. The essayist has so few baits with which to catch and hold the reader's attention. He has no story to arouse his curiosity and no rhyme to charm his ear: his space is so limited that he has but little room for movement, for changes of tone and pace. He cannot afford to make any mistakes. If he write tediously or carelessly or foolishly, the essay at once capsizes and sinks; the pleasure cruise is at an end, the reader is bored.

It is because of this razor edge between charm and boredom which so many essays balance on, that we might quarrel with Virginia Woolf's declaration that the essay should never arouse us, and declare instead that on occasions it does and should. Perhaps this is only true if we admit oratory and rhetoric into essay-writing, but if speeches be written to be read as well as to be heard, it is difficult to see how they can be excluded from this whole class of writings. Burke's speeches are superb essays, and so is Milton's *Areopagitica,* that great plea for the liberty of speech which, indeed, for the delight of direct intellectual and emotional and moral stimulus, in some of the most supple and sonorous cadences in the English language, remains unsurpassed. If I were to choose one sentence in the English language which is to myself the most kindling in its passion, and its idea and its expression, it would be one from the *Areopagitica.*

> I cannot praise a fugitive and cloister'd virtue, unexercis'd and unbreath'd, that never sallies out and sees her adversary, but slinks out of the race, where that immortal garland is to be run for, not without dust and heat.

The quality of that is the quality of the whole, and as a fur-

ther taste of it, I quote the famous passage on the life of books.

> I deny not, but that it is of greatest concernment in the Church and Commonwealth, to have a vigilant eye how Books demean themselves as well as men; and thereafter to confine, imprison, and do sharpest justice on them as malefactors: For Books are not absolutely dead things, but do contain a potency of life in them to be as active as that soul was whose progeny they are; nay, they do preserve as in a vial the purest efficacy and extraction of that living intellect that bred them. I know they are as lively, and as vigorously productive, as those fabulous Dragon's teeth; and being sown up and down, may chance to spring up armed men. And yet on the other hand, unless wariness be us'd, as good almost kill a Man as kill a good Book; who kills a Man kills a reasonable creature, God's Image; but he who destroys a good Book, kills reason itself, kills the Image of God, as it were in the eye. Many a man lives a burden to the Earth; but a good book is the precious life-blood of a master spirit, embalm'd and treasur'd up on purpose to a life beyond life.

It is true, however, that the class of writings which we usually mean when we speak of essays, does not have the rousing and animating quality of Burke or Milton. Its aim is much milder, its achievement quite different. The supreme art of the essay proper, that special type of writing which was originated and invented by Montaigne, and dates from the first publication of his *Essais* in March, 1571, is *to communicate personality.* The essay (the word was used by Montaigne simply to denote experiments in a new form of writing), is the most direct form of prose communication between author and reader: it is deliberate egotism and self-revelation. Montaigne wrote the epigraph for all essayists, 'these are fancies of my own, by which I do not pretend to discover things, but to lay open myself.' As Lamb said of him, 'his own character pervades the whole, and binds it sweetly together,' and it is significant that Coleridge said of Lamb himself, 'Charles Lamb has more totality and individuality of character than any other man I know.'

That is the character the perfect essayist requires. He says with Sir Thomas Browne: 'the world that I regard is myself; it is the microcosm of my own frame that I cast my eye on. For the other I use it but like my globe, and turn it round sometimes for my recreation.' The novelist or the dramatist requires to be detached from his own personality. He may be David Copperfield or Jane Eyre or Hamlet, but he must also be Dick Swiveller or Paul Emmuanuel or Lady Macbeth. But the essayist must never be more than one character. The personality with which he writes may not be entirely his own, but it must be a complete personality. Elia is not the whole of Charles Lamb, nor the Spectator the whole of Joseph Addison, but they are each a completely recognizable person. We can walk round them and feel we know them in the most actual and tangible way. And we must have this sense of intimacy with the essay-writer, it is the essential of his peculiar and difficult art. He must always be the same person, and we must never be out of his company. Whatever other personality or situation or circumstance he presents, whatever book or picture or actor he is discussing, he is at pains to remind us all the time that it is his vision of them we are sharing. The main interest is always shifted subtly from the subject of the essay, to the kind of mind and being—the personality—which is writing of that subject. Creative egotism is the secret of the essayist, an egotism which appears, in the hands of an artist, as if it were the most simple and natural thing in the world, while in reality it is never successful unless it is presented with supreme skill. Just as his subject matter appears desultory and meandering, and is really the most carefully conceived and constructed of unities.

Alexander Smith, a minor writer of the mid-nineteenth century, who wrote a good essay, "On the writing of essays," in a volume called *Dreamthorpe,* says that the essay resembles the lyric in that both are molded by some central mood, whimsical, serious or satirical. 'Give the mood, and the essay, from the first sentence to the last, grows round it as a cocoon grows round the silk-worm.' This is a good image of the essayist's art, and is a better starting point for the illustrating of essays than a mere history of the subject. But a few chronological landmarks are perhaps helpful.

Montaigne died in 1592, and the first ten of Bacon's essays appeared in print five years later, and were the first essays to be published in England. He increased the number to thirty-eight in the edition of 1612, and to fifty-eight in the final edition of 1625. But although Bacon must have taken the idea of the essay from Montaigne, nothing could be more different than the 'moods' from which each of the two spins his thread. Montaigne must always remain the perfect example of the essayist temperament—sympathetic, humorous, unexpected, lovable, passionately curious in his search after psychological truth—while Bacon takes this new instrument for writing of the world as it is seen through the eyes of a temperament, and manages to turn it into something completely inhuman. Montaigne is a warm flesh and blood figure, sitting at ease at his study writing-table underneath the beam on which is carved *I do not understand; I pause; I examine.* Bacon is a chilly statue of Wisdom, commenting on human life in the manner of a great judge in his robes and ermine, with the greatest brilliance and the greatest detachment. The subject is always perfectly planned and presented, but it is all entirely external and general. It has all been thought, never felt. . . .

It was not until Cowley's essays were published in 1668 that the tone of Montaigne crept into the English essay. Cowley's talent is a small one, his personality is not interesting or varied enough to bear very much exploitation of it: the vein is very soon worked out, but what there is of it is gold. In his essay "Of Myself" there is the true flavor—that intimacy and warmth of spirit, that fresh simplicity and apparent artlessness. It creates its own charm as it flows along: it is nothing, and yet it is delightful. . . .

Some of the essays of Sir William Temple (Dorothy Osborne's husband) have this same note, but it was the coming of the periodical newspaper which really established the essay in popularity. It created a market for it, which it has never lost, so that it was not only aristocratic dilet-

tantes who could afford to practise it; and it developed that easy, friendly manner which comes from the essayist's sense that he is writing for a familiar circle of readers who are in sympathy with him. It also encouraged the essayist to write on the subjects which make the best essays—incidents of daily life about him, the immediate, the personal, the tangible, not the abstract and indefinite. On April 12th, 1709, the first number of the *Tatler,* one little folded sheet of paper, appeared at the breakfast tables of the aristocracy and in the coffee-houses of the town, and from then onwards the eighteenth century was deluged with essays. To our modern taste, the majority of these essays are completely unreadable, except in small extracts, and indeed, the capacity of the reading public of the eighteenth century for swallowing pills in jam is one of the most surprising things about it. Why, with the example of that century before us, we continue to regard the Victorian age as the great age of moral lessons in literature, is a mystery. We are apt to think of the eighteenth century as a gay and wicked age, though it is difficult to know why. Perhaps because its greatest writers were satirists and its novelists much concerned about the sexual impulse in young men and the consequent danger of young women losing their virtue. But at no time did the daily and weekly reading of the majority concern itself so much with the moral conduct of life as it did in the eighteenth century. . . . The essay became the vehicle of platitude rather than of experience: the essayists will not let themselves be themselves because they are all so busy feeling they must be the Censor. And as a result, though it would be easy to make an anthology of first-rate passages from the eighteenth-century essayists, it is not surprising that the heart of the average student sinks when he is told that if he wants to write good prose he must give his days and nights to the study of Addison. Addison is a very dull writer, and the volumes of the *Tatler* and the *Spectator* are dull volumes, and there are many equally good writers of prose.

And yet it is not really because the eighteenth century is so concerned about problems of conduct that it is dull: it is because of the *way* in which the writers treat of them. We are all, as a matter of fact, interested in ethical questions and in reading about them, but we are not interested in having a purely conventional and general code of social and personal morality applied to every subject. It is that which stifles the individuality which is the breath of life to the essayist. Dr. Johnson's opinion of Addison fits many more than Addison: 'he thinks justly, but he thinks faintly.' There is nothing vigorous, energetic or personal in the moral values of these men. If, however, moral feeling be an essential part of the mood in which the essay is conceived—instead of being merely tacked on as an adjunct—it becomes an essential part of its total quality and effect, and we would not wish it otherwise. Ethical feeling can lap us round as securely as any other mood.

It is no longer the fashion now to read Robert Louis Stevenson. His vogue during his life and immediately after his early death was so great and glowing that a reaction was bound to set in. But his popularity will inevitably return. He was a second-rate novelist, for his creative gift was never substantial enough to write great novels, but he is a first-rate essayist. And the mood of all, or almost all, of his essays is an ethical one; he spins its thread around some problem of conduct or some tenet of his own individual faith. Stevenson had to struggle all his life with an incurable disease: he did his work unflinchingly against appalling odds. But the strange thing about his extraordinarily vivid personality was that it produced an attitude to life which, instead of being one of splendid stoical endurance of suffering, managed to be one of positive exhilaration. He justifies life because it is a battle: he loves positive values as much as Milton: 'To avoid an occasion for our virtues is a worse degree of failure than to push forward pluckily and make a fall.' It is only over-prudence and timidity which he finds paralyzing: 'There are some to whom never to forget their umbrella in a long life, is a higher and wiser achievement than to go smiling to the stake.' 'Youthful enthusiasm may be foolish, but it is better to be a fool than to be dead.'

> Whether we regard life as a lane leading to a dead wall, or whether we think of it as a vestibule or gymnasium, where we wait our turn and prepare our faculties for some more noble destiny; . . . whether we look justly for years of health and vigour, or are about to mount into a bath chair as a step towards the hearse; in each and all of these views and situations there is but one conclusion possible: that a man should stop his ears against paralysing terror, and run the race which is set before him with a single mind. . . . As courage and intelligence are the two qualities best worth a good man's cultivation, so it is the first part of intelligence to recognise our precarious state in life, and the first part of courage to be not at all abashed before the fact. A frank and somewhat headlong carriage, not looking too anxiously before, not dallying in maudlin regret over the past, stamps the man who is well armoured for this world.

Here we are very far removed from the bony conventional morality of the eighteenth century. We are in the company of a clear-cut, witty, courageous, sensitive personality, and we are in the presence of an artist in prose. Stevenson's confession that he learned his craft by playing 'the sedulous ape' to other writers has sometimes been taken to mean that his own use of language always remains imitative. Nothing is more untrue. His early work is inclined to be a little thin and mannered and over-ornamented, but his later essays—such essays as "Pulvis et Umbra," "The Lantern Bearers" or the once famous "A Christmas Sermon"—are the work of a complete and warmly-colored personality, communicating itself in a forthright, strong and warmly-colored prose. They lay us under a spell with the first word, and we wake refreshed with the last.

The moods in which the problems of human conduct are of supreme importance can therefore be the basis of the essayist's art as much as any other moods. But it is true that they very seldom do make thoroughly successful essays. If a personality is passionately concerned with such questions, it is ten to one that his calling will not be that of an essayist; he will be expressing his personality in some more immediately practical way. We may safely say that but for the accident of ill-health Stevenson would not have

been content to write essays. The essay which the man of such a temperament writes is seldom as we say 'pure literature.' It has an ulterior aim: it seeks to convert or persuade, to argue, to discuss, to analyze, to explain. It goes over into history or politics or criticism, like Macaulay or Carlyle or Arnold. But the pure essayist, as Virginia Woolf says, seeks only to give pleasure, and we read him with no ulterior aim ourselves. His own occupations and his own acquaintance are his subject matter, and we ask for nothing of more public or general importance.

Richard Burton

SOURCE: "The Essay as Mood and Form," in *Forces in Fiction, and Other Essays,* The Bowen-Merrill Company, 1902, pp. 85-99.

[*In the following essay, Burton surveys the history of the essay, tracing elements that contributed to the present form and focussing on the nineteenth-century familiar essayists of Britain and the United States.*]

It is odd that while the essay as a distinctive form in modern literature is so well cherished and enjoyable, it has received so little of expert attention. Books upon the drama, upon poetry in its many phases, upon the novel even—a thing comparatively of but yesterday—are as leaves on Vallombrosa for number; but books on the essay—where are they? It is high time the natural history of the essay was written, for here is a fascinating literary development which has had a vigorous, distinguished life of more than three hundred years in English and which counts among its cultivators some of the abiding names in our native literature. Here is a form, too, interesting because of its inter-filiations with such other forms as fiction which is connected with it by the bridge of the character-sketch; drama, whose dialogue the essay not seldom uses; and such later practical offshoots as the newspaper editorial and the book review.

This neglect of the essay is not altogether inexplicable. Scholars have been shy of it, I fancy, in part at least, because on the side of form (the natural and proper side to consider in studying the historical evolution of a literary genre) it has been thus fluent and expansive: a somewhat subtle, elusive thing. We can say, obviously, that an essay is a prose composition, but can we be more explicit than this rather gross mark of identification? The answer is not so easy. Moreover, the question has become further confused by a change in the use and meaning of the word within a century. A cursory glance at the history of the English essay will make this plain.

Lord Bacon was, by his own statement, fond of that passed master of the essay in French, Montaigne. It is small wonder then that, when at the end of the sixteenth century he put a name to his "dispersed meditations," he called them essays, after the Frenchman, using the word for the first time in our tongue. Not the name only but the thing was new. The form was slight, the expression pregnant and epigrammatic; there was no attempt at completeness. The aim of this early prince of essayists was to be suggestive rather than exhaustive—the latter a term too often synonymous with exhausting. Bacon's essays imply expanded note-book jottings; indeed, he so regarded them. In the matter of style, one has but to read contemporaries like Sidney, Lyly and Hooker, to see to what an extent Lord Bacon modernized the cumbersome, though often cloudily splendid, Elizabethan manner. He clarified and simplified the prevailing diction, using shorter words and crisper sentences with the result of closer knit, more sententious effect. In a word, Style became more idiomatic, and the relation of author and reader more intimate in the hands of this Elizabethan essay-maker. The point is full of significance for the history of this alluring form; its development ever since has been from this initiative. Slight, casual, rambling, confidential in tone, the manner much, the theme unimportant in itself, a mood to be vented rather than a thought to add to the sum of human knowledge; the frank revelation of a personality—such have been and are the head marks of the essay down to the present day. This fact is somewhat obscured by our careless use of the word at present to denote the formal paper, the treatise: the current definition of the essay admits this extension, and of course we bandy the word about in such meaning. But it is well to remember that the central idea of this form is what removes it forever from the treatise, from any piece of writing that is formal, impersonal and communicative of information. Little was done for the development of the essay, after Bacon, during the seventeenth century. But with Addison, Steele and the *Spectator* in the early eighteenth, the idea is reinforced and some of the essential features of this form brought the more clearly out. The social, chatty quality of the true essayist is emphasized; the writer enters into more confidential relations with his reader than ever he did with the stately Verulam; and the style approaches more nearly to the careless, easy elegance of the talk of good, but not stiff society. The *Spectator* papers unquestionably did more to shape the mold of essay writing in English than any other influence; at the same time, to speak as if Mr. Bickerstaff originated the form (as some critics do), is to overlook its origin with Bacon. The essay idea—this colloquial, dramatic, esoteric, altogether charming sort of screed, was cultivated quite steadily through the eighteenth century. It became, as a rule, more ponderous in the hands of Johnson and was in danger of taking on a didactic, hortatory tone foreign to its nature; yet occasionally in the *Rambler* papers, Johnson takes on a lightness of touch and tone that is surprising and suggests that we have perhaps regarded the dictator as too exclusively a wielder of sesquipedalian words. That this God of the Coffee House had a clear and correct idea of the essay is shown by his own description of it: "A loose sally of the mind," he says, "an irregular, indigested piece, not a regular and orderly performance."

Goldsmith, a light-horse soldier in contrast with Johnson, full panoplied and armed cap-a-pie, broadened the essay for literary and social discussion, although Grub Street necessity led him at times to become encyclopedic; and he was never happier than when, as in "The Revery at the Boar's Head" he played upon some whimsical theme, pizzicato, surcharging it with his genial personality. Minor writers, too, in the late eighteenth century had a hand in the development; none more so, to my mind, than the letter and fiction makers, Chesterfield and Walpole, Lady Mary Wortley Montagu and Fanny Burney—these and

that inimitable fuss and chronicler, Boswell. If one would know how society talked in the second half of that Tea Cup century, one must read—not the dialogue of the novelists where the art is too new to have caught quite the accent of life, but these off-hand epistles dashed off without a thought of print—to print were half way vulgar then—and hence possessing all the freshness and naturalness of life itself,—the ideal essay note. We may be thankful that as yet the habit of publishing everything, from one's thrills to one's table tastes, had not gained popularity,—those ladies and gentlemen could afford to be charmingly unreserved in their private correspondence. To-day in the very act of penning a note, intrudes the horrid thought that it may be incorporated as an integral part of one's "works."

The Letter, as a literary form, offers an interesting line of side inquiry in connection with the essay; it has influenced that form beyond doubt, is in a sense contributory to it. In the same way dialogue—a modern instance like Landor comes to mind—has had its share in shaping so protean a form.

But it was reserved for the nineteenth century to contribute in the person of Charles Lamb the most brilliant exemplar of the essay, prince of this special literary mood; not primarily a thinker, a knowledge-bringer, a critic, but just a unique personality expressing his ego in his own fascinating way, making the past pay rich toll, yet always himself; and finding the essay accommodative of his whimsical vagaries, his delicious inconsistencies, his deep-toned, lovable nature. And that incomparable manner of his! 'Tis at once richly complex and tremulously simple; an instrument of wide range from out whose keys a soul vibrant to the full meaning of humanity might call spirits of earth and heaven in exquisite evocations and cadences at times almost too piercing sweet. Turn to the Elia papers and see how perfectly this magic of Lamb's illustrates and supports the qualities of mood and form I am naming as typical of the essay as an historic growth. The themes, how desultory, audacious, trivial, even grotesque. The only possible justification for a dissertation on roast pig is the paper itself. Note, too, how brief some of the choicest essays are; half a dozen small pages, even less; and with what seeming carelessness they vary, stretching themselves at will to four times their normal length. Study the construction of any famous essay to see if it can be called close-knit, organic, and you shall find a lovely disregard of any such intention. The immortal Mrs. Battle on whist gives a capital example. If you turn to the end of that inimitable deliverance, you will find it to contain one of the most charming digressions in all literature. Lamb leaves that delicious old gentlewoman for a moment to speak of Cousin Bridget, Bridget Elia, the tragic sister Mary of his house, and playfully, tenderly, picturing their game at cards, forgets all else and never returns to Mrs. Battle. But who cares? Is not lack of organic connection (to call it by so harsh a name) more than justified by that homely-heartful picture of Charles and Mary Lamb, bent over their "mere shade of play,"—a game not for shillings but for fun—nay, for love. "Bridget and I should be ever playing," says he, and the reader is charmed and stirred clean out of all thought of Mrs. Battle. It is ever so with your essayist to the manner born! to wander and digress is with him a natural right. He is never happier than when he is playing mad pranks with logic, respectability and the mother tongue. Yet should his temperament be sensitive, his nature broad, deep and noble. The querulous-gentle Elia was surely of this race.

To turn from Lamb to any contemporary is an effect of anticlimax. None other was like to him for quality. Yet Hazlitt and Hunt were his helpers, doing good work in extending the gamut of this esoteric mood in literature. De Quincey, too, though losing the essay touch again and again because of didacticism and a sort of formal, stately eloquence, wrote papers in the true tradition of the essayist. Passages in the *Opium Eater* are of this peculiar tone and that great writer's intense subjectivity is always in his favor—since the genuine essay-maker must be frankly an egoist. Hunt is at times so charming, so light of touch, so atmospheric in quality that he deserves to be set high among essayists of the early century. A man who could produce such delicately graceful vignette work as his sketches of the Old Lady and the Old Gentleman, was a true commensal of Lamb. In such bits of writing the mood and manner are everything, the theme is naught; the man back of the theme is as important in the production of the essay as is the man back of the gun in warfare. Herein lies Hunt's chief claim on our grateful remembrance—here, and in certain of his verses, rather than in the more elaborate papers to be found in such a volume as *Fancy and Imagination*.

But already we must begin to recognize in writers like Hunt, Hazlitt and DeQuincy, and still more in latter men, a tendency distinctly modern and on the whole antagonistic to the peculiar virtues of the esoteric essay, the *causerie* of literature. It is moving fast toward the objective, rounded out, formally arranged treatise. It becomes argumentative, critical, acquisitive, logical, expository, laden with thought. Hence when we reach masters like Ruskin, Carlyle, Arnold, we see what is natural to them as essayists in one sense deflected into other (and no doubt quite as welcome) forms; one and all, they have messages, and missions. Now your bona fide essayist has nothing of the kind; he would simply button-hole you for a half hour while he talks garrulously, without a thought of purpose, about the world—and himself—especially the latter. Splendid blooms grow from out the soil which gives us our Ruskins and Carlyles; but when we are considering this sensitive plant of the literary garden, the essay, it were well to agree that it is another thing, and to save for its designation the word essay. Nor is this to deny essay touches, essay moments, essay qualities to Ruskin or Carlyle; it is only to make the point that their strenuous aim and habitual manner, so far as they went, were against the production of a very different kind of literature.

Earlier American literature has at least supplied one real essayist to the general body of English literature,—the genial Irving, who was nurtured on the best eighteenth century models and carried on the tradition of the *Spectator* and Goldsmith in papers which have just the desired tone of genteel talk, the air of good society. There are hints in Benjamin Franklin that had politics not engulfed him, as they afterward did Lowell, he might have shown himself

to the essay born. Irving is sometimes spoken of as a fictionist, but all his stories have the essay mood and manner; and he had the good sense practically never to abandon that gentle genre. His work always possesses the essay touch both in description and in the hitting off of character, thus offering an illustration of the fact that the essay, by way of the character sketch, debouches upon the broad and beaten highway of the novel,—the main road of our modern literature. There are plenty of Irving's papers which it is rather puzzling to name as essay or fiction; "The Fat Gentleman," for example. A later and very true American essayist, Dr. Holmes, furnishes the same puzzle in the Autocrat series: they have dialogue, dramatic characterization, even some slight story interest. Why not fiction then? Because the trail of the genuine essayist is everywhere; the characters, the dramatic setting, are but devices for the freer expression of Dr. Holmes's own delightful personality, which, as Mr. Howells testifies, Holmes liked to objectify. It is our intimate relation with him that we care about in converse with the essayist born; we sit down to enjoy his views. The fictionist's purpose, contrariwise, is to show life in a representative section of it and with dramatic interplay of personalities moving to a certain crescendo of interest called the climax.

And so Dr. Holmes remains one of our most distinctive and acceptable essayists of the social sort—possessing, I mean, that gift, perhaps best seen with the French, of making vivid one's sense of one's relation to other men and women in the social organism. It is the triumph of this kind of essay to be at once individualistic and social; without eccentricity, on the one hand, or vulgarity, on the other. Vulgarity, by the way, is a quality impossible to the heaven-called essayist; it can be better tolerated in poetry even. For the intimacy between the essayist and his reader (I say reader rather than audience with a feeling that the relation is a sort of solitude *à deux*) is greater than in the case of any other form of literary expression; hence, when one enters, as it were, the inner rooms of a friend's house, any hint of the *borné* is the more quickly detected, the more surely insufferable.

The voice of a natural essayist like Thoreau is somewhat muffled by being forced now and then into the public pulpit manner. Yet an essay-writer by instinct he certainly is; particularly in his journal, but often in the more formal chroniclings of his unique contact with nature. In Emerson, too, we encounter a writer with a vocation for the essay, but having other fish to fry,—doubtless a loftier aim but a different. No man, English or American, has a literary manner which makes the essay an inspired chat more than the Concord sage-singer; and the inspired chat comes close to being the beau ideal of your true-blue essayist. With less strenuousness of purpose and just a bit more of human frailty—or at least sympathy with the frail,—here were indeed a prince in this kind!

How much of the allurement of the essay style did Lowell keep, however scholarlike his quest, in papers literary, historical, even philological! In a veritable essay-subject like "On a Certain Condescension in Foreigners," he displays himself as of the right line of descent from Montaigne; there is in him then all that unforced, winsome, intimate, yet ever restrained revelation of self which is the essayist's model, and despair. In the love letters of the Brownings may be found some strictures by both Robert and Elizabeth upon an early book of this great American's which must pain the admirer of the Brownings as well as of Lowell. It displays a curious insensitiveness to just this power of the Cambridge man which made him of so much more value to the world than if he had been scholar and nothing more. One can hardly rise from anything like a complete examination of Lowell's prose without the regret that his fate did not lead him to cultivate more assiduously and single-eyed, this rare and precious gift for essay—a gift shared with very few fellow Americans.

A glance among later Victorian prose writers must convince the thoughtful that the essay in our special sense is gradually written less; that as information comes in at the door, the happy giving-forth of personality flies out at the window. It is in shy men like Alexander Smith or Richard Jefferies that we come on what we are looking for, in such as they, rather than the more noisily famed. Plenty of charming prosists in these latter days have been deflected by utility or emolument away from the essay; into criticism, like Lang and Gosse and Dobson and Pater; into preaching and play-making, like Bernard Shaw; into journalism like Barry Pain and Quiller-Couch; into a sort of forced union of poetry and fiction, as with Richard Le Gallienne. All of these, too, and others still have been touched by fiction for better or worse.

The younger Americans with potential essay ability are also for the most part swallowed up in more practical, "useful" ways of composition. Her old-fashioned devotion to the elder idea of the essay makes a writer like Miss Repplier stand out with a good deal of distinction, so few of her generation are willing or able to do likewise. There is no magazine in America to-day, with the honorable exception of *The Atlantic,* which desires from contributors essays that look back to the finer tradition. Mr. Howells has reached a position of such authority in American letters that what he produces in the essay manner is welcome—not because it is essay, but because it is he. His undeniable gift for the form is therefore all the better; often he strikes a gait happily reminiscent of what the essay in its traditions really is; the delightfully frank egoism of his manner covering genuine simplicity and modesty of nature. Since *Venetian Days* he has never ceased to be an essayist.

The twin dangers with the younger essayists of both the United States and England are didacticism and preciosity. The former I believe most prevalent in this country; and it is of course the death blow of the true essay. The danger of being too precious may be overcome with years: Max Beerbohm, for example, began by thinking and talking of himself, not for the reader's sake, but for self-love's sake. But of late he seems better to comprehend the essayist's proper subjectivity. We should not despair of essayists: no type of writer is rarer; the planets must conspire to make him; he must not be overwhelmed by life and drawn into other modes of expression.

Our generation has been lucky to possess one English essayist who has maintained and handed on the great tradition. I mean Stevenson. Although, in view of the extent

and vogue of his novels and tales, Stevenson's essay work may seem almost an aside, it really is most significant. He is in the line of Charles Lamb. Where a man like Pater writes with elegance and suggestion after the manner of the suave and thoroughly equipped critic, Stevenson does a vastly higher thing; he talks ruddily, with infinite grace, humor, pathos and happiness, about the largest of all themes,—human nature. From "Ordered South" to "Pulvis et Umbra," through many a gay mood of smile and sunshine to the very deeps of life's weltering sea, Stevenson runs the gamut of fancy and emotion, the fantasticality of his themes being in itself the sign manual of a true essayist. In the Letters no man using English speech has chatted more unreservedly, and with more essential charm; it is the undress of literature that always instinctively stops this side of etiquette, of decency. The Stevenson epistles drive us on a still-hunt outside of the mother-tongue for their equal, with little prospect of quarry save within French borders.

The essay is thus a literary creature to the making of which go mood and form—and the former would seem by far the paramount thing. Great and special gifts does it demand. 'Tis an Ariel among literary kinds, shy, airy, tricksy, elusive, vanishing in the garish light that beats down upon the arena where the big prizes of fiction are competed for amidst noise, confusion and éclat. But ever in its own slight, winsome way does it compel attention and gain hearts for its very own. 'Tis an aristocrat of letters; nowhere is it so hard to hide obvious antecedents. Many try, but few triumph in it. Therefore, when a real essayist arrives, let him be received with due acclaim and thanks special, since through him is handed on so ancient and honorable a form.

William Frank Bryan and Ronald S. Crane

SOURCE: An introduction to *The English Familiar Essay: Representative Texts,* edited by William Frank Bryan and Ronald S. Crane, Ginn and Company, 1916, pp. xi-lx.

[*Bryan and Crane were professors of English at Northwestern University. In the following excerpt, they discuss the major nineteenth-century writers of the familiar essay, drawing distinctions between the mature form of the familiar essay and its direct ancestor, the mid-seventeenth-century imitations of the* Tatler *and* Spectator.]

Within the early years of the nineteenth century the type of familiar essay was developed which has continued to the present. By 1825 it had largely supplanted the imitations of the *Tatler* and *Spectator,* and Lamb, Hunt, Hazlitt, De Quincey, and other writers had won for it a popularity that the essay had not enjoyed for a long time. The new type differed from the old in many essential respects.

In the first place, the new essay had a much wider range of subject than the old. It was no longer confined largely to "the Town," to the fashions and foibles of society, to problems of conduct and manners, or to the general principles of morality. There was, indeed, no general uniformity of topic. Each essayist wrote upon whatever presented itself to him as an attractive or congenial theme; his range of subject was determined only by the breadth or narrowness of his individual interests and sympathies. Lamb wrote of his schoolboy life, of his daily occupations, his vacation excursions, his friends and his family, his personal sympathies and antipathies; Leigh Hunt chatted about his reading, his fireside comforts, the interesting individuals or types he had observed or experiences he had encountered, or tried to discover compensation for the deaths of little children; Hazlitt lingered over his books or recalled his first meeting with poets later famous, recounted the delights of a solitary tramp in the open country and the evening comforts of an inn, presented the pleasures of painting or of hating, or considered the basis of his deepest feelings; De Quincey gossiped of his acquaintances or recalled gorgeous or terrible dream fancies. As many writers of the new essay, including Lamb and Hunt and Hazlitt, spent their most active years in London, they frequently, of course, wrote on some aspect of London life, but their subjects included such as had been in large measure beneath the sympathetic regard of the eighteenth-century essayists—chimney sweeps, the postman, clerks, artisans, and sailors.

In manner of presentation and purpose, too, the new essay was markedly different from the old. One of the most characteristic differences is that the essayist no longer hid his individuality behind the elaborately sustained figure of an invented Mr. Bickerstaff, or Mr. Spectator, or Chinese Traveler, but wrote in his own person. Even when through diffidence he employed the editorial plural or adopted a pen-name, he really expressed his own personality, and his thin disguise was easily penetrable. Many other long-used conventions were almost wholly discarded; for example, the machinery of clubs and correspondents, the visions and apologues, and the invented characters with classical or pseudo-classical names. The classics, too, and classical history were less drawn upon for mottoes and quotations and illustrations. In general, there was much less artificiality and much greater directness, and a strong tendency to rely for illustration upon the personal experience of the writer or of his acquaintances, upon contemporary events or those of comparatively recent history, and upon modern or native literature. Nor, as a rule, was the new essay marked by the satiric or didactic tone that generally pervaded the old. The eighteenth-century essay was largely social in character, and professed as its principal aim a reformation of the delinquencies and peccadillos of society. The new essay was just as distinctly individualistic; as a literary form it was not the vehicle of any propaganda. The character of each essayist's work as a whole was determined purely by his peculiar temperament, and any single essay might reflect his mood of a moment or the deeply grounded philosophy of his lifetime. The one property common to the essayists of the early nineteenth century is their egotism; they were chiefly interested in themselves, and were frank, though by no means offensively so, in the expression of this interest. This frankness of egotism, however, is characteristic of the period rather than of the literary type, although, of course, a strongly personal coloring is never absent from the familiar essay of the nineteenth century.

Of all the differences between the essay of the eighteenth

century and that of the nineteenth, the most obvious is the much greater length of the latter. As the content of a piece of writing is largely dependent upon the space it is to occupy, the greater length of the new essay is one of its essential characteristics. The eighteenth-century essay had space for only sketches and outlines or for the treatment of a very limited phase of a subject; the new essay could present full-length portraits or the development of ample themes, and it invited digression. The *Tatler* and *Spectator* papers, from their mode of publication and the temper of the particular reading public to whom they were directed, were very brief, ranging from about twelve hundred to fifteen hundred words each, and in this respect, as in others, they were followed by their imitators. Of the founders of the new essay, Leigh Hunt most closely resembled the writers of the preceding century in brevity; probably in part because of his temperament, and in part because, like the earlier essayists, he wrote principally for newspapers or for periodicals modeled upon the *Tatler*. Lamb was between the old and the new, the *Essays of Elia* averaging from one and a half to two times the length of the eighteenth-century periodical essay. The greater number of Hazlitt's essays were three or four times as long as those of the *Spectator* type; in this, as in so many other respects, they were wholly of the new order. Even within such expanded limits De Quincey was unable to confine himself, and some of his papers were inordinately long. Naturally, there cannot be any definitely fixed length for the essay, but so far as there is any standard, that set by Hazlitt became generally observed and is now usually followed. It permits the writer to treat his theme with reasonable fullness, but checks a presentation that would tax the capacity of the reader at a single sitting.

The changed character of the essay was the effect of a number of causes. The first was the progress of Romanticism, which, by 1820, throughout the world of literature had resulted in the expression of new interests or of those long dormant,—particularly the interest the individual felt in himself,—in the abandonment of old standards and conventions, and in experimentation with new or long-disused forms. Individualism had been strongly stimulated. The essayists were moved by the same forces as the poets. Indeed, in practically all essentials there is a manifest similarity between the new poetry and the new essay. The second cause is closely related to the first: the new forces in life and literature affected men of original and responsive genius, capable of developing a new type of essay, and by the success of their own efforts influential in establishing it in popular favor. The services of Lamb and Hunt and Hazlitt are exactly comparable to those of Wordsworth and Byron and Keats. A less general and somewhat more tangible influence was the greatly heightened interest in Montaigne. His *Essais,* in Cotton's translation, was one of the small stock of books identified as certainly belonging to Lamb; he was quoted or appreciatively referred to several times by Leigh Hunt; and Hazlitt was thoroughly familiar with the *Essais* and a consistent admirer of both their matter and their manner.

But the single factor of greatest moment in the development of the new type was the establishment of the modern literary magazine. At the beginning of the nineteenth century, publication of essays as independent periodicals after the fashion of the *Tatler* and the *Spectator* had largely given way to publication in newspapers and magazines. Obviously, the small news sheets could not provide space for any considerable expansion of the essay, which, moreover, was merely an excrescent growth upon them. Nor did the existing magazines, such as the *Gentleman's* and the *European,* offer much greater possibilities. They were literally magazines, overcrowded depositories of miscellaneous matter—meteorological data, tables of the values of stocks, parliamentary reports, records of births and deaths, cursory reviews, notes of the stage and the arts, letters from correspondents and answers to them, and curious information on a variety of topics. Literature was usually represented in a small section devoted to whatever of essays, sketches, verse, etc. the editor needed to fill out his ninety-odd pages, or had not the heart to reject. Rarely did a number of one of the old magazines have a single article of genuine literary merit or interest. And the critical reviews were even more hopelessly dull and wanting in originality. Both classes of periodicals were almost wholly the product of amateurs or of poorly paid drudges.

Vivification of the literary periodical first manifested itself in the critical reviews with the establishment of the *Edinburgh Review* in 1802 and the *Quarterly Review* in 1809, the former a Whig, the latter a Tory organ. From the first the rivalry between them was intense; and the liberal payments to contributors soon attracted to each a group of vigorous young writers, whose pronouncements upon the social, political, and literary questions of the day, whatever they lacked in depth and poise, certainly wanted nothing in assurance and energy. Both the *Edinburgh* and the *Quarterly* became immediately and dominantly popular.

The first notable effort to establish a distinctly literary magazine was made by Leigh Hunt in the *Reflector* (1811-1812). Lack of financial support, however, and other causes not now known made the venture abortive. But only a few years later the first modern magazine was actually founded. The success of the new reviews prompted William Blackwood, an active and astute Edinburgh publisher, to set up a magazine which should be equally different from the dull and characterless miscellanies then in existence. He was unfortunate, however, in the first selection of his staff, and the initial number of *Blackwood's Magazine,* which appeared in April, 1817, gave no real promise of originality or increased attractiveness. But with the October number John Wilson ("Christopher North"), together with Lockhart, joined Blackwood's forces; and the former, particularly, imparted to the magazine a character derived from his own freshness and high spirits. Almost instantly *Blackwood's* leaped into a more than local popularity.

The success of *Blackwood's* encouraged the establishment of the first magazine of similar character in London. This was the *London Magazine,* the initial number of which appeared in January, 1820. Its first editor, John Scott, was apparently given a free hand by the owners; he, in turn, threw open the pages of the *London* to good writing on almost any subject and paid for it liberally. As a result of this policy the *London* commanded the pens of original

and attractive writers and from the beginning was of interest and high standing. After the death of Scott in a duel, rapid changes in the control of the magazine ensued, the result of which was a swift descent in its fortunes. But it had shown the way to success and had set up a new standard for magazines. The conduct of the *New Monthly Magazine* illustrates the force of the example set by the *London.* The *New Monthly,* which was founded in 1814, during the first seven years of its existence was distinguished in no vital respect from the older miscellanies. In 1820, however, the popularity of the *London* forced a change of policy: it was placed under the editorship of Campbell, the poet, and inaugurating a new series with the first number for 1821, it became of the new order. Within a few more years many magazines of the older type had disappeared and very much the kind of magazine we know to-day had become definitely established.

Probably the most obvious contribution of the modern magazine to the development of the essay was the encouragement to expansion beyond the former narrow limits, an expansion impossible in the newspapers or in the older magazines, divided as they were into numerous crowded departments. The new magazines, unburdened with the traditions that hampered the old, and thus excluding much of the journalistic matter appearing in their predecessors, were able to provide not merely a page or two for an essay, but six or eight, and on occasion, ten or twelve or twenty pages. They thus made possible the changed content and manner of the essay, which could result only from an enlargement of its physical limits.

But increased length and all that goes with it was not the only indebtedness of the new essay to the new magazine. *Blackwood's* and the *London* could make a place for themselves only by being different from the long-established magazines, by surpassing them in literary interest and attractiveness; their editors and owners accordingly vied with one another in offering inducements to writers of original power, paying them with hitherto unexampled liberality and leaving them free to write as their own genius might direct. Finally, the very fact that these magazines were new, that they were unfettered by hampering precedents, was in itself a strong incentive to break away from existing conventions and to test new forms and modes. Lamb, Hunt, Hazlitt, Wilson, and De Quincey are chief among the founders of the new essay; though Hunt, the least modern of the group, owed comparatively little to the new magazines, even he departed from his eighteenth-century models for the first time in the *Reflector;* and *Blackwood's* produced Wilson's sketches, and the *London* stimulated Lamb, Hazlitt, and De Quincey to discover their peculiar genius and to give it expression. Extremely significant is the fact that the great body of familiar essays produced within the last century has been written for the modern magazine, the direct successor of *Blackwood's* and the *London.*

During the period within which the new essay was established Lamb, Hunt, and Hazlitt were the most notable writers—notable for their relations to the older type or for their influence upon the development of the new, as well as for the permanent interest and attractiveness of their writings.

Lamb's first essay, "The Londoner," was printed in the *Morning Post* for February 1, 1802. "The Londoner" promised to be the first of a series, but the promise was not carried out, and Lamb wrote no other essays until the establishment of Leigh Hunt's *Reflector*. To the four issues of this magazine, which appeared probably in 1811-1812, he contributed a number of short essays as well as two important critical papers. Consequent upon the death of the *Reflector* was a period of scant productivity, which lasted until the appearance of the *London Magazine* in 1820. Lamb's first contribution to this magazine, "The South Sea House," appeared in the number for August, 1820; his last, "Stage Illusion," in that for August, 1825. Between these two dates, writing over the pen-name "Elia," which he had appropriated from an Italian fellow clerk of the South Sea House, Lamb published in the *London* practically all his most characteristic essays. After 1820 he wrote but little except for the *London,* and after 1826 he practically ceased writing at all, his only considerable papers being three or four for the ephemeral *Englishman's Magazine* in 1831. Collections of Lamb's essays were made three times before his death in 1834: his *Works* (1818) contained most of his earlier pieces, and the *Essays of Elia* (1823) and the *Last Essays of Elia* (1833) included most of his contributions to the *London* as well as a few of both his earlier and his later papers.

Lamb's earlier essays were written under the influence of the long-established models. His first venture, "The Londoner," was obviously imitative, owing much in particular to the first number of the Spectator; and most of his brief papers in the *Reflector* were considerably indebted to the seventeenth-century "character" or to the *Tatler* and its successors. Moreover, even in the period of Lamb's most thoroughly original work, when Elia was doing much to establish the new type of familiar essay, he at times reverted to the manner of the old: the first part of "Poor Relations" is patterned after the seventeenth-century "character"; the first part of "The Wedding" is wholly in the manner of Steele's sketches of domestic life; and "A Vision of Horns," one of the *Essays of Elia* not reprinted by Lamb, he himself characterized as "resembling the most laboured papers in the *Spectator*."

But by far the greater number of the Elia essays were no more imitative than they are imitable; they were wholly original and the expression of Lamb's own personality. They were the very perfection of that kind of intimate writing which wins not merely interest for itself but affection for the writer. The content of these essays was varied. A few were playful fantasies, a few were serious musings; a small number presented Lamb's satirical observation and comment upon incongruities of conduct, a larger number, his humorous observation of incident and character; and seven or eight were critical papers on books and the stage. In almost every one of these papers, even those professedly critical, Lamb's personality was warmly reflected, and by far the greater number of his essays were undisguised autobiography and reminiscence, written in the first person. They recorded ingenuously his sympa-

thies and his prejudices, presented him and his family and his friends, disclosed his habits, and unveiled his memories. They formed almost a complete record of his life, together with an intimate and candid commentary upon it. In them appeared his tenderness and manliness, his tolerance of everything but pretence and priggishness and complacent stupidity, his intensely social nature, his liking for people with some harmless idiosyncrasy, his keen observation of the unexpected hidden amid the commonplace, his devotion to his old folios, and his half-humorous, half-pathetic attitude toward life.

Lamb's most fundamental characteristic was his humor—tender, playful, fantastic, never bitter, usually warming the reader's feeling or flashing a glimpse of a truth hitherto unconsidered. Very frequently the vehicle of this humor was a comparison startlingly unexpected, but perfectly appropriate and owing much of its happiness of effect to a suggestion of incongruity. The illustrative or figurative half of such a comparison was usually drawn from Lamb's familiar acquaintance with English literature of the late sixteenth and the seventeenth century—Shakespeare and the Elizabethan dramatists, Milton and Marvell, Burton and Browne and Fuller, and the Bible. From the same sources came the abundance of allusion that enriched every page, and the choice of word and turn of phrase that gave to his diction its archaic flavor. The result was not the affectation and artificiality that might have been expected, but what Lamb called a "self-pleasing quaintness," a style and manner peculiarly his own and perfectly expressive of his individuality.

About two years after the appearance of Lamb's "The Londoner," Leigh Hunt began to contribute his juvenile essays to the *Traveller* newspaper (1804-1805), and during the next fifty years, amid much ephemeral matter, largely critical or journalistic, a very considerable body of familiar essays appeared from his pen. Though in the *Reflector* (1811-1812) he made a notable attempt to found a literary magazine, yet the new type of magazine, when it was actually established, had much slighter effect upon his development than upon that of any of his contemporaries; by far the larger number of his essays were written for newspapers, family miscellanies, and independent sheets patterned somewhat closely after the *Tatler*. In fact, his most attractive and most characteristic work appeared in periodicals of the kind last mentioned. The most important of these was the earliest, the *Indicator,* which was issued weekly from October 13, 1819, to March 21, 1821. Similar in character were the *Companion* (1828) and *Leigh Hunt's London Journal* (1834-1835). No approximately full collection of Hunt's essays was made before his death, in 1859, nor, indeed, has any been made since. Selections from the *Indicator* and the *Companion* were reprinted in 1834; and the *Seer* (1840-1841), *Men, Women, and Books* (1847), and *Table Talk* (1851) contained a good deal of matter that had previously appeared.

The influence of the earlier types was even more pervasive and persistent in Hunt's work than in Lamb's. Hunt's papers in the *Traveller* were in avowed imitation of the *Connoisseur* (1754-1756), itself an imitation of the *Tatler* and the *Spectator*. In the *Reflector*, which he edited, most of his own essays, as well as many from other contributors, were similar in subject and manner to those of Addison and Goldsmith. A third literary venture of his, the *Round Table* papers in the *Examiner* (1815-1817), was confessedly designed after the *Tatler* and the *Spectator,* and most of Hunt's own writing was strongly suggestive of his reading in the essays of the eighteenth century. The influence of the early models persisted in a large proportion of even his most individual and most nearly original essays, such as those written for the *Indicator.* His "characters," particularly, a form which he cultivated as long as he wrote, owed much both to the seventeenth-century "characters" and to the more lifelike and dramatic studies of the *Tatler* and its successors.

Hunt's own everyday experiences and his observation of the everyday life about him formed the staple of his essays: he wrote upon books, the stage, clothes, manners and habits, the weather, animal pets, interesting types of character, the life of the London streets, the pleasures and the discomforts of a dweller in the suburbs, the joys and the sorrows of domestic life. Books were his chief interest, and his reading largely colored his observation. His distinctive manner first showed itself in "A Day by the Fire," in the last number of the *Reflector*—a cheery, familiarly gossiping presentation of a book lover's enjoyment of his snug fireside. Hunt's personality as revealed in his essays, unlike Lamb's, was not such as unfailingly to win the reader's appreciative sympathy, nor was he, like Hazlitt, keenly analytical or deeply reflective; he was merely a companionable sort of person who chatted entertainingly about everything that caught his own interest. His talk was sprightly, frequently interrupted to touch some topic that had suggested itself, now colored with sentiment, now shot through with gentle or tricksy humor. Few essayists have conveyed more perfectly than Hunt the sense of their own personality.

Hazlitt first appeared in the rôle of essayist as the principal associate of Leigh Hunt in the *Round Table* papers published in the *Examiner* between January 1, 1815, and January 5, 1817. After the somewhat abrupt termination of this series Hazlitt turned his energies for a few years very largely to the preparation of lectures on English literature, in the meantime writing a few brief essays for the *Edinburgh Magazine,* New Series (1818). With the establishment of the *London Magazine,* in 1820, the period of his most abundant and characteristic work as essayist began. In the periodicals to which he had been contributing he had been cramped for room; now he had space in which to write himself out upon his chosen topics, and his papers accordingly expanded to two or three times their former length. His first essay in the *London* appeared in June, 1820, and he wrote regularly for this magazine until December, 1821. In February of the following year he allied himself with the revivified *New Monthly Magazine,* to which he was a more or less regular contributor until his death, in 1830. He occasionally wrote also for other magazines, for newspapers, and for the miscellanies then coming into popularity.

These contributions to periodicals did not exhaust Hazlitt's fertility. In 1821-1822 he published under the title *Table Talk* thirty-three essays, twenty-six of which had not been printed previously; and in 1826, *The Plain Speaker,* in which thirteen of the thirty-two essays were new. These two collections contained a great deal of his most attractive and most characteristic writing. Except in the *Round Table* (1817), *Table Talk,* and *The Plain Speaker,* Hazlitt did not collect and republish his essays. In 1839 this was in part done by his son in *Winterslow* and *Essays and Sketches.*

In the *Round Table* paper on the *Tatler,* Hazlitt declared Montaigne to be "a most magnanimous and undisguised egotist." In a sense—not the commonly accepted one, to be sure—the first half of this characterization might be applied to Hazlitt as well as to Montaigne; the second half, without any qualification, would be applied to him by anyone who knew him. In the earlier papers of *Round Table* series his individuality showed strongly, although he wrote under the restraint of the editorial and collective we; in his later papers he broke through even this thin disguise and wrote freely and openly in his own person. Very few of his essays were purely autobiographic or reminiscent; and yet he wrote the whole body of them out of himself, and into them he wrote himself completely. It would be difficult to discover a single important circumstance of his life to which he did not refer in his writing, and equally difficult to find a paper of his in which he did not exhibit clearly some phase of his many-angled personality. As a young man Hazlitt studied painting, and although he was unsuccessful as an artist, painting and the great painters remained one of his passions. He was deeply rather than widely read—in Cervantes and Boccaccio, in certain French writers from Montaigne and Rabelais to Rousseau, and in English literature from the time of Shakespeare. His personal acquaintance included most of the writers of the time, for whom and for whose works he had strong—and usually mixed—feelings of attachment or aversion. He was a dramatic critic whose enthusiasm had not become sated or dulled. He fancied himself a metaphysician, and was much given to reflection upon philosophical and psychological problems and processes, particularly upon his own ideas and emotions. This speculative and reflective habit of mind produced his somewhat cynical observation of society, in which he concerned himself much more with the springs of conduct than with speech and dress and manners, though these details did not wholly escape his animadversion. Finally, he remained throughout his life a political Radical, preserving unchanged his hatred of repression and his faith in the doctrines and ideas of the French Revolution. Curiously enough, however, he saw in Napoleon the embodiment of these principles and made him the "god of his idolatry."

Although Hazlitt was almost never wholly promiscuous and desultory, yet, except in the briefer and earlier *Round Table* papers, he rarely presented a carefully ordered treatment of a subject. His essays had much of the discursive character of talk—but the talk of a thinker who is always master of his subject and is never mastered by it. His manner combined a good deal of Montaigne's reflective self-curiosity with Rousseau's naked self-revelation of feeling; he lacked, however, something of the latter's hectic sentimentalism as well as the former's open-mindedness. Hazlitt's style, though thoroughly individual, was unusually free from mannerisms; two particulars of it, however, were very striking. The first was his fondness for quotation, frequently remembered inexactly and almost as frequently somewhat changed to secure greater appositeness. The quotations were never paraded, and appeared as congruous and native as Hazlitt's own diction. The second was his favorite practice of beginning a paper, particularly one on a speculative or reflective theme, by some striking statement, epigrammatic or paradoxical. This was, of course, the device employed by Bacon and somewhat frequently by essayists of the seventeenth and eighteenth centuries. Hazlitt's work showed other occasional resemblances to the "character" and to the papers in the *Tatler,* but the indebtedness, even in his earliest essays, was actually very slight—Hazlitt was a thoroughgoing individualist, who never willingly conformed to any convention, literary or social.

Next to Lamb, Hunt, and Hazlitt, probably John Wilson ("Christopher North") and Thomas De Quincey were most influential in the establishment of the new type of familiar essay. Wilson joined the staff of *Blackwood's* with the number for October, 1817, and soon became the most important contributor to that magazine. The *Noctes Ambrosianæ,* which for the most part were written by him and by which his reputation was chiefly established, were a series of dialogues constituting a symposium upon the topics of the day, and cannot strictly be classed as familiar essays; but they possessed many of the features of the essay, and their popularity encouraged indirectly the cultivation of the type. In addition Wilson wrote for *Blackwood's* a number of papers after the general pattern that was being set by Lamb and Hazlitt.

De Quincey's first essay was the "Confessions of an English Opium-Eater," published in the *London Magazine* for September and October, 1821. It commanded immediate and lasting popularity. In the succeeding thirty years De Quincey wrote for a number of magazines particularly *Blackwood's* and *Tait's*; for the former, the "Suspiria de Profundis" (1845) and "The English Mail Coach" (1849); for the latter, many articles presenting sections of his autobiography and reminiscences of his literary friends and acquaintances. Most of the essays proper, such as the "Suspiria" and the "Confessions," were largely dream phantasmagoria, the real or feigned result of De Quincey's consumption of opium. They were characterized by their extreme length and discursiveness, and in many passages by a dignity of cadence and subtlety of rhythm hardly before attempted in English prose.

Though it is as a novelist that Dickens holds his place in literary history, yet it was as an essayist that he first attracted notice. His earliest departure from mere journalism was in the *Sketches by Boz,* the first of which was published in the *Monthly Magazine* for December, 1833, and others in the *Monthly* and in the *Evening Chronicle* during the next two years. Some of these sketches, particularly portrayals of characters, were apparently written under the influence of Leigh Hunt. A quarter of a century later Dickens began a new series of essays and sketches, first collected in the *Uncommercial Traveller* and issued in De-

cember, 1860. To this collection additions were made in 1868 and 1869.

But the chief figure among the essayists of the mid-century was Thackeray. A number of his contributions to *Punch* between 1846 and 1850—the *Snobs of England* (1846-1847), *Travels in London* (1847-1848), and *Mr. Brown's Letters to a Young Man about Town* (1849)—presented most of the features of the familiar essay, frequently differing from the type only in the excessive heightening of burlesque or satirical tone; and *The Proser* (1850) was really a series of familiar essays. They were written in the character of Dr. Solomon Pacifico, an "old Fogey" of kindly heart and much experience of the world and a very close relative of the later moralist of the *Roundabout Papers.* It is, however, to the *Roundabout Papers* in the *Cornhill Magazine* that Thackeray owes his place in the small group of writers who have given to the familiar essay in England its charm and distinction. When the *Cornhill* began publication in January, 1860, Thackeray was its editor, and he continued in this position until after the number for March, 1862. Then ill health and the irritating urgency of his editorial duties caused his resignation, though he remained a contributor to the magazine until his death, December 24, 1863. The first of the *Roundabout Papers* appeared in the initial number of the *Cornhill,* the last in the issue for November, 1863. The total number of essays included in the series is thirty-four, though six of them did not appear under this heading when they were first published in the *Cornhill.*

The various single *Roundabout Papers* rambled in such a pleasantly discursive fashion that they do not readily submit to any definite classification based on the subjects treated. A few were dream phantasmagoria; several were inspired by events or situations of contemporaneous interest; a goodly number were largely autobiographical or reminiscential, concerned particularly with Thackeray's boyhood, with his reading, and with his editorial trials and triumphs; but by far the largest part of the whole body consisted of reflections—humorous, satirical, sympathetic—based upon the writer's observation of human life and conduct and character. Indeed, in nearly every essay, whatever the professed subject, there were almost sure to be shrewd thrusts at sham and disingenuousness, or whole-hearted attacks upon baseness and meanness hidden behind respectability, or the sympathetic consideration of human weakness, or grateful appreciation of such simple virtues as manly strength and honor and womanly purity and charity. In Thackeray's consideration of the human comedy, his point of view was the same as in his novels, particularly the later ones—that of a member of the upper ranks of society, a man of breeding and position and knowledge of the world, whose experience had made him thoroughly cognizant of human frailty but had also mellowed him to a kindly tolerance. The audience to whom he especially directed himself were men of his own station and the members of their families; his sympathy embraced servants and workhouse inmates, but his attitude toward them was that of the considerate master and the genuinely charitable gentleman.

In the essayist's point of view, in the audience particularly addressed, and in the generally prevalent tone of social satire the *Roundabout Papers* were strongly suggestive of the eighteenth century. A further resemblance in detail appeared in the frequent use of illustrative characters with descriptive or suggestive names. But the differences were even more noteworthy than the resemblances. Unlike the eighteenth-century essayists Thackeray as a social satirist was concerned not with externals of taste and dress and manners, but with character and its expression in conduct. Further, in their greater length, in their discursiveness, and in their intimate revelations of personality, his essays were closely related to those of Montaigne and Lamb and Hazlitt. Montaigne was Thackeray's "bedtime book."

The *Roundabout Papers* owed almost as much of their attractiveness to their style as to the personality of the writer. They possessed the greatest charm of familiar writing—conversational ease that does not lack vigor or suppleness and still does not degenerate into vulgarity.

On the Essay's Discursive Nature:

In discursive writing . . . the law of the whole is not that of logical sequence; in it, the purpose is not to develop one single topic only, in an orderly way, to a definite conclusion. There may be, indeed, and there usually is, some dominating topic to which the writer recurs as often as he realizes himself to be in danger of drifting too far away from it; but the principle which chiefly prevails in discourse of this kind is that of the association of ideas.

The model for such writing is furnished by good talk in which the talkers drift from one topic to another, as usually happens when the talk is free and the talkers are sympathetic with one another; sympathetic temperamentally and in general, not necessarily, and indeed not probably, too much alike in their views on the topics discussed. Any one who has ever listened to a conversation between two or more good talkers, under favoring circumstances, knows how the talk drifts on and on, one topic or one remark suggesting another topic, until who knows how many topics have been glanced at, and some of them discussed before the evening is over; the evening, since, for the most part it is only after the business of the day is done that such talk is possible, in America, at least; the talkers and the listeners being alike persons who on that day, and on all their days, have had their abundant share in that business.

R. D. O'Leary, in The Essay, *Thomas Y. Crowell Company Publishers, 1928.*

Dr. John Brown, an active physician of Edinburgh and a valued friend of Thackeray's, occupies a small but significant position as essayist, chiefly by reason of his sketches of dog life and character. "Rab and his Friends," the best known of his works, was as much story as essay and claimed interest as much for its human figures as for its canine hero; but certain other very attractive papers were simply studies of the personality of dog companions by one who loved and understood them. Dr. Brown's essays

also included some delightfully fresh out-of-door pieces, such as "Minchmoor" and "The Enterkin" which in many respects anticipated the travel essays of Stevenson. His writings, of which only a part are properly familiar essays, were first collected in the three volumes of *Hora Subseciva,* published in 1858, 1861, and 1882, respectively.

Of the later nineteenth-century essayists Robert Louis Stevenson a fellow townsman of Dr. Brown's, was the most conspicuous—notable for the character of his own work and for the stimulus he gave both to the writing and to the reading of essays. Stevenson first appeared in print in a half-dozen papers written for the *Edinburgh University Magazine* (January-April, 1871). After the demise of this publication he practiced his art assiduously, but for some two and a half years he published nothing. Then, in December, 1873, an article of his entitled "Roads," which had been rejected by the *Saturday Review,* appeared in the *Portfolio.* In May, 1874, he contributed "Ordered South" to *Macmillan's Magazine,* and in the same year, through the discernment of Mr. Leslie Stephen, the editor of the *Cornhill,* his work was admitted to the pages of that magazine. From 1876 through 1882 the *Cornhill* was by far his most important medium of publication; after the latter year his writings appeared more at large. The most important body of essays of his later life was written for *Scribner's Magazine,* one paper appearing each month throughout 1888. In the summer of that year Stevenson sailed on his first voyage to the South Seas. Thereafter his voyages, the setting up of his establishment in Samoa and his interest in Samoan public affairs, letter writing, and absorption in fiction consumed his energies, and he published no essays.

Several small volumes of Stevenson's essays were collected and published before his death in 1894. The earliest of these, *Virginibus Puerisque* (1881), contained fourteen papers; *Memories and Portraits* (1887), sixteen; and *Across the Plains* (1892), twelve. All but three or four of the essays contained in these volumes had been printed previously in various periodicals. Even before *Virginibus Puerisque* two other slender volumes had appeared: *An Inland Voyage* (1878)—Stevenson's first book—and *Travels with a Donkey* (1879). The titles suggest narratives, but these little books were really series of travel essays, almost any one of which could be enjoyed separately, though the papers composing each volume were bound together by a slender thread of narrative. *Familiar Studies of Men and Books* (1882), despite its title, can hardly be considered a collection of familiar essays; it is rather a group of critical articles. For some years preceding Stevenson's death his essays were more widely read than were those of any one of his contemporaries; nevertheless, no full collection of them was issued before the publication of the first complete edition of his works in 1895.

Stevenson's essays presented chiefly four kinds of material: travel impressions, autobiography and reminiscence, moral and philosophical ideas, and a writer's interest in his craft. Probably Stevenson's most characteristic work was his development of the travel essay, the cultivation of this particular variety being the natural consequence of the nomadic habits which his search for health and his innate fondness for wandering confirmed in him. In his hands the travel sketch became not merely a narrative of travel or a description of places visited and objects and persons observed; it was both narrative and description combined with recollections, comments, reflections, and all interpenetrated by his personality.

The title *Memories and Portraits* indicates the character of a considerable number of Stevenson's essays other than those included in the volume to which it was affixed. The portraits ranged from those of beggars, the family gardener, and an old shepherd, to the friends of Stevenson's youth and the members of his own family. The memories were largely of his childhood and young manhood—and naturally so, as he had scarcely reached middle age when his last essay was written. The most highly individual papers of this kind were those in which Stevenson recalled his very early sensations and impressions, and interpreted the actions and emotions of childhood in very much the same sympathetic spirit as in his *Child's Garden of Verse.*

The essays in which were embodied Stevenson's ethical and philosophical ideas varied in content from an appreciation of wisely spent idleness or a study of the comic incongruities incident upon falling in love, to a resolute, almost stoical facing of man's ultimate fate. They manifested his conviction that life is well worth the living and that this world is a very good place in which to live it, his admiration for the active and unafraid, and his remoteness from that spirit which is actuated to well-doing merely by the hope of bread-and-butter success in this world or by a promised reward of immortality in another. Almost everywhere in Stevenson's essays the moralist appeared; not as the righteous Pharisee or the self-constituted reformer of society, but as an observer and thinker thoroughly human and richly endowed with a sense of humor.

Besides the distinctly critical articles a number of Stevenson's essays showed his interest in the craft of letters. These exhibited his contempt for slovenly and dishonest writing, and insisted upon the blindness of the note-taking realists who transcribe the bare apparent facts and ignore the poetry and romance of life. They also recounted his own efforts to learn to write and his unwearied pursuit of style. For no writer of English has been more consciously a stylist, or has considered more nicely the effects he aimed to produce. In the choice of word and phrase, as in the attitude toward his subject, he carried almost to the extreme what Mr. Leslie Stephen has characterized as a "hatred for the commonplace formula." His style was fluid, always in process of change, but there was a fairly consistent difference between that of his earlier and of his later essays. The earlier papers, those in the *Virginibus Puerisque* collection, for example, were the more mannered—Stevenson himself declared that they were written in a "neat, brisk little style"; the later, including most of the essays collected in *Across the Plains,* were less affected, less jaunty. While they were being written and afterwards, Stevenson was practicing what he called a "bald" style. He has named the models whom he chose to follow. Significantly enough, the eighteenth-century essayists are not included in the list; and equally significant is a statement of his that he "could never read a word" of Addison. But of Mon-

taigne and of Hazlitt—who of all the English essayists most resembles Montaigne—he was an eager and admiring student. And his relationship to these two was much closer than that of style in any narrowly restricted sense of the term.

With Stevenson the tale of the greater essayists of the nineteenth century is ended, and thus far in the twentieth century no one has appeared to match him in charm and distinction. As, moreover, no really important modification of the character of the familiar essay has occurred since his death, this sketch of the development of the type may well be concluded with the account of his work. But Stevenson is by no means the last of the English essayists; today Chesterton and Benson and Galsworthy are notable names. And despite the popularity of the short story, which during the last twenty-five years has come more and more to occupy the magazines, the essay holds its place secure, and promises to continue to give pleasant half hours to the thoughtful and unhurried reader.

Randolph Bourne

SOURCE: "The Light Essay," in *The Radical Will: Selected Writings, 1911-1918,* edited by Olaf Hansen, Urizen Books, 1977, pp. 506-10.

[*Bourne is widely considered one of the twentieth century's most astute and visionary critics of American life and letters. His writings established him as a leader of the youth movement that swept across American college campuses in the decade preceding World War I and which transformed New York's Greenwich Village into a mecca for modern artists and avant-garde intellectuals. In the following excerpt from a review originally published in the* Dial *in 1918, Bourne writes bemusedly of the "light essayists" of the recent past, emphasizing that the familiar essay is a key forum for middle-class rumination.*]

Perhaps it is hardly fair to relegate the light essay to the less creative forms of literature, to see it as journalism dressed up, as it were, for a literary party. Yet when you have begun to identify "creative" writing with novels, verse, and drama you find yourself belittling the essay as scarcely more than a subterfuge, an illegitimate method of securing the literary sensation without doing the genuine literary work. You suspect that the light essayist is a person who was born without the narrative style and the poetic gift, who has not had enough adventures or does not understand life well enough to write stories, and lacks the divine fire for verse. In spite of the august examples of the essay which our professors slowly brought us to admire, most of us would rather be a Maxim Gorky than a Lamb, or have written *The Brook Kerith* than the *Sketchbook* of Washington Irving. American writers especially seem to be compensating for their lack of novelistic talent by a striking artistic capacity for the light essay. They do not, like the protean Mr. Chesterton, simply toss it in as one of the many things they can do. They found whole literary careers on it. But you always feel something lacking, even in the piquant petulance of Miss Repplier, the sly charm of Dr. Crothers, the urbanity of Mr. Sedgwick, and even the inexhaustibly witty fooling of Simeon Strunsky. Just the last vivifying touch is absent. You feel that it is proper that most of these writers are middle-aged, and most of their readers too.

The youthful light essayist is usually a painful phenomenon. He is apt to be ostentatiously bright. The middle-aged mind is legitimately mellow, and its self-consciousness is rather pleasant. We know that it has ruminated over and is aware of a lot of things that happened before we were born. But vivid green shoots can't be mellow. The young essayist is afraid you will think he is unsophisticated, while the middle-aged doesn't much care if you do. And youth's idea of being whimsical is usually to nose about among the irrelevant, and be very bold with the trivial. The youthful essayist usually develops into the professional anecdotalist, with an active mind that is harnessed up to no real thinking but can only stream off from itself a futile current of amusing incident.

When Mr. Robert Cortes Holliday, therefore, in his *Walking-Stick Papers,* describes himself as a "pale, spectacled, middle-aged young man" you are prepossessed in his favor. A middle-aged young man ought to write pretty good light essays. He ought to be mellow without giving you the impression that life has no more adventures, and he ought to be as diverting as his youth and naivete will let him. The first requirement of the light essay is that it should amuse you. To be amused is to experience one of the really great pieces of good fortune in life. The trouble with most pretended amusement is the suddenness of your deflation. Mere wit and anecdote go out like a candle in the wind. But the good essay does not stale. You leave it refreshed and in a nice glow of pleasedness, and its flavor follows you. So that it is this quality of amusingness that finally saves the light essay from the non-creative reproach. But all the more ghastly are the efforts that fail. The light essay is a truly perilous thing.

Bonamy Dobrée

SOURCE: An introduction and "The Personal Essay," in *English Essayists,* Collins, 1946, pp. 7-9, 25-31.

[*An English historian and critic, Dobrée distinguished himself as a leading authority on Restoration drama and as a biographer who sought, through vivid depiction and style, to establish biography as a legitimate creative form. He is also known for his editing of* The Oxford History of English Literature *and* Writers and Their Work *series. In the following excerpt, he discusses the key nineteenth-century writers of the familiar essay, having first traced their literary roots to either the personal, individualist style of Montaigne or the experience-derived form of Francis Bacon.*]

Though the essay, a friendly, personal, informal piece of writing about anything you like, had existed from at least as early as the gay writings of Lucian in the second century B.C., the name in its everyday modern sense was first used when Montaigne published his *Essais* in 1580. Curious about the inner man, his purpose appeared to be no more than to give his friends a gossiping picture of his genial, sceptical mind; and in the slippered ease of his retirement, he looked into himself and wrote down what he found there. "I am myself the subject of my book," he told

the reader, and he may have chosen the name to indicate that he was trying the thing out. His work was soon made current in English; so when in 1600 Sir William Cornwallis published *Essays,* he in his turn declared that he was engaged in finding out what he really thought, progressing towards the 'land of light' from the darkness of 'opinion.' "I write therefore for myself, and my self profits from my writing." The essay, you were led to believe, claimed to put aside all pedantry, all learning crammed out of books, and merely gave you the reasonable decent man talking to you or me or anyone else of what he thought about life: or rather, the man was talking to himself and allowing anyone who cared to do so to overhear him.

But Bacon, when he issued his first ten *Essays* in 1597, did something quite different. It appears that he copied out, and put into some sort of form, the aphorisms he had jotted down in his commonplace-book, reflections upon life that had come to him out of his own experience or from the heads of others, writers classical and modern alike, and from the Bible. He probably had in mind the little writings of the Latin authors, Cicero, and especially Seneca. So the self hardly comes in; he is concerned with the world outside the individual; he is positive, not sceptical or musing. You might, indeed, call these essays collections of philosophical "wisecracks," based on learning and experience of the world. . . .

So what we shall here discuss are the kind of writing called 'essays' by Montaigne and Bacon, such things as have appeared in magazines or journals; or, where very early ones are concerned, would probably have appeared in magazines had they been invented; or which might well have appeared in that way later on. All issue from Montaigne or Bacon; some have more of the one in them, some more of the other. Some, like Lamb's, are purely and delightfully egotistical; they spring from Montaigne. Others, such as Arnold's, try to arrive at some definite truth or principle; they spring from Bacon. In nearly all there is a mixture; there are few examples of a pure type. Indeed the essay is the most varied form of writing. It can be descriptive, moralistic, whimsical, exhorting or pleadingly self-revealing, critical or historical; it can be anything you like. But all essays are aimed at the average reader, the 'common reader' to whom Virginia Woolf appealed in the essays she wrote under that title, though, like many of hers, they may be addressed to a reader assumed to be interested in a special subject. Essays, therefore, tend to be easy in style, and often they are deliberately familiar. There is something for everybody's palate in the rich array of English essays, something to pass away an idle moment, or something on which to spend three or four solid hours. They vary from the trivial to the portentous, from the wildly high-spirited to the gravely moral; at their most inconsequent they are idle amusement, at their best they are little gems of literature which give delight by their form, by what they have to tell us, and by the spirit they convey. . . .

By the third quarter of the eighteenth century, the essay had become a natural mode of communication, as befits a civilised age where real conversation, not the yaffle of the club-room or the tattle of the drawing-room, sets the tone.

From now on it tended to be lighter, more personal, the idea of its functions being widely accepted; thus Bacon was giving place to Montaigne. But though there was a continual flow of excellent writers, not at all dull or bad reading, there was no outstanding figure till we come to the nineteenth century, to that group which contains the names of Coleridge, Lamb, Hazlitt and De Quincey—together with those there is no space to enlarge upon—a group individually very various, but which represents a distinct stage. They are not moralistic in the obvious sense, so much as literary-philosophical, and again suddenly seem much closer to us than the eighteenth century essayists.

Man was getting tired of considering himself as a social creature only, and was trying to rediscover himself as an individual, whose interest for others, as well as for himself, lay precisely in his being different from other people.

Samuel Taylor Coleridge (1772-1834) is the most deeply philosophical, and in *The Friend* (1809; published as a book in 1818) we find the ethical and literary ideas which form part of the stock which give him his high position as thinker and critic of fundamental notions. And however much he may be based on the eighteenth, and indeed the seventeenth century, his political statements still strike home (since they really are fundamental), and the following passage might have been written in say, 1938, as justly as during the war in the middle of which he was writing:

> Little prospective wisdom can that man obtain, who hurrying onward with the current, or rather torrent, of events, feels no interest in their importance, except as far as his curiosity is excited by their novelty, and to whom all reflection and retrospect are wearisome. If ever there were a time when the formation of just public principles becomes a duty of private morality; when the principles of morality in general ought to be made to bear on our public suffrages, and to affect every great national determination; when, in short, his country should have a place by every Englishman's fireside; and when the feelings and truths which give dignity to the fireside and tranquillity to the deathbed, ought to be present and influensive in the cabinet and in the senate—that time is now with us. (*The Friend* I. 10.)

And who would say that the comment is not relevant now!

It is, however, Charles Lamb (1775-1834) who is the best known and best loved of this group, and who has had the widest influence on the essay. His famous *Essays of Elia* first appeared in *The London Magazine* from 1820 to 1823, a second series coming out some ten years later. It is the fashion nowadays to decry Lamb as being too mannered, too fanciful, altogether too egotistical and whimsical: but that is largely because his imitators—and people still imitate Lamb—have imitated the wrong thing. Imitators usually do. Because of his way of writing, a theory has grown up that the less an essay is 'about' the more perfect it is; the theory is a forcing to absurdity of the Montaigne position. Lamb's essays, nevertheless, are very definitely about something other than himself, though he seems always to be writing about himself alone. If one wanted to make a contrast between him and the usual run of eighteenth century essayists, one would say that whereas they were moralists, he was impressionistic; indeed he goes back further, and his style is Temple's rather than Addison's, though he has a literary sense and tact unknown to the retired ambassador.

He is egotistic in the sense that rather than seem to be uttering great truths about things, he gives his own feelings about them, and in the main he treats of small things (which after all make up most of our lives), preferring, as Hazlitt said of him, byeways to highways. But out of these small things he developed thoughts which spread over the whole of a personal life. Great issues do not figure in his titles; one is invited to read, rather, on subjects such as roast pig, or chimney sweepers, or Mrs. Battle's opinions on whist, but what you find implicit in what follows is an attitude towards life. He is at his best when he is reminiscent, while much of his writing is pervaded by a tenderness towards the helpless, the weak, or the oppressed, a tenderness which some find sentimental, but which, all the same, is invariably controlled. Steeped as he was in seventeenth century literature, he loved the strange striking word so much that its use almost became a vice with him. Yet how apt it seems, how it gives just that turn of whimsicality which is a defence against sentimentality, a whimsicality which it must be confessed itself sometimes came perilously near to being a vice. Yet look at the word 'nigritude' in the opening paragraph of his "In Praise of Chimney-Sweepers":

> I like to meet a sweep—understand me—not a grown sweeper—old chimney-sweepers are by no means attractive—but one of those tender novices, blooming through their first nigritude, the maternal washings not quite effaced from the cheek. . . .

Similar effects crop up everywhere.

But whatever archaic mannerisms (sometimes friendly parodies), or irrelevant eccentricities may here and there a little irritate you in Lamb, he is among the most intimate of our essayists; he really is like Montaigne. Although he was the close companion of the greatest literary figures of his day, we never feel as we read him that he is anything but a lovable ordinary man, lovable because he appreciates our actions, understands our feelings. In talking about "New Year's Eve," he tells us how he does not want to leave this life because "a new state of being staggers me," and:

> Sun, and sky, and breeze, and solitary walks, and summer holidays, and the greenness of fields, and the delicious juices of meats and fishes, and society, and the cheerful glass, and candle-light, and fireside conversations, and innocent vanities, and jests, and *irony itself*—do these things go out with life?
>
> Can a ghost laugh, or shake his gaunt sides, when you are pleasant with him?
>
> And you, my midnight darlings, my Folios; must I part with the intense delight of having you (huge armfuls) in my embraces? Must knowledge come to me, if it come at all, by some

awkward experiment of intuition, and no longer by the familiar process of reading?

> Shall I enjoy friendships there, wanting the smiling indications which point me to them here— the recognisable face—the 'sweet assurance of a look'?

As compared with his predecessors, with him we feel delightfully free of what he called the perpetual coxcombry of our moral pretensions.

Not that Lamb was always personal; his critical essays reach out beyond his own affairs, memories, and idiosyncrasies, to general principles, which are based, as all good criticism ultimately is, on what he feels he knows in his bones to be good. The essay on "The Artificial Comedy of the Last Century" was a landmark in the criticism of Restoration Comedy, for though its argument is false, it is freshly thought and eagerly argued. Perhaps Lamb is the sort of writer you either warm to very much, or ought to leave severely alone.

Owning some affinities with Lamb, whose portrait he painted, is William Hazlitt (1778-1830). Bagehot thought him the better essayist. He is to some degree a personal writer, whose subject is himself, but he is something of a bully to his reader, and is occasionally bad-tempered. He wrote for many reviews, including the *Edinburgh* . . . on all sorts of subjects, but his critical work is in many respects his best. He had a fine, clear, direct style, corresponding with a fine, clear, direct head, and he wrote memorably. One does not forget the portrait of Wordsworth in "My First Acquaintance with Poets," nor that of Jeremy Bentham in *The Spirit of the Age* (1825). He wrote also on more general subjects than Lamb was inclined to do, as a glance at the essays in *Winterslow* (posthumous) or *Table Talk, or Original Essays on Men and Manners* (1821-1822) will show, and he had a similar passion for the Elizabethan dramatists. Yet by way of embarking on a general disquisition he will often tell you of himself. Thus he begins "On Consistency of Opinion" with "Many people boast of being masters in their own house. I pretend to be master in my own mind." But equally often he shoots straight away at his target, as in "On Party Spirit":

> Party spirit is one of the *profoundnesses of Satan,* or, in modern language one of the dexterous *equivoques* and contrivances of our self-love, to prove that we, and those who agree with us, combine all that is excellent and praiseworthy in our own persons (as in a ring-fence), and that all the vices and deformity of human nature take refuge in those that differ from us. (*Winterslow* III.)

He can be scathing enough to make us look pretty closely into ourselves, as, in the same essay, "We may be intolerant even in advocating the cause of toleration, and so bent on making proselytes to freethinking as to allow no one to think freely but ourselves." Hazlitt was a widely read, widely thoughtful man, vigorous, combative, generous where he felt generosity was called for, biting where he thought reproof was needed.

Perhaps no short passage can give his quality better than the conclusion of a slashing attack on Byron in *The Spirit of the Age,* a collection consisting mainly of articles contributed to *The New Monthly Magazine*:

> We had written thus far when news came of the death of Lord Byron, and put an end at once to a strain of somewhat peevish invective, which was intended to meet his eye, not to insult his memory. Had we known that we were writing his epitaph, we must have done it with a different feeling. As it is, we must think it better, and more like himself, to let what we had written stand, than to take up our leaden shafts, and try to melt them into 'tears of sensibility', or mould them into dull praise and an affected show of candour. We were not silent during the author's lifetime, either for his reproof or encouragement (such as we could give, and *he* did not disdain to accept), nor can we now turn undertaker's men to fix the glittering plate upon his coffin, or fall into the procession of popular woe. Death cancels everything but truth, and strips a man of everything but genius and virtue. It is a sort of natural canonization. It makes the meanest of us sacred; it installs the poet in his immortality, and lifts him to the skies. Death is the great assayer of the sterling ore of talent. . . . We consign the least worthy qualities to oblivion, and cherish the nobler and imperishable nature with double pride and fondness. . . .

In spite of his familiarity he belongs to the Baconian rather than to the Montaigne family, arriving at a generalisation by applying hard thinking to every day, and in such a way that to read him is invigorating. One cannot rise from an essay of his without having thought about one's own self: when he is amusing, as he often is, it is not seldom at our own expense. Yet he is never dully moral; he does not ask you to fit yourself into a social scheme, to make yourself conform: you are for him an individual. To read him, then, is like bathing in the sea on a fine clear sunny day; but the water is cold, even a little rough: and there is plenty of salt in it.

If Coleridge is the profoundest of this group, Lamb the most intimate, and Hazlitt the most invigorating, Thomas De Quincey (1785-1859) is the most imaginative. He does not play delightfully with words as Lamb does, nor shoot them at you as Hazlitt is too often inclined to do; he satisfies you with them by means of an extraordinary music. Extremely learned in the more mysterious kinds of lore, which seems to have imbued his opium dreams, there is nearly always something a little startlingly fantastic about De Quincey. The obvious illustration is the most famous of his essays, "Murder Considered as one of the Fine Arts." (*Blackwood's* 1827). His criticism is not that of a man of letters, a man who knows the craft, so much as of an artist, intensely sensitive to what the work of art he is experiencing is doing to him. So he sees things that others do not see, and we may take as example the deeply probing little essay on "The Knocking at the Gate in Macbeth." But his most personal things are still his opium-haunted musings, such as "Levana, and Our Ladies of Sorrow." . . .

Sir John Squire

SOURCE: "The Essay," in *Flowers of Speech; Being Lectures in Words and Forms in Literature,* 1935. Reprint by Books for Libraries Press, Inc., 1967, pp. 108-15.

[*Squire was an English man of letters who, as a poet, lent his name to the "Squire-archy," a group of poets who struggled to maintain the Georgian poetry movement of the early twentieth century. He was also a prolific critic who was involved with many important English periodicals; he founded and edited the* London Mercury, *served as literary and, later, acting editor of the* New Statesman, *and contributed frequently to the* Illustrated London News *and the* Observer. *Squire's criticism, like his poetry, is considered traditional and good natured. In the following excerpt from a BBC radio lecture from the early 1930s, he defines and discusses the familiar essay, naming Abraham Cowley as the "first English essayist in the modern sense": the source from which sprang the nineteenth-century writers of the familiar essay.*]

The word "essay" is an intimidating one to the vast majority of the British population. It carries with it memories of efforts at school to compose one or two laborious pages on "How I Spent my Holidays," or "Which would you rather be, a Sailor or a Soldier?" It has, by the same token, painful associations for me. The first piece of really careful prose I ever remember writing was composed for a school essay on "Egypt." I thought of the Sphinx and the Pyramids, of Philae and the Valley of the Kings, of the Pharaohs going back into the mists of remote antiquity; I thought of the ancient Nile, rising in the mysterious Mountains of the Moon and flowing past all those monuments now, when they are crumbling, as of old when they were bright and new; and I laid myself out to write Ruskinian paragraphs full of colour and cadence, in which the words "illimitable" and "eternal" occurred much more frequently than I should allow them to occur now. "Well," thought I to myself complacently, "I can't imagine that anybody else has done anything like that." Did I get a prize? No; I wasn't even commended. All that happened was that I was taken aside by a master, who knitted his brows and bit his lips, and asked from what author I had copied out the passage on which I had dwelt most lovingly—the passage fullest of the venerable river, the immemorial sands, and the brooding spirit of antiquity. When I denied that I had copied it from anybody, I was invited to consider the old maxim that "lying only makes the offence worse," and I ended by narrowly escaping a beating for having the germs of a poet in me. This by the way; but I was trying to write one type of essay when another type was wanted. I was expected to write: "Egypt is a very old country. There was once a ruler there, a very wicked man called Pharaoh, who was drowned in the Red Sea for persecuting the Jews. The chief sights of Egypt are the Pyramids, which are not all the same size, and the Sphinx, which is a very large Sphinx."

Well, we are not talking about school essays. Nor are we talking about scientific, religious, political, and economic essays. Malthus wrote an *Essay on Population;* probably at this moment somebody is writing an *Essay on the most advantageous use of Phosphate Manures in Metalliferous*

Areas. The word "essay," in English, covers a multitude if not of sins at least of painstaking dullnesses. But when one talks of "The English Essay," one does not think of these or even of critical essays, however excellent, like Matthew Arnold's or Walter Bagehot's, but of a particular kind of wandering, personal thing which has flourished in England as nowhere else. . . .

The first English essayist in the modern sense was Abraham Cowley, whose essays (though in print at the Oxford University Press) are at the present time as neglected as his ingenious and, occasionally, lovely poems. "Who now reads Cowley?" asked Pope, more than two hundred years ago. The question might still be asked, but all the time he had had a few affectionate lovers. Listen to this, written in the middle of the seventeenth century—the beginning of an essay which at once shows Cowley's consciousness of whence his essays derived and forecasts the whole tone of the English essay from his day onward. It comes from his essay, *On Greatness.*

> Since we cannot attain to greatness, says the Sieur de Montaigne, let us have our revenge by railing at it: this he spoke but in jest. I believe he desired it no more than I do, and had less reason, for he enjoyed so plentiful and honourable a fortune in a most excellent country, as allowed him all the real conveniences of it, separated and purged from the incommodities. If I were but in his condition, I should think it hard measure, without being convinced of any crime, to be sequestered from it, and made one of the principal officers of state. But the reader may think that what I now say is of small authority, because I never was, nor ever shall be, put to the trial; I can therefore only make my protestation.
>
> > If ever I more riches did desire
> > Than cleanliness and quiet do require;
> > If e'er ambition did my fancy cheat,
> > With any wish so mean as to be great,
> > Continue, Heaven, still from me to remove
> > The humble blessings of that life I love.
>
> I know very many men will despise, and some pity me, for this humour, as a poor-spirited fellow; but I am content, and, like Horace, thank God for being so. . . . I confess I love littleness almost in all things. A little convenient estate, a little cheerful house, a little company, and a very little feast; and if I were ever to fall in love again (which is a great passion, and therefore I hope I have done with it), it would be, I think, with prettiness rather than with majestical beauty.

Honesty and whimsicality—and confidential buttonholing: there are all the things here that make people love Charles Lamb. The pedigree is straight from that to Hazlitt's *On Going a Journey:*

> The soul of a journey is liberty, perfect liberty, to think, feel, do just as one pleases. We go a journey chiefly to be free of all impediments and of all inconveniences; to leave ourselves behind, much more to get rid of others. It is because I want a little breathingspace to muse on indifferent matters . . . that I absent myself from the town for a while, without feeling at a loss the

moment I am left by myself. Instead of a friend in a post-chaise or in a Tilbury, to exchange good things with, and vary the same stale topics over again, for once let me have a truce with impertinence. Give me the clear blue sky over my head, and the green turf beneath my feet, a winding road before me, and a three hours' march to dinner—and then to thinking!

I may be doing a few people a service if I recommend a perusal of the essays of Abraham Cowley.

Since him, what a procession! There are obscurer men whom I might mention. I should like to send readers back to the neglected essays of Alexander Smith, whose *The Lark Ascending* (you may know his poem *Barbara* in the Oxford Book) is one of the most beautiful and thoughtful essays in English. But Addison, Steele, Johnson, Lamb, Hazlitt—it would require hours to celebrate adequately their contributions to our enjoyment. And in our own day Mr. Beerbohm, Mr. Lynd, Mr. Knox, Mr. Belloc, Mr. Lucas, Mr. Chesterton have continued the old tradition. We may regret that they mostly write so briefly: that cannot be helped; a contributor to periodicals has to write to the length required. All these authors would doubtless pour themselves out much more fully and ingeniously were they invited to write at Charles Lamb's length, and we may regret that (with the exception of Mr. Beerbohm) they do not. But it is agreeable to see spirit triumphing over matter, and posterity will take pleasure in the spectacle of men of letters of our own day continuing to compress their effusions within the limits of a newspaper column and still keep their freshness, their humour, their sense of beauty, and their capacity for exposing themselves as specimens of mankind.

Theodor W. Adorno

SOURCE: "The Essay as Form," in *Notes to Literature, Vol. 1,* edited by Rolf Tiedemann, translated by Sherry Weber Nicholsen, Columbia University Press, 1991, pp. 3-23.

[*In the following essay, originally published in 1958, Adorno offers a closely-engaged definitive essay on the essay.*]

That in Germany the essay is condemned as a hybrid, that the form has no compelling tradition, that its emphatic demands are met only intermittently—all this has been said, and censured, often enough. "The essay form has not yet, today, travelled the road to independence which its sister, poetry, covered long ago; the road of development from a primitive, undifferentiated unity with science, ethics, and art." But neither discomfort with this situation nor discomfort with the mentality that reacts to it by fencing off art as a preserve for irrationality, equating knowledge with organized science, and excluding anything that does not fit that antithesis as impure, has changed anything in the prejudice customary here in Germany. Even today, to praise someone as an *écrivain* is enough to keep him out of academia. Despite the telling insights that Simmel and the young Lukács, Kassner and Benjamin entrusted to the essay as speculation on specific, culturally pre-formed objects, the academic guild accepts as philosophy only what

is clothed in the dignity of the universal and the enduring—and today perhaps the originary. It gets involved with particular cultural artifacts only to the extent to which they can be used to exemplify universal categories, or to the extent to which the particular becomes transparent when seen in terms of them. The stubbornness with which this schema survives would be as puzzling as the emotions attached to it if it were not fed by motives stronger than the painful memory of the lack of cultivation in a culture in which the *homme de lettres* is practically unknown. In Germany the essay arouses resistance because it evokes intellectual freedom. Since the failure of an Enlightenment that has been lukewarm since Leibniz, even under present-day conditions of formal freedom, that intellectual freedom has never quite developed but has always been ready to proclaim its subordination to external authorities as its real concern. The essay, however, does not let its domain be prescribed for it. Instead of accomplishing something scientifically or creating something artistically, its efforts reflect the leisure of a childlike person who has no qualms about taking his inspiration from what others have done before him. The essay reflects what is loved and hated instead of presenting the mind as creation *ex nihilo* on the model of an unrestrained work ethic. Luck and play are essential to it. It starts not with Adam and Eve but with what it wants to talk about; it says what occurs to it in that context and stops when it feels finished rather than when there is nothing to say. Hence it is classified a trivial endeavor. Its concepts are not derived from a first principle, nor do they fill out to become ultimate principles. Its interpretations are not philologically definitive and conscientious; in principle they are over-interpretations—according to the mechanized verdict of the vigilant intellect that hires out to stupidity as a watchdog against the mind. Out of fear of negativity, the subject's efforts to penetrate what hides behind the facade under the name of objectivity are branded as irrelevant. It's much simpler than that, we are told. The person who interprets instead of accepting what is given and classifying it is marked with the yellow star of one who squanders his intelligence in impotent speculation, reading things in where there is nothing to interpret. A man with his feet on the ground or a man with his head in the clouds—those are the alternatives. But letting oneself be terrorized by the prohibition against saying more than was meant right then and there means complying with the false conceptions that people and things harbor concerning themselves. Interpretation then becomes nothing but removing an outer shell to find what the author wanted to say, or possibly the individual psychological impulses to which the phenomenon points. But since it is scarcely possible to determine what someone may have thought or felt at any particular point, nothing essential is to be gained through such insights. The author's impulses are extinguished in the objective substance they seize hold of. In order to be disclosed, however, the objective wealth of meanings encapsulated in every intellectual phenomenon demands of the recipient the same spontaneity of subjective fantasy that is castigated in the name of objective discipline. Nothing can be interpreted out of something that is not interpreted into it at the same time. The criteria for such interpretation are its compatibility with the text and with itself, and its power to give voice to the elements of the object in conjunction with one another. In this, the essay has something like an aesthetic autonomy that is easily accused of being simply derived from art, although it is distinguished from art by its medium, concepts, and by its claim to a truth devoid of aesthetic semblance. Lukács failed to recognize this when he called the essay an art form in the letter to Leo Popper that introduces *Soul and Form*. But the positivist maxim according to which what is written about art may in no way lay claim to artistic presentation, that is, autonomy of form, is no better. Here as elsewhere, the general positivist tendency to set every possible object, as an object of research, in stark opposition to the subject, does not go beyond the mere separation of form and content—for one can hardly speak of aesthetic matters unaesthetically, devoid of resemblance to the subject matter, without falling into philistinism and losing touch with the object a priori. In positivist practice, the content, once fixed on the model of the protocol sentence, is supposed to be neutral with respect to its presentation, which is supposed to be conventional and not determined by the subject. To the instinct of scientific purism, every expressive impulse in the presentation jeopardizes an objectivity that supposedly leaps forth when the subject has been removed. It thereby jeopardizes the authenticity of the object, which is all the better established the less it relies on support from the form, despite the fact that the criterion of form is whether it delivers the object pure and without admixture. In its allergy to forms as mere accidental attributes, the spirit of science and scholarship [*Wissenschaft*] comes to resemble that of rigid dogmatism. Positivism's irresponsibly sloppy language fancies that it documents responsibility in its object, and reflection on intellectual matters becomes the privilege of the mindless.

None of these offspring of resentment are pure falsehood. If the essay declines to begin by deriving cultural works from something underlying them, it embroils itself all too eagerly in the cultural enterprise promoting the prominence, success, and prestige of marketable products. Fictionalized biographies and all the related commercial writing that depend on them are not mere products of degeneration; they are a permanent temptation for a form whose suspiciousness of false profundity does not protect it from turning into slick superficiality. This can be seen even in Sainte-Beuve, from whom the genre of the modern essay derives. In products like Herbert Eulenberg's biographical silhouettes, the German prototype of a flood of cultural trash, and down to films about Rembrandt, Toulouse-Lautrec and the Bible, this involvement has promoted the neutralization of cultural works to commodities, a process that in recent intellectual history has irresistibly taken hold of what the Eastern bloc ignominiously calls "the heritage." The process is perhaps most obvious in Stefan Zweig, who produced several sophisticated essays in his youth and ended up descending to the psychology of the creative individual in his book on Balzac. This kind of writing does not criticize abstract fundamental concepts, aconceptual data, or habituated clichés; instead, it presupposes them, implicitly but by the same token with all the more complicity. The refuse of interpretive psychology is fused with current categories from the *Weltanschauung* of the cultural philistine, categories like "personality" or

"the irrational." Such essays confuse themselves with the same feuilleton with which the enemies of the essay form confuse it. Forcibly separated from the discipline of academic unfreedom, intellectual freedom itself becomes unfree and serves the socially preformed needs of its clientele. Irresponsibility, itself an aspect of all truth that does not exhaust itself in responsibility to the status quo, then justifies itself to the needs of established consciousness; bad essays are just as conformist as bad dissertations. Responsibility, however, respects not only authorities and committees, but also the object itself.

The essay form, however, bears some responsibility for the fact that the bad essay tells stories about people instead of elucidating the matter at hand. The separation of science and scholarship from art is irreversible. Only the naiveté of the manufacturer of literature takes no notice of it; he considers himself at least an organizational genius and grinds good works of art down into bad ones. With the objectification of the world in the course of progressive demythologization, art and science have separated. A consciousness for which intuition and concept, image and sign would be one and the same—if such a consciousness ever existed—cannot be magically restored, and its restitution would constitute a regression to chaos. Such a consciousness is conceivable only as the completion of the process of mediation, as utopia, conceived by the idealist philosophers since Kant under the name of *intellektuelle Anschauung*, intellectual intuition, something that broke down whenever actual knowledge appealed to it. Wherever philosophy imagines that by borrowing from literature it can abolish objectified thought and its history—what is commonly termed the antithesis of subject and object—and even hopes that Being itself will speak, in a *poésie* concocted of Parmenides and Jungnickel, it starts to turn into a washed-out cultural babble. With a peasant cunning that justifies itself as primordiality, it refuses to honor the obligations of conceptual thought, to which, however, it had subscribed when it used concepts in its propositions and judgments. At the same time, its aesthetic element consists merely of watered-down, second—hand reminiscences of Hölderlin or Expressionism, or perhaps *Jugendstil*, because no thought can entrust itself as absolutely and blindly to language as the notion of a primordial utterance would lead us to believe. From the violence that image and concept thereby do to one another springs the jargon of authenticity, in which words vibrate with emotion while keeping quiet about what has moved them. Language's ambitious transcendence of meaning ends up in a meaninglessness which can be easily seized upon by a positivism to which one feels superior; one plays into the hands of positivism through the very meaninglessness it criticizes, a meaninglessness which one shares by adopting its tokens. Under the spell of such developments, language comes, where it still dares to stir in scholarship and science, to resemble the handicrafts, and the researcher who resists language altogether and, instead of degrading language to a mere paraphrase of his numbers uses tables that unqualifiedly acknowledge the reification of consciousness, is the one who demonstrates, negatively, faithfulness to the aesthetic. In his charts he finds something like a form for that reification without apologetic borrowing from art. To be sure, art has always been so intertwined with the dominant tendencies of enlightenment that it has made use of scientific and scholarly findings in its techniques since classical antiquity. But quantity becomes quality. If technique is made absolute in the work of art; if construction becomes total and eradicates expression, its opposite and its motivating force; if art thus claims to be direct scientific knowledge and correct by scientific standards, it is sanctioning a preartistic manipulation of materials as devoid of meaning as only the "Seyn" [Being] of the philosophy departments can be. It is fraternizing with reification—against which it has been and still is the function of what is functionless, of art, to protest, however mute and reified that protest itself may be.

But although art and science became separate in the course of history, the opposition between them should not be hypostatized. Aversion to an anachronistic conflation of the two does not render a compartmentalized culture sacrosanct. For all their necessity, those compartments represent institutional confirmation of the renunciation of the whole truth. The ideals of purity and tidiness that are common to the enterprises of a veritable philosophy versed in eternal values, an airtight and thoroughly organized science, and an aconceptual intuitive art, bear the marks of a repressive order. A certificate of competency is required of the mind so that it will not transgress upon official culture by crossing culturally confirmed boundary lines. Presupposed in this is the notion that all knowledge can potentially be converted to science. The epistemologies that distinguish prescientific from scientific consciousness have one and all conceived the distinction solely as one of degree. The fact that it has gone no farther than the mere assurance of this convertibility, without living consciousness ever in actuality having been transformed into scientific consciousness, points up the precariousness of the transition, a qualitative difference. The simplest reflection on the life of consciousness would teach us to what a slight extent insights, which are by no means arbitrary hunches, can be fully captured within the net of science. The work of Marcel Proust, which is no more lacking in a scientific-positivist element than Bergson's, is an attempt to express necessary and compelling insights into human beings and social relations that are not readily accommodated within science and scholarship, despite the fact that their claim to objectivity is neither diminished nor abandoned to a vague plausibility. The measure of such objectivity is not the verification of assertions through repeated testing but rather individual human experience, maintained through hope and disillusionment. Such experience throws its observations into relief through confirmation or refutation in the process of recollection. But its individually synthesized unity, in which the whole nevertheless appears, cannot be distributed and recategorized under the separate persons and apparatuses of psychology and sociology. Under the pressure of the scientistic spirit and its desiderata, which are ubiquitous, in latent form, even in the artist, Proust tried, through a technique itself modeled on the sciences, a kind of experimental method, to salvage, or perhaps restore, what used to be thought of—in the days of bourgeois individualism, when individual consciousness still had confidence in itself and was not intimidated by organizational censorship—as the knowledge of a man of experience like the now extinct

homme de lettres, whom Proust conjures up as the highest form of the dilettante. It would not have occurred to anyone to dismiss what such a man of experience had to say as insignificant, arbitrary, and irrational on the grounds that it was only his own and could not simply be generalized in scientific fashion. Those of his findings that slip through the meshes of science most certainly elude science itself. As *Geisteswissenschaft,* literally the science of mind, scientific scholarship fails to deliver what it promises the mind: to illuminate its works from the inside. The young writer who wants to learn what a work of art is, what linguistic form, aesthetic quality, and even aesthetic technique are at college will usually learn about them only haphazardly, or at best receive information taken ready-made from whatever philosophy is in vogue and more or less arbitrarily applied to the content of the works in question. But if he turns to philosophical aesthetics he is besieged with abstract propositions that are not related to the works he wants to understand and do not in fact represent the content he is groping toward. The division of labor in the *kosmos noetikos,* the intellectual world, between art on the one hand and science and scholarship on the other, is not solely responsible for all that; its lines of demarcation cannot be set aside through good will and comprehensive planning. Rather, an intellect irrevocably modeled on the domination of nature and material production abandons the recollection of the stage it has overcome, a stage that promises a future one, the transcendence of rigidified relations of production; and this cripples its specialist's approach precisely when it comes to its specific objects.

In its relationship to scientific procedure and its philosophical grounding as method, the essay, in accordance with its idea, draws the fullest conclusions from the critique of system. Even empiricist theories, which give priority to experience that is open-ended and cannot be anticipated, as opposed to fixed conceptual ordering, remain systematic in that they deal with preconditions for knowledge that are conceived as more or less constant and develop them in as homogeneous a context as possible. Since Bacon—himself an essayist—empiricism has been as much a "method" as rationalism. In the realm of thought it is virtually the essay alone that has successfully raised doubts about the absolute privilege of method. The essay allows for the consciousness of nonidentity, without expressing it directly; it is radical in its non-radicalism, in refraining from any reduction to a principle, in its accentuation of the partial against the total, in its fragmentary character.

> Perhaps the great Sieur de Montaigne felt something like this when he gave his writings the wonderfully elegant and apt title of "Essay." The simple modesty of this word is an arrogant courtesy. The essayist dismisses his own proud hopes which sometimes lead him to believe that he has come close to the ultimate: he has, after all, no more to offer than explanations of the poems of others, or at best of his own ideas. But he ironically adapts himself to this smallness—the eternal smallness of the most profound work of the intellect in face of life—and even emphasizes it with ironic modesty.

The essay does not play by the rules of organized science and theory, according to which, in Spinoza's formulation, the order of things is the same as the order of ideas. Because the unbroken order of concepts is not equivalent to what exists, the essay does not aim at a closed deductive or inductive structure. In particular, it rebels against the doctrine, deeply rooted since Plato, that what is transient and ephemeral is unworthy of philosophy—that old injustice done to the transitory, whereby it is condemned again in the concept. The essay recoils from the violence in the dogma according to which the result of the process of abstraction, the concept, which, in contrast to the individual it grasps, is temporally invariant, should be granted ontological dignity. The fallacy that the *ordo idearum,* the order of ideas, is the *ordo rerum,* the order of things, is founded on the imputation of immediacy to something mediated. Just as something that is merely factual cannot be conceived without a concept, because to think it is always already to conceive it, so too the purest concept cannot be thought except in relation to facticity. Even the constructs of fantasy, presumably free of time and space, refer, if derivatively, to individual existence. This is why the essay refuses to be intimidated by the depraved profundity according to which truth and history are incompatible and opposed to one another. If truth has in fact a temporal core, then the full historical content becomes an integral moment in it; the a posteriori becomes the a priori concretely and not merely in general, as Fichte and his followers claimed. The relationship to experience—and the essay invests experience with as much substance as traditional theory does mere categories—is the relationship to all of history. Merely individual experience, which consciousness takes as its point of departure, since it is what is closest to it, is itself mediated by the overarching experience of historical humankind. The notion that the latter is mediated and one's own experience unmediated is mere self-deception on the part of an individualistic society and ideology. Hence the essay challenges the notion that what has been produced historically is not a fit object of theory. The distinction between a *prima philosophia,* a first philosophy, and a mere philosophy of culture that would presuppose that first philosophy and build upon it—the distinction used as a theoretical rationalization for the taboo on the essay—cannot be salvaged. An intellectual *modus operandi* that honors the division between the temporal and the atemporal as though it were canonical loses its authority. Higher levels of abstraction invest thought with neither greater sanctity nor metaphysical substance; on the contrary, the latter tends to evaporate with the advance of abstraction, and the essay tries to compensate for some of that. The customary objection that the essay is fragmentary and contingent itself postulates that totality is given, and with it the identity of subject and object, and acts as though one were in possession of the whole. The essay, however, does not try to seek the eternal in the transient and distill it out; it tries to render the transient eternal. Its weakness bears witness to the very nonidentity it had to express. It also testifies to an excess of intention over object and thereby to the utopia which is blocked by the partition of the world into the eternal and the transient. In the emphatic essay thought divests itself of the traditional idea of truth.

In doing so it also suspends the traditional concept of method. Thought's depth depends on how deeply it penetrates its object, not on the extent to which it reduces it to something else. The essay gives this a polemical turn by dealing with objects that would be considered derivative, without itself pursuing their ultimate derivation. It thinks conjointly and in freedom about things that meet in its freely chosen object. It does not insist on something beyond mediations—and those are the historical mediations in which the whole society is sedimented—but seeks the truth content in its objects, itself inherently historical. It does not seek any primordial given, thus spiting a societalized [*vergesellschaftete*] society that, because it does not tolerate anything that does not bear its stamp, tolerates least of all anything that reminds it of its own ubiquity, and inevitably cites as its ideological complement the very nature its praxis has completely eliminated. The essay quietly puts an end to the illusion that thought could break out of the sphere of *thesis,* culture, and move into that of *physis,* nature. Spellbound by what is fixed and acknowledged to be derivative, by artifacts, it honors nature by confirming that it no longer exists for human beings. Its alexandrinism is a response to the fact that by their very existence, lilacs and nightingales—where the universal net has permitted them to survive—make us believe that life is still alive. The essay abandons the royal road to the origins, which leads only to what is most derivative—Being, the ideology that duplicates what already exists, but the idea of immediacy, an idea posited in the meaning of mediation itself, does not disappear completely. For the essay all levels of mediation are immediate until it begins to reflect.

Just as the essay rejects primordial givens, so it rejects definition of its concepts. Philosophy has arrived at a thoroughgoing critique of definitions from the most divergent perspectives—in Kant, in Hegel, in Nietzsche. But science has never adopted this critique. Whereas the movement that begins with Kant, a movement against the scholastic residues in modern thought, replaces verbal definitions with an understanding of concepts in terms of the process through which they are produced, the individual sciences, in order to prevent the security of their operations from being disturbed, still insist on the pre-critical obligation to define. In this the neopositivists, who call the scientific method philosophy, are in agreement with scholasticism. The essay, on the other hand, incorporates the antisystematic impulse into its own way of proceeding and introduces concepts unceremoniously, "immediately," just as it receives them. They are made more precise only through their relationship to one another. In this, however, the essay finds support in the concepts themselves. For it is mere superstition on the part of a science that operates by processing raw materials to think that concepts as such are unspecified and become determinate only when defined. Science needs the notion of the concept as a *tabula rasa* to consolidate its claim to authority, its claim to be the sole power to occupy the head of the table. In actuality, all concepts are already implicitly concretized through the language in which they stand. The essay starts with these meanings, and, being essentially language itself, takes them farther; it wants to help language in its relation to concepts, to take them in reflection as they have been named unreflectingly in language. The phenomenological method of interpretive analysis embodies a sense of this, but it fetishizes the relationship of concepts to language. The essay is as skeptical about this as it is about the definition of concepts. Unapologetically it lays itself open to the objection that one does not know for sure how one is to understand its concepts. For it understands that the demand for strict definition has long served to eliminate—through stipulative manipulations of the meanings of concepts—the irritating and dangerous aspects of the things that live in the concepts. But the essay does not make do without general concepts—even language that does not fetishize concepts cannot do without them—nor does it deal with them arbitrarily. Hence it takes presentation more seriously than do modes of proceeding that separate method and object and are indifferent to the presentation of their objectified contents. The manner of expression is to salvage the precision sacrificed when definition is omitted, without betraying the subject matter to the arbitrariness of conceptual meanings decreed once and for all. In this, Benjamin was the unsurpassed master. This kind of precision, however, cannot remain atomistic. Not less but more than a definitional procedure, the essay presses for the reciprocal interaction of its concepts in the process of intellectual experience. In such experience, concepts do not form a continuum of operations. Thought does not progress in a single direction; instead, the moments are interwoven as in a carpet. The fruitfulness of the thoughts depends on the density of the texture. The thinker does not actually think but rather makes himself into an arena for intellectual experience, without unraveling it. While even traditional thought is fed by impulses from such experience, it eliminates the memory of the process by virtue of its form. The essay, however, takes this experience as its model without, as reflected form, simply imitating it. The experience is mediated through the essay's own conceptual organization; the essay proceeds, so to speak, methodically unmethodically.

The way the essay appropriates concepts can best be compared to the behavior of someone in a foreign country who is forced to speak its language instead of piecing it together out of its elements according to rules learned in school. Such a person will read without a dictionary. If he sees the same word thirty times in continually changing contexts, he will have ascertained its meaning better than if he had looked up all the meanings listed, which are usually too narrow in relation to the changes that occur with changing contexts and too vague in relation to the unmistakable nuances that the context gives rise to in every individual case. This kind of learning remains vulnerable to error, as does the essay as form; it has to pay for its affinity with open intellectual experience with a lack of security that the norm of established thought fears like death. It is not so much that the essay neglects indubitable certainty as that it abrogates it as an ideal. The essay becomes true in its progress, which drives it beyond itself, not in a treasure-hunting obsession with foundations. Its concepts receive their light from a *terminus ad quem* hidden from the essay itself, not from any obvious *terminus a quo,* and in this the method itself expresses its utopian intention. All its concepts are to be presented in such a way that they support one another, that each becomes articulated through its configuration with the others. In the essay discrete elements set off against one another come together to form a readable context; the essay erects no scaffolding and no structure. But the elements crystallize as a configuration through their motion. The constellation is a force field, just as every intellectual structure is necessarily transformed into a force field under the essay's gaze.

The essay gently challenges the ideal of *clara et distincta perceptio* and indubitable certainty. Altogether, it might be interpreted as a protest against the four rules established by Descartes' *Discourse on Method* at the beginning of modern Western science and its theory. The second of those rules, the division of the object into "as many parts as possible, and as might be necessary for its adequate solution," outlines the analysis of elements under whose sign traditional theory equates conceptual schemata of classification with the structure of being. Artifacts, however, which are the subject matter of the essay, do not yield to an analysis of elements and can be constructed only from their specific idea. Kant had good reasons for treating works of art and organisms as analogous in this respect, although at the same time, in unerring opposition to Romantic obscurantism, he took pains to distinguish them. The totality can no more be hypostatized as something primary than can elements, the product of analysis. In contrast to both, the essay orients itself to the idea of a reciprocal interaction that is as rigorously intolerant of the quest for elements as of that for the elementary. The specific moments are not to be simply derived from the whole, nor vice versa. The whole is a monad, and yet it is not; its moments, which as moments are conceptual in nature, point beyond the specific object in which they are assembled. But the essay does not pursue them to the point where they would legitimate themselves outside the specific object; if it did so, it would end up in an infinity of the wrong kind. Instead, it moves in so close to the *hic et nunc* of the object that the object becomes dissociated into the moments in which it has its life instead of being a mere object.

The third Cartesian rule, "to conduct my thoughts in such an order that, by commencing with objects the simplest and easiest to know, I might ascend by little and little, and, as it were, step by step, to the knowledge of the more complex," is in glaring contradiction to the essay form, in that the latter starts from the most complex, not from what is simplest and already familiar. The essay form maintains the attitude of someone who is beginning to study philosophy and somehow already has its idea in his mind. He will hardly begin by reading the most simple-minded writers, whose common sense for the most part simply babbles on past the points where one should linger; instead, he reaches for those who are allegedly the most difficult and who then cast their light backwards onto the simple things and illuminate them as an "attitude of thought toward objectivity." The naiveté of the student who finds difficult and formidable things good enough for him has more wisdom in it than a grown-up pedantry that shakes its finger at thought, warning it that it should understand the simple things before it tackles the complex ones, which, however, are the only ones that tempt it. Postponing knowledge in this way only obstructs it. In opposition to the cliché of "comprehensibility," the notion of truth as a casual relationship, the essay requires that one's thought about the matter be from the outset as complex as the object itself; it serves as a corrective to the stubborn primitiveness that always accompanies the prevailing form of reason. If science and scholarship, falsifying as is their custom, reduce what is difficult and complex in a reality that is antagonistic and split into monads to simplified models and then differentiate the models in terms of their ostensible material, the essay, in contrast, shakes off the illusion of a simple and fundamentally logical world, an illusion well suited to the defense of the status quo. The essay's differentiatedness is not something added to it but its medium. Established thought is quick to ascribe that differentiatedness to the mere psychology of the cognitive subjects and thinks that by doing so it has eliminated what is compelling in it. In reality, science and scholarship's self-righteous denunciations of oversophistication are aimed not at a precocious and unreliable method but at the upsetting aspects of the object that method makes manifest.

The fourth Cartesian rule, that one "should in every case institute such exhaustive enumerations and such general surveys" that one "is sure of leaving nothing out," the true principle of systematic thought, recurs unchanged in Kant's polemic against Aristotle's "rhapsodic" thought. This rule corresponds to the charge that the essay is, as the schoolmaster would put it, not exhaustive, while in fact every object, and certainly an intellectual one, encompasses an infinite number of aspects, and only the intention of the cognitive subject decides among them. A "general overview" would be possible only if it were established in advance that the object to be dealt with was fully grasped by the concepts used to treat it, that nothing would be left over that could not be anticipated from the concepts. The rule about the exhaustive enumeration of the individual parts claims, as a consequence of that first assumption, that the object can be presented in a seamless deductive system, a supposition of the philosophies of identity. As in the requirement of definition, the Cartesian rule has survived the rationalist theorem it was based on, in the form of a guide to practical thought: the comprehensive overview and continuity of presentation are demanded even of empirically open science. What in Descartes was to be an intellectual conscience monitoring the necessity of knowledge is thereby transformed into arbitrariness, the arbitrariness of a "frame of reference," an axiomatics to be established at the outset to satisfy a methodological need and for the sake of the plausibility of the whole, but no longer able to demonstrate its own validity or self-evidence. In the German version, this is the arbitrariness of an *Entwurf,* a project, that merely hides its subjective determinants under a pathos-laden quest for Being. The demand for continuity in one's train of thought tends to prejudge the inner coherence of the object, its own harmony. A presentation characterized by continuity would contradict an antagonistic subject matter unless it defined continuity as discontinuity at the same time. In the essay as a form, the need makes itself felt, unconsciously and atheoretically, to annul theoretically outdated claims to completeness and continuity in the concrete *modus operandi* of the mind as well. If the essay opposes, aesthetically, the mean-spirited method whose sole concern is not to leave anything out, it is following an epistemological impulse. The romantic conception of the fragment as a construction that is not complete but rather progresses onward into the infinite through self-reflection champions this anti-idealist motive in the midst of Idealism. Even in the manner of its presentation, the essay may not act as though it had deduced its object and there was nothing left to say about it. Its self-relativization is inherent in its form: it has to be constructed as though it could always break off at any point. It thinks in fragments, just as reality is fragmentary, and finds its unity in and through the breaks and not by glossing them over. An unequivocal logical order deceives us about the antagonistic nature of what that order is imposed upon. Discontinuity is essential to the essay; its subject matter is always a conflict brought to a standstill. While the essay coordinates concepts with one another by means of their function in the parallelogram of forces in its objects, it shrinks from any overarching concept to which they could all be subordinated. What such concepts give the illusion of achieving, their method knows to be impossible and yet tries to accomplish. The word *Versuch,* attempt or essay, in which thought's utopian vision of hitting the bullseye is united with the consciousness of its own fallibility and provisional character, indicates, as do most historically surviving terminologies, something about the form, something to be taken all the more seriously in that it takes place not systematically but rather as a characteristic of an intention groping its way. The essay has to cause the totality to be illuminated in a partial feature, whether the feature be chosen or merely happened upon, without asserting the presence of the totality. It corrects what is contingent and isolated in its insights in that they multiply, confirm, and qualify themselves, whether insights in that they multiply, confirm, and qualify themselves, whether in the further course of the essay itself or in a mosaiclike relationship to other essays, but not by a process of abstraction that ends in characteristic features derived from them. "This, then, is how the essay is distinguished from a treatise. The person who writes essayistically is the one who composes as he experiments, who turns his object around, questions it, feels it, tests it, reflects on it, who attacks it from different sides and assembles what he sees in his mind's eye and puts into words what the object allows one to see under the conditions created in the course of writing." There is both truth and untruth in the discomfort this procedure arouses, the feeling that it could continue on arbitrarily. Truth, because the essay does not in fact come to a conclusion and displays its own inability to do so as a parody of its own a priori. The essay is then saddled with the blame for something for which forms that erase all trace of arbitrariness are actually responsible. That discomfort also has its untruth, however, because the essay's constellation is not arbitrary in the way a philosophical subjectivism that displaces the constraint emanating from the object onto the conceptual order imagines it to be. What determines the essay is the unity of its object along with that of the theory and experience that have migrated into the object. The essay's openness is not the vague openness of feeling and mood; it is given contour by its substance. It resists the idea of a masterpiece, an idea which itself reflects the idea of creation and totality. Its form complies with the critical idea that the human being is not a creator and that nothing human is a creation. The essay, which is always directed toward something already created, does not present itself as creation, nor does it covet something all-encompassing whose totality would resemble that of creation. Its totality, the unity of a form developed immanently, is that of something not total, a totality that does not maintain as form the thesis of the identity of thought and its object that it rejects as content. At times, emancipation from the compulsion of identity gives the essay something that eludes official thought—a moment of something inextinguishable, of indelible color. Certain foreign words in Georg Simmel's work—cachet, attitude—reveal this intention, although it is not discussed in theoretical terms.

The essay is both more open and more closed than traditional thought would like. It is more open in that its structure negates system, and it satisfies its inherent requirements better the more rigorously it holds to that negation; residues of system in essays, through which they hope to make themselves respectable, as for instance the infiltration of literary studies by ready-made popular philosophical ideas, are as worthless as psychological trivialities. But the essay is also more closed, because it works emphatically at the form of its presentation. Consciousness of the non-identity of presentation and subject matter forces presentation to unremitting efforts. In this alone the essay resembles art. In other respects it is necessarily related to theory by virtue of the concepts that appear in it, bringing with them not only their meanings but also their theoretical contexts. To be sure, the essay behaves as cautiously toward theory as it does toward concepts. It does not deduce itself rigorously from theory—the chief flaw in all Lukács' later essayistic works—nor is it a down payment on future syntheses. The more it strives to consolidate itself as theory and to act as though it held the philosopher's stone in its hands, the more intellectual experience courts disaster. At the same time, by its very nature intellectual experience strives for such objectification. This antinomy is reflected in the essay. Just as it absorbs concepts and experiences from the outside, so too it absorbs theories. Its relationship to them, however, is not that of a "perspective." If in the essay the lack of a standpoint is no longer naive and in bondage to the prominence of its objects, if instead the essay uses its relationship to its objects as an antidote to the spell cast by the notion of a beginning, then the essay carries out, in the form of parody, thought's otherwise impotent polemic against a philosophy of mere "perspectives." The essay devours the theories that are close to it; its tendency is always to liquidate opinion, including the opinion it takes as its point of departure. The essay is what it was from the beginning, the critical form par excellence; as immanent critique of intellectual constructions, as a confrontation of what they are with their concept, it is critique of ideology.

> The essay is the form of the critical category of the mind. For the person who criticizes must necessarily experiment, he must create conditions under which an object becomes visible anew, and do so still differently than an author does; above all, the object's frailties must be tried and tested, and this is the meaning of the slight

variation the object experiences at the hands of its critic.

When the essay is charged with having no point of view of its own and accused of relativism because it does not acknowledge any standpoint outside itself, the notion of truth as something "fixed," a hierarchy of concepts, has come into play, the very notion that Hegel, who did not like points of view, had destroyed. Here the essay is in accord with its polar opposite, the philosophy of absolute knowledge. It wants to heal thought of its arbitrary character by incorporating arbitrariness reflectively into its own approach rather than disguising it as immediacy.

Idealist philosophy, to be sure, suffered from the inconsistency of criticizing an abstract overarching concept, a mere "result," in the name of process, which is inherently discontinuous, while at the same time talking about dialectical method in the manner of idealism. For this reason the essay is more dialectical than the dialectic is when the latter discourses on itself. The essay takes Hegelian logic at its word: the truth of the totality cannot be played off against individual judgments. Nor can truth be made finite in the form of an individual judgment; instead, singularity's claim to truth is taken literally, up to the point where its untruth becomes evident. The daring, anticipatory, and not fully redeemed aspect of every essayistic detail attracts other such details as its negation; the untruth in which the essay knowingly entangles itself is the element in which its truth resides. Certainly there is untruth in its very form as well; it relates to something culturally preformed and derivative as though it were an autonomous entity. But the more vigorously the essay suspends the notion of something primary and refuses to concoct culture out of nature, the more fundamentally it acknowledges the quasi-natural character of culture itself. Even now, the blind context of nature, myth, perpetuates itself in culture, and this is precisely what the essay reflects on: the relationship of nature and culture is its true theme. Instead of "reducing" cultural phenomena, the essay immerses itself in them as though in a second nature, a second immediacy, in order to negate and transcend the illusion of immediacy through its perseverance. It has no more illusions about the difference between culture and what lies beneath it than does the philosophy of origin. But for it culture is not an epiphenomenon that covers Being and should be destroyed; instead, what lies beneath culture is itself *thesis,* something constructed, the false society. This is why the origin has no more value for the essay than the superstructure. It owes its freedom in the choice of its objects, its sovereignty in the face of all priorities of fact or theory, to the fact that for it all objects are in a certain sense equally close to the center—equally close to the principle that casts its spell over all of them. It does not glorify concern with the original as more primordial than concern with what is mediated, because for it primordiality is itself an object of reflection, something negative. This corresponds to a situation in which primordiality, as a standpoint of the spirit in the midst of a societalized world, becomes a lie. The lie extends from the elevation of historical concepts in historical languages to primal words, to academic instruction in "creative writing," and to primitiveness pursued as a handicraft, to recorders and finger painting, in which pedagogical necessity acts as though it were a metaphysical virtue. Baudelaire's revolt of literature against nature as a social preserve does not spare thought. The paradises of thought too are now only artificial ones, and the essay strolls in them. Since, in Hegel's dictum, there is nothing between heaven and earth that is not mediated, thought remains faithful to the idea of immediacy only in and through what is mediated; conversely, it falls prey to the mediated as soon as it tries to grasp the unmediated directly. The essay cunningly anchors itself in texts as though they were simply there and had authority. In this way, without the deception of a first principle, the essay gets a ground, however dubious, under its feet, comparable to theological exegeses of sacred texts in earlier times. Its tendency, however, is the opposite, a critical one: to shatter culture's claims by confronting texts with their own emphatic concept, with the truth that each one intends even if it does not want to intend it, and to move culture to become mindful of its own untruth, of the ideological illusion in which culture reveals its bondage to nature. Under the essay's gaze second nature recognizes itself as first nature.

If the essay's truth gains its force from its untruth, that truth should be sought not in mere opposition to the dishonorable and proscribed element in the essay but rather within that element itself, in the essay's mobility, its lack of the solidity the demand for which science transferred from property relations to the mind. Those who believe that they have to defend the mind against lack of solidity are its enemies: the mind itself, once emancipated, is mobile. Once it wants more than the mere administrative duplication and processing of what has always already existed, the mind seems to have an exposed quality; abandoned by play, truth would be nothing but tautology. For historically the essay too is related to rhetoric, which the scientific mentality has wanted to get rid of since Bacon and Descartes—until, appropriately, in a scientific age it degenerated to a science *sui generis,* that of communications. Rhetoric was probably never anything but thought in its adaptation to communicative language. Such thought aimed at something unmediated: the vicarious gratification of the listeners. The essay retains, precisely in the autonomy of its presentation, which distinguishes it from scientific and scholarly information, traces of the communicative element such information dispenses with. In the essay the satisfactions that rhetoric tries to provide for the listener are sublimated into the idea of a happiness in freedom vis â vis the object, a freedom that gives the object more of what belongs to it than if it were mercilessly incorporated into the order of ideas. Scientific consciousness, which opposes all anthropomorphic conceptions, was always allied with the reality principle and, like the latter, antagonistic to happiness. While happiness is always supposed to be the aim of all domination of nature, it is always envisioned as a regression to mere nature. This is evident all the way up to the highest philosophies, even those of Kant and Hegel. These philosophies have their pathos in the absolute idea of reason, but at the same time they always denigrate it as insolent and disrespectful when it relativizes accepted values. In opposition to this tendency, the essay salvages a moment of sophistry. The hostility to happiness in official critical thought is especially marked

in Kant's transcendental dialectic, which wants to immortalize the line between understanding and speculation and prevent thought from "wandering off into intelligible worlds," as the characteristic metaphor expresses it. Whereas a self-critical reason should, according to Kant, have both feet firmly on the ground, should ground itself, it tends inherently to seal itself off from everything new and also from curiosity, the pleasure principle of thought, something existential ontology vilifies as well. What Kant saw, in terms of content, as the goal of reason, the creation of humankind, utopia, is hindered by the form of his thought, epistemology. It does not permit reason to go beyond the realm of experience, which, in the mechanism of mere material and invariant categories, shrinks to what has always already existed. The essay's object however, is the new in its newness, not as something that can be translated back into the old existing forms. By reflecting the object without violence, as it were, the essay mutely laments the fact that truth has betrayed happiness and itself along with it, and this lament provokes the rage directed against the essay. The persuasive element of communication is alienated from its original aim in the essay—just as the function of many musical features changes in autonomous music—and becomes a pure determinant of the presentation itself; it becomes the compelling element in its construction, whose aim is not to copy the object but to reconstitute it from its conceptual *membra disjecta*. The offensive transitions in rhetoric, in which association, verbal ambiguity, and a relaxation of logical synthesis made it easy for the listener and subjugated him, enfeebled, to the orator's will, are fused in the essay with the truth content. Its transitions repudiate conclusive deductions in favor of cross-connections between elements, something for which discursive logic has no place. The essay uses equivocations not out of sloppiness, nor in ignorance of the scientific ban on them, but to make it clear—something the critique of equivocation, which merely separates meanings, seldom succeeds in doing—that when a word covers different things they are not completely different; the unity of the word calls to mind a unity, however hidden, in the object itself. This unity, however, should not be mistaken for linguistic affinity, as is the practice of contemporary restorationist philosophies. Here too the essay approaches the logic of music, that stringent and yet aconceptual art of transition, in order to appropriate for verbal language something it forfeited under the domination of discursive logic—although that logic cannot be set aside but only outwitted within its own forms by dint of incisive subjective expression. For the essay does not stand in simple opposition to discursive procedure. It is not unlogical; it obeys logical criteria insofar as the totality of its propositions must fit together coherently. No mere contradictions may remain unless they are established as belonging to the object itself. But the essay does not develop its ideas in accordance with discursive logic. It neither makes deductions from a principle nor draws conclusions from coherent individual observations. It coordinates elements instead of subordinating them, and only the essence of its content, not the manner in which it is presented, is commensurable with logical criteria. In comparison with forms in which a preformed content is communicated indifferently, the essay is more dynamic than traditional thought by virtue of the tension between the presentation and the matter presented. But at the same time, as a constructed juxtaposition of elements it is more static. Its affinity with the image lies solely in this, except that the staticness of the essay is one in which relationships of tension have been brought, as it were, to a standstill. The slight elasticity of the essayist's train of thought forces him to greater intensity than discursive thought, because the essay does not proceed blindly and automatically, as the latter does, but must reflect on itself at every moment. This reflection extends not only to its relationship to established thought but also to its relationship with rhetoric and communication. Otherwise the essay, which fancies itself more than science, becomes fruitlessly prescientific.

The contemporary relevance of the essay is that of anachronism. The time is less favorable to it than ever. It is ground to pieces between an organized system of science and scholarship on the one side, in which everyone presumes to control everyone and everything and where everything not tailored to the current consensus is excluded while being praised hypocritically as "intuitive" or "stimulating," and on the other side a philosophy that has to make do with the empty and abstract remnants of what the scientific enterprise has not yet taken over and which thereby become the object of second-order operations on its part. The essay, however, is concerned with what is blind in its objects. It wants to use concepts to pry open the aspect of its objects that cannot be accommodated by concepts, the aspect that reveals, through the contradictions in which concepts become entangled, that the net of their objectivity is a merely subjective arrangement. It wants to polarize the opaque element and release the latent forces in it. Its efforts are directed toward concretizing a content defined in time and space; it constructs a complex of concepts interconnected in the same way it imagines them to be interconnected in the object. It eludes the dictates of the attributes that have been ascribed to ideas since Plato's definition in the *Symposium*, "existing eternally and neither coming into being nor passing away, neither changing nor diminishing," "a being in and for itself eternally uniform," and yet it remains idea in that it does not capitulate before the burden of what exists, does not submit to what merely is. The essay, however, judges what exists not against something eternal but by an enthusiastic fragment from Nietzsche's late period:

> If we affirm one single moment, we thus affirm not only ourselves but all existence. For nothing is self-sufficient, neither in us ourselves nor in things: and if our soul has trembled with happiness and sounded like a harp string just once, all eternity was needed to produce this one event—and in this single moment of affirmation all eternity was called good, redeemed, justified, and affirmed.

Except that the essay distrusts even this kind of justification and affirmation. It has no name but a negative one for the happiness that was sacred to Nietzsche. Even the highest manifestations of the spirit, which express this happiness, are always also guilty of obstructing happiness as long as they remain mere spirit. Hence the essay's innermost formal law is heresy. Through violations of the or-

thodoxy of thought, something in the object becomes visible which it is orthodoxy's secret and objective aim to keep invisible.

Georg Lukács

SOURCE: "On the Nature and Form of the Essay: A Letter to Leo Popper," in *Soul and Form*, translated by Anna Bostock, Merlin Press, 1974, pp. 1-18.

[*Lukács, a Hungarian literary critic and philosopher, was a leading proponent of Marxist thought. His development of Marxist ideology was part of a broader system of thought in which he sought to further the values of rationalism (peace and progress), humanism (socialist politics), and traditionalism (Realist literature) over the counter-values of irrationalism (war), totalitarianism (reactionary politics), and modernism (post-Realist literature). The subjects of his literary criticism are primarily the nineteenth-century Realists—Balzac and Tolstoy—and their twentieth-century counterparts—Gorky and Mann. In the following excerpt from an essay cast in the form of a letter to Leo Popper and first published in 1971, Lukács discourses on the nature of the essay: whether it is a form of art or of science. His essay begins by examining the critical essay, but moves by degrees to the essay in general.*]

To what extent have the really great writings which belong to this category been given literary form, and to what extent is this form of theirs an independent one? To what extent do the standpoint of such a work and the form given to this standpoint lift it out of the sphere of science and place it at the side of the arts, yet without blurring the frontiers of either? To what extent do they endow the work with the force necessary for a conceptual re-ordering of life, and yet distinguish it from the icy, final perfection of philosophy? That is the only profound apology to be made for such writings, as well as the only profound criticism to be addressed to them; for they are measured first and foremost by the yardstick of these questions, and the determining of such an objective will be the first step towards showing how far they fall short of attaining it.

The critique, the essay—call it provisionally what you will—as a work of art, a genre? I know you think the question tedious; you feel that all the arguments for and against have been exhausted long ago. Yet I believe that all the discussions have barely touched upon the essence of the real question: what is an essay? What is its intended form of expression, and what are the ways and means whereby this expression is accomplished? I believe that the aspect of "being well written" has been too one-sidedly emphasized in this context. It has been argued that the essay can be stylistically of equal value to a work of the imagination, and that, for this reason, it is unjust to speak of value differences at all. Yet what does that mean? Even if we consider criticism to be a work of art in this sense, we have not yet said anything at all about its essential nature. "Whatever is well written is a work of art." Is a well-written advertisement or news item a work of art? Here I can see what so disturbs you about such a view of criticism: it is anarchy, the denial of form in order that an intellect which believes itself to be sovereign may have free play with possibilities of every kind. But if I speak here of criticism as a form of art, I do so in the name of order (i.e. almost purely symbolically and non-essentially), and solely on the strength of my feeling that the essay has a form which separates it, with the rigour of a law, from all other art forms. I want to try and define the essay as strictly as is possible, precisely by describing it as an art form.

Let us not, therefore, speak of the essay's similarities with works of literary imagination, but of what divides it from them. Let any resemblance serve here merely as a background against which the differences stand out all the more sharply; the purpose of mentioning these resemblances at all will be to limit our attention to genuine essays, leaving aside those writings which, useful though they are, do not deserve to be described as essays because they can never give us anything more than information, facts and "relationships". Why, after all, do we read essays? Many are read as a source of instruction, but there are others whose attraction is to be found in something quite different. It is not difficult to identify these. Our view, our appreciation of classical tragedy is quite different today, is it not, from Lessing's in the *Dramaturgy;* Winckelmann's Greeks seem strange, almost incomprehensible to us, and soon we may feel the same about Burckhardt's Renaissance. And yet we read them: why? On the other hand there are critical writings which, like a hypothesis in natural science, like a design for a machine part, lose all their value at the precise moment when a new and better one becomes available. But if—as I hope and expect—someone were to write a new *Dramaturgy,* a *Dramaturgy* in favour of Corneille and against Shakespeare—how could it damage Lessing's? And what did Burckhardt and Pater, Rhode and Nietzsche do to change the effect upon us of Winckelmann's dreams of Greece?

"Of course, if criticism were a science . . ." writes Kerr. "But the imponderables are too strong. Criticism is, at the very best, an art." And if it were a science—it is not so impossible that it will become one—how would that change our problem? We are not concerned here with replacing something by something else, but with something essentially new, something that remains untouched by the complete or approximate attainment of scientific goals. Science affects us by its contents, art by its forms; science offers us facts and the relationships between facts, but art offers us souls and destinies. Here the ways part; here there is no replacement and no transition. In primitive, as yet undifferentiated epochs, science and art (and religion and ethics and politics) are integrated, they form a single whole; but as soon as science has become separate and independent, everything that has led up to it loses its value. Only when something has dissolved all its content in form, and thus become pure art, can it no longer become superfluous; but then its previous scientific nature altogether forgotten and emptied of meaning.

There is, then, a science of the arts; but there is also an entirely different kind of expression of the human temperament, which usually takes the form of writing about the arts. Usually, I say, for there are many writings which are engendered by such feelings without ever touching upon literature or art—writings in which the same life-problems

are raised as in the writings which call themselves criticism, but with the difference that here the questions are addressed directly to life itself: they do not need the mediation of literature or art. And it is precisely the writings of the greatest essayist which belong to this category: Plato's *Dialogues,* the texts of the mystics, Montaigne's Essays, Kierkegaard's imaginary diaries and short stories.

An endless series of almost imperceptible, subtle transitions leads from here to imaginative writing. Think of the last scene in the *Heracles* of Euripides: the tragedy is already over when Theseus appears and discovers everything that has happened—Hera's terrible vengeance on Heracles. Then begins the dialogue about life between the mourning Heracles and his friend; questions akin to those of the Socratic dialogues are asked, but the questioners are stiffer and less human, and their questions more conceptual, less related to direct experience than in Plato. Think of the last act of *Michael Kramer,* of the *Confessions of a Beautiful Soul,* of Dante, of *Everyman,* of Bunyan—must I quote further examples?

Doubtless you will say that the end of *Heracles* is undramatic and Bunyan is. . . . Certainly, certainly, but why? The *Heracles* is undramatic because every dramatic style has this natural corollary, that whatever happens within human souls is projected into human actions, movements and gestures and is thus made visible and palpable to the senses. Here you see Hera's vengeance overtaking Heracles, you see Heracles in the blissful enjoyment of victory before vengeance is upon him, you see his frenzied gestures in the madness which Hera has dealt to him and his wild despair after the storm, when he sees what has happened to him. But of what comes after you see nothing at all. Theseus comes—and you try in vain to determine by other than conceptual means what happens next: what you see and hear is no longer a true means of expression of the real event, and that the event occurs at all is deep down a matter of indifference to you. You see no more than that Theseus and Heracles leave the stage together. Prior to that some questions are asked: what is the true nature of the gods? Which gods may we believe in, and which not? What is life and what is the best way of bearing one's sufferings manfully? The concrete experience which has led up to these questions is lost in an infinite distance. And when the answers return once more into the world of facts, they are no longer answers to questions posed by real life—questions of what these men must do or refrain from doing in this particular situation. These answers cast a stranger's eye upon all facts, for they have come from life and from the gods and know scarcely anything of Heracles' pain or of its cause in Hera's vengeance. Drama, I know, also addresses questions to life, and in drama, too, the answer comes from destiny—and in the last analysis the questions and answers, even in drama, are tied to certain definite facts. But the true dramatist (so long as he is a true poet, a genuine representative of the poetic principle) will see *a life* as being so rich and so intense that almost imperceptibly it becomes *life.* Here, however, everything becomes undramatic because here the other principle comes into effect: for the life that here poses the question loses all its corporeality at the moment when the first word of the question is uttered.

There are, then, two types of reality of the soul: one is *life* and the other *living;* both are equally effective, but they can never be effective at the same time. Elements of both are contained in the lived experience of every human being, even if in always varying degrees of intensity and depth; in memory too, there is now one, now the other, but at any one moment we can only feel one of these two forms. Ever since there has been life and men have sought to understand and order life, there has been this duality in their lived experience. But the struggle for priority and pre-eminence between the two has mostly been fought out in philosophy, so that the battle-cries have always had a different sound, and for this reason have gone unrecognized by most men and have been unrecognizable to them. It would seem that the question was posed most clearly in the Middle Ages, when thinkers divided into two camps, the ones maintaining that the *universalia*—concepts, or Plato's Ideas if you will—were the sole true realities, while the others acknowledged them only as words, as names summarizing the sole true and distinct *things.*

The same duality also separates means of expression: the opposition here is between image and "significance". One principle is an image-creating one, the other a signifi-cance-supposing one. For one there exist only things, for the other only the relationships between them, only concepts and values. Poetry in itself knows of nothing beyond things; for it, every thing is serious and unique and incomparable. That is also why poetry knows no questions: you do not address questions to pure *things,* only to their relationships, for—as in fairy-tales—every question here turns again into a thing resembling the one that called it into being. The hero stands at the crossroads or in the midst of the struggle, but the crossroads and the struggle are not destinies about which questions may be asked and answers given; they are simply and literally struggles and crossroads. And the hero blows his miraculous horn and the expected miracle occurs: a thing which once more orders life. But in really profound criticism there is no life of things, no image, only transparency, only something that no image would be capable of expressing completely. An "imagelessness of all images" is the aim of all mystics, and Socrates speaks mockingly and contemptuously to Phaedrus of poets, who never have nor ever could worthily celebrate the true life of the soul. "For the great existence which the immortal part of the soul once lived is colourless and without form and impalpable, and only the soul's guide, the mind, can behold it."

You may perhaps reply that my poet is an empty abstraction and so, too, is my critic. You are right—both are abstractions, but not, perhaps, quite empty ones. They are abstractions because even Socrates must speak in images of his "world without form", his world on the far side of form, and even the German mystic's "imagelessness" is a metaphor. Nor is there any poetry without some ordering of things. Matthew Arnold once called it *criticism of life.* It represents the ultimate relationships between man and destiny and world, and without doubt it has its origin in those profound regions, even if, often, it is unaware of it. If poetry often refuses all questioning, all taking up of positions, is not the denial of all questions in itself an asking of questions, and is not the conscious rejection of any posi-

tion in itself a position? I shall go further: the separation of image and significance is itself an abstraction, for the significance is always wrapped in images and the reflection of a glow from beyond the image shines through every image. Every image belongs to our world and the joy of being in the world shines in its countenance; yet it also reminds us of something that was once there, at some time or another, a somewhere, its home, the only thing that, in the last analysis, has meaning and significance for the soul. Yes, in their naked purity they are merely abstractions, those two limits of human feeling, but only with the help of such abstractions can I define the two poles of possible literary expression. And the writings which most resolutely reject the image, which reach out most passionately for what lies behind the image, are the writings of the critics, the Platonists and the mystics.

But in saying this I have already explained why this kind of feeling calls for an art form of its own—why every expression of this kind of feeling must always disturb us when we find it in other forms, in poetry. It was you who once formulated the great demand which everything that has been given form must satisfy, the only absolutely universal demand, perhaps, but one that is inexorable and allows of no exception: the demand that everything in a work must be fashioned from the same material, that each of its parts must be visibly ordered from one single point. And because all writing aspires to both unity and multiplicity, this is the universal problem of style: to achieve equilibrium in a welter of disparate things, richness and articulation in a mass of uniform matter. Something that is viable in one art form is dead in another: here is practical, palpable proof of the inner divorce of forms. Do you remember how you explained to me the living quality of human figures in certain heavily stylized mural paintings? You said: these frescoes are painted between pillars, and even if the gestures of the men depicted in them are stiff like those of puppets and every facial expression is only a mask, still all this is more alive than the columns which frame the pictures and form a decorative unity with them. Only a little more alive, for the unity must be preserved; but more alive all the same, so that there may be an illusion of life. Here, however, the problem of equilibrium is posed in this way: the world and the beyond, image and transparency, idea and emanation lie in the two cups of a scale which is to remain balanced. The deeper down the question reaches—you need only compare the tragedy with the fairy-tale—the more linear the images become, the smaller the number of planes into which everything is compressed, the paler and more matt the radiance of the colours, the simpler the richness and multiplicity of the world, the more mask-like the expressions of the characters. But there are other experiences, for the expression of which even the simplest and most measured gesture would be too much—and too little; there are questions which are asked so softly that beside them the sound of the most toneless of events would be crude noise, not musical accompaniment; there are destiny-relationships which are so exclusively relationships between destinies as such that anything human would merely disturb their abstract purity and grandeur. I am not speaking here of subtlety or depth: those are value categories and are therefore valid only within a particular form. We are speaking of the fundamental principles which separate forms from one another—of the material from which the whole is constructed, of the standpoint, the world-view which gives unity to the entire work. Let me put it briefly: were one to compare the forms of literature with sunlight refracted in a prism, the writings of the essayists would be the ultra-violet rays.

There are experiences, then, which cannot be expressed by any gesture and which yet long for expression. From all that has been said you will know what experiences I mean and of what kind they are. I mean intellectuality, conceptuality as sensed experience, as immediate reality, as spontaneous principle of existence; the world-view in its undisguised purity as an event of the soul, as the motive force of life. The question is posed immediately: what is life, what is man, what is destiny? But posed as a question only: for the answer, here, does not supply a "solution" like one of the answers of science or, at purer heights, those of philosophy. Rather, as in poetry of every kind, it is symbol, destiny and tragedy. When a man experiences such things, then everything that is outward about him awaits in rigid immobility the outcome of the struggle between invisible forces to which the senses have no access. Any gesture with which such a man might wish to express something of his experience would falsify that experience, unless it ironically emphasized its own inadequacy and thus cancelled itself out. A man who experiences such things cannot be characterized by any outward feature—how then can he be given form in a work of literature? All writings represent the world in the symbolic terms of a destiny-relationship; everywhere, the problem of destiny determines the problem of form. This unity, this coexistence is so strong that neither element ever occurs without the other; here again a separation is possible only by way of abstraction. Therefore the separation which I am trying to accomplish here appears, in practice, merely as a shift of emphasis: poetry receives its profile and its form from destiny, and form in poetry appears always only as destiny; but in the works of the essayists form *becomes* destiny, it is the destiny-creating principle. This difference means the following: destiny lifts things up outside the world of things, accentuating the essential ones and eliminating the inessential; but form sets limits round a substance which otherwise would dissolve like air in the All. In other words, destiny comes from the same source as everything else, it is a thing among things, whereas form—seen as something finished, i.e. seen from outside—defines the limits of the immaterial. Because the destiny which orders things is flesh of their flesh and blood of their blood, destiny is not to be found in the writings of the essayists. For destiny, once stripped of its uniqueness and accidentality, is just as airy and immaterial as all the rest of the incorporeal matter of these writings, and is no more capable of giving them form than they themselves possess any natural inclination or possibility of condensing themselves into form.

That is why such writings speak of forms. The critic is one who glimpses destiny in forms: whose most profound experience is the soul-content which forms indirectly and unconsciously conceal within themselves. Form is his great experience, form—as immediate reality—is the image-element, the really living content of his writings.

This form, which springs from a symbolic contemplation of life-symbols, acquires a life of its own through the power of that experience. It becomes a world-view, a standpoint, an attitude vis-à-vis the life from which it sprang: a possibility of reshaping it, of creating it anew. The critic's moment of destiny, therefore, is that moment at which things become forms—the moment when all feelings and experiences on the near or the far side of form receive form, are melted down and condensed into form. It is the mystical moment of union between the outer and the inner, between soul and form. It is as mystical as the moment of destiny in tragedy when the hero meets his destiny, in the short story when accident and cosmic necessity coverage, in poetry when the soul and its world meet and coalesce into a new unity that can no more be divided, either in the past or in the future. Form is reality in the writings of critics; it is the voice with which they address their questions to life. That is the true and most profound reason why literature and art are the typical, natural subject-matter of criticism. For here the end-point of poetry can become a starting-point and a beginning; here form appears, even in its abstract conceptuality, as something surely and concretely real. But this is only the typical subject-matter of the essay, not the sole one. For the essayist needs form only as lived experience and he needs only its life, only the living soul-reality it contains. But this reality is to be found in every immediate sensual expression of life, it can be read out of and read into every such experience; life itself can be lived and given form through such a scheme of lived experience. Because literature, art and philosophy pursue forms openly and directly, whereas in life they are no more than the ideal demand of a certain kind of men and experiences, a lesser intensity of critical capacity is needed to experience something formed than to experience something lived; and that is why the reality of form-vision appears, at the first and most superficial glance, less problematic in the sphere of art than in life. But this only seems to be so at the first and most superficial glance, for the form of life is no more abstract than the form of a poem. Here as there, form becomes perceptible only through abstraction, and there as here the reality of form is no stronger than the force with which it is experienced. It would be superficial to distinguish between poems according to whether they take their subject-matter from life or elsewhere; for in any case the form-creating power of poetry breaks and scatters whatever is old, whatever has already been formed, and everything becomes unformed raw material in its hands. To draw such a distinction here seems to me just as superficial, for both ways of contemplating the world are merely standpoints taken up in relation to things, and each is applicable everywhere, although it is true that for both there exist certain things which, with a naturalness decreed by nature, submit themselves to one particular standpoint and others which can only be forced to do so by violent struggles and profound experiences.

As in every really essential relationship, natural effect and immediate usefulness coincide here: the experiences which the writings of the essayists were written to express become conscious in the minds of most people only when they look at the pictures or read the poem discussed and even then they rarely have a force that could move life itself. That is why most people have to believe that the writings of the essayists are produced only in order to explain books and pictures, to facilitate their understanding. Yet this relationship is profound and necessary, and it is precisely the indivisible and organic quality of this mixture of being-accidental and being-necessary which is at the root of that humour and that irony which we find in the writings of every truly great essayist—that peculiar humour which is so strong that to speak of it is almost indecent, for there is no use in pointing it out to someone who does not spontaneously feel it. And the irony I mean consists in the critic always speaking about the ultimate problems of life, but in a tone which implies that he is only discussing pictures and books, only the inessential and pretty ornaments of real life—and even then not their innermost substance but only their beautiful and useless surface. Thus each essay appears to be removed as far as possible from life, and the distance between them seems the greater, the more burningly and painfully we sense the actual closeness of the true essence of both. Perhaps the great Sieur de Montaigne felt something like this when he gave his writings the wonderfully elegant and apt title of "Essays". The simple modesty of this word is an arrogant courtesy. The essayist dismisses his own proud hopes which sometimes lead him to believe that he has come close to the ultimate: he has, after all, no more to offer than explanations of the poems of others, or at best of his own ideas. But he ironically adapts himself to this smallness—the eternal smallness of the most profound work of the intellect in face of life—and even emphasizes it with ironic modesty. In Plato, conceptuality is underlined by the irony of the small realities of life. Eryximachos cures Aristophanes of hiccups by making him sneeze before he can begin his deeply meaningful hymn to Eros. And Hippothales watches with anxious attention while Socrates questions his beloved Lysis—and little Lysis, with childish malice, asks Socrates to torment his friend Menexenos with questions just as he has tormented him. Rough guardians come and break up the gently scintillating dialogue, and drag the boys off home. Socrates, however, is more amused than anything else: "Socrates and the two boys wanted to be friends, yet were not even able to say what a friend really is." I see a similar irony in the vast scientific apparatus of certain modern essayists (think only of Weininger), and only a different expression of it in the discreetly reserved manner of a Dilthey. We can always find the same irony in every text by every great essayist, though admittedly always in a different form. The mystics of the Middle Ages are the only ones without inner irony—I surely need not tell you why.

We see, then, that criticism and the essay generally speak of pictures, books and ideas. What is their attitude towards the matter which is represented? People say that the critic must always speak the truth, whereas the poet is not obliged to tell the truth about his subject-matter. It is not our intention here to ask Pilate's question nor to enquire whether the poet, too, is not impelled towards an inner truthfulness and whether the truth of any criticism can be stronger or greater than this. I do not propose to ask these questions because I really do see a difference here, but once again a difference which is altogether pure, sharp and without transitions only at its abstract poles. When I

wrote about Kassner I pointed out that the essay always speaks of something that has already been given form, or at least something that has already been there at some time in the past; hence it is part of the nature of the essay that it does not create new things from an empty nothingness but only orders those which were once alive. And because it orders them anew and does not form something new out of formlessness, it is bound to them and must always speak "the truth" about them, must find expression for their essential nature. Perhaps the difference can be most briefly formulated thus: poetry takes its motifs from life (and art); the essay has its models in art (and life). Perhaps this is enough to define the difference: the paradoxy of the essay is almost the same as that of the portrait. You see why, do you not? In front of a landscape we never ask ourselves whether this mountain or that river really is as it is painted there; but in front of every portrait the question of likeness always forces itself willy-nilly upon us. Give a little more thought, therefore, to this problem of likeness—this problem which, foolish and superficial as it is, drives true artists to despair. You stand in front of a Velasquez portrait and you say: "What a marvellous likeness," and you feel that you have really said something about the painting. Likeness? Of whom? Of no one, of course. You have no idea whom it represents, perhaps you can never find out; and if you could, you would care very little. Yet you feel that it is a likeness. Other portraits produce their effect only by colour and line, and so you do not have this feeling. In other words, the really significant portraits give us, besides all other artistic sensations, also this: the life of a human being who once was really alive, forcing us to feel that his life was exactly as shown by the lines and colours of the painting. Only because we see painters in front of their models fight such a hard battle for this ideal expression—because the look and the battle-cry of this battle are such that it cannot be anything else than a battle for likeness—only for this reason do we give this name to the portrait's suggestion of real life, even though there is no one in the world whom the portrait could be like. For even if we know the person represented, whose portrait we may call "like" or "unlike"—is it not an abstraction to say of an arbitrarily chosen moment or expression that *this* is that person's likeness? And even if we know thousands of such moments or expressions, what do we know of the immeasurably large part of his life when we do not see him, what do we know of the inner light which burns within this "known" person, what of the way this inner light is reflected in others? And that, you see, is more or less how I imagine the truth of the essay to be. Here too there is a struggle for truth, for the incarnation of a life which someone has seen in a man, an epoch or a form; but it depends only on the intensity of the work and its vision whether the written text conveys to us this suggestion of that particular life.

The great difference, then, is this: poetry gives us the illusion of life of the person it represents; nowhere is there a conceivable someone or something against which the created work can be measured. The hero of the essay was once alive, and so his life must be given form; but this life, too, is as much inside the work as everything is in poetry. The essay has to create from within itself all the preconditions for the effectiveness and validity of its vision. Therefore two essays can never contradict one another: each creates a different world, and even when, in order to achieve a higher universality, it goes beyond that created world, it still remains inside it by its tone, colour and accent; that is to say, it leaves that world only in the inessential sense. It is simply not true that there exists an objective, external criterion of life and truth, e.g. that the truth of Grimm's, Dilthey's or Schlegel's Goethe can be tested against the "real" Goethe. It is not true because many Goethes, different from one another and each profoundly different from *our* Goethe, may convince us of their life: and, conversely, we are disappointed if our own visions are presented by others, yet without that vital breath which would give them autonomous life. It is true that the essay strives for truth: but just as Saul went out to look for his father's she-asses and found a kingdom, so the essayist who is really capable of looking for the truth will find at the end of his road the goal he was looking for: life.

The illusion of truth! Do not forget how slowly and with how much difficulty poetry abandoned that ideal. It happened not so very long ago, and it is highly questionable whether the disappearance of the illusion was entirely advantageous. It is highly questionable whether man should want the precise thing he sets out to attain, whether he has the right to walk towards his goal along straight and simple paths. Think of the chivalresque epics of the Middle Ages, think of the Greek tragedies, think of Giotto and you will see what I am trying to say. We are not speaking here of ordinary truth, the truth of naturalism which it would be more accurate to call the triviality of everyday life, but of the truth of the myth by whose power ancient tales and legends are kept alive for thousands of years. The true poets of myths looked only for the true meaning of their themes; they neither could nor wished to check their pragmatic reality. They saw these myths as sacred, mysterious hieroglyphics which it was their mission to read. But do you not see that both worlds can have a mythology of their own? It was Friedrich Schlegel who said long ago that the national gods of the Germans were not Hermann or Wotan but science and the arts. Admittedly, that is not true of the *whole* life of Germany, but it is all the more apt as a description of *part* of the life of every nation in every epoch—that part, precisely, of which we are speaking. That life, too, has its golden ages and its lost paradises; we find in it rich lives full of strange adventures and enigmatic punishments of dark sins; heroes of the sun appear and fight out their harsh feuds with the forces of darkness; here, too, the magic words of wise magicians and the tempting songs of beautiful sirens lead weaklings into perdition; here too there is original sin and redemption. All the struggles of life are present here, but the stuff of which everything is made is different from the stuff of the "other" life.

We want poets and critics to give us life-symbols and to mould the still-living myths and legends in the form of our questions. It is a subtle and poignant irony, is it not, when a great critic dreams our longing into early Florentine paintings or Greek torsos and, in that way, gets something out of them for us that we would have sought in vain everywhere else—and then speaks of the latest achievements of scientific research, of new methods and new facts? Facts are always there and everything is always contained in facts, but every epoch needs its own Greece, its own Middle Ages and its own Renaissance. Every age creates the age it needs, and only the next generation believes that its fathers' dreams were lies which must be fought with its own new "truths". The history of the effect of poetry follows the same course, and in criticism, too, the continuing life of the grandfather's dreams—not to mention those of earlier generations—is barely touched by the dreams of men alive today. Consequently the most varied "conceptions" of the Renaissance can live peacefully side by side with one another, just as a new poet's new phèdre, Siegfried or Tristan must always leave intact the Phèdre, Siegfried or Tristan of his predecessors.

Of course there is a science of the arts; there has to be one. The greatest essayists are precisely those who can least well do without it: what they create must be science, even when their vision of life has transcended the sphere of science. Sometimes its free flight is constrained by the unassailable facts of dry matter; sometimes it loses all scientific value because it is, after all, a vision, because it precedes facts and therefore handles them freely and arbitrarily. The essay form has not yet, today, travelled the road to independence which its sister, poetry, covered long ago—the road of development from a primitive, undifferentiated unity with science, ethics and art. Yet the beginning of that road was so tremendous that subsequent developments have rarely equalled it. I speak, of course, of Plato, the greatest essayist who ever lived or wrote, the one who wrested everything from life as it unfolded before his eyes and who therefore needed no mediating medium; the one who was able to connect his questions, the most profound questions ever asked, with life as lived. This greatest master of the form was also the happiest of all creators: man lived in his immediate proximity, man whose essence and destiny constituted the paradigmatic essence and destiny of his form. Perhaps they would have become paradigmatic in this way even if Plato's writing had consisted of the driest notations—not just because of his glorious form-giving—so strong was the concordance of life and form in this particular case. But Plato met Socrates and was able to give form to the myth of Socrates, to use Socrates' destiny as the vehicle for the questions he, Plato, wanted to address to life about destiny. The life of Socrates is the typical life for the essay form, as typical as hardly any other life is for any literary form—with the sole exception of Oedipus' life for tragedy. Socrates always lived in the ultimate questions; every other living reality was as little alive for him as his questions are alive for ordinary people. The concepts into which he poured the whole of his life were lived by him with the most direct and immediate life-energy; everything else was but a parable of that sole true reality, useful only as a means of expressing those experiences. His life rings with the sound of the deepest, the most hidden longing and is full of the most violent struggles; but that longing is—simply—longing, and the form in which it appears is the attempt to comprehend the nature of longing and to capture it in concepts, while the struggles are simply verbal battles fought solely in order to give more definite limits to a few concepts. Yet the longing fills that life completely and the struggles are always, quite literally, a matter of life and death. But despite everything the longing which seems to fill that life is not the essential thing about life, and neither Socrates' life nor his death was able to express those life-and-death struggles. If this had been possible, the death of Socrates would have been a martyrdom or a tragedy—which means that it could be represented in epic or dramatic form. But Plato knew exactly why he burned the tragedy he wrote in his youth. For a tragic life is crowned only by its end, only the end gives meaning, sense and form to the whole, and it is precisely the end which is always arbitrary and ironic here, in every dialogue and in Socrates' whole life. A question is thrown up and extended so far in depth that it becomes the question of all questions, but after that everything remains open; something comes from outside—from a reality which has no connection with the question nor with that which, as the possibility of an answer, brings forth a new question to meet it—and interrupts everything. This interruption is not an end, because it does not come from within, and yet it is the most profound ending because a conclusion from within would have been impossible. For Socrates every event was only an occasion for seeing concepts more clearly, his defence in front of the judges only a way of leading weak logicians *ad absurdum*—and his death? Death does not count here, it cannot be grasped by concepts, it interrupts the great dialogue—the only true reality—just as brutally, and merely from the outside, as those rough tutors who interrupted the conversation with Lysis. Such an interruption, however, can only be viewed humoristically, it has so little connection with that which it interrupts. But it is also a profound life-symbol—and, for that reason, still more profoundly humorous—that the essential is always interrupted by such things in such a way.

The Greeks felt each of the forms available to them as a reality, as a living thing and not as an abstraction. Alcibiades already saw clearly what Nietzsche was to emphasize centuries later—that Socrates was a new kind of man, profoundly different in his elusive essence from all other Greeks who lived before him. But Socrates, in the same dialogue, expressed the eternal ideal of men of his kind, an ideal which neither those whose way of feeling remains tied to the purely human nor those who are poets in their innermost being will ever understand: that tragedies and comedies should be written by the same man; that "tragic" and "comic" is entirely a matter of the chosen standpoint. In saying this, the critic expressed his deepest life-sense: the primacy of the standpoint, the concept, over feeling; and in saying it he formulated the profoundest anti-Greek thought.

Plato himself, as you see, was a "critic", although criticism, like everything else, was for him only an occasion, an ironic means of expressing himself. Later on, criticism became its own content; critics spoke only of poetry and art, and they never had the fortune to meet a Socrates whose life might have served them as a springboard to the ultimate. But Socrates was the first to condemn such critics. "It seems to me," he said to Protagoras, "that to make a poem the subject of a conversation is too reminiscent of those banquets which uneducated and vulgar people give in their houses. . . . Conversations like the one we are now enjoying—conversations among men such as most of us would claim to be—do not need outside voices or the presence of a poet. . . ."

Fortunately for us, the modern essay does not always have to speak of books or poets; but this freedom makes the essay even more problematic. It stands too high, it sees and connects too many things to be the simple exposition or explanation of a work; the title of every essay is preceded in invisible letters, by the words "Thoughts occasioned by. . . ." The essay has become too rich and independent for dedicated service, yet it is too intellectual and too multiform to acquire form out of its own self. Has it perhaps become even more problematic, even further removed from life-values than if it had continued to report faithfully on books?

When something has once become problematic—and the way of thinking that we speak of, and its way of expression, have not become problematic but have always been so—then salvation can only come from accentuating the problems to the maximum degree, from going radically to its root. The modern essay has lost that backdrop of life which gave Plato and the mystics their strength; nor does it any longer possess a naïve faith in the value of books and what can be said about them. The problematic of the situation has become accentuated almost to the point of demanding a certain frivolity of thought and expression, and this, for most critics, has become their life-mood. This has shown, however, that salvation is necessary and is therefore becoming possible and real. The essayist must now become conscious of his own self, must find himself and build something of his own out of himself. The essayist speaks of a picture or a book, but leaves it again at once—why? Because, I think, the idea of the picture or book has become predominant in his mind, because he has forgotten all that is concretely incidental about it, because he has used it only as a starting-point, a springboard. Poetry is older and greater—a larger, more important thing—than all the works of poetry: that was once the mood with which critics approached literature, but in our time it has had to become a conscious attitude. The critic has been sent into the world in order to bring to light this *a priori* primacy over great and small, to proclaim it, to judge every phenomenon by the scale of values glimpsed and grasped through this recognition. The idea is there before any of its expressions, it is a soul-value, a world-moving and life-forming force in itself: and that is why such criticism will always speak of life where it is most alive. The idea is the measure of everything that exists, and that is why the critic whose thinking is "occasioned by" something already created, and who reveals its idea, is the one who will write the truest and most profound criticism. Only something that is great and true can live in the proximity of the idea. When this magic word has been spoken, then everything that is brittle, small and unfinished falls apart, loses its usurped wisdom, its badly fitting essence. It does not have to be "criticism": the atmosphere of the idea is enough to judge and condemn it.

Yet it is now that the essayist's possibility of existence becomes profoundly problematic. He is delivered from the relative, the inessential, by the force of judgement of the idea he has glimpsed; but who gives him the right to judge?

It would be almost true to say that he seizes that right, that he creates his judgement-values from within himself. But nothing is separated from true judgement by a deeper abyss than its approximation, the squint-eyed category of complacent and self-satisfied knowledge. The criteria of the essayist's judgement are indeed created within him, but it is not he who awakens them to life and action: the one who whispers them into his ear is the great value-definer of aesthetics, the one who is always about to arrive, the one who is never quite yet there, the only one who has been called to judge. The essayist is a Schopenhauer who writes his *Parerga* while waiting for the arrival of his own (or another's) *The World as Will and Idea,* he is a John the Baptist who goes out to preach in the wilderness about another who is still to come, whose shoelace he is not worthy to untie. And if that other does not come—is not the essayist then without justification? And if the other does come, is he not made superfluous thereby? Has he not become entirely problematic by thus trying to justify himself? He is the pure type of the precursor, and it seems highly questionable whether, left entirely to himself—i.e., independent from the fate of that other of whom he is the herald—he could lay claim to any value or validity. To stand fast against those who deny his fulfilment within the great, redeeming system is easy enough: a true longing always triumphs over those who lack the energy to rise above the vulgar level of given facts and experiences; the existence of the longing is enough to decide the outcome. For it tears the mask off everything that is only apparently positive and immediate, reveals it as petty longing and cheap fulfilment, points to the measure and order to which even they who vainly and contemptibly deny its existence—because measure and order seem inaccessible to them—unconsciously aspire. The essay can calmly and proudly set its fragmentariness against the petty completeness of scientific exactitude or impressionistic freshness; but its purest fulfilment, its most vigorous accomplishment becomes powerless once the great aesthetic comes. Then all its creations are only an application of the measure which at last has become undeniable, it is then something merely provisional and occasional, its results can no longer be justified purely from within themselves. Here the essay seems truly and completely a mere precursor, and no independent value can be attached to it. But this longing for value and form, for measure and order and purpose, does not simply lead to an end that must be reached so that it may be cancelled out and become a presumptuous tautology. Every true end is a real end, the end of a road, and although road and end do not make a unity and do not stand side by side as equals, they nevertheless coexist: the end is unthinkable and unrealizable without the road being travelled again and again; the end is not standing still but arriving there, not resting but conquering a summit. Thus the essay seems justified as a necessary means to the ultimate end, the penultimate step in this hierarchy. This, however, is only the value of what it *does;* the fact of what it is has yet another, more independent value. For in the system of values yet to be found, the longing we spoke of would be satisfied and therefore abolished; but this longing is more than just something waiting for fulfilment, it is a fact of the soul with a value and existence of its own: an original and deep-rooted attitude towards the

whole of life, a final, irreducible category of possibilities of experience. Therefore it needs not only to be satisfied (and thus abolished) but also to be given form which will redeem and release its most essential and now indivisible substance into eternal value. That is what the essay does. Think again of the example of the *Parerga:* whether they occurred before or after the system is not a matter simply of a time-sequence; the time-historical difference is only a symbol of the difference between their two natures. The *Parerga* written before the system create their preconditions from within themselves, create the whole world out of their longing for the system, so that—it seems—they can give an example, a hint; immanently and inexpressibly, they contain the system and its connection with lived life. Therefore they must always occur before the system; even if the system had already been created, they would not be a mere application but always a new creation, a coming-alive in real experience. This "application" creates both that which judges and that which is judged, it encompasses a whole world in order to raise to eternity, in all its uniqueness, something that was once there. The essay is a judgement, but the essential, the value-determining thing about it is not the verdict (as is the case with the system) but the process of judging.

Only now may we write down the opening words: the essay is an art form, an autonomous and integral giving-of-form to an autonomous and complete life. Only now would it not be contradictory, ambiguous and false to call it a work of art and yet insist on emphasizing the thing that differentiates it from art: it faces life with the same gesture as the work of art, but only the gesture, the sovereignty of its attitude is the same; otherwise there is no correspondence between them.

OVERVIEW OF THE GENRE

Arthur C. Benson

SOURCE: "On Essays at Large," in *The Living Age,* Vol. XLVI, No. 3423, February 12, 1910, pp. 408-15.

[*Benson was an English educator and author. A prolific poet, novelist, and biographer, he is best known as an essayist. In the following excerpt from an essay originally published in the* Cornhill Magazine, *Benson approaches a definition of the essay and touches upon the accomplishment of several key writers of the familiar essay, including Lamb, Thackeray, and Stevenson.*]

There is no word which it seems harder to define than the word *Essay;* it seems as difficult to describe as the quality of justice in Plato's "Republic," which turned out to be the one indefinable and essential principle that was left, like Argon, when all the other qualities that go to the making up of the state were subtracted. Similarly, when all other forms of human composition have been classified, the essay is left. Almost the only quality that it seems possible to predicate of it is comparative brevity, and even that is not essential to it, for such a book as the "Anatomy of Melancholy" is little more than a gigantic essay, when all is said. The difficulty is that the word has travelled so far from its original meaning, which implied something tentative and evanescent. Yet if the word can be applied to Macaulay's Essays, the original conception falls to the ground at once, for Macaulay's Essays are certainly neither evanescent nor tentative, but some of the most positive and palpable documents in the archives of literature. The fact is that the word has been wrested from its meaning to cover any species of short study, biographical or historical. We do not, however, presume to plead that the word should be restored to its original meaning: words are our servants and not our masters; usage is more important than derivation, and it is mere pedantry to attempt to maintain the opposite. But for all that it is agreeable, even if it be useless, to discern and disentangle the proper qualities of things, and to play with literary values is as pretty a game as to toy with vintages.

The true essay, then, is a tentative and personal treatment of a subject; it is a kind of improvisation on a delicate theme; a species of soliloquy, as if a man were to speak aloud the slender and whimsical thoughts that come into his mind when he is alone on a winter evening before a warm fire, and, closing his book, abandons himself to the luxury of genial reverie. I remember once being in the studio of a great painter. He was at work on a portrait which for personal reasons I had been asked to criticize. After we had discussed the picture, he had taken up his palette and brush, and was adding some little touches. As he did this, he began to talk first about the methods, and then about the aims of art. He spoke as if almost unconscious of the presence of an auditor, in very simple, spontaneous language, as though he were thinking aloud. He suddenly broke off, with a half-blush, and said "These are some of the thoughts that come into my head as I stand at my work; I am ashamed to trouble you with them,"—and I could not induce him to resume. That was, I felt, a real essay in the making. I had seen the very telegraphy of the brain at work, the unseen soul at its business of thought, and I felt too, as I reflected, that I had understood it all perfectly, as I could not have understood a technical treatise; for the real stuff of thought is simple enough—it is the learned mind that complicates and embroiders. The theme itself matters little—the art of it lies in the treatment. And the important thing is that the essay should possess what may be called atmosphere and personality; and thus it may be held to be of the essence of the matter that the result should appear to be natural, by whatever expenditure of toil that quality may need to be achieved. In this sense it may be held that Bacon's Essays are hardly true essays, because they are too aphoristic—the bones are picked too clean, the definition is too superbly lucid and concise. Most essayists could not afford to spin their web as close as that—a single page of Bacon would furnish out themes and climaxes and ornaments for a whole essay of the more leisurely type. For the mark of the true essay is that the reader's thinking is all done for him. A thought is expanded in a dozen ways, until the most nebulous mind takes cognizance of it. The path winds and insinuates itself, like a little leafy lane among fields, with the hamlet-chimneys and the spire, which are its leisurely goal, appearing only by glimpses and vistas, to left or to right, just sufficiently to reassure the sauntering pilgrim as to the ultimate end of his enterprise. But the Essays of Bacon resemble more a series of stepping-stones, rigid, orderly, compact, the

progress across which must be wary and intent, admitting but little opportunity for desultory contemplation.

Again, the true essay must be, as we have said, tentative. It must never be authoritative. It must make no pronouncement, and draw no conclusion. The most the essayist may do is to venture to suggest. As a cicerone, he must not discourse professionally of dates and mouldings, but trifle gracefully with an historical association, or indicate an effect of light and shadow on a mellow wall. In fact the campanula that swings its lilac bells upon the broken ledge, or the orange rosettes of lichen on the weathered ashlar are more his concern than the origin and significance of the pile itself. His duty is rather to exhibit his subject from a dozen different points of view, and he must take thought of foreground and distance more than of elevation and perspective. If he convinces at all, it must be by persuasion and example, and not by precept or statute—but indeed his aim is never intellectual conviction, nor the unveiling of error; it is rather to show the poetical value of a thought, its suggestiveness, its gossamer connections, its emotional possibilities; and thus the breeze that stirs the surface of the pool is as important as the pool itself; the reflected images of tree and hill, that blend and waver as much his pre-occupation as the actual forms themselves—indeed more so; for, as I have said, atmosphere is the end of all his devices. Personality, then, is the characteristic of the essay; not necessarily egotistic personality, the mind regarding itself with absorbed delight, repeating and viewing and recording its own motions. That indeed is not forbidden to the essayist, for the essence of his art is zest in his subject; but greater still is the charm of personality unconscious of itself, and merely following its own contemplations with a delighted intentness, like the talk of a child. And here I think lies another characteristic of the true essayist, a certain childlike absorption in his subject. We all of us love trifles at heart; the shapes and aspects of things, the quality of sounds, the savors of food, the sweet and pungent odors of earth. We persuade ourselves, as life goes on, that these things are unimportant, and we dull our observation of them by disuse; but in all the essayists that I can think of, this elemental perception of things as they are is very strong and acute; and half their charm is that they recall to us things that we have forgotten, things which fell sharply and clearly on the perception of our young senses, or bring back to us in a flash that delicate wonder, that undimmed delight, when the dawn lay brightening about us, and when our limbs were restless and alert.

The mysterious quality called charm is thus another of the first requisites of the essayist; and here we are dealing with one of those ultimate and indivisible qualities which defy analysis. It brings us back to the naked principle of all criticism, that we like a thing, after all, because we do like it, and for no other reason; we may train and refine our taste, of course, but we only end by assimilating our taste to the perceptions of more richly endowed, more eager natures. But no artist can ever attain to charm by taking thought. What he can do is to improve and refine his methods, till he arrives at expressing the thought he conceives as closely as possible; he can get rid of clumsiness and hesitancy and obscurity, as the sculptor gets nearer at every stroke to the form concealed in the stone; but even so it is the form that is the ultimate and momentous thing, and not the polish of the surface—indeed that polish can be too high, too mechanical; the dint upon the stone, the rake-marks on the gravel, have an unconsidered charm, for they give the sense of the human hand at work.

It would be an ample task. but one that lies beyond the scope of this paper, to show how the seed of the essay sown by Montaigne in France not only did not flourish there, but was transplanted almost bodily to England, and became one of the chief glories of our literature. At first sight it would seem surprising. It would appear that the essay was a vehicle which would have exactly suited the subtle and suggestive temperament of the French, and was ill-adapted for the less imaginative if sturdier character of our own nation. Yet so it has been. In the hands of Addison and Steele, of Goldsmith and Johnson, the essay became perhaps the most characteristic product of English eighteenth-century literature, with its refined taste, its gentlemanly philosophy, and with just the touch of nature and sincerity that harmonized the whole. But with the romantic movement came a fresher impulse still; and the three great essayists of the early nineteenth century, Hazlitt, Lamb, and De Quincey, gave the essay both a breadth and an appeal which it had never hitherto known. Hazlitt was a great taster of the savors of life, and though a certain harshness and sombreness of nature made him perhaps more of a guide than a leader, yet the thought which caused him to say on his somewhat desolate death-bed, "Well, I have had a happy life," makes itself heard in his writings. De Quincey no doubt suffered from the hideous profusion in which his necessities and his circumstances impelled him to indulge. Never was there a noble and impassioned writer who so wallows at times in verbosity and ineptitude and yet who rises on the one hand to such authentic presentment of the very stuff of humanity, and on the other hand to such impassioned melody of thought and word. He tried perhaps to make prose do the work of poetry, but for all that he has contrived to baffle all who would clearly define the difference, and to leave among his myriad writings visions, where light and sound seem to blend magically into an essence for which no literary name can be found.

But the writer who, with no pretensions, no sacerdotal claims, winds himself subtly and firmly into the sovereignty of English essayists is Charles Lamb. Strangely enough it was late in life that he found his place. He had no ambitious range of subjects, nor had he the command of the organ-like melody which De Quincey owned. Perhaps this may be the reason why De Quincey, alone of notable critics, persistently descries Lamb's merits, accusing him of want of proportion and variety. But Charles Lamb brought to his work a largeness of heart and a sweetness of temper that survived both acute and wearing sorrows and a deepseated fragility of fame—"Saint Charles!" as Thackeray once said, putting a letter of Lamb's to his forehead. To this was added an extraordinary fineness of observation, and a delicate sensitiveness to the quality of experience that had slowly matured; and he had, too, a humor both whimsical and profound, which, into whatever extravagance it may have betrayed him in convivial mo-

ments, was always held in exquisite restraint when he came to write; and thus the essays have that rare balance of emotion, where pathos is kept from sickliness by a virile sense of absurdity, and where emotion preserves humor from the least touch of cynicism. It is not as if the two moods alternated, they co-existed; and a tact which was of the nature of genius kept the proportion exact. It is idle to say that Lamb can never be surpassed; but so perfect an adjustment of special faculties, combined with so limpid a style and so sincere a modesty of presentment, must of necessity be a rarity.

And now, "as in private duty bound" as the old bidding prayer runs, I may be allowed to touch upon a group of essayists who have been particularly connected with the pages of the *Cornhill Magazine*. It has from the first been the policy of the *Cornhill* to give prominence to the note of personal expression: and thus it has attracted to itself writers of this quality.

The output of Thackeray was so prodigious and his method so incredibly natural and spontaneous, that it is easy to say he was not an artist, just as pedantic critics used to say that his drawings were very amusing but undeniably amateurish. The truth is that Thackeray defied all rules. His wonderful eye saw everything, and his large heart had room for everything and everybody. He lived, and enjoyed life, with an absolutely unimpaired and childlike zest; and his brave, simple, tender spirit endured to the end. Where other men are connoisseurs of fine flavors and delicate *nuances,* Thackeray was a connoisseur of the broadest and biggest things of life—its pathos, its absurdity, its courage, its loyalty. As the French proverb says, he is *bon comme le pain.* His handling of humanity is so liberal that he puts one out of conceit with all uneasy devices, all nice assignments of epithets. He writes as the jovial Zeus of the *Iliad* might have written about the combats and the loves of men, sympathizing with and experiencing every passion and frailty, yet with a divine immunity from their penalties and shadows.

As Edward FitzGerald wrote of him in 1845—

> In the meanwhile old Thackeray laughs at all this; and goes on in his own way, writing hard for half a dozen reviews and newspapers all the morning; dining, drinking, and talking of a night; managing to preserve a fresh color and perpetual flow of spirits under a wear-and-tear of thinking and feeding that would have knocked up any other man I know two years ago at least.

And how characteristic it was of Thackeray that in his later days he could write, he confessed, anywhere better than in his own quiet study—in a club smoking-room or a bar-parlor, where he was in touch with the light and sound and even the scent of life!

The *Roundabout Papers* are perhaps among the greatest triumphs of the art of the essayist. It is impossible to say what they are all about—what are they not about? Yet the book is irresistible, and not to be laid aside; and, what is the strongest test of all, it is so contagious in style and manner that after reading it onc has a fatal tendency to try to imitate it; it produces a kind of mental intoxication, in which one feels *capable de tout*—of observing and loving and interpreting human nature in the same large and easy way.

Thackeray must have had the special gift of writing exactly as fast as he thought. If a man thinks faster than he writes, the result is abruptness of transition, a disconnected allusiveness, a sense of flying leaps and uneven progress. If he thinks slower than he writes, there is a sense of costive reluctance—he wades, as Tennyson said, in a sea of glue. But with Thackeray the word is the though; it has the sense of fluent talk without self-consciousness or strain.

It would be difficult to find a more complete contrast than that presented by Leslie Stephen to Thackeray. The *Hours in a Library* contain an immense amount of admirable literary appreciation, stated with a temperate justice and a reasonable candor which is above praise. These criticisms read like legal judgments passed upon writers by a man with a wide knowledge of the subject and distinct preferences of his own, before whom the cause of the writer has been pleaded by an advocate, on the one hand, of indiscriminate admiration and headlong eulogy, and on the other hand by an advocate of confessed hostility and whole-hearted contempt. The two extremes seem to be always in the mind of the presiding judge, and he delivers his decision with logical clearness and an extreme sense of responsibility. . . .

He was a man of very deep emotion and intense loyalty. But his sincerity and his candor deserted him in the presence of emotion. He was so afraid of sentiment, so ashamed of giving himself away, that he hung back at the very moment where his good sense would have been most valuable. No one desires a sacrifice of dignity, or a fatuous display of sentiment; but to deal with books and human beings, and to ignore the emotional framework, is a chilly business. And it is here that Thackeray strides ahead, because he was not ashamed to be known and seen to feel. Yet there is room for both; and Stephen's wholesome, manly, and dispassionate judgments are an excellent corrective of literary extravagance and sentimental preferences.

> **The essay does not set out to narrate or to prove; it has no dramatic purpose, no imaginative theme: its essence is a sympathetic self-revelation, just as in talk a man may speak frankly of his own experiences and feelings, and yet avoid any suspicion of egotism, if his confidences are designed to illustrate the thoughts of others rather than to provide a contrast and a self-glorification.**
>
> **—Arthur C. Benson**

The essays of Robert Louis Stevenson, many of which ap-

peared in the *Cornhill,* and were afterwards collected into the volume *Virginibus Puerisque,* are conceived and executed in a very different vein. They are confessedly and obviously elaborate writing, and the author seems to have worked in the spirit of the advice given by Keats to Shelley, "to load every rift with ore." The tone and temper of the essays are admirable; they are breezy without being boisterous, and brave without being *insouciant.* Perhaps it may be said of them that they are rather too deliberately buoyant, for there peeps in every now and then a touch of grim philosophy, not, indeed, foreign to the writer's experience, for even when they were written Stevenson had had, as Browning says, "trouble enough for one." It is better, I think, to read them in connection with their title. They are essentially youthful in spirit, but it may be doubted whether a certain maturity of temperament is not an almost necessary qualification in an essay-writer. He must have seen, so to speak, both sides of the coin. Stevenson had lived with zest, and he had begun to suffer, but he had not as yet lost interest in his sufferings: he had not yet begun to walk in that shadowy land, afterwards to become familiar to him, in which weakness takes the fight out of a man. In the early days of illness it is not without a certain lurid interest to have looked a spectre in the face, and to have shut the door upon him. Experience, after all, is always interesting, and the more disagreeable it is, the more zest it gives to hours of relief. To the young men and maidens who have glowed and thrilled over these manly, humorous, full-flavored essays, it adds a pleasant savor to life to peep into its afflicted places, its grated dungeons; and all the more so when one who has sojourned there comes out smiling, and assures his hearers that the dark corners were illuminated with courage and hope. But one grows a little older, and an uneasy suspicion falls upon one that the brisk performer on tabret and pipe is a little sick at heart, and that he is practising what is called in modern phrase "auto-suggestion," which consists in saying, like Mark Tapley, that everything is jolly, in the hope that one may seem a little less dreary than one feels. Still, the courage, the good temper, the determination to be pleased with life, qualities which lay at the very root of Stevenson's nature, here stand out in every page; and what is finer still, the conviction that, if one fails to be interested in life, it is one's own fault, and not the fault of life; and that one does not mend a bad business by whining and pleading exceptional justification for one's stupid and perverse blunders. The essay about the English Admirals, for instance, stirs the heart like the blast of a trumpet, with its splendid patriotism, its unreasonable courage. Still one may, I think, justly prefer Stevenson's letters to Stevenson's essays. In the letters one gets a freshness and spontaneity which one just misses in the essays. In the essays there is a construction of literary ornament; in the letters the construction is ornamented, and no more, by the literary flavor. Yet the essays, too, for all their spicy scent, have the intimacy of the true essay. You hear the talk and look into the eyes of a friend. You feel that nothing but the unhappy accidents of time and space kept you from swearing eternal brotherhood with a brave heart; and you end, as William Cory said so tenderly of Walter Scott, by hating the death that parts you from the beloved.

And here, too, may be mentioned the work of John Addington Symonds, some of whose most finished essays appeared in the *Cornhill*. He was a great friend of Stevenson's, and they were knit together by unity of temperament and trial. Opalstein and Firefly were the names they gave each other, this for the clouding gleams of fantastic brightness, and that for the swift lapses of lambent flame. Keen as Symonds' delight was in the joys and beauties of earth, quick and exact as his observation was, rich as his resources of language were, he had not quite the personal touch that wins the crown. It was a thwarted life, for all its energy and courage; and thwarted most of all in this, that be could never quite make his art obey his bidding. The passion of the scene, the memory, the experience mastered him; and though he could communicate delight, yet it was done more through a lavish profusion of detail than by the restrained economy of language that leaves the picture clean and firm and true. And this is all the more to be regretted, because Symonds never made the mistake of putting art before life. It was life and experience and emotion of which he was in search, and his writings are an attempt to establish relations, to bridge the gaps of life with confidences, to share his joy with other hearts. Yet the rhetorical vein in him just swept off that finest bloom, that sense of intimacy on which all depends.

And here, too, I may be permitted to add a word about a series of essays—the "Pages from a Private Diary." which claimed the affectionate regard of many readers of the *Cornhill*. There was no attempt made in them to strike an attitude or wind an adventurous horn; yet out of the simplest materials and the quietest outlook there came a delicately tinted picture of life, which, by its modest sincerity, its tranquil humor, would itself into the heart. And this is, perhaps, the best claim of all, to take a tract of life which is within the reach of everyone—a rustic landscape, a village street melting into orchards and pastures,—and so to render its serene charm, its blended green and gray, its misty distance, that its hidden life becomes audible, its even breath, its beating heart. And, further, to show that in these pastoral solitudes, where the year is marked by the rising of the wheat, the rustling of the leaf, the building of the rick, a life full of reflection and sympathy may be lived as in a firelit glow—this is to broaden the outlook of the heart, and to prove that it is the informing spirit more than the ample incident that makes the richness and the glow of life. It was Virgil's highest praise for the days of old that men were content with little; and it is still the crown of life, and its best hope, when that temper, as well as the adventurous heart, are found in due proportions in a nation's life.

And thus we end where we began, with the perception that of all the displays of art the essay is the most indefinable, the most subtle, because it has no scheme, no programme. It does not set out to narrate or to prove; it has no dramatic purpose, no imaginative theme: its essence is a sympathetic self-revelation, just as in talk a man may speak frankly of his own experiences and feelings, and yet avoid any suspicion of egotism, if his confidences are designed to illustrate the thoughts of others rather than to provide a contrast and a self-glorification. The essayist gives rather than claims; he compares rather than parades. He is led by his interest in others to be interested in himself, and it is as a man rather than as an individual that he takes the stage. He must be surprised at the discoveries he makes about himself, rather than complacent; he must condone his own discrepancies rather than exult in them. "One knocked," says the old fable, "at the Beloved's door, and cried 'Open!' 'Nay,' said the Beloved, 'I dare not open save to Love and God.' But the voice said 'Open then without fear, for I am both; I am thyself.' "

Francis N. Zabriskie

SOURCE: "The Essay as a Literary Form and Quality," in *The New Princeton Review,* Vol. IV, No. 5, September, 1887, pp. 227-45.

[In the following excerpt, Zabriskie surveys the prominent English and American writers of the familiar essay.]

In coming to the English essay of the nineteenth century, we dismiss at once an imposing phalanx of British reviewers and critics, whose works are commonly so classed. These masterful and often leonine vivisections of authors, these eloquent orations on paper, these able state papers, these splendid historical tapestries or biographical portraitures, have no more relation to the true essay than a Roman toga or a coat of mail has to a dressing-gown or a peajacket. Of course, we are not including Carlyle nor Professor Wilson. The latter has the essay touch in all he wrote, whether the story of a tramp among the lochs and moors, a swift silhouette of a contemporary, or a critique by wink and shrug and boisterous ha! ha! When Thomas Carlyle became possessed of his familiar spirit, Teufelsdröckh, he became a very Titan of essay. And yet Teufelsdröckh is but the intensified personality of Carlyle, manifesting itself in all his varied criticism of life, whether of men or books, of nations or individuals, of the past or the present, spurning all bondage to rules of logic or dictionaries or punctuation marks, a great intuitive, lightning-worded, self-disclosing soul.

Nothing could better illustrate the variety of style and the diversity of gifts which are included in the genius for essay, than the fact that the other great representative English essayist of the nineteenth century is Charles Lamb. Teufelsdröckh is as ungentle as Elia is "gentle." To read the former is like embarking on the rapids of Niagara; to read the latter is like an afternoon's row on the Thames in sight of London Bridge, and with the distant murmur of the Strand and Cheapside in our ears. The range of the former is from hero-worship and prophets to gigs and ballet-girls, from the Book of Job to "Tam O'Shanter," from Christianity to old clothes. Lamb never soars much higher than the chimney-pots of his beloved city, nor strays beyond its limits. He finds scope for his exquisite pathos and poetry, as well as humor, in its beggars and sweeps, its bookstalls and play-houses. And yet you will find this in common between the roar of the one and the dove-note of the other—they are the exact accent and dialect of the man at the moment.

We always associate Hazlitt and Leigh Hunt with Charles Lamb. The former must not be thought of too exclusively as a literary critic, though one of the most charming as well as keenest of book reviewers. The finest and most imperishable aroma of his genius is to be found in such essays as his "On the Want of Money," "Sitting for One's Picture," "Londoners and Country People," "Great and Little Things," and "Living to Oneself." Leigh Hunt is always Horace Skimpole in print. The subject seems to be utterly indifferent to him. It always starts him off on an airy, fanciful, and even fantastic talk on everything in earth and heaven, in Hampstead or at the world's end. He is preëminently the poet-essayist, as Horace Skimpole's Roman namesake was the essay-poet. We group about Lamb also Dr. John Brown, who has created a dogheaven, at least on earth; "Boz," who would be recognized as one of the greatest of essayists if he were not one of the greatest of novelists; Thackeray, who is recognized as one of the greatest of essayists despite his being one of the greatest of novelists. The genius of Landor has restored the dialogue essay of Plato and Xenophon and Fontenelle, and Sir Arthur Helps has transplanted it into the midst of the nineteenth century. Coleridge, in *Aids to Reflection* and *Table Talk,* and the Hares in *Guesses at Truth,* have paralleled the "Pensées" of Seneca and La Bruyère. The great Coleridge had his fits of essay in most of his writings, especially *The Friend* and *Biographia Literaria,* and he talked essay by the hour, "sitting on Ludgate Hill" or anywhere else that he could find an auditor. . . .

Washington Irving wrote his *Sketch-Book* and *Bracebridge Hall* under the spell of the *Spectator.* He once told Mr. Labouchère that he studied style by reading Addison's essays, and then writing them out from memory, and comparing his own phrases with the original. He even undertook, with his friend Paulding, to publish an American *Spectator.* Irving, however, advanced upon his English prototype by a criticism of life which could take account alike of town and country, of the Old World and the New. He also indicated the American tendency to a closer observation of nature.

N. P. Willis was a sparkling sketcher of the surface aspects both of nature and of society, and exhibits the forced gayety of Christopher North without his robust hilarity, and the sentimentality of Leigh Hunt without his delicacy of touch. Edwin P. Whipple's critical essays are informed with his personality, his observation, and his wit. Hawthorne, in his note-books and in such sketches as "A Rill from a Town Pump," must be reckoned among our essayists. Thoreau inaugurated the peculiarly American school of minute and meditative observers of nature. Emerson is quite alone in the sententious vein, and we have nothing answering to the French "Pensées" unless it be Colton's *Lacon.* . . .

But my space is covered. One cannot do more than sweep telescopically the crowded lights of the Milky Way. I must content myself with barely adding the names of Charles Lanman, Horace Bushnell, the late Dr. C. S. Henry, and "Timothy Titcomb," while still others, perhaps equally noteworthy, cannot even be mentioned.

W. E. Williams

SOURCE: "The Essay," in *The Craft of Literature,* International Publishers, 1925, pp. 140-47.

[In the following excerpt, Williams provides a brief overview of the familiar essay's nature and the key practitioners of the "pure" essay tradition.]

The didactic essay, or "paper," is a lesser channel of the essay-form; and even during the 19th century it was the non-critical or "literary" essay which left the deepest mark on non-narrative prose. Goldsmith had won a place in literature for the fancy-free style of the informal essay. Lamb consolidated its claim. He practised a kind of essay which is best described as the prose complement of the lyric, or rather, perhaps, of the ode. In an earlier [unexcerpted] chapter some illustrations were given to show how a certain subject-matter, considered by a variety of personalities, evokes a similar variety of lyrical ecstasy. Lamb and the "literary" essayists, working in the less sublime but more extensive medium of prose, react in a similar way to their subject-matter. A first view of an antique town, or the sound of church bells on a winter morning, releases from delicate sensibilities a flood of memories and fancies. The *subject* is of secondary importance: it is the gust of wind which sets ringing the thousand bits of glass that hang from the ridges of an oriental temple. Free from the strain of plot and characterisation, the essay can discover to its readers those "little things"—the whims, fancies, and turns of thought—which best reveal a personality.

It may (quite wrongly) be imagined that the "literary" essay, so strongly responsive to its writer's momentary mood, tends therefore to be an inconsequential farrago of fancy. The critical essay, it may be thought, developing an argument, must be logically set forth; while the other kind will be invertebrate and without design. An examination of Lamb's essays will destroy this mistaken notion. The Labyrinth of Gnossos is nothing but a maze to Theseus until he gets hold of the thread of silk that guides him to Ariadne. The thread of silk is there in each of Lamb's most labyrinthine essays.

Take, for example, "The Praise of Chimney Sweepers." The essay begins with a panegyric to the "matin lark"— the young sweep. Immediately afterwards, Lamb is recalling the thrill he felt as a boy when he saw a sweep's brush suddenly emerge from a chimney-top. The fifth paragraph is a parenthetic exhortation to the reader to give a penny to a sweep when he sees one. In the next paragraph, the maze takes what seems an incomprehensible turn, for it does nothing but describe a shop which sells sassafras tea; but soon we discover that this is the favourite beverage of sweeps. Then the essay takes a fresh turn, to mention those other stalls where the early workman gets his herbal beer. The following paragraph comes back to the sweep at the stall, where you are invited to stand him a drink and a snack. There we come into a new section of the maze, which begins most disconcertingly: "I am by nature extremely susceptible of street affronts," but which leads us on to consider the mischievous nature of sweeps. No sooner do we feel our way along than we come across a fresh and startling line: "I am by theory obdurate to the seductiveness of what are called, a fine set of teeth,"—but it directs us eventually to a consideration of the possibility that many sweeps are mislaid lordlings. We are led on to a pleasant story of one such romance. On the heels of that, we are without warning introduced to "my pleasant friend, Jem White," who however turns out to be a kind of patron saint of sweeps. One of his annual feeds for them is next described; and, just afterwards, we emerge unexpectedly to find that, Jem now dead, the sweeps lament his lost bounty.

From first to last the thread is there, and the shocks we get as we fancy ourselves lost from time to time, serve to heighten our pleasure at the constant return to the central idea.

Of this nature, as the student may find for himself, is the work of those modern essayists who follow the "pure" essay tradition: Stevenson, Jefferies, W. H. Hudson, Max Beerbohm, Chesterton, Robert Lynd, and E. V. Lucas. The essayist makes any approach he prefers, and pleases himself as to what turns his maze shall take. But a bird's-eye view of it reveals always a definite unity from first to last.

Most of the other characteristics of Lamb are shared, too, by the later essayists. The essay affords full scope for idiosyncrasy (Lamb's was a liking for the turns of phrase of Sir Thomas Browne and his fellows: G. K. Chesterton's is a mediæval zest for an extravagant phrase). It is the happy hunting ground of the whimsical fellows, who looking at life from odd angles, show us the wonder and drollness of it.

Joseph Epstein

SOURCE: "Piece Work: Writing the Essay," in *Plausible Prejudices: Essays on American Writing,* W. W. Norton & Company, 1985, pp. 397-411.

[*An American educator and the editor of the* American Scholar, *Epstein is considered one of the preeminent modern writers of the familiar essay. In the following excerpt from an essay originally published in the* New Criterion *in 1984, he defines and discusses the essay in form and intent, discoursing on several of the genre's foremost practitioners.*]

There has never been an Age of the Essay, but, in the modern era, there seem always to have been extraordinary essayists. Drawing on the English-speaking writers alone, permit me to read the honor roll: Francis Bacon, Sir Thomas Browne, Daniel Defoe; Addison, Steele, Swift; Oliver Goldsmith, Samuel Johnson, Sydney Smith; Lamb, Hazlitt, Cobbett; Carlyle, Arnold, Emerson; Beerbohm, Chesterton, Virginia Woolf; Mencken, Orwell, Edmund Wilson. This is not to mention—as I shall now do—some of the men and women who dropped in from other genres and fields of intellectual endeavor to work out on the essay: Hume and Mill, Thackeray and George Eliot, Bagehot and Macaulay, Mark Twain and Henry Adams, the brothers James and William Dean Howells, Oscar Wilde and Bernard Shaw, E. M. Forster, and John Maynard Keynes. Both lists could be easily extended, but I believe I have supplied the names of enough serious players to provide a pretty fair chooseup game.

Of all literary forms, the essay has perhaps changed least over the course of its life. Can this be because the form of the essay is itself so protean—because essays themselves have so little form? The formlessness of this very old form is part of its pleasure. A critic, comparing Bacon to Montaigne, who is the father of the essay and the Shakespeare of the genre, remarked that Bacon "never attained the freedom and ease, the seeming formlessness held in by an invisible chain" that is part of the pleasure of reading Montaigne and often distinguishes the essayist at his best. Samuel Johnson wrote rather sniffily of the essay as "an irregular, undigested piece." Aldous Huxley, with Montaigne in mind, once referred to the method of the essay as "free association artistically controlled"—the artistic control clearly being crucial. Rudely inserting myself into this august company, I recall being delighted when a reviewer of a volume of my essays once remarked that they reminded him of the comment that Kandinsky once made about his own method: "I take a line out for a walk."

That same reviewer then went on to lose all the ground he had gained by picturing me as the stereotypical writer of essays—in a phrase, the cliché essayist. We all know that figure: there he stands in plaster of paris, gentle chap, highly cultivated, a lover of nature, a man obviously in touch with the eternal verities. Sheathed in corduroy or tweed, suede patches at his elbows, he puffs reflectively on his pipe. A bit otherworldly perhaps, oblivious to the rush of contemporary events around him, shaped like a Bartlett pear, more full of Shakespeare and Emerson than *Bartlett's Book of Familiar Quotations,* he is, our cliché essayist, a bookish man to his papier-mâché fingertips. In recent incarnations, he might have written under the rubric of "The Easy Chair" or "The Peripatetic Reviewer" or "The Revolving Bookstand." Pipe-sucking, patch-wearing, proud to harken back to the leisurely culture of an older day—that's the good old cliché essayist, altogether out-of-it and not minding in the least.

It is a cliché—to use a cliché—that will not wash. Certainly, it fits none of the great figures of the form. Consider some among them: Charles Lamb, with his stutter and his dreary clerkship at East India House and his mad sister at home; William Hazlitt, with his passion and his sad marriage and his need to grind out a living through endless scribbling; H. L. Mencken, with his energy and his love of lambasting a phony and his joy in life despite his unshakable skepticism about finding the answers to any of its large questions; George Orwell, with his rough-cut cigarettes and his working-class get-up and his ideological battles; Edmund Wilson, with his loneliness during hot summers in his Talcottville stone house and his reading through insomniacal nights and living out his days like the character in "The Cask of Amontillado" imprisoned not by bricks but by books. No, not much evidence of the cliché essayist here.

If there is no standard type for the essayist, neither is there anything resembling a standard essay: no set style, no set length, no set subject matter. The essay is a pair of baggy pants into which nearly anyone and anything can fit. In the college catalogue of this term's offerings, it does not fall under "creative writing"; it is not, strictly speaking, even imaginative, though there has never been a want of imagination among its best practitioners. In range of interest, it is multivarious: there are literary essays, political essays, philosophical essays, and historical essays; there are formal essays and familiar essays. The essay is in large part defined by the general temperament of the essayist. The essayist is—or should be—ruminative. He isn't monomaniacal. He is without pedantry; he is not, as they say in university English departments, "in the profession." The essayist might be found almost anywhere, but the last place one is likely to find him is in the pages of the *PMLA*.

Along with essays, there are entities known as the article and the "piece"; let us also not forget journalism and criticism. Are these nomenclatural distinctions merely? Perhaps. No hard rules in this domain, where everyone is his own Adam, free to name the creatures about him as he thinks best. For myself, I hold the essay to be a piece of writing that is anywhere from three to fifty pages long, that can be read twice, that provides some of the pleasures of style, and that leaves the impression of a strong or at least interesting character. By this measure F. R. Leavis, though he might be writing at essay length, is always the critic, never the essayist. Max Beerbohm, even when he is writing criticism of the most ephemeral play, is perpetually the essayist.

A certain modesty of intention resides in the essay. It is a modesty inherent in the French verb that gives the form its name—*essayer:* to try, to attempt, to taste, to try on, to assay. However many words the essayist may avail himself of, he instinctively knows, or ought to know, that the last word cannot be his. If it is the last word an author wants, let him go write books. Not that the essayist need be light, a schmoozer, a kibitzer with a pen in his hand. As Percy A. Scholes, in *The Oxford Companion to Music,* characterizes Handel, so does the essayist aim to shape himself: "though facile he is never trivial." And sometimes the essayist can be profound. As Beethoven, quoted in the same *Oxford Companion to Music* article, remarked of Handel: "Go and learn of him how to achieve great effects with simple means."

Who becomes an essayist? What is the training? What aptitudes are required by the job? Nearly thirty years after attending a lecture by Stephen Potter, the one-upmanship man, I remain impressed by the answer Potter provided to a most woodenly phrased question from a graduate student in the audience. "Sir," this young man began, "you are a noted Coleridge scholar, a man of serious standing in the scholarly community, and this being so, I cannot help but wonder what it was that impelled you to write such works as *One-upmanship* and *Gamesmanship*—I cannot, sir, understand what strange turn in your intellectual life caused you to compose these most unusual books, whose philosophical implications, though interesting to be sure, are nonetheless puzzling in the extreme. My question, then, sir, not to put too fine a point on it, is, Why did you write these books?" Potter, who was got up for his lecture in the green suit and green tie and wore glasses with a green tint in them, the effect of all of which was to make his lank grayish hair also appear green, cleared his throat with a considerable harrumph and, straightfaced as a goat, replied: "Out of work, you know."

"Out of work, you know" strikes me as quite as good an explanation as any other for why certain highly talented men and women turn to the writing of essays. Many among the great essayists did not set out to become essayists. Hazlitt, we know, wished to be a painter and a philosopher. Matthew Arnold, who began as a poet, stopped writing poetry while still a young man and turned to the essay. Max Beerbohm, though a considerable draughtsman, was an even more considerable essayist. Orwell, had he his druthers, no doubt would have wished to be remembered as a novelist, though today it is for his essays that he is most highly regarded, at least among people whose regard seems to be most valued. My general point is that few people can have set out to be essayists because the essay had never enjoyed the prestige that other genres or forms of art have enjoyed.

The essayist is someone with a strong urge to write and no other place to exercise this urge but the essay. He wishes to leave the stamp of his personality on the page—and, with great good luck, who knows, on the age. But he has discovered that the concentrated language and heightened emotion that is at the heart of serious poetic creation is not for him; nor is the dramatizing imagination that is required, along with a great deal of patience, by the novel. He is probably someone of wide curiosity and sufficient egotism to think that what is curious to him will also be curious to all the world. Not probably but certainly he is someone who desires to exert his will on the life of his times and who demands to have a hand in directing the contemporary traffic in ideas, manners, and morals. All these deficiencies, desires, and demands he is able to pour into that shapeless, bottomless, lovely receptacle, the essay. . . .

In such essays as "On Familiar Style" and "On the Prose Style of Poets," Hazlitt set out his prescriptions for style in essay writing. "To write a genuine familiar or truly English style," he averred, "is to write as any one would speak in common conversation who had a thorough command and choice of words, or who could discourse with ease, force, and perspicuity, setting aside all pedantic and oratorical flourishes." On more than one occasion, Hazlitt, who with qualification much admired Johnson ("The man was superior to the author"), attacked Johnson's style for its pomp and uniformity. "His subjects are familiar, but the author is always upon stilts." He was prepared to allow the deliberate archaisms of Charles Lamb—"Mr. Lamb is the only imitator of old English style I can read with pleasure"—but for the rest he was for the plain style, in which "every word should be a blow; every thought should instantly grapple with its fellow." Because style and thought are unitary in Hazlitt, those who love the essay revere him to this day.

William Hazlitt was the first truly distinguished writer to earn his livelihood almost exclusively through the writing of essays. Then, as now, it was no easy row to hoe. Filled with strong opinions, political to the bone, never overly prudent about making enemies, Hazlitt took his living where he found it, writing for those papers and journals that could contain his strong views. (He was, after all, the author of an essay entitled "The Pleasure of Hating.") Yet, though much of Hazlitt's writing was done on the run, somehow much of it hangs together nicely: his writing on writers, his art criticism, his drama criticism, his familiar essays on such subjects as "The Fight," "The Indian Jugglers," "My First Acquaintance with Poets," to name only three among my own favorites. It all hangs together because it is all bound together by the glue of a courageous, complex, contentious character who, for all the obstacles life set before him, never ceased to love life. Love of life, in my reading of them, is one of the qualities that all the great essayists hold in common.

With the advent and then the wide spread of periodicals and magazines, the nature and limits of essay writing changed correspondingly. Story writers and poets, though they may write with an eye toward particular journals, are not nearly as hostage as essayists to editors and the confinements of space and time set by their journals. (Although here I am reminded of a writer in a story by George P. Elliott who turned out high-quality work of a perfectly unpublishable length: if memory serves, stories of ninety pages and poems of seventeen.) The essayist works under clear pressures, the pressures of prescribed length, the pressures of deadlines, the pressures of the possible prejudices of editors. One cannot read about the life of Hazlitt without a strong awareness of all these matters weighing down on him as he wrote. When his essays disappoint, which they sometimes do, my guess is that it is often because of the necessity of high production under these various pressures. Virginia Woolf remarked that many of Hazlitt's essays read like "fragments broken off from some larger book." Given the immensity of material Hazlitt produced—twenty-one volumes in the P. P. Howe edition of his collected writings—the wonder isn't that Hazlitt sometimes disappoints but that he is so frequently as good as he is.

It must also be said that these same pressures can have their advantages. The need to write for money may be a mixed blessing, but between writing for money and writing for no money, in my experience, writing for money is better. (Yet writing for larger sums does not necessarily give larger pleasure; there is also the quality of the audience one writes for to be considered.) Deadlines are of course damnable, but without them, as everyone who has written without them knows, less work would get done. Editors may have their prejudices, yet some are biased on behalf of intellectual tough-mindedness and can, in subtle ways, make even veteran writers write better. In this connection I have always been much taken by a passage in a letter Sydney Smith wrote to Francis Jeffrey, his editor at the *Edinburgh Review.* "I have three motives for writing reviews," Smith wrote. "1st the love of you; 2nd the habit of reviewing; 3rd the love of money—to which I may add a fourth, the love of punishing fraud or folly."

While the Victorians offer a glittering roster of names among practitioners of the essay, the essay itself, during the age of Victoria, became less intimate. It grew longer; it began to address itself directly to serious things. Where it felt the need to become political, in the wider, cultural sense of politics, it did not hesitate to do so—as in the essays of Arnold, Carlyle, Ruskin. In the latter part of the eighteenth century, *Gentleman's Magazine* initiated a "review of books" section, but it was in the nineteenth centu-

ry that books became, if not always the subject of, at least the occasion for, essays. Books provided the occasion, certainly, for many of the essays of Macaulay. The length at which such journals as the *Edinburgh Review* and *Blackwood's* allowed Macaulay to go on, for the most part cheerfully ignoring the book under review, cannot but be the envy of contemporary essayists, though it must be said of Macaulay's essays, as Johnson once said of *Paradise Lost,* that no one ever wished them longer.

Virginia Woolf, in an essay entitled "The Modern Essay," remarks on this loss of intimacy among essayists during the Victorian era, and feels that the essay went into exile with the death of Charles Lamb only to emerge again in the person of Max Beerbohm. Beerbohm was of course "Max" to his readers—"the incomparable Max," in Bernard Shaw's phrase—and it was he who brought personality back into the essay. As Virginia Woolf says, "Matthew Arnold was never to his readers Matt, nor Walter Pater affectionately abbreviated in a thousand homes to Wat." Virginia Woolf adored Max Beerbohm—as do I—and rightly gauges his gift: "He has brought personality into literature, not unconsciously and impurely, but so consciously and purely that we do not know whether there is any relation between Max the essayist and Mr. Beerbohm the man." Yet one wonders if "personality" is precisely the word. Beerbohm's great trick, and a fine trick it is, was to be consummately familiar without ever imposing the burden of being personal. This trick is also called charm, and, as Virginia Woolf knew, charm is available in literature only to those who write supremely well.

Charm, though, is given to few, and the intimacy of personality need not be the only voice in which the essayist speaks. None but the most pretentious ass among their admirers would ever think of referring to Orwell as George or Mencken as Henry. Virginia Woolf, in my view, has too pure, too constricted a conception of the essayist. In a lovely essay of hers on Addison, she compares his writing to that of the lutanist, implying, by analogy, that the lute is the perfect instrument of the essayist. This, too, seems too restrictive. Among essayists there have also been the kettle drums of Carlyle, the French horn of Macaulay, the violin of Pater, the cello of Arnold, the trumpet of Mencken, the rich viola of Virginia Woolf herself . . . but I had better stop before I assemble a full symphony orchestra. . . .

I have dwelt on [some of] the essayists who have meant most to me—this is, you might say, the essayist's prerogative—and left out at least two American essayists who are elsewhere much revered but to whose virtues I am apparently blind: Ralph Waldo Emerson and E. B. White. (And one other whom I do care about and to whose virtues I do not think I am blind—A. J. Liebling.) Emerson is too vatic for me; in his essays he takes such large bites yet leaves one with so little upon which to chew. He bounds from pronunciamento to pronunciamento, and while his generalities do often glitter, I believe that it is in its particularities that the truth of the essay resides. E. B. White writes a pellucid prose, but his subjects have never engaged me. Gertrude Stein once said about Glenway Westcott that his writing has a certain syrup but it does not pour; for me, the fluent essays of E. B. White pour and pour but no syrup comes out.

While there is not today a general essayist who gives the pleasure of Mencken, or a political essayist of the clean power of Orwell, or a literary essayist of the range of Edmund Wilson (Gore Vidal not long ago nominated himself for the latter post, though no one could be found to second the nomination), as a form the essay nonetheless seems to be flourishing. Here is a partial list of contemporary practitioners, as various in their interests as in their methods: V. S. Naipaul, Tom Wolfe, Joan Didion, Edward Hoagland, Cynthia Ozick, Elizabeth Hardwick, Lewis Thomas, Gore Vidal, Susan Sontag, and Wendell Berry. (In an earlier generation there had been Lionel Trilling, Robert Warshow, and the young James Baldwin.) Some of these are, in an odd sense, almost regional writers: Tom Wolfe is best on the Manhattan status life, Joan Didion is best on the cultures of California, Edward Hoagland is best outside city limits. A number of the writers I have named are also novelists, yet, with the exception of Naipaul, none is anywhere near so good in his fiction as in his essays. Why, one wonders, should this be so?

I wonder if it doesn't have something to do with the fact that the essay as a form is in the happy condition of having no avant-garde tradition. I say happy condition because, great though the benefits of the avant-garde tradition have been in poetry and fiction, this same avant-garde tradition—and I trust no one will think the juxtaposition of avant-garde and tradition is oxymoronic—can exert a tyrannous pull to keep changing, to do it as no one has done it before, to make it, perpetually and (as it sometimes seems) depressingly, new. The essay is under no such tyranny. The idea of an avant-garde essayist, far from being oxymoronic, is merely moronic.

Not that the essayist cannot dazzle, turn you around, knock your socks off. He can. Not that there haven't been radical changes in the way that essays have been written. There have. Yet in even the most experimental essay writing—some of the essays, for example, of William Gass—there is something old shoe about the relationship between the essayist and his reader. "It's just you and me, kid," the essayist implies when he puts pen to paper. "I realize that," the reader in effect responds. "What's your point in this essay, Bub?" However much art there may be in his writing, the essayist cannot hide behind the claim to be an artist. He must stand and deliver. He must provide instruction, entertainment, persuasion, or the reader, like the young woman in the joke about the seducer who took the time to put shoe trees in his shoes, will be gone.

I grew up at a time when the novelist was the great cultural hero, and the novel, if it was written with power or subtlety (or both), seemed the most heroic cultural act. But, for a complex of reasons, the novel seems to be going through a bad patch right now. The essay, though it can never replace the novel, does appear to be taking up some of the slack. It is a form with distinguished predecessors and a rich tradition, and within its generous boundaries one can do almost anything one wishes: report anecdotes, tell jokes, make literary criticisms, polemicize, bring in odd scraps of scholarship, recount human idiosyncrasy in

its full bountifulness, let the imagination roam free. Subjects are everywhere, and there is no shortage of cultivated and appreciative readers. Don't spread it around, but it's a sweet time to be an essayist.

Scott Russell Sanders

SOURCE: "The Singular First Person," in *The Sewanee Review,* Vol. XCVI, No. 4, Fall, 1988, pp. 658-72.

[*Sanders is an American educator and essayist. In the following excerpt, he discusses the characteristics and pitfalls of the personal, or familiar, essay.*]

The essay is a haven for the private idiosyncratic voice in an era of anonymous babble. Like the blandburgers served in their millions along our highways, most language served up in public these days is textureless tasteless mush. On television, over the phone, in the newspaper, wherever human beings bandy words, we encounter more and more abstractions, more empty formulas. Think of the pablum ladled out by politicians. Think of the fluffy white bread of advertising. Think, lord help us, of committee reports. By contrast the essay remains stubbornly concrete and particular: it confronts you with an oil-smeared toilet at the Sunoco station, a red vinyl purse shaped like a valentine heart, a bowlegged dentist hunting deer with an elephant gun. As Orwell forcefully argued, and as dictators seem to agree, such a bypassing of abstractions, such an insistence on the concrete, is a politically subversive act. Clinging to this door, that child, this grief, following the zigzag motions of an inquisitive mind, the essay renews language and clears trash from the springs of thought. A century and a half ago Emerson called on a new generation of writers to cast off the hand-me-down rhetoric of the day, to "pierce this rotten diction and fasten words again to visible things." The essayist aspires to do just that.

As if all these virtues were not enough to account for a renaissance of this protean genre, the essay has also taken over some of the territory abdicated by contemporary fiction. Pared down to the brittle bones of plot, camouflaged with irony, muttering in brief sentences and grade-school vocabulary, today's fashionable fiction avoids disclosing where the author stands on anything. Most of the trends in the novel and short story over the past twenty years have led away from candor—toward satire, artsy jokes, close-lipped coyness, metafictional hocus-pocus, anything but a direct statement of what the author thinks and feels. If you hide behind enough screens, no one will ever hold you to an opinion or demand from you a coherent vision or take you for a charlatan.

The essay is not fenced round by these literary inhibitions. You may speak without disguise of what moves and worries and excites you. In fact you had better speak from a region pretty close to the heart or the reader will detect the wind of phoniness whistling through your hollow phrases. In the essay you may be caught with your pants down, your ignorance and sentimentality showing, while you trot recklessly about on one of our hobbyhorses. You cannot stand back from the action, as Joyce instructed us to do, and pare your fingernails. You cannot palm off your cockamamy notions on some hapless character. If the words you put down are foolish, everyone knows precisely who the fool is.

To our list of the essay's contemporary attractions we should add the perennial ones of verbal play, mental adventure, and sheer anarchic high spirits. The writing of an essay is like finding one's way through a forest without being quite sure what game you are chasing, what landmark you are seeking. You sniff down one path until some heady smell tugs you in a new direction, and then off you go, dodging and circling, lured on by the songs of unfamiliar birds, puzzled by the tracks of strange beasts, leaping from stone to stone across rivers, barking up one tree after another. Much of the pleasure in writing an essay—and, when the writing is any good, the pleasure in reading it—comes from this dodging and leaping, this movement of the mind. It must not be idle movement, however, if the essay is to hold up; it must be driven by deep concerns. The surface of a river is alive with lights and reflections, the breaking of foam over rocks, but underneath that dazzle it is going somewhere. We should expect as much from an essay: the shimmer and play of mind on the surface and in the depths a strong current.

To see how the capricious mind can be led astray, consider my last paragraph, in which the making of essays is likened first to the romping of a dog and then to the surge of a river. That is bad enough, but it could have been worse. For example I began to draft a sentence in that paragraph with the following words: "More than once, in sitting down to beaver away at a narrative, felling trees of memory and dragging brush to build a dam that might slow down the waters of time. . . ." I had set out to make some innocent remark, and here I was gnawing down trees and building dams, all because I had let that *beaver* slip in. On this occasion I had the good sense to throw out the unruly word. I don't always, as no doubt you will have noticed. I might as well drag in another metaphor—and another unoffending animal—by saying that each doggy sentence, as it noses forward into the underbrush of thought, scatters a bunch of rabbits that go rushing off in all directions. The essayist can afford to chase more of those rabbits than the fiction writer can, but fewer than the poet. If you refuse to chase any of them, and keep plodding along in a straight line, you and your reader will have a dull outing. If you chase too many, you will soon wind up lost in a thicket of confusion with your tongue hanging out.

The pursuit of mental rabbits was strictly forbidden by the teachers who instructed me in English composition. For that matter nearly all the qualities of the personal essay, as I have been sketching them, violate the rules that many of us were taught in school. You recall we were supposed to begin with an outline and stick by it faithfully, like a train riding its rails, avoiding sidetracks. Each paragraph was to have a topic sentence pasted near the front, and these orderly paragraphs were to be coupled end-to-end like so many boxcars. Every item in those boxcars was to bear the stamp of some external authority, preferably a footnote referring to a thick book, although appeals to magazines and newspapers would do in a pinch. Our diction was to be formal, dignified, shunning the vernacular.

Polysyllabic words derived from Latin were preferable to the blunt lingo of the streets. Metaphors were to be used only in emergencies, and no two of them were to be mixed. And even in emergencies we could not speak in the first-person singular.

Already, as a schoolboy, I chafed against those rules. Now I break them shamelessly—in particular the taboo against using the lonely capital *I*. Just look at what I'm doing right now. My speculations about the state of the essay arise, needless to say, from my own practice as reader and writer, and they reflect my own tastes, no matter how I may pretend to gaze dispassionately down on the question from a hot-air baloon. As Thoreau declares in his brash manner on the opening page of *Walden:* "In most books the *I*, or first person, is omitted; in this it will be retained; that, in respect to egotism, is the main difference. We commonly do not remember that it is, after all, always the first person that is speaking. I should not talk so much about myself if there were anybody else whom I knew as well." True for the personal essay, it is doubly true for an essay about the essay: one speaks always and inescapably in the first-person singular.

We could sort out essays along a spectrum according to the degree to which the writer's ego is on display—with John McPhee, perhaps, at the extreme of self-effacement, and Norman Mailer at the opposite extreme of self-dramatization. Brassy or shy, stage-center or hanging back in the wings, the author's persona commands our attention. For the length of an essay, or a book of essays, we respond to that persona as we would to a friend caught up in a rapturous monologue. When the monologue is finished, we may not be able to say precisely what it was about, any more than we can draw conclusions from a piece of music. "Essays don't usually boil down to a summary, as articles do," notes Edward Hoagland, one of the least summarizable of companions, "and the style of the writer has a 'nap' to it, a combination of personality and originality and energetic loose ends that stand up like the nap of a piece of wool and can't be brushed flat." We make assumptions about that speaking voice, assumptions we cannot validly make about the narrators in fiction. Only a sophomore is permitted to ask how many children had Huckleberry Finn. But even literary sophisticates wonder in print about Thoreau's love life, Montaigne's domestic arrangements, De Quincey's opium habit, Virginia Woolf's depression.

Montaigne, who not only invented the form but perfected it as well, announced from the start that his true subject was himself. In his note "To the Reader," he slyly proclaimed:

> I want to be seen here in my simple, natural, ordinary fashion, without straining or artifice; for it is myself that I portray. My defects will here be read to the life, and also my natural form, as far as respect for the public has allowed. Had I been placed among those nations which are said to live still in the sweet freedom of nature's first laws, I assure you I should very gladly have portrayed myself here entire and wholly naked.

A few pages after this disarming introduction we are told

of the Emperor Maximilian, who was so prudish about displaying his private parts that he would not let a servant dress him or see him in the bath. The emperor went so far as to give orders that he be buried in his underdrawers. Having let us in on this intimacy about Maximilian, Montaigne then confessed that he himself, although "bold-mouthed," was equally prudish, and that "except under great stress of necessity or voluptuousness," he never allowed anyone to see him naked. Such modesty, he feared, was unbecoming in a soldier. But such honesty is quite becoming in an essayist. The very confession of his prudery is a far more revealing gesture than any doffing of clothes.

Every English major knows that the word *essay,* as adapted by Montaigne, means a trial or attempt. The Latin root carries the more vivid sense of a weighing out. In the days when that root was alive and green, merchants discovered the value of goods and alchemists discovered the composition of unknown metals by the use of scales. Just so the essay, as Montaigne was the first to show, is a weighing out, an inquiry into the value, meaning, and true nature of experience; it is a private experiment carried out in public. In each of three successive editions Montaigne inserted new material into his essays without revising the old material. Often the new statements contradicted the original ones, but Montaigne let them stand, since he believed that the only consistent fact about human beings is their inconsistency. Lewis Thomas has remarked of him that he was "fond of his mind, and affectionately entertained by everything in his head." Whatever Montaigne wrote about (and he wrote about everything under the sun—fears, smells, growing old, the pleasures of scratching) he weighed on the scales of his own character.

It is the *singularity* of the first person—its warts and crotchets and turn of voice—that lures many of us into reading essays, and that lingers with us after we finish. Consider the lonely melancholy persona of Loren Eiseley, forever wandering, forever brooding on our dim and bestial past, his lips frosty with the chill of the Ice Age. Consider the volatile dionysian persona of D. H. Lawrence, with his incandescent gaze, his habit of turning peasants into gods and trees into flames, his quick hatred and quicker love. Consider that philosophical farmer Wendell Berry, who speaks with a countryman's knowledge and a deacon's severity. Consider E. B. White, with his cheery affection for brown eggs and dachshunds, his unflappable way of herding geese while the radio warns of an approaching hurricane.

White, that engaging master of the genre, a champion of idiosyncrasy, introduced one of his own collections by admitting the danger of narcissism:

> I think some people find the essay the last resort of the egoist, a much too self-conscious and self-serving form for their taste; they feel that it is presumptuous of a writer to assume that his little excursions or his small observations will interest the reader. There is some justice in their complaint. I have always been aware that I am by nature self-absorbed and egoistical; to write of myself to the extent I have done indicates a too great attention to my own life, not enough to the lives of others.

Yet the self-absorbed Mr. White was in fact a delighted observer of the world, and shared that delight with us. Thus, after describing memorably how a circus girl practiced her bareback riding in the leisure moments between shows ("The Ring of Time"), he confessed: "As a writing man, or secretary, I have always felt charged with the safe-keeping of all unexpected items of worldly or unworldly enchantment, as though I might be held personally responsible if even a small one were to be lost." That may still be presumptuous, but it is presumption turned outward on the world. . . .

On that cocky first page of *Walden* Thoreau justified his own seeming self-absorption by saying that he wrote the book for the sake of his fellow citizens, who kept asking him to account for his peculiar experiment by the pond. There is at least a sliver of truth to this, since Thoreau, a town character, had been invited more than once to speak his mind at the public lectern. Most of us, however, cannot honestly say the townspeople have been clamoring for our words. I suspect that all writers of the essay, even Norman Mailer and Gore Vidal, must occasionally wonder if they are egomaniacs. For the essayist, in other words, the problem of authority is inescapable. By what right does one speak? Why should anyone listen? The traditional sources of authority no longer serve. You cannot justify your words by appealing to the Bible or some other holy text, you cannot merely stitch together a patchwork of quotations from classical authors, you cannot lean on a podium at the Atheneum and deliver your wisdom to a rapt audience.

In searching for your own soapbox, a sturdy platform from which to deliver your opinionated monologues, it helps if you have already distinguished yourself at making some other, less fishy form. When Yeats describes his longing for Maud Gonne or muses on Ireland's misty lore, everything he says is charged with the prior strength of his poetry. When Virginia Woolf, in *A Room of One's Own,* reflects on the status of women and the conditions necessary for making art, she speaks as the author of *Mrs. Dalloway* and *To the Lighthouse.* The essayist may also claim our attention by having lived through events or traveled through terrains that already bear a richness of meaning. When James Baldwin writes his *Notes of a Native Son,* he does not have to convince us that racism is a troubling reality. When Barry Lopez takes us on a meditative tour of the far north in *Arctic Dreams,* he can rely on our curiosity about that fabled and forbidding place. When Paul Theroux climbs aboard a train and invites us on a journey to some exotic destination, he can count on the romance of railroads and the allure of remote cities to bear us along.

Most essayists, however, cannot draw on any source of authority from beyond the page to lend force to the page itself. They can only use language to put themselves on display and to gesture at the world. When Annie Dillard tells us in the opening lines of *Pilgrim at Tinker Creek* about the tomcat with bloody paws who jumps through the window onto her chest, why should we listen? Well, because of the voice that goes on to say: "And some mornings I'd wake in daylight to find my body covered with paw prints in blood; I looked as though I'd been painted with roses."

Listen to her explaining a few pages later what she is up to in this book, this broody zestful record of her stay in the Roanoke Valley: "I propose to keep here what Thoreau called 'a meteorological journal of the mind,' telling some tales and describing some of the sights of this rather tamed valley, and exploring, in fear and trembling, some of the unmapped dim reaches and unholy fastnesses to which those tales and sights so dizzyingly lead." The sentence not only describes the method of her literary search, but also displays the breathless, often giddy, always eloquent and spiritually hungry soul who will do the searching. If you enjoy her company, you will relish Annie Dillard's essays; if you don't, you won't.

Listen to another voice which readers tend to find either captivating or insufferable:

> That summer I began to see, however dimly, that one of my ambitions, perhaps my governing ambition, was to belong fully to this place, to belong as the thrushes and the herons and the muskrats belonged, to be altogether at home here. That is still my ambition. But now I have come to see that it proposes an enormous labor. It is a spiritual ambition, like goodness. The wild creatures belong to the place by nature, but as a man I can belong to it only by understanding and by virtue. It is an ambition I cannot hope to succeed in wholly, but I have come to believe that it is the most worthy of all.

That is Wendell Berry writing about his patch of Kentucky. Once you have heard that stately, moralizing, cherishing voice, laced through with references to the land, you will not mistake it for anyone else's. Berry's themes are profound and arresting ones. But it is his voice, more than anything he speaks about, that either seizes us or drives us away.

Even so distinct a persona as Wendell Berry's or Annie Dillard's is still only a literary fabrication, of course. The first-person singular is too narrow a gate for the whole writer to pass through. What we meet on the page is not the flesh-and-blood author, but a simulacrum, a character who wears the label *I*. Introducing the lectures that became *A Room of One's Own*, Virginia Woolf reminded her listeners that " 'I' is only a convenient term for somebody who has no real being. Lies will flow from my lips, but there may perhaps be some truth mixed up with them; it is for you to seek out this truth and to decide whether any part of it is worth keeping." Here is a part I consider worth keeping: "Women have served all these centuries as looking-glasses possessing the magic and delicious power of reflecting the figure of man at twice its natural size." From such elegant revelatory sentences we build up our notion of the "I" who speaks to us under the name of Virginia Woolf.

What the essay tells us may not be true in any sense that would satisfy a court of law. As an example think of Orwell's brief narrative "A Hanging," which describes an execution in Burma. Anyone who has read it remembers how the condemned man as he walked to the gallows stepped aside to avoid a puddle. That is the sort of haunting detail only an eyewitness should be able to report. Alas, biographers, those zealous debunkers, have recently claimed that Orwell never saw such a hanging; that he reconstructed it from hearsay. What then do we make of his essay? Or has it become the sort of barefaced lie we prefer to call a story?

I don't much care what label we put on "A Hanging"—fiction or nonfiction: it is a powerful statement either way; but Orwell might have cared a great deal. I say this because not long ago I found one of my own essays treated in a scholarly article as a work of fiction, and when I got over the shock of finding any reference to my work at all, I was outraged. Here was my earnest report about growing up on a military base, my heartfelt rendering of indelible memories, being confused with the airy figments of novelists! To be sure, in writing the piece I had used dialogue, scenes, settings, character descriptions, the whole fictional bag of tricks; sure, I picked and chose among a thousand beckoning details; sure, I downplayed some facts and highlighted others; but I was writing about the actual, not the invented. I shaped the matter, but I did not make it up.

To explain my outrage I must break another taboo, which is to speak of the author's intention. My teachers warned me strenuously to avoid the intentional fallacy. They told me to regard poems and plays and stories as objects washed up on the page from some unknown and unknowable shores. Now that I am on the other side of the page, so to speak, I think quite recklessly of intention all the time. I believe that if we allow the question of intent in the case of murder, we should allow it in literature. The essay is distinguished from the short story not by the presence or absence of literary devices, not by tone or theme or subject, but by the writer's stance toward the material. In composing an essay about what it was like to grow up on that military base, I *meant* something quite different from what I mean when concocting a story. I meant to preserve and record and help give voice to a reality that existed independently of me. I meant to pay my respects to a minor passage of history in an out-of-the-way place. I felt responsible to the truth as known by other people. I wanted to speak directly out of my own life into the lives of others.

You can see I am teetering on the brink of metaphysics. One step farther and I will plunge into the void, wondering as I fall how to prove there is any external truth for the essayist to pay homage to. I draw back from the brink and simply declare that I believe one writes, in essays, with a regard for the actual world, with a respect for the shared substance of history, the autonomy of other lives, the being of nature, the mystery and majesty of a creation we have not made.

When it comes to speculating about the creation, I feel more at ease with physics than with metaphysics. According to certain bold and lyrical cosmologists, there is at the center of black holes a geometrical point, the tiniest conceivable speck, where all the matter of a collapsed star has been concentrated, and where everyday notions of time, space, and force break down. That point is called a singularity. The boldest and most poetic theories suggest that anything sucked into a singularity might be flung back out again, utterly changed, somewhere else in the universe. The lonely first person, the essayist's microcosmic "I," may be thought of as a verbal singularity at the center of the mind's black hole. The raw matter of experience, torn away from the axes of time and space, falls in constantly from all sides, undergoes the mind's inscrutable alchemy, and reemerges in the quirky unprecedented shape of an essay.

ELEMENTS OF FORM AND STYLE

William Hazlitt

SOURCE: "On Familiar Style," in *Romantic Prose of the Early Nineteenth Century,* edited by Carl H. Grabo, Charles Scribner's Sons, 1927, pp. 3-12.

[*Hazlitt was one of the leading essayists of the early nineteenth century. Influenced by the concise social commentary of Joseph Addison's* Spectator *essays and by the personal tone of Michel de Montaigne's essays, Hazlitt developed what became known as the familiar essay. Characterized by conversational diction and personal opinion on topics ranging from English poets to washerwomen, his familiar style is best represented by the essays in* The Round Table *(1817),* Table-Talk *(1821-22), and* The Plain Speaker *(1826). While he also produced an important body of critical works, Hazlitt's familiar essays are the most esteemed and successful of his writings. In the following essay, originally published in the second volume of* Table Talk *(1822), he defines the familiar essay's style.*]

It is not easy to write a familiar style. Many people mistake a familiar for a vulgar style, and suppose that to write without affectation is to write at random. On the contrary, there is nothing that requires more precision, and, if I may so say, purity of expression, than the style I am speaking of. It utterly rejects not only all unmeaning pomp, but all low, cant phrases, and loose, unconnected, *slipshod* allusions. It is not to take the first word that offers, but the best word in common use; it is not to throw words together in any combinations we please, but to follow and avail ourselves of the true idiom of the language. To write a genuine familiar or truly English style is to write as any one would speak in common conversation who had a thorough command and choice of words, or who could discourse with ease, force, and perspicuity, setting aside all pedantic and oratorical flourishes. Or to give another illustration, to write naturally is the same thing in regard to common conversation as to read naturally is in regard to common speech. It does not follow that it is an easy thing to give the true accent and inflection to the words you utter, because you do not attempt to rise above the level of ordinary life and colloquial speaking. You do not assume, indeed, the solemnity of the pulpit, or the tone of stage-declamation; neither are you at liberty to gabble on at a venture, without emphasis or discretion, or to resort to vulgar dialect or clownish pronunciation. You must steer a middle course. You are tied down to a given and appropriate articulation, which is determined by the habitual associations between sense and sound, and which you can only hit by entering into the author's meaning, as you must find the proper words and style to express yourself by fixing your thoughts on the subject you have to write

about. Any one may mouth out a passage with a theatrical cadence, or get upon stilts to tell his thoughts; but to write or speak with propriety and simplicity is a more difficult task. Thus it is easy to affect a pompous style, to use a word twice as big as the thing you want to express: it is not so easy to pitch upon the very word that exactly fits it. Out of eight or ten words equally common, equally intelligible, with nearly equal pretensions, it is a matter of some nicety and discrimination to pick out the very one, the preferableness of which is scarcely perceptible, but decisive. The reason why I object to Dr. Johnson's style is that there is no discrimination, no selection, no variety in it. He uses none but "tall, opaque words," taken from the "first row of the rubric"—words with the greatest number of syllables, or Latin phrases with merely English terminations. If a fine style depended on this sort of arbitrary pretension, it would be fair to judge of an author's elegance by the measurement of his words and the substitution of foreign circumlocutions (with no precise associations) for the mother-tongue. How simple it is to be dignified without ease, to be pompous without meaning! Surely it is but a mechanical rule for avoiding what is low, to be always pedantic and affected. It is clear you cannot use a vulgar English word, if you never use a common English word at all. A fine tact is shown in adhering to those which are perfectly common, and yet never falling into any expressions which are debased by disgusting circumstances, or which owe their signification and point to technical or professional allusions. A truly natural or familiar style can never be quaint or vulgar, for this reason, that it is of universal force and applicability, and that quaintness and vulgarity arise out of the immediate connection of certain words with coarse and disagreeable or with confined ideas. The last form what we understand by *cant* or *slang* phrases.—To give an example of what is not very clear in the general statement. I should say that the phrase *To cut with a knife,* or *To cut a piece of wood,* is perfectly free from vulgarity, because it is perfectly common; but to *cut an acquaintance* is not quite unexceptionable, because it is not perfectly common or intelligible, and has hardly yet escaped out of the limits of slang phraseology. I should hardly therefore use the word in this sense without putting it in italics as a license of expression, to be received *cum grano salis.* All provincial or bye-phrases come under the same mark of reprobation—all such as the writer transfers to the page from his fireside or a particular *coterie,* or that he invents for his own sole use and convenience. I conceive that words are like money, not the worse for being common, but that it is the stamp of custom alone that gives them circulation or value. I am fastidious in this respect, and would almost as soon coin the currency of the realm as counterfeit the King's English. I never invented or gave a new and unauthorised meaning to any word but one single one (the term *impersonal* applied to feelings) and that was in an abstruse metaphysical discussion to express a very difficult distinction. I have been (I know) loudly accused of revelling in vulgarisms and broken English. I cannot speak to that point; but so far I plead guilty to the determined use of acknowledged idioms and common elliptical expressions. I am not sure that the critics in question know the one from the other, that is, can distinguish any medium between formal pedantry and the most barbarous solecism. As an author, I endeavour to employ plain words and popular modes of construction, as, were I a chapman and dealer, I should, common weights and measures.

The proper force of words lies not in the words themselves, but in their application. A word may be a fine-sounding word, of an unusual length, and very imposing from its learning and novelty, and yet in the connection in which it is introduced may be quite pointless and irrelevant. It is not pomp or pretension, but the adaptation of the expression to the idea, that clenches a writer's meaning:—as it is not the size or glossiness of the materials, but their being fitted each to its place, that gives strength to the arch; or as the pegs and nails are as necessary to the support of the building as the larger timbers, and more so than the mere showy, unsubstantial ornaments. I hate anything that occupies more space than it is worth. I hate to see a load of band-boxes go along the street, and I hate to see a parcel of big words without anything in them. A person who does not deliberately dispose of all his thoughts alike in cumbrous draperies and flimsy disguises may strike out twenty varieties of familiar every-day language, each coming somewhat nearer to the feeling he wants to convey, and at last not hit upon that particular and only one which may be said to be identical with the exact impression in his mind. This would seem to show that Mr. Cobbett is hardly right in saying that the first word that occurs is always the best. It may be a very good one; and yet a better may present itself on reflection or from time to time. It should be suggested naturally, however, and spontaneously, from a fresh and lively conception of the subject. We seldom succeed by trying at improvement, or by merely substituting one word for another that we are not satisfied with, as we cannot recollect the name of a place or person by merely plaguing ourselves about it. We wander farther from the point by persisting in a wrong scent; but it starts up accidentally in the memory when we least expected it, by touching some link in the chain of previous association.

There are those who hoard up and make a cautious display of nothing but rich and rare phraseology—ancient medals, obscure coins, and Spanish pieces of eight. They are very curious to inspect, but I myself would neither offer nor take them in the course of exchange. A sprinkling of archaisms is not amiss, but a tissue of obsolete expressions is more fit *for keep than wear.* I do not say I would not use any phrase that had been brought into fashion before the middle or the end of the last century, but I should be shy of using any that had not been employed by any approved author during the whole of that time. Words, like clothes, get old-fashioned, or mean and ridiculous, when they have been for some time laid aside. Mr. Lamb is the only imitator of old English style I can read with pleasure; and he is so thoroughly imbued with the spirit of his authors that the idea of imitation is almost done away. There is an inward unction, a marrowy vein both in the thought and feeling, an intuition, deep and lively, of his subject, that carries off any quaintness or awkwardness arising from an antiquated style and dress. The matter is completely his own, though the manner is assumed. Perhaps his ideas are altogether so marked and individual as to require their

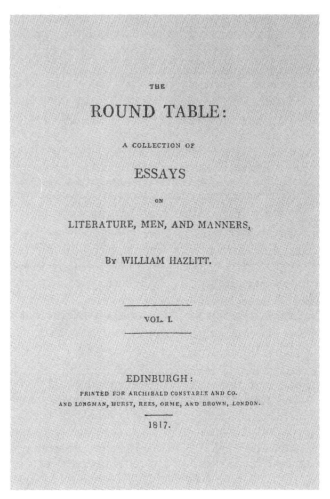

THE

ROUND TABLE:

A COLLECTION OF

ESSAYS

ON

LITERATURE, MEN, AND MANNERS,

BY WILLIAM HAZLITT.

VOL. I.

EDINBURGH:
PRINTED FOR ARCHIBALD CONSTABLE AND CO.
AND LONGMAN, HURST, REES, ORME, AND BROWN, LONDON.

1817.

Title page for the volume that collects the essays Hazlitt wrote for the Examiner *between 1814 and 1817.*

point and pungency to be neutralised by the affectation of a singular but traditional form of conveyance. Tricked out in the prevailing costume, they would probably seem more startling and out of the way. The old English authors, Burton, Fuller, Coryate, Sir Thomas Browne, are a kind of mediators between us and the more eccentric and whimsical modern, reconciling us to his peculiarities. I do not however know how far this is the case or not, till he condescends to write like one of us. I must confess that what I like best of his papers under the signature of Elia (still I do not presume, amidst such excellence, to decide what is most excellent) is the account of "Mrs. Battle's Opinions on Whist," which is also the most free from obsolete allusions and turns of expression—

A well of native English undefiled.

To those acquainted with his admired prototypes, these Essays of the ingenious and highly gifted author have the same sort of charm and relish that Erasmus's Colloquies or a fine piece of modern Latin have to the classical scholar. Certainly, I do not know any borrowed pencil that has more power or felicity of execution than the one of which I have here been speaking.

It is as easy to write a gaudy style without ideas as it is to spread a pallet of showy colours, or to smear in a flaunting transparency. "What do you read?"—"Words, words, words."—"What is the matter?"—*"Nothing,"* it might be answered. The florid style is the reverse of the familiar. The last is employed as an unvarnished medium to convey ideas; the first is resorted to as a spangled veil to conceal the want of them. When there is nothing to be set down but words, it costs little to have them fine. Look through the dictionary, and cull out a *florilegium,* rival the *tulippomania. Rouge* high enough, and never mind the natural complexion. The vulgar, who are not in the secret, will admire the look of preternatural health and vigour; and the fashionable, who regard only appearances, will be delighted with the imposition. Keep to your sounding generalities, your tinkling phrases, and all will be well. Swell out an unmeaning truism to a perfect tympany of style. A thought, a distinction is the rock on which all this brittle cargo of verbiage splits at once. Such writers have merely *verbal* imaginations, that retain nothing but words. Or their puny thoughts have dragon-wings, all green and gold. They soar far above the vulgar failing of the *Sermo humi obrepens*—their most ordinary speech is never short of an hyperbole, splendid, imposing, vague, incomprehensible, magniloquent, a cento of sounding common-places. If some of us, whose "ambition is more lowly," pry a little too narrowly into nooks and corners to pick up a number of "unconsidered trifles," they never once direct their eyes or lift their hands to seize on any but the most gorgeous, tarnished, thread-bare, patch-work set of phrases, the left-off finery of poetic extravagance, transmitted down through successive generations of barren pretenders. If they criticise actors and actresses, a huddled phantasmagoria of feathers, spangles, floods of light, and oceans of sound float before their morbid sense, which they paint in the style of Ancient Pistol. Not a glimpse can you get of the merits or defects of the performers: they are hidden in a profusion of barbarous epithets and wilful rhodomontade. Our hypercritics are not thinking of these little fantoccini beings—

That strut and fret their hour upon the stage—

but of tall phantoms of words, abstractions, *genera* and *species,* sweeping clauses, periods that unite the Poles, forced alliterations, astounding antitheses—

And on their pens *Fustian* sits plumed.

If they describe kings and queens, it is an Eastern pageant. The Coronation at either House is nothing to it. We get at four repeated images—a curtain, a throne, a sceptre, and a footstool. These are with them the wardrobe of a lofty imagination; and they turn their servile strains to servile uses. Do we read a description of pictures? It is not a reflection of tones and hues which "nature's own sweet and cunning hand laid on," but piles of precious stones, rubies, pearls, emeralds, Golconda's mines, and all the blazonry of art. Such persons are in fact besotted with words, and their brains are turned with the glittering but empty and sterile phantoms of things. Personifications, capital letters, seas of sunbeams, visions of glory, shining inscriptions, the figures of a transparency, Britannia with her shield, or Hope leaning on an anchor, make up their

stock-in-trade. They may be considered as *hieroglyphical* writers. Images stand out in their minds isolated and important merely in themselves, without any ground-work of feeling—there is no context in their imaginations. Words affect them in the same way, by the mere sound, that is, by their possible, not by their actual application to the subject in hand. They are fascinated by first appearances, and have no sense of consequences. Nothing more is meant by them than meets the ear: they understand or feel nothing more than meets their eye. The web and texture of the universe, and of the heart of man, is a mystery to them: they have no faculty that strikes a chord in unison with it. They cannot get beyond the daubings of fancy, the varnish of sentiment. Objects are not linked to feelings, words to things, but images revolve in splendid mockery, words represent themselves in their strange rhapsodies. The categories of such a mind are pride and ignorance— pride in outside show, to which they sacrifice every thing, and ignorance of the true worth and hidden structure both of words and things. With a sovereign contempt for what is familiar and natural, they are the slaves of vulgar affectation—of a routine of high-flown phrases. Scorning to imitate realities, they are unable to invent any thing, to strike out one original idea. They are not copyists of nature, it is true; but they are the poorest of all plagiarists, the plagiarists of words. All is farfetched, dear-bought, artificial, oriental in subject and allusion; all is mechanical, conventional, vapid, formal, pedantic in style and execution. They startle and confound the understanding of the reader by the remoteness and obscurity of their illustrations; they soothe the ear by the monotony of the same everlasting round of circuitous metaphors. They are the *mock-school* in poetry and prose. They flounder about between fustian in expression and bathos in sentiment. They tantalise the fancy, but never reach the head nor touch the heart. Their Temple of Fame is like a shadowy structure raised by Dulness to Vanity, or like Cowper's description of the Empress of Russia's palace of ice, "as worthless as in show 'twas glittering"—

It smiled, and it was cold!

Edgar Allan Poe

SOURCE: "Nathaniel Hawthorne," in *Essays and Reviews,* Library of America, 1984, pp. 568-88.

[*Considered one of America's most outstanding men of letters, Poe was a distinguished poet, novelist, essayist, journalist, short story writer, editor, and critic. He stressed an analytical, rather than emotive approach to literature and emphasized the specifics of style and construction in a work, instead of concentrating solely on the importance of ideological statement. Although Poe and his literary criticism were subject to controversy in his own lifetime, he is now valued for his literary theories. In the following excerpt from an 1842 review of Nathaniel Hawthorne's* Twice-Told Tales, *Poe defines the form of the familiar essay, comparing Hawthorne's essay style with that of Hazlitt, Hunt, Lamb, and Irving.*]

[Mr. Hawthorne's Essays, in his *Twice-Told Tales*] are each and all beautiful, without being characterised by the polish and adaptation so visible in the tales proper. A painter would at once note their leading or predominant feature, and style it *repose*. There is no attempt at effect. All is quiet, thoughtful, subdued. Yet this repose may exist simultaneously with high originality of thought; and Mr. Hawthorne has demonstrated the fact. At every turn we meet with novel combinations; yet these combinations never surpass the limits of the quiet. We are soothed as we read; and withal is a calm astonishment that ideas so apparently obvious have never occurred or been presented to us before. Herein our author differs materially from Lamb or Hunt or Hazlitt—who, with vivid originality of manner and expression, have less of the true novelty of thought than is generally supposed, and whose originality, at best, has an uneasy and meretricious quaintness, replete with startling effects unfounded in nature, and inducing trains of reflection which lead to no satisfactory result. The Essays of Hawthorne have much of the character of Irving, with more of originality, and less of finish; while, compared with the Spectator, they have a vast superiority at all points. The Spectator, Mr. Irving, and Mr. Hawthorne have in common that tranquil and subdued manner which we have chosen to denominate *repose;* but, in the case of the two former, this repose is attained rather by the absence of novel combination, or of originality, than otherwise, and consists chiefly in the calm, quiet, unostentatious expression of commonplace thoughts, in an unambitious unadulterated Saxon. In them, by strong effort, we are made to conceive the absence of all. In the essays before us the absence of effort is too obvious to be mistaken, and a strong undercurrent of *suggestion* runs continuously beneath the upper stream of the tranquil thesis. In short, these effusions of Mr. Hawthorne are the product of a truly imaginative intellect, restrained, and in some measure repressed, by fastidiousness of taste, by constitutional melancholy and by indolence.

Francis Thompson

SOURCE: "The Essay: Ancient and Modern," in *The Real Robert Louis Stevenson, and Other Critical Essays,* edited by Rev. Terence L. Connolly, University Publishers Incorporated, 1959, pp. 286-91.

[*Thompson was one of the most important poets of the Catholic Revival in nineteenth-century English literature. Like other writers of the fin de siècle period, Thompson wrote poetry and prose noted for rich verbal effects and a devotion to the values of aestheticism. In the following excerpt from a 1903 review of William Peacock's edition of* Selected English Essays, *he distinguishes the essay from the article, and laments the decline of the true essay.*]

The English Essayists! The very phrase has a delightful sound: outside fiction, it represents the most humane, the least formal, the most friendly, personal, and artlessly artistic mode of communication between writer and reader. Yet withal elastic, adjusting itself to the needs of individuality, so that in given hands it attains something of the grand style, and a more set structure: you have the *négligé* of Leigh Hunt, and the brilliantly elaborated balance of Macaulay, where the whole edifice is carefully proportioned, and nothing "wanders at its own sweet will." It

was the last word of art's endeavour to join hands with the multitude, before art degenerated into the article, a manufactured thing like the sausage or the sandwich. You cannot manufacture the essay. A manufactured essay is an apparent failure, like a manufactured poem; but a manufactured—veritably a hand-made—article may be a quite useful and workmanlike "article" of commerce. So one handles with interest, and one knows not what remembered perfumes from the sweet and goodly past of letters, Mr. Peacock's *Selected English Essays.* . . .

The modern essay is a new thing. It has forgotten the armchair attitude which is the leading trait of the essay as it was born with Montaigne. It has forgotten how to idle wisely, cultivatedly, or wittily. It has taken to be in rank earnest. It is purposeful—energetic, or critical, or what you please, but it nearly always has a purpose. Therewith comes a sense of form, and the obligation of form: it must be about something, and have beginning, middle, and end. To talk about a poker, and light upon a number of fascinating reflections, adorned with various knowledge, to the surprised contentment of your reader and yourself—this is impossible to your modern. His conscience would trouble him. Also his thoughts about a poker probably would not be worth the price of it. He could never get away from the poker. The original essay largely depended on the art of getting away from your subject. Nowadays, all a man can do with a subject is to write about it—which, after all, is what any fellow can do. The modern essay, in fact, began fatally to degenerate into the article, so that there is no real boundary-line between the two. Macaulay's essays—inadequately represented here by that on Goldsmith—are just long and brilliant articles. The same thing expanded becomes a biography, or biographical article, which in little was an essay. And in less it would be a "leader" or ordinary review. De Quincey is surely an article-writer rather than an essayist—when he is not writing those imaginative *bravuras* which range under no precedent at all. His famous "Murder as One of the Fine Arts" is no more an essay than some of Swift's ironic masterpieces, which Mr. Peacock has rejected for an unrepresentative essay on Style. Nor can the "Murder" be said to represent De Quincey, whose humour, unequal in this, is elsewhere weak. It would be to consider too curiously, however, were we absolutely to expunge these men from the ranks of essayists, in which they are a chief glory. The reader will not take our remarks too literally, or as more than an emphatic stressing of the change which has come over the modern essay. But there remains a band—Lamb, Hazlitt, and Hunt—who are essayists in the older sense. Hazlitt, indeed, is often of too energetic and purposeful a brilliance wholly to harmonize with the old tradition; but at times, as in essays here given, he is content to "laze," and is the very essayist—a fascinating essayist, too. As for Lamb, his delicious and sweet whimsicality is such that the essay seems born for him, not he for the essay. Hunt, with his amiable idle industry and gay flitting from sweet to sweet, keeps the secret of eighteenth century grace and lightness of touch as no man of his day kept it; and he too, in his limited, superficial, yet quite charming manner was an essayist born—nowadays, we think, too much underrated.

Of the moderns chosen by Mr. Peacock, Carlyle belongs to the strenuous order, nor do his lectures even profess to be essays. But Dr. John Brown ("Rab and his Friends"), Thackeray in the best of his *Roundabout Papers,* and R. L. S., in their several ways all have the roving spirit, the lightness of handling, which makes for the typical essay. The two latter both studied in the eighteenth century school, and with what accomplished grace Stevenson mastered its secret, adding the something of his own fascinating character, needs no telling. Addington Symonds is too deliberately accomplished, too studious of effect, to be quite the thing. But Matthew Arnold had the clarity and composed culture of the French essayists, and these four alone are sufficient to justify the essay in our day. Whether it can flourish in our twentieth century, so busied about many things, we greatly doubt. On living names we will not touch; but for the most part our best younger writers are either too prodigiously restless and eager to pack their work with effects, or frankly frivolous—which is quite another matter from the wise and airy leisure of the masters among the lighter essayists. Better the completion and purple patches of a Macaulay than *dilettante* frivolity. The advent of the democracy, which bodes ill for literature, bodes very ill, we fear, for the essay. The day is with the article. And the article may be made an excellent, a brilliant thing; but it is not the essay.

Charles E. Whitmore

SOURCE: "The Field of the Essay," in *PMLA,* Vol. XXXVI, No. 1, March, 1921, pp. 551-64.

[*In the following excerpt, Whitmore discusses the familiar essay (an imprecise term, in his estimation) in its several variations, having first differentiated it from the historical or critical essay (the "portrait") and the description of place or character (the "sketch").*]

For all practical purposes, . . . the essay in its modern aspect begins with Addison, and in his work we may first examine the adjustment of author's attitude to diversified material. We find in him . . . description, narration, and informal discussion; and we also find a class of essays characterized by *the inversion of a normal expository process.* That is, they expound a matter seemingly too trivial or absurd for serious exposition, or they expound it in an unexpected and whimsical way. The paper on the Fan (*Spectator,* No. 102) is a mock explanation of a process, soberly setting forth the workings of the academy which offers systematic drill in the management of the "little modish machine." The paper on the Cat-call (*ibid.,* No. 361) in reply to a letter inquiring the origin of the instrument, gives the various theories on the subject offered by learned friends, and discusses its applications in the writer's own day. So the proposal (*ibid.,* No. 251) to appoint a comptroller-general of the street-cries of London, which are duly divided into vocal and instrumental, with their relative sub-groups, is perfectly regular in development. In papers such as these the essay assumes a radically new shape, and discharges a novel function.

The same inversion, under a more bewildering stylistic cloak, can be traced in much of the most characteristic work of Lamb. "The Dissertation on Roast Pig"—if classification of that delicious whimsey be needed—is a mock process; "The Two Races of Men" is a mock division; "Imperfect Sympathies" is a thesis supported by deliberately humorous examples. We have also the mock encomium—a form which can trace its ancestry well back into classical times, and which was also practised in the Renaissance—in "The Praise of Chimney-sweepers" and "A Complaint of the Decay of Beggars." In his hands this subdivision of the essay makes steady progress in unexpectedness of topic, treatment, and style, until the second and third of these elements decisively prevail over the first. It is a method which obviously admits large amounts of paradox and parody, and may indeed employ them in excess, in which case the 'essay-quality' inevitably suffers, as it does with Mr. Chesterton. In Lamb, however, serious views usually underlie the discourse, however whimsical its outer aspect; and so they do in most of his successors who have adopted the type.

This method of inversion, it must be noted, necessarily falls in the domain of exposition, that is, on the intellectual side of writing; for the perception of unlikeness on which it rests involves comparison. An absurdity is not an absurdity to one who is unconscious of its conflict with ordinary experience; and in literature the wildest record of emotion, the most fantastic narrative, is in *method* indistinguishable from any other piece of description or narration. A fanciful story may be sober and closeknit like *Through the Looking-Glass,* or diffuse and rambling like *Water-Babies;* but only the reflective intelligence can distinguish either from a tale of common fact. So in general with inversion, paradox, irony: to the unreflective they are something quite other than what they are intended to be, and as unreflective readers abound, the puzzlement and irritation often caused by such methods are easily accounted for.

The unity of the essay, then, so far as it exists, is that of the essayist's point of view and manner of approach, not that of the several pieces, often radically different in method and temper, grouped under the term. Hence only resemblances between authors enable us to equate groups. The effort to discover a single continuous 'essay-tradition' in English is vain; I can see no reason to suppose that Lamb's work would have been in the slightest degree altered if Bacon had never written a line. Kinships between authors we can find; but they are exceedingly likely to cut across accepted literary divisions. Lamb derived much from Burton and Sir Thomas Browne; but can either be called an essayist in the sense that he is one? Dr. Holmes and Dr. Crothers have much in common; but surely the narrative interest in *The Autocrat* distinguishes it from *The Pardoner's Wallet.* In other words, the principle of classification is less that of literary form than that of author's attitude and intention.

Is it, however, possible to use this last criterion as the basis of a sounder division? I believe that it is; and in conclusion I wish to point out the various main groups which have come to light in the course of our survey, and to suggest names for them, so far as reliable practice supplies them. We have three main classes, with some sub-divisions, the relations of which will be clearest if they are arranged in quasi-tabular form.

I. The non-exhaustive treatment of a historical, biographical, or critical topic, the best general term for which is *study,* as in Froude's *Short Studies in Great Subjects,* Lord Bryce's *Studies in Contemporary Biography,* or Mr. Symons' *Studies in Prose and Verse.* Sometimes, in purely critical work, the term *estimate* appears, as in Professor Mather's *Estimates in Art,* or Mr. Drinkwater's *Swinburne: An Estimate.* In biography the variations of scope and treatment may justify the use of a separate term, the best, apparently, being *portrait,* as in Mr. Gamaliel Bradford's *Confederate Portraits* and *Union Portraits.*

II. The brief description of a place or a character, whether the latter be general, as in the older type, or specific. The best term for this is *sketch,* as in Irving's *Sketch-Book,* or Henry James' *Transatlantic Sketches.* The term *character,* however, will doubtless be retained in its technical sense with reference to the seventeenth-century type or to later work directly modelled on it.

III. The purely expository essay, of which we can distinguish three main types:

1) the essay which condenses the writer's experience and reading about a single topic, as in Bacon.

2) the essay which provides informal discussion of a point of manners or taste, as often in Addison and his successors.

3) the essay which inverts or whimsically applies a normal expository process, as in the examples cited from Addison and Lamb.

All three of these are sufficiently distinct to deserve separate names, especially the last; but I do not find that current practice justifies any. Certainly neither *informal* nor *familiar* can properly be restricted to either the second or the third class (neither fits the first); and there would seem to be a good opportunity for an inventor to supply us with the needed terms. Perhaps *commentary* might be revived to designate miscellaneous discussions of life in general; but it of course does not apply to any type of the essay proper.

It is now possible to see the lines by which the field of the essay is really divided. Brevity is at least highly desirable; informality has come to be largely taken for granted; tentativeness of approach and method, on the other hand, is a feature not necessarily restricted to the purely literary essay. As for the kinds of writing, the essayist's type of mind is most clearly reflected in the expository form, descriptive and narrative pieces being either subdued to it or given independent place, and argument given its own sphere in editorial or article. The literary essay as thus conceived has been well defined by Mr. D. T. Pottinger [in his prefatory remarks in *English Essays* (1917)] as "a written monologue or—in terms of another art—a personal letter addressed to the public." It might puzzle him to explain in what sense Pater's *Child in the House* (which he includes in his collection) is either. In truth, the portrait is obviously distinguished from the pure essay by the fact that it discards the direct approach of writer to reader, and

confines it self to the presentation of its real or imaginary subject; and the style which it adopts, whether rich and full-textured as in Pater, or keenly analytical in Mr. Bradford, is necessarily far removed from that of the *causerie.*

Thus we conclude that the unifying personality of the essayist, if sufficiently strong, can bring together a great variety of themes, and that the individual essay has free scope for variation. "We have to admit," says Mr. Ernest Rhys, "that so long as it obeys the law of being explicit, casually illuminative of its theme, and germane to the intellectual mood of its writer, then it may follow pretty much its own devices." But when it becomes interested in depicting a character or narrating an event for their own sakes, it begins to pass from the circle of the essay proper to that of the sketch or the protrait; in Irving's *Sketch-Book* no long scrutiny is needed to separate the real essays from the tales, and the task is fairly easy in many other cases. But the true province of the essay is in the setting forth—directly or invertedly—of its author's moods, tastes, predilections, aversions, and all other reactions to

---

J. Middleton Murry on the Essayist:

Though –the– novel and –the– essay do not exist, –the– novelist and –the– essayist do. The novelist is the writer who manages, through his prose fiction, to impose upon us the illusion of life. The life may be real of imaginary; he may have had quite another purpose in mind than to create the illusion: it does not matter; he is a novelist, because he is that and nothing else, not because we can find nothing else to call him. And the essayist is the writer who succeeds, in a prose which contains no narrative, in imposing upon us a sense of his living personality. It may be an intellectual personality; it may be spiritual; it may be carpet-slippered and convivial; but it must be living.

A distinction of this kind is vague, perhaps even arbitrary. Every tolerable piece of literature brings us into contact with a personality, if we have the knack of detecting the evidences. But the born essayist does not leave his personality to the mercies of detective criticism. Rather he exploits it, or, if "to exploit" be an unpleasant phrase, he employs it as an instrument for his purposes. He may go so far as to try to invent a personality, but that is a rash and dangerous method, adopted only by those second-rate writers who think, by imitating a manner, to emulate an effect. The personality which the true essayist employs is his own, but he is able to detach himself from it. He sees himself, as it were, in the round. And even when he is, as he often is, a critic of books, he is perpetually conscious of the personal equation in his judgments. If he does not copy Jules Lemaitre's rather painful trick of constantly recalling to our minds the obvious fact that all judgments are personal, he chooses the more delicate device of making us feel, by the very phrasing of his criticism, that his way of looking at things literary is of the same order as his taste in wine and waistcoats.

J. Middleton Murry, in The Nation and the Athenaeum, *1922.*

---

experience. "We might end," says Mr. Rhys again, "by claiming the essayists as dilute lyrists, engaged in pursuing a rhythm too subtle for verse, and life-like as common-room gossip." In a sense it is very true that the essay in the hands of such a writer as Lamb exemplifies the finest capacities of prose as a medium of self-expression precisely as lyric poetry expresses those of verse; but thereby an *Essay of Elia* and a pure lyric are as unlike as are the two media which they thus present at their most highly finished development; they are parallel, but unmistakably different, and neither could conceivably discharge the function of the other.

I do not suppose that any examination such as the present will result in a much more careful restriction of the term "essay"; the free and easy use has gone on too long to be easily discarded. None the less, the discrimination of the true essay from the study, the portrait, and the sketch is worth making, and a perception of the real distinctions between them may in time help to make usage a little more exact.

Virginia Woolf

SOURCE: "The Modern Essay," in *Collected Essays, Vol. II,* Harcourt Brace Jovanovich, 1925, pp. 41-50.

[*An English novelist, essayist, and short story writer, Woolf is considered one of the most prominent literary figures of twentieth-century English literature. Like her contemporary James Joyce, with whom she is often compared, she was one of the most innovative of the stream of consciousness novelists. Her critical essays cover almost the entire range of English literature and contain some of her finest prose. In the following excerpt from an essay originally published in 1922 in the* Times Literary Supplement, *she discusses the proper style and aim of the essayist, in a review of Ernest Rhys's five-volume edition of* Modern English Essays.]

The essay can be short or long, serious or trifling, about God and Spinoza, or about turtles and Cheapside. But as we turn over the pages of these five little volumes, [of *Modern English Essays,* edited by Ernest Rhys], containing essays written between 1870 and 1920, certain principles appear to control the chaos, and we detect in the short period under review something like the progress of history.

Of all forms of literature, however, the essay is the one which least calls for the use of long words. The principle which controls it is simply that it should give pleasure; the desire which impels us when we take it from the shelf is simply to receive pleasure. Everything in an essay must be subdued to that end. It should lay us under a spell with its first word, and we should only wake, refreshed, with its last. In the interval we may pass through the most various experiences of amusement, surprise, interest, indignation; we may soar to the heights of fantasy with Lamb or plunge to the depths of wisdom with Bacon, but we must never be roused. The essay must lap us about and draw its curtain across the world.

So great a feat is seldom accomplished, though the fault may well be as much on the reader's side as on the writer's.

Habit and lethargy have dulled his palate. A novel has a story, a poem rhyme; but what art can the essayist use in these short lengths of prose to sting us wide awake and fix us in a trance which is not sleep but rather an intensification of life—a basking, with every faculty alert, in the sun of pleasure? He must know—that is the first essential—how to write. . . . Literal truth-telling and finding fault with a culprit for his good are out of place in an essay, where everything should be for our good and rather for eternity than for the March number of the *Fortnightly Review.* But if the voice of the scold should never be heard in this narrow plot, there is another voice which is as a plague of locusts—the voice of a man stumbling drowsily among loose words, clutching aimlessly at vague ideas, the voice, for example, of Mr. Hutton in the following passage:

> Add to this that his married life was very brief, only seven years and a half, being unexpectedly cut short, and that his passionate reverence for his wife's memory and genius—in his own words, 'a religion'—was one which, as he must have been perfectly sensible, he could not make to appear otherwise than extravagant, not to say an hallucination, in the eyes of the rest of mankind, and yet that he was possessed by an irresistible yearning to attempt to embody it in all the tender and enthusiastic hyperbole of which it is so pathetic to find a man who gained his fame by his 'dry-light' a master, and it is impossible not to feel that the human incidents in Mr. Mill's career are very sad.

A book could take that blow, but it sinks an essay. A biography in two volumes is indeed the proper depository; for there, where the licence is so much wider, and hints and glimpses of outside things make part of the feast (we refer to the old type of Victorian volume), these yawns and stretches hardly matter, and have indeed some positive value of their own. But that value, which is contributed by the reader, perhaps illicitly, in his desire to get as much into the book from all possible sources as he can, must be ruled out here.

There is no room for the impurities of literature in an essay. Somehow or other, by dint of labour or bounty of nature, or both combined, the essay must be pure—pure like water or pure like wine, but pure from dullness, deadness, and deposits of extraneous matter. Of all writers in the first volume, Walter Pater best achieves this arduous task, because before setting out to write his essay ('Notes on Leonardo da Vinci') he has somehow contrived to get his material fused. He is a learned man, but it is not knowledge of Leonardo that remains with us, but a vision, such as we get in a good novel where everything contributes to bring the writer's conception as a whole before us. Only here, in the essay, where the bounds are so strict and facts have to be used in their nakedness, the true writer like Walter Pater makes these limitations yield their own quality. Truth will give it authority; from its narrow limits he will get shape and intensity; and then there is no more fitting place for some of those ornaments which the old writers loved and we, by calling them ornaments, presumably despise. Nowadays nobody would have the courage to embark on the once-famous description of Leonardo's lady who has

> learned the secrets of the grave; and has been a diver in deep seas and keeps their fallen day about her; and trafficked for strange webs with Eastern merchants; and, as Leda, was the mother of Helen of Troy, and, as Saint Anne, the mother of Mary . . .

The passage is too thumb-marked to slip naturally into the context. But when we come unexpectedly upon 'the smiling of women and the motion of great waters', or upon 'full of the refinement of the dead, in sad, earth-coloured raiment, set with pale stones', we suddenly remember that we have ears and we have eyes, and that the English language fills a long array of stout volumes with innumerable words, many of which are of more than one syllable. The only living Englishman who ever looks into these volumes is, of course, a gentleman of Polish extraction. But doubtless our abstention saves us much gush, much rhetoric, much high-stepping and cloud-prancing, and for the sake of the prevailing sobriety and hard-headedness we should be willing to barter the splendour of Sir Thomas Browne and the vigour of Swift.

Yet, if the essay admits more properly than biography or fiction of sudden boldness and metaphor, and can be polished till every atom of its surface shines, there are dangers in that too. We are soon in sight of ornament. Soon the current, which is the life-blood of literature, runs slow; and instead of sparkling and flashing or moving with a quieter impulse which has a deeper excitement, words coagulate together in frozen sprays which, like the grapes on a Christmas tree, glitter for a single night, but are dusty and garish the day after. The temptation to decorate is great where the theme may be of the slightest. What is there to interest another in the fact that one has enjoyed a walking tour, or has amused oneself by rambling down Cheapside and looking at the turtles in Mr. Sweeting's shop window? Stevenson and Samuel Butler chose very different methods of exciting our interest in these domestic themes. Stevenson, of course, trimmed and polished and set out his matter in a traditional eighteenth-century form. It is admirably done, but we cannot help feeling anxious, as the essay proceeds, lest the material may give out under the craftsman's fingers. The ingot is so small, the manipulation so incessant. And perhaps that is why the peroration—

> To sit still and contemplate—to remember the faces of women without desire, to be pleased by the great deeds of men without envy, to be everything and everywhere in sympathy and yet content to remain where and what you are—

has the sort of insubstantiality which suggests that by the time he got to the end he had left himself nothing solid to work with. Butler adopted the very opposite method. Think your own thoughts, he seems to say, and speak them as plainly as you can. These turtles in the shop window which appear to leak out of their shells through heads and feet suggest a fatal faithfulness to a fixed idea. And so, striding unconcernedly from one idea to the next, we traverse a large stretch of ground; observe that a would in the

solicitor is a very serious thing; that Mary Queen of Scots wears surgical boots and is subject to fits near the Horse Shoe in Tottenham Court Road; take it for granted that no one really cares about Æschylus; and so, with many amusing anecdotes and some profound reflections, reach the peroration, which is that, as he had been told not to see more in Cheapside than he could get into twelve pages of the *Universal Review,* he had better stop. And yet obviously Butler is at least as careful of our pleasure as Stevenson; and to write like oneself and call it not writing is a much harder exercise in style than to write like Addison and call it writing well. . . .

[We] suspect that the art of writing has for backbone some fierce attachment to an idea. It is on the back of an idea, something believed in with conviction or seen with precision and thus compelling words to its shape, that the diverse company which includes Lamb and Bacon, and Mr. Beerbohm and Hudson, and Vernon Lee and Mr. Conrad, and Leslie Stephen and Butler and Walter Pater reaches the farther shore. Very various talents have helped or hindered the passage of the idea into words. Some scrape through painfully; others fly with every wind favouring. But Mr. Belloc and Mr. Lucas and Mr. Squire are not fiercely attached to anything in itself. They share the contemporary dilemma—the lack of an obstinate conviction which lifts ephemeral sounds through the misty sphere of anybody's language to the land where there is a perpetual marriage, a perpetual union. Vague as all definitions are, a good essay must have this permanent quality about it; it must draw its curtain round us, but it must be a curtain that shuts us in, not out.

Robert Withington

SOURCE: "Of the Romantic Essay," in *South Atlantic Quarterly,* Vol. XXIII, No. 3, July, 1924, pp. 269-76.

[*In the following excerpt, Withington holds forth on the romantic essay—the essay concerned with "our emotions rather than our intellect," which "expresses itself in an emphasis on that which is distant, in time or place" and "deals with the supernatural often, or with the melancholic"—as a form of the familiar essay.*]

Our use of the term essay is vague enough at best; but even if we limit it to its "true province,"—the "setting forth . . . of its author's moods, tastes, predilections, aversions, and all other reactions to experience," as Dr. Whitmore phrases it—and exclude the "study," the "sketch," the "character," and the "portrait," we shall find plenty of room for humorous essays left. The term *romance,* too, is capable of many interpretations; it means one thing to the school-girl, and another to the critic of literature, but both of these meanings have a quality in common: and it is this quality which militates against humor.

Critics have found certain elements in that kind of writing which they term "romantic," and it might be well briefly to recall them. Broadly speaking, "romance" appeals to our emotions, rather than to our intellect; it expresses itself in an emphasis on that which is distant, in time or place; it deals with the supernatural often, or with the melancholic; with mediaeval ruins, with the uncanny, the eerie, the weird. It is essentially subjective. When Mark Twain takes a Connecticut Yankee to King Arthur's court, he finds no longer the romantic Camelot of Malory—or even of Tennyson; Thomas Ingoldsby's ghosts are not romantic; the cowboy is not romantic to the Wyoming sheriff, though he may be to a New York urchin or to a French peasant. Within certain limits the boundary may shift: the trenches were much more romantic to those who never saw them than to those who did—so was the Civil War, or the Commune; but the subjective, lyric outpouring of a poet's soul can never be anything but romantic. It is this self-revelation which lyric poet and essayist share in common, that gives us our starting-point; subjectivity is an important element of the romantic spirit.

From Montaigne on, essayists have voiced their moods in no argumentative or dogmatic way, but with an implicit— if not an expressed—tolerance of other people's moods and points of view. If essays are (as they have been called) "written monologues," or "personal letters addressed to the public," they are not propaganda, and aim neither to persuade nor to convince. Leaving out of account critical essays and such "non-exhaustive treatments" of historical, biographical, or even philosophical, topics (which Dr. Whitmore would call rather "studies" or "estimates"), as are sometimes included under this vaguely used term, there remains a residuum of expository essay, condensing the writer's experience (Bacon) or discussing informally a point of manners or taste (Addison); and the essay which inverts or whimsically applies a normal expository process (as often in Addison or Lamb.) Such is the classification of Whitmore. Not only does the personality of the writer tinge such essays with a romantic flavor (though in the case of Addison this is not common, as the *Spectator* is constantly objective), but the subject may often be romantic. . . .

In an illuminating chapter [in *The Essentials of Poetry*] on "Humor in Poetry," President Neilson points out "that in poetry of the romantic sort, and especially where the imagination is of the creative kind and works intensely, humor is often absent." If a given stanza contains both humor and poetry, "when the humor comes in, the poetry goes out." But Dr. Neilson does observe a few cases of humor in combination with true imaginative poetry, and cites a passage from *Measure for Measure* to illustrate his contention that the mutual exclusiveness of humor and imaginative poetry is not always absolute. Their harmony is made possible, he notes, through the element of sympathy—in itself largely imaginative—which enriches the poetry and lifts it above the level of satire that merely stings. This sympathetic element in humor brings it into its familiar relation with pathos; and just as Dr. Neilson finds the best example of that rare combination of humor with true poetry in Shakespeare, so we may find the unusual combination of humor with true romantic feeling in Lamb. In both combinations the humor is delicate, sympathetic, closely related to pathos, if you will; but it is none the less humor.

As Dr. Neilson shows, humor may be grim, pathetic, or merry. Such forms as irony or satire, directed as they are

to the intellect, cannot, of course, be considered even remotely romantic. Summing up the relation of humor to various types of poetry, Dr. Neilson concludes:

> In romantic poetry in general, poetry in which there is a marked predominance of imagination, we have found humor to be noticeably rare. . . . This has not been surprising. In real life everyone has observed the absence of humor in people of a strongly romantic tendency; and, in our own romantic moods, our flights into ideal realms are apt to be checked by the intrusion of even a momentary glimpse of ourselves as ludicrous. If it is difficult, as the philosophers have always said, to be in love and to be wise, it is still more difficult to be a romantic lover and retain a sense of humor.

It is needless to remark that the converse does not always hold: not everyone who lacks a sense of humor is necessarily in love.

What is true of romantic poetry is equally true of the romantic essay. When humor comes in, romance goes out; and if, in a given essay, both elements are found, those passages which are colored by one lose the other. A lover may have a sense of humor—but he does not have it in his most lover-like moods. We are apt to think that once a person has a sense of humor, he has it for all time; and we are sometimes surprised when he fails to show it.

When we find the tender, romantic humor which is made up of sympathy and a delicate perception of the ludicrous, we are midway between the satiric and the sentimental. It is not easy to walk such a path without getting over toward one extreme or the other, and we should not wonder at finding few writers who can combine the two qualities in just the right degree. When we do find such a one, however, we find a master of letters. Literature of this kind can rise to no greater heights than it attains in the pages of Elia, when, for instance, he yearns toward the dim specks—poor blots—innocent blacknesses, the young Africans of our own growth—these almost clergy imps, who sport their cloth without assumption; and from their little pulpits (the tops of chimneys), in the nipping air of a December morning, preach a lesson of patience to mankind. Or when he considers the best of Sapors—in the dish, his second cradle, how meek he lieth!—wouldst thou have had this innocent grow up to the grossness and indocility which too often accompany maturer swinehood? Or when (tenderest of all), he talks to the John and Alice who were nothing; less than nothing, and dreams . . . and when wakes to find himself quietly seated in his bachelor armchair, with the faithful Bridget unchanged by his side.

Such humor is like the happiness defined in a recent novel [A.S.M. Hatchinson's *This Freedom*].

> Happiness to be realized needs faint perception of sadness as needs the egg the touch of salt to manifest its flavour. Flashes of entertainment may enliven the most wretched of us; but that's pleasure; that's not happiness. One comes to know the only true and ideal happiness is happiness tinctured with faintest, vaguest hint of tears. It is peace; and who knows peace that has not come to it through storm . . . ?

The "flashes of entertainment" which are "pleasure" may be likened to wit, to satire; the happiness which is peace—which is "tinctured with faintest, vaguest hint of tears"—is the humor of the romantic essayist.

There are critics who scorn romanticism, in all of its manifestations, as if it were a plague; and undoubtedly if carried to excess it may become so. But all excesses are unhealthy, and the opposite extreme may be equally unwholesome. He who rules his life by intellect alone is no more pleasant to look upon than he whose imagination is "apt to startle" and turn a cow quietly grazing into a black horse without a head. *In media tutissimus ibis* remains ever sound advice; but if one must have an extreme, remember Stevenson's "It is better to be a fool than to be dead." The coldness of Bacon may hide a geyser of emotion—for Bacon lived and suffered; but if it does, we do not feel it, and most of us are attracted to writers who show more sympathy and less objectivity. Can one get a better idea of Thackeray's personality—hidden in his novels—than by reading the *Roundabout Papers?* "I dare say," begins his essay on "Ogres," "the reader has remarked that the upright and independent vowel, which stands in the vowel-list between E and O, has formed the subject of the main part of these essays." Montaigne presented "a well-meaning Booke" to his reader; "I desire therein to be delineated in mine owne genuine, simple and ordinarie fashion, without contention, art or study, for it is my selfe I pourtray." If Lamb is less obviously personal, he works on our sympathies, and his appeal is none the less romantic. The Breakfast Table papers of Holmes combine—as do Thackeray's essays—humor with that quality we call romanticism; but the idyl on Boston Common and the story of Iris show the sympathetic, delicate humor which fits the emotional appeal.

Laughter is a social emotion; we like to share our smiles, and for this reason we tell our stories to almost anyone who will listen to them—fellow-members of a club, or the stranger in the smoking-car. But we laugh best with our friends, as we laugh most heartily at those for whom we have little sympathy. No better distinction between romantic humor and its opposite can be drawn. At best, romantic humor is gentle; and when sympathy overflows upon us, our laughter fades.

No essay—in the true sense of the word—can be argumentative; indeed, no matter what his medium of expression, the artist should never argue. The observer, spectator, or whatever he may call himself, who stands outside his subject, looking at humanity objectively, may satirize manners and customs, but he cannot deal with subjects likely to arouse the antagonism of his readers or awaken his own bitterness. Tolerance, urbanity, humor, are the outstanding qualities of the objective essay; these may develop into sympathy, whimsicality, subjectivity. And when we find these qualities, we find romantic elements. *What* the subject is, is of minor importance; *how* it is dealt with, is what counts—the spirit of the essay gives it its classification. Often the qualities are felt, rather than observed; sometimes each paragraph has its distinctive flavor, and the essay as a whole can hardly be classified—though it can

be enjoyed. But if the essay is a "snapshot of a mood," why seek consistency?

One of the important characteristics of an essay is its style. To appreciate style, one has to use his intellect, it is true; but without analysis one can often feel a satisfaction in the way a writer expresses himself. When one is conscious of style, it is bad; for style is a window through which one looks at meaning—and one should never be aware of the glass. To deny romanticism any appeal to the intellect is, perhaps, unfair to romanticism; the approach to the intellect may, however, be made through the emotions; and when the emotions are aroused, the reader is not likely to analyze the means used to arouse them. If he becomes conscious of *tours de force,* his emotional response is weakened, and the romantic appeal of the essay is correspondingly lessened.

The romantic flavor of our essays can be traced back to Montaigne, whose chief aim was self-revelation. Bacon is the source of the objective essay—the handbook of conduct, which is in the back of the "Spectators" mind, as he satirizes his contemporaries in an endeavor to improve their behavior. Steele is a more sympathetic critic than his associate; and it does not need Thackeray's portrait of him in Henry Esmond to make him more romantic—and more lovable—than Addison. That "classical" writer is at his best on his death-bed; and the gentle scorn with which Mr. Roundabout and the Professor regard the spectacle is romanticism's answer to the humbug. Says Thackeray: "I like these little tales and sportive exercises. I had begun a little print collection once. I had Addison in his nightgown in bed at Holland House, requesting young Lord Warwick to remark how a Christian should die. . . ." "Addison," says Holmes, "gets up a *tableau* and utters an admirable sentiment,—or somebody makes the posthumous dying epigram for him."

For romanticism may preach and instruct—so long as it does so romantically; and romantic essayists may be permitted to sermonize occasionally, if they do not lose sympathy and tolerance in doing so. Propaganda kills romance, of all kinds; intolerance—that bane of the reformer—kills romance; but Mr. Roundabout, neither in nor out of his pulpit, professes to be bigger, or cleverer, or wiser, or better than any of his congregation; and Holmes admits that he has never yet met anyone who could teach him something. When the moralizer turns satirist, he is in danger of losing his title of romanticist (and much of his charm), because he is losing his sympathy.

J. B. Priestley

SOURCE: "In Defence," in *The Saturday Review,* London, Vol. 148, No. 3853, August 31, 1929, pp. 235-37.

[A highly prolific English man of letters, Priestley was the author of numerous popular novels that depict the world of everyday, middle-class England. His most notable critical work is Literature and Western Man *(1960), a survey of Western literature from the invention of movable type through the mid-twentieth century. In the following essay, Priestley defends the nature of the non-polemical familiar*

essay against charges of triviality launched by an article in the socialist periodical Clarion.]

It is not often that we essayists are attacked. This does not mean that our portion is praise. It is the custom to ignore us, and it is a mystery to me why we go on or why editors and publishers trouble to throw a few guineas our way. The large public demands that an essayist shall have been dead a long time or, alternatively, be an American journalist writing easy slop about the Open Road, before it condescends to buy and read him. The smaller and more intelligent public calls us charming fellows and then promptly thinks about something or somebody else. "Ah, yes," they say, "I saw a nice little thing of yours in the *Saturday* the other week. It was—er—about what-the-calling-it, you know, that thing." And when the volume arrives they bring out the small type and yawn through the same old tepid praise—"Variety of subjects—sense of humour—pleasant fancy—readable." For two weeks, sometimes three in a stirring season, the publisher puts your book in his advertisements—"Another charming volume," he says, wistfully. A schoolmaster in Newcastle and a retired civil servant in Dorset write to point out one or two mistakes in grammar. Six months later, an assistant professor in Saskatoon writes to ask if he may include the worst essay in the book in an anthology he is preparing. The rest is silence.

Being a vain man, I would rather be attacked than ignored, rather be thrown out than left unnoticed. Therefore I was glad to discover Mr. Stonier, who apparently contributes a literary causerie to the *Clarion,* the last number of which was sent to me the other day. This is not the *Clarion* I remember—it seems centuries ago—the penny weekly that was written by innumerable Blatchfords and had a passion for cycling clubs. (Many a time have I seen the *Clarion* enthusiasts streaming out, on fine Sunday mornings, in the West Riding of my childhood.) It is now a sixpenny monthly, quite handsome, and more dignified, though still rather dashing in the old cycling-club style. I read it all through and enjoyed it. But we must return to Mr. Stonier, who, in the course of a review of an "omnibus" book of essays, made the following observations:

> The conventional idea of an essay is this whimsical, childish-charming play with fancies. Almost all living essayists adopt this pose (sometimes successfully); with slight variations they present the same picture of an absent-minded, untidy, rambling, talkative but lovable amateur rather resembling Mr. Horace Skimpole. They write on the same topics without apparent effort every week in the literary reviews and book columns of newspapers. If only they had one word which they really felt bound to say, if only they did not spend all their time in practising a way of saying it! Mr. Belloc once wrote a book of essays which he called *On Nothing,* and though I have not read it, I am prepared to believe that the title described the book. There has been too much table-talk in recent essays, not enough of the pulpit or the soap-box. In short, what these writers lack is sincerity. . . .

Well, there is one essayist who has at last one word he feels bound to say, and that is "Boo!" And if this only calls up yet another "childish-charming fancy," namely, that Mr. Stonier is perhaps a goose, I cannot help it.

Let us first examine this pose that our critic says nearly all living essayists adopt. With one or two of the adjectives we cannot quarrel. It is true that we all pretend to be talkative. There may be essayists who pretend to be very taciturn, but of course we do not know anything about them, because their pose forbids them to write at all. As for being "lovable," the pretence, such as it is, is all the other way. Thus, Messrs. Belloc, Chesterton, Beerbohm, Lynd seem to me lovable men who are all pretending in their essays to be less lovable than they actually are. For the rest, I have not noticed Mr. Belloc's attempt to persuade us he is absent-minded, or Mr. Beerbohm's that he is untidy. But that, of course, is only the beginning. We must now face the charge expressed in the third sentence, in which, by the way, Mr. Stonier makes the mistake of assuming that essays appear in the book columns of newspapers. The charge is that we write on the same topics every week. Now that, it seems to me, is precisely what essayists do not do. Indeed, they are the only contributors to the Press or contemporary literature who do not write for ever on the same topics. Members of Parliament, leader-writers, women novelists, foreign correspondents, dramatic critics, stern young Socialists, retired Indian Army officers, clergymen, publicists, general busybodies, all these people can be discovered every day writing on the same old topics. But not the essayists. Heaven only knows what Mr. Chesterton or Mr. Lynd will be writing on next. The editor of this paper does not know what will be my next subject. I do not know myself. If Mr. Stonier knows, I wish he would drop me a line before next Tuesday.

He is prepared to believe that Mr. Belloc's title, *On Nothing,* describes the book. If so, he is prepared to believe anything. He tells us, with a frankness that does him credit (he must be new to the game), that he has not read this particular volume of essays. I find it difficult to believe that he has read any volume of essays by Mr. Belloc. If you wanted to suggest that men who write essays are vague-minded triflers, with no opinions, no beliefs, of their own, mere butterflies, could you find, in all the assembled literatures of Europe, a worse example, a more damning instance, than Mr. Belloc? Here is an essayist whose dense mass of opinion, whose arrogant conviction, almost crush the reader, and who affects at all times to be severely objective and concrete, and he of all men is singled out as an example of having nothing to say. I should have thought it obvious that a writer of some experience who dared to call a book *On Nothing,* knew very well—and assumed his readers knew very well—that he had something quite definite to say on nearly every subject under the sun. I have read books that really were on nothing, but they always bore such titles as 'The Decentralization of the Unconscious' or 'The Awareness of Graduality.' And no essayist ever wrote one.

To say there is too much table-talk in recent essays is to complain that there is too much meat in recent sausages. The essay, as we understand the essay nowadays, is table-talk in print. If Mr. Stonier does not like table-talk, then he does not like essays; and there is an end of it. Apparently, he favours the introduction of the pulpit and the soap-box. Here, he may congratulate himself, for he is with the majority. Most people prefer the pulpit and the soap-box in print to the dinner-table, and that is why essays are so comparatively unpopular and why some other kinds of writing pay so well. The popular Press has now said good-bye to the essay and the essayists, but it welcomes the preacher and the tub-thumper every morning. If an editor wants to have more than a million readers, he takes care to set up a pulpit and a soap-box on his leader-page. He also takes care to keep the table-talker out of the office. Is this because the table-talker, the essayist, is so insincere? Is the essayist insincere?

It is Mr. Stonier's word, this sincerity, and not mine. Perhaps because I have so little of the quality myself, perhaps for other and sounder reasons, I mistrust this word. It should be handled as carefully as dynamite. If the essayists, talking freely about themselves, their habits, their tastes, their hopes and fears, their weaknesses and little vanities, lack sincerity, what writers have it? Is it the possession of the philosophers, the critics, the historians, the biographers, the romancers? Why, they are even beginning to suspect the very prophets. Who has it, this sincerity? He that died o' Wednesday.

It is true that we essayists, even on Mr. Stonier's showing, have achieved something, for though, as he complains, we spend all our time practising a way of saying our nothings (sedulous apes to a man), yet, as he says, we write every week "without apparent effort." This means that we are very clever fellows, unless there happens to be a flaw in Mr. Stonier's logic, and it is not the business of one of your whimsical, fanciful, childish-charming laddies to suggest such a thing. But Mr. Stonier, I take it, is a man who likes philosophy, opinions, beliefs, a point of view, in a writer, and he misses these things in the essayists. But because he misses them he must not jump to the conclusion that they are not there. He has been in too much of a hurry, perhaps; a trifle deafened, it may be, by those pulpit and soap-box orations that he prefers. Table-talk has its own manner, and sometimes its nonsense is the sanest sense, just as the gravest or most passionate sense of the pulpit and the soap-box sometimes contrives, after being carried home to the table, to turn into the silliest nonsense.

Robert Lynd

SOURCE: "The Essay," in *Essays of the Year, 1930-1931,* The Argonaut Press, 1931, pp. xi-xix.

[*Lynd, an Irish journalist and author, served as literary editor of the* London News Chronicle, *and contributed regularly to the* New Statesman and Nation. *Primarily an essayist, Lynd cultivated the conversational style of Charles Lamb; his work is imaginative and gently whimsical. In the following essay, Lynd addresses the issue of the essay's ideal length.*]

Everyone who has hitherto attempted has failed to produce a satisfactory definition of the word "essay." The reason for this failure is simple enough: it is that an essay may be almost any kind of shortish piece of prose for which no other name can be discovered. Various critics have sought to limit the use of the word to short pieces in which the point of view is extremely personal, and in which even philosophy, if it appears, has the blood of autobiography in its veins. I know one admirable critic who would even exclude Bacon from the ranks of the essayists on the ground that his essays have nothing in common with those of Montaigne and Lamb. I cannot see much good in a definition which would compel us to rename the most memorable books of such writers as Bacon, Macaulay, Emerson, and Matthew Arnold.

It is true that if you heard someone saying that he liked (or loathed) essays, you would have a shrewd notion that he was not thinking of Locke's *Essay concerning Human Understanding,* or Bishop Berkeley's *Essay for Preventing the Ruin of Great Britain.* On the other hand, he might conceivably be a man who liked (or loathed) Bacon's string of epigrams on Truth equally with Lamb's deep well of memories in "Old China." Those who talk about the "true essay," as though only one kind of essay were "true," ignore the fact that even the individual essayist as a rule writes essays of more than one type. The essays of Addison, for example, sometimes resemble fiction, sometimes sermons, sometimes critical studies, and are sometimes the expressions of a humorous mind on the follies of the age or the follies of the ages. In *The Spectator,* Addison claimed perfect freedom to write as he chose on any subject that interested him. If his essays have survived, it is not because they conform to one type of "true essay," but because he was able to discourse like a man at his ease in good company on a variety of subjects in a variety of moods, grave and gay, anecdotal and philosophical. Hence, it seems to me that there is probably no such thing as a "true essay," just as there is no such thing as a "true letter." The only reasonable division of essays is into good, bad, and indifferent. And in regard to this it must be conceded that the majority of essays, like the majority of poems and the majority of novels, are either bad or indifferent.

Considering that the essay is so difficult of definition, it is no wonder that critics differ widely as to the date of its origin. Most of the authorities hold that the first essays were written by Montaigne in the sixteenth century; but Mr. F. H. Pritchard, in his anthology of the great essays of the world, has gone for his material as far back as the author of *Ecclesiastes,* and reckons even Aristotle among the essayists. It is, perhaps, a little extravagant to call a chapter of a book of philosophy an essay. And yet it may be argued with some show of reason that the earliest essays were themselves chapters of philosophy. In the essay we find philosophy grown familiar; and Bacon held that, though the name was new in his day, the essay itself was as old as Seneca. Didactic essays, such as Seneca's eulogy of clemency to the youthful Nero, are not in much favour today, but they are none the less essays on that account; and, in Greek, when Plutarch writes "On Having Many Friends" or "On Chance," he is obviously practising the same art that Bacon was afterwards to make famous in England. Montaigne, it is true, protested that in writing his essays he was not aiming at the service of his readers, as the familiar philosophers of earlier ages had done, and that he himself was the real matter of his book. But no one can read his book without seeing that in spirit it is an off-shoot of philosophy. Montaigne did not so much invent the essay as give it a new shape with his genius. He wrote the first essays in which philosophy and autobiography joined hands.

Nor, since his time, has the essay entirely lost its philosophic and didactic flavour. Addison was in much of his work a moralist of the coffee-house, and it was his ambition to improve society by entertaining it. Dr. Johnson wrote on such themes as the folly and inconvenience of affection, and the proper means of regulating sorrow. Hazlitt enjoyed a brief plunge into metaphysics no less than an excursion among things remembered. And so on, until in our own day Mr. G. K. Chesterton has again and again made the essay the vehicle of whatever religious, moral, and political ideas fired him when he sat down to write. The truth is that, contrary to a common notion, the immortality of the soul makes as good a subject for an essayist as does a broomstick. Swift has been much praised for having been able to write on a broomstick; but what is most astonishing in the business is that he did not write better on it. If Mr. Chesterton had written an essay on a broomstick, the broomstick would have burst into blossom like Tannhäuser's staff.

Since the essay became a branch of literary journalism, there has scarcely been a subject from the immortality of the soul down to broomsticks that it has not made its own. Its range has been as wide as that of conversation, and, at its best, it is often a kind of heightened conversation, whether grave or nonsensical, reminiscent or critical. When Hazlitt called a book of essays *Table Talk,* he came as near a definition of the popular essay of the last two centuries or so as is possible.

Literary puritans complain that the essay has been injured by the compulsion laid upon the essayist to talk on all manner of subjects at a moment's notice in the popular journals, and we are told that even the length of the essay has been dictated by the needs of journalism. We must judge by results, however, not by preconceived theories; and, if we do so, we shall find that the essay has been no more injured than the play or the novel by the call of the producer or printer, or the restrictions imposed by the paymaster. If a writer is a good writer, and is left free in his choice of subject and in his choice of treatment, his genius will find a means of expressing itself freely within the limits assigned to him. Pressure from without may even, within limits, be of service to an author's genius. Had it not been for the demands of journalism, we might never have had the *Essays of Elia.* Lamb's essays, like *The Pickwick Papers,* were commissioned work, and it is doubtful whether, but for the urgency of editors, Lamb would have had the incentive to write them. If there has never been a second Lamb, this is not due to the fact that conditions in journalism have changed; it is for the same reason that there has never been a second Shakespeare.

We are sometimes reminded that, while Lamb was permitted to expand his subject at will in the pages of a magazine, the modern essayist is confined to a narrower space in the columns of daily and weekly newspapers. But the fact is that the main tradition of the English essay has always been in favour of brevity, that Bacon wrote essays which would be dismissed as "snippets" by the advocates of length, and that Lamb himself voluntarily made many of his most delightful essays short enough to have appeared in a weekly review today. I was recently looking at Mr. J. B. Priestley's anthology *Essayists Past and Present,* and I could find no evidence that the essay has dwindled in size since the days of Steele. Steele's "Recollections of Childhood" occupies seven pages of the anthology; Mr. G. K. Chesterton's "A Piece of Chalk" also occupies seven. Addison's "Death of Sir Roger de Coverley" fills five pages; Mr. Belloc's "The Mowing of a Field" fills six. Johnson's and Goldsmith's essays run to about the same length. Lamb's "Old China," which is somewhat longer, takes up ten pages, but Mr. Lucas's "My Cousin the Bookbinder" takes up eleven. It is clear, then, that no novel vice of brevity has been forced upon the modern essayist. If a modern essayist has the genius to write as good an essay as "Old China" he has every opportunity to do so.

On the other hand, many of the great essays undoubtedly run far beyond the limit of two thousand words. I do not see how *Religio Medici* is to be described except as an essay, yet it fills a small book. Montaigne himself expanded the *Apology for Raymond Sebond* to the length of a booklet, while at other times he made an essay only a page or two pages long. Lamb's "Christ's Hospital Five-and-Thirty Years Ago" is about three times as long as "Dream Children." Hazlitt required generous space for "The Fight" and "My First Acquaintance with Poets." But it is an interesting fact that in the Victorian age, when the essayists took advantage of the greater elbow-room allowed to them, they failed to show any conspicuous advance on the briefer writers of the eighteenth century.

Obviously, it is as much an impossibility to lay down rules for the "right length" of an essay, as it would be to lay down rules for the "right length" of a novel. A good novel may be as short as *The Vicar of Wakefield* or as long as *War and Peace.* We instinctively feel that a line must be drawn somewhere both in regard to length and in regard to brevity; but when we complain that a novel is too short or too long, what we usually mean is merely that the novelist has not filled his space with the fiery energy of genius. And it is much the same with the essay. By its nature it must be shorter than the novel; and, just as an essay in a single sentence would cease to be an essay and become an epigram, so an essay in a large volume would cease to be an essay and become a treatise or a book of reminiscences. But the rules governing its length are as elastic as the rules governing the length of speeches.

On the whole, perhaps, we might be safe in saying that an essay should be of a length not likely to bore people who enjoy reading essays, and that both its matter and its manner should be of a kind not likely to bore people who enjoy reading essays. But that is about as far as a cautious man would care to go if he were asked for a good recipe for an essay. Probably it is more difficult to write a good recipe for an essay than it would be to write a good essay.

Harold C. Binkley

SOURCE: "Essays and Letter-Writing," in *PMLA,* Vol. XLI, No. 2, June, 1926, pp. 342-61.

[In the following excerpt, Binkley demonstrates close affinities between the familiar letter and the familiar essay, drawing on the works of Charles Lamb for examples.]

[There] is the sort of essay which, like the familiar letter, depends for its charm more on the familiar element than on any informative appeal. In this "familiar essay" the approach to the tone of the true familiar letter is so close that one can hardly discern the suble difference between them. But the distinctions are probably these: essays are likely to be abstract in their central theme, and letters are regularly concrete; essays, even in their most familiar manner, more than letters, are moulded to a sort of contour; both excite an æsthetic reaction in the reader, but the letter aims to evoke an *individual personal* reaction, while the essay reaches out towards a *multiple personal* reaction.

The fact that a final distinction can be beaten so fine leads one to wonder whether there is any fundamental difference between familiar letters and the modern familiar essay. Stevenson writing on the "Character of Dogs," Hazlitt on "Disagreeable People," or "Want of Money," or Lamb about "Poor Relations or Old China" come very near to the mood of the truly familiar letter. If one could but light on even a single instance in which an author carried a topic directly and smoothly from a genuine letter to an essay, we might finally conclude that there is a point where, without distortion, the mood and manner of the familiar letter merge into those of the essay.

Happily there are some excellent examples of this fusion. It is no accident that some of the princes among essay-writers of a century past have been also of the hierarchy of letter-writers. Consider Lamb. Or Stevenson. Both have left essays and letters which make to an astonishing degree the same sort of appeal. The casual reader feels this as quickly perhaps as the admirer and student, though he may not so deftly grasp the subtle distinctions. By looking more closely one sees that their essays are perhaps trimmed and shaped a little more carefully than their letters, omit details which are too intimate, or irrelevant to a chosen theme, focus a trifle more closely upon one idea, letting other suggestions—in a letter probably of equal importance—fall back to give the composition perspective. The letters, we might put it, are done in a single dimension with no shadows; the essays may be simple, carried through with stark economy of resource like an etching, yet having weight and depth and light and shadow to make them live, almost to move. Both, nevertheless, are lines upon paper, the same mediums, by the same hand, sometimes on identical subjects. This much we feel of more than one author who has left us work in both sorts.

But turning to a brief and more minute examination of this phase, we may find in Charles Lamb a most striking example of how an author may rework for publication ideas or anecdotes which he had already sent to friends in his letters. Sometimes the obligation of essay to letter is slight; the letter merely suggests a topic which had lodged in the author's mind and which sooner or later, when some incident stirs his recollection, emerges into an essay. Again, the letter may contain more ample material which is subsequently worked over into an article for Lamb's magazine public. Finally, there are two instances in which a letter or part of a letter is transferred to the printed page with only insignificant revision.

Let us imagine Lamb sitting in his "little back study in Bloomsbury" some evening well on in the year 1820, turning over his mind for an essay to be printed in the *London Magazine* for December. That afternoon Coleridge had taken away a volume—"Luster's Tables" as Becky, the maid, had it—and Lamb for the best of reasons resented it. Hadn't he always been pestered by friends who were more diligent in borrowing than in returning his precious volumes? Hadn't he once written Wordsworth something about chaining his books to his shelves "*More Bodleiano*" where people might "come and read them at chain's length?" "For of those who borrow," he added, "some read slow, some mean to read but don't read; and some neither read nor meant to read, but borrow to leave you an opinion of their sagacity." Well, borrowing was chronic with Coleridge and he might have a reminder this time, for, wrote Lamb, "My third shelf (northern compartment) from the top has two devilish gaps, where you have knocked out its two eye-teeth." And by the way, that letter finished, would not this nasty habit of borrowing books make a good subject for the essay? From his heart, we may believe, he began to write: "The human species, according to the best theory I can form of it, is composed of two distinct races, *the men who borrow, and the men who lend.*" And he is well on his way to a charming talk on this theme for some four or five pages of print. First he talks of borrowing in general, then of borrowing money, and finally he comes to his grievance against those who take away his treasures which are "cased in leather covers." He talks about C.—and "dear C." to whom the letter had been addressed, will probably recognize the author of the essay—but in a kindly tone, for "you are sure that he will make one hearty meal on your viands, if he can give no account of the platter after it." Yet, even this he tempers, for S.T.C. will surely return the volumes he takes "with usury; enriched with annotations tripling their value."

In this way a detail was taken from the letter, enlarged, remodelled—though in much the same style, even to the point of mentioning the authentic initials of the most recent offender—and converted into the more abstract and shapely reflection of the essay.

Another example reveals much the same process. In August, 1817, Lamb wrote to Barron Field, who was at that time in Sydney, New South Wales. The idea of writing to one so far away drew up in his mind a crowd of whimsical suggestions about the difficulties of keeping news fresh and authentic until his correspondent could read it. It is possible that as often as he wrote to Field he may have been struck by the futility of his "now's" and "will be's" when before they could be read they would long since be "has been's." However that may be, he printed in March, 1822 his essay on "Distant Correspondents," still "in a letter to B. F. Esq. at Sydney, New South Wales." Owing perhaps to the time which seems to have elapsed between the early idea and the later essay, there is a considerable and interesting difference in the style. The essay has grown from one short paragraph in the letter. Again, the letter is a collection of news items or quaint comment, all practically of equal value; the essay groups all the whimsical side play round the central theme of a remote correspondent, makes everything lead delicately towards that single idea, and comes to a close as it began with quaintly exaggerating the inconvenience of corresponding at such long range. The style of the essay is more polished, but it lacks just enough of the spontaneity of the letter to make us think that Field was probably more pleased to read the letter as he received it than he would have been to get it as it was published in full dress almost five years later.

One other theme of the letters we find repeated in the essays, one which appears to have hung heavy in Lamb's sensitive mind,—the execution for forgery of a banker, Fauntleroy by name. The day following the hanging Lamb wrote to Bernard Barton in a quaintly sad mood reminding Barton how very easy it was to make a trifling slip like the poor banker and end so. It is not hard to imagine that Lamb may at times have been dogged by a morbid fear of committing theft—a fear which itself had compelled him as a child to take a forbidden peach. There are four months between this letter to Barton and the publication of the essay which he called "The Last Peach." Here for a third time he takes the topic of a single paragraph in a previous letter as a nucleus about which to build a larger unit. But here, more than we have so far noted, there is a perfect identity of mood in the two versions, the same humorous droop of phrase, and the same wry twist of fanciful notions. It is not only then that ideas for essays are tucked away in earlier letters and there thoroughly at home; but even the *tilt of the mind* is carried over from one to the other—a literal transposition of the lyrical mood.

Similar to this and even more extended, is the relation of a letter from Lamb to Coleridge on March 9, 1822, to "The Dissertation upon Roast Pig," which appeared in the *London Magazine* for the following September. It is impossible that Lamb could have written these two pieces independent of each other; and the process was clearly one of development from the letter into the essay, not of condensation in the other direction. Lamb's letter consists of a single paragraph (barring a short concluding one), into which he packs a series of images which rise before him at the thought of roast pig. Thence he passes by means of a transition about the limits of generosity to the anecdote of his giving as a child his precious six-penny plum-cake to an old man he met on the way back to school. There is really little topical connection between the roast pig and the plumcake; consequently, no chance would be likely to throw them together on a second independent occasion.

The theme of the essay is the same as that of the letter— Roast Pig; and so it is labelled. It opens with a three-page apocryphal history of the discovery of the delicacy, which is not in the letter at all, and then point by point it picks up the mages of the early sentences of the letter and expands them into separate paragraphs, linking all together with the necessary transitions.

"They are interesting creatures at a certain age," says the letter. The essay reads:

> I speak not of your grown porkers—things between pig and pork—those hobbydehoys—but a young and tender suckling—under a moon old—guiltless as yet of the sty—with no original speck of the *amor immunditiae,* the hereditary failing of the first parent, yet manifest—his voice as yet not broken, but something between a childish treble, and a grumble—the mild forerunner, or *præludium* of a grunt.

To Coleridge Lamb suggests, "What a pity such buds should blow out into the maturity of rank bacon." For his public readers he builds out the idea:

> See him in the dish, this second cradle, how meek he lieth!—wouldst thou have had this innocent grow up to the grossness and indocility which too often accompany maturer swinehood? Ten to one he would have proved a glutton, a sloven, an obstinate, disagreeable animal— wallowing in all manner of filthy conversation— from these sins he is happily snatched away—
>
> > Ere sin could slight, or sorrow fade,
> > Death came with timely care—
>
> his memory is odoriferous—no clown curseth, while his stomach half rejecteth, the rank bacon—no coalheaver bolteth him in reeking sausages—he hath a fair sepulchre in the grateful stomach of the judicious epicure—and for such a tomb might be content to die.

"Was the crackling the colour of the ripe pomegranate?"

Lamb asks in the letter, and in the essay writes:

> There is no flavour comparable, I will contend, to that of the crisp, tawny, well-watched, not over-roasted, *crackling,* as it is well called—the very teeth are invited to their share of the pleasure at this banquet in overcoming the coy brittle resistance—with the adhesive oleaginous—O call it not fat—but an indefinable sweetness growing up to it—the tender blossoming of fat— fat cropped in the bud—taken in the shoot—in the first innocence—the cream and quintessence of the childpig's yet pure food—the lean, no lean, but a kind of animal manna—or rather, fat and lean (if it must be so) so blended and running into each other, that both together make but one ambrosial result, or common substance.

Other suggestions and images flit back and forth between the letter and essay until finally Lamb arrives at the transition from roast pig to six-penny plum-cake. In the letter Lamb wrote:

> To confess an honest truth, a pig is one of those things I could never think of sending away. Teals, wigeons, snipes, barn-door fowl, ducks, geese—your tame villatic things—Welsh mutton, collars of brawn, sturgeon, fresh or pickled, your potted char, Swiss cheese, French pies, early grapes, muscadines, I impart as freely unto my friends as to myself. They are but self-extended; but pardon me if I stop somewhere— where the fine feeling of benevolence giveth a

higher smack than the sensual rarity—there my friends (or any good man) may command me; but pigs are pigs, and I myself therein am nearest to myself. Nay I should think it an affront, an undervaluing done to Nature, who bestowed such a boon upon me, if in a churlish mood I parted with the precious gift.

In the essay we read:

> I am one of those who freely and ungrudgingly impart a share of the good things of this life which fall to their lot (few as mine are in this kind) to a friend. I protest I take as great an interest in my friend's pleasures, his relishes, and proper satisfactions, as in my own. "Presents," I often say, "endear Absents." Hares, pheasants, partridges, snipes, barn-door chicken (those "tame villatic fowl") capons, plovers, brawn, barrels of oysters, I dispense as freely as I receive them. I love to taste them, as it were, upon the tongue of my friend. But a stop must be put somewhere. One would not like Lear, "give every thing." I make my stand upon pig. Methinks it is an ingratitude to the Giver of all good flavours, to extra-domiciliate, or send out of the house, slightingly, (under pretext of friendship, or I know not what) a blessing so particularly adapted, predestined, I may say, to my individual palate—It argues an insensibility.

And here follows with somewhat less elaboration upon the passage in the letter the anecdote of Lamb's childhood generosity and his subsequent remorse for having disposed of the delicacy without a proper consideration for the sentiment behind the gift. After this digression he returns with unusual abruptness to the subject of pigs. Clearly this *exemplum* of the "impertinent spirit of alms-giving" is as remote from the central topic as in the letter it was from the delicious pig which Coleridge had dined upon. The letter carried him along from point to point, dictated the topics for his paragraphs, and when he arrived at the story of his boyhood experience, that too went into the mill. In relation to the rest of the essay, however, this episode is much less conspicuous than it was in the letter; it is so built about and closed in that it becomes finally just an odd stone in the structure.

Thus this letter is wholly assimilated to the plan of the larger structural unit without change of mood, and often without drastic revision of the style. In some instances we observe a suggestion drawn out into a filigree of delicate phrases. At other places, Lamb points his sentences with a trifle more skill, selects more carefully the words in the lists he so loves to compile, inserts a touch of more sophisticated humor to take the place of a purely personal quip, tints his style with a flatwash of subtle rhetorical dignity, and when all is done,—calls it an essay.

No examples could be found to illustrate more conclusively the practical relation of essay and letter which may exist in the trained literary consciousness of a writer. But to complete the evidence which this one author provides, mention may be made of a couple of essays which, with trifling, and from our immediate point of view wholly insignificant changes, have been taken intact from letters. In the former of these cases the authorship of the anonymous

essay was first established by noting its close resemblance to the letter. On February 1, 1806, Lamb had recounted in a letter to Wordsworth his conversation with a young man about the poet Spenser, and his discovery later that his companion had all the time been thinking of a contemporary figure, William Spencer, and making irrelevant comments under that misapprehension. With a few changes this anecdote served for an article in the *Reflector* five years later, entitled "On the Ambiguities Arising from Proper Names."

The last example I have to mention of any marked adaptation by Lamb of ideas in his letters to a subsequent use in published essays is that in which a letter to Henry Crabb Robinson of January 20, 1827, describing the death of Lamb's friend, Randall Norris, and making an appeal for Robinson's interest in the widow's behalf, was transferred with only the slightest revision to the columns of Hone's *Table Book* in the same year. Here it was entitled "A Death-Bed," with a subheading, "In a letter to R.H., Esq. of B." The trifle was re-reprinted again among the *Last Essays of Elia* in 1833. This delicate sketch is at one and the same time familiar letter and familiar essay. A complete identity, as here, of familiar correspondence with published literary expression is almost overproving our argument, for was it not agreed that publication with the vast extension of audience which it involved was antipathetic to certain qualities in a familiar letter? Certainly we must here grant an exception; and at the same time offer a reason which of itself is illuminating. When one looks more closely at this letter of Lamb's to Robinson about Norris, one finds there very little of Robinson. It is really an exquisite expression of Lamb's purely personal emotions in the circumstances of Norris's death. So long as nothing of the personality of the second person is infused into the letter, nothing can be lost by changing the identity of that second person,—as in reality we do when we throw letters open to the public. Anyone may read this prose lyric of Lamb's with much the same feelings as Robinson presumably felt. Lamb, the artist, achieves thus a complete reconciliation between all the essential conditions of the genuine familiar letter and the equally exacting conditions of the essay with all that they imply.

If this examination of the relation between letter-writing and the English essay has been to any purpose, it will be hard to deny what amounts to a positive obligation. Not only were the peculiar qualities of each dim and ambiguous in the early periods of the development of essay-writing, but in very recent times, as the essay culminated in a finely artistic prose genre, the technique and the spirit of them have been so similar as to permit a transfiltration through the thin bounds which ordinarily separate them. Furthermore, this is not a phenomenon which defies explanation. Analysis has shown that the essay temper differs from that of the letter not so much in a wholly new constitution as in a recomposition of the same elements. Perhaps all we have said does not prove beyond a doubt that between such vague and loosely constituted forms there has been a bond of definite obligation. And yet, considering the impossibility of ever proving by mathematical demonstration a case of literary relationship, we may, I believe, grant the case fairly conclusive.

Michael Hamburger

SOURCE: "An Essay on the Essay," in *Art as Second Nature: Occasional Pieces, 1950-74,* A Carcanet New Press Publication, 1975, pp. 3-5.

[*Hamburger is a German-born English poet, translator, and critic. An accomplished lyric poet in his own right, he has been widely praised for his translations of several German poets previously unfamiliar to English readers, including Friedrich Hoelderlin, Georg Trakl, and Hugo von Hofmannsthal. He has also written extensively on modern German literature. In the following excerpt from an essay originally published in 1965, Hamburger places the form of the familiar essay in the context of a leisurely amble—and thus, outside the sensibility of much of the modern world.*]

An Essay on the Essay

Even that isn't quite right: an essay really ought not to be on anything, to deal with anything, to define anything. An essay is a walk, an excursion, not a business trip. So if the title says 'on' that can only mean that this essay passes over a certain field—but with no intention of surveying it. This field will not be ploughed or cultivated. It will remain a meadow, wild. One walker is interested in wild flowers, another in the view, a third collects insects. Hunting butterflies is permitted. Everything is permitted—everything except the intentions of surveyors, farmers, speculators. And each walker is allowed to report whatever he happens to have observed about the field—even if that was no more than the birds that flew over it, the clouds that have still less to do with it, or only the transmutations of birds or clouds in his own head. But the person who drove there, sat there inside his car and then says he was there is no essayist. That's why the essay is an outmoded genre. ('Form' is what I almost wrote, but the essay is not a form, has no form; it is a game that creates its own rules.) . . .

The essay is not a form, but a style above all. Its individualism distinguishes it from pure, absolute or autonomous art. The point of an essay, like its justification and its style, always lies in the author's personality and always leads back to it. The essayist is as little concerned with pure, impersonal art as with his subject. Since the vast majority of so-called critical essays attaches primary importance to subjects, that is, to answers and judgements, the perpetuation of that genre does not prove that the essay has survived. Most critical essays are short treatises. With a genuine essay it makes no difference whether its title refers to a literary theme, whether to the origin of tragedy or the origin of roast pig.

ELEMENTS OF CONTENT

Alexander Smith

SOURCE: "On the Writing of Essays," in *A Book of Essays,* edited by Blanche Colton Williams, D. C. Heath and Company, 1931, pp. 243-61.

[*Smith was a respected nineteenth-century Scottish poet and familiar essayist. In the following excerpt from an essay included in his* Dreamthorpe: A Book of Essays

Written in the Country *(1863), he writes from a rustic retreat of the familiar essayist's subject matter and wide-ranging habit of mind.*]

Giddy people may think the life I lead here staid and humdrum, but they are mistaken. It is true, I hear no concerts, save those in which the thrushes are performers in the spring mornings. I see no pictures, save those painted on the wide sky-canvas with the colours of sunrise and sunset. I attend neither rout nor ball; I have no deeper dissipation than the tea-table; I hear no more exciting scandal than quiet village gossip. Yet I enjoy my concerts more than I would the great London ones. I like the pictures I see, and think them better painted, too, than those which adorn the walls of the Royal Academy; and the village gossip is more after my turn of mind than the scandals that convulse the clubs. It is wonderful how the whole world reflects itself in the simple village life. The people around me are full of their own affairs and interests; were they of imperial magnitude, they could not be excited more strongly. Farmer Worthy is anxious about the next market; the likelihood of a fall in the price of butter and eggs hardly allows him to sleep o' nights. The village doctor—happily we have only one—skirrs hither and thither in his gig, as if man could neither die nor be born without his assistance. He is continually standing on the confines of existence, welcoming the newcomer, bidding farewell to the goer-away. And the robustious fellow who sits at the head of the table when the Jolly Swillers meet at the Blue Lion on Wednesday evenings is a great politician, sound of lung metal, and wields the village in the taproom, as my Lord Palmerston wields the nation in the House. His listeners think him a wiser personage than the Premier, and he is inclined to lean to that opinion himself. I find everything here that other men find in the big world. London is but a magnified Dreamthorp.

And just as the Rev. Mr. White took note of the ongoings of the seasons in and around Hampshire Selborne, watched the colonies of the rooks in the tall elms, looked after the swallows in the cottage and rectory eaves, played the affectionate spy on the private lives of chaffinch and hedge-sparrow, was eavesdropper to the solitary cuckoo; so here I keep eye and ear open; take note of man, woman, and child; find many a pregnant text imbedded in the commonplace of village life; and, out of what I see and hear, weave in my own room my essays as solitarily as the spider weaves his web in the darkened corner. The essay, as a literary form, resembles the lyric, in so far as it is moulded by some central mood—whimsical, serious, or satirical. Give the mood, and the essay, from the first sentence to the last, grows around it as the cocoon grows around the silkworm. The essay-writer is a chartered libertine, and a law unto himself. A quick ear and eye, an ability to discern the infinite suggestiveness of common things, a brooding meditative spirit, are all that the essayist requires to start business with. Jaques, in *As You Like It,* had the makings of a charming essayist. It is not the essayist's duty to inform, to build pathways through metaphysical morasses, to cancel abuses, any more than it is the duty of the poet to do these things. Incidentally he may do something in that way, just as the poet may, but it is not his duty, and should not be expected of him. Skylarks are primarily created to sing, although a whole choir of them may be baked in pies and brought to table; they were born to make music, although they may incidentally stay the pangs of vulgar hunger. The essayist is a kind of poet in prose, and if questioned harshly as to his uses, he might be unable to render a better apology for his existence than a flower might. The essay should be pure literature as the poem is pure literature. The essayist wears a lance, but he cares more for the sharpness of its point than for the pennon that flutters on it, than for the banner of the captain under whom he serves. He plays with death as Hamlet plays with Yorick's skull, and he reads the morals—strangely stern, often, for such fragrant lodging—which are folded up in the bosoms of roses. He has no pride, and is deficient in a sense of the congruity and fitness of things. He lifts a pebble from the ground, and puts it aside more carefully than any gem; and on a nail in a cottage-door he will hang the mantle of his thought heavily brocaded with the gold of rhetoric. He finds his way into the Elysian fields through portals the most shabby and commonplace.

The essayist plays with his subject, now in whimsical, now in grave, now in melancholy mood. He lies upon the idle grassy bank, like Jaques, letting the world flow past him, and from this thing and the other he extracts his mirth and his moralities. His main gift is an eye to discover the suggestiveness of common things; to find a sermon in the most unpromising texts. Beyond the vital hint, the first step, his discourses are not beholden to their titles. Let him take up the most trivial subject, and it will lead him away to the great questions over which the serious imagination loves to brood—fortune, mutability, death—just as inevitably as the runnel, trickling among the summer hills, on which sheep are bleating, leads you to the sea; or as, turning down the first street you come to in the city, you are led finally, albeit by many an intricacy, out into the open country, with its waste places and its woods, where you are lost in a sense of strangeness and solitariness. The world is to the meditative man what the mulberry plant is to the silkworm. The essay-writer has no lack of subject-matter. He has the day that is passing over his head; and, if unsatisfied with that, he has the world's six thousand years to depasture his gay or serious humour upon. I idle away my time here, and I am finding new subjects every hour. Everything I see or hear is an essay in bud. The world is everywhere whispering essays, and one need only be the world's amanuensis. The proverbial expression which last evening the clown dropped as he trudged homeward to supper, the light of the setting sun on his face, expands before me to a dozen pages. The coffin of the pauper, which today I saw carried carelessly along, is as good a subject as the funeral procession of an emperor. Craped drum and banner add nothing to death; penury and disrespect take nothing away. Incontinently my thought moves like a slow-paced hearse with sable nodding plumes. Two rustic lovers, whispering between the darkening hedges, are as potent to project my mind into the tender passion as if I had seen Romeo touch the cheek of Juliet in the moonlight garden. Seeing a curly-headed child asleep in the sunshine before a cottage-door is sufficient excuse for a discourse on childhood; quite as good as if I had seen infant Cain asleep in the lap of Eve with Adam looking on. A lark cannot rise to heaven without raising as many thoughts as there are notes in its song. Dawn cannot pour its white light on my village without starting from their dim lair a hundred reminiscences; nor can sunset burn above yonder trees in the west without attracting to itself the melancholy of a lifetime. When spring unfolds her green leaves I would be provoked to indite an essay on hope and youth, were it not that it is already writ in the carols of the birds; and I might be tempted in autumn to improve the occasion, were it not for the rustle of the withered leaves as I walk through the woods. Compared with that simple music, the saddest-cadenced words have but a shallow meaning.

The essayist who feeds his thoughts upon the segment of the world which surrounds him cannot avoid being an egotist; but then his egotism is not unpleasing. If he be without taint of boastfulness, of self-sufficiency, of hungry vanity, the world will not press the charge home. If a man discourses continually of his wines, his plate, his titled acquaintances, the number and quality of his horses, his men-servants and maid-servants, he must discourse very skilfully indeed if he escapes being called a coxcomb. If a man speaks of death—tells you that the idea of it continually haunts him, that he has the most insatiable curiosity as to death and dying, that his thought mines in churchyards like a 'demon-mole'—no one is specially offended, and that this is a dull fellow is the hardest thing likely to be said of him. Only, the egotism that over-crows you is offensive, that exalts trifles and takes pleasure in them, that suggests superiority in matters of equipage and furniture; and the egotism is offensive, because it runs counter to and jostles your self-complacency. The egotism which rises no higher than the grave is of a solitary and hermit kind—it crosses no man's path, it disturbs no man's *amour proper*. You may offend a man if you say you are as rich as he, as wise as he, as handsome as he. You offend no man if you tell him that, like him, you have to die. The king, in his crown and coronation robes, will allow the beggar to claim that relationship with him. To have to die is a distinction of which no man is proud. The speaking about one's self is not necessarily offensive. A modest, truthful man speaks better about himself than about anything else, and on that subject his speech is likely to be most profitable to his hearers. Certainly, there is no subject with which he is better acquainted, and on which he has a better title to be heard. And it is this egotism, this perpetual reference to self, in which the charm of the essayist resides. If a man is worth knowing at all, he is worth knowing well. The essayist gives you his thoughts, and lets you know, in addition, how he came by them. He has nothing to conceal; he throws open his doors and windows, and lets him enter who will. You like to walk round peculiar or important men as you like to walk round a building, to view it from different points, and in different lights. Of the essayist, when his mood is communicative, you obtain a full picture. You are made his contemporary and familiar friend. You enter into his humours and his seriousness. You are made heir of his whims, prejudices, and playfulness. You walk through the whole nature of him, as you walk through the streets of Pompeii, looking into the interior of stately mansions, reading the satirical scribblings on the walls. And the essayist's habit of not only giving you his thoughts, but telling you how he came by them, is interesting, because it shews you by what alchemy the ruder world becomes transmuted into the finer. We like to know the lineage of ideas, just as we like to know the lineage of great earls and swift race-horses. We like to know that the discovery of the law of gravitation was born of the fall of an apple in an English garden on a summer afternoon. Essays written after this fashion are racy of the soil in which they grow, as you taste the lava in the vines grown on the slopes of Etna, they say. There is a healthy Gascon flavour in Montaigne's Essays; and Charles Lamb's are scented with the primroses of Covent Garden.

The essayist does not usually appear early in the literary history of a country: he comes naturally after the poet and the chronicler. His habit of mind is leisurely; he does not write from any special stress of passionate impulse; he does not create material so much as he comments upon material already existing. It is essential for him that books should have been written, and that they should, at least to some extent, have been read and digested. He is usually full of allusions and references, and these his reader must be able to follow and understand.

E. H. Lacon Watson

SOURCE: "The Essay Considered from an Artistic Point of View," in *The Westminster Review,* Vol. CXLI, No. 5, May, 1894, pp. 559-65.

[In the excerpt below, Lacon Watson outlines the pleasure-giving, defining features of the familiar essay.]

In the history of the world, as in the history of individual man, each age will have its own especial type of literature. The favourite may co-exist with several others, but it will none the less be the favourite. At the present time it is clear that the commonest mode of expression is in the novel, and I suppose that the age—in England at all events—is gradually drifting in the direction of lyric poetry, conjoined with the short sketch or story. The epic and the drama may be safely regarded as tranced, or even dead. History has a fair hold on the educated. The essay, in its various forms, still breaks out sporadically now and again, stray flowerets from a seedling long discontinued, or like the rare sparks flying from a burnt-out firebrand.

I confess to a more than sneaking kindness for the Essay, in most of her moods. A book of these detached thoughts makes no too pressing demands upon the reader; he may take it up for a spare half-hour or so, and leave it with unconcern to attend to other matters, with no harassing anxiety as to finding the place when he returns. For in a book of this kind there is no continuity of thought, no definite plan. It will go hard with us if we cannot pick out one or two essays out of two dozen that give some pleasure, or that have some message for us. So that it is better, to my mind, for the subjects to be varied as much as possible, and the treatment. I am no great friend to this modern style, introduced by Macaulay, of lengthy book reviews and historical disquisitions. They are good reading, but a trifle too solid for the times when one would fain turn to some delicate, yet not worthless, trifling. As good read a volume of history or a biography as some of these. There are seasons

when the reader instinctively lays his hand upon Montaigne, or Lamb, or Stevenson's *Virginibus Puerisque,* and lazily, with pipe in mouth, listens to their quaint conceits and moralisings. Even a Lowell may be too serious for us at times, too full of information. A model essay should contain its fair proportion of useful knowledge, but it should be concealed so delicately; like the onion in the salad, it should be unseen, but permeate the whole. Defoe had a good notion of this, who said, "Thus may we wheedle men into knowledge of the world, who rather than take more pains would be content with their ignorance." The substratum of fact should be there, like the trellis-work on which a creeper grows, but the flowering luxuriance of fancy should clothe it so completely that we hardly guess its presence.

The idea of an essay was, with Bacon, the elaboration of a single thought. But though this is strictly in accordance with the meaning of the word—essay is identical with assay, and should signify merely a careful weighing or examination—yet it is not our conception of the real thing. Montaigne is the true founder of the essay proper, and the early writers in the *Tatler, Spectator, Rambler* and so forth were his disciples. Like a good talker, he roams from subject to subject, led by some chance association, and by this means we get the delicate play of his fancy on various points: each discourse is a diamond glittering with a thousand facets, and we are not wearied by too sustained argument upon any one theme. It is this that now and again the wearied student longs for—this delightful inconsequence. When we pick up a volume of his, or of Lamb's, we have left the beaten road and wandered into some charming maze of inextricable forest paths. Dry and dusty facts are left behind, or covered over with the green turf. Here is the place to lounge in on a summer's day, and we stroll along none too hurriedly, resting, as the mood takes us, against the trunk of some giant tree of thought. It is the touch of egotism that marks the ideal writer in this form—a touch, however, that should not be overdone. I doubt whether Thackeray allowed quite sufficient of himself to appear in his *Roundabout Papers,* and it is possible that Leigh Hunt showed a trifle too much. Like the lyric poem, the essay should contain a suspicion of the writer's personality, and should also have the look of careless ease, but the look merely, like a thin glittering sheet of ice over deep waters. It should be desultory, but not too desultory; there should be some slight thread of connection running through the whole, to lead us insensibly from point to point. For it is annoying in the highest degree to meet on a sudden with some abrupt change of thought for which no reason is discoverable. It jars the mind, and puts the reader out of conceit with himself, as if in strolling along our woodland path he should strike his foot against some hidden rock. The author should gossip, but there should be purpose in his seeming divagations. He may decorate with arabesques the line on which he travels, but there must be a line, even though the shortest and slenderest. Indeed, the slenderest peg will serve for the true essayist to hang his disquisition upon. The subject should be not too narrowly defined. In good hands a book or an author will be no mere dull review; but for the less practised writer, the more ordinary craftsman, it were perhaps safer to take some more general subject as his starting-point. I like best in Lamb those rambling discourses where he makes some imaginary acquaintance the text for his sermon, as with Captain Jackson in his cottage on the Bath Road, or the redoubtable Sarah Battle, tutelary goddess of the whist-table. Indeed, a touch of character-drawing, though not perhaps strictly proper to the style, has been ever found a useful adjunct. Addison, of course, has his worthy knight and his satellites, and Johnson, in his *Idler,* would occasionally introduce imaginary friends to the public, as his Drugget and Minim. And it is noticeable that this does, in fact, give a lighter tone, and that the commonly heavy doctor does attain to some degree of sprightly vivacity in the employment of this machinery, that distinguishes these sketches plainly enough from their more ponderous companions. . . .

The ideal essayist, I imagine, has yet to be evolved, the man who shall combine in his own person the original power of Bacon, the grace of Addison, the transcendental insight of Emerson, the gay fancy of Charles Lamb, with any unconsidered trifles that he may chance to pick up from other essayists. But, until we see his work, we may well be content with his component parts, which, after all, may possibly afford us more pleasure separately than they would in ever so cunning a combination. . . .

It gives an agreeable sensation to feel that our time is not being altogether spent on mere relaxation. It is for this reason also that a certain amount of useful information should be sprinkled over the pages of the essayist, to the end that the reader may feel that he is insensibly acquiring knowledge, sucking it in, as it were, through every pore. It is true that the general essay is not over-popular just now. Of book reviews and criticism of all sorts we have a sufficiency; but the old fanciful dissertations of Lamb have few successors. It is characteristic of the true essayist that he can write pleasantly upon any subject. The common house-fly will furnish him with a theme expanding under his treatment to unimaginable heights. It matters not in the smallest degree from what point he starts, his province is none the less the wide unmeasured heaven of imagination. He takes the whole arena of knowledge as his lawful kingdom, and nothing of the varied complexities of human life is foreign to him. I confess that I should like to see more of this true catholicity in range of subject among our essayists of to-day. For, after all, books and the authors of books do not make up the whole sum of human life, and there are other aspects of the world to be noticed besides those which are seen from Fleet Street or the Strand. Dickens and Thackeray have been discussed enough, even the perennial fount of Johnsonian criticism is running muddy towards its close. I would respectfully suggest to all British essayists of the present day to leave these worthy gentlemen in peace, and try their hand in a somewhat wider field.

Carl Van Doren

SOURCE: "A Note on the Essay," in *Essays of Our Times,* edited by Sharon Brown, Scott, Foresman and Company, 1928, pp. 396-98.

[*Van Doren is considered one of the most perceptive critics of the first half of the twentieth century. He worked for many years as a professor of English at Columbia University and served as literary editor and critic of the* Nation *and the* Century *during the 1920s. A founder of the Literary Guild and author or editor of several American literary histories, Van Doren was also a critically acclaimed historian and biographer. In the following excerpt, he defines the unique nature of the familiar essay.*]

The sonnet has a standard form very much as a man has. Leave off the sestet of your sonnet and you do about what a god does when he leaves the legs off a man. The drama has a standard form very much as a rendezvous has. Write a drama in which no spark is exchanged between the audience and the action, and you have done what fate does when it keeps lovers from their meeting. The novel has a standard form very much as a road has. You may set out anywhere you like and go wherever you please, at any gait, but you must go somewhere, or you have made what is no more a novel than some engineer's road would be a road if it had neither beginning, end, nor direction. But the essay! It may be of any length, breadth, depth, weight, density, color, savor, odor, appearance, importance, value, or uselessness which you can or will give it. The epigram bounds it on one side and the treatise on the other, but it has in its time encroached upon the territory of both of them, and it doubtless will do so again. Or, to look at the essay from another angle, it is bounded on one side by the hell-fire sermon and on the other by the geometrical demonstration; and yet it ranges easily between these extremes of heat and cold and occasionally steals from both of them. It differs from a letter by being written to more—happily a great many more—than one person. It differs from talk chiefly by being written at all.

Having to obey no regulations as to form, the essay is very free to choose its matter. The sonnet, by reason of its form, tends to deal with solemn and not with gay themes. The drama, for the same reason, tends to look for intense and not for casual incidents. The novel tends to feel that it must carry a considerable amount of human life on its back. The essay may be as fastidious as a collector of carved emeralds or as open-minded as a garbage-gatherer. Nothing human, as the platitude says, is alien to it. The essay, however, goes beyond the platitude and dares to choose matter from numerous non-human sources. Think of the naturalists and their essays. Think, further, of the range of topics for essayists at large. Theodore Roosevelt in an essay urges the strenuous life; Max Beerbohm in an essay defends cosmetics. De Quincey expounds the fine art of murder, Thoreau the pleasures of economy, William Law the blisses of prayer, Hudson the sense of smell in men and in animals, Schopenhauer the ugliness of women, Bacon the advantages of a garden, Plutarch the traits of curiosity, and A. C. Benson the felicity of having nothing much in the mind. All, in fact, an essayist needs to start with is something, anything, to say. He gets up each morning and finds the world spread out before him, as the world was spread out before Adam and Eve the day they left paradise. With the cosmos, past, present, and future, to pick from, the essayist goes to work. If he finds a topic good enough he may write a good essay, no matter how he writes it.

He may. There is still, however, the question of his manner. Thousands of dull men have written millions of true things which no one but their proof-readers, wives, or pupils ever read. If each essayist could take out a patent on each subject into which he dips his pen, and could prevent any other pen from ever dipping into it after him, he might have better luck. But there are no monopolists in this department. Would research find in all the hoards of books or all the morgues of manuscripts a single observation which has never been made twice? Competition in such affairs is free and endless. The only law which gives an essayist a right to his material is the law which rules that the best man wins. The law does not say in what fashion he must be best. Any fashion will do. Let him be more sententious, like Bacon; or more harmonious, like Sir Thomas Browne; or more elegant, like Addison; or more direct, like Swift; or more hearty, like Fielding; or more whimsical, like Lamb; or more impassioned, like Hazlitt; or more encouraging, like Emerson; or more Olympian, like Arnold; or more funny, like Mark Twain; or more musical, like Pater; or more impish, like Max Beerbohm; or more devastating, like Mencken. Let the essayist be any of these things and he may have a copyright till someone takes it away from him. What matters is the manner. If he has good matter, he *may* write a good essay; if he has a good manner he probably *will* write a good essay.

An essay is a communication. If the subject of the discourse were the whole affair, it would be enough for the essayist to be an adequate conduit. If the manner were the whole affair, any versatile fellow might try all the manners and have a universal triumph. But back of matter and manner both lies the item which is really significant. The person who communicates anything in any way must be a person. His truth must have a tone, his speech must have a rhythm which are his and solely his. His knowledge or opinions must have lain long enough inside him to have taken root there; and when they come away they must bring some of the soil clinging to them. They must, too, have been shaped by that soil—as plants are which grow in cellars, on housetops, on hillsides, in the wide fields, under shade in forests. Many kinds of men, many kinds of essays! Important essays come from important men.

William M. Tanner and D. Barrett Tanner

SOURCE: An introduction to *Modern Familiar Essays*, edited by William M. Tanner and D. Barrett Tanner, Little, Brown, and Company, 1927, pp. 3-11.

[*In the following excerpt from an essay originally published in 1927, the critics provide a brief overview of the familiar essay's elements.*]

In the evolution of literary types the essay, like lyric poetry, appears late. The essayist follows the epic poet, the dramatist, the story-teller, and the historian. It is not his function to chronicle actions and events, real or imaginary, but to interpret as much as he can of life and human conduct and to comment on the significance of what he discovers in himself and in those about him. He is an interested observer, a leisurely, meditative thinker. No "special stress of passionate impulse" actuates him to write, for,

unlike the epic poet and the dramatist, he does not seek to produce in his readers and hearers a strong emotional response. His appeal is to those persons who enjoy using their memories, their minds, and their imagination, and who recognize in him an entertaining companion in contemplative thinking. He creates little, but appraises what men have done and felt and thought and said. He needs, therefore, as part of his material, the work of his predecessors and contemporaries. Besides his understanding of people, he possesses an easy familiarity with literature and other of the fine arts, and he presupposes a like understanding and familiarity in his readers. For this reason the essayist does not develop in a primitive society. He demands as his proper environment "a certain ripeness of civilization, a certain growth of culture." It is not surprising, then, that the essay, as a recognized literary type, dates back hardly more than three centuries to Montaigne in France and Bacon in England.

The history and the development of the essay have so often been traced that it seems unnecessary to do more than call to the attention of the reader a few of its more important characteristics as a literary genre. Broadly defined, an essay is a relatively short piece of meditative writing, expository in nature and usually prose in form. It is a tentative and personal treatment of a subject. It is not an exhaustive treatise elaborately composed in accord with the principles of strict logic, but is rather the personal expression of the author's thoughts, moods, fancies, and opinions concerning his subject. . . .

The familiar essay has for its immediate purpose the entertainment of the reader, though it may, as it often does, contribute indirectly to his information. It is addressed to the senses, the memory, the emotions, and the imagination, as well as to the intellect. The personality of the familiar essayist, the mood he creates, the conversational intimacy of his style, and the individuality of his diction are of much greater importance than are subject matter, theme, and structure. The familiar essay, said the late Mr. A. C. Benson, "is a kind of improvisation on a delicate theme; a species of soliloquy, as if a man were to speak aloud the slender and whimsical thoughts that come into his mind when he is alone on a winter evening before a warm fire, and, closing his book, abandons himself to the luxury of genial reverie." Examples of the familiar essay are to be found in the writings of such earlier essayists as Montaigne, Abraham Cowley, Addison, Steele, Samuel Johnson, Goldsmith, Lamb, Leigh Hunt, William Hazlitt, Thackeray, Stevenson, and Oliver Wendell Holmes. The present collection contains familiar essays from a large number of representative British and American authors of our own time.

The familiar essay is essentially personal writing. The point of view is usually that of the first person. The subject, the theme, the material, and the mood are all personally chosen. Individuality of thought and originality of expression, together with the revelation of pleasing literary personality, are the chief characteristics of the familiar essay. "The point of the essay is not the subject, [writes Benson] for any subject will suffice, but the charm of personality. . . . The essential thing is that the writer shall have formed his own impression, and that it shall have taken shape in his own mind. The charm of the essay depends upon the charm of the mind that has conceived and recorded the impression." By personality in the familiar essay is not meant an obtrusive egotistic personality but rather one that is unconscious of itself.

> Essayists are intensely interested in themselves [writes Charles Leonard Moore] and in everything that happens to them. Why is it that such egotism does not revolt us? They fling themselves upon our interest with the most naïve confidence, and we receive them with open arms. The more they tell us the more we want to know. . . . To unbosom oneself seems to be a short cut to the affection of the world, which likes to play the part of a priest in a confessional and hearken to sins and peccadilloes, vauntings, and vaporings. That is the secret of the perennial charm of memoris. . . . The great essayists mingle their egotism with modesty and geniality and humor. It is their enormous enjoyment of life that they communicate to us.

Certainly no reader has failed to find pleasure in the charm of personality as it is expressed in the inimitable *Essays of Elia*. Likewise, he has enjoyed the confidential self-revelation that forms so great a share of the appeal of lesser writers who trace their lineage from Montaigne and Lamb, many of whom are represented in the present volume. Though essays and essayists vary in the degree of personality that they reveal, the real art of the familiar essayist lies in his personal treatment of his subject.

Closely allied to the charm of personality is the mood that characterizes the familiar essay. It represents the author's attitude of mind, his mental or emotional point of view, and it determines the vein in which he writes. In the reader he attempts to create a similar mood as an aid to pleasurable communication. In a sense, a familiar essay, like a lyric poem, is moulded by a central mood, which helps to give it unity or completeness. The moods of essayists vary as freely as do the moods of men and women in real life: in dealing with one subject the mood may be serious; with another, humorous; with another, whimsical; with another, mildly satirical; and so on. To a very great extent the individual temperament of the author and his immediate purpose in writing will determine the mood that he employs in presenting his ideas. . . .

Rarely have familiar essayists other than Charles Lamb, in whose literary personality humor and seriousness were admirably blent, exhibited more than a single mood in an essay.

The coherent structure of a familiar essay, as well as its scope, is mainly determined by the theme or the one central idea that the writer develops. The title, which serves as a name for the essay, may suggest the theme, but rarely does it state it specifically. The theme is the subject, the nucleus, or the core of meaning, of the essay. The formality of structure required in the didactic essay is not in accord with the mood, the discursive treatment, and the conversational style of the familiar essay. Hence, the impression of unity that a reader gets from an informal essay is the result of oneness of mood, singleness of theme, and rel-

evancy of material. Though the familiar essayist is privileged to pursue a desultory meandering course and to digress freely, he is careful to see that all he includes bears some relationship to the theme. Seldom do we find that the author has stated his theme, but it is implied at least and pervades the entire essay. It is usually possible to state it clearly in one's own words, often in a single sentence. For example, it is easy to discover the theme of Mr. [Henry Seidel] Canby's "Red Brick Literature": The writers of red brick literature suffer from a lack of air, space, light, repose, meditation, and solitude as a result of living the artificial and rather sordid life of the modern large city. The theme of Mr. Benson's "On Growing Older" is this: The advantages of growing older outweigh the disadvantages. That of Mr. [Don] Marquis's "Preface to a Book of Fishhooks" is expressed by the author: In fishing, I prefer to put all the exertion up to the fish.

"Just as we may say there is a lyric tongue, which the true poets of that kind have contributed to form," observes Mr. Ernest Rhys, "so there is an essayist's style or way with words—something between talking and writing." Such a style may almost be called "a talking mode of writing," but its ideal is the best kind of conversation. "The essay does not achieve genuine success," says Mr. Edmund Gosse, "unless it is written in the language spoken to-day by those who employ it with the maximum of purity and grace. It should be a model of current cultivated ease of expression and a mirror of the best conversation." The familiar essay, in its easy naturalness and refined intimacy of expression, resembles the letters of cultured people. Its style is personal, informal, discursive, and confidential. In the essays of such writers as Montaigne, Charles Lamb, Mr. E. V. Lucas, Mr. A. C. Benson, and Mr. Charles S. Brooks we find such a style admirably illustrated. The great essayists exhibit a nice adaptation of style to personality, mood, and theme. They seem hardly conscious of writing, but express themselves in simple, spontaneous language, almost as if they were thinking aloud. The impression of spontaneity they communicate through their apparent zest in their subjects and the gusto with which they write. We feel that they have greatly enjoyed writing, so easily and naturally do they express themselves, though in reality they may have expended great toil in achieving such ease and naturalness. In the familiar essay there should be no hint of laborious effort or self-consciousness on the part of the author, no matter how long and painstakingly he has worked in the process of composition. A genial personality revealed through a pleasingly individual style constitutes the chief appeal of the familiar essay, and in this type of literature, more than in any other, style is the man. The familiar essayist's style, as Mr. Ernest Rhys has truly said, "is partly a question of art, partly of temperament; and indeed, paraphrasing Steele, we may say that the success of an essay depends upon the make of the body and the formation of the mind, of him who writes it."

The art of the familiar essayist has been well summed up in the paragraph here quoted:

> I have little doubt in my own mind that the charm of the familiar essayist depends upon his power of giving the sense of a goodhumored,

gracious, and reasonable personality and establishing a sort of pleasant friendship with his reader. One does not go to an essayist with a desire for information, or with an expectation of finding a clear statement of a complicated subject; that is not the mood in which one takes up a volume of essays. What one rather expects to find is a companionable treatment of that vast mass of little problems and floating ideas which are aroused and evoked by our passage through the world, our daily employment, our leisure hours, our amusements and diversions, and above all by our relations with other people—all the unexpected, inconsistent, various, simple stuff of life; the essayist ought to be able to impart a certain beauty and order into it, to delineate, let us say, the vague emotions aroused in solitude or in company by the sight of scenery, the aspect of towns, the impressions of art and books, the interplay of human qualities and characteristics, the half-formed hopes and desires and fears and joys that form so large a part of our daily thoughts.

The essayist ought to be able to indicate a case or a problem that is apt to occur in ordinary life and suggest the theory of it, to guess what it is that makes our moods resolute or fitful, why we act consistently or inconsistently, what it is that repels or attracts us in our dealings with other people, what our private fancies are. The good essayist is the man who makes a reader say: "Well, I have often thought all those things, but I have never discerned before any connection between them, nor got so far as to put them into words." And thus the essayist must have a great and far-reaching curiosity; he must be interested rather than displeased by the differences of human beings and by their varied theories. He must recognize the fact that most people's convictions are not the result of reason, but a mass of associations, traditions, things half-understood, phrases, examples, loyalties, whims. He must care more about the inconsistency of humanity than about its dignity; and he must study more what people actually do think about than what they ought to think about. He must not be ashamed of human weaknesses or shocked by them, and still less disgusted by them; but at the same time he must keep in mind the flashes of fine idealism, the passionate visions, the irresponsible humors, the salient peculiarities, that shoot like sun rays through the dull cloudiness of so many human minds, and make one realize that humanity is at once above itself and in itself, and that we are greater than we know; for the interest of the world to the ardent student of it is that we most of us seem to have got hold of something that is bigger than we quite know how to deal with; something remote and far off, which we have seen in a distant vision, which we cannot always remember or keep clear in our minds.

The supreme fact of human nature is its duality, its tendency to pull different ways, the tug-of-war between Devil and Baker which lies inside our restless brains. And the confessed aim of the essayist is to make people interested in life and in themselves and in the part they can take in life; and he does that best if he convinces men and women that life is a fine sort of a game, in which they can take a hand; and that every existence, however confined and restricted, is full of outlets and pulsing channels, and that the interest and joy of it is not confined to the politician or the millionaire, but is pretty fairly distributed, so long as one has time to attend to it, and is not preoccupied in some concrete aim or vulgar ambition. Because the great secret which the true essayist whispers in our ears is that the worth of experience is not measured by what is called success, but rather resides in a fulness of life; that success tends rather to obscure and to diminish experience, and that we may miss the point of life by being too important; and that the end of it all is the degree in which we give rather than receive.

G. K. Chesterton

SOURCE: "On Essays," in *Come to Think of It . . . ,* Dodd, Mead & Company, 1931, pp. 1-6.

[*Regarded as one of England's premier men of letters during the first half of the twentieth century, Chesterton is best known today as a colorful bon vivant, a witty essayist, and as the creator of the Father Brown mysteries and the fantasy* The Man Who Was Thursday (1908). *His essays are characterized by their humor, frequent use of paradox, and chatty, rambling style. In the following essay, originally published in 1929 in the* Illustrated London News, *Chesterton touches upon the essays of Robert Louis Stevenson and William Hazlitt to illustrate his belief that the essay as a genre, a development of the modern age, lends itself to inexactitude and the propagation of pleasant-sounding untruths, unlike its medieval counterpart, the thesis.*]

There are dark and morbid moods in which I am tempted to feel that Evil re-entered the world in the form of Essays. The Essay is like the Serpent, smooth and graceful and easy of movement, also wavering or wandering. Besides, I suppose that the very word Essay had the original meaning of "trying it on." The serpent was in every sense of the word tentative. The tempter is always feeling his way, and finding out how much other people will stand. That misleading air of irresponsibility about the Essay is very disarming through appearing to be disarmed. But the serpent can strike without claws, as it can run without legs. It is the emblem of all those arts which are elusive, evasive, impressionistic, and shading away from tint to tint. I suppose that the Essay, so far as England at least is concerned, was almost invented by Francis Bacon. I can well believe it. I always thought he was the villain of English history.

It may be well to explain that I do not really regard all Essayists as wicked men. I have myself been an essayist or tried to be an essayist; or pretended to be an essayist. Nor do I in the least dislike essays. I take perhaps my greatest literary pleasure in reading them; after such really serious necessities of the intellect as detective stories and tracts written by madmen. There is no better reading in the world than some contemporary essays, like those of Mr. E. V. Lucas or Mr. Robert Lynd. And though, unlike Mr.

Lucas and Mr. Lynd, I am quite incapable of writing a really good essay, the motive of my dark suggestion is not a diabolic jealousy or envy. It is merely a natural taste for exaggeration, when dealing with a point too subtle to permit of exactitude. If I may myself imitate the timid and tentative tone of the true essayist, I will confine myself to saying that there is something in what I say. There is really an element in modern letters which is at once indefinite and dangerous.

What I mean is this. The distinction between certain old forms and certain relatively recent forms of literature is that the old were limited by a logical purpose. The Drama and the Sonnet were of the old kind; the Essay and the Novel are of the new. If a sonnet breaks out of the sonnet form, it ceases to be a sonnet. It may become a wild and inspiring specimen of free verse; but you do not have to call it a sonnet because you have nothing else to call it. But in the case of the new sort of novel, you do very often have to call it a novel because you have nothing else to call it. It is sometimes called a novel when it is hardly even a narrative. There is nothing to test or define it, except that it is not spaced like an epic poem, and often has even less of a story. The same applies to the apparently attractive leisure and liberty of the essay. By its very nature it does not exactly explain what it is trying to do, and thus escapes a decisive judgment about whether it has really done it. But in the case of the essay there is a practical peril; precisely because it deals so often with theoretical matters. It is always dealing with theoretical matters without the responsibility of being theoretical, or of propounding a theory.

For instance, there is any amount of sense and nonsense talked both for and against what is called mediævalism. There is also any amount of sense and nonsense talked for and against what is called modernism. I have occasionally tried to talk a little of the sense, with the result that I have been generally credited with all the nonsense. But if a man wanted one real and rational test, which really does distinguish the mediæval from the modern mood, it might be stated thus. The mediæval man thought in terms of the Thesis, where the modern man thinks in terms of the Essay. It would be unfair, perhaps, to say that the modern man only essays to think—or, in other words, makes a desperate attempt to think. But it would be true to say that the modern man often only essays, or attempts, to come to a conclusion. Whereas the mediæval man hardly thought it worth while to think at all, unless he could come to a conclusion. That is why he took a definite thing called a Thesis, and proposed to prove it. That is why Martin Luther, a very mediæval man in most ways, nailed up on the door the theses he proposed to prove. Many people suppose that he was doing something revolutionary, and even modernist, in doing this. In fact, he was doing exactly what all the other mediæval students and doctors had done ever since the twilight of the Dark Ages. If the really modern Modernist attempted to do it, he would probably find that he had never arranged his thoughts in the forms of theses at all. Well, it is quite an error to suppose, so far as I am concerned, that it is any question of restoring the rigid apparatus of the mediæval system. But

I do think that the Essay has wandered too far away from the Thesis.

There is a sort of irrational and indefensible quality in many of the most brilliant phrases of the most beautiful essays. There is no essayist I enjoy more than Stevenson; there is probably no man now alive who admires Stevenson more than I. But if we take some favourite and frequently quoted sentence, such as, "To travel hopefully is better than to arrive," we shall see that it gives a loophole for every sort of sophistry and unreason. If it could be stated as a thesis, it could not be defended as a thought. A man would not travel hopefully at all, if he thought that the goal would be disappointing as compared with the travels. It is tenable that travel is the more enjoyable; but in that case it cannot be called hopeful. For the traveller is here presumed to hope for the end of travel, not merely for its continuance.

Now, of course, I do not mean that pleasant paradoxes of this sort have not a place in literature; and because of them the essay has a place in literature. There is room for the merely idle and wandering essayist, as for the merely idle and wandering traveller. The trouble is that the essayists have become the only ethical philosophers. The wandering thinkers have become the wandering preachers, and our only substitute for preaching friars. And whether our system is to be materialist or moralist, or sceptical or transcendental, we need more of a system than that. After a certain amount of wandering the mind wants either to get there or to go home. It is one thing to travel hopefully, and say half in jest that it is better than to arrive. It is another thing to travel hopelessly, because you know you will never arrive.

I was struck by the same tendency in re-reading some of the best essays ever written, which were especially enjoyed by Stevenson—the essays of Hazlitt. "You can live like a gentleman on Hazlitt's ideas," as Mr. Augustine Birrell truly remarked; but even in these we see the beginning of this inconsistent and irresponsible temper. For instance, Hazlitt was a Radical and constantly railed at Tories for not trusting men or mobs. I think it was he who lectured Walter Scott for so small a matter as making the mediæval mob in *Ivanhoe* jeer ungenerously at the retreat of the Templars. Anyhow, from any number of passages, one would infer that Hazlitt offered himself as a friend of the people. But he offered himself most furiously as an enemy of the Public. When he began to write about the Public he described exactly the same many-headed monster of ignorance and cowardice and cruelty which the worst Tories called the Mob. Now, if Hazlitt had been obliged to set forth his thoughts on Democracy in the theses of a mediæval schoolman, he would have had to think much more clearly and make up his mind much more decisively. I will leave the last word with the essayist; and admit that I am not sure whether he would have written such good essays.

Hilaire Belloc

SOURCE: "By Way of Preface: An Essay upon Essays

upon Essays," in *One Thing or Another,* edited by Patrick Cahill, Hollis & Carter, 1955, pp. 11-14.

[At the turn of the century, Belloc was considered a provocative essayist and one of England's premier men of letters. His characteristically truculent stance as a proponent of Roman Catholicism and economic reform—and his equally characteristic clever humor—drew either strong support or harsh attacks from his audience. In such collections as On Nothing *(1908) and* On Everything *(1909), Belloc proved that he could write convincing and forceful essays on nearly any subject, as either controversialist or defender of the status quo, in a prose style marked by clarity and wit. In the following excerpt from an essay originally published in the* New Statesman *in 1929, he rebuts the critical charge that the familiar essay is flooding English periodicals with triviality.]*

There has been a pretty little quarrel lately—it will probably be forgotten by the time this appears, but no matter—a quarrel between those who write essays and those who have written an essay or two to show that the writing of essays is futile. These last seem to be particularly annoyed by the foison of essays in the present generation. They say it has burst all restraint and is choking us under a flood.

Of old, the essay appeared here and there in some stately weekly paper. Then it dignified once a week some of the more solemn of the daily papers. Then it appeared in another, and another more vulgar. Then, not once a week, but twice a week, in these last: finally, every day. And now (say they) it is everywhere. And the enemies of the essay—or at least of this excess of essays, this spate of essays, this monstrous regiment of essays—are particularly annoyed by the gathering of the same into little books, which they think a further shocking sin against taste. It is bad enough (they say) to drivel away week by week, or even day after day, for your living, but you may be excused (poor devil!), for a living you must get. What is quite unpardonable is to give this drivel the dignity of covers and to place it upon shelves.

The enemies of the modern essay go on to say that it cannot possibly find sufficient subject-matter for so excessive an output. And so on.

Now here let me break modern convention at once, and say that I am a good witness and in a good position also to plead in the matter. I have written this sort of essay for many weary years. I know the motive, I know the method, I know the weakness, but also all that is to be said for it. And I think that, upon the whole, the modern practice is to be supported.

I certainly do not say that with enthusiasm. It would be better for literature, no doubt, and for the casual reader (who reads a great deal too much), if the output were less. It would certainly be better for the writer if he could afford to restrict that output. But I know that, in the first place, the level remains remarkably high in this country (where there are a dozen such things turned out to one in any other), and that it does so remain high is an argument in favour of the medium. For a sufficient standard maintained in any form of writing should be proof that there

is material and effort sufficient to that form: that there is a need for that form to supply, and that it is supplied.

These modern essays of ours may be compared to conversation, without which mankind has never been satisfied, which is ever diverse (though continually moving through the same themes), and which finds in the unending multiplicity of the world unending matter for discussion and contemplation. It lacks the chief value of conversation, which is the alternative outlook—the reply. That cannot be helped. But I fancy the reader supplies this somewhat in his own mind, by the movements of appreciation or indignation with which he receives what is put before him. Indeed, sometimes his indignation moves him to provide free copy in protest; though I am afraid that the corresponding pleasure does not get the same chance of expression. I do indeed note, especially in the daily papers nowadays, continual letters from correspondents approving (usually) the more horribly commonplace pronouncements, or those which have been put in to order, as part of some propaganda or other undertaken by the owner of the sheet. These letters I suspect. I believe they are arranged for. But the letters of indignation are certainly genuine, and editors get a good many more than they print. When such letters are written in disapproval of what I myself have written, I nearly always agree with them.

I can also claim to give evidence as a reader of other people's essays. For I can read this kind of matter with less disgust than any other in the modern press. Yes, I prefer it even to murders. And I cannot tell you how much I prefer it to ignorant comment upon the affairs of Europe or conventional rubbish upon affairs domestic: the presentation of little men as great, of falsehood as truth, of imaginaries as realities.

As for a dearth of subject, I see no sign of it at all. If I consider any one man of that half-dozen or so whom I read regularly, my colleagues in this same trade, I can name no one except myself who tends to repetition. And there is no reason why a fairly well-read man, still active and enjoying occasional travel, let alone the infinite experience of daily life, should lack a subject. Stuff is infinite. The danger lies not in the drying up of matter but in the fossilization of manner. Nor do I find much trace of *that* in my contemporaries.

G. Douglas Atkins

SOURCE: "In Other Words: Gardening for Love—The Work of the Essayist," in *Estranging the Familiar: Toward a Revitalized Critical Writing,* The University of Georgia Press, 1992, pp. 18-33.

[In the following essay, Atkins discursively examines the essayist's craft as that of a gardener of words and affirmer of life.]

Essayists, teachers, or both, we typically, indeed unavoidably, use various metaphors in attempting to describe this baggy, perhaps unwieldy, seemingly (but only seemingly) shapeless, in any case lovable, thing, the essay. We keep trying to capture it in words, this slippery, elusive shape, though as Elizabeth Hardwick says, it's a little like trying to catch a fish in the open hand. That we keep trying, posing new metaphors, putting the matter in other words, says something, though I'm not sure quite what, besides that a virtual subgenre exists of essays on the essay. "In other words": essayists put it *otherwise*—that's what essayists do, when, so often, they write about the essay, trying on one, then another metaphor in an effort to describe, to capture, its handsome, comely, beckoning, teasing, essence. It is impossible to do, of course, and that is one reason, a major one, for the continuing, happy, respectful effort. I am obviously implicated in the attempt, this essay in one sense acknowledging the failure of the previous chapter. "In other words": I'm adding mine to the conversation, to the stream of voices that have spoken for so long so well about the form they love.

It's hard to do better than Joseph Epstein, in "Piece Work: Writing the Essay," collected in his *Plausible Prejudices* and significantly positioned last in that volume of essays on American writing. At the risk of simplifying and reducing the importance of his rich and informed if somewhat surly account, I want only to suggest how much is packed into Epstein's title, which even he doesn't fully exploit: "piece work." How appropriate for the essay, for, thinking of its openness and amiableness, I hear "peace work"; and of course "piece work" alludes to everything from the irregular and poorly paying, temporary jobs sometimes available in factories and print shops to the art and craft of quilting, the province of women in the last century and continued, by women, largely in rural areas in this century as at once an outlet for their artistic skills and often a necessity for survival. Essay writing is certainly irregular and poorly paying work; in a number of ways the form seems (to me at least) feminine, and writing it resembles the piecing together of rags and remnants from hither and yon, discarded, thought to be no longer of any use. As in so much else concerning the essay, Montaigne led the way, cleared the path, asking in "Of Friendship," "And what are these things of mine, in truth, but grotesque and monstrous bodies, pieced together of divers members?" and elsewhere (in "Of Vanity") referring to his *essais* as "only an ill-fitted patchwork." The essay often seems, in fact, more a crazy quilt than an organic growth (which may help to account for its disfavor during the heyday of the New Criticism). And like quilting, the essay dropped out of fashion (though I sense that quilting too is enjoying a renascence, surviving mainly as a self-conscious craft and appearing in such phenomena as Whitney Otto's best-selling novel *How to Make an American Quilt*).

Applied to essays, the metaphor of piece work as quilting points up just how dependent these things are on quotation, cut from the full cloth of other text(ile)s. Here William H. Gass, philosopher-novelist-essayist, is best:

> Born of books, nourished by books, a book for its body, the essay is more often than not a confluence of such little blocks and strips of texts. Let me tell you, it says, what I have just read, looked up, or remembered of my reading. Horace, Virgil, Ovid, Cicero, Lucretius meet on a page of Montaigne. Emerson allows Othello and Emilia words, but in a moment asks of Jacobi, an obscure reformer and now no more than a

note, a bigger speech. A strange thing happens. Hazlitt does not quote Shakespeare but Henry VI, whose voice is then lined up to sing in concert with the rest: the living and the dead, the real and the fictitious, each has a part and a place. Virginia Woolf writes of Addison by writing of Macaulay writing of Addison, of whom Pope and Johnson and Thackeray have also written. On and On. In this way the essay confirms the continuity, the contemporaneity, the reality of writing. The words of Flaubert (in a letter), those of Madame Bovary (in her novel), the opinions of Gide (in his *Journal*), of Roger Fry, of Gertrude Stein, of Rilke, of Baudelaire (one can almost imagine the essay's subject and slant from the racy cast of characters), they form a new milieu—the context of citation. And what is citation but an attempt to use a phrase, a line, a paragraph, like a word, and lend it further uses, another identity, apart from the hometown it hails from?

Like those once-familiar things, quilts, essays offer comfort and warmth.

Continuing with Gass: the essay, he says, in the way it pieces together quotations "convokes a community of writers" and "uses any and each and all of them like instruments in an orchestra." (Metaphors abound.) The essayist plunders texts—like a quilter rummaging around in a treasured bag of remnants, scraps left over or cut from other serviceable items: shirts and sheets, pants and tablecloths, dresses and curtains, the fabric in which we live our daily lives. Why? why do essayists plunder texts? "Precisely because they are sacred." Thus the essayist's work of quoting (or quilting) needs to be distinguished from that of the article writer, who also quotes. The method of the essayist, "we are essay-bound to observe," writes Gass,

> is quite different from that of the Scholastics, who quoted authorities in order to acquire their imprimaturs, or from that of the scholar, who quote[s] in order to provide himself with a set of subjects, object lessons, and other people's errors, convenient examples, confirming facts, and laboratory data. However, in the essay, most often passages are repeated out of pleasure and for praise; because the great essayist is not merely [!] making a face at the ideas of others, but a big belly-bumper and exclaimer aloud; the sort who is always saying, "Listen to this! Look there! Feel this touchstone! Hear that!" "By necessity, by proclivity,—and by delight, we all quote," Emerson says. You can be assured you are reading an excellent essay when you find yourself relishing quotations as much as the text that contains them, as one welcomes the chips of chocolate in those celebrated cookies. The apt quotation is one of the essayist's greatest gifts, and, like the good gift, congratulates the giver.

Quoting . . . quilting—they *do* sound somewhat alike, don't they?

Remembered, picked up, and dropped or sewed in, these bits and pieces, these strips and shards, of texts may, Gass seems to suggest, grow, even take on a life of their own, not overwhelming an essay the way weeds take over a flower bed or untended land, but nonetheless sometimes coming to be relished almost as much as the text in which they have been planted. The language thus shifts; our metaphors turn, almost in spite of ourselves, like flowers toward the sun (helio*tropes*), toward nature as ground. If the essay seems pieced and patched together like a quilt, it also seems natural—in several important ways. It appears at once as both a natural growth and a constructed thing. It is, in more than one respect, a threshold being, an "in-between" thing, hanging indeterminately—but not unhappily—between knowledge and art, creation and cognition, thought and things, writing and living, nature and cultivation, involving a little of both and all. Maybe *that's* one reason why it evades our grasp, is so difficult to describe. Could it also help to account for its staying power, its appeal?

A couple of years ago a lady friend gave me a book entitled *Gardening for Love: The Market Bulletins.* The book, handsome in design and full of rich surprises, is a posthumously published collection of the writings of one Elizabeth Lawrence on a variety of topics having to do with gardening, compiled by Allen Lacy, himself the author of such books as *Ground Work: A Gardener's Miscellany.* Lawrence writes, simply but often gracefully, of her love affair with plants, of the "market bulletins" she eagerly sought (a product of another age, these are classified ads in which gardeners hawk their herbs and ornamental perennials), of the letters she received in response to her replies to those ads.

Not until several months had passed, the seeds perhaps having had time to germinate, did I really come to appreciate the title of Elizabeth Lawrence's book. And then all at once it struck me that "gardening for love" nicely describes the work of the essayist: the essayist's labor resembles gardening in part because both proceed from love, bodied forth in their very manners. Alice Walker makes the point movingly in the passage from "In Search of Our Mothers' Gardens" that I adduced as an epigraph. And I think, too, of Sir William Temple's tender "Upon the Gardens of Epicurus; or, of Gardening, in the Year 1685," a virtually paradigmatic essay on gardening.

Love links gardening and essay writing. You don't rush love—we, at least many of us, have the scars about our hearts to prove it. Tiresome platitudes concerning "love at first sight" and romance versions of tempestuous "love" notwithstanding, love, which certainly involves hormonal response though without being identified with it, takes time, develops over time, requires time for hearts, minds, and not least bodies to become finely attuned, atoned, atoned. It grows "slowly, precariously," not unlike the tender peach trees I grew up with in South Carolina, susceptible to early frosts that can destroy an entire crop. In a relationship between two people, always fragile and far more delicate than we care to admit to each other and to ourselves, chance or accident is important: some relationships blossom and grow to maturity, others fade, wither, and die. We all know that. Love requires not only time but also nurture and cultivation: it doesn't just develop on its own, free of attention and work. You don't maintain and devel-

op a relationship, any more than you grow full-bodied, variegated, and delicately scented American Beauty roses, by ignoring the coloration of response to your caress, the almost-imperceptible whisper of need, the appearance of dis-ease, or signs of boredom, the strength of attachment, the nature and depth of roots. Love*making,* so central to love even if slighted in our contemporary (over-)emphasis on sex, figures the problem (and opportunity): slow, careful nurturing, marked by attention, concern, and response, produces the best yields. Time matters: it bodies forth respect—for the other. You have to take the time, be patient, and *love.* Love is incommensurate with haste, inseparable from nurture. The same may be said of the essay.

Nature and nurture: they belong together as much as quilting and quoting. What is there about the essay as form that links it to nature? Many of the great nature writers, of course, have been essayists, many of the great essayists nature writers: I think not just of Emerson and Thoreau, John Muir and John Hay, and before any of them William Bartram, but also of Noel Perrin, David Rains Wallace, Ann Zwinger, Wendell Berry, Peter Matthiesen, Barry Lopez, Sue Hubbell, Gretel Ehrlich, Robert Finch, David Quammen, Edward Abbey, Edward Hoagland, John McPhee, Annie Dillard—the list is not endless but certainly long and distinguished. Sometimes technical, this nature writing is also artful (I think too of Richard Selzer, writing about that aspect of nature that is the human body under conditions of surgery); it is, as a matter of fact, as respectful of the reader, language, and form as it is of the earth and the creatures that populate it. There is, in other words, represented in much of this writing stewardship of both land and language.

To repeat: What is there about the essay that links it to nature?

In *The Observing Self: Rediscovering the Essay* Graham Good opens a path toward an answer. Good distinguishes four "principal types" of the essay: the travel, the moral, the critical, and the autobiographical, which, he admits, are neither mutually exclusive nor exhaustive categorizations. Corresponding to these types or forms are "the main essayistic activities: traveling, pondering, reading, and remembering." Often the travel essay, notes Good, simply narrates a *walk,* and he goes on to claim that "the essay is *essentially* a peripatetic or ambulatory form. The mixture of self-preoccupation and observation, the role of chance in providing sights and encounters, the ease of changing pace, direction, and goal, make walking the perfect analog of 'essaying.'" The history of commentary on the essay, by essayists (whose opinions weigh heavily), confirms Good's thesis.

Unhurried, taken by all the flora and fauna fortunately come upon, more interested, in fact, in the journey, in journeying, than in any destination finally reached, the essay is a walk (and at the same time a garden of delights made of its adventures). Hazlitt's "On Going a Journey" is a classic example of the peripatetic nature of the essay, an account of a walk that itself meanders, that truly offers the reader the experience of journeying. In a *Sewanee Review* celebration of the essay, a tribute collectively entitled "Sallies of the Mind," William Howarth elaborates on this notion (and motion). Though all texts are journeys, Howarth suggests, without quite saying it, the essay seems paradigmatic, even quintessential writing. At any rate, the essay's itinerancy is a matter of process, indeed natural process, subject to the vicissitudes of chance, entailing accident and thriving on serendipity. Such writing—according to Howarth, who has written so well elsewhere of McPhee's writing way—is "motion, a journey through constantly recurring cycles. The circuit spins repeatedly, through steps of gathering material, compiling and arranging it, then synthesizing a draft. Successive revisions follow, a learning process that reveals what to say and how to find a form—often a form that rehearses the writing journey. This faith in continuity values loose and imprecise forms, devoted to an ecological web of relationships rather than strict hierarchies." Constituted by movement, the essay is related to the cycles of nature, rooted in an awareness of the ebb and flow of life, constructed in accordance with seasonal change, planting seeds here, carefully nurturing saplings there, harvesting at some point, lying peacefully limp and fallow at another. It paces, but the essay also knows *about* pace, how to pace itself. Probably thought of most often as an autumnal, even mature creature, the essay is not always bursting with life, it is true, yet alive it certainly is, redolent of the stages and processes of natural growth and the life cycle.

Discussing Montaigne's "originating" efforts, Graham Good shrewdly notes, "The starting-point of the essay was the mind's *natural* desire for knowledge. The task is to bring that desire back to Nature in a wiser and more accepting condition. To do this, thought has to stay close to life, rather than constituting a separate world." Rooted in the world, the essay is anti-Gnostic: thought "has to be re-applied to the experience in which it originates and of which it is a part. Thought should enhance the process of living rather than erode or ignore it." Since Montaigne, the essay has been physical, material, taking the body very much into account. For Montaigne, of course, "the body's existence in time is the very basis of existence. . . . Montaigne rejects asceticism or any other view" that Gnostically "emphasizes the split in man between divine and earthly, rational and irrational, virtuous and sinful."

Let me try to make all this a little clearer, the link between nature and the essay a little more socure. I will do so via Wordsworth and Geoffrey Hartman's understanding of the poet whose early career (leading up to *The Prelude* in 1805) represents an attempt to understand the relation of mind or imagination and nature. By the time of his great autobiographical poem, according to Hartman, Wordsworth "took literally the concept of *culture* as *cultivation*," having moved beyond a certain radicalism, having returned, in fact, "from revolutionary schism to the idea of a ground out of which things grew slowly, precariously; where accident was important, some grew and some didn't, but where there were, for humanity generically considered, infinite chances of birth and rebirth. The literalism of 'Fair seed-time had my soul' (*Prelude* I 301) shocks us into a view of culture as nature." In describing this relation to nature, Hartman uses the Hebraic term *akedah,* which literally means "binding" and which he opposes to the (Christian) notion of "apocalypse." The latter term denotes the haste and impatience manifest in the *uncultivated* mind or imagination.

Implied, maybe even made explicit, by "culture as nature" is the idea of *slow* growth, careful and responsive nurturing—what has to be respected, then, because it deserves no less, and cultivated: fertilized, weeded, watered, caressed, even pampered, brought along at its own pace, which must be discovered and can only be by a heart responsive, a soul prepared. For Hartman, such ideas link up with the essence of the humanities, with due process, and with what he calls "delay time," voided in our mad rush toward communication, meaning, and intimacy. He says it best, I think, in *Easy Pieces*. Describing the humanities as "always in 'slow motion' compared to the sciences or to the immediate demands of the practical world," Hartman writes of their "calendar" as might the *Farmer's Almanac* of the seasons: the humanities calendar, he says, "allows the store of experience to come before us once again, as we incline—fast and forgetful—into the future. Here and there contact is made between these calendars or wheels moving at different speeds; and the meshing that occurs, which can be very powerful indeed, not only at the point of contact but as it provides a design for mutual and coordinated work, is what we call experience." As usual, Hartman has reference to Wordsworth, and as we read him, we may find springing to mind such contemporary naturalists or, better, environmentalists as Wendell Berry, Wes Jackson, and Gary Paul Nabhan. Wordsworth attacked, writes Hartman, "in what he named *lyrical* ballads, the very concept of the newsworthy event, composing lyrics that were anything but sensational. They displaced the avid reader's attention from the unusual or fantastic incident to the sensitive response that an ordinary life might elicit. His almost plotless ballads are our first instance of minimalist art. But they are not yet abstract like that art: they surround familiar thoughts and happenings with an imaginative aura. The strange subtlety of Wordsworth's poems was intended to retain ear, eye, and imagination, to wean them from the age's degrading thirst after 'outrageous stimulation.' "

Enter, then, the quotidian or "ordinary," familiar existence. At the heart of Wordsworthian realism lies what? Respect for time, the capacity to abide time, *and so* the ability to find in everyday life the materials of romance. No vampish rush after immediate gratification, either. It's a *negative* capability, like what Keats described as the ability to abide "uncertainties, Mysteries, doubts, without any irritable reaching after fact and reason" and therefore to rest content "with half knowledge." The impulse clearly resembles that which prompts the realistic novel. In perhaps the *locus classicus* of apologies for that effort, George Eliot (in *Adam Bede*) allegorically expresses her preference for Dutch "genre" paintings: "I turn without shrinking," she writes, "from cloud-borne angels, from prophets, sibyls, and heroic warriors, to an old woman bending over her flower-pot, or eating her solitary dinner, while the noonday light, softened perhaps by a screen of leaves, falls on her mob-cap, and just touches the rim of her spinning-wheel, and her stone-jug, and all those cheap common things which are the precious necessaries of life to her." Graham Good, who quotes this passage, comments as follows: "The sensibility described here, with its ability to find significance and beauty in the detail of a small world and little-regarded people and things, is often found in the essay, which also turns aside from the grand design and the imposing statement for minor truths." Minor truths perhaps from some transcendent perspective, but major ones for those of us embroiled in the inevitable pains and frequent pleasures of day-to-day living.

Lacking the muscle, strength, girth, and power of a novel or the wound tightness and intensity of a poem, the essay is modest, unpretentious, often all too willing to acknowledge, even to accept, what E. B. White called its second-class citizenship. Which is not to say that it gives up on being artful. On the contrary, the essay is secure enough in its own being to be artful on its own terms, in its own admittedly limited, fragile way, of inviting its readers to share in its artistry, not marvel at or stare in awe and amazement, but instead to feel reassured that its maker was an artisan who, precisely in the lack of show, showed her art. That's part of what is meant, I gather, by the term *"familiar* essay": not only are its subjects ordinary, quotidian, but its tone and mode of address, the nature of the voice heard in the narrative and along the rise and fall of the sentences, are such that you know a good deal about that of which the essayist speaks. He or she speaks to you, moreover, as someone known, recognized, familiar. The familiarity bred is, however, neither quick nor vampish: as in all good, effective, loving relationships the essayist preserves an identity while allowing you yours; the essayist engages in conversation with you and though, like Edward Hoagland, 'Phillip Lopate, and—even more—Nancy Mairs, he or she can be open, candid, and at times brutally frank, there is usually no lust for intimacy. If it comes, fine, but only after you've gotten to know each other. Rather than in bed, you feel more like in a garden, walking and talking with someone you know, like, and respect, teasing a little, perhaps flirting some, but also discussing situations and ideas and perhaps admitting emotions that matter to you in both your everyday and your inner life.

Whether or not it is quite yours, the essayist's garden through which you both stroll, sometimes arm in arm (the essay *is* a dia-logue), the garden that *is* the essay is marked by those qualities Alexander Pope famously prescribed for gardens (and writing!)—utility rather than show, and "naturalness," not excessive order or signs of manipulated diversity and apertures. "Unaffected simplicity"—that was Pope's goal (and achievement in both his own garden at Twickenham and his best poetry), and it is the goal of the essay as well as its achievement in the hands of those who well (at)tend the form. This is Pope "On Gardens" in the *Guardian* no. 173 (29 September 1713), edited by the essayist Joseph Addison: "There is certainly something in the amiable Simplicity of unadorned Nature, that spreads over the Mind a more noble sort of Tranquility, and a loftier Sensation of Pleasure, than can be raised from the nicer Scenes of Art." In stark contrast, Pope claims, to such simplicity "is the modern Practice of Gardening; we seem to make it our Study to recede from Nature, not only in the Tonsure of Greens into the most regular and formal Shapes, but even in monstrous Attempts beyond

the reach of the Art it self: We run into Sculpture, and are yet better pleas'd to have our Trees in the most awkward Figures of Men and Animals, than in the most regular of their own." The garden is, thus, artful precisely in its imitation of nature. It is a product of cooperation between us forked creatures and nature, not so unlike the way the essay appears as both a natural and a constructed thing.

Listen to E. B. White on the essayist. He's writing in the foreword to his collected essays. In what he says, you can hear many of the themes threading their way through the foregoing account. White *exemplifies,* in fact, the work of the essayist. Catch the rhythm of the thought, the cadence of his sentences. Note how White lingers over notions, caresses them in the structure of his language, stays with language, in fact. He's in no hurry: he's gardening for love. "The essayist is a self-liberated man, sustained by the childish belief that everything he thinks about, everything that happens to him, is of general interest. He is a fellow who thoroughly enjoys his work, just as people who take bird walks enjoy theirs. Each new excursion of the essayist, each new 'attempt,' differs from the last and takes him into new country. Only a person who is congenitally self-centered has the effrontery and the stamina to write essays." Perhaps, we say in response to White's quietly joyful and perambulating self-criticism, which is quite attractive, if not positively seductive. It is affirmative, perhaps egotistical, in its very criticism of self-centeredness. What a strange effect! What a wonderful thing, the essay!

Continuing, not exactly rambling on, White turns to the work of the essayist, meaning himself, of course. "There are," he begins, "as many kinds of essays as there are human attitudes or poses, as many essay flavors as there are Howard Johnson's ice creams. The essayist arises in the morning and, if he has work to do [!], selects his garb from an unusually extensive wardrobe: he can pull on any sort of shirt, be any sort of person, according to his mood or his subject matter—philosopher, scold, jester, raconteur, confidant, pundit, devil's advocate, enthusiast." Immediately White becomes more personal, all the more engaging—the turn from the general to the personal is neither sharp nor modulated and is, therefore, exemplary. "I like the essay," he writes (and then proceeds to indict himself for imposing his love, even as he details the effects of that love), "have always liked it, and even as a child at work, attempting to inflict my young thoughts and experiences on others by putting them on paper. I early broke into print in the pages of *St. Nicholas.* I tend still to fall back on the essay form (or lack of form) when an idea strikes me, but I am not fooled about the place of the essay in twentieth-century American letters—it stands a short distance down the line." And it does, of course, still does, but since White wrote in 1977 the essay has advanced some distance in popularity and prestige, even as Howard Johnson's myriad flavors of ice cream have given way to Baskin-Robbins as a cultural landmark.

Still, White is clear-sighted, not really plaintive, certainly not resentful of the essay's status. It is, after all—or so it pretends, as White does here so beautifully—a slight thing, almost a trifle. Thus the essayist, "unlike the novelist, the poet, and the playwright, must be content in his self-imposed role of second-class citizen. A writer who has his sights trained on the Nobel Prize or other earthly trumphs," advises White, "had best write a novel, a poem, or a play, and leave the essayist to ramble about, content with living a free life and enjoying the satisfactions of a somewhat undisciplined existence."

White goes on to claim—"argue" is not quite the right word—that what matters most is the essayist's honesty.

> There is one thing the essayist cannot do, though—he cannot indulge himself in deceit or in concealment, for he will be found out in no time. Desmond McCarthy . . . observes that Montaigne "had the gift of natural candour. . . ." It is the basic ingredient. And even the essayist's escape from discipline is only a partial escape: the essay, although a relaxed form, imposes its own disciplines, raises its own problems, and these disciplines and problems soon become apparent and (we all hope) act as a deterrent to anyone wielding a pen merely because he entertains random thoughts or is in a happy or wandering mood.

The candor we experience in essays, including White's here, is a matter of integrity, of being honest with and faithful to what one is writing. The honesty is artistic, and the ironic self-deprecation is that virtually endemic to the essay—it is already there in Montaigne, and it persists through the centuries, though with modifications in form. In Edward Hoagland's words: "an essayist soon discovers that he doesn't have to tell the whole truth and nothing but the truth; he can shape or share his memories, as long as the purpose is served of elucidating a truthful point." And that fact advances somewhat, at least in my judgment, the essay's status along the line of art forms.

At the end of his brief account, White circles back to what has exercised him from the beginning, the matter of the essayistic ego. Whether he did then, White now understands how much it is precisely a question of the essayistic ego, even if he does not (of course) use that rather unessayistic term. If he remains critical of his own self-involvement, the presumption appears in perspective; the essayistic now seems special, as indeed it is—both modest and presumptuous, self-denying and affirming, critical of self and *thereby* assertive of self. A delicate balance is needed, and justice is nothing if not a complex and problematic thing:

> I think some people find the essay the last resort of the egoist, a much too self-conscious and self-serving form for their taste; they feel that it is presumptuous of a writer to assume that his little excursions or his small observations will interest the reader. There is some justice in their complaint. I have always been aware that I am by nature self-absorbed and egotistical; to write of myself to the extent I have done indicates a too great attention to my own life, not enough to the lives of others. I have worn many shirts, and not all of them have been a good fit. But when I am discouraged or downcast I need only fling open the door of my closet, and there, hidden behind everything else, hangs the mantle of Michel de Montaigne, smelling slightly of camphor.

The voice we hear here, and in essays generally, may be a construction rather than the unalloyed representation of the flesh-and-blood human being, but still, something genuinely good, warm, human and humane, generous of spirit, and good-hearted can be heard in that voice, felt in the prose. No matter how created the pose, you want to believe the man or woman wears it comfortably. Who but one attentive to others and interested in people, affairs, feelings, geese, a dying pig, yellow roses, Kansas sunsets (had he the privilege of observing them), the sun, the moon, and the stars can be so critical as White is of not attending enough to the lives of others? The essayist is so involved in life—Joseph Epstein says, "love of life . . . is one of the qualities that all the great essayists hold in common"—so sensitive to the balance that makes it good that he or she feels intensely when the scale is tipped ever so slightly and so must attempt to redress the balance, even if the terms of the attempt seem to us, who are less sensitive, unbalanced.

In "Being Familiar" Sam Pickering joins the effort to describe the essay, suggesting that it is a product of both wander and wonder: "Scholarly writing and the familiar essay are very different. Instead of driving hard to prove a point, the essay saunters, letting the writer follow the vagaries of his willful curiosity. Instead of reaching conclusions, the essay ruminates and wonders. Rather than being right or informative, it is thoughtful. Instead of being serious, it is often lighthearted, pondering subjects like the breeding habits of beetles, and, alas, of people. Of course as a person ages it becomes increasingly difficult to be scholarly or definitive." Of course, "being definitive" is the goal of article writing; "being familiar," the heart, never merely the goal, of essay writing. Pickering goes on: "Truth seems beside the point, or at least amid the many doings of a day it seems to have progressively less to do with living. Years have passed since I have read a study advertised as definitive. Being definitive, and perhaps even clever, is an activity for youth. Certainly it was in my case." "Being definitive" is also a matter of reaching conclusions. It contrasts with the skepticism and what I have called the "negative capability" of the essay. Being particular in the way the essayist is, Pickering helpfully illustrates: "Not long ago a university press that just reprinted an academic book I wrote in fresher days rejected a new manuscript. 'You don't reach enough conclusions,' the editor explained; 'writing essays seems to have affected your scholarship.' The editor was right; I now have trouble reaching conclusions. Instead of cudgeling stray dogs along the route I travel . . . I stop and pet them. If they could talk, I'd probably sit down, start chatting, and forget about the race."

Reading Sam Pickering, I recall E. B. White describing an ideal reader of *Walden,* probably the quintessential nature book in our literature. As Susan Allen Toth has written in her tribute to White, included in *How to Prepare for Your High-School Reunion,* his essay "A Slight Sound at Evening" works because, a mix—I might say, a quilt as well as a garden—of Thoreau, *Walden,* and White, it embodies the commentator's excitement about the author and his work and in so doing provides reason sufficient why "our hearts beat faster when we read him." White's response to Thoreau is human—that's what it comes down to.

Here is White on *Walden*'s ideal reader, one who has approached perhaps Sam Pickering's "negative capability": "I think it is some advantage to encounter the book at a period in one's life when the normal anxieties and enthusiasms and rebellions of youth closely resemble those of Thoreau in that spring of 1845 when he borrowed an ax, went out to the woods, and began to whack down some trees for timber. Received at such a juncture, the book is like an invitation to life's dance, assuring the troubled recipient that no matter what befalls him in the way of success or failure he will always be welcome at the party— that the music is played for him, too, if he will but listen and move his feet." The essay may *be for* those who have achieved some age, maturity, and judgment (many commentators think so), for whom "outrageous stimulation" is neither required nor desired. (If it is, and I doubt that the essay's real appeal is limited to us middle-aged folk, but *if* it is, then we're obviously and sadly mistaken in making it the cornerstone of freshman comp.) *In any case,* and age is no necessary prerequisite for maturity, the essay persists as "an invitation to life's dance." It represents, in other words, neither quiescence nor acquiescence in the face of increasing age, sagging breasts, and graying hair. It is, instead, a celebration and a thanksgiving, figured by both May and November: an invitation to life's *dance.*

"Invitation" also deserves emphasis, for essays smile. Being familiar, they welcome, enjoin you. They are not always happy, of course (think of Dr. Johnson's *Rambler* essays or, differently, Hazlitt's), though they manage, somehow, to remain affirmative, affirmative in the way Keats's "negative capability" is affirmative: that affirmation, if not joy, derives from and perhaps only by means of experienced pain. The essay is thus experienced, though—pace Sam Pickering—not sad. It recalls the Wordsworthian knowledge that "lies too deep for tears."

I repeat: essays smile. The skin around the eyes crinkles (a sign of age?); the eyes, soft and warm (probably brown), may not dance, though they can twinkle. And the smile appears genuine; the face makes you feel comfortable. It offers recognition, and you feel positively invited to respond.

Whether or not they make you smile in turn, essays can make you feel good, comfortable, at ease. They're familiar and personal. It's impossible to be with them long and remain tight or glum. You want, in fact need, to spend time with them, more and more time. You can become dependent. It's like with a lover.

You and essays: a relationship develops. If, as has often been claimed, the essayist is an *amat*eur, it is surely in the root, the most basic sense of the word: the essayist is one who loves, who understands the value of nurture and cultivation. The smile that creases the face of the gardener-essayist betokens love.

THE COCKNEYS: HAZLITT, LAMB, AND HUNT

Orlo Williams

SOURCE: "III" and "IV," in *The Essay,* Martin Secker, 1915, pp. 36-47, 48-63.

[*In the following excerpt, Williams discusses the accomplishment of the major nineteenth-century English essayists and posits the defining characteristics of the true essayist.*]

Towards the end of the eighteenth century, by some miracle that has been variously explained, the civilized world, which had been modern before, suddenly became modern again after some eighty years of being old-fashioned. There is no need to recall the astounding wonders of that time—the French Revolution, the rise of Napoleon, the mortal convulsions of Europe, the Romantic movement, the new fountain of English poetry, the beginning of industrialism and so forth. It is enough for our purpose to notice that, among other marvels, the English essay reached a perfection to be found neither before nor afterwards. This is not to say that more people wrote good essays: it was rather the case that fewer people wrote better ones. The stream that had formed that rather stagnant pool of fifty volumes was now divided into several channels. Political pamphlets and squibs carried off some of the waters; others went, with everincreasing flow, into the daily papers, which became more important, fuller and more literary, thus beginning the flood of occasional journalism which has swamped the essay in our own day. A third runnel was diverted into the critical reviews and magazines which were a new portent of the age. First arose the *Quarterly,* then the *Edinburgh.* Into these went the solid criticism of history, art and literature from the pen of a Southey, a Gifford, or a Croker whose articles were extended reviews of particular books or treatises on particular subjects. None of these streams produced the essay proper and they call for no further comment. The waters of the true essay, though they too were attracted by the magazines, ran from a few notable heads—Charles Lamb, William Hazlitt, Leigh Hunt and Thomas de Quincey—though there were doubtless other contributory trickles whose individuality is no longer remembered.

Of these four writers Leigh Hunt is by far the least important. He was a genial, facile writer, ever ready to turn out agreeable prose or verse, but there is nothing very remarkable about his essays, which could easily be equalled by the occasional articles on light subjects that appear daily or weekly in our periodicals. De Quincey, as I have said, was a true essayist who wrote but few true essays. Much of his prose work consists of serious criticism, and other parts of it are pure fantasy. One of his best, "The English Mail Coach," which has all its author's spirited *élan,* only leads up to a narration of his neurotic dreams, and even "Murder as a Fine Art," for all its boisterous fun, is a trifle too long and too insistent on details unpleasant in themselves to be a perfect essay. Undoubtedly de Quincey formally debars himself from fuller consideration here by having thrown so much of his finest essay-matter into *"The Confessions of an Opium Eater,"* a work of consummate genius full of splendid passages that leave an ineffaceable impression. With regret I leave his incorrigibly discursive humour and his vividly coloured style, but there is no more warrant for lingering over the "Opium Eater" than over "Tristram Shandy." With regard to Hazlitt there are fewer limitations to be made. His essays are mostly true essays, and even where their subject is literary or æsthetic criticism he contrives to be neither heavy nor professorial, but, while fashioning the essay into the nicest engine for his critical purpose, to preserve its essential lightness and mobility. It has been said with truth that Hazlitt is a perfect model for all young writers. In him there is not a fault to be reprehended nor even a *culpable* deficiency. He is tolerant, broad-minded, highly cultivated, endowed with the most enlightened views on art, eloquent, humorous, and very human; his style is smooth and brilliant, yet he has the charm of seeming intimately conversational; he can soar on the wings of eloquence, yet his common sense is unimpeachable. Perhaps, if he had always reached the level of his essay "On Going a Journey," which all walkers should know by heart, no restraint could be put upon admiration. But his other moments have not quite this happiness. If one reads his essays on "The Past and the Future," "Genius and Common Sense," or "Living to Oneself," there is nothing to be said in criticism of them but this: "How much better Lamb would have handled these subjects!" There are solid reasons for holding Hazlitt the more perfect writer of the two, but there it is—the comment rises instinctively to one's lips. It comes, possibly, to this: that Hazlitt, as an essayist, was absolutely proficient, but Charles Lamb was a genius.

This shy, stuttering little clerk of the East India House, who looked like a Quaker in his dark coat, and in uncongenial company behaved as awkwardly as one of those poor relations whom he satirized, who often smoked too much and drank too much, who lived so bravely under the shadow of insanity and bore its reality (in the case of his unlucky sister) with such angelic devotion, who was—in the parlance of the world—an oddity, and whose friends—Coleridge, George Dyer, Burnett, Godwin, John Fenwick, Jem White—were oddities too, "in the world's eye a ragged regiment," who failed as a poet, a dramatist, and a journalist—this man, whom nature and circumstance had shabbily stinted and yet of whom his friend, Bryan Procter, wrote: "When he did speak his words had a flavour in them beyond any that I have heard elsewhere," brought to the essay a mind incomparably fitted for that form. It was a fertile mind, with a natural affinity to letters, that in the course of years had become richly planted and yielded richly; it was a wonderfully assimilative mind, which made the matter devotedly acquired so inseparably its own, that its possessor had no need of a note-book, since reminiscences, cadences, instances, half-quotations poured themselves out from this storehouse with perfect appositeness; it was a mind of unusual delicacy, capable of discerning the most elusive sentiments and of exquisitely appreciating character whether in life or in literary art; it was a mind endowed with tolerance, with sympathy, with singularly pure taste and yet with a faculty of glowing enthusiasm for its individual preferences; it was a mind by turns jovial, genial, witty, tender, wistful; it was a companionable mind, a loving mind, for "he hated no one whom

he had once met"; it had been through the fire and yet preserved the original imp; it was a rare mind, a precious mind, a mind of innumerable facets and infinite elasticity. Lamb himself describes, not its virtues, but its dynamic qualities in "Imperfect Sympathies":

> The owners of the sort of faculties I allude to have minds rather suggestive than comprehensive. They have no pretences to much clearness or precision in their ideas, or in their manner of expressing them. Their intellectual wardrobe (to confess fairly) has few whole pieces in it. They are content with fragments and scattered pieces of truth. She presents no full front to them—a feature or side-face at most. Hints and glimpses, germs and crude essays at a system, is the utmost they can pretend to. They beat up a little game peradventure—and leave it to knottier heads, more robust constitutions, to run it down. The light that lights them is not steady and polar, but mutable and shifting: waxing, and again waning. Their conversation is accordingly. They will throw out a random word in or out of season, and be content to let it pass for what it is worth. They cannot speak always as if they were on their oath—but must be understood, speaking or writing, with some abatement. They seldom wait to mature a proposition, but e'en bring it to market in the green ear. They delight to impart their defective discoveries as they arise, without waiting for their full development.

Even this passage must be understood "with some abatement," and those who are inclined to set Lamb down as an idle babbler, a mere agreeable rattle, may read "The Artificial Comedy of the Last Century" or the analysis of character in *Twelfth Night* in "Some of the Old Actors," and make their recantation: but it expresses the electric mental activity, irreducible to the service of exactitude, which made him an unsatisfactory journalist and the king of essayists.

On the Individuality of the English familiar essayists:

One looks in vain in the essays of Lamb, Hazlitt, Hunt, and de Quincey for any uniformity of theme or attitude. Each man wrote according to his own tastes and abilities and appealed to that segment of the public that was sympathetic to his views. They all kept only one quality in common—their individuality. Each essayist asserted his bias, rode his hobby, or aired his prejudices with complete confidence in the worth of his opinions.

Homer C. Combs, in A Book of the Essay, from Montaigne to E. B. White, *edited by Homer C. Combs, Charles Scribner's Sons, 1950.*

It is almost impossible to criticize Hazlitt's essays: this is also true of Elia's, with the added fact that, in every case, one is convinced of their being unsurpassable, so limpid and delicate is their style, their art so cunningly finished, so apparently careless. Lamb called them "a sort of unlicked, incondite things—villainously pranked out in an affected array of antique modes and phrases," but he was laughing at the pedants. It is true that his mouth is ever full of snatches from Burton, Fuller and Sir Thomas Browne, that his sentences are punctuated with quaint interjections, and that his wit leaps hither and thither like "Ariel and all his quality." His essays may be called unmethodical, their logical skeletons may not be obvious, passages may defy precise parsing, but it is the business of the essayist to flit and not to pad. He should be a man overcrowded with matter, who must cram a quantity into a small space; he must force the pace and keep the reader a little breathless, only resting him now and then with a halt in the shade or a station before a fair prospect. Lamb performs this task of a pacemaker with consummate ingenuity, never flagging himself nor allowing the reader to flag, but ever tempting him on with new delights.

To begin giving instances of Lamb's perfection is a dangerous step, for one would lief quote every essay entire, and to make a choice is bewildering. In his work, as in that of a great painter, there are infinite gradations of light and shade. From the whimsical brightness of "All Fools' Day" or "A Dissertation on Roast Pig," to the melancholy of "Blakesmoor in Hertfordshire" or "Confessions of a Drunkard," there stretches the whole spectrum of sentiment. It is impossible to decide in what mood Elia is most enchanting. When one reads Bridget Elia's speech in "Old China":

> "Do you remember the brown suit, which you made to hang upon you, till all your friends cried shame upon you, it grew so threadbare—and all because of that folio Beaumont and Fletcher, which you dragged home late at night from Barker's in Covent Garden? Do you remember how we eyed it for weeks before we could make up our minds to the purchase, and had not come to a determination till it was near ten o'clock of the Saturday night, when you set off from Islington, fearing you would be too late—and when the old bookseller with some grumbling opened his shop, and by the twinkling taper (for he was setting bedwards) lighted out the relic from his dusty treasures—and when you lugged it home, wishing it were twice as cumbersome—and when you presented it to me—and when we were exploring the perfectness of it (*collating* you called it)—and while I was repairing some of the loose leaves with paste, which your impatience would not suffer to be left till daybreak—was there no pleasure in being a poor man? Or can those neat black clothes which you wear now, and are so careful to keep brushed, since we have become rich and finical, give you half the honest vanity, with which you flaunted it about in that overworn suit—your old corbeau—for four or five weeks longer than you should have done, to pacify your conscience for the mighty sum of fifteen—or sixteen shillings was it?—a great affair we thought it then—which you had lavished on the old folio?"

When one reads this speech or Elia's answer to it in the same essay, or the pathetic vision, inspired by Lamb's first love, in "Dream Children," or "Mackery End," or "A Superannuated Man," or "Christ's Hospital Thirtyfive Years Ago," one would swear that Lamb excelled most in the mood of wistful reminiscence. But the oath would not be binding. At another time one's love goes out to his marvellous portraits, those of Samuel Salt and Lovell in "The Old Benchers of the Inner Temple," of George Dyer in "Oxford in the Vacation," of his brother in "My Relations," of Ralph Bigod in "Two Races of Men," of Sarah Battle and of the ghostly South-Sea House with its phantom clerks, Evans, John Tipp, the polished Man and rattling Walter Plumer: at another one will extol his graceful satires such as "The Old and New Schoolmaster," "Modern Gallantry" or "A Bachelor's Complaint of the Behaviour of Married People." Then, again, one cherishes his moments of dashing absurdity as in "All Fools' Day," "Newspapers Thirty-Five Years Ago," or "Popular Fallacies," those inimitable examples of comic brevity, and one comes to the conclusion that Lamb is most himself in such passages as this from "Grace Before Meat":

> "I am no Quaker at my food. I confess I am not indifferent to the kinds of it. Those unctuous morsels of deer's flesh were not made to be received with dispassionate services. I hate a man who swallows it, affecting not to know what he is eating. I suspect his taste in higher matters. I shrink instinctively from one who professes to like minced veal. There is a physiognomical character in the tastes for food. C——— holds that a man cannot have a pure mind who refuses apple-dumplings. I am not certain but he is right. With the decay of my first innocence, I confess a less and less relish daily for those innocuous cates. The whole vegetable tribe have lost their gust for me. Only I stick to asparagus, which still seems to inspire gentle thoughts,"

or in such a characteristic uplifting as the *finale* of "A Chapter on Ears," where Elia recounts his sensations at the organ-playing of Novello:

> "I stagger under the weight of harmony, reeling to and fro at my wits' end;—clouds, as of frankincense, oppress me—priests, altars, censers, dazzle before me—the genius of *his* religion hath me in her toils—a shadowy triple tiara invests the brow of my friend, late so naked, so ingenuous—he is Pope—and by him sits, like as in the anomaly of dreams, a she-Pope too,—tricoroneted like himself!—I am converted, and yet a Protestant;—at once *malleus hereticorum,* and myself grand heresiarch: or three heresies centre in my person:—I am Marcion, Ebion, and Cerinthus—Gog and Magog—what not?—till the coming in of the friendly supper-tray dissipates the figment, and a draught of true Lutheran beer (in which my friend shows himself no bigot) at once reconciles me to the rationalities of a purer faith; and restores me to the genuine unterrifying aspects of my pleasant-countenanced host and hostess."

But it is no use: one might read through the *Essays of Elia* every month of a year, and then be unable to pick one's favourite. Elia responds to almost any mood. Nobody, as he says, would take up the *Faerie Queen* as a stopgap nor deny that "Milton almost requires a solemn service of music before you take him up"; but Elia himself, whether read at leisure or in hasty snatches, is fascinating at all times. Other essayists, before or since Charles Lamb, have equalled him in some of his excellences, but taken all in all he stands without a rival. To imitate him is as impossible as wholly to explain him, for he followed no school and founded none: yet if I were asked for a subtle test of profound acquaintance with the essential qualities of English prose literature, I should find it difficult to devise any more searching than the task of giving lucidly a judicious appreciation of the *Essays of Elia.*

Lamb there has been no essayist entirely worthy to place by his side, though Robert Louis Stevenson may, perhaps, be classed with Hazlitt. To guard once more against misconception, let me not be supposed to deny that the nineteenth century has had its great masters of English prose. One may enjoy and admire Macaulay, Matthew Arnold, Carlyle, Ruskin, Walter Pater and John Addington Symonds, while refusing them a place among the English essayists. Macaulay called his critical writings essays, but the reason for his exclusion and that of other critical writers has already been given. Macaulay's vivid discussions of history and letters, with their glittering antitheses and the stately glamour of their evocations, were contributions to knowledge, not *divertissements.* He is always the historian or the critic lecturing to a fascinated audience; his eye is always on the main purpose, that of settling somebody's case; his business was not to be leisurely and discursive, but to lead his theme up to an effective climax. One may read Macaulay's essays, I grant, purely for the sake of æsthetic delectation, but it is a delectation entirely different from that induced by reading Lamb, with whom Macaulay, except for using a common language, had no point of contact. The same kind of consideration applies to Carlyle and Ruskin. Their eloquent discourses—the rough force of the one and the magnificent declamation of the other—must be called rhapsodies rather than essays. As for Walter Pater, he was an admirable craftsman in constructing mosaics of musical speech, a subtle appreciator of beauty, a great stylist, if you will, but a fine style and an exquisite taste do not make an essayist if a certain magic sympathy with common humanity be wanting. On account of his popularity in England it would not be fitting to omit the name of Emerson, who was a lofty thinker with a finished style: but his essays are too consistently lectures to the aspiring. Really to enjoy Emerson implies a considerable moral and intellectual thirstiness: those who do not pant for these uplifting waterbrooks, preferring a potion with more body and flavour, find in them an alkaline flatness which, like the springs of Contrexéville, is excellent as a corrective, insipid as a beverage.

Robert Louis Stevenson certainly had in him the stuff of an essayist. He knew the meaning of zest. He was a man of wide human sympathies and a capacious, intellectual appetite. "Times change," he wrote to W. E. Henley in the preface to *Virginibus Puerisque,* "opinions vary to their opposite, and still this world appears a brave gymnasium, full of sea-bathing, and horse exercise and bracing, manly virtues"—a promising outlook for an essayist. In spite of his carefully polished style, there is nothing cold or hard in Stevenson's essays: he lavishes on them his own bright, lovable, mercurial personality. The best of them are a plea-

sure to read and a pleasure to remember. The one on "Walking Tours," for instance, is as perfect as Hazlitt's "On Going a Journey," full of the joy of limbs healthily wearied, ecstatically reposed.

> You lean from the window, your last pipe reeking whitely in the darkness, your body full of delicious pains, your mind enthroned in the seventh circle of content; when suddenly the mood changes, the weathercock goes about, and you ask yourself one question more: whether, for the interval, you have been the wisest philosopher or the most egregious of donkeys? Human experience is not yet able to reply; but at least you have had a fine moment, and looked down upon all the kingdoms of the earth. And whether it was wise or foolish, to-morrow's travel will carry you, body and mind, into some different parish of the infinite.

Such a passage as that, or the brilliant sketches of physiognomy in the first essay on "Talk and Talkers," or parts of *Travels with a Donkey,* place Stevenson in the first rank of English essayists. Yet it cannot be said that he always attains so high a level. There are many essays of his that tickle the ear but do not arrest the memory. His gentle moralizings on love and life and death that fill so much of *Virginibus Puerisque,* gay upon the surface, inwardly melancholy, pass out of the mind like a tuneful song heard faintly upon the water. For all their attractiveness of form they are a trifle sentimental, a trifle commonplace, a trifle wanting in a firm grasp of reality; they are the headwaters feeding that shallow pool wherein the Narcissus of to-day, Mr. A. C. Benson, yearns with half-ashamed admiration over his own image. Stevenson's great defect as an essayist is his constancy of feature. The reader's mental picture of him seldom varies: those expressive lips have always a wistful smile, those large eyes are ever so lightly filmed with mist. He read his own heart and the hearts of others with understanding, but he shrank from really groping in either. In writing about life he gives the impression of sparing the boys and girls of his title the knowledge that devastating passion, blighting foolishness and hideous hypocrisy are among its ingredients. Charles Lamb did not often seriously moralize, but the gentle Elia could be tragically poignant, whereas in Stevenson's philosophic view there is something of the hopeless prettiness to be found in Leader's landscapes. If an essayist is going on the moral tack, he must do so ruthlessly, giving himself away and showing up everybody else.

Leslie Stephen

SOURCE: "The Essayist," in *Men, Books, and Mountains: Essays by Leslie Stephen,* edited by S. O. A. Ullmann, University of Minnesota Press, 1956, pp. 45-73.

[Stephen is considered one of the most important English literary critics of the late Victorian and early Edwardian era. In his criticism, which was often moralistic, Stephen argued that all literature is nothing more than an imaginative rendering, in concrete terms, of a writer's philosophy or beliefs. It is the role of criticism, he contended, to translate into intellectual terms what the writer has told the reader

through character, symbol, and plot. Stephen's analyses often include biographical judgements of the writer as well as the work. In the following excerpt from an essay originally published in the Cornhill Magazine *in 1881, he examines the strengths and weaknesses of Hazlitt and Lamb as representatives of the "cockneys," whose work, to Stephen, represented a return to the essay tradition of Addison and Steele.*]

The essay writer is the lay preacher upon that vague mass of doctrine which we dignify by the name of knowledge of life or of human nature. He has to do with the science in which we all graduate as we grow old, when we try to pack our personal observations into a few sententious aphorisms not quite identical with the old formulæ. It is a strange experience which happens to some people to grow old in a day, and to find that some good old saying— "vanity of vanities," for example—which you have been repeating ever since you first left college and gave yourself the airs of a man of the world, has suddenly become a vivid and striking impression of a novel truth, and has all the force of a sudden discovery. In one of Poe's stories, a clever man hides an important document by placing it exactly in the most obvious and conspicuous place in the room. That is the principle, it would sometimes seem, which accounts for the preservation of certain important secrets of life. They are hidden from the uninitiated just because the phrases in which they are couched are so familiar. We fancy, in our youth, that our elders must either be humbugs—which is the pleasantest and most obvious theory— or that they must have some little store of esoteric wisdom which they keep carefully to themselves. The initiated become aware that neither hypothesis is true. Experience teaches some real lessons; but they are taught in the old words. The change required is in the mind of the thinker, not in the symbols of his thought. Wordly wisdom is summed up in the familiar currency which has passed from hand to hand through the centuries; and we find on some catastrophe, or by the gradual process of advancing years, that mystic properties lurk unsuspected in the domestic halfpenny.

The essayist should be able, more or less, to anticipate this change, and make us see what is before our eyes. It is easy enough for the mere hawker of sterile platitudes to imitate his procedure, and to put on airs of superhuman wisdom when retailing the barren *exuviæ* of other men's thought. But there are some rare books, in reading which we slowly become aware that we have to do with the man who has done all that can be done in this direction—that is, redis- covered the old discoveries for himself. . . .

Essays may be mentioned which, though less popular than some downright twaddle, have a better chance of endurance. But, apart from the most modern performances, some of the very best of English essays came from the school which in some sense continued the old traditions. The "cockneys" of the first quarter of the century, still talked about the "town," as a distinct entity. Charles Lamb's supper parties were probably the last representatives of the old-fashioned club. Lamb, indeed, was the pet of a little clique of familiars, standing apart from the great world—not like Addison, the favourite of a society, in-

cluding the chief political and social leaders of the day. The cockneys formed only a small and a rather despised section of society; but they had not been swamped and over-whelmed in the crowd. London was not a shifting caravanserai, a vague aggregate of human beings, from which all traces of organic unity had disappeared. Names like Kensington or Hampstead still suggested real places, with oldest inhabitants and local associations, not confusing paraphrases for arbitrary fragments of S. or N.W. The Temple had its old benchers, men who had lived there under the eyes of neighbours, and whose personal characteristics were known as accurately as in any country village. The theatre of Lamb's day was not one amongst many places of amusement, with only such claims as may be derived from the star of the moment; but a body with imposing historical associations, which could trace back its continuity through a dynasty of managers, from Sheridan to Garrick, and so to Cibber and Betterton, and the companies which exulted in the name of the King's servants. When sitting in the pit, he seemed to be taking the very place of Steele, and might still listen to the old "artificial comedy," for which we have become too moral or too squeamish. To read Elia's essays is to breathe that atmosphere again; and to see that if Lamb did not write for so definite a circle as the old essayists, he is still representing a class with cherished associations, and a distinctive character. One should be a bit of a cockney fully to enjoy his writing; to be able to reconstruct the picturesque old London with its quaint and grotesque aspects. For Lamb is nowhere more himself than in the humorous pathos with which he dwells upon the rapidly vanishing peculiarities of the old-fashioned world.

Lamb, Leigh Hunt, and Hazlitt may be taken to represent this last phase of the old town life before the town had become a wilderness. They have all written admirable essays, though Hunt's pure taste and graceful style scarcely atone for the want of force or idiosyncrasy. No such criticism could be made against his friends. Lamb was not only the pet of his own clique, but the pet of all subsequent critics. To say anything against him would be to provoke indignant remonstrance. An attack upon him would resemble an insult to a child. Yet I will venture to confess that Lamb has some of the faults from which no favourite of a little circle is ever quite free. He is always on the verge of affectation, and sometimes trespasses beyond the verge. There is a self-consciousness about him which in some moods is provoking. There is a certain bigotry about most humourists (as of a spoilt child) which has become a little tiresome. People have come to talk as if a sense of humour were one of the cardinal virtues. To have it is to be free of a privileged class, possessed of an esoteric system of critical wisdom. To be without it is to be a wretched matter-of-fact utilitarian pedant. The professed humorist considers the rest of mankind as though they were deprived of a faculty, incapable of a relish for the finest literary flavours. Lamb was one of the first representatives of this theory, and is always tacitly warning off the profane vulgar, typified by the prosaic Scotchman who pointed out that his wish to see Burns instead of Burns' son was impracticable, inasmuch as the poet himself was dead. The pretension is, of course, put forward by Lamb in the most amiable way, but it remains a pretension. Most people are

A manuscript page from Lamb's essay "A Dissertation upon Roast Pig."

docile enough to accept at his own valuation, or at that of his admirers, any man who claims a special privilege, and think it wise to hold their tongues if they do not perceive it to be fully justified by the facts. But I admit that, after a certain quantity of Lamb, I begin to feel a sympathy for the unimaginative Scotchman. I think that he has something to say for himself. Lamb, for example, was a most exquisite critic of the authors in whom he delighted. Nobody has said such admirable things about the old English dramatists, and a little exaggeration may be forgiven to so genuine a worshipper. But he helped to start the nuisance of "appreciative criticism," which proceeds on the assumptive fancy that it necessarily shows equal insight and geniality to pick up pebbles or real jewels from the rubbish-heaps of time. Lamb certainly is not to be blamed for the extravagance of his followers. But this exaltation of the tastes or fancies of a little coterie has always its dangers, and that is what limits one's affection for Lamb. Nobody can delight too much in the essay upon roast pig—the apologue in which contains as much sound philosophy as fine humour—or in Mrs. Battle's opinions upon whist, or the description of Christ's Hospital, or the old benchers of the Temple, or Oxford in the Long Vacation. Only I cannot get rid of the feeling which besets me when I am ordered to worship the idol of any small sect. Accept their shibboleths, and everything will go pleasantly. The underlying conceit and dogmatism will only turn its pleasanter side towards you, and show itself in tinging the admirable sentiments with a slight affectation. Yet, one wants a little more fresh air, and one does not like to admire upon compulsion. Lamb's manner is inimitably graceful; but it reminds one just a little too much of an ancient beau, retailing his exquisite compliments, and putting his hearers on their best behaviour. Perhaps it shows the corruption of human nature, but I should be glad if now and then he could drop his falsetto and come out of his little entrenchment of elaborate reserve. I should feel certain that I see the natural man. "I am all over sophisticated," says Lamb, accounting for his imperfect sympathy with Quakers, "with humours, fancies craving hourly sympathy. I must have books, pictures, theatres, chitchat, scandal, jokes, antiquities, and a thousand whimwhams which their simpler taste could do without." There are times when the simpler taste is a pleasant relief to the most skilful dandling of whimwhams; and it is at those times that one revolts not exactly against Lamb, but against the intolerance of true Lamb worshippers.

The reader who is tired of Lamb's delicate confections, and wants a bit of genuine nature, a straightforward uncompromising utterance of antipathy and indignation, need not go far. Hazlitt will serve his turn; and for that reason I can very often read Hazlitt with admiration when Lamb rather palls upon me. If Hazlitt has the weaknesses of a cockney, they take a very different form. He could hardly have been the ideal of any sect which did not enjoy frequent slaps in the face from the object of its worship. He has acquired, to an irritating degree, the temper characteristic of a narrow provincial sect. He has cherished and brooded over the antipathies with which he started, and, from time to time, has added new dislikes and taken up grudges against his old friends. He has not sufficient culture to understand fully the bearing of his own theories;

and quarrels with those who should be his allies. He has another characteristic which, to my mind, is less pardonable. He is not only egotistical, which one may forgive, but there is something rather ungentlemanlike about his egotism. There is a rather offensive tone of self-assertion, thickly masked as self-depreciation. I should be slow to say that he was envious, for that is one of the accusations most easily made and least capable of being proved, against anyone who takes an independent view of contemporary celebrities; but he has the tone of a man with a grievance; and the grievances are the shocks which his vanity has received from a want of general appreciation. There is something petty in the spirit which takes the world into its confidence upon such matters; and his want of reticence takes at times a more offensive form. He is one of the earliest "interviewers," and revenges himself upon men who have been more popular than himself by cutting portraits of them as they appeared to him. Altogether he is a man whom it is impossible to regard without a certain distrust; and that, as I fancy, is the true reason for his want of popularity. No literary skill will make average readers take kindly to a man who does not attract by some amiable quality.

In fact, some explanation is needed, for otherwise we could hardly account for the comparative neglect of some of the ablest essays in the language. We may be very fine fellows now, but we cannot write like Hazlitt, says a critic who is more likely than anyone to falsify his own assertions. And when I take up one of Hazlitt's volumes of essays, I am very much inclined at times to agree with the assertion. They are apt, it is true, to leave a rather unpleasant flavour upon the palate. There is a certain acidity; a rather petulant putting forwards of little crotchets or personal dislikes; the arrogance belonging to all cliquishness is not softened into tacit assumption, but rather dashed in your face. But, putting this aside, the nervous vigour of the writing, the tone of strong conviction and passion which vibrates through his phrases, the genuine enthusiasm with which he celebrates the books and pictures which he really loves; the intense enjoyment of the beauties which he really comprehends, has in it something inspiring and contagious. There is at any rate nothing finicking or affected; if he is crotchety, he really believes in his crotchets; if he deals in paradoxes, it is not that he wishes to exhibit his skill, or to insinuate a claim to originality, but that he is a vehement and passionate believer in certain prejudices which have sunk into his mind or become ingrained in his nature. If every essayist is bound to be a dealer in commonplace or in the inverse commonplace which we call a paradox, Hazlitt succeeds in giving them an interest, by a new method. It is not that he is a man of ripened meditative wisdom who has thought over them and tested them for himself; nor a man of delicate sensibility from whose lips they come with the freshness of perfect simplicity; nor a man of strong sense, who tears away the conventional illusions by which we work ourselves into complacency; not a gentle humourist, who is playing with absurdities and appeals to us to share his enjoyable consciousness of his own nonsense; it is simply that he is a man of marked idiosyncrasy whose feelings are so strong, though confined within narrow channels, that his utterances have always the emphatic ring of true passion. When he talks about one of his favourites, whether Rousseau or Mrs. Inchbald, he has not perhaps much to add to the established criticisms, but he speaks as one who knows the book by heart, who has pored over it like a lover, come to it again and again, relished the little touches which escape the hasty reader, and in writing about it is reviving the old passionate gush of admiration. He cannot make such fine remarks as Lamb; and his judgments are still more personal and dependent upon the accidents of his early studies. But they stimulate still more strongly the illusion that one has only to turn to the original in order to enjoy a similar rapture. Lamb speaks as the epicure; and lets one know that one must be a man of taste to share his fine discrimination. But Hazlitt speaks of his old enjoyments as a traveller might speak of the gush of fresh water which saved him from dying of thirst in the wilderness. The delight seems so spontaneous and natural that we fancy—very erroneously for the most part—that the spring must be as refreshing to our lips as it was to his. We are ashamed after it when we are bored by the *Nouvelle Héloïse*.

There is the same kind of charm in the non-critical essays. We share for the moment Hazlitt's enthusiasm for the Indian jugglers, or for Cavanagh, the fives-player, whom he celebrates with an enthusiasm astonishing in pre-athletic days, and which could hardly be rivalled by a boyish idolater of Dr. Grace. We forget all our acquired prejudices to throw ourselves into the sport of the famous prize-fight between the gasman and Bill Neate; and see no incongruity between the pleasure of seeing one side of Mr. Hickman's face dashed into "a red ruin" by a single blow, and of taking a volume of Rousseau's sentimentalism in your pocket to solace the necessary hours of waiting.

It is the same, again, when Hazlitt comes to deal with the well-worn topics of commonplace essayists. He preaches upon threadbare texts, but they always have for him a strong personal interest. A commonplace maxim occurs to him, not to be calmly considered or to be ornamented with fresh illustrations, but as if it were incarnated in a flesh and blood representative, to be grappled, wrestled with, overthrown, and trampled under foot. He talks about the conduct of life to his son, and begins with the proper aphorisms about industry, civility, and so forth, but as he warms to his work, he grows passionate and pours out his own prejudices with the energy of personal conviction. He talks about "effeminacy," about the "fear of death," about the "main chance," about "envy," about "egotism," about "success in life," about "depth and superficiality," and a dozen other equally unpromising subjects. We know too well what dreary and edifying meditations they would suggest to some popular essayists, and how prettily others might play with them. But nothing turns to platitude with Hazlitt; he is always idiosyncratic, racy, vigorous, and intensely eager, not so much to convince you, perhaps, as to get the better of you as presumably an antagonist. He does not address himself to the gentle reader of more popular writers, but to an imaginary opponent always ready to take up the gauntlet and to get the worst of it. Most people rather object to assuming that position, and to be pounded as if it were a matter of course that they were priggish adherents of some objectionable theory. But if you can take him for the nonce on his own

terms and enjoy conversation which courts contradiction, you may be sure of a good bout in the intellectual ring. And even his paradoxes are more than mere wanton desire to dazzle. Read, for example, the characteristic essay upon "The Pleasure of Hating," with its perverse vindication of infidelity to our old friends, and old books, and you feel that Hazlitt, though arguing himself for the moment into a conviction which he cannot seriously hold, has really given utterance to a genuine sentiment which is more impressive than many a volume of average reflection. A more frequent contrast of general sentiment might, indeed, be agreeable. And yet, in spite of the undertone of rather sullen melancholy, we must be hard to please if we are not charmed with the occasional occurrence of such passages as these:

> I remember once strolling along the margin of a stream, skirted with willows and flashing ridges, in one of those sequestered valleys on Salisbury plain, where the monks of former ages had planted chapels and built hermit's cells. There was a little parish church near, but tall elms and quivering alders hid it from my sight; when, all of a sudden, I was startled by the sound of a full organ pealing on the ear, accompanied by the rustic voices and the rolling quire of village maids and children. It rose, indeed, like an inhalation of rich distilled perfumes. The dew from a thousand pastures was gathered in its softness, the silence of a thousand years spoke in it. It came upon the heart like the calm beauty of death; fancy caught the sound and faith mounted on it to the skies. It filled the valley like a mist, and still poured out its endless chant, and still it swells upon the ear and wraps me in a golden trance, drowning the noisy tumult of the world.

If the spirit of clique were invariably productive of good essay-writing, we should never be in danger of any deficiency in our supplies. But our modern cliques are so anxious to be cosmopolitan, and on a level with the last new utterance of the accepted prophet, that somehow their disquisitions seem to be wanting in individual flavour. Perhaps we have unknown prophets amongst us whose works will be valued by our grandchildren. But I will not now venture upon the dangerous ground of contemporary criticism.

John Dennis

SOURCE: "The Art of Essay Writing," in *The National Review,* London, Vol. I, No. 5, July, 1883, pp. 744-57.

[*Dennis was a minor English man of letters who is esteemed for his astute, wide-ranging literary criticism. However, his several unusually abusive attacks on the character and writings of Alexander Pope have largely diminished his posthumous status in the field. In the following excerpt, Dennis identifies the eighteenth century as the golden age of the essay and states that of the nineteenth-century essayists only Charles Lamb is comparable in achievement to the genre's preeminent practitioner, Joseph Addison.*]

With a few exceptions, the Essay, as it comes from the hands of Steele and Addison, of Goldsmith and Chesterfield, is a species of literature which belongs to the eighteenth century. At the beginning of that century it was born, and before the end of it the art had nearly ceased to exist. The essays that enlighten, and sometimes burden our own age, belong to a different order. They deal frequently with the profoundest problems of life, with science, with philosophy, and with a criticism unknown to our forefathers. The weightiest, the ripest, and, may I not add, the crudest thought of the age appears in periodicals. For the most part, the fare presented in our best reviews and magazines is of solid quality, and compressed, like tinned meats, within a narrow space. Like those meats, too, it is often more nourishing than grateful. Beef and plum-pudding are good in their way, but we sometimes prefer strawberries or grapes. The age is too busy and too earnest, I do not say too sensible, to enjoy the sportive humour and kindly satire so welcome in the reign of good Queen Anne and her immediate successors. How indeed can men "laugh and shake in Rabelais' easy chair" now that they have lost the leisure which made laughter so delightful? How, in the mighty growth and complexity of society, can they attempt to correct its errors with the humorous but gentle wisdom of Addison, and the genial sprightliness of Steele? . . .

I do not propose attempting to weigh the merits of essayists who belong to our own age. There is not space enough for such a review, neither is it necessary. We do not compare the masters of the Dutch school with the spiritual conceptions of Raphael, or with the landscapes of Turner. Something appropriate could be said, perhaps, of Leigh Hunt and Hazlitt, and a tribute almost affectionate might be paid to the memory of Sir Arthur Helps, whose cheerfully wise volumes are refreshing as the earliest blossoms of Spring. The author of *Friends in Council,* however, does not belong at all, and Hazlitt and Hunt belong in but slight measure, to the tribe of writers known as the old English essayists. Charles Lamb, although of our century by accident of birth, belongs in spirit to an earlier time, and it is impossible to touch on the art of essay writing without some recognition of a master who surpasses all his predecessors. In humorous conception, in tenderness of feeling, in that intuitive apprehension of what is fittest to say which is the prerogative of genius, in playfulness of fancy, and in the under-current of sadness that gives humanity to mirth, the author of *Elia* has no rival. His essays, in one respect, resemble fine poetry, for they will bear reading again and again, and out of each perusal some fresh charm may be extracted. And in Lamb's writings, as in that of his predecessors in the delightful art, it is the treatment and not the subject which gives vitality to an essay. He is discursive like Montaigne, and like him exhibits the easy frankness which makes a writer companionable. His latest and best biographer has justly said that a large portion of Lamb's history might be constructed from the essays alone, but his confidences are idealised and the glow of a rich imagination gives its colour to the homeliest fact. His style is not so natural as Addison's, or rather does not seem so natural, for in both cases "the art itself is nature." As Mr. Ainger observes: "It evades analysis. One might as well seek to account for the perfume of lavender or the

flavour of quince. It is in truth an essence prepared from flowers and herbs gathered in fields where the ordinary reader does not often range." No allusion is made by Mr. Ainger to Addison, but this apt illustration of Elia's style reminds us that a very different image would be needed to illustrate the simple charm of the *Spectator*. Each is perfect of its kind, and in both the style is the outward and visible sign of an interior beauty. England has greater names in literature than the names of Addison and Lamb, but few that are more dear; and he who would understand and enjoy the exquisite art of which they are masters, will find the best guidance and the most unfailing delight in the study of their works.

J. H. Lobban

SOURCE: An introduction to *English Essays,* edited by J. H. Lobban, 1896. Reprint by Blackie & Son, Limited, 1903, pp. ix-lxi.

[*In the following excerpt from his introduction to* English Essays, *originally published in 1896, Lobban focuses on the essay characteristics and accomplishment of Hunt, Hazlitt, and Lamb.*]

By the beginning of this century the face of society had changed, and the essay could no longer afford to confine its scope to "the town". As much as poetry the essay reflects the spirit of the age, and while the former was striking many new notes, the other, leaving aside antiquated scandal and pinchbeck sentimentalism, was being pressed into the service of political and philosophical exposition. When Leigh Hunt commenced to write essays, he was plainly under the spell of a past age, and the *Connoisseur* [a Georgian periodical edited by Colman and Thornton] was admittedly his model. Nor did he ever wholly succeed in throwing off the faded garments of the eighteenth century, and there is always present in his style a touch of archaism which makes one rank him with the earlier essayists rather than with his own vigorous contemporaries. In 1812 he was known only as an unusually capable dramatic critic, and it was not till seven years later that he began in the *Indicator* to revive the essay on the lines of Addison and Goldsmith. He cannot, however, be placed in the first rank of English essayists. In all his work there is a lack of virility, and he had no special endowment of pathos or of humour. When it is said that he could write commonplace gracefully, his merits and defects are summarized. His essays bear nowhere the impress of a strong personality, they contain no fresh creations, and they scarcely ever deviate from one level of unemotional calm. Yet he had indubitable skill in writing on familiar subjects, and he wielded a simple style that on rare occasions became even eloquent. The essays "On Sleep," and "On the Deaths of Little Children" are his finest pieces of word-painting. The former, if disfigured by some patches of cheap moralizing, concludes with two paragraphs of singular beauty, while the other, though not displaying Steele's pathos, nor Lamb's April blending of tears and smiles, is a masterpiece of tender imagery and artistic restraint. Leigh Hunt was a genuine man of letters, with no very strong feelings and with but little imagination, loving books and flowers, and able to treat any subject in a pleasant and cultured style.

The indisputable decline of his reputation is to be accounted for by his want of any striking originality, and by his being overshadowed by his greater contemporaries. Prior to the appearance of the *Indicator,* Hazlitt had done some of his best critical work, while Lamb, having given the results of his loving study of the early dramatists, was on the point of coming forward in the character of Elia. The exclusion of critical papers necessarily gives a totally inadequate representation of Hazlitt, who wrote his best only when art or literature was his theme. In him, much more distinctly than in Hunt or Lamb, a modern spirit is apparent. Save for a certain exuberance of style, there is nothing in his essays to suggest even now the flavour of antiquity; he approached his subjects with perfect originality and freshness; his style cannot be definitely linked to any prototype; and, as critics of his own day were quick to observe, "his taste was not the creature of schools and canons, it was begotten of Enthusiasm by Thought". It is enthusiasm, indeed, that is the most obvious characteristic of the essays—and they are his best essays—which he contributed between 1820 and 1830 to the *Examiner* and other papers. The traditional limits of the periodical essay, however, were somewhat narrow for the full display of Hazlitt's genius. He craved for "more elbow-room and fewer encumbrances", and, as Professor Saintsbury has said, "what he could do, as hardly any other man has ever done in England, was a *causerie* of about the same length as Sainte-Beuve's". None of his writings display those emotional qualities on which the reputation of the chief English essayists is based, and his success must be attributed to the virile excellence of his style, and to his passionate and unaffected love of letters. "My sun", he wrote, "arose with the first dawn of liberty. . . . The new impulse to ardour given to men's minds imparted a congenial warmth and glow to mine; we were strong to run a race together." Burke was the one author whom he never wearied of commending, and it was at the torch of Burke's eloquence that the fire of his own style was kindled. Fortunately for literature, it was to it and not to politics that Hazlitt directed his enthusiasm, with the result that, in spite of some prejudices and exaggerations, his writings are unrivalled as a stimulating introduction to the study of literature. His knowledge of books was as extensive as his devotion was profound; they were to him "the first and last, the most home-felt, the most heart-felt of all our enjoyments". Hazlitt's position among the essayists depends on the fact that he devoted himself less to the delineation of character than to the exposition of literature. If not the first, he was the most influential of those who bent the essay to this purely literary purpose, and he may be regarded as standing midway between the old essayists and the new. It was a fashion in his own time, and one that has often since been followed, to insist too strongly on Hazlitt's limitations as a critic. Yet, after all has been said, his method was essentially the same as Sainte-Beuve's, and his essays cannot even now be safely neglected by students of the literary developments with which they deal. It is impossible to read them without catching something of the ardour of his own enthusiasm, and it says much for the soundness of his taste and judgement that the great majority of his criticisms emerged undistorted from the glowing crucible of his thought.

While there is a strong egotism in his essays, Hazlitt can scarcely be called a "personal essayist", for he had no Jonsonian "humour", and he rode no Shandean hobby-horse. With him, indeed, any survey of the essay's history might end, for it would be possible to trace some affinity between him or some of his predecessors, and any of those who have subsequently used the essay form. At least one exception must be made in favour of Charles Lamb, who occupies in so many ways a unique place in the development, and who more closely than any other went back to the practice of Montaigne in allowing his personality to colour everything he wrote. The *Essays of Elia* began in 1822, at a time when Sydney Smith had already a secure reputation as a wit, and Christopher North was beginning to make the fame of *Blackwood's Magazine* by his riotous humour. Unlike either of these, Lamb was an anachronism. Everywhere around him literature was striking out new channels, and exaggerated protests were being made against the alleged artificiality of the previous century. Except at the demands of private friendship Lamb took little interest in contemporary writing; he remained constant to his first love for the past, and drew his inspiration from the pure wells of Elizabethan literature. He had mined deeply in Burton and in Fuller, in the old dramatists, and in the writers of artificial comedy; their idioms became his idioms, and he unconsciously brocaded his language with their quaint conceits and similitudes. "He evades the present", in the words of Hazlitt, "he mocks the future. . . . He pitches his tent in the suburbs of existing manners . . . and occupies that nice point between egotism and disinterested humanity." In his own phrase, he venerated an honest obliquity of understanding, and due weight must always be attached to the influence of his idiosyncrasies upon his style. As the works of Goldsmith and Hood derive new meaning when interpreted in the light of the records of their lives, so the *Essays of Elia* must be viewed against the tragic background of their author's life, before due appreciation can be made of the delicacy of their humour and of the infinte tenderness of their unobtrusive pathos. It leads rather to a misconception of Lamb to associate him only with so hackneyed an essay as the "Dissertation on Roast Pig". Exquisite fooling, no doubt, it is, but it has not the recondite beauties, the quaint paradoxes, the felicitous characterization, the intermingling of humour and pathos, that are everywhere apparent in his best essays. The descriptions of "Mrs. Battle" and of the "Convalescent" are masterpieces which more readily than most of his essays can be directly compared with the work of Addison and Goldsmith; "Dream-Children" is typical of Lamb's whimsical pathos and of the extreme delicacy of his touch; "Thoughts on Books" is the most charming confession extant of a literary creed; while "All Fools' Day" and the "New Year's Coming of Age" depict him in his most fantastic mood, toying with his subject, and wresting from it innumerable pleasantries. Lamb can scarcely be classed along with any other essayist; the archness and piquancy of his humour, if they sometimes remind one of Sterne, had for the most part an ancestry older than Addison and Steele, and it is only by going back to the writers of the seventeenth century that one fully detects the atavism of his style. "There is an inward unction, a marrowy vein both in the thought and feeling, an intuition deep and lively of his subject, that carries off any quaintness or awkwardness arising from an antiquated style and dress." In these happy words Hazlitt has pointed out the most indefinable feature in Lamb's essays—the rich marrowiness of their style. With their extra-ordinary nimbleness of fancy and grace of expression the *Essays of Elia* are indeed "a paradise of dainty devices", redolent of the sweetness and old-world air of Cowley. His quaint paradoxes, too, seem to rise naturally from the subject and do not grate on the ear with the metallic ring of modern epigram. The obliquity of Lamb's genius precluded in his own day, as it still precludes, the possibility of successful imitation; he created no new school of essayists, and he left no abiding mark on the development of English prose; but he is within certain well-defined limits one of the most artistic exponents of the essay, and the power of fully appreciating the delicacy of his work is one of the surest indications of a literary epicure.

In the case of a continuous development, as that of the essay must necessarily be, it is inevitable that one of the boundaries of the field surveyed should be arbitrarily imposed. The latter half of this century has shown little regard for the older style of essays on abstract subjects; the essay has more and more become associated with literary criticism; and it might almost be said that fiction has again entered into combat with it, and in the form of the short story has ousted it from popular regard. Yet, in spite of powerful rivals, the essay is still a vital literary form. What the sonnet is to the poet, the same and more is the essay to the prose artist, requiring similar compression of thought, and affording similar scope for brilliancy of execution. It would be hazardous to suppose that criticism of the future will regard the present age as marking a revival in the history of the development; but it is tolerably certain that no future collection of the best British essayists will ignore the work of Robert Louis Stevenson. . . . The real history of the essay coincides with the period of a century and a half which elapsed between the appearance of the *Tatler* and the year of Leigh Hunt's death. During that time its progress was more than once arrested, and it is a gain to clearness with small sacrifice of accuracy to regard the three critical periods in the essay's history as being the beginning, the middle, and the end of the eighteenth century—periods connected with the names of Steele and Addison, Johnson and Goldsmith, Hazlitt and Lamb. If not the greatest, the essay is certainly the most characteristic literary form of the eighteenth century. It owed its origin to the club-life of Queen Anne society, and true to its original purpose, it faithfully mirrored the manners of the day, when fiction presented nothing but ideals, and artificial comedy only caricature. It may be doubted, too, if any other literary development has been so prolific of results. No doubt the essay's greatest secondary achievement was the fillip it gave to the inauguration of the novel, but it founded, also, a requisite medium for literary criticism and created the miscellaneous magazine. Not, however, that the fame of the essay requires to be propped up by that of its various descendants. It has been the favourite medium of many of the greatest masters of English prose, who have lavished on it the best of their artistic skill and all the resources of their wisdom and humour. There is no end to the variety of subjects which the English essayists

have handled; no foible escaped their laughter, no abuse their scorn; for their motto has been, as it must continue to be, that which Steele selected for the first English periodical—

Quicquid agunt homines . . . . .
. . . . nostri est farrago libelli.

Elizabeth Drew

SOURCE: "The Essay," in *The Enjoyment of Literature*, W. W. Norton & Company, Inc., 1935, pp. 38-61.

[*In the following excerpt, Drew discusses and illustrates the significance of Hazlitt and Lamb in the familiar essay's development. She concludes by comparing their accomplishment with that of late-nineteenth and early-twentieth-century essayists, notably Max Beerbohm.*]

From very early days, when minor seventeenth-century writers wrote 'characters,' which, in general, were nothing but wooden descriptions of commonplace types, the essayist was fond of the character sketch. It lends itself naturally to the essay, and . . . the Sir Roger papers hold a unique place among early essays. Goldsmith did something of the same sort in his pictures of Beau Tibbs, and Lamb's 'Captain Jackson' is a little masterpiece in that style. These, however, are all very simple in their method of presentation, and a more complex treatment, which is indeed a most masterly illustration of the technique of the essay, is Hazlitt's My 'First Acquaintance with Poets'. It is a long essay—twenty-five pages in the edition I have of it—but once started upon it, there is no one, I think, who has any interest in the literary personalities of the early nineteenth century, who could possibly want to stop. It opens without preamble, and we are at once in the atmosphere of living presences.

> My father was a Dissenting Minister at Wem in Shropshire; and in the year 1798 . . . Mr. Coleridge came to Shrewsbury, to succeed Mr. Rowe in the spiritual charge of a Unitarian congregation there. He did not come till late on the Saturday afternoon before he was to preach; and Mr. Rowe, who himself went down to the coach in a state of anxiety and expectation to look for the arrival of his successor, could find no one at all answering the description but a round-faced man in a short black coat (like a shooting-jacket) which hardly seemed to have been made for him, but who seemed to be talking at a great rate to his fellow-passengers. Mr. Rowe had scarce returned to give an account of his disappointment, when the round-faced man in black entered, and dissipated all doubts on the subject, by beginning to talk. He did not cease while he stayed; nor has he since, that I know of. . . .

To Hazlitt, Coleridge's talk came as a revelation:

> A sound was in my ears as of a Siren's song; I was stunned, startled with it, as from deep sleep; but I had no notion then that I should ever be able to express my admiration to others in motley imagery or quaint allusion, till the light of his genius shone into my soul, like the sun's rays glittering in the puddles of the road. I was at that

time dumb, inarticulate, helpless, like a worm by the wayside, crushed, bleeding, lifeless; but now, bursting from the deadly bands that

bound them, With Styx nine times round them,

my ideas float on winged words, and as they expand their plumes, catch the golden light of other years. My soul has indeed remained in its original bondage, dark, obscure, with longing deep and unsatisfied; my heart, shut up in the prison-house of this rude clay, has never found, nor will it ever find, a heart to speak to; but that my understanding also did not remain dumb and brutish, or at length found a language to express itself, I owe to Coleridge. But this is not to my purpose.

It is very much to the purpose of the essay, however, for blended throughout with the sense of the actual presences of these men of genius in all the glory of their youth and hope, is the peculiar egotism of Hazlitt himself, the conviction that somehow he is the victim of an unfair fate, and the sense of almost unbearable regret and wistfulness with which he is looking back and remembering.

The scene of the sermon which Coleridge preached, and Hazlitt listened to, on the following day, follows, and then they are joined by the presence of Hazlitt's father, and the three of them sit eating their dinner and talking together in the warmest spirit of good fellowship. 'I remember the leg of Welsh mutton and the turnips on the table that day had the finest flavour imaginable.' When Coleridge has to leave, Hazlitt walks six miles with him on his way and again they talk, and something of the miracle of Coleridge's talk does take shape before us, and the magic of his personality as a young man, and the change, alas, which the years have brought. All through that winter, the magic dwelt with the young Hazlitt. One thought, he says, blotted out everything, *'I was to visit Coleridge in the spring.'* As a matter of fact he did not get there till the autumn, when we walk the journey with him, and get wet at Tewkesbury, and stop at the inn where he sat up all night reading *Paul and Virginia*. The next day he arrived.

> The country about Nether Stowey is beautiful, green and hilly, and near the sea-shore. I saw it but the other day, after an interval of twenty years, from a hill near Taunton. How was the map of my life spread out before me, as the map of the country lay at my feet. In the afternoon Coleridge took me over to All-Foxden . . . where Wordsworth lived. . . . Wordsworth himself was from home, but his sister kept house, and set before us a frugal repast; and we had free access to her brother's poems, the *Lyrical Ballads,* which were still in manuscript. . . .
>
> In the outset of life (and particularly at this time I felt it so) our imagination has a body to it. We are in a state between sleeping and waking, and have indistinct but glorious glimpses of strange shapes, and there is always something to come better than what we see. As in our dreams, the fullness of the blood gives warmth and reality to the coinage of the brain, so in youth our ideas are clothed, and fed, and pampered with our good spirits; we breathe thick with thoughtless

> happiness, the weight of future years presses on the strong pulses of the heart, and we repose with undisturbed faith in truth and good. As we advance, we exhaust our fund of enjoyment and of hope. We are no longer wrapped in lamb's-wool, lulled in Elysium. As we taste the pleasures of life, their spirit evaporates, the sense palls; and nothing is left but the phantoms, the lifeless shadows of what *has been!*
>
> . . . The next day Wordsworth arrived from Bristol at Coleridge's cottage. I think I see him now. He answered in some degree to his friend's description of him, but was more gaunt and Don Quixote-like. He was quaintly dressed . . . in a brown fustian jacket and striped pantaloons. There was something of a roll, a lounge in his gait, not unlike his own Peter Bell. There was a severe, worn pressure of thought about his temples, a fire in his eye (as if he saw something in objects more than the outward appearance), an intense high narrow forehead, a Roman nose, cheeks furrowed by strong purpose and feeling, and a convulsive inclination to laughter about the mouth, a good deal at variance with the solemn, stately expression of the rest of his face. . . . He sat down and talked very naturally and freely, with a mixture of clear gushing accents in his voice, a deep guttural intonation, and a strong tincture of the northern *burr,* like the crust on wine. He instantly began to make havoc of the half of a Cheshire cheese on the table. . . .

They all went over again to All-Foxden, and we hear them reading poetry aloud in the open air, and talking endlessly; and we see them sitting in the low latticed window, or in the garden, and again talking endlessly, and we hear that Coleridge likes to compose walking over uneven ground, or breaking through the straggling branches of a copse wood: whereas Wordsworth always wrote, if he could, 'walking up and down a straight gravel path, or in some spot where the continuity of his verse met with no collateral interruption.'

Then they left Dorothy behind, and set off on a walking tour down the coast to Lynton, staying in sweet country inns, and listening to the fisher-folk, and talking away among themselves as hard as ever. When they returned, Hazlitt set out for his home again, and Coleridge for Germany, and the scenes fade out. . . . For a moment Lamb looks in and makes a remark, and then the essay ends.

The reader is so caught up and carried along by the writing, that it is not until the whole is analyzed and anatomized that we realize the brilliance of the artistry with which its varied strands are knit together, its varied emotions fused into a unity of effect. It appeals to so much of the total human consciousness: to purely intellectual interests, to dramatic emotions, to the sense of common curiosity, to reverence and admiration, to laughter and pity, to eye and ear and physical sensation, and to the ache in the heart of every human being who has lost his youth and its dreams.

It is time to say something of the greatest artist among English essay-writers—Charles Lamb. It would be interesting to work out a comparison between his essay on "Old China" and Hazlitt's "My First Acquaintance with Poets," and to note in detail the different methods of two artists, with widely different personalities, dealing with something of the same sort of theme. Both create extraordinarily living figures and both intertwine the past and the present to gain a particular effect. Lamb writes in a mood of comedy, Hazlitt in one of disillusion; Lamb uses the dramatic method, Hazlitt the descriptive; and each essay is a masterpiece of its kind. But something more general must be said of Lamb.

I suspect there are times when all readers who do not regard Lamb as 'Saint Charles' find his exaggerated 'quaintness' irritating; when his description of his own writings as 'villainously prank't in an affected array of antique modes and phrases,' seems justly to sum up their weakness; when his so carefully created personality palls. But these are definitely, I think, some of those occasions when the reader is at fault, when 'habit and lethargy have dulled his palate.' For to come freshly and without prejudice to Lamb is to confess that, within the limits of the essay, he is perfection. This perfection is partly the result of a unique temperament, partly the effect of a unique kind of learning and thinking, and partly sheer technical mastery of his medium. One great element in his success is the tangibility, the concreteness of the world he creates. Lamb is sometimes spoken of as if he were a shy, elusive, almost dim figure. He was, of course, shy and retiring in life; he stammered and was insignificant-looking; he hated publicity and 'occasions.' But there is no one who is more clearly embodied in his writing. There the outline of his own figure is cleanedged, firm and sure, projected in the round, unlike the figure of anybody else; significant, unique.

> In proportion as the years both lessen and shorten, I set more count upon their periods, and would fain lay my ineffectual finger upon the spoke of the great wheel. I am not content to pass away, 'like a weaver's shuttle.' Those metaphors solace me not, nor sweeten the unpalatable draught of mortality. I care not to be carried with the tide, that smoothly bears human life to eternity; and reluct at the inevitable course of destiny. I am in love with this green earth; the face of town and country; the unspeakable rural solitudes, and the sweet security of streets. I would set up my tabernacle here. I am content to stand still at the age to which I am arrived; I, and my friends: to be no younger, no richer, no handsomer. I do not want to be weaned by age; or drop, like mellow fruit, as they say, into the grave.—Any alteration, on this earth of mine, in diet or in lodging, puzzles and discomposes me. My household-gods plant a terrible fixed foot, and are not rooted up without blood. They do not willingly seek Lavinian shores. A new state of being staggers me.

> Sun, and sky, and breeze, and solitary walks, and summer holidays, and the greenness of fields, and the delicious juices of meats and fishes, and society, and the cheerful glass, and candle-light, and fireside conversations, and innocent vanities, and jests, and *irony itself*—do these things go out with life?

> Can a ghost laugh, or shake his gaunt sides, when you are pleasant with him?
> And you, my midnight darlings, my Folios! must I part with the intense delight of having you (huge armfuls) in my embraces? Must knowledge come to me, if it come at all, by some awkward experiment of intuition, and not linger by this familiar process of reading?

We know Lamb as perhaps we know no other writer of essays. The precision and clarity and grace of his presentation of himself delight the sensuous imagination everywhere. We have glimpses of the childhood of some of the other essayists, of Cowley, of Steele, of Hazlitt, but we know none of them as we know the child Elia. We see him turning over the pages of the old illustrated Bible, putting his fingers through the picture of the Ark, and shuddering over the Witch of Endor calling up Samuel: we see him at the rapture of his first play, or reading Cowley in the hot window seat of the storeroom at Blakesmoor, with the hum and flapping of the solitary wasp; we know him wandering in the green lanes at Mackery End, or as a schoolboy bathing all day long, like an otter, in the New River at Newington.

It is with the same clear outline that the reader sees his relations and friends, his own adult life, and indeed, everything his pen touches—Captain Jackson helping himself cheerfully to cheese-rind, or Mrs. Battle sitting bolt upright with her cards; Bridget Elia slicing French beans, or the tired little chimney-sweep asleep on the freshly laundered aristocratic sheets. But the extreme clarity of outline with which we see everything that Lamb wants us to see, is perhaps inclined to make us forget that there are a number of things which he does not wish us to see. We know him so well where we do know him, that we take no account of the gaps in our knowledge. But Lamb never speaks about himself in the way Hazlitt, for instance, does: we are completely ignorant of what he really thinks or of what he really feels about his own life, and its course and its conditions.

Nevertheless, we find more of a complete man in the essays of Elia than in any other English essays. We have his finely cut, keen and original mind, his leaping freakish nonsense, his tenderness, his irrational prejudices, his myriad moods of grave and gay. Like almost all great artists Lamb has created an unmistakable world of his own in his art. His style composes, as it were, a new element, in which we live and move and breathe while we read him; an atmosphere which is formed by that peculiar and unique use of language of his, and which seals the reader from the familiar and commonplace. Words are his slaves. There is never the slightest danger in Lamb of the atmosphere being dispersed by his lack of the skill to sustain it. There is no blurring or feebleness or fumbling. He can make his instrument communicate exactly what he wishes it to, whether he is criticizing the tragedies of Shakespeare, or wandering through Oxford in the vacation, or describing a poor relation. His language can be as sumptuous and sonorous as Milton or as simple as Steele, and his power of enlarging his effects with the subtleties and suggestion of quotation and allusion might be compared with that modern master of the same art, Mr. T. S. Eliot.

There are very few essayists whose creation of personality can be spoken of in the same breath with Lamb. Some create mannerisms by which we recognize them easily, some—Macaulay and Pater and G. K. Chesterton, for example—have a peculiar character of mind which stamps everything they write and gives it a vitality of its own, but that is not the same thing as the creative egotism of the pure essayist. The only modern writer who touches that particular quality is Max Beerbohm. His essays have not the width and variety of Lamb; he has none of Lamb's vast reading, his marrowy meditative vein, his direct humanity. He is detached, sophisticated in his simplicity, sly and very quiet in his humor and wit. The unity of his work is not the unifying of a wide diversity of moods into one personality, but rather the unifying of a whole personality into a single mood. The tone of his voice never changes, but it is an individual voice of great polish and distinction.

> It is not easy (says Hazlitt) to write a familiar style. Many people mistake a familiar for a vulgar style, and suppose that to write without affectation is to write at random. On the contrary, there is nothing that requires more precision, and, if I may so say, purity of expression, than the style I am speaking of. . . . It is not to throw words together in any combination we please, but to follow and avail ourselves of the true idiom of the language.

There could not be a better description of the writing of Max Beerbohm. It reads as if it were the easiest thing in the world, but no one else has done it. His great talent in that style is the character sketch and the anecdote, and it must, I think, be noticeable to all readers, that it is undeniable that the more the essay tends towards biography, autobiography or fiction, the better we are pleased. The pure exploitation of personality is a ticklish business. As Montaigne says:

> 'Tis a rugged road, more so than it seems, to follow a pace so rambling and uncertain, as that of the soul; . . . to choose and lay hold of so many little nimble motions.

The soul, indeed, is so elusive and so difficult to capture in words that it almost always escapes, and either leaves the mind to comment, or has its place taken by a trivial and wordy egotism. The mind produces articles and treatises and critical essays which appeal to other minds, and provide intellectual stimulus, but a second-rate egotism produces that most tedious of all poor literature—the poor essay. And the fact that the average reader does, undoubtedly, find essays in general dull reading, leads us to an inescapable conclusion: the conclusion that the essay does not today satisfy many of the needs which literature does satisfy, or at any rate does not satisfy them nearly so well as either biography or fiction.

Melvin R. Watson

SOURCE: "The Familiar Essay and the Tradition," in *Magazine Serials and the Essay Tradition: 1746-1820,* Louisiana State University Press, 1956, pp. 69-86.

[*In the following excerpt, Watson discourses on the flowering of the familiar essay and on Hunt, Lamb, and Hazlitt as its preeminent authors.*]

Despite numerous studies of the familiar essay and essayists, the relationship between the development of Lamb, Hazlitt, and Hunt and the essay tradition of Addison and Steele has never been fully treated. The reason for this situation is obvious. Attention has been focused principally upon the mature work of these writers where the familiar essay has completely flowered. By 1820, except in the writings of Leigh Hunt, who remained fairly loyal to Addison and Steele throughout his life, the tradition had been completely transformed into a new creation which had few resemblances to the old; but from 1802 on, and especially during the decade after 1810, these men were experimenting, just as other essay serialists had done, and they started on the firm foundation of the tradition.

During this experimental period it was Leigh Hunt who was the daring entrepreneur and who furnished the laboratories in which these literary scientists could work. In the *Examiner* and *Reflector* the freedom which Lamb, Hazlitt, and even Hunt himself needed was provided. John and Leigh Hunt founded the *Examiner* in 1808 with the objects of assisting "in producing Reform in Parliament, liberality of opinion in general . . . and a fusion of literary taste into all subjects whatsoever"; but except for a few scattered essays from Leigh Hunt's pen and the department called "Theatrical Examiner," it was not until 1814 that this Sunday paper became an important repository for the literary periodical, though it still retained its general character of a miscellany. Several years after the establishment of the *Examiner,* John Hunt projected a literary journal which his brother edited. Leigh Hunt's "Prospectus" throws light on the attitude toward contemporary magazines and promises the reader a different kind of fare:

> The *Reflector* will be an attempt to improve upon the general character of Magazines, and all the town knows, that much improvement of this kind may be effected without any great talent. Reform of periodical writing is as much wanted in Magazines, as it formerly was in Reviews, and still is in Newspapers. . . . The old Magazines are notorious in their dotage; and as to the new ones, that have lately appeared, they have returned to the infancy of their species—to pattern-drawing, doll-dressing, and a song about Philips. . . . The principal feature of [the *Reflector*] will be *Miscellaneous Literature,* consisting of Essays on Men and Manners, Enquiries into past and present Literature, and all subjects relative to Wit, Morals, and a true Refinement.

Of this group of three writers, Leigh Hunt has the closest affinity to the essay tradition, and from its influence he never completely escaped. From "The Traveller" (1804-1805) to "The Occasional" (1859), he was often engaged in writing essay serials which show indebtedness to their eighteenth-century prototypes. Of the early essayists he preferred "open-hearted Steele with all his faults, to Addison with all his essays"; but he lays many tributes at the feet of the latter, and unlike Lamb and Hazlitt he mentions with praise the *Rambler, Idler, Adventurer, Connoisseur, Mirror,* and *Lounger.* His first venture in essay writing, as a matter of fact, was inspired, not by the *Tatler* or *Spectator,* but by George Colman and Bonnell Thornton's *Connoisseur,* which "gave me an entirely fresh and delightful sense of the merits of essay-writing." The resulting series of papers, published as "The Traveller" in an evening paper of the same name under the signature of "Mr. Town, *junior,* Critic and Censor-general" has not survived and is known to us only through the references in the *Autobiography;* but Hunt is frank enough to confess that they "were little read" and "were not at all noticed in public."

At first glance, Leigh Hunt's essays in the *Reflector* seem completely revolutionary. Here he seems to be scorning limitations and soaring freely wherever he will for as long as he pleases, but the revolution is more apparent than real. True, he took advantage of the freedom from space limitations—as Lamb did not—and wrote longer essays, one of which extends to nineteen octavo pages, and the subjects he chose have some originality and individuality; but the technique is familiar. Excluding the strictly political essays and the continuation of Voltaire's "Travels of Reason," there are four full-length papers and one short piece. And in them there are two dreams, an imaginary dialogue, and an oriental apologue, and all but one are thoroughly didactic. "On the Spirit Proper for a Young Artist" contains impersonal, fatherly advice and concludes with a dialogue on money-making; "An Analogical Essay on the Treatment of Intellectual Disorders, together with an Account of a Surprising Cure performed therein by the Writer when asleep" is cleverly conceived but is carried through, even to the long, didactic dream, in a traditional manner; and "The True Enjoyment of Splendour," the story of the poor man who enjoys vicariously the jewels worn by the royal favorite, breaks away from the habit of using pseudo-Oriental names but is caught in the toils of the formalized diction associated with eighteenth-century oriental style.

There remain the two essays which Hunt reprinted in the 1817 collected edition of the *Round Table.* One, the "Account of a Familiar Spirit, who visited and conversed with the Author, in a manner equally new and forcible, showing the Carnivorous Duties of all Rational Beings and the true end of Philosophy," later titled, with greater effectiveness, "On the Night-mare," introduces, after a long and serious philosophical discussion, the Prince of Nightmares who discourses on men and his connection with them. Granted that Hunt here gives a slight twist to the dream device and that he succeeds in writing an entertaining and sprightly essay in which the didactic element is only implicit, yet the foundation of the paper remains traditional. "A Day by the Fire," on the other hand, approaches the precincts of the familiar essay. The paper is a composite picture, comparable to "L'Allegro," of how a person might spend an ideal day indoors. The casual tone, especially of the opening, the use of "I" and of such phrases as "I frankly confess" or "I must not scruple to confess," and the occasional brief digressions show how close Hunt came to the familiar essay; but the intimate tone and the self-revealing mood are seldom achieved and never sustained. It is, I believe, the best example available of the essay in transition, but it is not the full-fledged familiar essay.

Although Hunt—at least until 1820—never approached any closer to the genuine familiar essay than he had in "A Day by the Fire," he was intermittently projecting in the *Examiner* new ideas for essays, including four serials. The "Round Table" is the only one of these which is remembered today—and that primarily because of Hazlitt's work—but the others are important for indicating where Hunt's sympathies lay. In the second issue of the journal he began "The Literary and Philosophical Examiner" with an introductory paper on periodical essays which praises his predecessors in a conventional manner, admits that "the age of periodical philosophy is perhaps gone by," but contends that "it will be my endeavor to avoid those subjects which have been already handled in periodical works, or at any rate if I should be tempted to use them, I will exert myself to give them a new air and recommendation." Other matters, however, attracted Hunt, and the serial was not continued. Later in the same year he inaugurated another series, "Miscellaneous Sketches," for which, in addition to factual, biographical, and historical sketches, he wrote three clever satirical essays. But "Upon the Heterogeneous Whimsicality of Names," "Breakfast Sympathies upon the Miseries of War," and "An Analytical Inquiry into the Intellectual and Inspiring Qualities of Wood" could have been written by a number of eighteenth-century essayists. In fact, the light, bantering tone and thoroughly objective attitude are typical of the better magazine serialists such as "Momus" or "Harlequin".

In 1813, yet another serial was started. "Table Talk," its title perhaps suggested by John Selden's work, was to be primarily a collection of notes on interesting subjects and is remembered today for Lamb's scattered contributions; but one paper by Hunt should be noticed. "May Weather," though in length allied to the eighteenth-century essay, is clearly transitional. Within the limits of less than a page, Hunt plays with the idea of typical May weather, explains the poor weather during early May in his time by the change of the calendar, quotes lines from John Milton's "On May Morning," digresses to Charles II, and concludes facetiously: "But hey-day! Where am I running to? I had almost forgotten this prepossessing thick wall,—this taking romantic spot of my own, ycleped Horsemonger Lane."

If for no other reason, Leigh Hunt's name should live because of the "Round Table" and his collaboration therein with Hazlitt. For the final issue of the 1814 volume of the *Examiner,* Hunt wrote a new prospectus, giving the plans for the coming year which include "a series of Articles, comprising subjects of Miscellaneous Interest, Literature, Manners, etc., headed the GENERAL EXAMINER." Regardless of how the serial developed, it started as a traditional imitation. In the advertisement to the collected edition Hazlitt records: "It was proposed by my friend, Mr. Hunt, to publish a series of papers in the *Examiner,* in the manner of the early periodical Essayists, the Spectator and Tatler." But Hunt in the introductory paper had already acknowledged the debt to his predecessors: "There has now been a sufficient distance of time since the publication of our good old periodical works, and a sufficient change in matters worthy of social observation, to warrant the appearance of a similar set of papers." The principal change proposed was the dropping of fictitious disguises, but this was no innovation in essay serials. Then despite this avowal, the essayists became "Knights" of the "Round Table." Though the disguises are thin and the machinery is nonessential, the framework remains to place this work squarely in the tradition. Nor is there anything novel in the length of the essays, the suggestions to correspondents, or the announced subject matter. Furthermore, in discarding the more artificial devices and in refraining largely from didacticism and satire, Hunt and Hazlitt allied themselves, perhaps unconsciously, with the later development of the tradition.

The essays by Hunt, as might be expected, are more completely in the tradition than those by Hazlitt, these sixteen papers containing much of the conventional material found in the series. Especially do we find this characteristic in the letters: the request for admission as Squire to the Knights of the Round Table; the plea for advice from the Journeyman Mechanic who has been advised against marriage by a convert to Malthusian economics; the two contracted views in the rejoinders to former papers on the ability of women; and the remarks on various correspondence with an extract from a second letter by the would-be Squire—all are done in the eighteenth-century spirit and manner. "On Commonplace People" and "On Talking Nonsense" in their lightness and sprightliness of tone and their circular approach to the subject employ a well-established technique; and the three didactic lectures, on egotism, in defense of women, and on death and burial, contain no novel methods. Finally, the two critical papers, interesting as their subject matter is, are old-fashioned in treatment.

Three papers, three pictures of characters, show Hunt departing slightly from the tradition. His different conception of the character sketch is expressed in a long introduction to the essay "On Washerwomen," in which he advocates "direct picture-making . . . in detached sketches of men and things." The portrait of the washerwomen with its splendid bits of dialogue and its racy descriptions of the washerwomen's work is a masterful vignette. The other two, however, are composite portraits of types: "The Old Lady" and "The Maid Servant" differ from most previous characters in that there is no satire and that the general environment, the life, and activity are stressed rather than merely the personality traits; but these sketches lack any genuine vitality or individuality.

But in spite of their traditional nature, the literary worth of these essays must be recognized. They are well written, and the best of them possess a spontaneity, a vivacity, a good-naturedness that characterize much of Hunt's writing. His subjects are often clever adaptations of oft-told themes into which he infuses new life; but his general method and technique make no effort to break away from the essay tradition of the preceding century. In his own writing before 1820, Hunt did little to foreshadow the familiar essay.

Actually, Lamb started his essay career before Hunt did. In the *Morning Post* for February 1, 1802, appeared "The Londoner, No. 1," the beginning of what was obviously intended to be an essay serial, though it never got beyond this first number. According to well-established tradition, Lamb starts with his autobiography, which, though characterized by sprightliness and realistic detail, is conventional in method. But it was not until eight years later that Lamb was offered the chance to show his abilities in the essay form. As E. V. Lucas cogently remarks: "The *Reflector* gave Lamb his first encouragement to spread his wings with some of the freedom that an essayist demands." Yet, in spite of this freedom of space and subject matter, Lamb continued in the tradition.

With the exception of two critical essays, which are in a class by themselves, Lamb's contributions to the *Reflector* fall into a well-defined pattern using the devices of fictitious correspondents and character sketches. Under such names as "Pensilis," "Crito," "Moriturus," and "Edax," Lamb complains of the inconveniences of being hanged and of confusing moral and personal deformity; ponders on burial societies; and pleads for a sympathetic understanding of a voracious appetite. There are character sketches of an undertaker and a good clerk, done in a mixture of seventeenth-century method and eighteenth-century manner; there are handbills, one of which is probably genuine, and one undoubtedly fictitious, and there is even a club—of damned authors. Throughout, the tone is Lamb's own with a gentle whimsy substituted for satire, but the light, humorous touches, which are a dominant feature of these papers, are equally as characteristic of Addison and Steele; and the method is completely conventional.

The three delightful letters published in the last number of the *Reflector* are representative. "A Bachelor's Complaint of the Behaviour of Married People" begins in a conventional manner: "I am a single man not quite turned of forty, who have spent a good deal of my time in noting down the infirmities of Married People"; and then protests against those couples who are too loving, against their "excessive airs," and against the stratagems which many wives employ to wean their husbands away from former friends. In enumerating some of the "mortifications" suffered from such wives, "Innuptus" uses the time-honored Romanized names of "Testacea" and "Cerasia." Even the final paragraph is in the best essay-periodical manner: "But I am weary of stringing up all my married acquaintance under Roman denominations. Let them amend and change their manners, or I promise to send you the full-length English of their names, to be recorded to the terror of all such desperate offenders in future." "Edax" proposes "to lay before you a case of the most iniquitous persecution that ever poor devil suffered," the persecution of an all-consuming appetite, which is constantly misunderstood by all his friends and which will surely be responsible for his ultimate downfall. The literary allusions and quotations, the gross exaggeration of situation, the broad humor—seasoned with a dash of pathos—instantly classify "Edax on Appetite." "Hospita on the immoderate Indulgence of the Pleasures of the Palate" is a companion piece to "Edax" and records—again with exaggeration—the trials of a household in which such a man as Edax is a regular visitor. Hospita's account immediately calls to mind the innumerable domestic problems thrown into the laps of essay-periodical editors. To be sure, there is a great deal of Lamb in the most conventional of these essays; but it is essential to remember that the *Elia* papers did not burst full-grown from the brow of their creator. They are the result of training which started with the century-old essay tradition.

Lamb's second attempt at an essay serial suffered the same fate as his earlier one. "Theatralia" started out brilliantly with one of Lamb's finest critical essays, "On Garrick, and Acting; and the plays of Shakespeare, considered with reference to their fitness for Stage Representation," a lengthy development of the famous paradox "that the plays of Shakespeare are less calculated for performance on a stage, than those of almost any other dramatist whatever." But his concluding promise that "in some future Number I propose to extend this inquiry to his [Shakespeare's] Comedies; and to shew why Falstaff, Shallow, Sir Hugh Evans, and the rest, are equally incompatible with stage representation" was thwarted by the cessation of the magazine. The other critical essay in the *Reflector,* "On the Genius and Character of Hogarth," shows the same mastery of method and technique as the paper on Shakespeare. Since they are about three times as long as the other essays, these two critiques contrast strangely with Lamb's other contributions. The only logical conclusion seems to be that by 1811, Lamb had attained mastery of the critical essay but was still in the experimental stage of the familiar essay.

"Confessions of a Drunkard," "On Christ's Hospital and the Character of the Christ's Hospital Boys," and "On the Melancholy of Tailors," the only three essays published by Lamb between 1811 and August 1820, when he made his first appearance in the *London Magazine,* are still transitional. The first, though in letter form, is unsigned and is slightly longer than similar *Reflector* papers; but in tone and technique it is entirely comparable to "Edax on Appetite." The last, signed "Burton, Junior," is brief and written in the same tone as "On the Danger of Confounding Moral with Personal Deformity." But the other is the most interesting, since it can be compared with an *Elia* essay on the same subject. The earlier recollections were written with a definite purpose in mind: to defend the governors of Christ's Hospital against "the public charges of favouritism and the undue distribution of influence." This fact may account for the excessive objectivity and impersonality—in spite of personal reminiscence—which strike one immediately. The character sketches lack the vividness and the anecdotes have little of the intimacy which characterize Lamb's mature essays. "Christ's Hospital Five and Thirty Years Ago," on the other hand, is in one way complementary to the earlier paper. According to Elia, the former essay is a "magnificent eulogy" in which Lamb "has contrived to bring together whatever can be said in praise of [the cloisters], dropping all the other side of the argument most ingeniously." Elia's reminiscences mix the bitter with the sweet. From the mild irony of the beginning, in which Lamb is characterized as a favored, fortunate schoolboy, to the catalogue of "Grecians," this is Lamb at his best—chatty, vivid, intimate. The early essays have many virtues, but they are most important for showing Lamb as an artist in transition.

Though Hazlitt was over thirty-five when he started writing for the *Examiner,* he still had to experiment for several years before he hit the right combination which produced such essays as "My First Acquaintance with the Poets," "On Going a Journey," or "On the Pleasure of Hating." Like Leigh Hunt, he started his essay career as a devotee of the Steelean essay: "Of all the periodical Essayists, (our ingenious predecessors,) the *Tatler* has always appeared to us the most accomplished and agreeable. . . . We have always preferred the *Tatler* to the *Spectator.* . . . The *Tatler* contains only half the number of volumes, and we venture to say, at least an equal quantity of sterling wit and sense." But, unlike Hunt, he had no appreciation for the eighteenth-century imitators. The *Rambler* is "a collection of moral Essays, or scholastic theses" in which the charm of the earlier periodicals is quite lost; the *Adventurer* is "completely trite and vapid"; the *World* and *Connoisseur* are "a little better"; but the *Lounger* and *Mirrour* need only be mentioned to show their inferiority. Yet despite Hazlitt's admiration for the "first sprightly runnings," the "freshness," the "strokes of humor" of the *Tatler,* he was unable to imitate it.

The advertisement to the 1817 edition of the *Round Table* makes clear that imitation of the tradition was the aim. Hazlitt attempts to explain the failure of this aim when he says: "Our plan had been no sooner arranged and entered upon, than Bonaparte landed at Frejus, *et voila la Table Ronde dissoute.* Our little congress was broken up as well as the great one: Politics called off the attention of the Editor from the Belles Lettres; and the task of continuing the work fell chiefly upon the person who was least able to give life and spirit to the original design. A want of variety in the subjects and mode of treating them, is, perhaps, the least disadvantage resulting from this circumstance." But to recognize that the serial is not a successful imitation of the *Tatler* does not deny its place in the tradition. As a matter of fact, Hazlitt's early essays depart relatively little from the traditional subject matter and method. His ideas, his attitude toward life and literature were formed early and changed little, but his style and his method in the essay altered greatly about 1820.

The half-dozen attempts to write social satire are perhaps the most significant evidence of his unsuccessful imitation of the tradition. There is little doubt that in these essays Hazlitt would have liked to laugh at the foibles he was attacking, but indignation invariably mastered him. In his writing he was too intense, too good a hater to smile genially at what he considered vices. "On Good-Nature," for example, is an impassioned attack on what its author believes is a hypocritical attitude. The good-natured person cares only for his own comfort and is content to let the world alone so long as he is not troubled. The generalized character sketches of the good-natured man and the well-meaning man, his near kinsman, are severe and biting. The same technique appears in "Respectable People," for respectability to Hazlitt "means a man's situation and success in life, not his character or conduct." The concluding sentence is typical Hazlittian satire: "To be an Edinburgh Reviewer is, I suspect, the highest rank in modern literary society." But perhaps the best illustration of this tendency is "On Fashion," which contrasts strangely with

Steele's skirmishes on the same subject, the difference, however, being more one of means than of end. Hazlitt is heavy and serious, Steele is light and humorous; Hazlitt pounds with a bludgeon, Steele thrusts deftly with a rapier. And the other essays in this group reinforce this conclusion.

Most of the other essays tend to be matter-of-fact, straight-forward, analytical, impersonal, and often slightly didactic discussions. Sometimes the subject brings up memories of the eighteenth-century serials; sometimes for brief moments there are hints of the essayist-to-be; often new light is thrown on a topic by a freshness of approach; but only in several isolated instances is the reader struck forcibly by the difference of treatment. The two articles on manner are a good illustration. Formed as an elaboration of Lord Chesterfield's dictum that manner is of more importance than matter, the first paper stresses the importance of how a thing is done and the essential qualities of good humor and spirit. It concludes with a paragraph on grace, "the outward expression of the inward harmony of the soul." The second part begins with an illustration of the difference of manner in two objects when the matter remains the same, drawn from a comparison of the "Flower and the Leaf " and Dryden's paraphrase; continues with Chesterfield's character of the Duke of Marlborough, a good example of the general theory of manner; includes a paragraph on grace as an essential quality in women; and concludes with the acknowledgment that manner is not everything. Several characteristics should be noted. In the first place, everything is orderly and has its place in the general structure. The section on manner and matter is a digression, but a self-conscious one which was omitted in the 1817 edition. In the second place, the personal allusions, to "one of the most pleasant and least tiresome persons of our acquaintance" and "another friend of ours," are not in the least intimate. The core of the essays is drawn from reading, not from experience. Finally, the discussion, which originally occupied two numbers of the "Round Table," was condensed into one number in the collected edition.

An even better example of this impersonal, didactic tendency is "On the Love of Life," Hazlitt's first contribution to the "Round Table." "It is our intention," he begins, "in the course of these papers, occasionally to expose certain vulgar errors, which have crept into many of our reasonings on men and manners." Then in the most concise, traditional way possible he contends that "the love of life is, in general, the effect not of our enjoyments, but of our passions. We are not attached to it so much for its sake, or as it is connected with happiness, as because it is necessary to action." Inserted into this brief essay are acknowledged quotations from Addison, Jeremy Taylor, and Milton and unacknowledged ones from Spenser, Henry Fielding, Wordsworth, and possibly Bacon. With a didactic aim and a formal manner familiarity is hardly to be expected.

Despite the scarcity of "familiarity" in these essays, all of them are by no means so barren of interest as the preceding paragraphs may imply. As in the satirical papers, the reader can always be fascinated by Hazlitt's vituperative powers, especially by the milder form exemplified in "The

Tendency of Sects" and "Nicknames"; or by a sudden flaring up of anti-intellectualism, similar to eighteenth-century attacks on pedants, in "The Ignorance of the Learned." But most interesting and significant are those papers in which Hazlitt approaches the preserves of the familiar essay. In this group the qualities which make the familiar essay a distinctive literary genre are seen creeping into Hazlitt's writing. Intimate details, personal reminiscences, digressive passages indicate a change in attitude toward the essay and in method of composition.

"On the Love of Nature" begins as an urbane attempt to explain the phenomenon psychologically but develops into a sincere tribute to the effect of nature on a sympathetic spirit. A different method is employed in "Different Sorts of Fame." After a quotation from William Melmoth's *Fitz-Osborn's Letters* on the futility of posthumous fame and comments on the inherent sophism in the statement and the reputation achieved by Junius and James Elphinston, the translator of the *Rambler* mottoes, a personal confession is quite unobtrusively introduced: "For our own parts, one object which we have in writing these Essays, is to send them in a volume to a person who took some notice of us when children, and who augured perhaps better of us than we deserved." That Hazlitt grew to realize the value of informality, of personal reminiscences, and of fancy is shown too in "Actors and Acting." The first part, a justification of the stage as a refiner of manners, a teacher of morals, and a source of amusement, makes no preparation for the section on actors, where Hazlitt recalls the actors he has seen, imagines the consequences if all the great actors of the past should appear in London during a single season, and acknowledges that for him the early career of an actor, the provincial engagements, would be more exciting than London triumphs. What begins as an old-fashioned defense of the stage turns into a familiar essay.

Several other times too Hazlitt foreshadows his future triumphs. The charm of "On Pedantry" rests on its different definition of pedantry, its chatty tone, its use of digressions, and its personal allusions. For Hazlitt, pedantry is "the power of attaching an interest to the most trifling or painful pursuits. . . . He who is not in some measure a pedant, though he may be a wise, cannot be a very happy man." The discussion takes up two numbers and skips happily from topic to topic, touching lightly on the charm of old novels, the professional jargon of physicians, the decline in the use of original texts by divines, the disuse of ancient languages, the policy followed by the *Tatler* and *Spectator* of sacrificing learning to the graces, Chaucer's description of the "Clerk of Oxenford," the slight profit to the arts from "universal diffusion of accomplishment and pretension," the relativity of the term "gentleman," and chivalrous and romantic love. No idea, it seems, comes amiss, and space is even found for an allusion to the impressiveness of the weighty volumes of the *Fratres Poloni* as they stood on the shelves of the Hazlitt library. It is, on the other hand, the liveliness, the enthusiasm, the gusto of the writing that make "Character of the Country People" notable. This paper, the last written by Hazlitt before he started contributing to the *London Magazine,* shows that he was moving rapidly toward the familiar essay. Composed at Winterslow Hut, it treats actual experiences with the rustics and the conclusions drawn from these experiences. It is studded with allusions to the author, his friends, and his neighbors and shows his mature method of incorporating quotations from various sources into the body of the text. Doubtless, Hazlitt wrote more genial and charming essays than this one but none that is more typical of his development.

Over a third of his papers included in the 1817 edition of the *Round Table* deal with the arts and are critical; but since most of these are personal appreciations of individual works of art, allied in method to Steele's impressionistic criticism, or individualistic treatments of theoretical problems, they seem nearer the familiar essay and present no such problems as the ones already discussed. There are papers on *Lycidas*, John Amory's *John Buncle, Midsummer Night's Dream,* William Hogarth's *Marriage à la Mode,* Wordsworth's *Excursion,* and the *Beggar's Opera;* there are analyses of Milton's versification, the character of Milton's Eve, and Edmund Kean's interpretation of Iago; and there are general discussions of beauty, imitation, and gusto in art. Though the technique used here is similar to that of some of Addison's and Steele's criticism, the content and style show that, like Lamb, Hazlitt achieved the familiar tone in the critical essays much earlier than elsewhere.

Finally, the use of the character and the letter should be briefly noted. Though Hazlitt admired the light, urbane, satirical sketches of the *Tatler,* he indulged only in serious analysis of character. Thus he maintained that William Pitt's power consisted entirely in the artful use of words and a certain dexterity of logical arrangement, and that the mainspring of Rousseau's personality was an extreme sensibility. His sketches of "John Bull" and the good-natured man, on the other hand, are not so sympathetic, reminding the reader more of Pope's satire than of Steele's. The letter form appears rarely in these early essays. In one instance Hazlitt dropped the letter disguise on republishing the essay; yet in another place he added it. But that he seldom used the device is sufficient proof that he felt little need for artificial objectivity in his essays.

Though hampered in its development for a century by the rule of the *Spectator* tradition, the familiar essay came into its kingdom about 1820, after the leaders had served a long apprenticeship under the ruling dynasty. Then, aided by the new periodicals, the temper of the age, and their own personalities, they became joint rulers in the kingdom of the essay; and under their beneficent rule it was legal for the essayist to express freely his inmost thoughts, his preferences and his prejudices, his sympathies and his antipathies, his reminiscences and his dreams.

STATUS OF THE GENRE

Agnes Repplier

SOURCE: "The Passing of the Essay," in *In the Dozy Hours, and Other Papers,* Houghton, Mifflin and Company, 1894, pp. 226-35.

[*Repplier was an American essayist during the late nineteenth and early twentieth centuries. A prolific writer, she published thirteen volumes of familiar essays. In the following work, Repplier claims that reports of the familiar essay's death are exaggerated.*]

It is the curious custom of modern men of letters to talk to the world a great deal about their work; to explain its conditions, to uphold its value, to protest against adverse criticism, and to interpret the needs and aspirations of mankind through the narrow medium of their own resources. A good many years have passed since Mr. Arnold noticed the growing tendency to express the very ordinary desires of very ordinary people by such imposing phrases as "laws of human progress" and "edicts of the national mind." To-day, if a new story or a new play meets with unusual approbation, it is at once attributed to some sudden mental development of society, to some distinct change in our methods of regarding existence. We are assured without hesitation that all stories and all plays in the near future will be built up upon these favored models.

To a few of us, perhaps, such prophetic voices have but a dismal ring. We listen to their repeated cry, "The old order passeth away," and we are sorry in our hearts, having loved it well for years, and feeling no absolute confidence in its successor. Then some fine afternoon we look abroad, and are amazed to see so much of the old order still remaining, and apparently disinclined to pass away, even when it is told plainly to go. How many times have we been warned that poetry is shaking off its shackles, and that rhyme and rhythm have had their little day? Yet now, as in the past, poets are dancing cheerfully in fetters, with a harmonious sound which is most agreeable to our ears. How many times have we been told that Sir Walter Scott's novels are dead, stone dead; that their grave has been dug, and their epitaph written? Yet new and beautiful editions are following each other so rapidly from the press, that the most ardent enthusiast wonders wistfully who are the happy men with money enough to buy them. How many times have we been assured that realistic and psychological fiction has supplanted its gay brother of romance? Yet never was there a day when writers of romantic stories sprang so rapidly and so easily into fame. Stevenson leads the line, but Conan Doyle and Stanley Weyman follow close behind; while as for Mr. Rider Haggard, he is a problem which defies any reasonable solution. The fabulous prices paid by syndicates for his tales, the thousands of readers who wait breathlessly from week to week for the carefully doled-out chapters, the humiliating fact that *She* is as well known throughout two continents as *Robert Elsmere,*—these uncontrovertible witnesses of success would seem to indicate that what people really hunger for is not realism, nor sober truthfulness, but the maddest and wildest impossibilities which the human brain is capable of conceiving.

And so when I am told, among other prophetic items, that the "light essay" is passing rapidly away, and that, in view of its approaching death-bed, it cannot be safely recommended as "a good opening for enterprise," I am fain, before acquiescing gloomily in such a decree, to take heart of grace, and look a little around me. It is discouraging, doubtless, for the essayist to be suddenly informed that his work is *in articulo mortis*. He feels as a carpenter might feel were he told that chairs and doors and tables are going out of fashion, and that he had better turn his attention to mining engineering, or a new food for infants. Perhaps he endeavors to explain that a great many chairs were sold in the past week, that they are not without utility, and that they seem to him as much in favor as ever. Such feeble arguments meet with no response. Furniture, he is assured,—on the authority of the speaker,—is distinctly out of date. The spirit of the time calls for something different, and the "best business talent"—delightful phrase, and equally applicable to a window-frame or an epic—is moving in another direction. This is what Mr. Lowell used to call the conclusive style of judgment, "which consists simply in belonging to the other parish;" but parish boundaries are the same convincing things now that they were forty years ago.

Is the essay, then, in such immediate and distressing danger? Is it unwritten, unpublished, or unread? Just ten years have passed since a well-printed little book was offered carelessly to the great English public. It was anonymous. It was hampered by a Latin title which attracted the few and repelled the many. It contained seven of the very lightest essays that ever glided into print. It grappled with no problems, social or spiritual; it touched but one of the vital issues of the day. It was not serious, and it was not written with any very definite view, save to give entertainment and pleasure to its readers. By all the laws of modern mentors, it should have been consigned to speedy and merited oblivion. Yet what happened? I chanced to see that book within a few months of its publication, and sent at once to London for a copy, thinking to easily secure a first edition. I received a fourth, and, with it, the comforting assurance that the first was already commanding a heavy premium. In another week the American reprints of *Obiter Dicta* lay on all the book counters of our land. The author's name was given to the world. A second volume of essays followed the first; a third, the second; a fourth, the third. The last are so exceedingly light as to be little more than brief notices and reviews. All have sold well, and Mr. Birrell has established—surely with no great effort—his reputation as a man of letters. Editors of magazines are glad to print his work; readers of magazines are glad to see it; newspapers are delighted when they have any personal gossip about the author to tell a curious world. This is what "the best business talent" must call success, for these are the tests by which it is accustomed to judge. The light essay has a great deal of hardihood to flaunt and flourish in this shameless manner, when it has been severely warned that it is not in accord with the spirit of the age, and that its day is on the wane.

It is curious, too, to see how new and charming editions of *Virginibus Puerisque* meet with a ready sale. Mr. Stevenson has done better work than in this volume of scattered papers, which are more suggestive than satisfactory; yet there are always readers ready to exult over the valorous "Admirals," or dream away a glad half-hour to the seductive music of "Pan's Pipes." Mr. Lang's *Essays in Little* and *Letters to Dead Authors* have reached thousands of people who have never read his admirable translations

from the Greek. Mr. Peter's essays—which, however, are not light—are far better known than his beautiful *Marius the Epicurean*. Lamb's *Elia* is more widely read than are his letters, though it would seem a heart-breaking matter to choose between them. Hazlitt's essays are still rich mines of pleasure, as well as fine correctives for much modern nonsense. The first series of Mr. Arnold's *Essays in Criticism* remains his most popular book, and the one which has done more than all the rest to show the great half-educated public what is meant by distinction of mind. Indeed, there never was a day when by-roads to culture were more diligently sought for than now by people disinclined for long travel or much toil, and the essay is the smoothest little path which runs in that direction. It offers no instruction, save through the medium of enjoyment, and one saunters lazily along with a charming unconsciousness of effort. Great results are not to be gained in this fashion, but it should sometimes be play-hour for us all. Moreover, there are still readers keenly alive to the pleasure which literary art can give; and the essayists, from Addison down to Mr. Arnold and Mr. Pater, have recognized the value of form, the powerful and persuasive eloquence of style. Consequently, an appreciation of the essay is the natural result of reading it. Like virtue, it is its own reward. "Culture," says Mr. Addington Symonds, "makes a man to be something. It does not teach him to create anything." Most of us in this busy world are far more interested in what we can learn to do than in what we can hope to become; but it may be that those who content themselves with strengthening their own faculties, and broadening their own sympathies for all that is finest and best, are of greater service to their tired and downcast neighbors than are the unwearied toilers who urge us so relentlessly to the field.

A few critics of an especially judicial turn are wont to assure us now and then that the essay ended with Emerson, or with Sainte-Beuve, or with Addison, or with Montaigne,—a more remote date than this being inaccessible, unless, like Eve in the old riddle, it died before it was born. Montaigne is commonly selected as the idol of this exclusive worship. "I don't care for any essayist later than Montaigne." It has a classic sound, and the same air of intellectual discrimination as another very popular remark: "I don't read any modern novelist, except George Meredith." Hearing these verdicts, one is tempted to say, with Marianne Dashwood, "This is admiration of a very particular kind." To minds of a more commonplace order, it would seem that a love for Montaigne should lead insensibly to an appreciation of Sainte-Beuve; that an appreciation of Sainte-Beuve awakens in turn a sympathy for Mr. Matthew Arnold; that a sympathy for Mr. Arnold paves the way to a keen enjoyment of Mr. Emerson or Mr. Peter. It is a linked chain, and, though all parts are not of equal strength and beauty, all are of service to the whole. "Let neither the peculiar quality of anything nor its value escape thee," counsels Marcus Aurelius; and if we seek our profit wherever it may be found, we insensibly acquire that which is needful for our growth. Under any circumstances, it is seldom wise to confuse the preferences or prejudices of a portion of mankind with the irresistible progress of the ages. Rhymes may go, but they are with us still. Romantic fiction may be submerged, but at present it is well above water. The essay may die, but just now it possesses a lively and encouraging vitality. Whether we regard it as a means of culture or as a field for the "best business talent," we are fain to remark, in the words of Sancho Panza, "This youth, considering his weak state, hath left in him an amazing power of speech."

William Dean Howells

SOURCE: "Editor's Easy Chair," in *Harper's Monthly Magazine,* Vol. CV, No. 629, October, 1902, pp. 802-05.

[*Howells was the chief progenitor of American realism and an influential American literary critic during the late nineteenth and early twentieth centuries. In the following excerpt, Howells laments the development of the "old-fashioned essay," with its lyrical, dramatic, epical, and ethical sense, into the structured, thesis-bound "article."*]

The old-fashioned essay, as we had it in Montaigne, and almost as we had it in Bacon, obeyed a law as subjective as that of the gypsy music which the Hungarian bands made so popular with us ten or fifteen years ago. Wandering airs of thought strayed through it, owning no allegiance stricter than that which bound the wild chords to a central motive. Often there was apparently no central motive in the essay; it seemed to begin where it would, and end where it liked. The author was bound to give it a name, but it did not hold him bound otherwise. It could not very well take for title a first line, or part of a first line, like those poems, now rarely written, which opened with some such phrase-as, When those bright eyes; or, Had I the wings; or, If yon sweet star. If it could, that would have been the right way of naming most of the essays which have loitered down to us from antiquity, as well as those which help to date the revival of polite learning. Such a custom would have befitted nearly all the papers in the *Spectator* and the *Tatler* and the *Rambler,* and the other periodicals illustrating the heyday of the English essay. These, indeed, preserved an essential liberty by setting out from no subject more severely ascertained than that which lurked in some quotation from the classics, and unless there was an allegory or an apologue in hand, gadded about at their pleasure, and stopped as far from it as they chose. That gave them their charm, and kept them lyrical, far from the dread perhaps of turning out a sermon, when the only duty they had was to turn out a song.

Just how or why the essay should have departed from this elder ideal, and begun to have a conscience about having a beginning, a middle and an ending, like a drama, or a firstly, secondly, and thirdly, like a homily, it would not be easy to say, though we feel pretty sure that it was not from any occasion of Charles Lamb's, or Leigh Hunt's, or William Hazlitt's, or their compeers, in bearing down to our day the graceful tradition which seems now to have been lost. We suspect that the change may have happened through the greater length to which the essay has run in modern times. You may sing a song for a certain period, but if you keep on you have an opera, which you are bound to give obvious form. At any rate, the moment came when the essay began to confuse itself with the article, and to assume an obligation of constancy to premises and conclu-

sions, with the effect of so depraving the general taste that the article is now desired more and more, and the essay less and less. It is doubtful, the corruption has gone so far, whether there is enough of the lyrical sense left in the reader to appreciate the right essay; whether the right essay would now be suffered; whether if any writer indulged its wilding nature, he would not be suspected of an inability to cultivate the growths that perceptibly nourish, not to say fatten, the intellect. We have forgotten, in this matter, that there are senses to which errant odors and flying flavors minister, as grosser succulences satisfy hunger. There is a lyrical sense, as well as a dramatic, an epical, an ethical sense, and it was that which the old-fashioned essay delighted.

Orlo Williams

SOURCE: "IV," in *The Essay,* Martin Secker, 1915, pp. 48-63.

[*In the following excerpt, Williams cites the hurried, deadline-driven modern world as the source of the familiar essay's decline, seeing little hope for the genre's resurrection.*]

So often with [our modern essayists] a good idea is spoiled by hasty thought and hasty composition, or they are obviously striving to raise fruit from a barren inspiration. They are compelled—and we are all to blame for it—to write a specified number of words at specified intervals, and, seeing that the greedy public makes no distinction between their best and their worst, act humanly upon this painful fact, and gaily collect this taskwork of theirs at the end of the year into pretty little books that save us the trouble of looking for Christmas presents.

In fact, the enormous demand for what is called occasional journalism has destroyed the essay as a work of art. Writers must live, and since "articles" that attract jaded readers for five minutes are well paid for, it is natural that few should spend hours polishing an essay that needs leisure and a cultivated mind for its enjoyment, when the result of their labour is certain to be rejected by any editor as not being topical or as wanting human interest. The huge development of journalistic enterprise to-day has its advantages, nor is it to be deplored that the best equipped writers of an age should contribute to the newspapers, but, the paramount influences in editorial offices being what they are, it is hopeless to look to journalism for permanent works of art. The editor's sole concern is with what his readers are thinking of now: the past is nothing to him, the extreme limit of his future is next week. His success lies in catching the particular; the universal spells ruin. If a man has in him an idea that hits the moments he must drag it out and fling it down in an hour or so, crude and ragged, or its season has passed for ever. The late Richard Middleton put the case well at the beginning of his little book *Monologues,* when he wrote, deploring the decay of the essay:

> The fact is, that essays are bad journalism in the literal sense of that elastic word, because they take no count of time, while it is the function of journalism to tear the heart out of to-day. A

good essay should start and end in a moment as long as eternity; it should have the apparent aimlessness of life, and, like life, it should have its secret purpose. Perhaps the perfect essay would take a lifetime to write and a lifetime to comprehend; but, in their essence, essays . . . ignore time and negate it. They cannot be read in railway trains by travellers who intend to get out at a certain station, for the mere thought of a settled destination will prevent the reader from achieving the proper leisurely frame of mind. Nor can they be written for a livelihood, for a man who sits down to write an essay should be careless as to whether his task shall ever be finished or not.

These words were written by a man who had in him both an essayist and a poet, yet failed to make a livelihood: and they are true. Writing is now too highly organized a trade for occasional incursions to be encouraged, and now that reading is regarded far more as a narcotic than a stimulus, readers have no discrimination. If an elderly administrator sat down to imitate Montaigne to-day he would have to publish at his own risk and to his certain loss, no matter how great his art, while any ancient numbskull who can string together tedious "Memoirs of a Busy Life," with anecdotes of a few prominent persons, is sure of a large library circulation. And what magazine would accept the "Essays of Elia" to-day? Lamb would be told that he was far too obscure and elusive, and that if he had anything of interest to say about the old South-Sea House, it must be written in a "chatty" manner without exclamation marks. As for "Mackery End" or "Old China" or "Thoughts on Books and Reading," nobody would look at them. Newspapers and periodicals do not want discursiveness, whence it follows that the essay is not to be sought in them, and since it is difficult to get essays published the impulses of the potential essayist are inevitably checked.

A revival of the true essay would have many advantages. It would purge other forms of literature of their humours, it would maintain the fine standard of English prose style which is in sad danger of declining, and it would perpetuate a particularly English form of literary art which is of the highest intrinsic value. But it is to be feared that in this case hope can derive small encouragement from present circumstance. Readers are too restless, writers have become too agile. Life, which was once reckoned by days, is now reckoned by moments which the future threatens with still further subdivision. As the image of a continuous flow of water, when projected through a shutter revolving with intense rapidity, appears on the screen to fall in single drops, so the continuous stream of time in our day appears a jerky procession of unconnected particles. Under such conditions the essay cannot come to being. In Mr. Wells' latest Utopia men, being absolutely free from material struggle, again find leisure to fight duels for a woman's beauty. In that day, perhaps, the essay may be born again.

Richard Le Gallienne

SOURCE: "Sad Demise of Pleasurable Reading," in *Facts and Ideas for Students of English Composition,* John O.

Beaty, Ernest E. Leisy, Mary Lamar, eds., F. S. Crofts & Co., 1930, pp. 225-32.

[In the following excerpt from an essay originally published in 1923, Le Gallienne bemoans the emphasis on cleverness and over-seriousness in modern literature, outlining the technique of the best essayists in crafting pleasurable essays.]

We are so serious nowadays that we are in danger of forgetting that reading is among the pleasures; that indeed pleasure, and not profit, is the first satisfaction we expect from literature, and from some of the finest forms of literature the whole satisfaction. That certain books of accurately stated and melodiously arranged fact, or of thought clearly and inspiringly formulated, bring us a certain kind of pleasure is true enough, but that pleasure, except in the case of a few masterpieces, is not primarily a literary pleasure. Literary pleasure, pure and undefiled by information or intellectual or moral purpose, comes of our enjoyment of words so chosen and arranged by the literary artist who uses them, and so animated by his individual spirit that it is a delight to read them for their own sake, as one delights in a piece of tapestry, a glass of old wine, or a pipe of perfect tobacco. One might have added a perfect piece of music, but that music, of late, has become so intellectualized, in common with all the arts, that one cannot safely use it as an illustration of simple, complete and unadulterated pleasure. All literary masterpieces, whatever other inspirations or satisfactions they bring us, are first of all, a pleasure to read, whether they be a great tragedy, the *Bacchae,* say, or *Hamlet,* or a great elegy, such as *Lycidas,* or whether they be but a romance by Alexandre Dumas, or an essay by Charles Lamb. We have the same complete, simply analyzed, immediate, unthinking impression of enjoyment in reading them as we get from a bird singing. The first good they do us, whatever the other good may be, is that they make us happy. They are—pleasure. . . .

Though novel writing has become largely a branch of scientific research, psychological, psycho-analytical, sociological and "ological" in other fearsome ways, there still remain kindly benefactors of the human race who write novels to give their readers pleasure, that pleasure for which the novel was invented, the pleasure of a story beguilingly told. The poem and essay, however, are all but sunk under the burdens of the "cerebral" demands made upon them. Poetry is no longer asked, or even allowed, to be beautiful, but is valued for the amount of "cerebralism"—ugly and unnecessary word lately added to the cant-vocabulary of modish criticism—that disfigures it. A thing of beauty is no longer a joy forever, and unless a poet wears his brains on his sleeve he is not credited with possessing any. His "singing-coat" must be worn inside out, so that all its seams, and the manner of its tailoring, are evident; the art that parades, rather than conceals, art, and is therefore no art at all, is our only wear. It is the wrong side of the pattern we would seem to be after. And the essay is in much the same case. Indeed, in the pleasure-sense of the word the essay is all but extinct. It still lingers in one or two of the older magazines, which still keep up the tradition of an "easy chair," where we may still listen to a good talker-of-the-pen for the pleasure of hearing him talk, and once in a rare while a volume is published in which an essayist dances his wayward round merely to bring enjoyment "to your moments as they pass, and simply for those moments' sake." Such pleasure as we used to find in *The Spectator,* or in Goldsmith's *Citizen of the World*—pleasure still abounding there for those who care to seek it—in De Quincey, Lamb, Hazlitt and Leigh Hunt, even in Washington Irving and Oliver Wendell Holmes, pleasure still in the world while Pater, Matthew Arnold, Stevenson and Andrew Lang yet wielded their persuasive pens—where is that pleasure to be found today? Perhaps Anatole France is the last master in that kind left to us, humane survivor of the stock of Montaigne and Voltaire. Where are all the humane friendly writers gone to?

> Nay, never ask this week, fair lord,
> Where they are gone, nor yet this year,
> Save with thus much for an overword—
> But where are the snows of yester-year?

Though the word "essay" has long since taken on an inclusiveness not contemplated by its inventor, it is the personal element which constituted its originality in the hands of Montaigne that still determines the character of the true essay as distinct from the various forms of miscellaneous writing generally and loosely so-called. Pamphlets with a purpose, informatory treatises, historical disquisitions, biographical studies, critical appreciations, frequently partake of the character of the essay proper, in so far as they are impregnated by the individuality of their writers, or have an esthetic quality over and above the matters of which they treat. Macaulay, Carlyle, Emerson and Thoreau, and numerous other purposeful prose writers, have written such essays, in which subject and treatment are so combined as to bring us spiritual and intellectual stimulus as well as the enjoyment of vigorous and beautiful writing. But, used in this sense, the word "essay" is so inclusive that it may be said to cover all forms of prose writing that do not attain the dimensions of a book, but are rather sketches of, excursions into their subjects, than complete surveys. Therefore, it is not narrow or academic to try and distinguish from the multifarious variety of the offshoots of the essay, the central and original type now almost lost sight of under this vast efflorescence. The present condition of the essay is analogous to that of the lyric. The word "lyric" is used to cover all manner of poetry except the epic and dramatic, yet when we speak of "a lyric" we do not first think of a "dramatic lyric" by Browning, though a long poem like Shelley's "Ode to the West Wind" may be as properly called a lyric as Shakespeare's "Under the greenwood tree." So when we say "an essay" we rather think of a meditation such as Cowley's essay "On Myself," a piece of verbal tapestry such as De Quincey's "Ladies of Sorrow," or a familiar confidence such as Lamb's essay on "Old China," rather than even an essay on Leonardo da Vinci by Walter Pater. In these examples the personality of the writer and the charm of the treatment preponderate over the subject matter, which is general and not particular in its nature—not informative, not "cerebral."

There is an old saying that a clever cook should be able to make good soup out of a dish-rag, and was it Morris who wrote of poets "who make their honey out of

nought"? The essayist is just such an artist. In his case treatment is pretty nearly everything, subject matter—anything or nothing. That is, his subject matter becomes important only by his manipulation of it and because his choice of it serves to reveal himself, his individual attitudes and moods. Essay writing is a form of autobiography, the egoism of a writer who by reason of personal charm makes it seem natural and pleasing for him to talk of himself and by the exercise of a peculiar tact so identifies himself with his reader that his egoism becomes what we may call a generalized egoism, an egoism not for himself alone, but the expression of the humanity in him appealing to the humanity in us all. He is, first and last, a friendly writer, and companionably assumes that you feel as he feels about things. His writing is a form of hobnobbing with an imaginary crony, and it is not that he considers his own tastes and experiences as important merely because they are his, but because, as he hopes, they are yours as well. He writes because he wants the sympathy of a fellow human being.

Leigh Hunt, one of the most natural of essayists, spoke for all true essayists when he said: "The little of myself that pleases myself I could wish to be accounted worth pleasing others." Essays written in this spirit are thus but so many letters of introduction to the reader. Over and above their intrinsic wisdom and beauty and humor, the final success of say the essays of Montaigne and Lamb lies in their making us so entirely acquainted with their writers that we know them far more intimately than we know the people of our daily lives. So Samuel Pepys, apparently writing for no eye but his own, has contrived to present us with a completely known human being, a Samuel Pepys far better known to us than to his contemporaries over two centuries ago. It follows, therefore, that the essayist's most important asset is himself. More perhaps than in any other forms of writing, it is the man behind the pen that determines for us the value of his essays. How much of a human being is he? Is he the kind of person we want to know and listen to? We have got to like him, or he has failed. If he is a pragmatic, self-opinionated fellow, "egoistic" in the usual weary sense of that word, we shall not remain long in his company. We must take to him, or, however clever he may be, we will soon, as Lamb said of "Zimmerman on Solitude," leave him to himself. Of course, there are exceptions, crotchety "eccentrics," who have value for us as curiosities of human nature, but even these usually strike some kindred chord of perversity in ourselves by which they hold our attention.

First, then, our essayist must be a personality of one kind or another, an individualist who, in analyzing and presenting himself, brings us face to face with one who is "sui generis," some one the like of whom we have not met before and yet who, paradoxically, will be ourselves too. Such personalities are not common, and they need conditions for their growth which cannot be made. They are no hasty products, and their development comes of processes that cannot be formulated. They have selected from life only that which interests them, quite independent of the valuations of others or of the times in which they chance to live. They have strong instinctive likes and dislikes, and, as Lamb said, their "household gods have terribly rooted feet." No less than the poet, the essayist is born and not made. The haste and superficiality of modern life, its feverish "seriousness" also, are not conducive to their occurrence. They are aristocratic, not democratic, growths. Usually they need old soil to grow in, the soil of old cultures, well fertilized with "the humanities." And one condition, that of leisure, leisure at least of the brooding spirit, is of paramount importance to them. They are imperfectly "contemporary," and what goes on in their own minds is of more importance to them than any current events however "epoch-making," or whatever else is going on in the keen adventurous intelligences of the moment. Their world is their own, not that of contemporary politicians, fashionable philosophers, or revolutionizing men of science. Their pet cat is more to them than the whole of Russia, and an old playbook—"that folio, Beaumont and Fletcher, which you dragged home late at night from Barker's in Covent Garden"—is "modern" enough literature for their tastes. From the multitudinous chaos of human life and history they create their own microcosm, into which they invite you to enjoy it with them.

This is to speak of the great creative essayists, but all true essayists, in a degree, succeed in a like manner, by the simple fact of their being themselves, and of writing sincerely, and even naïvely, of what alone interests them, writing of them in their own way, none daring to make them afraid. And here is an important point. While an essayist must be essentially self-conscious, he must be so in an entirely withdrawn way, and even while, as we said, he invites the sympathy of his audience, he must never be afraid of it. In this he resembles a good actor. He must think, and yet not think, of how it is looking from the front. He must never get stage fright. He must never suddenly fear that perhaps his audience is not with him, never suddenly be overcome with the sense that perhaps he is too intimate, too much himself. He must take himself for granted, and it must never occur to him to wonder if he is failing to interest his reader. He must have instinctive faith in his own interest, and never doubt that what he cares to write his reader will be equally anxious to read. He must be quite at home with his audience, "at ease in mine inn." Like a good talker, he must be agreeably and unobtrusively confident that he has "the floor." Under no other conditions can he exercise his charm.

To be at his ease with himself and his reader, we said, is one of the first conditions of the essayist's art; but the case must not be that of self-satisfied complacence or of that coxcombical arrogance affected, for example, by some contemporary British essayists, at present sitting in the seats of the vanished mighty, who ostentatiously posture in their dressing gowns or some other form of negligée, with an air that anything becomes them, and anything they condescend to hand out is good enough for their readers. The case I mean cannot be affected. It only comes of being to the manner born. However odd, or quaint, or paradoxical the essayist's manner, or point of view, it is only valid when it is natural. Deliberate harlequinade is merely a bore, and to be a trick writer is not to be an essayist. For that reason Mr. Bernard Shaw, however we may regard him, is much nearer to being a true essayist than Mr. G. K. Chesterton. Mr. Shaw is a reality, of sorts. He

is quite naturally himself. But it is not natural for any one to be a Chesterton.

John P. Waters

SOURCE: "A Little Old Lady Passes Away," in *Forum and Century,* Vol. 90, No. 1, July, 1933, pp. 27-9.

[*In the following essay, Waters ascribes the death of the familiar essay to its popularity and artlessness, and to its having become, in practice, the domain of adolescents and misfits.*]

The essay, that lavender-scented little old lady of literature, has passed away. Search the magazines for her sparrowy whimseys, and in all but one or two of them you will find, in her stead, crisp articles, blatant exposés, or statistic-laden surveys. Even in the few that admit her pale ghost to their circle of economists, sociologists, and Washington correspondents, her position is decidedly subordinate: a scant column or two near the insurance advertisements at the back of the book. Her mourners—and there still are many—wonder why. There was a time. . . .

There was a time when the familiar essay was important; so important that The Atlantic Monthly Press issued four printings of a book explaining its characteristics and construction; so important that Christopher Morley, the little old lady's favorite American nephew, took time off to anthologize her for admiring high-school teachers and their victims in English I-II, who were often led to believe that all literature, like all Gaul, was divided into three parts: fiction, poetry (pronounced poy'tree), and the familiar essay, with the familiar essay far in the lead as a literary form.

This last, this classifying it as a form, was not always easy to do. Those who tried usually gave Montaigne the credit for originating it and traced its development through Abraham Cowley, Thomas Browne, *Blackwood's Magazine,* Lamb, Hazlitt, and Thackeray. In tone and content, however, the essays of these pioneers little resembled the ones that this generation of readers remembers. Indeed, about all that links them is the common note of personal expression, the feeling that behind the words is a human being and not an omniscient voice. Yet even in this quality there is a difference between the old and the new.

In the former, though one was aware of personality, one was still conscious of the writer's dignity, of a slight barrier that he raised between himself and his audience. In the latter, this dignity was all too often missing, discarded for buttonholing intimacy, crackerbarrel philosophizing, and Winnie-the-Pooh whimsey.

What brought about this change? Why did so many modern essayists err in carrying familiarity too far? To find the answer, we must consider what the modern form was like at its best, and why it was popular.

At its best, the familiar essay was "a kind of improvisation on a delicate theme, a species of soliloquy; as if a man were to speak aloud the slender and whimsical thoughts that come to his mind when he is alone on a winter evening before a warm fire."

Intimacy, reverie, whimsey—these were the qualities that won it thousands of devoted readers, that made it kindly relief from frowning treatises, ramrod sermons, and all the high and mighty didacticism our fathers were flayed with before its advent. It was warm and human, unconcerned with life's granite problems but fascinated with the trifles, moods, and humors that colored the lives of its readers. It was comfortable literature, muddying no quiet pools with a stirred-up sense of sin, goading no laggard ambition to be something. Instead, it chatted easily and urbanely, graceful successor to the gradually dying art of conversation.

With so much in its favor, what caused its downfall? The answer is: the same qualities that made it popular—intimacy, reverie, whimsey. These qualities elicited so many gurgles of, "How charming! What a delightfully helpless fellow the author must be!" from sisters, wives, and maiden aunts, that literarily inclined gentlemen who had not been gushed over for years immediately concluded that the way to become inundated in gush was to put themselves in print as quaint old fuss-budgets. As a consequence, starveling hacks raced bony clergymen to the mailboxes with manuscripts that would make them "dears" and "darlings" to the petticoated portion of the populace.

They succeeded, of course, for the trick was easy. One had only to empty his mind of all knowledge, all common-sense, all everything, except tender quotations from Horace and Tennyson, and start reacting. Anything was a fit subject, the simpler and more far-fetched the better. For example, Mr. Percival Biggs—a six-foot giant who had played tackle for Yale in the days when football was played with the feet—would suddenly develop all the cute physical attributes of a pansy when confronted by the relatively simple problem of stoking his hot-air furnace. Instead of being a harmless cylinder of sheet-metal, it became "an insatiable scarlet-mawed monster." His modest two tons of winter coal became "sable diamonds" to be "immolated thrice daily." He himself was transformed from a lazy suburbanite to a "quaking panderer to Zoroaster." He wallowed in self-pity.

There were other schools, too. The mellowists, for example, did not want to be darlings. They wanted to be ripe, winey. Young men of twenty, green as quinces, ripened overnight. No Village attic lacked its fireside philosopher with his bowl of russet apples, his October cider, his Sherlock Holmes pipe, and his tin of Craven's Mixture—as unmellow a blend of grass and red-pepper, by the way, as Britain's abominable tobacconists ever foisted upon gullible Anglophiles. Reverie took the place of all other mental functions, and bookish archaisms from Evelyn and Pepys bid fair to drive out all other words from thesaurus and dictionary.

Worst of all, however, were the coy writers, the ones who defined death-strangulation with little tinklings called "An' Him Went Home to Him's Muvver." Others of these twitterers delighted in tickling the risqué with the feather end of their pens. Never boorishly, of course. A mild *damn*—in quotation marks—perhaps. Or the impish suggestion that they—pagans that they were—sometimes

didn't quite close their shower-curtains all the way. This group was especially dear to schoolmarms from Brookline, Mass., who—during the months that Columbia Summer School was open—made life on the West Side subway utterly unbearable for native-born New Yorkers by staring them into nervous fits in an effort to gather first-hand material for hellish little papers on "The Typical New Yorker—Poor Thing."

At first, of course, these insect pests were few in number, and their buzzings were harmless enough. But when ever-increasing hordes discovered that writing the familiar essay was the ovaltine their egos needed, the end was near. No literature that is peopled exclusively with doddering loons afraid of sewing-machine flywheels, bewildered by the complex mechanics of hot-water faucets, and hero-stricken with such worthies as tympani thumpers, elevator starters, scissor grinders, and street cleaners can survive long.

The final axe fell when the high schools, with well-meaning but pitifully misdirected affection, took to teaching the fragile art to their fuzzy-lipped brats. Where there was one asinine but educated gush-hunter before, there were now whole herds of pubescent illiterates to annoy friends, relatives, and editors with misspelled masterpieces patterned after, or swiped from, the models their texts supplied.

For texts were essential paraphernalia in the tax-supported essay mills. Though the ninth-grade savants brashly disregarded the fact that the only endurable familiar essayist is a person with well-digested learning, impeccable syntax, urbane humor, pleasant sophistication, and indisputable savoir-faire, they were realistic to the extent that they provided inspiration for off-days when their darlings were not quite equal to scintillating out a three-hundred-word tiara for Miss Sophie Spragg to display at the next Parent-Teacher meeting. Consequently, they selected texts that made plagiary as easy as possible by presenting carefully preserved specimens in neatly labelled blocs: "Essays of Type I—Personal Experiences, Confessions, Self-Analyses; Essays of Type II—Reflections on Life, Human Nature, Customs, and Experience; Essays of Type III—Observations and Discoveries in the familiar and the Commonplace; Essays of Type IV—Nature Essays; Essays of Type V—General Observations, Comments, and Opinions of the Author."

Yet helpful as this break-down was, it was only preliminary and padding to the real meat of the book—the Appendix, which listed some two hundred and fifty "suggested titles." These were always added apologetically; for of course out of the adolescents' wide reading, mature wisdom, and glowing personalities would flow so many "topics" that such a list was almost an insult. Still, to be on the safe side, the text-writers always left it there; and it is remarkable how hungrily, and thankfully, the mute inglorious Morleys swallowed its insults and wrote, as per suggestion, on "My Ailments" (No. 27), "On Being Small" (No. 38), "Why the Dessert Course Last?" (No. 67), "Nature's Languages" (No. 174), or—supreme inspiration—"Diddling" (No. 225).

With such near-Beerbohm flowing into it, no form, let alone the most delicate, could retain its sparkle. Worse still, the public's palate became corrupted. Those who did not turn away in disgust either preferred the spurious stuff to the vintage products of the Morleys, Conrads, and McFees or took to regarding all essays and all essayists with stiffnecked contempt. And why not? Weren't they themselves able to bat out essays by the yard? Didn't they know all the tricks the masters used in building up their effects? And what, pray, was so wonderful about Hilaire Belloc? Anybody could do as well; and because anybody could, nobody wanted to.

What else, then, could the little old lady do but die as unobtrusively as possible? The children who had gathered around her hassock to hear her thin little musings had all grown up and gone away—or remained to mock her quaintness with their new-found wisdom. Radio, prohibition, and prosperity were stinging their senses with more peppery fare. A new and dizzyingly complex world had roared across the quiet hearth; and listeners once sure of their philosophies and content to roam in the pleasant meadows of reverie now groped bewilderedly for *facts*, explanations, anything to help them realign their lives before new discoveries, new techniques, drove out all meaning from life itself. Reverie, whimsey, and humor were out; they didn't get you anywhere.

Hence, gradually, the little old lady deserted her familiar haunts and faded away. Occasionally a sentimental editor, remembering her pleasant tea-table chatter, invites her fluttery ghost to visit his prim Caslon pages. There, politely baffled by the loud talk of collectivism and social trends and economic determinism all about her, she sits a while and muses with her old friends. Then she leaves and does not come back for months at a time. One day, perhaps, her pale ghost will not appear at all, and the hard young sociologists can have her pages all to themselves. But I hope not. For all their cocksure *-ologies,* they cannot comfort us the way she did—when she was at her best.

Henry Seidel Canby

SOURCE: "A Disappearing Art," in *The Saturday Review of Literature,* Vol. IX, No. 1, July 23, 1932, p. 1.

[*Canby was a professor of English at Yale and one of the founders of the* Saturday Review of Literature, *where he served as editor in chief from 1924 to 1936. He was the author of many books, including* The Short Story in English *(1909), a history of that genre which was long considered the standard text for college students. In the following unsigned essay, he laments the decline of the familiar essay in the face of a fast-paced society which lacks the patience to engage with the works of "amiable fellows with a charitable, if sometimes amused, outlook on life."* . . .]

Time was when the essay was one of the most honored devices of literature. Only so lately as the 'nineties of the last century it was still flourishing, finding its way with little difficulty into the magazine and emerging through it eventually in book form. But the temper of our day seems to be **against** it. We have substituted for it the informative or controversial article, the discussion of some problem of immediate import, the analysis of a trend, or the exposition of a point of view. That pleasant dalliance with things of small significance, the whimsical trifling with the routine of daily living, and the nimble tossing about of ideas and impressions that lent the essay its appeal seem to be out of tune with the time. We demand sterner stuff, or, for our hours of leisure, more exciting literature than the essay affords.

For it is of the very essence of the essay that it be gentle, discursive, non-propagandist. Conceived in tranquility, it grows of contemplation, and matures by mellowness of spirit. Nothing is too trivial to be transmuted by it into significance, nothing too immense for it to catch and transform into a personal matter. Few literary forms bring the author and his reader into so direct communion or establish so intimate a relationship between them. Few partake so largely of the informality of conversational intercourse, with its wanderings into the by-lanes opening up from the main path of interest and its excursions into the unexpected and the remembered.

The mood and tempo of present-day civilization are, we fear, little likely to restore the essayist to his lost popularity. We live too fast, think too little, are too impatient of the speculative, and too avid of accomplishment to tolerate the ruminative discursiveness of the easy chair philosopher. The war startled us out of the pleasant places of thought into a horrified awareness of the maladjustments of political society, and the peace thrust us into an era of rebellion against the smugness which had accepted a prewar world as one to rejoice in. Suddenly the essayists vanished; they were no longer amiable fellows with a charitable, if sometimes amused, outlook on life, but crusaders with missions to fulfil or fallacies to expose. They fulminated instead of wooed the fancy, expounded instead of diverted, lived in the moment instead of in time.

It is a pity, indeed, that they should have so disappeared and that publishers, or at least most of them, should shy away from the attempt to restore them. At best, the essay that interests the publisher today is the essay in criticism which, if broadly handled, allows, of course, some leeway for general discussion. But it is necessarily focussed about a book, or an idea or group of ideas, and permits of little latitude for that browsing among fancies and feelings which in the past has so often lent amenity to literature. We need the mildness of mood of the essayist sadly, and his perspective on life and living. For part of what ails society today is that it lives so fiercely in the instant, is so extravagantly buoyed up by confidence when things go well, so despairingly cast down by fears when they go ill. A little admixture of the essayist's habit of mind would help us all, a little of that detachment which holds itself remote enough from the turmoil of the moment to see its world, sunflecked now, now in shadow, a thing of infinite possibilities, a little of that mellowness of feeling which loves even when it jests at humanity, a little of that agility of fancy which uses a commonplace as a springboard to adventures of the spirit. "Philosophy is a good horse in the stable," and essayists are philosophers of a most approachable kind.

Katharine Fullerton Gerould

SOURCE: "An Essay on Essays," in *The North American Review,* Vol. CCXL, No. 3, December, 1935, pp. 409-18.

[Gerould was an American short story writer during the first half of the twentieth century. In the essay below, published as world events indicated the approach of World War II, she discusses the familiar essay as a form of writing out of fashion at a time when essay writing has been supplanted by propagandizing.]

Some of the rhetoric books my generation used in college went back to Aristotle for many of their definitions. "Rhetoric," he says, "may be defined as a faculty of discovering all the possible means of persuasion in any subject." Persuasion, indeed, is more starkly and simply the purpose of the essay than of fiction or poetry, since the essay deals always with an idea. No true essay, however desultory or informal, but states a proposition which the writer hopes, temporarily at least, to make the reader accept. Though it be only the defense of a mood, subject and predicate are the bare bones of any essay. It may be of a complex nature (like many of Emerson's) stating several propositions; but unless it states at least one, it is not an essay. It may be a dream or a dithyramb; I repeat, it is not an essay.

Let us neglect the old rhetorical distinctions between exposition and argument. To sort all essays into those two types of writing would be more troublesome a task than the wicked stepmother ever set her stepdaughter in a fairytale. We can no more do it without the help of magic than could the poor princess. When is an essay argument, and when is it exposition? That way lie aridity and the carving of cummin. In so far as the essay attempts to persuade, it partakes of the nature of argument. Yet who would call Lamb's "Dream Children" an argument? Or who shall say it is not an essay? It contains a proposition, if you will only look for it; yet to associate Lamb's persuading process with the forum would be preposterous. All writing presupposes an audience (which some of our younger writers seem to forget) but formal argument presupposes opponents, and I cannot find the faintest scent of an enemy at hand in "Dream Children."

I am sorry to kick the dust of the Schools about, even in this half-hearted way, yet some salutation had to be made to rhetoric, which is a noble science, too much neglected. Let us now forget the rhetoricians, and use our own terminology (our common sense too, if we have any). Let us say, first, that the object of the essay is, explicitly, persuasion; and that the essay states a proposition. Indeed, we need to be as rigorously simple as that, if we are going to consider briefly a type that is supposed to include Bacon's "Of Truth," De Quincey's "Murder as a Fine Art," Lamb's "In Praise of Chimney Sweeps," Hazlitt's "On Going a Journey," Irving's "Bachelors," Hunt's "Getting up on Cold Mornings," Poe's "The Poetic Principle," Emerson's "Self-Reliance," Arnold's "Function of Criticism," Stevenson's "Penny Plain and Twopence Coloured," Paul Elmer More's "The Demon of the Absolute," Chesterton's "On Leisure," Max Beerbohm's "No. 2, The Pines,"

Stephen Leacock's "People we Know," and James Truslow Adams' "The Mucker Pose."

The foregoing list, in itself, confesses our main difficulty in delimiting the essay. The most popular kind of essay, perhaps, is that known as "familiar." When people deplore the passing of the essay from the pages of our magazines, it is usually this that they are regretting. They are thinking wistfully of pieces of prose like Lamb's "Sarah Battle on Whist," Leigh Hunt's "The Old Gentleman," Stevenson's "El Dorado," Max Beerbohm's "Mobled King." They mean the essay that is largely descriptive, more or less sentimental or humorous, in which it is sometimes difficult to find a stated proposition. This kind of prose has not been very popular since the war, and I, for one, am not regretting it. It will come back—as long as the ghost of Montaigne is permitted to revisit the glimpses of the moon. But the familiar-essay-which-is-hardly-an-essay can be spared for a few years if necessary, since it demands literary gifts of a very high order, and the authors mentioned have at present no competitors in this field. If the bones of the essay are to be weak, the flesh must be exceeding fair and firm.

Are we to admit, at all, that "Sarah Battle" and "The Old Gentleman," and "El Dorado" and "Mobled King" are essays? Do they state a proposition to which they attempt to persuade us? Well, we can twist them to a proposition, if we are very keen on our definition—though I think most of us would admit that they are chiefly descriptive and that they are only gently directed to the creation of opinion. Must we then deny that they are essays? No. I think they are essays, though it is obvious that the familiar essayist goes about his business far otherwise than Arnold or Emerson or Macaulay. He attempts rather to sharpen our perceptions than to convince us of a statement; to win our sympathy rather than our suffrage. His proposition is less important to him than his mood. If put to it, we can sift a proposition out of each one of these—and they were especially chosen because they put our definition on its defense. Lamb states, if you like, that to abide by the rigor of the game is in its way an admirable thing; Leigh Hunt states, if you like, that growing old is a melancholy business; Stevenson states that it is better to travel hopefully than to arrive; Max Beerbohm states that no man is worthy to be reproduced as a statue. But the author's proposition, in such essays, is not our main interest. This brings us to another consideration which may clarify the matter.

Though an essay must state a proposition, there are other requirements to be fulfilled. The bones of subject and predicate must be clothed in a certain way. The basis of the essay is mediation, and it must in a measure admit the reader to the meditative process. (This procedure is frankly hinted in all those titles that used to begin with "Of" or "On": "Of Truth," "Of Riches," "On the Graces and Anxieties of Pig-Driving," "On the Knocking at the Gate in 'Macbeth'," "On the Enjoyment of Unpleasant Places"). An essay, to some extent, thinks aloud; though not in the loose and pointless way to which the "stream of consciousness" addicts have accustomed us. The author must have made up his mind—otherwise, where is his proposition? But the essay, I think, should show how and why he made up his mind as he did; should engagingly rehearse the steps by which he came to his conclusions. ("Francis of Verulam reasoned thus with himself ".) Meditation; but an oriented and fruitful meditation.

This is the most intimate of forms, because it permits you to see a mind at work. On the quality and temper of that mind depends the goodness of the production. Now, if the essay is essentially meditative, it cannot be polemical. No one, I think, would call Cicero's first oration against Catiline an essay; or Burke's Speech on the Conciliation of America; hardly more could we call Swift's "Modest Proposal" a true essay. The author must have made up his mind, but when he has made it up with a vengeance, he will not produce an essay. Because the process is meditative, the manner should be courteous; he should always, by implication, admit that there are good people who may not agree with him; his irony should never turn to the sardonic. Reasonableness, urbanity (as Matthew Arnold would have said) are prerequisites for a form whose temper is meditative rather than polemical.

We have said that this is the most intimate of forms. Not only for technical reasons, though obviously the essayist is less sharply controlled by his structure than the dramatist or the sonneteer or even the novelist. It is the most intimate because it is the most subjective. When people talk of "creative" and "critical" writing—dividing all literature thus—they always call the essay critical. In spite of Oscar Wilde, to call it critical is probably correct; for creation implies objectivity. The created thing, though the author have torn its raw substance from his very vitals, ends by being separate from its creator. The essay, however, is incurably subjective; even "Wuthering Heights" or "Manfred" is less subjective—strange though it sound—than "The Function of Criticism" or "The Poetic Principle." What Oscar Wilde really meant in "The Critic as Artist"—if, that is, you hold him back from his own perversities—is not that Pater's essay on Leonardo da Vinci was more creative than many a novel, but that it was more subjective than any novel; that Pater, by virtue of his style and his mentality, made of his conception of the Mona Lisa something that we could be interested in, regardless of our opinion of the painting. I do not remember that Pater saw himself as doing more than explain to us what he thought Leonardo had done—Pater, I think, would never have regarded his purple page as other than criticism. I, myself—because I like the fall of Pater's words, and do not much care for Mona Lisa's feline face—prefer Pater's page to Leonardo's portrait; but I am quite aware that I am merely preferring criticism, in this instance, to the thing criticized. I am, if you like, preferring Mr. Pecksniff's drunken dream—"Mrs. Todgers's idea of a wooden leg"—to the wooden leg itself. Anything (I say to myself) rather than a wooden leg!

A lot of nineteenth century "impressionistic" criticism—Jules Lemaître, Anatole France, etc.—is more delightful than the prose or verse that is being criticized. It is none the less criticism. The famous definition of "the adventures of a soul among the masterpieces" does not put those adventures into the "creative" category; it merely stresses their subjectivity. Wilde is to some extent right when he says that criticism is the only civilized form of autobiography; but he is not so right when he says that the highest criticism is more creative than creation. No one would deny that the purple page Wilde quotes tells us more about Pater than it does about Leonardo, or even about Mona Lisa—as Macaulay's Essay on Milton conceivably tells us more about Macaulay than about the author of *Paradise Lost.* All Bacon's essays together but build up a portrait of Bacon—Francis of Verulam reasoning with himself; and what is the substance of the *Essays of Elia,* but Elia? "Subjective" is the word, however, rather than "creative."

It is this subjectivity—Montaigne's first of all, perhaps—that has confused many minds. It is subjectivity run wild that has tempted many people to believe that the familiar essay alone *is* the essay; which would make some people contend that an essay does not necessarily state a proposition. But we are talking of the essay itself; not of those bits of whimsical prose which are to the true essay what expanded anecdote is to the short story.

The essay, then, having persuasion for its object, states a proposition; its method is meditation; it is subjective rather than objective, critical rather than creative. It can never be a mere marshaling of facts; for it struggles, in one way or another, for truth; and truth is something one arrives at by the help of facts, not the facts themselves. Meditating on facts may bring one to truth; facts alone will not. Nor can there be an essay without a point of view and a personality. A geometrical proposition cannot be an essay, since, though it arranges facts in a certain pattern, there is involved no personal meditative process, conditioned by the individuality of the author. A geometrical proposition is not subjective. One is even tempted to say that its tone is not urbane!

Perhaps—with the essay thus defined—we shall understand without effort why it is being so little written at present. Dorothy Thompson said the other day that Germany is living in a state of war. The whole world is living more or less in a state of war; and a state of war produces any literary form more easily than the essay. It is not hard to see why. People in a state of war, whether the war be military or economic, express themselves polemically. A wise man said to me, many years ago, that, in his opinion, the worst by-product of the World War was propaganda. Many times, in the course of the years, I have had occasion to recall that statement. There are perhaps times and places where propaganda is justified—it is not for me to say. But I think we should all agree that the increasing habit of using the technique of propaganda is corrupting the human mind in its most secret and delicate processes. Propaganda has, in common with all other expression, the object of persuasion; but it pursues that legitimate object by illegitimate means—by *suggestio falsi* and *suppressio veri;* by the *argumentum ad hominem* and hitting below the belt; by demagogic appeal and the disregard of right reason. The victim of propaganda is not intellectually persuaded, but intellectually—if not emotionally—coerced. The essayist, whatever the limitations of his intelligence, is bound over to be honest; the propagandist is always dishonest.

To qualify a large number of the articles and pseudoessays

that appear at present in our serious periodicals, British and American, as "dishonest" calls for a little explaining. When one says that the propagandist is always dishonest, one means this: He is a man so convinced of the truth of a certain proposition that he dissembles the facts that tell against it. Occasionally, he is dishonest through ignorance—he is verily unaware of any facts save those that argue for him. Sometimes, having approached his subject with his decision already made, he is unable to appreciate the value of hostile facts, even though he is aware of them. In the latter case, instead of presenting those hostile facts fairly, he tends to suppress or distort them because he is afraid that his audience, readers or listeners, will not react to them precisely as he has done. The propagandist believes (when he is not a paid prostitute) that his conclusions are right; but, no more than any other demagogue, does he like to give other men and women a fair chance to decide for themselves. The last thing he will show them is Francis of Verulam reasoning with himself. He cannot encourage the meditative process. He is, at best, the special pleader.

It can have escaped no reader of British and American periodicals that there is very little urbane meditation going on in print. Half the articles published are propaganda—political, economic, social; the other half are purely informational, mere catalogues of fact. The essay is nowhere. Either there is no proposition, or evidence is suppressed. Above all, there is no meditation—no urbanity. All this is characteristic of the state of war in which we are unfortunately living; that state of war which, alas! permits us few unprejudiced hours.

Yet I think many people would agree that we need those unprejudiced hours rather particularly, just now. We need the essay rather particularly, just now, since fiction and poetry have suffered even more cruelly than critical prose from the corruption of propaganda on the one hand and the rage for "fact-finding" on the other. We need to get away from polemics; we even need to get away from statistics. Granted that we are in a state of war: are we positively so badly off that we must permit every sense save the economic to be atrophied; that we cannot afford to think about life in any terms except those of bread? The desperate determination to guarantee bread to every one—which seems to be the basis of all our political and economic quarreling—is perhaps our major duty. And after? as the French say. Is it not worth our while to keep ourselves complex and civilized, so that, when bread for every one is guaranteed, we shall be capable of entertaining other interest?

The preoccupation with bread alone is a savage's preoccupation; even when it concerns itself altruistically with other people's bread, it is still a savage's preoccupation. The preoccupation with facts to the exclusion of what can be done with them, and the incapacity for logical thinking, are both savage. Until a man begins to think—not merely to lose his temper or to learn by heart—he is, mentally, clothed in the skins of beasts. We are, I fear, under economic stress, de-civilizing ourselves. Between propaganda and "dope" there is little room for the meditative process and the subtler propositions.

I am not urging that we play the flute while Rome burns. I recall the sad entry in Dorothy Wordsworth's journal: "William wasted his mind all day in the magazines." I am not asking the magazines to waste the minds of our Williams. . . . The fact that the familiar essay of the whimsical type is not at the moment popular—that when people wish to be diverted, they prefer Wodehouse to Leacock, let us say—does not disturb me. But it seems a pity that meditative prose should suffer a total eclipse, if only because meditation is highly contagious. A good essay inevitably sets the reader to thinking. Just because it expresses a point of view, is limited by one personality, and cannot be exhaustive or wholly authoritative, it invites the reader to collaboration. A good essay is neither intoxicant nor purge nor anodyne; it is a mental stimulant.

Poetry may be, indeed, as Arnold said, "a criticism of life." But most of us need a different training in critical thinking than that which is offered to us by the poets. A vast amount of the detail of life, detail which preoccupies and concerns us all, is left out of great poetry. We do not spend all our time on the heights, or in the depths, and if we are to live we must reflect on many matters rather temporal than eternal. The essayist says, "Come, let us reason together." That is an invitation—whether given by word of mouth or on the printed page—that civilized people must encourage and, as often as possible in their burdened lives, accept.

Walter Prichard Eaton

SOURCE: "On Burying the Essay," in *The Virginia Quarterly Review,* Vol. 24, No. 4, Autumn, 1948, pp. 574-83.

[*In the following excerpt, Eaton laments the passing of the familiar essay from contemporary periodical literature in favor of the thesis-driven expository essay.*]

I have attended more than one gathering known as a Writers' Conference. These gatherings generally consist of ten or a dozen professional authors, editors, and agents, called the staff, and perhaps a hundred would-be writers, many of whom have brought with them samples of their efforts in prose or verse, and who for two weeks listen to talks on the craft of writing (and selling), and meet for conferences with whatever member of the staff has been assigned to read their effusions. . . .

At the most recent conference I attended the entire group were severely taken to task in a lecture by one of the staff for their preoccupation with themselves, their own emotions and reminiscences, and their failure, as he saw it, to throw their weight against the world's wrongs, cops with a pen instead of a night stick. To these five-score would-be writers, these women (and a few men) verging on middle age, these people of small talent perhaps, but with something in them which struggled for expression, the lecturer declared: "You must not write about yourselves. The personal essay is dead and done for. There is no market for it in the magazines and no place for it in the modern world. You must ally your art with the great forces of democratic progress, illuminate evils, combat them. . . ."

That, at least, is the gist of his words. Only the phrase "the personal essay is dead and done for" can I affirm is a direct quotation. I remember those words well for they hit me with an unpleasant shock, filled me with an immediate and rather violent dislike for the speaker, and started my mind off on several tracks, so that it was some-time before I found myself listening to the lecturer again.

He was now telling the conferees what, specifically, to write about. It seems the lumber barons have their plans laid to separate the finest remaining stand of Douglas fir in America from the Olympic National Park, and of course to cut it down. Up and at them, conferees! Authors of America unite! You have nothing to lose but your firs. This timber grab was, of course, what the lecturer was just then writing about, I presume with specific knowledge. None of his auditors had such specific knowledge, and the only effective (possibly effective) writing they could do would be a letter to their congressman. It was difficult to see why they could not write such a letter and also continue the composition of a "personal" essay on the peculiarities of their grandmothers or the return of the petticoat. Then I began asking myself why this man was so intent upon rescuing the fir forest from the axe; what had made him conscious of the beauty and value of the Olympic wilderness, or of any of our national parks—if he was conscious, and not, as I no doubt unworthily suspected, animated by a kind of socialist zeal. But I gave him the benefit of the doubt, again ceased to listen to him, and tried to answer my own question.

The answer wasn't hard to find, and in light of his opening declaration not unamusing. What made him—and us—conscious of the value and beauty of the wilderness, and of the scenic glories of our national parks, was the personal essay. To be sure, there has always been a crude and inexpressive love of the wilderness in the pioneer American, combined, however, with a love of the chase, of the material benefits to be secured, especially timber, and of freedom from restraint. But anything which could be called a conscious aesthetic appreciation, and a realization of the relation between such an appreciation and a philosophy of civilized living, awaited the vision of a man named Thoreau, who embodied it in personal essays if ever there were such things. It was a momentous week that Henry spent on the Concord and Merrimack Rivers, though the world little knew it then. In later days much has been written about Thoreau's doctrine of civil disobedience, about his transcendentalism, about his attempted escape from a life of "quiet desperation," about his qualities as a field naturalist; but the fact remains that probably his chief contribution to us, his later countrymen, and a contribution made as much by indirection through personal essays by his disciples as through direct contact with his own lean prose, has been an appreciation of Nature, a love of woods and fields and flowers, and an accompanying desire to preserve the natural beauty around us. Thoreau wrote constantly of these things, and always in personal terms. Was there ever a more egregiously personal book than *Walden?*

While Thoreau still lived, there was a student at the University of Wisconsin who attracted attention by inventing an alarm clock which tipped his bed over at a designated hour. After college he tramped into Canada and found the calypso in flower, which he later said was one of the two most memorable meetings of his life. (The other was with Ralph Waldo Emerson, a writer of personal essays.) This man was some time in finding himself. He drifted to California and became a sawyer in the Yosemite Valley. There he discovered his mission, not as a sawyer of giant trees, but as savior. He climbed, with a loaf of bread and a pocket-full of raisins for all provision, into the high places. He rejoiced as the mountain hurricane lashed the tops of the giant sequoias making a mighty music. He wrote endlessly, and not easily, of the beauties he found in rugged nature, of the physical and spiritual refreshment they brought him. He wrote personal essays about them.

His name, of course, was John Muir. The time came when he had to enter the lists with polemical articles, to get the Yosemite under National Park protection, or later to try to save portions of it from being grabbed back. But he had paved the way by his personal essays. It was the spirit of John Muir made manifest in his essays which caused other eyes to open and other voices to back his pleas for conservation. I didn't have to labor this point with myself, but my mind wandered into a high meadow where the Sierra snows were melting on the encircling peaks and the Alpine flowers were in bloom, so the lecturer had reached his conclusion when I began to listen again. Soon the conferees' were filing out, some of them perhaps determined to plunge into the arena of important controversy, forgetful of self. A few, I must say, looked a bit bewildered as if wondering in just what important controversy they were sufficiently informed to plunge. And a few were frowning as if they didn't want anything to do with important controversies. These may have been the lyric poets.

I was reminded of another lecture I had recently heard in a college hall, delivered by a visiting poet of some contemporary distinction. He divided poetry into that which spoke with a private voice, and that which spoke with a public voice. As I recall, Milton was the last poet to employ a public voice until the arrival of the moderns, including, no doubt, the lecturer. All the poetry that came between was dismissed as of no interest or value any more. I was reminded of a parody I had recently heard:

> The world is too much with us, late and soon,
> Auden and Spender we lay waste our
>   powers. . . .

I was also perplexed by the obvious fact that the poetry which speaks with a public voice reaches only a tiny and very private audience, while the poetry which employs a private voice is quoted and beloved by a very large public indeed. Infinitely more people know how Keats felt when he explored Chapman's Homer than know their way around the Waste Land, and it is barely possible are the better for it. At any rate, there was the lecturer's paradox gnawing at my mind, and I sat out the lecture to see if he would resolve it; but he didn't.

And here at the conference were five score yearning writers confronted with the inescapable fact that what moves most of us to poetic expression is personal emotion, what urges us to write a story is a sense of drama and a curiosity about human character, what we can put into an essay of any value whatsoever is what we have felt and known. What we know best is ourselves. Politics, sociology, international relations, can be written about with profit only by experts, and seldom even at their hands can literature result. Such polemical writing is necessary to the world, no doubt, and we all have to read it, often to our exceeding weariness. But the writer who has some urge, however dim, to contribute his mite to the great body of literature has instinctively to turn within for his material, and with what skill and charm he may command, body forth the dignity and the dreams of the individual man.

Nor does he do this, of course, by talking about it. He does it by revelation. Indeed, he cannot help himself. What has made Tennessee Williams' play, *A Streetcar Named Desire,* so great a success is neither its well-constructed story nor the skill of the performers nor its social implications, but the profound pity which the play evokes because that sense of pity, that human compassion, is the author's contribution to his age. Revealing that, he accomplishes far more for understanding among peoples than he ever could by a polemic article about social relations in a changing society. The tensions of politics and race relations are in the long run resolved only by tolerance, sympathy, understanding, by respect for human rights and dignities; and it is in the arts and literature that these things are made manifest and moving. For writers to turn from their proper task of revelation, to forsake the humanities for the arena, would in most cases benefit nobody.

No doubt I am being a bit unfair to the lecturer who started me off on these reflections. By the "personal" essay he probably had in mind neither the self-revelations of Montaigne (who created the essay, or at any rate named it) nor the nature writings of Thoreau, but rather the pleasant piffle of those who, in remote imitation of Charles Lamb, confect little pieces, desperately "literary," about the trivia of their lives. When Christopher Morley's book called *Mince Pie* was issued, a critic rather cruelly remarked it should have been called "Lamb Stew." Like many writers of great talent, Lamb was responsible for a host of imitators to the point of weariness. It was the fashion to take any subject, the more trivial the better, and embroider it with wit, with literary graces, and thus become an essayist. How hard these essayists worked at their task! How they sought for paradoxical moral reflections to achieve a sense of weight! How unspontaneous sometimes was their wit, like too many of Dr. Holmes' puns! How tiresome, often, was their product! No doubt a serious-minded man, without much humor, and imbued with a conviction (born of thunder on the Left) that art is justified, anyway, only as propaganda, would turn from them in scorn.

Yet there was nothing wrong with the method. It was the method of Montaigne, who by it revealed to the modern world an ideal of tolerance. It was the method of Lamb, who by it revealed a sweet and gentle and urbane soul we are the richer for knowing. It was the method of Thoreau whose trivia were beans and bull frogs which he translated into translated into transcendental symbols. It was the method of self-revelation, and when it failed that was because the self revealed was not worth the knowing. Dr. Johnson defined the essay, meaning the personal essay, as

"A loose sally of the mind; an irregular, undigested piece; not a regular and orderly performance." Doubtless he was thinking of the essays of Montaigne. But Dr. Johnson lives today largely by the loose sallies of his own mind rather than by his forbiddingly orderly performances in the so-called formal essay, because they best reveal the man we like to know. "Throughout the entire history of the essay," says Tanner, "personality has been a most important characteristic." The Scotsman, Alexander Smith, himself a charming essayist, remarks in his essay "On the Writing of Essays":

> A modest, truthful man speaks better about himself than about anything else, and on that subject his speech is likely to be most profitable to his hearers. Certainly there is no subject with which he is better acquainted, and on which he has better title to be heard. . . . If a man is worth knowing at all, he is worth knowing well. The essayist gives you his thoughts and lets you know, in addition, how he came by them . . . Of the essayist, when his mood is communicative, you obtain a full picture. You are made his contemporary and familiar friend.

We read biography not to pay tribute to great men, but to understand them. We read fiction to enlarge our understanding of character. (Here, perhaps, I am a trifle optimistic.) We read personal essays to enjoy the acquaintance of Charles Lamb, of Max Beerbohm, of the late Simeon Strunsky, whose personal essays for so many years leavened the editorial page of the *New York Times.* (It was Simeon Strunsky who many years ago had at Theodore Roosevelt, then become an editor of *The Outlook,* in a series of playful essays called "Through the Outlooking Glass," causing the ex-president to ask F. P. A. what sort of a man Strunsky was. Very intelligent, Mr. Adams informed him. "That's what I thought," replied Mr. Roosevelt. "He seems the most intelligent of my opponents. In fact, he seems so intelligent that I cannot understand his being an opponent.")

I for one wish that we could read such essays more often in our magazines which today are so portentous with polemics. I could feel more cheerful about the future of the human race after becoming "the contemporary and familiar friend" of a modern Montaigne or Lamb or Hazlitt than after struggling through a mass of predictions by "experts" on everything from the devaluation of the franc to the establishment of a full-fledged law school in Oklahoma over the week-end. At any rate, I'm quite confident that among the scores of conferees who listened to the funeral oration at the grave of the familiar essay were some whose thoughts and fancies, whose self-revelations, might with proper guidance in the arts of expression have proved interesting; and I am equally sure that neither I nor anybody else would have cared to hear them on the subject of Soviet relations in Southern Manchuria.

Then there is the subject of criticism—if I may consider this a personal essay and let my mind make a loose sally in that direction. I have of late made some febrile attempts to understand the criticism in some of our more highbrow publications, especially when it concerned literature which I had struggled dutifully to assimilate. But I have found so much of this criticism written in a jargon which I can only assume is the "public" speech of a very private coterie of the elect, that I have given up the effort to understand. It has generally been assumed by the ignorant that criticism is designed to clarify rather than obfuscate, to put the pieces of the puzzle together rather than to dump them off the table. That ignorance I continue to share, and have, indeed, reached the age when I can afford even to be a little cocky about it. At any rate, I take more satisfaction and secure more nourishment in the criticisms of men and manners, no less than of literature, which I find in the personal essays of those whom I respect. Their criticism is impressionistic, to be sure, but is perhaps the more honest for that, and is not dictated by cults and coteries, or for that matter by an ambition to impress a gathering of the Modern Language Association.

I have in mind one of the most delightful of personal essays by E. B. White. (In fairness I should state that it first appeared in *Harper's Magazine*.) It begins, "Miss Nims, take a letter to Henry David Thoreau. Dear Henry: I thought of you the other afternoon as I was approaching Concord doing fifty on Route 62. . . ." And it goes on to describe Mr. White's pilgrimage to the shrine at Walden, where "from beneath the flattened popcorn wrapper *(granum explosum)* peeped the frail violet." The essay is a smilingly ironic picture of what happens in our modern age when you turn a horde of picnickers loose in a place of beauty which you thought to conserve. Under the smile is a certain bitterness about the human race which travels about so easily in motor cars and is so far from the spirit of Henry Thoreau. But Mr. White is not unaware of certain difficulties in Thoreau's position. In pleasant parody of *Walden* he lists at the end of his letter what his sojourn in Concord cost him, a modest $7.70; but that included 25 cents for a bat and $1.25 for a left-handed fielder's glove, "gifts to take back to a boy." He apologizes to Henry for these items. "You must remember," he says in closing, "that the house where you practiced the sort of economy which I respect was haunted only by mice and squirrels. You never had to cope with a shortstop."

Is this any less valid criticism of Thoreau, the Concord eremite, as a guide to the common man seeking a way of life among his kind, because it chances to be charming and witty, because it makes us smile, and even follow in our thoughts the writer's journey in reverse over Route 62 in order to witness the reception of that left-handed fielder's glove by his offspring? Is it any less penetrating because it is found in a delightful personal essay, written by a man whom we are happy to know and whose every self-revelation betrays a spirit of understanding and tolerance for all things not mean and evil? In short, is it any the worse for being literature instead of pedantic jargon?

These be what I was taught in school to call rhetorical questions. May I have the privilege of asking another? Would our serious magazines be any the worse for a few more such essays, any the less readable, any the less influential in fostering the humanistic spirit? If an essay by Charles Lamb, delayed in the mails (as is perfectly possible these days) were to reach an editor's desk, would it be

rejected as something dead and done for? As somebody always says somewhere in every new play, "I wonder."

Clifton Fadiman

SOURCE: "A Gentle Dirge for the Familiar Essay," in *Party of One: The Selected Writings of Clifton Fadiman,* The World Publishing Company, 1955, pp. 349-53.

[*Fadiman became one of the most prominent American literary critics during the 1930s with his insightful and often caustic book reviews for the* Nation *and the* New Yorker *magazines. In the following excerpt from an essay originally published in* Holiday, *he laments the decline of the familiar essay.*]

Say what you will of our manners, surely our essays grow less familiar. With such masters as E. B. White, Christopher Morley, Bernard DeVoto, and John Mason Brown exerting their delaying action the eclipse of the familiar essay will be slow. Nonetheless it is setting to the horizon, along with its whole constellation: formal manners, apt quotation, Greek and Latin, clear speech, conversation, the gentleman's library, the gentleman's income, the gentleman. . . .

Explaining the decline of the familiar essay is one of the few pleasures now available to the familiar essayist. One will blame the creeping politicalization of man, and it is true that different bloods course through the veins of the political animal and the polite essayist. Another will heave his halfbrick at the big, black giant, Science, seeing in him the foe of the personal and the informal. The critic David Daiches points out that "there are too few people who know enough about enough matters to afford an audience for the attractive discussion which is expert without being specialized." Here the guilt is placed not so much on the shortcomings of our education as on the wildfire spread of our knowledge. There is something to the notion that the intimate discourse, bright with its thousand flowers of allusion, grows more richly in the climate of *omne scibile,* or at least in one in which a large number of people all know the same things. In the country of the specialist the merely educated man is lost.

The world of the personal essay is small. It has its own limits. They resemble neither the hard bounds of that vaster world in which all the answers are given, nor the blurred ones of that equally vast world in which no questions are asked. The familiar essay is not argument and it is more than entertainment. It was invented to seduce the reader into mental play during those intervals in which his mind prefers to hover like Mohammed's coffin between the purposive and the passive.

With the death of that kind of mind the familiar essay will die too. As the areas of both the purposive and the passive enlarge, the familiar essay's plot of ground narrows. It offers little to us when, hot for certainties, we read to improve ourselves, or compete with our neighbors, or bring ourselves up-to-date. And it offers even less when, swinging toward passivity, we cast about for the soft ottomans of print, finding them in the comics, the columns, and the picture magazines. Being neither quite useful nor quite trivial the familiar essay ends by being, like all outmoded reminders of a vaguely recalled lost paradise, somehow exasperating.

Almost 400 years ago in 1580 Montaigne laid down its pair of lenient laws. "What do I know?" he asked his own skeptic mind, and for an answer came up only with "It is my self I portray." The question marked out the method of the familiar essay, digressive and noncommitting. The answer marked out its subject matter, the ego of the essayist.

Its method, to those who think of words as either mental weapons or mental lullabies, seems quaint. So too does its subject matter.

The familiar essayist invites me to rest in the shade of the perpendicular pronoun. His connection with me is a personal one, chancy and fragile, a friendship sustained only by a few dozen paragraphs. He does not raise, much less settle, the kind of issue known as crucial. He is full of opinions and void of conclusions. He has the impertinence to solicit my interest in such useless topics as old china or getting respected at inns or the feats of Indian jugglers. By a cunning display of his personality he seduces me into a co-consideration of these small matters. He exerts charm, not that he may persuade me to anything, but solely for the pleasure of it. He demands only that I do my best to march with the humor or eccentricity of his mind. If I cannot follow him, the devil take me. He wants to involve me but not if it means truckling to my prejudices, streamlining his style for my greater ease, or pretending that in the veined shell of his paragraphs lies hidden the pearl of the Truth. The familiar essayist is his own man. At no price will he be mine.

His kind of ego is out of fashion. Others are in. We can and do admire the grand strut of the politician and the general. From the fact that they deal with important matters, such as war and politics, we conclude that their egos are of corresponding weight. The peacocking confessionals of film stars and odd-larynxed crooners attract us too, though differently. Since they live in a world so fabulous that no road leads from it to our own workaday one, the play of their egos becomes pure exciting spectacle, committing us to no response beyond gap-mouthed wonder and the pleasure of vicariously sharing in fairyland. . . .

The ego of a twentieth-century "personality" is a kind of public utility, developed and expanded systematically by the techniques of publicity. In a way all of us feel that we own a small piece of Senator McCarthy or Debbie Reynolds. But the ego of a Charles Lamb or a Robert Louis Stevenson is a private non-utility. No matter how frankly it exposes itself, it never in either sense quite gives itself away.

The transformation of the private ego of the typical Renaissance hero into the public ego of the typical modern "leader" is reflected in our conversation. On all sides we hear talk about "the individual" and "individualism," talk inconceivable at the Mermaid Tavern or the court of Lorenzo de' Medici. Individuals don't champion individualism. They live it.

Of all the forms of writing it is the familiar essay, I think, that has suffered most from this transformation. The novelist can mount a soapbox and so compete with other public egos. The playwright, by the very nature of his trade, has always been half-public, half-private. The poet can retire into the fastness of himself, or content himself with talking to other poets. The essayist of another stripe—the travel essayist, the historical essayist, the propaganda essayist, the formal literary critic—can find his proper audience and remain, however perilously, in business. But to whom shall a man talk if he has some notions to advance on the decline of the walking stick? Who listens to the man who, varying the outburst of the old lady in the nursery rhyme, cries

> Lawk a mercy on me,
> This is some of I!

Joseph Wood Krutch

SOURCE: "No Essays, Please!" in *The Saturday Review of Literature*, Vol. XXXIV, No. 10, March 10, 1951, pp. 18-19, 35.

[*Krutch is widely regarded as one of America's most respected literary and drama critics. A conservative and idealistic thinker, he was a consistent proponent of human dignity and the preeminence of literary art. His literary criticism is characterized by such concerns. In the following excerpt, Krutch discourses upon the decline and disapearance of the familiar essay—in the style of the familiar essay.*]

Every now and then someone regrets publicly the passing of the familiar essay. Perhaps such regretters are usually in possession of a recent rejection slip; in any event there are not enough of them to impress editors. The very word "essay" has fallen into such disfavor that it is avoided with horror, and anything which is not fiction is usually called either an "article," a "story," or just "a piece." When *The Atlantic Monthly*, once the last refuge of a dying tradition, now finds it advisable to go in for such "articles" as its recent "What Night Playing Has Done to Baseball" it is obvious that not merely the genteel tradition but a whole literary form is dead.

I am sure that the books on how to become a writer in ten easy lessons have been stressing this fact for a long time now. If *I* were writing such a book I certainly should, and I think that I could give some very practical advice. To begin with I should say something like the following:

Suppose that you have drawn a subject out of your mental box and you find that it is "Fish." Now if you were living in the time of Henry Van Dyke and Thomas Bailey Aldrich your best lead would be: "Many of my friends are ardent disciples of Isaac Walton," That would have had the appropriate personal touch and the requisite not too recondite literary allusion. But today of course no live-wire editor would read any further, not because this sounds like a dull familiar essay but simply because it sounds like a familiar essay. But "Fish" is still a perfectly usable subject provided you remember that salable nonfiction "pieces" almost invariably fall into one of three categories: the factual, the polemic, and what we now call—

though I don't know why we have to deviate into French—*reportage.*

If you decide to be factual a good beginning would be: "Four million trout flies were manufactured last year by the three leading sports-supply houses." That is the sort of thing which makes almost any editor sit up and take notice. But it is no better than certain other possible beginnings. The polemic article ought to start: "Despite all the efforts of our department of wild life conservation, the number of game fish in American lakes and streams continues to decline steadily." Probably this kind of beginning to this kind of article is best of all because it sounds alarming and because nowadays (and for understandable reasons) whatever sounds alarming is generally taken to be true. However, if you want to go in for the trickier *reportage* start off with a sentence something like this: " 'Cap' Bill Hanks, a lean, silent, wryly humorous down-Easterner, probably knows more about the strange habits of the American fisherman than any man alive."

Of course, no one will ever inquire where you got your statistics about the trout flies, whether the fish population really is declining, or whether "Cap" Bill Hanks really exists. In fact, one of the best and lengthiest "Profiles" *The New Yorker* ever ran turned out to be about a "character" at the Fulton Fishmarket who didn't. Whatever looks like official fact or on-the-spot reporting is taken at face value and will be widely quoted. The important thing is that the editor first and the reader afterwards shall get the feeling that what he is being offered is not mere literature but the real low-down on something or other—whether that something or other is or is not anything he cares much about.

Fling your facts around, never qualify anything (qualifications arouse distrust), and adopt an air of jolly omniscience. Remember that "essays" are written by introverts, "articles" by extroverts, and that the reader is going to resent anything which comes between him and that low-down which it is your principal function to supply. "Personalities," the more eccentric the better, are fine subjects for *reportage.* Manufacture or get hold of a good one and you may be able to do a "profile." But no one wants any personality to show in the magazine writer, whose business it is to be all-knowing, shrewd, and detached almost to the point of non-existence. This means, of course, that your style should have no quality which belongs to you, only the qualities appropriate to the magazine for which you are writing. The most successful of all the magazines functioning in America today seldom print anything which is not anonymous and apparently owe a considerable part of their success to the fact that nearly everything which appears in them achieves the manner of *Life, Time,* or *Fortune,* as the case may be, but never by any chance any characteristic which would enable the most sensitive analyst of style to discover who had written it.

The ideal is obviously a kind of writing which seems to have been produced not by a man but by some sort of electronic machine. Perhaps in time it will actually be produced that way, since such machines now solve differential equations and that is harder to do than to write the average magazine article. Probably if Vannevar Bush were

to put his mind to the problem he could replace the whole interminable list of editors, assistant editors, and research assistants employed by the Luce publications with a contraption less elaborate than that now used to calculate the trajectory of a rocket. Meanwhile the general effect of mechanical impersonality can be achieved by a system of collaboration in the course of which such personalities as the individual collaborators may have are made to cancel one another out.

This system works best when these collaborators are divided into two groups called respectively "researchers" and "writers"—or, in other words, those who know something but don't write and those who don't know anything but do. This assures at the very outset that the actual writers shall have no dangerous interest in or even relation to what they write and that any individuality of approach which might tend to manifest itself in one of them will be canceled out by the others. If you then pass the end-result through the hands of one or more senior editors for further regularization you will obviously get finally something from which every trace of what might be called handwork has disappeared.

Obviously, few publications can afford the elaborate machinery which the Luce organization has set up. However, a great many strive to achieve something of the same effect by simpler means, and they expect their contributors to cooperate by recognizing the ideal and by coming as close to the realization of it as is possible for an individual to come. The circulations achieved by these publications seem to indicate how wise from one point of view their policy is. Those which still permit or even encourage a certain amount of individuality in their writers—even those which still offer a certain amount of non-fiction which is to some extent personal and reflective as opposed to the factual and the bleaky expository—must content themselves with relatively small circulations. Moreover, since they also print a good deal of the other sort of thing they create the suspicion that they survive in spite of rather than because of their limited hospitality to the man-made as opposed to the machine-made article.

No doubt the kind of essay which *The Atlantic* and the old *Century* once went in for died of anemia. It came to represent the genteel tradition at its feeblest. No one need be surprised that it did not survive. But what is significant is the fact that, whereas the genteel novel was succeeded by novels of a different sort and genteel poetry by poetry in a different manner, the familiar essay died without issue, so that what disappeared was a once important literary form for which changed times found no use. And the result is that there disappeared with it the best opportunity to consider in an effective way an area of human interest.

Because the "article" is impersonal it can deal only with subjects which exist in an impersonal realm. If its subject is not ominous, usually it must be desperately trivial; and just as the best-selling books are likely to have for title either something like "The World in Crisis" or "My Grandmother Did a Strip Tease," so the magazine articles which are not heavy are very likely to be inconsequential. I doubt that anyone was ever quite as eccentric as almost every subject of a *New Yorker* "Profile" is made to seem; but if a topic cannot be made "devastating" the next best thing is "fabulous."

Perhaps what disappeared with the familiar essay was not merely a form, not merely even an attitude, but a whole subject matter. For the familiar essay affords what is probably the best method of discussing those subjects which are neither obviously momentous nor merely silly. And, since no really good life is composed exclusively of problems and farce, either the reading of most people today does not actually concern itself with some of the most important aspects of their lives or those lives are impoverished to a degree which the members of any really civilized society would find it difficult to understand. Just as genuine conversation—by which I mean something distinguishable from disputation, lamentation, and joke-telling—has tended to disappear from social gatherings, so anything comparable to it has tended to disappear from the printed page. By no means all of the Most-of-My-Friends essays caught it. But the best of them caught something which nowadays hardly gets into print at all.

Somehow we have got into the habit of assuming that even the so-called "human problems" are best discussed in terms as inhuman as possible. Just how one can profitably consider dispassionately so passionate a creature as man I do not know, but that seems to be the enterprise to which we have committed ourselves. The magazines are full of articles dealing statistically with, for example, the alleged failure or success of marriage. Lawyers discuss the law, sociologists publish statistics, and psychologists discuss case histories. Those are the methods by which we deal with the behavior of animals since animals can't talk. But men can—or at least once could—communicate, and one man's "familiar essay" on love and marriage might get closer to some all-important realities than any number of "studies" could.

No one is, to take another example, naive enough to suppose that all the current discussions of the welfare state are actually as "objective" as most of them pretend to be. Personal tastes, even simple self-interest, obviously influence most of them but only insofar as they introduce distortions between the lines. Everybody who writes for or against the competitive society tries to write as though he did not live in it, had had no personal experience of what living in it is like, and was dealing only with a question in which he had no personal interest. This is the way one talks about how to keep bees or raise the Black Angus. It is not the way either the bees or the Black Angus would discuss the good life as it affected them, and it is a singularly unrealistic way of considering anything which would affect us. Even the objective studies would be better and more objective if their authors permitted themselves freely to express elsewhere their "familiar" reaction to conditions and prospects instead of working in these feelings disguised as logical argument or scientific deduction.

All the sciences which deal with man have a tendency to depersonalize him for the simple reason that they tend to disregard everything which a particular science cannot deal with. Just as medicine confessedly deals with the physical man and economics confessedly deals not with Man but with the simplification officially designated as

The Economic Man, so psychiatry deals with a fictitious man of whom there would be nothing more to be said if he were "normal," and one branch of psychology deals with what might be called the I.Q. man whose only significant aspect is his ability to solve puzzles.

Literature is the only thing which deals with the whole complex phenomenon at once, and if all literature were to cease to exist the result would probably be that in the end whatever is not considered by one or another of the sciences would no longer be taken into account at all and would perhaps almost cease to exist. Then Man would no longer be—or at least no longer be observed to be—anything different from the mechanical sum of the Economic man, the I.Q. man, and the other partial men with whom the various partial sciences deal. Faced with that prospect we may well look with dismay at the disappearance of any usable literary form and wonder whether or not we have now entered upon a stage during which man's lingering but still complex individuality finds itself more and more completely deprived of the opportunity not only to express itself in living but even to discover corresponding individualities revealing themselves in the spoken or the written word.

That the situation could be radically altered by the cultivation of the familiar essay I am hardly prepared to maintain. Its disappearance is only a minor symptom. Or perhaps it is just a little bit more than that. At least there are a number of subjects which might profitably be discussed by fewer experts and more human beings. They might achieve a different kind of understanding of certain problems and they might lead to more humanly acceptable conclusions. "Most of my friends seem to feel that . . . ."

David Daiches

SOURCE: "Reflections on the Essay," in *A Century of the Essay, British and American,* edited by David Daiches, Harcourt Brace Jovanovich, 1951, pp. 1-8.

[*Daiches is a prominent English scholar and critic who has written extensively on English and American literature. In the following excerpt, Daiches discusses the evolution of the familiar essay through its synthesis with the critical essay, holding that the successful modern essay retains the stamp of the genre's earlier style.*]

To write an essay on the essay: the prospect has a certain charm, for the essay is the most selfindulgent of literary forms, and to talk about it calls for an intellectual ease, a relaxed and quizzical attitude, which modern literary critics, whether academic or merely esoteric, generally feel it their duty to avoid. Yet when we think of the essay in this way we are ignoring some of the major forms it has assumed in the last hundred years. The personal or familiar essay—Dr. Johnson's "loose sally"—from Montaigne to Charles Lamb is, I suppose, the essay *par excellence;* it is this kind of essay which established the form as a literary *genre* and gave it its name. Montaigne in 1580 called his confessional discourses *Essais,* that is, attempts, tentative and suggestive remarks, and there is a long line of essay writers who take their cue from him. But the characteristic modern essay is an altogether more serious affair. William James discussing pragmatism, T. S. Eliot appraising Andrew Marvell, Edmund Wilson analyzing A. E. Housman—there is nothing here of the tentative personal confession: these writers are telling the truth as they see it, cogently, urgently, and with high seriousness. The modern essay writer tends to be both more concerned and more *committed* than his predecessor.

Of course, there have been serious philosophical essays from very early times—the Greeks were particularly good at that kind of writing, and it can be found in English literature throughout the seventeenth and eighteenth centuries—but the essay as a recognized literary form, as a kind of writing agreeable for its own sake and enjoyable apart from its message, was a century ago more likely to be the kind of thing done by Montaigne or Abraham Cowley (whose essay, "Of Myself," published posthumously with his other essays in 1668, is one of the first truly confessional short pieces of prose in English) or Addison or Goldsmith or Charles Lamb. While the familiar essay has by no means disappeared in the last hundred years, it has become a thin trickle indeed when compared with the stream of serious critical and philosophical discussions in our time. One might venture a preposterous generalization, and say that ever since the middle of the last century writers have become increasingly worried, have taken themselves and their readers ever more seriously, have more and more lost interest in the light play of ideas, so that the essays they produce are, like Matthew Arnold's or Bertrand Russell's or George Orwell's, searching investigations of troubling problems or earnest exhortations to the gentiles. . . .

Western man has become increasingly concerned about himself in the last hundred years (with good cause, it might be added), and this concern is reflected in the growing seriousness of the vast majority of essays. It may be objected that I am here using the term "essay" for two very different kinds of writing, that on the one hand we have the familiar essay, read for its stylistic grace and confessional charm, and on the other we have the serious prose discussion, which can handle any subject, can be of any length, and is often of interest only to those who have a previous interest in the subject handled. Thus, it might be maintained, all that I am saying is that the essay has in some measure given way to the critical discussion, a quite different form of writing, which has existed for a much longer period of time than the essay proper. But the fact is that the line between the professional treatise and the personal chat is a continuous one, and while it is easy enough to distinguish between the extremes, there is a middle ground—the critical essays of Hazlitt, for example—where impressionistic confession and objective exposition of ideas mingle, and even reinforce each other. The element of personality is never wholly absent from any of the discussions included in the present anthology, and so long as that element is present, reinforcing the argument with all kinds of overtones and implied attitudes, the link between the personal essay and the serious monograph is maintained, and we have a right to continue the use of the term "essay."

The serious philosophical essay—Locke's *Essay Concern-*

ing Human Understanding, for example—of the seventeenth or eighteenth century is indeed not an essay in the sense in which I am using the term; but with the growth of periodicals which offered a vehicle for the shorter and less professional prose discussion something of the style and tone of the familiar essay inevitably crept in, so that even T. S. Eliot, for all his repudiation of personality in literature, projects himself in his critical essays in a highly idiosyncratic way, and we see the man reflected in the prose much more immediately and directly than we do in the essays of David Hume or of other professional philosophers. This combination of earnest exposition with revelation—conscious or unconscious—of personality is to be found in the more serious of Addison's *Spectator* essays and is a feature of periodical literature from Addison's day to our own.

There is, however, a difference between the kind of thing that earlier periodical writers were doing and what we often find in modern journals. The growth of specialization has produced more and more specialized periodicals, each addressed to experts, and each using a jargon unintelligible to even the most cultured layman. The decline of the essay in present-day America—and there can be no doubt that, in spite of the fact that good examples of the form can be found without much difficulty, it has declined—is largely due to the decline of the layman, of the non-specialist inquirer, the intelligent and well-read man of large general curiosity. If the essay, however serious and objective in intention, can be defined as a reasonably short prose discussion in which the personality of the author in some degree shapes the style and tone of the argument, and in which the writer's skill in the handling of prose exposition is impressive in its own right and pleasing for the reader to watch in operation, then the treatise in the specialized professional journal today is certainly very far from being an essay: it is most often a set of harsh shorthand notes meant to be translated by the expert reader who can fit it into its context and make sense (if not charm) out of it in relation to that context.

The art of the essay, like that of conversation, has declined in the last century because there are too few people who know enough about enough matters to afford an audience for the attractive discussion which is expert without being specialized. The secret of Dr. Johnson's conversation was that, considering himself an educated man, he had a clearly defined opinion on whatever might be brought to his attention, and was prepared to express it forcefully in the language of educated men, not gracelessly and hermetically in the language of technical experts. The serious prose discussion can only remain an essay if the author is similarly at ease in the world of human thought and is prepared to see the infinite relevance of any particular arguments he might present. That is why Emerson and Arnold and Bertrand Russell and Eliot remain essayists, experts though they are in their way. They write in an atmosphere of luminous intelligence, not in the blinding darkness of technical footnoting.

With human knowledge increasingly broken up into fragments and distributed among experts, the essay which appeals to the "general reader" tends to get ever thinner and triter, talking down to a common ignorance or a common set of prejudices, as far too many newspaper editorials do today. In such an atmosphere, the good essayist renders a very special service: he reminds us of the importance of general intelligence, demonstrating by the example of his own practice that the terms "general" and "intelligence" are not contradictory. The technical expert with his special jargon may be necessary (though this is arguable) if we are to continue to extend the limits of human knowledge in specific areas, but it can be claimed for the essayist that it is he who integrates this knowledge with the pattern of culture of his day, who airs it and demonstrates its relevance to our daily thinking and its general significance in the intellectual climate of our time.

The essayist can perform this function with varying degrees of solemnity. The sense of concern and commitment which we get in Eliot's critical essays is very different from the witty exploitation of ideas we get in an essay by Aldous Huxley, and both these writers have nothing in their tone and attitude that remotely resembles, say, the relaxed and discursive intelligence of Christopher Morley. Yet all are performing a similar kind of service; they are handling ideas effectively in prose in such a way as both to please the reader by the aptness of the expression (by their style, that is to say) and to arouse him to an awareness of the implications for human intelligence of what is being discussed. There is no activity more civilized and more civilizing.

If we can distinguish—at their extremes—between the serious prose discussion addressed to those already interested in the subject and the familiar essay which appeals by the grace with which the author projects his personality, and if we make this distinction only to realize that there is an important middle ground where elements of both come together, we have still left no place for recognition of the kind of essay whose function is simply to demonstrate a certain kind of mastery over prose. The "Character" writers of the seventeenth century, who wrote cleverly phrased descriptions of character types in order to show the aptness of their phrasing, have their heirs in nineteenth-century essayists who are simply professional wielders of a graceful pen. The early Stevenson is often in this category. Stevenson wanted to be a writer before he had anything to say—he even undertook journeys solely in order to be able to write about them skillfully when they were over—and in his earliest phase produced many accomplished essays which, if we take a musical analogy, can be compared to *études* rather than pieces. They are exercises in the handling of English prose, often quite brilliant in their way, and fascinating reading for anyone interested in the potentialities of the medium. This kind of essayist has diminished almost to non-existence, which is a pity, for the essay as *étude* demonstrates and encourages a concern with craftsmanship in exposition of which the present generation stands all too much in need.

One must beware, however, of making too hard and fast a separation between the essay as *étude* and the essay as full composition. Just as the short treatise and the personal essay can merge into each other, so, and to an even greater degree, the essay as exhibition of mere craftsman-ship can transform itself imperceptibly into a significant treatment of some phase of human thought or experience. Stevenson wrote "Walking Tours" primarily as an exercise in English prose; but it emerges as more than that, and we read it as much for its pleasing rendition of a state of mind and its effective capturing of the tone of personality as for the modulation of its prose rhythms. Indeed, modulation of prose rhythms, or any other aspect of literary craftsmanship, can be seen as effective only to the degree that it gives life to some content, for the arrangement of words is successful in proportion as it communicates the full implications of what the author has to say. In literature (and perhaps in music, too) there can never be a pure *étude*.

So one sets up distinctions between different kinds of essays in order to break them down again. Not, of course, that these distinctions are unreal: one does not need to demonstrate that E. B. White is doing something very different from what Oliver Wendell Holmes did, or even that the humorous essay of Thurber is very far away, in tone, style, and general purpose, from the equally (but differently) humorous essay by Max Beerbohm. But distinctions can be seen and appreciated without the setting up of rigid categories, even if such categories are helpful in the initial clearing of one's mind. Let us by all means read the essays in this collection for what they are, recognizing individuality of style and purpose, noting different degrees of seriousness, appreciating humor, whimsicality, gracefulness, profundity, wit, irony, compassion, shrewdness, and whatever other qualities come through to us, conveyed by the appropriate handling of prose; but there is no harm, either, in recognizing the common purpose that runs through even such a disparate group of essays as this. Here are intelligent and civilized men using the medium of English prose in order to set ideas happily in a context of human awareness. The ideas may be deliberately trivial or preposterous, or they may be profound and challenging, or they may lie anywhere between these extremes. But in each case the author conveys them in appropriate language, organizes them deftly, and presents them in such a way that we can take some delight in the presentation at the same time we respond as intelligent and thoughtful readers to the implications of what is said.

Something in the present state of civilization has made most of us far too defensive about our interests and our pleasures. Do we need to apologize for reading what thoughtful men have said well, whether of description, argument, or self-revelation? Do I need to write another essay explaining the value of this sort of thing? If the reader does not see that the answer to both these questions is a resounding "No!" he is beyond salvation by essays or by any other kind of literature.

Michael Hamburger

SOURCE: "An Essay on the Essay," in *Art as Second Nature: Occasional Pieces, 1950-74,* A Carcanet New Press Publication, 1975, pp. 3-5.

[In the following excerpt from an essay originally published in 1965, Hamburger cites the familiar essay, with its inher-

ent aimlessness and leisureliness, as a casualty of the mechanized, hurrying modern world.]

The essay is just as outmoded as the art of letter-writing, the art of conversation, the art of walking for pleasure. Ever since Montaigne the essay has been highly individualistic, but at the same time it presupposes a society that not only tolerates individualism but enjoys it—a society leisured and cultivated enough to do without information. The whole spirit of essay-writing is contained in the first sentence of the first great collection of English essays—Francis Bacon's of 1597: 'What is *Truth;* said jesting *Pilate;* And would not stay for an Answer.' A jesting Pilate who asks questions but doesn't wait for answers is the archetypal personification of the essay, of essay-writing and essayists. The English essay flourished for three centuries, even when the earnestness of the Victorian age had begun

---

The essay is a form with distinguished predecessors and a rich tradition, and within its generous boundaries one can do almost anything one wishes: report anecdotes, tell jokes, make literary criticisms, polemicize, bring in odd scraps of scholarship, recount human idiosyncrasy in its full bountifulness, let the imagination roam free. Subjects are everywhere, and there is no shortage of cultivated and appreciative readers. Don't spread it around, but it's a sweet time to be an essayist.

—Joseph Epstein

---

to question its peculiar relation to truth. Only the totalitarian systems of this century turned walking without a purpose into a crime. Since the time of G. K. Chesterton and Virginia Woolf the essay has been a dead genre. Needless to say, people continued—and still continue—to write prose pieces which they call essays; but already George Orwell was too 'committed', too puritanical, too much aware of a crisis to take walks without a bad conscience. . . .

The spirit of essay-writing walks on irresistibly, even over the corpse of the essay, and is glimpsed now here, now there, in novels, stories, poems or articles, from time to time in the very parkland of philosophy, formidably walled and strictly guarded though it may seem, the parkland from which it escaped centuries ago to wander about in the wild meadow. But it is never glimpsed where that wild meadow has been banned from human consciousness even as a memory or possibility, where walls have become absolute and walking itself has become a round of compulsion and routine. It has come to terms with the overcrowded streets of large cities, but hardly with factories, barracks, offices, not at all with prison yards and extermination camps. Anyone who can never get these out of his

mind cannot tolerate the aimlessness and evasiveness of essay-writing, but calls it shameless, egotistic and insolent. But somewhere or other the spirit of essay-writing is walking on; and no one knows where it will turn up. Perhaps in the essay again, one day?

FURTHER READING

Benson, Arthur Christopher. "The Art of the Essayist." In *Contemporary Essays,* edited by Odell Shepard, pp. 14-25. New York: Charles Scribner's Sons, 1929.
　　Discursive reflections on the essayist's role, concluding that "He [the essayist] works . . . on what is called the analytic method, observing, recording, interpreting, just as things strike him, and letting his fancy play over their beauty and significance; the end of it all being this: that he is deeply concerned with the charm and quality of things, and desires to put it all in the clearest and gentlest light, so that at least he may make others love life a little better, and prepare them for its infinite variety and alike for its joyful and mournful surprises."

Blunden, Edmund. *Leigh Hunt's "Examiner" Examined.* Cobden Sanderson, 1928, 263 p.
　　Examines the controversies and persons, including the principal English familiar essayists, who contributed to Hunt's *Examiner* from 1808 to 1825. Blunden reprints selections by or concerning Hunt, Lamb, John Keats, Percy Bysshe Shelley, and Lord Byron.

Brooks, Charles S. "Lazy Ink-Pots." In his *Like Summer's Coud: A Book of Essays,* pp. 183-93. New York: Harcourt, Brace and Co., 1925.
　　Exults in the joy of languid meditation and of writing essays on the subjects of one's meditation.

Freeman, John. "The English Essay—Francis Bacon to George Saintsbury." *The Bookman* (London) 65, No. 38 (December 1923): 349-52.
　　Overview of the essay's history, with short references to Lamb and Hazlitt as the successors of Samuel Johnson and Oliver Goldsmith and as writers who effected "a new development of the essay."

Huxley, Aldous. Preface to *Collected Essays,* pp. v-ix. New York: Harper and Brothers, 1959.
　　Discusses the nature of the best-crafted essay, defining it as a combination of three different types of essay, among them—and predominantly—the personal (familiar) essay.

O'Leary, R. D. "What Is an Essay?" In his *The Essay,* pp. 1-43. New York: Thomas Y. Crowell Co., 1928.
　　Discourses at length on the form of the essay and on the need for brevity by the essayist, in a book written for students of English composition.

Orage, A. R. "On Essay Writing." In his *Selected Essays and Critical Writings,* edited by Herbert Read and Denis Saurat, pp. 46-50. London: Stanley Nott, 1935.
　　Commentary on a modern essay which demonstrates the extent to which the personal essay has changed in the direction of impersonality and bluntness since the time of Hunt, Hazlitt, and Lamb.

Priestley, J. B. "A Grossly Egotistical Matter." In his *I for One*, pp. 241-48. 1923. Reprint. Freeport, N.Y.: Books for Libraries Press, 1967.

> Laments the potential essays lost after Priestley burned a pocket notebook filled with scraps of ideas for familiar essays.

————. Introduction to *Essayists Past and Present: A Selection of English Essays*, pp. 7-32. 1925. Reprint. Freeport, N.Y.: Books for Libraries Press, 1967.

> Overview of the essay's history, from Montaigne to Robert Lynd, with significant discussion of the role of Hazlitt and Lamb in the essay tradition.

Squire, J. C. "An Essay on Essays." in *Essays of the Year (1929-1930)*, pp. ix-xvii. London: Argonaut Press, 1930.

> Rambling discourse on the stream-of-consciousness nature of the familiar essay, with special regard given the writings of Lamb, Hilaire Belloc, and Robert Lynd.

Stewart, John L. "Familiar Essays: Comment." In *The Essay: A Critical Anthology*, pp. 530-31. New York: Prentice-Hall, 1952.

> Pedagogical introduction to the familiar essay's tonal, thematic, and stylistic characteristics.

Walker, Hugh. *The English Essay and Essayists*. London and Toronto: J. M. Dent & Sons, 1928, 343 p.

> Discursive history of the English essay from its beginnings through the early twentieth century, focusing upon the key editors, practitioners, and periodicals in which their work appeared.

Nineteenth-Century Historical Fiction

INTRODUCTION

The genre of nineteenth-century historical fiction includes novels and romances written about the distant past, about the recent past, or about the time period contemporary with an author's experience. Although they agree about the general characteristics of the genre, critics debate the degree to which historical accuracy or realistic representation should be present in a work of historical fiction. Depending on the novelist's motives, historical fiction may emphasize realistic depiction of historical facts throughout the novel, truthful portrayal of the spirit of an age, or correctness in the representation of specific historical movements or themes. Nineteenth-century novelists, including Sir Walter Scott, Edward Bulwer-Lytton, George Eliot, Nathaniel Hawthorne, Charles Dickens, and Benito Pérez Galdós, wrote historical fiction in order to demonstrate similarities between the past and the present, to initiate social reform, to change readers' views about historical persons or events, and to supplement and encourage the formal study of history.

Most critics agree that Sir Walter Scott became "the father of the historical novel" in 1814 when he wrote *Waverly*, a novel about life in the Scottish borderlands. *Waverly* achieved enormous popular and critical success and sparked the public's interest in history, and many commentators hold it as the standard by which historical fiction ought to be judged. Scott followed *Waverly* with several more historical romances, including *Ivanhoe* (1819). As the popularity of the genre increased, so did the critics' and the public's desire for historical accuracy. Scott and his numerous imitators were criticized by essayist and historian Thomas Carlyle and others who frowned on novels written solely for the sake of readers' amusement. Many commentators held that authors had a responsibility to ensure factual accuracy within their work. In 1846, George Henry Lewes praised Scott's achievement in *Waverly*, stating that "no grave historian ever succeeded better in painting the character of the epoch." Throughout the 1830s and 1840s readers and critics alike began to look to historical fiction as a necessary complement to historical studies. Novels produced at this time include Bulwer-Lytton's extensively researched *Rienzi, The Last of the Tribunes* (1835) and Harriet Martineau's *The Hour and the Man* (1841), both of which provided detailed evaluations of historical figures and eras. However, there was growing concern among scholars that with so many historical novels being written, readers would start to view historical fiction as a substitute for, rather than a supplement to, the formal study of history. Concurrent with these developments was the trend among some authors to write novels about contemporary social issues, with the aim of realistically representing the problems in Victorian England. Dickens's *Oliver Twist* (1838), for example, examines the cruelty experienced by children in workhouses. During the 1850s and 1860s, the public's interest in the genre dwindled, partly in response to the high volume of historical novels being published. Similarly, critical sentiment toward historical fiction ranged from skepticism to hostility, although highly esteemed historical novels such as Dickens's *A Tale of Two Cities* (1859) and Eliot's *Romola* (1862) were still being published. By the 1860s, as James Simmons has written, "the vogue for historical fiction had expended itself."

Many scholars have noted that in nineteenth-century America historical novelists often romanticized aspects of the past to some degree in order to accomplish their aims. Some American novelists wrote about colonial America in an attempt, some critics have argued, to redefine or to reemphasize nineteenth-century national values. According to Beverly Seaton, many novels about the colonial period assured white readers of their racial superiority. William Gilmore Simms's *The Yemassee* (1835), for example, centered around conflicts with Native Americans in which white settlers are depicted as virtuous while Native Americans are rendered as cruel and dishonest. Novels such as Paul Leicester Ford's *Janice Meredith* (1899) and S. Weir Mitchell's *Hugh Wynne, Free Quaker* (1897) incorporate analyses of religious fanaticism in colonial times in order to remind nineteenth-century readers of the importance of supporting liberalism in organized religion. Pauline Hopkins, in *Contending Forces: A Romance Illustrative of Negro Life North and South* (1899), uses the motifs of traditional nineteenth-century romances—such as ending the novel with the heroine's happy marriage—in order to interest both African American and white readers. After capturing the attention of this larger audience, Hopkins then focuses on the realities of African American history. Still other novelists, rather than detailing specific movements, events, or themes, chose to characterize a time and place, as Hawthorne does with his depiction of seventeenth-century Puritan New England in *The Scarlet Letter* (1850).

Critics continue to debate the definition and attributes of historical fiction. Harry E. Shaw has maintained that a "minimal" definition of the genre is necessary to accommodate the variety of views on history. Brander Matthews has claimed that novelists who wrote about their own time period produced the most "trustworthy" historical fiction. Joseph Turner has admitted that defining the genre is problematic, and has categorized historical fiction in terms of the novelist's treatment of past. Modern scholars have also studied nineteenth-century historical fiction with a view to understanding how each novelist addressed the social issues of his or her day through his or her treatment of the past.

REPRESENTATIVE WORKS

Eligio Ancona
   El filibustero 1866
Edward Bulwer-Lytton
   Rienzi, The Last of the Tribunes 1835
   The Last of the Barons 1843
James Fenimore Cooper
   The Prarie 1823
   Pioneers 1827
Charles Dickens
   Oliver Twist 1838
   A Tale of Two Cities 1859
George Eliot
   Scenes of Clerical Life 1858
   Romola 1862
Paul Leicester Ford
   Janice Meredith 1899
Benito Pérez Galdós
   Episodios nacionales, Series I and II 1873-79
Nathaniel Hawthorne
   The Scarlet Letter 1850
Pauline Hopkins
   *Contending Forces: A Romance Illustrative of Negro
      Life North and South* 1899
Charles Kingsley
   Westward Ho! 1855
Harriet Martineau
   The Hour and the Man 1841
S. Weir Mitchell
   Hugh Wynne, Free Quaker 1897
Charles Reade
   The Cloister and the Hearth 1861
Sir Walter Scott
   Waverley 1814
   Ivanhoe 1819
William Gilmore Simms
   The Yemassee 1835
Daniel Pierce Thompson
   The Green Mountain Boys 1839

DEFINITIONS AND CHARACTERISTICS

George Henry Lewes

SOURCE: A review of "The Foster Brother: A Tale of the
War of Chiozza," in *The Westminster Review*, Vol. XLV,
No. 1, March, 1846, pp. 34-54.

[*Lewes was one of the most versatile men of letters in the
Victorian era. A prominent English journalist, he was the
founder, with Leigh Hunt, of* The Leader, *a radical political journal that he edited from 1851 to 1854. He served as
the first editor of the* Fortnightly Review *from 1865 to
1866, a journal which he also helped to establish. Critics
often cite Lewes's influence on the novelist George Eliot, to
whom he was companion and mentor, as his principal contribution to English letters, but they also credit him with*

*critical acumen in his literary commentary, most notably
in his dramatic criticism. In the following excerpt, Lewes
harshly criticizes authors of some historical romances for
their inclusion of "useless" information and for their failure to capture the spirit of the time period about which they
were writing.*]

To judge from the number yearly published, one may presume that there is a great demand for historical romances;
and to judge from the quality of those published, one may
suppose the readers very good-natured, or very ignorant;
or both. We believe they are both.

To write a good historical romance is no easy task; to write
such as are published (with an exception here and there)
is, we believe, one of the easiest of all literary tasks. Were
it otherwise, how could Mr James and Alexandre Dumas
pour forth their novels with such amazing rapidity? One
announces that he finished a volume in twelve days; the
other has recently signed an agreement to limit himself to
twenty volumes in the year! Were it otherwise, how could
the great quantity of yearly publications be kept up? Few
will be bold enough to assert that the great mass of novelists display any remarkable talent; yet the great mass of
novels are historical; *ergo,* we conclude that the historical
novel is one wherein mediocrity is at its ease. Must it not
be so? In the domestic novel mediocrity cannot escape dulness and twaddle; in the art-novel it cannot escape rant
and maudlin; in the *roman intime* it degenerates into utter
drivel; and in the satirical novel it is in the plight of one
endeavouring to be witty, and sinking into mere pertness
and personality. For the domestic novel a man needs
knowledge of character, power of truthful painting, pathos, and good sense. For the art-novel he needs imagination, style, and a knowledge of art. For the *roman intime*
he needs a mastery over mental analysis, passion, and lyrical feeling. For the satirical novel he needs wit, and knowledge of the world. But for the historical novel, as it is generally written, he needs no style, no imagination, no fancy,
no knowledge of the world, no wit, no pathos; he needs
only to study Scott, and the historical novelists; to "cram"
for the necessary information about costumes, antiquated
forms of speech, and the leading political events of the
epoch chosen; and to add thereto the art, so easily learned,
of complicating a plot with adventures, imprisonments,
and escapes. As for character, he need give himself no
trouble about it: his predecessors have already furnished
him with *types;* these he can christen anew. Probability he
may utterly scorn. If he has any reflections to make, he
need only give them a sententious turn; truth, novelty, or
depth, are unimportant. Sprinkle largely with love and
heroism; keep up the mystery overhanging the hero's
birth, till the last chapter; and have a good stage villain,
scheming and scowling through two volumes and a half,
to be utterly exposed and defeated at last—and the historical novel is complete.

The writers of this bastard species are of two kinds: the
one kind has a mere surface-knowledge of history, picked
up from other novels, and from Hume, or Sismondi. The
other has "crammed" for the occasion: knows much, but
knows it ill: is minutely tedious, because he insists on
teaching you to-day what he himself learned yesterday. He

reads chronicles only to quote them, and endeavours by *notes* to supply the want of that mastery of the subject, which long familiarity alone can give, and which alone enables a man to paint an epoch. This false erudition, joined to a false imagination, produces an abortion, to which we prefer the flimsiest of novels.

Yet the public evidently encourages historical romance, even such historical romance as is afforded it. We have already hinted two reasons for this; and to them we could add a third, viz.: It is thought easier and pleasanter to read history in romance, than to read it in those respectable russia-bound octavos, "which no gentleman's library should be without." Idleness;—a wish to get at knowledge by a royal route; and a pleasant self-sophistication, that reading such novels is not "a waste of time,"—these are the great encouragers of historical novels. What is the consequence? The consequence is, that we have false history, and a bad story, palmed upon us for a novel. Now we are of those, albeit accustomed to grave studies, who utterly deny the fact of a novel being a waste of time: certainly a bad novel is; but so is every bad book. Think of the delight a good novel will give; think of the emotions it excites, the trains of thought it suggests; think also of the influence exercised upon mental culture by the perusal of novels. This influence may be good or bad, according to the truth or falsehood of the works; but in stating the case for novels, we have a right to speak only of the good. The question is not, are *bad* novels waste of time? No one doubts it. We confess, then, to a high relish for novels. If we seldom read them, it is because the good are rare. We confess to a high opinion of their influence; and so far from thinking them a "waste of time" (which is the frequent assertion of some very frivolous people, trying to look profound) we believe few works more capable of fulfilling the highest aim of books. There is but one indispensable condition: they must be true. Of course by truth we do not mean *literality;* few tales are so false as those "founded upon facts"; the truth we speak of is truth of character and feeling.

It is your bad historical romance, the reading of which is waste of time. No-knowledge is better than mis-knowledge; and the scraps of history picked up from a novel are just sufficient to mislead the indolent into the idea of their possessing "information." Either history is worth knowing, or it is not: if worth knowing, then worth studying in proper sources; if not, then surely a great incumbrance to a tale. We suggest this to worthy mammas, and tutors, who only allow young people to read *historical* romances, because *there* some good "information" is to be gained. We know a lady who piques herself upon her strictness, and who, while refusing to allow her daughter, aged sixteen, to read novels, allowed her to read St Simon's 'Mémories'—because they were historical! This is a good instance of the error we are combating; it is indeed a type. Worthy mammas! Excellent tutors! Is there no other sort of "information," but that of "facts"? Are there no things under the sun worth learning, besides the erudition of 'Mangnall's Questions?' Is knowledge of the human heart not information? Are your children to live in the world, to battle with it, and not to know it? Are they to mix with men and women, and rather than learn the na-

tures of men and women, in the best way they can, to "cram" up a certain amount of "information" of mere externals, of names and dates, and those ancient names and dates? This is poor wisdom; but akin to the wisdom which devotes the long and precious years of youth to the study of that which they will never (in nine cases out of ten) need in after-life.

Let not the reader suppose that we cast any slight upon historical romance. Our object has been solely to point attention to the fallacy of supposing that bad historical romances—and very few good ones are published—can be less a waste of time than other romances. The conjunction of two such elements as history and fiction may be excellent, provided the history be good and the fiction good. But if the history be bad, or superficial, it is an excrescence. The story, after all, is the main thing; and if history be joined to it, it is only on the privilege of adding a new interest to the story.

When we speak of bad and false history, we mean useless, or worse than useless handling of past times, characters, and events. Those sticklers for truth, who reproach Scott with having falsified history because he wilfully confused dates, forget the far greater truth which that wonderful writer generally presented. If, for his purposes, he disarranged the order of events a little; no grave historian ever succeeded better in painting the character of the epoch. He committed errors of detail enough to make Mrs Markham shudder. He divined important historical truths which had escaped the sagacity of all historians. A great authority, Augustin Thierry, has pronounced Scott the greatest of all historical divinators. All Europe has pronounced him to be the greatest of modern romance writers.

When, therefore, a writer has so familiarized himself with the inward spirit and outward form of an epoch, as to be able to paint it with accuracy and with ease, he may make that epoch a very useful and entertaining scene for his story: and then if his story be good, he will have written a good historical romance. Unfortunately it is only the outward form that most writers study; thinking with this outward form to compose splendid accessories. But after all, what are accessories? Very much what splendid processions, gorgeous scenery, numerous attendants, and spangled dresses are to a tragedy: a panoply of ennui.

Admitting the utility of history to romance, when history is properly understood, there is, we think, still one caution necessary. Let a man be thoroughly versed in the epoch, and perfectly capable of painting it, there is one danger he must always avoid: the danger of misrepresenting historical personages. In a former paper on the historical drama, we attempted to prove the almost insuperable difficulty of representing well-known historical persons, except as subordinate actors in the drama. The dramatist is forced to falsify history. The novelist is not quite so badly situated, but the danger is considerable. He may sketch portraits; but he must be wary how he makes the persons act and speak. His safety lies in entrusting the main action of his story to imaginary actors, and bringing known persons forward as only slightly connected with the plot. Of course, this applies only to such persons whose characters are tolerably known to us. If the epoch be remote, and the characters dimly perceived, the novelist has perfect licence; for such epochs verge upon the domain of the fabulous, wherein imagination may roam at will. But this, which is an obstacle to the historian, is an assistance to the novelist. Assured that we must be as ignorant as himself, he can invent his materials and create his characters. Shakspeare was at liberty to create a character for Macbeth, for Hamlet, or for Lear. No such licence could be allowed to one who treated of Elizabeth, Charles I., Strafford, or Louis XIV.

Brander Matthews

SOURCE: "The Historical Novel," in *The Historical Novel and Other Essays,* Charles Scribner's Sons, 1901, pp. 3-28.

[*An American critic, playwright, and novelist, Matthews wrote extensively on world drama and served for a quarter century at Columbia University as professor of dramatic literature; he was the first to hold that title at an American university. Matthews was also a founding member and president of the National Institute of Arts and Letters. Because his criticism is deemed both witty and informative, Matthews has been called "perhaps the last of the gentlemanly school of critics and essayists" in America. In the following essay written in 1897, Matthews argues that the only truly representative and "trustworthy" historical novel is that whose subject matter is contemporary with the author's experience.*]

When Robert Louis Stevenson wrote his 'Note on Realism,' and declared that "the historical novel is dead," he did not think he would live to be the author of the *Master of Ballantrae.* But when Prosper Mérimée expressed to a correspondent his belief that the historical novel was a "bastard form," he could look back without reproach upon his own *Chronique de Charles IX*—one of the finest examples of the kind of fiction he chose to despise. Whether or not most readers of English fiction at the end of the nineteenth century approve Mérimée opinion that the historical novel is illegitimate by birth, few of them will agree with Stevenson in deeming it defunct. If we can judge by the welcome it receives from the writers of newspaper notices, it is not moribund even; and if we are influenced by the immense sale of *Ben-Hur* and by the broadening vogue of *Quo Vadis,* we may go so far as to believe that it was never stronger or fuller of life.

We might even suggest that the liking for historical fiction is now so keen that the public is not at all particular as to the veracity of the history out of which the fiction has been manufactured, since it accepts the invented facts of the Chronicles of Zenda quite as eagerly as it receives the better-documented *Memoirs of a Minister of France.*

More than any other British author of his years, Stevenson worked in accord with the theories of art which have been elaborated and expounded in France; and it may be that when he declared the historical novel to be dead he was thinking rather of French literature than of English. There is no doubt that in France the historical novel is not cherished. No one of the living masters of fiction in France has attempted any but contemporary studies. M. Daudet, M.

Zola, M. Bourget, find all the subjects they need in the life of their own times. Flaubert's fame is due to his masterly *Madame Bovary,* and not to his splendid *Salmmbô.* So sharp is the French reaction against Romanticism that even impressionist critics like M. Jules Lemaître and M. Anatole France do not overpraise the gay romances of the elder Dumas, as Stevenson did. In France the historical novel has no standing in the court of serious criticism. As Mérimée wrote in the correspondence from which one quotation has already been made, "History, in my eyes, is a sacred thing."

Historical fiction suffers in France from the same discredit as historical painting, and for the same reasons. It is either too easy to be worth while—a French critic might say—or so difficult as to be impossible. When a young man once went to Courbet for advice, saying that his vocation was to be a historical painter, the artist promptly responded: "I don't doubt it; and therefore begin by giving three months to making a portrait of your father!"

Perhaps French opinion is nowhere more accurately voiced than by M. Anatole France in the 'Jardin d'Épicure':

> We cannot reproduce with any accuracy what no longer exists. When we see that a painter has to take all the trouble in the world to represent to us, more or less exactly, a scene in the time of Louis Philippe, we may despair of his ever being able to give us the slightest idea of an event contemporary with Saint Louis or Augustus. We weary ourselves copying armor and old chests; but the artists of the past did not worry themselves about so empty an exactness. They lent to the hero of legend or history the costume and the looks of their own contemporaries; and thus they depicted naturally their own soul and their own century. Now what can an artist do better?

In other words, Paul Veronese's *Marriage at Cana* is frankly a revelation of the Italian Renascence; and this revelation is not contaminated by any fifteenth-century guess at the manners and customs of Judea in the first century. It is difficult to surmise how some of the laboriously archeological pictures of the nineteenth century will affect an observer of the twenty-first century. As in painting, so in the drama: Shakspere made no effort to suggest the primitive manners and customs of Scotland to the spectators of his *Macbeth*; and if the characters of *Julius Caesar* are Roman, it is chiefly because of the local color that chanced to leak through from North's Plutarch. What Shakspere aimed at was the creation of living men and women—interesting because of their intense humanity, eternal because of their truth and vitality. He never sought to differentiate Scotchmen and Danes of the past from Englishmen of the present. He lent to all his personages the vocabulary, the laws, the usages, the costumes which were familiar to the playgoers that flocked to applaud his pieces. Archeology was unknown to him and to them; anachronism did not affright them or him. Probably he would have brushed aside any demand for exactness of fact as an attempt to impose an unfair restraint upon the liberty of the dramatist—whose business it was to write plays to be acted in a theater, and not to prepare lectures to be delivered in a college hall. Shakspere and Veronese, each in his own art, worked freely, as though wholly unconscious of any difference between their own contemporaries and the subjects of the Caesars.

The compilers of the 'Gesta Romanorum' had no conception of the elements of either geography or chronology; and the authors of the Romances of Chivalry seem to have been as ignorant, although their scientific nihilism is perhaps wilful—like Stockton's when he tells us a 'Tale of Negative Gravity.' The essential likeness of the Romances of Chivalry to the Waverley Novels has been pointed out more than once; and in each group of tales we find the hero, or the technical hero's rescuing friend, omnipresent, omniscient, and almost omnipotent. The essential difference between the two kinds of fiction is quite as obvious also: it lies in the fact that Scott and his followers know what history is, and that even when they vary from it they are aware of what they are doing.

The historical novel, as we understand it today, like the historical drama and like historical painting, could not come into being until after history had established itself, and after chronology and geography had lent to history their indispensable aid. Nowadays the novelist and the dramatist and the painter are conscious that people do not talk and dress and behave as they did a hundred years ago, or a thousand. They do not know precisely how the people of those days did feel and think and act: they cannot know these things. The most they can do is to study the records of the past and make a guess, the success of which depends on their equipment and insight. They accept their obligation to history and to its handmaids—an obligation which Shakspere and Veronese would have denied quite as frankly as the compilers of the 'Gesta Romanorum' or the writers of the Romances of Chivalry. Scott was appealing to a circle of more or less sophisticated readers, any one of whom might be an antiquary: he was to be tried by a jury of his peers. But the author of *Amadis of Gaul,* for example, wrote for a public that cared as little as he himself did about the actual facts of the countries or of the periods his hero traversed in search of strange adventure.

Although it is not difficult to detect here and there in Scott's predecessors the more or less fragmentary hints of which he availed himself, it would be absurd to deny that Scott is really the inventor of the historical novel, just as Poe was afterward the inventor of the detective story. In the *Castle of Otranto* Horace Walpole essayed to recall to life the Gothic period as he understood it; but—if we may judge by Mrs. Radcliffe and the rest of his immediate imitators—it was the tale of mystery he succeeded in writing and not the true historical novel. For this last, Walpole was without two things which Scott possessed abundantly—the gift of story-telling and an intimate knowledge of more than one epoch of the past.

And Scott had also two other qualifications which Walpole lacked: he was a poet and he was a humorist. As it happens, the steps that led Scott to the Waverley Novels are not hard to count. He began by collecting the ballads of the Border; and soon he wrote new ballads in the old manner. Then he linked ballads together, and so made *Marmion* and the *Lady of the Lake.* When he thought that

the public was weary of his verse, he told one of these ballad tales in prose, and so made *Waverley.* But he had read Miss Edgeworth, and he wished to do for the Scottish peasant what she had done for the Irish: thus it is that the prose tales contained sketches of character at once robust and delicate. In time, when he tired of Scotch subjects, he crossed the Border; and in *Ivanhoe* he first applied to an English subject the formula he had invented for use in North Britain, helped in his handling of a medieval theme by his recollections of the *Götz von Berlichingen* of Goethe, which he had translated in his prentice days. After a while he crossed the Channel, and found that the method acquired in telling the Scotch stories enabled him to write *Quentin Durward,* a story of France, and the *Talisman,* a story of Palestine. Although he had to forego his main advantage when he left his native land, Scott did not abandon his humor; and these later tales contain more than one memorable character, even if they reveal none so unforgetable as are a dozen or more in the Scotch stories.

Probably the immense vogue of the Waverley Novels, as they came forth swiftly one after another in the first quarter of the nineteenth century, was due rather to the qualities they had in common with the *Castle of Otranto* than to the qualities they had in common with *Castle Rackrent.* No doubt it was the union of the merits of both schools that broadened the audience to which the Waverley Novels appealed; but, in attaining his contemporary triumph, Scott owed more to Horace Walpole than to Maria Edgeworth. He surpassed Walpole immeasurably, because he was a man of deeper knowledge and broader sympathy. His audience was far wider than Miss Edgeworth's, because he infused into his Scottish tales a romantic flavor which she carefully excluded from her veracious portrayals of Irish character.

Yet it may be suggested that the stories of Scott most likely to survive the centenary of their publication and to retain readers in the first quarter of the twentieth century are perhaps those in which he best withstands the comparison with Miss Edgeworth—the stories in which he has recorded types of Scottish character, with its mingled humor and pathos. For mere excitement our liking is eternal: but the fashion thereof is fickle; and we prefer our romantic adventures cut this way to-day and another way to-morrow. Our interest in our fellow-man subsists unchanged forever, and we take a perennial delight in the revelation of the subtleties of human nature. It is in the *Antiquary* and in the *Heart of Midlothian* that Scott is seen at his best; and it is by creating characters like Caleb Balderstone and Dugald Dalgetty and Wandering Willie that he has deserved to endure.

In work of this kind Scott showed himself a Realist. He revealed himself as a humorist with a compassionate understanding of his fellow-creatures. He gave play to that sense of reality which Bagehot praises as one of the most valuable of his characteristics. When he is dealing with medieval life,—which he knew not at first hand, as he knew his Scottish peasants, but afar off from books,—the result is unreal. He was as well read in history as any man of his time; and he himself explained his superiority over the host of imitators who encompassed him about, by saying that they read to write, while he wrote because he had read. But this knowledge was second-hand, at best: it was not like his day-in-day-out acquaintance with the men of his own time; and this is why the unreality of *Ivanhoe,* for instance, is becoming more and more obvious to us. The breaking of the lances in the lists of Ashby-de-la-Zouch is to us a hollow sham, like the polite tournament at Eglinton. The deeds of daring of Ivanhoe and of the Black Knight and of Robin Hood still appeal to the boy in us; but they are less and less convincing to the man.

Although Ivanhoe and Robin Hood and the Black Knight are boldly projected figures, their psychology is summary. How could it be anything else? With all his genius, Scott was emphatically a man of his own time and of his own country, with the limitations and the prejudices of the eighteenth century and of the British Isles. Few of his warmest admirers would venture to suggest that he was as broad in sympathy as Shakspere, or as universal in his vision; and yet he was trying to reconstruct the past for us, in deed and feeling and thought—the very thing that Shakspere never attempted. The author of *Much Ado about Nothing* and of the *Comedy of Errors* was content to people the foreign plots he borrowed so lightly with the Elizabethans he knew so well. The author of *Ivanhoe* and of the *Talisman* made a strenuous effort to body forth the very spirit of epochs and of lands wholly unlike the spirit of the eighteenth century in the British Isles. It is a proof of Scott's genius that he came so near success; but failure was inevitable. "After all," said Taine, "his characters, to whatever age he transports them, are his neighbors—canny farmers, vain lairds, gloved gentlemen, young marriageable ladies, all more or less commonplace, that is, well ordered by education and character, hundreds of miles away from the voluptuous fools of the Restoration or the heroic brutes and forcible beasts of the Middle Ages."

The fact is that no man can step off his own shadow. By no effort of the will can he thrust himself backward into the past and shed his share of the accumulations of the ages, of all the myriad accretions of thought and sentiment and knowledge, stored up in the centuries that lie between him and the time he is trying to treat. Of necessity he puts into his picture of days gone by more or less of the days in which he is living. Shakspere frankly accepted the situation: Scott attempted the impossible. Racine wrote tragedies on Greek subjects; and he submitted to be bound by rules which he supposed to have been laid down by a great Greek critic. To the spectator who saw these plays when they were first produced, they may have seemed Greek; but to us, two hundred years later, they appear to be perhaps the most typical product of the age of Louis XIV; and a great French critic has suggested that to bring out their full flavor they should be performed nowadays by actors wearing, not the flowing draperies of Athens, but the elaborate court-dress of Versailles. *Phèdre* is interesting to us to-day, not because it is Greek, but because it is French; and some of Scott's stories, hailed on their publication as faithful reproductions of medieval manners, will doubtless have another interest, in time, as illustrations of what the beginning of the nineteenth century believed the Middle Ages to be.

Not only is it impossible for a man to get away from his own country, but it is equally impossible for him to get away from his own nationality. How rarely has an author been able to create a character of a different stock from his own! Certainly most of the great figures of fiction are compatriots of their makers. We have had many carpetbag novelists of late—men and women who go forth gaily and study a foreign country from the platform of a parlor-car; and some of these are able to spin yarns which hold the attention of listening thousands. What the people of the foreign countries think of these superficial tales we can measure when we recall the contempt in which we Americans hold the efforts made by one and another of the British novelists to lay the scene of a story here in the United States. Dickens and Trollope and Reade were men of varied gifts, keen observers all of them; but how lamentable the spectacle when they endeavored to portray an American! Probably most American endeavors to portray an Englishman are quite as foolish in the eyes of the British. Dickens twice chose to compete with the carpet-bag novelists; and if we Americans are unwilling to see a correct picture of our life in *Martin Chuzzlewit,* we may be sure that the French are as unwilling to acknowledge the *Tale of Two Cities* as an accurate portrayal of the most dramatic epoch in their history. There are those who think it was a piece of impertinence for a Londoner like Dickens to suppose that he could escape the inexorable limitations of his birth and education and hope to see Americans or Frenchman as they really are; finer artists than Dickens have failed in this—artists of a far more exquisite touch.

The masterpieces of the great painters instantly declare the race to which the limner himself belonged. Rubens and Velasquez and Titian traveled and saw the world; they have left us portraits of men of many nationalities: and yet every man and woman Rubens painted seems to us Dutch; every man and woman Velasquez painted seems to us Spanish; every man and woman Titian painted seems to us Italian. The artists of our own time, for all their cosmopolitanism, are no better off; and when M. Bonnat has for sitters Americans of marked characteristics he cannot help reproducing them on canvas as though they had been reflected in a Gallic mirror. In short, a man can no more escape from his race than he can escape from his century; it is the misfortune of the historical novelist that he must try to do both.

The *Atalanta in Calydon* of Mr. Swinburne has been praised as the most Greek of all modern attempts to reproduce Greek tragedy; and it may deserve this eulogy—but what of it? It may be the most Greek of the modern plays, but is it really Greek after all? Would not an ancient Greek have found in it many things quite incomprehensible to him? Even if it is more or less Greek, is it as Greek as the plays the Greeks themselves wrote? Why should an Englishman pride himself on having written a Greek play? At best he has but accomplished a feat of main strength, a *tour de force,* an exercise in literary gymnastics! A *pastiche,* a paste jewel, is not a precious possession. A Greek play written by a modern Englishman remains absolutely outside the current of contemporary literature. It is a kind of thing the Greeks never dreamed of doing; they wrote Greek plays because they were Greeks and could do nothing else; they did not imitate the literature of the Assyrians nor that of the Egyptians; they swam in the full center of the current of their own time. If Sophocles were a modern Englishman, who can doubt that he would write English plays, with no backward glance toward Greek tragedy? The lucidity, the sobriety, the elevation of the Greeks we may borrow from them, if we can, without taking over also the mere external forms due to the accidents of their age.

Art has difficulties enough without imposing on it limitations no longer needful. Let the dead past bury its dead. This has been the motto of every great artist, ancient and modern, of Dante, of Shakspere, and of Molière. A man who has work to do in the world does not embarrass himself by using a dead language to convey his ideas. Milton's Latin verse may be as elegant as its admirers assert; but if he had written nothing else, this page might need a footnote to explain who he was. If a layman may venture an opinion, the use of Gothic architecture in America at the end of the nineteenth century seems an equivalent anachronism. Gothic is a dead language; and no man to-day in the United States uses it naturally, as he does the vernacular. One of the most accomplished of American architects recently drew attention to the fact that "such a perfect composition and exquisite design as M. Vaudremer's church of Montrouge, Paris, unquestionably the best and ablest attempt in our time to revive medieval art, is considered cold even by his own pupils"; and then Mr. Hastings explains that "this is because it lacks the life we are living, and at the same time is without the real medieval life." Gothic was at its finest when it was the only architecture that was known, and when it was used naturally and handled freely and unconsciously—just as the best Greek plays were written by the Greeks.

In other words, the really trustworthy historical novels are those which were a-writing while the history was a-making. If the *Tale of Two Cities* misrepresents the Paris of 1789, the *Pickwick Papers* represents with amazing humor and with photographic fidelity certain aspects of the London of 1837. The one gives us what Dickens guessed about France in the preceding century, and the other tells us what he saw in England in his own time. Historical novel for historical novel, *Pickwick* is superior to the *Tale of Two Cities,* and *Nicholas Nickleby* to *Barnaby Rudge.* No historical novelist will ever be able to set before us the state of affairs in the South in the decade preceding the Civil War with the variety and the veracity of *Uncle Tom's Cabin,* written in that decade. No American historian has a more minute acquaintance with the men who made the United States than Mr. Paul Leicester Ford; and yet one may venture to predict that Mr. Ford will never write a historical novel having a tithe of the historical value possessed by his suggestive study of the conditions of contemporary politics in New York city, the *Honorable Peter Stirling.* Nevertheless there are few librarians bold enough to catalogue *Pickwick* and *Uncle Tom* and *Peter Stirling* under historical fiction.

One of the foremost merits of the novel, as of the drama, is that it enlarges our sympathy. It compels us to shift our point of view, and often to assume that antithetic to our custom. It forces us to see not only how the other half lives, but also how it feels and how it thinks. We learn not merely what the author meant to teach us: we absorb, in addition, a host of things he did not know he was putting in—things he took for granted, some of them, and things he implied as a matter of course. This unconscious richness of instruction cannot but be absent from the historical novel—or at best it is so obscured as to be almost nonexistent.

In *Anna Karénina* one can see Russian life in the end of this century as Tolstoy knows it, having beheld it with his own eyes: in *War and Peace* we have Russian life in the beginning of this century as Tolstoy supposes it to have been, not having seen it. One is the testimony of an eyewitness: the other is given on information and belief. *Pendennis* and the *Newcomes* and *Vanity Fair*—for all that the last includes the battle of Waterloo, fought when Thackeray was but a boy—are written out of the fulness of knowledge: *Henry Esmond* is written out of the fulness of learning only. In the former there is an unconscious accuracy of reproduction, while in the latter unconsciousness is impossible. The historical novel cannot help being what the French call *voulu*—a word that denotes both effort and artificiality. The story-teller who deals honestly with his own time achieves, without taking thought, a fidelity simply impossible to the story-teller who deals with the past, no matter how laboriously the latter may toil after it.

In fact, the more he labors, the less life is there likely to be in the tale he is telling: humanity is choked by archeology. It calls for no research to set forth the unending conflict of duty and desire, for example. If we examine carefully the best of the stories usually classed under historical fiction we shall find those to be the most satisfactory in which the history is of least importance, in which it is present only as a background. The examination may lead to a subdivision of the class of historical fiction into the actual historical novel and the novel in which history is wholly subordinate, not to say merely incidental.

A British critic, Professor George Saintsbury, has laid down the law that "the true historical novelist employs the reader's presumed interest in historical scene and character as an instrument to make his own work attractive." Although it would be easy to dissent from this dictum, it may be used to explain the distinction drawn in the preceding paragraph. A tale of the past is not necessarily a true historical novel: it is a true historical novel only when the historical events are woven into the texture of the story. Applying this test, we see that the *Bride of Lammermoor* is not a true historical novel; and this is perhaps the reason why it is held in high esteem by all lovers of genuine Romance. By the same token, the *Scarlet Letter* is not a true historical novel.

Neither in the *Bride of Lammermoor* nor in the *Scarlet Letter* is there any reliance upon historical scene or character for attraction. Scott was narrating again a legend of an inexplicable mystery: but although the period of its occurrence was long past when he wrote, he presented simply the characters enmeshed in the fateful adventure, and relied for the attractiveness of his story upon the inherent interest of the weird climax toward which the reader is hurried breathless under the weight of impending doom. Hawthorne was captivated by a study of conscience, the incidents of which could be brought out more conveniently and more effectively by throwing back the time of the tale into the remote past.

In another story of Scott's, not equal to the *Bride of Lammermoor* in its tragic intensity, but superb in its resolute handling of emotion, the *Heart of Midlothian,* there is perhaps a stiffer infusion of actual history; but it would be rash to suggest that in its composition the author relied on historical scene or character to make his work attractive. The attraction of the *Heart of Midlothian* lies in its presentation of character at the crisis of its existence. So in the *Romola* of George Eliot, although the author obviously spent her strength in trying to transmute the annals of Florence into her narrative, the historical part is unconvincing; the episode of Savonarola is seen to be an excrescence; and what remains erect now is a wholly imaginary trinity—the noble figure of Romola, the pretty womanliness of little Tessa, and the easy-going Tito, with his moral fiber slowly disintegrating under successive temptations. Tito is one of the great triumphs of modern fiction, not because he is a Greek of the Renascence, but because he is eternal and to be found whenever and wherever man lacks strength to resist himself.

If we were thus to go down the list of so-called historical novels, one by one, we might discover that those which were most solidly rooted in our regard and affection are to be included in the subdivision wherein history itself is only a casual framework for a searching study of human character, and that they are cherished for the very same qualities as are possessed by the great novels of modern life. Without going so far as to say that the best historical novel is that which has the least history, we may at least confess the frank inferiority of the other subdivision in which the author has been rash enough to employ historical scene and character to make his own work attractive. What gives charm and value to *Henry Esmond* is exactly what gives charm and value to *Vanity Fair*—Thackeray's understanding of his fellow-man, his sympathetic insight into human nature, his happy faculty for dramatically revealing character by situation. Perhaps the eighteenth-century atmosphere, with which Thackeray was able to surround Esmond only by infinite skill, is not breathed comfortably by the most of those who enjoy the book for its manly qualities. One feels that the author has won his wager—but at what a cost, and at what a risk!

Some logical readers of this essay may be moved to put two and two together, and to accuse the present writer of a desire to disparage the historical novel, because he has tried to show, first, that the novelists cannot reproduce in their pages the men and women of another epoch as these really thought and felt, and, second, that the novelists who have attempted historical fiction have best succeeded when they brought the fiction to the center of the stage and left the history in the background. But to draw this conclusion would be unjust, since the writer really agrees with the views of Sainte-Beuve as expressed in a letter to Champfleury: "The novel is a vast field of experiment, open to all the forms of genius. It is the future epic, the only one,

probably, that modern manners will hereafter justify. Let us not bind it too tightly; let us not lay down its theory too rigidly; let us not organize it."

To point out that a historical novel is great—when it is great—because of its possession of the identical qualities that give validity to a study of modern life, is not to suggest that only the contemporary novel is legitimate. To dwell on the deficiencies of the historical novel is not to propose that only realistic fiction be tolerated hereafter. But perhaps a due consideration of these inherent defects of the historical novel may lead the disinterested reader to confess its essential inferiority to the more authentic fiction, in which the story-teller reports on humanity as he actually sees it. And if Romance is preferred to Realism, Romance is purest when purged of all affection.

Genuine Romance is always as delightful as shoddy Romanticism is always detestable. Fantasy is ever beautiful, when it presents itself frankly as fantasy. *Undine* does not pretend to accuracy; and the *Arabian Nights* never vaunted itself as founded on the facts of Haroun-al-Rashid's career. Stevenson's romances, artistically truthful, though they contradict the vulgar facts of every-day existence,—*Markheim,* for example, and the *Strange Case of Dr. Jekyll and Mr. Hyde,*—bid fair to outlive his Romanticist admixtures of Scott and Dumas; and the *New Arabian Nights,* with its matter-of-fact impossibility, will outweigh the *Master of Ballantrae* a dozen times over. But pure Romance and frank fantasy are strangely rare; there are very few Hoffmanns and Fouqués, Poes and Stevensons, in a century—and only one Hawthorne.

Not long ago an enterprising American journalist wrote to some twoscore of the story-tellers of Great Britain and of the United States to inquire what, in their opinion, the object of the novel was. Half a dozen of the replies declared that it was "to realize life"; and the rest—an immense majority—were satisfied to say that it was "to amuse." Here we see the practitioners of the art divided in defining its purpose; and a like diversity of opinion can be detected among the vast army of novel-readers. Some think that fiction ought to be literature, and that "literature is a criticism of life." Some hold that fiction is mere story-telling—the stringing together of adventure, the heaping up of excitement, with the wish of forgetting life as it is, of getting outside of the sorry narrowness of sordid and commonplace existence into a fairy-land of dreams where Cinderella always marries Prince Charming and where the haughty sisters always meet with their just punishment. It is to readers of this second class that the ordinary historical novel appeals with peculiar force; for it provides the drug they desire, while they can salve their conscience during this dissipation with the belief that they are, at the same time, improving their minds. The historical novel is aureoled with a pseudo-sanctity, in that it purports to be more instructive than a mere story: it claims—or at least the claim is made in its behalf—that it is teaching history. There are those who think that it thus adds hypocrisy to its other faults.

Bagehot—and there is no acuter critic of men and books, and none with less literary bias—Bagehot suggested that the immense popularity of *Ivanhoe* was due to the fact that "it describes the Middle Ages as we should wish them to be." This falsification characteristic of the historical novel in general is one of its chief charms in the eyes of those who like to be ravished out of themselves into an illusion of a world better than the one they, unfortunately, have to live in. "All sensible people know that the Middle Ages must have been very uncomfortable," continues Bagehot. "No one knew the abstract facts on which this conclusion rests better than Scott; but his delineation gives no general idea of the result: a thoughtless reader rises with the impression that the Middle Ages had the same elements of happiness which we have at present, and that they had fighting besides." Scott knew better, of course; but though "when aroused, he could take a distinct view of the opposing facts, he liked his own mind to rest for the most part in the same pleasing illusion." Perhaps Bagehot might have agreed with some later critics who have held that many of Scott's novels are immoral because of this falsification of historic truth—a charge which receives no support from the *Bride of Lammermoor,* for example, nor from the *Heart of Midlothian,* and half a dozen other of his stories, in which Scott's strong sense of reality and his fine feeling for Romance are displayed in perfect harmony.

Alfred Tresidder Sheppard

SOURCE: "The Germ and the Plot," in *The Art & Practice of Historical Fiction,* Humphrey Toulmin, 1930, 81-94.

[*In the excerpt that follows, Sheppard discusses the sources and ideas that inspired such historical novels as Charles Dickens's* A Tale of Two Cities, *Sir Walter Scott's* Woodstock, *and George Eliot's* Romola.]

"A little Plote of my simple penning."—LORD DARNLEY (1554).

I

That indefatigable antiquary, folklorist, historian, ecclesiast and writer of historical (and other) fiction, the Rev. Sabine Baring-Gould, made it a rule to read no reviews, and possibly because of that his work suffered. George Henry Lewes, treating George Eliot much as if she were a Grand Lama, was careful to keep from her knowledge any adverse criticisms of her work. Charles Dickens read very few novels. When he wrote *A Tale of Two Cities* he was staggered . . . at the cart-load of books on the Revolution sent to his door in response to his suggestion by Carlyle.

I think myself that anyone anxious to attempt the historical novel will be well advised to know nothing of an *Index Expurgatorius*. Victor Hugo's mother was wiser than her world thought her when she allowed her boy to roam at large among books, good, indifferent, and bad. It is useful to know what has been done in the same field, to trace origins and developments, and to study criticisms. One should, of course, be ready to criticize the critics, some of whom I propose to criticize by and by. A wide reading of the historical novel in all its stages aided by the estimates of men competent to judge is immensely useful. One can see how this writer and that have dealt with situations,

problems, difficulties; one can distinguish between failure and success, and perhaps see the causes of each.

I have endeavoured to trace very roughly the development of the historical novel from the early legends, anecdotes, *chansons de geste,* and mediæval romances, to the present day, because I am convinced that many writers fail through ignorance of the work that has preceded them. One need not be a sedulous ape, but example, good or bad, is better than precept where it is a case of avoiding pitfalls, or attempting to do better than the best. There have been very great historical novels. The perfect historical novel has never yet been written, and may never be. It must preserve the merits and avoid the demerits of the great writers, and even then draw something from lesser writers where the great have failed. It must preserve dignity and avoid grandiloquence, preserve atmosphere and avoid the archaic carried to extremes, preserve accuracy of background and avoid the crowding out of the human interest, preserve strength and avoid the needlessly coarse and ruthless and morbid, preserve the dramatic without being melodramatic, preserve proportion without sacrificing detail. Whether it will ever be written I do not know. There is no great historical novel without obvious and even glaring faults. Those who essay this form will, unless by a miracle, fail themselves; but at least they should at the outset attempt the miracle of throwing the rope of the wagon across a star.

II

An eminent historian writing of the Middle Ages has said that every country has possessed in its own primeval literature the first germ of romance. Just as in the rude epic of our forefathers, in the snatch of song in which modern rhyme was preceded by primitive means of arresting the ear, in the nursery tale or legend with its simple but often very effective plot (take, for instance, the ancient story of the spinning girl helped by, and then circumventing, the power of evil) are to be found the germs of our modern historical fiction, so each novel begins in the mind of its author with a germ from which the whole book is finally to grow. I remember having a long discussion once on this subject with an historical novelist who endeavoured to show how different books had sprung from a still-traceable germ, and held the theory that every great book could be set down in essence in a few words. A postcard (it was urged) ought to hold even *The Grand Cyrus*. Recently I was reminded of this by a reference in Lytton to authors who take the germs of their novels from history, and by another comment by a critic that the germ of a novel and the content of it should be reducible to a dozen or a score of words.

How does any historical novel, great or small, have its origin and take shape and bulk from that first beginning?

Lytton wrote himself, in another passage, "To my mind a writer should sit down to compose a fiction as a painter prepares to compose a picture. His first care should be the conception of a whole as lofty as intellect can grasp." Stevenson said, "A work of art is first cloudily conceived in the mind." One of our most popular modern novelists has said that the idea of his most famous book came to him from a train journey and the sight of someone sitting opposite him in the carriage round whom a hazy story began to weave itself. In *The Young Duke* Disraeli (Lord Beaconsfield) gave a receipt for writing a novel: "Take a pair of pistols, a pack of cards, a cookery-book, and a set of new quadrilles; mix them up with half an intrigue and a whole marriage, and divide them into three equal portions." (It was, of course, the day of the three-decker.) Alexander Pope once wrote a recipe for an epic poem, treating it as if a plum-pudding were in the making; an important ingredient was the "fable" or plot, which could be taken out of any "old poem, history book, romance, or legend."

We have in a Book of Memoranda by Charles Dickens the germ of *A Tale of Two Cities,* but it would be impossible to construct from it the novel as it finally appeared; his first idea, which could easily go onto a postcard, ran:

> How as to a story in two periods—with a lapse of
> time between, like a French drama?

This first indefinite "germ-idea" was followed by "Titles for such a notion." He had always great difficulties with his titles, and took immense, though certainly not wasted, time in making a final choice. Here are the first efforts at a title for the story in two periods which became the *Tale of Two Cities*:

TIME! THE LEAVES OF THE FOREST. SCATTERED LEAVES. THE GREAT WHEEL. ROUND AND ROUND. OLD LEAVES. SO LONG AGO. FAR APART. FALLEN LEAVES. FIVE AND TWENTY YEARS. YEARS AND YEARS. ROLLING YEARS. DAY AFTER DAY. FELLED TREES. MEMORY CARTON. ROLLING STONES. TWO GENERATIONS.

For some time the idea was laid aside, though evidently a book was shaping gradually. "One of These Days," "Buried Alive," "The Thread of Gold," "The Doctor of Beauvais," were considered and rejected. In March, 1859, he wrote "This is to certify that I have got exactly the name for the story that is wanted; exactly what will fit the opening to a T: A Tale of Two Cities."

Alexandre Dumas attached far more importance to the idea and conception of a novel than to the actual execution: this, he thought, of quite minor importance. Before putting pen to paper he gave the closest attention to the planning of his book. When success had come to him, he would lie silent for days, it is said, on the deck of his yacht imagining, thinking, planning, until the plot had taken clear shape from the germinal idea, and everything had been carefully arranged. He wrote very rapidly when the actual penmanship began. Once he accepted a challenge to prove this; he was to write the first volume of the *Chevalier de Maison Rouge* (the plot having already matured) in sixty-two hours, including sufficient time for sleep and food; the book was to fill seventy-five pages, with forty-five lines to each page. He finished his task in less than the appointed time. Some of his historical novels were built up from an anecdote.

The greatest difficulty which any novelist, but especially the historical novelist, has to face is the difficulty of selection. What the Right Hon. H. A. L. Fisher said recently

about the art of literature consisting in omissions seems to me not only tersely put but important and, to a large extent, true. As a matter of fact, Stevenson had said the same thing. It is not, or should not be, hard to find the germ or even the plot for novels. It is hard to find the germ or plot for *a* novel. When a journalist complained to Lord Northcliffe about the difficulty of finding ideas for articles, he was told that a bus-ride down Fleet Street ought to supply ideas enough to fill a newspaper; which is perfectly true, given the eye that can see what the ordinary eye misses. O. Henry said that you had only to knock at any door and say "All is discovered!" to find a story. In every period of history, in every episode, in a fragment of stone, in an old weapon, in a name on a desolate grave, in a scrap of verse, is the germ of an historical novel. The difficulty is, or should be, selection. The selection of title is a difficulty. The selection of character and incident is a difficulty. And it is as important to know what to reject as what to select.

Perhaps I may be forgiven here if, by way of illustration, I give some scraps from my own experience. The germ of my first novel, *The Red Cravat,* lay in a paragraph in Carlyle's *Frederick the Great,* where Frederick William of Prussia gives a letter to a girl which is really an order for her instant marriage to one of his giant grenadiers; she discovers or suspects this, and hands it to an old woman who is promptly married when it is delivered. In my book the grenadier became English, the letter or order after vicissitudes secured his marriage to an English girl with whom he was in love. (But almost always one wanders much farther than this from the germinal idea, which sometimes, when the book is finished, seems altogether lost. The Red King cried out, when Alice, coming through the Looking Glass, took hold of the end of his pencil, "It writes all manner of things that I don't intend.") *Running Horse Inn* began with the idea of writing a novel round a little wooden inn I knew at Herne Bay, calling it by another name, and part of the germinal idea included a certain episode in a trial for murder, early in the nineteenth century, when a scrap of torn newspaper used as the wad of a gun proved guilt. *The Rise of Ledgar Dunstan* and *The Quest of Ledgar Dunstan* were based on the hypothesis that the world war might have been the secret and unintentional work of one obscure individual. *A Son of the Manse* might have been summed up in a few words as a study of the results in certain cases of harsh, procincial Nonconformity on sensitive natures. Consciously or unconsciously it undoubtedly owed something to George Douglas Brown's powerful but gloomy *The House with the Green Shutters.* *The Autobiography of Judas Iscariot* was inspired by a scrap of legend and a little story by Anatole France. *Brave Earth* was the result of a paragraph read in an old copy of *Baker's Chronicle* picked up on a Cambridge bookstall. This paragraph described the unexpected fate of a Bodmin man during the Western Insurrection under Humphry Arundell in 1549, but the novel drifted far beyond this one episode, which had, in the end, no essential connection with the plot or book. *Here Comes an Old Sailor* was based on an old legend; the scenes were placed chiefly at Fordwich, because that tiny forgotten port of Canterbury had caught my imagination during a visit long before the book came to be written. *Queen Dick* first began to take shape after reading some verses about *Queen Dick*—Richard

Cromwell—among some contemporary tracts and broadsheets.

In every case, the book itself was, in the end, very different from my first intention—in more ways, unfortunately, than one. In my short stories germinal ideas have come, I find on reflection, from the suggestions of friends (one was based on a description of the game of Pool) on a chance remark made by a chambermaid in a French hotel about a neighbouring circus, on newspaper paragraphs, on a journey in the tube when the lights went out suddenly and unexpectedly, on memories attached to a certain old wooden seat at a watering-place long ago, on scraps in old chronicles and histories, on an incident in school life which I transferred to Napoleonic days, with grown men instead of boys for the actors. There is no reason to reject anything because one finds it first in a modern setting. What happens in a modern liner may (unless one is attempting another story like "The Ship that Found Herself"—and perhaps even then) be made to happen in a Spanish galleon, a Cinque-Port ship, a Viking-ship, a coracle. A train may become a stage coach. A tank of today's warfare may be the wooden horse of Troy.

I do not know whether it is the experience of most authors that books drift very far from the first intention, but probably in the majority of cases the final result is far indeed from the preliminary nutshell form, or even from a carefully elaborated plot. With Scott this was certainly the case, though he was careful to warn young writers that he did not advise them to imitate his own methods. He said often that he could never adhere to a written-out careful plot; ideas rose as he wrote. When he was at work on *Woodstock*—a novel which I have heard one distinguished critic describe as the best of Scott's novels, though I am far from agreeing with him—he reports in his *Journal,* "This morning I had some good ideas respecting Woodstock which will make the story better. The devil of a difficulty is that one puzzles the skein in order to excite curiosity, and then cannot disentangle it for the satisfaction of the prying fiend they have raised." On the 12th of February, 1826, he wrote again: "Having ended the second volume of *Woodstock* last night I have to begin the third this morning. Now I have not the slightest idea how the story is to be wound up to a catastrophe. I am just in the same case as I used to be when I lost myself in former days in some country to which I was a stranger. I always pushed for the pleasantest road, and either found or made it the nearest. . . . I only tried to make that which I was actually writing diverting and interesting, leaving the rest to fate. A perilous style, but I cannot help it. I would not have young writers imitate my carelessness, however."

In spite of his faults and foibles, Scott was too essentially modest to be unaware of his own faults; or of many of them. While engaged on one of his novels he broke off to have a nap, first urging his readers to do the same—at all events, in his *Journal,* to which he confided his difficulties and dissatisfactions. Publication in parts, or in three-volume form, itself led to a certain looseness in the work of most of our earlier novelists. J. R. Lowell once said that he himself could not write a novel, nor conceive how anyone else was able to, and he would sooner be hanged than

begin to print anything before he had wholly finished it. "Moreover," he added, "what can a man do when he is a treadmill?" Scott, when ill-health and his noble effort to redeem his fortunes made his work largely a treadmill business, certainly wrote many a careless and dreary page, but I think there is still some truth in what a once popular Scottish writer, Mrs. Grant of Laggan, who knew him well, wrote. Quoting an old proverb of the North, "King's caff is better than ither folks' corn," she said: "Though the 'caff' (chaff) may abound, it is still *King's* caff."

III

The first thing, then, in writing an historical novel is the germ from which it is to grow into something which may—or may not—bear some final resemblance to its origin; a "germ" which may be reducible to writing in a few words, or may be almost formless, like Stevenson's cloudy conception in the mind. Nathaniel Hawthorne, who was at once more and less an historical novelist because, as someone has written of him, he saw *everything* double, and never saw the surface of things without seeing beneath the surface, wrote down carefully in brief abstract his stories before he set seriously to work; here, for instance, are a few of the ideas he jotted down in his notes for tales and essays:

> "The History of an Almshouse in a country village from the eve ofits foundation downwards." (He elaborates this postcard "germ" by suggesting the vicissitudes of fortune such a history might show; the rich of one generation becoming the poor of the next; perhaps the son and heir of the founder being glad to enter as an inmate; a gleam of occasional sunshine being given to the

Portrait of Sir Walter Scott by Sir Edwin Landseer

tale by the good fortune of some inmate, for instance a nameless infant being discovered the child of wealthy parents.)

"A young woman in England poisoned by an East Indian barbed dart which her brother had brought home as a curiosity."

"A story, the principal characters of which shall always seem on the point of entering on the scene, but shall never appear."

"For a child's story—imagine all sorts of wonderful playthings."

The world is so full of a number of things that every way one turns there are novels and short stories for those with eyes to see, and all the world's history offers backgrounds. Scott, Dumas, Stevenson, Hardy, all the great historical novelists had note-books constantly at hand. (Hardy even scribbled notes on leaves and chips of wood.) Reade devoted a large part of his working day to note-books and cuttings. An idea or the broad outlines of a plot may come at any moment and in any place; even from a dream, as Stevenson and Walpole found—though dreamland is perhaps the most unsatisfactory country from which the novelist can draw his inspiration. Too often there is disillusion on full awakening, as Jebb (not famous as a novelist) found once when suffering from typhoid fever; he dreamed a dream which seemed to make the plan of a most amazing and admirable novel, only to find it resolve itself into sheer nonsense in daylight. Lytton dreamed, or said that he dreamed, verse—but it was nonsense verse. *Dr. Jekyll and Mr. Hyde,* though the best dream-story ever written, suffers from its origin; there is at least a grain of truth in Watts-Dunton's criticism, that had it not been for the influence upon him of the healthiest of all writers except Chaucer—Sir Walter Scott—Stevenson might have been in the ranks of the pompous problem-mongers of fiction and the stage, who do their best to make life hideous.

He and we were spared that, and Stevenson escaped another peril; he tells us he wrote *Kidnapped* partly for a lark, partly as a pot-boiler, but suddenly it moved, David and Alan stepped out of the canvas, and he found himself in another world. It is a little disconcerting to find that one very great historical novel, Kingsley's *Westward Ho!* (there was an earlier *Westward Ho!* by the way, by James Kirke Paulding, the American novelist, published in 1832) was written partly as a pot-boiler; fine story as it is, it might have been better still if no other influence had been at work than love of his story for his story's sake. As he admitted frankly, he had one eye upon his public; but for all that *Westward Ho!* stands in my opinion high above *Hypatia* (written after prolonged study of Egypt in literature) or *Hereward the Wake* (splendid in parts, but not to be taken too seriously as history). In *Westward Ho!* the prejudice and bigotries of the days he described, and the sturdy patriotism made truculent by the pretensions of Spain, exactly suited Kingsley's own temperament. Early and later days in Clovelly, Bideford, and that countryside, and memories of his grandfather's stirring yarns of adventure and the sea, first inspired him and then gave him zest to write this epic of the spacious days of Queen Elizabeth. The storm was drawn from his own knowledge and experi-

ence on the wild North Devon coast. It is interesting, by the way, to compare John Masefield's fine and too little appreciated book *Captain Margaret* with Kingsley's great story.

I first read *Westward Ho!* years back on Bideford Quay, and *Lorna Doone* is another Devon book as good, to me, "as clotted cream, almost"; even if nowadays one is more critical, and some of the verdicts of history are being revised.

Kingsley's book, written as he said for immediate popularity, and to make men (and boys, he might have added) fight, might possibly be a hundred times better, and quite certainly he was right when he said that with more care and time he himself might have made it twice as good. Yet it is a fine book, steeped in the spirit of the strong and stalwart Elizabethan gallants. And here perhaps one may make an aside about the number of great historical novelists who have been essentially poets; Kingsley was one, Blackmore one (some magnificent lines of his, at the time of their rediscovery anonymous, were retrieved for the end of the *Oxford Book of English Verse* by that fine critic Sir Arthur Quiller-Couch), Scott of course first became famous as a poet, Lytton wrote verse, Victor Hugo was more notably poet than novelist, and more recent instances are Stevenson, M. E. Coleridge, Eden Phillpotts, Thomas Hardy, Rudyard Kipling, and Maurice Hewlett. "The truth is I write everything and approach everything as a poet," said Hewlett—"history, psychology, romance, novels, everything. I use the poetic method entirely—stuff myself with the subject, drench myself, and then let it pour out as it will. I trust to inspiration or what is called inspiration absolutely. I never put anxious or deliberate brain-work into a book; such as there may be of that is done in sleep." If any distinction is to be made between an historical novel and a romance, Blackmore has made it in his one great book, *Lorna Doone;* but even in the structure of its sentences and paragraphs it may be as properly called a poem; the words over and again, without any alteration or addition, shape themselves into blank verse.

There has been considerable discussion as to the foundations of actual fact on which this book stands. I remember hearing years back from a relative of Blackmore's that the novelist explored the Devon countryside to gather material, with his brother-in-law, but it was evidently no very strenuous expedition, as most of the excursions seem to have been made easily, by carriage. Eighteen years before *Lorna Doone* was published, *Cooper's Guide to Lynton* referred to a certain ruined village of eleven deserted cottages in a North Devon valley; the Doones, once a family of distinction impoverished during the Stuart troubles, were said to have occupied them. The leader or founder of the Doone family at this time had fought as a private soldier at Sedgemoor on Monmouth's side, and had escaped from the brutalities of Jeffreys. They made themselves a terror for miles around, escaping, when pressed, with their booty to Bagworthy, few daring to follow them across the wild fastnesses of Exmoor. The last of the Doones were an old man and his granddaughter who perished in the snow while singing Christmas carols for pence in 1800. In 1863 the legend of the Doones was a current tale among boys in Devon. Three or four years before *Lorna Doone* appeared a tale entitled *The Doones of Exmoor* was published in *The Leisure Hour,* and Blackmore, who saw it, probably was incited by it to write his own greater story.

IV

Environment—the fascination of some district known and loved—has been the first inspiration of many an historical novel. James Payn wrote once, "To the story-teller the germ is everything," and said that it might be put into half a dozen lines. If he had put in half a dozen words the germ of his *Lost Sir Massingberd* he might have written "Man Lost in a Hollow Tree." It was the sight of a hollow tree, and the possibilities it suggested, that led to his most popular book. But there is a curious foot-note to this story. In the Diaries of Sir Mountstuart Grant Duff I came across an account told by Jean Ingelow—the poet, and a finer poet than the modern world has yet quite discovered—of a visit she paid in girlhood to an uncle; he had been guardian to a young Mr. Massingberd, heir to a great estate, who had mysteriously disappeared and was never found. This may quite probably have made James Payn search for an explanation of the mystery.

George Eliot might have stated the germ of *Romola* in two words: "Florence—Savonarola." She found the City of Flowers more stimulating to the imagination than even Rome—and I think this is not an uncommon experience. Unfortunately a few weeks sojourn is not sufficient, even aided by prodigious reading of Florentine historians, to enable one to catch the spirit of the city, or of the age she describes. Leslie Stephen, so often wrong, was largely right when he described *Romola* as "a magnificent piece of cram." A few famous scenes in fiction which gripped the imagination in youth leave one colder in more mature years. I cannot quite recapture the thrill of the first reading of the assassination of the Marquis, or even the death of Carton, in *A Tale of Two Cities,* though I am still convinced that it is a greater book than many modern critics would have us believe. Hypatia's murder is less bloodcurdling than of old; and in the same way, the banquet scene in *Romola,* which held one breathless in boyhood, has lost much of its fascination. Her characters are indeed, in *Romola,* fifteenth-century figures in Victorian dress; her Florence is the Florence of the student-tourist. Merezhkowski in *The Forerunner* paints a Florence at once more vivid and more true. During her brief stay George Eliot made it part of her work to capture the essence of the Florentine character. In a month or two, even perhaps in a year or two, it cannot be captured. Towards the end of a year's stay I myself still made daily and surprising discoveries. The Florentine, who must be today very much in some ways as he was in the Renaissance—and yet in some ways very different—is unlike the Sienese, the Pisans, the Genoese, the Romans, the Neapolitans. He does not wear all his heart on his sleeve, and no doubt found some sly amusement in the English woman-novelist taking her diligent notes in his shops and markets, and poked sly fun at her (as the Florentine loves to do) when she had passed. . . . No; though Lewes preferred its serial publication because it was a book to be read solemnly and slow-

ly—though the payment for it was so enormous—though in writing it George Eliot passed from youth to age—I would sacrifice *Romola* for a few more chapters of the Aunts in *The Mill on the Floss,* or a few more chapters like the opening chapters of *Adam Bede.*

Harry E. Shaw

SOURCE: "An Approach to the Historical Novel," in *The Forms of Historical Fiction: Sir Walter Scott and His Successors,* Cornell, 1983, pp. 19-50.

[*In the excerpt that follows, Shaw argues that a "negative, minimal definition of historical fiction" is necessary in order to accommodate the variety of interpretations regarding the role of history in the historical novel's structure.*]

When critics discuss literary groups and genres, they are usually doing more than indulging in the pleasures of the taxonomical imagination. Genres help us sense the lay of the literary land. They imply questions and sometimes answers: we see a forest, or at least clumps of trees, instead of trees. In other parts of life, we constantly make distinctions that are like generic distinctions in literary studies, and they matter. As we know, an attempt to correct social injustice may dictate very different actions depending on the groups it singles out for attention. Debates between microhistorians and macrohistorians hinge on the same problem; they also remind us that the time span we choose to think about has a significant impact on the conclusions we draw about a given topic. It may be true that in the long run, we are all dead, but such a perspective is more useful to a mystic than to a mercenary. When we experience a work of literature, we employ in a refined and complex way our general ability to see the world in terms of significant groups and patterns. Making sense of a work rests upon knowing what to expect from it, understanding how to take it in. This in turn implies that we have a sense of what sort of thing it is, how it works, what its rules are. Beyond that, generic assumptions allow us—indeed, force us—to focus on some things at the expense of others; they can make certain aspects of a text disappear or seem trivial. . . .

What is the historical novel? In attempting to answer this question, it would seem advisable, before plunging into speculations about historiography and the nature of a truly historical outlook, to ask what sort of term "the historical novel" is in the first place. How does it differ from other groups of novels—the picaresque novel, the industrial novel, the sentimental novel, the eighteenth-century novel? Which is it most like? A simple but accurate answer is that the term historical novel denotes a kind of novel which can be differentiated from other groups of novels not in terms of a defining compositional technique (the picaresque novel), nor through its power to evoke a set of emotions (the gothic or sentimental novel), and certainly not in terms of the period in which it was written (the eighteenth-century novel). Instead, the principle of differentiation involves the milieu represented, which makes the closest parallel in our list the industrial novel. Though it seems fair to say that the industrial novel is a narrower category, it is the same sort of category as the historical novel.

A convenient way of extending this simple, intuitive notion that historical novels are works that in some way represent historical milieux is to speak in terms of fictional probability. A character or incident in a novel can be probable in either or both of two ways. We usually think of probability as involving fidelity to the external world that a work represents. Some eighteenth-century readers of *Clarissa* found Mrs. Sinclair's house in London improbable because they could not believe that such carefully contrived dens of iniquity actually existed. One might complain that Clarissa herself violates probability in this sense because she is too good to be true—we have never met anyone like her in the world in which we live. In the historical novel, anachronisms and mistakes of historical fact are responsible for breaches of probability in this sense. But probability can also depend upon how consistently a work follows its own internal rules and patterns. Soliloquies in drama are probable in this second sense, but not in the sense of being faithful reproductions of the behavior we expect from our fellows in their everyday affairs. In general, the more stylized a work becomes, the more these two kinds of probability diverge; the more directly mimetic it is, the more they coalesce. Probability involves our sense of a novel's "fit," both the way it fits the world it imitates and the way its parts fit together to produce a unified whole. A novel's power to illuminate life and its intrinsic beauty as a formed work of art depend in large measure on its probability in both senses.

The concept of fictional probability implies a way of defining historical fiction. We can say that while in most novels probability stems from our general ideas about life and society, in historical novels the major source of probability is specifically historical. Though many kinds of novels may incorporate a sense of history, in historical novels history is, as the Russian Formalists would put it, "foregrounded." When we read historical novels, we take their events, characters, settings, and language to be historical in one or both of two ways. They may represent societies, modes of speech, or events that in very fact existed in the past, in which case their probability points outward from the work to the world it represents; or they may promote some sort of historical effect within the work, such as providing an entry for the reader into the past, in which case the probability points inward, to the design of the work itself. In *Waverly,* Fergus MacIvor has both internal and external probability, while Edward Waverley's probability rests primarily on the way in which he furthers the novel's historical design. Fergus is a faithful composite picture of the Highland Jacobite nobility, providing a good external portrait of them and also representing the historical weaknesses that in Scott's opinion doomed their movement. Waverly, on the other hand, is the reader's entry into the novel. He functions primarily as a fictional device, allowing the historical import of the novel to be felt with maximum force. The idea of internal probability allows us to see why a work can become more historical, not less historical, if it rearranges individual aspects of the historical record for the sake of demonstrating a larger pattern.

Historical novels, then, are works in which historical probability reaches a certain level of structural prominence. This may seem an impotent and lame conclusion, objectionable on several counts. It is negative and minimal. It is vague in terms of what counts as historical. It creates distinctions of degree, not kind; and in particular, it does not indicate the kind of prominence history must have in the structure of a truly historical novel. In fact, these qualities are virtues. Because the definition is vague in terms of what counts as historical, it leaves open the possibility that history may mean different things in different works. The definition works in terms of differences of degree, not kind, but it should: the modern historical novel arose as part of the rise of historicism, which made a sense of history part of the cultural mainstream and hence available to novels in general, not simply to historical novels. But the definition's greatest strength is that it does not specify what role history must play in a novel's structure if we are to consider that novel a work of historical fiction. One of my main contentions is that we cannot make sense of historical fiction unless we recognize that history plays a number of distinctly different roles in historical novels. . . . A negative, minimal definition of historical fiction leaves the way clear for these necessary distinctions.

In most respects, historical fiction depends upon the formal techniques and cultural assumptions of the main traditions of the novel. Because of this dependence, it does not have a significant history apart from the history of the novel as a whole. What is often called the classical historical novel begins with Scott; but the important line of fictional development runs not from Scott to the historical novelists who followed him, but instead from Scott to such masters of European fiction as Balzac, Dickens, and even (so argues Louis Maigron [in *Le roman historique à l'époque romantique: Essai sur l'influence de Walter Scott,* 1898]) Flaubert. The authors who produce the best historical novels after Scott tend, with the exception of Cooper and Tolstoy, to be masters of other kinds of writing, who enter the field with one or two attempts, as Dickens, Thackeray, and Hugo do. Georg Lukács [in *The Historical Novel,* 1937] is in my opinion essentially accurate in describing the history of the novel as a great stream from which tributaries branch off, only to rejoin and further enrich it in due course. Scott's works form such a tributary: he branches off from the eighteenth-century novel, discovers in artistic terms the rich significance of history, and then reunites with the mainstream of nineteenth-century fiction through his influence on Balzac, enriching it with new materials, insights, and techniques.

Since they lack a history of their own, the most useful way to group historical novels historically is in terms of coherent movements of the novel as a whole, and of the esthetic and cultural presuppositions that underlie them. The realist novel, which begins with Richardson and finds its greatest achievement in the works of Eliot and Balzac and Tolstoy, is such a movement. I shall call such works "standard" novels; the group of historical novels which derives its unity from its relationship with standard fiction then becomes "standard historical novels. . . ." They all employ the formal techniques of standard fiction, and in particular, they use the plotted action, which creates in the reader a pattern of hopes and fears for one or more protagonists, as their formal basis. They also share with the standard novel a set of broad cultural assumptions that provide the grounds for their intelligibility and are the ultimate source of their "realism." The situation of historical fiction in our own century becomes more complex. As the novel in general changes, new forms of historical fiction emerge. But strong continuities with nineteenth-century forms also persist in such distinguished historical novelists as Marguerite Yourcenar or H. F. M. Prescott.

I have suggested that no single quality of historical insight defines historical fiction. But since we have narrowed our sights to the standard historical novel, can't we say something more specific about the kind or kinds of historical vision they embody? We can indeed, but only within limits. The historian Herbert Butterfield and the literary critic Avrom Fleishman have both tried in different ways to define the quality historical novels share, and their discussions are useful here. Both define historical fiction by differentiating it from historiography. For Butterfield [in *The Historical Novel,* 1924], historiography attempts to "make a generalisation, to find a formula," because it views history as "the whole process of development that leads up to the present." The historical novel, by contrast, attempts to "reconstruct a world, to particularise, to catch a glimpse of human nature." The task of the historical novelist is to render the unique "atmosphere" of an age in the past, to "recapture the fleeting moment." For Fleishman [in *The English Historical Novel: Walter Scott to Virginia Woolf,* 1971], by contrast, the historical novelist accomplishes something more like the task Butterfield sets the historian: "What makes a historical novel historical is the active presence of a concept of history as a shaping force." Both critics are clearly drawing on the achievements of historicism for their definitions, a procedure that seems entirely in order since the rise of the historical novel is bound up with the rise of historicism in general. But Butterfield invokes what we might call a minimal historicist vision; Fleishman, historicism at its most powerful and dignified.

Identifying the historicity of historical novels with "the active presence of a concept of history as a shaping force" seems to have much to recommend it. Probably the most important aspect of the historicist view of the past is its recognition that history shapes human beings through specific and unique social mediations. This need not imply the view often attributed to Hegel—the idea that history is a vast teleological progression leading relentlessly toward one divine event—though such a belief is one of its extreme potentialities. It does involve a sociological sense of both past and present, a recognition that societies are interrelated systems which change through time and that individuals are profoundly affected by their places within those systems. The greatest modern critics of nineteenth-century fiction from a historical point of view, whatever their other differences, agree that the creation of this grasp of social-historical milieux is its principal achievement. For Erich Auerbach, it is the prerequisite for a fully serious treatment of everyday life; for Lukács, it involves a fundamental discovery concerning the meaning of histori-

cal process itself. Both critics describe this development as the discovery of "the present as history," a phrase which derives ultimately from Hegel. In asserting that historical novels are defined by their sense of "history as a shaping force," Fleishman would thus appear to have rendered them an important service: he has acquitted them of the charge of portraying mere local color, finding in them instead the historical insights we associate with historicism at its most developed.

But Butterfield, writing at a time when valuing historical particularity caused critics less embarrassment than it does now, is closer to the truth about the historical probability that serves as a basis for the standard historical novel. The problem with Fleishman's mode of definition is that it saves too much too quickly, giving historical fiction a cognitive dignity that is unearned. The works of Harrison Ainsworth betray no insight whatever into "history as a shaping force," but we unhesitatingly call them historical novels. Fleishman's discussion quickly slides from defining historical fiction to finding a criterion for "authentic" historical fiction, a separate issue for which his maximal kind of definition is entirely appropriate.

The recognition that human beings are part of a larger historical process is not the source of the distinctively historical probability that distinguishes standard historical fiction, though the best historical novels certainly convey it. The probability that distinguishes standard historical novels rests on a simpler notion—the realization that history is comprised of ages and societies that are significantly different from our own. We can call this idea the recognition of "the past as past" (Ainsworth's fiction doesn't really measure up to this criterion either, but it is at least possible to recognize in his sensationalistic use of historical atmosphere a debased version of it, whereas any connection whatever with a notion of historical process or the present as history is in his case unimaginable.) The recognition of the past as past can lead to a sense of history as a process, and perhaps it ought to, but in fact it has not always done so in historical fiction.

By arguing that historical fiction need not view history as a process, I am parting company not only with Fleishman but with Lukács as well, though in a different way. For Lukács, the historical novel arises in the works of Scott when Scott discovers on an esthetic level that history is a process in which the past acts as the necessary precondition for the present. Unlike Butterfield or Fleishman, however, Lukács simply isn't interested in the problem of defining historical fiction, and given his distrust of "mere formalism," it is hard to see how he could be. He pursues instead the question of how the historical spirit comes to consciousness in literature. With more consistency than other writers who hold similar views concerning what is truly historical about historical novels, Lukács believes that historical fiction does not constitute a genre separate from the European realist novel as a whole. In his version of Marxist esthetics, a truly separate genre can arise only from a new vision of reality, and the truly historical novel shares (and in fact helped to create) the vision of reality we find in genuinely realistic novels. Historical fiction is thus part of a larger fictional genre, realist fiction, which is characterized by the mode of knowledge it embodies. This mode of knowledge provides, in the process he calls "preparatory esthetic processing," a necessary but not sufficient condition for the creation of realist fiction.

My discussions of Lukács, Butterfield, and Fleishman have revealed a number of fundamental differences among them, but they are united in believing historical fiction to be fundamentally a mode of knowledge. Such a view has its attractions. Who would want to deny that the best historical fiction can add to the richness of our sense of history, or that the structuring of history in great historical fiction may have cognitive value? Narrativist philosophers of history have recently argued with some persuasiveness that historical understanding itself may proceed according to the logic of narrative discourse, not of science. But it seems important for a number of reasons to oppose the idea that historical novels, or even standard historical novels, embody a defining vision of history in more than a minimal way.

Such an idea can become quickly and narrowly prescriptive in practice, blinding us to the workings of novels that embody a vision of history we do not respect. It is tempting to say that works which embody a historical vision we find uninteresting or unacceptable, or that seem to have no historical vision at all, are not "really" historical novels. But it is more useful to discriminate between great and mediocre historical novels than to exclude imperfect works from the group—a procedure that logically tends to produce a group containing one and only one true member. A different consequence appears in Fleishman's criticism. As we have seen, he believes that historical novels are characterized by "the active presence of a concept of history as a shaping force." He is also interested in tracing the history of historical fiction in England, which of course implies that there is a significant history to trace. Each of these premises raises problems. Combined, they cause him to exaggerate and homogenize the level of historical consciousness in the works he considers. Only by doing so can he produce a developing tradition of English historical fiction.

The search for a specific way of perceiving history which defines historical fiction is in my view a local manifestation of the understandable but unacceptable desire to separate literary discourse from "scientific discourse" and thus to save for literature its own distinct significance. This view, which places great stress on differentiating between true and false poetic modes, is most familiar as one of the cornerstones of the New Criticism as practiced by Cleanth Brooks and others. Lukács from his Marxist point of view has come up with a similar if somewhat more elegant procedure involving three levels of discourse—everyday speech, scientific discourse, and (mediating between the two on a whole series of intermediate levels) the language of literature. This is not the place to weigh the merits of such views extensively. I shall merely say that in my view "scientific discourse" in the sense required by Brooks and the others has been shown not to exist; their argument is based upon a false dichotomy. Literary works in general do not embody a distinct mode of knowledge, though they certainly can impart knowledge. Though literary works

can have cognitive claims, they are in the first instance verbal constructions designed to create certain effects through the disposition of their parts.

For our present purposes, the idea that historical fiction is a mode of telling the truth about history is objectionable chiefly because it does not account for the very different formal status that visions of history have in fact assumed in historical fiction. Such a definition excludes works we all call historical novels. Furthermore, if we adopt such a definition, we must conclude that most great nineteenth-century novels are historical novels, which renders the concept "historical novel" useless as a conceptual aid and falsifies the strong intuitive impression that leads readers to give the group a name in the first place. In practice, such an emphasis also tends to exclude or preclude problems of artistic form and effect, operating as if historical novels conveyed unmediated historical doctrine. Finally, the idea that historical fiction is a mode of historical knowledge leaves as a complete mystery what is surely the most striking fact about these works.

Joseph W. Turner

SOURCE: "The Kinds of Historical Fiction: An Essay in Definition and Methodology," in *Genre,* Vol. XII, No. 3, Fall, 1979, pp. 333-55.

[*In the following essay, Turner identifies three categories of historical fiction—documented, invented, and disguised historical novels—and discusses the boundaries between history and fiction.*]

"Everyone knows what a historical novel is; perhaps that is why few have volunteered to define it in print" [Avrom Fleishman, *The English Historical Novel: Walter Scott to Virginia Woolf,* 1971]. So begins Avrom Fleishman's foray into the morass of defining historical fiction. Now there is, without doubt, a significant portion of truth in this disarming gambit: except for an occasional skirmish over how far back a novel must be set to count as history, critics have assumed that the term "historical novel" effectively explains itself. But the remainder of Fleishman's theoretical discussion—not to mention the ensuing chapters on individual novels—attests to a fundamental problem this appeal to common sense only serves to mask: namely, that neither history nor fiction is itself a stable, universally agreed upon, concept. Small wonder, then, that as soon as Fleishman moves beyond the conventional definition and tries to distinguish between history and fiction, he creates as many problems as he solves. Not only does the whole discussion threaten to founder, but it usually circumvents that danger by presuming greater unanimity about what history actually is than exists among historians. Thus we find Fleishman asserting, for example, that "most philosophers of history" subscribe to the "covering law" theory of Popper and Hempel, when in fact there is anything but agreement on the question of the authority of historical explanations. Worse yet is the way Fleishman selectively appeals to contending schools of historiography when trying to argue his thesis that history and fiction can be differentiated according to "their similarities of aim and differences of means." Using Collingwood, Gallie, and Dilthey to assert the affinity between history and fiction, only to bring in Popper and Hempel to insist on the points of divergence, creates a tortuous, even if not altogether loaded, argument. We might just as easily juggle the contending schools differently and arrive at the contrary thesis: that history and fiction share the same means but have quite different ends. There is, for that matter, no reason to rule out the other two possible combinations in between.

My point, I should perhaps hastily add, is not that Professor Fleishman has nothing to tell us about historical fiction. His chapters on individual novels are often quite good. But his attempt at definition confuses as much as it clarifies. The problem with the opening chapter, moreover, is not simply one of definition, although it proves inadequate even for Fleishman's own purposes. Rather, the confusion inheres in his basic method, and in this regard he is by no means alone. Despite their divergent conclusions, in fact, nearly every commentator on the genre has opted for the same procedure: starting out with a comparison of history and fiction, they arrive at (depending on their preferences or presuppositions) a conception of historical fiction that revolves around either what fiction shares with history or what fiction claims for itself. Thus Georg Lukács and Harry Henderson build their critical approaches, although quite different, on the observation that history and fiction possess certain common traits. Conversely, Lion Feuchtwanger and Floyd C. Watkins erect their conceptions of the genre, although again quite different, on the argument that history and fiction are first and foremost distinct.

Now much has been accomplished in this manner, to be sure; but I question the advisability of adopting any method that depends for its success on the assumption that we can all agree on precisely what history is, much less how fiction relates to it. Either one of these questions is enough to detain discussion for a very long time; take them together and we shall never get out of the starting blocks. For with two such essentially contested concepts as history and fiction, comparison only compounds the contention.

Despite what common sense would appear to tell us,. . . . definition *is* a problem with the historical novel. Despite what the composite nature of the genre would seem to require, moreover, comparison is *not* the solution. But if not by distinguishing between history and fiction, you might ask, how are we to characterize the genre? Not, I think, by setting out formal elements shared by its members. First, because there is an inevitable circularity, if not a certain pseudo-empiricism, in such attempts at generic description: isolating common denominators restricts us, by and large, to recapitulating an a priori definition. Secondly, because formal properties may not be the genre's distinguishing characteristic: it is the content more than the form, after all, that sets historical novels off from other fiction. Finally, and perhaps most importantly, because the very diversity of the genre frustrates our rage to generalize, and condemns our results—should we persist—to triviality: for there are at least three distinct kinds of historical novels (those that invent a past, those that disguise a documented past, and those that re-create a documented past), and therefore no single description can blanket all

three without losing most of its significance. We can succeed, then, if we wish, in forcing the genre to conform to a single conception of fiction or of history, but only at considerable costs. For the impulse to create historical fiction comes from incredibly disparate sources; it finds expression, moreover, in an equal variety of fictional forms. Similarly, the motives for reading historical fiction are manifold, and the satisfactions it provides are just as varied. Aside from the tautology of common sense (all historical novels are novels about history), in short, all we can say in general about the genre is that it resists generalization.

Rather than thinking in terms of necessary formal features, therefore, we need to begin with a question: exactly what do readers decide when they place a novel within the category of historical fiction? Notice that their decision entails two choices: whether they will consider the text a *historical* novel, and whether they will consider it a historical *novel*. There are, in other words, two boundaries to be set if we are to define the genre: one between historical novels and other fiction, one between historical novels and narrative history. Instead of trying to establish them simultaneously, however—which is precisely what the comparison of history and fiction in previous discussions was meant to do—we would do well to take up the boundaries one at a time. Instead of trying to establish them for all historical novels, moreover, the boundaries must be redrawn (and in different ways) for each of the three types of historical fiction. With these two strictures in mind, then, return for a moment to Avrom Fleishman's formulation of the commonly accepted definition. He mentions the need for a past setting ("beyond an arbitrary number of years" as he puts it) and for a number of historical events ("particularly those in the public sphere," he adds), but he insists that to be genuinely historical a novel must contain "a real person among the fictitious ones." Now it is clear, as many reviewers have pointed out, that this last requirement is simply arbitrary: it excludes from the genre, among other works, *Middlemarch* and *Absalom, Absalom!,* which is more than enough to raise a few hackles. Even Fleishman chafes under the restrictions of his own definition, as time goes on, arguing for example that *Nostromo* "is more solidly historical than many novels that more neatly fit the definition." But the point to be drawn from this contradiction is not, as Murray Baumgarten would have it [in "Novel: Some Postulates," *Clio,* 4 (1975)], that Fleishman has thereby "reduced his own, elsewhere insisted upon, generic definition" to shambles. Rather, confusion results only because of the failure to differentiate between kinds of historical novels. Thus the definition can be put to good use—and not just salvaged—with but the slightest of changes: each member of the genre need only meet some, and not all, of the requirements. The presence of a real person in a novel may not be a necessary condition, for example, but it comes very close to being a sufficient one. When we read a novel about actual people from the past, we automatically assume that we have a historical novel. And though it may well be that in rare instances we might finally reject that initial assumption, even that possibility in no way disturbs our definition, for we have not posited any necessary condition. Generally speaking, then, novels with an actual historical character can be considered historical fiction. Novels of this type I should like to call documented historical novels, to emphasize their direct links with recorded history.

The justification for this distinction, as Fleishman points out, is that having actual people in a novel raises the problem of the ontological status of "real" as opposed to "invented" characters. I shall return to this issue shortly; all I wish to stress here is that its very presence sets off documented historical novels from other fiction. Not only do these actual characters set the stage for much of the quarreling over historical "accuracy" (as in William Styron's *The Confessions of Nat Turner,* say), but their non-fictive status creates a series of narrative problems that do not arise when the novelist is working entirely with his own inventions. Thus documented historical novels require separate consideration. Then, too, this distinction has the further advantage of helping to explain some of the inconsistencies that crop up in categorizing historical fiction. Novels set in the author's own lifetime—Robert Coover's *The Public Burning,* say—or even novels that are more nearly autobiographical—Norman Mailer's *Armies of the Night,* for example—are frequently thought of as historical novels, even though they violate one or more of the criteria in the commonly accepted definition. The explanation, of course, is that both these works partake of many of the same qualities, and raise many of the same difficulties, as documented historical novels; they both have enough specific links to actual persons and events—particularly those in the public sphere—that we tend to think of them as providing historical interpretations. Now we could, to be sure, deplore the inconsistency and cling tenaciously to the definition; but that would be to ignore the way certain novels align themselves with obvious members of the genre, thereby engaging historical as well as generic expectations.

In any case, on the fiction side of the boundary between narrative histories and historical fiction stands the documented historical novel. Delaying for the moment the problem of deciding how to make that demarcation, let us move away from narrative histories along a theoretical continuum in the direction of novels generally. At some point, by no means imperceptible, we pass from documented historical novels to what I shall call disguised historical novels. Robert Penn Warren's *All the King's Men* will serve as an example. In contrast to something like *The Confessions of Nat Turner,* Warren's novel includes no actual characters or events. Nevertheless the work stands somewhere between documented history and conventional fiction: Willie Stark may be Warren's invention, but the parallels between the careers of Huey Long and Willie Stark are so close that we find ourselves reading the novel as a disguised account of a documented past. The critical issue here, therefore, entails defining the novel's relationship to recorded history and determining what aesthetic significance it might have. The very fact that Warren has chosen to transform the figure of Huey Long, after all, might warrant the conclusion that the whole question is irrelevant: by changing the name of the historical character, you might say, Warren circumvents the reader's impulse to judge the novel as a historical re-creation. Thus you could argue, and with some conviction, that within

the terms that the novel sets for itself *All the King's Men* has nothing to do with Huey Long.

Despite this formalist argument and the fictional disguise on which it depends, historical questions persist. Although the name has been changed to protect the fiction, the striking similarities between the novel and recorded history continually tease the reader beyond the novel itself. Perhaps the closest, although not altogether satisfactory, analogy would be to the dynamics of allegory, for in both cases it is up to the reader to supply the identifications that lie outside the text. In contrast to the way allegory normally works, however, *All the King's Men* does not insist on a dual interest. Warren is perfectly willing—indeed, would almost prefer—to leave the Huey Long question aside. And for good reason: to insist on the historical re-creation brings the fictional disguise under attack. Thus once having decided to translate history into his own terms, Warren is better off not calling attention to that fact. If he is to maintain the autonomy of his fiction, he must assert its independence from history by presenting Willie Stark as if he were a completely fictitious character. Still, the parallels exist to qualify the fictional claim: even with the disguise, we can read *All the King's Men* as an interpretation of Huey Long, though it is not exclusively (nor perhaps even primarily) that. The link to past actuality may be attenuated, but it is nevertheless there. Neither drawn directly from recorded history nor composed as an outright fiction, Warren's disguised historical novel situates itself half-way between documented and invented history. Now it is possible, certainly, to imagine a disguised historical novel in which the camouflage is so complete or the historical antecedents so obscure that the reader never recognizes the disguise. And it is equally possible to imagine a disguised historical novel in which the historical parallels are so extensive and precise that the reader wonders why there should be any disguise at all. But between these two extremes, there is a good deal of historical fiction that operates in the manner of *All the King's Men,* simultaneously striking the reader as being completely new creation and disguised re-creation. Because of this peculiarly double focus (and the variety of ways that a novelist might engage it), moreover, the disguised historical novel exhibits certain distinctive characteristics, which here again merit separate consideration.

Thus only in the final stage of the continuum—which I shall call the invented historical novel—do we face any real problem establishing the boundary between historical novels and other fiction. Here, since the principal characters and events are all invented, any insistence on a generic distinction must contend with the fact that most novels are presented as if they were history. More often than not, as Henry James points out, the realistic novelist aspires to the authority of history: "It is impossible to imagine what a novelist takes himself to be unless he regards himself as an historian and his narrative as a history. . . . As a narrator of fictitious events he is nowhere; to insert into his attempt a back-bone of logic, he must relate events that are assumed to be real" [*Partial Portraits,* 1888]. Thus it would seem that all novels, or at least all realistic ones, are "historical." Interestingly enough, in fact, Georg

Lukács—in his seminal work on the genre—argues that historical novels are no different from any others:

> If then we look at the problem of genre seriously, our question might be: which facts of life underlie the historical novel and how do they differ from those which give rise to the genre of the novel in general? I believe that when the question is put in this way, there can only be one answer—none. An analysis of the work of the important realists will show that there is not a single, fundamental problem of structure, characterization, etc. in their historical novels which is lacking in their other novels, and vice versa. . . . The ultimate principles are in either case the same. [*The Historical Novel,* 1937]

Such a conflation of realistic and historical novels, though true enough perhaps in the sense that Lukács formulates it, nevertheless confuses the distinction between genres and kinds: the "ultimate principles" may well be the same, for they are indeed both novels, but finer discriminations at a lower level of generality (and with a less organic conception of literary forms) can still be made. In this instance, the novel's setting and the author's relationship to it become the determining factors. The farther back in time the fiction is set, that is, the more likely we are to treat it as an invented historical novel. Here, then, we must almost insist on a temporal requirement: either Fleishman's suggestion of an admittedly arbitrary "two generations" or Harry Henderson's less-restricted notion of "the world that existed before the author was born" [*Versions of the Past: The Historical Imagination in American Fiction,* 1974]. Removed thus from the author's experience, the characters and events—though invented—begin to require the exercise of a distinctively historical imagination.

On these grounds alone, then, we might differentiate between this last type and fiction generally. In addition, however, invented historical novels are frequently structured to highlight the problems of historical interpretation. William Faulkner's *Absalom, Absalom!,* for example, is not only set in the unexperienced past but also examines the nature of historical inquiry. Admittedly, Quentin's attempt to learn the truth about Thomas Sutpen involves something that is historical only within the artifice of Faulkner's fiction. But with all the conflicting interpretations that stand between Quentin and the "real" Sutpen, his narrative stance takes on a historical significance that it does not have in realistic fiction. Much more than the illusion of verisimilitude is involved; indeed, the meaning of history and the possibility of recovering it become the primary concerns in Faulkner's novel. Determinations of fact, assessments of documents and oral reports, interpretations of motive—these are all methodological issues for the historian, as they are for Quentin. Thus by predicating a gap between the narrator and his story, Faulkner raises the issue of how it is to be closed. Herein lies the difference between many invented historical novels and other fiction: in realistic novels, though the narrator may pose as a historian, attention is usually diverted from the problem of how the narrator can know his story; in invented historical novels, by contrast, that very possibility is often brought into question, turning the novel into a reflection on the way we know history. Generally speaking, then, unless

they have such a complex narrative structure, invented historical novels remain distinct from other fiction only by placing the action far enough into the past as to claim for themselves the status of a historical reconstruction.

To summarize, then, historical novels fall into three different categories, which represent distinct stages along the continuum (although individual novels may combine elements of all three). Each of the three kinds, moreover, can be distinguished from other fiction (albeit with decreasing ease as we move from documented, through disguised, to invented historical novels) in terms of the kind of characters and events that predominate. In setting the other boundary, quite naturally, the problematic is reversed. Neither invented nor disguised historical novels seem to run any risk of being confused with the works of narrative historians. Admittedly, these two kinds *pretend* to be referential; we can, to be sure, even judge the adequacy of their historical re-creation. But we do not, with invented historical novels anyway, expect to find these fictional creations mentioned in any historical documents. We are being presented with fictional, not historical, events— events that never were observable outside the text, nor ever can be, since they do not exist before or apart from the words that create them. Then, too, with disguised historical novels—if we accept the translation on its own terms—the same ontological difference obtains: the very act of the disguise asserts a fundamental discontinuity between the novel and recorded history, amounting to an insistence on the fictional status of the characters and events. With documented historical novels, however, the conventional distinction between history and fiction threatens to collapse, for the novelist and the historian share the same event. By drawing on recorded history rather than disguising it or inventing his own, moreover, the novelist appears (by virtue of eschewing these generic alternatives) to be making the historian's claim to re-create an extra-textual reality.

Certainly, the precise nature of this apparent claim to historical truth has been the subject of most of the debate surrounding the documented historical novel. On the one hand, it is argued that the novelist is not a historian and that no one expects him to be: thus so long as he does not violate our sense of what Robert Penn Warren has called "the spirit of his history," he is free to change facts and invent whatever he needs to tell his story. Whether or not his novel is "good history" does not matter; the important requirement, as Warren and others have insisted, is that it should make "historical sense" in a thematic or symbolic way. On the other hand, it has been argued that once the novelist moves into the arena of history he must comport himself as a historian: thus he must restrain his inventiveness, work within the existing evidence. The fact that he is a novelist is not relevant; he has pretended to be a historian, and therefore owes allegiance to the documents. Now neither of these positions in isolation, nor the very way of posing the issue, illuminates very much, except that there is a tension inherent in the genre (expressed in the oxymoron of the name itself). Readers conventionally expect, in other words, that a novelist will adhere fairly closely to his sources—why else call it "historical"? At the same time, however, they also assume that the novelist can take greater liberties than the historian—why else call it "fiction"? Where the problem lies, therefore, is that these expectations represent conflicting commitments, which can never be simply (nor ever finally) resolved. For so long as we look for a single answer, we are forced to privilege one of the two conventional expectations; and no matter which we choose to emphasize, neither the dependence on or independence of recorded history, there are documented historical novels aplenty to contradict the choice. Almost inevitably so: not only does a tension exist within the terms of the genre, but there is a further complication built into the way a novelist can work either within or against these conventional expectations. Thus to argue that documented historical novels are or are not valuable because they do or do not stick to the "facts" amounts to something of a false problem.

Instead of trying to decide once and for all about the question of fidelity to history, then, we need to consider the status of historical events in fiction. This issue, which has occupied the attention of theorists since Aristotle, has frequently been resolved by arguing that historical events are transformed the very moment they take their place in the poetic fiction. Thus, as Aristotle formulates it, the poet can take his subject from history, but in doing so he "is none the less a poet for that; since some historic occurrences may very well be in the probable and possible order of things; and it is in that aspect of them [rather than in their 'actual' aspect] that he is their poet." Aristotle insists here on the autonomy of all fictions, even historical ones. Murray Krieger, in commenting on the *Poetics,* explains the point this way:

> Every element taken from [historical] reality— an incident, a character, an idea, even words and their normal meanings—must be newly justified by the role it must play in that closed teleological pattern. As a result, that element must change its meaning, indeed its very nature and ontological status, by virtue of these interlocked functions. ["Fiction, History, and Empirical Reality," *Critical Inquiry,* I (1974)]

Thus the responsibility of the documented historical novelist, according to this view, would be not to history but to the teleology of his poetic fiction. It would follow, then, that even documented historical novels are discontinuous from history and thus no different than disguised or invented historical novels.

The argument for autonomy, in short, provides a way of securing the distinction between narrative histories and documented historical novels, but at the cost of collapsing the one between documented and other types of historical fiction. Far more debilitating, however, is the way that Krieger's argument minimizes the dynamics of aesthetic response: while it may well be that every historical character and event must be "newly justified by the role it must play in that closed teleological pattern," there is still a resistance to that very process built into the distinct ontological status of the historical material. Consider in this light a slight variation on L.C. Knights' argument for aesthetic autonomy, the proverbial "How many children had Lady Macbeth?" Now in an invented or disguised historical novel, Knights' premise would hold: Faulkner, for example, can tell us that Rosa Coldfield never bore children, and there is the end to the question. But if a novelist were to write about Queen Elizabeth, the reader would expect from the very first that Elizabeth bore no legitimate children and that the crown was passed on to James I. It is precisely this sort of historical expectation that the argument for autonomy, with its synchronic formal analysis, does not take into account; and it is precisely along these lines that we can describe the differences between documented historical novels and other fiction, even other historical fiction. Faulkner could just as easily have decided to arrange for Rosa to marry Sutpen and bear his coveted male heir. That would be quite a different novel from *Absalom, Absalom!,* to be sure, but no one would know what they were missing. In a novel about Queen Elizabeth, by contrast, the rhetorical situation is not the same: the reader expects certain things to happen and will no doubt be surprised—perhaps even disappointed—if they do not. Now that is not to rule out the possibility—it should be stressed—that a novelist might create, and convince his readers to accept, a story about Queen Elizabeth's hitherto unknown illegitimate son. Rather, it suggests only there may well be resistance on the part of some readers to tampering with recorded history. Mary Renault explains why: "One can at least desire the truth; and it is inconceivable to me how anyone can decide deliberately to betray it; to alter some fact which was central to the life of a real human being, however long it is since he ceased to live, in order to make a smoother story, or to exploit him as propaganda for some cause." Whereas Renault is committed to historical accuracy as a fundamental requirement of good historical fiction, however, I wish only to insist on it as a conventional expectation. The point, then, is not to try to legislate how readers *should* react to a novelist's divergence from recorded history; it is, rather, simply to assert that the reader will in all probability *react,* and that this reaction—whether it leads to insight or disappointment—is different from any provoked in invented or even disguised historical novels. For only by dealing directly with historical events does the novelist create the expectation that he will follow what actually happened; and only when this expectation exists does compliance with (or divergence from) recorded history take on internal significance.

Insofar as he generates historical expectations, then, the documented historical novelist is in a position similar to the historian's; but because he is writing fiction, and not history, the documented historical novelist operates within a different set of generic conventions. Crudely put, the difference is that the historian is supposed to restrict himself to historical events, while the documented historical novelist need not. The novelist is free, more so than the historian, to fill in with imagined details the gaps in recorded history. Admittedly, this distinction is basically a matter of degree: historians have never been prohibited from speculating, nor have they even been prevented from inventing characters (usually to stand for representative types). Nevertheless, the historian conventionally must identify his speculations and inventions, refer them to what documents exist, and defend them against previous interpretations. The documented historical novelist, by contrast, usually slips in his inventions and speculations unannounced. The reason for this, as we shall see, is that the novelist conventionally does not wish to call attention to himself or to the fact that his "history" is part fiction. For the moment, though, the important point is that the boundary between documented historical novels and narrative history needs to be drawn along the lines of generic conventions, and not in terms of Aristotle's universality and particularity (which so much of the previous criticism on the genre has invoked).

Once having recognized the importance of conventions and expectations in documented historical novels, moreover, we find that a critical approach to all of historical fiction immediately presents itself: namely, reader-response criticism. In contrast to the synchronic formalist model, a theory of aesthetic response obviates the need to define in advance what history is or how a novel should relate to it; instead, it allows us to follow the way the implied reader adjusts his conception of history to the one the novelist is creating. Its focus on the actions involved in responding to a literary text is thus ideally suited to the process of expectation and revision that is engaged when novelists write about the past. Furthermore, it should also be clear that the number and kinds of historical expectations increase as we move along the theoretical continuum from invented, through disguised, to documented historical novels. Aside from the idea that each of the three types generates historical expectations differently, all that remains to be observed is that it is possible, even within a single kind, for a novelist to bring generic expectations to bear on historical ones in a great many ways.

Before proceeding further, then, we need a general sketch of the respective generic conventions. Invented historical novels exhibit very little that is unique. Generally, they rely on novelistic forms that can be loosely termed realistic—avoiding, that is, anything that might draw attention to the fact that they are not history but fiction. Thus invented historical novels avoid any self-conscious reflections on their ontological status; instead, the narrator comports himself as a historian, pretending that his statements refer to an extra-textual reality. Thus whatever historical expectations the reader brings to such texts are fairly generalized; since they can only be applied indirectly to these fictitious characters and events, moveover, the invented historical novel retains much, if not all, of the conventional autonomy of fiction.

With disguised historical novels, the same preference for realistic forms presents itself. The same conventions hold therefore, with one addition: the reader is expected to grant the novelist's right to disguise history and then do with it what he will. The critical difficulty in analyzing this kind of historical novel, however, has less to do with defining its conventions than with explaining the double articulation of the text—its autonomy and its historical referents—and the resulting double role of the reader. In principle, at least, the effect of the generic conventions would be to inhibit historical expectations. In a situation where anything is possible reader expectations tend to be minimal or non-existent; and since the disguise signals the author's privilege to change history in any way he should choose, it becomes rather difficult for the reader to know

in advance what will happen. As time goes on, of course, the reader may begin to discern certain patterns or tendencies in the disguise; and from this interpretive process, he may even begin to develop assurances about what to expect. But the reader can never be certain if, or when, the pattern might be broken. Moreover, he really has no grounds on which to object to any of the changes, no reason for being disappointed in the way that one might be disappointed by a documented historical novel that recounted Custer's victory at Little Bighorn. Perhaps, then, we should posit a certain passivity on the part of readers of disguised historical novels, less an anticipating of the disguise than a waiting to see how it is developed. We might say, in other words, that in conventional examples of this type of historical fiction the reader interprets the referential component of the novel retrospectively. Having followed the story of Willie Stark, as it were, we can superimpose it on what we know of Huey Long; but we almost have to wait until we have gotten Willie's story before we can make the comparison. Granted, some of this goes on all along, and the reader does have expectations generated within the terms of the fiction itself. So we might, from this perspective, conceive of the reader being engaged in a process of constantly measuring these internal and forward-looking glances against what he knows to have actually happened. But even in this more complicated model, the reader is operating on two distinct levels—the historical and the fictional; he is in fact reinforcing his sense of the separation. Thus it is not until the end of the book that the two can ever quite be brought together with any assurity. All the while, moreover, the awareness of the disguise is focusing the reader's attention on the design of the novel itself. Thus we might say that the disguise points more to the closed teleological pattern of the novel than it does to history. And to this extent, it could be argued, disguised historical fiction maintains a conventional autonomy.

Beyond these tentative hypotheses, however, we would do well to stick to individual cases, noting only that a position of this kind on the theoretical continuum makes one of two distinct rhetorical strategies likely. There are, in other words, some disguised historical novels—*All the King's Men* is a good example—that are written in much the same way as invented historical novels. Here, although the disguise may be obvious, it is never insisted upon. The novel proceeds as if its characters and events were entirely fictitious. In direct contrast, there are some disguised historical novels—E. L. Doctorow's *The Book of Daniel* is a good example—that self-consciously flaunt the fact of their double status, that force the reader constantly to engage the disguise. A brief comparison of the two novels should clarify this distinction.

Doctorow's disguised account of the Rosenberg trial and its aftermath presumes the same generic conventions than operate in Warren's novel. In *The Book of Daniel* Susan Isaacson loses her parents when they are electrocuted for conspiring against the United States. She eventually responds to this childhood trauma by attempting suicide and then willing her death. Now the generic conventions prevent us from objecting to this narrative premise on the grounds that it does not comport with what actually happened. To this extent, and it is no small matter, *The Book of Daniel* shares the same autonomy as *All the King's Men*. The way that Susan's story sheds light on the experience of the Rosenbergs, therefore, is oblique and retrospective: having been convinced by Doctorow's fiction that Susan's suicide is inevitable, we are left to wonder about the fact that the Rosenberg children did not respond in the same way.

Despite this important resemblance, however, the generic status of *The Book of Daniel* is far more problematical than that of *All the King's Men*. At the same time as the disguise preserves the autonomy of the novel, Doctorow tries to generate the kinds of historical expectations that are created when a novelist deals directly with recorded history. Rather than invented historical fiction, which is what Warren's novel resembles, Doctorow's novel keeps moving in the direction of documented historical fiction, as evidenced by the way Doctorow manipulates his narrator, Susan's brother Daniel. Notice, for example, the elaborate game of hide-and-seek that Daniel plays with his implied reader at the beginning of the novel. At first he uses his adopted name, Daniel Lewin, and for the first twenty pages he enjoys his anonymity, even going so far as to entertain himself with ironies that only he can appreciate. In this process of toying with the reader, of course, Daniel is dropping clues to his public identity, which he reveals before too long by recounting his appearance at a rally in New York to free the Isaacsons. Daniel insures that his reader makes the identification by self-consciously referring to the game that he has been playing:

> Oh, baby, you know it now. We done played enough games for you, ain't we. You a smart lil fucker. You know where it's at now, don' you big daddy. You got the picture. This the story of a fucking, right? You pullin' out yo lit-er-ary map, mutha? *You know where we goin', right muthafuck?* (My emphasis)

The shift in tone and diction that occurs here points to an emotional involvement in his story that has been controlled up to this point in the novel. For Daniel to display his aggression and outrage is itself striking; that he should turn it against his audience, by mocking the reader's sense of discovery, is altogether disconcerting.

Even more importantly, however, Daniel's self-conscious reference to his public identity brings the fictional disguise into play in a radical fashion. Within the terms of Daniel's story, Paul and Rochelle Isaacson are actual historical characters. Thus when Daniel finally identifies his parents, he can be sure that his imagined readers will "know where we goin'." But for the actual reader of *The Book of Daniel*, as opposed to the one Daniel pretends to address, this passage elicits a more complicated response. Since the Isaacsons never really existed before the novel was written, the reader must first make the connections to the Rosenbergs before he can make any sense out of Daniel's remarks. Without the identification there can be no expectations. Thus to the extent that Daniel believes his reader already knows his story, the actual reader must interpret the novel on two levels: for if he is to occupy the same position as the audience that Daniel addresses, he must continually translate, even as he willingly accepts, the fictional dis-

guise that stands between him and the history that Daniel purports to be recounting.

Therein lies Doctorow's unconventional strategy. Unlike *All the King's Men,* which never *depends* on the existence of Huey Long for its meaning or its effect, *The Book of Daniel* cannot be read without taking the Rosenbergs into account. Doctorow insists, in short, that we do and do not accept the disguise. Clearly, the risks are considerable, for he is threatening the very nature of the generic contract. No matter how hard he pushes the disguised historical novel in the direction of documented history, in fact, there is a resistance to that transformation built into the conventions of this fictional kind. And besides, there are places where he needs our acceptance of the disguise. Thus Doctorow all but faces the same rhetorical problem as the little boy who cried "wolf" one too many times: if he expects the reader to accept the disguise in some places, then he had better not subvert it at others, and vice versa. That is not to say, however, that the novel fails; the self-consciousness with which Doctorow points to the problem anticipates, and partially defuses, the reader's objections. But it does suggest the conventional affinities between disguised and invented historical novels, as well as account for much of the confusion expressed by reviewers of the novel. In addition, it highlights the potential impact of playing historical expectations off against generic conventions, since whatever its flaws *The Book of Daniel* is a powerful novel and at least part of its success comes from the rhetorical risks that Doctorow takes.

Turning now to the conventions of documented historical fiction, we find the same basic principles operating. Most of the generic conventions are designed to preserve the autonomy of the fiction. Thus, as we have said, the novelist is traditionally allowed greater freedom than the historian to speculate in order to create what history has failed to provide, an unbroken record of the past. At the same time, the novelist is not required to disturb his illusion by identifying his inventions. More specifically, however, we find a number of strategies designed to help circumvent the problems created by the distinct ontological status of historical and fictional events. More than relying on realistic forms to lend their fictions the illusion of historicity, for example, documented historical novelists frequently center the narrative on their own invented characters. Observing this pattern in the novels of Sir Walter Scott, Georg Lukács even raises it to the level of a critical precept, arguing that world-historical figures are not an appropriate subject for the novelist and so should be kept in the background of the fiction. Now Lukács' reasons for insisting on this "classical form of the historical novel" have as much to do with his Marxist interpretation of history as they do with any inherently formal limitations or requirements of the genre. But even without broaching the issue of Marxist historiography, we might quarrel with Lukács' restrictive definition on the grounds that there are, quite simply, many good historical novels that take major historical figures as their prime subject (George Garrett's *Death of the Fox,* for example). Nevertheless, Lukács has drawn our attention to an important point: that the subordination of history to fiction is a frequent strategy, since it has the advantage of freeing the novelist to do what he presumably does best—invent. This movement toward invented historical fiction permits the novelist, in effect, to recover much of the autonomy that he has sacrificed to history. But even with a preponderance of invention, the problem of handling the interaction of history and fiction persists. Indeed, to some extent it is actually exacerbated by the compartmentalizing strategy. The farther you keep actual and fictitious characters apart, that is, the more you remind the reader of the difference, and the more you deprive yourself of one of the great advantages of documented historical fiction—the tendency for the novelist's inventions to accrue historicity from their very proximity to historical events. Once history and fiction are rigidly separated, moreover, there are limitations imposed on the way they can interact: generally speaking, at least, history must invade the fiction rather than the reverse if the illusion of historicity is to be preserved.

This elaboration of the basic conventions and strategies could be extended, but the underlying principle is clear: if his fiction is to carry the weight of history, the novelist does well to distract any attention from himself or the artifice he has created, to gesture through his text to the past he seeks to recapture. In recent years, however, various writers of historical fiction—such as John Barth, Thomas Berger, and Ishmael Reed—have taken the opposite tack, creating what might be called comic historical fiction (by which I mean, less that they engage in humorous treatment of certain historical materials, although they do, than that they create their comic perspectives on history by poking fun at these generic conventions, playing delightful variations on the interaction of their fictions with history, and generally flaunting the inescapable artifice of their creations). This trend toward self-reflexive historical fiction merits careful attention: its connections with both conventional historical novels and other recent self-conscious fiction are historically and artistically significant. But rather than broaching that enormous subject here, I should like to take a brief look at one of the more conventional examples of recent historical fiction, William Styron's *The Confessions of Nat Turner*, if only because any satisfactory approach to the genre should be able to bring some coherence, even if not consensus, to the Nat Turner controversy.

Certainly, a great many issues are brought into focus by Styron's novel, ranging anywhere from disputations of "fact" to the ideological content of historical fiction. Just as certainly, the controversy itself merits critical and historical analysis, here again ranging anywhere from the details of a particular interpretation to reflections on the political dynamics of culture. Not only are all these matters worth pursuing, moreover, but they suggest something of the complexities of literary, historical, and cultural analysis required by many documented historical novels. I shall have to restrict myself here, however, to the question of artistic value, particularly as it relates to Styron's handling of generic conventions. Let us begin, then, with Styron's own conception of historical fiction, which he boldly sets forth in his prefatory note (and which he was later to defend with appeals to the authority of Lukács). As Styron conceives it, the virtue of historical fiction resides in the novelist's conventional freedom to speculate and invent:

During the narrative that follows I have rarely departed from the *known* facts about Nat Turner and the revolt of which he was the leader. However, in those areas where there is little knowledge in regard to Nat, his early life, and the motivations for the revolt (and such knowledge is lacking most of the time), I have allowed myself the utmost freedom of imagination in reconstructing events—yet I trust remaining within the bounds of what meager enlightenment history has left us about the institution of slavery. [*The Confessions of Nat Turner*, 1967]

Though we might well question whether the enlightenment that history affords is as "meager" as Styron believes it to be, I shall leave that argument to the professional historian. I only wish to pursue the artistic consequences of Styron's decision to speculate "in those areas where there is little knowledge."

In itself, Styron's strategy is neither unusual nor problematical; the conventions of the documented historical novel clearly countenance it, and the practice of a great many historical novelists makes it even predictable. But we might ask whether Styron has taken that conventional freedom too far. The entire credibility of the novel, after all, hinges on the illusion that it is the actual Nat Turner who speaks to us. Putting aside the stylistic problems this creates, there are still extraordinary difficulties built into the attempt to know the mind of a historical character. Much has been said about the daring—some would say foolhardiness, or worse—of a white author attempting to render the thoughts of a black revolutionary. Perhaps more needs to be said about the existentialist perspective that Styron brings to Nat Turner's religious convictions. But even after the opinions from both sides are in (and notice how much depends on the critic's own conception of what a "true" account would be), we still need to examine Styron's formal solutions to the rhetorical difficulties presented by his subject.

Styron thinks, to be sure, of *The Confessions of Nat Turner* as an unconventional historical novel; he calls it a "meditation on history" as opposed, presumably, to a simple chronicle of events. But what he has given us is the height of conventionality, a documented historical novel that not only presumes almost unlimited freedom to speculate, but one that asks the reader to accept without question the pseudo-historicity of its autobiographical form. The critical issue, therefore, is not whether Styron is entitled to speculate and invent, but whether the form he has chosen for the novel allows him to reflect on his own historical reconstruction. And it must be said, I would contend, that it does not. While the novel is clearly a meditation—in the sense that it is Styron's imaginative re-creation—it is not presented in the form of a meditation. In fact, any time the reader becomes aware that it is Styron's meditation the novel's necessary illusion has slipped, for it asks us to believe that Nat is doing the telling. Now precisely how well Styron succeeds in creating or maintaining that illusion has been, and will no doubt continue to be, endlessly disputed. Whether it convinces or not, however, the strategy of the first-person narrative builds into the novel an unresolvable contradiction: for if it *is* Nat Turner's "Confessions," then it cannot be Styron's "meditation," and vice versa. The difficulty, therefore, goes beyond the inevitable problem of convincing the reader that Nat Turner is speaking, to a deeper irony: that to succeed, Styron must efface himself completely, forfeit any attempt at "meditation."

My point, in short, is not that Styron should have fettered his imagination, given up any hope of penetrating the veil of mystery that stands between him and this particular past. On the contrary, the historical novelist is obligated to exercise his imagination to the full. But the more one's historical subject stands shrouded in mystery, the greater one's responsibility to create a formal correlative for the necessary expense of imagination. There is, to be sure, a little of this in Styron's *Confessions;* and I do not wish to underestimate his achievement. Clearly, he has created a striking, albeit controversial, image of the conditions of slavery. Nevertheless, Styron's own essay, "This Quiet Dust," is a far superior "meditation" on that same history. In that autobiographical sketch he wrestles with the difficulty, yet necessity, of recovering this past; captures the relevance, as well as many of the ambivalences and complications, of his own involvement in the historical recreation; and explores the significance of both. Yet such self-conscious reflections run directly counter to the heavily conventional strategies and design of his own novel. It is almost as if Styron has been seduced by the very lack of historical documentation, betrayed by the very freedom conventionally allowed the novelist. Whatever the cause, however, what is missing from *The Confessions of Nat Turner* is any formal representation of the limits of historical knowledge, any acknowledgment of his own wrestlings with the recalcitrance of history.

To judge Styron's *Confessions* lacking in this respect and therefore seriously flawed does not, I think, impose an irrelevant criterion on the novel, nor does it amount to a reversion to the idea that the novelist is bound by existing historical evidence. Rather, it implies only that historical novelists—particularly those who re-create an actual past—invite historical judgments; and further that one of the primary concerns in such evaluations revolves around the novelist's conception of his own relationship to the past. In much the same way, therefore, as Hegel distinguished among three classes of historical consciousness (Original, Reflective, and Philosophical), we need to draw similar divisions among historical novelists: those who write in the Original mode, where the principal concern is to create a compelling picture of the past—history primarily *in itself;* those who write in the Reflective mode, where the chasm between past and present is recognized only to be bridged—history *in and for itself;* and those who write in the Philosophical mode, where the primary concern becomes how, or if, history itself is possible—history *in and for,* but primarily *about itself.*

This new set of categories attributes value, to be sure; there is no avoiding it, nor would we want to. The best historical fiction, in my view, is ultimately about itself, about the meaning and making of history, about man's fate to live in history and his attempt to live in awareness of it. While I would be willing to defend that view, I have sought to avoid imposing it on the theoretical problems of

definition and methodology. There are many *good* historical novels (and Styron's is only one of them) that either do not achieve, or more often never even aspire to, the Philosophical mode. There are even—lest it seem that I have unwittingly privileged self-consciousness—a good many self-reflexive historical novels (Thomas Berger's *Little Big Man,* for example) that remain almost entirely within the Reflective mode. There are, for that matter, novels in the Philosophical mode (George Garrett's *Death of the Fox,* for instance) that share much of Styron's commitment to imaginative invention, while resisting most of the comedy of Barth's self-reflection in *The Sot-Weed Factor.* It would be a mistake, then, to define the genre in such a way as to privilege the Philosophical mode, and I would stress that the initial categories of analysis (invented, disguised, and documented historical novels) are value-neutral: whatever sense there may be of a progression along the continuum relates only to the increasingly distinctive interpretive problems that arise as we move closer to the boundary with narrative history. We should be wary (as much as it is possible), moreover, about confusing the value of a novel with the amount of analytical criticism that it requires or the specifically theoretical issues that it raises. It should be observed, then, that the Hegelian categories of historical consciousness just introduced do not align themselves with the purely descriptive generic categories that I proposed at the start. Faulkner's *Absalom, Absalom!* is as much in the Philosophical mode as John Barth's *The Sot-Weed Factor,* though the first is invented and the second documented. Nor is any absolute hierarchy of value intended: there is no reason why we cannot appreciate novels in the Original or Reflective modes for what they have to offer.

Finally, it should be noted that these two sets of categories, and my discussion, have touched only briefly, if at all, on other important issues. There are, for example, historical problems to be faced when dealing with nineteenth-century historical fiction. I have side-stepped the issue here by drawing my examples from modern, predominantly contemporary, fiction. But there is more than enough flexibility within an aesthetics of reader response to accommodate the historically conditioned shifts in conceptions of history and the novelist's relationship to it. Still other questions remain—the novelist's ideological commitments, his affinity for a particular type of historical explanation, his ideas on the nature or course of history, his conception of the relevance of his work. Depending on our interpretive concerns, therefore, other discriminations, along somewhat different lines, would need to be made. In particular, if we wished to pursue primarily historiographical issues (such as the role of narrative in historical explanations, for example, as in *The Sot-Weed Factor*), we would find not only that thematic categories are far more appropriate, but that they cut across the original differentiations into kinds. The necessity for the categories of invented, disguised, and documented historical novels, therefore, is exclusively interpretive, a matter of differing expectations and conventions involved in our reading. Similarly, the real advantage of the categories derived from Hegel is evaluative: that they point to what I take to be the central issue, the meaning and making of history. And while metahistory is by no means all there is to history, nor all that there is to historical fiction, it remains the subject that has engaged all the great historians. A historical novelist—even a literary critic in search of definition and methodology—could do much worse.

Helen Cam on the utility of the historical novel:

The function . . . of the historical novel is to awaken the incurious, especially the young, to interest in the past, widening the horizons of all and enticing a minority to serious study. For such it can arouse the critical faculty and stimulate investigation for the verification or disproof of unfamiliar facts, leading to first-hand acquaintance with original sources. It can enlarge the sympathies by compelling the reader to see abstract generalizations, whether political, social or economic, in terms of the human individual. The historical novelist has resources . . . from which the scientific historian is debarred. He may fill in the lamentable hiatuses with his own inventions. But he must keep the rules. His inventions must not be incompatible with the temper of the age—its morals and its psychology no less than its material conditions—and they must not be incompatible with the established facts of history. The novel that can do all this is a good historical novel.

Helen Cam in Historical Novels, *Routledge & Kegan Paul, 1961.*

VICTORIAN HISTORICAL FICTION

Sir John Marriott

SOURCE: "The Victorian Era: Social Reform in Fact and Fiction," in *English History in English Fiction,* 1940. Reprint by Kennikat Press, 1970, pp. 251-69.

[*In the following excerpt, Marriott presents an overview of nineteenth-century historical fiction, noting that its authors were concerned with portraying the Victorian way of life and discussing the social issues of that time.*]

At each stage of our journey the way becomes more arduous, the impedimenta heavier, the problems more baffling. That is pre-eminently true of the Victorian era. The embarrassment is, however, to some extent relieved by the fact that not all the great Victorian novelists dealt with contemporary affairs. Thackeray's (1811-63) history, for instance, belongs to the eighteenth century. The best-beloved characters of Charles Dickens (1812-70) are very early if not prae-Victorian. Even George Eliot (1819-80), though she herself had more of the *Zeit-geist* than any of her contemporaries, drew inspiration for her best work from her reminiscences of childhood and early life. Yet, in fact, her recollections were tinged as much by the scientific spirit of Darwinism as by the moral problems which never ceased to haunt a mind permeated by the evangelical

teaching imbibed in youth. Of the Anglican Establishment in mid-Victorian days, Anthony Trollope is among novelists the most faithful analyst; of the difficulties which, in the scientific era, were beginning to beset clergy and laity alike, there is no better illustration than that of Mrs. Humphry Ward's Robert Elsmere.

The reign of Queen Victoria, in respect of fiction as of politics, divides into three periods: (i) a period of unrest, agitation, and depression extending from the Queen's accession (1837) to the "Hungry Forties", to the Irish Famine (1845), and the "Young Ireland Rebellion" (1848); (ii) the period of ever-expanding prosperity in trade and agriculture, and the political ascendancy of the middle classes (1846-85), and (iii) the Imperialist revival which began about 1885 and culminated in the "Diamond Jubilee" of 1897. The last four years of the reign were an unhappy anticlimax.

This [essay] is concerned with the middle period marked by the ascendancy of the "Manchester School", whose policy was based on the physiocratic formula of *laissez-faire, laissez-aller.* The free-trade experiment initiated by Peel (1841-46), and steadily pursued until the Great War of 1914-18, was only one manifestation of that policy. Not that any policy is ever in England carried to its logical extreme. If abuses obtrude themselves they must be remedied without regard to philosophic dogmas. If *laissez-faire* led to scandalous conditions in the coal mines and the cot-

Drawing of George Eliot by Samuel Laurence, 1860.

ton-mills, the State must interfere to protect the women and children who were sacrificed by unscrupulous employers on the altar of Mammon. If *laissez-faire* had allowed the new factory towns to grow up in drab ugliness, without regard to amenities or even to decency and sanitation, in order to enrich greedy builders and ground-landlords; if it permitted brave sailors in the Merchant Service to pursue their arduous calling in unseaworthy ships; if it refused to interfere between capitalist employers and the wage-earners, and permitted the exploitation of the most defenceless workers by sweating, and by unrestricted hours of labour; if it allowed new generations of children to grow up to manhood without the rudiments of education, and excessive drinking to undermine the health and morale of a considerable section of the adult population—if in the sacred name of Liberty all such things were permitted, retribution was bound to fall upon the whole community, and reaction to embody itself in legislation and administration.

The result was a strong encroachment (as some regard it) of the State upon the free action of individual citizens, and an ever increasing volume of legislation designed to correct abuses which wise prevision might altogether have avoided.

The pace at first was slow; advance was exceedingly cautious. But it gathered momentum as the reign went on. Enquiries were instituted by Select Committees and Royal Commissions, notably in regard to the employment of women and children underground and in cotton mills. The revelations appalled the public conscience. Children under five were sent into mines and into factories. Not least to be pitied were the "apprentices" who were sent off by the parish authorities from London and the southern counties by wagon loads at a time to be apprenticed to the millowners in Lancashire, there to be "used up" as the "cheapest raw material in the market". Even more pathetic, perhaps, because more unnatural, was the lot of children forced into the mills by the poverty of parents. Such were the children of whom M. T. Sadler tells in *The Factory Girl's Last Day,* a simple little poem that makes an even stronger appeal than Mrs. Browning's more elaborate *Cry of the Children:* for Sadler summarizes a mass of firsthand evidence which, with "Dick" Oastler, he was foremost in collecting. The new middle-class electorate turned Sadler out of Parliament in 1832, but not even the Report of the Royal Commission did more than that philanthropic Tory to secure the passing of Lord Shaftesbury's *Ten Hours' Act* of 1847. The Act, though its terms went only half way, really settled the principle that in the interests of the community the State was not merely entitled but was bound to protect the weak and restrain the avarice of the strong.

Factory legislation affords only one illustration of a movement which with ever increasing force and velocity has now almost entirely obliterated all traces of *laissez-faire.*

In the course of a century nothing less than a social revolution has been effected. By this means the abuses arising from the economic revolution which preceded it have been to a large extent corrected. No longer could Carlyle complain that "in the midst of plethoric plenty the people perish". If there is no plethora of wealth, such as remains is

more equally distributed. Great fortunes are still made, but it is increasingly difficult to transmit them to heirs. There is, moreover, general appreciation of the truth that great accumulations of wealth are as a rule due to the exceptional abilities of organizers of industry, that it were suicidal to penalize them, and that such fortunes represent not a deduction from the wages of labour but an addition to the wealth of the community.

The wide sweep of such developments does not afford appropriate subjects for prose fiction. Just as the landscape painter looks for his subject not to a great range of snow-capped mountains, but to a clump of fir trees on some gentle eminence, to the water-lilies covering the surface of a pond, to cattle chewing the cud, or to a flock of sheep on a mountainside, so the novelist seizes upon an incident apparently isolated, and demonstrates the effect of great movements, political or economic, by their reactions upon individuals.

Take, for instance, the subject of trade unionism and strikes, as treated respectively by the social historian and the novelist. The historian explains how both the Common Law and Statutes innumerable operated to prevent combination among workmen, and how economic pressure gradually wore down the resistance of legislative restraints; how the outrages committed by trade-unionists in industrial centres in the winter of 1866-7 compelled the attention of Parliament, and how the legislation of 1871-76 not only gave to trade union funds the benefit of the Friendly Societies Acts, but put combinations in furtherance of trade disputes in a position legally privileged.

That is not the way of the novelist. Mrs. Gaskell in *Mary Barton* shows how a trade dispute led to the murder of Harry Carson, a young, thoughtless but not ungenerous employer, to the trial and almost to the conviction of Jem Wilson, a young workman; how John Barton drew the lot which to his dismay made him an assassin. Very temperately and impartially Mrs. Gaskell puts the case for and against both sides: blaming the masters less for avarice than for want of imagination, and showing how the men were driven to the fatal weapon of the strike for lack of the information as to trade conditions which the masters refused to impart to them. Even more clearly is the same lesson taught in *North and South*. In that deeply pathetic story a beautiful contact is established between Thornton, the self-made highly successful cotton lord, and the gentle scholarly Hale who, driven by conscientious doubts to resign his living in the New Forest, has settled in the "Cotton" town as a private tutor. Equally beautiful is the contact between the parson's daughter, Margaret Hale, tender-hearted and gently nurtured, and Nicholas Higgins, weaver and trade-unionist, and his consumptive daughter. Of masters and men Thornton and Higgins are admirable representatives. Though deemed to be a "hard man", and uncompromising in his views as to the part which capital and management must play in industry, Thornton is, in fact, as thoughtful for his men's interests as for his own, so long as they don't meddle in matters that the masters can alone decide. Higgins holds the views of his class about the strike weapon. Farm labourers, so Margaret Hale assures him, do not strike. "I know naught of your ways down south," he retorts. "I have heard they're a pack of spiritless, downtrodden men; welly clemmed to death; too much dazed wi' clemming to know when they're put upon. Now it's not so here. We know when we're put upon; and we'en too much blood in us to stand it. We just take our hands fro' our looms, and say, 'Yo' may clem us, but yo'll not put upon, my masters!' And be danged to 'em, they shant."

That is the men's case in a nutshell. There is, however, another side to the picture. Charles Reade had no such first-hand knowledge of industrial conditions as Mrs. Gaskell, but he studied blue books with all the fervour of a scholar engaged in research. Some of the results are embodied in *Put Yourself in his Place*—where we see Henry Little, young and manly, waging single-handed a successful fight against the cruel and heartless tyranny of the trade union.

The essential difference between the novelist and the historian is one of method. The historian deals with facts, in the general; the novelist must illustrate their reaction upon individuals. Thus, Mrs. Henry Birchenough in her excellent story, *Potsherds,* tells us nothing about the "evolution of the potter's industry" (as the historian would). She tells the story of William Handley, a successful potter, who having, by sheer hard work, sagacity, and courage, made a little fortune, bought out his old master's daughter (foreseeing difficulties ahead) and presently turned the business into a limited liability concern. In an equally good novel, *Probation,* Jessie Fothergill tells the story (again in reference to the actors rather than the action) of the quiet but heroic courage with which the working men of Lancashire faced (1861-63) the calamity of the cotton famine. In 1862, Cobden estimated the loss in wages at £7,000,000 per annum. Yet through it all the cotton operatives adhered to the cause of the Northern States, though it was Abraham Lincoln's blockade of the Southern ports that brought the famine upon Lancashire. The men had convinced themselves that the North was fighting in the cause of righteousness and freedom, and not all their sufferings induced them to waver in their devotion to the North.

Another illustration. There are at least three novels dealing with a half-forgotten incident in the social history of South Wales. S. Baring Gould's *In Dewisland,* K. L. Montgomery's *The Gate-Openers* and Violet Jacobs' *The Sheep-Stealers* all deal with the "Rebecca Riots" of 1843. The following passage from *The Sheep-Stealers* explains the position. "At this time a wave of wrath which had a considerable foundation of justice was surging over South Wales. By a General Highway Act, a new principle of road-government had been brought in under which the trustees of turnpike roads might raise money through tolls sufficient to pay the interest of the debts and keep the highways in repair. The gates had in some cases been taken by professional toll-renters, men who came from a distance, and who were consequently regarded with suspicion by the intensely conservative population of the rural districts. These people having higher rents to make up had refused to give credit to farmers, or to allow them to compound for tolls on easy terms as had been formerly their custom. The effect of all this had been to rouse the public to a state of fury which had resulted, in many places, in serious

riots. In carrying out the provisions of their respective acts, the trustees were under little or no control; they erected fresh gates, interpreted the laws as they thought fit, and there was no appeal from their decisions." The first riot had broken out at Carmarthen, where the methods adopted by "Rebecca and her children" met with remarkable success. The name "Rebecca" had been chosen by a bible-reading community in reference to a text in Genesis (xxiv-60): "And they blessed Rebekah and said unto her . . . let thy seed possess the gate of those which hate them." Rhys Walters, a substantial young farmer, was chosen to be captain of one of the many bands of rioters. Like other "Rebeccas" young Walters disguised himself by wearing a woman's clothes; and so effectual and popular did the disguise prove that Rebecca and her children "grew bolder and bolder: they possessed many of the gates of those which hated them, and spread terror throughout many parts of Central and South Wales. The leaders were never caught, and the few followers who were arrested were treated with leniency. The Government issued a commission to enquire into the grievances and as a result the toll-bars in many districts of Central Wales were abolished. Disorder, however, especially if successful, is infectious: "Rebecca's reputation did not suffer from lack of imitators."

No discerning reader can read the above passage from *The Sheep-Stealers* without perceiving that the "Rebecca Riots" afford a good illustration of the debt which history owes to fiction. Many histories of the period contain a brief and arid reference to the riots: but they do not supply the touches by which the novelist gives to the incident—not, admittedly of the first importance—a real, living and human interest.

Charles Reade (1814-84) dramatist, Bohemian, country-gentleman, Fellow of Magdalen College, Oxford, has a place of his own in the history of Victorian fiction. Not all his novels are didactic or historical. In *Griffith Gaunt,* for example (generally accounted his masterpiece) the interest is psychological. But between 1856 and 1884 he devoted novel after novel to the exposure of some economic or social scandal. W. L. Courtney, a fine critic, deemed Charles Reade worthy to be ranked with such literary giants as Thackeray, Dickens and George Eliot. But his gifts were dissimilar. "He was not," says Courtney, "an artist like Thackeray: he had not the undeniable genius and prodigality of power which is found in Dickens; nor had he the gift of keen analysis or the profound thoughtfulness of George Eliot. Here and there he has the note of Dickens, witness the magnificent funeral scene of Edward Josephs in *It is Never too late to Mend* (Chapter XXVII)," but in his conscientious accumulation of evidence he excels them all. Among historical novels Reade's *The Cloister and the Hearth* is among the greatest, but it is outside the scope of the present survey. Others not merely come within but illustrate with exceptional clarity the central thesis of this book. Here is Reade's own apology for the method he adopted. "I have taken a few undeniable truths out of many, and have laboured to make my readers realize those appalling facts of the day which most men know, but not one in a thousand comprehends, and not one in a hundred thousand realises until fiction . . . comes to his aid, studies, penetrates, digests the hard facts of chronicles and blue-books, and makes the dry bones live."

Reade's plea is, surely, irresistible. A fellow-craftsman bears testimony to his success. "Mr. Reade . . . can make a blue-book live and yet be a blue-book still. . . . The reader is not conscious that he is going through the boiled-down contents of a blue-book. He has no aggrieved sense of being entrapped into the dry details of some harassing social question. The reality reads like romance; the romance lives like reality."

Thus *It is Never too late to Mend* is based upon disclosures of the cruelties which disgraced the administration of the prison-system. The gaol described by Reade was at Winson Green, Birmingham, and Warder Brown is a portrait of Warder Evans. Francis Eden, the courageous and sympathetic chaplain, equally no doubt had an original. From English prisons Reade's story moves off to the gold-fields lately (1851) discovered at Ballarat in Victoria. No more vivid description of the wild confusion that followed the frenzied rush alike of "emancipists" (ex-convicts) and free settlers was ever penned. There is poetry and pathos, too, even in a novel dealing primarily with prisons and convicts. Witness the scene of the gold-diggers at Ballarat gathering round one Sunday morning to listen to the skylark: "These shaggy men, full of oaths, strife, and cupidity had once been white-headed boys and strolled about the English fields with little sisters and little brothers, and seen the lark rise and heard him sing this very song. . . . And so for a moment or two years of vice rolled away like a dark cloud from the memory and the past shone out in the song-shine; they came back, bright as the immortal notes that lighted them, those faded pictures, and those fleeted days; the cottage, the old mother's tears . . . the village church and its simple chimes; . . . the chubby playmates that never grew to be wicked, the sweet hours of youth—and innocence—and home."

Hard Cash turns upon the iniquities of private lunatic asylums and of the doctors who by their venality and gullibility played into the hands of those who found those institutions a convenient means of gratifying spite or greed. Alfred Hardie, the hero of *Hard Cash,* a young man of refinement and culture "with an indefinable air of Eton and Oxford about him", the victim of an unnatural father, finds a staunch ally in Dr. Sampson against the conspiracy against his liberty, supported by "the most venal class (in Reade's judgment) upon earth". A subsidiary interest in *Hard Cash* is the panic that resulted from the bursting of the Bubble induced by the wild speculation in railway shares. Up to 1844 the annual expenditure on railways had not exceeded £5,000,000. During the next three years it was £185,000,000. Sir Robert Peel was greatly concerned for the financial stability of the country, and in November, 1845, *The Times* (apparently at his instance) sounded a note of alarm at the revelation that the railways, completed, under construction, and projected, were seeking to raise no less than £700,000,000. *Hard Cash* (1863) illustrates the results of the gigantic gamble. And who, but for Charles Reade, would to-day recall it, or take warning by that disastrous incident?

Charles Dickens is, in the present connexion, more diffi-

cult to "place" than Charles Reade. His one indisputably historical novel commands the admiration of many readers to whom the rest of his novels make but slight appeal. But the deeply moving *Tale of Two Cities* is outside the scope of this survey. *Barnaby Rudge* contains a vivid account of that curious and almost isolated outburst of Protestant fanaticism known as the Lord George Gordon riots. Sir George Savile's Bill for the removal of certain penalties imposed on Roman Catholics had received the assent of Parliament in 1775. Scotland had successfully opposed its application to the Northern Kingdom. Protestant zealots in London hoped by violence to secure its repeal in England. For nearly a week, 2nd-7th June, 1780, London was in the hands of the mob. An attack was made on Lord North's official residence in Downing Street; Catholic chapels were burnt down; prisons were broken open; the Bank of England was threatened. Only the courage and firmness of King George III saved the situation. "There shall be at least one magistrate in the kingdom," he declared, "who will do his duty." By his orders the military acted with effect. Nearly three hundred lives were lost and the hospitals were filled with the wounded; but despite the lamentable weakness of the Government and the magistracy, London was saved from wholesale incendiarism. Gordon himself became a Jew and ultimately died insane in Newgate.

But for *Barnaby Rudge* this disgraceful episode would, for the public at large, have passed into oblivion. In other novels Dickens was concerned less with history than with the amendment of contemporary abuses. *American Notes* (1842) and *Martin Chuzzlewit* (1844) reflect his bitter disappointment with the "Great Republic". "We must be cracked up," says Hannibal Chollop, speaking of his fellow countrymen in *Martin Chuzzlewit*. Dickens failed to come up to expectations. The *American Notes* he dedicated "to those friends in America who giving me a welcome which I must ever gratefully and proudly remember left my judgment free". His judgment might be left free, but the expression of his views on international copyright, on American slavery, and above all on the experiences of Martin Chuzzlewit, the younger, and Mark Tapley in New York and in "the thriving City of Eden" (Chapters XVI and XXI) gave bitter offence. Perhaps Dickens kept too constantly in mind the advice given by old Weller to Sam when he proposed to get a "pianner" to carry Mr. Pickwick out of the Fleet prison: "There ain't no vurks in it (whispered his father). It'll hold him easy with his hat and shoes on, and breathe through the legs vich his holler. Have a passage ready taken for 'Merriker. The 'Merrikin Government will never give him up ven once they find as he's got money to spend, Sammy. Let the guv'nor stop there till Mrs. Bardell's dead, or Mr. Dodson and Fogg hung . . . then let him come back and write a book about the 'Merrikins, as'll pay all his expenses and more if he blows 'em up enough." Dickens certainly "blew 'em up enough" in 1842–44, and deeply they resented it. But it is pleasant to recall that when he returned to lecture there in the winter of 1867–8, he had a magnificent reception and came home with £19,000 in his pocket.

To come nearer home. *Oliver Twist* (1838), was written with the express purpose of exposing the cruelties practised on a workhouse child as punishment for "the impious and profane offence of asking for more", and the still greater cruelties inflicted on the child who fell into a den of thieves. More definitely it was Dickens's object to provide an antidote to Gay's *Macheath* and Lytton's *Paul Clifford*. He deemed it a social duty to "draw a knot of such associates in crime as really did exist; to paint them in all their deformity . . . in all the squalid misery of their lives . . . with the great black ghastly gallows closing up the prospect". That duty he effectively discharged in *Oliver Twist*. In *Nicholas Nickleby* (1839), the tyranny of the ignorant proprietor of a private academy was the object of his denunciation. *Bleak House* (1853) was written to show how the law's delays in such a suit as "Jarndyce versus Jarndyce"—a "monument of Chancery practice"—inflicted "monstrous wrong" upon long suffering litigants. Dickens had been assured by an eminent Chancery Judge that the Court "despite a trivial blemish or so in its rate of progress" was, in the administration of justice "almost immaculate". Armed with the facts of a case, still undecided (in August, 1853), after twenty years of litigation, involving £70,000 in costs, Dickens resolved by *Bleak House* to disturb the complacency of the distinguished lawyer. *Hard Times* (1854) popularized Carlyle's impeachment of the economics of the "Manchester School". Mr. Bounderby is an unlovely figure, and Thomas Gradgrind the pedagogue is not much better. "A man of realities, a man of facts and calculations. A man who proceeds upon the principle that two and two are four, and nothing over." The picture is a caricature, but as there is no smoke without fire, so caricature would lose its appeal if not based upon a substratum of truth.

Little Dorrit (1855–7) has historically a twofold interest: the administrative muddle which inflicted such suffering upon British soldiers in the trenches before Sebastopol led to Dickens's castigation of the "Circumlocution Office"; his own personal experiences are recalled in those of William Dorrit, the "Father of the Marshalsea" and his brother Frederick. Dickens's savage portrayal of the unreformed Civil Service may be compared with the not dissimilar pictures in Trollope's *Autobiography* and in his *The Three Clerks* (1857). Mr. Sadleir has described Trollope's as "an inexpert picture of a vanished age". The age had not vanished in 1855–7 when Dickens was writing *Little Dorrit*. Reform began, indeed, in 1855: it had not come when, in 1853, Sir Stafford Northcote and Sir Charles Trevelyan reported that "admission to the Civil Service was, indeed, eagerly sought after, but it was for the incompetent, indolent or incapable that it was chiefly desired". Patronage was evidently the root of the evil: their report virtually got rid of it, though it was not until 1870 that the competitive test was definitely imposed. That Dickens and Trollope contributed substantially to the reform of a gross abuse is indisputable. *David Copperfield* also proved how deeply Dickens felt for the debtor's unhappy lot. In Mr. Micawber he drew a portrait of his own father, who was committed to the Marshalsea, and in the very words of Mr. Micawber warned his son "to take warning by the Marshalsea, and to observe that if a man had twenty pounds a year and spent nineteen pounds, nineteen shillings and sixpence he would be happy, but that a shilling spent the other way would make him

wretched". Mr Dickens senior may well have derived consolation as did Mr. Dorrit, from the reflection that an imprisoned debtor knew "the worst of it". "We have got to the bottom, we can't fall, and what have we found? Peace. That's the word for it. . . ." "We are quiet here; we don't get badgered here; there's no knocker here to be hammered at by creditors and bring a man's heart into his mouth. Nobody comes here to ask if a man's at home and to say he'll stand on the doorstep till he is. . . . It's freedom, sir, it's freedom." "Freedom" it was in all cases, and in the case of wealthy debtors who refused to pay imprisonment involved little if any discomfort. But with the majority it was otherwise, and the picture of Little Dorrit, the complacent debtor's devoted daughter, is evidently drawn from life. Nor did Dickens ever draw a more pathetic figure. But by the time *Little Dorrit* was published the Marshalsea had disappeared. An *Act* of 1844, though not entirely abolishing imprisonment for debt remedied all the worst abuses connected with the old system.

In Dickens, then, we have one of the best examples of the novelist who throws light upon some special incident or some particular feature of past days that deserves to be borne in mind, even though not of the first historical importance. "Works of fiction indirectly are great instructors of this world; and we can hardly exaggerate the debt which we owe to a Charles Dickens." So said Benjamin Jowett, preaching the funeral sermon on Dickens in Westminster Abbey.

The debt which the historian owes to George Eliot is of a totally different order. She was not a social reformer but a psychologist. Her one strictly historical novel was one of her less successful efforts. Anyway, *Romola,* dealing with Florentine history, does not concern us. The *Scenes of Clerical Life,* on the contrary, *Felix Holt, Middlemarch, Silas Marner, Mill on the Floss* and *Adam Bede* no historian of the nineteenth century can ignore.

Though all George Eliot's novels were written during the last twenty years of her life, all that was best in them was supplied by recollections of the days when, after her mother's death, the charge of her father's household and the farm devolved upon her. Nevertheless her novels clearly bear the impress of the circumstances of her later life. Again and again as we read of the lives of the squires, the parsons and the farmers, of the doctors and the tradesmen of rural England and provincial towns, we are sharply reminded that the novels were written by a woman who had left all that early life behind her, who had become a brilliant star in a firmament of intellectuals, who had translated Strauss's *Leben Jesu,* had helped to edit the *Westminster Review,* and shared the home of George Henry Lewes.

Born at Arbury Farm, Chilvers Coton, near Warwick, in 1819, Marian Evans was (as some one has said) "saturated with the racy sap of the English Midlands". Her father, Robert Evans, was the son of a carpenter and builder and he himself started life in the same business but rose to be land agent to Sir Roger Newdigate in Warwickshire. Entirely trusted by his employers, greatly respected and liked by their tenants, Robert Evans was the original of Caleb Garth and supplied traits—all of them wholly admirable—to the characters of Adam Bede and Mr. Hackit. Of

Mrs. Evans there are traces in the Dodson family, in Mrs. Hackit and above all in Mrs. Poyser. She was a woman of clock-work regularity—all her farm work was done by 9 O'clock, and of any irregularity—even in the natural world—she was wholly intolerant. "She brought out her furs on the first of November, whatever might be the temperature. If the season didn't know what it ought to do, Mrs. Hackit did." Marian's earliest views on religion were largely derived from an aunt, Mrs. Samuel Evans, who was the prototype of Dinah Morris, and told her niece the story which supplied the germ of *Adam Bede*. Though country bred, devoted to the work of the farm, and especially skilled (as we should guess from the picture of Mrs. Poyser's dairy) in butter-making, Marian had all the instincts of a scholar. When she was about one-and-twenty she became intimate with a family (the Brays of Coventry) who held strong secularist views, and it was in this alien atmosphere that George Eliot first inbibed doubts (deepened by her task of translating Strauss's *Leben Jesu*) concerning her early evangelicalism. The period of blank agnosticism was, however, transient. Thus, in 1862, she writes to a friend: "Please don't ask me ever again not to rob a man of his religious belief, as if you thought that my mind tended to such robbery. I have too profound a conviction of the efficacy that lies in all sincere faith, and the spiritual blight that comes with no faith, to have negative propaganda in me." Most vigorously she protested against what she well described as the "quackery of infidelity", and insisted on the contrary that "the great thing is reverence, reverence for the hard won inheritance of the ages".

Thus as an historical authority George Eliot holds a twofold position. Herself "the authentic voice of Darwinism", her novels, though descriptive of country life in the 'thirties, re-echoed the scientific spirit and the intellectual unsettlement of a generation that was profoundly influenced by the teaching of the biologists. That the later work of George Eliot was overweighted by her philosophy is undeniable, yet R. H. Hutton was surely right when he said: "What is remarkable in George Eliot is the striking combination in her of very deep speculative power with a very great and realistic imagination. It is rare to find an intellect skilled in the analysis of the deepest psychological problems so completely at home in the conception and delineation of real characters."

The explanation is that the characters *were* real and the scenes in which they played their part were those familiar to George Eliot from childhood. "Shepperton" was Chilvers Coton and the curate, the Rev. John Gwyther, was the original of the Rev. Amos Barton, who served three churches and maintained a wife and six children on a stipend of £80 a year. Cheverel Manor is Arbury Hall and its owner, Sir Christopher Cheverel, is a portrait of Sir Roger Newdigate, some of whose traits reappear in Sir James Chetham of *Middlemarch,* if not in Mr. Brookes, the kindly but fatuous uncle of Dorothea—Mr. Casaubon's unhappy wife. In the long gallery of George Eliot's parsons, Mr. Casaubon, the self-centred scholar squarson stands apart; but Mr. Cadwallader, the lovable devotee of trout-fishing, has much in common with the Rev. Augustus Debarry, the sporting Rector of Treby Magna, something less with his colleague, Mr. Farebrother (the most

admirable of all George Eliot's parsons) and hardly more with Parson Irwine in *Adam Bede*. Old Mr. Crewe, the Curate of Milby who in a "brown Brutus wig delivered inaudible sermons on a Sunday, and on a week day imparted the education of a gentleman . . . to three pupils in the upper Grammar School" is sharply contrasted with Mr. Tryan, the zealous evangelical who brought comfort to poor Janet Dempster. All these different types are brought together at the Milby clerical meeting, and each is as perfectly discriminated from the others as are Jane Austen's parsons. George Eliot's specific contribution to the religious history of the nineteenth century is, however, her appreciation of the beauty and power of the Evangelical movement, within and without the Established Church. Of course she perceived and exposed its failings. But the woman who could compose Dinah Morris's sermon in *Adam Bede,* who could pray as Rufus Lyon prays in *Felix Holt,* who could minister comfort to the stricken soul of Silas Marner as did Dolly Winthrop, with her simple creed of faith and love—that woman, sceptic though she believed herself to be, was not far from the Kingdom of God.

Of George Eliot's novels the one most definitely permeated by politics is *Felix Holt the Radical*. It gives a vivid account of an election contest under the old system of open voting and a long drawn out poll, and, all through, the private lives of the persons of the drama are inextricably mixed up with, and largely determined by, the public events attending on the Reform battle of 1830—32.

The Reform Bill also plays a considerable part in *Middlemarch*. Nevertheless, the real historical value of George Eliot's novels consists less in such incidents, and much more in her faithful picture of the rural and provincial life of England a century ago.

George Eliot enjoyed, of course, no monopoly. Interested readers may seek additional information from M. Betham Edwards's *The Lord of the Harvest, A Suffolk Courtship, A Humble Lover* and *Mock Beggars Hall,* which specially illustrate rural conditions in East Anglia. They must not ignore Lytton's *The Caxtons, My Novel* and *Kenelm Chillingly,* nor some of Henry Kingsley's works; least of all can anyone afford to neglect the works of Anthony Trollope. Trollope's prolific pen ranged from England to Australia, from St. Martin's le Grand to Barchester, but it is on his delineation of "county" and Cathedral society in mid-Victorian days that his title to be a genuine historical authority will rest. For widely as Trollope ranged his social outlook was narrow.

Except so far as he came across them in the hunting field he knew little of any class below that of the squires and the parsons—except, indeed, in Ireland where for nearly twenty years he went in and out among all classes: peasants and farmers, peers and squireens, priests, gombeen men and the rest. His Irish novels are in fact political pamphlets in the guise of fiction. In *Can you Forgive Her? Phineas Finn, Phineas Redux, The Eustace Diamonds, The Prime Minister* and *The Duke's Children,* the Background is parliamentary, and some of the characters are recognizable. Daubeny, the Tory leader, was on Trollope's admission Disraeli, whom he detested as a man, a politician, and a novelist. Turnbull was John Bright, Phineas Finn was in part Joe Parkinson, an English journalist who married a millionaire's daughter, and in part John Pope Hennessy, a young Irish politician who was taken up by Disraeli.

If, however, the wider definition of "Historical" be accepted, these political novels are perhaps less historical than the Chronicles of Barsetshire and many others.

Barchester has taken so strong a hold on popular imagination that Trollope's work has come to be identified with the Anglican Establishment, with Bishop (and Mrs.) Proudie, with Archdeacon Grantley, his imposing presence and hot temper; with Mr. Harding, the gentle, humble-minded warden of Hiram's Hospital; with Mr. Roberts, the weak but well-meaning parson of Framley; with poor Mr. Crawley of Hogglestock, driven to desperation by poverty; with Mr. Ovid, the saintly and scholarly Tractarian, and the rest of the cloth. Rightly so. But if Trollope is preeminently the chronicler of the Church, as by law established and comfortably if unevenly endowed, it is the Church as an integral part of a coherent social system that he is concerned with.

His theme is rural England centred on the cathedral city which is also the county town. Trollope has been happily described as "the supreme novelist of acquiescence". If that means that he carefully analysed, shrewdly observed, and accurately described, but studiously refrained from passing judgment, it is true. Trollope is never, like George Eliot or Thackeray, didactic. He sums up the evidence with impartiality: the verdict he leaves to the reader.

Some of the novels such as *He Knew He was Right* (1869), and *The Way We Live Now* (1875) may perhaps be cited as exceptions: but if more censorious than the earlier novels, they are not less truly historical. The last-named may, indeed, be said to mark the beginning of the transition from the England of Trollope to the England of Galsworthy, from squirearchy to plutocracy, from dignified comfort to pushful restlessness. But *The Forsyte Saga* has a further significance. As the domestic counterpart of the Imperialist revival, it illustrates the last period of the Victorian era.

James C. Simmons

SOURCE: "The Romancers and Historic Truth: The Question of Responsibility," "The Novelist as Historian: An Unexplored Tract of Victorian Historiography" and "The Decline of a Literary Fashion: The Historical Romance After 1850," in *The Novelist as Historian: Essays on the Victorian Historical Novel,* Mouton de Gruyter, 1973, pp. 22-33, 34-54, 55-63.

[*In the following excerpt, Simmons analyzes the changing role of historical accuracy in the Victorian historical novel.*]

THE ROMANCERS AND HISTORIC TRUTH:
THE QUESTION OF RESPONSIBILITY

As many Victorian novelists gravitated toward the social, political, and religious issues of their age, critical hostility increased towards previous and contemporary writers who were thought not serious enough for the changed

Edward Bulwer-Lytton.

temper of the times. For most Victorians Scott's position as the chief of the English novelists remained secured and unquestioned. His novels continued to enjoy wide popular sales and continued critical support. He served for many as the touchstone by which subsequent novelists were tested and often found wanting. Furthermore, Scott's popularity, based in part on his exemplary life, was expanded and secured by the frank biography of his son-in-law.

But Scott proved an easy target for those more earnest critics who were opposed on general principles to any literature which professed merely to entertain its readers. He himself had repeatedly voiced opinions to the effect that the novel form was woefully unsuited to any serious endeavor, and for this reason considered it inferior to both drama and poetry. He continued to express skepticism toward the defense of fiction that rested upon its presumed moral influence. "The professed moral of a piece", he stated in an essay on Fielding, "is usually what the reader is least interested in; it is like the mendicant, who cripples after some splendid and gay procession, and in vain solicits the attention of those who have been gazing upon it." He then went on to insist that the novel was

> a mere elegance, a luxury contrived for the amusement of polished life, and the gratification of that half love of literature, which pervades all ranks in an advanced state of society, and are read much more for amusement, than with the least hope of deriving instruction from them. [*The Lives of Eminent Novelists and Dramatists,* 1887]

And in the introductory epistle to *The Fortunes of Nigel* [1893] he trumpeted, almost as a challenge: "I care not who knows it—I write for general amusement."

But an increasing number of readers found Scott's professed goal of amusement to be inadequate in light of the newer emphasis upon the seriousness of the artist's responsibility to his public. A dissentient minority of important Victorian thinkers and critics took issue with the popular consensus and began censuring him on grounds that distinctly reflected the changed temper of the post-Scott years. For the first time his novels were scrutinized for their philosophy and history. In each case there were those who found the Wizard of the North sadly lacking in those qualities they held to be essential to great literature.

Thomas Carlyle was one of those writers who insisted upon the seriousness of the literary endeavor and reacted accordingly in his evaluation of Scott's fiction. His statement, made in a lengthy review of Lockhart's *Life* in 1838, is generally taken as definitive of the Victorian hostility toward Scott. Here he amplified a charge recorded in the privacy of his notebooks over a decade before when he labelled the novelist "the great *Restaurateur* of Europe". "What is his novel, any of them?" he had asked sarcastically. And the answer had come back, "A bout of champagne, claret, port or even ale drinking. Are we wiser, better, holier, stronger? No; we *have been—amused* [*Two Notebooks,* 1898].

In his lengthy evaluation of Scott for *The Westminster Review* Carlyle took him to task for being a "mere entertainer" who had "no message whatever to deliver to the world". His novels, Carlyle insisted, were

> Not profitable for doctrine, for reproof, for edification, for building up or elevating, in any shape! The sick heart will find no healing here, the darkly-struggling heart no guidance: the Heroic that is in all men no divine awakening voice. We say, therefore, that they do not found themselves on deep interests, but on comparatively trivial ones.

As such, Carlyle felt, Sir Walter Scott participated in his age, the spiritual emptiness of his writings merely reflecting the spiritual vacuum of the early nineteenth century, an age "fallen languid, destitute of faith and terrified at scepticism".

As James Hillhouse has pointed out, this criticism of Scott was nothing new by 1838. Rather Carlyle, writing from a Scottish Calvinist background, was only giving more eloquent expression to charges that had been leveled against the novelist for the past decade by other critics working within the Evangelical and Utilitarian frameworks. John Stuart Mill, writing a decade earlier in *The Westminster Review,* attacked the Waverley novels on much the same grounds. "There is no one of [Scott's] productions", he concluded, "from which, unless it be by chance, any one useful lesson can be derived" [*Westminster Review,* (April, 1824)]. And at the same time F. D. Maurice expressed the regret that men of such obvious genius, such as Scott, "instead of doing something to reform their age, should submit themselves to the meanest eddies of that current which

they might have turned from its wanderings" [*The Athenaeum,* 11 March, 1828].

Harriet Martineau perhaps best points up the changing attitude toward Scott. Shortly after his death she wrote two essays, "The Genius of Scott" and "The Achievement of Scott", which are a sympathetic evaluation of his measure as a writer and a hope for a new fiction based on the techniques initiated by him but refined for new ends. Unlike Maurice and Carlyle, Miss Martineau did not feel that Scott's novels merely amused "indolent languid old men". Rather they exerted a strong moral force and taught all men "the power of fiction as an agent of morals and philosophy". Scott was for her both a "vindicator of genius and an unconscious prophet of [fiction's] future achievements". She called upon the new generation of writers to refine upon his techniques to produce "the philosophical romance". She went on to criticize the "spurious brethen", those imitators of Scott who had taken over his techniques for the historical romance without adapting them to meet the new demands of the changing times and of a reading public, which on the scent of utility, "cannot be interested without a larger share of philosophy, or a graver purpose in fiction, than formerly". As Richard Stang has observed [in *The Theory of the Novel in England, 1850-1870,* 1959], such criticism embodies a radically different view of fiction and the role it is to play than that expressed by Scott and his contemporaries.

Scott's defense, when such criticism was sometimes brought to his attention late in his life, was that if a historical romancer avoided a too gross confusion of the manners of various peoples and periods, presented a reasonably accurate portraiture of the historical characters, and in general maintained a sense of credulity, the author could not in all fairness be assigned to the company of "the light and frivoulous associates with whom a careless observer would be disposed to ally him", but would "take his seat on the bench of the historians of his time and country". And in the prefatory remarks affixed to *Peveril of the Peak* Scott defended his novels against the charges of corrupting history and misguiding his readers, asserting that his historical fictions encouraged in his readers an interest in formal histories. At the very least, the less ambitious reader would quit one of his romances "with a degree of knowledge, not perhaps of the most accurate kind, but such as he might not otherwise have acquired". The possibility that the historical romance might be utilized for the serious instruction of the reader in history was recognized quite early by both Scott and his advocates as a chief potential in this form of fiction. This, however, was due to Scott's innovation of introducing historical events and personages into his narratives. Previous historical romancers had generally been content with setting their stories in a distant time without any real concern for the manners, costumes, events, and people of the earlier period.

As it turned out, this proved to be one of the most common defenses of Scott's fictions and historical fiction in general throughout the Victorian years. Archibald Alison, the historian, asserted in a eulogistic appraisal of the historical romance that it was one of "the most delightful and instructive species of composition . . . and can give the truth of history without its monotony" ["The Historical Romance", *Blackwood's Edinburgh Magazine* LVIII (September, 1845)]. And in the mid-1860s another critic insisted that

> After reading Sir Walter Scott's "Kenilworth", we are irresistibly led to consult history to learn if he has given a faithful representation of Elizabeth and Leicester, and we are influenced in precisely the same way by Bulwer, Dickens, and others ["Is the Perusal of Works of Fiction Right or Wrong?", *The British Controversialist, and Literary Magazine* (1865)].

There is some indication that exactly this happened. John G. Lockhart noted that each of his father-in-law's novels had been followed by the re-issue of the principal sources for the work. The popularity of *Quentin Durward,* for example, led to the re-publication of Philip de Comines, which enjoyed a brisk sale in its new edition. But the evidence is overwhelming that the majority of readers of Scott and the romancers who followed after him were content to get their history from the historical romances and did not use them as stepping stones into the more academic treatments of the subject. There is no doubt that one of the chief reasons for the phenomenal popularity of the historical romance throughout the early decades of the Victorian period was that readers had convinced themselves that with a minimum of effort and a maximum of pleasure they could learn history while reading an entertaining story. As has often been observed, the nineteenth century was a time of increased historical consciousness when men for the first time became aware of the past as being profoundly different from the present. And in England this developing awareness was nurtured and encouraged by the profusion of historical romances which provided many Victorian readers with their sense of the historical past. The volumes of Turner, Hallam, Palgrave, Grote, and Thirlwall, unread, collected dust on the library shelves, while readers turned with interest to the latest historical romance. In 1836 a critic in *Blackwood's* commented upon the extent to which his contemporaries were indebted to Scott for their sense of the past, asking rhetorically, ". . . who is there who must not have observed in general conversation, that the notions of bygone times and characters, most interesting to us from a national point of view, are more often taken from the unperishable novels of Sir Walter Scott and others, rather than from the documents of more sober research?" ["Irish Tales," *Blackwood's Edinburgh Magazine* XXXIX (May, 1836)]. Even as late as 1876 the prominent historian Edward A. Freeman noted that a chief error which any historian of the twelfth century had to contend against was "the notion that for many generations . . . after the Norman Conquest, there was a broadly marked line, recognized on both sides, between 'Normans' and 'Saxons' ". He traced this misconception back to Scott's *Ivanhoe* and admitted that no amount of argument by prominent historians to the contrary had been successful in putting down this popular belief, indicating the extent to which the general reader derived his impressions of a past epoch from the historical romances rather than the histories.

There were several reasons for this state of affairs. George

Henry Lewes was no doubt correct when he asserted that a chief factor was "Idleness;—a wish to get at knowledge by a royal route" ["The Historical Romance", *Westminster Review* XLV (March, 1846)]. But things were more complex than Lewes realized. A much more significant reason was that these novels introduced the reading public to an aspect of historical studies almost wholly neglected by the formal historians of the 1820s and '30s. As a critic in *The Edinburgh Review* observed in 1832, Scott took his readers "below that surface on which float the great events and stately pageants of the time" and acquainted them "with the minor details and with the habits, condition, and opinions of former races". The result was that readers could now "institute a closer comparison between the complexion of their times and that of our own" ["The Waverley Novels", *Edinburgh Review* LV (April, 1832)]. Even Carlyle conceded this point, admitting that Scott's novels "taught all men this truth . . . that the bygone ages of the world were actually filled by living men, not by protocols, state-papers, controversies and abstractions of men. . . . History will henceforth have to take thought of it." In short, many readers found in Scott's fictions an aspect of history that appealed strongly to them and was conspicuously absent from the formal histories of the day.

A further stimulus to the readiness of readers to gain their history from romances lay in the fact that historical instruction had not yet been allotted a place in the educational systems of most English schools. Thomas Arnold's introduction into the curriculum at Rugby of a broad range of historical studies proved to be a major innovation in the early 1830s and the cause of considerable controversy in the years following the adoption. The situation was little better in the major universities at Oxford and Cambridge. At Cambridge, for example, there were only two triposes in the first half of the century, one in mathematics, natural religion, and moral philosophy with the emphasis upon mathematics, and a second in classical studies. Once again it was Thomas Arnold who was chiefly responsible for the introduction of historical studies into the curricula of the higher schools. In August of 1841, the year before his death, he was appointed to the Regius Chair of Modern History at Oxford and proved to be the first holder of the chair to take his title literally and lecture on modern history. The lectures, enormously successful, marked the "beginning of the effective teaching of modern history in both Universities" [G. M. D. Henderson-Howatt, "Thomas Arnold and the Teaching of History", *Quarterly Review* CCCII (April, 1964)]. Within the following decade historical studies had become a formal part of the curricula at both universities: Cambridge in 1848, Oxford in 1852.

The unimportance of historical studies in the universities is underscored by the fact that the major historians of the first fifty years of the century lived and worked outside of the academic communities of Oxford and Cambridge. George Grote was a London banker and a Member of Parliament; Connop Thirlwall, a bishop in the Anglican Church; Thomas Carlyle, a man of letters; Thomas Macaulay, a Member of Parliament; and Sir Francis Palgrave, a civil servant, lawyer, and Keeper of the Records. After 1860 this all changed, so that the major historians of the latter half of the century, Edward Freeman, William Stubbs, John Green, and Lord Acton, were all formally connected with the faculties of one of the major universities.

History, then, for the first half of the nineteenth century was an area of study conspicuous both for the intense interest it aroused and its absence from the formal curricula of virtually all the schools in the island. If it was to be learned at all, the knowledge had to be gained through a program of independent study. A man's understanding of history, both ancient and modern, was then a measure of both his own interests and his personal initiative. But this was the time of self-education and self-help, of Mechanics Institutes and the Library of Useful Knowledge. Given the background, it is not surprising that so many people turned to the historical romances for the historical knowledge they thought could be gained from them.

With historical romances being read by so many people in place of the more formal histories, it soon became apparent to many Victorian critics that the authors of historical fiction were under a special obligation to their readers to insure the accuracy of the historical portions of their narratives. A reviewer in *Blackwood's* in 1836 argued that "writers of historical romances, tales, and novels [are] under a greater moral responsibility than the compilers of real history". The reason for this was that fact and fiction in their works are so subtly interwoven that the majority of the readers will be quite unable to distinguish the two. Care must thus be taken not to falsify or misrepresent historical personages and events.

The problem was rendered more acute by the disregard of historical accuracy by the historical romancers of the day. Scott and his followers were frequently bound by the popular conception of the past, what Herbert Butterfield has called the "picture-gallery of the past"—a popular impression built up over the years from a general blurring of history, ballads, Biblical stories, local traditions, poetry, and romance. Instead of correcting this romantic and popular sense of the past, as some Victorian critics felt they should, the historical romancers frequently catered to it. "No-knowledge is better than mis-knowledge", asserted George Henry Lewes and insisted that it was the latter that most readers picked up from the historical fictions of the day.

Numerous critics now attacked Scott's novels and those of his followers on the grounds of historical inaccuracy and misrepresentation. This is a note peculiarly Victorian. In Scott's own day there had been little discussion of the merit of the historical aspects of his novels and little demand for a precise attention to the niceties of historical fact. He would, no doubt, have agreed with Nassau Senior in his article on the Waverley novels in *The Quarterly Review* of 1821 when he said of history in Scott's romances that

> We do not object to Sir Walter's alterations of facts and characters, on account of their tendency to produce false historical impressions. The object of a novel is not to instruct; and the reader who is absurd enough to look into fiction for truth, cannot hope even to be pitied for having

been led into error ["Sir Walter Scott", reprinted in *Essays on Fiction,* 1864].

But by the time of Scott's death critics had become increasingly less tolerant of such laxity toward historical fact. H. A. Taine, writing much later, observed that "From Walter Scott we learned history. And yet is this history? All these pictures of a distant age are false [*History of English Literature,* trans. H. VanLaun, 1883]." And Sir Francis Palgrave, the historian and Keeper of the Records, stated in 1851 that "Historical novels are mortal enemies to history", and then attacked Scott's *Ivanhoe* as "out of time, out of place, out of season, out of reason, ideal or impossible" [*The History of Normandy and of England,* 1851]. It was largely due to historical fiction, Palgrave argued, that the British reading public had come to consider English history as little more than "a splendid melodrama, set to the sound of kettledrums and trumpets".

Even had Scott wished to have been more precise, he would have found himself at a disadvantage in relation to his successors. Much new material was opened up in the 1820s and '30s, well after he had written most of his novels, but in ample time for those who wrote in the early decades of the Victorian era. This was indeed a time of histories. Sir Francis Palgrave's massive studies began appearing in the late 1820s. His efforts and those of Nicholas Nicolas resulted in many of the records of the Public Records Office being catalogued and made available for the first time to scholars. The volume of historical research swelled to such proportions that Charles Knight noted in 1854 that for the thirty-five year period between 1816 and 1851 books on history and geography far outstripped fiction, titles in the latter category being a full third fewer than in the former.

In accordance with this increased interest in history (aroused ironically enough by Scott's own romances), critics and novelists began paying increased attention to the historical element of historical fiction. The historical novelists in the earlier Victorian decades found an entirely new critical attitude awaiting them. No longer was the factual looseness tolerated by Scott and his contemporaries going unchallenged. As *Blackwood's* noted in 1863:

> It is harder work now to write a historical romance than it used to be in the days of Sir Walter, when it cost the romancer no scruple of conscience to put a new saint into the calender for the sake of a handy oath that would rhyme; and when the great novelist could venture to transport us bodily into the previous centuries, upon his own absolute authority, without citing witnesses, or stopping in the tide of the narrative to prove minutely that he could not be wrong [*Blackwood's Edinburgh Magazine* XCIV (November 1863)].

Scott's imitators were continually flayed throughout this period for their misrepresentations and falsifications of history. In 1833 Sir John F. W. Herschel in a speech before the subscribers to the Windsor and Eton Public Library castigated

> the desperate attempts to novelize history which

the herd of Scott's imitators have put forth, which have left no epoch since the creation untenanted by modern antiques-and no character in history unfalsified.

Such sentiments were echoed by scores of periodical reviewers who flayed the contemporary historical romancers for their gross inaccuracies and crude distortions of history. A critic in *The Athenaeum* in 1835 spent over half of his review setting straight the historical inaccuracies in the portrayal of Richard III in a minor novel of the day. "These remarks may seem somewhat out of place in the review of a novel", he concluded, "but historic truth is of more importance than the novel itself." [*The Athenaeum*, 20 June 1835]

The upshot of this criticism was a pressure on all writers to insure the accuracy of the historical elements in their romances and to discourage the more flagrant abuses of chronology and fact that had occurred in many of Scott's romances. Historical novelists now made readier use of prefaces, footnotes, and appendices to defend their own interpretations, trace a detail back to its source, and attack other historians. The attitude of many was now a most defensive one. Edward George Howard in his *Sir Henry Morgan, the Buccaneer* (1844), a factual biographical historical romance, included in the next a lengthy resume of his sources and his reasons for selecting one over another when the two conflicted. This was done, he insisted, "in order to guard against cavils concerning our accuracy as biographers". And in 1862 we find George Eliot destroying the first draft of her manuscript of *Romola* and beginning again because of the numerous mistakes in the historical aspects of the story.

To sum up, in the 1820s through the 1840s we find that many critics and readers looked upon the historical romance as a potential rival to formal history, and that indeed for much of the reading public the historical fiction from *Waverley* on was so employed. . . . [These] newer demands for a historical romance that was neither frivolous nor grossly inaccurate forced historical fiction to assume a radically new shape, as it responded to the demands of the age.

THE NOVELIST AS HISTORIAN: AN UNEXPLORED TRACT OF VICTORIAN HISTORIOGRAPHY

In 1852 a critic for *Fraser's Magazine,* reviewing the third and fourth volumes of Macaulay's *History of England,* commented upon the incredible reception accorded the work by the British peoples. It was, he noted, a bulky work of several thick volumes on a subject which the great mass of readers "might have been expected to turn from, at the very outset, as special and scientific". Why, he wondered, this intense interest in the *History?* The reviewer offered several possible explanations. The steady, ever increasing spread of a liberal education and the recent admission of large sections of the British populace into the active political mainstream had, he felt, stimulated both historical writing and reading. Then he offered a third suggestion, the proliferation of works of "light history" that had in recent years filled the bookstalls. These

works making at all events some pretension to the name of histories, have to a great extent driven books of mere fiction out of the market; purveyors of what used, not long since, to be called light literature, are now become purveyors of light history [*Fraser's Magazine* LIII (February, 1856)].

It was, he argued, chiefly this indulgence by large numbers of readers in "light histories" that had created for Macaulay an audience more extensive and responsive to his *History* than otherwise would have been the case.

As I suggested [previously], a principal source of this "light history" in the early decades of the Victorian era was the historical romance, which in terms of sheer bulk dominated the fiction market throughout the period and eventually stimulated the public appetite for some of the more formal histories. As one reads through this flood of historical romances published in the 1830s and '40s, he soon becomes aware of its schismatic nature. On the one hand, he finds a large body of writers who faithfully followed the formula for the historical romance developed and popularized by Sir Walter Scott in such novels as *Ivanhoe* and *Quentin Durward*. Writers such as Wm. Harrison Ainsworth and G. P. R. James were imitative rather than original, and content to follow Scott at a distance. Their novels were invariably adventure tales, depicting the actions of fictitious personages played out against a historical backdrop. The historical element generally took the form of excessive attention to costume and pageantry, occasionally punctuated by the introduction of historical events and personages. Like Scott, they all saw their role primarily as that of entertainers, allowing themselves the customary latitude in regard to historical facts and chronology.

But throughout the 1830s and '40s many Victorian reviewers leveled considerable criticism at Scott and his followers, objecting both to the lack of any real intellectual substance in their fictions and to the innumerable liberties taken with historical fact. Such criticism was distinctly Victorian and reflected the new earnestness of an age imbued with the Utilitarian demands for a literature that consciously instructed its readers. Because of these newer pressures for a historical romance that was neither frivolous nor grossly inaccurate, some historical fiction in the 1830s assumed a radically new shape, as it responded to the demands of the age. A handful of writers—significantly, all of them historians in one capacity or another—did produce a type of historical fiction, which, although it flourished for a short time only, does represent the first substantial attempt to meet the demands of the age. They did so in the easiest and most logical manner, one which would suggest itself naturally to men and women accustomed to work as historians. They all emphasized the historical aspect of the genre at the expense of the fictive and wrote as historians rather than romancers. For them the historical romance became a vehicle for the popularization and commercialization of the most recent findings of historical research. These writers were not content to go to history for an exciting backdrop nor to portray an age merely through a representation of its costumes, manners, and architecture. The historical novel in their hands became a vehicle for the exegesis of a historical period, an exegesis from the perspective of a historian, not a romancer.

Such a solution—the emphasis of history over romance—entailed a drastic change in the form of historical fiction as it had been developed by Scott. He usually set his imaginary characters and episodes in the foreground, preferring to keep the actual historical elements in the background and allowing them only occasional prominence. Scott was generally quite unconcerned with the accuracy of the historical portions of his romances, always permitting himself considerable liberty in regard to the facts and never feeling himself under any real obligation toward a fidelity to historical accuracy.

However, with this later generation of historical novelists the artist's responsibility became that of a close factual fidelity to the historical material. Their novels are about historical personages and events, each treated from the point of view of the historian rather than the romancer. Their works were carefully researched, and scholarly accuracy was one of their goals. Rigidly excluding those elements of tradition, legend, and fantasy that Scott had utilized so extensively and following only bona fide historical sources, these writers reconstructed an earlier period with the deliberate patience and care of an archaeologist fitting together the fragments of some shattered pot. They maintained a strict control over all the fictional elements introduced, never permitting them to dominate. History was not compromised for the sake of the story at hand, as was true of the novels of Scott and his imitators. The goal of these later writers was emphatically not entertainment but rather the instruction of the reading public in the important moments of the past. Edward Bulwer Lytton in *Rienzi, the Last of the Tribunes* (1835), *The Last of the Barons* (1843), and *Harold, the Last of the Saxon Kings* (1848), Harriet Martineau in *The Hour and the Man* (1841), Edward George Howard in *Sir Henry Morgan, the Buccaneer* (1842), and Charles Macfarlane in *The Camp of Refuge* (1844) utilized the historical novel as a ready means of forcing a re-evaluation of a particular historical personage, hitherto looked upon unfavorably. Frederick Chamier found in the historical romance the surest means of reminding the reading public of the finer moments of British naval history during the Napoleonic wars. The historian and Keeper of the Records Sir Francis Palgrave turned to the historical tale in *Truths and Fictions of the Middle Ages: The Merchant and the Friar* (1837) and the unfinished *Three Generations of an Imaginary Norfolk Family* to popularize his recent findings in fourteenth century British jurisprudence and Parliamentary procedure. The Reverend Richard Cobbold utilized two carefully researched biographically oriented romances, *The History of Margaret Catchpole* (1845) and *Mary Anne Wellington, the Soldier's Daughter, Wife, and Widow* (1846), to treat the impact of historical events on ordinary people. They all wrote "light history". As a group they flourished for a short time only, about fifteen years; by 1850 they were themselves a part of literary history.

Thus, there developed in the 1830s and '40s the concept of the historian-novelist. Writers such as Bulwer, Macfarlane, and Palgrave saw themselves in competition, not with their contemporary romancers, but with the formal historians of their day. The factual literalness and heavy scholarship of their novels gave added weight to the authors' claims that such books were to be taken as a loose kind of history by their readers.

It would be a mistake, however, to see these historian-novelists as an isolated and freakish phenomenon on the Victorian literary scene. Rather they are but one aspect of the general and pervasive movement toward a consciously didactic fiction. The literary tastes of many Victorian readers ran pre-eminently in favor of what T. H. S. Escott called "the literature of positive information and instructive fact" [*England, Her People, Polity, and Pursuits,* 1880]. This was the time of the ascendancy of Bulwer's Mr. Bluff, "the sensible, *practical* man", the embodiment of vulgar Utilitarianism. Mr. Bluff, as Bulwer made clear in *England and the English* [1833], was a most prominent type by 1833. He was the individual who "hates both poets and philosophers . . . has a great love of facts . . . does not observe how the facts are applied to the theory . . . [and] only wants the facts for themselves". The Bluffs, and their near relations, the Gradgrinds and the Bounderbys, exerted a crucial influence on the literature of the period, especially, the novel, in their drive for facts, facts, and more facts. As early as 1831 Mrs. Gore, the novelist, could lament that "Nothing but books or plays administrant to unnatural excitement, or of a nature to gratify the outcry for useful knowledge, have now any vogue in London."

Thus, those historical novelists who emphasized the historical side of the genre and utilized the form for the elucidation of specific historical personages and events were part of a much larger phenomenon in the Victorian world. By focusing upon factual rather than imaginative experiences, they managed to escape the evangelical and Utilitarian strictures against a literature of "mere entertainment" and produced a series of novels which appealed to an instruction-oriented reading public, imbued with its responsibilities for self-education. They too wrote their novels of purpose. And though their purpose was academic rather than social, religious, or political, their affinity to Kingsley, Disraeli, Froude, and Gaskell should not be overlooked.

The fact that the claims of these authors to the status of historians rather than romancers were honored by their contemporary critics and the reading public alike should not appear too surprising. This acceptance reflects the unsettled state of English historiography in the early decades of the Victorian era, a time in which the historiographic theories and practices of Carlyle, Froude, and Macaulay were in the ascendant, while the stricter standards of the "scientific" school of German historiography, laid down by Neibuhr and Ranke, were still relatively unknown in England.

Indeed, it is advantageous to think of these historian-novelists as representing an extension of those principles of romantic historiography as practiced by the literary historians of both England and France. The difference between a historical novel by a Bulwer or a Macfarlane and a more formal history by a Froude or a Macaulay is one of degree rather than kind. For all these historians the emphasis fell upon a concept of history as a narration rather than a dissertation. They represent a reaction against the analytical, abstract, and stylistically "dead" histories of Sharon Turner, Henry Hallam, James Mill, and other professionals. The progression was away from a concept of history as abstract exposition toward an idea of history as a fully developed narrative drama. Carlyle, for instance, wished to reinstate the historian as the teller of tales, whose finished works, reconstructing the past in the most graphic, dramatic, and detailed manner possible, permitted the reader to experience history, to be made contemporary with the facts, acquiring them with the ingenuous spirit of a contemporary. To this end all the literary historians stressed the importance of the imagination to the historian. "Stern Accuracy in inquiring, bold Imagination in expounding and filling-up", wrote Carlyle, "these are the two pinions on which History soars." Carlyle, Froude, and Macaulay all used their artistic imaginations to flesh in the "dry bones" of research, to create a sense of suspense and tension and mood on the part of the reader. There was a pronounced tendency in all their historical writings to see history almost exclusively as drama, color, and passion, and by focusing on these elements they sometimes excluded or subordinated the less picturesque but more consequential matters. Macaulay wrote in his journal in 1853 that his technique was to pass quickly over all that was dull and to dwell at length upon that which was dramatic. This desire for picturesqueness frequently dictated extensive treatment of incidents of negligible historical importance. All these historians are content to describe, but rarely do they explain. The surface is covered with an unprecedented thoroughness, but little attempt is made to explore the depths. We leave their histories with a sense of vivid tableaux indelibly etched on our memories, but with little real understanding of the events detailed and the personages represented. "To exalt the drama is to condemn the history" [*History and Historians in the Nineteenth Century* 1935]. G. P. Gooch said this of Carlyle's *French Revolution,* but it applies to all these literary historians.

Thus, by writing history in a vivid, dramatic, and imaginative fashion, Macaulay, Carlyle, and Froude produced historical narratives that rivalled the historical romances both in readability and popular sales. One result was that the distinction, hitherto clearly defined, between historical fiction and formal history broke down completely at this time. Bulwer's historical novels were treated by the reviewers as history, not fiction, and judged as such. And at least one journal, *The Gentleman's Magazine,* in a series of reviews on Froude's volumes of his *History of England* refused to consider them as history, but did think them excellent romance and compared him to Ainsworth in his treatment of the sixteenth century. However, the exact nature of this aspect of Victorian historiography and historical fiction can be best appreciated through a close examination of the novels of Edward Bulwer Lytton, Edward Howard, and Harriet Martineau.

Edward Bulwer Lytton (1830-1873) was the innovator and the foremost exponent of the new type of historical fiction based on extensive research, careful attention to factual accuracy, and the depiction of historical events and personages. His novel *Rienzi* initiated the new vogue in 1835 and his *Harold* marked its close in 1848. Of all the men and women to work in historical fiction, Bulwer Lytton enjoyed the highest reputation among his contemporaries. His major historical novels represent the most scholarly and complex use of history by any Victorian novelist.

Of all the men to work with the post-Scott historical novel, Bulwer evolved the most comprehensive and articulate theory of the composition of the historical romance. He was perhaps more acutely aware than his contemporaries of the various paths open to him. He wrote in his preface to *Harold* that he had early realized there were two options available to him:

> the one consists in lending to ideal personages to an imaginary fable the additional interest to be derived from historical groupings; the other, in extracting the main interest of romantic narrative from History itself.

Bulwer had taken up the first option in his first three historical romances, *The Disowned* (1828), *Devereux* (1829), and *The Last Days of Pompeii* (1834). However, he felt uneasy about the possibility of factual distortions slipping into his fictions when the historical portions were subordinated to a melodramatic narrative. Therefore, he abandoned it for the alternate means of using romance in the service of history, an approach Bulwer claimed to have initiated.

In his three major historical novels Bulwer was less interested in the portrayal of "mere manners" which modern scholarship and the multitude of historical romancers had already rendered familiar to the reading public. Instead he concentrated upon developing the great personages of past epochs whom he felt had been "carelessly dismissed in the long and loose record of [the] centuries". He set famous historical figures at the nucleus of his works and attempted to show how the dynamic, powerful, and continually vital makers of history went about their work.

Bulwer not only selected major historical personages for his fictions, but he looked also for those periods of tremendous social upheaval when the men involved were placed under the abnormal stress of cataclysmic events. He favored epochs of momentous change, when an older order was giving away to a newer, and a country's history was being decisively settled for the next several hundred years. Scott, too, had frequently chosen periods of transition; but, as he made clear in his preface to *The Fortunes of Nigel,* this was for the increased possibility of picturesque development available to the novelist working in these periods. Bulwer, uninterested in picturesque contrast and juxtaposition, went to these periods of violent change for other reasons. The portrayal of the historical characters at those times presented the greatest challenge to his powers as a novelist and historian. The juxtaposition of the old against the new threw the representative qualities of each period into the clearest relief for historical analysis.

Bulwer, in thus taking upon himself the task of dramatizing great and famous personages and significant moments

Harriet Martineau in 1833.

from history, broke completely with the tradition established by Scott. The role he accepted for himself was that of historian, not novelist. His chief problem was "how to produce the greatest amount of dramatic effect at the least expense of historical truth". This difficulty was first grappled with in *Rienzi* in 1835, and the success of that "experiment" confirmed him in his belief that

> the true mode of employing history in the service of romance, is to study diligently the materials *as* history; conform to such views of the facts as the author would adopt, if he related them in the dry character of the historian.

Such a method, Bulwer stressed, placed the writer under close restrictions. The chief events of the narrative are set and the characters already drawn; they cannot be tampered with by the author. Imaginative speculation is permitted only in the development of the "inner, not outer, history of man". That is, the author is free to conjecture about private passions and motivations, but this must always be speculation hedged about by close historical scholarship. In all these novels Bulwer was careful to insist that he took no liberties with the facts, but rather constructed his stories upon the real facts: "[My] boldest inventions are but deductions from the amplest evidence [I] could gather."

> For the main materials of the three Historical Romances I have composed, I consulted the original authorities of the time with a care as scrupulous as if intending to write, not a fiction,

but a history. And having formed the best judgment I could of the events and characters of the age, I adhered faithfully to what, as an Historian, I should have held to be the true course and true causes of the great political events, and the essential attributes of the principal agents.

For his three major historical novels, then, Bulwer assumed the mantle of the historian. In each case he was convinced by his own extensive investigation that a particular man or event had been misjudged by contemporary historians, and he wished to set the record straight. In *Rienzi* he was primarily concerned with salvaging the Tribune's character from the "superficial and unfair" treatment by Gibbon:

> I regarded the completion of these volumes, indeed, as a kind of duty;- for having had the occasion to read the original authorities from which modern historians have drawn their accounts of the life of Rienzi, I was led to believe that a very remarkable man had been superficially judged, and a very important period crudely examined.

The novel, which was originally intended to be a history, was in fact the first comprehensive treatment of Rienzi to appear in England and sustained Bulwer's promise that the reader would gain "a more full and detailed account of the rise and fall of Rienzi, than in any English work of which I am aware".

In *The Last of the Barons* Bulwer undertook to explicate the complicated events of the latter half of the English fifteenth century:

> I venture to think that the general reader will obtain from these pages a better notion of the important age, characterized by the decline of the feudal system, and immediately preceding that great change in society which we usually date from the accession of Henry VIII, than he could otherwise gather, without wading through a vast mass of neglected chronicles and antiquarian dissertations.

Hume's judgments on the period are constantly attacked in the notes to the novel as "hasty", "inaccurate", and "more than ordinarily incorrect". The novel also contains considerable scholarly speculation regarding both the character of Richard III ("I think I shall give a new reading of Richard the Third's crimes and character-new, but I hope not untrue") and the reasons behind the sudden and desisive rupture between Edward IV and his baron Warwick in February of 1470, an aspect of their relationship that had long been obscured in histories. Bulwer's final resolution was that Edward had foolishly attempted the virtue of one of Warwick's daughters, but he did not arrive at this solution of the rupture because it was the most satisfying in terms of a romance situation. Rather he came to this conclusion only after painstaking and exhausting research into the chronicles. Since this represented an original interpretation of a crucial moment, and one at odds with the opinions of most former scholars on the period, Bulwer was careful to present his argument with an extensive annotation of sources to support his thesis.

Bulwer was equally explicative in *Harold, the Last of the*

Saxon Kings. There he detailed the political, social, and intellectual features of the age, so that the reader would understand "why England was conquered, and how England survived the Conquest". And to this end he devoted much of his leisure time for close to a decade in doing research.

Bulwer always stressed the accuracy of the history in his fictions. He did considerable research and was proud of the pictures and explications of past periods that he crammed into his novels. He never took an "unwarranted liberty with the real facts", but rather constructed his tales on the historical facts. Bulwer himself traced the popularity of his historical fiction to his "faithful narration of historical facts" rather than to any fictional elements he might have employed in the composition of the novels. Confident of his researches and the suppositions he drew, he stood by the validity of his historical novels as history:

> Nay, [the author] ventures to believe, that whoever hereafter shall write the history of Edward IV. will not disdain to avail himself of some of the suggestions scattered throughout these volumes, and tending to throw new light upon the events of that intricate but important period.

And it should be stressed that Bulwer's research for his novels was extensive and thorough. Before attempting to write, he systematically studied all available material, both ancient and modern, on his subject. Bulwer's general technique in regard to his sources was to rely heavily and narrowly upon a single work for a particular section of the novel at hand, going to other sources only when some secondary circumstance, which lacked support in the main reference work, could be found elsewhere. When a particular source coincided with his own interpretation of a person or an event, Bulwer generally followed it with close exactitude. In this respect he shares in the general attitudes and practices of the literary historians of his day. Macaulay, for instance, had often argued that there was no reason why, with the proper research and restraint, the formal historian could not portray a historical figure such as Elizabeth with a vividness comparable to Scott's portraiture in *Kenilworth* and "without employing a single text not authenticated by ample testimony" ["History", in *Miscellaneous Essays and the Lays of Rome*, 1910].

Bulwer, like the literary historiographers, insisted upon the importance of imagination in breathing life into the facts of history. "Fiction", he asserted, "when aspiring to something higher than mere Romance, does not pervert, but elucidate Facts." Bulwer here echoes Carlyle's dictum that "Stern accuracy in inquiring, bold Imagination in expounding and filling-up, these are the two pinions on which History soars." For Bulwer, as for the other literary historians, the artist in history should exercise his imagination to flesh in "the cold outlines of the rapid chronicler", achieving immediacy through color and detail.

In Bulwer's historical novels the fictional element is rigidly restricted to the depiction of the "inward life" of his historical personages, specifically in regard to determining their motives. All is worked toward a more complete understanding of the "genuine natures of the beings who actually lived [in order] to restore the warmth of the human heart to the images recalled from the grave". The purely imaginary characters, when they are introduced, are always few in number and so ordered as not to interfere with the actual historical events and motivations. Always these wholly fictitious characters are merely the passive sufferers in the panorama of history and never its active agents. Furthermore, we find that most of these minor characters exist less as fully realized individuals and more as academic abstractions. Writing as a historian and wishing to examine each age as fully as possible, Bulwer frequently set up his minor characters to embody some particular force he felt to be at work in the epoch in which he was interested. Therefore, if Nicholas in *The Last of the Barons* represents the incipient middle and commercial classes coming into prominence at the end of the fifteenth century, then we can assume that Nicholas' destiny is that of his class, for he takes his validity as a representative of a historical type rather than as an individual.

This readiness to see character as abstraction, together with Bulwer's selection of epochs of transition, led to another characteristic feature of his historical fiction: namely, the artificial balancing of characters, one against the other, the older order up against the new. This is most evident in *The Last of the Barons* where we find the dichotomy expressed chiefly in the figures of Warwick (representing the feudal order of a landed aristocracy) and Edward IV (standing for that segment of the aristocracy allied with the new commercial classes). The same division is carried out on other levels. Marmaduke, a retainer in Warwick's household, and Nicholas Alwyn, an ambitious merchant and the future mayor of London, repeat the Warwick-Edward axis. Other characters are set up, however, to illuminate various aspects of this division. Adam Warner represents the forces of modern science and knowledge incipient at this time; he is juxtaposed with Friar Bungay, who embodies medieval superstition and finally works the destruction of the scholar.

In his own day Bulwer's historical fictions were received by most critics and readers as worthy additions to the historical publications of the age. Henry Crabb Robinson, a voracious reader, worked through Bulwer's historical novels in 1843 and noted in his journal that "I could not but consider [them] as instructive as the general history of Hume". The long hostile *Fraser's Magazine* took a kinder view of *Harold* and found that in spite of too much unassimilated history in the narrative, it still gave "a better account of the causes which led to the Norman Conquest than any book we know". Edward A. Freeman in his *History of the Norman Conquest of England* observed that *Harold* was a work "which, if the sentiment and super-natural parts be struck out, forms a narrative more accurate than most so-called histories of the time" and insisted that Bulwer's treatment of the age was superior to that of Palgrave in the latter's multi-volume study of Saxon England. And at a number of points in his own history Freeman acknowledges debts to Bulwer's novel. Even as late as 1914 an American critic could call *The Last of the Barons* "indispensable to the student of English history" [E. G. Bell, *Introduction to the Prose Romances, Plays, and Comedies of Edward Bulwer, Lord Lytton*, 1914].

Bulwer's books thus capitalized upon the demand of many Victorian readers for a historical narrative that was dramatic, entertaining, and accurate. And the popular success enjoyed by his books encouraged other novelists to follow his lead and use the historical romance as a vehicle for their own historical speculations and researches. One of the most successful imitations was that of Edward George Greville Howard (?-1841), *Sir Henry Morgan, the Buccaneer,* which appeared posthumously in 1842. The book reflects Howard's long career as a naval officer. Upon retiring, he became a member of Captain Frederick Marryat's circle and worked for a time in editorial capacities with several magazines when not writing his own naval novels that enjoyed a moderate popularity with the reading public of the day.

Howard chose as the subject of this, his final novel, the life of the most famous British buccaneer. This man of the mid-seventeenth century rose from a position as an obscure indentured servant in the West Indies to become one of the most powerful men in the hemisphere. Through a combination of genius, skill, and daring he collected a fleet of 36 ships and 1846 men under his command, and with them proved to be for a number of years the major threat to Spanish commerce in the American area. His most famous exploit was the march across the Isthmus of Panama and the subsequent capture and sacking of Panama City, then the richest and most important city in the Spanish colonial empire. Regardless of the difference of opinion regarding Morgan's character, there is no doubt that this feat was the result of brilliant leadership and martial skill. For his exploits against the Spanish authorities, Morgan was knighted by the English king and appointed governor of Jamaica.

Howard's attitude toward Morgan vacillates throughout the novel. In the earlier portions of the book the pirate is seen as "more a demon than a man". The author is repelled by the ruthless cruelty and brutality of the buccaneer, especially in the early days of Morgan's career. But, as the story progresses, Howard finds himself caught up in the adventures of his subject. The author then holds the reader back from a condemnation of Morgan, many of whose actions are now explained and extenuated by constant reference to the wholly corrupt Jamaican society. The epic sacking of Panama City, a triumph against unbelievable odds, firmly establishes Morgan as a hero in Howard's eyes. Now we find the author referring to his subject as "our hero" and insisting that the capture of the city was

> one of the most wonderful military achievements on record. There was no surprise, no treachery. The conquest was gained by the most consummate generalship, and a courage that was never surpassed. If deeds of war can confer honour, Morgan and his associates must stand pre-eminent amongst mankind. They had to contend with and conquer a brave and cautious enemy. England should be proud of these men, though they have been stigmatized as pirates; and glory in their achievements.

The apotheosis is now complete. Morgan's band of cut-throats, bandits, and pirates has become his "associates". His achievements at Panama City now place him on a

level with the greatest of English military heroes. Howard continually defends Morgan's character against charges made by the French and Spanish historians. From the middle of the second volume the author's chief purpose is to use his novel as a vehicle for a general re-evaluation of Morgan's place in history. And from here to the end of the book Howard takes a generally uncritical approach to his hero. Even Morgan's slide into a state of perpetual drunkenness and licentiousness while governor of Jamaica does not shake his faith.

Howard did considerable research for his novel. Virtually nothing is known of Morgan's youth in Wales, and the novelist's account is pure fiction. Howard gives Morgan a frustrating love affair and a rivalry with a Spanish duke washed to the Welsh shores after a shipwreck. But this unpromising opening soon gives way to a more interesting, and certainly less orthodox, treatment of his subject once Howard begins the narration of Morgan's life about which more is known. Now he follows the facts of his career closely. Numerous documents relating to the important moments of Morgan's life are quoted from at length. For instance, at the close of the book Howard inserts in full the official report of Sir Hans Sloane, Morgan's personal physician, in his own account of the pirate's death. For many of the details of Morgan's exploits, especially the accounts of the storming of the fort at Chagre and the siege of Panama City, Howard relied heavily upon the narrative of John Esquemeling, *The Buccaneers of America*. Esquemeling had served as a physician under Morgan and had participated in the numerous actions described. Howard accepts the validity of his account of events but quarrels with him on the nature of Morgan's character.

As the novel progresses, Howard takes his task more seriously. His purpose becomes less that of writing an entertaining novel and more that of biographer striving to salvage his subject from the unfair treatment of earlier historians. Thus, we find Howard viewing himself as a novelist in the earlier portions of the book, but as a biographer and historian in the latter. As his concept of his task becomes more serious, Howard allows himself decreasingly less liberty in regard to the facts. Not only does he examine numerous authorities, but he also strives to achieve some sort of critical evaluation of each source in an attempt to find that which is the most accurate. There is greater hesitation to fill in those areas about which his authorities tell him little. This greater sense of scholarly objectivity is perhaps present more in theory than practice. But Howard continues to insist upon his identity as a historian:

> We well know that the writer of a romance is expected to know every undivulged emotion of the characters of his creation, and also to be able to account for every incident. This responsibility must not be thrown upon us, for these especial reasons: the first is, that we are writing biography, and speak only from authorities, many of them dubious, we must confess, and from what our hero has himself divulged in occasional conversations; and the second, that many of the transactions-must we call them atrocities?-that have been imputed to him, he resolutely denies. These atrocities we are forced to record, and let the reader himself judge, by the manner in which

we relate them, whether or not they may justly
be attributed to him.

In other words, Howard will refuse the license allotted to
romancers to modify history for the ends of drama and
hold himself to a faithful depiction of the facts. He follows
his lengthy description of the battle for Panama City with
a testimonial to the reader assuring him of the accuracy
of his account. He has, he insists, "collated numerous authorities and many manuscripts in the British Museum"
to achieve "as faithful a record as any that history can produce of a remote transaction". All this is done "in order
to guard against cavils concerning our accuracy as biographers".

Howard's novel then is essentially a biography of Morgan
and an evaluation of his place in the history of the time
and area. As one contemporary reviewer noted, the book
was more a history than a romance: "The book is fearfully
and painfully true to the actual history of its extraordinary
hero, and may be regarded quite as much in the light of
a 'Life' of Morgan the Buccaneer, as of a 'Romance'"
[*New Monthly Magazine* LXIV (March, 1842)].

Much the same could be said of Harriet Martineau's carefully researched biographical novel *The Hour and the
Man* (1841) which took as its subject the life of Toussaint
L'Ouverture. Martineau (1802-1876) was strongly committed to the idea that didacticism was perhaps the surest
index to an author's importance. In her essays on literature she continued to remind her contemporary authors
that the temper of their times demanded a strong, unequivocal commitment to the principles of the Utilitarian
value of literature. Her own writings were almost exclusively didactic, written to serve a specific end in the cause
at hand. Possessing the two-fold ability to grasp abstract
principles and embody them simply and clearly in illustrative fictional narratives, Harriet Martineau was one of the
most successful of the Victorian popularizers.

The Hour and the Man reflects her ideas on the importance of utility and serious purpose in fiction. The book
was one of her "philosophical romances", heavily burdened with the author's ideas on morality and politics.
The plot, supplied to her by history, concerned the emergence of Toussaint L'Ouverture as the liberator of the
slaves in the French colony of Haiti. The novel is a document in the abolitionist movement; here Martineau pleaded the cause of the Negro. In Toussaint L'Ouverture she
gave to the anti-slavery forces a black hero for their cause.

In August of 1791 the Haitian slaves revolted. Their struggle was singularly ineffectual until Toussaint L'Ouverture
emerged as their leader a few months later. A slave himself
for the first forty-five years of his life, he was a self-
educated black with a deep commitment to the progress
of his race. As the circumstances demonstrated, he proved
to be a master at military and political organization. Within a short time he had worked his ragged and ill-
disciplined force of ex-slaves into the finest army in the
Western Hemisphere. In a series of brilliantly executed
campaigns, he defeated the two foremost military powers
of Europe, virtually annihilating vastly superior English
and French forces. As absolute ruler of the Haitian people,

Toussaint proved to be a force for moderation, bringing
peace and prosperity to the country.

Such was the man who captured Martineau's imagination.
In her biographical novel Toussaint emerges as an idealized embodiment of the Noble Savage recast in terms of
the abolitionist agitation of the early Victorian years, an
Oronookoo crossed with an Uncle Tom. All this represented a sharp departure from the traditional attitude toward the man, most historians before Martineau regarding Toussiant as a man blessed by a natural genius for both
politics and war, but hypocritical and treacherous, "in all
affairs, the prince of dissemblers". However, Martineau
concluded after considerable investigation that the man
had been unfairly judged, that in fact he was "an honest,
a religious, and a mild and merciful man".

In Martineau's depiction of the man and his life she continually insists upon his Christian ethics of love and patience. When the revolt first erupts, he does not lend it his
support, for he feels that, though slavery is wrong, revenge
and lawlessness are not the solution: "'. . . if [the whites]
have oppressed their negroes, as they too often have, our
duty is clear,—to bear and forbear, to do them good in return for their evil.'" He joins the revolution only when he
learns that the revolutionary government in Paris has conferred upon the Negroes their freedom and the rights of
French citizenship; thus, it is the slave-owners, not the
blacks, who are against the law of France. As leader of the
blacks he is a constant and unswerving force for moderation, justice, and racial harmony; as governor of the island
his cardinal principle is *"No Retaliation"*. A racial holo-
caust is thus averted. A man of honor, Toussaint remains
completely impartial in his fulfillment of his duties; he
himself has no private interests, no concern for anything
but the good of all the people under his rule. Martineau
continually contrasts him with the thoroughly unscrupulous, treacherous, and cruel whites who succeed in capturing him only through a Machiavellian duplicity.

Martineau thus idealized her Toussaint out of all credibility. Carlyle wrote to Emerson to complain how she had
made a "Washington-Christ-Macready . . . of a rough-
handed, hard-headed, semi-articulate gabbing Negro".
Carlyle's criticism was valid to the extent that Martineau
had deliberatedly idealized her Toussaint, but then he had
always been unsympathetic to the abolitionist movement.
In actual fact, there is much in common between the historiographic methods of *The Hour and the Man* and those
Carlyle employed in his own biographies of Sterling, Frederick the Great, and Cromwell. Both biographers wrote
around a principal idea and ideals and the result was more
an abstraction than a recognizable character of individual
distinction, a quasi-historical icon for the reader's contemplation. Both were ready to apotheosize their subjects and
Carlyle especially fell far short of detached objectivity,
ruthlessly suppressing everything that might jeopardize
the heroic stature of his subjects.

Thus, Carlyle's disgust over *The Hour and the Man* was
finally little more than Caliban's rage at seeing his own
face in the mirror. Indeed, it is advantageous to think of
all those authors who undertook to write historical novels
that were factually accurate as representing an extension

into the realm of fiction of the theories and practices of romantic historiography and biography and, as such, their works of "light history" all share to varying degrees in the strengths and weaknesses of romantic historiography: its nationalism, partiality, hero worship, and the lack of a truly critical spirit. Like Macaulay, Carlyle, Froude, these historian-novelists were all amateurs and men of letters, who looked upon history as an adjunct to *belles lettres,* rather than a science as did Neibuhr, Ranke, and their followers in England. These men were primarily interested in the depiction of individuals and events and avoided the discussion of the more abstract questions of economic, political, social, religious issues. By slighting opportunities for reflection, generalization, and the discussion of more abstract matters, these historians reduced history to a well-told tale. Behind the approach of Macaulay, Carlyle, and Froude was a firm conviction that a factual story may be, and should be, told as agreeably as a fictitious one, that the incidents of real life, both domestic and political, may be so arranged without subsequent corruption of accuracy to command all the interest hitherto allotted to a fictional story. And a novel such as Bulwer's *Rienzi,* H. Martineau's *The Hour and the Man,* or Howard's *Sir Henry Morgan* finally realized the ultimate implications embedded within the theory and practice of romantic historiography.

THE DECLINE OF A LITERARY FASHION:
THE HISTORICAL ROMANCE AFTER 1850

In Benjamin Disraeli's *The Infernal Marriage* [1881] a bored Proserpine inquires of Tiresias what books he has that she might read. When he offers her some historical novels, her reply is sharply critical:

> Oh! if you mean those things as full of costumes as a fancy ball and almost as devoid of sense, I'll have none of them. Close the curtains; even visions of the Furies are preferable to these insipidities.

When this first appeared in *The New Monthly Magazine* in 1834, Disraeli and Proserpine were considerably in advance of their age, for the vogue for historical fiction was then at its height. But when the novelette was reprinted in book form in 1853, such sentiments were common. By then the fashion for historical fictions of all kinds was well into its decline and the critical reaction to the form was strongly hostile.

In a way this is paradoxical, for by 1850 the major Victorian historical novels had yet to be published; Thackeray's *Henry Esmond* appeared in 1852; Newman's *Callista* in 1856; Kingsley's *Hypatia* in 1852-1853, *Westward Ho!* in 1855, and *Hereward the Wake* in 1865; Dickens' *A Tale of Two Cities* in 1859; Reade's *The Cloister and the Hearth* in 1861; and George Eliot's *Romola* in 1862-1863. It is surprising, then, to find that the most prominent and successful efforts in the field came during this decade and a half when the vogue for historical fiction had expended itself and these writers could no longer count on the tide of literary fashion to insure the popularity of their books with the reading public. Indeed there was even a considerable risk for a major artist to turn to the genre at this time. Anthony Trollope in 1857 encountered this changed attitude toward the historical romance. In that year when he was going from publisher to publisher seeking an outlet for the manuscript to his novel *The Three Clerks,* he was advised by one house: "Whatever you do, don't be historical; your historical novel [*La Vendée,* 1850] is not worth a damn." The advice suggests the waning of public interest in the form and the hesitancy of publishers to take the risk on a second or third-rate specimen, even though a few years before they turned them out by the score.

Further evidence of this decline exists in abundant measure in the reviews of the periodicals in the latter half of the century. *The Quarterly Review* in 1868 felt it a matter of duty to run a lengthy article on Lockhart's *Life of Scott* in a futile attempt to counter the sharp decline of Scott's popularity among the readers of the day: ". . . not Lockhart only, but Scott himself, both as a man and as a writer, seems to be in danger of passing—we cannot conceive why—out of the knowledge of the rising generation." This was looked upon as "a great public misfortune" [*Quarterly Review* CXXIV (January, 1868)]. And Leslie Stephen in an essay written on the hundredth anniversary of Scott's birth observed that many people in private freely admitted that "Scott is dull" and that his books ("most amusing nonsense") had been moved from the library to the schoolroom.

The Victorian critics were now for the first time able to gain a perspective on the deluge of historical romances that had appeared in the 1830s and '40s. For many of them it was the clarity of mind one gains upon emerging from a long, irrational, and exhausting binge. *The Athenaeum* in an obituary of G. P. R. James in 1860 found upon looking back that it was not "one of the least curious features in literary history, that during a prolonged period there was a public and a popularity for second and even third-rate romancers who could present the sovereigns, generals, and statesman of past times and foreign countries, if only in name" [*The Athenaeum,* 23 June 1860]. And in 1892 the Oliphants saw fit to congratulate their age upon the fact that since the death of James Grant, no professional historical romancer had arisen to take his place. This was, they felt, a definite sign of progress in the development of readers' tastes. But by that time no writer with any pretense to importance (with the exception of Robert Louis Stevenson) thought in terms of the historical romance. The state of the genre in the last decades of the century was neatly summed up by William Sharp writing in *The Academy* in 1889.

> The historical novel is at a low ebb. It is unpopular with the highly cultured reader, for it must almost inevitably annoy him with more or less gross and disillusioning anachronisms; it is wearisome to the mass of library subscribers, for it deals with episodes of no present significance and with personages of alien speech and manners; and it is of no strong appeal to those who love to have their wine of literature diluted with the water of instructive facts. No writer who has gained the ear of the public can afford to indulge in a historical romance unless he have very good ground, indeed, for his conviction that he can be weighed in the balance of public estimation and not be found wanting [William Sharp in a review

of Arthur Sherburne Hardy's *Passe Rose* in *The Academy,* 13 July 1889].

The most obvious reason for the decline of interest in the historical romance would appear to be the innumerable and incompetent imitations of Scott that flooded the market for a thirty year period and surfeited the public taste for the form. This was the explanation offered by *The British Quarterly Review* in 1859: "We are scarcely surprised that the public should of late years have turned away from this class of fiction when we remember the many wretched imitations—weak sketches in washy water-colours" ["Novels and Novelists", *The British Quarterly Review* XXX (October, 1859)].

It was this, but also much more. No longer were people accepting the original premise that readers could learn history through the historical romance, no matter how carefully researched the work may be. The genre, in a word, ceased to be a rival to history, both in theory and in practice. In the late 1850s and the 1860s the ascendancy of the historiographic methods of Germanic scientific scholarship was secured, as Freeman, Stubbs, and Green began publishing. The earlier forms of literary historiography came under increasingly heavy critical attack as the amateur historian gave way to the professional.

A critic for *The Edinburgh Review* in 1859, referring to historical fiction weighted on the side of history, called it "not a novel but a loose kind of history . . . written with the license of fiction, an unsound kind of production and dangerous to the integrity of historic truth" [*Edinburgh Review* CX (October, 1859)]. The complaint was always the same: "How is the reader to know when the author is giving us fact, and when fiction?" [*Edinburgh Review* CXX, July, 1864]. And this was asked not only of Bulwer and his followers but also of Macaulay, Carlyle, and Froude. In a way it represents the logical extension of the earlier criticism of historical fiction which violated the facts of chronology, biography, and circumstances. But whereas the earlier critics had been appeased by a new kind of historical fiction that kept strictly to the facts and allowed only a minimal excercise of the imagination, these later critics, imbued with the stricter demands of the new scientific historiography, applied the same vise even more harshly to both the historical romance and the romantic historiography.

Furthermore, the Utilitarian antagonism to imaginative literature and its insistence upon facts, facts, and more facts came under increasing attack. In 1846 George Henry Lewes sharply questioned the relevance of facts as the Utilitarians saw them.

> Is there no other sort of "information", but that of "facts"? Are there no things under the sun worth learning, besides the erudition of "Mangnall's Questions?" Is knowledge of the human heart not information? Are your children to live in the world, to battle with it, and not to know it? Are they to mix with men and women, and rather than learn the natures of men and women, in the best way they can, to "cram" up a certain amount of "information" of mere externals, of names and dates, and those ancient names and

dates? ["The Historical Romance", *Westminster Review* XLV (March, 1846)].

And the reading public concurred. The sales of Bulwer's *Harold,* appearing two years later, fell off sharply. Bentley, the book's publisher, had earlier advised the author to edit severely the lengthy passages of factual exposition so prominent in that novel. Bulwer declined the advice, but later came to see the soundness of the criticism. Henceforth, he wrote Bentley afterwards, a writer must include only *"unperceived* research . . . to avoid the *appearance* of erudition which perhaps impeded the popularity of *Harold"*.

Perhaps the most significant reason for the lapse of interest in the historical romance was the ascendency of the realistic novel in the 1840s. Romance, especially the historical romance, became yesterday's fashion and there were few buyers around to take it. *Fraser's Magazine* in a gently critical review of G. P. R. James' *The Woodsman* in 1849 advised him to give up the genre, for "the day of mere romance has gone by" [*Fraser's Magazine* XL (December 1849)]. And *The Athenaeum* noted, somewhat prematurely in 1841, the decline of romance and attributed it to the charged temper of the age:

> . . . a romance is at variance with the spirit of the present age. The nineteenth century is distinguished by a craving for the positive and the real—it is essentially an age of analysis and of criticism. [*The Athenaeum,* 25 December 1841].

Whether as the Newgate fiction or as the historical, naval, fashionable, or oriental tale, the romance had dominated the fiction of the 1830s and '40s. The common reader was interested in the extraordinary rather than the ordinary, and the novel dealing with domestic middle-class life was an exception and a definite risk, insofar as any publisher was concerned. In her *Autobiography* Harriet Martineau recounted the numerous obstacles she encountered in 1838 when she sought to place her manuscript of *Deerbrook,* a tranquil story of middle-class life in a small English town. John Murray rejected the novel because he felt that the bulk of the readers, desirous only of "high life in novels, and low life, and ancient life", would not accept "a presentiment of the familiar life of every day".

But the demand for realism gained impetus throughout the 1840s, strengthened by the critical response accorded the novels of Thackeray. By the 1850s a new cycle had begun in English fiction and romance had been replaced by the new realism. An "atmosphere of complacent domesticity" dominated the fiction of that decade with such novels as Elizabeth Gaskell's Cranford, Mrs. Oliphant's *The Chronicles of Carlingford,* George Eliot's *Scenes of Clerical Life,* and Anthony Trollope's *The Warden* and *Barchester Towers* riding high on the best seller lists [Lionel Stevenson, *The English Novel: A Panorama, Boston* 1960]. Critics now lauded the "hearth-stone narrative", and demanded novels "perfectly quiet, domestic, and truthful . . . undisturbed by artificial agitations . . . [wherein there] is nothing irreconcilable with everyday experience" [*Fraser's Magazine* XLIV (October, 1851)]. This change in emphasis is most apparent in Bulwer's canon. *Rienzi* in 1835 initiated a new phase of historical fiction, and *Harold* in 1848 marked its close. With his usual acumen for detecting shifts in popular tastes, Bulwer abandoned the historical romance for *My Novel,* a work treating middle-class life.

The romance was now suspect in many critical quarters. The realist Thackeray, who "would have History familiar rather than heroic", expunged the melodramatic and extraordinary elements from his historical novel *Henry Esmond.* An aging Charles Macfarlane, writing his autobiography shortly before his death in 1858, complained of a new generation of readers who appeared to be "getting rather too fond of realities, and much too indifferent to romance and sentiment", and asked that writers give their younger readers "more generous, more glowing, more ideal pictures; and set up the heroes and heroines of our tales on the pedestal of romance." Much later Stevenson would observe that the "historical novel is forgotten" in the critical and popular emphasis upon a photographic realism.

Stevenson was exaggerating, for the historical novel was not forgotten. It continued to be written and read although its numbers had diminished considerably since the 1840s. The genre was temporarily absorbed with the thesis novels of the 1850s. Charles Kingsley utilized it for the purposes of patriotism and muscular Christianity; Newman and Wiseman, for the bland introduction to Catholic doctrine; Dickens, for social analysis. But these novels all represent the tail-end of one tradition, the final playing out of a cycle going back in somewhat different form to the Waverley novels.

In the 1850s and '60s readers and critics evolved a new set of demands for historical fiction, demands considerably different from those of earlier decades. Historical fiction ceased to be considered ancillary to formal history and became accepted on its own as light literature with little pretension to anything weightier. The American historian William H. Prescott had said much earlier that history and romance were "too near akin ever to be lawfully united" and urged that it was enough "for the novelist if he be true to the spirit" of a past age. In the latter half of the century this became the general attitude toward the romancer's responsibility toward the historical portions of his novels. The historical novelist, insisted a critic in *Bentley's Miscellany,* "must follow rather the poetry of history than its chronology: his business is not to be the slave of dates; he ought to be faithful to the character of the epoch". He then noted the innumerable inaccuracies in de Vigny' *Cinq-Mars,* but went on quickly to add: ". . . after all the value of historical, as well as other fictions, must be measured . . . by the power and skill it displays, rather than by the historical accuracy or importance of the events and persons introduced" ["The Historical Novel," *Bentley's Miscellany* XLVI (1859)]. Critics and readers ceased to be bothered by historical anachronisms, and there were now hostile comments about the occasional "hypercriticism" and the "captious and nibbling critic" who dared to intrude such remarks as had been common a decade earlier. Antiquarian research and concern with the trifles of costume, armor, and architecture were now both unnecessary and unwanted. Leslie Stephen noted that his fellow countrymen had lost their love for buff jerkins and other scraps from the medieval collections in museums, and Anthony Trollope, rereading *Old Mortality* in 1873, found the historical essays and background material tedious.

Thus, there was a shift in the last three decades of the century away from the historical element in the genre and a general agreement on the part of novelists, critics, and readers alike that the romancer's chief obligation was not to history but to the free exercise of his artistic imagination, unfettered by any demands for factual accuracy. There was no longer any need for practioners of the historical romance to demonstrate their scholarly control over historical portions of their novels. Richard Blackmore, Robert Louis Stevenson, Arthur Conan Doyle, and Thomas Hewlett no longer paraded facts and research before their readers, as had been the common practice of writers in the 1830s and '40s. Stevenson remarked in the preface to *Kidnapped,* "how little I am touched by the desire of accuracy". Footnotes, scholarly prefaces, and appendices disappeared entirely from their historical romances. Relieved from the burden of antiquarianism and the padding of superfluous details gleaned from exhaustive hours spent in thorough research, the historical romance in their hands discovered a new vitality, an ease and lightness hitherto completely unknown to the genre. The historical romances of the latter half of the century were unabashedly entertainment. The novelists now wrote for the pure love of exotic adventure in distant lands and times. They wrote to amuse and no longer felt defensive about a lack of any intellectual substance to their works. Stevenson, expressing this new attitude, advised the reader of *Kidnapped* that this work was "no furniture for the scholar's library, but a book for the winter evening schoolroom when the tasks are over and the hour for bed draws near". Once again the historical novelist was, as in the days of Scott, the teller of tales.

Andrew Sanders

SOURCE: An introduction to *The Victorian Historical Novel, 1840-1880,* Macmillan, London, 1978, pp. 1-31.

[*In this excerpt, Sanders examines the impact of Sir Walter Scott's work on later historical novelists, discussing in detail the advances made within the genre by such writers as Charles Reade and George Eliot.*]

Despite the sharp decline in Scott's critical reputation in this century, the Waverley novels have not lacked powerful friends and committed advocates, notable amongst them being Georg Lukács, a critic himself moulded by his study of Hegel and Marx. To Lukács, Scott's art is both progressive and in a true sense revolutionary, structured on the economic and ideological basis of the European reaction to the Revolution in France. Scott's inherent conservatism, which Lukács readily acknowledges, is seen as giving him a special kind of objectivity as a social critic, for by studying conflict, and by seeking to balance political opposites, Scott emerges as a dialectical thinker looking forward to Hegel and Marx. To Lukács, the 'classical form of the historical novel' evolved by Scott shows a real understanding of the 'progressive' nature of a compromise which leads to evolution, Hegel's 'dialectic of transition':

> He attempts by fathoming historically the whole of English development to find a 'middle way' for himself between warring extremes. He finds in English history the consolation that the most violent vicissitudes of class struggle have always finally calmed down into a glorious 'middle way'. Thus, out of the struggle of the Saxons and Normans there arose the English nation, neither Saxon nor Norman; in the same way the bloody Wars of the Roses gave rise to the illustrious reign of the House of Tudor, especially that of Queen Elizabeth; and those class struggles which manifested themselves in the Cromwellian Revolution were finally evened out in the England of today, after a long period of uncertainity and civil war, by the 'Glorious Revolution' and its aftermath [*The Historical Novel*].

Scott's conservative 'middle way' allows for a broad view which stretches panoramically from Scotland, through England, to Europe beyond. But the essence of his compromise lies in his use of what Lukács styles a 'neutral' hero, a figure caught up, like Edward Waverley, in a political crisis, and coming into immediate contact with men and causes which represent the extremes of political division. The neutral hero stands as the representative of society as a whole, and is able to learn from the extremes he sees and from the humanised historical figures he meets, not as heroes but as men among men.

Lukács is a forceful apologist, despite the fact that his analysis tends to distort or under-rate the work of Scott's major successors in the English tradition. He sees the historical novel as the recorder of social evolution and of 'the life of the people' and he is led to trace a line running through Stendhal, Balzac and Tolstoi rather than one which can readily accommodate a Dickensian or Thackerayan dissent or even the determined 'provinciality' of much nineteenth-century English fiction. This bias towards 'social realism' in Lukács's work properly excludes the escapism of a novelist like Harrison Ainsworth, but it also manages to avoid mention of George Eliot's concern with individual spiritual evolution. His philosophical bias insists on seeing history as progressive and that the relevance of a given historical period is dependent upon its meaning to the present, but it blinds him to the real diversity of Victorian historical fiction, and, moreover, to the advances of the twentieth-century novel, breaking away from the well-explored confines of social realism.

Lukács fails to appreciate that the very distinctiveness of English history, and of the inherited tradition in fiction, made for an equally distinctive and varied response to Scott, one which can necessarily be paralleled by developments on the Continent. The prejudices moulded by a bourgeois democracy in a nation which had not experienced invasion since the eleventh century and which had produced a typical compromise in its reaction to the Reformation, made in turn for 'provincial' fictional treatment of subjects derived from incidents in the French Revolution, or the Norman Conquest, or in the religious conflicts of the sixteenth and seventeenth centuries. Victorian his-

torical novelists chose individual solutions to problems they found suggested in the Waverley novels, and they felt free either to take what they wanted from Scott's example or to adapt Scott's formulae to their particular ends.

To Nassau Senior, writing in 1821, Scott's novels 'from their number, their merit, their originality, and their diffusion, have more influence than is exercised by any others within the whole scope of our literature'. That influence helped to shift Victorian fiction as a whole away from experiment and away from the diversity of eighteenth-century narrative forms, into a determined realism which saw man as a social animal with pre-eminent social responsibilities. Although they have most often been seen as both symptoms and causes of Romanticism, the Waverley novels examined man in an essentially un-Romantic sense, as gregarious rather than solitary, detached but involved in mankind, viewing society as determining rather than wrecking the individual's destiny, and the individual himself as commonsensical instead of possessed. Scott's central characters may admire the flamboyant gestures of rebels or questors, but they come to acknowledge the need for conformity in the interests of the majority. Although the organisers of the Eglinton Tournament, and later, Mark Twain, considered *Ivanhoe* to be a call for the revival of chivalry, Scott himself made it plain that his novel was a critique of an absent crusading king and of the divisions perpetuated by a false sense of honour. If we can now see the Victorian novel as, in some degree, a reaction against the wilder excesses of Romanticism, Scott had played an important part in making it so, though he can also be accused of giving it a narrower purpose within the boundaries of realism. The new wave of English fiction in the late 1830s and early 1840s showed itself to be freshly alert to social problems, concerned with local colour, and actively determined to prove that, through the novel, history had a place in modern life. *Waverley* and its successors had quickened a creative impulse while giving the novel a new prestige and popularity.

Although its influence can be felt through the entire range of Victorian fiction, *Waverley*'s importance for the historical novel lies in what it demonstrated of a means of examining the life of a period separated from the present by at least a full generation, or, in terms of its sub-title, by some sixty years. Scott's later work dealt with far earlier periods, but *Waverley* had established a pattern of accounting for social change, and explaining even comparatively recent changes to a world that was beginning to lose touch with its past. 'To elder persons', Scott told his readers in 1814, 'it will recall scenes and characters familiar to their youth; and to the rising generation the tale may present some idea of the manners of their forefathers.' Certainly, for the novelist himself, details of his story had to be researched rather than remembered or simply invented. Beyond *Waverley* Scott stretched further into the dark backward of Scottish, then English, then European time, adapting his heroes and their social environment accordingly. Just as he had made the past present and the distant near to historians like Macaulay and Carlyle, so, to a new generation of novelists, Scott seemed a precedent, a challenge, and an example. Themes of revolution, dissent, war, violence, transition and decay which had been constants in the Waverley novels were consequently to find a readier place in the historical novels of the later nineteenth century than they were to do in stories concerned with contemporary life. The past could be seen to reflect the present, and, as a consequence, modern problems could be judged more detachedly for being considered within an historical perspective. Victorian historical novels are not, as a rule, escapes into a romantic past, but an attempt to prove that man and his society develop as part of a process which includes and envelops the present. At their best, the historical novels of the period deserve to stand beside the major triumphs of Victorian fiction, a place that was certainly granted to them in their own time but which has been often denied them since by changing critical and literary fashions.

Among critics of the first half of the nineteenth century there is evidence of a widespread optimism as to the potential of the historical novel and to the challenge it presented to the aspiring novelist. 'All who choose to take the trouble can possess themselves of the antiquarian facts,' wrote J. A. Heraud in the *Quarterly Review* in 1827, 'but the novelist undertakes something more than merely to transcribe from the old documents. . . . He is to go beyond the letter that kills, and to give us the spirit that makes alive' [Vol. 35 (March 1827)]. Such *dicta* were to be regularly echoed. Writing eleven years later in the *Monthly Chronicle,* Edward Bulwer-Lytton urged that prose fiction now formed 'so wide and essential a part of the popular literature of Europe' that it was appropriate to set out laws as a guide to future progress [Vol. I]. Of the historical novelist in particular, he demanded 'a perfect acquaintance' with the characteristics and spirit of the past, and affirmed that the novelist's art 'will be evinced in the illustrations he selects, and the skill with which they are managed'. Perverse as it might seem to any reader familiar with the drudgery of Bulwer's own historical fiction, he goes on to insist that the novelist should 'avoid all antiquarian dissertations not essentially necessary to the conduct of his tale', simply because 'minuteness is not accuracy'. Bulwer ends by hinting at his own ambitions for, he tells us, an historical novelist who continues from where Scott had left off would have to 'deeply consider all the features of the time, and select those neglected by his predecessor;—would carefully note all the deficiencies of the author of *Kenilworth,* and seize at once upon the ground which that versatile genius omitted to consecrate to himself.'

It was, with others', Bulwer-Lytton's youthful work as the recorder of the vices, crimes, and whims of his own times, both from a 'silver fork' and a 'Newgate' angle, which appears to have most offended the superior-minded Archibald Allison, taking 'The Historical Romance' as the subject of an article in *Blackwood's Magazine* in 1845. The Victorian novelist, Allison objected, had a vocation beyond that of an illustrator of low-life subjects:

We protest against the doctrine, that the lofty art of romance is to be lowered to the delineating the manners of cheesemongers and grocers, of crop-head charity boys, and smart haberdashers' and milliners' apprentices of doubtful reputation. If we wish to see the manners of such classes, we have only to get into a railway or steam-

boat; the sight of them at breakfast or dinner will probably be enough for any person accustomed to the habits of good society. [*Blackwood's Edinburgh Magazine* LVIII (September 1845)]

Such disdain is worthy of Lord Melbourne, reacting in a similar manner to *Oliver Twist,* but for Allison the real strength of modern fiction lay in its power of evoking history, for as such the novel could take its place 'beside the plays of Shakespeare'. The effect of the publication of *Waverley* thirty years previously, he notes, with an appropriately Shakespearean simile, was 'like the invention of gunpowder or steam (sic)' and worked a similar change in the 'moral world'. He proceeds, waxing yet more effusively pompous:

From that moment the historical romance was born for mankind. One of the most delightful and instructive species of composition was created; which unites the learning of the historian with the fancy of the poet; which discards from human annals their years of tedium and brings prominently forward their eras of interest; which teaches morality by example, and conveys information by giving pleasure; and which, combining the charms of imagination with the treasures of research, founds the ideal upon its only solid and durable base—the real.

Having thus announced his reasons for considering the historical novel to be intellectually serious, he goes on to stress its moral seriousness: 'Considered in its highest aspect, no art was ever attempted by man more elevated and ennobling than the historical romance. It may be doubted whether it is inferior even to the lofty flights of the epic, or the heart-rending pathos of the dramatic muse.' He seeks to cap his claim by arguing, somewhat more spuriously, from the evidence of popularity—'Homer and Tasso never, in an equal time, had nearly so many readers as Scott'—and he notes that it will probably prove to be impossible to estimate the influence of 'the fascinating art' of the historical novelist over future ages. He does, however, remark on one happy influence already evident, one that would doubtless have delighted Sir Walter, for we are told that the Waverley novels have 'gone far to neutralize the dangers of the Reform Bill'.

Like Bulwer, Allison was also anxious to define rules for the future writer, and to extract 'principles', in truly Aristotelian manner, from extant examples and evidence. The romance should be above all things 'elevating and yet interesting in subject', and ideally its subject should be drawn from national history, or at least based 'on incidents cousin-german . . . to those of its own national existence'. As a consequence he prefers *Ivanhoe* to *Anne of Geierstein,* and *The Last of the Barons* to *The Last Days of Pompeii,* and ends by praising Fenimore Cooper's *The Last of the Mohicans* and the 'admirable delineation of the manners, ideas, hopes and fears, joys and sorrows, of humble life' which he found in Manzoni's *I Promessi Sposi.* To Allison, as to Bulwer or to Charles Reade, 'the real' and 'truth to nature' find their highest and most accurate expression in historical fiction, with history giving a vital and epic dimension to social realism.

This confidence about the future was not necessarily justified by the evidence of the present, for in the following year, 1846, G. H. Lewes was to complain bitterly of the 'mediocrity' of most of the numerous progeny of the Waverley novels. Lewes excepts Scott—'that wonderful writer'—from his strictures, but he finds most of the historical fiction of the 1840s to be served up according to a cheap commercial recipe, the secret of which he divulges: 'Sprinkle largely with love and heroism, keep up the mystery overhanging the hero's birth till the last chapter; and have a good stage villain, scheming and scowling through two volumes and a half, to be utterly exposed and defeated at last—and the historical novel is complete.'

But the repetitiveness, ignorance and incompetence of Scott's imitators disturbed an unknown reviewer of 1847 in *Fraser's Magazine* less than the prospect of further fictional challenges to the authority of the conventional historian. Posing the question 'Walter Scott—Has History gained by his writings?', he argued that the historical novel had wrecked a reader's proper detachment:

> It is very difficult to take up a volume of Scott in anything like a spirit of critical examination. One cannot read him in cold blood. He sets all one's tastes and sympathies working at once to the dire distraction of the reason. Flooded by his humour, and exhilarated by his heartiness and freshness, one lingers in the company of his gloriously life-like creations about as much disposed to question their title to the name they bear, as the opium-smoker to doubt the existence of his imaginary Houries.

It is an indirect compliment to the power of the Waverley novels, but it is hard to imagine such ideals standing up in the face of the emotive force of the prejudices and style of a Gibbon, a Carlyle or a Macaulay. Nevertheless, the critic does not go further in his censure of Scott's method, though he voices a suspicion of imaginative literature which sets him in an honourably Platonic tradition; instead he transfers his venom to the work of Scott's shabbier successors, and especially to G. P. R. James. It would be vain to attempt to shield James from the attack, but it is interesting to note that this antipathy to the 'dandy littérateurs' was shared by serious historical novelists as disparate as Bulwer, Kingsley and Thackeray, all of whom were offended that Scott's image should have been so recklessly defaced, and his reputation so tarnished. For all three, however, the answer to the impertinent question as to whether or not history had gained from Scott's novels was an emphatic 'Yes'.

By the late 1850s there was good evidence of fresh invention and renewed energy in English historical fiction, and it was understandable that a critic should proclaim that the novel was by now the 'essential' complement to the study of history. Academic history on its own, readers were told, was insufficient to bring out 'the nature and power of a people's genius—what they thought, hated, loved'. The attraction of historical fiction lay 'not in any facility which it affords for the construction of a better story, nor any superior interest that attaches to the known and prominent characters with which it deals, or to the events it describes: but rather the occasion it gives for

making us familiar with the every-day life of the age and country in which the scene is laid.'

By suggesting that the strength of any novel lay in its power to evoke 'every-day life', we sense that the reviewer acknowledges both the importance of realism and the consequent variety of response to a variety of situations. Indeed, by the time of the review, Thackeray had brilliantly dispensed with Scott's historic detachment in his *Esmond*, Kingsley had looked intently at the puckered face of a long-dead Alexandria in his *Hypatia*, and Dickens was already serialising his very personal response to the French Revolution in *A Tale of Two Cities*. All of them had first established their literary bearings in novels dealing with the world of their contemporaries, but history had given each a new dimension. The 1860s were to be marked by the acclaim accorded to George Eliot's *Romola* and to Reade's *The Cloister and the Hearth*, and by the comparatively muted response to Mrs Gaskell's *Sylvia's Lovers*. The very fact that so many of the major artists of the period had turned to history for subjects, and that novelists in particular chose to attempt stories set in the past, can be seen to stem from Scott's continuing authority over an age so acutely aware of the value and relevance of an historical sense.

Lukács's definition of a 'classical form' based on the novels of Scott, with a neutral hero and a movement towards a balance of opposites, is, generally speaking, a useful one, even though it is restrictive in terms of an appreciation of the variety of character and structure in the Waverley novels themselves. If *Waverley* is taken as the type case, its pattern can hardly be said to have been followed in some of its most admired successors—Old *Mortality* or *The Antiquary*, for example. *Rob Roy*, it is true, only slightly varies its shape, moving Francis Osbaldistone into Edward Waverley's role as the Englishman caught up in an especially Scottish aspect of the political conflict which affects the combined fortunes of Scotland and England. A second, but more significant variation on the idea is that of the Scotsman in England, Nigel Olifaunt in *The Fortunes of Nigel* for example, or the Scotsman abroad in *Quentin Durward*, or even the Englishman abroad, as in Scott's last, floundering novel, *Count Robert of Paris*. A further important adaptation is to see a Briton mixed up in an alien political struggle within his homeland, as happens in *Ivanhoe, The Betrothed, Woodstock* and *Redgauntlet*, and which is a device borrowed later by Stevenson in his most Scott-like novels. Finally, there is the epic, exploratory experience of Jeanie Deans, journeying out into a wider world in *The Heart of Midlothian*, and symbolically reconciling Scotland to the Union and to a Hanoverian dynasty in London. In all the novels a comparatively innocent, but intelligent, central character learns, matures, and independently works out a kind of resolution of the opposed forces that he or she encounters, either through an acceptance of the *status quo* or through a commitment to a progressive new order. In some prominent cases, notably *Ivanhoe* and *Woodstock*, a concluding marriage brings personal fulfilment to the hero while also standing as a public sign of social reconciliation. In the great majority of Scott's novels—though *The Talisman* is a possible exception—the hero is neutral because he is also fictional and therefore a free agent, able to form decisions which are not necessarily tied by the restrictive need to follow the events of recorded history. The neutral heroes meet, admire, dislike, follow or reject the 'great men' of history by first seeing them as fallible and human. His heroes can be drawn emotionally, like Scott himself, to Jacobitism and Popery, or to Royalist, Saxon or Highland resistance to change, but like their creator, they are also likely to come to acknowledge the historic inevitability of change. They see rights and wrongs on both sides, and they become involved as rounded human beings, aware of conflicting loyalties, and of family or romantic obligations, while still moving towards a recognition of the creativity and practicality of commitment.

Scott's successors and imitators were able to vary this flexible enough 'classical form' as it best suited their tastes and fictional ends, though they did so at times conscious that they were aiming at a broader and more ambitious kind of historical novel. Tolstoi's variation on the Scott pattern, for example, might at first seem complex, though it is really only an exceptionally subtle and expressive duplication of the *Waverley*-type, giving *War and Peace* a shape based on parallel heroes and families, caught up severally, then together, in the Napoleonic disruption of Russian life. In England the fifty years following Scott's death witnessed a considerable amount of experimental activity, rarely the tired, scholarly imitation which has been all too often assumed. Harrison Ainsworth's novels have much to answer for in having given historical fiction a bad name, but they in fact tend to ignore Scott's precedent in an attempt to restore and re-embellish the Gothic fiction of the early century. Despite his considerable initial success, Ainsworth proved to be incapable of development or of sustaining his achievement; he ransacked English history for likely plots, and often he ended up with unlikely ones; he looked to sensationalism to sell his novels, and he pleased neither his early critics nor a later and more critical audience. By the 1850s Ainsworth had already outwritten the fashion for the kind of romance he had hoped to rejuvenate. Bulwer-Lytton's drab, learned, and aristocratic historical novels form a surprising contemporary contrast to Ainsworth's and to those of G. P. R. James. Bulwer aimed high, and meditated long and publicly about what he should be doing; he saw Scott as deficient in accuracy and guilty of distortions of chronology and character, and he attempted instead to restore the academic prestige of the novel, making it worthy of serious study. He had a real enough respect for Scott's achievement, however, as the shape of his enduringly popular *The Last Days of Pompeii* suggests, with its forward looking conclusion and its range of characters invented from miscellaneous archaeological details. Bulwer's later novels took Scott's pattern to an extreme by attempting to function as imaginative, and only partly fictional, biographies of the great men of history. Despite the fecundity of his ideas, he had little talent as a story-teller, and scarcely any at all as a writer of English, and as a consequence his novels remain cramped by their musty artificiality.

Of the abler novelists of the first half of the nineteenth century only Charles Kingsley followed Bulwer in experimenting with the biography of a known historical figure presented as a kind of *Heldenleben,* though in the case of *Hereward the Wake* he was lucky to have chosen a hero who was far more shadowy than Bulwer's King Harold. Kingsley's development as a novelist reveals a movement away from the use of a central character who is not so much neutral as opaque (Philammon in *Hypatia*), towards a muscular Christian type (Amyas Leigh) and finally to a primitive nordic ideal. Like Carlyle, Kingsley believed in heroes and in the virtues of modern hero-worship, and his novels expound ideas which he considered to be vital to the troubled world of his own times. If he now strikes us as a clumsy Jingoist or a blood-curdler it is perhaps because Kingsley reflects precisely those Victorian attitudes which have proved to be least accessible to the post-Victorians.

The thinning of the neutral *Waverley* hero to a state of semi-opacity had already been attempted by Dickens in his *Barnaby Rudge* of 1841. In his novel Dickens had set out to show states of mental disturbance, not simply in his rabble-rousing villain, but also on a wider, public level in the excesses of the mob and in a general intolerance and lack of social will. With an imbecile prominent amongst his characters, and the one from whom the book is named, the novelist added a new dimension to his theme, for Barnaby is at once exploitable, and capable, because vulnerable, of accentuating both innocence and guilt. With Barnaby's imbecility compensated for by the growing awareness of the commonsensical Gabriel Varden (who was originally to have been the title character), the novel is a far more masterly and intelligent historical study than it has often been credited with being. It is nevertheless remarkable that when Dickens returned to historical fiction, and to the problem of popular unrest and revolution in *A Tale of Two Cities,* he chose a more individual form to express his by now more developed ideas. Like *Quentin Durward, A Tale of Two Cities* moves Britons abroad to France and observes their reactions to a foreign political crisis; unlike Scott's novel, however, it includes no well-known historical figures amongst its characters, and, as its title suggests, it considers phenomena which are common to both London and Paris, even though it shows that the Parisian inheritance of hatred and disorder is the more disastrous. Dickens's knot of fictional characters are only partly detached from the Revolution which overtakes them, but the novel takes family connections, private histories, and the ties of responsibility, and uses them as a means of explaining, and then privately resolving, the public divisions between philosophies, classes, and nations. Dickens uses his plot as a kind of myth which can contain and fulfil the historical problem examined in his novel. Whatever *A Tale of Two Cities* may be said to lack in comparison to its author's other mature novels, it compensates by transferring a Dickensian formula, a private resolution of a public challenge, into an emotionally charged historical context.

Dickens's posing of a private answer to a general question resembles the solutions evolved intellectually in two very different novels, George Eliot's *Romola* and J. H. Newman's *Callista*. In *Romola* George Eliot explored the central theme of her work, the individual's moral choice between egotism and altruism, within an historical perspective provided by the diversity of Renaissance Florence. Newman's *Callista,* set in third-century North Africa, is a far less impressive achievement but it too looks at moral choice, and considers the struggle of an intelligent woman for belief in an alien world. Both novels are shaped around the progress of the heroine, and, as many contemporary commentators recognised, the struggles of both Romola and Callista project a very Victorian *Ahnung* backwards into history. The yearning of the individual for purpose is seen as a constant human aspiration rather than as the product of specific historical circumstances, but the growth of the heroine's awareness is taken as a token of the parallel between the progress of the soul and the forward movement of humanity.

The shift away from the 'classical form' is yet more pronounced in two novels centred in provincial communities rather than in a political vortex. Thackeray had dispensed with the heroic in *Henry Esmond,* but both Mrs Gaskell in *Sylvia's Lovers* and Hardy in *The Trumpet-Major* looked at societies in which the possibility of heroism is restricted by the milieu of the province. Both novels consider the historical process as it touches the lives of ordinary men and women, troubled by war and the rumour of war, but rarely probing the meaning of their experience or able to see the long-term consequence of it. For Mrs Gaskell and Hardy, village or small-town society has changed only in outward circumstances in the sixty years which separate the writer from his subject, but both take as a central idea the real edge of violence added to maritime life in the Napoleonic Wars by the presence of the press-gang. 'Great men' only marginally involve themselves, but their

Charles Reade

decisions interfere indirectly with the patterns of life otherwise determined by the seasons or by landscape. *Sylvia's Lovers* and *The Trumpet-Major* are primarily love-stories in which private malice, the pains of unrequited love or simply jealousy, find a new dimension in the violence of war. Both writers, from their very different points of view, offer a new stress on the private worlds of their characters, minutely recording the overlappings of private and communal pasts, or recorded and unrecorded history, or of tradition and 'unhistoric' action. Simple men and women are seen to contribute as fully to the slow progress of humanity as the kings and the generals.

Nevertheless, the most radical departure from the *Waverley* from in the fifty years following Scott's death remains Thackeray's *Henry Esmond* of 1852. Thackeray saw history not as a charted stream but as a series of currents and eddies moving slackly forwards. But his real challenge to the Scott norm lies in his choice of an autobiographical narrator, a moody, sensitive, and involved character who can only describe what has happened to him from the point of view of his own 'uniscience'. The 'history' witnessed by Henry Esmond is vivid and significant enough, ranging from the 'Glorious Revolution' and the Seven Years War to the succession of the Hanoverians, but because Esmond is telling his own story as well, he can never have the detachment of Scott's omniscient narrator. As a further consequence of his chosen form Thackeray rejects the tidy resolutions of the Waverley novels, leaving us instead with his hero's withdrawal from the political arena, still, it seems, divided in his loyalties but married to the woman he never suspected he loved. There is a chance of private happiness, but, as with most human observers, many other aspects of experience are left unresolved, avoided, forgotten or abandoned by the wayside. In the end the 'hero' of an 'unheroic' but virtuous life leaves for a traditionless new world in Virginia. For Esmond history is an act of memory, and as an alert, but frequently biassed, narrator he views the heroic and the tragic through the quotidian, acknowledging the equal importance for the individual of the petty and inconsequential decision as well as of political or social resolve. History emerges in Thackeray's disconcerting scheme as a series of arbitrary acts, not as a determined progress, and, for the novelist, art alone gives shape and meaning because it tells a human truth.

To many Victorian critics, however, the most successful and innovatory historical novel of the century was Charles Reade's *The Cloister and the Hearth.* To modern readers it might well seem to have a claim to have been the most overrated English novel of the age, and even George Orwell, a rare twentieth-century admirer of Reade's, considered it the novelist's bad luck 'to be remembered by this particular book, rather as Mark Twain, thanks to the films, is chiefly remembered by *A Connecticut Yankee at King Arthur's Court'.* Nonetheless, when *The Cloister and the Hearth* first appeared in 1861, the *Saturday Review* proclaimed that Reade had achieved what scarcely any other Englishman of his generation had shown himself able to do. He had written an historical novel 'that is pleasant and touching to read'. The story was declared to be not unworthy of comparison to one of Scott's, but, the reviewer went on to note, time had begun to expose Scott's shortcomings:

> There is a certain thinness—not a poverty, but a scantiness—in the *Waverley Novels,* which modern readers, turning back to them after the interest of the first reading has long passed away, can scarcely fail to feel. There are heroes in Scott's historical novels, there are attempts to paint and analyse character, there are many passages introduced in order to bring before us the historical era as the author conceives it. But there is much that is left sketchy and in outline in all this. The heroes are amiable dummies, and so are the heroines. Their feelings, and the feelings of their friends and enemies, are mostly on the surface. It is astonishing in how very few pages we come to the end of even the best scenes of Scott.

It is a rare Victorian response, though a valid enough one, but the reviewer continues by remarking on the rapid development of new literary styles and attitudes; 'modern romances of the highest class', he told his readers, 'are more thorough and elaborate':

> Sir Edward Lytton has shown us what industry and a power of combination can do in this way although the great inferiority of his conception of character will not permit us to rank him as an historical novelist with Mr. Reade. What we have gained, so far as it is a gain, since Scott wrote, has been gained by the greater minuteness of reflection, analysis, and knowledge which we have cultivated during the last thirty years [*Saturday Review* LXXVII (1862)].

Reade is seen, then, as reflecting advances in fictional and historical investigation. Some months later the *Westminster Review* added its own acclaim. 'There are some novels', it remarked, 'of which the general excellence is so conspicuous, that judges need not hesitate about stamping them with the seal of their approbation.' Reade's characters merited like praise: 'No creation of modern fiction is more true to nature and, at the same time, a more loveable character' than Margaret Brandt; Catherine, Gerard's mother, bore 'a certain resemblance to Mrs Poyser', while Denys was nothing short of a French Falstaff. To Swinburne, in an essay still republished as a Preface to the Everyman edition of the novel, it was difficult to find 'a story better conceived or better composed, better constructed or better related.'

Such adulation was not unmitigated, even some admiring critics complained of the novel's excessive length, but *The Cloister and the Hearth* continued to be thought of by many readers as the greatest English historical novel until well into the twentieth century. Since its decline in popularity it has, like the rest of Reade's output, been, not always unjustly, neglected. It is certainly now a hard book to appreciate as heartily as its original audience appreciated it, impeded as it is by melodramatic twists, digressive excursions into aspects of mediaeval life, and by a painfully artificial dialogue. But *The Cloister and the Hearth* remains typical of its period as a serious and ambitious historical novel of the second rank, one which neither broke new ground nor consolidated familiar fictional territory.

Its interest lies in its Englishness, for despite its Continental setting and Reade's cosmopolitan reading, it is quirky, untidy, provincial, and lacking in real philosophical or intellectual direction. Reade's contemporaries mistook its bittiness for a varied and accurate account of life in the period before the Reformation, but it is more likely to strike a modern audience as ragged and uneven, learned and lyrical by turns, but as often frenetic and more than a little vulgar.

The novel's loose structure gave Reade's encyclopaedic mind full play, and its central wandering movement from the Netherlands to Italy and back again allowed for an episodic treatment of jarring characters, ideas, and cultures. Its structure, so strangely admired by Swinburne, depends upon discord, and Reade attempts to balance the settled, domestic life of his Dutch family against the southward wanderings of their alienated son. It is a balance which Reade's digressive and woolly mind finds it hard to maintain. *The Cloister and the Hearth* has a variety and freedom which might well have appalled Scott, but it sadly lacks the order and developed resolution of the best of the Waverley novels, and it falls short of the looser control over the elements of an historical plot evolved after Scott by Thackeray, Dickens or George Eliot.

Reade proclaimed his purpose at the outset:

> Not a day passes over earth, but men and women of no note do great deeds, speak great words, and suffer noble sorrows. Of these obscure heroes, philosophers, and martyrs, the greater part will never be known till that hour, when many that are great shall be small, and the small great; but of others the world's knowledge may be said to sleep: their lives and characters lie hidden from nations in the annals that record them. The general reader cannot feel them, they are presented so curtly and coldly: they are not like breathing stories appealing to his heart, but little historic hailstones striking him but to glance off his bosom: nor can he understand them; for epitomes are not narratives, as skeletons are not human figures.

> Thus records of prime truths remain a dead letter to plain folk: the writers have left so much to the imagination, and imaginationis so rare a gift. Here, then, the writer of fiction may be of use to the public—as an interpreter.

Reade is not mourning the silence of village Hampdens, for, like Thackeray, he is aspiring to a history which is 'familiar rather than heroic', or like George Eliot in the Finale to *Middlemarch* he is proclaiming his faith in 'unhistoric acts'. Like his greater contemporaries he is doubting the Carlylean historical thesis and looking to the novel as an amplifier of conventional history. But *The Cloister and the Hearth* only partly justifies this opening statement of intent, for Reade undermines his stated intention by giving us, if not the history of a great man, at least the history of a great man's parents. Gerard's and Margaret's experience is given a fresh relevance at the end of the story by the revelation of the future destiny of their son. Like Tolstoi in *War and Peace,* though with hardly any of Tolstoi's deftness, Reade suggests that the future will develop dramatically in the period after the close of the narrative. Erasmus looms over the novel's last pages, and a sudden flash illuminates our understanding of what has gone before, but the 'little historic hail-stones' cease simply to glance off our bosoms once we are bidden to look up to the Reformation storm-cloud.

The musty chronicle, 'written in intolerable Latin', which the novelist mentions as his source for the story in his third paragraph proves to be Erasmus's by no means ill-written or obscure autobiographical fragment published posthumously as the *Compendium Vitae* at Leiden in 1615. Indeed, at the end of the narrative Reade himself admits to having derived some of his best scenes from Erasmus's 'mediaeval pen', having borrowed both ideas and details directly from the *Colloquies* and the *Encomium Moriae*. It is an excusable enough sleight of hand and even the initial dismissal of the 'musty chronicle' helps to maintain the secret of the real future identity of young Gerard. Otherwise Reade emerges from all of his novels, and not just *The Cloister and the Hearth,* as much a determined 'truth-teller' in fiction as Bulwer-Lytton. While he was working on his historical novel, Reade remarked on the relationship between fact, fiction, and history, citing Erasmus's *Colloquies* as supporting evidence: 'They are a mine of erudition and observation; but so are most of his works; but in the 'colloquies' there is fiction, and its charm, superadded to his learning, language, method, and philosophy—as in the immortal Macaulay.' It is a clumsy and somewhat illogical sentence, but it is one which is attempting to link the philosopher to the historian and to the writer of fiction—the interpreter of dead letters to plain folk: 'Where things so rare and solid as long and profound research, lucid arrangement, and empire over language, meet in an historian, there he has a good chance of immortality; but, where he blends with these rare virtues the seductive colours of fiction, he turns that good chance into a certainty.' Reade balances uneasily, and probably unwittingly, between two distinct schools of thought; on the one hand, he sides with 'the immortal Macaulay' as an historian first and an inventor of history second; on the other, he feels himself one with Thackeray as an accurate storyteller, incorporating facts into fiction. Reade does not go on to explain himself further, nor does his historical novel suggest what he believed the real distinction between an historian and an historical novelist to be. He does not even appear to recognise any distinct philosophy of history. Like Bulwer, he claims equality and respect for the novelist's contribution to the study of the past, but he blurs definitions and claims to sovereignty to leave his readers instead with the impression of a vacillating and unsteady mind.

Like most of Scott's successors, however, Reade devoutly trusted in the virtues of 'realism' and in the developing æsthetic doctrine of 'truth to nature'. With George Eliot and Sir David Wilkie, though not with Ruskin, he admired the popular domesticity of the seventeenth-century Dutch genre painters; his artist-figure in the earlier *Christie Johnstone,* having expressed solidarity with 'Gerard Dow and Cuyp and Pierre de Hoogh', goes on to proclaim loudly in italics:

> *The resources of our art are still unfathomed! Pictures are yet to be painted that shall refresh men's inner souls, and help their hearts against the artificial world; and charm the fiend away, like David's harp!! The world, after centuries of lies, will give nature and truth a trial. What a paradise art will be, when truths, instead of lies, shall be told on paper, on marble, on canvas, and on the boards!!!*

As some early critics of Reade suggested, it is the mediaeval Dutch school which most touches *The Cloister and the Hearth,* and the novelist even goes to the length of introducing artists and paintings into his tale. But Reade's doctrine of accuracy went deeper than a desire to describe interiors or the circumstances of fifteenth-century scullery-maids; he believed in the radiance of the commonplace, and in the intensity of ordinary experience. Like Jan van Eyck, who appears briefly in the novel, he crowds his canvas with people and things, but each part is intended to capture and express the wholeness and wonder of creation. The novel takes the details of a lost world, from its faith to its fleas, and makes a picture of them. Reade assumes that his picture will have a natural unity simply because it is true to life. The pains he took to compose *A Good Fight,* the fragmentary original of *The Cloister and the Hearth,* were stressed by the tired but proud novelist in a letter to James Fields:

> You may well be surprised that I am so long over 'Good Fight', but the fact is, it is not the writing but the reading which makes me slow. It may perhaps give you an idea of the system in which I write fiction, if I get down the list of books I have read, skimmed, or studied to write this little misery.

He then lists the titles of some seventy-nine volumes, adding 'etc., etc.,' when he had done. 'Surely this *must* be the right method,' he commented with a hint of desperation. There was, in fact, nothing unique about his method; *Romola* left George Eliot 'an old woman', and even Dickens claimed to have consulted a 'cartload' of reference books in the preparation of *A Tale of Two Cities,* but like a literary Pre-Raphaelite Brother, Reade seemed to trust solely to the efficacy of detail, and to the idea that accuracy imparted life to his art.

Each episode in the novel is arranged by another, not purely for dramatic effect, or for contrast, or as a means of moving his plot forward, but because each 'tells the truth' about the particular aspect of mediaeval life he wants to describe. *The Cloister and the Hearth* is really little more than an assemblage of not always harmonious parts; plot, for Reade, comes second to cumulative experience, and, rather than let his characters shape his narrative, or find their destiny in themselves, he lets them wander until he sees fit to nudge them back into the loose arching pattern provided by his love-story. Reade never keeps an idea or a theme steadily before us and, as a consequence, his story neither holds us while we read it, nor brings us to a point of rest when we have finished it.

If Reade had models in mind for *The Cloister and the Hearth* they were probably the comic novels of Fielding and, before him, of Cervantes. Unlike most Victorian historical novels, Reade's remains in an eighteenth-century picaresque tradition. Nonetheless, Fielding's notion of a comic epic in prose in *Tom Jones* had derived as much from the Homeric and Virgilian epic shape as it had from Cervantes, providing his novel with its twelve books and its tripartite structure. Tom's journey to London merely forms the second third of the narrative account of his developing fortunes and moral awareness, sandwiched as it is between sections which establish him first as Squire All-worthy's ward, then as an independent man in Town. As Coleridge was to acknowledge, Fielding's complex and neat plot gives the novel much of its distinction. Reade possessed neither Fielding's ordering imagination, nor a hero to match Cervantes's. If he can be said to have aimed at 'unity by inclusion', he really has so vague a sense of architectural design, that his details habitually impede our appreciation of his whole. Gerard discovers little during his lengthy journey away from Holland, but if, like Thackeray in *Henry Esmond,* Reade had wished to persuade us of the arbitrary nature of experience, it would have greatly assisted his scheme if, like Thackeray, he had first determined the balance of art to learning, and fiction to fact. *The Cloister and the Hearth* attempts too much, and tries to be too many kinds of novel, without ever managing to persuade us of its own consistency and its own conviction.

In common with Thackeray, however, and later, with Mrs Gaskell and Hardy, Reade was proposing a view of history in his novel which ran counter to Carlyle's. His anti-Carlyleanism is most blatantly stated in *Christie John-stone,* where the novelist's mouth-piece, Lord Ipsden, loudly but somewhat clumsily attacks a mediaeval enthusiast's opinion of past and present, suggesting that

> 'Five hundred years added to a world's life made it just five hundred years older, not younger,— and if older, greyer,—and if greyer, wiser.

> 'Of Abbot Sampson,' said he, 'whom I confess both a great and good man, his author, who with all his talent belongs to the class muddle-head, tells us, that when he had been two years in authority his red hair had turned grey, fighting against the spirit of his age; how the deuce, then, could he be a sample of the spirit of his age? . . .

> 'The earnest men of former ages are not extinct in this. . . . There still exist in parts of America, rivers on whose banks are earnest men, who shall take your scalp, the wife's of your bosom, and the innocent child's of her bosom. . . .

> 'Moreover, he who has the sense to see that questions have three sides is no longer so intellectually as well as morally degraded as to be able to cut every throat that utters an opinion contrary-to his own.'

However much Reade may be distorting, or simply misunderstanding the thread of the argument of *Past and Present,* Lord Ipsden's words do manage to suggest why the novelist came to treat mediaeval history as he did in *The Cloister and the Hearth.* He saw the 'spirit of the age' expressed in common life, not in the thoughts and actions of the world-historical hero, and he saw earnestness as responsible for intolerance, bigotry, and cruelty. Trust as he

might in progress, Reade believes in Erasmus's satiric darts rather than Luther's or Knox's cudgels. Firm convictions make heroes and martyrs, but they also contribute to antagonism and oppression. Modern man should be open to the three sides of any given question. Reade's historic heroes are limited by the narrowness of their own times and, in their passivity, represent the true spirit of the world he is describing.

Nevertheless, as its title suggests, *The Cloister and the Hearth* deals with the tension that Reade saw as symptomatic of the end of the Middle Ages, that between the Church and the family, between celibacy and marriage, and between the contemplative and the active life. The novel's comment on mediaeval religion and, by extension, on a romanticised view of the pre-Reformation Church, is as deliberate and critical as its opposition to the 'heroic' view of history. The central tragedy of the story derives from the Church's imposition of celibacy on its clergy, and this Reade sees both as a restriction of personal freedom and as a perversion of human sexuality. Celibacy distorts relationships and infects public morality. To the novelist himself, his enforced bachelorhood as the Fellow of an unreformed Oxford College was a vexing survival of a defunct prejudice. At the end of his novel his anger breaks through the otherwise tolerant surface:

> Thus, after life's fitful fever these true lovers were at peace. The grave, kinder to them than the Church, united them for ever; and now a man of another age and nation, touched with their fate, has laboured to built their tombstone, and rescue them from long and unmerited oblivion.

> He asks for them your sympathy, but not your pity.

> No, put this story to a wholesome use. . . .

> I ask your sympathy, then, for their rare constancy and pure affection, and their cruel separation by a vile heresy in the bosom of the Church; but not your pity for their early but happy end.

The vile heresy is celibacy—'an invention truly fiendish'— and the story is intended to stand as a warning to a freer and maturer age, one that has outgrown the restrictions accepted by its benighted ancestors. Like Kingsley in his *Hypatia,* Reade finds a relevant modern message in a study of pre-Reformation Christianity; he assents to progress which moves men away from superstition, and he hints at the dangers to the nineteenth century of a revival of monasticism. Unlike the yet more rabid and unbalanced Kingsley, however, Reade might strike us elsewhere as being suprisingly tolerant of the abuses he attacks; he implies criticism rather than attempting frontal assaults on moral patterns that his characters take for granted. Gerard and Margaret accept the state of society in which they find themselves, they see its shortcomings and argue over them; they suffer, but they submit only to love each other at a distance.

The novel moves forward to its key, the revelation that the house in the Brede Kirk Straet will eventually bear the inscription: '*Haec est parva domus natus qua magnus Eras-*

mus' and we know that Erasmus will herald the changes of the sixteenth century. But, in the course of his narrative, Reade has suggested that change is already in the wind. In Rome, Gerard's semi-pagan friend and patron, Fra Colonna, seems determined to prove that the Church's order and its ceremonies derive from only partly suppressed heathen mysteries. As a man of the Renaissance, Colonna is convinced that he lives in a fallen world, and that ancient virtues are to be preferred to modern ones; at times he is little more than yet another of the novelist's mouthpieces—'Thou seest, the heathen were not *all* fools. No more are we. Not *all.'* Although Gerard's journey to Rome does not prove to be a quest, it at least seems to give him sufficient strength and resource to emerge from the temporary atheism, occasioned by the news of Margaret's death, into a quieter, empirical faith. Gerard's rational religion, though we never determine its source and inspiration, looks forward to his son's. In Chapter XCVI he urges the dying Margaret not to invoke a saint as an intercessor, but to turn to Him 'to whom the saints themselves do pray'. She expires with the name Jesu on her lips, to be echoed some time later, at the same hour, by her pining, faithful lover. For Reade the pair have worked out a simple, practical, rational faith which gives some kind of meaning to their muddled, cruel and credulous world. 'To their early death', readers are warned, 'apply your Reason and your Faith, by way of exercise and preparation.' We are also, it seems, being asked to look forward to a temperate Protestantism and to the nineteenth century which is reaping the benefits of the Reformation.

In its time *The Cloister and the Hearth* was often compared favourably to *Romola;* both novels are set in the late fifteenth century, and consider a society which is seeking new directions; both Reade and George Eliot look to some kind of spiritual progress to provide meaning to the hurly-burly of history. Swinburne's essay on Reade attempted, not very successfully, to chart a *via media* between an excessive admiration of *Romola* and, as it now seems, the extraordinary view that George Eliot had been inspired and influenced by the earlier novel. Swinburne affirmed that no rational admirer would dispute the assertion that the author of *The Cloister and the Hearth* 'could not have completed—could not have conceived—so delicate a study in scientific psychology as the idlest or least sympathetic reader of *Romola* must recognise and admire in the figure of Tito', but he urged that there was a 'well-nigh puerile insufficiency of some of the resources by which the story has to be pushed forward or warped round before it can be got into harbour'. Even if he were posing as a strict realist, Swinburne is unnecessarily harsh, but one could hardly expect him to sympathise with the reasons *why* George Eliot manhandles her heroine's boat into the harbour of the plague-stricken village. Romola is capable of growing, maturing, breaking and growing again; for all the vividness of their setting, Read's characters are comparatively static and bland. To George Eliot the human psyche contains an infinite complexity and potential for choice; to Reade the details of a confused, irrational, and various external world present the only reality that an artist can paint. George Eliot is sure of her moral bearings, and she makes sense of history because of it; Reade looks at fragmentary experience, and takes the design of the whole for

granted without caring to explain what the design means. Arthur Conan Doyle is said to have paid tribute to *The Cloister and the Hearth* by describing it as like 'going through the Dark Ages with a dark lantern'. The dimness of Reade's kindly guiding light now only allows us the odd glimpse of the faded brightness of his historical vision.

'It has been said', Samuel Butler remarked in an aside in *Erewhon Revisited,* 'that though God cannot alter the past, historians can; it is perhaps because they can be useful to Him in this respect that He tolerates their existence.' Butler's theological premisses might now strike us as soundly based, but to most nineteenth-century readers an historian was not simply tolerated by Heaven, he was an inspired unfolder and explainer of the ways of God to man. To an age of progress and ringing grooves of change, the study of history offered proof that men were moving efficiently and inexorably onwards, drawn towards the climax of Creation by a divine force. If God, for a growing number, did not exist, it proved intellectually convenient to replace Him with a new faith in an evolving, progressing, creative humanity. The two propositions were not mutually exclusive, even though a religious man might be tempted to settle for social passivity, while the atheist opted for revolution; both were interpreting and expressing the *ens realissimum,* and both were proving useful to their God.

In literature a more significant moral and cultural gulf now divided those who continued to believe in an unchanging human condition, from those who held, with Sir Walter Scott, that man was conditioned by his environment. It was an argument that had ancient roots in the Pelagian controversy of the fourth and fifth centuries, and it is still shaping branching opinions in our own. Henry Fielding's eighteenth-century lawyer in *Joseph Andrews* is 'not only alive, but hath been so these four thousand years'. In the Dedicatory Epistle to *Ivanhoe,* however, Scott suggested that for the majority of his readers it was easier to accept the foreignness of a backward and distant country than that of another age. A modern gentleman reader 'surrounded by all the comforts of an Englishman's fireside' was

> not half so much disposed to believe that his own ancestors led a very different life from himself; that the shattered tower, which now forms a vista from his window, once held a baron who would have hung up at his own door without any form of trial; that the hinds, by whom his little pet-farm is managed, a few centuries ago would have been his slaves; and that the complete influence of feudal tyranny once extended over the neighbouring village, where the attorney is now a man of more importance than the lord of the manor.

Fielding's English lawyer might, but for his buckle-shoes, have been recognised on the Athenian stage; Scott's attorney has a social function that changes with time and with shifts in power. The past is another country and as circumstances alter so does the individual's world-view; the novelist's role is not simply to describe mankind in general, but to show how specific men have been moulded by specific historical manners. Fielding spoke with and to the moral prejudices of a neo-classical age; Scott and his successors expressed the confident moralising spirit of their own age.

To the Victorian historical novelists the past was not frozen by eternity, nor was it, unlike the scenes of Keats's Grecian Urn, rendered eternal, silent, and unravished by art. To Scott's successors history was contemporary, synchronic and enveloping; it was living and vibrating in the present, and the artist represented its reality as if it were an act of personal memory. The past reinforced rather than undermined the present. Though to many Victorians the past, like the sea lapping Tennyson's Ithaca, moaned with many voices, those voices seemed to call for continued advance into the future.

An anonymous critic discusses the role of history in historical fiction:

We have ever considered writers of historical romances, tales, and novels, to be under a greater moral responsibility than the compilers of real history. For the reader, yielding to their profession, is, at the outset, disarmed of his enquiring spirit; and as an almost unbounded liberty of blending truth and fiction is assumed, the points of pretension are not very easily tangible. The business of such writers being to illustrate truth by invention, they have a wide field for incidents which, vividly and for effect, artificially put together, are the means of making impressions (true or false), whether of particular characters or times. And, as they are not tied down to any necessary chain or succession of facts, they may make many incidents so bear upon *one* as to give it a peculiar force, and so engage the affections or interest of the reader as to make the impressions almost indelible. So much has the taste of the day run into these historical fictions, that we suspect that ideas received from general history are becoming more vague, and in the minds of many, superseded by such as have arisen from the more engaging narratives of those picturesque authors. History has in this respect, perhaps, been losing ground, retreating back to her old regions of poetry, and laying aside the mantle of everyday truth for the fanciful vestments of theatrical representation.

From "Irish Tales," in Blackwood's Edinburgh Magazine, *May, 1836.*

AMERICAN HISTORICAL FICTION

Ernest E. Leisy

SOURCE: "Colonial America," in *The American Historical Novel,* University of Oklahoma Press, 1950, pp. 21-67.

[*In the excerpt that follows, Leisy describes a number of historical novels written about the American colonies, main-*

taining that a majority of them focus on themes such as Puritanism, conflicts with Native Americans, and witchcraft.]

The Southern Colonies

In the colonial South there was an abundance of incidents to invite romantic treatment by novelists. The arrival of the first white settlers in Virginia, the Carolinas, and Maryland; the Smith-Pocahontas romance; the Virginia Massacre of 1622; life in Jamestown under Governor Berkeley at the time of Bacon's Rebellion; events at the capital of Williamsburg; the Yemassee wars in Carolina—these, as well as the romantic careers of Virginia's Governor Spotswood and young Washington, were each the subject of historical fiction at one time or another.

The primacy of the Old Dominion made her a natural favorite among writers of the historical novel. The Virginia depicted in American fiction was a highly romantic land, a land of cavaliers, in contrast to the haven of criminals depicted by Defoe and the Elizabethan dramatists. . . .

The episode which appealed to novelists more than any other in the early history of Virginia was the rescue of Captain John Smith by the Indian maid Pocahontas. Whether fact or legend (Smith first recalled the story after Pocahontas appeared at the Court of St. James's), here was the essence of romance—the flower of chivalry saved from a cruel beheading by a radiant daughter of nature. John Davis, an English traveler, touched on the theme in *The First Settlers of Virginia* (1802); John Esten Cooke, under the pseudonym Anas Todkill, contributed a "memoir," *My Lady Pocahontas* (1885); and an Englishman, David Garnett, published the most detailed account as *Pocahontas* (1933).

Davis, after a sojourn of several years in Virginia, the Carolinas, and Georgia, briefly mentioned the episode in his *Travels* (1802). He refurbished it in *The First Settlers of Virginia, an Historical Novel* (1802), and expanded it in *Captain Smith and Princess Pocahontas* (1805), with historical material copied almost verbatim from Robertson and Belknap. From the slightness of the plot it is clear that Davis little sensed the dramatic values inherent in his materials. The episode in which Pocahontas intervenes in the Captain's behalf is brief, comes too early, and is treated without suspense. After Smith's supposed death, Pocahontas is comforted by John Rolfe, whom she later marries. The couple leave with their little son for England, where Pocahontas attracts much attention, but soon succumbs to a fever. The book, though it bears the subtitle of "historical novel," is really a plotless chronicle of travel, embellished with romantic sidelights on the Indians and the boundless forests.

Cooke's account of Smith includes glimpses of Shakespeare's England prior to and after the founding of Jamestown. Couched in the semiarchaic style of the Puritan Anas Todkill, the memoir is mainly a love tragedy, a tribute to the devotion of a gentle maid to a courageous cavalier. But dark days are ahead. There are the machinations of three leaders, who, by disputing Smith's authority, force him to go back to England. Pocahontas, supposing Smith dead, assuages her sorrow by serving the infant colony as a protecting deity. But she is seized by the buccaneer Argall, who thus hopes to curb the power of her father, Powhatan. Eventually Rolfe wins her, and takes her with him to England. There she is admired by royalty. On a chance meeting with Smith at the Globe Theater she sees William Shakespeare, who confesses she served as inspiration for his Miranda! Fanciful as this memoir is, it carefully follows Smith's own account in *The Generall Historie of Virginia,* and it conveys the atmosphere of the period. . . .

The Virginia Massacre in 1622 was the next episode in Virginia history to appeal to writers of fiction. It might be observed in passing that "massacre" was a euphemism applied whenever the Indians got the upper hand in combat between the two races; if the reverse was true, it was dubbed a "bloody victory." The "massacre" of 1622, following the period of good will engendered by Smith and Powhatan, came at a time when the settlers around Jamestown had let their fortifications fall into disuse. After Powhatan's death in 1618, his brother Opechancanough felt that the whites should be expelled before it might be too late. Accordingly, he rallied the tribes and raided the outlying plantations, killing some four hundred persons and devastating much property.

This massacre furnished the background of two short romances, *Ruth Emsley* (1850), by William H. Carpenter, and *The Head of a Hundred* (1895), by Maud Wilder Goodwin. In *Ruth Emsley,* the betrothed of George Pierce is taken captive during the general uprising, but is rescued in the nick of time by a young chief—an intervention which enables George and Ruth to be happily united.

The Head of a Hundred resorts to the courtly style of Elizabethan romance in relating the fortunes of a young physician who comes to Jamestown after having been flouted in England by the spirited Elizabeth Romney. Shortly after, she too arrives with a shipload of maids as wives for the settlers. On the voyage she has had the misfortune to break her arm, which offers the physician an opportunity to help her. She spurns further advances, although at his insistence she accepts custodianship of his ancestral ring while he is away on a mission to King Accomac. On the way, his boat picks up John Rolfe and his motherless son. The story comes to its climax during the devastating massacre, when the love of the "head of a hundred" for Elizabeth finally triumphs. Despite conventional plots, both novels blend history and fiction fairly well. . . .

The next group of novels on colonial Virginia center about Bacon's Rebellion in 1676. This rebel attack on excessive taxation and arbitrary government came, significantly enough, just a century before the colonies united in revolt against royal authority. In the course of the long reign of Sir William Berkeley as the royal governor, the conflict between his will and that of the people was heading toward a crisis. The immediate provocation of the uprising was the dilatory policy of the Governor about Indian depredations. Some even accused him of trading with the Indians for personal profit. Whatever truth there may have been in the accusations, the young rebel Bacon, by rallying the people against the forces of despotism, became a symbol of warning for the future in colonial affairs.

In William A. Caruthers' story based on this event, *The Cavaliers of Virginia, or the Recluse of Jamestown* (1834), the Governor is anxious for a leading beauty, Virginia Fairfax, to marry his adopted son, Frank Beverly. This hope is challenged by the young cavalier Bacon, who is leading the people's cause against the royal governor. In the struggle which ensues, Bacon is thrown into prison to await death, but public opinion rallies to his defense, forces Berkeley into temporary retirement, and enables Bacon to win the celebrated beauty.

Although the author based his story on Burk's *History of Virginia,* he adapted his material considerably to meet the requirements of romance. According to the record, Bacon, instead of being awarded the lovely Miss Fairfax, died from a fever at the point of victory. The Gothic subplot of Caruthers' story transfers, on doubtful authority, the regicide Whalley from New England to a cave near Jamestown, where he may serve conveniently as an ally to the cavaliers. The allies of Bacon were really not cavaliers at all, but small farmers. In these respects, as well as in his verbose, rhetorical style, Caruthers was writing under the direct influence of Sir Walter Scott. He deserves credit for managing his double plot with no little dexterity, but it is obvious that he was more interested in his role as storyteller than as historian. His imaginary Virginia, with its absurd mysteries and melodramatic villains, had little basis in reality.

A more realistic version of the Bacon-Berkeley quarrel appeared in St. George Tucker's *Hansford* (1857). Tucker, the grandson of the Revolutionary jurist, tried to reconcile the diverse opinions concerning Sir William handed down by history, but relied mainly on Kercheval's *History of the Valley of Virginia.* He considered Berkeley a brave cavalier who was warped to bloody excesses by his insane loyalty to Charles II. When, after Bacon's death, Berkeley recovered power for a short time, he put to death so many leaders in the rebellion that even Charles, on replacing him, exclaimed, "That old fool has killed more people in that naked country than I have done for the murder of my father."

According to the novel, Thomas Hansford, a rebel friend of Nathaniel Bacon, is betrothed to Virginia Temple, the charming daughter of a member of the House of Burgesses. The Temple family is opposed to the match and favors the courtly Alfred Bernard, a villainous rival. When the temporizing policy of the Governor results in open rebellion, Hansford is dismissed by the family, while Bernard shines at the birthnight ball. Then Bacon's men defeat the Indians; but the Governor rescinds the young man's commission. The attack on the government follows, with the rebels routing the cavaliers and forcing Berkeley to leave. Unable to hold the town for long, they set it afire. Three months later Bacon dies from dysentery, and Hansford's romance ends in tragedy. On a secret visit to Virginia, Hansford is trapped by Bernard, who turns out to be his illegitimate brother. Although Bernard expresses remorse for his brother's execution, he soon sails for England with Berkeley, and dies later in a popish plot. Virginia, another conventionally tragic heroine, accepts her fate.

In summing up his view of the rebellion, Tucker expresses

the opinion that Bacon was impelled in his course by his intense desire for fame. In style as well as in point of view, *Hansford* reflects a growing sense of realism in the writing of historical fiction.

Half a century later, Mary Johnston based her romance, *Prisoners of Hope* (1898), on this same uprising of bondservants and slaves against Governor Berkeley. On the plantation of Colonel Verney, the tobacco king, Godfrey Landless, bondservant from Newgate, has fallen in love with the Colonel's daughter Patricia. She is also being formally courted by her cousin, Sir Charles Carew, who has come from England to replenish his fortune, though he is now engrossed by her beauty. After Patricia spurns Landless, he heads an insurrectionary organization. This action leads to his imprisonment and to Patricia's abduction by the Indians. On her recapture by Landless, she confesses her love for him; but her father bans the rebellious bondsman to the forest, while Patricia, in the key of sentimental romance, vows eternal celibacy. The atmosphere of the period is well conveyed, with its laced and brocaded ladies, its silk-stockinged men, its convicts and slaves, and its scenes in the House of Burgesses, at the Governor's ball, and in tobacco fields. Matters of topical interest are discussed, like the Act of Uniformity and the Navigation Laws, and a fresh point of view emerges in the commoner's asserting himself; but the work as a whole is in the romantic manner of an age before realism set in. . . .

The valley of the Shenandoah held the greatest romantic appeal for John Esten Cooke, a native of the region. In *The Virginia Comedians* (1854) he drew a mellow picture of its brocaded gentry in the days immediately preceding the Revolution. He depicted such diversions as the earliest theater in the colonies, fox hunts, cavalier balls, the Williamsburg fair and the Jamestown races. But the center of interest is the love story.

While horseback riding near his ancestral home, Effingham Hall, a short distance from Williamsburg, young Champ Effingham, a blasé Oxonian, meets Beatrice Hallam of Hallam's theatrical troupe, recently arrived from London. He calls on her at the Raleigh Tavern, falls madly in love with her, and even joins the cast. His father naturally is incensed, for Champ might easily marry Clare Lee, a gentleman's daughter. Worse, Beatrice has the hardihood to reject the Byronic young gentleman in favor of the proletarian Charles Waters, who has chanced to save her life when her boat capsizes. Later, in desperation, Champ tries to abduct her, stabs Charles, and is obliged to leave the country. Waters recovers, however, and Beatrice eventually marries him, while Champ, after a sojourn in Europe, returns to marry Clare. In the second volume the interest shifts from Beatrice, who goes into a fatal decline, to the middle-class Waters family. The story closes on the aroused opposition to the Stamp Act, led by "the man in the red cloak," Patrick Henry.

A sequel, *Henry St. John* (1856), notes the strong undercurrent of colonial revolt, in which Virginians were the leaders. "Charles Waters was the *brain,* Henry the tongue, Jefferson the pen, and Washington the sword of the Revolution." St. John, a great-grandson of Pocahontas, expresses the general opposition to Lord Dunmore after the haughty governor dissolves the House of Burgesses. Following a duel over the beautiful Bonnybel Vane, and following Dunmore's refusal to give him a commission, St. John in final desperation leaves for the frontier. The novel, based on Campbell's *Virginia* and on early files of the *Virginia Gazette,* blends history and romance better than its predecessor, but it is too attenuated for the modern reader. As romancer and historian, Cooke did "more than any other to popularize the legendary view of Revolutionary Virginia. His intimate knowledge of historical details did not correct his view of colonial life, but only served to make his picture of it seem more real to those who read him. Not only has he impressed his conception of colonial life upon untrained historians like Page and novelists like Mary Johnston and Hallie Ermine Rives; he has even influenced so well trained a historian as John Fiske, who in his *Old Virginia and Her Neighbors* betrays the influence of Cooke's *Virginia: A History of the People* (1883). . . .

The beginnings of another colony, Maryland, are the theme of *Sir Christopher* (1901), by Maud Wilder Goodwin. This romance of a Maryland manor in 1644 pictures the life of the immediate descendants of the people in her earlier book, *The Head of a Hundred.* Sir Christopher Neville, a Roundhead, after being refused by the young widow Elinor Calvert because of religious differences, comes to Maryland as overseer of a seven-thousand-acre estate given by Lord Baltimore to Mrs. Calvert and her young son. Neville further incurs the dislike of the Calverts, who are fairly hospitable to persons of other faiths, when he is thought to have killed Father Mohl. Then the pirate Ingle on his deathbed confesses the murder, and the way is open for Elinor and Sir Christopher to wed. Among the historical characters introduced are Giles Brent, deputy governor, Councilor Claiborne, and Sir William Berkeley. The work is one of few on the Papist-Protestant conflict along the border between Maryland and Virginia, but it has barely survived the generation that produced it.

An earlier and much livelier novel of colonial Maryland, *Rob of the Bowl* (1838), by John P. Kennedy, pictures the conflict between Protestants and Catholics at a slightly later date (1681) than in *Sir Christopher.* When King Charles orders all Catholic officers in the province to be replaced by Protestants, there is a flare-up. Blanche Warden, however, has troubles of her own, for she is loved by Albert Verheyden, Lord Baltimore's secretary, as well as by Cocklecroft, member of a smuggling ring. A duel fails to materialize, but one rainy night Albert loses his way and arrives at a deserted house on the seashore, known as the Wizard's Chapel. At this smugglers' rendezvous he is taken captive, but the mysterious cripple Rob, who transports himself on a bowl, recognizes Albert as his own long-lost son and helps him to escape. Later, when Rob publicly confesses his paternity and repents his smuggling activities, the council forgives him and jails Cocklescroft. As the story closes, Blanche and Albert are to be married.

Clearly the importance of this book does not lie in originality of plot or characters. The introduction of the smugglers, and the author's manner of alternating history with fiction and then blending the two, mark Kennedy as a devoted follower of Scott, although his style is more brisk.

There are overtones, also, of Elizabethan drama. Garret Weasel and his wife, keepers of the Crow and Archer, are well realized, and the scenes at the fisherman's hut are excellent. Albert appears too saintly, but the proprietary, Lord Calvert, is well portrayed. He is tolerant toward Protestants, even though their active antagonism is shown to underlie much of the trouble in the colony. The things, then, that make *Rob of the Bowl* a satisfying work for the reader of historical romance are a beautiful heroine, a hero with clouded ancestry, smugglers plying their trade, picturesque tavern scenes, an abduction and a rescue, excitement, and a happy ending. All this is presented in a style that knows no lassitude, and the story is readily enjoyable today.

The beginnings of South Carolina have been ably described by her leading novelist, William Gilmore Simms. In *The Yemassee* (1835) the theme is the conflict between the early settlers and the powerful Yemassee Indians, abetted by designing Spaniards in Florida. The setting of the romance is Pocota-ligo, ancient seat of the tribe, headed in 1715 by Sanutee and his wife Matiwan. Their son, Occonestoga, has been bribed into betraying the tribe to the encroaching whites, after which his mother in a moving scene kills him rather than have him publicly dishonored. The love story centers about Gabriel Harrison, who is really Governor Craven, and Bess Matthews, daughter of a Puritan preacher. This use of an "unknown" character Simms borrows from Scott, while the exciting attack upon the blockhouse comes from Cooper. His Indians, like Cooper's, lament their unhappy fate in metaphorical language, but they are more realistic, more ferocious, and shrewder than Cooper's. Some of the incidents come from legends told Simms by his grandmother, but the vividness of the setting is the result of the author's alert personal observation. *The Yemassee* is a thrilling story, as is natural where men surrounded by danger battle for survival. Simms, in telling it, displays unusual gifts of narrative.

Some twenty years later, Simms wrote another colonial romance of South Carolina, *The Cassique of Kiawah* (1859). The narrative skips lightly over an Indian insurrection to describe pioneer life and smuggling activities in and about infant Charleston in 1684. The scene shifts from the deck of a privateer to the low drinking houses on the Ashley and then to the fashionable masquerades of the town. The cassique, Sir Edward Berkeley, brother of the Virginia governor, has built a spacious house at Kiawah for his family, consisting of his wife Olive, his infant son, and his domineering mother-in-law. Olive has been in love with his younger brother, Harry, a buccaneer of the Drake and Cavendish school, and has married Edward only after being assured that Harry has been lost at sea. Tortured by the realization that she cannot love her husband and nagged by her mother, she becomes a melancholiac with visions of her lover at night. When Harry returns as the Captain Calvert who supplied the colony with Spanish booty, he brings with him his Spanish wife, Zulieme, who before long becomes the belle of Charleston society. One night Sir Edward and Olive meet Harry, but before the old love is revived, Olive dies in an Indian attack, and Harry Zulieme have an heir.

Although the history is of subsidiary interest and the action drags in places, there is a skillful contrast of personalities in the fun-loving Zulieme and her matter-of-fact husband, as well as in the idealistic cassique and his pensive wife. The Indians are not so well individualized as in *The Yemassee,* but the corrupt governor in his relation with smugglers is well characterized, and the early life of Charleston is ably depicted. Simms, despite his fondness for the melodramatic, was a true raconteur.

The New England Colonies

Life in colonial New England presented a bleak contrast to the gay, sophisticated round of activities in the southern colonies. The northern colonists were interested in the salvation of men's souls, rather than in social frivolities or business, although they seem not to have been averse to driving a shrewd bargain with the Indians or with one of their countrymen. Themes which have stirred the imagination of novelists are: Puritanism, with its religious conflicts; Indian life and insurrections; the trouble with the regicides; the loss of the Connecticut charter; and the witchcraft frenzy. Besides these subjects from the seventeenth century, there were others, such as smuggling, the land-grant controversy between New York and New Hampshire, and the French and Indian Wars, which led up to exciting events in pre-Revolutionary Boston.

Puritan life is glimpsed in an early novel entitled *A Peep at the Pilgrims in Sixteen Hundred Thirty-Six* (1824), by Mrs. Harriet V. Cheney. Her two-volume "peep" is fairly comprehensive, extending from Plymouth to Boston, New Amsterdam, and Hartford, as it follows the romance of a newly arrived Anglican and a Puritan maid. It enables the reader to meet the affable Miles Standish and the waggish Peregrine White, as well as to hear Governor Winslow and Governor Winthrop discuss political and religious dissensions; and, for good measure, it lets him attend Governor Kieft's ball with the hero, before assisting Captain Mason in a hairbreadth rescue of the heroine from the Pequods. Obviously, Mrs. Cheney was trying to incorporate in her plot too much history, gleaned from Morton, Neal, and Irving, and it impeded the progress of her narrative. A plethora of historical matter was a problem that was to plague novelists for many a year.

A thorn in the side of the Plymouth colony was the roisterer Thomas Morton. When he was not annoying them with selling rum and firearms to the Indians, he appears to have been in league with Sir Philip Gardiner in some of his dark schemes. John Lothrop Motley, before becoming a famous historian, wrote a fantasy about these men of mischief and their conflict with the colonists, which he called *Merry-Mount* (1849). According to this account, the cavalier Morton had been obliged to leave England because of indiscretions involving love and money, and, dissatisfied on reaching Virginia, had come up to Plymouth, where with a set of lawless resolutes he lords it over the Pilgrims at Merry-Mount near by. The merrymaking this spouter of Horace and his greenwood crew indulge in is at such variance with the austere code of his neighbors that Morton soon finds himself in the hands of Captain Standish. But the good-humored man frees himself and once more commands his roisterers in a greenwood fortress before he is finally deported. Meanwhile, Sir Philip saves the heroine from a wolf, but is prevented from winning her hand, even though he fights a duel in her behalf. Clearly, the grim Puritans were winning the day, and the most intolerant of all was Governor Endicott at Naumkeak.

Motley had Morton's own account, *The New English Canaan* (1637), as source. Evidently, too, he had read the Stratford playwright, not only for the hawking scene and the scene in the fortress, but for such low comedy types in the ribald crew as the sprawling Rednape, the clumsy Bootefish, Canary Bird, and Peter Cakebread. The Elizabethan period was not remote, and these characters and scenes might be transferred with slight change of atmosphere. Rich as the story was in local color and vivid factional strife, it never attained the compact force of Hawthorne's contemporary tale, "The May-Pole of Merry Mount." . . .

The outstanding romance about colonial New England is of course Hawthorne's *The Scarlet Letter* (1850). This distinction belongs to it by virtue of a thorough assimilation of historical fact, together with the unfolding of a perennially interesting human story, one motivated at every point by the conditions and circumstances of the times. Minister Dimmesdale's sin of concealing an adulterous relation with Hester Prynne is set against the reverence of the populace for the man of God. Adultery is conceived of not as an affair of the civil order, but as a problem that concerns the immortal soul. The minister can find peace only through expiation; Hester, because of the public ignominy she has endured, is prepared for a larger view.

The Scarlet Letter, as a tale of human responsibility in terms of Calvinistic preoccupation with the problem of evil, possesses the very stuff of Greek tragedy. Three scenes of communal coloring outline the drama. The opening tableau shows the condemned adulteress led to the scaffold to receive the magistrates' sentence. Then, at the Governor's Hall the magistrates seek to take Hester's child from her while she is confronted by both the minister and her fiendish husband. Finally, after seven years of penance, climaxed by the holiday scene and the election sermon, it is clear that conformity is better than nature's lawless law. The story owes its somber understanding to the author's latent Puritanism—an insight modified by the critical perspective of a fourth-or fifth-generation descendant. To Hawthorne passion was of a higher order than intellect; even the church, disregarding the very nature of man, had relied too much on laws and on learning. As a work of art, this gaunt, powerful romance demonstrates that it is not necessary for a historical novel to be cluttered up with historical names and events in order to be effective. If it is true to the spirit of the times, that is sufficient; if, in addition, the action delineated is universal and timeless, the work is a masterpiece.

Before Hawthorne wrote *The Scarlet Letter,* he had made a number of short excursions into the New England of the seventeenth century. In one of these, "The Gentle Boy," he introduced the theme of sectarian conflict by depicting the fate of a winsome Quaker child left helpless among the Puritans. A number of minor novels dealt with sectarian strife. Eliza Buckminster Lee's *Naomi* (1848), although evincing no conspicuous creative ability, is a fair and accurate story of Quaker persecution. *Margaret Smith's Journal* (1849), by John Greenleaf Whittier, is in the form of a pretended diary of an English girl visiting her relatives in the Bay Colony during 1678—79. The main thread of the narrative tells of Rebecca Rawson's jilting a noble youth in favor of a baronet's son. The baronetcy proves spurious, however, and the husband a bigamist who deserts her in England. Interpolated in the diary are various historical references: to the persecution of Quakers and witches, to Sir Christopher Gardiner, John Eliot, Cotton Mather, and Michael Wigglesworth. In general, historical and fictitious elements are interwoven in much the style of Hawthorne's "The Gentle Boy."

Joseph Banvard's *Priscilla, or the Trials for the Truth* (1854) tells of a girl who escapes to America in order to avoid proselyting by Anglicans, only to discover Puritans equally in tolerant. With her family, she finally takes refuge among the Baptists of Rhode Island. *The Knight of the Golden Melice* (1856), by John Turvill Adams, connects the mysterious Sir Christopher Gardiner with plans to establish Catholicism in 1630 in the Massachusetts Bay Colony. Governor Winthrop, though he differs from Gardiner in creed, respects him highly, and trusts his relations with the Pequots. In other versions, as for example, Miss Sedgwick's *Hope Leslie,* Sir Christopher is regarded with suspicion. In Motley's *Merry-Mount* he appears a Puritan saint in Plymouth and a worldly plotter at Merry-Mount.

Yet another novel to bring out Puritan intolerance was J. G. Holland's *The Bay-Path* (1857). At Agawam (Springfield), about 1650, Magistrate Pynchon is banished by Cotton and Norton for writing an unorthodox book about Puritanism, and a young woman whom he has befriended is accused of witchcraft and executed. Holland, editor of the *Springfield Republican,* and later the first editor of *Scribner's Monthly,* knew local legend thoroughly but chafed under the restrictions imposed upon him by history, and he wrote rather verbosely.

The second generation of Puritans, according to Esther Forbes's *Paradise* (1937), were not altogether pious and gloomy, but were earthy men and women, contriving, eating, lusting, and, on occasion, warring with the Indians. In the novel, Jude Parre, gentleman, in 1639 acquires from the Indians a large tract of land some twenty miles inland from Boston. Here he founds the town of Canaan, builds his estate, Paradise, rears his family of five children, and is looked up to by the community. But troubles are ahead, both in the family and with the Indians. Fenton, Jude's lusty son, brings home a siren, Bathsheba, causing the gawky Salome, who admires him, to commit adultery with his brother Christopher. The public branding of the couple hurts Jude, who serves as justice for Canaan, and he dies. Bathsheba develops into a mad schizophrenic, while Fenton goes on to martial and amatory exploits as a squire extraordinary. His fine-grained, passionate sister, Jazan, has a frustrated marriage with a fanatical preacher, Forethought Fearing, who dares, however, to defend Bathsheba in public. The Indian troubles, culminating in King Philip's War, hurl the community into a maelstrom of death, from which the group at Paradise emerge, though not without scars. In this fast-moving story, history and romance are deftly interwoven, with due regard for social, political, and religious tensions, and without a trace of sentimentalism. But the characters are typed, and considering their apparent sophistication, undermotivated. A story pivoted on adultery and branding unfortunately courts comparison with *The Scarlet Letter,* a classic that not merely interprets the past, but illuminates human nature regardless of fashions in psychology.

Most of the novels about early New England revolve about the relations of the whites with the Indians. By the eighteen twenties, when the first of these novels appeared, red men in that region were no longer a menace. As a result, there developed a sentimental attitude toward them. Young women novelists speculated on what kind of husband an Indian would make. That is the question in Lydia M. Child's *Hobomok* (1824) and in Catherine M. Sedgwick's *Hope Leslie* (1827). Young Hobomok, living at Naumkeak (Salem), is so "unwarped by the artifices of civilized life" that he gives up his white wife and infant upon the unexpected return of her betrothed, long mourned as dead. This is probably as well, for the author's picturing of domestic life is better than her handling of her noble red man.

Miss Sedgwick, a preceptress and distinguished literary lady of western Massachusetts, conceived of her task in *Hope Leslie* as illustrating for juvenile readers domestic manners in the seventeenth century. Hope is an orphan, the ward of her uncle Fletcher, with whose son Everell she falls in love. Magawisca, an Indian maiden of high lineage, and also a member of the Fletcher household, becomes so attached to Everell that, during an Indian raid, when he is about to be executed by her tribe, she outdoes Pocahontas by catching a blow which lops off her arm.

Seven years later the scene shifts to Governor Winthrop's household in Boston, where the villain, Sir Philip Gardiner, abetted by Thomas Morton of Merry-Mount, has designs on Hope; but when he attempts to abduct her, his "page" warns her of her danger from the Papist and notorious bigamist. In the further development of this overinvolved plot, Hope almost loses the man she really loves, but the end comes out all right. Aside from presenting the trials of the young people, this highly moral tale depicts the persecution of the Indians by the Puritan oligarchy. The author consulted the leading authorities, Hubbard, Trumbull, and Heckewelder, with a view to illustrating, as she says, "not the history, but the character of the times." She has succeeded in doing this without impeding her narrative. *Hope Leslie,* though diffuse and sentimental, is plausible; it rightly enjoyed wide popularity in its day.

The strained relations between the Indians and the whites in New England culminated in King Philip's War, 1675–76. This conflict marked the final desperate effort of the Indians to preserve their hunting grounds and to keep the whites from imposing their form of civilization upon them. James Fenimore Cooper, in *The Last of the Mohicans,* had dealt with the red man's final stand in New York, and he now undertook to picture the tragic fate of this race in New England. *The Wept of Wish-ton-Wish*

(1829), based in the main on Trumbull's *History of Connecticut,* was laid in the infant settlement of Hartford. The outpost of the stalwart Puritan, Mark Heathcote, is attacked and his daughter Ruth taken captive by the Indians. She is long wept for, but when, years later, hope for her return has been abandoned, she is discovered to be the wife of Conanchet, sachem of the Narragansets, to whom she has borne a child. Her life ends in tragedy, for after disowning her family, she loses her husband at the hands of Uncas, the Mohican chieftain. Cooper was quite in his element in this novel in depicting the Indian raids on the defenseless villages and farms, in particular the attack on the blockhouse. The leader of the villagers against the Indian attack is Goffe, the regicide, who figures in several romantic novels thereafter. Unfortunately, the author had a deep-seated antipathy for the Puritan character, and in this novel harps on their absurdities, especially the hypocrisies of one Rev. Meek Wolfe. So constantly is this worthy made to reprimand his followers that some readers have thought him intended as a caricature of Cotton Mather, but Mather is referred to in another connection. *The Wept of Wish-ton-Wish* is not one of Cooper's best efforts.

Two other early novels which concentrated on King Philip's War were *Mount Hope* (1851) by G. H. Hollister, a Connecticut lawyer and diplomat, and *The Doomed Chief* (1860) by Daniel P. Thompson, a Vermont novelist of the mid-century. Hollister focused attention on King Philip rather than on the regicides, but lacked imaginative power to bring out the dramatic aspects of his tale. Thompson was hardly more successful. In *The Doomed Chief,* Deacon Mudridge of Plymouth orders some Indians hanged for a crime they did not commit—an act which so incenses Metacom (King Philip) that he threatens bloody warfare. Meanwhile, the zealous Deacon attempts to have his nephew Sniffkin marry Madian, a girl beloved by Vane Willis. In the warfare which follows, Vane, because he is stigmatized as a Quaker, is unable to obtain a commission. Mudridge even accuses him of having made away with Madian. Finally, Vane helps inflict a severe defeat upon the Indians, pushing them as far as Mount Hope and confusing them to the extent that King Philip is slain and Queen Wetamoo drowns herself. Madian is found at last, and the Deacon punished. Thompson appears to have regarded the war an infliction from God for decadent manners. Despite his use of Mather's *Magnalia,* Sparks's *Life of Eliot,* Thatcher's *Indian Biography,* Carver's *Travels,* and possibly Mason's *History of the Pequot War* and Hubbard's *Narratives,* he could not draw a fair picture of the Puritans. His portraits of King Philip, John Eliot, and Roger Williams are acceptable, but in general he lacked imagination to transmute the events of history.

The fate of the regicides in New England was the subject of several works of fiction. Cooper's *The Wept of Wish-ton-Wish . . .* [has] already been mentioned. Upon the restoration of Charles II after the Commonwealth period, three men who had signed the death warrant of Charles I—Goffe, Whalley, and Dixwell—fled England and spent the remainder of their lives hiding in Puritan havens in the New World. The first novelist to use the regicide theme was Sir Walter Scott in *The Peveril of the Peak* (1822). Doubtless the popularity of this work inspired one of his ardent disciples, James McHenry, but lately come from Ireland to Baltimore, to use the theme in *The Spectre of the Forest* (1823). His pictures of Goffe's activities in Connecticut were spectral, however, rather than historical, and were designed to heighten the Gothic effects of his narrative. The few historical events—Sir Edmund Andros's attack upon Frontenac and the witchcraft episode (which McHenry asserted had been suppressed by Connecticut historians), as well as the escapades of Goffe—were employed merely to vary and complicate the machinery of horror in a rather slight novel. Writers in other media did comparatively better. Delia Bacon's "The Regicides," Hawthorne's short story "The Grey Champion," and J. N. Barker's play *Superstition* (1826) certainly were in no way inferior to the novels on the theme of the regicides.

The loss of the Connecticut charter in 1687 was the subject of one novel, *The Romance of the Charter Oak* (1871). Its author was William Seton, a military officer and scholar. After creating interest in Lydia Goffe, the author turned aside to show how the Connecticut colony sought a union with Massachusetts rather than with New York. At the request of James II, Governor Andros demanded that the people of Connecticut return the liberal charter which Charles II had given them in 1662. He was unable to obtain the document, however, since the people had hidden it in the hollow trunk of an old tree. The story, based on colonial records, Palfrey's *History of New England,* and Bulkeley's *Will and Doom,* combines with an account of political events, interesting observations on the costumes, furniture, and architecture of the period. The narrative lacks animation, however, and is mentioned here only because it memorializes an episode which other novelists overlooked.

A more popular subject for writers of fiction was the witchcraft delusion. Superstition had long been a scourge in Europe, and the mania found its way into Massachusetts and Connecticut toward the end of the seventeenth century. Salem was the principal seat of the delusion. In 1693, after nineteen victims of the craze had been hanged, a revulsion of feeling led to the liberation of all accused persons. The first novel to treat witchcraft in New England was *Rachel Dyer* (1828), by John Neal. This "North American Story," written for English readers, was not a narrative so much as a series of violent, incoherent accusations, and refutations made by Mather, Phips, and Sewall during the trials of Martha Cory, Samuel Parres, Sarah Good, Elizabeth and Rachel Dyer, and the hero-victim, George Burroughs. The author conceded the sincerity of the Puritans, but charged their gloomy state of mind with facilitating belief in witchcraft; once hallucinations sprang up, they quickly multiplied.

Neal declared that "the time was at hand for a Declaration of Independence in the great Republic of Letters," and that knowing that in the view of Englishmen, Irving was only "the American Addison" and Cooper had "just enough reputation not to hazard it by stepping aside into a new path," he, who had too little respect for authorship to risk anything, thought he might call the attention of American "novel writers to what is undoubtedly native

and peculiar." Instead of gaining American followers, however, the egregious Neal, who had recently "exposed" American writers in *Blackwood's Magazine,* attracted the attention of those English critics who were only too ready to accept his assertion that roughness and turgidity were distinctive characteristics of American writers and his grotesque characters truly representative of American life. The most distinct impression left by *Rachel Dyer* is of a too liberal peppering of dashes and exclamation points.

John W. DeForest, a well-known novelist of the mid-nineteenth century, dealt with the Salem delusion in a novelette, *Witching Times,* which appeared in *Putnam's Magazine,* 1856–57. Henry More, after fighting the superstition of the period, is executed for his zeal. His daughter Rachel is also condemned, but is rescued by her husband in a realistic scene. Among the historical figures introduced are Elder Noyse, with his passion for Rachel, the "tyrant" Elder Parris, Judge Hathorne, ancestor of the novelist, and Cotton Mather, who seizes his opportunity for advancement among the clerical oligarchy then in power. DeForest's sense of the historical is not sufficiently imaginative to keep the narrative from dragging. The scene in which Giles Corey is executed by being pressed to death is the only vivid episode in the book. . . .

The eighteenth century found New England either in conflict over boundary disputes, as in the quarrel between Vermont and the York gentry over the Hampshire Grants, or engaged in the French and Indian Wars of the pre-Revolutionary struggle. One novel, *Agnes Surriage* (1886), by Edwin L. Bynner, may serve as a transition between those novels already discussed and those about to follow. It touches on witchcraft, but has more to do with smuggling. In the main, however, it is a love romance, based on the legend of Sir Harry Frankland, previously used by Oliver Wendell Holmes in his ballad "Agnes." According to the story, the young collector of the port of Boston in 1745 falls in love with a beautiful servant at an inn in Marblehead. Agnes, this daughter of a poor fisherman, apparently lives with him for a while in sin, but after they go to Europe and she helps him escape from the wreckage of the earthquake at Lisbon, he marries her in gratitude. John Fiske praised the book as "one of the greatest of American historical novels."

For generations Yankees and Yorkers contested with each other for control of the borderlands between the Connecticut and the Hudson, Yankees contending that Yorkers were solvenly, uneducated, godless folk, and Yorkers convinced that Yankees were pushing, miserly hypocrites. As a matter of fact, Yankees did penetrate into the lands of the Yorkers, and honeycombed upstate New York with their ideas and institutions. By the time of the Revolution the boundary dispute had turned into a class war between landlords and tenants engaged in an agrarian struggle. This controversy over the land was joined with the Revolutionary campaigns of Ethan Allen and Seth Warner in a very popular novel, *The Green Mountain Boys* (1839), by Daniel Pierce Thompson.

Judge Thompson, Vermonter born and bred, considered these episodes in the early history of his state in themselves romantic "with the use of little more fiction than was deemed sufficient to weave them together and impart to the tissue a connected interest." According to his racy account, the Vermonters drove the York state men from the Grants, but the tool of the land-jobbers vowed he would take revenge on the greenwood hero's sweetheart. While her lover was away helping heroic Ethan Allen take Fort Ticonderoga, the villain won over the girl's neutral father, and by calumny secured the defection of the daughter. After Allen was captured, the hero, Seth Warner, joined St. Clair against Burgoyne, who was then descending from the north. During this expedition the young man vindicated himself by rescuing the girl and her father.

Thompson was able to relate his story with something of the animation and suspense which actually characterized the strife because he had the story directly from aged participants. Ethan Allen, St. Clair, Seth Warner, Schuyler, Benedict Arnold, and others move through these scenes freely and humanly—an important advance in historical fiction over such stiff and shadowy portraitures as Cooper's Washington and John Paul Jones. Perhaps the greatest charm of the narrative lies in the piquancy of its provincialism, which triumphs over occasional lapses in idiom. These mountaineer kinsmen of Thompson were fighting, not for adventure merely, but for defense of home. It is only natural that such a stirring appeal to patriotism should have caused the book to run through many editions.

The French and Indian Wars, 1754–63, were fought largely outside the borders of New England. But in *Haverhill, or the Memoirs of an Officer in the Army of Wolfe* (1831), James A. Jones linked mid-eighteenth century Yankee manners with the conflict when he told of the rise of a humble youth from Cape Cod. When Lynn Haverhill's love for Mary Danvers is thwarted by the girl's aristocratic father, who wants her to marry her wealthy cousin Charles, the unhappy youth seeks to prove his worth by going to sea. After rescue in a storm and a period of imprisonment in an Indian camp, he joins Wolfe's army at Quebec. Following the victory on the Plains of Abraham, he comes home to find his mother and his brother dead and his wayward sister gone—reportedly to the West Indies. During his fruitless search for her, he becomes infatuated with a Creole, Margaretta, only to find that his former rival Charles has prior claims, which leaves him free to marry his first love. In spite of its use of the long arm of coincidence, the book is still worth reading. The fact that the narrative is in the first person gives the reader a sense of actual participation in the events. General Wolfe is shown as unpretentious as a clerk in banter, but unsurpassed when energy and decision are required, and noble in the hour of death. No previous author has related with such detail the manners of a New England community— its shooting matches, husking bees, quilting frolics, sleighing parties, wrestling matches, horse races, favorite dishes, courtships, gossip, and superstitions. The style is fluent and seasoned with homely wit, and for once the characters are not impeccable.

Wolfe's defeat of Montcalm at Quebec was only one of the three objectives for which the French and Indian Wars were waged. The others were Louisburg and Ticonderoga.

In the Champlain region there fought a romantic American hero, Major Robert Rogers, whose exploits have been recorded by the historian Francis Parkman, and in fiction by Sir Gilbert Parker in *The Seats of the Mighty* (1896). . . .

Beverly Seaton

SOURCE: "A Pedigree for a New Century: The Colonial Experience in Popular Historical Novels, 1890-1910," in *The Colonial Revival in America,* edited by Alan Axelrod, W. W. Norton & Company, 1985, pp. 278-93.

[*In the following excerpt, Seaton discusses some common characteristics of colonial American historical novels, asserting that they were especially popular among middle-class Americans and that they provided "a spiritual ancestry for liberal religion, patterns for social behavior, comforting reminders of . . . 'racial purity,' and delightful glimpses of a sumptuous style of life.'*]

Between 1890 and 1910, historical novels about the colonial period were very popular with American middle-class readers. During this time, six appeared on the best-seller lists: *Hugh Wynne, Free Quaker* by S. Weir Mitchell, *Richard Carvel* by Winston Churchill, *Janice Meredith* by Paul Leicester Ford, *To Have and to Hold* and *Audrey* by Mary Johnston, and *Alice of Old Vincennes* by Maurice Thompson. In addition, many other popular novelists published colonial historical novels during this period, notably Robert W. Chambers, Maud Wilder Goodwin, Sarah Orne Jewett, Robert Neilson Stephens, and Mary Hartwell Catherwood. For juvenile readers, there were Amanda Douglas's Little Girl series (*A Little Girl in Old New York,* and so on), adventure novels for boys by Everett Tomlinson, Mary Wells Smith's Boy Captive and Young Puritans series, and the fictionalized biographies of Jefferson, Franklin, William Penn, and Lafayette by Hezekiah Butterworth (the editor of *Youth's Companion*). Readers interested in the colonial period also made a successful author of Alice Morse Earle, whose twelve books, published between 1891 and 1903, cover various aspects of colonial life. Publishers capitalized on the current interest in American history by reissuing such colonial historical novels of the past as Henry Peterson's *Pemberton* and *Dulcibel,* Daniel Thompson's *Green Mountain Boys,* and J. G. Holland's *Bay Path,* a novel about the Puritans which in its 1899 Homewood edition is indiscriminately illustrated with hundreds of stereotyped images of the American colonial experience, many not at all related to the period of the story.

In *A Season of Youth,* Michael Kammen pointed out the popularity of historical novels about the American Revolution at the turn of our century and said that this period, like others when such novels were popular, was a time of "cultural indirection" when "national values needed to be defined or redefined" [Michael Kammen, *A Season of Youth: The American Revolution and the Historical Imagination,* 1978]. Certainly we will all agree that at the beginning of the twentieth century all sorts of social and economic changes were apparent. My analysis of these popular books about American colonial life shows that their authors were shaping their perspective on history to an-swer new questions and meet new challenges. These books have many elements in common, which suggest what the American colonial experience must have meant to their readers.

Of course, some of the elements of these books are shared with popular fiction in general. Before focusing on signifi-cant aspects of the colonial theme, therefore, we need to clear the ground of these more general features. One of them is the extensive use of young heroes and heroines, who typically marry at the end of the story. In using young men and women as the main characters, "colonial" writers followed the pattern of most popular novels. Like-wise, the hero is often unusually sympathetic to women, interested in their costumes, fond of reading and flowers (of course, he is also an excellent swordsman and a coura-geous fighter). In popular fiction, the reader identifies with the main character, and if the novelist expects to attract readers of both sexes (and most novelists did at the turn of the century), he must create characters with whom both sexes can identify. Melodramatic elements have been a constant component of popular fiction since its begin-nings, and there is no more stereotyped melodramatic plot element than mysterious parentage, which is very com-mon in these historical novels. Also, dastardly villains and cruel, selfish parents are common melodramatic charac-ters. Colonial historical novels also share two significant stylistic conventions with the general run of popular his-torical novels: the use of the first person to give an element of authenticity and cameo appearances by major historical figures.

While not all the popular historical novels about Ameri-can colonial life focused on the Revolutionary period, most did. Of the biggest best-sellers, for example, only the two by Mary Johnston—*To Have and to Hold* and *Au-drey*—are not set during the Revolution. And these two novels, as well as the historical novels of Maud Wilder Goodwin, are set in the swashbuckling Old South. Mary Catherwood's novels concern the French in the Midwest. Conspicuously missing are novels about the Puritans, who had had their chroniclers among earlier historical novel-ists J. G. Holland, Catharine Maria Sedgwick, Henry Peterson, and Lydia Maria Child.

The absence of novels about the Puritans may be associat-ed with a significant aspect of the fiction I am discussing, the unsympathetic treatment of strict, old-fashioned reli-gion. In *Janice Meredith* [1899], Janice's mother, once pleasant and cheerful, becomes depressed by the loss of her other children and turns to hellfire religion. She wants the fifteen-year-old Janice to marry a Presbyterian clergy-man, a widower with five children. In a Victorian ro-mance, the motherly warnings she gives Janice about her behavior and the state of her soul would have been an ex-pression of the novel's major point of view, but Paul Lei-cester Ford made them the vehicle of fanaticism and de-pression—one more sign of the victory of Henry Ward Beecher over his father, Lyman. Hugh Wynne's stern Quaker father lapses into religious fanaticism also, albeit the Quaker version rather than the Presbyterian. Hugh's father objects to his son's fighting in the Revolution and

to his participation in wordly activities generally. He is dismissed from meeting on July 4, 1776. Similarly, Douw Mauverensen, the Dutch hero of Harold Frederic's *In the Valley,* renounces the strict Calvinism of his clergyman fa-ther.

Even in those novels in which religion is not made an issue, its very absence is a sign that the novelist is not look-ing at our history as the work of God's providential hand. In several of the novels, the only visible representative of religion is a corrupt clergyman—Reverend Allen, Richard Carvel's tutor, for example. Plainly, readers at the turn of the century were not looking for reassurance that God was at work in American history; rather, they were looking for a version of our past that accorded better with contempo-rary views of religion.

By the turn of the century, the victory of liberal Protes-tantism as represented by Henry Ward Beecher over the strict religion of old New England was an acknowledged aspect of our cultural life. Religion had its place, of course, but the strongly morbid tone of Calvinistic theology was unpopular and considered misguided. In *Child Life in Co-lonial Days* [1899], Alice Morse Earle referred to Puritan children pictured in the books of those times as "short-lived and morbid young Christians" and called Isaac Watts "a bigoted old bachelor" and Richard Coddington, author of *For the Instructing of the Younger Sorts of Maids and Boarders at Schools,* a "tiresome old bore." When writing of the books written for Puritan children, she said, "I will not give any of the accounts in full, for the expres-sion of religious thought shown therein is so contrary to the sentiment of today that it would not be pleasing to modern readers." Earlier novelists such as Henry Peter-son and Catharine Maria Sedgwick had shown the harsher aspects of Puritan culture, notably the witchcraft trials and related issues, but only as the darker side of a general-ly positive culture.

The novelists of 1890–1910 ask us to look toward the non-Puritan colonists for our heritage. Their view of Puritan thinking is expressed in an outburst of Gideon Darden, the drunken Church of England clergyman in Mary John-ston's *Audrey* [1902]. Darden attacks Mr. Eliot, a minister from New England who dares to preach a sermon directed at Audrey, an innocent with a damaged reputation: " 'Ye beggarly Scot!' [Darden] exclaimed thickly. 'Ye evil-thinking saint from Salem way, that know the very lining of the Lord's mind, and yet, walking through his earth, see but a poisonous weed in his every harmless flower! Shame on you to beat down the flower that never did you harm!' "

That the author's sympathy here is with a drunken clergy-man reflects another aspect of these novels, one related to the issue of nineteenth-century religion. The authors make very clear that back in colonial days men swore and drank a lot and that perhaps loose women were prominent in good circles; they always explain in some way that times were different then, and we must be understanding. In-stead of showing a past age of sinless men and women, they hasten to display our ancestors as people of the world in every sense. While turn-of-the-century readers might have had more refined manners, they were plainly expect-ed to be worldly as well, to accept such an explanation as this typical one in *Hugh Wynne* [1897]. Wynne recalls the merrymaking of his fellow apprentices: "I liked it well, and, with my aunt's warning in mind, drank but little, and listened to the talk, which was too free at times, as was the bad custom of that day." Hugh was warned by his aunt, incidentally, because he had been drinking too much, a fault which later gets him into much trouble. Many of the young heroes of these novels get drunk, and almost all of them indulge in duels. Readers of the time were very fond of the kind of romantic and exciting action characterized by the duel, and some of the other popular historical novels of the period that were not about American history also featured such high-tempered behavior—Charles Major's *When Knighthood Was in Flower,* for instance, or Henryk Sienkiewicz's *Quo Vadis.*

In characterizing the heroes as young men of liberal habits and quick tempers, our novelists were distancing them from the tamer heroes of Victorian romances. The dashing hero, whether in costume of the Continental army officer or the Virginia Cavalier of the seventeenth century, served as a historical model for a new man, less the Victorian gentleman, more the twentieth-century man-about-town. Our novelists used historical models to justify those changes in manners that were beginning to appear in their own time. Their interest in the hero as a "new man" was less intense, however, than their concern with the heroine.

One of the most striking features of these novels is the uniformity of the characterization of the heroines. Almost without exception, they could be called minxes, a term actually used in most of the books. When we first meet Janice Meredith, for instance, she is being scolded for reading novels, and we see that she is far from repentant after her mother's remarks. We have the same introduction to Alice Roussillon, of *Alice of Old Vincennes.* She, too, is reading romances and reacts to an old priest's chastising by arguing with him. These "new women" are argumentative, willful, courageous, and, above all, flirtatious. As young girls they are tomboys—running races, for example, as do the heroines of *Audrey* and *Cardigan;* besting the hero at throwing the tomahawk, as does the heroine of *The Maid-at-Arms;* or even winning a dueling match with the hero, as Alice does. But when they become women, they are most marked by their impatient willfulness. Some of them are willful to the point of arrogance, as Stephens's heroines Elizabeth Phillipse (*The Continental Dragoon*) or Margaret Winwood (*Philip Winwood*); the same can certainly be said of the younger Janice Meredith. Margaret Winwood goes so far as to engage in spying against the army of Washington, in which her husband serves. Perhaps the two women who love Richard Carvel, Patty Swain and Dolly Manners, best illustrate the old and the new in style of heroine. Patty is the apotheosis of the Victorian heroine—quiet, domestic, fair-minded—while Dolly is the proud and clever woman of the world. Naturally, Richard loves Dolly, although Patty is so much more worthy of his devotion. Worth, in fact, is a very much outmoded concept in feminine attractions when these novelists work out their plots. Beauty, wit, and spirit are the major qualities looked for in the heroines.

I was much struck with a recurring scene in these novels,

which might be called the young woman's rite of passage—her first social appearances dressed in the clothes of a grown woman. The heroine is often a childhood companion of the young hero who fails to realize that the girl has become a woman until he sees her descending the stairs in full regalia. The astonishment of the hero and the triumph of the girl is a set piece in most of these novels. When fourteen-year-old Dolly Manners appears dressed for the Christmas party at Carvel Hall, for instance, Richard's grandfather says, " 'Richard, she has outstripped you, fair and square. You are only an awkward lad, and she—why i'faith, in two years she'll be beyond my protection' " [Winston Churchill, *Richard Carvel,* 1899]. Michael Cardigan is so upset when he first sees Silver Heels (Felicity Warren) dressed up that he engages in a disastrous flirtation with another girl. When Dorothy Varick of *The Maid-at-Arms* appears in her best outfit, the hero does not even recognize her. Alice Roussillon wears her only fancy gown to a ball in order to impress Fitzhugh Beverley, the Virginia gentleman who later marries her and takes her back to a big white house in Virginia (where she belongs, by the way—her real name is Tarleton).

A tragic version of the great scene appears in *Audrey,* when the hero, drunk and angry, causes his young ward Audrey to be dressed up to dance with him at the governor's ball at Williamsburg. Since the town has been speculating that she is his mistress, she is treated with extreme rudeness. Meanwhile he suddenly realizes that she has become a woman and falls in love with her. Clothes do indeed make the woman. Our novelists dwell on the details of clothing and hairstyles, even when the first-person narrator is a male. Hugh Wynne, for instance, explains his unusual interest in women's dress: "If you should wonder how, at this distant day, I can recall her dress, I may say that one of my aunt's lessons was that a man should notice how a woman dressed, and not fail at times to compliment a gown, or a pretty fashion of hair" [Mitchell, *Hugh Wynne*].

The heroines are of course all extremely beautiful, Janice Meredith and Dolly Manners so much so as to test the reader's belief. All of fashionable London is at Dolly's feet; and Janice is loved by every man she meets, perhaps even George Washington (although nothing scandalous is intended). Such prodigious sex appeal annoyed one reader at least, who wrote on the flyleaf of a copy of *Janice Meredith,* owned by Frederick Dickson, "The heroine, Janice, is an insufferable piece of baggage, that every man apparently, for some unknown reason, wants to marry, and she at times is evidently ready to marry any or all of them." Our heroines are not stupid girls; wit naturally demands intelligence. But looks, rather than their minds, are their fortunes. Whether they were in agreement with the hero's politics from the first or had to be won over, they all find happiness in a romantic love scene far from the setting of ordinary domestic life. Janice Meredith, after all the trials to which she is subjected as she is pulled from one Revolutionary battle to another, speaks this testimonial to her maturity: " 'O mommy—isn't it a relief to be told what to do, and not to have to worry one's self. He didn't make us think once.' "

Frances Ellen Watkins Harper

Whereas the Victorian gentlewoman found a historic pattern for behavior in the Puritan maiden, the young woman of the turn of the century could find a model of worldliness and sprightly behavior in these colonial dames outside the Puritan tradition. While some young women of the time were only momentarily touched by the "Janice Meredith hairdo" and danced briefly to the "Janice Meredith Waltz," others were more enduringly influenced by the model of feminine behavior described in the book. Many novelists were interested in the question of the "new woman," who wanted to ride a bicycle, vote, and work in business offices. In the face of such challenges, some popular novelists, such as Harold Bell Wright, labored to show that the old-fashioned Victorian pattern of womanhood was best. Yet, plainly, America's concepts of proper womanly behavior were changing, and the colonial minxes gave historic sanction to some of the aspects of the change.

An interesting contrast to the minx is the version of the colonial woman given in the work of Alice Morse Earle. This author tried to support changes in women's behavior differently, concentrating more on responsibility, maturity, and intelligence than on beauty and "spirit," in such books as *Colonial Dames and Goodwives, Margaret Winthrop,* and *Home Life in Colonial Days.* Her work shows a tendency to look for historic precedents for the roles taken by her contemporaries, with an emphasis on the se-

rious. The more popular novelists, in contrast, allow women new frivolities but little else.

Changes in religious attitudes and the roles of women were alterations within the middle classes, but the tides of southern European immigration transformed American society from the outside. While the cultural and ethnic demography of America was altered by the new immigrants, Americans of the dominant "native" culture were finding many ways to fortify their own sense of nationality. Kammen has pointed out that the Revolutionary historical novels of the turn of the century emphasize elitism and stress our ties with England in response to America's perception of a threat to its "racial purity." There is abundant evidence that the idea of "racial purity," which perhaps reached its peak during the presidency of Theodore Roosevelt, was a popular concept. I will examine some of the dimensions of the elitism shown in these novels.

Most obvious is the upper-class status of many of the heroes and heroines. Once in a while, it is true, the hero is a lower-class individual who rises in the world, succeeding as well in working out his role in the politics of the time or winning the heroine. Douw Mauverensen of *In the Valley* is one of those with the greatest social mobility, some of which he owes to his upbringing by his foster father, a peer of Sir John Johnson. The hero of *Janice Meredith* is John Brereton, whom we first meet as an indentured servant just off the boat; of course he turns out to be a youth of good English family and ends the war as an American general. (The unhappy reader of Frederick Dickson's copy caviled at the plausibility of this: "A man might resign from the British army and emigrate to distant lands because he did not approve of his mother's conduct, but with plenty of money at his command, he would *not* sell himself as a slave.") The hero of Mary Johnston's *Prisoners of Hope* is also first met just off the boat, an indentured servant of the heroine's father. Although he turns out to be a gentleman, he fails to get the girl because of his politics. (But she will always love him.)

The more typical hero, however, is a youth of the upper classes, and the successful heroine (the one who gets to marry the hero) is also almost always of such a family. The most notable exception is Audrey, whose beauty wins the heart of one of colonial Virginia's finest young gentleman, one loved by Col. William Byrd's own daughter; yet she is killed in the final scene, the novelist thus preventing a most unsuitable marriage. Readers are expected to sympathize with the upper classes, and the advice given to Richard Carvel is followed by most of the heroes: " 'Seek no company . . . beyond that circle in which you were born.' " Paul Leicester Ford apologizes for a scene in his *Janice Meredith* which shows the blue-blooded Janice working alongside the servants—in those days people were much more familiar with their servants than we should think of being. Likewise, the "tall, blond, stalwart, blue-eyed" Lt. John Seymour Seymour, "of an old and distinguished Philadelphia family, so proud of its name that in his instance they had doubled it," who is the hero in Cyrus T. Brady's truly awful novel *For Love of Country* [1899], verges on caricature for us—but was taken seriously by readers of that time.

Many of the novels have scenes in London, allowing the novelist to provide cameo appearances of famous eighteenth-century Englishmen and to emphasize the English origin of our national heritage. Wrote Winston Churchill, "Ah, London town, by what subtleties are you tied to the hearts of those born across the sea? That is one of the mysteries of race." As Kammen has shown, many of the novels promote the idea that the Revolution did not really pit America against England, but Englishmen against other Englishmen. In keeping with the general tone of Anglophilia, there are many English officers and colonial aristocrats of old Virginia who do not favor the forces of democracy, yet are treated favorably by the novelists. Of course there are the evil ones, too—exaggerated portraits, many of them. Robert W. Chambers's portrayal of Walter Butler makes him a truly black-hearted villain. In *Cardigan* [1901], Chambers described Lord Dunmore (who is pictured as a degenerate fop lusting after the beautiful Silver Heels) as "for all the world like a white cat dancing through hell fire." My own favorite among the foppish villains is Lord Carnel, of *To Have and to Hold,* who came to Virginia after Jocelyn Leigh, the heroine, to force her to marry him. He dresses in red and black and is accompanied by an Italian doctor who specializes in subtle poisons.

There are plenty of villains among the ordinary citizens, and in general the populace is depicted as cowardly and mean-minded. Paradoxically, the novels that have the rise of democracy as a theme (whether set during the Revolution or in some early Southern rebellion) usually present aristocratic leaders among common folk who, in contrast to the altruistic leaders, foment rebellion only in their own selfish interests without regard for the general good. *Janice Meredith* is most vehement in this, picturing the ordinary Jerseymen of the day in the worst possible light. Many of the historical characters such as Washington and Major André (to cite the most popular) are shown as exemplars of their class, while John Paul Jones's troubles are related to his low origins in *Richard Carvel* and *The Tory Lover.*

Racism is so obvious in these novels that it needs little commentary. Blacks are nowhere considered of any importance, except as a threat in some of the Southern novels, and Indians are seldom treated favorably. In *Alice,* for instance, Thompson said of Indians, "Their innate repulsiveness is so great that, like the snake's charm, it may fascinate; yet an indescribable, haunting disgust goes with it. And, after all, if Alice had been asked to tell just how she felt toward the Indian she had labored so hard to save, she would promptly have said, 'I loathe him as I do a toad.' " Anti-Semitism is especially marked in *Richard Carvel.* One of Richard's new friends in London, a charming but dissipated gambler, asks Richard, " 'Do you have Jews in America?' " The gambler has set aside a special waiting room in his quarters which he calls "the Jerusalem Chamber, where I keep my Israelites"—that is, money lenders trying to collect on loans. Irish, Poles, Italians, and Greeks are conspicuous by their absence (excepting Lord Carnal's Italian physician), while the French are treated with suspicion, and Germans are most often represented one-dimensionally as the Hessian troops. The cheerful mixture of American immigrants described in James Feni-

more Cooper's *Pioneers* is quite unlike what we find in these later novels.

A further aspect of the elitism of these novels can be seen in their descriptions of homes and gardens. The use of colonial artifacts as adjuncts to gracious living is one of the most familiar facts about the colonial revival, and these historical novels fully participate in this popular movement, tying the objects to persons of culture and refinement. In some of her books, Earle related some personal experiences of collecting china; perhaps more familiar are the stories Robert and Elizabeth Shackleton told in their popular tales of collecting colonial materials. They would ride around the countryside in a horse-drawn buggy, stopping at farmhouses where they would try to buy Washington pitchers and mahogany mirrors for dimes and quarters, often succeeding. One striking aspect of their narratives of such ventures is the tone of ridicule adopted to describe the farm homes and farm people. While their rural hosts had a genuine connection with the past, it was not one to elicit any sympathy; rather, these collectors wanted to rescue the old china or furniture from these modern peasants and give it an honored place in their own magnificent homes. Although Earle lovingly described the household cares of the colonial wife in many books, she had little good to say about the contemporary version of such a woman.

When we look back at the Puritans or the early settlers on any of our frontiers, we do not find a high standard of living. But the colonial aristocrats, either of the Old South or of eighteenth-century Philadelphia or New York, provided a historical precedent and sanction for living on an opulent scale. The idealized life-styles mirrored in the pages of *Country Life in America* had their genealogy traced in these works of fiction. Not much attention was given to the nineteenth-century state of the old homes or the area that surrounded them. *Alice of Old Vincennes* sometimes compares the scenes of the past with contemporary Vincennes, using the Roussillon cherry tree as a significant landmark. In the fictional foreword to *Richard Carvel,* Daniel Clapsaddle Carvel of Pennsylvania says that Mr. Carvel's town house in Annapolis "stands to-day, with its neighbours, a mournful relic of a glory that is past," while the interior furnishings of these homes have "gone to decorate Mr. Centennial's home in New York or lie with a tag in the window of some curio shop." Anthony Gresham of Groton, Connecticut, hero of Chauncey Hotchkiss's *In Defiance of the King,* provides a footnote to architectural history: "In the days of my greatest activity our house was considered somewhat pretentious, but at this writing (1830) it is looked upon as a fair type of the style known as Colonial, and has fallen from its former prestige." But as in most genealogy, greatest attention is given to the past rather than the present state of the "family." To call attention to the decay of mansions or neighborhoods would introduce a theme of change and development which had no part in these historical romances.

Most of the descriptions of homes and gardens simply revel in the magnificence of it all, many writers romanticizing even the homely details of colonial housekeeping. Lionel Carvel's estate on the Eastern Shore is a central presence in *Richard Carvel,* and the early chapters give a detailed account of the life of young Richard, spent between the estate and the Annapolis town house. *Hugh Wynne* describes gracious living in Old Philadelphia, both in the Wynne home and in that of his aunt Gainor Wynne, who is not a Quaker and thus lives a more worldly life. Central to the plot of *Janice Meredith* is Greenwood, the title character's home near New Brunswick, New Jersey. Phillipse Manor is of similar importance as the principal setting of Robert Neilson Stephens's *Continental Dragoon.*

Humbler homes were described in Amelia E. Barr's two novels of early New York, *A Maid of Old New York* and *The House on Cherry Street,* which show the homes of well-to-do Dutch burghers, whose wives did their own work. The writers presented standard house and room description, giving such details as the contents of the bookshelves and the kind of furniture and pictures found in the rooms, and tended to show happy family scenes related to the decor. In *Hugh Wynne,* for example, Mrs. Wynne takes young Hugh to see the patterns she had traced in the sand of her dining room:

> The great room where we took our meals is still clear in my mind. The floor was two inches deep in white sand, in which were carefully traced zigzag lines, with odd patterns in the corners. A bare table of well-rubbed mahogany stood in the middle, with a thin board or two laid on the sand that the table might be set without disturbing the patterns. In the corners were glass-covered buffets, full of silver and Delft ware; and a punchbowl of Chelsea was on the broad window-ledge, with a silver-mounted cocoanut ladle.

Perhaps no book has more feeling in its descriptions of colonial homes and gardens, though, than *Audrey.* The hero and heroine spend much time in the garden of the hero's estate, Fair View, in tidewater Virginia, and sundials, roses, paved walks, and box hedges are prominent images. *Audrey* was published in 1902, two years after the great success of *To Have and to Hold,* the profits from which Mary Johnston spent building herself a palatial country home in Warm Springs, Virginia. The profits from some other historical romances went into the creation of fine homes, too. Paul Leicester Ford bought a fine city home; Robert Chambers furnished an old home at Broadalbin, New York, with antiques; and Winston Churchill built Harlakenden House at Cornish, New Hampshire. Using the proceeds from the sales of their books, authors built the homes they had described, the homes they had made America's increasingly affluent middle class dream of.

The popular historical novels written for children during this period reflect some of the same ideas that we find in the adult novels and teach lessons in patriotism and good behavior. While Mary Wells Smith published several books about young Puritans, which emphasize the adventures of their lives and show little sympathy for the conservative elders in the stories, most of the popular books for children concern life around the time of the Revolution or slightly after it. None of Amanda Douglas's Little Girl books is set in Puritan New England—not even *A Little Girl in Old Salem*—and Douglas showed scant respect for the old-time religious characters in her stories. In *A Little*

Girl in Old Boston [1898], she mildly ridicules old Puritan ways, especially in the character of Mrs. Leverett, writing, "The intangible change to liberalness puzzled her." Mary Smith wrote patronizingly that, "Despite their grimness, there was plenty of human nature in the Puritans" (whatever that means). The prevailing sentiment in the stories is that bright, cheerful, *worldly* people are the best and the most attractive to the children who are characters in the stories. Religion is little discussed, except to comment on its grimness.

Young heroes are the juvenile images of the heroes of the adult romances, especially the swashbuckling Noah Dare, hero of several of Everett Tomlinson's works. The young heroines are similar to the minxes of the adult works, much given to pretty clothes, spirited skirmishes with other children, and flirtations with grim old uncles. All of the Little Girls, for instance, are similar to one another in character, despite their different backgrounds and locations. The Little Girl books tend to trace the heroine from her arrival in the city—often as an orphan come to live with relatives—until the time of her marriage. And dressing up is important to them. In *A Little Girl in Old Washington* [1900], one of the girls warns a young admirer, " 'Wait until you see me in the gorgeousness of a train and top-knot. You will wonder at my dignity. Perhaps you will not even recognize me.' "

Certainly the children's books share the racism and bigotry of the adult novels. Indians are the villains in Mary Smith's stories of the Deerfield massacre and the siege of Hadley. Catholics are unfavorably treated in *A Little Girl in Old Detroit,* in which the mother of our heroine is a religious fanatic who has entered a convent. The church tries to entrap the bright and vibrant young girl, but she is rescued by her father. Unlike the characters in the adult stories, however, those in the children's books are often middle class rather than aristocrats. The life of the past is often described in more detail than in the adult novels, with more emphasis on the way people used to do things rather than on fashion and manners.

Hezekiah Butterworth emphasized historical facts and persons more than the other writers did, while Amanda Douglas often frankly compared past ways with those of the present, usually to the detriment of the past. "When people sigh for the good old times they forget the hardships and the inconveniences," she wrote of bathing in the kitchen. Douglas usually ended her books with praise of the modern city, as in this typical passage:

> Old Pittsburg did not vanish with the little girl, however. But she went on her way steadily, industriously. The new century came in with great acclaim. Shipbuilding prospered. Iron foundries sprang up. The glass works went from the eight pots and the capacity of three boxes at a blowing to double that number, then doubled it again. The primitive structure erected by George Anshuts before the century ended was the progenitor of many others sending their smoke defiantly up in the clear sky. And all along the Monongahela valley as well as in other places the earth gave up its stores of coal as it had given up its stores of iron.

And in 1816 Pittsburg was incorporated as a city and had a mayor and aldermen and her own bank. It was a new Pittsburg then, a hive of human industry, where one business after another gathered and where fortunes were evolved from real work, and labor reaps a rich reward.

This mixture of pleasure in thinking of old ways even as we recognize the superiority of modern American life is generally the same as what we find in the adult novels. "Sitting in the liberal geniality of the nineteenth century's sunset glow," wrote Maurice Thompson, "we insist upon having our grumble at the times and the manners of our generation; but if we had to exchange places, periods and experiences with the people who lived in America through the last quarter of the eighteenth century, there would be good ground for despairing ululations."

In his study of the Revolution as cultural icon, Kammen concluded that Americans have generally regarded the War of Independence as a rite of passage. Traditionally, the rite of passage marks the transition from youth to adulthood; using this model, we can say that the popular novels of 1890—1910 treated the colonial period as the childhood of the successful, productive adult America of the nineteenth century. Childhood is normally romanticized, yet few adults want to return to it. This state of affairs adequately represents the novelists' perspective on the period they were portraying. They looked back on it with pride and pleasure from the superiority of the adult considering the child he has been.

The source of their pride is revealed in their continual emphasis on the social quality of our colonial ancestors. Rather than searching the family tree for the workmanly traits of ambition, initiative, or independence, the novelists demonstrate that America had her colonial Aristocracy. An almost direct contrast can be found in the popular twentieth-century novels about the frontier experience—mostly the western frontier of the nineteenth century—which emphasize the concepts and personalities that created modern America. The colonial period as seen in turn-of-the-century novels, however, does not show action so much as situation: our significant colonial ancestors were significant for their social and economic situation, not for character or deeds.

This reading of the colonial experience served its purpose in its time. In the pages of these novels, readers found a spiritual ancestry for liberal religion, patterns for social behavior, comforting reminders of our "racial purity," and delightful glimpses of a sumptuous style of life. The readers of these novels were the same persons who made that "retired" Congregational minister Wallace Nutting a rich man by buying his platinum prints of women in colonial costume pouring tea or doing needlework while seated in authentic Windsor chairs in authentic colonial drawing rooms. Devotees of colonial revival fiction hung these pictures on the walls of their little suburban homes where they lived through the challenges of a new century.

Jane Campbell

SOURCE: "Female Paradigms in Frances Harper's *Iola*

Leroy and Pauline Hopkins's *Contending Forces*," in *Mythic Black Fiction: The Transformation of History*, The University of Tennessee Press, Knoxville, 1986, pp. 18-41.

[*In the following excerpt, Campbell discusses the works of two African–American novelists, Frances Ellen Watkins Harper and Harriet E. Wilson, arguing that while they mythologized the lives of African Americans in their romances, Harper and Wilson also used their novels to discuss realities of African-American history.*]

The period between the first publication of *Clotel* (1853) and that of Frances Ellen Watkins Harper's *Iola Leroy; or Shadows Uplifted* (1892) was a dormant one for black romancers. One major work emerged: Harriet E. Wilson's *Our Nig; or Sketches from the Life of a Free Black* (1859), the first black romance published in this country, explores the plight of a woman whose life as an indentured servant duplicates that of her enslaved sisters. That blacks produced little fiction during this period should not be surprising; social conditions did not lend themselves to literary productivity. Freed by the Emancipation Proclamation, blacks found that in some ways life proved even more difficult than it had before the Civil War. Many freed men and women, released from bondage with few skills except those of field labor, went to work on plantations leased by former Southern planters. August Meier and Elliot Rudwick have shown that though "a significant number of ex-slaves bought farms after the war," many more black laborers worked for very poor wages on these leased plantations.

> In some arrangements, blacks were paid partly in food, clothing, and medical care, but lessees had endless opportunities to fleece the Negroes of what little they had, and medical care was practically never provided. Government agents interested in the Black's welfare attempted to draw up regulations to mitigate the problems, but at best these were compromises with the demands of the plantation owners and the lessees. At worst they were flagrantly ignored. [August Meier and Elliott Rudwick, *From Plantation to Ghetto*, 1976]

Such conditions are fictionalized by W.E.B. Du Bois in *The Quest of the Silver Fleece* (1911), but more than forty years of such suffering preceded the transformation into fiction.

Other conditions following the war evolved from the despair, rage, and frustration of white Southerners propelled into a way of life entirely foreign to them. Raised under a strict caste system, they were suddenly forced to overturn their perceptions of themselves and of blacks, to reverse behavior to which they were conditioned. Such demand asked for more than the old racist code could handle; thus, Southerners set about reinstituting the old South under the facade of Northern mercantilism and industrialization. The sharecropping system provided one strategy for this reinstitution, and the Black Codes provided another. Under these statutes, enacted in 1865 and 1866, unemployed blacks were declared vagrants. Contracts between laborers and employers often emphasized their relationship through use of the terms "master" and "servant";

blacks could not own firearms. Other efforts toward reinstating the old order involved violence in the form of race riots (more properly, pogroms) and harassment by the Klan. These efforts, in conjunction with Northern disenchantment at the lack of immediate "progress" by blacks, culminated in the Compromise of 1877, legislation that withdrew Federal troops from the South, more or less abandoned the ideal of total equality, and ushered in the post-Reconstruction period about which Pauline Hopkins, Sutton Griggs, Charles Chesnutt, and W. E. B. Du Bois write.

A series of court cases followed the compromise, reflecting what C. Vann Woodward calls "The cumulative weakening of resistance to racism" [C. Vann Woodward, *The Strange Career of Jim Crow,* 1966]. In the *Civil Rights Cases of 1883* the Supreme Court decided that the Fourteenth Amendment allowed Congress to prohibit states, but not individuals, from racial discrimination. This and other court decisions attest to the climate of the late 1890s, one in which aggression toward blacks reached a new high. Various signs from American culture served to legitimize such aggression: conciliatory Northerners, an imperialist national temper, and the submissive philosophy of Booker T. Washington. Although Washington intended to better the situation for blacks, it is probable that the concepts expressed in his Atlanta Compromise Address of 1895, in which he warned against forcing political or professional goals, suggested that he himself felt blacks were inferior. With a major spokesman for black people implying black inferiority, one gets a sense of racism's pervasiveness at the time. Not only politicians, but historians, anthropologists, and sociologists enunciated racist views. To underscore notions of Afro-America's inadequacy, authors of popular literature mapped out the plantation tradition, whipping up the emotions of any reader entertaining doubts about the mood's legitimacy. Joel Chandler Harris and Thomas Nelson Page, popularizers of the stereotypes of benevolent masters, comic darkies, tainted mulattoes, and loyal mammies, surfaced partly as a result of the South's desire to return to a mythically ideal past and partly because the Genteel Tradition demanded denial of ugly reality in favor of mawkish fantasy. The loyal mammy, in particular, deserves mention here, for this stereotypically adamantine, kind, unattractive, and sexless woman was beloved by white Southerners immersed in nostalgia for the antebellum South. The mammy, as Barbara Christian has pointed out, served as a correlate for the mythically dainty, "refined" plantation mistress, a being supposedly far above the vulgar duties of nursing babies or performing the menial tasks associated with childcare [Barbara Christian, *Black Women Novelists: The Development of a Tradition, 1892-1976*].

The mammy stereotype, one which typified stoic endurance, was, of course, both limited and harmful, justifying abusive treatment of black women on the grounds that they were impervious to pain. The stereotype of the promiscuous black woman, closely akin to the mammy stereotype, likewise justified the historical sexual exploitation of black women, a practice as old as slavery. After the Civil War, when black men by the score experienced lynching for allegedly violating white women, black

women writers and lecturers continued to testify to the reality of the situation: black, not white, women were more often the victims of interracial coercive sex, brutality, and rape. Whereas white women did indeed suffer sexual exploitation, such exploitation occurred more often within their own race than it did between the races. It would be naive to assume that sex never happened between black males and white females. But crucial to the racist attitude is whites' flat refusal to acknowledge that sex between black men and white women could be mutually voluntary, that white women were seldom victims. "Not all of those innocents existed in reality," Trudier Harris writes. "But all acquired innocence in the white male imagination" [Trudier Harris, *Exorcising Blackness: Historical and Literary Lynching and Burning Rituals,* 1984]. Ultimately, most sex between white and black victimized blacks, not whites. The white female suffered few legal consequences from voluntary liaisons, whereas the black male could be put to death at the whisper of a rumor. At the same time, numerous black women, assertive enough to speak for the legions who suffered similar fates, report repeated sexual harassment by slave owners and employers, as well as more direct attack in the form of rape, an ultimate violation used as a weapon of terror for centuries. Whether wielded as an expression of dominance by an individual or launched as a tool for mass subjugation by a gang, rape of black women by white men swells the annals of black history. Not only did white men systematically assault black women during slavery, but rapes accompanied riots of the 1890s and the blood baths engendered by the Klan. Regardless of the degree of force and violence involved, such sexual exploitation posited its justification on the myth of the promiscuous black woman. Although Harris and Page cannot be held responsible for perpetuating the image of the oversexed black woman, an image that would have marred the facile surface of the genteel plantation living they depicted, Christian notes that not only was this image present in post-Civil War popular literature, but in Southern white women's diaries. In any case, the image of the black "wench" persists today, sanctioning abuse on the grounds that the victim elicits it.

Both Frances Harper and Pauline Hopkins write in direct response to these historical conditions and cultural images, but in many ways their mythmaking hearkens back to *Clotel.* Thus they provide a bridge between Brown and the male post-Reconstruction writers Sutton Griggs and Charles Chesnutt. Like Brown, Harper and Hopkins set as their task the reification of Afro-American humanity, and they laud many of the same white American ideals with as much enthusiasm as their predecessor: a Caucasian standard of beauty, high regard for industry, uncritical admiration for Anglo-Saxon "culture" and "refinement," and firm belief that education will allow blacks to surmount prejudice and attain equality. Yet, they write their romances forty years after *Clotel's* publication, and as a result, *Iola Leroy* and *Contending Forces* reveal post-Reconstruction's influence. Harper and Hopkins touch on the problems of lynching, of voting disenfranchisement, of the difficulties of educated blacks finding and retaining employment, and of expatriation to Africa. *Iola Leroy* and *Contending Forces* exhibit other striking similarities as well. Pivotal to Harper and Hopkins are their outrage at women's victimization and their notion that black women must resist such victimization whenever possible. Reverence for motherhood also informs their romances. In accordance with their sanctification of motherhood, both writers celebrate the reunion of families splintered by slavery and underscore the need for the black extended family to stabilize. A final similarity which deserves notice is the relative critical neglect which Harper and Hopkins have suffered; this obscurity must be attributed, at least in part, to the fact that they were women.

Contending Forces; a Romance Illustrative of Negro Life North and South, originally published in 1899, might appear at first glance to be a traditional historical romance, one that fictionalizes the past, for its action begins during slavery and jumps to post-Reconstruction, just as *Iola Leroy* begins during slavery and moves to the Reconstruction period immediately after the war. As with most black historical romancers of the nineteenth and early twentieth centuries, however, Harper and Hopkins find mythmaking incompatible with a detailed depiction of slavery, given its attendant humiliations. Thus, although they do fictionalize the antebellum South, and Harper applauds blacks' participation in the Civil War, their treatment of slavery is brief and symbolic, their romances moving rather quickly to the period after emancipation. Consequently, the central characters' enslavement receives short shrift. Harper never presents the lives of Iola and her mother as property, and Iola's bondage appears to last a few months, at most. Grace Montfort dies almost immediately after she is remanded to slavery in *Contending Forces,* and Hopkins glosses over the slave experience of Grace's two sons. Moreover, the enslaved characters are all so light-skinned as to pass for white, so that the romances focus more clearly on the tragic irony of mulattoes suffering along with dark-skinned Afro-Americans than they focus on the questions of slavery's horrors for multitudes of black people.

Harper infuses *Iola Leroy* with the central notion that black women possess the power to effect historical transformation. In order to change history, however, black women must insist on their dignity, shunning victimization and excoriating racist stereotypes. But it is not enough for black women to shape history through enhancing their own self-worth, Harper argues. Black women should embrace the role of motherhood, acting as culture bearers while simultaneously fostering pride in their children so that future generations can serve as race leaders. Finally, by playing an equal role with the black man in engineering social reform and racial equality, the black woman can come to view herself as the apotheosis of intelligence, courage, and self-sacrifice, instrumental in the historical process.

Harper's strategies for relaying these fictional messages parallel those of her literary contemporaries, black and white, male and female. Commingling woman's romance conventions with Afro-American historical concerns, she coaxes her audience into accepting the innate significance of black women. Proclaiming the need for women to acquire marketable job training, her heroine Iola serves as a black feminist prototype in fiction, despite Harper's tendency to assign her artificially feminine characteristics such as fragility. Iola, a talented and predictably tragic octoroon cast out of the white mainstream and into black culture, functions as a messianic figure (notwithstanding her sentimental treatment) by choosing to identify with blackness. Tapping the romance for its inherent faith in the remarkable, Harper avows that the black family, though estranged during slavery, can reunite, allowing women to assume their proper historical role. Harper's very real rhetorical talents, admirably displayed in her lectures, do not translate well into fiction, resulting in a work that resembles a series of political debates. Yet *Iola Leroy* is at least as good as *Clotel,* and Harper's romance deserves more critical attention than it has heretofore received.

Iola Leroy begins during the Civil War, when black men and women eagerly took up the opportunity to participate in a conflict they believed would eliminate slavery. Twenty years before the war, Iola's mother, Marie, has been freed and married by her master. Despite Marie's protests, her husband Eugene Leroy insists on "protecting" their three children from knowledge of their black heritage; thus all three children grow up believing themselves to be white. As soon as Eugene dies, his reprehensible cousin finds loopholes in Marie's marriage contract and manumission, takes possession of the Leroy plantation, and remands Marie and her children to slavery. When the reader first encounters Iola, she has been freed from enslavement to serve as a nurse in the war. Soon afterward, she rejects a white doctor's suggestion that she marry him and pass for white, her rejection based on two principles: first, she has decided to identify with her blackness, and, second, she has determined to embark on a quest for her mother after the war. Subsequently, Iola reunites her family and marries a mulatto doctor, both of them dedicating their lives to crusading for the race.

Harper's historical concerns are imbued with romantic elements. Her characters are extraordinary mulattoes created to transform whites' notions of blacks. According to Iola, Dr. Frank Latimer, her fiancé, exemplifies "high, heroic manhood." In fact, she declares, "he belongs to the days of chivalry." Dr. Latimer's veins run with "the blood of a proud, aristocratic [white] ancestry," but it is his black mother who aids him in his highest achievement, for after being freed from slavery in the early 1800s, she works for thirty years so that he can become a doctor. Eventually, he attains the title of "The Good Doctor," signalling his mythic status. Not satisfied with confining his influence to medicine, Dr. Latimer is "a true patriot" and "a leader in every reform movement for the benefit of the community." Evidently, Iola's beau serves as the model of race leadership.

Despite Dr. Latimer's heroic qualities, it is Iola in whom reside the central tenets of Harper's mythmaking. Harper, a dedicated abolitionist and feminist, herself boasted a long career of leadership. During her illustrious tenure as a lecturer, she toured for such organizations as the State Anti-Slavery Society of Maine and helped to found the National Association of Colored Women. From Harper's point of view, "it is the women of a country who help to mold its character and to influence if not determine its destiny."

Iola epitomizes the qualities Harper envisions as fundamental for a messianic woman. Highly intelligent and well-educated, she is also self-sacrificing, devoting her life to a series of jobs that prove her bravery and selflessness: nursing wounded soldiers, teaching poor children, instructing Sunday school students, and helping a young pastor. Independent and assertive, she speaks out against oppression without regard for censure. And although educated in private schools, she makes clear that she has attained her education at the expense of black people, whose unpaid labor has made possible her privileges. Her decision to refuse a white man's marriage proposal and decline to pass for white further reinforces her heroism, as do her indignant rejections of white men who assume her sexual availability during her enslavement. Enraged by the historical sexual exploitation of black women, Harper repeatedly underlines Iola's virtue, at the same time clarifying, for her white readers in particular, the coercion involved in sex between master and slave. Furthermore, Harper insists that such sex, proceeding from woman's powerlessness, degrades white men more than it does black women. As Iola puts it: "I have heard men talk glibly of the degradation of the negro, but there is a vast difference between abasement of condition and degradation of character. I was abased, but the men who trampled on me were the degraded ones." Black women, Harper believes, must view themselves as actors in, rather than victims of, history. Thus, although Harper does not directly depict slavery, she does anticipate later reflections on it by writers of the mid-to-late twentieth century, her ruminations on slavery offering the beginnings of revisionist history from a feminist perspective.

Hampered by racism, Harper's mythmaking has of necessity to fuse the refutation of deplorably stereotypic views of black women with the romance conventions of her day, thus leading her into the same traps that ensnared Brown and, later, Hopkins and Chesnutt. In order to telegraph Iola's singularity to an audience surrounded with images of black females as either unattractive superwomen or comely "wenches," Harper fuses the motif of the tragic mulatto with that of the Sentimental Heroine. Despite Iola's initial description as a "spitfire," she is at the same time "a trembling dove [snatched] from the gory vulture's nest" when a young black soldier named Tom Anderson rescues her from her lascivious slavemaster. Until she reunites with her family, Iola remains heart-broken, "homeless and alone," by her own admission, animated by a terrible secret sorrow. In the tradition of the tragic mulatta, Iola has blue eyes and is indecipherable from a white woman. Her beauty, which Harper repeatedly emphasizes, earmarks her as extraordinary, but it also reinforces the concept that one must be white to be beautiful, a distressing idea for a writer dedicated to racial equality. *Iola Leroy's* heroine decides to turn down the white doctor's suggestion to pass for white early in Harper's romance; yet Iola harbors a disconcertingly ambivalent attitude toward her lineage throughout most of the book. Although declaring the best blood in her veins to be African, when she decides to pass in order to get a job, she believes it unnec-

essary to announce that her great-grandmother was an Afro-American, evidently forgetting for the moment that she has dedicated herself to insisting her grandmother, her mother, and she herself are Afro-Americans as well and that they should identify with that heritage. Recounting her slave experience to her future husband, Iola maintains, "you cannot conceive what it must have been to be hurled from a home of love and light into the dark abyss of slavery; to be compelled to take your place among a people you have learned to look upon as inferiors and social outcasts." One gets the sense that it is Iola's reversal of fortune that marks her as more noble than she might have been were she born among her "inferiors," as she expresses it. In the same vein, one apprehends that Harper milks Iola's transformation (Iola changes from a girl who defends her father's slave ownership into a young woman who speaks out against slavery) in order to appeal primarily to white women who had mixed feelings about the "peculiar institution" before emancipation.

Another influence signalling the mythmaking qualities of *Iola Leroy* and at the same time marring it is that of the Genteel Tradition, a flaw typifying black historical romance from Brown to Du Bois. Aside from repeated references to Iola's "refinement" and Dr. Latimer's "aristocratic" lineage, Harper points to her central characters' gentility by way of their regal bearing and courtly manners. Their associates are often intellectual, well-turned-out, and well bred, obvious especially at the *conversazione*, as Harper calls a gathering in which they hash out Reconstruction issues. Here, race leaders convene to present papers on expatriation, the black mother's moral responsibilities, the meaning of patriotism in a racist country, and the prejudice of the courts. Stilted, painfully learned dialogue predominates, characters occasionally slipping into allusion, as when Marie remarks, "the true strength of a race means purity in women and uprightness in men; who can say, with Sir Galahad: 'My strength is the strength of ten / Because my heart is pure.' " Elsewhere Harper's presentation of history exhibits the marks of excessive decorum; lynching is "perfectly alarming," while housing discrimination against Iola's brother is attributed to the discovery that he is not white but a member of "an unfashionable and unpopular race." But the passages which display most tellingly Harper's struggles to present history in a genteel manner are those involving Iola's experiences as a slave, which she declines to describe to her own mother because this "fearful siege of suffering . . . would only harrow up [Marie's] soul to hear." Considering that Marie, too, suffered enslavement, Iola's discretion seems unnecessary. But for Harper, mythic history demanded characters epitomizing gentility and erudition, characters who could furnish a counter-statement to the demeaning visions of Afro-America that permeated white culture. During an era when literacy among blacks in general, and black women in particular, was exceptional, Harper's intellectual female characters transmit important messages.

Another device Harper employs in her mythologizing of history is that of coincidence, a romance strategy well suited to communicating to her audience that blacks can surmount hardship and forge meaningful lives. The disruption of black families is emblematic of the mendaciousness of the "peculiar institution," a system which reduced human beings to property bought and sold according to economic considerations, reinforcing a sense of powerlessness and subjugation. Yet, *Iola Leroy* abounds with improbable reunions between members of families that slavery has torn apart. While nursing soldier Robert Johnson, Iola sings him a tune she learned from her family, thus setting in motion a chain of events leading to the discovery that Robert is Iola's uncle, whom she has never before met. After the war, when the two embark on a quest for their mothers, they easily discover Robert's forbear at a meeting held in a black settlement. That this meeting, called primarily for the purpose of fellowship, appears to be the only one Iola and Robert attend testifies to the unlikelihood of Robert's reunion with his mother. That she is the first speaker at the meeting to recount the story of watching her small children wrenched from her arms and sold points up the romantic quality of Harper's book. An equally remarkable twist of fate enables Iola's mother to find her son Harry, wounded in a hospital where she just happens to visit. Their moment of mutual recognition occurs when Marie, equipped with fruit and flowers, bends over Harry's bed to comfort the anonymous young man she has inexplicably selected to receive her gifts. Coincidence follows coincidence when Harry encounters Iola at a conference where she reveals her identity by narrating her personal history to the assembled company. Harper chooses to fictionalize family reunions at such meetings in true romance fashion, ignoring the realistic necessity for Afro-Americans to attend dozens, perhaps hundreds, of such meetings, attendance which produced infrequent reunions. Yet Harper, writing in the tradition of black historical romancers, fictionalizes the historical truth that some families did reunite by this method; thus, she reformulates history, simultaneously encouraging readers to continue seeking lost family members.

Harper also can be credited with a prodigious feat: refuting dehumanizing images of black women by presenting a heroine strong enough to change the course of history yet at the same time genteel and fragile. In order to succeed at this herculean effort, she merges historical concerns with the conventions of nineteenth-century women's fiction. Nina Baym, in her study of women's novels and romances written between 1820 and 1870, has noted patterns that one may observe even in later fiction of the century [Nina Baym, *Woman's Fiction: A Guide to Novels by and about Women in America, 1820-1870,* 1978]. Although Baym suggests that the pure genre of women's fiction, as she defines it, disappears after the Civil War, many of the individual characteristics she identifies persist in popular romances today. Such fiction usually centers on a heroine who is either an orphan or has experienced separation from her family. As has been shown, Harper fictionalizes the historical reality of families fragmented during slavery by presenting a lonely, alienated young woman whose mother has been sold away from her. Like most nineteenth-century heroines, Iola suffers abuse, in her case from cruel slavemasters who seek to sexually exploit her. For the most part, this abuse is reported rather than shown, Harper recoiling from fictionalizing such demeaning experiences in connection with her rarefied heroine. Ultimately, Iola claims that her suffering has enhanced

her character, a given for much nineteenth-century fiction. Typical of most heroines of her day, Iola escapes her potentially disastrous fate with the aid of a guardian figure, Tom Anderson. When Tom dies from battle wounds, Iola eventually re-encounters Tom's friend Robert Johnson, who acts as another guardian, supporting her efforts to find her mother and to locate employment, which Iola insists a woman must have, whether married or single. In women's fiction of the 1800s, Baym notes, the function of the guardian, or surrogate father or brother, supersedes that of the aspiring suitors, some of whom pursue the heroine for spurious reasons. Usually, the heroine sees through such unscrupulous suitors and refuses their advances. Not only does Iola reject sexual advances, she turns down a marriage proposal, well-meaning though it is, that threatens to repeat her mother's history, Dr. Gresham offering her the tenuous security of posing as a white woman. Women's fiction of Harper's era generally concludes with the heroine triumphantly successful, having transcended her misfortune by dint of her own talents, character, and efforts. Although Iola does receive aid in escaping slavery, Harper bases her heroine's subsequent good fortune on her mythic qualities. From her graduation speech, which reduces every member of her audience to tears, to her work at the hospital, where Dr. Gresham describes her as quintessentially tireless and devoted, to her visionary expression as she rhapsodizes about a race leader's responsibilities, Iola remains a mythic character.

Iola's mythic capabilities stand her in good stead even after her marriage; rather than offering her an identity, Iola's marriage provides her with a partner in her struggle to bring about racial equality, allowing her to devote herself to educating mothers and children for Afro-America's benefit. Throughout *Iola Leroy,* Harper synthesizes woman's historical role with these fictional conventions, clarifying the need for black females to set their sights beyond their personal happiness and contribute to a better world. That Iola, married to a successful doctor, has the luxury of working without pay rather than toiling at domestic service, field labor, or the narrow range of other occupations open to the majority of black women of her time who struggled to feed themselves and their children may suggest that her audience was comprised primarily of middle-class white females. Yet for those black women who read *Iola Leroy* in 1892, and for those who read it today, Harper's insistence that black women must change the course of history deserves commendation. For even those readers who see their lives as circumscribed by economic and familial concerns can take notice of the primary tenet of Harper's mythmaking: the value of motherhood.

Naturally, many contemporary feminists would deplore the relegation of women to the domestic life that Harper's romance appears to sanction. Yet, given the few avenues open to Afro-American females in Harper's day, one must regard her sanctification of motherhood as ingenious, a way of telegraphing to nineteenth-century black women that child rearing designated them as instrumental in historical process. Celebration of motherhood inheres in nineteenth-century fiction, but Harper infuses this convention with the respect for motherhood central to Afro-American culture, placing her firmly in the mythmaking tradition of black historical romance. Harper, writing from within Afro-American culture, had plenty of opportunity to base *Iola Leroy* on motherhood's significance to that culture, where, as Robert Staples has noted, "motherhood represents maturity and the fulfillment of one's function as a woman" [Robert Staples, *The Black Woman in America: Sex, Marriage, and the Family,* 1978]. Although, as Christian points out, motherhood is a mixed blessing, serving as "a battleground for racist and sexist ideology," reverence for motherhood is so pivotal to both black and white nineteenth-century women readers as to represent a fortuitous choice for Harper's historical romance [Barbara Christian, *Black Feminist Criticism: Perspectives on Black Women Writers,* 1985].

The value of motherhood takes various forms in Harper's mythmaking. Several characters sanctify this role. During the war, one man decides not to join the fight for emancipation, though he fervently wants to do so, because becoming a soldier would force him to leave his mother behind. Robert never loses a chance to remind his companions that being sold away from his mother constitutes the greatest catastrophe of his life, equating loss of mother with loss of self. Since for Harper one of slavery's primary injustices was its destruction of families, Robert's repeated references to this experience simultaneously decry injustice and exalt motherhood. Iola and Robert's quest for their mothers comprises a large portion of the narrative, fleshing out the concept that Robert enunciates and transforming the romantic rescue of a damsel in distress to the rescue of the estranged mother. Marie elucidates one of Harper's views of black women's exploitation during slavery when she laments that black women who bear illegitimate children by their white masters are as victimized as their children because the mothers are denied all respect due them; instead, they are branded as temptresses. Obviously, Harper avers, slavery, by its very nature, mitigated against reverence for motherhood, thus depriving black women of self-respect and happiness.

Writing her romance after slavery's demise, however, Harper concerns herself with how her black sisters can redress these past injustices, turning around their victimization. Iola, who admires a young female's efforts to initiate a school to train future wives and mothers, herself delivers a paper on educating mothers. From her perspective, mothers can change history by passing on appropriate values to their children, thus enlightening future generations about racism and how to combat it. Harper interweaves this view of mothers' role with her adulation for education in general, which she envisions as blacks' primary hope. Deploring the ignorance and uncouthness of her own pupils during her brief stint as a public school teacher, Iola, like Harper, insists that educated blacks must "elevate" those without education.

Although beset by post-Reconstruction demons such as lynching, disenfranchisement, and stereotyping, Harper manages to formulate a positive concept of history. She realizes that emancipation has not inaugurated the joyous era envisioned by Brown but has installed slavery in new guises. Yet she feels blacks must resist the temptation to adopt corrupt white cultural values, supplanting greed,

ruthlessness, and racism with selflessness, generosity, and love. Harper remains convinced, in fact, that blacks, given the power, would overshadow whites, and she contends that eventually the Afro-American civilization will surpass the Anglo-Saxon, black America led by partnerships of women and men such as Iola and her husband. For, Harper writes, "the world cannot move without woman's sharing in the movement, and to help give a right impetus to that movement is woman's highest privilege." Harper's evolutionary concept of history, assuming that Afro-Americans will lead Anglo-Americans to a higher state of being, is not, however, based on militant or separatist principles. Instead, Harper espouses a union of "the best of both races," together forging a new culture deriving from equality rather than expediency. Investing her mythmaking with religious fervor, Harper maintains that whites can progress at the same rate as blacks if they emulate Christian virtues.

Pauline Hopkins's *Contending Forces,* like *Iola Leroy,* mythologizes black history of the 1890s; and Hopkins also reveals a preoccupation with the after-effects of slavery without devoting a great deal of space to depicting slavery. Hopkins introduces the reader to the Montforts, an extravagantly wealthy couple living in Bermuda in the year 1800. When Charles and Grace Montfort agree to relocate their plantation and their seven hundred slaves to North Carolina, friends enjoin them to reconsider, given the South's barbarity at the time. Unfortunately, Charles ignores this plea, moving to the States, where the family passes for white. Not long afterward, the white community, who suspects that the Montforts are mulattoes, gets wind of Charles' plan to emancipate his slaves gradually and conspires to subvert this plan. Murdering Charles, the whites seize the plantation along with its human cargo and remand to slavery Grace and her children, Charles, Jr., and Jesse. Driven to near insanity, Grace drowns herself, resulting in Charles, Jr., and Jesse being left alone with Anson Pollack, the malevolent character who has spearheaded the plot to destroy the Montfort family. Subsequently, an Englishman buys the young man Charles from Pollack, taking him to Great Britain and freeing him. Jesse, who has also reached adulthood, manages to escape, fleeing to Boston. *Contending Forces* then leaps from 1800 to 1896, where a new generation, Jesse Montfort's grandchildren, live comfortably with their mother, "Ma" Smith, in Boston. The vast majority of Hopkins's book centers on the post-Reconstruction lives of these grandchildren, Will and Dora Smith, and their friend Sappho Clark. Sappho, who resides at the Smith boarding house, falls in love with Will, but their engagement founders when John Langley, Dora's fiancé, a scoundrel determined to seduce Sappho at any cost, blackmails Sappho. When Langley convinces Sappho that Will would reject her if he knew she had an illegitimate son, she secretly leaves Boston for New Orleans, repairing to a convent with her child. Meanwhile, Dora and Will learn that Sappho's son has resulted from an abduction by a white man, and they agree on her innocence. Dora breaks her engagement to the scheming Langley, and Will pledges himself to marry no one but Sappho. Several years later, a British citizen named Charles Montfort Withington appears to announce his kinship with the Smiths: a direct descendant of Charles Montfort, Withington is the Smiths' cousin. Sometime after this joyous family reunion, Withington helps the Smiths recover their stolen inheritance of $150,000. When Will by chance finds Sappho in New Orleans and marries her, *Contending Forces* concludes happily.

To some degree, one might view Hopkins as a pioneer, for *Contending Forces* encourages interest in and repect for investigating personal history, anticipating contemporary writers such as Alex Haley, Toni Morrison, and David Bradley. Hopkins enlists her audience to consider the possibility that history can repeat itself by her daring to provide a glimpse of black women's humiliation during slavery at the same time as she cautions black women to prevent sexual exploitation from recurring in the present. Renouncing racist myths that erode self-respect, myths posited on the alleged wantonness of black Americans, Hopkins challenges her readers to contextualize those myths in order to understand the historical origins of them. She urges solidarity among women for the purpose of engendering self-esteem and historical transformation. At the same time as she excoriates white America for its mistreatment of blacks, however, she props up her mythmaking with inflated reverence for Anglo-American culture.

Hopkins's predominant mythmaking strategy is the romance typical of popular nineteenth-century white women writers. *Contending Forces* abounds with the trappings of domestic fiction: Hopkins juxtaposes imperiled heroines, concupiscent villains, and tragic misunderstandings with serene domestic scenes symbolizing cosmic harmony. At the same time, rhetorical devices with serious political implications permeate this apparent melodrama. The central heroine of *Contending Forces* may possess predictable beauty, but Hopkins uses Sappho's attractiveness to suggest the victimization that has accompanied beauty for black women in a racist society. Her villains perpetrate crimes against Afro-America, be it sexual coercion of women or ritualized murder of men. And Hopkins infuses the cult of domesticity with political messages, so that seemingly innocuous gatherings of women proclaim the significance of the black women's club movement, and joyous reunions among kin betoken the vibrancy of the black family. Sad to say, not only does she transmit assimilationist concepts through the devices of tragic mulatto and Genteel Tradition (motifs Brown, Harper, and Chesnutt employ with equal vigor), she allows her narrator to relay white supremist cant. Finally, *Contending Forces* reflects the deep confusion post-Reconstruction racism engendered in its writers, for Hopkins also affirms the need for mulattoes to take pride in their African lineage. Compared with the other writers of her day, Hopkins is quite a skillful author, managing an adroit fusion of women's romance and black historical concerns; and given her attempts at revisionist history, it is time she received recognition.

Hopkins transforms history into a cloak and dagger romance designed to keep a wide audience spellbound. Basing the early chapters involving the Montforts on an actual occurrence, she entwines fact with fancy to craft a mythic history. Through the romance, Hopkins's central concerns, the disruption of the black family during slavery

and the sexual abuse of black women, emerge. Coincidences abound: the Englishman Charles Montfort Withington happens upon the Smiths when he meets Will purely by chance in Boston. Meretricious John Langley, whose unrequited lust for Sappho drives him to wreak havoc with her life, turns out to be the grandnephew of Anson Pollack, who two generations before punctured Grace Montfort's tranquility because she refused to encourage his sexual advances. And Sappho Clark's tragic story of being sold into prostitution by her white uncle surfaces when a stranger narrates the story to the American Colored League, unaware that Sappho sits in the audience.

Another device of romance, the supernatural, plays an important part in *Contending Forces*. Madame Frances, Sappho's aunt and a highly esteemed fortune teller, predicts several characters' futures when they consult her. Had Langley heeded her prognostications, he might have prevented a disastrous chain of occurrences: his loss of Sappho, his jilting by Dora, and his freezing to death in the Arctic, a fate he has seen suggested on the magic screen of Madame Frances. Buttressing the miraculous quality of romance, the supernatural also serves to remind Hopkins's audience of Afro-America's latent power, for as the narrator notes, "the occult arts . . . were once the glory of the freshly imported African." Hopkins believes that Afro-American culture would benefit if blacks could resurrect this power.

Aiming "to raise the stigma of degradation from [the] race," as Hopkins points out in her preface, she lit upon the strategies evident in nineteenth-century women's fiction, novels and romances whose popularity surpassed all other fiction of their day. Using these strategies, Hopkins hoped, as did Harper, to garner the largest possible audience for her mythmaking. In the manner of Harper and other women writers, Hopkins fashions a romance about a lonely young orphan with a violent, subterranean past who must prove her virtue through additional suffering and is eventually rewarded with an ideal husband. Mabelle Beaubean, alias Sappho Clark, functions to acquaint her audience with the grim historical convergence of racism and sexism at the same time as she serves as a paradigm of black womanhood, a counterimage to the same stereotypes that plagued Frances Harper. Perhaps even more than Harper, Hopkins is appalled by the myth that black women invite sexual overtures. No one could imagine a less consciously seductive heroine than Sappho Clark, who views her beauty as a curse rather than an asset, and whose son has resulted from rape and enforced prostitution when Mabelle is only fourteen. Highly cultivated, Sappho is variously described as a saint and a Madonna. A vulnerable woman with a slight frame, tiny hands, and a frail constitution, the heroine of this romance is the antithesis of the earthy siren so beloved by racist ideology. Sappho, who with other rape victims shares guilt about her victimization, tries to make amends by her cool distance in the presence of men, whom she freezes out when they approach her with any behavior that one might construe as dishonorable. For example, when she discovers that Will Smith has repeatedly entered her room in her absence to make fires for her, she indignantly orders him to cease. Her responses to Langley's unscrupulous advances demonstrate her ethics as well, since he is engaged to Dora. Furthermore, her shrewd assessment of him transmits the notion that women can intuit truth and thereby control their fates. From the outset, Sappho dislikes the necessity of hiding her past from Will, and when she departs for Boston, despite her love for him, she does so in order to preserve his family's respectability. In short, Sappho testifies to the innate morality of black women who have suffered sexual abuse.

Emblematic of her virtue is Sappho's beauty, which Hopkins has wrought by means of the tragic mulatto motif intertwined with the Sentimental Heroine formula. Her hair has a golden cast; her skin boasts the attributes of a lily. This demure heroine can be recognized by her "aquiline nose, rosebud mouth, soft brown eyes veiled by long, dark lashes which swept her cheek, just now covered with a delicate rose flush." True to form for such a heroine, Sappho not only blushes prettily but trembles, faints, or weeps under pressure.

At the same time Hopkins mines the Sentimental Heroine device, however, she invests her romance with feminist leanings. Not only does Sappho's personal history emphasize the interplay of sexism and racism; Sappho herself stands as a counterimage for Dora, her foil. For while Dora exults in her good fortune at not having to work outside the home, Sappho recounts stories of her own problems keeping jobs, fictionalizing the difficulties blacks have faced in a white male dominated marketplace. Whereas Dora serves as a mouthpiece for the ideas espoused by her friend and eventual husband Arthur, a Booker T. Washington figure, Sappho denounces Arthur's faith that "industrial education and the exclusion of politics will cure all our race troubles." Dora confesses that the subject is "a little deep" for her and admits that she accepts whatever values men subscribe to, a fortunate position since Arthur "thinks women should be seen and not heard" with regard to political discussion. Sappho is disgusted.

Further inklings of feminism mingle with the sentimental depiction of Grace Montfort, who experiences a sadistic whipping only moments after being remanded to slavery. It is interesting to compare Hopkins's mythmaking with regard to Grace's beating with Bontemps's vision of Juba in *Black Thunder,* Juba refusing to cry or flinch as she suffers the same fate as Grace. The victim in *Contending Forces,* on the other hand, shrieks for her husband, whom she knows to be dead, to save her, as the lash descends on her "frail and shrinking form." Not satisfied with allowing Grace to lapse into unconsciousness once, Hopkins subjects her to a series of "fainting fit[s]." The reader may wish that Hopkins had created a more stoic heroine, a woman more akin to Juba, in order to fictionalize the suffering and humiliation of hundreds of thousands of black women during slavery. Yet, she navigates a nearly impossible course: the communication of the agony of black women during a time when most writers chose to ignore slavery entirely because it interfered with mythmaking. In an effort to provide a counterstatement to the notion of the invulnerable black woman, she goes a bit too far. One must remember, however, that Hopkins generates her romance out of the conventions of her time, as do her male

literary peers. Moreover, as Baym notes in her analysis of fiction of Hopkins's day, female writers committed themselves to illustrating woman's dilemma: "mistreatment, unfairness, disadvantage, and powerlessness, recurrent injustices occasioned by her status as female. . . ." Hopkins's impulse to infuse the conventions of white women's fiction with the particulars of black women's history is noteworthy.

Hopkins's mythmaking, like Harper's, resorts to the Genteel Tradition. Although the modern reader may find the earmarks of this tradition comical, one must appreciate the degradation whites sought to visit upon blacks during the 1890s and the necessity for providing rebuttal to such degradation. In an era when popular literature, from Thomas Nelson Page to Mark Twain, insisted on Afro-Americans' "primitiveness," ignorance, and illiteracy, Hopkins may be forgiven for contriving characters who curtsy, lapse into verse, and otherwise proclaim their refinement and intellect. If today one chortles at Charles Montfort "cast[ing] himself upon the velvet turf," or "myriad stars . . . bespangling the firmament," he or she must remember Hopkins's literary models. As will become obvious in analysis of Sutton Griggs, Charles Chesnutt, and W. E. B. Du Bois, such devices prevailed as a result of a painfully constrictive socio-political climate, and mythmaking was impossible without such devices.

Another aspect of romance, the presence of villains lying in wait for unsuspecting victims, is evident in *Contending Forces.* In every case such villains are men seeking to exploit black women; inevitably, these men evince admiration for the victim's charms while harboring violent hatred. When Anson Pollack approaches Grace Montfort, her rejection spurs him to revenge, so that his victory involves her being whipped nearly to death. Sappho's white uncle, who appears "extremely fond" of her, sells his niece into prostitution. Whether he himself rapes her is unclear; however, his "fondness" clearly involves lust mixed with hatred. John Langley, Pollack's grandnephew, likewise appears wildly in love with Sappho, yet his real aim is to secure her sexual favors while he marries Dora for her fortune. Underneath Langley's desire, "he longed to crush her . . ." and he achieves his aim when Sappho cowers in terror before him as he threatens to expose her to Will Smith. To accuse Hopkins of melodrama circumvents her wish to admonish women that what passes for love often masks hate; in the case of white men, black women must exercise special caution. Hopkins's mythmaking goes even further than Harper's in cautioning readers to ruminate on black history, for she not only decries black woman's sexual exploitation, based as it is on the myth of her sexual availability, she illuminates its companion myth: the black rapist.

Several chapters of *Contending Forces* center on reaction to a lynching involving skinning and dismembering the victim for his purported rape of a white woman. White and black speakers urge Boston's American Colored League to excuse the white community for these atrocities. Two black speakers, Luke Sawyer and Will Smith, register their alarm, however, at this accommodationist stance. Narrating the story of Mabelle Beaubean, Luke offers an

Shall The Race Have a Fair Chance?

Contending Forces.

A Romance of Negro Life

NORTH AND SOUTH

BY

PAULINE E. HOPKINS,

The Popular Colored Writer.

Author of "Talma Gordon," "General Washington," etc.

With original illustrations and cover design by R. Emmett Owen.

Over 400 pages, 8vo. Price, $1.50.

" *The civility of no race can be perfect whilst another race is degraded.*"— EMERSON.

A most fascinating story that is pre-eminently a race-work, dedicated to the best interest of the Negro everywhere. It holds you as by a spell, from start to finish.

A book that will arouse intense interest wherever shown, as it is the most powerful narrative yet published, of the wrongs and injustice perpetrated on the race. Startling in the array of facts shown and logical in the arguments it presents.

The incidents portrayed HAVE ACTUALLY OCCURRED, ample proof of which may be found in the archives of the Court House at Newbern, N. C., and at the seat of government at Washington, D. C.

The author tells an impartial story, leaving it to the reader to draw conclusions. She has presented both sides of the dark picture — lynching and concubinage — truthfully and without vituperation, introducing enough of the exquisitely droll humor peculiar to the Negro to give a bright touch to an otherwise gruesome subject.

It is a book that will not only appeal strongly to the race everywhere, but will have a large sale among the whites. The book mailed postpaid to any address on receipt of $1.50.

AGENTS WANTED EVERYWHERE. LIBERAL COMMISSION.

Many of our Agents are making from $15.00 to $25.00 a week. You can do the same. Address at once for full particulars and special territory,

The Colored Co-operative Publishing Company,

5 Park Square, BOSTON, MASS.

An advertisement for Pauline Hopkins's Contending Forces, *1899.*

oral history about the violation of black, rather than white, womanhood, violation that he feels must be avenged. In response to Sawyer's story, Will Smith proclaims that the notion that black men pose a serious threat to white women represents a subterfuge justifying lynching. The truth is, Will continues, "lynching was instituted to crush the manhood of the enfranchised black. . . . Irony of ironies! *The men who created the mulatto race, who recruit its ranks year after year by the very means which they invoked lynch law to suppress,* bewailing the sorrows of violated womanhood!" In order for Afro-Americans to understand the impetus for lynching, Hopkins insists, they must dissolve the cant surrounding lynching. Angela Y. Davis revoices Hopkins's analysis: "In the history of the United States, the fraudulent rape charge stands as one of the most formidable artifices invented by racism. The myth of the black rapist has been methodically conjured up whenever recurrent waves of violence and terror against the Black community have required convincing justifications" [Angela Y. Davis, *Women, Race, and Class,* 1981]. The reality of black women's violation stands as bitter reminder that whites have rewritten history for their own benefit. Hopkins insists that black women must beware white men, for underneath burns "a living fire of hatred." Such men, Hopkins implies, project their lust, their obsession with domination, onto black men, the latter of whom are allegedly consumed with desire for white women. At the same time, white men project their appetites onto black women, branding them as lascivious. Such binary thinking, conveniently equating blacks with "evil" sexuality and whites with "virtuous" chastity, inverts the historical reality of racism, suggesting that Afro-Americans are ruled by savage instincts. For Hopkins as well as for Harper, black women must refuse to capitulate to this oppressive set of myths.

Contending Forces fictionalizes women's collective efforts to create a countermythology. In the chapter entitled "The Sewing Circle," a large group of women gather to make garments for a church fair. Mrs. Willis, who plays a significant role in this chapter, serves as the embodiment of the black women's club movement. Although women's organizations existed before the Civil War, during the 1890s these clubs, led by such esteemed members as Frances Harper, Mary Church Terrell, and Fannie Barrier Williams, achieved greater prominence than they had earlier, in part because of the formation of the National Association of Colored Women in 1896. Gerda Lerner notes that it is unclear whether this association spawned new clubs or whether existing clubs began to attain recognition; nevertheless, the club movement as a whole deserves credit for uniting black women in the crusades against lynching and Jim Crow and for integration [Gerda Lerner, ed., *Black Women in White America: A Documentary History,* 1972]. When characters in the sewing circle discuss woman's role in racial upbuilding, they turn to Mrs. Willis for direction. Mrs. Willis echoes Harper's injunction that mothers, as culture bearers, constitute black America's future, and she applauds African women's native virtue, suggesting that black American women, by extension, are innately virtuous. She goes on to caution her listeners that black women must not assume responsibility for the sexu-

al exploitation of their ancestors and themselves. With this chapter, Harper charts black woman's role in changing history through her solidarity with other women, who help her to forge a new vision that runs counter to the one white culture promulgates. At the same time, the cult of domesticity, a motif pervading *Contending Forces,* enshrines the possibilities inherent in the home, where a sewing circle can become a political forum.

Hopkins's concept of history, exhibited in the aforementioned chapter and elsewhere, presupposes an educated, "cultured" class of leaders who will foster the rest of Afro-America so that it may evolve into ideal humanity. Patronizing as her mythmaking seems, it mirrors the attitudes of other post-Reconstruction black writers in its evolutionary concept of history. Unlike Harper, however, Hopkins conveys no notion that blacks are inherently more moral than whites or that black leaders will enhance white evolution. If anything, Hopkins hazards the idea that racial intermixture with Anglo-Saxons, however much it exploits women, has improved Afro-Americans, infusing blacks with characteristics of "the higher race." This blatant endorsement of racial supremacy has been responsible, in part, for the critical neglect of Hopkins' fiction; whether she was collapsing under the weight of the dominant cultural ideology or merely appealing to a white audience fails to excuse her. Yet paradoxically, Hopkins insists that, regardless of skin color, African descent people must identify with Afro-America. In addition, she avows in her epigraph from Emerson that whites have debased themselves by racial oppression. Finally, *Contending Forces* challenges "the best" of both races to consolidate in order to bring about historical change. Denouncing violence for agitation, Hopkins seeks to arouse moral urgency in black and white readers alike.

Struggling under the suffocating mantle of post-Reconstruction, Harper and Hopkins fashion romances that reveal their vital awareness of history, even while they employ the cult of domesticity, lauding the family as the circle within which moral harmony can reign. *Contending Forces* concludes with the two branches of the Montfort family—English and American—reunited after years of estrangement. As if to retrieve their European heritage, Dora and her husband, Dr. Lewis, "Ma" Smith, Will, Sappho, and her son Alphonse embark on a trip to England, underscoring the significance of the family unit. Hopkins sanctifies motherhood as vigorously as did Harper, for Sappho has reclaimed Alphonse, exulting in her renewed role; in fact, under her influence Alphonse blossoms despite his previous years of neglect. *Iola Leroy* and *Contending Forces* resemble each other in additional ways. Wrestling to abolish dehumanizing stereotypes, both writers create legendary heroines who surmount historical difficulties without jeopardizing their much vaunted gentility or femininity. As orphans victimized by racism, Iola and Sappho triumph over the vicissitudes of personal history through nearly superhuman virtue, offering radiant hope to women who have endured similar fates. Able to pass for white, these heroines decry the need to do so and ally themselves with Afro-America, to some extent at least. Both romances end with marriage to enterprising, peerless suitors, but *Iola Leroy* and *Contending Forces* should not be dismissed as "love stories" or "domestic fiction," for both authors speak out against racial oppression and mythologize history. Amidst attention to other issues, Harper reminds her readers that those Afro-Americans who fought and nursed during the Civil War deserve equality. That these books end optimistically, despite being composed during one of the most oppressive eras in black history, invites charges of escapism; however, writers respond differently to oppression. In an effort to reach a wide female audience, these two authors relied on the formula plots of nineteenth-century women's fiction, literature that inevitably ended with marriage. Heroic roles for women were limited in the 1890s; faced with mob rule, Jim Crow humiliation, and sexual exploitation, Harper and Hopkins took refuge in a mythic future, hoping to communicate the transformational possibilities of marriage and motherhood to readers—both black and white—at the same time as they infused their narratives with the realities of black history.

REALISM IN HISTORICAL FICTION

D. A. Williams

SOURCE: "The Practice of Realism," in *The Monster in the Mirror: Studies in Nineteenth-Century Realism,* edited by D. A. Williams, Oxford University Press, Oxford, 1978, pp. 257-79.

[*In the following excerpt, Williams briefly discusses the handling of time period and the role of historical accuracy in several Realist novels.*]

The Realist pays close attention to the physical and historical setting as well as to the social context. . . . Balzac may claim that the physical environment has a determinative influence on behaviour but, most typically the physical setting can be read as effect rather than cause, an indication of rather than an influence upon character. There is a widespread tendency . . . to exploit the symbolic potential of the physical setting, although this need not necessarily detract from its authenticity. Attentiveness to the physical setting grows, too, out of an 'archaeological' interest in the shape of things in the past. Although it is commonly assumed that the Realist deals with the present, . . . [many] novelists . . . set the action on average between ten and twenty years in the past. [Ivan] Turgenev, in setting the action only two years earlier and [George] Eliot and [Giovanni] Verga in making the action begin over forty years in the past, represent two extremes. The existence of a temporal gap allows the distinction between now and then, *hoc tempus* and *illud tempus* to be underlined, the past to be objectified and the understanding between narrator and reader who together look back on it to be strengthened. The straw bonnet which Eliot says 'our contemporaries might look at with conjectural curiosity as at an obsolete form of basket' and the 'refinements' of Rosanette's apartment 'which would seem paltry to Rosanette's present-day counterparts' are presented as museum pieces which provoke a certain degree of mirth

or scorn. 'Those days', Strindberg observes, very rapidly become mythologized as 'the good old days'. The most obvious explanation of the Realist's preference for the recent past is that the retrospective view makes for a clearer understanding of how society works. Also, as Stoneman suggests, 'research and documentation could be more easily accomplished at a distance in time, when records were more easily available and judgement had the benefit of perspective'. In some cases setting the novel in the past allows the writer to 'pull his punches' (Holmes) or to avoid, like Verga, a critical period in the history of his country. On the other hand, moving back in time takes Flaubert into the thick of one of the most turbulent periods of French history out of which no group or class emerged unblemished. Setting the novel in the recent past does, however, simplify the novelist's task, since it allows him to leave out whatever might interfere with or complicate the working of his model of society, without causing the reader to object. And as well as allowing him to be selective it also allows him to be evasive. Eagleton has pointed [out in *Criticism and Ideology,* 1976] that in some respects *Middlemarch* is lacking in historical substance: 'The Reform Bill, the railways, the cholera, machine-breaking; these "real" historical forces do no more than impinge on its margins.' Turgenev's silence about Bazarov's past and his possible connections with other radicals might seem a more serious omission to the reader of the time, who would like some indication of the strength of the faction he represents.

It could be argued that the Realist, whilst appearing to be concerned with the past, is in fact mainly preoccupied with the present. A period of twenty years earlier is sufficiently distant to admit the simplification and stylization necessary for his purpose but at the same time is sufficiently close for more up-to-date issues not to seem anachronistic when projected back into it. The commercialization of literature was particularly acute in the thirties but its backdating to the twenties in *Lost Illusions* allows it to be isolated and visualized more clearly in the context of an age whose contours, since the Revolution of 1830, have become sharper and more schematized. Likewise the rise of Gesualdo may, Gatt-Rutter points out, have been put a decade or two too far back in history but this allows the 'drive to monopoly' to emerge more powerfully as the salient characteristic of a new class, since the contrast between old and new becomes accentuated.

In some cases the effort to bring out the specificity of an earlier phase of history is perfunctory. There are some surprising omissions from Balzac's account of the year 1821-2 and Verga, in fact, confuses the years 1820 and 1821. Balzac, Mount argues, is concerned only with the general features of the age, not with precise details. On the other hand a novelist like Flaubert feels the historian's compulsion to make sure the factual details are correct and in documenting himself for his novel proceeds very much like a historian. Too much historical material, however, can be an embarrassment and Flaubert was worried that his insipid hero would be eclipsed by colourful historical figures such as Lamartine. The common practice, adopted by Eliot, Strindberg, Galdós, and Fontane is to avoid the two extremes represented by Balzac and Flaubert, making passing reference to the major events and figures of the age in which the novel is set, whilst omitting references to more transient phenomena and figures of the kind that Flaubert inserted into the political discussions of *Sentimental Education.* The balance between the historical accuracy to which the Realist is ostensibly committed and the 'de-historicizing' to which his interest in 'perennial' problems and 'basic' human nature conduces, is always a delicate one. It is not clear, Gatt-Rutter argues, whether Verga sees Gesualdo as a particular embodiment of a timeless, universal figure, 'homo economicus', or as the embodiment of a unique moment in the evolution of society. Flaubert's attitude to Frédéric is also ambiguous; on the one hand, he illustrates the deleterious effects of the Romantic legacy, on the other, his psychological state is viewed as a permanent possibility.

There is one way in which the Realist can avoid 'overloading' when integrating historical material into his model and that is to 'use history as a means of characterization' (Macklin) by setting up parallels between what happens in the public, historical sphere and what happens in the private, fictional sphere. It may simply be a question of making developments in the fictional microcosm conform with what is happening in society at large, as when George Eliot writes: 'While Lydgate . . . felt himself struggling for Medical Reform against Middlemarch, Middlemarch was becoming more and more conscious of the national struggle for another kind of Reform'. Subtler parallels may be engineered between political and emotional régimes. These are present in *Middlemarch* but more carefully orchestrated in *Fortunata and facinta* and *Sentimental Education.* In both cases changes of political régime are aligned with changes of heart in the hero. In *Fortunata and facinta* 'Juanito's oscillations between mistress and wife are an image of Spain's swing from order to revolution, from anarchy to peace.' In *Sentimental Education* each of Frédéric's affairs is closely associated with a distinct phase of French history. In both cases a jocular analogy is drawn by the character himself; Frédéric's 'I'm following the fashion. I've reformed' is akin to Juanito's 'Anyway, I can't stand any more and this improper relationship is going to end today. Down with the republic!' In *Fortunata and facinta* the country alternates between 'intermittent fevers of revolution and peace' just as Juanito switches backwards and forwards between Fortunata and Jacinta but in *Sentimental Education* the movement does not seem reversible. The drama of profanation in both spheres prevents the swing back to earlier hopes and aspirations and the reactionary movement, when it comes, is decisive. Whilst Galdós emphasizes the basic instability of both political régimes and marriage, Flaubert stresses the necessary deterioration and gradual impoverishment which overtake both high political hopes and high emotional enterprise.

Despite the rich diversity of contexts in which the various [Realist] novels are produced, there is clearly much that they have in common—the technique of impersonality, the movement towards a more dramatic presentation, an elaborate though rarely obtrusive patterning, a profound understanding of the way society works and affects the individual, an interest in the forces and changes which characterize different phases of historical development. These various features will not necessarily all be found in any single novel nor, when they are present, need they be identical. There is, however, much to be gained from viewing Realism as a family likeness which . . . undoubtedly exists between novelists working at different times and in different places throughout the nineteenth century.

George Lukács

SOURCE: "Balzac and Stendhal," in *Studies in European Realism: A Sociological Survey of the Writings of Balzac, Stendhal, Zola, Tolstoy, Gorki, and Others,* translated by Edith Bone, Hillway Publishing Co., 1950, pp. 65-84.

[*Lukács, a Hungarian literary critic and philosopher, is acknowledged as a leading proponent of Marxist thought. His development of Marxist ideology was part of a broader system of thought in which he sought to further the values of rationalism (peace and progress), humanism (socialist politics), and traditionalism (Realist literature) over the counter-values of irrationalism (war), totalitarianism (reactionary politics), and modernism (post-Realist literature). The subjects of his literary criticism are primarily the nineteenth-century Realists and their twentieth-century counterparts. In major works such as* Studies in European Realism *(1950) and* The Historical Novel *(1955), Lukács explicated his belief that "unless art can be made creatively consonant with history and human needs, it will always offer a counterworld of escape and marvelous waste." In the following excerpt, Lukács compares Balzac's views on romanticism and realism with those of Stendhal as evidenced through their novels and correspondence.*]

In September 1840, Balzac, then at the zenith of his glory published an enthusiastic and most profound review of *The Monastery of Parma* by Stendhal, an as yet quite unknown author. In October Stendhal replied to this review in a long and detailed letter, in which he listed the points on which he accepted Balzac's criticism and those in reference to which he wished to defend his own creative method in opposition to Balzac. This encounter, which brought the two greatest writers of the XIXth century face to face in the arena of literature, is of the greatest importance, although—as we will show later—Stendhal's letter was more guarded and less candid in expressing his objections than Balzac's review. Nevertheless it is clear from the review and the letter that the two great men were essentially in agreement as to their view of the central problems of realism and also of the diverging paths which each of them pursued in search of realism.

Balzac's review is a model for the concrete analysis of a great work of art. In the whole field of literary criticism there are few other examples of such a detailed, sympathetic and sensitive revelation of the beauty of a work of art. It is a model of criticism by a great and thinking artist who knows his own craft inside out. The significance of this criticism is not in the least diminished by the fact—which we propose to show in the course of our argument—that despite the admirable intuition with which Balzac understood and interpreted Stendhal's intentions, he yet remained blind to Stendhal's chief aim and attempted to foist on the latter his own creative method.

These limitations, however, are not limitations of Balzac's own personality. The reason why the comments of great artists on their own works and the works of others are so instructive is precisely because such comments are always based on the inevitable and productive single-mindedness. But we can really benefit by such criticisms only if we do not regard them as abstract canons but uncover the specific point of view from which they spring. For the single-mindedness of so great an artist as Balzac, is as we have already said, both inevitable and productive; it is precisely this single-mindedness which enables him to conjure up before us life in all its fullness.

The urge to clarify his attitude to the only contemporary writer he regarded as his equal caused Balzac to define at the very beginning of his review with more than his accustomed precision, his own position in reference to the development of the novel, i.e. his own place in the history of literature. In the introduction to *The Human Comedy* he confined himself in the main to establishing his own position in relation to Sir Walter Scott, mentioning only the features he regarded as a continuation of Scott's life-work and those which transcended it. But in his review of *The Monastery of Parma* he gives a most profound analysis of all the trends of style existing in the novel of his time. The concrete depth of this analysis of style will not be diminished in the eyes of the intelligent reader by the fact that Balzac's terminology is rather loose and sometimes misleading.

The essential content of this analysis could be summed up as follows: Balzac distinguishes three principal trends of style in the novel. These trends are: the "literature of ideas" by which he means chiefly the literature of the French enlightenment. Voltaire and Le Sage among the old and Stendhal and Mérimée among the new writers are in his view the greatest representatives of this trend. Another trend is the "literature of images," represented mainly by the romantics Chateaubriand, Lamartine, Victor Hugo and others. The third trend, to which he himself adheres, strives for a synthesis of both the other trends. Balzac—rather unfortunately—calls this trend "literary eclecticism." (The source of this unfortunate term is probably his over-estimation of the idealist philosophers of his time, such as Royer-Collard). Balzac enumerates Sir Walter Scott, Mme. de Stael, Fennimore Cooper and George Sand as representing this trend. The list shows clearly how lonely Balzac felt in his own time. What he has to say about these writers—for instance his most interesting review of Fennimore Cooper's works which he published in the *Revue Parisienne,* show that his agreement with them regarding the deeper problems of creative methods did not go very far. But in the Stendhal review, when he wanted to justify his own creative method, as a great historical trend, in the eyes of the only contemporary writer whom he regarded as his equal, he felt compelled to point to a galaxy of precursors, of writers striving towards similar goals.

Balzac works out the contrast between his own trend and the "literature of ideas" most pointedly and this is understandable enough because his opposition to Stendhal shows itself here more clearly than anywhere else. Balzac says: "I don't believe that it is possible to depict modern society by the methods of seventeenth-century and eighteenth-century literature. I think pictures, images, descriptions, the use of dramatic elements of dialogue are indispensable to the modern writers. Let us admit frankly that the form of Gil Blas is tiring and that there is something infertile in the piling up of events and ideas." When immediately after this he extols Stendhal's novel as a masterpiece of the "literature of ideas," he stresses at the same time that Stendhal has made certain concessions to the other two schools of literature. We shall see in the following that Balzac understood with exceptional sensitivity that it was impossible for Stendhal to make concessions in artistic detail either to romanticism or to the trend represented by Balzac himself; on the other hand we shall also see that when discussing the final problems of composition, the problems which already almost touch on basic problems of *Weltanschauung,* he censured Stendhal precisely for his failure to make concessions.

What is at issue here is the central problem of the nineteenth-century world-view and style: the attitude to romanticism. No great writer living after the French revolution could avoid this issue. Its discussion began already in the Weimar period of Goethe and Schiller and reached its culminating point in Heine's critique of romanticism. The basic problem in dealing with this issue was that romanticism was by no means a purely literary trend; it was the expression of a deep and spontaneous revolt against rapidly developing capitalism, although, naturally in very contradictory forms. The extreme romanticists soon turned into feudalist reactionaries and obscurantists. But the background of the whole movement is nevertheless a spontaneous revolt against capitalism. All this provided a strange dilemma for the great writers of the age, who, while they were unable to rise above the *bourgeois* horizon, yet strove to create a world-picture that would be both comprehensive and real. They could not be romanticists in the strict sense of the word; had they been that, they could not have understood and followed the forward movement of their age. On the other hand they could not disregard the criticism levelled by the romanticists at capitalism and capitalist culture, without exposing themselves to the danger of becoming blind extollers of *bourgeois* society, and apologists of capitalism. They therefore had to attempt to overcome romanticism (in the Hegelian sense), i.e. to fight against it, preserve it and raise it to a higher level all at the same time. (This was a general tendency of the time and by no means required acquaintance with Hegel's philosophy, which Balzac himself lacked.) We must add that this synthesis was not achieved completely and without contradictions by any of the great writers of the age. Their greatest virtues as writers rested on contradictions in their social and intellectual position, contradictions which they boldly followed through to their logical conclusion, but which they could not objectively solve.

Balzac may also be counted among the writers who while accepting romanticism, at the same time consciously and vigorously strove to overcome it. Stendhal's attitude to romanticism is on the contrary a complete rejection. He is a true disciple of the philosophers of the Enlightenment. This difference between the two writers is of course manifest in their creative methods. Stendhal for instance advises a novice author not to read modern authors; if he wanted to learn to write good French he should study, if possible, books written before 1700; if he wanted to learn to think correctly, he should read Helvetius' "De l'esprit" and Jeremy Bentham.

Balzac on the contrary admired such outstanding romanticists as Chénier and Chateaubriand, although not uncritically. We shall see later that it is this divergence of opinion that lies at the root of the decisive controversy between them.

We must stress this divergence from the start, for unless we are clear on this point we cannot assess the true significance of the praise Balzac gave to Stendhal's book. For the feeling, the wealth of thought and the perfect absence of envy with which Balzac championed his only real rival is admirable not only as a personal attitude,—although the history of *bourgeois* literature knows very few examples of a similar objective tribute. Balzac's review and his enthusiasm are so admirable because by them he strove to ensure the success of a work which was in diametrical opposition to his own most cherished aims. Again and again Balzac stresses the streamlined, concentrated structure of Stendhal's novel. He describes this structure with some justification as dramatic, and claims that in this incorporation of a dramatic element Stendhal's style is related to his own. Following this train of thought he praises Stendhal for not embellishing his novel with "hors d'oeuvres", with insertions. "No, the persons act, reflect and feel and the drama goes forward all the time. The poet, a dramatist in his thoughts, does not stray from his path to pick any little flower; everything has a dithyrambic speed." All along Balzac stresses the absence of episode, the directness, and frugality of Stendhal's composition. In this praise a certain community of tendencies inherent in both writers is made manifest. Superficially it would be precisely in this sphere that the contrast in style between Stendhal's "enlightenist" severity and Balzac's romantically many-coloured and almost inextricably rich and chaotic mode of composition is greatest. Yet this contrast conceals a deep affinity as well; in his better novels Balzac also does not stoop to pick a flower by the roadside; he, too, depicts the essential and nothing but the essential. The difference and the contrast is in what Balzac and Stendhal, each for his part, consider essential. Balzac's conception of the essential is far more intricate and far less concentrated into a few great moments than Stendhal's.

This passionate striving for the essential, this passionate contempt for all trivial realism is the artistic link that unites these two great writers in spite of the polar divergence of their philosophies and creative methods. That is why Balzac, in his analysis of Stendhal's novel, could not refrain from touching upon the deepest problems of form—problems which are highly topical to this day. Balzac the artist sees quite clearly the indissoluble connection between a felicitous choice of subject and successful composition. He therefore considers it most important to explain in detail the consummate artistry shown by Stendhal in setting the scene of his novel in a little Italian court. Balzac, quite rightly, stresses the point that Stendhal's picture

grows far beyond the framework of petty court intrigues in a small Italian duchy. What he shows in his novel is the typical structure of modern autocracy. He brings before us in their most characteristic manifestation the eternal types produced by this form of social existence. "He has written the modern *Il Principe*," says Balzac, "the novel that Macchiavelli would have written had he been exiled to nineteenth-century Italy. *The Monastery of Parma* is a typical book in the best sense of the word. Finally it brilliantly lays before the reader all the sufferings inflicted on Richelieu by the *camarilla* of Louis XIII."

In Balzac's view Stendhal's novel achieves its comprehensive typicality precisely because its scene is laid in Parma, on a stage of trivial interests and petty intrigues. For—Balzac continues to present such vast interests as those which occupied the cabinets of Louis XIV or Napoleon would necessarily require so wide a stage, so much objective explanation, as would greatly impede the end,—the period following upon the return of Count Mosca and the Duchess of Sanseverina to Parma, the story of the love between Fabrice and Clelia and Fabrice's withdrawal to the monastery.

Here Balzac would like to impose his own method of composition on Stendhal. Most of the Balzac novels have a much rounder plot and their predominant atmosphere is much more of one piece than is found in Stendhal or in the novels of the eighteenth century. Balzac mostly depicts some catastrophe tensely concentrated both in time and space or else shows us a chain of catastrophes, and tints the picture with the magic of a mood that is never inconsistent or out of tune. Thus does he seek artistic escape from the flabby shapelessness of modern bourgeois life by embodying certain compositional features of the Shakespearean drama and of the classical *novella* in the structure of his novels. A necessary result of this mode of composition is that many characters in such a novel cannot fulfil their destinies within its limits. The Balzacian principle of cyclic structure rests on the assumption that such unfinished and incomplete characters will reappear as the central figures of some other story in which the mood and atmosphere are appropriate to their occupying a central position. This principle has nothing in common with later forms of the cyclic novel, such as we find in the works of Zola. One should think of how Balzac makes Vautrin, Rastignac, Nucingen, Maxime de Trailles and others appear as episodic figures in "Le Pere Goriot," but find their true fulfilment in other novels. Balzac's world is, like Hegel's, a circle consisting entirely of circles.

Stendhal's principle of composition is diametrically opposed to Balzac's. He too, like Balzac, strives to present a totality, but always tries to crowd the essential features of a whole epoch into the personal biography of some individual type (the period of the Bourbon restoration in *Le Rouge et le Noir*, the absolutism of the small Italian states in *The Monastery of Parma* and the July monarchy on *Lucien Leuwen*). In adopting this biographical form Stendhal followed his predecessors, but endowed it with a different, quite specific meaning. Throughout his career as a writer he always presented a certain type of man and all representatives of this type, despite their clear-cut individuality, and the wide divergences in their class position and circumstances, are at the core of their being and in their attitude to Stendhal's whole epoch are very closely related to each other (Julien Sorel, Fabrice del Dongo, Lucien Leuwen). The fate of these characters is intended to reflect the vileness, the squalid loathsomeness of the whole epoch—an epoch in which there is no longer room for the great, noble-minded descendants of the heroic phase of *bourgeois* history, the age of the revolution and Napoleon. All Stendhal heroes save their mental and moral integrity from the taint of their time by escaping from life. Stendhal deliberately represents the death of Julien Sorel on the scaffold as a form of suicide and Fabrice and Lucien withdraw from life in a similar way, if less dramatically and with less pathos.

Balzac entirely failed to notice this decisive point in Stendhal's world-view when he suggested that *The Monastery of Parma* ought to be concentrated around and restricted to the struggles at the court of Parma. But all that Balzac considered superfluous from the viewpoint of his own method of composition were for Stendhal matters of primary importance. Thus, to begin with, the opening of *The Monastery of Parma*—the Napoleonic age, Eugene Beauharnais' glittering, colourful viceregal court, as the decisive influence determining Fabrice's whole mentality and development, and in contrast to it the vivid satirical description of the vile, contemptible Austrian tyranny and the portrayal of the Del Dongos, the rich Italian aristocrats demeaning themselves to act as spies of the hated Austrian enemy—all these things were absolute essentials to Stendhal, and for the same reason the same applies to the end of the novel, Fabrice's final evolution.

True to his own principles of composition, Balzac suggests that Fabrice might be made the hero of a further novel under the title: "Fabrice or the Italian of the Nineteenth Century.". "But if this young man is made the principal figure of the drama," says Balzac, "then the author is under the obligation to inspire him with some great idea, give him some quality which ensures his superiority over the great figures surrounding him—and such a quality is lacking here." Balzac failed to see that according to Stendhal's conception of the world and his method of composition, Fabrice did possess the quality which entitled him to be the principal hero of the novel. Mosca and Ferrante Palla are far more characteristic representatives of the type Balzac wanted to see, i.e. of the nineteenth-century Italian, than is Fabrice. The reason why Fabrice is nevertheless the hero of Stendhal's novel is that, despite his constant adaptation of himself to realities in his external way of life, he nevertheless represents that final refusal to accept a compromise, to formulate which was Stendhal's essential poetic objective. (I mention only *en passant* Balzac's almost comic misunderstanding of Fabrice's withdrawal to a monastery which he, Balzac, would have liked to see motivated on a religious, preferably Catholic basis. Such a possibility, quite feasible in the case of Balzac—we need only to recall the conversion of Mlle. de la Touche in *Beatrix*—is quite foreign to the world created by Stendhal.)

Things being thus, one may well understand that Balzac's

criticism roused very conflicting emotions in Stendhal. As an artist unrecognised or misunderstood in his own time and hoping for recognition and understanding only in a distant future, he was naturally deeply moved by the passionate enthusiasm with which the greatest living writer had acclaimed his book. He realised, too, that Balzac was the only man who had on many points recognized his own deepest creative aspirations and paid tribute to them in a brilliant analysis. He was especially gratified by the part of Balzac's analysis which dealt with his choice of subject and the setting of the scene in a little Italian court. But in spite of the sincere pleasure he felt at Balzac's review, he yet voiced objectively his very sharp opposition, although in a very polite and diplomatic form, especially to Balzac's strictures on his style. Balzac, at the end of his review, criticized Stendhal's style rather severely, although he again showed his deep appreciation of Stendhal's great literary qualities, especially his ability to characterize people and bring out their essential traits by very few words. "Few words suffice M. Beyle; he characterizes his figures by action and dialogue; he does not fatigue the reader with descriptions but hurries forward towards the dramatic climax—and achieves it by a word, a single remark." In this sphere, therefore, Balzac accepted Stendhal as his equal, although—specifically in respect of characterization—he often mercilessly criticized other authors, even those whom he regarded as belonging to his own trend of thought. Thus he frequently criticizes Sir Walter Scott's dialogue and, in the *Revue Parisienne,* deplored Cooper's proneness to characterize his personages by a few constantly recurring phrases. He pointed out that examples of this can be found in Scott's writings too, "but the great Scotsman never abused this device which indicates an aridity, an infertility of the mind. Genius consists in throwing light on every situation by words which reveal the character of the figures, and not in muffling the personages in phrases which might apply to anything." (This remark is still most pertinent, for since the days of naturalism and through the influence of Richard Wagner and others, the leitmotiv-like stereotyped characterization of figures is still in vogue. Balzac rightly stresses that this is merely a means of concealing the inability to create lifelike characters in their movement and evolution.)

But although Balzac greatly appreciates Stendhal's capacity for characterizing his figures succinctly and yet profoundly by the words he puts in their mouths, he yet expresses considerable dissatisfaction with the style of his novel. He quotes a number of lapses of style and even grammar. But his criticism goes further than this. He demands that Stendhal should subject his novel to very extensive editing, and argues that Chateaubriand and De Maistre often rewrote some of their works. He concludes with the hope that Stendhal's novel, thus rewritten, "would be enriched by that ineffable beauty with which Chateaubriand and De Maistre endowed their favourite books."

Stendhal's every artistic instinct and conviction revolted against this conception of style. He readily admitted slovenliness of style. Many pages of the novel were dictated and sent to the publisher without revision. "I say what children say: 'I won't do it again'." But his acquiescence in the criticism of his style is almost entirely limited to this one point. He heartily despises the models of style quoted by Balzac. He writes: "Never, not even in 1802 . . . could I read even twenty pages of Chateaubriand. . . . I find M. De Maistre unbearable. The reason why I write badly is probably that I am too fond of logic." In defence of his style he adds the further remark: "If Mme. Sand had translated the *Monastery* into French, it would have been a great success. But in order to express all that is contained in the present two volumes, she would have needed three or four. Please consider this." The style of Chateaubriand and his companions he characterizes in these terms: "1. Very many small pleasant things which it was quite superfluous to say. . . . 2. Very many small lies which are pleasant to hear."

As we see, Stendhal's criticism of the romantic style is very severe indeed, although he by no means said all that he thought about Balzac as a stylist and as a critic of style. He seizes the opportunity of hinting, when he makes these polemical remarks, that he has the greatest admiration for certain writings of Balzac (*The Lily in the Valley, Old Goriot*), and naturally this was not mere politeness. But at the same time he passes over in silence, with understandable diplomacy, the fact that he despises the romantic traits in Balzac's style just as much as the style of the romanticists proper. Thus he once said about Balzac: "I can quite believe that he writes his novels twice. First he writes them sensibly and the second time he decorates them in a nice neologistic style with '*Pâtiments de l'âme,*' '*il neige dans son cœur*' and similar charming things." Nor does he mention how deeply he despises himself for every concession he makes to the neologistic style. Once he wrote of Fabrice: "He went for a walk, listening to the silence." On the margin of his own copy he apologised for this phrase to "the reader of 1880" in these terms: 'In order that an author should find readers in 1838 he had to write such things as "listening to the silence." ' This shows that Stendhal had no intention of concealing his dislikes, he merely refrained from expressing them and drawing conclusions from them as radically and explicitly as he felt them.

To this negative criticism he appends a positive admission: "Sometimes I consider for a quarter of an hour whether I should put the adjective before or after the noun. I try to relate clearly and truthfully what is in my heart. I know only one rule: to express myself clearly. If I cannot speak clearly, my whole world is annihilated." From this point of view he condemns the greatest French writers, such as Voltaire, Racine and others, for filling their lines with empty words for the sake of a rhyme. 'These verses,' says Stendhal, 'fill up all the spaces that rightly belong to the true little facts.' This ideal of style he finds realized in his positive models. 'The memoirs of Gouvion-St.-Cyr are my Homer. Montesquieu and Fénelon's *Dialogues of the Dead* are I believe very well written. . . . I often read Ariosto, I like his narrative style.'

It is thus obvious that in matters of style Balzac and Stendhal represent two diametrically opposed trends, and this conflict manifests itself sharply on every individual issue. Balzac, in criticizing Stendhal's style, says of him: "His long sentences are ill-constructed, his short sentences are not rounded off. He writes approximately in Diderot's manner, who was not a writer." (Here Balzac's sharp opposition to Stendhal's style drives him into an absurd paradox; in other reviews he judges Diderot with far more justice.) It is true, however, that even this paradoxical utterance expresses a trend of style really existing in Balzac. To it, Stendhal replies: "As for the beauty, roundness, and rhythm of sentences (as in the funeral oration in *Jaques the Fatalist*) I often consider that a fault."

What is revealed in these problems is a conflict of style between the two great trends in French realism. During the subsequent evolution of French realism the principles of Stendhal fall ever more into disuse.

Flaubert, the greatest figure among the post-1848 French realists, is an even more enthusiastic admirer of Chateaubriand's beauties of style than was Balzac. And Flaubert no longer had any understanding at all of Stendhal's greatness as a writer. The Goncourts relate in their diary that Flaubert flew into fits of rage every time 'M. Beyle' was described as a writer. And it is obvious without any special analysis that the style of the greater representatives of later French realism, of Zola, Daudet, the Goncourts, etc. was determined by their acceptance of the romanticist ideals and not at all by a Stendhal-like rejection of the romantic 'neologisms.' Zola, of course, thought his teacher Flaubert's worship of Chateaubriand a fad, but this did not prevent him from modelling his own style on that of another great romanticist, Victor Hugo.

The reason for the contrast in style between Balzac and Stendhal is at core one of world-view. We recapitulate: the attitude to romanticism of the great realists of the period, the attempt to turn it into a sublimated element of a greater realism is, as we have already said, no mere question of style. Romanticism, in the more general sense of the word, is no mere literary or artistic trend, but the expression of the attitude taken up towards the post-revolutionary development of *bourgeois* society. The capitalist forces liberated by the revolution and the Napoleonic empire are deployed on an ever widening scale and their deployment gives birth to a working class of ever more decidedly developing class-consciousness. Balzac's and Stendhal's careers as writers extend to the period of the first great movements of the working class (e.g. the rising in Lyons). This is also the time when the Socialist world-view was born, the time of the first Socialist critics of *bourgeois* society, the time of the great Utopians St. Simon and Fourier. It is also the time when, parallel with the Utopian-Socialist criticism of capitalism, its romanticist criticism also reaches its theoretical culminating point (Sismondi). This is the age of religious-feudalist Socialist theories (Lamennais). And it is this period which reveals the pre-history of *bourgeois* society as a permanent class war (Thiers, Guizot, etc.).

The deepest disagreement between Balzac and Stendhal rests on the fact that Balzac's world-view was essentially influenced by all these newer trends, while Stendhal's world-view was at bottom an interesting and consistent extension of the ideology of pre-revolutionary Enlightenment. Thus Stendhal's world-view is much clearer and more progressive than that of Balzac, who was influenced both by romantic, mystic Catholicism and a feudalist Socialism and strove in vain to reconcile these trends with a political monarchism based on English models and with a poetic interpretation of Geoffroy de Saint Hilaire's dialectic of spontaneous evolution.

This difference of world-view is quite in keeping with the fact that Balzac's last novels were full of a profound pessimism about society and apocalyptic forebodings regarding culture, while Stendhal, who was very pessimistic regarding the present and criticized it so wittily and with such profound contempt, optimistically expected his hopes regarding *bourgeois* culture to be realized around 1880. Stendhal's hopes were no mere wistful dreams of a poet unappreciated by his own time; they were pregnant with a definite conception of the evolution of *bourgeois* society, although of course an illusory conception. In Stendhal's view, in pre-revolutionary times there had been a culture and a section of society able to appreciate and judge cultural products. But after the revolution, the aristocracy goes in eternal fear of another 1793 and has hence lost all its capacity for sound judgment. The new rich, on the other hand, are a mob of self-seeking and ignorant upstarts indifferent to cultural values. Not until 1880 did Stendhal expect *bourgeois* society to have reached the stage again permitting a revival of culture—a culture conceived in the spirit of enlightenment, as a continuation of the philosophy of enlightenment.

It is a curious result of this strange dialectic of history and of the unequal growth of ideologies, that Balzac—with his confused and often quite reactionary world-view—mirrored the period between 1789 and 1848 much more completely and profoundly than his much more clear-thinking and progressive rival. True, Balzac criticized capitalism from the right, from the feudal, romantic viewpoint, and his clairvoyant hatred of the nascent capitalist world order has its source in that viewpoint. But nevertheless this hatred itself becomes the source of such eternal types of capitalist society as Nucingen and Crevel. One need only contrast these characters with old Leuwen, the only capitalist ever portrayed by Stendhal, in order to see how much less profound and comprehensive Stendhal is in this sphere. The figure itself, the embodiment of a superior spirit and superior culture, with an adventurous gift for finance, is a very lifelike transposition of the pre-revolutionary traits of the Enlightenment into the world of the July monarchy. But however delicately portrayed and lifelike the figure is, Leuwen is an exception among capitalists and hence greatly inferior to Nucingen as a type.

We can observe the same contrast in the portrayal of the main types of the restoration period. Stendhal hates the restoration and regards it as the era of petty baseness, which has unworthily supplanted the heroic epoch of the revolution and Napoleon. Balzac in contrast, is personally an adherent of the restoration, and although he flays the policy of the nobility, he does so only because he thinks it was not the policy by means of which the nobility could have prevented the July revolution. But matters stand quite otherwise when we turn to the worlds created by the pens of the two great writers. Balzac the writer understands that the restoration is merely a backdrop for the increasing capitalisation of France and that this process of capitalisation is carrying the nobility along with it with irresistible force. So he proceeds to put before us all the grotesque, tragic, comic and tragicomic types engendered by this capitalist development. He shows how the demoralising effect of this process must of necessity involve the whole of society and corrupt it to the core. Balzac the monarchist can find decent and sincere adherents of the ancient regime only among *borné* and outdated provincials, such as old d'Esgrignon in the *Cabinet of Antiques* and old Du Guenic in *Beatrix*. The ruling aristocrats, who keep up with the times, have only smiles for the honourably narrow-minded backwardness of these types. They themselves are concerned only with making the best use of their rank and privileges in order to derive the greatest possible personal advantages from this capitalist development. Balzac the monarchist depicts his beloved nobles as a gang of gifted or ungifted careerists and climbers, empty-headed nitwits, aristocratic harlots, etc.

Stendhal's restoration novel, *Le Rouge et le Noir,* exhales a fierce hatred of this period. And yet Balzac has never created so positive a type of romantic monarchist youth as Stendhal's Mathilde de la Mole. Mathilde de la Mole is a sincere convinced monarchist who is passionately devoted to romantic monarchist ideals and who despises her own class because it lacks the devoted and passionate faith which burns in her own soul. She prefers the plebeian Julien Sorel, the passionate Jacobin and Napoleon-admirer, to the men of her own station. In a passage, most characteristic of Stendhal, she explains her enthusiasm for the romantic monarchist ideals. ' "The time of League wars was the most heroic period of French history," she said to him (Julien Sorel) one day, her eyes flashing with passion and enthusiasm. "In those days everyone fought for a cause they chose for themselves. They fought to help their own party to win, not just in order to collect decorations, as in the days of your precious Emperor. Admit that there was less self-seeking and pettiness then. I love the cinquecento." ' This Mathilde de la Mole counters Julien's enthusiasm for the heroic Napoleonic epoch with a reference to another, in her eyes even more heroic, period of history. The whole story of Mathilde's and Julien's love is painted with the greatest possible authenticity and accuracy. Nevertheless Mathilde de la Mole as a representative of the young aristocrats of the restoration period is by no means as truly typical as is Balzac's Diane de Maufrigneuse.

Here we come back again to the central problem of Balzac's criticism of Stendhal: to the question of characterization and in connection with it to the ultimate principles of composition applied by the two great writers to their novels. Both Balzac and Stendhal chose as central characters that generation of gifted young people on whose thoughts and emotions the storms of the heroic period have left deep traces and who at first felt out of place in the sordid baseness of the restoration world.

The qualification "at first" really applies only to Balzac. For he depicts precisely the catastrophe, the material, moral and intellectual crises in the course of which his young men do finally find their bearings in a French society rapidly evolving towards capitalism and who then conquer or attempt to conquer a place for themselves (Rastignac, Lucien de Rubempré, etc.). Balzac knew perfectly well the price that had to be paid for finding a niche in the society of the restoration period. It is not by accident that the almost superhuman figure of Vautrin appears twice, like another Mephistopheles, to tempt the heroes struggling in a desperate crisis onto the path of "reality," or, in other words, the path of capitalist corruption and unprincipled careerism. Nor is it by accident that Vautrin succeeds in this on both occasions. What Balzac painted here is how the rise of capitalism to the undisputed economic domination of society carries the human and moral degradation and debasement of men into the innermost depths of their hearts.

Stendhal's composition is quite different. As a great realist, he of course sees all the essential phenomena of his time no less clearly than Balzac. It is certainly no accident and probably not due to Balzac's influences that Count Mosca, in his advice to Fabrice, says much the same about the part played by ethics in society as Vautrin does in his advice to Lucien de Rubempré when he compares life with a card game, in which he who wants to play cannot first investigate the rules of the game as to their rightness, their moral and other values. Stendhal saw all this very clearly, sometimes with even greater contempt and cynicism (in the Ricardian sense) than Balzac. And as the great realist that he is, he allows his hero to take part in the game of corruption and careerism, to wade through all the filth of growing capitalism, to learn, and apply, sometimes even skilfully, the rules of the game as expounded by Mosca and Vautrin. But it is interesting to note that none of his principal characters is at heart sullied or corrupted by this participation in the "game." A pure and passionate ardour, an inexorable search for truth preserves from contamination the souls of these men as they wade through the mire, and helps them to shake off the dirt at the end of their career (but still in the prime of their youth), although it is true that by so doing they cease to be participants in the life of their time and withdraw from it in one way or another.

This is the deeply romantic element in the world-view of Stendhal the enlightened atheist and bitter opponent of romanticism. (The term 'romanticism' is of course used here in the widest, least dogmatic sense). It is in the last instance due to Stendhal's refusal to accept the fact that the heroic period of the *bourgeoisie* was ended and that the 'antediluvian colossi'—to us a Marxian phrase—had perished for ever. Every slightest trace of such heroic trends as he can find in the present (although mostly only in his own heroic, uncompromising soul) he exaggerates into proud reality and contrasts it satirico-elegiacally with the wretched dishonesty of his time.

Thus the Stendhalian conception comes into being; a gallery of heroes who idealistically and romantically exaggerate mere tendencies and dawnings into realities and hence can never attain the social typicality which so superbly permeates *The Human Comedy.* It would be quite wrong, however, to overlook the great historical typicality of Stendhal's heroes because of this romantic trait. The

mourning for the disappearance of the heroic age is present throughout the whole of French romanticism. The romantic cult of passion, the romantic worship of the Renaissance all spring from this grief, from this desperate search for inspiring examples of great passions which could be opposed to the paltry, mercenary present. But the only true fulfiller of this romantic longing is Stendhal himself, precisely because he nevertheless always remained faithful to realism. He translates into reality all that Victor Hugo tried to express in many of his plays and novels. But Victor Hugo gave us only abstract skeletons dressed in the purple mantle of rhetoric, while Stendhal created flesh and blood, the destinies of real men and women. What makes these men and women typical—although regarded superficially they are all extreme individual cases—is that these extreme cases incarnate the deepest longings of the best sons of the post-revolutionary *bourgeois* class. Stendhal differs sharply from all romanticists in two respects: firstly, in that he is quite aware of the exceptional, extreme character of his personages and renders this very exceptionality with incomparable realism by the aura of loneliness with which he surrounds his heroes; secondly, in that he depicts with admirable realism the inevitable catastrophe of these types, their inevitable defeat in the struggle against the dominating forces of the age, their necessary withdrawal from life or more accurately their necessary rejection by the world of their time.

These characters possess so great a historical typicality that a similar conception of human destinies was put forward in post-revolutionary Europe quite independently by many writers who knew nothing of each other. We find this conception in Schiller's *Wallenstein,* when Max Piccolomini rides to his death. Hoelderlin's Hyperion and Empedocles abandon life in the same way. Such, too, is the fate of more than one of Byron's heroes. It is therefore not a chase after literary paradoxes, but merely an intellectual expression of the dialectic of class evolution itself, if we here set Stendhal the great realist side by side with such writers as Schiller and Hoelderlin. However profound are the differences between them in all points relating to creative method (the reason for which is the difference in French and German social evolution) the affinity of basic conception is no less profound. The accents of Schiller's elegiac 'such is the fate of beauty upon earth' are echoed in the accents with which Stendhal accompanies his Julien Sorel to the scaffold and his Fabrice del Dongo to the monastery. Finally it must be said that not all these accents were purely romantic, even in Schiller. The affinity of the conception of hero and destiny in all these writers derives from the general affinity of their conception of the evolution of their own class, from a humanism that despairs of the present, from a steadfast adherence to the great ideals of the rising *bourgeoisie* and from the hope that a time would come when these ideals would be realized after all (Stendhal's hopes of the year 1880).

Stendhal differs from Schiller and Hoelderlin in that his dissatisfaction with the present does not manifest itself in lyrical elegiae forms (like Hoelderlin's) nor limit itself to an abstract-philosophical judgment on the present (like Schiller's) but provides the foundation for his portrayal of the present with a magnificent, profound and sharply satirical realism.

The reason for this is that Stendhal's France had recently experienced revolution and the Napoleonic empire and live revolutionary forces had actually taken the field in opposition to the Restoration, while Schiller and Hoelderlin, living in a Germany as yet socially and economically unchanged, a Germany that had not yet had its *bourgeois* revolution, could only dream of developments, the real motive forces of which necessarily remained unknown to them. Hence Stendhal's satirical realism, hence the elegiac lyricality of the Germans. What nevertheless lends Stendhal's writings a wonderful depth and richness, is that despite all pessimism in regard to the present he never abandoned his humanist ideals. The hopes Stendhal harboured in conjunction with *bourgeois* society as it would be in 1880, was a pure illusion, but because it was an historically legitimate, basically progressive illusion, it could become the source of his literary fertility. One should not forget that Stendhal was also a contemporary of Blanqui's risings, by which that heroic revolutionary attempted merely to renew a plebeian-Jacobin dictatorship. But Stendhal did not live to see the distortion of *bourgeois* Jacobinism into a travesty of itself, the transformation which turned the best revolutionaries from citizens into proletarians. His attitude to the working-class unrest of his time (see *Lucien Leuwen*) was democratic-revolutionary; he condemned the July monarchy for its ruthless bludgeoning of the workers; but did not and could not see the part the prole-

tariat was to play in the creation of a new society, nor the perspectives opened up by socialism and by a new type of democracy.

As we have already seen, Balzac's illusions, his incorrect conception of social evolution, were of a totally different nature. That is why he does not conjure up, and oppose to the present, the 'antediluvian' monsters of a past heroic age. What he did was to depict the typical characters of his own time, while enlarging them to dimensions so gigantic as in the reality of a capitalist world can never pertain to single human beings, only to social forces.

Because of his attitude to life Balzac is the greater realist of the two and, despite the wider acceptance of romantic elements in his world-view and style, he is in the final count the less romantic too.

In their attitude to the development of *bourgeois* society in the period between 1789 and 1848, Balzac and Stendhal represent two important extremes in the gamut of possible attitudes. Each of them built a whole world of characters, an extensive and animated reflection of the whole of social evolution, and each of them did so from his own distinct angle. Where their point of contact lies is in their deep understanding and their contempt of the trivial tricks of mere naturalistic realism and of the mere rhetorical treatment of man and destiny. A further point of contact is that they both regard realism as transcending the trivial and average, because for both of them realism is a search for that deeper essence of reality that is hidden under the surface. Where they diverge widely is in their conception of what this essence is. They represent two diametrically opposed, although historically equally legitimate, attitudes towards the stage of human development reached in their time. Hence, in their literary activities—with the one exception of the general problem of the essence of reality—they must of necessity follow diametrically opposite paths.

Thus the profound understanding and appreciation of Stendhal shown by Balzac in spite of all divergencies, is more than a mere piece of fine literary criticism. The meeting of these two great realists is one of the outstanding events of literary history. We might compare it with the meeting of Goethe and Schiller, even though it did not lead to so fruitful a co-operation as that of those two other great men.

J. Lloyd Read

SOURCE: "From the Reform Movement to the Beginning of Realism," in *The Mexican Historical Novel, 1826-1910,* Instituto de las Españas, 1939, pp. 134-252.

[*In the following excerpt, Read discusses the trend toward greater realism in the late-nineteenth-century Mexican historical novels of several authors.*]

In the late [eighteen] fifties there began a struggle without possibility of compromise between two opposite points of view, the liberal and the reactionary. The heat of that struggle separated the population into two camps, both radical in their attitudes and bent on extermination, each unaware of its own weaknesses. Mexico was a nation seething with hatreds, wherein moderation scarcely exist-

Portrait of Charles Dickens.

ed. In that period every fireside was a forum for fierce outbursts; all eyes were blinded by swirling storms of passion, and all ears were filled with the roar of fanaticisms. But for the first time in Mexican history the issue was clearly defined and understood, and for the first time the liberals had a clear conception of their own program.

It is significant that the outstanding leaders of the liberals were Indians and *mestizos,* representatives of the majority of the population, and that the reactionaries were creoles forming themselves around the church as a nucleus.

Speaking in general of conditions in Mexico during that period, and in particular of the inefficiency of the republican group, Jesús Agras exclaimed:

> *¿Qué es y ha sido México desde el gran día de su independencia?... el pueblo más desgraciado de la tierra... Víctima sucesivamente o de la ciega tiranía militar o del desenfreno de la demagogia, ni un solo día ha disfrutado los goces de una verdadera sociedad ... todas y cada uno de los mexicanos ... han visto irse destruyendo hasta extinguirse todo aquello que forma el atractivo de la vida social [Reflecciones sobre la naturaleze y origen de los males y trastornos Que han producido la decadencia en México, 1864].*

> [What is Mexico and what has she been since the great day of her independence? . . . the most unhappy nation on earth . . . The victim successively either of blind military tyranny or of the license of demagoguery, not for a single day has she enjoyed the fruits of a true society . . . every Mexican has seen everything that contributes to the attractiveness of social life destroyed.]

He charged that Mexico was worse than a nomadic society, for in the forests at least people would not be plagued with

> *. . . una mentida civilización, los odios, las venganzas, las miserias, las pasiones todas, en fin, de una reunión monstruosa sin leyes eficaces, sin autoridad verdadera, sin obediencia, sin moralidad pública y sin amor procomunal.*

> [. . . the false civilization, the hatreds, the vengeance, all the passions . . . of a monstruous hoard without efficacious laws, without true authority, without discipline, without public morality and without public loyalty.]

One of the most damaging bits of testimony concerning society in Mexico in that epoch is the statement of the Empress Charlotte:

> Your majesty perhaps believes, as I did, that nothingness is incorporeal; on the contrary, in this country one stumbles upon it at every step, and it is made of granite, it is more powerful than the spirit of man, and God alone can bend it . . . one has to struggle against the wilderness, the distances, the roads, and the most utter chaos [Egon Caesar Corti, *Maximilian and Charlotte of Mexico,* 1929].

Altamirano protested that literary gatherings were of no interest to people, the theatres were unattended, except by the few who had no other way to escape from the sight of the poverty, degradation, filth, and prosaic barbarism of the human ant-hill. The capital he thought melancholy, anemic, with the squalor, nakedness, indolence, starvation and abysmal depravity of the proletariat overbalancing the attractions of *El Zócalo* and *Plateros* Avenue. The social functions of the higher class were stagnant. There was neither initiative nor variety, even among the leaders of society who held their roles by divine right rather than by merit. There were no critics, only eulogizers.

Such conditions could not stimulate or even support literary production. Juan Díaz Covarrubias, aware of the futility of writing for such a public in such stressful times, wrote to Luis G. Ortiz:

> *Tal vez habrá muchos que digan que sólo un niño o un loco es el que piensa escribir en México en esta época aciaga de desmoronamiento social, y pretende ser leído a la luz rojiza del incendio y al estruendo de los cañones.*

> [There will perhaps be those who will say that nobody but a child or a crazy man would think of writing in Mexico in this unfortunate period of social disintegration, and hope to be read by the red glow of incendiarism and to the accompaniment of roaring canons.]

Though, as previously stated, education in Mexico was in general still ineffective at the time of the Reform movement, in fact was to continue so to be throughout the century, there had developed a group of thinkers and teachers whose love for liberalism amounted to religious ardor. This group, beginning with Ignacio Ramírez, the intellectual whip of his generation, and including such men as Ignacio Manuel Altamirano and Justo Sierra, did more to renovate Mexican society and literature than all other educational agencies combined; in fact they constituted the only progressive factor in education.

Ramírez, widely known by his pseudonym *El Nigromante,* while still a student showed his rebellious and independent temperament by defending the thesis "There is no God; all animate nature is self-sustaining." That heretical pronouncement was not the prattle of an undisciplined student; it was a declaration of war against practically all traditionally consecrate attitudes on the part of one of the sharpest intellects Mexico has produced. As an orator, as a journalist, and as a teacher, Ramírez became the implacable destroyer of everything associated with the old regime. He became the guiding spirit of a group of young intellectuals into whose minds he planted ideas that constituted the basis of the reform movement.

As the mentor of liberalism Ignacio Ramírez represented the tardy application of a true cosmopolitanism to the social problems of Mexico. Though his attitudes were stimulated largely by extensive reading of foreign literatures, they were not the uncritical products of that reading. That he had only disdain for the superficial liberalism that manifested itself in the repetition of catch phrases taken from superficial foreign thinkers is shown by such statements as the following:

> *Devoramos en las ciencias a los vulgarizadores*

enciclopédicos, sin notar que no son extensos en sus tratados, sino porque son superficiales.

[We devour in the sciences the works of encyclopedic quacks, without noticing that they are not extensive in their treatises, but because they are superficial.]

He was unerring in his diagnosis of Mexico's intellectual ills as results of ignorance and undigested erudition.

The ideals of Ramírez and of his disciples systematized the movement for reform and culminated in the Constitution of 1857 and the Reform Laws, the two most important achievements of Mexican history in that they laid bare the basic ills of the nation and pointed out the road to progress.

With Benito Juárez, the exponent of the political ideals of this group, we have little to do here; but of Ignacio Manuel Altamirano, the literary preceptor of his generation, we must take account at the proper time, for it was he that indoctrinated Mexican writers in literary nationalism and became teacher and personal adviser to a whole generation of amateur novelists and poets.

ELIGIO ANCONA

Eligio Ancona was born in Mérida, Yucatan, in 1836. He studied law at the *Universidad Literaria del Estado*. Like many other literary figures of Mexico, he was prominent in political affairs, serving as governor *pro tem.* of his native state, judge in a circuit court, judge of the Supreme Court of Mexico, and as deputy to the national congress. As a journalist he used the columns of *La Píldora* and *Yucatán* in defense of the liberal cause against the regime instituted by the imperialists. He was recognized by the learned societies of his time as one of Mexico's important erudites. His contribution to the history of Yucatan is largely contained in his *Historia de Yucatán.*

Acona wrote six novels, of which five are historical: *La cruz y la espada* and *El filibustero*, 1866; *Los mártires del Anáhuac*, 1870; *El Conde de Peñalva*, 1879; and *Memorias de un alférez,* published in 1904, eleven years after the author's death. All of these historical novels have two volumes each except *El Conde de Peñalva.*

El filibustero is the story of Leonel, an orphan left in infancy on the doorstep of D. Gonzalo Villagómez, a rich *encomendero* of Valladolid. D. Gonzalo and his wife, doña Blanca, loved the child as if he were their own until the birth of a daughter, Berenguela, four years later; then they grew strangely cold toward him.

Leonel learned rapidly under the instruction of Father Hernando of the Franciscan convent of Sisal and became the self-appointed tutor to Berenguela. The two fell in love; but their plans to marry met the determined opposition of D. Gonzalo and his wife, who had arranged Berenguela's marriage to a nobleman. Leonel challenged his rival to a duel, but instead of fighting him attempted to save him from a mob. In the confusion the fiancé of Berenguela was killed and Leonel was wounded.

Intent on keeping the two lovers separated, doña Blanca and Father Hernando had Leonel thrown into prison.

When the latter was released he learned that Berenguela had married. He left home and became a pirate, assuming the name Barbillas.

In one of his raids the pirate Barbillas and his men captured the Captain General of the provine of Yucatan and several political dignitaries traveling in his company, among whom was the husband of Berenguela. Later, when Berenguela was free from her husband, Leonel wanted to marry her. Father Hernando, his old teacher, imprisoned the girl in a convent; but in the face of the threat of Leonel to take her by force the friar revealed to him that his lover was in reality his half sister, for Leonel was the son of Father Hernando and doña Blanca.

Leonel in desperation visited a man unjustly condemned by the Inquisition to prison for the remainder of his life, exchanged clothes with him and permitted him to escape, taking thus on himself the sentence he allowed the other to avoid.

The story is somewhat emotional in tone. In one case it was said of Leonel:

> *El se llevaría aquel cadáver que nadie había visto, escogería un rincón ignorado del mundo para sepultarlo, construiría junto a la tumba una cabaña, y allí al lado de Berenguela . . . conversando diariamente con ella, esperaría tranquilo y feliz el fin de sus días.*
>
> [He would carry away that corpse which nobody had seen; he would choose an unknown corner of the world in which to bury it; he would build a cabin close to the tomb, and there at Berenguela's side . . . talking to her every day, he would await serene and happy the end of his days.]

Other traces of romantic subjectivism are apparent in the violence of reactions, in extraordinary situations, in the mystery surrounding the origin of the chief character, in the interest in the distant past, in the resort to piracy, and in the manipulation of plot for the sake of effect. Berenguela is like the typical romantic heroine, beautiful, helpless, and self-effacing; Leonel is the perfect lover driven by desperation to piracy.

There is in this work a tendency to give free reign to fancy in the manner of dealing with historical facts. Historical accuracy was wisely rejected as a criterion by the author. His aim was creation within a very loose framework of historical trends. Characters such as he presented in this work never existed except in his fancy, but they had real existence there.

The author, furthermore, capitalized his personal reactions to the institutions of the colonial regime to add effectiveness to his interpretation. Those institutions and their personnel furnished the element of difficulty or dramatic conflict in the story. Justice and virtue are augmented in attractiveness by such descriptions of their opposites as the following:

> *Al valiente conquistador . . . ha sucedido el indolente encomendero que . . . sólo cuida de explotar al miserable indígena.*
>
> *Al celoso misionero . . . ha sucedido el fraile o*

el cura convertido en publicano, que gasta la mayor parte de su tiempo en inspeccionar el cobro de sus rentas.

A los grandes aventureros . . . han sucedido los gobernadores y capitanes generales, que con muy honrosas excepciones sólo se dedican a sacar de su posición toda la utilidad posible.

[The valiant *conquistador* has been succeeded by the indolent landholder whose only interest is the exploitation of the natives.

The zealous missionary has been supplanted by the friar and the priest turned publican, who spends most of his time overseeing the collection of dues.

The great adventurers have been followed by governors and captains general, who, with honorable exceptions, dedicate themselves to wresting from their positions all the gains they can.]

There is something of pathos in his description of his own native state of Yucatan as one of the most unhappy places of Spanish America, partly because of its subjection to repeated attacks of pirates who established their base at Belice.

The author injected something of the holy zeal of a crusader into his attacks on the Inquisition and on ecclesiastical organizations in general. These were developed in the role of opposition to the realization of the legitimate aspiration of the chief characters. Without concerning ourselves with the accuracy of his characterization, the reader can accept the depiction for artistic purposes. Whether fair or not, Ancona's satire and ridicule are part of the effectiveness of the story. Especially indicative of his use of these literary tools is his treatment of the customs of honoring saints with bull fights, and of trying men before the Inquisition on charges of being Mohammedans because they never drank wine, and on charges of being Jews because they bathed themselves and changed clothes on Saturday. The latter charge was brought against the innocent Cifuentes by a priest's niece, with the result that Cifuentes was found guilty and sent to prison. Ancona related with convincing indignation that the goods of heretics were accursed, that their possessions would corrupt any Christian except the inquisitors themselves. He included in this story a rather vivid description of the Inquisition's instruments of torture and the use to which they were put.

An interesting manifestation of Ancona's zeal to find virtue and value in unsanctified places and to uncover conventionalized abuses among official spokesmen of authoritative bodies is seen in the statement he put into the mouth of a pirate:

. . . esa sociedad perversa en donde el hermano vende al hermano, en donde el que debe protegeros sacrifica a sus infames pasiones, en donde las más dulces y las más santas afecciones ceden a la insaciable codicia del oro o al vil influjo del poder.

[. . . that perverse society in which brother sells brother, in which the one whose duty it is to protect sacrifices you to his vile passions, in which the sweetest and most saintly affections give way to insatiable greed for gold or to the evil influence of power.]

In the formation of his interest it was natural that Ancona feel the influence of his famous fellow-townsman, Justo Sierra. Not only did Ancona absorb much of Sierra's interest in the history of Yucatan, but he was the first Mexican novelist to follow the lead offered in *Un año en el Hospital de San Lázaro* by writing a novel based on the pirates that infested the coast of Yucatan. So strongly was he impressed with Sierra's use of colonial history as a field for the novel that three of his stories deal with the same generation as *La hija del judío*. Leaving out Payno's *El hombre de la situación*, Ancona's *El filibustero* is the first full length novel after Sierra to deal with the pre-independence period; and, counting *Jicoténcal* as a Mexican novel, it is the third Mexican novel to deal with that epoch.

Ancona owed more than general fields of interest to Sierra; he was indebted to his predecessor for his zeal for liberal institutions and his antagonistic attitude toward the old regime. The Inquisition assumes in Ancona's work much the same aspect and role as in *La hija del judío*. The same is true of other institutions and of conditions in general in the province of Yucatan. But Ancona is more subjective than Sierra; his attacks against the colonial regime are more direct. His portrayals are interesting; indeed *El filibustero* is of interest even to the reader of today.

In the same year that *El filibustero* was published there appeared another historical novel of Ancona under the title *La cruz y la espada,* in two volumes of 296 and 312 pages respectively.

Four years later, in 1870, he published his *Los mártires del Anáhuac* in two volumes of 326 and 322 pages respectively. Since writing *El filibustero*, Ancona had acquired a more definite conception of the technique and material of the historical novel. In *Los mártires del Anáhuac* the progression of the story is more logical, the plan is clear and is more carefully followed, and there is less to offend one's sense of reality. Out of the mass of details connected with the conquest of Mexico Ancona chose a few and developed them in such a manner as to leave a clear impression of the significant aspects of the struggle.

Because Ancona emphasized the importance of Cortés' strategy in utilizing the dissidence existing among the Amerinds rather than attributing the success of the invader to superhuman bravery and prowess, the novel has more verisimilitude than the accounts of some of the professional chroniclers of the conquest. It gains in plausibility by attributing much of the success of Cortés to the internal disintegrating forces that had destroyed the solidarity of the Aztec empire before the coming of the Spaniards. Cortés' genius stands out more clearly in the dextrous manipulation of local forces than in superhuman military exploits.

His success was made more natural by the fact that the superstitious Amerinds, bewildered by the horses and cannons of the invaders, and restrained for some time by the belief that Cortés was the returned spirit of Netzahualcoyotl, delayed their resistance long enough to permit the invader to win for himself the support of some influential local leaders.

So natural and inevitable does the course of events seem that the reader is almost prepared to agree with the Aztec priests that the gods had decreed the destruction of Aná-huac; and that the strange beared invaders were merely catalytic agents, intrinsically insignificant, furnishing only the impetus for the long and tragic processes of reduction. Ancona utilized this situation in creating a dramatic sense of impending doom, with the bearded captain playing constantly the role of villain and hero. The entire work has a good balance of dramatized history and novelistic elements.

In no other Mexican historical novel is the reader made to sympathize with both the contending forces so much as in this one. The daring band of Spaniards, led by a brave adventurer into the territory of a people capable of crushing them with an army of a quarter of a million men, excites admiration; and the intrepidity shown in the burning of their only means of escape is a true epic not surpassed by the exploits of all the imaginary knights of literature. Yet sympathy of Cortés is tempered by a like feeling for the Amerinds, superstitious, defeated by themselves and threatened with the most humiliating fate ever experienced by a people. Their grief for Anáhuac is like the lament of the Jews over the fall of Jerusalem: "By the waters of Babylon we sat down and wept," and like the song of the Babylonians: "Babylon is fallen, is fallen to rise no more." The reader is made to regret that the proud race was to be swept into the ignominy of practical slavery and spiritual annihilation.

But not all is admiration and sympathy. The Amerinds are despicable at times for their weakness and cowardice, and Cortés changes his role from that of hero to that of cruel and treacherous schemer, then back to that of hero. He is at once a genius of unsurpassed bravery and a monster of inhumanity, admired and hated by the reader.

There are a few contradictions in the story; for example, in relating the story of Tizoc's father the author has the Aztecs furnish beautiful maidens for the enjoyment of the sacrificial victim during the period of preparation for the sacrifice. This fornication is sanctioned by the priests and by the people; but later, sex irregularity is branded as the most heinous crime in the eyes of the Aztecs and their gods, punishable by crushing the heads of the guilty parties. Gelitzli, the daughter of Montezuma, whom Cortés violated after giving her a powerful drug, was cursed forever by the gods; and although she was not a willing party to the act, the people determined to sacrifice her.

The chronology is not always accurate. But the discrepancies the work contains are few and not serious, for Ancona was quite familiar with the general facts of the conquest and subsequent domination. In this story the author has aided popular appreciation of the basic social forces involved, and what is more important, has used the historical background as materials for an interesting bit of literary creation.

By pointing out the fact that the introduction of Christianity into Mexico was aided greatly by the similarity be-

tween the religion of the Amerinds and Christianity, Ancona creates a feeling of the basic similarities of human aspirations of all races, however widely dispersed. Some of the factors of each are pathetic, some are admirable; but in essence they are all human and therefore similar. Both emphasized the device of pleasing God by the infliction of suffering on human beings, especially on those considered to be enemies or heretics. In both religions that sacrifice at times went to the extreme of taking human life. The author does not descend to the plane of polemics by attempting to show the fallacies of one and the credibility of the other; he uses both to build his situations as his purposes demand.

Missing entirely the beauty of symbolism of Christian ceremonies, the aborigines had no difficulty in substituting the statues of saints for their idols and the various members of the Holy Family for their deities. Santiago, the patron saint of warriors, fitted into the place of Huitzilopochtli; San Isidro, the patron of harvests, was easily confused with Matlacueye and Centectl. Even the idea of the Trinity caused the Amerinds no trouble, its acceptance being a matter of changing names.

The system of *encomiendas* and *repartimientos* is described as a device conceived for the protection of the natives but one that resulted in their practical enslavement. It was a Don Quijote who had left the shepherd lad in the hands of Juan Haldudo for protection.

The style of *Los mártires del Anáhuac* is not attractive; it is common-place, distinctly inferior to that of the better Spanish novelists and to that of Altamirano. Indeed its lack of variety and sparkle would render a less interesting plot quite boresome.

Several of the characters are well drawn and convincing; especially is this true of Cortés and Moteuczoma. The Spanish soldiers, fired by zeal for adventure and gold, the Amerinds, astonished and bewildered, both European and native made cautious by superstition, all are interesting as literary characters.

Concha Meléndez calls attention [in *El libro y el pueblo*, 1932, Vol. X, No. 5] to the fact that *Los mártires del Anáhuac* is the first Mexican novel based on the conquest, but acceptance of her statement must be deferred until the authorship of *Jicoténcal* is definitely established. The latter work, however, was probably unknown to Mexican authors of the latter half of the century. The Cuban, Gertrudis Gómez de Avellaneda's *Guatimozín* (Madrid, 1846 and Mexico, 1853 and 1857) had acquired considerable popularity, however, and was still widely read at the time when Ancona was writing *Los mártires del Anáhuac*.

Las memorias de un alférez, published in Mérida in 1904, is a historical novel dealing with the attempts of a minor official of the Spanish army stationed in Yucatan to solve the mystery of the murder of the Captain-General of the colony. His activities brought him into conflict with the family of the girl he loved.

The plot is weakened by useless manipulations, v. gr., in one instance the protagonist was captured in a forest, bound, gagged, blindfolded and searched by a group of assassins who then disappeared, leaving him alone. Later they returned, searched him again, carried him a little farther into the woods and left him. The work abounds in unusual actions and situations. It is not entirely plausible that the protagonist should fall casually in love with a woman connected with those who were scheming to kill him, nor that without knowing her name, station or family he should call her "the one whom I loved most in all the world" twenty-four hours after seeing her for the first time. Neither is it natural that a letter found in the drawer of an old desk should be torn by chance in all the places that contained names and other data that could clear up a murder mystery. The reader cannot be expected to believe that a total stranger should be sufficiently interested in a local murder scandal to become terror-stricken, have his heart action impeded and his hair raised on his head by reading a letter written by the murderers, who probably would never have written such an incriminating document in the first place. And surely no sane man would be so indiscreet in the face of threats of death from a secret enemy as the protagonist was.

The work does contain, however, some interesting recreation of the epoch involved. Attention is called to the scarcity of books in the province as the result of censorship and import restrictions. The author compares the forces of justice to degenerate Roman nobles equipped with shields and steel swords fighting blindfolded slaves armed with wooden weapons.

Occasional statements reveal the author's tendency to seek the cause for attitudes and actions, for example:

> . . . *pero es tan hermoso desempeñar el papel de redentor.*
>
> [. . . but it is so thrilling to assume the role of redeemer.]
>
> . . . *ese egoísmo de la naturaleza humana que tiende a buscar en otras personas el origen de las desgracias que acaso nos acarreamos con nuestra propia imprudencia.*
>
> [. . . that egoism of human nature which tends to seek in others the origin of the misfortunes which we perhaps bring on ourselves by our own imprudence.]
>
> . . . *El valor en el hombre se halla en razón directa de la salud que disfruta.*
>
> [. . . Courage exists in a man in direct ratio with the health that he enjoys.]

Ancona incorporated into this work a few paragraphs on the primitive state of man and the delights of freedom in the wilds of nature that sound much like Rousseau's writing.

La cruz y la espada, 1866, a story of the love of Alonso de Benavides and Doña Beatriz, into which Zuhuy-Kak, the daughter of an Amerind king is injected, contains practically all of the abuses of the early historical novels of Spain and France. Benavides wounded his lover's father while trying to elope with her. After the young man fled to America, Doña Beatriz followed him disguised as a man. She appeared in time to save him from the Amerinds, who were in the act of sacrificing him on a stone altar. Zuhuy-Kak had fallen in love with Benavides; but she was killed by an Amerind woman in order to prevent her marriage to a Spaniard. Benavides' troubles were removed when he learned that Beatriz' father was not her father at all and had desisted from his attempts to keep the two lovers apart.

There are evidences of poor imitation of Cooper and of Chateaubriand, and an abundance of illogical imagination. Even the life of the Amerinds, which might have saved the work from complete oblivion if it had been well portrayed, has no appeal, even in fancy. It, along with the plot, lacks the semblance of reality that is necessary even in a fantastic work.

El Conde de Peñalva is an historical novel published in 1879; but it is not available for study. Though *La mestiza,* 1891, is not historical, its emphasis on the conflict between the whites on one hand and the Amerinds and *mestizos* on the other is in keeping with Ancona's preoccupation with the indigenous racial spirit.

IGNACIO MANUEL ALTAMIRANO

Ignacio Manuel Altamirano was born in Tixtla, in what is now the state of Guerrero, December 12, 1834. His family, of pure Indian stock, was given a Spanish name by the Spaniard who baptized them. The poverty common to Indians of Mexico was no stranger to Altamirano. González Obregón remarked that the boy lived to the age of fourteen like all Indian boys, ignorant, speaking only the tribal dialect of his people, untamed and occupied only with hunting and childish combats.

Ignacio Manuel's father was elected *alcalde* of the little village. This distinction aroused in the local schoolmaster an interest in the boy's education. Then Manuel started on his remarkable career as a student.

By virtue of his excellence, demonstrated in competitive examinations, he won a scholarship that intitled him to free instruction in the *Instituto Literario de Toluca.* In 1849 he took up the study of Spanish, Latin, French and philosophy in that school. His abilities engenered respect for him among his teachers and fellows to such an extent that he was made librarian of the school.

González Obregón considers the contact with books given him by his duties as librarian one of the most important influences of his career, for "there it was that he fed his soul on knowledge and erudition."

The sharp-witted scourge of authoritarianism and obscurantism in Mexico, Ignacio Ramírez, noticing this young Indian seated often outside the door of his classroom listening to his lectures, invited him in. The fiery liberalism of the teacher was the orienting force in the early attitude of the student.

Later Altamirano was given board and room at a private college in Toluca for his services as teacher of a class in French. But he was poor and impatient. He became a wanderer, trying his hand at teaching and even at production of a mediocre dramatic work, *Morelos en Cuauhtla,* which he had composed.

He entered the *Colegio de San Juan Letrán,* but his work was interrupted in 1854 by participation in the revolution. Though he was a good soldier, he realized that he was more of a student than a military man and soon resumed his study of law with the ambition of reforming the legal codes and the political machine. But even this was not enough to occupy all his attention. He became the leader of a group of young journalists interested in general social reform and in the improvement of literature. His private room became "the editorial office of a newspaper, a reformist club and a literary center which grew with the attendance of numerous students and partisans of the revolution."

His role as teacher of Latin brought him a close acquaintance with classical literature from which emanated much of his grace and good taste.

When the Congress met in 1861, after the War of Reform had stirred anew the political passions of the nation, Altamirano went to that body as a deputy. When the amnesty bill came up for discussion, Altamirano, who had already acquired fame as an orator, asked for recognition on the floor. The effect of his speech is known to most school children of Mexico today. As an example of oral eloquence it has no superior in Mexican literature.

After the triumph of the liberals under the leadership of Benito Juárez, Altamirano, Ignacio Ramírez and Guillermo Prieto founded *El Correo de México.* (González Obregón is authority for the statement that Altamirano had already founded *El Eco de la Reforma* and *La Voz del Pueblo* in the state of Guerrero.) He and Manuel Payno established *El Federalista, La Tribuna* and *La República,* the directorship of which he gave up in 1881.

In 1869 Altamirano founded *El Renacimiento,* a weekly literary magazine of considerable influence in the development of literary trends of the latter half of the nineteenth century. Altamirano was editor of *El Siglo xix, El Monitor Republicano* and *La Libertad.* He contributed generously to *El Domingo, El Artista, El Semanario Ilustrado, El Federalista, El Liceo Mexicano* and many provincial and foreign magazines.

But Altamirano's activities did not stop here. He was the center of several literary societies. He revived the defunct *Liceo Hidalgo,* was Secretary and Vice-President of *La Sociedad Mexicana de Geografía y Estadística,* founded the *Sociedad Gorostiza* composed of dramatic authors, was President of *Escritores Públicos* and of the *Sociedad Netzahualcoyotl.* He was a member of many foreign scientific and literary societies.

In political circles Altamirano was prominent, serving at various times as Fiscal de la Suprema Corte de Justicia, Procurador General de la Nación, Oficial Mayor de la Secretaría de Fomento and deputy to the National Congress.

In the field of education he was Professor of Administrative Law in the National School of Commerce, Professor of General and Mexican History in the School of Jurisprudence and Professor of Philosophy in the last named insti-

tution. In the latter part of his life his chief interest was education.

> *Leer y enseñar, y conversar sin descanso: tales fueron sus últimos afanes; los libros y la juventud, sus fieles amigos y sus hijos predilectos.*

> [To read and to teach, and to converse without ceasing; such were his greatest desires; books and youth, his faithful friends and his favorite sons.]

In 1889 Altamirano was appointed Mexican Consul General in Spain. Later he held the same post in France, having exchanged places with Manuel Payno because of his poor health. He died in San Remo February 13, 1893.

López Portillo y Rojas pronounced Altamirano's *Clemencia* the best Mexican novel of its time. It was written after the author's return from the military campaign described in the work, a campaign in which he himself had taken part. It is an expansion of a story Altamirano told one night to a group of ladies who later insisted that he put it in novel form. The first chapter appeared in *El Renacimiento* in 1869 as a part of *Cuentos de invierno,* and the remainder followed in the same magazine in serial form. In the same year Díaz de León y Santiago White printed a very attractive second edition with good photographs by Cruces y Campa and with several excellent drawings. The popularity of the second edition was so great that it was sold in a few days. *Clemencia* was later reproduced in serial form by the *Grand Journal de Pérou,* a French-Spanish newspaper of Lima. The fourth edition was printed by Mr. Armas, director of a New York illustrated newspaper called *El Ateneo,* in the first volume of his paper. The fifth edition is that which appeared with *Las tres flores, Julia,* and *La navidad en las montañas* in a collection called *Cuentos de invierno,* printed by F. Mata in Mexico in 1880. Another edition appeared in Mexico and in Paris, no date, and still another in Valencia, no date.

The setting of the story is the region around Guadalajara in December, 1863, the year of the French occupation of Mexico. The historical material serves only as a frame for the actions of two officers in the army of the republic, one handsome and with an unusual appeal for women, talented and cultured, but at heart a coward and traitor; the other unattractive, but diligent, loyal and decent. A conflict developed over the affections of a beautiful woman, with a none too pleasant result.

The characterization of the four chief personages is well done, but the most attractive features of the work are the depiction of natural scenery and the pleasing style. There is a tone of genuine artistic dignity that contrasts sharply with the perorative style of most Mexican authors of the times. The fact that occasional excesses of inflated language creep in does not destroy the general impression of artistic discretion and sincerity. It is not too much to say that this novel and others of Altamirano incorporate the best aesthetic judgment and balance to be found in the Mexican novel up to the dates of their respective compositions.

In his narrative the author knew only one vein, that of constantly serious narration in which everything conforms to the sweet sadness of his temperament. At times the effect could be heightened if he had shed his seriousness long enough to relieve the strain.

He could not escape a constant preoccupation with the sense of tragedy of human life, the melancholy that was a part of his racial heritage and that made romanticism so attractive to him and his compatriots.

Altamirano's genius was too short of flight to create full-length novels, and he lacked the organizing ability necessary to present his excellent material in impressive plots. As a result, his works are little more than short stories. But his poetic genius gave a magic touch of life to nature and laid bare the beauties of the realm beyond superficial facts of the world and human nature. It is on this penetration into the soul of things that his fame is based. His was no surface world, but one of beauty hidden from the eyes of the unworthy; and he succeeded in painting that world with beauty and grace.

Altamirano's influence in the novel was primarily that of a preceptor who illustrated his teachings with short models. His stories were too few and too scant of plot to serve as complete novels; but his teachings gave encouragement and orientation to an inexperienced generation of writers, many of whom, however, needed much more than advice.

Altamirano sensed the increase of interest in literature that followed the fall of the empire of Maximilian and attempted to turn that interest into national channels. In the press, with which he was closely connected throughout his long career, in the classroom, from the lecture platform and in gatherings of literary men he preached consistently that Mexican authors should apply the best technique of universal art to Mexican life with the interpretation of the soul of their country as an ideal. Something of his spirit of patriotism may be seen in the following statements quoted from one of his critical essays:

> *¿Acaso en nuestra patria no hay un campo vastísimo de que puede sacar provecho el novelista . . . ?*
>
> *¡Oh! si algo es rico en elementos para el literato, es este país, del mismo modo que lo es para el minero, para el agricultor y para el industrial.*
>
> *La historia antigua de México es una mina inagotable . . . Los tres siglos de la dominación española son un manantial de leyendas poéticas y magníficas . ..*
>
> *Nuestras guerras de independencia son fecundas en grandes hechos y en terribles dramas. Nuestras guerras civiles son ricas de episodios, y notables por sus resultados . . .*
>
> *Nuestra era republicana se presenta a los ojos del observador interesantísima . . .*
>
> *¿Y el último imperio? ¿Pues se quiere además de las guerras de nuestra independencia un asunto mejor para la epopeya? . . . Este pueblo mísero y despreciado, levantándose poderoso y enérgico, sin auxilio, sin dirección y sin elementos, despedazando el trono para levantar con sus restos un cadalso . . .*

[Is there not perchance, in our country a vast field from which the novelist can profitably draw materials?

Oh! if anything is rich in material for the writer, it is this country, just as for the miner, for the farmer and for the industrialist.

The ancient history of Mexico is an inexhaustible mine . . . The three centuries of Spanish rule are a veritable spring of poetic and magnificent legends.

Our wars of independence abound in great deeds and terrible dramas. Our civil wars are rich in episodes and notable for their results.

Our republican era is exceedingly interesting to the observer.

And the last empire? Does one wish in addition to the wars of our independence a better subject for epic literature? This people, miserable and despised, arousing itself, powerful and energetic, without help, without direction and without equipment, destroying the throne to raise from its debris a scaffold . . .]

But not only in Mexican history did Altamirano see a field rich in material for the writer; in the country's natural scenery and in its picturesque human types he saw an inexhaustible field that had scarcely been touched. He deplored the fact that since the days of Fernández de Lizardi and Manuel Payno Mexican writers had neglected this richest of all sources of inspiration. He called attention to the progress that had been made in other important Spanish American countries, where writers

> *Cantan su América del Sur, su hermosa virgen, morena, de ojos de gacela y de cabellera salvaje. No hacen de ella ni una dama española de mantilla, ni una* entretenue *francesa envuelta en encajes de Flandes.*
>
> *Esos poetas cantan sus Andes, su Plata, su Magdalena, su Apurimac, sus pampas, sus gauchos, sus pichireyes; trasportan a uno bajo la sombra del ombú, o al pie de las ruinas de sus templos del Sol, o al borde de sus pavorosos abismos o al fondo de sus bosques inmensos, . . . le hacen. . . escuchar el rugido de sus fieras terribles . . . y meditar a orillas de sus mares. . . .*

[They sing their South America, their beautiful virgin, dark with gazelle-like eyes and luxuriant hair. They make of her neither a Spanish lady with a mantilla nor a French entretenue wrapped in Flemish lace.

Those poets sing their Andes, their River Platte, their Magdalena, their Apurimac, their pampas, their gauchos, their *pichireyes;* they transport one to the shade of the *ombú* tree, or to the foot of the ruins of the temple of the sun god, or to the brink of their awe-inspiring abysses or to the depths of their immense forests, or they make him hear the roar of terrible wild beasts and meditate on the shore of their seas.]

As is to be expected, Altamirano saw as the chief obstacle to the proper development of this national material the habit of imitating slavishly the European models with which Mexico was flooded. He did not go to the extreme of advocating lack of attention to foreign literature; indeed he insisted that the literature of the older civilizations must be taken as a guide in the acquisition of good taste.

> *No negamos la gran utilidad de estudiar todas las escuelas literarias del mundo civilizado; seríamos incapaces de este desatino, nosotros que adoramos los recuerdos clásicos . . . No: al contrario, creemos que estos estudios son indispensables; pero deseamos que se cree una literatura absolutamente nuestra, como todos los pueblos tienen, los cuales también estudian los monumentos de los otros, pero no fundan su orgullo en imitarlos servilmente.*

> [We do not deny the great profit of studying all literary schools of the civilized world; we would be incapable of such folly, we who adore the memory of the classics . . . No; on the contrary, we believe that these studies are indispensable; but we wish for the creation of a literature entirely ours, like all peoples have, each of which also studies the literary monuments of the others, but does not base its pride on servile imitation of them.]

He expressed profound respect for such masters of the novel as Walter Scott, Cooper, Richardson, Dickens, Hugo, Balzac, and Dumas, and considered the study of their works essential to any novelist.

But he contended that foreign works were valuable to Mexican writers only for instruction in the general procedure and technique of composition, and not as sources whose materials were to be imitated. The author's attitude in this regard is best expressed in his own words:

> *En cuanto a la novela nacional, a la novela mexicana, con su color americano propio, nacerá bella, interesante, maravillosa. Mientras que nos limitemos a imitar la novela francesa, cuya forma es inadaptable a nuestras costumbres y a nuestro modo de ser, no haremos sino pálidas y mezquinas imitaciones, así como no hemos producido más que cantos débiles imitando a los trovadores españoles y a los poetas ingleses y a los franceses . . .*

> *Nosotros todavía tenemos mucho apego a esa literatura hermafrodita que se ha formado de la mezcla monstruosa de las escuelas española y francesa en que hemos aprendido, y que sólo será bastante a expulsar y a extinguir la poderosa e invencible sátira de Ramírez, que él sí es tan original y tan consumado como habrá pocos en el nuevo continente.*

> [As for the national novel, the Mexican novel, with its distinctively American color, it will be born beautiful, interesting, marvelous. As long as we limit ourselves to the imitation of the French novel, whose form is inadaptable to our customs and to our spirit, we shall produce only pale and mediocre imitations, just as we have produced only weak poetry while imitating Spanish, English and French poets . . .

We still have much fondness for that hermaph-

rodite literature which is made up of a monstrous mixture of the Spanish and French schools in which we have learned, and which can be expelled and extinguished only by the powerful and invincible satire of Ramírez, who is indeed as original and as nearly perfect as few others in the New World.]

Altamirano called attention to the recent tendency toward expansion of the novel to such a degree that it had become a medium for the presentation of historical facts, intellectual and moral viewpoints, philosophical positions, and social, political, and religious propaganda. It had come to be "the best vehicle of propaganda."

Reasoning from his major premise that morality is the most desirable characteristic of any people, and from his contention that the novel was the school of the people, he came to the conclusion that the chief duty of the novelist is to guide the masses in the formation of virtuous and wholesome attitudes. Hence, the novelist was to concern himself with teaching patriotism, chastity, industry, honesty, and order. In this connection he cited the success that had attended the church's policy of indoctrinating the public by an educational program adapted to the end it sought, and advocated the pursuit of the same policy by the novelist.

Granted the wisdom of the procedure of the church in religious instruction and the fact that art does have a moral mission to perform, such advice given to unseasoned writers of a nation without literary orientation and experience had some unfortunate results, as will appear in the examination of many subsequent works whose authors were dominated by the desire to indoctrinate their fellow countrymen. It was easy for writers of an immature society to substitute superficial conventionalities for the deep moral principles Altamirano had in mind. By morality he meant what Plato meant when he used the word; but unfortunately, not all of his followers had the philosophical background necessary for a complete understanding of its true nature.

But in spite of his views concerning the duty of the novelist to indoctrinate, he persisted in his demand for impartiality and careful study of facts.

> *En las novelas de costumbres se necesita tan grande dosis de fina observación y de exactitud, como para las novelas históricas se necesitan instrucción y criterio. De otro modo sólo se producirán monstruosidades ridículas . . . [La crítica literaria en México, 1907].*

> [In the novels of customs one needs a wealth of fine observation and accuracy and for historical novels, knowledge and sound criteria are indispensable. Otherwise there will be produced only ridiculous monstrosities . . .]

Statements concerning Altamirano's contribution to Mexican literature as critic and guide of his own and the following generations abound in the works of historians of Mexican literature. Morena Cora wrote concerning him:

> *Altamirano más que ningún otro escritor ejerció grande influencia en la juventud estudiosa de su patria.*

[Altamirano more than any other writer exercised great influence on the studious youth of his country.]

Jiménez Rueda wrote:

> *Poeta, novelista, maestro, ejerció en su tiempo una influencia decisiva en la marcha de los acontecimientos* [*Historia de la literatura mexicana*, 1928].

[Poet, novelist, teacher, in his time he had a decisive influence on the march of events.]

González Peña is not less enthusiastic in his praise:

> *Altamirano es el más grande escritor de su tiempo.*

[Altamirano is the greatest writer of his time.]

> *. . . realiza una de las más extraordinarias carreras que la historia de nuestras letras registra; es el maestro de dos generaciones; trabaja activamente en la prensa; da el tono en la crítica literaria; estimula y alienta a los que comienzan . . .*

[. . . he made for himself one of the most extraordinary careers that the history of our literature records; he is the teacher of two generations; he works actively in the press; he gives guidance in literary criticism; he stimulates and encourages those who are beginning . . .]

An examination of his literary prose, poetry and critical articles and a study of his activities in originating and directing literary societies composed of writers justify the statements quoted. But as a critic Altamirano's kind, fatherly feeling led him to praise some young writers to their hurt. His desire to encourage kept him from being as severe as his role demanded. In discussing Florencio del Castillo's work, for instance, he called the young writer:

> *. . . un escritor distinguido que fué honra de las bellas letras mexicanas . . .*

[. . . a distinguished writer who was the honor of Mexican belles lettres. . .]

Such empty phrase-making indicates that Altamirano was too prone to let his kindness soften his criticism.

Madeleine de Gogorza Fletcher

SOURCE: "The *Episodio Nacional:* An Approach to the Genre," in *The Spanish Historical Novel, 1870-1970,* Tamesis Books Limited, 1973, pp. 1-10.

[*In the following excerpt, de Gogorza Fletcher differentiates between two kinds of historical fiction in Spanish literature—the* episodio nacional *and the traditional historical novel.*]

Spanish literature in the nineteenth and twentieth centuries has developed a new genre, the *episodio nacional,* or the historical novel of the recent past, of which two types may be discerned: (1) the novel of a recent historical period prior to the writer's experience and (2) the novel of historical events contemporary with the writer's own lifetime.

The fact that prominent critics have disputed the term "historical novel" as applied to [Benito Pérez] Galdós' *Episodios* and have seen a fundamental similarity between the *Episodios* and Galdós' other novels opens up the question of genre which we shall try to clarify briefly. Amado Alonso, "Lo español y lo universal en Galdós", in his *Materia y forma en poesía* (1955), referring to the real life origin of some of the characters in the *Novelas contemporáneas,* notes that real life characters and invented ones and real historical circumstances and fictional ones are present in both the *Episodios nacionales* and the *Novelas contemporáneas.* He also points out that novels which deal with the period of the author's own lifetime are not generally called historical novels. Joaquín Casalduero in his definitive book, *Vida y obra de Galdós* (1943), states the fundamental similarity between the *Episodios* and Galdós' other novels:

> Por último, *Episodios nacionales* es título con que (Galdós) agrupaba en colección una serie de obras que fundamentalmente en nada se diferencian del resto de sus novelas.

The Marxist critic George Lukács in his general study *The Historical Novel,* trans. Hannah and Stanley Mitchell (1963), points to this lack of differentiation as a general phenomenon, concluding that the best novels of each type (the realistic novel of contemporary society and the realistic historical novel) are precisely those in which the characteristics of the two genres are most mingled.

Having said this much, we must insist that the *Episodios* do fulfill a different function from Galdós' other novels. Initially, Galdós intended them to teach the Spanish people of their history, and indeed, the *Episodios* reached a wider audience than the other novels and sold more copies. The more pedestrian tone of the opinions in the first *Episodios* (especially Series I) as contrasted to the other novels written in the same period show that Galdós was consciously addressing himself to this wider audience, using his powers of persuasion as well as of artistic judgment in the selection of his material. Contrasting *Episodios* I and II with *Doña Perfecta* for example, we see that Galdós is careful not to offend religious sentiment in the *Episodios.* The type of pious moralizing which he puts in the mouths of his two domestic females who are made to triumph over the revolutionary character in each series, Inés in Series I who verges on smugness in her advice to her dying father, the revolutionary Santorcaz and Soledad in Series II who gives lessons in Christian charity to the revolutionary Pedro Sarmiento and even lectures Monsalud, shows not only Galdós' desire at that period for moderation but also the submission of his own views (more like those of the liberal heroes) to the prevailing views of the average Spanish middle class individual (represented by the women). Joaquín Casalduero (*Vida y obra*) contrasts the symbolic value of Salvador Monsalud with that of Pepe Rey, noting that while Pepe Rey represents the philosophical-religious aspect of the struggle, Monsalud is only concerned with the political world. This is an important difference between the other novels and the *Episodios.* It is the concrete practical aspect of the national problem which comes to the fore in Galdós' *Episodios* rather than philosophical-religious theorizing. In the works of the novelists who followed Galdós in writing *episodios* we can find a strong politico-didactic element and a tendency to focus on historically significant public events occurring in the recent past or even in the author's own life time. These characteristics make it possible to differentiate the *episodio nacional* from the novel of contemporary society.

I distinguish the *episodio nacional* from the historical novel of the distant past (the traditional historical novel) only on the basis of subject matter. There is no noteworthy difference in form between the two genres as such. They differ only in content, that is, in the nature of the historical subject matter itself. Recent national history (the province of the *episodio nacional*) exerts a stronger emotional pull on the author than remoter history does and makes the author reveal his political beliefs and his expectations for the future of his country. Recent history is more alive for him, more emotionally charged than events of the distant past. Because the historical period which he describes is recent, he automatically understands many of its customs, ideas, and preoccupations and thereby avoids some of the pitfalls confronting the author of the historical novel of the distant past.

An example illustrating the difference between the *episodio nacional* and the traditional historical novel can be taken from the work of Ramón Sender, who wrote historical novels of both kinds. *Míster Witt en el cantón,* Sender's *episodio* written about the Spanish revolutionary experiment of Cartagena in 1873, reflects the emotional warmth of his current preoccupation with the contemporary revolutionary situation of Spain in 1934, and the similarities between the two situations deepen his understanding of the past. On the other hand, his five or six traditional historical novels are colder, and in them Sender's treatment of the historical subject matter, with which he is less directly acquainted, is less convincing.

. . . [Formalistic] developments in the style of an author are seen to reflect changes in the attitude of the author toward his subject matter. Of course this is an oversimplification of the complex relationship between form and content, but it is intended as a challenge to habits of critical thought which have been working mechanically on the basis of formalistic assumptions. The nature of this experimental point of view can be seen most clearly in . . . Valle-Inclán, because, of all the writers discussed, he is the most concerned with style and the most inventive and fecund in stylistic innovation. An examination of Valle-Inclán's work reveals four major phases: (1) the *Sonatas,* (2) the *Comedias bárbaras,* (3) the last two novels of the Carlist trilogy, and (4) the *Ruedo ibérico.* Each of these four phases is characterized by a change in historical perspective and a parallel change in stylistic expression.

In the historical novels discussed here, the content often seems to impose a form. There is a shape to content, to the extent even that one may ask whether style and content in the historical novel are not practically the same thing. For example, in Unamuno's *Paz en la guerra* the paradoxical nature of the philosophical content makes for discontinuity in style. Unamuno's basic ideas, in this novel as elsewhere, are paradoxical aphorisms metaphorically combining several different levels of experience, . . . where the

two ideas contained in the title *Paz en la guerra,* "peace in war", are analyzed.

When Unamuno's paradoxical ideas are extended and magnified in a realistic novel, their lack of coherence tends to separate elements of dialogue, realistic description, philosophical generalization, historical information, and so on. In spite of being related to the same subject matter, these elements do not cast light on each other. Indeed they often seem to be in contradiction. In Unamuno's work the ideas that "fighting leads to love and mutual comprehension" or that "the conflict between regionalism and centralism leads eventually to a peaceful internationalism," often contradict the experience of the fictional characters or the concrete historical events described. Elements which are interesting in themselves are forced into false relationships with other elements for the sake of the philosophical unity represented in the title.

The genre of the *episodio nacional* was initiated by the greatest Spanish novelist of the nineteenth century, Benito Pérez Galdós. In his *Episodios nacionales,* which are the first and most extensive example of the genre, there are two slightly different categories of recent history. Series I and II and part of Series III reconstruct the period of his parents' and grandparents' generation and thus belong to the first type of *episodio nacional* mentioned above. Part of Series III and Series IV and V deal with the history of Spain during Galdós' own lifetime and cannot be totally separated from his own personal reminiscences, or even perhaps from his view of contemporary society in his *Novelas contemporáneas.* Accordingly, these novels belong to the second type of *episodio.*

Corresponding to Galdós' first Episodios—that is, recent but not contemporary history—are Baroja's *Memorias de un hombre de acción,* Valle-Inclán's *Ruedo ibérico* (one would also tend to include his trilogy on the second Carlist war, since it took place when he was only seven years old), Unamuno's *Paz en la guerra* (he was nine at the time of the same war), Sender's *Míster Witt en el cantón,* and Juan Goytisolo's *Señas de identidad.* Some of these novels attempt to understand the present in historical context or to draw the lessons of the past for the future; others represent a flight from the present to a more congenial past.

The second group of novels in this category, those which correspond to Galdós' later *Episodios* (that is, novels dealing with national history during the writer's own lifetime), includes novels written about the Civil War of 1936-39 by men who took part in the conflict as adults, among them Ramón Sender (*Los cinco libros de Ariadna*), José María Gironella (*Los cipreses creen en Dios, Un millón de muertos, Ha estallado la paz*), Max Aub (*Campo cerrado, Campo abierto, Campo de sangre, Campo francés, Campo del moro, Campo de los almendros*), and Camilo José Cela (*San Camilo,* 1936). In writing about the war, none of these Spanish novelists has the exalted and poetic vision of Hemingway and other foreigners, because the foreign writers see the Spanish war as a crusade, and it is the symbolic role of Spain in the international conflict which determines their emotional attitude.

FURTHER READING

Butterfield, H. *The Historical Novel: An Essay.* Cambridge: Cambridge University Press, 1924, 113 p.
  Analyzes the relationship between the writing of historical novels and the study of history.

Cahalan, James M. *Great Hatred, Little Room: The Irish Historical Novel.* Syracuse: Syracuse University Press, 1983, 240 p.
  Traces the development of the genre in Ireland and provides analysis of Sir Walter Scott's influence on Irish historical fiction.

Chapman, Raymond. *The Sense of the Past in Victorian Literature.* Beckenham: Croom Helm, 1986, 212 p.
  Discusses the depiction of English history in Victorian literature.

Dekker, George. *The American Historical Romance.* Cambridge: Cambridge University Press, 1987, 376 p.
  Provides an in-depth study of the American historical romance including discussion on regionalism, the role of the hero and heroine, and historical romances of the South.

Fleishman, Avrom. *The English Historical Novel: Walter Scott to Virginia Woolf.* Baltimore: Johns Hopkins Press, 1971, 262 p.
  Analyzes the history and criticism of English historical fiction from the birth of the genre through the twentieth century.

Henderson, Harry. *Versions of the Past: the Historical Imagination in American Fiction.* New York: Oxford University Press, 1974, 344 p.
  Offers a detailed analysis of American historical fiction.

Kerr, James. *Fiction against History: Scott as Storyteller.* Cambridge: Cambridge University Press, 1989, 142 p.
  Examines the relationship between fiction and history in Sir Walter Scott's Waverley novels.

Lukács, Georg. *The Historical Novel.* Translated by Hannah and Stanley Mitchell. London, Merlin Press, 1962, 363 p.
  Theoretical examination of the genre from a Marxist viewpoint emphasizing the impact of social and economic developments on historical fiction.

Mizruchi, Susan L. *The Power of Historical Knowledge: Narrating the Past in Hawthorne, James, and Dreiser.* Princeton: Princeton University Press, 1988, 313 p.
  Analyzes "the problem of history" in American literature and historiography and discusses the role of history in the works of Hawthorne, James, and Dreiser.

Petrey, Sandy. *Realism and Revolution: Balzac, Stendhal, Zola, and the Performances of History.* Ithaca: Cornell University Press, 1988, 211 p.
  Discusses works of Balzac, Stendhal, and Zola as representative of the French realist novel.

Urey, Diane Faye. *The Novel Histories of Galdós.* Princeton: Princeton University Press, 1988, 267 p.
  Discusses the historical novels, known as *episodios nacionales*, of Spain's Benito Pérez Galdós.

White, Hayden. "Four Kinds of Realism in Nineteenth-Century Historical Writing." In *Metahistory: The Historical Imagination in Nineteenth-Century Europe.* Baltimore: Johns Hopkins University Press, 1973, 448 p.
  Analyzes historical realism as romance, comedy, tragedy, and satire, based on the views of four historians, including Alexis de Tocqueville.

Women's Diaries

INTRODUCTION

Historically, women kept records of their families' economic transactions, their husbands' accomplishments, and the births and deaths of family members. During the Victorian era, however, these records became more personal. At a time when individual rights and liberties were emphasized, women wrote more often of their own feelings: their opinions of the institution of marriage, their political beliefs, their aspirations. Until recently, the study of nineteenth-century women's diaries focused primarily on figures such as Jane Welsh Carlyle and Dorothy Wordsworth, both of whom were related to and acquainted with members of the literary canon. Scholars also read diaries to study the accomplishments of writers such as Louisa May Alcott, Elizabeth Barrett Browning, George Eliot, George Sand, and Mary Shelley, or to witness the political dealings of people like Doroteya Kristoforovna Lieven and Queen Victoria. However, diaries of seemingly ordinary women are now being studied because they make apparent the thoughts of nineteenth-century women, enlarging the history of the era. Women's private writings are thus recognized as valuable tools to understanding fully the nineteenth century.

REPRESENTATIVE WORKS

Louisa May Alcott
  Louisa May Alcott: Her Life, Letters, and Journals, 1889
Marie Bashkirtseff
  Le journal de Marie Bashkirtseff, 1887
  [*The Journal of Marie Bashkirtseff,* 1890]
Elizabeth Barrett Browning
  Diary by E.B.B.: The Unpublished Diary of Elizabeth Barrett Barrett, 1831-1832, 1969
Fanny Burney
  Diary and Letters of Madame d'Arblay. 7 vols. 1842-1846
  The Early Diary of Frances Burney, 1768-1778. 2 vols. 1889
  The Journals and Letters of Fanny Burney (Madame d'Arblay). 12 vols. 1972-1984
Lady Charlotte Bury
  Diary Illustrative of the Times of George the Fourth. 4 vols. 1838-1839
Jane Welsh Carlyle
  Letters and Memorials of Jane Welsh Carlyle. 3 vols. 1883
Mary Boykin Chesnut
  A Diary from Dixie, 1905
George Eliot [Mary Ann Evans]

George Eliot's Life as Related in Her Letters and Journals. 3 vols. 1885
Emily Hawley Gillespie
  "A Secret to Be Burried": The Diary and Life of Emily Hawley Gillespie, 1858-1888, 1989
Fanny Kemble
  Journal of F. A. Butler. 2 vols. 1835
  Journal of a Residence on a Georgian Plantation in 1838-1839, 1863
Doroteya Kristoforovna Lieven
  The Unpublished Diary and Political Sketches of Princess Lieven, 1925
George Sand [Amandine-Aurore-Lucile Dupin Dudevant]
  Journal intime (posthume) publié par Aurore Sand, 1926
  [*The Intimate Journal of George Sand,* 1929]
Lady Charlotte Elizabeth Guest Schreiber
  Lady Charlotte Guest: Extracts from Her Journal, 1833-1852, 1950
Mary Wollstonecraft Shelley
  Mary Shelley's Journal, 1947
Victoria, Queen of England
  Leaves from the Journal of Our Life in the Highlands, from 1848 to 1861, 1867
  More Leaves from the Journal of a Life in the Highlands, from 1862 to 1882, 1884
Dorothy Wordsworth
  Journals of Dorothy Wordsworth. 2 vols. 1897

OVERVIEW

Cynthia Huff (essay date 1985)

SOURCE: An introduction to *British Women's Diaries: A Descriptive Bibliography of Selected Nineteenth-Century Women's Manuscript Diaries,* AMS Press, 1985, pp. ix-xxxvi.

[*In the following excerpt, Huff describes commonalities of form, structure, and content among nineteenth-century women's diaries.*]

Not long after the close of the nineteenth century, Virginia Woolf speculated about the form and content of diaries while writing her own. Characteristically, she decided that she would like hers "to resemble some deep old desk, or capacious hold-all, in which one flings a mass of odds and ends." Yet she realized too that the diary could not be shapeless, for "looseness quickly becomes slovenly," and she feared her own diary writing "becoming slack and untidy." Woolf's comments in many ways capture the impulse and practice of diary writing for nineteenth-century British women. Women in the last century wrote diaries because they wished to embrace the flux of life, to store its nuances in a place of safe keeping, so that when the time came they could sift and evaluate the past, whether it was measured by the recurrence of birth and death or by the tallying of accounts. As Woolf realized, creating a diary is a skill which requires the manipulation of the vastness of experience. By deciding what to enter in her diary and which form to use to encase the record of her life, each [diarist] tells her own story in her own way.

Recently scholars have recognized our need to hear the stories told by little-known or neglected women, for only by hearing their voices can we rightfully evaluate our own past and their place within it. Echoing Virginia Woolf, Elaine Showalter [in *A Literature of Their Own*] emphasizes that the extraordinary woman must be viewed in relation to her contemporaries, and, furthermore, that the study of women's lives provides new pathways for the investigation of numerous other disciplines. Her comments are generally confirmed by scholars of women's studies, who are keenly aware of the necessity for uncovering the writings of women, not only because these are fascinating accounts, but also because these records contain much information about medical practices, the configuration of the family, recreational activities, child care, political events, and social customs. . . .

Nineteenth-century British women's manuscript diaries are of two types: those kept in a printed format and those whose format is self-determined. The self-determined volumes are usually bound, although in a few cases the diary keeping impulse exerts so much influence that the writer creates a makeshift journal of single sheets of paper folded together. In the self-determined diary the writer is free to choose the format, which can vary from daily to yearly entries and may include newspaper clippings, sketches, and poems, as well as notations of expenditures or addresses. The printed format is imposed on the diarist, although the writer often ignores and violates the rules, spaces, dates, and arrangements dictated by the diary publishers.

One of the primary features of diaries with printed formats is their compendium of useful information, since they were intended by their publishers to function simultaneously as personal records, almanacs, and account books. The blurring of the distinctions between the monetary and the personal, as well as between the public and the private, is especially strong in volumes with printed formats, where the diarist enters her comments alongside pages for accounts. Such an ordering facilitates an equation of monetary reckoning and personal evaluation. Furthermore, the inclusion in diaries with printed formats of certain types of public information and features of popular entertainment provide a direction and framework for the diarist's rendition of her life.

The contents of diaries with printed formats changed over the course of the century. As entertainment began increasingly to center on the acquisition of goods, the rebusses, charades, and Vauxhall songs which were common in the first few decades gave way to a spate of advertisements at the close of the Victorian era. Such a change betokens the different attitudes at the beginning and the end of the nineteenth century, and indicates as well how the study of diaries with printed formats can help the social historian determine trends.

Analyzing the format of these diaries helps determine the writer's self-conception and social class. . . . By selecting a volume entitled a "Ladies' Diary," a writer provides a possible clue to her class, and certainly to her self-image, while the printed contents of such volumes indicate what the general interests of ladies were supposed to be. The publishers of these diaries felt their buying public would be entertained by color foldouts, especially common at the beginning of the century, but they also thought information would attract their audience. In accord with Virginia Woolf's idea of the diary as a catch-all, printed diaries list facts about virtually everything from foreign postage to taxes on lunatics. Interestingly, many of the advertisements in printed volumes feature other diaries.

In addition to the printed contents of diaries, the writer's use of such a volume is significant. The spaces for the diarist's comments in volumes with printed formats are ordinarily quite restricted, and the majority of the writers reacted to this by spilling their remarks into the spaces designated for other entries or by continuing certain entries at the back of the volume. Occasionally diarists failed to compose entries in the spaces allotted to a particular day, and in such instances the writer merely redated the entries. A lack of spacing between entries or comments entered both vertically and horizontally are common in some self-determined volumes.

Yet another feature common to both self-determined diaries and diaries with printed formats is the summary and anniversary entry. The memoranda space in many diaries with printed formats is meant to function as an ordering device, an opportunity for the diarist to review her actions, but frequently the space is not used by the writer for this purpose. Instead, diarists write summary and anniversary entries when noteworthy or recurrent events take place. Childbearing, family deaths, birthdays, wedding anniversaries, and the end of the year serve as pauses in the diarist's life and occasions for composing retrospective entries. Entries which merely summarize a period of time during which the writer has been unable to compose her diary usually occur after childbirth or a family death. In such cases the diarist primarily recounts the event. However, the purpose of entries written on anniversaries is usually self-evaluation and reflection, for here the diarist considers the past year's texture and activities as well as her recent behavior, and looks forward to the coming year.

If diaries were merely composed diurnally they might be the untidy creations which Virginia Woolf feared, but instead their narrative structure shows recurrent traits which provide them with a discernible form. Rather, diaries are structured by significant events in the writer's life whose occurrence must be considered when determining the arrangement of the individual diary and the perimeters of the genre. Anniversary and summary entries serve an important function in the diary's arrangement, since they act as divisions which are roughly analogous to chapters in a novel or stanzas in a poem.

These nineteenth-century manuscript diaries also exhibit common stylistic properties. . . . Diaries have often been considered highly personal, almost solipsistic, compositions whose secretive quality is symbolized by a lock. However, such a conception of the diary is at odds with the stylistic features of nineteenth-century manuscripts, where the use of the first person plural pronoun indicates that diaries were often written as family documents. Diarists frequently employ "we" rather than "I," and their common omission of the singular pronoun makes their entries seem distanced rather than intimate. The collective quality captured by the use of "we" points to a society where the family rather than the individual was often the most important unit, and where women in particular were expected to subsume their identity in the familial configuration. "We" is also employed by diarists when they are composing their works as travelogues where its use again shows its collective function.

A reading of nineteenth-century manuscripts indicates the self-reflexive qualities of the genre. Many diarists appear to be aware of an audience, for they often begin their journals by addressing a possible future reader, often themselves at some later date, or a family member. Because a woman was frequently the designated chronicler of family records, she copied out the diaries of family members, but she might also render another's diary because of its importance for herself. One way of learning about the thoughts and activities of a friend or relative was to read her diary or to hear it read aloud. The well-established practice of diary reading may help account for the frequent use of "we," since this is a narrative device which includes the reader or listener and which, consequently, was often used by nineteenth-century novelists.

Yet other stylistic features point to the conscious craft of diary writing and indicate that Virginia Woolf's sense of the diary as both a carefully considered product and a catch-all captures its seemingly contradictory essence. Diarists apparently often reread their journals and edited them, since additional comments and crossed-through words and phrases appear in the manuscripts. These changes indicate the writer's awareness of an audience just as their tendency to use circumlocutions does. When the diarists considered a word or phrase objectionable, they wrote in a foreign language or employed dots and dashes. Their inclination to mark over pencilled entries with ink also indicates the diarists' sense of their creations as something permanent.

Diarists' habitual use of standard narrative techniques helps give their writing a literary tone and quality. In many diaries the writer narrates one or more deathbed scenes, and to capture the drama of the moment, uses quotation marks throughout the dialogue. Long narrative accounts of important events or conversations are a staple in many journals. Diarists often relate anecdotes with a novelistic verve, providing punch lines, moral plots, character delineations, and well-constructed scenes.

The tone and intent of diaries can change rapidly from humorous to solemn, as the author switches from narrating a fascinating incident to addressing God. The direct addresses to the Lord, which occur most commonly in sum-

mary and anniversary entries, seem closely related to the sermons and prayers which were a daily ingredient in the lives of nineteenth-century women. In addition to addressing God about spiritual matters, diarists also sought His help during dire circumstances such as childbirth, illness, or death. In such instances their sentence length and structure usually varies from its normal pattern. The change in the structure and length of sentences often signals a shift in import in the diaries, just as it does in other kinds of narrative. Diarists who write more about their inner lives tend to write longer sentences and entries, while the women who concentrate on outside events construct more fragments and shorter entries. The latter may occur partly because so many fragmentary phrases and terse entries are frequently extensions of account books.

The content of nineteenth-century British women's manuscripts is as wide-ranging as the concept of the diary as a "capacious hold-all" would imply. At one end of the spectrum of possible journal forms stands the account book. Some of the manuscripts included in this bibliography are primarily account books, though women often combined the rendering of accounts with comments about their daily lives or their spiritual progress. The variety of items listed in even a short volume employed for keeping accounts is staggering; and this type of diary indicates the complexity and diversity of nineteenth-century life as well as the numerous discrepancies between it and our own. The cost of hair oil, chimney pots, and mahogany screens, as well as of staple items such as coal, beer, and sugar commonly appear in diaries, which are an excellent source for the expenditures of everyday life in the last century. Naturally, the items or expenses which occur in diaries changed somewhat over the course of the century. It is common in diaries written during the first few decades of the nineteenth century to see listings of amounts won or lost at cards, while later diarists include the cost of train travel. Women also frequently record the cost of hiring servants and laborers.

The extensive keeping of accounts in diaries shows the scope of women's managerial functions and business acumen. Since women frequently employed their diaries to keep track of the estate's affairs, they were often responsible for recording variables such as weather changes, harvest yields, and the acquisition of animals. In fact, comments about the weather form such a regular feature in the diaries that they are not noted in the index.

Another type of diary represented in the bibliography is the travel journal. Often, the travelogue forms only a part of the diarists' record, since many simply used the same volume to record their activities at home and during their journeys. At home or traveling, the diarists commonly noted who visited or dined, and what entertainments they attended, but there are some features unique to the travel journal. Travel narratives frequently include sketches and postcards, and the more interesting accounts reveal the writer's attitude toward foreigners. On the whole the British diarists were quite xenophobic, and contrast unfavorably the customs of others with their own. The elasticity of the diary form permits the capturing of diverse experiences and the molding of opinion, both concomitants of travel. Diarists often wrote accounts of their sojourns for the enjoyment and information of family and friends as well as for their own recollection; and when their diaries assume the configuration of travelogues they become similar to the accounts of tours so popular during the Victorian era and one of the forerunners of modern travel brochures.

Since they primarily record things, whether expenditures or daily activities, both travel journals and account books are outer-directed diaries. Outer-directed diaries concentrate not so much on the writer's reactions to events, but on the events themselves, and the diarist's comments about physical possessions are ordinarily rendered without any indication of how these relate to her life. Outer-directed diaries focus on the accoutrements of the writer, whether her collection of objects takes the form of places visited or the acquisition of goods. The outer-directed diary accords with Woolf's definition of the form as a "capacious hold-all," for it places side-by-side "a mass of odds and ends," without necessarily indicating their relationship to one another or to the diarist.

If travelogues and account books stand at one end of the spectrum of diary forms, the religious record, which presents inner rather than outer experience, stands at the other. Like account books and travelogues, the religious diary is constructed with a definite purpose. Even though the religious impulse may not dominate the entire diary, writers often become more spiritually inclined after the occurrence of momentous events. Nineteenth-century British women frequently set out to compose diaries whose primary intent was to evaluate their spiritual progress and to cite their participation in religious observances and activities. The Quakers in particular wrote diaries which record their attendance at monthly meetings, visits to the faithful and to possible converts, and spiritual tribulations and triumphs. Since important religious activities are repeated at specified times and the Quakers' experiences are related to their religious and social commitment, much of the content of their journals is relatively predictable.

Other religious diarists tend to follow similar patterns. Intensely spiritual diarists tend to see God's hand everywhere, and to view others as exemplars. Most diarists consider some relatives or friends as exemplary; and, especially when a loved one has died, she may eulogize the noble characteristics of this individual. In their zeal to improve their behavior and become more worthy Christians, religious diarists consistently compare themselves, usually to their disparagement, to some worthy individual. The esteemed person is often the diarist's minister, but it can also be Christ, a Biblical character, or a dying person.

Especially if they had suffered intensely and patiently, the dying were considered particularly saintly. One of the major activities of religious diarists is visiting the terminally ill. Since this was a form of charity considered appropriate to the female domain and sensibilities, providing solace to the dying was not restricted to any one group of women. But those who were religious were especially committed to this pursuit. Their records are filled with deathbed scenes which emphasize the beauty of death and its release

from worldly trials into perpetual bliss. Religious diarists narrated deathbed scenes for much the same reason that they held up others as exemplars: in both cases the diarists wished to alter their own behavior to accord with spiritual teachings.

Diaries kept by very religious women are geared toward altering the self and relating personal experience; like other inner-directed diaries, they tend to be structured around personally significant events. Anniversaries serve as milestones which afford the diarist an opportunity to review her past, to anticipate the future, and to evaluate her behavior. Yearly anniversaries necessitate a periodic review of the diarist's self, which underscores and accentuates the journal's purpose of shaping behavior.

Religious diaries are not the only type of personal record designed to effect moral reformation. Nineteenth-century British children were encouraged by their parents to write diaries, and journals were given as gifts to both children and servants. It is common to read in manuscript diaries that a young child is told to keep an account of his or her life so that he or she can recall past actions and hence learn to correct mistakes and use time wisely.

Perhaps the extreme example of the diary's use in molding the behavior of children occurs when a governess details her pupil's progress. Since the teacher not only records the ratings achieved in various subjects by the student, but also comments obliquely on her relationship with her pupil and employer, behavior book diaries reveal as much about the governess as about the pupil. Although behavior books may have an ostensibly objective purpose in mind, they imply much about the governess's social position, and her educational expectations and beliefs. They serve as excellent source material about the role of the governess in the last century; and their rhetorical construction is complex enough to reward students fascinated by this unusual autobiographical form.

For many women, the diaristic impulse is less directed than account books or religious records. The journals composed by nineteenth-century women tend instead to amalgamate the qualities of inner- and outer-directed diaries. Entries vary from sketchy listings to long, personally revealing descriptions of important events. Such diaries are a good source for an examination of the genre's form and content, as they include a wide spectrum of topics, styles, and structures. Areas of interest and common configurations recur in the diary, and certain events ordinarily experienced by nineteenth-century women provide the key to both the form and content of most manuscript journals. A woman's depiction of her life varies, of course, depending on her age and the years in which she wrote. Younger women are more preoccupied with marriage while older women focus on death. Given such variables, the diaries include comments about marriage and men, service and self-identity, public events and family experiences.

Children may begin writing about their lives because their parents urge it, but even diaries which are initiated through a sense of duty usually only continue if they help the writer evaluate her life. The diary allows its creator to sift and mold her existence, and the very act of writing gave nineteenth-century women a sense of control and identity they might otherwise have lacked. Keeping a diary enabled women to enter their achievements and failures, sort out their relationships, and converse with an understanding friend, a role the diary often filled. Although these processes are intrinsic to the very act of composing a diary, they are most prevalent in the accounts maintained by girls and young women.

Two topics which surface again and again in diaries written early in life are marriage and the desire to be male. In the last century girls were painfully aware both of the inferior status of their sex, and of men's inability to live up to their exalted position. Young women commonly imagined what they would do had they been born male, for many desired to make their mark in the world. The accident of birth prevented them from pursuing many of their goals, because women's social and political power was limited in the last century. Young women most resented their lack of freedom. Some fantasized about being missionaries in India to convert unbelievers, but many, attracted by pomp and glory, wished to become soldiers, and virtually all desired the escape from confinement which they felt males enjoyed. Young women in the nineteenth century, of course, saw their brothers reap the benefits of an education far superior to their own, and experienced as well the restrictions of chaperonage.

Accompanying women's expression of their wish for greater influence was a gnawing sense that men's superior status was largely a social construction. Men and the relationship between the sexes are frequent subjects in nineteenth-century women's diaries, though some modern readers may be startled that such topics were discussed not only by radical feminists but by ordinary women as well. Despite some acceptance of stereotypes of female purity and passivity and male worldliness and aggressiveness, the diarists saw men as considerably more flawed than the ideal of the omniscient, benevolent patriarch would suggest. One diarist commented that men failed to see the humanity of the Indian servants they despised, while another expressed her disdain for the opposite sex by writing "men" in minuscule letters. Though aware that men were supposed to posses superior attributes, she commented that all the ones she knew were mean and ignoble. Even though young women tended to criticize men in general, they often made exceptions for brothers and husbands.

The relationship between brothers and sisters in the last century was complex, and further study might help unravel the intricacies of nineteenth-century family structures. Because males had a superior education and greater physical freedom, sisters often had to rely on their brothers for knowledge. Too, the closeness of siblings encouraged a sense of companionship between sisters and brothers, and throughout their lives women frequently asked their brothers for assistance rather than their husbands. Circumstances would encourage a young woman to consider her brothers, especially the eldest, as more exemplary than other males. The eldest brother frequently achieved this position by tutoring his sisters. Some diaries detail these methods of instruction as well as the diarist's desire to ad-

here to the moral code her oldest brother exemplified. There are instances where a sister's adoration of an elder brother resembles her love of Christ; her diary is a monument to his achievements.

But their diaries serve too as a means of enabling women to cope with marriage, a momentous change which frequently symbolized loss and death. Young women dreaded marriage because it meant leaving the family home and the security of close and long-established relationships and a familiar milieu. Many agonized about the advent of marriage and came to accept betrothal only by exalting the superior qualities of the husband, who to some extent psychologically replaced the eldest brother. Most young women knew their husbands merely cursorily before they married, and many congratulate themselves if during the new couple's honeymoon they socially act like brother and sister.

Marriage structures nineteenth-century British women's manuscript diaries. The diarists' detailed descriptions and their recognition of their altered position indicates the importance of the wedding day. Entries depicting the day of the wedding are quite long, and note the guests at the wedding breakfast and service, the exact time and place of the ceremony, her behavior throughout, and, most significantly, her new status as wife. The diarists express their awareness of their new identity by referring to their husbands by their Christian names for the first time.

In the last century childbirth usually closely followed marriage. Parturition served as another important chapter in many diarists' lives and enabled women to shape their accounts. Childbirth constituted a journey into fear and anxiety for nineteenth-century women, as the dangers of disease and death were great. Understandably, Victorian women did not distinguish between childbirth and other bodily disorders; and given the fact that women had ample reason to fear for their lives, it is not surprising that they used their diaries to prepare themselves for the momentous event and to record their symptoms. Two sisters, who were both expecting their first child, passed a series of secret notes back and forth. This practice, which is recorded in one sister's diary, must have mitigated the anguish and pain of pregnancy by helping to establish and maintain female solidarity. Since diaries were commonly read by female friends and relatives, the similarities in the way pregnant women constructed their entries may point to an existing ritual bond among women.

The account of the birth itself is especially significant, for this is virtually always a summary entry which provides an important pause in the diary and the diarist's life, and, like the descriptions of marriage, follows a pattern. Although the entry detailing the birth may be written several months later, the mother is very scrupulous about noting when she was taken ill, who attended the confinement, the precise time of the birth, and her reactions to it. Yet another common feature of the entries about parturition is the expression of fear and anxiety, and to avoid further alarming family members, mothers often confided their distress to their diaries.

When not engaged in the process of childbearing, nineteenth-century women often nursed the sick and assisted other women during childbirth. Since diaries were used to record these activities, they serve now, as they did then, as compendia of details about parturition and disease. Many accounts become primarily descriptions of the illnesses undergone by friends and relatives. They serve other purposes too. Because diaries were commonly read by others, they were apparently a source for much medical information and helped women reinforce their prescribed roles as nurses. Diaries also enabled women to mold themselves according to the community's expectations and to play their proper part in the support system provided by women during childbirth. Ironically, nineteenth-century women's ability to use their diaries to cope with the ordeals of disease and childbirth may have hindered us from properly judging their social contributions. Contrary to popular belief, Victorian women were not idle or mere trophies exhibited by their husbands, for the large role disease played in their lives, either through childbirth or nursing, forced them continually to employ their time usefully.

Women in the last century were not always involved in nursing or childbirth. Manuscript diaries indicate that women participated in the public life of Britain, even though they did so less than men. Because women could not vote, their interest in politics was largely vicarious. Some diarists followed political developments closely, especially if a relative were active in Parliament, and virtually all noted particularly newsworthy events in the government. The condemnation of Napoleon is a common strain in diaries written early in the century, as are comments about social unrest, which indicate class bias.

Women's perception of the significant cultural events and activities which helped mold nineteenth-century society provides a more complete portrait of the age. Diaries written in the middle years of the century contain descriptions of and reactions to the Great Exhibition and the coming of the railroad. Then as now, London epitomized Britain, and whether a diarist called it her home or was merely a sojourner, she recorded London plays and exhibitions, sights, such as the British Museum or the Bank, and lectures, public readings, and religious services. The last were not activities confined to London since all are staples in nineteenth-century manuscript diaries. Remarks about reading and sports are also prevalent. Riding horseback was common for women throughout the century, while towards the end croquet and tennis came into vogue. Many diaries contain lengthy lists of the writer's reading, and often women used their accounts to respond to character delineation, especially of women.

Although women were certainly a part of male cultural and recreational activities, their role and their identity centered on serving others. Entertainment and educational endeavors often fell under the rubric of service, since women escorted children to enlightening and amusing events or supervised these at home. But clearer expressions of service were performing secretarial duties, dispensing charity, and nursing the sick and dying. Diaries may function partly as account books because wives and unmarried daughters often acted as secretaries for the head of the household, though occasionally a young woman would perform these duties for her mother. Consequently, manuscript diaries contain notations of letters written, bills paid, and household items procured. The diaries also show women's participation in an extensive system of charity, for they describe distributing coal and blankets to the poor, giving money to the needy, and teaching and supervising in schools for destitute children.

As the professions began to assume their twentieth-century configuration and as more of the functions of service were taken over by the state, the diversity of duties engaged in by women started to diminish. This trend may have accounted in part for the inaccurate contemporary view of nineteenth-century women as useless. However, as their diaries attest, the life of women revolved around the duties of service. Writing and re-reading their diaries must have made women conscious of their identity through the rendering of service and confident about their place in nineteenth-century society.

Because much of a woman's life was spent nursing the sick and dying, deaths and illnesses form a large portion of nineteenth-century manuscript diaries. Writers often used their journals to cope with the loss occasioned by the demise of friends and relatives. Older women, in particular, concentrated on the loss of loved ones, and their diaries seem to have helped them prepare for their own deaths as well.

Diaries and their composition still served as a bastion against the finality of death, even though accounts often end because either the writer or a loved one has died. By exhibiting the indelible stamp of each woman's existence and the ways in which she wished to present her being, diaries act as a monument to, and a recreation of, the life of their writer. British women's manuscript diaries are not the untidy, shapeless creations Virginia Woolf feared. Through their diverse subject matter and a variety of forms and styles, these diaries nonetheless exhibit recurrent patterns which indicate how each writer evaluated her milieu and herself, and chose to construct a record which mitigated against the chaos of death.

Margaret Willy on the relationship between women and diary-writing:

The keeping of diaries, as demonstrated by men from Pepys and Evelyn onwards, is by no means a mainly feminine province. Nevertheless there is something in the activity which strongly appeals to female instinct and inclination. The figure of the young girl writing up her private journal in her room late at night is a familiar one in fiction. And in fact, although we might hesitate to go as far as the writer who suggested 'that women make more refreshing, more effective diarists than men,' the art of the English diary has been enriched by a good many notable contributions on the distaff side.

Margaret Willy, in an introduction to Three Women Diarists: Celia Fiennes, Dorothy Wordsworth, Katherine Mansfield, *Longmans, Green & Co., 1964.*

DIARY AS HISTORY

Lillian Schlissel   (essay date 1982)

SOURCE: An introduction to *Women's Diaries of the Westward Journey,* revised edition, Schocken Books, 1992, pp. 9-17.

[*In the introduction to* Women's Diaries of the Westward Journey, *Schlissel describes nineteenth-century women's diaries as sources for a more complete and accurate history of the American Western expansion.*]

[*Women's Diaries of the Westward Journey*] began with a fascination for the diaries of the overland women, with the detail of their lives and the dramatic dimensions of their everyday existence. These were ordinary women who were caught up in a momentous event of history. Between 1840 and 1870, a quarter of a million Americans crossed the continental United States, some twenty-four hundred miles of it, in one of the great migrations of modern times. They went West to claim free land in the Oregon and California Territories, and they went West to strike it rich by mining gold and silver. Men and women knew they were engaged in nothing less than extending American possession of the continent from ocean to ocean. No other event of the century except the Civil War evoked so many personal accounts as the overland passage. Young people and even children kept diaries and felt that their lives, briefly, had become part of history. The mundane events of each day—the accidents and the mishaps and the small victories—had grown significant. In the case of women, suddenly, because of their diaries, their daily lives became accessible, where so much of the life of nineteenth-century women has disappeared from view.

The westward movement was a major transplanting of young families. All the kinfolk who could be gathered assembled to make that hazardous passage together. Women were part of the journey because their fathers, husbands, and brothers had determined to go. They went West because there was no way for them *not* to go once the decision was made.

The emigrants came from Missouri, Illinois, Iowa, and Indiana, and some all the way from New York and New Hampshire. Most of them had moved to "free land" at least once before, and their parents and grandparents before them had similarly made several removals during their lifetime. These were a class of "peasant proprietors." They had owned land before and would own land again. They were young and consumed with boundless confidence, believing the better life tomorrow could be won by the hard work of today. Emblematic of their determination was Barsina French, who fastidiously copied penmanship and grammatical exercises into her diary as the oxen led her parents' wagon across the empty plains.

The journey started in the towns along the Missouri River between St. Joseph and Council Bluffs. These settlements came to be known as the "jumping-off places." In the winter months emigrants gathered to join wagon parties and to wait for the arrival of kin. It was an audacious journey through territory that was virtually unknown. Guidebooks promised that the adventure would take no more than three to four months time—a mere summer's vacation. But the guidebooks were wrong. Often there was no one in a wagon train who really knew what the roads would bring, or if there were any roads at all. Starting when the mud of the roads began to harden in mid-April, the emigrants would discover that the overland passage took every ounce of ingenuity and tenacity they possessed. For many, it would mean six to eight months of grueling travel, in a wagon with no springs, under a canvas that heated up to 110° by midday, through drenching rains and summer storms. It would mean swimming cattle across rivers and living for months at a time in tents.

Over eight hundred diaries and day journals kept by those who made the overland journey have been published or catalogued in archives, and many more are still in family collections. As a general category, the nineteenth-century diary is something like a family history, a souvenir meant to be shared like a Bible, handed down through generations, to be viewed not as an individual's story but as the history of a family's growth and course through time. Overland diaries were a special kind of diary, often meant to be published in county newspapers or sent to relatives intending to make the same journey the following season. Many of them are filled with information about the route, the watering places, the places where one could feed the cattle and oxen, and the quality of the grasses along the way. Such diaries seldom contain expression of intimate feelings, but there are occasions when emotions flash out, beyond control and sharp.

The story of the Overland Trail has been told many times, and emigrant diaries have been used before in these histories. Merrill Mattes, in his study *The Great Platte River Road,* drew upon some six hundred diaries as he described the Trail from the Missouri to the South Pass of the Rockies. And other historians, among them John Faragher [in *Women and Men on the Overland Trail*], Howard Lamar [in "Rites of Passage: Young Men and Their Families in the Overland Trail Experience, 1843-69," in *Soul-Butter and Hog Wash and Other Essays on the American West*], Julie Roy Jeffrey [in *Frontier Women: The Trans-Mississippi West, 1840-1880*], and John Unruh [in *The Plains Across: The Overland Emigrants and the Trans–Mississippi West, 1840–1880*], have used such diaries as the bases for revisions of different aspects of the West's history. No study, though, has been woven entirely out of the stuff of the women's writing in order to assess whether our picture of this single event of history, the overland experience, is in significant manner altered by the perception of the women.

Working with personal papers—letters and diaries—presents the historian with special problems. As documents, these items are the accounts of singularities. They record the particular moment and the personal response. Therefore it is necessary to determine whether they are merely idiosyncratic and anomalous, or whether they form part of a larger configuration that contains and explains disparate events. Only when the patterns emerge with regularity can one believe the responses are representative.

[*Women's Diaries of the Westward Journey*] is made of the diaries, reminiscences, and letters of 103 women, a random sample among the thousands of women who went West. These are the diaries of white women, many of them daughters of second and third generation American families. Some attempt is made to include the experiences of black women, many of whom went West as slaves. White or black, these women neither directed events nor affected the course of the journey. They were ordinary women in ordinary families, and the question is whether, as their story unfolds, the historical event takes on new dimension.

What I have looked for in reading these diaries were places where the women seemed to see something different than their men saw. What I asked was whether the overland experience, studied so many times before, would be revealed in a new aspect through the writings of women, and whether such perspective as the women bring might prove to be historically valuable.

The first step was to reconstruct from the diaries in fine detail the daily lives of the women, to separate out of the diaries those writings that pertained to the "woman's sphere." In the course of describing the daily life of the women, I came to see the design of the emigrant family and something of the dimensions of its emotional balances and work roles. For while it is true that family history cannot be reconstructed from women's writings alone, nevertheless the women were the shapers of the family, and it is they who provide us with primary access to the internal dynamics of households.

Certain dimensions emerged simply and easily. For example, marriage was the social norm accepted by both men and women, although within the structure of marriage men were considerably more free. Great numbers of men went West, leaving their wives and children at home; women, in contrast, almost always traveled within a family structure.

Most marriages seemed companionable. They were entered into in recognition that farming and particularly the work of making a farm out of a frontier was work that required a large family if it were to succeed. Dynamics within the family, what historian John Faragher has termed the "political economy of sex," was determined by the work of each partner, but the balance of power always followed upon the strong prescriptions of patriarchy. Men were the heads of households, and while frontier women were often called upon to perform "men's work," those additional chores did not yield them any extra perquisites.

On the Overland Trail, women strove to be equal to the demands of the day. They asked no special help or treatment. They responded to the spectacular beauty of the land, and they took keen interest in the economies of the road, recording the costs of ferriage and food supplies. They were as knowledgeable as men about the qualities of grasses for the animals. They understood what was expected of them and endeavored to do their share of the work of each day.

The women on the Overland Trail did the domestic chores: they prepared the meals and washed the clothes and cared for the children. But they also drove the ox teams and collected pieces of dung they called "buffalo chips" to fuel their fires when there was no wood. And when there were no buffalo chips, they walked in clouds of dust behind the wagons, collecting weeds. They searched for wild berries and managed to roll some dough on a wagon seat and bake a pie over hot rocks in order to lift meals out of the tedium of beans and coffee.

For women traveling with small children, the overland experience could be nerve-wracking. Children fell out of the wagons. They got lost among the hundreds of families and oxen and sheep. Children suffered all the usual childhood ills—measles, fevers, toothaches, diarrhea. But on the Trail, children who were drenched by days of heavy rains or burned by hot sun could be especially irritable and hard to care for. Free from supervision, older children were full of excitement and mischief. Their mothers worried constantly that Indians would steal them.

For women who were pregnant, the overland crossing could be a nightmare. One never knew for certain where labor might begin: in Indian territory, or in the mountains, or in drenching rain. One might be alone, with no women to help, and only fear at hand. The birth might be simple, or it might be complicated and tortuous. Among rural Americans of the nineteenth century, pregnancy and impending birth were not reasons to defer the decision to move, not when free land lay at the journey's end.

It has been suggested by historian Howard Lamar and psychiatrist Daniel Levinson [in "Mid-Life Transition: A Period in Adult Psychosocial Development"] that the overland passage played a vital role in the life cycle of men, corresponding to "breaking away," improving, or bettering oneself, the stages that mark a man's life. If experiences attain mythic dimension because some pattern in all the endless variety reverberates against the fixed frame of human needs and yearnings, if the westward migration became an expression of testing and reaching for men, then it surely must have been an "anti-mythic" journey for women. It came when the physical demands of their lives drained their energies into other directions. The severity of the dislocation of the journey can be gauged in the knowledge that about one of every five overland women was seized by some stage of pregnancy, and virtually every married woman traveled with small children. When women wrote of the decision to leave their homes, it was almost always with anguish, a note conspicuously absent from the diaries of men.

The diaries of men and women carry certain predictable characteristics, with men writing of "fight, conflict and competition and . . . hunting," and women writing of their concerns with "family and relational values." But it is not true, as some have concluded, that the diaries of men and of women are essentially alike. Although many women, along with the men, wrote of the splendors of the landscape and the rigors of the road, although many overland diaries seem tediously interchangeable, there are not only important distinctions, but distinctions so profound as to raise the question whether women did not ultimately perceive the westward trek differently. Traveling side by side, sitting in the very same wagons, crossing the continent in response to the call for free land, women did not always see the venture in the clear light of the expectation of success. There were often shadows in their minds, areas of dark reservation and opposition. The diaries of women differ from the accounts of the men in both simple and in subtle ways. In the diaries of the women for example, the Indians are described as helpful guides and purveyors of services far more often than they are described as enemies. Although the women universally feared the Indians, they nevertheless tell, with some amusement, that their farmer-husbands were not always good buffalo hunters, coming back to the wagon parties empty-handed and later trading shirts with the Indians for salmon and dried buffalo meat. The women, in the naturalness of their telling, offer a new perception of the relations between the emigrants and the Indians. Having no special stake in asserting their bravery, having no special need to affirm their prowess, the women correct the historical record as they write of the daily exchanges by which the Indians were part of life of the road.

New configurations continue to appear when one reads the women's diaries closely. One of the commonplaces of rural life was the absence of men for periods that varied from weeks to months and years. Many of the men who traveled the Oregon Trail alone had left behind them their wives and their children, and they might be gone for two years or more. During these periods women were expected to serve as head of the household as well as of the farm or of any commercial enterprise—a mill or a store—that the family owned. On the Overland Trail, when a woman was widowed, she was expected to continue with her children and to file her claim alone. No widow ever placed her wagon and her family under the protection of another family. The expectation was that women would direct the family enterprise independently when need arose. There are indices that in the patriarchal values of rural communities there were interfaces where women were more independent—and independent in more ways—than has been commonly assumed.

In another aspect the women's diaries differ from the diaries written by men. As ritual caretakers of the stick and the dying, the women saw the real enemies of the road as disease and accident. It is women's diaries that we are reminded that the heaviest emigration of the Overland Trail was accomplished during years of cholera epidemic. As travelers hurried across the continent to the "rag towns" of California and Nevada in order to pan the clear streams for gold, cholera swept over the Trail.

Nowhere in the world could it have been more bleak to be stricken than on an open and unmarked road, to be left by the side of the Trail either to recover or to die. The women write of the deaths and the burials. They tell of typhoid, mountain fever, measles, dysentery and drownings. The women knew that disease and accident killed more emigrants than did Indians. The women, whose job it was to care for the dying, carefully noted the cost of the westward movement in human life. Whereas men recorded the death in aggregate numbers, the women knew death as personal catastrophe and noted the particulars of each

grave site, whether it was newly dug or old, whether of a young person or an adult, whether it had been disturbed by wolves or by Indians. The women were the actuaries of the road, tallying the miles with the lives that were lost. One must suspect, finally, that many women judged the heroic adventure of their men as some kind of outrageous folly thrust upon them by obedience to patriarchal ritual.

In their accommodation to the life of the road, the women tried to weave a fabric of accustomed design, a semblance of their usual domestic circle. Out of the disorder of traveling, the women created and held on to some order and routine. Against all odds, they managed to feed their families, do the wash, and care for the scattering children. They strove to calm the quarreling men, to keep a diary record of passing friends and families, to note who took the children when parents died on the road, to note carefully the names on the grave markers. The women even managed to bear new life on the crest of the journey's upheaval.

In the end, a woman who came through the journey felt she had won her own victory. The test of the journey was whether or not she had been equal to the task of holding her family together against the sheer physical forces that threatened to spin them to the four winds of chance. It was against the continual threat of dissolution that the women had striven. If ever there was a time when men and women turned their psychic energies toward opposite visions, the overland journey was that time. Sitting side by side on a wagon seat, a man and a woman felt different needs as they started at the endless road that led into the New Country.

Overland women recorded their pride in having preserved the integrity of family life intact in the names they gave to the children born on the Trail. Gertrude Columbia was born on the shores of the surging Columbia River. Alice Nevada drew first breath in the rocky lands of the Sierra Nevada. Gila Parrish was born somewhere along the Gila River in Arizona. Two children lived, and one child died. The New Country, the women knew in a profound way, was a bittersweet promise that took its own toll of hope and of optimism.

In the very commonplace of their observations, the women bring us a new vision of the overland experience; they bring it closer to our own lives. They do not write of trailblazing or of adventure but of those facets of living that are unchanging. In reading their diaries we come

---

William Matthews on the historical importance of studying diaries:

Sentiment and sentimentality, fancy, conformity, annoyance, vanity, the spirit of the moment and the occasion, are the soul of social history, but it is only in diaries and their like that the soul may be found.

William Matthews, in a preface to British Diaries: An Annotated Bibliography of British Diaries Written between 1442 and 1942, *University of California Press, 1950.*

closer to understanding how historical drama translates into human experience. Through the eyes of the women we begin to see history as the stuff of daily struggle.

Virginia Walcott Beauchamp   (essay date 1987)

SOURCE: An introduction to *A Private War: Letters and Diaries of Madge Preston, 1862-1867,* Rutgers University Press, 1987, pp. xiii-xxxviii.

[*In the following excerpt, Beauchamp tries to establish the historical importance of studying diaries written by average people, and specifically her own scholarship on the private writings of Madge Preston.*]

When the three of [Madge Preston's] diaries in the collection of the Maryland Historical Society were acquired, they were characterized in the inventory as dealing with trivial events. Similarly Jessie Bernard deplores "the trivia and banalities of daily life" that constituted the major content of letters she exchanged with her son [*Self-Portrait of a Family*]. Yet in rereading their communications Bernard discovered that the letters gave "a perspective to the times in which they were written." She notes how "war and fear of war did, in fact, run like a red thread through the letters. I was surprised to find how much they intruded in our lives."

Both judgments are founded on an unexpressed assumption in the word *trivial* about what we mean by history. Somehow it encompasses great events—disruptions of large populations, conflicts between and within governments, structures of power. But when we read the personal papers of those who lived in such times, we discover that we stand history on its head. As Robert Fothergill, from his reading of diaries of the past, so well appreciates:

> They were so concretely *there,* so firmly embedded in the centre of their own existence, each consciousness composing all the elements of its experience into a unique and incommunicable set of relations, with itself as the focal point of history. One's sense of the substance of history is turned inside out. Where one habitually thought of "ordinary lives" forming a vast background to historical "events," now one's vision is of the great events dimly passing behind the immediate realities that comprise an individual's experience. [*Private Chronicles: A Study of English Diaries*]

The urge is in fact compelling to know that single life. Joanna Field describes once observing a woman from a train window: "I was seized with an impulse to know more about her. . . . I wanted to know that woman as a person, a unique individual, not a specimen. . . . [I]t seemed to be just the unique qualities of particular experience that I wanted" [*A Life of One's Own*]. And another psychologist, Gordon Allport, reinforces Field's view: "A person is a self-regarding focus of value. What we *want* to know is what life does look like from this focus of value . . . and a document produced precisely from this point of view is exactly what we desire" [*Personal Documents*].

The reality of American experience has only occasionally encompassed war. Throughout most of the centuries of the building of this nation, people have gone about their daily lives in wholly personal ways. But what were those ways? And how did those people regard their lives? As the scholarly field of women's history opens up, our desire to know seems insatiable.

Out of this desire came my impulse to browse through the files of letters, handwritten in faded ink, that fill out the two collections of Preston family papers from which [*A Private War: Letters and Diaries of Madge Preston, 1862-1867*] is drawn, and to open Madge's diaries, with their crumbling leather covers. Out of these pages come tumbling forth [what Fothergill calls] all the "multitude of details about daily thoughts, emotions, and actions" which make our lives as we live them—inconsistent, rapidly fading, obsessive, or circling back. Reading nineteenth-century women's diaries and letters highlights how separate were the men's and women's cultures of that time and how sharply both men and women of our own century have been cut off from those earlier women's lives. Conventional history speaks of the world of our male forebears—and then most usually of the elite group that wielded power. But for all people outside such groups, to discover their own history is to empower themselves. Through women's history, all of us can learn to respect the women who went before us—drawing strength from their examples of endurance and from the structures and models of relatedness in the female culture that supported them.

But the reading of diaries takes a special kind of detective work. One cannot peruse them as one reads a novel where the writer has arranged details and imagery in consciously patterned ways. In diaries some of the mysteries they contain—workings of the unconscious mind—are unfathomed as well by the writer. Other mysteries, of names unidentified, of references assumed, come about because the writer—who is also often the intended reader—knows them all too well. Hindsight helps to break the code of the mysteries of the psyche. . . .

The popularity of diary keeping as a literary activity exploded during the nineteenth century. In part this new literature reflected a new kind of consciousness "shaped by print culture," as Walter Ong has observed [in *Orality and Literacy: The Technologizing of the Word*]. Diary keeping reflected also a new concern with individualism which was finding expression in democratic modes of government, in the Romantic movement in literature, and in laissez-faire capitalism. The diary also reflected a new, and modern, conceptualization of time. Yet for nineteenth-century women—cut off from the means men drew on in the larger world of commerce, government, and the arts to develop their individual potential—the diary was the quintessentially female form: no document could be more private and therefore modest. Yet in the very tangibleness of its form, it could preserve for an unknown posterity the record of a life lived, of thoughts registered on a living mind. It could outlast the oblivion of death.

Judy Nolte Lensink   (essay date 1989)

SOURCE: An introduction to *"A Secret to Be Burried":
The Diary and Life of Emily Hawley Gillespie, 1858-1888,*
edited by Judy Nolte Lensink, University of Iowa Press,
1989, pp. xi-xxvi.

[*In the following excerpt, Lensink uses the diary of Emily
Hawley Gillespie to argue that diaries are a valuable means
to reconstructing women's history.*]

The sound of nineteenth-century women, once thought
lost to us, is alive because ordinary women like Emily
Hawley Gillespie gave voice to their thoughts in their diaries. For years these books, intended for private use, lay
buried in family storage places. At the turn of the century
historian Henry Adams unwittingly lamented [in *The Education of Henry Adams*], "The woman who is known only
through a man is known wrong, and excepting one or two
. . . no woman has pictured herself. . . . and all this is
pure loss to history, for the American woman of the nineteenth century was much better company than the American man." The pictures that women created of themselves
lay buried in their diaries. Now over a century later we are
finally ready to appreciate them. "Women's unpublished
collections constitute gifts from the Fates," historian Carroll Smith-Rosenberg observes [in *Disorderly Conduct*],
"precious for having been preserved despite their very anonymity and supposed insignificance."

The Victorian era has been called the apogee of diary writing. The rising rate of female literacy in the nineteenth
century gave women access to this private form of expression. While seventeenth-century diarists had been primarily concerned with the "useful Exercise" of methodically
tracing their daily relationship to God, by the mid-
eighteenth century the emergence of secular self-
consciousness meant some diarists were recording events
they wanted to remember rather than those they needed
to. The combination of discipline and indulgence involved
in daily self-examination could be appealing to nineteenth-
century women: "Here I may review my feelings, mourn
over my numerous imperfections. . . . Veiled from the
world I vent my feelings on paper for I do find relief in recording the exercises of my mind," Sophronia Grout
wrote in her 1823 journal. Emily Hawley Gillespie fondly
called her journal her "only confident."

Even the diaries of men enshrined in traditional history
like John Quincy Adams and William Byrd tell us far
more about personal life, with its myriad moods, occurrences, and interactions, than about the public events and
achievements for which they are noted. Robert Fothergill
read a multitude of British diaries and noted their effect
on our conception of history:

> One's sense of the substance of history is turned
> inside out. Where one habitually thought of "or-
> dinary lives" forming a vast background to his-
> torical "events", now one's vision is of the great
> events dimly passing behind the immediate reali-
> ties that comprise an individual's experience. In
> diary after diary events like the Old Pretender's
> rebellion in 1715, or the battle of Waterloo a cen-
> tury later, float by like rumours. Indeed, the very
> notion of an historical "event" becomes obscure

and begins to seem like an abstraction, a fantasy.
In the foreground is the individual consciousness, absolutely resisting the insistence of future
historians that it should experience itself as peripheral. [*Private Chronicles*]

Ordinary women who would never have considered writing for the public record left volumes of journals that further challenge our perception of history. They provide authentic viewpoints that Joseph Wilder finds missing in traditional history: "The antinomy of life and thought, felt
as a gap in our knowledge of ourselves and others, means
that history is a conceptual reconstruction, never an intact
resurrection of lived experience. History, then, is oriented
toward impersonal, collective development, at the loss of
the individual, affective climate of the experience being re-
thought. It is this orientation which allows the historical
voice—the interpretation of the historian—to evade the
plurality of perspectives which persists at the level of individuals" [*Politics and History*]. Women's voices, no longer
peripheral "secrets to be buried," challenge the dominant
voice of the scholar and present female perspectives in
texts that require innovative ways of reading and interdisciplinary methodology so that we may begin to rewrite
history.

A long diary like the one Emily Hawley Gillespie kept for
thirty years is an extensive and intensive life history which
turns our sense of Victorian womanhood inside out. No
longer a figure frozen in sepia portraits of the past, the diarist becomes a living being immersed in the now. Emily
Gillespie felt the power within her journal, which she
called "the history of my life," as she reread passages written a decade earlier: "have been writing off some more of
my old Diary, it seems almost like living my life over
again." Diaries contain both life and history, as James
Boswell sensed when he wrote in his diary, "My wife, who
does not like journalizing, said it was leaving myself embo-
welled to posterity—a good strong figure. But I think it
is rather leaving myself embalmed. It is certainly preserving myself."

If, as anthropologist Franz Boas argued, each person is the
locus of culture, the crucible of interaction between the individual and social ideology, then the diary of an ordinary
woman like Emily Hawley Gillespie, kept without literary
or historical pretense, is an ideal ethnographical record.
It provides the breadth of a thirty-year-long account (a
"longitudinal study") with the depth of a single cultural
informant's perspective. Her journal points "both outward to the world of recorded experience and inward to
the reflective consciousness," maintaining in its immediacy the "tension between the individual text and social context" that Albert Stone finds in the best autobiographical
writing [*American Autobiography*].

When anthropologists elicit a life history, they listen for
the informant's interpretation as well as recall, knowing
that interpretation changes the substance of a story. Boas
questioned the empirical usefulness of such personal documents: "They are valuable rather as useful material for a
study of the perversion of truth brought about by the play
of memory with the past." The liberties that the informant
uses in telling a life history are the creative elements that

interest literary critics of autobiography. . . . The diary form minimizes this play of memory upon experience because of its immediacy.

Diaries are not, however, direct records of real life. Each diarist has motives for undertaking her writing and is selective in creating the account of her days. These drives change over time and are often not explicit, although scholars have tried to classify them. Robert Fothergill, for example, categorizes diarists' rationales as profit (self-improvement), pleasure, egotism, compensation, and communication. Nineteen-year-old Michigan farm girl Emily Hawley began her journal in 1858 without a statement of her intent:

> March 29 Monday: Breakfast at 7. help Mother wash. at ten Mr. Barnum (the Presbyterian preacher) came along from Medina. I rode with him as far as the church then went on foot to Mr. Farsts, made Harriet a visit; after tea Cal Acker came there. I stayed with sister Edna at Charles Blanchards all night. Cyrus & Lowell Baldwin call to see their nephew (Orphas baby-boy).

We know what she did on the day and whom she encountered, but not what she felt or thought. Only gradually did Emily Hawley, stimulated by experience, begin to write a commentary on the day's events and characters, letting her ego and voice emerge in her book.

Emily Hawley Gillespie set down her life story in her own words, without the prompting or influence of an ethnographer. But a century separates the diarist and her readers. We are faced with the difficult effort of trying to understand Gillespie across the gulfs created by both time and culture. From the onset of life history collection, anthropologists have been aware of the necessity to know the subject in context and to avoid as much as possible the ethnographer's own world view. While no scholar intervened between Emily Hawley Gillespie and her private book, there is no live interaction in which we can further question Gillespie on certain points, clarify issues, be corrected and informed by her. We are left with her journal, our self-conscious subjectivity, and a responsibility to understand Emily Hawley Gillespie within the now-lost world she describes.

What we earn from the effort is insight into how women themselves defined the contexts of their daily lives. Diaries document and confirm the findings of feminist scholarship in several disciplines. Women have what Smith-Rosenberg calls "sociological otherness." Scholars working with a wide variety of diaries have noted the different worlds of women and men. John Faragher's [*Women and Men on the Overland Trail*] demonstrated that while two-thirds of the topics in journals were the same for both genders, one-third differed. Women wrote about their families, their homes, and other women, while men's distinctive focus was on violence, aggressive feelings, and competition. Faragher's findings are similar to Robert Fothergill's conclusions from reading English diaries: ordinary women showed less "self-assertion and ego" than their male contemporaries in the nineteenth century. My study of a small sample of midwestern diaries showed that men perceived of themselves as individuals, while women

wrote about themselves *and* their families. Lillian Schlissel's [*Women's Diaries of the Westward Journey*] stage shows differences between the worlds of young and older women. Future comparative studies of women in various ethnic groups and classes will no doubt further illuminate the diversity among women's perceptions.

An overall contextual pattern emerges from private journals and life histories that defines women's perceptions of their world. In ["Women's Life Histories"] Susan Geiger concludes, "Regardless of differences in culture, class, race, ethnicity, or religion, women seem to share a condition of familial 'embeddedness' that is central to the way we, as women, experience and construct the social world." Emily Hawley Gillespie indeed most often defined herself within family relationships as a daughter, wife, and mother. In 600 B.C. Confucius noted that woman's status was derived from her affiliation with a triad of men (her father, her husband, and, finally, her son), and Gillespie's language acknowledges this power of men in her life; she writes about her father's house, her husband's farm. Instructed by feminist history, we also study her relationships with women, for Gillespie was deeply attached to her mother and her daughter, and thus we find the emotionally rich context that informed her life and diary.

We can begin to understand Emily Gillespie because for the past two decades women's historians have suggested a variety of useful theoretical perspectives for studying women's experiences. Very few women in American history fit into the political/military model of human existence. Women have inhabited a separate sphere, a concept that has characterized Western thought about sexual difference. Linda K. Kerber says, "Much of the history of relations between the sexes in modern times can be written in terms of a continuing struggle to maintain or redefine the boundaries of women's sphere." In ["Separate Spheres"], Kerber suggests this rhetorical concept of separate spheres has both aided historians studying women and confined the creativity of historical inquiry.

Research into Victorian prescriptive literature in the 1960s, for example, found an ideology that promoted a "cult of True Womanhood" for correct female behavior in the private sphere of the home. This historical view generally assumed that ideology unilaterally acted upon women who internalized ideals that entrapped them in purity, piety, domesticity, and submissiveness. However, a second view into separate spheres that relied on women's private writings suggested that they were creative actors who helped defined domestic roles to empower their lives. In *The Bonds of Womanhood*, Nancy F. Cott concluded, "The more historians have relied on women's personal documents the more positively they have evaluated women's sphere." Diarists like Emily Gillespie defined themselves in a variety of ways—pure and unappreciated daughter, anxious young wife, moral guide of children—that reflected the multiplicity of their roles and the limitations of the notion of "a" woman's sphere. Kerber suggests, "The ideology of separate spheres could be both instrumental and prescriptive; it is this double character that has made it so difficult for historians to work with."

Indeed, once feminist historians entered the private literature by women, they uncovered complex networks of support and emotion, a "female world of love and ritual." This research, pioneered by Carroll Smith-Rosenberg, focused on women's desire to be autonomous actors rather than on the embeddedness of their lives lived amidst families dominated by fathers, husbands, and male children. Marilyn Ferris Motz's [*True Sisterhood*] shows both the functional role of the "female family" and the ongoing struggle and negotiation involved in maintaining such networks.

The far more difficult and dynamic history of women we are now writing describes them in fuller context and includes their complex relationships with men. Questions of how much actual power women had within the domestic sphere, of the economic as well as emotional sources of woman's agency, have been central to the best recent women's history. Attention to women's personal documents enables us to now see the nineteenth century from the female actors' point of view. This history of gender interaction suggests "an ongoing struggle between women and men actors for control of the script, a struggle that ultimately transforms the play, the players—even the theater itself," Smith-Rosenberg notes.

The script of Emily Hawley Gillespie's life is recorded in her diary and illuminates this dynamic of a woman enacting Victorian ideology while using, questioning, and stretching its boundaries. Gillespie was not a victim of this ideology, although she read conventional sentimental novels about the roles of the sexes. Nor was she a heroine who aggressively defended women's rights. (She could not even imagine getting the horse and wagon herself in order to attend a Susan B. Anthony lecture in town.) She was simply a woman who described her daily encounters with expectations that came not only from her family and community but from her own aspirations. We witness the ongoing internalization of cultural values that formed Emily Gillespie and women like her into dutiful daughters and diligent mothers of the nineteenth century who attended church, supported community organizations, raised their children, and were buried as "wife of." "Simply because they failed in resisting dominant social currents does not mean they lacked character or courage," historian Altina Waller writes in [*Reverend Beecher and Mrs. Tilton*]. Waller was impressed by "the intense pressures that had to be exerted before Elizabeth Tilton, Eunice Beecher, and others like them were 'domesticated.'" Gillespie's diary reflects these pressures.

The work of several feminist historians has provided models for telling this complex story of the tension between nineteenth-century ideals and the reality women faced. A particularly rich theater in which gender ideology and dynamics are enacted is marriage. [In "Review Essay: American History"] Barbara Sicherman notes, "The disparities between expectations and reality, between stereotypes and actual behavior, are often highlighted in the emotional context of marriage." While intriguing work has been done on the strains facing notable nineteenth-century women with supportive husbands, the bold face of gender ideology is to be found in studying traditional marriages. In Emily Hawley Gillespie's case, the relative isolation of

farm life in pioneer Iowa further magnified the importance of her husband as a working partner and put particular pressures on the marital roles of lover and companion. As we learn more about the experiences of individual women and form theories that account for historical moment, class, and ethnicity, we will be able to judge how typical the graphically depicted ruptures within the Gillespie family were.

It was this mixture of typicality and atypicality that first attracted me to Emily Hawley Gillespie and her diary. Gillespie shared many characteristics and experiences with her midwestern contemporaries, making her a sort of rural Everywoman. She came to Iowa from the old Northwest Territory, she married at age twenty-four (the high end of the acceptable average), and she bore three children. Gillespie was active in community and agricultural affairs and was concerned about moral reform issues that interested many women.

But other traits emerged from the Gillespie diary that distinguished her from her peers and hinted at her questioning nature. She had youthful aspirations to be a painter or writer and showed some artistic talent. She was a Universalist and liberal in her ideas about the individual's power and natural dignity before God. A close reading between the lines of the diary showed that her small family was not accidental. She read *Woodhull and Claflin's Weekly,* a radical women's rights journal. Yet like all people who wish to get along, Gillespie inwardly suffered for the gulf she saw between what should have been her ideal performances as daughter, mother, and wife and what was. Perhaps it was the memory of some misdeed—a deed so bad she could not even confess it to her private journal—that plagued her to the end: "I have written *many* things in my journal. but the worst is a secret to be burried when I shall cease to be."

This diary reveals the private thoughts of a woman who lived a "dual life," like Edna in Kate Chopin's *The Awakening:* "that outward existence which conforms, the inward life which questions." Gillespie's diary is the result of a Faustian bargain she seems to have made for surviv-

---

Arthur Ponsonby on the value of diaries to historical scholarship:

There may be superior persons who condemn diaries as frivolous and negligible unless they deal with historical incidents. People who attach more importance to the actual than to the human may agree. But every event, every historical fact, is composed in its essence of purely human elements. Anything, therefore, which contributes to a knowledge of humanity, not only prominent humanity, but humble humanity, ought not to be ignored by historians, or indeed by philosophers and psychologists.

Arthur Ponsonby, in an introduction to English Diaries: A Review of English Diaries from the Sixteenth to the Twentieth Century, *Methuen & Co. Ltd, 1927.*

al—she would try to conform if she could express her rebellious questions in her private journal. And as many a
woman diarist learns, according to Thomas Mallon, "the
cultivated inner life can be a much more powerful and
dangerous weapon. . . . It may be in her diary that she
discovers how to keep part of herself back, and to take revenge on those who have wounded what part of her has
been exposed" [*A Book of One's Own*]. Thus Gillespie's
book is both her reaction to her daily role as a woman and
her subversive action of questioning the script.

Suzanne L. Bunkers   (essay date 1988)

SOURCE: "Midwestern Diaries and Journals: What
Women Were (Not) Saying in the Late 1800s," in *Studies
in Autobiography,* edited by James Olney, Oxford University Press, Inc., 1988, pp. 190-210.

[*In the following excerpt, Bunkers explores the unpublished
diaries of several nineteenth-century women for insight into
their lives.*]

The late 1800s found Americans reading not only such
works as George Washington Cable's *The Grandissimes,*
Henry James's *The Portrait of a Lady,* and William Dean
Howells's *A Modern Instance* but also Sarah Orne Jewett's
A Country Doctor and Mary Murfree's *The Prophet of the
Great Smoky Mountains.* Critics and readers alike were
awakening to the literature of American women writers
whose works contributed to the growing effort to portray
American life realistically. In actuality, however, the majority of fiction published in the United States during these
decades offered a realistic assessment of the lives of only
a small percentage of Americans. To understand better
what women's lives were like during the late 1800s, we
must examine their autobiographical texts, for it was in diaries, journals, letters, and memoirs that many women expressed their attitudes, opinions, and beliefs concerning
their lives in late nineteenth-century America.

Such was the case particularly in the Midwestern United
States, where most women writing in the 1800s were not
famous literary or historical figures but unknown women
writing privately about the events of their everyday lives.
Thanks to the recent work of women's historians, we no
longer view these women in terms of stereotypes such as
the "saint in the sunbonnet" or the "little woman," patient
and long-suffering, who followed her man west into the
wilderness. Instead, we are beginning to explore the diversity of women's lives and experiences as presented to us
in their autobiographical writings.

Women's diaries and journals chart unmapped territory
in such an exploration because they challenge the reader
to formulate a more inclusive definition of autobiography
than has traditionally been used to delineate the boundaries of the genre. Unlike a traditional autobiography, a
diary or journal is written day by day, often with no editor
but the writer herself, with brief (if any) statements about
purpose or intended audience, and with few preconcep-
tions about the form the finished text might take. A diary
or journal is not written as a retrospective narration and
interpretation of a life already lived but as a commentary
on life as it *is* lived, that is, on life as process rather than

as product. It might well be argued that the diary or journal can rightly be considered the most authentic form of
autobiography because it is least subject to outside editing
and censorship and because it most fully represents life as
process.

My examination of this form of autobiography is based on
my study over the past five years of the unpublished diaries and journals of approximately fifty women who lived
and worked in Minnesota, Iowa, and Wisconsin from approximately 1840 to 1900. Among these unpublished writings are several texts that shed useful light on what some
American women were thinking, feeling, saying, and
doing during this period of time. . . .

My work has led me to concur with other scholars of
women's history that the central strategy of the women
who wrote these diaries and journals was the selective use
of speech and silence. What remained unsaid was every bit
as important as—and, in some cases, more important
than—what was said.

To examine this issue, it is important to locate these diaries and journals within their cultural and historical milieu. By the late 1800s in Minnesota, Iowa, and Wisconsin,
the American Indian population, while still substantial,
was for the most part confined to reservations, and the
small black American population was centered primarily
in larger Midwestern cities. In these three Upper Midwestern states, immigrants from Norway, Sweden, Germany, Luxembourg, Holland, and Ireland predominated,
having established cities, towns, villages, and homesteads
among the lakes, rolling hills, and prairie farmlands.

Not surprisingly, most of the diaries and journals I examined have been those of Caucasian women of the middle
to upper-middle class, many with access to at least some
education, particularly if they lived in larger towns or cities. In many rural areas, education was much harder to
obtain, especially for the daughters of immigrant women.
Some of these daughters were able to attend "country
school" for a few years; most could speak English but not
read or write it well.

The form and content of Midwestern women's private
writings were shaped by the writers' experiences of four
interwoven contexts: the geographical, the cultural, and
socioeconomic, and the situational. A few words follow
concerning each of these contexts. Women in Minnesota,
Iowa, and Wisconsin lived in more varied geographical
settings than might initially be assumed. Women in northern Minnesota or Wisconsin, for instance, dwelled in small
lumber towns and mining villages, in woodland, lakeland,
and farming areas, and in larger cities. Women in the
southern parts of these states as well as in most of Iowa
lived in ethnically segregated farming villages, on homesteads ranging from acreages to farms of several hundred
acres, or in towns like Mankato, Minnesota; Fort Dodge,
Iowa; and Janesville, Wisconsin. Women in urban centers
such as Milwaukee, Des Moines, and Minneapolis-St.
Paul might have been members of the founding families,
but they could just as easily have been schoolteachers,
seamstresses, or homemakers. Wherever these women
lived, however, their lives were affected by extremes of

Midwestern weather as well as by the region's topography. Thus, the diversity of living conditions experienced by women in the Upper Midwest during this era was an important factor in their writing in a variety of autobiographical forms such as calendar inscriptions, three-line daily reports, lengthy introspective journal entries, and carefully structured retrospective memoirs.

As I have noted, in the predominant Midwestern culture of the times, women of color were a silenced and nearly invisible presence, particularly as reflected in historical accounts and in autobiographical records extant in historical societies today. A Caucasian, second- or third-generation, Euro-American woman was far more likely than a woman of color to have kept a diary or journal; and her socioeconomic status had a major influence on whether she did any autobiographical writing at all.

Simply stated, the more economic resources available to a woman, the greater her opportunity for education. The greater her opportunity for education, the greater her ease with writing, her familiarity with texts that might serve as models, her free time for writing, and her money for writing materials. Predictably, a good number of the diaries and journals I have studied have been those written by young women from financially secure families whose descendants donated family papers, among them these diaries and journals, to state, county, and local historical societies during the early to mid 1900s. A Midwestern woman's class played a central role in determining not only whether she wrote diaries and journals but also whether her autobiographical writings were considered worth saving and donating to historical society archives.

Finally, we cannot examine these diaries and journals without recognizing that a specific situational context existed for each entry. The form of a woman's autobiographical writings was shaped both by her purpose and by her perception of her intended audience. A homesteading woman might have recorded her daily observations on the weather so that she and her husband could keep track of weather patterns that would yield information on crop development. A first-year teacher in a small-town elementary school might have described her interactions with students both to reassure herself of her capabilities and to create a record of activities for her superiors. An older woman might have referred to her diary as her friend or confidante not as a literary convention but as a means of making herself more comfortable with expressing her thoughts and feelings in what she hoped would be a safe place. Certainly, the situational context surrounding a woman's writings, while one of the most difficult aspects for a researcher to reconstruct, is one of the most fascinating areas for examination because it yields a sense of the writer's character and personality as she shapes her self-image through her writing. . . .

Four primary themes emerge in these autobiographical texts. First, each writer expressed a need to view the use of her time and energies as worthwhile. It might, of course, be argued that simply by recording her activities, any writer asserts the belief that what one does is important, yet the tone of many of these diaries and journals reveals that their writers felt the need to explain their activi-

ties in detail, not so much as a means of filling pages but as a way of justifying to themselves that they were using their time well and that their activities were appreciated by others. The activities recorded in a diary or journal function as the individual writer's attempt to validate her work and, by extension, her sense of self. The October 16, 1883, journal entry of Abbie T. Griffin, a Minneapolis seamstress, is representative of such attempts:

> This day I am thirty-two years old and a quiet day it has been. This morning I did up my work, bought eight bushels of Beauty of Hebron potatoes and this afternoon bought 2 1/2 tons of nut coal & 1/2 ton of Ill. Lump of N.W. Fuel Co. Went over to Nellie's and she cut me a velvet vest for my black broadcloth jacket. It is a cold stormy windy night.

The writer's comment here might appear self-deprecatory in its passing reference to her birthday amidst the recitation of chores completed. The fact that she noted the date at all, however, indicates that her birthday was important to her, even though she spent the day working rather than celebrating.

Abbie T. Griffin's diary, which she kept from January 1882 until May 1885, is structured around her daily reports on her work as a seamstress and as a nurse for her ailing mother. Specific entries recount her sewing projects, her attempts to find work, the weather, visits to and from friends, and her mother's worsening condition. On June 11, 1882, Abbie wrote of meeting Clint Dike, who visited her home with a mutual friend. Abbie and Clint's courtship apparently began soon afterwards, although Abbie generally wrote sparingly, if at all, about her suitor in subsequent diary entries, such as this one from August 7, 1882: "Hot until noon and then a shower cooled the air. Went to the store early and worked hard at the dress all day, began at four o'clock this morning. Mr. Dike saw me safely home. He goes with Ettie in the morning to Dodge county Minn."

Abbie's reference to "Ettie" in this entry concerns Clint Dike's young daughter Etta Dike, who came to Minneapolis to board with Abbie later in 1882, after living for some time with her father's brother and sister-in-law, Morrel and Jemima Dike, and their three children near Big Lake, Minnesota. Clint Dike had apparently been widowed sometime after 1872, when Etta was born, and before 1880, when the state census listed Etta as part of her uncle and aunt's household in Sherburne County. By 1882, he had arranged for his nine-year-old daughter to live with Abbie, whose growing affection for the girl is reflected in diary entries such as that made on November 4, 1882: "Sat up late and worked on Ettie's dress, but did not finish it but made her a pair of flannel panties, very pretty ones of red with a little frill embroidered with black."

While specific entries describe Abbie's relationship with Etta, her work, and social activities, the diarist said little about her relationship with Clint until an entry made in early 1885. On January 26, after not writing in her diary for three months, Abbie matter-of-factly described her wedding to Mr. Dike:

> I have determined to write a Journal once more

& record many transactions. Last Tuesday night at 11:50 P.M. we had a very interesting ceremony here. For two weeks mother had been very low and on that night we gave up all hope of her and feeling her end was approaching she felt as if she would like to see us married. Clint went directly to get cousin Ed and they went together to get a licence came back hunted a minister and were ready. I had only a common dress and it was a dark grey trimmed with pipings of crimson, just a full skirt and slashed basque. The Rev. Archibald Hadden transformed me from Miss G. to Mrs. S. C. Dike. Mother has been very low and is so still. Last night was the first night for eighteen nights that I could sleep all night. Mrs. Hull came & watched with mother. Nettie Sullivan wrote us a letter today and I received one from Poughkeepsie.

The wedding, which occurred shortly before the death of Abbie's mother on February 5, 1885, was recorded by the diarist in much the same way as she had reported on her daily work and activities. Because the entry reflects Abbie's preoccupation with her mother's decline and says little about her new husband, it is difficult to infer how Abbie felt about marrying Clint. The writer's selective use of speech and silence in encoding her message is evident here, not so much in what she has said as in what she has not said.

Abbie's two final entries, one from February 10, 1885, and the other from May 25, 1885, tell of her collapse from arthritis and exhaustion following her mother's death and of her attempts to recover her physical and emotional health. Ironically, the last sentence in Abbie's diary reads: "I hope to write more now." But Abbie T. Griffin wrote nothing more about her daily activities, her husband and stepdaughter, or her health. We can only speculate about what direction her life took after May 1885, yet we can view her diary as representative of many kept by Midwestern women during the 1880s in its emphasis on sense of self as defined by the recording of the writer's daily work and activities.

Like Abbie T. Griffin, fifty-eight-year-old Maria Merrill wrote often in her journal about her work, first on a farm near Sechlersville, Wisconsin, and later in Winona, Minnesota, where she moved with her son so that he could attend the State Normal School to become a teacher. Maria's journal entry on October 31, 1890, is representative of her many commentaries on her life as a widow raising her children on a small Wisconsin farm:

> We threshed the 21st and 22nd of August. We had 128 bushels of wheat and 542 bushels of oats and about 50 bushels of potatoes which were very poor. Our corn is good and yields well. We have not got it all husked yet. It is not very dry this year. Waldo had to build a new crib to hold all the corn. We have sold all the hogs, except four little pigs, and we bought a sow for breeding purposes. . . . Clara has been husking corn a long time and I have done the housework.

It is evident from what Maria wrote here that she played an integral role in the operation of the farm and that her work contributed to her sense of worth as a person. Wit-

ness this journal entry made shortly after Maria and her son Waldo had rented out the farm and moved to Winona in late 1894:

> It was a great sacrifice to me to break up my home where I had lived so long and go among strangers in my feeble old age but I thought that perhaps I ought to give [Waldo] all the chance I could for an education. . . . I can't say that I have enjoyed life much since I have been here. It seems as if it would be all that I would ask in this life if we could all be back on the farm again and have everything as it used to be but since it cannot be I try very hard to bear it patiently.

Maria Merrill, like Abbie T. Griffin, used speech and silence selectively to encode her feelings into her journal entries. She tried to mitigate her sense of personal unhappiness with an admonition to herself to be patient and accept her lot, but the undercurrent in the entry above is one of dissatisfaction and great sadness at having lost her identity as a farm woman. Regardless of differences in age and environment, Abbie T. Griffin and Maria Merrill displayed in their writing one notable similarity: the need to validate their lives and develop some sense of self through the recording of their daily work and activities.

While Midwestern diarists and journalers of the late 1800s clearly needed to view themselves and their work as important, a second major thematic focus in their writing is the need for connection with other human beings. For these women, the diary or journal became a place to write about relationships with others, thereby validating themselves as members of communities. In her diary, kept during the first several months of 1888, Ida M. Bliss, a fourteen-year-old schoolgirl from Janesville, Wisconsin, wrote often about her activities with family and friends. Typical entries reported on Ida's lessons at school; and some entries, like the two that follow, offer hints about how she was feeling:

> *January 3, 1888.* School commenced today. I went, of course. Miss Green is our teacher she is the same one we had last term. It has been very cold all day. Our Holiday vacation is gone and I don't know whether to be glad or sorry.

> *January 11, 1888.* I went to school and did nothing else worth speaking of. It is as cold as ever and no signs as yet of moderation. I am reading hospital sketches by Miss Alcott.

These entries do more than simply report on the weather and on Ida's ambivalence toward school. They also let us know that, although she was reading Alcott's work, Ida viewed her reading and her other daily activities as "nothing else worth speaking of." Again, as in Abbie T. Griffin's birthday entry, a self-deprecatory tone appears, a tone that might reflect only an offhand remark, or which might function as a purposeful strategy for encoding a pattern into a text. Whether or not this was the case with Ida M. Bliss's diary, the writer's repetition of daily activities, broken only by references to friends' visits, provides evidence that much of Ida's self-concept as an adolescent was formed as the result of her interactions with others. Her diary is important because it reflects the day-by-day process by which that self-concept was formed.

Ida's diary entries stopped abruptly on April 3, 1888, and the diary's pages remained blank until June 20, 1888, when the writer penned this cryptic entry:

> I begin my diary again on the 20 day of June; after skipping about two months. It has been one of the most wreatched days in the short fourteen years of my life.
>
> Continued in Memoran.

The implications of this brief entry become even more fascinating when one turns to the back of Ida's diary to the pages labeled "Memorandum" and finds that the page on which she had continued this entry had been torn out. Evidently, Ida's encoding of her message by writing it in the "Memorandum" pages proved insufficient for her or whoever else removed this page from her diary. Whatever was written there must have been so private or so taboo that it had to be expurgated. Such an act offers perhaps the clearest indication thus far of how speech and silence could be used selectively in a diary or journal by a young woman writing during the late 1800s.

A third theme emerging in women's diaries and journals of this era is the writer's need for an outlet for emotions such as intense grief and anger, which her culture did not deem appropriate for public expression by a woman. In many circumstances, the diary or journal functioned as a friend or confidante whom the writer could trust with her innermost feelings and secrets. Such is the case with Martha Smith Brewster of Mankato, Minnesota, who began keeping a diary in 1876, shortly after the death of her young son, Georgie, and who continued writing in it until early 1880. In several entries, such as this one from March 14, 1876, Martha spoke of the difficulties she faced in dealing with her sorrow over her son's death: "Somehow I feel sad & lonely this evening. I can't write nor work guess had better to go to bed."

Martha's references to her grief were more often oblique than direct, yet throughout the diary she made a consistent effort to come to terms with her emotions while at the same time not say too much. It is as if she did not want to give herself away, not even to herself. Specifically, the first entry in Martha's diary made careful use of encoding to express grief in a culturally acceptable manner. Martha began by writing a prayer to "Our Blessed Master," but she soon changed direction, writing, "Four weeks ago on Sabbath night my little boy. . . ." She went no further, however. She carefully crossed out those words before continuing: "What a comfort this assurance of the saviour is to us when we are called upon to part from our little ones." The writer's use of a prayer to begin her diary entry might seem appropriate, given the circumstances, but it is significant that she chose to delete any personal reference to the loss of her son and instead to encode her grief in the formal, stylized language of prayer.

Few entries in Martha Smith Brewster's diary speak directly of her grief, yet the pervasive tone of sadness in the diary cannot be overlooked. This is a form of autobiography that records how a woman worked through the grieving process over a period of several years. Even in Martha's final diary entry, almost four years after Georgie's death, there is a muted expression of that same grief:

> *October 20, 1879.* Georgie's 6th birthday. It is a beautiful summer day so warm. This year I have had a dollar for Missions for Georgie's birthday gift again. Dear child how distinctly I can remember him both from voice & expression of features.

This diary is characteristic of many nineteenth-century diaries and journals by both women and men that recount the writer's loss of a loved one, either by death or by separation, and which fulfill the writer's intense need for an outlet for the expression of grief. As twentieth-century theorists have observed, several stages comprise the grieving process. For women such as Martha Smith Brewster, who lived in an environment where the infant mortality rate was high but where most survivors had little time or opportunity to express their grief, the diary or journal became an indispensable tool for a partial or complete working through of the grieving process.

In addition to the three themes discussed thus far, Midwestern women's diaries and journals of the late 1800s embody a fourth: the writer's need for a forum for commentary on such subjects as marriage, religion, politics, and world events. Contrary to popular myth, Midwestern women were not isolated and unaware of what was going on in the world. In fact, many of these women used their diaries and journals as places for expression of their opinions on social issues. Abbie T. Griffin, for example, wrote this terse journal entry, which expressed her shock at an event that had outraged her community:

> *Friday April 28, 1882.* A terrible thing happened here on Fourth Ave. S yesterday a man Frank McManus decoyed off a little daughter of Jason Spear & outraged her & at night a group of vigilantes took him out of jail & hung him up.

Another diarist, Emily Hawley Gillespie, who lived in rural Iowa and whose ten-volume journal spanned the period from 1858 to 1888, regularly recorded details of life on the family farm near Manchester. In one entry dated July 29, 1877, Emily wrote this in response to receiving the news that a neighbor woman had been committed to an asylum:

> I only wonder that more women do not have to be taken to that asylum, especially farmers' wives. No society except hired men to eat their meals. Hard work from the beginning to the end of the year. Their only happiness lies in their children with the fond hope that *they* may rise higher.

Emily's journal entries functioned not only as a measure of her awareness of the potential isolation of farm women but also as an indictment of her culture's failure to treat such women with more understanding and compassion.

As the years passed, Emily Hawley Gillespie used her journal as a place to record her activities in the temperance movement, her interests in writing and phrenology, and her attendance at agricultural association meetings.

Emily Hawley Gillespie.

Certain entries made from 1880 to 1885, however, concerned her deteriorating relationship with her husband of twenty years, James Gillespie. At one point during 1883, Emily commented, "When a man lays his hands hold of his wife & children I think tis time something was done." Her use of the third-person rather than the first-person forms in this entry functioned as an encoding strategy by which Emily could break the silence about her husband's violence and at the same time distance herself from it.

By 1885, Emily's comments on her domestic situation had become more direct. On April 26, 1885, she wrote:

> I only hope that [Sarah] may not see the trouble I have. Ah, *marriage is a lottery,* how full of deceit do they come with their false tongues and "*there is no one as dear as thee*" until one is married then "*you are mine now we have something else to do besides silly kissing.*"

What makes entries such as this even more interesting is the fact that, due to Emily's worsening dropsy (edema), her daughter Sarah took over writing some journal entries for her mother in 1886 and thus had the opportunity to read earlier entries as well as those she recorded for Emily. How much of Emily's journal was written with the pur-

pose of providing a record of her life for her daughter is an intriguing, if unanswerable, question. Emily Hawley Gillespie's journal ended with her death in 1888. Today it remains one of the most comprehensive longitudinal documents on the life of a nineteenth-century Midwestern American woman.

Much remains to be said about the diaries and journals of women writing during the late 1800s, and more work needs to be done in unearthing these forgotten but nonetheless significant source materials. As a form of autobiography, these texts serve an important function: They enable us to alter our field of vision and enlarge our perspective on the expanding boundaries of the genre. Through an analysis of the writers' selective use of speech and silence to encode messages into their texts, we can see how these women shaped their autobiographical writings to record a sense of a changing, growing self. Texts like these require that we reexamine traditional assumptions about what women's lives were like in nineteenth-century America. They encourage new approaches to studying the lives of women who were not well known and whose diaries and journals were in many cases the only autobiographical statements they left behind.

Diaries and journals such as those by Abbie T. Griffin, Maria Merrill, Ida M. Bliss, Martha Smith Brewster, and Emily Hawley Gillespie are indeed worth reading as one form of autobiography written by nineteenth-century women, not only because they provide an accurate accounting of women's lives during that era but also because they point the way toward Virginia Woolf's *A Writer's Diary,* Joanna Field's *A Life of One's Own,* Anne Frank's *The Diary of a Young Girl,* and countless other diaries and journals being written by women today.

THE SOCIOLOGY OF DIARIES

Margo Culley (essay date 1985)

SOURCE: An introduction to *A Day at a Time: The Diary Literature of American Women from 1764 to the Present,* The Feminist Press at the City University of New York, 1985, pp. 3-26.

[*In the introduction to* A Day at a Time: The Diary Literature of American Women from 1764 to the Present, *Culley discusses how the conception of the self changed over the course of the nineteenth century and how this affected diary writing.*]

As all the standard bibliographical sources show, American men kept journals in numbers far exceeding those kept by women until well past the middle of the nineteenth century. One of the most fascinating questions about American diary literature is, therefore, how, in the twentieth century, the diary came to be a form of writing practiced predominantly by women writers. The reasons why women continued to choose periodic life-writing and men began to abandon the form are complex. The reason is not, as some writers about autobiography have suggested, that women's lives are fragmented and thus so are the forms of their writing. Nor is the reason that other avenues of literary expression were closed to women writers. The first argument embodies a type of life/art fallacy for which feminist critics must invent a pithy name in order to stop its easy use; the second, as abundant evidence now indicates, is also simply not true.

An important part of the answer to how and why diary literature became the province of women writers is the emergence of the self as the subject of the diary. If we come to the reading of diaries with only the modern idea of the diary as the arena of the "secret" inner life, we will distort or be disappointed in what we find in the journal pages written by American women throughout their history. It is only relatively recently (roughly in the last one hundred years) that the content of the diary has been a record of private thoughts and feelings to be kept hidden from others' eyes. Many eighteenth- and nineteenth-century diaries were semi-public documents intended to be read by an audience. Those kept by men, in particular, record a public life or are imbued with a sense of public purpose or audience. In the course of the nineteenth century, as a split between the public and private spheres came increasingly to shape the lives of women and men, those aspects of culture associated with the private became the domain of women. Simultaneously, changing ideas of the self, influenced by romanticism, the industrial revolution, and the "discovery" of the unconscious contributed to changes in the content and function of the diary. As the modern idea of the secular diary as a "secret" record of an inner life evolved, that inner life—the life of personal reflection and emotion—became an important aspect of the "private sphere" and women continued to turn to the diary as one place where they were permitted, indeed encouraged, to indulge full "self-centeredness." American men, unused to probing and expressing this inner life in any but religious terms found, as the secular self emerged as the necessary subject of the diary, the form less and less amenable to them.

Also, toward the end of the nineteenth century, diary keeping in America became associated with gentility, and keeping a life-record among a "lady's" accomplishments. Etiquette books of the period containing prescriptive material about diary keeping suggest ways in which the genre became "feminized" ("Dear Diary"). Of course, the basic requirements of literacy and a modicum of leisure are the strongest determinants of who did and did not keep journals, and we can demonstrate how the ideology of "refinement" shaped the authorship in terms of class and race as well as gender.

The Changing Function and Content of the Diary

The American diary has its roots in the spiritual autobiography that charts the progress of the pilgrim's soul toward God, a function the diary still serves for some today. But throughout the eighteenth and nineteenth centuries in America, the secular journal served a number of semi-public purposes and the writers of many of these secular journals intended them to be read. Women diarists in particular wrote as family and community historians. They recorded in exquisite detail the births, deaths, illnesses, visits, travel, marriages, work, and unusual occurrences that made up the fabric of their lives. Women for whom

that fabric had been torn, who emigrated to this country, traveled as part of the westward migration, joined their husbands on whaling ships, or went to distant lands as missionaries, used journals to maintain kin and community networks. The diaries kept by these women functioned as extended letters often actually sent to those left behind.

If we look at two examples . . . , we can chart the changes from diarist as family and social historian to the modern diarist whose principal subject is the self. Mary Vial Holyoke (1737-1802) and Mary MacLane (1881-1929) kept their journals at opposite ends of the continent, but they are also separated from each other by the romantic discovery of the secular self, the split between the private and the public spheres emphasized by the industrial revolution, and the psychoanalytic celebration of individual consciousness. Here is the record of Mary Vial Holyoke for the months of April and May 1770 in Salem, Massachusetts:

> Apr. 7. Mr. Fisk Buried.
> 23. Went with Mr. Eppes to Mrs. Thomas. Took Down Beds.
> 26. Put Sals Coat in ye frame.
> 27. Made mead. At the assembly.
> May 14. Mrs. Mascarene here & Mrs. Crowninshield. Taken very ill. The Doctor bled me. Took an anodyne.
> 15. Kept my Bed all day.
> 17. Brought to Bed at 12 of a son.
> 19. The Baby taken with fits the same as ye others. Nurse came. Mrs. Vans Died.
> 20. The Baby very ill. I first got up.
> 21. It Died at II clock A.M. Was opened. The Disorder was found to Be in the Bowels. Aunt Holyoke died.
> 22. Training. Mother Pickman here. Mrs. Sarjant yesterday.
> 23. My dear Baby buried.
> 28. Mrs. Pickman, Miss Dowse Drank tea here. Mrs. Jones, Lowell, Brown, Cotnam, Miss Cotnam & Miss Gardner Called to see me.
> 29. Wrote to Boston and Cambridge. Mrs. Savage Brought to Bed. The widow Ward lost 2 children with ye Throat Distemper from May 25th to May 29th.
> 30. Cato went to Boston and returned. [*The Holyoke Diaries, 1709-1856.*]

Nearly 150 years later in Butte, Montana, Mary MacLane introduces herself in her journal with this Whitmanesque catalogue:

> And at this point I meet Me face to face.
> I am Mary MacLane: of no importance to the wide bright world and dearly and damnably important to Me.
> Face to face I look at Me with some hatred, with despair and with great intentness.
> I put Me in a crucible of my own making and set it in the flaming trivial Inferno of my mind. And I assay thus:
> I am rare—I am in some ways exquisite.
> I am pagan within and without.
> I am vain and shallow and false.
> I am a specialized being, deeply myself.
> I am of woman-sex and most things that go with that, with some other *pointes*

I am dynamic but devastated, laid waste in spirit.
I'm like a leopard and I'm like a poet and I'm
like a religieuse and I'm like an outlaw.
I have a potent weird sense of humor—a saving
and a demoralizing grace.
I have brain, cerebration—not powerful but fine
and of a remarkable quality.
I am scornful-tempered and I am brave.
I am slender in body and someway fragile and
firm-fleshed and sweet.
I am oddly a fool and a strange complex liar and
a spiritual vagabond.
I am strong, individual in my falseness: waver-
ing, faint, fanciful in my truth.
I am eternally self-conscious but sincere in it.
I am ultra-modern, very old-fashioned: savagely
incongruous.
I am young, but not very young.
I am wistful—I am infamous.
In brief, I am a human being.
I am presciently and analytically egotistic, with
some arresting dead-feeling genius.
And were I not so tensely tiredly sane I would
say that I am mad. [*I, Mary Maclane: A Diary
of Human Days*]

The contrast between these two journal entries illustrates clearly the changes in the content, function, and form of the diary as created by American women writers in the last two hundred years. Eighteenth-century Mary Holyoke keeps her record as one might enter births and deaths in the family Bible. Her diary is typical of the period—a chronicle of who visited, who was ill, who was born, and who died, with events traditionally considered "histori-cal," such as the military training she mentions, very much in the background. She begins this journal when she marries as though to become the family and community historian is one of the duties of her new station in life. Her record with its factual fragments of sentences could not be more different from the later effusions of Mary MacLane. Mary Holyoke uses the first person pronoun only once in this two-month section. And one might say that the only evidence of a subjective reaction to the events she men-tions is in the line where she uses the one adjective, "My *dear* Baby buried." In this single word is the germ of "self" that explodes in the pages of Mary MacLane's diary. What we do get in the Holyoke record that is utterly absent in the later text is a picture of family and communi-ty life, particularly the associations between the women of the community as they attend one another in the rituals of childbirth, illness, and death. This is not to say that the diary contains no record of an individual consciousness. Indeed in her very preoccupation with these details emerges her unique history. Mary Holyoke, though the wife of a prominent Salem physician, lost eight children in childbirth, a fact strongly influencing the selection of detail for her record.

The Mary MacLane diary, intended for publication when written, chronicles pure "Ego." Her favorite pronoun is the first person, as in the lines above, where "I am" is like a chant with "me" and "my" echoing choruses. But though she focuses intensely and exclusively on her own consciousness, we, ironically, know almost nothing about her. The diary contains no mention of routine daily activi-ty, of family, of friends other than "the anemone lady." Utterly absent in this diary is the sense of self as part of a social fabric.

The self in Mary MacLane's record is no longer witness and chronicler but the *subject* of the record. In her exclu-sive focus on her own exquisitely analyzed individual sen-sibility, MacLane writes under the general influence of European romanticism, the specific tradition of the French *journal intime,* and in the context of the impact of Freud; but her most important predecessor, whom she mentions early in her journal, is Marie Bashkirtseff, a young Russian painter whose diary of utter self-absorption [*Marie Bashkirtseff: The Journal of a Young Artist, 1860-1884*] was first published in France in 1887. Marie Bashkirtseff always felt she would die young and she did succumb to tuberculosis in her mid-twenties. She undertook her diary with the hope that, if her painting did not bring her fame and immortality, the diary would. Again, she was correct. When edited by her mother from the eighty-four volumes Marie wrote, the published jour-nal became phenomenally popular. With its translation into English in 1889 a kind of Marie Bashkirtseff cult de-veloped in America. Women from Old Deerfield, Massa-chusetts to Butte, Montana began keeping journals with the explicit expectation that their journals would make them famous, too. (One who took exception to the Bash-kirtseff rage was Alice James, who refused to read the infa-mous journal and called Bashkirtseff "the perverse of the perverse.") Marie Bashkirtseff readily admitted to "im-mense egotism" for which she was both adored and de-spised. But the wide popularity of her journal in America clearly gave American women "permission" to pay that kind of sustained attention to the self.

Reasons for "Keeping a Diary"

Marie Bashkirtseff's enthusiastic self-regard coupled with her acute consciousness of the passage of time identify two crucial, related, often unconscious motives for keeping a diary. In the year of her death, Bashkirtseff wrote a Pref-ace to her diary in which she said: "The record of a woman's life, written down day by day, without any at-tempt at concealment, as if no one in the world were ever to read it, yet with the purpose of being read, is always in-teresting; for I am certain that I shall be found sympathet-ic, and I write down everything, everything, everything. Otherwise why should I write?" Though few women dia-rists express such irrepressible self-admiration, keeping a diary, one could argue, always begins with a sense of self-worth, a conviction that one's individual experience is somehow *remark*able. Even the most self-deprecating of women's diaries are grounded in some sense of the impor-tance of making a record of the life. As Bashkirtseff states, the writing act itself implies an audience and this audience will be the vehicle of preserving the life-record (in the act of reading) despite the passage of time and inevitable change. Even the phrase "keeping a diary" suggests this resistance to time, change, and ultimately, death. Though rarely expressed as directly as in Bashkirtseff's text, the essence of the impulse to keep a diary is captured in "I write, therefore I am." And will be.

Some American women diarists write explicitly for an imagined future audience who will survive them, as does Mollie Sanford on the Nebraska and Colorado frontiers, declaring, Bashkirtseff-like, "I do not want to be forgotten" [*Mollie: The Journal of Mollie Dorsey Sanford in Nebraska and Colorado Territories, 1857-1866*]. Most diarists do not write consciously or explicitly in defiance of death or what Bashkirtseff calls "oblivion"; but we can see how the smaller "deaths" or dislocations have often prompted journal keeping. Marriage, travel, and widowhood are all occasions creating a sense of a discontinuity of self—I was that, now I am this; I was there, now I am here. Keeping a life record can be an attempt to preserve continuity seemingly broken or lost. This can most clearly be seen in the numbers of women who left family and friends to travel West and used journals as a vehicle for maintaining severed networks. They were strongly informed by a sense of audience that shapes their accounts of wondrous and unfamiliar sights and their efforts to come to grips with a new life. Laura Downs Clark, who traveled with her new husband to the Firelands region of Ohio, kept a journal for her mother left behind. The diary reveals a tension between an objective record of daily events and her subjective response to her situation. Most of the entries are short: "June 24 [1818] Wednesday rained hard in the middle of the day—Salted down our pork & hung our fish up to dry." But every time her husband leaves her alone for any period of time, she records long entries that, in her words, "give full vent to my feelings."

> July 10th . . . O! that parting moment when I was seated in the waggon to take (perhaps) a final farewell of all this world holds dear to me when I bid Grandmother farewell as she stood with weeping eyes to take her last look & I turned my back upon them (O! how my heart aches & the tears bedew my cheeks whilst writing this scene) it seems now as if that this moment was not realized enough at the time & it surely was not by me though no mortal tongue can express my feelings at that time how I catched the last glimmer of the Dear old habitation—the fields the trees & everything else seemed to wear a gloomy aspect at my departure was the ways of heaven ever more dark than in my leaving you—when I think of the little probability I have of seeing you again it seems as if I must fly! instantly fly to you. . . . ["The Original Diary of Mrs. Laura (Downs) Clark, of Wakeman, Ohio," *The Firelands Pioneer,* January, 1920]

The next entry returns to her earlier mode: "July 11th Saturday got out shingle enough to finish the roof and side up the end I had to cook for my men kept school & made a slipper for Mrs. Canfields baby—very hot weather indeed and very dry—." In this 1818 diary, we can almost feel the pressure of the internal, emotional life displacing social history as the necessary subject of the diary. Her usual entries are short and matter-of-fact. Those where she records her feelings are long, intense passages written while she is thinking of her mother, that is, in the *imagined* company of women.

Many diaries, of course, are not written for others' eyes, but for an audience who is the diarist herself. Charlotte Forten gives as complete an account of why she is keeping a diary as any woman in the mid-nineteenth century. In 1854, she writes:

> A wish to record the passing events of my life, which, even if quite unimportant to others, naturally possess great interest to myself, and of which it will be pleasant to have some remembrance, has induced me to commence this journal. I feel that keeping a diary will be a pleasant and profitable employment of my leisure hours, and will afford me much pleasure in after years, by recalling to my mind the memories of other days, thoughts of much-loved friends from whom I may be separated . . . the interesting books that I read; and the different people, places and things that I am permitted to see. Besides this, it will doubtless enable me to judge correctly the growth and improvement from year to year. [*The Journal of Charlotte Forten*]

Her phrase "even if quite unimportant to others" suggests the possibility in her mind that others *might* find her record of interest, but her stated purpose is to establish continuity between present and future selves.

Constructing the Self

As invaluable as women's life-records are as historical sources containing a kind of "truth" about women's lives not found in other places, we must remember that diaries and journals are texts, that is, verbal constructs. The process of selection and arrangement of detail in the text raises an array of concerns appropriately "literary," including questions of audience (real or implied), narrative, shape and structure, persona, voice, imagistic and thematic repetition, and what James Olney calls "metaphors of self " [in *Metaphors of Self: The Meaning of Autobiography*]. The act of autobiographical writing, particularly that which occurs in a periodic structure, involves the writer in complex literary as well as psychological processes. It is a paradox that the process whose frequent goal is to establish self-continuity involves at its heart a dislocation from the self, or a turning of subject into object. Even in some of the earliest American women's diaries we can see this kind of "double consciousness," as the self stands apart to view the self. Rebekah Dickinson, a single woman living in Hatfield, Massachusetts in 1787, is very much conscious of herself as different from those around her and she fills the pages of her journal with this sense of "otherness": " . . . wondered how my lot fell by Self alone how it Came about that others and all the world was in Possession of Children and friends and a hous and homes and i was so od as to Sit here alone . . ." She writes of herself being "as lonely as tho i was Cast out from all the rest of the People and was a gasing stock for the old and young to gaze upon." In using her journal as a vehicle for religious self-examination, Dickinson knows herself as God would know her (completely, truly, and from within) and also views herself from the imagined position of those around her. The painful sense of "otherness" that fills the pages of this journal is borne of her awareness of being alone as she experiences it subjectively, compounded by her sense that others view her as an odd object.

An important vehicle in this process of objectifying the self is the audience of the journal. Some journals, as we have seen, are intended for real audiences but in many more the audience is implied. In some instances, the diary itself takes on this role as it is personified. "Dear diary" is a direct address to an ideal audience: always available, always listening, always sympathetic. Charlotte Forten addresses this audience on the last day of 1856: "Once more my beloved Journal, who are become a part of myself,—I say to thee, and to the Old Year,—Farewell!" Later she writes: "And now farewell, farewell to thee! my dear old friend, my *Only confidant!*—my journal!" In another passage where she seems to be speaking to a loved one, she is also speaking to the diary itself. "What name shall I give to thee, oh *ami inconnue?* It will be safer to give merely an initial—A. And so, dear A., I will tell you a little of my life for the past two years."

Others who have given their journals names include Helen Ward Brandreth, a young upper-class girl in New York state, who in 1876 begins her diary: "I have determined to keep a journal. I shall call it Fannie Fern." She cautions Fannie, questions her, and apologizes to her ("I am afraid that you will think me dead or that something awful has happened to me"). Carol Potter, who has written about this diary kept by her great-grandmother, says in her own diary: "Most people would laugh to think that a personal diary was of such significance to a person, but this one is to me. When Nellie [Brandreth] writes—my dearest darling Fan—over and over, I know how she felt about that little book. It was a friend and so is this dumpy little blue notebook. How I wish I had started in a really nice bound notebook. But one never knows what will become of a first meeting or even a few."

A contemporary diarist who knows what the relationship between writer and journal may become writes: "This notebook becomes my own little cheerleader, conscience, reckoner. You said it, now do it, it yells—OK, OK. WHAT?? It says—what's holding you up? What's the paralysis?" (March 1, 1977). Two days later she writes: "This journal has become my friend, my compulsion also . . . I need this writing. It is saving me . . . releasing me . . . But there is no one here to hold me, to tell me it's alright and yes—you can do it!—Right about now I feel the biggest, grandest need to be mothered."

The importance of the audience, real or implied, conscious or unconscious, of what is usually thought of as a private genre cannot be overstated. The presence of a sense of audience, in this form of writing as in all others, has a crucial influence over what is said and how it is said. Friend, lover, mother, God, a future self—whatever role the audience assumes for the writer—that presence becomes a powerful "thou" to the "I" of the diarist. It shapes the selection and arrangement of detail within the journal and determines more than anything else the kind of self-construction the diarist presents. In naming her diary after the popular novelist Fanny Fern, Helen Ward Brandreth casts herself in its pages as the heroine of a piece of romantic fiction. She describes to "Fan" her "spooners," her flirtations, her engagement to the "wrong man," and her scheming to free herself for the "right man."

I danced with him about six times; then he asked me to go out on the stoop with him. Of course I went and when we got out there he took off his glove and wanted to hold my hand. I resisted the temptation for awhile, but, O Fan, I am *so* ashamed; at last I yielded. My hand trembled so that I was afraid he would notice it. O Fan, Fan!! I will die if he marries Birdie, For he does like her more than anybody else. At present.

As we read Brandreth's journal we can see how its pages contain not *self* in any total sense, but a self which is to some degree a fiction, a construction. Even Mary MacLane, who attempts to write *everything,* is aware of this phenomenon and the crucial role of audience in the process. "I am trying my utmost to show everything—to reveal every petty vanity and weakness, every phase of feeling, every desire. It is a remarkably hard thing to do, I find, to probe my soul to its depths, to expose its shades and half-lights." She later concludes: "I am in no small degree, I find, a sham—a player to the gallery" [*The Story of Mary MacLane*]. Whether "the gallery" is the personified diary, a real or implied audience, all diarists are involved in a process, even if largely unconscious, of selecting details to create a persona. The presence of the "gallery" is strongly felt in the journal of Alice James, brilliant and tortured invalid, who casts herself in her journal as an ironic social satirist. In what Robert Fothergill calls "the unique instance in the genre of a self-presentation which is almost unremittingly comic" [*Private Chronicles: A Study of English Diaries*], we see clearly the distance possible between the character created in the diary and the far more complex life lived.

The pages of the diary might be thought of as a kind of mirror before which the diarist stands assuming this posture or that. One might even draw analogies between the process of psychoanalysis and the process of periodic life-writing, where the transference is made to the pages of the journal. But unlike the many oral forms of self-presentation, the self-constructions in the pages of a diary are fixed in time and space, available to the diarist for later viewing. Evidence abounds in all periods that women read and reread their diaries, a reality that renders the self-construction and reconstruction even more complex. Some diarists record comments upon previous entries, some emend them, some copy over entire diaries and edit them. One Amherst, Massachusetts woman in rewriting her diary omits an entire year and comments: "We had such a hard year in 1905 that I destroyed my diary did not want to read it—." Mary MacLane, very aware of the charged experience of encountering past selves in the pages of her journal writes: "I write this book for my own reading. / It is my postulate to myself. / As I read it makes me clench my teeth savagely: and coldly tranquilly close my eyelids: it makes me love and loathe Me, Soul and bones" [*I, Mary MacLane*]. As modern psychoanalysis has demonstrated, such dialogue with aspects of the self is a potent process capable of unlocking mysteries of the human psyche and becoming the occasion of profound knowledge, growth, and change.

This power may explain why numbers of diarists record that periodic life-writing becomes addictive. Even in some early diaries we find comments like that of Lydia Smith in 1805: "I find that my idle habit of scribbling interferes so much with all regularity that I have determined to relinquish it, tho not entirely, yet I must so constrain it as to pursue my duties and studies, etc. I must wean myself by degrees for I have not strength to quit at once" ["Lydia Smith's Journal, 1805-1806," *Proceedings of the Massachusetts Historical Society,* 1914-15]. For those who do not wean themselves from the writing, diaries may be kept for a lifetime, and in some cases seem to be understood as synonymous with the life itself. In 1899, knowing she is near death, Cynthia Carlton writes: "I am not very well. Tried to straighten diary" [*Cynthia: Excerpts from the Diaries of Cynthia Brown Carlton, 1841-1900*]. And the well-known last entry in Alice James's journal is by her companion Katherine Loring, who writes: "One of the last things she said to me was to make a correction in the sentence of March 4th 'moral discords and nervous horrors.' This dictation of March 4th was rushing about in her brain all day, and although she was very weak and it tired her much to dictate, she could not get her head quiet until she had it written: then she was relieved . . ." For these women it is almost as though the life cannot be ended until the diary is finished. After her death in 1848, Elizabeth Ann Cooley's husband makes this final entry in her journal: "This journal is done! The author being Elizabeth A. McClure died March 28, 1848. Tho happy in Christ Jesus being the only consolation left me!! She was 22 years 7 months and 12 days old" ["From Virginia to Missouri in 1846: The Journal of Elizabeth Ann Cooley," *Missouri Historical Review,* January 1966]. In the spirit of the diarist, he does not begin the entry saying she has died, but that the journal is done.

This conflation of the journal and the life itself may indeed be an accurate rendering of a complex dialectic. Some evidence exists that the persona in the pages of the diary shapes the life lived as well as the reverse. As Mary Mac-Lane comments: "I don't know whether I write this because I wear two plain dresses or whether I wear two plain dresses because I write it." The statement makes one ask to what extent Helen Ward Brandreth "plots" the romantic episodes of her life in order that they be available to "Fannie Fern" and whether Alice James views the world as ironic social satirist *because* of the persona in her journal or vice versa.

Reading a Diary: The Manuscript

The ideal way to study a diary is to have the manuscript itself in your hand because all the material aspects of a diary create important impressions. Is the cover ornate? Are the edges gilt? Does it have a lock? Or was the writing done on the least expensive of notebooks whose covers have barely survived? Perhaps no notebook at all was available and the diarist wrote between printed lines of poetry in a book she owned. Or perhaps the diarist is using a book manufactured for the purpose; volumes such as "A Line A Day" dramatically influence the form of the written record.

The most intriguing state in which to find a manuscript is the one complete with all the bits and pieces the diarist placed inside: clippings from newspapers, dried flowers,

mementos from friends. Each detail adds a bit of knowledge or suggests a mystery. Jennie E. Greson's journal of her "grand tour in 1877" stands apart from the numbers of similar accounts with its collection of hotel cards, theater tickets, and flowers picked "inside the coliseum," "on the grounds of Hampton Court," and "on the grounds of the Royal Academy, Amsterdam."

Handwriting tells stories, too. What do we make of the tiny, almost invisible because written in pencil script of a mill girl in Easthampton, Massachusetts, who kept a diary in 1863? Or of the dramatic changes in handwriting matching changes in tone in the 1901 entry of Elizabeth Hudson? Would we read the passage where she is angry at her husband in the same way if we had not seen the uncharacteristically large and bold letters and the dark impression of a pen pressed hard against the page? Would the passage in a contemporary journal: "Another goddamn idiot evening with Amy crapping around about going to sleep. . . . I am so pissed I started her to bed at 8 and she is still up at 9:25! No more naps! . . . I have so much to do. SHIT. ANGER. FRUSTRATION" read the same neatly printed on a page as it does scrawled across the pages of a notebook in increasingly larger block letters?

The Edited Diary

But, of course, we most often do not have the advantage of the information contained in the material object as we read a diary. The diaries available to the general reading public are the ones that have been published and the process of publication has almost always involved the process of editing. The editor may or may not be the author herself, but as Arthur Ponsonby, the well-known critic and historian of English diaries, has written, "No editor can be trusted not to spoil a diary" [*English Diaries: A Review of English Diaries from the Sixteenth to the Twentieth Century*]. Only a pair of examples are needed to underline his point. Eliza Frances Andrews, who edited her Civil War diary for publication fifty years after it was written, writes in her introduction:

> To edit oneself after the lapse of nearly half a century is like taking an appeal from Philip drunk to Philip sober. The changes of thought and feeling between the middle of the nineteenth and the beginning of the twentieth century are so great that the impulsive young person who penned the following record and the white-haired woman who edits it, are no more the same than were Philip drunk with the wine of youth and passion and Philip sobered by the lessons of age and experience. The author's lot was cast amid the tempest and fury of war, and if her utterances are sometimes out of accord with the spirit of our own happier time, it is because she belonged to an era which, though but of yesterday, as men of ages count history, is separated from our own by a social and intellectual chasm as broad as the lapse of a thousand years. [*The War-Time Journal of a Georgia Girl, 1864-1865*]

Andrews's sense of the sharp discontinuity of the past and present, including past and present selves, is not the only force shaping the published document. As have many diarists, Andrews destroyed a large part of the diary she kept over a ten-year period "in those periodic fits of disgust and self-abasement that come to every keeper of an honest diary in saner moments." A relative who expressed an interest in the Civil War portion of her diary saved that volume from a similar fate. But Andrews admits, "So little importance did the writer attach to the documents even then, that the only revision made in changing it from a personal to a family history, was to tear out bodily whole paragraphs, and even pages, that were considered too personal for other eyes than her own. In this way the manuscript was mutilated, in some places, beyond recovery." Such lessons learned, however, are rarely learned forever, and in preparation of her manuscript for publication, Andrews states that she omitted "Matters strictly personal," explaining "a natural averseness to the publication of anything that would too emphatically 'write me down to an ass.'"

The diary and letters of Maria Mitchell, Nantucket astronomer and educator, edited by her sister Phebe M. Kendall, met a similar fate. Of her sister, Kendall writes: "She had no secretiveness, and in looking over her letters it has been almost impossible to find one which did not contain too much that was personal, either about herself or others, to make it proper; especially as she herself would be very unwilling to make the affairs of others public" [*Maria Mitchell: Life, Letters and Journal*]. The contemporary reader, living in an age that values "the personal" in ways that neither Andrews nor Kendall would have understood, will find such editorial decisions unforgivable.

Indeed, even small changes that are nothing like such major butchering can change the impression of a passage. Punctuation marks where there were none or inconsistent capital letters regularized all alter the record of the diarist. Even spaces on a page can communicate, but few editors of a diary can afford to leave them. Many editors will be tempted to omit repetitious material, but in fact it is precisely in what *is* repeated that we find the preoccupations, the obsessions, the "metaphors of self" of the diarist. So, the first problem for the reader of a published diary is the integrity of the text, and she or he will want to know as much as possible about the editorial history of any given text.

That is not to say that the reader should be entirely cynical about the diary that has been edited. Most published diaries, just like published fiction, have gone through an editorial process in shaping the manuscript for an audience different from the one for whom the record was originally kept. The reader's instinctive suspicion of this process is grounded in the sense of the immediacy and verisimilitude claimed by the genre. But the reader should remember that the original record is itself a reconstruction of reality and not "truth" in any absolute sense. Perhaps then the reader can think of the editorial process as an activity separate and distinct from the production of the life-record, one that may be creative and artistic in its own right.

The challenge to the editor in transforming a manuscript diary to a published one is to render both an accurate and accessible version of the original text and to make known as fully as possible the methods by which those goals were pursued. Most talented editors will operate with a combi-

nation of clear guidelines and good instincts that can be subject to scrutiny through comparisons with the original text. Some diaries lend themselves to publication in their entirety with complete verbatim transcription or even facsimile reproduction, but many (because of length, for example) do not. Readers who would object to any changes in an original record must remember that without the editorial process, many diaries that have been made available to a reading public would be resting in archives and read only by research specialists.

Diaries as Literature: The Writer as Protagonist

How, then, do we read a diary, whether an original manuscript or an edited version, with an awareness that it is a verbal construct with important relationships to other forms of literature such as autobiography and even fiction? First, we must attend to the main subject of any diary, the author herself, mirrored directly or mirrored slant in its pages. Here we can test Robert Fothergill's hypothesis about women as protagonists in their diaries:

> . . . the need to project an ego-image does not appear to be a leading motive in diaries written by women. This is not to say that the personalities of women are rendered any less vividly or variously in the diary imprint than men's, but that the projection of self as dramatic protagonist is not the mode which the imprint commonly takes. There should be nothing very surprising in this. It is the merest platitude to observe that the position of women in society has tended to preclude the assertion of individual ego. . . . Egotism in men and pre-occupation with an effective self-image have been accepted and rewarded; in women they have been discouraged. A woman cannot easily cast herself as protagonist, when society and the controlling personal relationships of her life demand proficiency in exclusively supporting roles. Nor does it follow that she might therefore tend to project a more rather than less assertive ego in the diary. . . . Hence one does not find in past centuries women diarists who strut and perform and descant on their own singularity.

Mary MacLane certainly does "strut and perform and descant on her own singularity," and the memorable self-portraits created by Abigail Abbot Bailey, Nancy Shippen Livingston, Charlotte Forten, Alice James, Molly Sanford, Helen Ward Brandreth, to name just a few, suggest that Fothergill's conclusions need further examination in relation to American texts. He may be quite correct in asserting that "ego" in women rests on principles other than contest and dramatic self-assertion. If so, women's diaries will be a rich territory for study of the female construction of self and its literary representation.

In the accumulation of selected detail, particularly in the repetitions, preoccupations, even obsessions of the diarist, we find what James Olney calls the "metaphors of self." In reading a diary we must interrogate such metaphors in order to reveal their principles of construction. What organizing ideas, conscious or unconscious, shape the persona? What symbols come to represent the subject? Rebekah Dickinson, like many eighteenth-century diarists, finds these ideas and symbols in Scripture. She presents herself as a "stranger in a strange land," the entries in her diary echoing each other with the words "lonesome," "alone," "forsaken." Mary Dodge Woodward, a widow building a new life with her adult children on the Dakota plains, finds her self-reference in ordinary flowers. A rose geranium she has brought from home is the frequent subject of a diary entry. "The sitting room is full of sunshine and I am alone with the exception of Roxy, our dog, and my old rose geranium which really seems like a thing of life, it looks so much like home. I tend the plants with the greatest care fearful lest I might lose them." When she is sick, she notes that the rose geranium has "drooped"; when the temperature drops to forty below she writes: "There are still plenty of leaves on the old geranium which, with the help of the big coal stove has braved a Dakota winter." The plant comes from home, is old, and does not grow naturally on the prairie. And when she writes about a peony plant that she brought from her mother's home in Vermont, planted in Wisconsin where she lived with her husband, and which now blooms in the Dakota Territory, her comment, "anything that can live in this cold country should be reverenced," is about the persistent flower but it is also about herself [*The Checkered Years*].

Mary Holyoke's litany of childbirths and deaths, Elizabeth Fuller's accounting of work in her father's household, and Sarah Nichols's record of her walking tours are also such imprints of self. Even a record of the weather may tell us much about the diarist who chose to record it. Elizabeth Dixon Smith Geer, on an overland journey from Indiana to Oregon, sends this report to friends left at home:

> Nov. 30 [1847] Raining. This morning I ran about trying to get a house to get into with my sick husband. At last I found a small, leaky concern, with two families already in it . . . My children and I carried up a bed. The distance was nearly a quarter of a mile. Made it down on the floor in the mud. I got some men to carry my husband up through the rain and lay him on it. . . . There are so many of us sick that I cannot write any more at present. I have not time to write much, but I thought it would be interesting to know what kind of weather we have in the winter.

Two months later, her sick husband has died and the weather continues to be the emblem of her condition: "Today we buried my earthly companion. Now I know what none but widows know; that is, how comfortless is that of a widow's life, especially when left in a strange land, without money or friends, and the care of seven children. Cloudy" ["Diary of Mrs. Elizabeth Dixon Smith Geer," *Transactions of the Oregon Pioneer Association,* 1907].

Time and Narrative Structures

While the novel and autobiography may be thought of as artistic wholes, the diary is always in process, always in some sense a fragment. That is not to say that diaries do not have distinct shapes, but that their shapes derive from their existence in time passing. Some are shaped by external events in the diarist's life, which, even from the writer's point of view, have a beginning, middle, and end.

Courtship diaries ending with a marriage and travel diaries ending with the arrival at a destination are examples of such texts.

Because diaries are periodic in creation and structure, incremental repetition is an important aspect of the structure of most journals, and the dynamic of reading the periodic life-record involves attending to what is repeated. Repeated actions large and small build tension as they advance the "plot." Will beloved Sister Mary Ermeline in the convent school diary of Suzette Pierce be waiting in the hall again today? Will she take her arm again and speak of friendship and love? Will the wagon train in the diary of Amelia Stewart Knight make it across this next, even more dangerous river?

The calendar year provides the structural rhythms of many diaries. Frequently diarists mark the end of each calendar year with repeated rituals; early diaries often end the year with a list of persons who died during that year, later ones with reflections and resolutions. Many women diarists mark holidays and personal anniversaries as does Mary Dodge Woodward:

> Thanksgiving Day. This used to be a day of unusual gladness, for on this day Walter was born, and he has proved a great blessing to me. We used to try, after the fashion of New Englanders, to be all at home on Thanksgiving if it were possible. I have been very happy with my family around the table many years—how happy, I did not realize until that sad day on which the father was taken from us and I was left alone with the children. Never since then have all the children been with me on this day. It is our fourth Thanksgiving in Dakota. The turkey is roasted and eaten, and the day has gone; I am thankful.

Time and the Reader

A novel creates a fictional world complete unto itself, while an autobiography or memoir looks back from a fixed point in time which is the terminus of the retrospective. A diary, on the other hand, is created in and represents a continuous present. And as we have seen, many diarists reread previous entries before writing a current one, creating a complexly layered present to which a version of the past is immediately available. From entry to entry, the text incorporates its future as it reconstructs its past.

While analogies may be drawn between the construction of self in a diary and an autobiography, and even between the creation of a persona in a diary and a novel, the unique demands made of the reader of a diary derive from its periodic creation and structure. The writer's relationship to "real time" and representation of "time passing" in the text itself, create formal tensions and ironies not found in texts generated from an illusion of a fixed point in time. What is known as well as what is *unknown* to the writer underscore the unique dynamic of the periodic text. Further, what is known and unknown to the *reader* of the journal text determine the unusually active role demanded of that reader. Again, periodicity is the key phenomenon determining the relationship of the writer and the reader to the text, and to each other, within both real and imaged time.

While diaries may have narrative structures approximating those of other forms of verbal art—action moving toward an end creating anticipation around the question of what happens next—the obvious difference in the "plots" of diaries and those of most other narratives is that the novelist, poet, oral storyteller, or writer of an autobiographical memoir knows what happens next and directs the reader's response at every point. Most diaries, on the other hand, are a series of surprises to writer and reader alike, one source of the immediacy of the genre. For example, eighteen-year-old Helen Marnie Stewart kept a journal on her family's trip to Oregon in 1853. She writes: "it being raining the road is extremely slippy and there is very steep hills to go up and down and that makes it difficult and hard   there was neer us a grave that had been dug open and a women head was layin and a come sticking in her hair   it seems rather hard." Though the last line, indeed the understatement of the entire passage, suggests the extent to which Helen Stewart and her party had become inured to horror, the reader experiences something of the sharp intake of breath in coming unprepared upon the grave in the diary text that Helen Stewart felt in seeing it along the road.

Surprises, Mysteries, and Silences of Diaries

The surprises, the mysteries, and the silences of diaries must all be considered in relation to what is known and unknown to both writer and reader. Though a diary may have been intended for a real audience, it was likely not created for its current reader. Some of the diary, at least on first reading, may mean nothing to the reader. (This is one reason why it is so hard to imitate a diary in fictional form. The temptation of the author to tell too much makes the reader realize immediately, as in *The Diary of a Shirtwaist Striker,* by Theresa Serber Malkiel, for example, that the diary is not an authentic one.) As a result the reader must take a rather active role in the creation of the world within the diary. One source of the engagement of reading a private, periodic record is precisely this activity, which can be akin to putting together pieces of a puzzle—remembering clues and supplying the missing pieces, linking details apparently unrelated in the diarist's mind, and decoding "encoded" materials.

This process is complicated by the fact that while the diarist almost always has more knowledge about her world than the reader has, the reader may have some knowledge unavailable to the diarist. What we know about the outcome of the Civil War creates, in part, the you-can't-put-it-down quality of many narratives from that period. What we know about the continuing struggle for women's rights intensifies our reactions to Abigail Bailey's account of kidnapping by her husband and Mary Ann Sims's account of her brother-in-law's attempt to take her property away upon the death of her husband ["Private Journal of Mary Ann Own Sims," *Arkansas Historical Quarterly,* Summer and Autumn 1976].

All diarists operate within the limits of their own self-knowledge, limits the reader may be able to transcend. As Mary MacLane writes: "I have analyzed and analyzed, and I have gotten down to some extremely fine points—and yet there are still things upon my horizon that go be-

yond me" [*The Story of Mary MacLane*]. The repeated patterns of a life may escape the writer recording them while they do not escape an aware reader. In a very real sense the contemporary reader may know more about the source of anguish felt by Rebekah Dickinson, more about Charlotte Forten's drive to prove she was as capable as any white person, more about the racism of Eliza Frances Andrews than the diarist did herself.

One task for the reader of any diary is to identify the "silences" of the text. What the diarist did not, could not, or would not write sometimes shrieks from the page. Adrienne Rich's poem, "Cartographies of Silence," illuminates:

> The technology of silence
> the rituals, etiquette
>
> the blurring of terms
> silence not absence
>
> of words or music or even
> raw sounds
>
> Silence can be a plan
> rigorously executed
> the blueprint to a life
>
> It is a presence
> it has a history a form
>
> Do not confuse it
> with any kind of absence

> ["Cartographies of Silence," *The Dream of a
> Common Language, Poems 1974-1977*]

The task of the reader of a diary is to identify these presences: their technology, ritual, etiquette, plan, history, and form. One of the loudest silences in the diaries of American women surrounds the line written by Mary Holyoke on September 1, 1782: "My Dear Child Died 9 A.M., which makes the 8th Child." This woman, who gave birth to twelve children, three of whom survived, records no grief, no terrified anticipation of childbirth, no mention of pregnancy, no mention (of course) of sex. Only the careful record of babies born to herself and others in her community and of babies dead and buried. Most diaries contain such silences created by choices, conscious and unconscious, made by the writer in her time.

Sometimes the diarist indicates the things she will not say in her written record. Helen Ward Brandreth's last New Year's resolution for 1877 is a wonderful example:

This is my greatest *sin*. O Fan, if I could only stop but it is *so* hard. I have made more good resolutions about it than anything else and when I think I have entirely recovered from it I do it over again. The last time I did it was Dec. 14, 1877, only a little bit of a while ago. I would tell you what it is only it is so horridly awfully vile and then some one *might* read this and O horrors! what would they think of me. I would be disgraced for life.

The diary contains no entry for Dec. 14, 1877, and so the reader is left with only this suggestive mystery.

Another example is the contemporary diarist who writes freely about sex, but adds, "But, I am finding it tricky to write about my attractions to women . . . I will leave that private." Her comment reveals her assumption that somehow the diary, even in an age where it is usually thought to be, is not, in fact, private. Such silences when so identified indicate the presence of an implied or potential audience, who even if not a conscious presence, exerts a powerful shaping influence on the text.

The Reader's Journey

Today's reader of the text, another powerful shaping audience, recreates the journal in the act of reading. The words "journal" and "journey," like the word "diary," have their roots in the French word for "day." So we might think of all diaries as travel diaries and the overriding metaphor of all journals as the journey, a journey from one "place" in time to another. The journey becomes a parallel one for writer and reader in more than one sense. The vividness of the self-created character in many journal pages derives in part from the concrete, distinct, and peculiar detail she reports along her journey. The unique specificity of most journals creates the effect sought by writers of other forms of verbal art—an entire world whose closed borders the reader may enter for a time. For the reader who may never have had thirteen children, or traveled in a wagon to Oregon, or sailed to Africa as a black American, the journey recorded in the diary becomes the reader's journey.

Further, the special demands made upon the reader for active participation in the recreation of the writer's journey affirm the reader's like capacities of imagination. The text created in a continuous presence but now fixed in time, must be re-created by a reader in a new, continuous present. The reader's consciousness of time passing may be, in part, what makes reading the journal a compelling experience. As the journal pages construct continuity out of the apparent discontinuity created by time passing in the writer's life, the act of reading may generate a parallel process for the reader. The participation of the reader means that the writing act has indeed succeeded in defying time; and the text, in turn, grants the active reader the conviction, "they wrote, therefore, I am."

DIARIES AS PSYCHOLOGICAL SCHOLARSHIP

Martha Tomhave Blauvelt   (essay date 1993)

SOURCE: " 'This Altogather Precious tho Wholy Worthless Book': The Diary of Mary Guion, 1800-1852," in *Anxious Power: Reading, Writing, and Ambivalence in Narrative by Women,* edited by Carol J. Singley and Susan Elizabeth Sweeney, State University of New York Press, 1993, pp. 125-141.

[*In the following essay, Blauvelt uses the diary of Mary Guion (1782-1871) to explore from a feminist critical perspective issues that affected nineteenth-century women as a whole: the reasons some kept diaries, the ways diaries functioned in their lives, and the interplay between diary-writing and popular literature of the time.*]

At the turn of the nineteenth century, Mary Guion (1782-1871), a seventeen-year-old living in rural Westchester

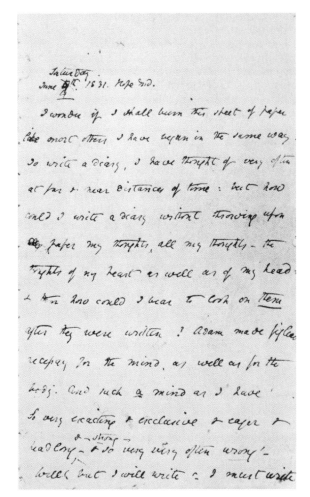

An entry from the diary of Elizabeth Barrett Browning.

County, New York, began to keep a diary. Like many young women, she began with brief, unrevealing entries; but her journal, unlike most, burgeoned into 387 closely written pages, 340 of them covering her courtship years from 1800 to 1807. Guion chronicled the everyday life of a young woman of the early American republic in almost overwhelming detail: who came to tea, what they said, where she went, whom she danced with, how she spent her day. It is impossible to read this flood of words without asking why Guion needed to record her life in such detail. What did writing mean to her? Did she experience the ambivalence or "anxious power" so common to female writers? [The essays in *Anxious Power* have as their uniting principle the belief that female authors can experience both empowerment and anxiety when writing. Blauvelt and the other essayists insist that while such women are enfranchised by their self-expression, language itself, because of its inherent patriarchy, simultaneously disenfranchises them.]

As an historian interested in women's writing, I believe that we can find its meaning in precisely those details of everyday life which Guion's diary described. Texts can be understood only in terms of context: the experience of writing had specific meaning in the early nineteenth century, in America, for a woman, and for those engaged in courtship. An examination of Guion's 1800-1807 courtship diary suggests the origins of both the anxiety and the power of writing. At first, Guion's journal functioned as an educational tool: it represented her desire to "improve" her intellectual abilities at the same time that it raised fears that her diary lacked "geniues." But as Guion entered her twenties and made marriage her central concern, her diary gained a new function: it became a means of empowerment that helped her to analyze men's motivations and strengthened her resolve in relationships with them. In sum, the meaning of writing changed as the circumstances of Guion's life changed.

Directly related to the role of writing in Guion's education and courtship is the role of reading. Throughout her journal, books—especially novels—both invited Guion to write and set the literary standards she anxiously tried to imitate. At the same time, their plots provided warnings about men's behavior and advice essential to successful courtship. In Mary Guion's case, "anxious power" characterized reading as well as writing. Both "precious" and "worthless," her diary captures the interplay of reading and writing in the context of everyday life in early nineteenth-century America.

That Mary Guion began a diary at all suggests that she possessed an important initial power: the freedom to write. Her particular class, family, and historical era provide the immediate context in which we must interpret her writing. Born in 1782 into a prosperous North Castle, New York, family, she enjoyed the leisure both to read others' literary creations and to produce her own. In her diary Guion records periodic spinning, woolcarding, milking, candle-making, knitting, and sewing, yet she regularly spent nights at balls, and days immersed in reading or writing, without any suggestion of their interference with important tasks. Undoubtedly the fact that she had four sisters lessened the household labor of each. Within two days' journey from New York City, the Guion family could also purchase many goods rather than make them; Guion's journal itself may have been purchased in the city.

If the Guion family's class and location provided leisure time, its atmosphere also encouraged writing. Guion's father and mother were, as she said, "the best and most indu[l]gent of Parents." They willingly provided the material needs for writing by buying her pen and paper and grating her privacy. At a time when many parents discouraged their daughters' interest in literary enterprises, her father and brothers regularly borrowed novels for Guion and joined her in reading them aloud. Happily situated in a circle which mirrored the family ideal of the early republic, Guion enjoyed great latitude, from how she behaved with men to whether she went to church and how she spent her time. Her family's respect and love for her is reflected in Guion's conviction that her life merited a book.

Leisure and encouragement created the possibility for writing, but the fact that Mary Guion grew up during the late eighteenth century gave the practice of writing particular meaning. The early republic was an era of enthusiasm for women's education, an enthusiasm that had significant implications for diary keeping. This educational reform movement was not motivated by any overriding concern for women's right to develop their minds: rather, they were to learn in order to become better companions to their husbands and better mothers to their sons. Nor did it transform educational practice. The irregular spelling, erratic capitalization and idiosyncratic punctuation of Guion's journal—not uncommon in women's writing of the time—suggest the limits of female education during this period. Yet the early republic had a marked effect on female education in that it validated women's desire for self-improvement. "Improvement," with its image of progressive attainment of knowledge, was a favorite word of both educational theorists and young women such as Mary Guion. Guion apparently spent few years in school, but she maintained that "it would be impossible for any to prise an education higher than I" and was proud of her past academic performance. "I was envied by all the little misses at school for receiving the premium at the expiration of the Quarter," she recalled in 1804. And long after she finished her formal education, Guion sought opportunities to polish her basic skills. In 1801, for example, she began studying grammar with her brother James. Two years later, at age twenty, she went back to school to study arithmetic. Her comment that "the Schollars were all quite small so they had not power to draw my attention from [m]y book" suggests both the incongruity of her situation and her determination to learn. It is unclear how frequently she attended school, but as late as 1806 she went to night classes, set aside days to study geography and ciphering, and vowed "to improve every moment to some kind of useful study."

Writing was an integral part of Guion's effort to continue her education beyond school. It provided a freedom of subject, style, and structure which encouraged self-expression as well as literary expertise. For young women eager to "improve" themselves, journals also promised privacy in education; through them women could polish their writing without school or correspondent. Guion may have known that journal keeping, with its habits of daily writing and observation, was a common assignment in female academies; by keeping a diary she privately participated in a practice of the most elite schools of her time. She noted that "the less I practise the worse I write," and over time her prose became more polished and her entries more reflective. A penchant for self-improvement through writing was partly responsible for the marked increase in the number and quality of diaries by women such as Guion during the early national period.

Equally important in encouraging Guion and other women to write was the early republic's expanding book market. . . . At the turn of the century imports and American editions were available in higher numbers than ever before. Recognizing that many of the most avid readers were young women who could not afford to purchase books, entrepreneurs founded lending libraries where for a modest fee local patrons could borrow books of all kinds. Mary Guion and her family regularly borrowed volumes from these libraries, as well as from literary friends. "I wish it was as customary for every family to have a good library as it is to have a bed in their house", she wrote in 1806. Reading was an integral part of Guion's social life:

she and her brother regularly read out loud to each other, and Guion delighted in a "smart confab" over books with her suitors. Between 1800 and 1807 Guion read an amazing number of works, including novels such as *The Children of the Abbey, The Fool of Quality, Charlotte Temple,* and *The Man of Feeling*; sentimental poetry such as Young's *Night Thoughts*; popular philosophy; and many magazines.

The novels Guion read were especially important in encouraging her and other women to become writers. [In *Mothers of the Novel: 100 Good Woman Writers Before Jane Austen,*] Dale Spender estimates that female novelists outnumbered male authors by two- and perhaps three-to-one during the century before Jane Austen, as the female author became a public figure for the first time. More important is the frequency with which eighteenth-century literature, especially sentimental fiction, represents women at their writing desks, composing letters or keeping diaries. More than in any other period, the fictional heroine of the eighteenth century is a writer. Often her writings carried the plot, and women's private compositions became public fiction: a substantial proportion of English and American novels were epistolary works which prominently featured women's letters, and many epistolary novels included diary entries as a narrative device. . . . Even third-person narratives often had the fragmented quality of letters and diaries; as Janet Todd notes [in *Sensibility: An Introduction*], "missing chapters, torn sentences or mutilated letters" form gaps in the prose, as if the novel were a private manuscript, a diary-like fragment of private life. In all these cases, women appear in the act of writing and often tell their own stories.

Sentimental heroines not only told their own stories, but told them well. As [Cathy N.] Davidson points out [in *Revolution and the World: The Rise of the Novel in America*], novels demonstrated "that an unblemished prose style was as proper to a would-be heroine as a spotless reputation or a winsome smile" (73). The sentimental heroine was as well-educated as she was well-spoken. Fictional heroines regularly engaged in philosophical asides and talked knowingly about the works of Locke, Hume, and Rousseau. Readers such as Guion had ample reason for believing that "people might very much improve the understanding by a sereous attention to" novels. Sentimental fiction in effect provided an education in how to write about oneself and how to write well. Guion was only one of many female readers who attempted to imitate the prose of sentimental fiction in their private first-person narratives.

But if both the diary and the novel promised Guion "improvement," the process of writing itself raised doubts about her intellectual abilities. Her diary mirrors this ambivalence. On the one hand, a journal is preeminently a "book of the self " [Robert A. Fothergill, *Private Chronicles: A Study of English Diaries*], and in its inception, scope and detail, Mary Guion's diary is an overt assertion of self. It is based on the assumption that her life is worth recording, deserves to be remembered, and merits a second existence on paper. But the creation of another self put her in a peculiarly painful situation. In a word she used repeated-

ly, it "exposed" her. Above all, it exposed her relative lack of education and called into question her intellectual self-worth. Guion often deprecated "this Silly Simple nonscence" which gave "but a very imperf[e]c't idea to what I should wish it might be." Guion repeatedly called herself "illiterate" and lamented, "I really wish I was in possession of an education or a geniues sufficient to inscribe something that would afford if to no one els' to myself a real pleasure and satisfaction." With these mixed feelings, she characterized her journal as "this altogather precious tho wholy worthless book."

Guion's embarrassment and pride in her other self are reflected alternately in her fear that someone would read her book and her hope that it would find an audience. She went to great lengths to assure that no one would see her diary and typically wrote when her family was asleep. When others were near, she wrote in fear of interruption: "am siting by the fire all a lone writing expecting every moment some intruder to discover me & expose my work." When company came she often "stole" outside with her journal, and when visiting relatives she withdrew to a "hovel for retirement" to write. On one cold November day in 1803, she summed up her secrecy with the words: "al alone writing for no one to read." Yet Guion clearly expected someone to read her diary. She frequently prefaced entries with "if there ever is a reader to this paper" or "what will the candid reader thinck of me." Occasionally she playfully invited the reader to guess with whom she had danced or what her feelings were. Several times she expressed the hope that she would "entertain" her reader, although she typically despaired of edifying anyone.

Usually Guion's references were to future readers, but occasionally she also offered opportunities for contemporaries to study her diary. Her behavior suggests that her references to readers were not simply a literary device. One night after retiring she realized she had left her journal by the fire, where her brothers might find it. In what seems an extended flirtation with exposure, she decided to wait until morning to retrieve it. "I believe it ran in [my] thots all night for I had a curious sort of Dream and awoke with the first dawn of day," she reported. On going below, she found "it had not been disturbed." It is hard to tell if she was disappointed or relieved at this discovery.

Guion had escaped "exposure" that time but, inevitably, someone read her journal: her adored older brother James. In a long account dating from late July 1801, Guion described her intense reaction to this self-revelation. At that point she had been writing her diary for over a year. She began with an acute juxtaposition: "Friday I was a Scrubing the floor   James was In the study   he stepd in the Parlour & said to me Polly I never know[n] you kept a Journal befor." Rising to stop him, Guion wished she "had never a wroat it" and was filled with "Shame," especially for a lovesick acrostic she had written. She told James that she had meant no one to read her diary, but he replied that he could see no harm in it. At this point Guion "said no mor" despite "a kind of febleness & trembleng thoro Shame." Her desire to know what he thought of her diary had overcome her initial reluctance to be exposed.

Fortunately, her first reader "seemd to aplaud it" and offered to buy her a new journal so she could continue writing. Torn between pleasure and embarrassment, Guion ended her account on an ambivalent note: she found "great satisfaction" in her brother's reaction, but judged it "undeservingly" bestowed.

Guion's mixed feelings towards her literary creation never entirely abated. A desire both to assert and improve herself had motivated her writing, but even as the process of writing expressed her self-worth, the seemingly inadequate result undercut her self-confidence. Emotionally, the diary was "precious" to her; intellectually, it seemed often insufficient and even "worthless." In many ways Guion's deprecation of her intellect was similar to that of contemporary female English autobiographers. Like Mary, they engaged in self-presentation, belittled their intellects, and both feared and desired an audience. What distinguishes the reactions of diarists such as Guion from those of female autobiographers of her time is how gender intersects with their respective literary forms. The autobiography, as a public form, exposed female writers to the gender expectations of a public audience and ignited fears of deficiency. As Patricia Meyer Spacks shows [in *Imagining a Self: Autobiography and Novel in Eighteenth-Century England*], female autobiographers were acutely aware that in simply publishing their life histories, they had revealed themselves as unfeminine. They compensated for this outrageous act by writing defensively and belittling themselves. By contrast, Guion, facing at best a private or future audience, feared intellectual deficiency more than feminine deficiency. Private writing did not assume male privilege the way public writing did, and her self-criticisms typically appear in the context of a desire for more education and greater intellectual ability, rather than an effort to appear deferential. She had not escaped the oppression of gender—it had limited her educational opportunities—but no "angel in the house" seems to have suggested that writing was inappropriate for her sex. Instead, Guion offered her writing on its own terms: a flawed literary creation that others might not find worth reading, but which she, in her struggle for improvement, found worth writing.

The desire to be educated and the fear that she was not provide the basic ambivalence in Mary Guion's diary. But her journal served another function: an instrument to help her decide whom to marry. As such, it took her diary in new directions. Novel reading, which had encouraged her writing, provided themes and a self-understanding which shaped her courtship. At the same time, her diary became a representation of the ideal man she sought in courtship. As she moved toward marriage in 1807, Guion lost her fear of self-exposure and began to use her diary to expose the machinations of men. In the complex interplay of these factors, Guion's diary empowered her as she negotiated her way in a patriarchal society.

When she began her diary at age seventeen, Guion was already well launched on the search for a spouse. In a pattern of advance and retreat that characterized the dance figures of her day, dozens of young men move through her diary. Guion captured the pairing and unpairing in a brief entry from June, 1800: "I went to Meeting   two Young Gentlemen came home with us staid & drank tea   one of them went away and another took his pla[c]e in the evening." As many historians have observed, courtship was the most crucial period of a woman's life, and she had best choose a partner carefully. Under common law husbands controlled family money, and women had few legal rights; a wrong choice meant not only personal unhappiness but possible economic disaster. Guion's own family provided a telling example of the dangers of marrying the wrong man. Her sister Sally's husband not only neglected Sally when she was sick and ridiculed her before others, but blamed his wife when someone tried to rape her, trafficked in stolen goods, and spent his earnings on drink, leaving his family in poverty. "How much do I pity her hard lot—!" Guion exclaimed; "much sooner would I meet with Death than live with a person of th[a]t discription." Her brother James, on the other hand, was a supremely considerate husband. Guion understandably wondered which would be her fate, and as a result, hers is primarily a courtship diary in which she compared suitors.

Women had undoubtedly always wondered whom they would marry, but courtship diaries such as Mary Guion's were not common until the rise of a reading public in the late eighteenth century. Guion and her contemporaries were avid readers of a sentimental fiction which was often written specifically for female readers and typically focused on a young woman whose name furnished the book's title. Variously subjected to handsome rakes, nasty husbands, and money-hungry parents determined to marry her to a brute, the heroine made her way to a fate of either seduction and death, or virtue and bliss. These seemingly farfetched plots accurately captured women's vulnerable social and economic position, in which unwed pregnancy meant social if not literal death, and a wise marital choice was crucial to happiness. Guion's sister Sally's life offered ample proof of these fictional themes. In this sense these novels were, as their authors maintained, "founded on fact." As such, they provided their female readers opportunities to consider appropriate responses to male courtship and marital behavior without suffering the consequences.

Sentimental fiction inevitably influenced another form of literature "founded on fact": the diary. The realism of these novels, and their focus on women, encouraged female readers to incorporate elements of plot and theme into their own "books": diarists quickly assumed the place of fictional heroines, made their own courtships the chief subject of their entries, and acutely analyzed male behavior. Novel reading was especially important in encouraging women to continue journal writing once they had started. Frequently women became discouraged over the fragmented nature of diary keeping; if they could not find a pattern to their entries, they often quit. As extraordinary a diarist as she was, Guion occasionally became mired in lists of who came to tea and periodically abandoned her journal. The plots of novels both provided shape to the sprawl of everyday life and endowed the domestic with literary significance. Guion recognized the influence of fiction when she, much like a novelist, included conversations in her entries. Originally fiction had appropriated the letter and the diary; in a complex dialogue of reinterpretation and reinforcement, the diary reappropriated the novel and fostered the journal of courtship.

Guion's diary recalls sentimental fiction in its plot (whom will she marry?), characters, and themes. Immediately recognizable to any novel reader was the man to whom she devoted many entries: Captain Jasup, a wealthy middleaged widower who, despite his protestations of innocence, turned out to be a shameless rake. Guion and Jasup met at a wedding in 1804 where, Mary breathlessly reported, Jasup "seamed to wish to be very familiar took his seat next me & even ventured to put his arm round me wich quite ambaresed me." On meeting again, Jasup shocked Guion by openly embracing her, "teling me at the same time he wanted me to know him next time I seen him what must I thinck of his fredom did he not behave thus to se if I had wit suficient to resent it." Significantly, Guion drew on a favorite sentimental novel in her reaction: "I thot of it several times of makeing the same speach to him as Evelina did to Clement [in Fanny Burney's 1778 novel (*Evelina*)] 'Your fredom Sir were you are more acquainted may perhaps be better accepted' but did not speak it."

Despite her reservations, Guion, like the heroine of any seduction and betrayal novel, was quite taken with Jasup. She danced with him, went sleighing, allowed him to visit her, and flirted. But having recently read *Charlotte Temple,* she decided to investigate his character. Guion discovered that Jasup drank, gambled, had "strange transactions" with his housekeeper and "had contracted an acquaintance with a fashionable tho despisable disorder." He was, in short, a villain. "I believe the Gentlemen thinck it an honour to then to tell as many Fictious stories to the Ladies as their imagination can invent," Guion remonstrated. "Adieu! Adieu! for ever, I will endevour to never write, speak, and even thinck, of him more." In this account Guion cast herself in the role of innocent heroine, a potential victim to the villainous fictional males over whose escapades she had wept. But in her diary she had an opportunity to rewrite the often unhappy endings of sentimental novels. Here novel reading and diary writing at first parallel each other, but then diverge: her familiarity with novels warned Mary Guion away from her seducer and in her book women escape their literary fate.

Throughout her diary the question of whom Guion will marry is intimately related to a theme prominent in sentimental fiction: whom can a woman trust? Her journal provided the means to distinguish reality from flattery, words from intentions. The theme that men's words are false appears on the first surviving page of Guion's journal. There a young gentleman, Jotham Smith, promised to take her to a ball but never came for her. Over the next few years "the inconstant young Sycopha[n]t" repeatedly promised to visit Guion at certain appointed times but failed to appear. Occasionally she retaliated by snubbing him, but more typically she accepted his excuses and fell into his trap: "after all this I once more concented for him to come again wich I hartily repent of," Guion wrote in wonderment, "how strange it is I shoul[d] act so different to my Reason." Other men treated her no better.

By the time Guion met Captain Jasup in 1804, she had

concluded that "two fac[e]d Gentlemen are quite common now a day" and wondered, "can an inocent female account for the meaning of so much discimulation in the other sex." Even before she investigated Jasup's character, she suspected his intentions. When Jasup proposed that they write to each other, Guion knowingly reported, "to that I would not consent for I am very sensible it is an easy matter for the pen to write expresions that the heart never experienced . . . and as I detest flattery so much I would not with my own consent indulge him with so fair an oportunity of that kind." Looking back at their relationship, Guion concluded that it was only Jasup's age which had lent credibility to "the reality of his words."

Guion was no more sure of her own feelings than those of her suitors. She repeatedly used her diary to puzzle over whom she loved best and therefore should marry. This question was especially difficult because Guion could not settle what role feelings should play in her decision. She found herself caught between two "companions": "reason" and "fancy." In her philosophical moments she usually favored reason and cited the republican truism, "let reason be my guide." Reason told her that Jasup was too old for her and that no "sober woman" wanted a rake. "But I have another companion that I call Fancy wich is apt to intrude itself unless I keep a wachful eye," she realized. "Fancy" seemed to have a strong sexual component: her entries on Jotham Smith and Captain Jasup, the men to whom fancy drew her, emphasized the former's looks and the latter's outrageous advances. With both Smith and Jasup she had allowed fancy momentarily to triumph, only to be deceived and ill-treated. Not unlike the heroines of sentimental fiction, she found passion left her a victim.

Guion resolved her conflict between fancy and reason by deciding that the proper basis for marriage was friendship, which incorporated the warm, affective element of fancy without its sexual dangers and recognized the good sense of reason without its coldheartedness. Like many early republicans, she idealized marriage as the union of kindred, feeling souls living in harmony, equality, and sympathy, " 'where every thought is anticipated before it escapes from the lips; where advice, consolation, succour, are reciprocally given and received.' " Guion glimpsed such a relationship in her brother's union, but it was her sister Sally's unhappy marriage which cemented her firm belief that "those who list in the conjugal state are designed as help mates for each other not as tirants."

Yet as Mary Guion discovered during her courtship, even when she had determined her true feelings, it was not always possible to express them. How was she forthrightly to convey her feelings when the entire community scrutinized her courtships? Guion frequently reported rumors that she would marry whichever young man was currently visiting her, a practice that made her reluctant to open her heart to anyone. A too frank preference for one man might also endanger her reputation. The customs of the period similarly set limits to honesty in courtship. After entertaining an unwanted suitor, Guion complained, "the Gentlemen have much the advantage of the Ladies for they need only go were they choose but we must stay at home and pretend to be pleased with the company of such persons whose absence would be a relief to us."

Guion found this situation particularly painful. Throughout her diary she characterized herself as "partial to plain dealing" and "candid." During her years of courtship she became more and more desperate in her search for a man she could trust. Drawn more to men than to her own sex, Guion lacked the close female friendships which sustained other women in her position. As she suffered repeated disappointments, her affection grew for her one trusted confidante: her diary. During the years from 1800 to 1807 Guion increasingly recognized the role her journal played in her life. "Wen I amuse myself with my pen or a book I always find that I have very agreeable & entertaining company & that wich never Cloys," she wrote in 1804, undoubtedly thinking of the tedious young gentlemen she had been compelled to entertain. The following year, when she struggled with her feelings for Captain Jasup, she repeatedly praised her diary. "I believe my pen will always expose my thots what a tell tale has it ever been and still continues to be . . . by placing them in so external a point of vieu that I can read them at leisure, wich tho simple as they are often afford me real pleasure." "I conseal nothing from this paper," she maintained. "So different am I from many others that I find a real pleasure in it when my mind is animated, and a sympathising friend when dejected." "My two reall friends," Guion concluded in 1805, were "my boock & pen."

In short, with her diary Guion developed the affectionate, confiding, egalitarian relationship she idealized for husbands and wives. If novels warned her away from villains, her journal embodied the alternative. In that sense, she anticipated the relationship she finally developed with the man she would marry: Samuel Brown. Brown first appeared in Guion's diary in December 1800 and by 1802 she reported rumors that they would marry. At this point she was drawn to him, but Smith, Jasup, and others caught her fancy. When she gave up Jasup in 1805, her attention returned to Brown. In him she at last found "candid speach" and "a reasonable and a constant heart." But by then she was herself reluctant to speak frankly. For two years she temporized, unable to either refuse or accept Brown, overcome with anxiety at the prospect of making a wrong choice. In a striking metaphor, she felt she stood "upon a precipice," hardly knowing "which path to chuse." Acutely aware that on her decision would depend her "happiness or misery" and unsure which way to turn, she "artfully . . . disguised my fealings and every emotion of my heart when in [Brown's] company," confining her feelings to her faithful journal.

Bit by bit, Brown broke down her reticence, and Guion in March 1807 "at last determined [to] marry none but him." But this marked no unthinking capitulation. Guion had spent the last two years "observing his discourse and behaveour for before marriage people can hardly be too critical." Having given reason its due, Guion could then allow fancy some leeway. In the months prior to her wedding she and Brown engaged in much sexual banter: clearly he had won her heart as well as her head. Guion recognized his place in her life by characterizing him in exactly

the same terms she had described her journal in 1805. Brown was, she felt, "a Sympathsi[zing] friend." Guion now had not two but three friends: "my book my Pen and my—Lover."

Guion's grouping of her book, pen and lover captures for us the intertwining of reading, writing and courtship that were crucial for her diary. As I have shown, there are many parallels between the plots, themes and subjects of novels and diaries. But the relationship between reading and writing can be understood in a different, more ironic sense if we focus on the process common to both: the interplay of fiction and reality. The novels Guion read were fictional constructs of reality. That was part of their appeal: from the safety of her seat by the fire, Guion could analyze imagined aspects of her own life. The warnings embedded in that fiction potentially enhanced her safety: they told her of the dangers of certain types of behavior and men. In this sense, sentimental fiction was a reading of and a guide to reality. But throughout her diary, Guion understood fiction in another sense: the "Fictious" words of men whose intentions were dishonorable. This type of fiction had portended ruin for her sister. Sally had mistaken "appearances"—fiction—for reality, and disaster had ensued. Throughout her years of courtship, it was Mary Guion's aim to avoid a similar fate. To do so, she must distinguish the fictions around her and accurately "read" men's behavior.

Guion solved this problem of reading through writing. In turning to a diary she in a sense created yet another fiction, in that her journal was a partial vision of reality and often an echo of sentimental literature. But she recognized that her journal placed her thoughts "in so external a point of view" that she could read them "at leisure." Her diary helped distance her from life, from reality, much as novels did, so that she could safely analyze its meaning and choose how to act. In a sense, her diary made her both author and audience, writer and reader. In those roles she could both vent her emotions and explore them, be the subject of an often unmanageable life and control that life, recognize her fancies and counter them with reason. Her creation of that partial fiction, that rereading of her life, helped bring her courtship to a happy conclusion.

But if the interaction of book, pen and lover helped Mary Guion through the perils of courtship, that same combination led to the decline of her journal: after her marriage, Guion would never again keep her diary with the faithfulness that had characterized her single years. Only forty-seven pages cover the years from 1807 to 1852. The particular circumstances of daily life which had initially encouraged her to write—leisure time, a supportive family, the influence of novels and the freedom to "improve" herself—ended with marriage and motherhood. Submerged in care for her husband and four daughters, Guion gave up novel reading, embraced religion, and became a devout matron. Context hastened the decline of her journal, just as it had shaped its beginning. But Guion did not forget how essential writing had been to her happiness. In 1822, at the age of forty, she reread her courtship diary and was at first so appalled by its seeming triviality that she began to burn it. But in a final assertion of her writing's worth, she could not bring herself to destroy the entire manuscript. Although writing would never again occupy a central place in her development, this last reluctance to burn her literary creation suggests that Guion recognized that her journal was more "precious" than "worthless," and that it had once been a source of power in her life. Its surviving pages remind us how the concrete details of everyday life shape the meaning of writing for women.

Mary Guion on diary-writing:

"I believe my pen will always expose my thots what a tell tale has it ever been and still continues to be . . . by placing them in so external a point of vieu that I can read them at leisure, wich tho simple as they are often afford me real pleasure."

Mary Guion, in a diary entry of 1804.

Robert Coles   (essay date 1968)

SOURCE: "Psychoanalytical Observations on Elizabeth Barrett Barrett's Diary," in *Diary by E. B. B.: The Unpublished Diary of Elizabeth Barrett Barrett, 1831-1832,* edited by Philip Kelley and Ronald Hudson, Ohio University Press, 1969, pp. xxxix-xlv.

[*In the following essay, Coles, a psychiatrist, cautions against applying rigorous psychoanalytic methods to diaries.*]

Freud's discoveries did not only come as a consequence of his work as a psychiatrist whose very sick and very troubled and very confusing patients eventually inspired books such as *Studies on Hysteria* and the great *Interpretation of Dreams.* Like Elizabeth Barrett Browning, and any number of other 19th-century figures, he was a determined correspondent, particularly in the years that preceded his great break-through—his realization that dreams harken back to childhood experiences and can be quite rationally analysed, that repressed sexual conflict has a critical role in the life of the mind, that doctors receive from patients feelings once meant for (and likely as not, kept from) parents. In fact, we now know a lot of what was going through his mind as he made his psychoanalytic formulations. He had all along been writing to a close friend and fellow doctor, Wilhelm Fliess, who lived in Berlin. Again and again he shared his thoughts and feelings with Dr. Fliess, to the point that some analysts today become embarrassed—all that fervor, passion, despair. Scientists ought to have more restrained and orderly minds as they go about their business!

Clearly Freud needed a correspondent, needed someone to read his ideas and respond to them. He also needed to learn from himself, to write out his guesses and convictions and thus give them a form of permanence, an existence that can be welcomed or challenged by others. For that matter, in both *The Interpretation of Dreams* and *The Psychopathology of Everyday Life* he took pains to indicate his interest in explaining what goes on in minds like his own and those of people who have no symptoms. He could find a dream of his, a letter of his, as revelatory as the bizarre "associations" of a thoroughly disturbed patient. Put differently, he saw all of us, finally, more alike than not.

As for the artist or writer—men like Michelangelo, Leonardo da Vinci, Dostoyevsky—Freud made no claim to an understanding of their *genius,* their particularly inspired ability to instruct and arouse our minds and hearts. He did take an interest in the lives of great men, and was willing on more than one occasion to make a highly speculative generalization about a person he would never, could never, see and hear and question. Diaries, notebooks, letters had been left—or novels—and Freud looked at them as psychoanalytically interesting—but only that. He never intended that his way of putting things, his viewpoint, his chosen phrases be used to "explain" (or explain *away*) an artist's work, or sully and defame his name.

Of course, a major part of Freud's life was given over to a *search,* an effort to plumb the depths, to go deep, to uncover the hidden, to turn the obvious around so that the secret, the forbidden, the denied would come to light. Only later did he have time to see how powerfully we are influenced (yes, in our unconscious, too) by the world we live in, by customs, habits and conventions, by the time-bound, class-bound nature of our lives. It is foolish to call him "wrong" for emphasizing so long and so hard the psycho*pathology* of everyday life. Discoverers struggle against whatever darkness *they* face, something later generations tend to forget. In 1900 everyday life had all sorts of surfaces, many of them troubling indeed. But nothing "superficial" could quite satisfy Freud, or command his attention and his reverence. He had to ignore the obvious psychological importance of rituals or beliefs in order to explore the unobvious, in order to be the "conquistador" he later called himself. Freud pushed aside contemporary knowledge and made his own, only to hear it charged (and in a way, to find out himself) that there were indeed other worlds—the market-place, the public arena, with its books, cultivated styles, tastes and all too powerful symbols—than the one he had conquered, all of which did not embarrass, humiliate or even surprise him. It is some of his doctrinaire, religious-minded followers who can make him seem dated. They cling to his every word, his every theoretical statement, however tentative, speculative or purely clarifying its purpose. They want to stop the clock of history, to make dogma out of one man's brilliant effort to resolve and clarify the intellectual problems of *his* day. One can only say that we all have it in us to do that, to convert abstractions into real and enduring things, to attribute an unassailable substance or permanence to ideas, to fight for a chosen leader until the end of time.

I say all this here because I cannot avoid thinking what certain psychoanalysts might have done a few years back with Elizabeth Barrett Barrett's diary. There she was, at age twenty-five, very much isolated from the world, nervous, moody, excitable, fearfully attached to her father, and not in the best state of health by any means. For some reason in June of 1831 she started a diary, and for some reason in the spring of 1832 she abruptly stopped making further entries. No matter that she is not here to be questioned; the diary lets us know that the "facts" are obvious. She had a strong "super-ego," a conscience that curbed her, admonished her, lacerated her, and made her feel exceedingly timorous and shameful on occasion. Her "ego" was intact enough; she was, after all, a poet and in general a very intelligent, cultivated woman. She saw the world sensitively and in fact made sharp comments on the hypocrisy and foolishness of others. (Again, her conscience did not let others off its hook any more than she herself was spared.) But what of her "id"? What did she do with all her "libido," her unconscious sexual and aggressive "drives"?

Well, to answer the kind of psychoanalyst who would put the question that way, she held all that energy *in check*, as any upper-class 19th century lady *ought* to have done. Obviously a vibrant, even tempestuous person, she largely kept to herself. Amid all sorts of daily activities and in the presence of a large family she was in spirit very much alone. In 1831 her mother was dead and her father quite hard-pressed—not by poverty, but by the incredible burdens of wealth. Hope End, a magnificent estate in sight of the Malvern Hills, required more money than Mr. Edward Barrett could summon, and in 1832 the house had to be surrendered. In the last months Mr. Barrett spent little time there; he was desperately trying to straighten out and come on top of his financial difficulties, and London was the scene of his struggle. Elizabeth, the oldest child, always very close to her parents, and particularly a favorite of her father's, was in a sense orphaned.

Elizabeth Barrett Browning

The diary shows her loneliness, but also her almost defiant effort to know someone more than superficially, more than properly or conventionally or routinely. The diary gives a fascinating account of the day-to-day activities that kept the English gentry *going* in the early 19th century. Henry James has shown once and for all how significant and revealing customs and traditions can be; what happens in the living-room or the drawing-room can be as "revealing" and "profound" as anything that takes place in the bedroom, that temple of revelation which right now obsesses psychiatrists, not to mention a nondescript collection of American novelists, movie producers, television directors and playwrights. Elizabeth Barrett took in her fair share of luncheons, teas and walks, and into all of them she managed to put herself, her wishes and fears—rather in the fashion and tradition of lovers, or of the philosophers and psychiatrists who are engaged in today's eventfully described conversations, called "dialogues."

Well, who was the "self," the "person" who emerges in this short-lived, breezy, fitfully serious, occasionally frantic and passionate diary? Once her class is declared, her intellectual achievements and artistic promise (at twenty-five) recognized, we are left with her "mind," which somehow felt the need of a diary late one spring day and somehow—after a summer, a fall and a winter—allowed the diary to die. Of course, from the very start Miss Barrett had her doubts or misgivings—today called "ambivalence": "I wonder if I shall burn this sheet of paper like most others I have begun in the same way." Interestingly enough her hesitation was precisely the kind that psychoanalysts know so very well: "To write a diary, I have thought of very often at far and near distances of time: but how could I write a diary without throwing upon paper my thoughts, all my thoughts—the thoughts of my heart as well as of my head?—and then how could I bear to look on *them* after they were written?" How's that for a prelude to Freud's psychoanalytic method, some three-quarters of a century early? The woman who wrote those words knew already that "everyday life" has its "psychopathology." That is, she knew how devious yet revealing the mind can be—so that any sustained commitment to writing is inevitably self-revealing, and thus painful.

What matters is not that we find in these pages of hers all sorts of dramatic and satisfying "complexes" or "problems" or "neurotic trends." Frankly (and it may have taken us too long to do so) a good number of psychiatrists have at last given up pouncing on this or that fragment of behavior and making it an awesome, clinical and categorical generalization. Yes, Dostoyevsky may have secretly, unwittingly yearned to do away with his father; Leonardo da Vinci surely did have quite enough "latent homosexuality"; and in this case, Miss Barrett's considerable "involvement" with her "beloved Papa," her "dear, dear Papa," stands clear. Yet, the really important thing (so we have come to think) is not the presence of violence and one or another passion, but the *use* a particular mind makes of its various urges, conflicts, difficulties, or whatever. In other words, if I am to say that Elizabeth Barrett had an "Oedipus complex," or more exactly, an "Electra complex," I am under an obligation to go on, in fact to show what in heaven's name made me single out this particular person for that rather common and unremarkable condition. To assert, then, that Elizabeth Barrett loved her father and feared him, and may ("deep down" or "way underneath") have wished for his death is to offer a commonplace.

More interesting is the part both Mr. Barrett and Hugh Stuart Boyd played in Miss Barrett's development as an observer and particularly a writer—the reason, after all, we find her thoughts, daily or otherwise, so valuable today. We know that in 1819 a father sent his thirteen-year-old daughter's poem to the printer. Fifty copies of *The Battle of Marathon* were made, and the father described it as a "great epic of eleven or twelve years old, in four books." They were very much companions, Mr. Barrett and Elizabeth. The world well knows what happened later, when Robert Browning came upon the scene, and the master of 50 Wimpole Street said no to him, no to the prospect that *any* of his children would marry. Meanwhile, Elizabeth spent years adoring, placating and appeasing her father before September 12, 1846, when she and another poet were married in the face of Mr. Barrett's angry refusal of sanction. I do not think it is stretching things to say she was encouraged by her father to have a mind that enjoyed wide freedom—so long as her body, her life as a woman, remained safely out of any suitor's reach. Under such circumstances she did not become a constricted, fearful, impossibly shy and suspicious woman. Protected enough from romances, she yet became a romantic, as a poet, letter-writer, and briefly, a diarist.

Page after page of the diary shows just how alive, how yearning, how sensitive and alert was this strangely distant and gifted young woman. She reads voraciously in the classics, but she is very much aware of contemporary English politics. She attends church, reads the paper, reads Greek, writes, awaits anxiously her daily mail, and through it all reveals herself a very shrewd observer of people—and of herself. Certainly the woman who wrote the following words would not find Sigmund Freud's discoveries either surprising or shocking: "I dreamt last night,—for night dreams are as well worth recording as day dreams—that I was re-writing the Warren-blacking lines,—and inserted in some part of them the following—'Fame o'er him flashed her meteor wing—/and *he*—he was a King.' What king I was writing of, is out of my head." And at another point she observes: "Arabel dreamt last night that *he* was dead, and that *I* was laughing! Foolish dream!—and more foolish I who could think of it in the storm!—" Her sense of irony may not have been "consciously" intended, but there can be no doubt that she would have been a very apt "analysand." When one of my patients calls a dream foolish, then goes on to point out its lingering presence in her thoughts, I know she only awaits another's permission to acknowledge the glimmers of her own mind's awareness.

If Elizabeth Barrett was pretty much able to sense a number of things going on in her psychological life, she probably did not—could not—stop and think about the strong and complicated "meaning" of her "relationship" with Hugh Stuart Boyd. Today, we can swoop down on a life such as hers and make our statements: she "transferred"

her devotion from her father to Mr. Boyd, twenty-five years older, blind, highly educated and—rather like Mr. Barrett—able to be a literary companion. Much of this happened, moreover, when Elizabeth Barrett was quite without parents. Her mother died when she was twenty-two—three years before the diary began—and her father, as mentioned, spent increasing lengths of time away in London. She needed someone, even as she kept her distance from just anyone. Yes, there were brothers and sisters, and they come up again and again in the diary; but Elizabeth was the first-born child of devoted, possessive parents and apparently she was not about to consider the kind of strength and reassurance she had learned to expect from them as lost forever.

A major share of her diary is given over to Mr. Boyd, to her efforts to please him, to see him, to feel herself his good friend. I suppose it was all very "neurotic," the young lady sick with a variety of aches and pains, and her old, blind friend. There weren't even *other* friends. She is generally impatient with people, and with herself, too. She speaks of her boredom, her unwillingness to risk herself with people. Friendship is something very special—reserved it seems for Mr. Boyd almost alone. There are times when she can relax a little and glimpse the intensity of her feelings toward him, and there are even times when others seem able to twit her ever so gently on the matter: "Very soon after breakfast Eliza Cliffe came; but still sooner Bummy said to me laughingly, 'Are you going to see Mr. Boyd today?' And laughing was my answer—'Yes! If *you* will come too.' Then grave was her observation 'But you know you can go tomorrow.' 'Go tomorrow. Oh I think not.' (*Oh I wish I could!* was what my heart *assided*). 'Why certainly Mr. Boyd may not like your going quite so often.' How could I help saying 'If I thought Mr. Boyd did not like my going *very often,* I would not go at all.'"

There are moments when she is not so detached. She fears his silences, wonders how he will be at the next visit, and in general adjusts her mood to what she judges the success or failure of their precious friendship. Very simply—but also not so simply—she loved him, and he her. Nor is their love to be considered some bit of extravagant psychopathology. They shared ideas; they gave one another all sorts of information; they inspired one another. If psychiatrists have not yet come to the point that they can appreciate the dignity and worth of such a relationship, then there is indeed more for us to learn than even we appreciate—and the most arrogant psychiatrist will usually preface his remarks with a declaration of humility and an avowal of relative ignorance.

In point of fact Mr. Boyd was to Miss Barrett what Dr. Fliess was to Dr. Freud: a mind whose company made the world seem more hopeful, responsive and encouraging. The Elizabeth Barrett who sought after Mr. Boyd so persistently was trying hard to be a poet, a writer, a classical scholar, and thus a person apart from others. The Sigmund Freud who relied almost passionately—I put in "almost" where it is not necessary, and even misleading, out of my own shyness—on the correspondence with Dr. Fliess and on the "congresses," the walks and talks they had from time to time, was very much like Miss Barrett, a "loner," a person desperately trying to live with a particularly intense and gifted mind that needed at least one "other" person to receive ideas and feelings. Perhaps every writer is secretly speaking to someone; and every painter wants one other person to watch what he puts on canvas. I have had "creative" patients tell me that they can almost feel themselves talking as they work—silently and alone. Now, I am not trying to make yet another attempt to "explain" the writer or painter "at work." I am simply trying to suggest that a number of very significant men and women in the history of literature, the arts, and the sciences too, have at critical moments in their lives *turned to somebody,* and done so in a way that reveals not only neurosis (I suppose any time we get involved with another human being *that* can happen) but an effort to find—well, use whatever word is congenial: reassurance, support, sanction, the grace that comes when two people speak, when one person listens to another.

In a sense then, Elizabeth Barrett's diary can be "summarized" psychologically in a sentence or two, or be seen as one more example of how utterly, persistently (and wonderfully) elusive are the sources of the human mind's energies. In 1831, when there was no telephone to give a person's thoughts quick but strictly passing expression, Miss Barrett made her various moods and ideas submit to the permanence of a diary. (There were also, of course, letters.) She talked to herself, shunned many others, and found in Mr. Boyd reason enough to feel lonely but not alone. She also revealed how very much a large, intimate and well-to-do family can mean to a supposedly reserved or distant young woman. Freud, after all, mainly saw those Victorians who had fallen apart—at a time when the Victorian Age itself was coming to an end. We do not know enough about the very considerable strengths that characterized the family-life of some of the prudish or "repressed" people who lived in the 19th century. It is true that they didn't know what we know about atoms and molecules or the workings of the unconscious—so that to us they seem to have lived terribly in the dark, groping where we understand, faltering where we can see and cure. Yet, Freud himself came out of that century—he was born before Mrs. Robert Browning died—as did Wordsworth, Balzac and Tolstoy. It is hard to believe that a few psychoanalytic formulations, a few electron microscopes or space-capsules, make our life all that more knowing, all that different in its essentially comic, frivolous and importantly tragic nature.

To me the Elizabeth Barrett [that appears in her diary] is best thought of as a *defiant writer*—self-centered and proud as anyone is who dares ask others to read, to listen, to pay heed. A social historian would find her diary a valuable introduction to a kind of living now almost gone. (Obviously there are remnants that persist, and not only in England.) And as for a psychiatrist, he has to take note of the tensions that crop up repeatedly in the young lady's written comments—but then go on to remind himself what she did with those tensions in the full course of her fifty-five years of life.

DIARY AS AUTOBIOGRAPHY

Francis Anne Kemble (essay date 1835)

SOURCE: A preface to *Journal of a Residence in America,* A. and W. Galignani and Co., 1835, pp. v-vi.

[*In the following excerpt, Kemble explains the purpose and composition of her published diary.*]

A preface appears to me necessary to this book, in order that the expectation with which the English reader might open it should not be disappointed.

Some curiosity has of late been excited in England with regard to America: its political existence is a momentous experiment, upon which many eyes are fixed, in anxious watching of the result; and such accounts as have been published of the customs and manners of its societies, and the natural wonders and beauties of its scenery, have been received and read with considerable interest in Europe. This being the case, I should be loth to present these volumes to the English public without disclaiming both the intention and the capability of adding the slightest detail of any interest to those which other travellers have already furnished upon these subjects.

This book is, what it professes to be, my personal journal, and not a history or a description of men and manners in the United States.

Engaged in an arduous profession, and travelling from city to city in its exercise, my leisure and my opportunities would have been alike inadequate to such a task. The portion of America which I have visited has been a very small one, and, I imagine, by no means that from which the most interesting details are to be drawn. I have been neither to the south nor to the west; consequently have had no opportunity of seeing two large portions of the population of this country,—the enterprising explorers of the late wildernesses on the shores of the Mississippi,—and the black race of the slave states,—both classes of men presenting peculiarities of infinite interest to the traveller: the one, a source of energy and growing strength, the other, of disease and decay, in this vast political body.

My sphere of observation has been confined to the Atlantic cities, whose astonishing mercantile prosperity, and motley mongrel societies, though curious under many aspects, are interesting but under few.

What I registered were my immediate impressions of what I saw and heard; of course, liable to all the errors attendant upon first perceptions, and want of time and occasion for maturer investigation. The notes I have added while preparing the text for the press; and such opinions and details as they contain are the result of a longer residence in this country, and a somewhat better acquaintance with the people of it.

Written, as my journal was, day by day, and often after the fatigues of a laborious evening's duty at the theatre, it has infinite sins of carelessness to answer for; and but that it would have taken less time and trouble to re–write the whole book, or rather write a better, I would have endeavoured to correct them. . . .

However, my purpose is not to write an apology for my book, or its defects, but simply to warn the English reader, before he is betrayed into its perusal, that it is a purely egotistical record, and by no means a history of America.

Cynthia Huff   (essay date 1987)

SOURCE: "From Faceless Chronicler to Self-Creator: The Diary of Louisa Galton, 1830-1896," in *Biography: An Interdisciplinary Quarterly* Vol. 10, No. 2, Spring, 1987, pp. 95-106.

[*In the following essay, Huff argues that although Louisa Galton's diary was originally intended to be a family history and a record of her husband's achievements, she uses the diary instead to assert her own personality in various ways.*]

William Gass is one of the many male writers and contemporary critics who defines art in sexual terms. In *Fiction and the Figures of Life* he comments that

> ordinary language ought to be like the gray inaudible wife who services the great man: an ideal engine, utterly self-effacing, devoted without remainder to its task; but when language is used as an art it is no longer used merely to communicate.

Gass wrote this almost a century after Louisa Galton was composing her unpublished *Annual Record,* which was intended to be a tribute to the accomplishments of her husband Francis Galton, an eminent Victorian scientist.

Frances Anne Kemble.

However, Gass's metaphor defines the role Louisa was expected to assume, that of the inarticulate and mechanical wife who serves the genius, whether sexually or linguistically; and the connections between Gass's definition of literature and Louisa Galton's prescribed role as the chronicler of her husband's achievements indicate the inferior status often ascribed to women and their writing, particularly their composition of diaries.

There seems little doubt that Louisa was expected to serve her husband as the scribe who recorded his successes for posterity, a role she inherited from the women in Francis's family. From birth Francis Galton was groomed by his family, particularly its female members, to be a scientific genius. According to his biographer, the young Galton's education and nurturance were the focal point of his mother and four sisters' existence, as they each defined themselves largely according to the role they played in his development. Francis's eldest sister, Elizabeth, served as his surrogate mother from the time of his infancy until her own marriage, and after this his older sister, Emma, nurtured Francis.

But Elizabeth bequeathed yet another and equally important legacy to Emma. Originally the recorder of the family history, Elizabeth passed on this duty as well. The family records of the Galtons noted the significant events of communal life such as births, deaths, and marriages, and their maintenance by the female members defined the roles the sisters were to play in the family mythology. [In *The Politics of the Family,*] R. D. Laing emphasizes the importance of certain stories for the reaffirmation and continuance of family structure, since mutually agreed upon interpretations provide the cues which direct the actions of each family member. In the case of the Galton family, Elizabeth and then Emma learned their roles partly by acting as the keepers of the family history. Both Galton sisters served the family mythology by acting as its inarticulate chroniclers. Although Elizabeth's record has apparently been lost, Emma's has not, and an examination of it helps to untangle the role of women as scribes in the Galton tradition and elucidate too the weight of the familial text Louisa Galton must have felt after her marriage to Francis.

The focal point of Emma's record is the paterfamilias: first, her father Samuel Tertius Galton, and then Francis. Samuel Tertius Galton, like his father, was interested in science, and Francis's destiny was, it seems, to fill the place occupied by his grandfather and father, though the youngest male Galton was expected to achieve greater scientific eminence than his predecessors. The role Francis was to play in the family mythology and the ordering of that story within the familial text were the primary concerns of Emma Galton once she inherited the nurturance of Francis and the inscription of her brother's history.

Emma's rendition of the line of inheritance stands out in the familial text she wrote. Her record does not proceed chronologically, but associationally, and the starting point for her first train of associations is her father's death in 1844, even though the earliest events Emma mentions occur in 1829. Emma's entries are generally brief and rather oblique, but she carefully notes the details of her father's death: its place and exact time, the day on which the corpse was removed from the family home, and the date of the funeral. The death of Samuel Tertius Galton altered the familial configuration both spatially and psychologically. The family coach was sold; Elizabeth and Adele Galton married; and the remaining women in the family left the patriarchal household.

The changes within the family structure are reflected in Emma's record, particularly in her use of the word "blank." Emma often composed her family record by quoting others, as she does when she cites Elizabeth's letter to her aunt in which Elizabeth characterizes the impact of her father's death:

> Yet none but his children can know what a daily, what an hourly loss he is to them. All our occupations and pleasures were so connected with him, that everything now seems a blank and it will be a very long time before we shall cease to be constantly reminded of him in everything we do.

The use of the term "blank" to indicate death and a severing of familial connections appears frequently in the journals and correspondence of many of the Galtons.

Although deaths, especially of men, often instigate and order diaries written by nineteenth-century British women, in the case of the Galtons death was another catalyst as well. Death brought about a blank space both within the family structure and within the familial text. As inarticulate chroniclers the women in the Galton family were expected to fill in space, to inscribe the blank by relating the history of a new patriarch. Emma played her role accordingly. Once her father died she transferred the focus of the family history to Francis, its heir, and retold in a slightly different refrain the story of the scientific prowess of her grandfather and father.

The familiar and familial story, however, gained in stature and refinement. Francis Galton was heralded by his contemporaries as well as by his family, and it must have seemed only fitting to his dutiful sister Emma that the pages of the family history primarily record his achievements. Emma died before her prominent brother; and her rendition of the family record always focused on him. She commented on *his* scientific pursuits and achievements, *his* journeys abroad, *his* illness and recovery in 1852, and *his* marriage to Louisa. Other family members are mentioned in Emma's account and she relates some details about herself as well. Still, Emma remains in her role as the inarticulate scribe who lauds the heir's achievements. She does not dwell on the publication of her own book, *The Unprotected,* where she gives financial advice to unmarried women, nor does her account express her own fears and anxieties, her hopes and wishes. She remains in the background, merely a player in the family drama, a minor part of the family record whose voice is subsumed by the "we" of the collective narrative. Against this backdrop Francis stands out.

Emma inscribed the family mythology and the successes of Francis in one volume, just as her sister Elizabeth had before her. Convinced of her son's intellectual prowess,

Mrs. Galton maintained yet another volume containing the biographical record of the first eight years of his life in which she detailed Francis's development and accomplishments. Like her daughters, Mrs. Galton was merely the recorder of the patriarch's power, merely a woman who thought of herself and her family in relation to her eminent son. Apparently she expected her new daughter-in-law Louisa to place herself in this position as well, for it is in the volume where Mrs. Galton recorded her son's early years that Louisa Butler commenced her *Annual Record.*

When Louisa, the daughter of a former headmaster of Harrow and Dean of Peterborough, married Francis Galton in 1853, she was expected to serve the great man by chronicling and assisting his development. She did so, at least initially, for at the time of her marriage Louisa filled in the yearly gaps between the end of Mrs. Galton's biography of her son and her own marriage to him. Louisa began her *Annual Record* by composing a retrospective survey which included only brief details for the years 1830 to 1834. But from 1835 until the year of their marriage Louisa wrote slightly longer accounts of her own and her husband's lives on separate pages, labeling one "Frank's Life" and the other "Louisa's Life."

What is most interesting and revealing initially about Louisa's *Annual Record* is the form it takes. Louisa did not backdate her yearly entries to correspond with her birth, but rather to match the record of Frank's activities; hence she started the account in 1830, the year Mrs. Galton's biography of her son ends. Louisa designated the left-hand page as Frank's and the right-hand page as hers; and significantly, when she composed the entries on Frank's page she assumed different voices. In some of the entries referring to Francis, Louisa called him by his Christian name; at other times she assumed his voice and wrote "I"; and sometimes she deleted the subject. Louisa, whether consciously or subconsciously, appears to be struggling with her designated position as the gray inaudible wife, for at times she subsumed her identity by adopting that of her husband and lived vicariously through him. Even in this early phase of her role as mechanical chronicler, though, Louisa chafes against the boundaries imposed by familial expectations and by the tradition of the familial text as a vehicle in which women serve others by memorializing their achievements. Certainly Louisa's deletion of the subject signifies her resistance toward becoming Francis. When she refers to him by his Christian name she maintains a distance between herself and her husband by symbolically refusing to merge her identity with his and become a mute chronicler.

Louisa's sense of herself as an individual and her opposition to the ideal of service symbolized by the role of inarticulate chronicler asserts itself rather quickly. At first her accounts of Francis's youth are more complete than her own, but as the record nears the year of their marriage this process is reversed. Louisa's earliest entries are brief and associational and follow the tradition adhered to by Emma. But when she begins to record the events of her life more fully the short phrases are replaced by full sentences. Furthermore, when Louisa first enters a joint account for the newly-married couple, she does so not on Frank's page, but on her own. It seems clear that as Louisa jotted down the summaries of Frank's life and her life between 1830 and 1853, she decided that hers was as valid as Frank's, perhaps more so, and that their union did not belong under Frank's jurisdiction as symbolized by his page, but rather under hers. This decision was not a momentary one on Louisa's part, as the entries for the four years after their marriage are written on Louisa's page, the right-hand one. Finally, beginning in 1858, Louisa uses both the right- and left-hand pages to detail her life with Francis.

Louisa's symbolic altering of the familial text was an important decision. By creating a blank space where the entries for Frank's life were to have been she began psychologically to re-evaluate her relationship with her husband and his family and to define in her own terms the familial script she would create. Although her decision was probably not a conscious one, Louisa did, nevertheless, assume the power to utilize the space within the familial text as she saw fit when she chose to express nothing on Frank's page, to say nothing through his voice. This act was the first step in her quiet challenge of the primacy of the patriarch's life within the familial record and her first assertion that her own voice was not entirely muted by the acclaim of her husband's scientific prowess.

But if Louisa escaped somewhat from the confinement imposed by her role as the faceless and voiceless recorder of her husband's successes, she continued to use her *Annual Record* to register the achievements and activities of her extended family. Louisa never had any children as she was expected to, but like other unpublished nineteenth-century British women's accounts, hers records the life-events of a family, such as births, deaths, and marriages. These life-events assume more significance than they might otherwise because her diary is yearly, not daily. It is obvious from reading the entries written shortly after her marriage that her family is important to Louisa, for she does not give over the tradition of recording family events in favor of chronicling her own.

In fact her *Annual Record* seems to move from focusing on Francis to centering on her extended family. Such a practice was in keeping with the ideal of service enjoined for women in the last century, since it too placed them in the background, rather than the foreground, and hence confined their expressive impulses within socially defined limits of conduct. Even though Louisa was not submerging her voice and her identity in her husband's, she was defining herself as part of the family setting. By inscribing her own part within the context of a familial story Louisa was playing the role traditionally assigned to nineteenth-century British women: namely, to consider their conduct and their lives in relation to others rather than to laud their own accomplishments. Louisa's 1859 entry typifies this tendency, for here she refers to the visit of her sister-in-law, Emma, and the election of her brother, Montague, as headmaster of Harrow, as the principal events of the year. In 1869 Louisa first mentions her illness, the theme which characterizes the second volume of the *Annual Record* and establishes her confinement from ill health.

But this foreboding is overshadowed by family matters, for the yearly entries between 1870 and 1874 are dominated by Louisa's accounts of familial grief and concern, specifically the deaths of her own and Francis's mothers and the anguish occasioned by Emma Galton's operation. In 1872 Louisa details the death of her mother by noting the exact number of days between the onset of her illness and her death, its cause, and the setting for the funeral. Such specificity was a common practice in nineteenth-century British women's journals whenever the diarists recorded life-events of any kind, and surely this habit caused the diarist to view herself as merely a part of a large detailed picture composed of familial events. In 1873 Mrs. Galton died, and in her 1874 yearly summary Louisa characterizes the impact of this familial event: "Uneasy from the very beginning about dear Mrs. Galton, Frank went to see her early in Feb ʸ & she died Feb ʸ 12th aged 90. This coming so soon after my dear Mother's made a sad blank, both houses gone." Such an entry shows that Louisa's identity continued to reside at least partly within the family structure, and presages too the note of loss which characterizes much of Louisa's record, especially in her later years. Yet the cessation of both houses frees Louisa somewhat from the constraints imposed on the chronicler of family records. The blank space brought about by death allowed Louisa more latitude for self-expression, probably because the ties within the extended family structure were loosened.

Almost immediately Louisa began to inscribe her story of the familial text left vacant by Mrs. Galton's death. Louisa may have felt freer to create her own place within the family mythology once her mother-in-law died precisely because the older Mrs. Galton helped initiate Louisa into the position of inarticulate scribe, thus re-enacting the relationship of Francis and his mother. However, the 1874 entry indicates that Louisa had no intention of playing such a part, and furthermore that she wished to modify her relationship with her husband. In the autumn of 1874 Louisa was confined to her sick room. But instead of chafing against the strictures occasioned by illness, Louisa writes of the peace and happiness she experienced. Although she mentions that friends and relatives solaced her, the main source of comfort she notes is Francis. His care of her made Louisa feel "sustained by love." Here Francis is serving his wife, whose illness paradoxically allows her some escape from the familial designation of the wife who effaces herself to assist the great man. Louisa's confinement from sickness gradually becomes a major theme in the second volume of the *Annual Record*. Instead of being trapped within the boundaries mapped out by the Galton family configuration and the text which legitimized and perpetuated her subservient position, Louisa instead began to inscribe her confinement onto the text, thus making her own story as much a part of the family history as her husband's scientific discoveries.

Louisa inscribes the second volume of her *Annual Record* "A Continuation of Our Yearly Summary," but in many senses the "our" is a misnomer, since the second volume tells her story more than Francis's or her family's. Beginning a new book helped release Louisa from the Galton family tradition of chronicling, which the first volume symbolized. The tone of the second volume is more personal, as are the themes of her entries. Instead of seeing herself as part of the family drama, Louisa begins more and more to view others in relation to herself, and specifically in relation to her declining health.

Physical confinement becomes for Louisa both a restriction and a liberation. Louisa Galton's confinement derived as much from age and ill health as from the constraint of nineteenth-century women's spheres, and she poignantly realizes that she no longer has the social opportunities of a young woman. In 1878 when Louisa is fifty-six years old she writes:

> A year of no great mark for ourselves and families. My health has gone on improving, but greatly narrows our life or rather lives, as I lose so many opportunities of making friends & of mixing myself with the stirring interests of the day by refusing all dinner invitations and yet I am so much stronger that I always hope I shall be able to resume old habits, still years go on.

Louisa's ill health resulted from problems with her stomach and sphincter, which were constricted to only a fraction of their normal size at the time of her death. Her maladies brought her much discomfort, as her record attests, yet they also caused Louisa to be more introspective, partly because she was prevented from attending social functions. As she becomes distanced from the public world, her record increasingly assumes the tone and texture of a personal, inner-directed diary. Louisa writes more and more about herself, and hence her diary moves from a mere rendition of events to a consideration of her intimate relationships. Although she is confined physically, she is no longer imprisoned as inarticulate, for she speaks in her own voice about her own concerns. As her health deteriorates it becomes the fulcrum on which the familial record pivots.

By 1883, when Louisa was sixty-two, she was writing more and more frequently that there are "few events to record," but paradoxically her entries become longer as she increasingly uses the *Annual Record* to validate her existence and provide her with the self-esteem she feels she is losing as she ages. Her friends and family die, and Francis becomes increasingly deaf; and although the diary never ceases entirely to be a record of Francis's accomplishments and family activities, she turns to it more and more as she might to a friend, thus transforming it from a recording of occurrences outside herself to a rendering of her feelings.

The entry for 1883 is especially significant, since it indicates the diary's primary function as Louisa's psychological support, and establishes the pattern of the entries. Throughout her married life, Louisa's existence was ordered to correspond with Francis's intellectual pursuits, and generally her concerns seem to have meant little to him. Hence she uses the *Annual Record* to voice her problems with servants, and more and more to write of her frustration and her sense of loss and doom. Her 1883 entry keynotes this tendency, for here Louisa tells us that "events for me are fewer and fewer as health impedes my doing much," and proceeds to relate the "frightful blow"

she experienced because of her two sisters-in-law's deaths. The very act of expressing her feelings in the *Annual Record* allows Louisa to cope with the disintegration of her family through death and to prepare herself for death as well. Even when Louisa relates public events, these seem to reflect the melancholy tone of her personal life. In 1878 when Francis is ill, Louisa is suffering acutely, and their friend Mr. Gurney dies, she writes: "There is a good deal of distress & depression, many failures of Banks." Ironically enough, Louisa develops a self through preparing to lose one, as she consistently views the outside world in terms of her own sense of disintegration and confinement.

One way she does this is through poetic descriptions. In her entry of 1882 she personifies the fog in an almost Dickensian manner by speaking of how it "brought on my pain & kept me in its grasp more or less for 6 weeks." Louisa here seems almost obsessed with her struggle against confinement as she expresses how the weather hampers and controls her through determining her physical condition. In much the same way Louisa considers herself governed by servants. In the same entry she mentions the joy she experiences because she has been "free from cook embroglios." Louisa's utterances are not always so directly linked to home events or to her illness. Even a short journey can evoke emotions of abiding demise. In her 1892 entry Louisa describes a trip to Leamington as "a chill autumnal day, wind wailing, dead leaves falling, decay all around of what had been." Louisa's ability to characterize her environment in terms of her own sense of dissolution simultaneously confines her and frees her from confinement. Throughout the latter part of the second volume of her *Annual Record* Louisa's tone and imagery clearly presage death; but it is this very preoccupation with the inevitable decay of all things which helps free Louisa from the restraints of her prescribed role as family chronicler and allows her to recreate the familial text in her own image.

As Louisa nears death her entries change in significant ways. Primarily they began to assume a definite closure, though too she chafes at the dependency her physical disabilities occasion. There seem to be several reasons for the latter. First, problems with her stomach prevented Louisa at times from traveling abroad, a pleasure she felt freed her from the irksome obligations of supervising servants. Travel to the sunnier climates of Europe also improved Louisa's health, and the contrast between the dark, confining atmosphere of England and the light, invigorating ambience of Switzerland and Italy becomes a staple in her account. The older Louisa gets, the more she seems to want to escape the stays of life, and the more she desires self-sufficiency. She chastises herself occasionally for her inability to serve others because of her debilitating health, but the reason for her unhappiness derives less from any desire to adhere to her expected role as the gray, inarticulate wife whose identity is determined by fulfilling obligations, than from Louisa's insistence that she not cause trouble and hence be bound to others through her sickness.

The final entries in the *Annual Record* indicate Louisa's preparation for death and her realization that she is in a transitional period between the confinement which ill health and her familial role represent and the awesome yet thrilling freedom which the future holds. As Louisa anticipates the future the years seem shorter, and in 1890 for the first time her entry exhibits closure. The ending of the 1890 entry quietly invokes Louisa's sense of finality, but it is her 1891 entry where she writes that she "feel[s] our life closing in & the dim great future looming ever & ever nearer." Louisa begins to address God at the end of each entry and her closing prayers to Him show her solemn preparation for death.

Louisa, however, dreads that death will take her unawares or create obstacles, for she painfully reflects upon the consequences of "what may come to either of us after 44 years of happy union" [1894]. She fears too that she will quickly by replaced by another. In her final entry of 1896 Louisa writes: "Darwin announced his engagement to Miss Cumberland, which gave me a pang to think how soon a dear life companion could be forgotten for the sake of comfort & companionship." Still, as Louisa realizes only too poignantly, change and replacement are inevitable. Her final remarks in the *Annual Record,* which refer to the death of a valued friend, have a Biblical ring: "So surely do good good things come to us & pass from us." In her *Annual Record,* however, Louisa mitigated against her own oblivion. She chronicled not her husband's life, as she was meant to do, but her own, and even her acutely distressing thoughts about death indicate the strength of a woman who faced the boundaries of her existence.

Not only are Francis's achievements displaced by Louisa's intimations of mortality, but the very framework of the Galton family record has been rehabilitated by Louisa. The form of the 1883 entry definitively establishes the pattern of Louisa's yearly recordings in the second volume. Louisa begins her summaries by describing her illness and her reactions to it in some detail, and only later does she mention family activities or her husband's work. Once Louisa has detailed her illness she writes of her travels, usually on the Continent; and it is significant that this follows her descriptions of illness, since Louisa realized that escaping the confinement of the damp English climate was tantamount to enjoying better health. Louisa's choice of subject matter, her placing of personally relevant topics in the primary positions, and her inclusion of more material about herself than about others, indicate that the *Annual Record* becomes no longer the chronicle written by the gray inaudible wife, but rather a portrait of a woman hemmed in by confinement but escaping from it, by telling her own story and allotting herself a major role in the familial script.

Perhaps the best evidence to support this interpretation comes from Francis Galton. When he was asked by a publisher in 1907 to write his autobiography, he told a relative: "I *have* Louisa's diaries, but they refer little to myself." Louisa's last entry is for 1896, and Francis continues the *Annual Record* only one more year. In it he writes of Louisa's death, but the greater memorial to her is his perhaps unconscious following of the pattern she had established. Like Louisa, Francis writes first of her poor health. Ironically, Louisa's fatal illness occurs abroad, and Fran-

cis follows his comments about her decline with details about the symptoms which result in her death. Remarks about Louisa's debilitated condition make up the bulk of the entry, just as they did when Louisa kept the family account. Only at the end of the 1897 entry does Francis mention family activities and his own work. Francis's adherence to the ordering of the entries created by Louisa signifies, albeit momentarily, that the *Annual Record* is not so much the tribute to the great man, but instead the rendering of the ways in which an unknown woman defined herself.

Louisa Galton's *Annual Record* stands as an exemplum of the restrictions placed on women who write and of the means which can be used to break through these restrictions. Even though women have traditionally been assigned the role of chronicler, not of creator, by critics such as Gass, Louisa Galton, like other nineteenth-century women diarists, created her own story by taking possession of the familial text which was designed to memorialize others, especially men. Nor was she atypical when she chose not to limit herself to the role of the gray inaudible wife, for other women of the last century also worked within and overcame the constraints of the familial record to emerge as creators of their own stories. Their success indicates our need to uncover the stories of these forgotten women, to read their scripts, and to forge the links between their histories and our own.

Catherine Wilmot on her diary:

"I will every now and then record the events of the day so that like a snail wherever I crawl I may be known by the trail I shall leave smeared behind me in this book."

Quoted by Arthur Ponsonby, in Scottish and Irish Diaries from the Sixteenth to the Nineteenth Century, *Methuen & Co. Ltd., 1927.*

DIARY AS LITERATURE

Judy Nolte Lensink   (essay date 1987)

SOURCE: "Expanding the Boundaries of Criticism: The Diary as Female Autobiography," in *Women's Studies: An Interdisciplinary Journal,* Vol. 14, 1987, pp. 39-53.

[*In the following essay, Lensink argues for the importance of diaries as literary artifacts.*]

In recent years, a few American women's autobiographies have entered the boundaries of the curricular canon, particularly in Women's Studies courses. The life stories of notables like Elizabeth Cady Stanton and autobiographically-grounded texts like Tillie Olsen's "Silences" and Adrienne Rich's *Of Woman Born* have become classics. This acceptance of autobiography as a means for teaching about American lives began approximately a generation ago in interdisciplinary courses where such diverse texts as *The Education of Henry Adams* and *Black Boy* were read as case studies in intellectual history. But along with hard-won acceptance by the academy came limitations, as autobiographical texts were subjected to traditional literary criteria.

The current study of autobiography has moved steadily away from readings of what James Olney calls "the simplest and commonest of writing propositions" to increasingly literary forms of the genre such as Vladimir Nabokov's *Speak, Memory* and Maxine Hong Kingston's pastiche of myth and memory, *The Woman Warrior*. The autobiographies of ordinary people like Lucy Larcom and "plain" Anne Ellis are defined as historical/social documents rather than as literature from distinctive American voices. Autobiography scholarship has become established, complete with high-ranking theoretical scholars, classic essays, a canon of heavily-studied texts—and boundaries.

The diary, that form of written personal narrative least colored by artifice, closest to the American life, truly "the story of a distinctive culture from within," that autobiography was once touted to be, is outside the interest of most scholars. The few diaries included in the canon are read for their content, rather than for their innovative literary form. For it is content writ large—significant periods in our military/political history, famous people encountered—that permits a few "important" diaries inside the boundaries. The only diary extensively studied for its form is Anais Nin's, which is certainly atypical of this genre. Thus the diary is acknowledged as a legitimate autobiographical text only when either the times recorded are extraordinary—William Byrd's, Mary Chesnut's—or the writer is extraordinarily established in literature—Henry Thoreau, Anais Nin.

Why are the estimated 100,000 American diaries, which record that dynamic interaction of the individual and society we seek in American Studies and Women's Studies, virtually ignored as both literary and cultural texts by the very scholars who once expanded the critical boundaries of history and literature to encompass autobiography? Partially it is because we have yet to establish the critical tools that will make the unwieldy form of the diary accessible. It is also because we were trained as scholars to see the stories within ordinary peoples' diaries as inherently less interesting than those told by Henry James, Henry Thoreau, or Henry Adams. But on a deeper level, I would argue, the diary is resisted because in both form and content it comes closest to a female version of autobiography. As more about female psychology, language and historical experience is illuminated by theorists such as Carol Gilligan, Suzanne Juhasz and Carroll Smith-Rosenberg, the diary is emerging as a female text. The narrative of an American life that is both female *and* ordinary, the diary remains marginal. Mary Jane Moffat has ironically linked the terms that both women and their diaries engender: ". . . emotional, fragmentary, interrupted, modest, not to be taken seriously, private, restricted, daily, trivial, formless, concerned with self . . . endless . . ." [*Revelations: Diaries of Women*].

We can invert the critique of diaries that excludes them as too problematic for literary/historical study and find

that the insistence upon an obviously literary Design in autobiography obstructs our reading of a separate "Truth" as told by female diarists. By crossing many of the formalist "bindaries" of published autobiography, I would argue, diarists both tell their truth *and* create female design—a supersubtle design, similar to a quilt's, made up of incremental stitches that define a pattern. How can we as scholars, brought up on the canon, trained by the academy's fathers, learn to read these designs? First, we can look anew at the diary's characteristic language, content and narrative structure, then reassess it *sui generis,* as itself, rather than as "deficient" autobiography.

The language of ordinary people's diaries is considered tedious because it is often literal and repetitive. As Elizabeth Hampsten noted in [*Read This Only to Yourself: The Private Writings of Midwestern Women, 1880-1910*]—and as I have found in the 4,000-page diary I am studying—intensity of experience is usually signaled by quantity of language rather than by metaphor. But if the public literary language of metaphor is indeed a male tongue, as Helene Cixous argues, [in "The Laugh of the Medusa," *The Signs Reader*], then the private, plain-speaking voice within a woman's diary may be close to her true tongue. Using a both/and strategy, we can look at diary language as both a truer rendering of "real life" via real speech, and yet as design.

If quantity of concrete language is characteristic of the prose, content analysis is one way to find out, literally, what "counted" in women's diaries. Note that I said diaries and not lives, for there is not always a correlation between what a diarist writes about and what really matters. In fact, topics upon which most diarists were virtually silent—sexuality, birth control—were probably so important that they were taboo. Therefore we need to read between the lines as well as count sentences. While content analysis such as that done by John Faragher [in *Women and Men on the Overland Trail*] is still vulnerable to a scholar's interpretation, it is one route beyond the limitations of infinite individual texts to conclusions based on a body of literature.

When the language within a diary is excessively metaphoric, on the other hand, it may obscure rather than inscribe true emotion, just as it may so fetchingly in public autobiography. Ann Douglas has argued [in *The Feminization of American Culture*] that lush metaphor in nineteenth-century women's prose about death and children, for example, is obfuscation, a camouflage of pat imagery provided by a culture that no longer values the very things it sentimentalizes in language. The sanctioned images that diarists use to cope with death, for example, perhaps employ metaphor to stop raw emotion from pouring out onto the page.

Finally, a diarist's language may form a design of unconscious metaphor. For example, in almost every middle-class nineteenth-century woman's diary I have read, the image of *Home* recurs. I will return to this particular iconography later to show its function as a unifying metaphor in the diary I am studying. The deceptively simple language of the diary, then, can be denotative, consciously literary, or approach the truth "slant" through its unselfconscious choice of imagery chosen from daily life.

In the critical literature on the content of autobiography, certain criteria recur: coherence, significance, and systematic retrospection. This view of the self and life, transposed to the writing of the life, is an androcentric one, as Patricia Meyer Spacks [in "Reflecting Women," *Yale Review,* 1973] and Suzanne Juhasz [in " 'Some Deep Old Desk or Capacious Hold-All': Form and Women's Autobiography," *College English,* Feb. 1978] have argued. Diarists write around these criteria and still create cohesive autobiographies, as I will show.

The initial sense of incoherence one gets when reading an ordinary woman's diary—comments on the weather, health, tomato canning, followed by a stanza of sentimental poetry—occurs because we are used to constructed books rather than those that "happened," as Thomas Mallon defines diaries [in *A Book of One's Own*]. Anais Nin called them organic texts, rather than the imposed texts that result from a controlling intelligence [*The Novel of the Future*]. On the other hand, the diary is obviously not a literal transcription of a day. The diarist too selects what to describe and creates what I call "diary time"—giving a full page to a lover's single sentence, while describing fourteen hours of the day with the single telling phrase, "did usual work." In fact, diary-writing is one way in which women have made coherent their experiential lives. Paul Rosenblatt observes, "As one writes about what has happened and how one feels, one is defining the situation and one's reactions. The act of defining may be seen as an act of controlling, delineating, and shaping . . ." [*Bitter, Bitter Tears: Nineteenth-century Diaries and Twentieth-century Grief Theories*]. Within the text of the diary, then, a coherent world formed by the writer's perceptions exists: populated by reappearing characters, mappable, even if only the size of a household. The changes that occur across time form the natural plot of the diary. While women's life stories generally do not fit the individualistic, linear narrative form of men's, as feminist scholars have noted, they do move forward within a subtle sequence of relational cycles. Rather than playing the mannikin who arrives at multiplicity from chaos, a woman may see *herself* as multiplicity—daughter, wife, mother, teacher, widow. This lack of closure, of denouement, gives the diary a form similar to life itself and renders autobiography the more lifeless form. Anais Nin, a writer in several genres, described why she preferred the diary form:

> The diary made me aware of organic and perpetual motion, perpetual change in character. When you write a novel or a short story [or an autobiography?] you are arresting motion for a period of that story, a span of time. There is something static about that. . . . And so in many cases, reading novels, I had the feeling of still life rather than a perpetual motion.

In the classic autobiography, the author attempts, as Yeats did, "to stand apart" from his life in order to "judge." The diary, by contrast, demands everyday composition, an immersion in the text which parallels the immersion in life. The significance demanded by Goethe, who avoided in his autobiography "the incoherent realia

strewn about [that] must necessarily disturb the good effect" is the antithesis of the contextual diary, rich with realia, that reflects a different view of life. Reading *from* the diary, rather than discarding it or editing it to show some applied concept of significance, we might discover a different *bios,* a life lived by women, as did psychologist Carol Gilligan when she listened to women's words rather than to men's theories:

> When one begins with the study of women and derives developmental constructs from their lives, the outline of a moral conception . . . begins to emerge and informs a different description of development. In this conception, the moral problem arises from conflicting responsibilities rather than from competing rights and requires for its resolution a mode of thinking that is contextual and narrative rather than formal and abstract. [*In a Different Voice: Psychological Theory and Women's Development*]

Likewise, the diary-writer, less concerned with "significance," can create a more vital version of her life, in situ, rather than pulling one out of context with some intellectualizing forceps to be examined "objectively" in the light of significance.

The critics' insistence on "the retrospective stance" is still considered essential to truth in personal history, laments Albert Stone [in *The American Autobiography*]. Yet it must soon crumble, as autobiographers like Maya Angelou and Maxine Hong Kingston write perceptively about their childhoods and young adult lives with white-hot immediacy. Angelou's multi-volume life story, told by a still-evolving persona, forms a serial autobiography not unlike that formed by the diary.

In reassessing our ideas of what constitutes legitimate autobiographical design, we can elicit a nearer truth from diary texts. I liken reading a diary to watching a young child at play. If you can catch her in a private moment, you come close to hearing her real voice; once she knows you are listening, however, that voice becomes adulterated, then becomes even more modified for a larger audience. It still poses as a child's, but the private voice was much better. A study of diaries may reformulate our ideas of how ordinary women spoke, thought, and perceived their worlds. Once diaries are considered texts (no longer subtexts), we can use them to read women's culture—no longer seen as a subculture.

> A study of diaries may reformulate our ideas of how ordinary women spoke, thought, and perceived their worlds. Once diaries are considered texts (no longer subtexts), we can use them to read women's culture—no longer seen as a subculture.

—*Judy Nolte Lensink*

By way of illustration, I would like to turn to my study of a long diary to show how it is both autobiography, with thematic purpose, persona and imagery, and something more—a document that traces at great length an ordinary individual's encounter with ideology. When read intertextually with other women's narratives, this type of diary will help us rewrite nineteenth-century women's history through their own autobiographies.

The diary was written faithfully by Emily Hawley Gillespie, a Midwestern woman, for thirty years—from 1858, just before she turned twenty, to 1888, the year of her death. It tells the story of an idealistic young woman who courts selectively, marries hopefully, and works ceaselessly on an Iowa farm, only to see her labor, her dreams and eventually herself discarded.

The purpose of the diary, as stated on its opening page, is to give "reminiscences of the life, from day to day, of Miss Emmie E. Hawley." The use of "reminiscences" at the start of a diary can alert us to as many meanings as Henry Adams' use of "mannikin." It could signal a conscious selectivity operative in the diary, a sign at the outset that this writer will record what she wishes to remember, rather than the whole story. We can expect and do find flattering suitors, personal triumphs, and incidents that vindicate the diarist. In a later volume opened with a poem, the autobiographer is again signaling the theme and bias of her text: "Another book is added to my journal of life/May it not be filled with sorrow and strife. Let pure & undefiled Virtue, its pages unfold/May our hearts be as pure & bright as fine Gold."

The rather literary term "reminiscences" might also indicate Hawley's lofty plans to start a book. And, indeed, the diary graduates from loose sheets of foolscap, to tied "booklets," to account notebooks, and finally leatherbound journals. If such a youthful diarist was intending to author a bona fide book, as chapter headings like "Home" and "Virtue" show at one point, rather than an ephemeral record, then questions of audience would arise, as they do in her very first volume. In one incident she asks "dear reader" if she should not be pitied, a form of authorial address straight out of sentimental fiction. She also early shows a strong sense of privacy. While she elliptically refers to an event as a memory aid, she keeps details away from the public realm of language. She writes, "George . . . and I went to take a walk; we went perhaps forty rods from the house and sat on a log beneath a beautiful shade tree and talked,—well never mind what about."

This explicit show of the "author-ity" to omit perhaps the most important events of her life (which may have been sexual, since she was also coding her menstrual cycle in the diary's margins with exclamation marks) shows both the strength of diaries—their refreshing honesty about their own construction—and their ultimate limitation, like all autobiography, as documents about "reality." Later in her life, when the tale of romance has become instead a painful chronicle of a wronged woman, Gillespie still withholds the most unpleasant aspects of her story from the eyes of whatever audience she anticipates. After detailing her husband's cruelties, she declares, "I have

written *many* things in my journal, but the worst is a secret to be buried when I shall cease to be." This reluctance shows what a powerful entity the diary has become. Rather than bury the book because it tells all, she will take her agony to her grave so that the diary itself will never "cease to be."

In Gillespie's diary, the goal to reminisce increasingly wars with the desire to have an "undefiled" book, despite her unhappiness. She insists on remembering, however, drawing small Victorian-style hands in the book's margins to point to entries for quick reference: death dates, proud moments in her children's lives. She also threads together her life by intra-textual reference, noting on a certain date where she was ten years earlier, according to her diary. This leads to a type of internal closure which this diarist seems to have desired, as she links together thematically significant events far apart in time: comets observed, the history of a piece of fabric, her teaching salary of two decades ago compared to her daughter's. And while she never stands apart from herself to judge, as did many formal autobiographers of her era, she does rather ruthlessly objectify others, as does every diarist who portrays people via language.

Another, more cynical reading of the term "reminiscences" would alert the scholar to the possibility that the title was applied after the moment of the diary's origin, perhaps years later when the writer reread her journals, as Gillespie noted doing. Almost no century-old personal document remains unaltered by either an author with second thoughts, a nervous relative, or the elements. Indeed, practically every published diary I have encountered, from Mary Chesnut's to the more obscure Samuella Curd's, contains the editor's explanation of alternations detected in the manuscript. This inability to leave well enough alone suggests that an autobiographical impulse to potentially go public lurks within those who persist in keeping a diary.

While the need to remember stays consistent throughout the composition of Gillespie's book, the narrative's purpose—and therefore her choice of literary form—changes across three decades. Her book, definitely not a still-life, is a meta-autobiography. It opens in a sentimental vein. Emily quotes her many suitors on the same pages in which she refers to sentimental fiction like [Mary Jane Holmes'] *Tempest and Sunshine,* wishing perhaps in her diary's pages to mirror the trysts of novels. She describes the courtship methods and failings of men with drinking habits, fiery tempers and speech defects, saving herself for "*the* one" who will honor her ideal of a husband and lover. As she moves to Iowa to live and work in her uncle's inn, the diary briefly lapses into the form and language of a travel account, for which there were many published models. After her arrival in Iowa, the diary returns to the sentimental mode, with Emily playing the orphan alone in the wide, wide world of the Far West.

Early in her marriage to wealthy James Gillespie, her choice as she neared her twenty-fourth birthday, the romance drops out of the diary, as entries like this show: "do my wash,—finish shirt—my cow has a calf this morning. James chop wood & kill the calf." Or perhaps Emily Gillespie decided that as a wife she should record less frivolous memories and instead emphasize financial accounts, an element in her diary all along. The diary soon becomes the couple's book; Emily mentions several times asking her husband at day's end what she should write for him. This literal "accounting" for Gillespie's time fits her belief that those who work hard will see their wealth—and happiness—accumulate.

When the two Gillespie children become old enough to appreciate Emily's life plan for them as "young folks"—academy educations, minimal farm chores, fancy dress clothes—her diary becomes a record of their mother's deeds and beliefs. Again, the diary follows a tradition, that of the memento book. Anne Bradstreet's autobiography was dedicated "To My Dear Children" and began with her wish that the book would in some way show her children "their mother's heart." Soon Emily's and James' activities take up less diary space, the children's activities and virtues more. The egotism necessary to write a diary, at war with the altruism Gillespie feels for her children, is resolved in the act of dedicating the books (as she did her life) to her offspring.

As Emily Gillespie's heart becomes more embittered by strife with James, her late diary increasingly resembles the accounts of "injured females" like Elizabeth Ashbridge's, which were popular in England during the eighteenth century. In this genre, drama and religious messages were combined in tales wherein women played the Christians and their husbands the lion, according to [Daniel B. Shea's *Spiritual Autobiography in Early America*]. James, Emily now reveals in a narrative of much different tone, had never been an ideal husband; now she records his unnatural failure as a father in the diary kept to burn memories into her children's minds as well as her own. The diary becomes so vital a "confidant" and family member that when she is ill the children take dictation for it. After her death, both children wrote their own observations in the diary margins after reading it. Sixty years later, daughter Sarah devoted much time transcribing the diary's early sections into more permanent books and in essence "publishing" it by placing copies in several historical archives.

Despite the grotesque mutation that domestic dreams take in Gillespie's life and the changing form of her diary, her narrator's voice remains almost rigidly consistent, as did Franklin's in his autobiography. Thomas Mallon has described this type of older diary persona as "horizontal," in that one's personality is perceived as staying consistent across time. Like the Puritans, Gillespie asks in her diary, "How well was I myself today?" (Modern diarists of the psychoanalytic age usually envision themselves as mutable, moving vertically through time. They ask, "Who am I today, compared to myself two years ago?") Gillespie's diary, however, does not completely follow the earlier religious model of daily self-criticism. She is quite well-pleased with herself, often defending her viewpoint in her book. Her diary, then, is a transitional one, as reflected in its persona.

Because Gillespie views her life through the lens of relationship, her persistent persona—the striving sufferer—is often portrayed relationally. At the diary's start, she is an undersesteemed daughter who obeys her mother's warning about going to New York for art training and agrees to stay home. As a betrothed young woman, she describes a nightmare in which she finds it impossible to please her fiancé and his parents. Then she strives to be the perfect mother, castigating herself in her diary for chastising her children, writing prayers that ask for more patience. Later she describes herself as the unappreciated wife of a farmer, the misunderstood daughter of an elderly resident father, the maligned sister of jealous siblings. Only at the very end of her diary does she begin to look beyond relationships, to criticize the social structure that has predetermined the pattern of her life and book, rather than the individual antagonists. Ironically, this insight comes via personal relationships. When a dear neighbor woman is institutionalized, Gillespie writes, "I only wonder that more women do not have to be taken to that asylum. Especially farmer's wives. No society except hired men to eat their meals. Hard work from the beginning to the end of the year." Later, she worries when her daughter is courted by an attractive man and again goes from the specific relationship to the generalization: "Ah, marriage is a lottery."

Gillespie's creation of "characters" in the diary is clearest in her evolving depiction of James. In the early years, his activities are seen as heroic, his moods as "fine temperment," his words as quite romantic. In the last years, he is described as insane; when Emily quotes him, she writes his words in the dialect of a rube. While her self-portraiture is more consistent, her persona does develop an increasingly vigorous voice. My content analysis shows that her use of evaluative commentary, both positive and negative, rises dramatically as she ages. Her ego emerges, reinforcing my earlier interpretation—that this never was intended to be a diary that recorded life. Rather, it was a book in which to frame an author-ized version of life—selective, mutable as the ideology driving it, eventually vocal and judgmental.

If we accept this diary as constructed autobiography then, rather than mere recorded narrative, certain images can be traced that serve as metaphors for Gillespie. One such that I alluded to earlier, *Home,* informs her book, as it did dozens of other women's diaries and the prescriptive literature of the nineteenth century. Gillespie's book shows how difficult it was to enact an idealized image with real-life people.

For young Emily Hawley, home was called "father's" and it was clear that a dependent unmarried daughter must leave it. Never "at home" at her uncle's inn, forced then to live in a wing of her new father-in-law's house, Gillespie finally delights in a rented place of her own: "we are at home enjoying life finely." When adorable children are added to this home, she thanks the Lord for her "happy family circle." While neighbors succumb to the agricultural depression of the mid-1870's, the Gillespies build a large house and Emily receives a deed to the entire farm from her husband. (The autobiographer's interpretation of this incident changes with her marriage: at the time of the event, the present of the deed is treated as a great honor from James. Only later, in the embittered years, does Gillespie write that James deeded over the farm to protect it from creditors.) Later, as a carpenter completes an addition to the home, the entire family argues over money; when a Brussels carpet and new furniture are put in the parlor, Emily excludes James from her image of the home, noting that the finery is too nice for him. "Home" also turns upon Emily Gillespie, who complains about the social isolation of the farm which causes her to "always be at home," a phrase she wrote with such pleasure ten years earlier. When the marriage explodes and she is forced to rent her own home from James, Gillespie sees the embodiment of her life's round of "usual work" slipping away. Moved as an invalid to a rented house in town, where she had always wanted to live for the society, she is ultimately confined to a bedroom. Having achieved the ideal home for only a few years of her life, Gillespie records through its imagery the diminishment of her dreams that could find no residence. Her diary, an unrelenting descriptive document, stands as a stark counterpoint to the home so touted by writers like the Beechers, balancing our view of women as seen through prescriptive literature. By first reading within diaries, and then conducting an intertextual analysis, we can begin to understand what happened to Victorian women living among icons of children, church, and home.

Another image in the Gillespie diary, that of perpetual motion, connects stunningly with Anais Nin's use of the same conceit 117 years later for her own diary, that "novel of the future." It seems almost inevitable that a pioneer woman immersed in the "usual work" of daily routine might arrive at the image of perpetual motion in a complaint. But for Gillespie, the image appears in an unearthly dream that shows her desire to exist on a higher plane, to somehow profit from the "perpetual motion" that was her life:

> Oh how grand it would be if one could live two hundred years, live to see the wonders wrought, to see the progress in art & science. *not* live for mere life alone. it almost enraptures us in reverie of thought to even have an idea of such a life. *There is one invention which I do believe can be made to be a perfect success, and that is perpetual-motion as I dreamed it about 15 or 18 years* ago. it must be done by weight and pressure by springs on an inclined plane, similar to a machine used by putting a horse into into a sort of tread-mill—

> The frame was silver and sparkling stones,
> The horse was gold-tied with a golden chain,
> Beneath his feet was an inclined plane
> So bright, as it turned beneath his tread,
> That it seemed too real to be only a dream.
> Within the golden horses feet, cut in notched form
> Were diamonds, to fit & drive the bars of gold
> On which were notched plates of dazling brightness.
> Standing near this wonder of art and skill
> Was the inventor: his raiment—gold and silver thread,
> A cloak embroidered with glistening diamonds.
> Right proud he was, of his rare invention.
> I too—for once—was dressed in gorgeous array

> If *twere* in a *dream*. Aye three times this presentiment.
> As I stood beside him I asked "What's the name of this?"
> With uplifted hand he answered "Perpetual Motion."

The way that Emily Gillespie made sense of real-life perpetual motion was to recount daily what her drudgery amounted to, both literally in her financial records—and emotionally in the record of her children's developing character. Gillespie's diary, then, is a self-kept tally of how she did indeed account for something. Her chosen persona of the sufferer was perfectly enacted in the autobiographical form of the diary, kept privately and relentlessly while she silently endured life's hardships. When she was ultimately silenced by death, her diary, passed through generations, would proclaim her angelic sacrifice more movingly than any words on a headstone. Emily Gillespie at last could speak and be appreciated through the accumulative narrative that paralleled the pattern of her life.

What I hope this . . . suggests is that rich autobiographical texts reside in ordinary women's diaries. If we can see the gender-blindness of the current literary criteria that disregard diaries, and overcome our fear of new forms when faced with dusty, scribbled narratives, I predict that we will again expand the boundaries of our reading and thinking to include new literature about American lives.

FURTHER READING

Andrews, Matthew Page. *The Women of the South in War Times.* Baltimore: Norman, Remington, 1920, 466 p.
> Discusses Southern women's roles in the Civil War and World War I.

Arksey, Laura, Nancy Pries, and Marcia Reed. *American Diaries—An Annotated Bibliography of Published American Diaries and Journals,* Vol. 1, *Diaries Written from 1492 to 1844.* Detroit: Gale Research Co., 1983, 311 p.
> Comprehensive bibliography of published American diaries and journals from 1492 to 1844. Entries are arranged chronologically, and some are annotated. The book includes name, subject, and geographic indexes.

———. *American Diaries—An Annotated Bibliography of Published American Diaries and Journals,* Vol. 2, *Diaries Written from 1845 to 1980.* Detroit: Gale Research Co., 1987, 501 p.
> Comprehensive bibliography of published American diaries and journals from 1845 to 1980. Entries are arranged chronologically, and some are annotated. The book includes name, subject, and geographic indexes.

Drury, Clifford Merrill. *First White Women over the Rockies: Diaries, Letters and Biographical Sketches of the Six Women of the Oregon Mission Who Made the Overland Journey in 1836 and 1838.* Glendale, Calif.: Arthur H. Clark, 1963-1966. Three vols.
> Chronicles the lives of the first six white American women to cross the Rocky Mountains. The books re-

print parts of the women's diaries and letters, and include Drury's biographic and historical commentary.

Godfrey, Kenneth W., Audrey M. Godfrey, and Jill Mulvay Derr. *Women's Voices: An Untold History of the Latter-day Saints, 1830-1900.* Salt Lake City: Deseret Book Co., 1982, 448 p.
> Excerpts portions of nineteenth-century Mormon women's diaries.

Havlice, Patricia Pate. *And So to Bed: A Bibliography of Diaries Published in English.* Metuchen, New Jersey: Scarecrow Press, 1987, 698 p.
> Bibliography of diaries published in English.

Hellerstein, Erna Olafson, Leslie Parker Hume, and Karen M. Offen, eds. *Victorian Women: A Documentary Account of Women's Lives in Nineteenth-Century England, France, and the United States.* Stanford, California: Stanford University Press, 1981, 534 p.
> Historical study that utilizes diaries, letters, medical writings, government documents, and sociological analyses to investigate the lives and attitudes of Victorian women.

Hinding, Andrea, ed. *Women's History Sources: A Guide to Archives and Manuscript Collections in the United States.* New York: R. R. Bowker Co., 1979. Two vols.
> Extensive guide to manuscript collections, arranged according to state and city. Each entry contains a short description of the specific holdings of each collection. The second volume is an index to the first volume.

Hoffman, Nancy. *Woman's "True" Profession: Voices from the History of Teaching.* Old Westbury, N.Y.: Feminist Press, 1981, 327 p.
> Collection of diaries, letters, poetry, photographs, short stories, and scholarly essays about women and their place in education.

Jones, Katharine M., ed. *Heroines of Dixie: Confederate Women Tell Their Story of the War.* Indianapolis: Bobbs-Merrill, 1955, 430 p.
> Presents sections from women's diaries pertaining to the Civil War.

Luchetti, Cathy. *Women of the West.* St. George, Utah: Antelope Island Press, 1982, 240 p.
> Reprints selections from several diaries written by women pioneers. The book includes introductions to each excerpt, photographs, a bibliography, and a discussion of minority women.

Matthews, William. *British Diaries: An Annotated Bibliography of British Diaries Written between 1442 and 1942.* Berkeley: University of California Press, 1950, 339 p.
> Bibliography of published and unpublished British diaries, arranged chronologically according to the date of their first entries.

———. *American Diaries in Manuscript, 1850-1954: A Descriptive Bibliography.* Athens, Georgia: University of Georgia Press, 1974, 176 p.
> Bibliography of unpublished or partially published American diaries, arranged chronologically. Each entry gives the author's name, the period covered in the diary, a brief description, and the location of the manuscript.

Ponsonby, Arthur. *English Diaries: A Review of English Diaries from the Sixteenth to the Twentieth Century.* London: Methuen & Co. Ltd., 1923, 447 p.
> Quotes extensively from and reviews several important published diaries. Ponsonby summarizes the contents of two diaries by nineteenth-century English women.

———. *Scottish and Irish Diaries from the Sixteenth to the Nineteenth Century.* London: Methuen & Co. Ltd., 1927, 192 p.
> Quotes extensively from and reviews several important published diaries, including summarizing the contents of four diaries by nineteenth-century Scottish women.

Schlissel, Lillian. *Women's Diaries of the Westward Journey.* New York: Schocken Books, 1992, 278 p.
> Historical study of the westward journey using diaries as a means to understanding women's roles. The book includes Schlissel's commentary and excerpts from nineteenth-century women's diaries. A portion of this book is excerpted in the entry above.

Williams, Ora G. "Muskets and Magnolias: Four Civil War Diaries by Louisiana Girls." *Louisiana Studies* IV, No. 3 (1965): 187-97.
> Explores the attitudes expressed by four women diarists toward slavery and work in the Civil-War South.

Nineteenth-Century Literature Criticism

Cumulative Indexes
Volumes 1-48

How to Use This Index

The main references

Calvino, Italo
1923-1985.....CLC 5, 8, 11, 22, 33, 39,
73; SSC 3

list all author entries in the following Gale Literary Criticism series:

BLC = Black Literature Criticism
CLC = Contemporary Literary Criticism
CLR = Children's Literature Review
CMLC = Classical and Medieval Literature Criticism
DA = DISCovering Authors
DC = Drama Criticism
HLC = Hispanic Literature Criticism
LC = Literature Criticism from 1400 to 1800
NCLC = Nineteenth-Century Literature Criticism
PC = Poetry Criticism
SSC = Short Story Criticism
TCLC = Twentieth-Century Literary Criticism
WLC = World Literature Criticism, 1500 to the Present

The cross-references

See also CANR 23; CA 85-88;
obituary CA 116

list all author entries in the following Gale biographical and literary sources:

AAYA = Authors & Artists for Young Adults
AITN = Authors in the News
BEST = Bestsellers
BW = Black Writers
CA = Contemporary Authors
CAAS = Contemporary Authors Autobiography Series
CABS = Contemporary Authors Bibliographical Series
CANR = Contemporary Authors New Revision Series
CAP = Contemporary Authors Permanent Series
CDALB = Concise Dictionary of American Literary Biography
CDBLB = Concise Dictionary of British Literary Biography
DLB = Dictionary of Literary Biography
DLBD = Dictionary of Literary Biography Documentary Series
DLBY = Dictionary of Literary Biography Yearbook
HW = Hispanic Writers
JRDA = Junior DISCovering Authors
MAICYA = Major Authors and Illustrators for Children and Young Adults
MTCW = Major 20th-Century Writers
NNAL = Native North American Literature
SAAS = Something about the Author Autobiography Series
SATA = Something about the Author
YABC – Yesterday's Authors of Books for Children

Literary Criticism Series
Cumulative Author Index

Aldiss, Brian W(ilson)
1925- .... **CLC 5, 14, 40**
See also CA 5-8R; CAAS 2; CANR 5, 28;
DLB 14; MTCW; SATA 34

Alegria, Claribel 1924-............ **CLC 75**
See also CA 131; CAAS 15; DLB 145; HW

Alegria, Fernando 1918-.......... **CLC 57**
See also CA 9-12R; CANR 5, 32; HW

Aleichem, Sholom .... **TCLC 1, 35**
See also Rabinovitch, Sholem

Aleixandre, Vicente 1898-1984 ... **CLC 9, 36**
See also CA 85-88; 114; CANR 26;
DLB 108; HW; MTCW

Alepoudelis, Odysseus
See Elytis, Odysseus

Aleshkovsky, Joseph 1929-
See Aleshkovsky, Yuz
See also CA 121; 128

Aleshkovsky, Yuz .... **CLC 44**
See also Aleshkovsky, Joseph

Alexander, Lloyd (Chudley) 1924- .. **CLC 35**
See also AAYA 1; CA 1-4R; CANR 1, 24,
38; CLR 1, 5; DLB 52; JRDA; MAICYA;
MTCW; SAAS 19; SATA 3, 49, 81

Alfau, Felipe 1902-.............. **CLC 66**
See also CA 137

Alger, Horatio, Jr. 1832-1899 ..... **NCLC 8**
See also DLB 42; SATA 16

Algren, Nelson 1909-1981 .... **CLC 4, 10, 33**
See also CA 13-16R; 103; CANR 20;
CDALB 1941-1968; DLB 9; DLBY 81,
82; MTCW

Ali, Ahmed 1910- .... **CLC 69**
See also CA 25-28R; CANR 15, 34

Alighieri, Dante 1265-1321 .... **CMLC 3**

Allan, John B.
See Westlake, Donald E(dwin)

Allen, Edward 1948-.............. **CLC 59**

Allen, Paula Gunn 1939- .... **CLC 84**
See also CA 112; 143; NNAL

Allen, Roland
See Ayckbourn, Alan

Allen, Sarah A.
See Hopkins, Pauline Elizabeth

Allen, Woody 1935- .... **CLC 16, 52**
See also AAYA 10; CA 33-36R; CANR 27,
38; DLB 44; MTCW

Allende, Isabel 1942- .... **CLC 39, 57; HLC**
See also CA 125; 130; DLB 145; HW;
MTCW

Alleyn, Ellen
See Rossetti, Christina (Georgina)

Allingham, Margery (Louise)
1904-1966 .... **CLC 19**
See also CA 5-8R; 25-28R; CANR 4;
DLB 77; MTCW

Allingham, William 1824-1889 ... **NCLC 25**
See also DLB 35

Allison, Dorothy E. 1949- .... **CLC 78**
See also CA 140

Allston, Washington 1779-1843 .... **NCLC 2**
See also DLB 1

Almedingen, E. M. .... **CLC 12**
See also Almedingen, Martha Edith von
See also SATA 3

Almedingen, Martha Edith von 1898-1971
See Almedingen, E. M.
See also CA 1-4R; CANR 1

Almqvist, Carl Jonas Love
1793-1866 .... **NCLC 42**

Alonso, Damaso 1898-1990 .... **CLC 14**
See also CA 110; 131; 130; DLB 108; HW

Alov
See Gogol, Nikolai (Vasilyevich)

Alta 1942-..................... **CLC 19**
See also CA 57-60

Alter, Robert B(ernard) 1935-...... **CLC 34**
See also CA 49-52; CANR 1, 47

Alther, Lisa 1944-.............. **CLC 7, 41**
See also CA 65-68; CANR 12, 30; MTCW

Altman, Robert 1925-............. **CLC 16**
See also CA 73-76; CANR 43

Alvarez, A(lfred) 1929-.......... **CLC 5, 13**
See also CA 1-4R; CANR 3, 33; DLB 14,
40

Alvarez, Alejandro Rodriguez 1903-1965
See Casona, Alejandro
See also CA 131; 93-96; HW

Amado, Jorge 1912-..... **CLC 13, 40; HLC**
See also CA 77-80; CANR 35; DLB 113;
MTCW

Ambler, Eric 1909-............ **CLC 4, 6, 9**
See also CA 9-12R; CANR 7, 38; DLB 77;
MTCW

Amichai, Yehuda 1924- ...... **CLC 9, 22, 57**
See also CA 85-88; CANR 46, 46; MTCW

Amiel, Henri Frederic 1821-1881 .. **NCLC 4**

Amis, Kingsley (William)
1922- .. **CLC 1, 2, 3, 5, 8, 13, 40, 44; DA**
See also AITN 2; CA 9-12R; CANR 8, 28;
CDBLB 1945-1960; DLB 15, 27, 100, 139;
MTCW

Amis, Martin (Louis)
1949- .... **CLC 4, 9, 38, 62**
See also BEST 90:3; CA 65-68; CANR 8,
27; DLB 14

Ammons, A(rchie) R(andolph)
1926-......... **CLC 2, 3, 5, 8, 9, 25, 57**
See also AITN 1; CA 9-12R; CANR 6, 36;
DLB 5; MTCW

Amo, Tauraatua i
See Adams, Henry (Brooks)

Anand, Mulk Raj 1905-.......... **CLC 23**
See also CA 65-68; CANR 32; MTCW

Anatol
See Schnitzler, Arthur

Anaya, Rudolfo A(lfonso)
1937- .... **CLC 23; HLC**
See also CA 45-48; CAAS 4; CANR 1, 32;
DLB 82; HW 1; MTCW

Andersen, Hans Christian
1805-1875 .. **NCLC 7; DA; SSC 6; WLC**
See also CLR 6; MAICYA; YABC 1

Anderson, C. Farley
See Mencken, H(enry) L(ouis); Nathan,
George Jean

Anderson, Jessica (Margaret) Queale
.... **CLC 37**
See also CA 9-12R; CANR 4

Anderson, Jon (Victor) 1940- .... **CLC 9**
See also CA 25-28R; CANR 20

Anderson, Lindsay (Gordon)
1923-1994 .... **CLC 20**
See also CA 125; 128; 146

Anderson, Maxwell 1888-1959 ..... **TCLC 2**
See also CA 105; DLB 7

Anderson, Poul (William) 1926- .... **CLC 15**
See also AAYA 5; CA 1-4R; CAAS 2;
CANR 2, 15, 34; DLB 8; MTCW;
SATA-Brief 39

Anderson, Robert (Woodruff)
1917-..................... **CLC 23**
See also AITN 1; CA 21-24R; CANR 32;
DLB 7

Anderson, Sherwood
1876-1941 .... **TCLC 1, 10, 24; DA;**
SSC 1; WLC
See also CA 104; 121; CDALB 1917-1929;
DLB 4, 9, 86; DLBD 1; MTCW

Andouard
See Giraudoux, (Hippolyte) Jean

Andrade, Carlos Drummond de ...... **CLC 18**
See also Drummond de Andrade, Carlos

Andrade, Mario de 1893-1945..... **TCLC 43**

Andreas-Salome, Lou 1861-1937... **TCLC 56**
See also DLB 66

Andrewes, Lancelot 1555-1626 .... **LC 5**

Andrews, Cicily Fairfield
See West, Rebecca

Andrews, Elton V.
See Pohl, Frederik

Andreyev, Leonid (Nikolaevich)
1871-1919 .... **TCLC 3**
See also CA 104

Andric, Ivo 1892-1975 .... **CLC 8**
See also CA 81-84; 57-60; CANR 43;
DLB 147; MTCW

Angelique, Pierre
See Bataille, Georges

Angell, Roger 1920-.............. **CLC 26**
See also CA 57-60; CANR 13, 44

Angelou, Maya
1928- .... **CLC 12, 35, 64, 77; BLC; DA**
See also AAYA 7; BW 2; CA 65-68;
CANR 19, 42; DLB 38; MTCW;
SATA 49

Annensky, Innokenty Fyodorovich
1856-1909 .... **TCLC 14**
See also CA 110

Anon, Charles Robert
See Pessoa, Fernando (Antonio Nogueira)

Anouilh, Jean (Marie Lucien Pierre)
1910-1987 ...... **CLC 1, 3, 8, 13, 40, 50**
See also CA 17-20R; 123; CANR 32;
MTCW

Anthony, Florence
See Ai

Anthony, John
See Ciardi, John (Anthony)

Anthony, Peter
  See Shaffer, Anthony (Joshua); Shaffer,
    Peter (Levin)

Anthony, Piers 1934- .... **CLC 35**
  See also AAYA 11; CA 21-24R; CANR 28;
    DLB 8; MTCW

Antoine, Marc
  See Proust, (Valentin-Louis-George-Eugene-)
    Marcel

Antoninus, Brother
  See Everson, William (Oliver)

Antonioni, Michelangelo 1912- ..... **CLC 20**
  See also CA 73-76; CANR 45

Antschel, Paul 1920-1970
  See Celan, Paul
  See also CA 85-88; CANR 33; MTCW

Anwar, Chairil 1922-1949 .... **TCLC 22**
  See also CA 121

Apollinaire, Guillaume .. **TCLC 3, 8, 51; PC 7**
  See also Kostrowitzki, Wilhelm Apollinaris
    de

Appelfeld, Aharon 1932- .... **CLC 23, 47**
  See also CA 112; 133

Apple, Max (Isaac) 1941- .... **CLC 9, 33**
  See also CA 81-84; CANR 19; DLB 130

Appleman, Philip (Dean) 1926- ..... **CLC 51**
  See also CA 13-16R; CAAS 18; CANR 6,
    29

Appleton, Lawrence
  See Lovecraft, H(oward) P(hillips)

Apteryx
  See Eliot, T(homas) S(tearns)

Apuleius, (Lucius Madaurensis)
  125(?)-175(?) .... **CMLC 1**

Aquin, Hubert 1929-1977 .... **CLC 15**
  See also CA 105; DLB 53

Aragon, Louis 1897-1982 .... **CLC 3, 22**
  See also CA 69-72; 108; CANR 28;
    DLB 72; MTCW

Arany, Janos 1817-1882 .... **NCLC 34**

Arbuthnot, John 1667-1735 .... **LC 1**
  See also DLB 101

Archer, Herbert Winslow
  See Mencken, H(enry) L(ouis)

Archer, Jeffrey (Howard) 1940- .... **CLC 28**
  See also BEST 89:3; CA 77-80; CANR 22

Archer, Jules 1915- .... **CLC 12**
  See also CA 9-12R; CANR 6; SAAS 5;
    SATA 4

Archer, Lee
  See Ellison, Harlan (Jay)

Arden, John 1930- .... **CLC 6, 13, 15**
  See also CA 13-16R; CAAS 4; CANR 31;
    DLB 13; MTCW

Arenas, Reinaldo
  1943-1990 .... **CLC 41; HLC**
  See also CA 124; 128; 133; DLB 145; HW

Arendt, Hannah 1906-1975 .... **CLC 66**
  See also CA 17-20R; 61-64; CANR 26;
    MTCW

Aretino, Pietro 1492-1556 .... **LC 12**

Arghezi, Tudor.................... **CLC 80**
  See also Theodorescu, Ion N.

Arguedas, Jose Maria
  1911-1969 .... **CLC 10, 18**
  See also CA 89-92; DLB 113; HW

Argueta, Manlio 1936- .... **CLC 31**
  See also CA 131; DLB 145; HW

Ariosto, Ludovico 1474-1533........ **LC 6**

Aristides
  See Epstein, Joseph

Aristophanes
  450B.C.-385B.C.... **CMLC 4; DA; DC 2**

Arlt, Roberto (Godofredo Christophersen)
  1900-1942 .... **TCLC 29; HLC**
  See also CA 123; 131; HW

Armah, Ayi Kwei 1939- .... **CLC 5, 33; BLC**
  See also BW 1; CA 61-64; CANR 21;
    DLB 117; MTCW

Armatrading, Joan 1950- .... **CLC 17**
  See also CA 114

Arnette, Robert
  See Silverberg, Robert

Arnim, Achim von (Ludwig Joachim von
    Arnim) 1781-1831 .... **NCLC 5**
  See also DLB 90

Arnim, Bettina von 1785-1859.... **NCLC 38**
  See also DLB 90

Arnold, Matthew
  1822-1888 ..... **NCLC 6, 29; DA; PC 5;**
                                          WLC
  See also CDBLB 1832-1890; DLB 32, 57

Arnold, Thomas 1795-1842 ...... **NCLC 18**
  See also DLB 55

Arnow, Harriette (Louisa) Simpson
  1908-1986 .... **CLC 2, 7, 18**
  See also CA 9-12R; 118; CANR 14; DLB 6;
    MTCW; SATA 42; SATA-Obit 47

Arp, Hans
  See Arp, Jean

Arp, Jean 1887-1966............... **CLC 5**
  See also CA 81-84; 25-28R; CANR 42

Arrabal
  See Arrabal, Fernando

Arrabal, Fernando 1932- ... **CLC 2, 9, 18, 58**
  See also CA 9-12R; CANR 15

Arrick, Fran.................... **CLC 30**

Artaud, Antonin 1896-1948 ..... **TCLC 3, 36**
  See also CA 104

Arthur, Ruth M(abel) 1905-1979.... **CLC 12**
  See also CA 9-12R; 85-88; CANR 4;
    SATA 7, 26

Artsybashev, Mikhail (Petrovich)
  1878-1927 .... **TCLC 31**

Arundel, Honor (Morfydd)
  1919-1973 .... **CLC 17**
  See also CA 21-22; 41-44R; CAP 2;
    CLR 35; SATA 4; SATA-Obit 24

Asch, Sholem 1880-1957 .... **TCLC 3**
  See also CA 105

Ash, Shalom
  See Asch, Sholem

Ashbery, John (Lawrence)
  1927- ...... **CLC 2, 3, 4, 6, 9, 13, 15, 25,**
                                          41, 77
  See also CA 5-8R; CANR 9, 37; DLB 5;
    DLBY 81; MTCW

Ashdown, Clifford
  See Freeman, R(ichard) Austin

Ashe, Gordon
  See Creasey, John

Ashton-Warner, Sylvia (Constance)
  1908-1984 .... **CLC 19**
  See also CA 69-72; 112; CANR 29; MTCW

Asimov, Isaac
  1920-1992 ..... **CLC 1, 3, 9, 19, 26, 76**
  See also AAYA 13; BEST 90:2; CA 1-4R;
    137; CANR 2, 19, 36; CLR 12; DLB 8;
    DLBY 92; JRDA; MAICYA; MTCW;
    SATA 1, 26, 74

Astley, Thea (Beatrice May)
  1925- .... **CLC 41**
  See also CA 65-68; CANR 11, 43

Aston, James
  See White, T(erence) H(anbury)

Asturias, Miguel Angel
  1899-1974 .... **CLC 3, 8, 13; HLC**
  See also CA 25-28; 49-52; CANR 32;
    CAP 2; DLB 113; HW; MTCW

Atares, Carlos Saura
  See Saura (Atares), Carlos

Atheling, William
  See Pound, Ezra (Weston Loomis)

Atheling, William, Jr.
  See Blish, James (Benjamin)

Atherton, Gertrude (Franklin Horn)
  1857-1948 .... **TCLC 2**
  See also CA 104; DLB 9, 78

Atherton, Lucius
  See Masters, Edgar Lee

Atkins, Jack
  See Harris, Mark

Atticus
  See Fleming, Ian (Lancaster)

Atwood, Margaret (Eleanor)
  1939- ..... **CLC 2, 3, 4, 8, 13, 15, 25, 44,**
                             84; DA; PC 8; SSC 2; WLC
  See also AAYA 12; BEST 89:2; CA 49-52;
    CANR 3, 24, 33; DLB 53; MTCW;
    SATA 50

Aubigny, Pierre d'
  See Mencken, H(enry) L(ouis)

Aubin, Penelope 1685-1731(?)........ **LC 9**
  See also DLB 39

Auchincloss, Louis (Stanton)
  1917- .... **CLC 4, 6, 9, 18, 45**
  See also CA 1-4R; CANR 6, 29; DLB 2;
    DLBY 80; MTCW

Auden, W(ystan) H(ugh)
  1907-1973 ...... **CLC 1, 2, 3, 4, 6, 9, 11,**
                             14, 43; DA; PC 1; WLC
  See also CA 9-12R; 45-48; CANR 5;
    CDBLB 1914-1945; DLB 10, 20; MTCW

Audiberti, Jacques 1900-1965 ...... **CLC 38**
  See also CA 25-28R

Audubon, John James
  1785-1851 .... **NCLC 47**

Auel, Jean M(arie) 1936- .... **CLC 31**
  See also AAYA 7; BEST 90:4; CA 103;
    CANR 21

Auerbach, Erich 1892-1957 .... **TCLC 43**
  See also CA 118

Behrman, S(amuel) N(athaniel)
1893-1973 . . . . **CLC 40**
See also CA 13-16; 45-48; CAP 1; DLB 7,
44

Belasco, David 1853-1931 . . . . **TCLC 3**
See also CA 104; DLB 7

Belcheva, Elisaveta 1893- . . . . **CLC 10**
See also Bagryana, Elisaveta

Beldone, Phil "Cheech"
See Ellison, Harlan (Jay)

Beleno
See Azuela, Mariano

Belinski, Vissarion Grigoryevich
1811-1848 . . . . **NCLC 5**

Belitt, Ben 1911- . . . . **CLC 22**
See also CA 13-16R; CAAS 4; CANR 7;
DLB 5

Bell, James Madison
1826-1902 . . . . **TCLC 43; BLC**
See also BW 1; CA 122; 124; DLB 50

Bell, Madison (Smartt) 1957- . . . . . . **CLC 41**
See also CA 111; CANR 28

Bell, Marvin (Hartley) 1937- . . . . . **CLC 8, 31**
See also CA 21-24R; CAAS 14; DLB 5;
MTCW

Bell, W. L. D.
See Mencken, H(enry) L(ouis)

Bellamy, Atwood C.
See Mencken, H(enry) L(ouis)

Bellamy, Edward 1850-1898 . . . . . . **NCLC 4**
See also DLB 12

Bellin, Edward J.
See Kuttner, Henry

Belloc, (Joseph) Hilaire (Pierre)
1870-1953 . . . . **TCLC 7, 18**
See also CA 106; DLB 19, 100, 141;
YABC 1

Belloc, Joseph Peter Rene Hilaire
See Belloc, (Joseph) Hilaire (Pierre)

Belloc, Joseph Pierre Hilaire
See Belloc, (Joseph) Hilaire (Pierre)

Belloc, M. A.
See Lowndes, Marie Adelaide (Belloc)

Bellow, Saul
1915- . . . . . . **CLC 1, 2, 3, 6, 8, 10, 13, 15,**
25, 33, 34, 63, 79; DA; SSC 14; WLC
See also AITN 2; BEST 89:3; CA 5-8R;
CABS 1; CANR 29; CDALB 1941-1968;
DLB 2, 28; DLBD 3; DLBY 82; MTCW

Bely, Andrey . . . . **TCLC 7; PC 11**
See also Bugayev, Boris Nikolayevich

Benary, Margot
See Benary-Isbert, Margot

Benary-Isbert, Margot 1889-1979 . . . **CLC 12**
See also CA 5-8R; 89-92; CANR 4;
CLR 12; MAICYA; SATA 2;
SATA-Obit 21

Benavente (y Martinez), Jacinto
1866-1954 . . . . **TCLC 3**
See also CA 106; 131; HW; MTCW

Benchley, Peter (Bradford)
1940- . . . . **CLC 4, 8**
See also AAYA 14; AITN 2; CA 17-20R;
CANR 12, 35; MTCW; SATA 3

Benchley, Robert (Charles)
1889-1945 . . . . **TCLC 1, 55**
See also CA 105; DLB 11

Benedikt, Michael 1935- . . . . **CLC 4, 14**
See also CA 13-16R; CANR 7; DLB 5

Benet, Juan 1927- . . . . **CLC 28**
See also CA 143

Benet, Stephen Vincent
1898-1943 . . . . **TCLC 7; SSC 10**
See also CA 104; DLB 4, 48, 102; YABC 1

Benet, William Rose 1886-1950 . . . **TCLC 28**
See also CA 118; DLB 45

Benford, Gregory (Albert) 1941- . . . . **CLC 52**
See also CA 69-72; CANR 12, 24;
DLBY 82

Bengtsson, Frans (Gunnar)
1894-1954 . . . . **TCLC 48**

Benjamin, David
See Slavitt, David R(ytman)

Benjamin, Lois
See Gould, Lois

Benjamin, Walter 1892-1940 . . . . . **TCLC 39**

Benn, Gottfried 1886-1956 . . . . **TCLC 3**
See also CA 106; DLB 56

Bennett, Alan 1934- . . . . **CLC 45, 77**
See also CA 103; CANR 35; MTCW

Bennett, (Enoch) Arnold
1867-1931 . . . . **TCLC 5, 20**
See also CA 106; CDBLB 1890-1914;
DLB 10, 34, 98

Bennett, Elizabeth
See Mitchell, Margaret (Munnerlyn)

Bennett, George Harold 1930-
See Bennett, Hal
See also BW 1; CA 97-100

Bennett, Hal . . . . **CLC 5**
See also Bennett, George Harold
See also DLB 33

Bennett, Jay 1912- . . . . **CLC 35**
See also AAYA 10; CA 69-72; CANR 11,
42; JRDA; SAAS 4; SATA 41;
SATA-Brief 27

Bennett, Louise (Simone)
1919- . . . . **CLC 28; BLC**
See also BW 2; DLB 117

Benson, E(dward) F(rederic)
1867-1940 . . . . **TCLC 27**
See also CA 114; DLB 135

Benson, Jackson J. 1930- . . . . **CLC 34**
See also CA 25-28R; DLB 111

Benson, Sally 1900-1972 . . . . **CLC 17**
See also CA 19-20; 37-40R; CAP 1;
SATA 1, 35; SATA-Obit 27

Benson, Stella 1892-1933 . . . . **TCLC 17**
See also CA 117; DLB 36

Bentham, Jeremy 1748-1832 . . . . . **NCLC 38**
See also DLB 107

Bentley, E(dmund) C(lerihew)
1875-1956 . . . . **TCLC 12**
See also CA 108; DLB 70

Bentley, Eric (Russell) 1916- . . . . **CLC 24**
See also CA 5-8R; CANR 6

Beranger, Pierre Jean de
1780-1857 . . . . **NCLC 34**

Berendt, John (Lawrence) 1939- . . . . **CLC 86**
See also CA 146

Berger, Colonel
See Malraux, (Georges-)Andre

Berger, John (Peter) 1926- . . . . . . **CLC 2, 19**
See also CA 81-84; DLB 14

Berger, Melvin H. 1927- . . . . **CLC 12**
See also CA 5-8R; CANR 4; CLR 32;
SAAS 2; SATA 5

Berger, Thomas (Louis)
1924- . . . . **CLC 3, 5, 8, 11, 18, 38**
See also CA 1-4R; CANR 5, 28; DLB 2;
DLBY 80; MTCW

Bergman, (Ernst) Ingmar
1918- . . . . **CLC 16, 72**
See also CA 81-84; CANR 33

Bergson, Henri 1859-1941 . . . . **TCLC 32**

Bergstein, Eleanor 1938- . . . . **CLC 4**
See also CA 53-56; CANR 5

Berkoff, Steven 1937- . . . . **CLC 56**
See also CA 104

Bermant, Chaim (Icyk) 1929- . . . . . . **CLC 40**
See also CA 57-60; CANR 6, 31

Bern, Victoria
See Fisher, M(ary) F(rances) K(ennedy)

Bernanos, (Paul Louis) Georges
1888-1948 . . . . **TCLC 3**
See also CA 104; 130; DLB 72

Bernard, April 1956- . . . . **CLC 59**
See also CA 131

Berne, Victoria
See Fisher, M(ary) F(rances) K(ennedy)

Bernhard, Thomas
1931-1989 . . . . **CLC 3, 32, 61**
See also CA 85-88; 127; CANR 32;
DLB 85, 124; MTCW

Berriault, Gina 1926- . . . . **CLC 54**
See also CA 116; 129; DLB 130

Berrigan, Daniel 1921- . . . . **CLC 4**
See also CA 33-36R; CAAS 1; CANR 11,
43; DLB 5

Berrigan, Edmund Joseph Michael, Jr.
1934-1983
See Berrigan, Ted
See also CA 61-64; 110; CANR 14

Berrigan, Ted . . . . **CLC 37**
See also Berrigan, Edmund Joseph Michael,
Jr.
See also DLB 5

Berry, Charles Edward Anderson 1931-
See Berry, Chuck
See also CA 115

Berry, Chuck . . . . **CLC 17**
See also Berry, Charles Edward Anderson

Berry, Jonas
See Ashbery, John (Lawrence)

Berry, Wendell (Erdman)
1934- . . . . **CLC 4, 6, 8, 27, 46**
See also AITN 1; CA 73-76; DLB 5, 6

Berryman, John
1914-1972 . . . . . . **CLC 1, 2, 3, 4, 6, 8, 10,**
13, 25, 62
See also CA 13-16; 33-36R; CABS 2;
CANR 35; CAP 1; CDALB 1941-1968;
DLB 48; MTCW

Bertolucci, Bernardo 1940- . . . . **CLC 16**
See also CA 106

Bertrand, Aloysius 1807-1841 . . . . **NCLC 31**

Bertran de Born c. 1140-1215 . . . . . **CMLC 5**

Besant, Annie (Wood) 1847-1933 . . . **TCLC 9**
See also CA 105

Bessie, Alvah 1904-1985 . . . . **CLC 23**
See also CA 5-8R; 116; CANR 2; DLB 26

Bethlen, T. D.
See Silverberg, Robert

Beti, Mongo . . . . **CLC 27; BLC**
See also Biyidi, Alexandre

Betjeman, John
1906-1984 . . . . **CLC 2, 6, 10, 34, 43**
See also CA 9-12R; 112; CANR 33;
CDBLB 1945-1960; DLB 20; DLBY 84;
MTCW

Bettelheim, Bruno 1903-1990 . . . . . . **CLC 79**
See also CA 81-84; 131; CANR 23; MTCW

Betti, Ugo 1892-1953 . . . . **TCLC 5**
See also CA 104

Betts, Doris (Waugh) 1932- . . . . **CLC 3, 6, 28**
See also CA 13-16R; CANR 9; DLBY 82

Bevan, Alistair
See Roberts, Keith (John Kingston)

Bialik, Chaim Nachman
1873-1934 . . . . **TCLC 25**

Bickerstaff, Isaac
See Swift, Jonathan

Bidart, Frank 1939- . . . . **CLC 33**
See also CA 140

Bienek, Horst 1930- . . . . **CLC 7, 11**
See also CA 73-76; DLB 75

Bierce, Ambrose (Gwinett)
1842-1914(?) . . . . **TCLC 1, 7, 44; DA;**
SSC 9; WLC
See also CA 104; 139; CDALB 1865-1917;
DLB 11, 12, 23, 71, 74

Billings, Josh
See Shaw, Henry Wheeler

Billington, (Lady) Rachel (Mary)
1942- . . . . **CLC 43**
See also AITN 2; CA 33-36R; CANR 44

Binyon, T(imothy) J(ohn) 1936- . . . . **CLC 34**
See also CA 111; CANR 28

Bioy Casares, Adolfo
1914- . . . . . . **CLC 4, 8, 13; HLC; SSC 17**
See also CA 29-32R; CANR 19, 43;
DLB 113; HW; MTCW

Bird, Cordwainer
See Ellison, Harlan (Jay)

Bird, Robert Montgomery
1806-1854 . . . . **NCLC 1**

Birney, (Alfred) Earle
1904- . . . . **CLC 1, 4, 6, 11**
See also CA 1-4R; CANR 5, 20; DLB 88;
MTCW

Bishop, Elizabeth
1911-1979 . . . . . . **CLC 1, 4, 9, 13, 15, 32;**
DA; PC 3
See also CA 5-8R; 89-92; CABS 2;
CANR 26; CDALB 1968-1988; DLB 5;
MTCW; SATA-Obit 24

Bishop, John 1935- . . . . **CLC 10**
See also CA 105

Bissett, Bill 1939- . . . . **CLC 18**
See also CA 69-72; CAAS 19; CANR 15;
DLB 53; MTCW

Bitov, Andrei (Georgievich) 1937- . . . **CLC 57**
See also CA 142

Biyidi, Alexandre 1932-
See Beti, Mongo
See also BW 1; CA 114; 124; MTCW

Bjarme, Brynjolf
See Ibsen, Henrik (Johan)

Bjornson, Bjornstjerne (Martinius)
1832-1910 . . . . **TCLC 7, 37**
See also CA 104

Black, Robert
See Holdstock, Robert P.

Blackburn, Paul 1926-1971 . . . . . . **CLC 9, 43**
See also CA 81-84; 33-36R; CANR 34;
DLB 16; DLBY 81

Black Elk 1863-1950 . . . . **TCLC 33**
See also CA 144; NNAL

Black Hobart
See Sanders, (James) Ed(ward)

Blacklin, Malcolm
See Chambers, Aidan

Blackmore, R(ichard) D(oddridge)
1825-1900 . . . . **TCLC 27**
See also CA 120; DLB 18

Blackmur, R(ichard) P(almer)
1904-1965 . . . . **CLC 2, 24**
See also CA 11-12; 25-28R; CAP 1; DLB 63

Black Tarantula, The
See Acker, Kathy

Blackwood, Algernon (Henry)
1869-1951 . . . . **TCLC 5**
See also CA 105

Blackwood, Caroline 1931- . . . . . . **CLC 6, 9**
See also CA 85-88; CANR 32; DLB 14;
MTCW

Blade, Alexander
See Hamilton, Edmond; Silverberg, Robert

Blaga, Lucian 1895-1961 . . . . **CLC 75**

Blair, Eric (Arthur) 1903-1950
See Orwell, George
See also CA 104; 132; DA; MTCW;
SATA 29

Blais, Marie-Claire
1939- . . . . **CLC 2, 4, 6, 13, 22**
See also CA 21-24R; CAAS 4; CANR 38;
DLB 53; MTCW

Blaise, Clark 1940- . . . . **CLC 29**
See also AITN 2; CA 53-56; CAAS 3;
CANR 5; DLB 53

Blake, Nicholas
See Day Lewis, C(ecil)
See also DLB 77

Blake, William
1757-1827 . . . . . **NCLC 13, 37; DA; WLC**
See also CDBLB 1789-1832; DLB 93;
MAICYA; SATA 30

Blasco Ibanez, Vicente
1867-1928 . . . . **TCLC 12**
See also CA 110; 131; HW; MTCW

Blatty, William Peter 1928- . . . . **CLC 2**
See also CA 5-8R; CANR 9

Bleeck, Oliver
See Thomas, Ross (Elmore)

Blessing, Lee 1949- . . . . **CLC 54**

Blish, James (Benjamin)
1921-1975 . . . . **CLC 14**
See also CA 1-4R; 57-60; CANR 3; DLB 8;
MTCW; SATA 66

Bliss, Reginald
See Wells, H(erbert) G(eorge)

Blixen, Karen (Christentze Dinesen)
1885-1962
See Dinesen, Isak
See also CA 25-28; CANR 22; CAP 2;
MTCW; SATA 44

Bloch, Robert (Albert) 1917-1994 . . . **CLC 33**
See also CA 5-8R; 146; CAAS 20; CANR 5;
DLB 44; SATA 12

Blok, Alexander (Alexandrovich)
1880-1921 . . . . **TCLC 5**
See also CA 104

Blom, Jan
See Breytenbach, Breyten

Bloom, Harold 1930- . . . . **CLC 24**
See also CA 13-16R; CANR 39; DLB 67

Bloomfield, Aurelius
See Bourne, Randolph S(illiman)

Blount, Roy (Alton), Jr. 1941- . . . . . **CLC 38**
See also CA 53-56; CANR 10, 28; MTCW

Bloy, Leon 1846-1917 . . . . **TCLC 22**
See also CA 121; DLB 123

Blume, Judy (Sussman) 1938- . . . **CLC 12, 30**
See also AAYA 3; CA 29-32R; CANR 13,
37; CLR 2, 15; DLB 52; JRDA;
MAICYA; MTCW; SATA 2, 31, 79

Blunden, Edmund (Charles)
1896-1974 . . . . **CLC 2, 56**
See also CA 17-18; 45-48; CAP 2; DLB 20,
100; MTCW

Bly, Robert (Elwood)
1926- . . . . **CLC 1, 2, 5, 10, 15, 38**
See also CA 5-8R; CANR 41; DLB 5;
MTCW

Boas, Franz 1858-1942 . . . . **TCLC 56**
See also CA 115

Bobette
See Simenon, Georges (Jacques Christian)

Boccaccio, Giovanni
1313-1375 . . . . **CMLC 13; SSC 10**

Bochco, Steven 1943- . . . . **CLC 35**
See also AAYA 11; CA 124; 138

Bodenheim, Maxwell 1892-1954 . . . **TCLC 44**
See also CA 110; DLB 9, 45

Bodker, Cecil 1927- . . . . **CLC 21**
See also CA 73-76; CANR 13, 44; CLR 23;
MAICYA; SATA 14

Boell, Heinrich (Theodor)
1917-1985 . . . . **CLC 2, 3, 6, 9, 11, 15, 27,**
32, 72; DA; WLC
See also CA 21-24R; 116; CANR 24;
DLB 69; DLBY 85; MTCW

Boerne, Alfred
See Doeblin, Alfred

Browne, (Clyde) Jackson 1948(?)-... **CLC 21**
See also CA 120

Browning, Elizabeth Barrett
1806-1861 ..... **NCLC 1, 16; DA; PC 6;
WLC**
See also CDBLB 1832-1890; DLB 32

Browning, Robert
1812-1889 .... **NCLC 19; DA; PC 2**
See also CDBLB 1832-1890; DLB 32;
YABC 1

Browning, Tod 1882-1962 .... **CLC 16**
See also CA 141; 117

Bruccoli, Matthew J(oseph) 1931- .. **CLC 34**
See also CA 9-12R; CANR 7; DLB 103

Bruce, Lenny .... **CLC 21**
See also Schneider, Leonard Alfred

Bruin, John
See Brutus, Dennis

Brulard, Henri
See Stendhal

Brulls, Christian
See Simenon, Georges (Jacques Christian)

Brunner, John (Kilian Houston)
1934- .... **CLC 8, 10**
See also CA 1-4R; CAAS 8; CANR 2, 37;
MTCW

Bruno, Giordano 1548-1600 .... **LC 27**

Brutus, Dennis 1924- .... **CLC 43; BLC**
See also BW 2; CA 49-52; CAAS 14;
CANR 2, 27, 42; DLB 117

Bryan, C(ourtlandt) D(ixon) B(arnes)
1936- .... **CLC 29**
See also CA 73-76; CANR 13

Bryan, Michael
See Moore, Brian

Bryant, William Cullen
1794-1878 .... **NCLC 6, 46; DA**
See also CDALB 1640-1865; DLB 3, 43, 59

Bryusov, Valery Yakovlevich
1873-1924 .... **TCLC 10**
See also CA 107

Buchan, John 1875-1940 .... **TCLC 41**
See also CA 108; 145; DLB 34, 70; YABC 2

Buchanan, George 1506-1582 .... **LC 4**

Buchheim, Lothar-Guenther 1918- ... **CLC 6**
See also CA 85-88

Buchner, (Karl) Georg
1813-1837 .... **NCLC 26**

Buchwald, Art(hur) 1925-.......... **CLC 33**
See also AITN 1; CA 5-8R; CANR 21;
MTCW; SATA 10

Buck, Pearl S(ydenstricker)
1892-1973 .... **CLC 7, 11, 18; DA**
See also AITN 1; CA 1-4R; 41-44R;
CANR 1, 34; DLB 9, 102; MTCW;
SATA 1, 25

Buckler, Ernest 1908-1984 .... **CLC 13**
See also CA 11-12; 114; CAP 1; DLB 68;
SATA 47

Buckley, Vincent (Thomas)
1925-1988 .... **CLC 57**
See also CA 101

Buckley, William F(rank), Jr.
1925- .... **CLC 7, 18, 37**
See also AITN 1; CA 1-4R; CANR 1, 24;
DLB 137; DLBY 80; MTCW

Buechner, (Carl) Frederick
1926- .... **CLC 2, 4, 6, 9**
See also CA 13-16R; CANR 11, 39;
DLBY 80; MTCW

Buell, John (Edward) 1927-........ **CLC 10**
See also CA 1-4R; DLB 53

Buero Vallejo, Antonio 1916- ... **CLC 15, 46**
See also CA 106; CANR 24; HW; MTCW

Bufalino, Gesualdo 1920(?)-........ **CLC 74**

Bugayev, Boris Nikolayevich 1880-1934
See Bely, Andrey
See also CA 104

Bukowski, Charles
1920-1994 .... **CLC 2, 5, 9, 41, 82**
See also CA 17-20R; 144; CANR 40;
DLB 5, 130; MTCW

Bulgakov, Mikhail (Afanas'evich)
1891-1940 .... **TCLC 2, 16; SSC 18**
See also CA 105

Bulgya, Alexander Alexandrovich
1901-1956 .... **TCLC 53**
See also Fadeyev, Alexander
See also CA 117

Bullins, Ed 1935- .... **CLC 1, 5, 7; BLC**
See also BW 2; CA 49-52; CAAS 16;
CANR 24, 46, 46; DLB 7, 38; MTCW

Bulwer-Lytton, Edward (George Earle Lytton)
1803-1873 .... **NCLC 1, 45**
See also DLB 21

Bunin, Ivan Alexeyevich
1870-1953 .... **TCLC 6; SSC 5**
See also CA 104

Bunting, Basil 1900-1985 .... **CLC 10, 39, 47**
See also CA 53-56; 115; CANR 7; DLB 20

Bunuel, Luis 1900-1983 .. **CLC 16, 80; HLC**
See also CA 101; 110; CANR 32; HW

Bunyan, John 1628-1688 .. **LC 4; DA; WLC**
See also CDBLB 1660-1789; DLB 39

Burford, Eleanor
See Hibbert, Eleanor Alice Burford

Burgess, Anthony
**CLC 1, 2, 4, 5, 8, 10, 13, 15, 22, 40, 62,
81**
See also Wilson, John (Anthony) Burgess
See also AITN 1; CDBLB 1960 to Present;
DLB 14

Burke, Edmund
1729(?)-1797 .... **LC 7; DA; WLC**
See also DLB 104

Burke, Kenneth (Duva)
1897-1993 .... **CLC 2, 24**
See also CA 5-8R; 143; CANR 39; DLB 45,
63; MTCW

Burke, Leda
See Garnett, David

Burke, Ralph
See Silverberg, Robert

Burney, Fanny 1752-1840 .... **NCLC 12**
See also DLB 39

Burns, Robert
1759-1796 ...... **LC 3; DA; PC 6; WLC**
See also CDBLB 1789-1832; DLB 109

Burns, Tex
See L'Amour, Louis (Dearborn)

Burnshaw, Stanley 1906-..... **CLC 3, 13, 44**
See also CA 9-12R; DLB 48

Burr, Anne 1937- .... **CLC 6**
See also CA 25-28R

Burroughs, Edgar Rice
1875-1950 .... **TCLC 2, 32**
See also AAYA 11; CA 104; 132; DLB 8;
MTCW; SATA 41

Burroughs, William S(eward)
1914- .... **CLC 1, 2, 5, 15, 22, 42, 75;
DA; WLC**
See also AITN 2; CA 9-12R; CANR 20;
DLB 2, 8, 16; DLBY 81; MTCW

Burton, Richard F. 1821-1890.... **NCLC 42**
See also DLB 55

Busch, Frederick 1941- ... **CLC 7, 10, 18, 47**
See also CA 33-36R; CAAS 1; CANR 45;
DLB 6

Bush, Ronald 1946- .... **CLC 34**
See also CA 136

Bustos, F(rancisco)
See Borges, Jorge Luis

Bustos Domecq, H(onorio)
See Bioy Casares, Adolfo; Borges, Jorge
Luis

Butler, Octavia E(stelle) 1947- ..... **CLC 38**
See also BW 2; CA 73-76; CANR 12, 24,
38; DLB 33; MTCW

Butler, Robert Olen (Jr.) 1945-..... **CLC 81**
See also CA 112

Butler, Samuel 1612-1680 .... **LC 16**
See also DLB 101, 126

Butler, Samuel
1835-1902 ...... **TCLC 1, 33; DA; WLC**
See also CA 143; CDBLB 1890-1914;
DLB 18, 57

Butler, Walter C.
See Faust, Frederick (Schiller)

Butor, Michel (Marie Francois)
1926- .... **CLC 1, 3, 8, 11, 15**
See also CA 9-12R; CANR 33; DLB 83;
MTCW

Buzo, Alexander (John) 1944-...... **CLC 61**
See also CA 97-100; CANR 17, 39

Buzzati, Dino 1906-1972 .... **CLC 36**
See also CA 33-36R

Byars, Betsy (Cromer) 1928-....... **CLC 35**
See also CA 33-36R; CANR 18, 36; CLR 1,
16; DLB 52; JRDA; MAICYA; MTCW;
SAAS 1; SATA 4, 46, 80

Byatt, A(ntonia) S(usan Drabble)
1936- .... **CLC 19, 65**
See also CA 13-16R; CANR 13, 33;
DLB 14; MTCW

Byrne, David 1952-............... **CLC 26**
See also CA 127

Byrne, John Keyes 1926-
See Leonard, Hugh
See also CA 102

Byron, George Gordon (Noel)
1788-1824 . . . . . **NCLC 2, 12; DA; WLC**
See also CDBLB 1789-1832; DLB 96, 110

C. 3. 3.
See Wilde, Oscar (Fingal O'Flahertie Wills)

Caballero, Fernan 1796-1877. . . . . **NCLC 10**

Cabell, James Branch 1879-1958 . . . **TCLC 6**
See also CA 105; DLB 9, 78

Cable, George Washington
1844-1925 . . . . **TCLC 4; SSC 4**
See also CA 104; DLB 12, 74

Cabral de Melo Neto, Joao 1920- . . . **CLC 76**

Cabrera Infante, G(uillermo)
1929- . . . . **CLC 5, 25, 45; HLC**
See also CA 85-88; CANR 29; DLB 113;
HW; MTCW

Cade, Toni
See Bambara, Toni Cade

Cadmus and Harmonia
See Buchan, John

Caedmon fl. 658-680. . . . . **CMLC 7**
See also DLB 146

Caeiro, Alberto
See Pessoa, Fernando (Antonio Nogueira)

Cage, John (Milton, Jr.) 1912- . . . . . **CLC 41**
See also CA 13-16R; CANR 9

Cain, G.
See Cabrera Infante, G(uillermo)

Cain, Guillermo
See Cabrera Infante, G(uillermo)

Cain, James M(allahan)
1892-1977 . . . . **CLC 3, 11, 28**
See also AITN 1; CA 17-20R; 73-76;
CANR 8, 34; MTCW

Caine, Mark
See Raphael, Frederic (Michael)

Calasso, Roberto 1941- . . . . **CLC 81**
See also CA 143

Calderon de la Barca, Pedro
1600-1681 . . . . **LC 23; DC 3**

Caldwell, Erskine (Preston)
1903-1987 . . . . **CLC 1, 8, 14, 50, 60**
See also AITN 1; CA 1-4R; 121; CAAS 1;
CANR 2, 33; DLB 9, 86; MTCW

Caldwell, (Janet Miriam) Taylor (Holland)
1900-1985 . . . . **CLC 2, 28, 39**
See also CA 5-8R; 116; CANR 5

Calhoun, John Caldwell
1782-1850 . . . . **NCLC 15**
See also DLB 3

Calisher, Hortense
1911- . . . . **CLC 2, 4, 8, 38; SSC 15**
See also CA 1-4R; CANR 1, 22; DLB 2;
MTCW

Callaghan, Morley Edward
1903-1990. . . . . **CLC 3, 14, 41, 65**
See also CA 9-12R; 132; CANR 33;
DLB 68; MTCW

Calvino, Italo
1923-1985 . . . . . **CLC 5, 8, 11, 22, 33, 39,**
73; SSC 3
See also CA 85-88; 116; CANR 23; MTCW

Cameron, Carey 1952- . . . . **CLC 59**
See also CA 135

Cameron, Peter 1959- . . . . **CLC 44**
See also CA 125

Campana, Dino 1885-1932. . . . . . . **TCLC 20**
See also CA 117; DLB 114

Campbell, John W(ood, Jr.)
1910-1971 . . . . **CLC 32**
See also CA 21-22; 29-32R; CANR 34;
CAP 2; DLB 8; MTCW

Campbell, Joseph 1904-1987 . . . . **CLC 69**
See also AAYA 3; BEST 89:2; CA 1-4R;
124; CANR 3, 28; MTCW

Campbell, Maria 1940-. . . . . **CLC 85**
See also CA 102; NNAL

Campbell, (John) Ramsey 1946- . . . . **CLC 42**
See also CA 57-60; CANR 7

Campbell, (Ignatius) Roy (Dunnachie)
1901-1957 . . . . **TCLC 5**
See also CA 104; DLB 20

Campbell, Thomas 1777-1844 . . . . **NCLC 19**
See also DLB 93; 144

Campbell, Wilfred . . . . **TCLC 9**
See also Campbell, William

Campbell, William 1858(?)-1918
See Campbell, Wilfred
See also CA 106; DLB 92

Campos, Alvaro de
See Pessoa, Fernando (Antonio Nogueira)

Camus, Albert
1913-1960 . . . . **CLC 1, 2, 4, 9, 11, 14, 32,**
63, 69; DA; DC 2; SSC 9; WLC
See also CA 89-92; DLB 72; MTCW

Canby, Vincent 1924-. . . . . **CLC 13**
See also CA 81-84

Cancale
See Desnos, Robert

Canetti, Elias
1905-1994 . . . . . . **CLC 3, 14, 25, 75, 86**
See also CA 21-24R; 146; CANR 23;
DLB 85, 124; MTCW

Canin, Ethan 1960-. . . . . **CLC 55**
See also CA 131; 135

Cannon, Curt
See Hunter, Evan

Cape, Judith
See Page, P(atricia) K(athleen)

Capek, Karel
1890-1938 . . . . . **TCLC 6, 37; DA; DC 1;**
WLC
See also CA 104; 140

Capote, Truman
1924-1984 . . . . . **CLC 1, 3, 8, 13, 19, 34,**
38, 58; DA; SSC 2; WLC
See also CA 5-8R; 113; CANR 18;
CDALB 1941-1968; DLB 2; DLBY 80,
84; MTCW

Capra, Frank 1897-1991. . . . . **CLC 16**
See also CA 61-64; 135

Caputo, Philip 1941-. . . . . **CLC 32**
See also CA 73-76; CANR 40

Card, Orson Scott 1951- . . . . **CLC 44, 47, 50**
See also AAYA 11; CA 102; CANR 27, 47;
MTCW

Cardenal (Martinez), Ernesto
1925- . . . . **CLC 31; HLC**
See also CA 49-52; CANR 2, 32; HW;
MTCW

Carducci, Giosue 1835-1907. . . . . . **TCLC 32**

Carew, Thomas 1595(?)-1640. . . . . . . **LC 13**
See also DLB 126

Carey, Ernestine Gilbreth 1908- . . . . **CLC 17**
See also CA 5-8R; SATA 2

Carey, Peter 1943- . . . . **CLC 40, 55**
See also CA 123; 127; MTCW

Carleton, William 1794-1869. . . . . . **NCLC 3**

Carlisle, Henry (Coffin) 1926-. . . . . . **CLC 33**
See also CA 13-16R; CANR 15

Carlsen, Chris
See Holdstock, Robert P.

Carlson, Ron(ald F.) 1947-. . . . . **CLC 54**
See also CA 105; CANR 27

Carlyle, Thomas 1795-1881 . . **NCLC 22; DA**
See also CDBLB 1789-1832; DLB 55; 144

Carman, (William) Bliss
1861-1929 . . . . **TCLC 7**
See also CA 104; DLB 92

Carnegie, Dale 1888-1955 . . . . **TCLC 53**

Carossa, Hans 1878-1956. . . . . **TCLC 48**
See also DLB 66

Carpenter, Don(ald Richard)
1931- . . . . **CLC 41**
See also CA 45-48; CANR 1

Carpentier (y Valmont), Alejo
1904-1980 . . . . **CLC 8, 11, 38; HLC**
See also CA 65-68; 97-100; CANR 11;
DLB 113; HW

Carr, Caleb 1955(?)-. . . . . **CLC 86**

Carr, Emily 1871-1945. . . . . **TCLC 32**
See also DLB 68

Carr, John Dickson 1906-1977 . . . . . . **CLC 3**
See also CA 49-52; 69-72; CANR 3, 33;
MTCW

Carr, Philippa
See Hibbert, Eleanor Alice Burford

Carr, Virginia Spencer 1929-. . . . . . . **CLC 34**
See also CA 61-64; DLB 111

Carrier, Roch 1937-. . . . . **CLC 13, 78**
See also CA 130; DLB 53

Carroll, James P. 1943(?)-. . . . . **CLC 38**
See also CA 81-84

Carroll, Jim 1951- . . . . **CLC 35**
See also CA 45-48; CANR 42

Carroll, Lewis . . . . **NCLC 2; WLC**
See also Dodgson, Charles Lutwidge
See also CDBLB 1832-1890; CLR 2, 18;
DLB 18; JRDA

Carroll, Paul Vincent 1900-1968. . . . **CLC 10**
See also CA 9-12R; 25-28R; DLB 10

Carruth, Hayden
1921- . . . . . . **CLC 4, 7, 10, 18, 84; PC 10**
See also CA 9-12R; CANR 4, 38; DLB 5;
MTCW; SATA 47

Carson, Rachel Louise 1907-1964 . . . **CLC 71**
See also CA 77-80; CANR 35; MTCW;
SATA 23

Chatterji, Saratchandra . . . . TCLC 13
See also Chatterje, Sarat Chandra

Chatterton, Thomas 1752-1770 . . . . LC 3
See also DLB 109

Chatwin, (Charles) Bruce
1940-1989 . . . . CLC 28, 57, 59
See also AAYA 4; BEST 90:1; CA 85-88;
127

Chaucer, Daniel
See Ford, Ford Madox

Chaucer, Geoffrey
1340(?)-1400 . . . . LC 17; DA
See also CDBLB Before 1660; DLB 146

Chaviaras, Strates 1935-
See Haviaras, Stratis
See also CA 105

Chayefsky, Paddy . . . . CLC 23
See also Chayefsky, Sidney
See also DLB 7, 44; DLBY 81

Chayefsky, Sidney 1923-1981
See Chayefsky, Paddy
See also CA 9-12R; 104; CANR 18

Chedid, Andree 1920- . . . . CLC 47
See also CA 145

Cheever, John
1912-1982 . . . . . . CLC 3, 7, 8, 11, 15, 25,
64; DA; SSC 1; WLC
See also CA 5-8R; 106; CABS 1; CANR 5,
27; CDALB 1941-1968; DLB 2, 102;
DLBY 80, 82; MTCW

Cheever, Susan 1943- . . . . CLC 18, 48
See also CA 103; CANR 27; DLBY 82

Chekhonte, Antosha
See Chekhov, Anton (Pavlovich)

Chekhov, Anton (Pavlovich)
1860-1904 . . . . . TCLC 3, 10, 31, 55; DA;
SSC 2; WLC
See also CA 104; 124

Chernyshevsky, Nikolay Gavrilovich
1828-1889 . . . . NCLC 1

Cherry, Carolyn Janice 1942-
See Cherryh, C. J.
See also CA 65-68; CANR 10

Cherryh, C. J. . . . . CLC 35
See also Cherry, Carolyn Janice
See also DLBY 80

Chesnutt, Charles W(addell)
1858-1932 . . . . TCLC 5, 39; BLC; SSC 7
See also BW 1; CA 106; 125; DLB 12, 50,
78; MTCW

Chester, Alfred 1929(?)-1971 . . . . CLC 49
See also CA 33-36R; DLB 130

Chesterton, G(ilbert) K(eith)
1874-1936 . . . . TCLC 1, 6; SSC 1
See also CA 104; 132; CDBLB 1914-1945;
DLB 10, 19, 34, 70, 98; MTCW;
SATA 27

Chiang Pin-chin 1904-1986
See Ding Ling
See also CA 118

Ch'ien Chung-shu 1910- . . . . CLC 22
See also CA 130; MTCW

Child, L. Maria
See Child, Lydia Maria

Child, Lydia Maria 1802-1880 . . . . NCLC 6
See also DLB 1, 74; SATA 67

Child, Mrs.
See Child, Lydia Maria

Child, Philip 1898-1978 . . . . CLC 19, 68
See also CA 13-14; CAP 1; SATA 47

Childress, Alice
1920-1994 . . CLC 12, 15, 86; BLC; DC 4
See also AAYA 8; BW 2; CA 45-48; 146;
CANR 3, 27; CLR 14; DLB 7, 38; JRDA;
MAICYA; MTCW; SATA 7, 48, 81

Chislett, (Margaret) Anne 1943- . . . . CLC 34

Chitty, Thomas Willes 1926- . . . . CLC 11
See also Hinde, Thomas
See also CA 5-8R

Chomette, Rene Lucien 1898-1981
See Clair, Rene
See also CA 103

Chopin, Kate . . . . TCLC 5, 14; DA; SSC 8
See also Chopin, Katherine
See also CDALB 1865-1917; DLB 12, 78

Chopin, Katherine 1851-1904
See Chopin, Kate
See also CA 104; 122

Chretien de Troyes
c. 12th cent. - . . . . CMLC 10

Christie
See Ichikawa, Kon

Christie, Agatha (Mary Clarissa)
1890-1976 . . . . . . CLC 1, 6, 8, 12, 39, 48
See also AAYA 9; AITN 1, 2; CA 17-20R;
61-64; CANR 10, 37; CDBLB 1914-1945;
DLB 13, 77; MTCW; SATA 36

Christie, (Ann) Philippa
See Pearce, Philippa
See also CA 5-8R; CANR 4

Christine de Pizan 1365(?)-1431(?) . . . . LC 9

Chubb, Elmer
See Masters, Edgar Lee

Chulkov, Mikhail Dmitrievich
1743-1792 . . . . LC 2

Churchill, Caryl 1938- . . . CLC 31, 55; DC 5
See also CA 102; CANR 22, 46; DLB 13;
MTCW

Churchill, Charles 1731-1764 . . . . LC 3
See also DLB 109

Chute, Carolyn 1947- . . . . CLC 39
See also CA 123

Ciardi, John (Anthony)
1916-1986 . . . . CLC 10, 40, 44
See also CA 5-8R; 118; CAAS 2; CANR 5,
33; CLR 19; DLB 5; DLBY 86;
MAICYA; MTCW; SATA 1, 65;
SATA-Obit 46

Cicero, Marcus Tullius
106B.C.-43B.C. . . . . CMLC 3

Cimino, Michael 1943- . . . . CLC 16
See also CA 105

Cioran, E(mil) M. 1911- . . . . CLC 64
See also CA 25-28R

Cisneros, Sandra 1954- . . . . . . CLC 69; HLC
See also AAYA 9; CA 131; DLB 122; HW

Clair, Rene . . . . CLC 20
See also Chomette, Rene Lucien

Clampitt, Amy 1920-1994 . . . . CLC 32
See also CA 110; 146; CANR 29; DLB 105

Clancy, Thomas L., Jr. 1947-
See Clancy, Tom
See also CA 125; 131; MTCW

Clancy, Tom . . . . CLC 45
See also Clancy, Thomas L., Jr.
See also AAYA 9; BEST 89:1, 90:1

Clare, John 1793-1864 . . . . NCLC 9
See also DLB 55, 96

Clarin
See Alas (y Urena), Leopoldo (Enrique
Garcia)

Clark, Al C.
See Goines, Donald

Clark, (Robert) Brian 1932- . . . . CLC 29
See also CA 41-44R

Clark, Curt
See Westlake, Donald E(dwin)

Clark, Eleanor 1913- . . . . CLC 5, 19
See also CA 9-12R; CANR 41; DLB 6

Clark, J. P.
See Clark, John Pepper
See also DLB 117

Clark, John Pepper
1935- . . . . CLC 38; BLC; DC 5
See also Clark, J. P.
See also BW 1; CA 65-68; CANR 16

Clark, M. R.
See Clark, Mavis Thorpe

Clark, Mavis Thorpe 1909- . . . . CLC 12
See also CA 57-60; CANR 8, 37; CLR 30;
MAICYA; SAAS 5; SATA 8, 74

Clark, Walter Van Tilburg
1909-1971 . . . . CLC 28
See also CA 9-12R; 33-36R; DLB 9;
SATA 8

Clarke, Arthur C(harles)
1917- . . . . CLC 1, 4, 13, 18, 35; SSC 3
See also AAYA 4; CA 1-4R; CANR 2, 28;
JRDA; MAICYA; MTCW; SATA 13, 70

Clarke, Austin 1896-1974 . . . . CLC 6, 9
See also CA 29-32; 49-52; CAP 2; DLB 10,
20

Clarke, Austin C(hesterfield)
1934- . . . . CLC 8, 53; BLC
See also BW 1; CA 25-28R; CAAS 16;
CANR 14, 32; DLB 53, 125

Clarke, Gillian 1937- . . . . CLC 61
See also CA 106; DLB 40

Clarke, Marcus (Andrew Hislop)
1846-1881 . . . . NCLC 19

Clarke, Shirley 1925- . . . . CLC 16

Clash, The
See Headon, (Nicky) Topper; Jones, Mick;
Simonon, Paul; Strummer, Joe

Claudel, Paul (Louis Charles Marie)
1868-1955 . . . . TCLC 2, 10
See also CA 104

Clavell, James (duMaresq)
1925-1994 . . . . CLC 6, 25
See also CA 25-28R; 146; CANR 26;
MTCW

Cooper, Douglas 1960- . . . . **CLC 86**

Cooper, Henry St. John
See Creasey, John

Cooper, J. California. . . . . **CLC 56**
See also AAYA 12; BW 1; CA 125

Cooper, James Fenimore
1789-1851 . . . . **NCLC 1, 27**
See also CDALB 1640-1865; DLB 3;
SATA 19

Coover, Robert (Lowell)
1932- . . . . . **CLC 3, 7, 15, 32, 46; SSC 15**
See also CA 45-48; CANR 3, 37; DLB 2;
DLBY 81; MTCW

Copeland, Stewart (Armstrong)
1952- . . . . **CLC 26**

Coppard, A(lfred) E(dgar)
1878-1957 . . . . **TCLC 5**
See also CA 114; YABC 1

Coppee, Francois 1842-1908 . . . . . . **TCLC 25**

Coppola, Francis Ford 1939- . . . . **CLC 16**
See also CA 77-80; CANR 40; DLB 44

Corbiere, Tristan 1845-1875 . . . . . **NCLC 43**

Corcoran, Barbara 1911- . . . . **CLC 17**
See also AAYA 14; CA 21-24R; CAAS 2;
CANR 11, 28; DLB 52; JRDA; SATA 3,
77

Cordelier, Maurice
See Giraudoux, (Hippolyte) Jean

Corelli, Marie 1855-1924. . . . . **TCLC 51**
See also Mackay, Mary
See also DLB 34

Corman, Cid. . . . . **CLC 9**
See also Corman, Sidney
See also CAAS 2; DLB 5

Corman, Sidney 1924-
See Corman, Cid
See also CA 85-88; CANR 44

Cormier, Robert (Edmund)
1925- . . . . **CLC 12, 30; DA**
See also AAYA 3; CA 1-4R; CANR 5, 23;
CDALB 1968-1988; CLR 12; DLB 52;
JRDA; MAICYA; MTCW; SATA 10, 45

Corn, Alfred (DeWitt III) 1943- . . . . **CLC 33**
See also CA 104; CANR 44; DLB 120;
DLBY 80

Cornwell, David (John Moore)
1931- . . . . **CLC 9, 15**
See also le Carre, John
See also CA 5-8R; CANR 13, 33; MTCW

Corso, (Nunzio) Gregory 1930- . . . **CLC 1, 11**
See also CA 5-8R; CANR 41; DLB 5, 16;
MTCW

Cortazar, Julio
1914-1984 . . . . . . **CLC 2, 3, 5, 10, 13, 15,**
33, 34; HLC; SSC 7
See also CA 21-24R; CANR 12, 32;
DLB 113; HW; MTCW

Corwin, Cecil
See Kornbluth, C(yril) M.

Cosic, Dobrica 1921- . . . . **CLC 14**
See also CA 122; 138

Costain, Thomas B(ertram)
1885-1965 . . . . **CLC 30**
See also CA 5-8R; 25-28R; DLB 9

Costantini, Humberto
1924(?)-1987 . . . . **CLC 49**
See also CA 131; 122; HW

Costello, Elvis 1955- . . . . **CLC 21**

Cotter, Joseph Seamon Sr.
1861-1949 . . . . **TCLC 28; BLC**
See also BW 1; CA 124; DLB 50

Couch, Arthur Thomas Quiller
See Quiller-Couch, Arthur Thomas

Coulton, James
See Hansen, Joseph

Couperus, Louis (Marie Anne)
1863-1923 . . . . **TCLC 15**
See also CA 115

Coupland, Douglas 1961- . . . . **CLC 85**
See also CA 142

Court, Wesli
See Turco, Lewis (Putnam)

Courtenay, Bryce 1933- . . . . **CLC 59**
See also CA 138

Courtney, Robert
See Ellison, Harlan (Jay)

Cousteau, Jacques-Yves 1910- . . . . . . **CLC 30**
See also CA 65-68; CANR 15; MTCW;
SATA 38

Coward, Noel (Peirce)
1899-1973 . . . . **CLC 1, 9, 29, 51**
See also AITN 1; CA 17-18; 41-44R;
CANR 35; CAP 2; CDBLB 1914-1945;
DLB 10; MTCW

Cowley, Malcolm 1898-1989 . . . . **CLC 39**
See also CA 5-8R; 128; CANR 3; DLB 4,
48; DLBY 81, 89; MTCW

Cowper, William 1731-1800 . . . . **NCLC 8**
See also DLB 104, 109

Cox, William Trevor 1928- . . . **CLC 9, 14, 71**
See also Trevor, William
See also CA 9-12R; CANR 4, 37; DLB 14;
MTCW

Coyne, P. J.
See Masters, Hilary

Cozzens, James Gould
1903-1978 . . . . **CLC 1, 4, 11**
See also CA 9-12R; 81-84; CANR 19;
CDALB 1941-1968; DLB 9; DLBD 2;
DLBY 84; MTCW

Crabbe, George 1754-1832. . . . . . . **NCLC 26**
See also DLB 93

Craig, A. A.
See Anderson, Poul (William)

Craik, Dinah Maria (Mulock)
1826-1887 . . . . **NCLC 38**
See also DLB 35; MAICYA; SATA 34

Cram, Ralph Adams 1863-1942 . . . . **TCLC 45**

Crane, (Harold) Hart
1899-1932 . . . . **TCLC 2, 5; DA; PC 3;**
WLC
See also CA 104; 127; CDALB 1917-1929;
DLB 4, 48; MTCW

Crane, R(onald) S(almon)
1886-1967 . . . . **CLC 27**
See also CA 85-88; DLB 63

Crane, Stephen (Townley)
1871-1900 . . . . . . **TCLC 11, 17, 32; DA;**
SSC 7; WLC
See also CA 109; 140; CDALB 1865-1917;
DLB 12, 54, 78; YABC 2

Crase, Douglas 1944- . . . . **CLC 58**
See also CA 106

Crashaw, Richard 1612(?)-1649 . . . . . . **LC 24**
See also DLB 126

Craven, Margaret 1901-1980 . . . . **CLC 17**
See also CA 103

Crawford, F(rancis) Marion
1854-1909 . . . . **TCLC 10**
See also CA 107; DLB 71

Crawford, Isabella Valancy
1850-1887 . . . . **NCLC 12**
See also DLB 92

Crayon, Geoffrey
See Irving, Washington

Creasey, John 1908-1973. . . . . **CLC 11**
See also CA 5-8R; 41-44R; CANR 8;
DLB 77; MTCW

Crebillon, Claude Prosper Jolyot de (fils)
1707-1777 . . . . **LC 1**

Credo
See Creasey, John

Creeley, Robert (White)
1926- . . . . . **CLC 1, 2, 4, 8, 11, 15, 36, 78**
See also CA 1-4R; CAAS 10; CANR 23, 43;
DLB 5, 16; MTCW

Crews, Harry (Eugene)
1935- . . . . **CLC 6, 23, 49**
See also AITN 1; CA 25-28R; CANR 20;
DLB 6, 143; MTCW

Crichton, (John) Michael
1942- . . . . **CLC 2, 6, 54**
See also AAYA 10; AITN 2; CA 25-28R;
CANR 13, 40; DLBY 81; JRDA;
MTCW; SATA 9

Crispin, Edmund . . . . **CLC 22**
See also Montgomery, (Robert) Bruce
See also DLB 87

Cristofer, Michael 1945(?)- . . . . **CLC 28**
See also CA 110; DLB 7

Croce, Benedetto 1866-1952 . . . . . . **TCLC 37**
See also CA 120

Crockett, David 1786-1836 . . . . **NCLC 8**
See also DLB 3, 11

Crockett, Davy
See Crockett, David

Crofts, Freeman Wills
1879-1957 . . . . **TCLC 55**
See also CA 115; DLB 77

Croker, John Wilson 1780-1857 . . **NCLC 10**
See also DLB 110

Crommelynck, Fernand 1885-1970 . . **CLC 75**
See also CA 89-92

Cronin, A(rchibald) J(oseph)
1896-1981 . . . . **CLC 32**
See also CA 1-4R; 102; CANR 5; SATA 47;
SATA-Obit 25

Cross, Amanda
See Heilbrun, Carolyn G(old)

Crothers, Rachel 1878(?)-1958 . . . . . **TCLC 19**
See also CA 113; DLB 7

Croves, Hal
See Traven, B.

Crowfield, Christopher
See Stowe, Harriet (Elizabeth) Beecher

Crowley, Aleister..................**TCLC 7**
See also Crowley, Edward Alexander

Crowley, Edward Alexander 1875-1947
See Crowley, Aleister
See also CA 104

Crowley, John 1942-.............**CLC 57**
See also CA 61-64; CANR 43; DLBY 82;
SATA 65

Crud
See Crumb, R(obert)

Crumarums
See Crumb, R(obert)

Crumb, R(obert) 1943-...........**CLC 17**
See also CA 106

Crumbum
See Crumb, R(obert)

Crumski
See Crumb, R(obert)

Crum the Bum
See Crumb, R(obert)

Crunk
See Crumb, R(obert)

Crustt
See Crumb, R(obert)

Cryer, Gretchen (Kiger) 1935-......**CLC 21**
See also CA 114; 123

Csath, Geza 1887-1919..........**TCLC 13**
See also CA 111

Cudlip, David 1933-..............**CLC 34**

Cullen, Countee
1903-1946......**TCLC 4, 37; BLC; DA**
See also BW 1; CA 108; 124;
CDALB 1917-1929; DLB 4, 48, 51;
MTCW; SATA 18

Cum, R.
See Crumb, R(obert)

Cummings, Bruce F(rederick) 1889-1919
See Barbellion, W. N. P.
See also CA 123

Cummings, E(dward) E(stlin)
1894-1962......**CLC 1, 3, 8, 12, 15, 68;**
DA; PC 5; WLC 2
See also CA 73-76; CANR 31;
CDALB 1929-1941; DLB 4, 48; MTCW

Cunha, Euclides (Rodrigues Pimenta) da
1866-1909..................**TCLC 24**
See also CA 123

Cunningham, E. V.
See Fast, Howard (Melvin)

Cunningham, J(ames) V(incent)
1911-1985................**CLC 3, 31**
See also CA 1-4R; 115; CANR 1; DLB 5

Cunningham, Julia (Woolfolk)
1916-......................**CLC 12**
See also CA 9-12R; CANR 4, 19, 36;
JRDA; MAICYA; SAAS 2; SATA 1, 26

Cunningham, Michael 1952-.......**CLC 34**
See also CA 136

Cunninghame Graham, R(obert) B(ontine)
1852-1936..................**TCLC 19**
See also Graham, R(obert) B(ontine)
Cunninghame
See also CA 119; DLB 98

Currie, Ellen 19(?)-..............**CLC 44**

Curtin, Philip
See Lowndes, Marie Adelaide (Belloc)

Curtis, Price
See Ellison, Harlan (Jay)

Cutrate, Joe
See Spiegelman, Art

Czaczkes, Shmuel Yosef
See Agnon, S(hmuel) Y(osef Halevi)

Dabrowska, Maria (Szumska)
1889-1965..................**CLC 15**
See also CA 106

Dabydeen, David 1955-...........**CLC 34**
See also BW 1; CA 125

Dacey, Philip 1939-..............**CLC 51**
See also CA 37-40R; CAAS 17; CANR 14,
32; DLB 105

Dagerman, Stig (Halvard)
1923-1954..................**TCLC 17**
See also CA 117

Dahl, Roald 1916-1990.....**CLC 1, 6, 18, 79**
See also CA 1-4R; 133; CANR 6, 32, 37;
CLR 1, 7; DLB 139; JRDA; MAICYA;
MTCW; SATA 1, 26, 73; SATA-Obit 65

Dahlberg, Edward 1900-1977...**CLC 1, 7, 14**
See also CA 9-12R; 69-72; CANR 31;
DLB 48; MTCW

Dale, Colin.....................**TCLC 18**
See also Lawrence, T(homas) E(dward)

Dale, George E.
See Asimov, Isaac

Daly, Elizabeth 1878-1967........**CLC 52**
See also CA 23-24; 25-28R; CAP 2

Daly, Maureen 1921-.............**CLC 17**
See also AAYA 5; CANR 37; JRDA;
MAICYA; SAAS 1; SATA 2

Damas, Leon-Gontran 1912-1978 ...**CLC 84**
See also BW 1; CA 125; 73-76

Daniel, Samuel 1562(?)-1619.......**LC 24**
See also DLB 62

Daniels, Brett
See Adler, Renata

Dannay, Frederic 1905-1982.......**CLC 11**
See also Queen, Ellery
See also CA 1-4R; 107; CANR 1, 39;
DLB 137; MTCW

D'Annunzio, Gabriele
1863-1938................**TCLC 6, 40**
See also CA 104

d'Antibes, Germain
See Simenon, Georges (Jacques Christian)

Danvers, Dennis 1947-...........**CLC 70**

Danziger, Paula 1944-...........**CLC 21**
See also AAYA 4; CA 112; 115; CANR 37;
CLR 20; JRDA; MAICYA; SATA 30,
36, 63

Dario, Ruben 1867-1916 ....**TCLC 4; HLC**
See also CA 131; HW; MTCW

Darley, George 1795-1846........**NCLC 2**
See also DLB 96

Daryush, Elizabeth 1887-1977....**CLC 6, 19**
See also CA 49-52; CANR 3; DLB 20

Daudet, (Louis Marie) Alphonse
1840-1897..................**NCLC 1**
See also DLB 123

Daumal, Rene 1908-1944........**TCLC 14**
See also CA 114

Davenport, Guy (Mattison, Jr.)
1927-..........**CLC 6, 14, 38; SSC 16**
See also CA 33-36R; CANR 23; DLB 130

Davidson, Avram 1923-
See Queen, Ellery
See also CA 101; CANR 26; DLB 8

Davidson, Donald (Grady)
1893-1968............**CLC 2, 13, 19**
See also CA 5-8R; 25-28R; CANR 4;
DLB 45

Davidson, Hugh
See Hamilton, Edmond

Davidson, John 1857-1909........**TCLC 24**
See also CA 118; DLB 19

Davidson, Sara 1943-..............**CLC 9**
See also CA 81-84; CANR 44

Davie, Donald (Alfred)
1922-................**CLC 5, 8, 10, 31**
See also CA 1-4R; CAAS 3; CANR 1, 44;
DLB 27; MTCW

Davies, Ray(mond Douglas) 1944- ..**CLC 21**
See also CA 116

Davies, Rhys 1903-1978...........**CLC 23**
See also CA 9-12R; 81-84; CANR 4;
DLB 139

Davies, (William) Robertson
1913-.....**CLC 2, 7, 13, 25, 42, 75; DA;**
WLC
See also BEST 89:2; CA 33-36R; CANR 17,
42; DLB 68; MTCW

Davies, W(illiam) H(enry)
1871-1940..................**TCLC 5**
See also CA 104; DLB 19

Davies, Walter C.
See Kornbluth, C(yril) M.

Davis, Angela (Yvonne) 1944-......**CLC 77**
See also BW 2; CA 57-60; CANR 10

Davis, B. Lynch
See Bioy Casares, Adolfo; Borges, Jorge
Luis

Davis, Gordon
See Hunt, E(verette) Howard, (Jr.)

Davis, Harold Lenoir 1896-1960....**CLC 49**
See also CA 89-92; DLB 9

Davis, Rebecca (Blaine) Harding
1831-1910..................**TCLC 6**
See also CA 104; DLB 74

Davis, Richard Harding
1864-1916..................**TCLC 24**
See also CA 114; DLB 12, 23, 78, 79

Davison, Frank Dalby 1893-1970 ...**CLC 15**
See also CA 116

Davison, Lawrence H.
See Lawrence, D(avid) H(erbert Richards)

Davison, Peter (Hubert) 1928- ..... **CLC 28**
See also CA 9-12R; CAAS 4; CANR 3, 43;
DLB 5

Davys, Mary 1674-1732............. **LC 1**
See also DLB 39

Dawson, Fielding 1930-............ **CLC 6**
See also CA 85-88; DLB 130

Dawson, Peter
See Faust, Frederick (Schiller)

Day, Clarence (Shepard, Jr.)
1874-1935 .... **TCLC 25**
See also CA 108; DLB 11

Day, Thomas 1748-1789............. **LC 1**
See also DLB 39; YABC 1

Day Lewis, C(ecil)
1904-1972 .... **CLC 1, 6, 10; PC 11**
See also Blake, Nicholas
See also CA 13-16; 33-36R; CANR 34;
CAP 1; DLB 15, 20; MTCW

Dazai, Osamu .... **TCLC 11**
See also Tsushima, Shuji

de Andrade, Carlos Drummond
See Drummond de Andrade, Carlos

Deane, Norman
See Creasey, John

de Beauvoir, Simone (Lucie Ernestine Marie
Bertrand)
See Beauvoir, Simone (Lucie Ernestine
Marie Bertrand) de

de Brissac, Malcolm
See Dickinson, Peter (Malcolm)

de Chardin, Pierre Teilhard
See Teilhard de Chardin, (Marie Joseph)
Pierre

Dee, John 1527-1608 .... **LC 20**

Deer, Sandra 1940-.............. **CLC 45**

De Ferrari, Gabriella .... **CLC 65**

Defoe, Daniel
1660(?)-1731 .... **LC 1; DA; WLC**
See also CDBLB 1660-1789; DLB 39, 95,
101; JRDA; MAICYA; SATA 22

de Gourmont, Remy
See Gourmont, Remy de

de Hartog, Jan 1914-............. **CLC 19**
See also CA 1-4R; CANR 1

de Hostos, E. M.
See Hostos (y Bonilla), Eugenio Maria de

de Hostos, Eugenio M.
See Hostos (y Bonilla), Eugenio Maria de

Deighton, Len .... **CLC 4, 7, 22, 46**
See also Deighton, Leonard Cyril
See also AAYA 6; BEST 89:2;
CDBLB 1960 to Present; DLB 87

Deighton, Leonard Cyril 1929-
See Deighton, Len
See also CA 9-12R; CANR 19, 33; MTCW

Dekker, Thomas 1572(?)-1632....... **LC 22**
See also CDBLB Before 1660; DLB 62

de la Mare, Walter (John)
1873-1956 .. **TCLC 4, 53; SSC 14; WLC**
See also CDBLB 1914-1945; CLR 23;
DLB 19; SATA 16

Delaney, Franey
See O'Hara, John (Henry)

Delaney, Shelagh 1939-........... **CLC 29**
See also CA 17-20R; CANR 30;
CDBLB 1960 to Present; DLB 13;
MTCW

Delany, Mary (Granville Pendarves)
1700-1788 .... **LC 12**

Delany, Samuel R(ay, Jr.)
1942-............ **CLC 8, 14, 38; BLC**
See also BW 2; CA 81-84; CANR 27, 43;
DLB 8, 33; MTCW

De La Ramee, (Marie) Louise 1839-1908
See Ouida
See also SATA 20

de la Roche, Mazo 1879-1961...... **CLC 14**
See also CA 85-88; CANR 30; DLB 68;
SATA 64

Delbanco, Nicholas (Franklin)
1942-.................... **CLC 6, 13**
See also CA 17-20R; CAAS 2; CANR 29;
DLB 6

del Castillo, Michel 1933-......... **CLC 38**
See also CA 109

Deledda, Grazia (Cosima)
1875(?)-1936 .... **TCLC 23**
See also CA 123

Delibes, Miguel .... **CLC 8, 18**
See also Delibes Setien, Miguel

Delibes Setien, Miguel 1920-
See Delibes, Miguel
See also CA 45-48; CANR 1, 32; HW;
MTCW

DeLillo, Don
1936- ..... **CLC 8, 10, 13, 27, 39, 54, 76**
See also BEST 89:1; CA 81-84; CANR 21;
DLB 6; MTCW

de Lisser, H. G.
See De Lisser, Herbert George
See also DLB 117

De Lisser, Herbert George
1878-1944 .... **TCLC 12**
See also de Lisser, H. G.
See also BW 2; CA 109

Deloria, Vine (Victor), Jr. 1933-.... **CLC 21**
See also CA 53-56; CANR 5, 20; MTCW;
NNAL; SATA 21

Del Vecchio, John M(ichael)
1947-...................... **CLC 29**
See also CA 110; DLBD 9

de Man, Paul (Adolph Michel)
1919-1983 .... **CLC 55**
See also CA 128; 111; DLB 67; MTCW

De Marinis, Rick 1934-........... **CLC 54**
See also CA 57-60; CANR 9, 25

Demby, William 1922-....... **CLC 53; BLC**
See also BW 1; CA 81-84; DLB 33

Demijohn, Thom
See Disch, Thomas M(ichael)

de Montherlant, Henry (Milon)
See Montherlant, Henry (Milon) de

Demosthenes 384B.C.-322B.C. ... **CMLC 13**

de Natale, Francine
See Malzberg, Barry N(athaniel)

Denby, Edwin (Orr) 1903-1983 ..... **CLC 48**
See also CA 138; 110

Denis, Julio
See Cortazar, Julio

Denmark, Harrison
See Zelazny, Roger (Joseph)

Dennis, John 1658-1734........... **LC 11**
See also DLB 101

Dennis, Nigel (Forbes) 1912-1989.... **CLC 8**
See also CA 25-28R; 129; DLB 13, 15;
MTCW

De Palma, Brian (Russell) 1940-.... **CLC 20**
See also CA 109

De Quincey, Thomas 1785-1859 ... **NCLC 4**
See also CDBLB 1789-1832; DLB 110; 144

Deren, Eleanora 1908(?)-1961
See Deren, Maya
See also CA 111

Deren, Maya .... **CLC 16**
See also Deren, Eleanora

Derleth, August (William)
1909-1971 .... **CLC 31**
See also CA 1-4R; 29-32R; CANR 4;
DLB 9; SATA 5

Der Nister 1884-1950........... **TCLC 56**

de Routisie, Albert
See Aragon, Louis

Derrida, Jacques 1930-........... **CLC 24**
See also CA 124; 127

Derry Down Derry
See Lear, Edward

Dersonnes, Jacques
See Simenon, Georges (Jacques Christian)

Desai, Anita 1937-............ **CLC 19, 37**
See also CA 81-84; CANR 33; MTCW;
SATA 63

de Saint-Luc, Jean
See Glassco, John

de Saint Roman, Arnaud
See Aragon, Louis

Descartes, Rene 1596-1650 .... **LC 20**

De Sica, Vittorio 1901(?)-1974 ..... **CLC 20**
See also CA 117

Desnos, Robert 1900-1945........ **TCLC 22**
See also CA 121

Destouches, Louis-Ferdinand
1894-1961 .... **CLC 9, 15**
See also Celine, Louis-Ferdinand
See also CA 85-88; CANR 28; MTCW

Deutsch, Babette 1895-1982 .... **CLC 18**
See also CA 1-4R; 108; CANR 4; DLB 45;
SATA 1; SATA-Obit 33

Devenant, William 1606-1649 ...... **LC 13**

Devkota, Laxmiprasad
1909-1959 .... **TCLC 23**
See also CA 123

De Voto, Bernard (Augustine)
1897-1955 .... **TCLC 29**
See also CA 113; DLB 9

De Vries, Peter
1910-1993 .... **CLC 1, 2, 3, 7, 10, 28, 46**
See also CA 17-20R; 142; CANR 41;
DLB 6; DLBY 82; MTCW

Dexter, Martin
See Faust, Frederick (Schiller)

Dowson, Ernest Christopher
1867-1900 .... **TCLC 4**
See also CA 105; DLB 19, 135

Doyle, A. Conan
See Doyle, Arthur Conan

Doyle, Arthur Conan
1859-1930 .... **TCLC 7; DA; SSC 12;**
WLC
See also AAYA 14; CA 104; 122;
CDBLB 1890-1914; DLB 18, 70; MTCW;
SATA 24

Doyle, Conan
See Doyle, Arthur Conan

Doyle, John
See Graves, Robert (von Ranke)

Doyle, Roddy 1958(?)- .... **CLC 81**
See also AAYA 14; CA 143

Doyle, Sir A. Conan
See Doyle, Arthur Conan

Doyle, Sir Arthur Conan
See Doyle, Arthur Conan

Dr. A
See Asimov, Isaac; Silverstein, Alvin

Drabble, Margaret
1939- .... **CLC 2, 3, 5, 8, 10, 22, 53**
See also CA 13-16R; CANR 18, 35;
CDBLB 1960 to Present; DLB 14;
MTCW; SATA 48

Drapier, M. B.
See Swift, Jonathan

Drayham, James
See Mencken, H(enry) L(ouis)

Drayton, Michael 1563-1631 .... **LC 8**

Dreadstone, Carl
See Campbell, (John) Ramsey

Dreiser, Theodore (Herman Albert)
1871-1945 ...... **TCLC 10, 18, 35; DA;**
WLC
See also CA 106; 132; CDALB 1865-1917;
DLB 9, 12, 102, 137; DLBD 1; MTCW

Drexler, Rosalyn 1926- .... **CLC 2, 6**
See also CA 81-84

Dreyer, Carl Theodor 1889-1968 .... **CLC 16**
See also CA 116

Drieu la Rochelle, Pierre(-Eugene)
1893-1945 .... **TCLC 21**
See also CA 117; DLB 72

Drinkwater, John 1882-1937 ..... **TCLC 57**
See also CA 109; DLB 10, 19

Drop Shot
See Cable, George Washington

Droste-Hulshoff, Annette Freiin von
1797-1848 .... **NCLC 3**
See also DLB 133

Drummond, Walter
See Silverberg, Robert

Drummond, William Henry
1854-1907 .... **TCLC 25**
See also DLB 92

Drummond de Andrade, Carlos
1902-1987 .... **CLC 18**
See also Andrade, Carlos Drummond de
See also CA 132; 123

Drury, Allen (Stuart) 1918- .... **CLC 37**
See also CA 57-60; CANR 18

Dryden, John
1631-1700 ... **LC 3, 21; DA; DC 3; WLC**
See also CDBLB 1660-1789; DLB 80, 101,
131

Duberman, Martin 1930- .... **CLC 8**
See also CA 1-4R; CANR 2

Dubie, Norman (Evans) 1945- ...... **CLC 36**
See also CA 69-72; CANR 12; DLB 120

Du Bois, W(illiam) E(dward) B(urghardt)
1868-1963 ...... **CLC 1, 2, 13, 64; BLC;**
DA; WLC
See also BW 1; CA 85-88; CANR 34;
CDALB 1865-1917; DLB 47, 50, 91;
MTCW; SATA 42

Dubus, Andre 1936- ... **CLC 13, 36; SSC 15**
See also CA 21-24R; CANR 17; DLB 130

Duca Minimo
See D'Annunzio, Gabriele

Ducharme, Rejean 1941- .... **CLC 74**
See also DLB 60

Duclos, Charles Pinot 1704-1772 ..... **LC 1**

Dudek, Louis 1918- .... **CLC 11, 19**
See also CA 45-48; CAAS 14; CANR 1;
DLB 88

Duerrenmatt, Friedrich
1921-1990 ...... **CLC 1, 4, 8, 11, 15, 43**
See also CA 17-20R; CANR 33; DLB 69,
124; MTCW

Duffy, Bruce (?)- .... **CLC 50**

Duffy, Maureen 1933- .... **CLC 37**
See also CA 25-28R; CANR 33; DLB 14;
MTCW

Dugan, Alan 1923- .... **CLC 2, 6**
See also CA 81-84; DLB 5

du Gard, Roger Martin
See Martin du Gard, Roger

Duhamel, Georges 1884-1966 .... **CLC 8**
See also CA 81-84; 25-28R; CANR 35;
DLB 65; MTCW

Dujardin, Edouard (Emile Louis)
1861-1949 .... **TCLC 13**
See also CA 109; DLB 123

Dumas, Alexandre (Davy de la Pailleterie)
1802-1870 .... **NCLC 11; DA; WLC**
See also DLB 119; SATA 18

Dumas, Alexandre
1824-1895 .... **NCLC 9; DC 1**

Dumas, Claudine
See Malzberg, Barry N(athaniel)

Dumas, Henry L. 1934-1968 ..... **CLC 6, 62**
See also BW 1; CA 85-88; DLB 41

du Maurier, Daphne
1907-1989 ...... **CLC 6, 11, 59; SSC 18**
See also CA 5-8R; 128; CANR 6; MTCW;
SATA 27; SATA-Obit 60

Dunbar, Paul Laurence
1872-1906 ...... **TCLC 2, 12; BLC; DA;**
PC 5; SSC 8; WLC
See also BW 1; CA 104; 124;
CDALB 1865-1917; DLB 50, 54, 78;
SATA 34

Dunbar, William 1460(?)-1530(?) .... **LC 20**
See also DLB 132, 146

Duncan, Lois 1934- .... **CLC 26**
See also AAYA 4; CA 1-4R; CANR 2, 23,
36; CLR 29; JRDA; MAICYA; SAAS 2;
SATA 1, 36, 75

Duncan, Robert (Edward)
1919-1988 .... **CLC 1, 2, 4, 7, 15, 41, 55;**
PC 2
See also CA 9-12R; 124; CANR 28; DLB 5,
16; MTCW

Dunlap, William 1766-1839 .... **NCLC 2**
See also DLB 30, 37, 59

Dunn, Douglas (Eaglesham)
1942- .... **CLC 6, 40**
See also CA 45-48; CANR 2, 33; DLB 40;
MTCW

Dunn, Katherine (Karen) 1945- ..... **CLC 71**
See also CA 33-36R

Dunn, Stephen 1939- .... **CLC 36**
See also CA 33-36R; CANR 12; DLB 105

Dunne, Finley Peter 1867-1936 .... **TCLC 28**
See also CA 108; DLB 11, 23

Dunne, John Gregory 1932- .... **CLC 28**
See also CA 25-28R; CANR 14; DLBY 80

Dunsany, Edward John Moreton Drax
Plunkett 1878-1957
See Dunsany, Lord
See also CA 104; DLB 10

Dunsany, Lord .... **TCLC 2**
See also Dunsany, Edward John Moreton
Drax Plunkett
See also DLB 77

du Perry, Jean
See Simenon, Georges (Jacques Christian)

Durang, Christopher (Ferdinand)
1949- .... **CLC 27, 38**
See also CA 105

Duras, Marguerite
1914- ...... **CLC 3, 6, 11, 20, 34, 40, 68**
See also CA 25-28R; DLB 83; MTCW

Durban, (Rosa) Pam 1947- .... **CLC 39**
See also CA 123

Durcan, Paul 1944- .... **CLC 43, 70**
See also CA 134

Durkheim, Emile 1858-1917 ...... **TCLC 55**

Durrell, Lawrence (George)
1912-1990 .... **CLC 1, 4, 6, 8, 13, 27, 41**
See also CA 9-12R; 132; CANR 40;
CDBLB 1945-1960; DLB 15, 27;
DLBY 90; MTCW

Durrenmatt, Friedrich
See Duerrenmatt, Friedrich

Dutt, Toru 1856-1877 .... **NCLC 29**

Dwight, Timothy 1752-1817 ...... **NCLC 13**
See also DLB 37

Dworkin, Andrea 1946- .... **CLC 43**
See also CA 77-80; CANR 16, 39; MTCW

Dwyer, Deanna
See Koontz, Dean R(ay)

Dwyer, K. R.
See Koontz, Dean R(ay)

Dylan, Bob 1941- ...... **CLC 3, 4, 6, 12, 77**
See also CA 41-44R; DLB 16

Elytis, Odysseus 1911- .... **CLC 15, 49**
See also CA 102; MTCW

Emecheta, (Florence Onye) Buchi
1944- .... **CLC 14, 48; BLC**
See also BW 2; CA 81-84; CANR 27;
DLB 117; MTCW; SATA 66

Emerson, Ralph Waldo
1803-1882 ...... **NCLC 1, 38; DA; WLC**
See also CDALB 1640-1865; DLB 1, 59, 73

Eminescu, Mihail 1850-1889 ..... **NCLC 33**

Empson, William
1906-1984 .... **CLC 3, 8, 19, 33, 34**
See also CA 17-20R; 112; CANR 31;
DLB 20; MTCW

Enchi Fumiko (Ueda) 1905-1986.... **CLC 31**
See also CA 129; 121

Ende, Michael (Andreas Helmuth)
1929- .... **CLC 31**
See also CA 118; 124; CANR 36; CLR 14;
DLB 75; MAICYA; SATA 42, 61

Endo, Shusaku 1923- ..... **CLC 7, 14, 19, 54**
See also CA 29-32R; CANR 21; MTCW

Engel, Marian 1933-1985......... **CLC 36**
See also CA 25-28R; CANR 12; DLB 53

Engelhardt, Frederick
See Hubbard, L(afayette) Ron(ald)

Enright, D(ennis) J(oseph)
1920- .... **CLC 4, 8, 31**
See also CA 1-4R; CANR 1, 42; DLB 27;
SATA 25

Enzensberger, Hans Magnus
1929- .... **CLC 43**
See also CA 116; 119

Ephron, Nora 1941- .... **CLC 17, 31**
See also AITN 2; CA 65-68; CANR 12, 39

Epsilon
See Betjeman, John

Epstein, Daniel Mark 1948- .... **CLC 7**
See also CA 49-52; CANR 2

Epstein, Jacob 1956- .... **CLC 19**
See also CA 114

Epstein, Joseph 1937-............ **CLC 39**
See also CA 112; 119

Epstein, Leslie 1938- .... **CLC 27**
See also CA 73-76; CAAS 12; CANR 23

Equiano, Olaudah
1745(?)-1797 .... **LC 16; BLC**
See also DLB 37, 50

Erasmus, Desiderius 1469(?)-1536.... **LC 16**

Erdman, Paul E(mil) 1932- .... **CLC 25**
See also AITN 1; CA 61-64; CANR 13, 43

Erdrich, Louise 1954-.......... **CLC 39, 54**
See also AAYA 10; BEST 89:1; CA 114;
CANR 41; MTCW; NNAL

Erenburg, Ilya (Grigoryevich)
See Ehrenburg, Ilya (Grigoryevich)

Erickson, Stephen Michael 1950-
See Erickson, Steve
See also CA 129

Erickson, Steve .... **CLC 64**
See also Erickson, Stephen Michael

Ericson, Walter
See Fast, Howard (Melvin)

Eriksson, Buntel
See Bergman, (Ernst) Ingmar

Eschenbach, Wolfram von
See Wolfram von Eschenbach

Eseki, Bruno
See Mphahlele, Ezekiel

Esenin, Sergei (Alexandrovich)
1895-1925 .... **TCLC 4**
See also CA 104

Eshleman, Clayton 1935-........... **CLC 7**
See also CA 33-36R; CAAS 6; DLB 5

Espriella, Don Manuel Alvarez
See Southey, Robert

Espriu, Salvador 1913-1985........ **CLC 9**
See also CA 115; DLB 134

Espronceda, Jose de 1808-1842... **NCLC 39**

Esse, James
See Stephens, James

Esterbrook, Tom
See Hubbard, L(afayette) Ron(ald)

Estleman, Loren D. 1952- .... **CLC 48**
See also CA 85-88; CANR 27; MTCW

Eugenides, Jeffrey 1960(?)-........ **CLC 81**
See also CA 144

Euripides c. 485B.C.-406B.C. .... **DC 4**
See also DA

Evan, Evin
See Faust, Frederick (Schiller)

Evans, Evan
See Faust, Frederick (Schiller)

Evans, Marian
See Eliot, George

Evans, Mary Ann
See Eliot, George

Evarts, Esther
See Benson, Sally

Everett, Percival L. 1956- .... **CLC 57**
See also BW 2; CA 129

Everson, R(onald) G(ilmour)
1903- .... **CLC 27**
See also CA 17-20R; DLB 88

Everson, William (Oliver)
1912-1994 .... **CLC 1, 5, 14**
See also CA 9-12R; 145; CANR 20; DLB 5,
16; MTCW

Evtushenko, Evgenii Aleksandrovich
See Yevtushenko, Yevgeny (Alexandrovich)

Ewart, Gavin (Buchanan)
1916- .... **CLC 13, 46**
See also CA 89-92; CANR 17, 46, 46;
DLB 40; MTCW

Ewers, Hanns Heinz 1871-1943 ... **TCLC 12**
See also CA 109

Ewing, Frederick R.
See Sturgeon, Theodore (Hamilton)

Exley, Frederick (Earl)
1929-1992 .... **CLC 6, 11**
See also AITN 2; CA 81-84; 138; DLB 143;
DLBY 81

Eynhardt, Guillermo
See Quiroga, Horacio (Sylvestre)

Ezekiel, Nissim 1924-............ **CLC 61**
See also CA 61-64

Ezekiel, Tish O'Dowd 1943-....... **CLC 34**
See also CA 129

Fadeyev, A.
See Bulgya, Alexander Alexandrovich

Fadeyev, Alexander.............. **TCLC 53**
See also Bulgya, Alexander Alexandrovich

Fagen, Donald 1948-............. **CLC 26**

Fainzilberg, Ilya Arnoldovich 1897-1937
See Ilf, Ilya
See also CA 120

Fair, Ronald L. 1932-............. **CLC 18**
See also BW 1; CA 69-72; CANR 25;
DLB 33

Fairbairns, Zoe (Ann) 1948- .... **CLC 32**
See also CA 103; CANR 21

Falco, Gian
See Papini, Giovanni

Falconer, James
See Kirkup, James

Falconer, Kenneth
See Kornbluth, C(yril) M.

Falkland, Samuel
See Heijermans, Herman

Fallaci, Oriana 1930-............. **CLC 11**
See also CA 77-80; CANR 15; MTCW

Faludy, George 1913-............. **CLC 42**
See also CA 21-24R

Faludy, Gyoergy
See Faludy, George

Fanon, Frantz 1925-1961..... **CLC 74; BLC**
See also BW 1; CA 116; 89-92

Fanshawe, Ann 1625-1680.......... **LC 11**

Fante, John (Thomas) 1911-1983 ... **CLC 60**
See also CA 69-72; 109; CANR 23;
DLB 130; DLBY 83

Farah, Nuruddin 1945-....... **CLC 53; BLC**
See also BW 2; CA 106; DLB 125

Fargue, Leon-Paul 1876(?)-1947 ... **TCLC 11**
See also CA 109

Farigoule, Louis
See Romains, Jules

Farina, Richard 1936(?)-1966 .... **CLC 9**
See also CA 81-84; 25-28R

Farley, Walter (Lorimer)
1915-1989 .... **CLC 17**
See also CA 17-20R; CANR 8, 29; DLB 22;
JRDA; MAICYA; SATA 2, 43

Farmer, Philip Jose 1918-....... **CLC 1, 19**
See also CA 1-4R; CANR 4, 35; DLB 8;
MTCW

Farquhar, George 1677-1707........ **LC 21**
See also DLB 84

Farrell, J(ames) G(ordon)
1935-1979 .... **CLC 6**
See also CA 73-76; 89-92; CANR 36;
DLB 14; MTCW

Farrell, James T(homas)
1904-1979 .... **CLC 1, 4, 8, 11, 66**
See also CA 5-8R; 89-92; CANR 9; DLB 4,
9, 86; DLBD 2; MTCW

Farren, Richard J.
See Betjeman, John

Folke, Will
See Bloch, Robert (Albert)

Follett, Ken(neth Martin) 1949- .... **CLC 18**
See also AAYA 6; BEST 89:4; CA 81-84;
CANR 13, 33; DLB 87; DLBY 81;
MTCW

Fontane, Theodor 1819-1898..... **NCLC 26**
See also DLB 129

Foote, Horton 1916-.............. **CLC 51**
See also CA 73-76; CANR 34; DLB 26

Foote, Shelby 1916- .... **CLC 75**
See also CA 5-8R; CANR 3, 45; DLB 2, 17

Forbes, Esther 1891-1967.......... **CLC 12**
See also CA 13-14; 25-28R; CAP 1;
CLR 27; DLB 22; JRDA; MAICYA;
SATA 2

Forche, Carolyn (Louise)
1950- .... **CLC 25, 83, 86; PC 10**
See also CA 109; 117; DLB 5

Ford, Elbur
See Hibbert, Eleanor Alice Burford

Ford, Ford Madox
1873-1939 .... **TCLC 1, 15, 39, 57**
See also CA 104; 132; CDBLB 1914-1945;
DLB 34, 98; MTCW

Ford, John 1895-1973............. **CLC 16**
See also CA 45-48

Ford, Richard 1944-.............. **CLC 46**
See also CA 69-72; CANR 11, 47

Ford, Webster
See Masters, Edgar Lee

Foreman, Richard 1937-.......... **CLC 50**
See also CA 65-68; CANR 32

Forester, C(ecil) S(cott)
1899-1966 .... **CLC 35**
See also CA 73-76; 25-28R; SATA 13

Forez
See Mauriac, Francois (Charles)

Forman, James Douglas 1932-...... **CLC 21**
See also CA 9-12R; CANR 4, 19, 42;
JRDA; MAICYA; SATA 8, 70

Fornes, Maria Irene 1930-...... **CLC 39, 61**
See also CA 25-28R; CANR 28; DLB 7;
HW; MTCW

Forrest, Leon 1937- .... **CLC 4**
See also BW 2; CA 89-92; CAAS 7;
CANR 25; DLB 33

Forster, E(dward) M(organ)
1879-1970 ..... **CLC 1, 2, 3, 4, 9, 10, 13,
15, 22, 45, 77; DA; WLC**
See also AAYA 2; CA 13-14; 25-28R;
CANR 45; CAP 1; CDBLB 1914-1945;
DLB 34, 98; DLBD 10; MTCW;
SATA 57

Forster, John 1812-1876 .... **NCLC 11**
See also DLB 144

Forsyth, Frederick 1938-...... **CLC 2, 5, 36**
See also BEST 89:4; CA 85-88; CANR 38;
DLB 87; MTCW

Forten, Charlotte L. .... **TCLC 16; BLC**
See also Grimke, Charlotte L(ottie) Forten
See also DLB 50

Foscolo, Ugo 1778-1827......... **NCLC 8**

Fosse, Bob .... **CLC 20**
See also Fosse, Robert Louis

Fosse, Robert Louis 1927-1987
See Fosse, Bob
See also CA 110; 123

Foster, Stephen Collins
1826-1864 .... **NCLC 26**

Foucault, Michel
1926-1984 .... **CLC 31, 34, 69**
See also CA 105; 113; CANR 34; MTCW

Fouque, Friedrich (Heinrich Karl) de la Motte
1777-1843 .... **NCLC 2**
See also DLB 90

Fournier, Henri Alban 1886-1914
See Alain-Fournier
See also CA 104

Fournier, Pierre 1916- .... **CLC 11**
See also Gascar, Pierre
See also CA 89-92; CANR 16, 40

Fowles, John
1926- .... **CLC 1, 2, 3, 4, 6, 9, 10, 15, 33**
See also CA 5-8R; CANR 25; CDBLB 1960
to Present; DLB 14, 139; MTCW;
SATA 22

Fox, Paula 1923-................. **CLC 2, 8**
See also AAYA 3; CA 73-76; CANR 20,
36; CLR 1; DLB 52; JRDA; MAICYA;
MTCW; SATA 17, 60

Fox, William Price (Jr.) 1926- ..... **CLC 22**
See also CA 17-20R; CAAS 19; CANR 11;
DLB 2; DLBY 81

Foxe, John 1516(?)-1587 .... **LC 14**

Frame, Janet .... **CLC 2, 3, 6, 22, 66**
See also Clutha, Janet Paterson Frame

France, Anatole................... **TCLC 9**
See also Thibault, Jacques Anatole Francois
See also DLB 123

Francis, Claude 19(?)- .... **CLC 50**

Francis, Dick 1920- .... **CLC 2, 22, 42**
See also AAYA 5; BEST 89:3; CA 5-8R;
CANR 9, 42; CDBLB 1960 to Present;
DLB 87; MTCW

Francis, Robert (Churchill)
1901-1987 .... **CLC 15**
See also CA 1-4R; 123; CANR 1

Frank, Anne(lies Marie)
1929-1945 .... **TCLC 17; DA; WLC**
See also AAYA 12; CA 113; 133; MTCW;
SATA 42

Frank, Elizabeth 1945-............ **CLC 39**
See also CA 121; 126

Franklin, Benjamin
See Hasek, Jaroslav (Matej Frantisek)

Franklin, Benjamin 1706-1790... **LC 25; DA**
See also CDALB 1640-1865; DLB 24, 43,
73

Franklin, (Stella Maraia Sarah) Miles
1879-1954 .... **TCLC 7**
See also CA 104

Fraser, (Lady) Antonia (Pakenham)
1932- .... **CLC 32**
See also CA 85-88; CANR 44; MTCW;
SATA 32

Fraser, George MacDonald 1925-.... **CLC 7**
See also CA 45-48; CANR 2

Fraser, Sylvia 1935-.............. **CLC 64**
See also CA 45-48; CANR 1, 16

Frayn, Michael 1933-...... **CLC 3, 7, 31, 47**
See also CA 5-8R; CANR 30; DLB 13, 14;
MTCW

Fraze, Candida (Merrill) 1945-..... **CLC 50**
See also CA 126

Frazer, J(ames) G(eorge)
1854-1941 .... **TCLC 32**
See also CA 118

Frazer, Robert Caine
See Creasey, John

Frazer, Sir James George
See Frazer, J(ames) G(eorge)

Frazier, Ian 1951-................ **CLC 46**
See also CA 130

Frederic, Harold 1856-1898...... **NCLC 10**
See also DLB 12, 23

Frederick, John
See Faust, Frederick (Schiller)

Frederick the Great 1712-1786 ...... **LC 14**

Fredro, Aleksander 1793-1876..... **NCLC 8**

Freeling, Nicolas 1927- .... **CLC 38**
See also CA 49-52; CAAS 12; CANR 1, 17;
DLB 87

Freeman, Douglas Southall
1886-1953 .... **TCLC 11**
See also CA 109; DLB 17

Freeman, Judith 1946-............ **CLC 55**

Freeman, Mary Eleanor Wilkins
1852-1930 .... **TCLC 9; SSC 1**
See also CA 106; DLB 12, 78

Freeman, R(ichard) Austin
1862-1943 .... **TCLC 21**
See also CA 113; DLB 70

French, Albert 1944(?)- .... **CLC 86**

French, Marilyn 1929-...... **CLC 10, 18, 60**
See also CA 69-72; CANR 3, 31; MTCW

French, Paul
See Asimov, Isaac

Freneau, Philip Morin 1752-1832.. **NCLC 1**
See also DLB 37, 43

Freud, Sigmund 1856-1939 .... **TCLC 52**
See also CA 115; 133; MTCW

Friedan, Betty (Naomi) 1921-...... **CLC 74**
See also CA 65-68; CANR 18, 45; MTCW

Friedman, B(ernard) H(arper)
1926- .... **CLC 7**
See also CA 1-4R; CANR 3

Friedman, Bruce Jay 1930-.... **CLC 3, 5, 56**
See also CA 9-12R; CANR 25; DLB 2, 28

Friel, Brian 1929-.......... **CLC 5, 42, 59**
See also CA 21-24R; CANR 33; DLB 13;
MTCW

Friis-Baastad, Babbis Ellinor
1921-1970 .... **CLC 12**
See also CA 17-20R; 134; SATA 7

Frisch, Max (Rudolf)
1911-1991 ..... **CLC 3, 9, 14, 18, 32, 44**
See also CA 85-88; 134; CANR 32;
DLB 69, 124; MTCW

Fromentin, Eugene (Samuel Auguste)
1820-1876 .... **NCLC 10**
See also DLB 123

Frost, Frederick
See Faust, Frederick (Schiller)

Frost, Robert (Lee)
1874-1963 . . . . CLC 1, 3, 4, 9, 10, 13, 15,
26, 34, 44; DA; PC 1; WLC
See also CA 89-92; CANR 33;
CDALB 1917-1929; DLB 54; DLBD 7;
MTCW; SATA 14

Froude, James Anthony
1818-1894 . . . . NCLC 43
See also DLB 18, 57, 144

Froy, Herald
See Waterhouse, Keith (Spencer)

Fry, Christopher 1907- . . . . CLC 2, 10, 14
See also CA 17-20R; CANR 9, 30; DLB 13;
MTCW; SATA 66

Frye, (Herman) Northrop
1912-1991 . . . . CLC 24, 70
See also CA 5-8R; 133; CANR 8, 37;
DLB 67, 68; MTCW

Fuchs, Daniel 1909-1993 . . . . CLC 8, 22
See also CA 81-84; 142; CAAS 5;
CANR 40; DLB 9, 26, 28; DLBY 93

Fuchs, Daniel 1934- . . . . CLC 34
See also CA 37-40R; CANR 14

Fuentes, Carlos
1928- . . . . . . CLC 3, 8, 10, 13, 22, 41, 60;
DA; HLC; WLC
See also AAYA 4; AITN 2; CA 69-72;
CANR 10, 32; DLB 113; HW; MTCW

Fuentes, Gregorio Lopez y
See Lopez y Fuentes, Gregorio

Fugard, (Harold) Athol
1932- . . . . CLC 5, 9, 14, 25, 40, 80; DC 3
See also CA 85-88; CANR 32; MTCW

Fugard, Sheila 1932- . . . . CLC 48
See also CA 125

Fuller, Charles (H., Jr.)
1939- . . . . CLC 25; BLC; DC 1
See also BW 2; CA 108; 112; DLB 38;
MTCW

Fuller, John (Leopold) 1937- . . . . CLC 62
See also CA 21-24R; CANR 9, 44; DLB 40

Fuller, Margaret . . . . NCLC 5
See also Ossoli, Sarah Margaret (Fuller
marchesa d')

Fuller, Roy (Broadbent)
1912-1991 . . . . CLC 4, 28
See also CA 5-8R; 135; CAAS 10; DLB 15,
20

Fulton, Alice 1952- . . . . CLC 52
See also CA 116

Furphy, Joseph 1843-1912 . . . . TCLC 25

Fussell, Paul 1924- . . . . CLC 74
See also BEST 90:1; CA 17-20R; CANR 8,
21, 35; MTCW

Futabatei, Shimei 1864-1909 . . . . . TCLC 44

Futrelle, Jacques 1875-1912 . . . . . . TCLC 19
See also CA 113

Gaboriau, Emile 1835-1873 . . . . . . NCLC 14

Gadda, Carlo Emilio 1893-1973 . . . . CLC 11
See also CA 89-92

Gaddis, William
1922- . . . . . CLC 1, 3, 6, 8, 10, 19, 43, 86
See also CA 17-20R; CANR 21; DLB 2;
MTCW

Gaines, Ernest J(ames)
1933- . . . . CLC 3, 11, 18, 86; BLC
See also AITN 1; BW 2; CA 9-12R;
CANR 6, 24, 42; CDALB 1968-1988;
DLB 2, 33; DLBY 80; MTCW

Gaitskill, Mary 1954- . . . . CLC 69
See also CA 128

Galdos, Benito Perez
See Perez Galdos, Benito

Gale, Zona 1874-1938 . . . . TCLC 7
See also CA 105; DLB 9, 78

Galeano, Eduardo (Hughes) 1940- . . . CLC 72
See also CA 29-32R; CANR 13, 32; HW

Galiano, Juan Valera y Alcala
See Valera y Alcala-Galiano, Juan

Gallagher, Tess 1943- . . . . CLC 18, 63; PC 9
See also CA 106; DLB 120

Gallant, Mavis
1922- . . . . CLC 7, 18, 38; SSC 5
See also CA 69-72; CANR 29; DLB 53;
MTCW

Gallant, Roy A(rthur) 1924- . . . . CLC 17
See also CA 5-8R; CANR 4, 29; CLR 30;
MAICYA; SATA 4, 68

Gallico, Paul (William) 1897-1976 . . . CLC 2
See also AITN 1; CA 5-8R; 69-72;
CANR 23; DLB 9; MAICYA; SATA 13

Gallup, Ralph
See Whitemore, Hugh (John)

Galsworthy, John
1867-1933 . . . . TCLC 1, 45; DA; WLC 2
See also CA 104; 141; CDBLB 1890-1914;
DLB 10, 34, 98

Galt, John 1779-1839 . . . . NCLC 1
See also DLB 99, 116

Galvin, James 1951- . . . . CLC 38
See also CA 108; CANR 26

Gamboa, Federico 1864-1939 . . . . . . TCLC 36

Gann, Ernest Kellogg 1910-1991 . . . . CLC 23
See also AITN 1; CA 1-4R; 136; CANR 1

Garcia, Cristina 1958- . . . . CLC 76
See also CA 141

Garcia Lorca, Federico
1898-1936 . . . . TCLC 1, 7, 49; DA;
DC 2; HLC; PC 3; WLC
See also CA 104; 131; DLB 108; HW;
MTCW

Garcia Marquez, Gabriel (Jose)
1928- . . . . CLC 2, 3, 8, 10, 15, 27, 47, 55,
68; DA; HLC; SSC 8; WLC
See also AAYA 3; BEST 89:1, 90:4;
CA 33-36R; CANR 10, 28; DLB 113;
HW; MTCW

Gard, Janice
See Latham, Jean Lee

Gard, Roger Martin du
See Martin du Gard, Roger

Gardam, Jane 1928- . . . . CLC 43
See also CA 49-52; CANR 2, 18, 33;
CLR 12; DLB 14; MAICYA; MTCW;
SAAS 9; SATA 28, 39, 76

Gardner, Herb . . . . CLC 44

Gardner, John (Champlin), Jr.
1933-1982 . . . . . CLC 2, 3, 5, 7, 8, 10, 18,
28, 34; SSC 7
See also AITN 1; CA 65-68; 107;
CANR 33; DLB 2; DLBY 82; MTCW;
SATA 40; SATA-Obit 31

Gardner, John (Edmund) 1926- . . . . . CLC 30
See also CA 103; CANR 15; MTCW

Gardner, Noel
See Kuttner, Henry

Gardons, S. S.
See Snodgrass, W(illiam) D(e Witt)

Garfield, Leon 1921- . . . . CLC 12
See also AAYA 8; CA 17-20R; CANR 38,
41; CLR 21; JRDA; MAICYA; SATA 1,
32, 76

Garland, (Hannibal) Hamlin
1860-1940 . . . . TCLC 3; SSC 18
See also CA 104; DLB 12, 71, 78

Garneau, (Hector de) Saint-Denys
1912-1943 . . . . TCLC 13
See also CA 111; DLB 88

Garner, Alan 1934- . . . . CLC 17
See also CA 73-76; CANR 15; CLR 20;
MAICYA; MTCW; SATA 18, 69

Garner, Hugh 1913-1979 . . . . CLC 13
See also CA 69-72; CANR 31; DLB 68

Garnett, David 1892-1981 . . . . CLC 3
See also CA 5-8R; 103; CANR 17; DLB 34

Garos, Stephanie
See Katz, Steve

Garrett, George (Palmer)
1929- . . . . CLC 3, 11, 51
See also CA 1-4R; CAAS 5; CANR 1, 42;
DLB 2, 5, 130; DLBY 83

Garrick, David 1717-1779 . . . . LC 15
See also DLB 84

Garrigue, Jean 1914-1972 . . . . CLC 2, 8
See also CA 5-8R; 37-40R; CANR 20

Garrison, Frederick
See Sinclair, Upton (Beall)

Garth, Will
See Hamilton, Edmond; Kuttner, Henry

Garvey, Marcus (Moziah, Jr.)
1887-1940 . . . . TCLC 41; BLC
See also BW 1; CA 120; 124

Gary, Romain . . . . CLC 25
See also Kacew, Romain
See also DLB 83

Gascar, Pierre . . . . CLC 11
See also Fournier, Pierre

Gascoyne, David (Emery) 1916- . . . . CLC 45
See also CA 65-68; CANR 10, 28; DLB 20;
MTCW

Gaskell, Elizabeth Cleghorn
1810-1865 . . . . NCLC 5
See also CDBLB 1832-1890; DLB 21, 144

Gass, William H(oward)
1924- . . . CLC 1, 2, 8, 11, 15, 39; SSC 12
See also CA 17-20R; CANR 30; DLB 2;
MTCW

Gasset, Jose Ortega y
See Ortega y Gasset, Jose

Gates, Henry Louis, Jr. 1950-...... **CLC 65**
See also BW 2; CA 109; CANR 25; DLB 67

Gautier, Theophile 1811-1872 ..... **NCLC 1**
See also DLB 119

Gawsworth, John
See Bates, H(erbert) E(rnest)

Gaye, Marvin (Penze) 1939-1984 ... **CLC 26**
See also CA 112

Gebler, Carlo (Ernest) 1954-....... **CLC 39**
See also CA 119; 133

Gee, Maggie (Mary) 1948-......... **CLC 57**
See also CA 130

Gee, Maurice (Gough) 1931-...... **CLC 29**
See also CA 97-100; SATA 46

Gelbart, Larry (Simon) 1923-... **CLC 21, 61**
See also CA 73-76; CANR 45

Gelber, Jack 1932-........ **CLC 1, 6, 14, 79**
See also CA 1-4R; CANR 2; DLB 7

Gellhorn, Martha (Ellis) 1908-.. **CLC 14, 60**
See also CA 77-80; CANR 44; DLBY 82

Genet, Jean
1910-1986 ... **CLC 1, 2, 5, 10, 14, 44, 46**
See also CA 13-16R; CANR 18; DLB 72;
DLBY 86; MTCW

Gent, Peter 1942-................ **CLC 29**
See also AITN 1; CA 89-92; DLBY 82

Gentlewoman in New England, A
See Bradstreet, Anne

Gentlewoman in Those Parts, A
See Bradstreet, Anne

George, Jean Craighead 1919-...... **CLC 35**
See also AAYA 8; CA 5-8R; CANR 25;
CLR 1; DLB 52; JRDA; MAICYA;
SATA 2, 68

George, Stefan (Anton)
1868-1933 .... **TCLC 2, 14**
See also CA 104

Georges, Georges Martin
See Simenon, Georges (Jacques Christian)

Gerhardi, William Alexander
See Gerhardie, William Alexander

Gerhardie, William Alexander
1895-1977 .... **CLC 5**
See also CA 25-28R; 73-76; CANR 18;
DLB 36

Gerstler, Amy 1956-.............. **CLC 70**

Gertler, T. .... **CLC 34**
See also CA 116; 121

Ghalib 1797-1869 .... **NCLC 39**

Ghelderode, Michel de
1898-1962 .... **CLC 6, 11**
See also CA 85-88; CANR 40

Ghiselin, Brewster 1903-.......... **CLC 23**
See also CA 13-16R; CAAS 10; CANR 13

Ghose, Zulfikar 1935-............. **CLC 42**
See also CA 65-68

Ghosh, Amitav 1956-.............. **CLC 44**

Giacosa, Giuseppe 1847-1906 ...... **TCLC 7**
See also CA 104

Gibb, Lee
See Waterhouse, Keith (Spencer)

Gibbon, Lewis Grassic .... **TCLC 4**
See also Mitchell, James Leslie

Gibbons, Kaye 1960- .... **CLC 50**

Gibran, Kahlil
1883-1931 .... **TCLC 1, 9; PC 9**
See also CA 104

Gibson, William 1914-........ **CLC 23; DA**
See also CA 9-12R; CANR 9, 42; DLB 7;
SATA 66

Gibson, William (Ford) 1948-... **CLC 39, 63**
See also AAYA 12; CA 126; 133

Gide, Andre (Paul Guillaume)
1869-1951 .... **TCLC 5, 12, 36; DA;**
SSC 13; WLC
See also CA 104; 124; DLB 65; MTCW

Gifford, Barry (Colby) 1946-....... **CLC 34**
See also CA 65-68; CANR 9, 30, 40

Gilbert, W(illiam) S(chwenck)
1836-1911 .... **TCLC 3**
See also CA 104; SATA 36

Gilbreth, Frank B., Jr. 1911-....... **CLC 17**
See also CA 9-12R; SATA 2

Gilchrist, Ellen 1935-... **CLC 34, 48; SSC 14**
See also CA 113; 116; CANR 41; DLB 130;
MTCW

Giles, Molly 1942- .... **CLC 39**
See also CA 126

Gill, Patrick
See Creasey, John

Gilliam, Terry (Vance) 1940-....... **CLC 21**
See also Monty Python
See also CA 108; 113; CANR 35

Gillian, Jerry
See Gilliam, Terry (Vance)

Gilliatt, Penelope (Ann Douglass)
1932-1993 .... **CLC 2, 10, 13, 53**
See also AITN 2; CA 13-16R; 141; DLB 14

Gilman, Charlotte (Anna) Perkins (Stetson)
1860-1935 .... **TCLC 9, 37; SSC 13**
See also CA 106

Gilmour, David 1949-............. **CLC 35**
See also CA 138

Gilpin, William 1724-1804....... **NCLC 30**

Gilray, J. D.
See Mencken, H(enry) L(ouis)

Gilroy, Frank D(aniel) 1925-........ **CLC 2**
See also CA 81-84; CANR 32; DLB 7

Ginsberg, Allen
1926- ...... **CLC 1, 2, 3, 4, 6, 13, 36, 69;**
DA; PC 4; WLC 3
See also AITN 1; CA 1-4R; CANR 2, 41;
CDALB 1941-1968; DLB 5, 16; MTCW

Ginzburg, Natalia
1916-1991 .... **CLC 5, 11, 54, 70**
See also CA 85-88; 135; CANR 33; MTCW

Giono, Jean 1895-1970......... **CLC 4, 11**
See also CA 45-48; 29-32R; CANR 2, 35;
DLB 72; MTCW

Giovanni, Nikki
1943- ...... **CLC 2, 4, 19, 64; BLC; DA**
See also AITN 1; BW 2; CA 29-32R;
CAAS 6; CANR 18, 41; CLR 6; DLB 5,
41; MAICYA; MTCW; SATA 24

Giovene, Andrea 1904-............ **CLC 7**
See also CA 85-88

Gippius, Zinaida (Nikolayevna) 1869-1945
See Hippius, Zinaida
See also CA 106

Giraudoux, (Hippolyte) Jean
1882-1944 .... **TCLC 2, 7**
See also CA 104; DLB 65

Gironella, Jose Maria 1917-....... **CLC 11**
See also CA 101

Gissing, George (Robert)
1857-1903 .... **TCLC 3, 24, 47**
See also CA 105; DLB 18, 135

Giurlani, Aldo
See Palazzeschi, Aldo

Gladkov, Fyodor (Vasilyevich)
1883-1958 .... **TCLC 27**

Glanville, Brian (Lester) 1931-...... **CLC 6**
See also CA 5-8R; CAAS 9; CANR 3;
DLB 15, 139; SATA 42

Glasgow, Ellen (Anderson Gholson)
1873(?)-1945 .... **TCLC 2, 7**
See also CA 104; DLB 9, 12

Glaspell, Susan (Keating)
1882(?)-1948 .... **TCLC 55**
See also CA 110; DLB 7, 9, 78; YABC 2

Glassco, John 1909-1981 .... **CLC 9**
See also CA 13-16R; 102; CANR 15;
DLB 68

Glasscock, Amnesia
See Steinbeck, John (Ernst)

Glasser, Ronald J. 1940(?)-........ **CLC 37**

Glassman, Joyce
See Johnson, Joyce

Glendinning, Victoria 1937-........ **CLC 50**
See also CA 120; 127

Glissant, Edouard 1928-........ **CLC 10, 68**

Gloag, Julian 1930- .... **CLC 40**
See also AITN 1; CA 65-68; CANR 10

Glowacki, Aleksander
See Prus, Boleslaw

Glueck, Louise (Elisabeth)
1943- .... **CLC 7, 22, 44, 81**
See also CA 33-36R; CANR 40; DLB 5

Gobineau, Joseph Arthur (Comte) de
1816-1882 .... **NCLC 17**
See also DLB 123

Godard, Jean-Luc 1930-.......... **CLC 20**
See also CA 93-96

Godden, (Margaret) Rumer 1907-... **CLC 53**
See also AAYA 6; CA 5-8R; CANR 4, 27,
36; CLR 20; MAICYA; SAAS 12;
SATA 3, 36

Godoy Alcayaga, Lucila 1889-1957
See Mistral, Gabriela
See also BW 2; CA 104; 131; HW; MTCW

Godwin, Gail (Kathleen)
1937- .... **CLC 5, 8, 22, 31, 69**
See also CA 29-32R; CANR 15, 43; DLB 6;
MTCW

Godwin, William 1756-1836...... **NCLC 14**
See also CDBLB 1789-1832; DLB 39, 104,
142

Harris, George Washington
1814-1869 . . . . NCLC **23**
See also DLB 3, 11

Harris, Joel Chandler 1848-1908 . . . TCLC **2**
See also CA 104; 137; DLB 11, 23, 42, 78,
91; MAICYA; YABC 1

Harris, John (Wyndham Parkes Lucas)
Beynon 1903-1969
See Wyndham, John
See also CA 102; 89-92

Harris, MacDonald . . . . CLC **9**
See also Heiney, Donald (William)

Harris, Mark 1922- . . . . CLC **19**
See also CA 5-8R; CAAS 3; CANR 2;
DLB 2; DLBY 80

Harris, (Theodore) Wilson 1921-. . . . CLC **25**
See also BW 2; CA 65-68; CAAS 16;
CANR 11, 27; DLB 117; MTCW

Harrison, Elizabeth Cavanna 1909-
See Cavanna, Betty
See also CA 9-12R; CANR 6, 27

Harrison, Harry (Max) 1925- . . . . . . CLC **42**
See also CA 1-4R; CANR 5, 21; DLB 8;
SATA 4

Harrison, James (Thomas)
1937- . . . . CLC **6, 14, 33, 66**
See also CA 13-16R; CANR 8; DLBY 82

Harrison, Jim
See Harrison, James (Thomas)

Harrison, Kathryn 1961- . . . . CLC **70**
See also CA 144

Harrison, Tony 1937-. . . . . CLC **43**
See also CA 65-68; CANR 44; DLB 40;
MTCW

Harriss, Will(ard Irvin) 1922- . . . . . . CLC **34**
See also CA 111

Harson, Sley
See Ellison, Harlan (Jay)

Hart, Ellis
See Ellison, Harlan (Jay)

Hart, Josephine 1942(?)- . . . . CLC **70**
See also CA 138

Hart, Moss 1904-1961 . . . . CLC **66**
See also CA 109; 89-92; DLB 7

Harte, (Francis) Bret(t)
1836(?)-1902 . . . . TCLC **1, 25; DA;**
SSC 8; WLC
See also CA 104; 140; CDALB 1865-1917;
DLB 12, 64, 74, 79; SATA 26

Hartley, L(eslie) P(oles)
1895-1972 . . . . CLC **2, 22**
See also CA 45-48; 37-40R; CANR 33;
DLB 15, 139; MTCW

Hartman, Geoffrey H. 1929-. . . . . . . CLC **27**
See also CA 117; 125; DLB 67

Haruf, Kent 19(?)- . . . . CLC **34**

Harwood, Ronald 1934-. . . . . CLC **32**
See also CA 1-4R; CANR 4; DLB 13

Hasek, Jaroslav (Matej Frantisek)
1883-1923 . . . . TCLC **4**
See also CA 104; 129; MTCW

Hass, Robert 1941-. . . . . CLC **18, 39**
See also CA 111; CANR 30; DLB 105

Hastings, Hudson
See Kuttner, Henry

Hastings, Selina. . . . . CLC **44**

Hatteras, Amelia
See Mencken, H(enry) L(ouis)

Hatteras, Owen . . . . TCLC **18**
See also Mencken, H(enry) L(ouis); Nathan,
George Jean

Hauptmann, Gerhart (Johann Robert)
1862-1946 . . . . TCLC **4**
See also CA 104; DLB 66, 118

Havel, Vaclav 1936-. . . . . . . CLC **25, 58, 65**
See also CA 104; CANR 36; MTCW

Haviaras, Stratis. . . . . CLC **33**
See also Chaviaras, Strates

Hawes, Stephen 1475(?)-1523(?) . . . . . LC **17**

Hawkes, John (Clendennin Burne, Jr.)
1925- . . . . . . CLC **1, 2, 3, 4, 7, 9, 14, 15,**
27, 49
See also CA 1-4R; CANR 2, 47; DLB 2, 7;
DLBY 80; MTCW

Hawking, S. W.
See Hawking, Stephen W(illiam)

Hawking, Stephen W(illiam)
1942- . . . . CLC **63**
See also AAYA 13; BEST 89:1; CA 126;
129

Hawthorne, Julian 1846-1934 . . . . . TCLC **25**

Hawthorne, Nathaniel
1804-1864 . . . . . . NCLC **39; DA; SSC 3;**
WLC
See also CDALB 1640-1865; DLB 1, 74;
YABC 2

Haxton, Josephine Ayres 1921-
See Douglas, Ellen
See also CA 115; CANR 41

Hayaseca y Eizaguirre, Jorge
See Echegaray (y Eizaguirre), Jose (Maria
Waldo)

Hayashi Fumiko 1904-1951. . . . . . . TCLC **27**

Haycraft, Anna
See Ellis, Alice Thomas
See also CA 122

Hayden, Robert E(arl)
1913-1980 . . . . . . CLC **5, 9, 14, 37; BLC;**
DA; PC 6
See also BW 1; CA 69-72; 97-100; CABS 2;
CANR 24; CDALB 1941-1968; DLB 5,
76; MTCW; SATA 19; SATA-Obit 26

Hayford, J(oseph) E(phraim) Casely
See Casely-Hayford, J(oseph) E(phraim)

Hayman, Ronald 1932-. . . . . CLC **44**
See also CA 25-28R; CANR 18

Haywood, Eliza (Fowler)
1693(?)-1756 . . . . LC **1**

Hazlitt, William 1778-1830 . . . . . . NCLC **29**
See also DLB 110

Hazzard, Shirley 1931- . . . . CLC **18**
See also CA 9-12R; CANR 4; DLBY 82;
MTCW

Head, Bessie 1937-1986. . . CLC **25, 67; BLC**
See also BW 2; CA 29-32R; 119; CANR 25;
DLB 117; MTCW

Headon, (Nicky) Topper 1956(?)- . . . CLC **30**

Heaney, Seamus (Justin)
1939- . . . . CLC **5, 7, 14, 25, 37, 74**
See also CA 85-88; CANR 25;
CDBLB 1960 to Present; DLB 40;
MTCW

Hearn, (Patricio) Lafcadio (Tessima Carlos)
1850-1904 . . . . TCLC **9**
See also CA 105; DLB 12, 78

Hearne, Vicki 1946-. . . . . CLC **56**
See also CA 139

Hearon, Shelby 1931-. . . . . CLC **63**
See also AITN 2; CA 25-28R; CANR 18

Heat-Moon, William Least. . . . . CLC **29**
See also Trogdon, William (Lewis)
See also AAYA 9

Hebbel, Friedrich 1813-1863 . . . . . NCLC **43**
See also DLB 129

Hebert, Anne 1916- . . . . CLC **4, 13, 29**
See also CA 85-88; DLB 68; MTCW

Hecht, Anthony (Evan)
1923-. . . . . CLC **8, 13, 19**
See also CA 9-12R; CANR 6; DLB 5

Hecht, Ben 1894-1964 . . . . CLC **8**
See also CA 85-88; DLB 7, 9, 25, 26, 28, 86

Hedayat, Sadeq 1903-1951. . . . . . . TCLC **21**
See also CA 120

Hegel, Georg Wilhelm Friedrich
1770-1831 . . . . NCLC **46**
See also DLB 90

Heidegger, Martin 1889-1976 . . . . . . CLC **24**
See also CA 81-84; 65-68; CANR 34;
MTCW

Heidenstam, (Carl Gustaf) Verner von
1859-1940 . . . . TCLC **5**
See also CA 104

Heifner, Jack 1946-. . . . . CLC **11**
See also CA 105; CANR 47

Heijermans, Herman 1864-1924 . . . TCLC **24**
See also CA 123

Heilbrun, Carolyn G(old) 1926-. . . . . CLC **25**
See also CA 45-48; CANR 1, 28

Heine, Heinrich 1797-1856 . . . . NCLC **4**
See also DLB 90

Heinemann, Larry (Curtiss) 1944- . . CLC **50**
See also CA 110; CANR 31; DLBD 9

Heiney, Donald (William) 1921-1993
See Harris, MacDonald
See also CA 1-4R; 142; CANR 3

Heinlein, Robert A(nson)
1907-1988 . . . . . . CLC **1, 3, 8, 14, 26, 55**
See also CA 1-4R; 125; CANR 1, 20;
DLB 8; JRDA; MAICYA; MTCW;
SATA 9, 69; SATA-Obit 56

Helforth, John
See Doolittle, Hilda

Hellenhofferu, Vojtech Kapristian z
See Hasek, Jaroslav (Matej Frantisek)

Heller, Joseph
1923- . . . . CLC **1, 3, 5, 8, 11, 36, 63; DA;**
WLC
See also AITN 1; CA 5-8R; CABS 1;
CANR 8, 42; DLB 2, 28; DLBY 80;
MTCW

Hirsch, E(ric) D(onald), Jr. 1928-... **CLC 79**
See also CA 25-28R; CANR 27; DLB 67;
MTCW

Hirsch, Edward 1950- .... **CLC 31, 50**
See also CA 104; CANR 20, 42; DLB 120

Hitchcock, Alfred (Joseph)
1899-1980 .... **CLC 16**
See also CA 97-100; SATA 27;
SATA-Obit 24

Hitler, Adolf 1889-1945......... **TCLC 53**
See also CA 117

Hoagland, Edward 1932- .... **CLC 28**
See also CA 1-4R; CANR 2, 31; DLB 6;
SATA 51

Hoban, Russell (Conwell) 1925- .. **CLC 7, 25**
See also CA 5-8R; CANR 23, 37; CLR 3;
DLB 52; MAICYA; MTCW; SATA 1,
40, 78

Hobbs, Perry
See Blackmur, R(ichard) P(almer)

Hobson, Laura Z(ametkin)
1900-1986 .... **CLC 7, 25**
See also CA 17-20R; 118; DLB 28;
SATA 52

Hochhuth, Rolf 1931-........ **CLC 4, 11, 18**
See also CA 5-8R; CANR 33; DLB 124;
MTCW

Hochman, Sandra 1936-......... **CLC 3, 8**
See also CA 5-8R; DLB 5

Hochwaelder, Fritz 1911-1986...... **CLC 36**
See also CA 29-32R; 120; CANR 42;
MTCW

Hochwalder, Fritz
See Hochwaelder, Fritz

Hocking, Mary (Eunice) 1921- ..... **CLC 13**
See also CA 101; CANR 18, 40

Hodgins, Jack 1938-............. **CLC 23**
See also CA 93-96; DLB 60

Hodgson, William Hope
1877(?)-1918 .... **TCLC 13**
See also CA 111; DLB 70

Hoffman, Alice 1952-............ **CLC 51**
See also CA 77-80; CANR 34; MTCW

Hoffman, Daniel (Gerard)
1923- .... **CLC 6, 13, 23**
See also CA 1-4R; CANR 4; DLB 5

Hoffman, Stanley 1944-........... **CLC 5**
See also CA 77-80

Hoffman, William M(oses) 1939- ... **CLC 40**
See also CA 57-60; CANR 11

Hoffmann, E(rnst) T(heodor) A(madeus)
1776-1822 .... **NCLC 2; SSC 13**
See also DLB 90; SATA 27

Hofmann, Gert 1931-............ **CLC 54**
See also CA 128

Hofmannsthal, Hugo von
1874-1929 .... **TCLC 11; DC 4**
See also CA 106; DLB 81, 118

Hogan, Linda 1947- .... **CLC 73**
See also CA 120; CANR 45; NNAL

Hogarth, Charles
See Creasey, John

Hogg, James 1770-1835......... **NCLC 4**
See also DLB 93, 116

Holbach, Paul Henri Thiry Baron
1723-1789 .... **LC 14**

Holberg, Ludvig 1684-1754 .... **LC 6**

Holden, Ursula 1921-............ **CLC 18**
See also CA 101; CAAS 8; CANR 22

Holderlin, (Johann Christian) Friedrich
1770-1843 .... **NCLC 16; PC 4**

Holdstock, Robert
See Holdstock, Robert P.

Holdstock, Robert P. 1948-........ **CLC 39**
See also CA 131

Holland, Isabelle 1920- .... **CLC 21**
See also AAYA 11; CA 21-24R; CANR 10,
25, 47; JRDA; MAICYA; SATA 8, 70

Holland, Marcus
See Caldwell, (Janet Miriam) Taylor
(Holland)

Hollander, John 1929- ...... **CLC 2, 5, 8, 14**
See also CA 1-4R; CANR 1; DLB 5;
SATA 13

Hollander, Paul
See Silverberg, Robert

Holleran, Andrew 1943(?)-......... **CLC 38**
See also CA 144

Hollinghurst, Alan 1954- .... **CLC 55**
See also CA 114

Hollis, Jim
See Summers, Hollis (Spurgeon, Jr.)

Holmes, John
See Souster, (Holmes) Raymond

Holmes, John Clellon 1926-1988.... **CLC 56**
See also CA 9-12R; 125; CANR 4; DLB 16

Holmes, Oliver Wendell
1809-1894 .... **NCLC 14**
See also CDALB 1640-1865; DLB 1;
SATA 34

Holmes, Raymond
See Souster, (Holmes) Raymond

Holt, Victoria
See Hibbert, Eleanor Alice Burford

Holub, Miroslav 1923-............ **CLC 4**
See also CA 21-24R; CANR 10

Homer c. 8th cent. B.C.- ..... **CMLC 1; DA**

Honig, Edwin 1919- .... **CLC 33**
See also CA 5-8R; CAAS 8; CANR 4, 45;
DLB 5

Hood, Hugh (John Blagdon)
1928- .... **CLC 15, 28**
See also CA 49-52; CAAS 17; CANR 1, 33;
DLB 53

Hood, Thomas 1799-1845........ **NCLC 16**
See also DLB 96

Hooker, (Peter) Jeremy 1941-...... **CLC 43**
See also CA 77-80; CANR 22; DLB 40

Hope, A(lec) D(erwent) 1907- .... **CLC 3, 51**
See also CA 21-24R; CANR 33; MTCW

Hope, Brian
See Creasey, John

Hope, Christopher (David Tully)
1944- .... **CLC 52**
See also CA 106; CANR 47; SATA 62

Hopkins, Gerard Manley
1844-1889 .... **NCLC 17; DA; WLC**
See also CDBLB 1890-1914; DLB 35, 57

Hopkins, John (Richard) 1931-...... **CLC 4**
See also CA 85-88

Hopkins, Pauline Elizabeth
1859-1930 .... **TCLC 28; BLC**
See also BW 2; CA 141; DLB 50

Hopkinson, Francis 1737-1791 ...... **LC 25**
See also DLB 31

Hopley-Woolrich, Cornell George 1903-1968
See Woolrich, Cornell
See also CA 13-14; CAP 1

Horatio
See Proust, (Valentin-Louis-George-Eugene-)
Marcel

Horgan, Paul 1903- .... **CLC 9, 53**
See also CA 13-16R; CANR 9, 35;
DLB 102; DLBY 85; MTCW; SATA 13

Horn, Peter
See Kuttner, Henry

Hornem, Horace Esq.
See Byron, George Gordon (Noel)

Horovitz, Israel (Arthur) 1939-..... **CLC 56**
See also CA 33-36R; CANR 46; DLB 7

Horvath, Odon von
See Horvath, Oedoen von
See also DLB 85, 124

Horvath, Oedoen von 1901-1938... **TCLC 45**
See also Horvath, Odon von
See also CA 118

Horwitz, Julius 1920-1986......... **CLC 14**
See also CA 9-12R; 119; CANR 12

Hospital, Janette Turner 1942-..... **CLC 42**
See also CA 108

Hostos, E. M. de
See Hostos (y Bonilla), Eugenio Maria de

Hostos, Eugenio M. de
See Hostos (y Bonilla), Eugenio Maria de

Hostos, Eugenio Maria
See Hostos (y Bonilla), Eugenio Maria de

Hostos (y Bonilla), Eugenio Maria de
1839-1903 .... **TCLC 24**
See also CA 123; 131; HW

Houdini
See Lovecraft, H(oward) P(hillips)

Hougan, Carolyn 1943- .... **CLC 34**
See also CA 139

Household, Geoffrey (Edward West)
1900-1988 .... **CLC 11**
See also CA 77-80; 126; DLB 87; SATA 14;
SATA-Obit 59

Housman, A(lfred) E(dward)
1859-1936 ...... **TCLC 1, 10; DA; PC 2**
See also CA 104; 125; DLB 19; MTCW

Housman, Laurence 1865-1959 ..... **TCLC 7**
See also CA 106; DLB 10; SATA 25

Howard, Elizabeth Jane 1923- ... **CLC 7, 29**
See also CA 5-8R; CANR 8

Howard, Maureen 1930- ..... **CLC 5, 14, 46**
See also CA 53-56; CANR 31; DLBY 83;
MTCW

Kallman, Chester (Simon)
1921-1975 . . . . **CLC 2**
See also CA 45-48; 53-56; CANR 3

Kaminsky, Melvin 1926-
See Brooks, Mel
See also CA 65-68; CANR 16

Kaminsky, Stuart M(elvin) 1934- . . . **CLC 59**
See also CA 73-76; CANR 29

Kane, Paul
See Simon, Paul

Kane, Wilson
See Bloch, Robert (Albert)

Kanin, Garson 1912- . . . . **CLC 22**
See also AITN 1; CA 5-8R; CANR 7;
DLB 7

Kaniuk, Yoram 1930- . . . . **CLC 19**
See also CA 134

Kant, Immanuel 1724-1804 . . . . . . **NCLC 27**
See also DLB 94

Kantor, MacKinlay 1904-1977 . . . . . . **CLC 7**
See also CA 61-64; 73-76; DLB 9, 102

Kaplan, David Michael 1946- . . . . . . **CLC 50**

Kaplan, James 1951- . . . . **CLC 59**
See also CA 135

Karageorge, Michael
See Anderson, Poul (William)

Karamzin, Nikolai Mikhailovich
1766-1826 . . . . **NCLC 3**

Karapanou, Margarita 1946- . . . . **CLC 13**
See also CA 101

Karinthy, Frigyes 1887-1938 . . . . . . **TCLC 47**

Karl, Frederick R(obert) 1927- . . . . . **CLC 34**
See also CA 5-8R; CANR 3, 44

Kastel, Warren
See Silverberg, Robert

Kataev, Evgeny Petrovich 1903-1942
See Petrov, Evgeny
See also CA 120

Kataphusin
See Ruskin, John

Katz, Steve 1935- . . . . **CLC 47**
See also CA 25-28R; CAAS 14; CANR 12;
DLBY 83

Kauffman, Janet 1945- . . . . **CLC 42**
See also CA 117; CANR 43; DLBY 86

Kaufman, Bob (Garnell)
1925-1986 . . . . **CLC 49**
See also BW 1; CA 41-44R; 118; CANR 22;
DLB 16, 41

Kaufman, George S. 1889-1961 . . . . . **CLC 38**
See also CA 108; 93-96; DLB 7

Kaufman, Sue . . . . **CLC 3, 8**
See also Barondess, Sue K(aufman)

Kavafis, Konstantinos Petrou 1863-1933
See Cavafy, C(onstantine) P(eter)
See also CA 104

Kavan, Anna 1901-1968 . . . . . . **CLC 5, 13, 82**
See also CA 5-8R; CANR 6; MTCW

Kavanagh, Dan
See Barnes, Julian

Kavanagh, Patrick (Joseph)
1904-1967 . . . . **CLC 22**
See also CA 123; 25-28R; DLB 15, 20;
MTCW

Kawabata, Yasunari
1899-1972 . . . . . **CLC 2, 5, 9, 18; SSC 17**
See also CA 93-96; 33-36R

Kaye, M(ary) M(argaret) 1909- . . . . . **CLC 28**
See also CA 89-92; CANR 24; MTCW;
SATA 62

Kaye, Mollie
See Kaye, M(ary) M(argaret)

Kaye-Smith, Sheila 1887-1956 . . . . . **TCLC 20**
See also CA 118; DLB 36

Kaymor, Patrice Maguilene
See Senghor, Leopold Sedar

Kazan, Elia 1909- . . . . **CLC 6, 16, 63**
See also CA 21-24R; CANR 32

Kazantzakis, Nikos
1883(?)-1957 . . . . **TCLC 2, 5, 33**
See also CA 105; 132; MTCW

Kazin, Alfred 1915- . . . . **CLC 34, 38**
See also CA 1-4R; CAAS 7; CANR 1, 45;
DLB 67

Keane, Mary Nesta (Skrine) 1904-
See Keane, Molly
See also CA 108; 114

Keane, Molly . . . . **CLC 31**
See also Keane, Mary Nesta (Skrine)

Keates, Jonathan 19(?)- . . . . . ; . . . . . **CLC 34**

Keaton, Buster 1895-1966 . . . . **CLC 20**

Keats, John
1795-1821 . . . **NCLC 8; DA; PC 1; WLC**
See also CDBLB 1789-1832; DLB 96, 110

Keene, Donald 1922- . . . . **CLC 34**
See also CA 1-4R; CANR 5

Keillor, Garrison . . . . **CLC 40**
See also Keillor, Gary (Edward)
See also AAYA 2; BEST 89:3; DLBY 87;
SATA 58

Keillor, Gary (Edward) 1942-
See Keillor, Garrison
See also CA 111; 117; CANR 36; MTCW

Keith, Michael
See Hubbard, L(afayette) Ron(ald)

Keller, Gottfried 1819-1890 . . . . **NCLC 2**
See also DLB 129

Kellerman, Jonathan 1949- . . . . **CLC 44**
See also BEST 90:1; CA 106; CANR 29

Kelley, William Melvin 1937- . . . . . . **CLC 22**
See also BW 1; CA 77-80; CANR 27;
DLB 33

Kellogg, Marjorie 1922- . . . . **CLC 2**
See also CA 81-84

Kellow, Kathleen
See Hibbert, Eleanor Alice Burford

Kelly, M(ilton) T(erry) 1947- . . . . **CLC 55**
See also CA 97-100; CANR 19, 43

Kelman, James 1946- . . . . **CLC 58, 86**

Kemal, Yashar 1923- . . . . **CLC 14, 29**
See also CA 89-92; CANR 44

Kemble, Fanny 1809-1893 . . . . **NCLC 18**
See also DLB 32

Kemelman, Harry 1908- . . . . **CLC 2**
See also AITN 1; CA 9-12R; CANR 6;
DLB 28

Kempe, Margery 1373(?)-1440(?) . . . . . **LC 6**
See also DLB 146

Kempis, Thomas a 1380-1471 . . . . **LC 11**

Kendall, Henry 1839-1882 . . . . **NCLC 12**

Keneally, Thomas (Michael)
1935- . . . . . . **CLC 5, 8, 10, 14, 19, 27, 43**
See also CA 85-88; CANR 10; MTCW

Kennedy, Adrienne (Lita)
1931- . . . . **CLC 66; BLC; DC 5**
See also BW 2; CA 103; CAAS 20; CABS 3;
CANR 26; DLB 38

Kennedy, John Pendleton
1795-1870 . . . . **NCLC 2**
See also DLB 3

Kennedy, Joseph Charles 1929-
See Kennedy, X. J.
See also CA 1-4R; CANR 4, 30, 40;
SATA 14

Kennedy, William 1928- . . . **CLC 6, 28, 34, 53**
See also AAYA 1; CA 85-88; CANR 14,
31; DLB 143; DLBY 85; MTCW;
SATA 57

Kennedy, X. J. . . . . **CLC 8, 42**
See also Kennedy, Joseph Charles
See also CAAS 9; CLR 27; DLB 5

Kent, Kelvin
See Kuttner, Henry

Kenton, Maxwell
See Southern, Terry

Kenyon, Robert O.
See Kuttner, Henry

Kerouac, Jack . . . . . **CLC 1, 2, 3, 5, 14, 29, 61**
See also Kerouac, Jean-Louis Lebris de
See also CDALB 1941-1968; DLB 2, 16;
DLBD 3

Kerouac, Jean-Louis Lebris de 1922-1969
See Kerouac, Jack
See also AITN 1; CA 5-8R; 25-28R;
CANR 26; DA; MTCW; WLC

Kerr, Jean 1923- . . . . **CLC 22**
See also CA 5-8R; CANR 7

Kerr, M. E. **CLC 12, 35**
See also Meaker, Marijane (Agnes)
See also AAYA 2; CLR 29; SAAS 1

Kerr, Robert . . . . **CLC 55**

Kerrigan, (Thomas) Anthony
1918- . . . . **CLC 4, 6**
See also CA 49-52; CAAS 11; CANR 4

Kerry, Lois
See Duncan, Lois

Kesey, Ken (Elton)
1935- . . . . . . **CLC 1, 3, 6, 11, 46, 64; DA;
WLC**
See also CA 1-4R; CANR 22, 38;
CDALB 1968-1988; DLB 2, 16; MTCW;
SATA 66

Kesselring, Joseph (Otto)
1902-1967 . . . . **CLC 45**

Kessler, Jascha (Frederick) 1929- . . . . **CLC 4**
See also CA 17-20R; CANR 8

Kornbluth, C(yril) M. 1923-1958. . . . **TCLC 8**
  See also CA 105; DLB 8

Korolenko, V. G.
  See Korolenko, Vladimir Galaktionovich

Korolenko, Vladimir
  See Korolenko, Vladimir Galaktionovich

Korolenko, Vladimir G.
  See Korolenko, Vladimir Galaktionovich

Korolenko, Vladimir Galaktionovich
  1853-1921 . . . . **TCLC 22**
  See also CA 121

Kosinski, Jerzy (Nikodem)
  1933-1991 . . . . **CLC 1, 2, 3, 6, 10, 15, 53,
                                                    70**
  See also CA 17-20R; 134; CANR 9, 46, 46;
  DLB 2; DLBY 82; MTCW

Kostelanetz, Richard (Cory) 1940- . . **CLC 28**
  See also CA 13-16R; CAAS 8; CANR 38

Kostrowitzki, Wilhelm Apollinaris de
  1880-1918
  See Apollinaire, Guillaume
  See also CA 104

Kotlowitz, Robert 1924- . . . . **CLC 4**
  See also CA 33-36R; CANR 36

Kotzebue, August (Friedrich Ferdinand) von
  1761-1819 . . . . **NCLC 25**
  See also DLB 94

Kotzwinkle, William 1938- . . . **CLC 5, 14, 35**
  See also CA 45-48; CANR 3, 44; CLR 6;
  MAICYA; SATA 24, 70

Kozol, Jonathan 1936- . . . . **CLC 17**
  See also CA 61-64; CANR 16, 45

Kozoll, Michael 1940(?)- . . . . **CLC 35**

Kramer, Kathryn 19(?)- . . . . **CLC 34**

Kramer, Larry 1935- . . . . **CLC 42**
  See also CA 124; 126

Krasicki, Ignacy 1735-1801 . . . . . . **NCLC 8**

Krasinski, Zygmunt 1812-1859 . . . . **NCLC 4**

Kraus, Karl 1874-1936 . . . . **TCLC 5**
  See also CA 104; DLB 118

Kreve (Mickevicius), Vincas
  1882-1954 . . . . **TCLC 27**

Kristeva, Julia 1941- . . . . **CLC 77**

Kristofferson, Kris 1936- . . . . **CLC 26**
  See also CA 104

Krizanc, John 1956- . . . . **CLC 57**

Krleza, Miroslav 1893-1981 . . . . **CLC 8**
  See also CA 97-100; 105; DLB 147

Kroetsch, Robert 1927- . . . . . . **CLC 5, 23, 57**
  See also CA 17-20R; CANR 8, 38; DLB 53;
  MTCW

Kroetz, Franz
  See Kroetz, Franz Xaver

Kroetz, Franz Xaver 1946- . . . . **CLC 41**
  See also CA 130

Kroker, Arthur 1945- . . . . **CLC 77**

Kropotkin, Peter (Alekseievich)
  1842-1921 . . . . **TCLC 36**
  See also CA 119

Krotkov, Yuri 1917- . . . . **CLC 19**
  See also CA 102

Krumb
  See Crumb, R(obert)

Krumgold, Joseph (Quincy)
  1908-1980 . . . . **CLC 12**
  See also CA 9-12R; 101; CANR 7;
  MAICYA; SATA 1, 48; SATA-Obit 23

Krumwitz
  See Crumb, R(obert)

Krutch, Joseph Wood 1893-1970. . . . **CLC 24**
  See also CA 1-4R; 25-28R; CANR 4;
  DLB 63

Krutzch, Gus
  See Eliot, T(homas) S(tearns)

Krylov, Ivan Andreevich
  1768(?)-1844 . . . . **NCLC 1**

Kubin, Alfred 1877-1959 . . . . **TCLC 23**
  See also CA 112; DLB 81

Kubrick, Stanley 1928- . . . . **CLC 16**
  See also CA 81-84; CANR 33; DLB 26

Kumin, Maxine (Winokur)
  1925- . . . . **CLC 5, 13, 28**
  See also AITN 2; CA 1-4R; CAAS 8;
  CANR 1, 21; DLB 5; MTCW; SATA 12

Kundera, Milan
  1929- . . . . **CLC 4, 9, 19, 32, 68**
  See also AAYA 2; CA 85-88; CANR 19;
  MTCW

Kunene, Mazisi (Raymond) 1930- . . . **CLC 85**
  See also BW 1; CA 125; DLB 117

Kunitz, Stanley (Jasspon)
  1905- . . . . **CLC 6, 11, 14**
  See also CA 41-44R; CANR 26; DLB 48;
  MTCW

Kunze, Reiner 1933- . . . . **CLC 10**
  See also CA 93-96; DLB 75

Kuprin, Aleksandr Ivanovich
  1870-1938 . . . . **TCLC 5**
  See also CA 104

Kureishi, Hanif 1954(?)- . . . . **CLC 64**
  See also CA 139

Kurosawa, Akira 1910- . . . . **CLC 16**
  See also AAYA 11; CA 101; CANR 46, 46

Kushner, Tony 1957(?)- . . . . **CLC 81**
  See also CA 144

Kuttner, Henry 1915-1958 . . . . **TCLC 10**
  See also CA 107; DLB 8

Kuzma, Greg 1944- . . . . **CLC 7**
  See also CA 33-36R

Kuzmin, Mikhail 1872(?)-1936 . . . . **TCLC 40**

Kyd, Thomas 1558-1594 . . . . . . **LC 22; DC 3**
  See also DLB 62

Kyprianos, Iossif
  See Samarakis, Antonis

La Bruyere, Jean de 1645-1696 . . . . . . **LC 17**

Lacan, Jacques (Marie Emile)
  1901-1981 . . . . **CLC 75**
  See also CA 121; 104

Laclos, Pierre Ambroise Francois Choderlos
  de 1741-1803 . . . . **NCLC 4**

Lacolere, Francois
  See Aragon, Louis

La Colere, Francois
  See Aragon, Louis

La Deshabilleuse
  See Simenon, Georges (Jacques Christian)

Lady Gregory
  See Gregory, Isabella Augusta (Persse)

Lady of Quality, A
  See Bagnold, Enid

La Fayette, Marie (Madelaine Pioche de la
  Vergne Comtes 1634-1693 . . . . . . **LC 2**

Lafayette, Rene
  See Hubbard, L(afayette) Ron(ald)

Laforgue, Jules 1860-1887 . . . . **NCLC 5**

Lagerkvist, Paer (Fabian)
  1891-1974 . . . . **CLC 7, 10, 13, 54**
  See also Lagerkvist, Par
  See also CA 85-88; 49-52; MTCW

Lagerkvist, Par
  See Lagerkvist, Paer (Fabian)
  See also SSC 12

Lagerloef, Selma (Ottiliana Lovisa)
  1858-1940 . . . . **TCLC 4, 36**
  See also Lagerlof, Selma (Ottiliana Lovisa)
  See also CA 108; SATA 15

Lagerlof, Selma (Ottiliana Lovisa)
  See Lagerloef, Selma (Ottiliana Lovisa)
  See also CLR 7; SATA 15

La Guma, (Justin) Alex(ander)
  1925-1985 . . . . **CLC 19**
  See also BW 1; CA 49-52; 118; CANR 25;
  DLB 117; MTCW

Laidlaw, A. K.
  See Grieve, C(hristopher) M(urray)

Lainez, Manuel Mujica
  See Mujica Lainez, Manuel
  See also HW

Lamartine, Alphonse (Marie Louis Prat) de
  1790-1869 . . . . **NCLC 11**

Lamb, Charles
  1775-1834 . . . . **NCLC 10; DA; WLC**
  See also CDBLB 1789-1832; DLB 93, 107;
  SATA 17

Lamb, Lady Caroline 1785-1828 . . **NCLC 38**
  See also DLB 116

Lamming, George (William)
  1927- . . . . **CLC 2, 4, 66; BLC**
  See also BW 2; CA 85-88; CANR 26;
  DLB 125; MTCW

L'Amour, Louis (Dearborn)
  1908-1988 . . . . **CLC 25, 55**
  See also AITN 2; BEST 89:2; CA 1-4R;
  125; CANR 3, 25, 40; DLBY 80; MTCW

Lampedusa, Giuseppe (Tomasi) di . . . **TCLC 13**
  See also Tomasi di Lampedusa, Giuseppe

Lampman, Archibald 1861-1899 . . **NCLC 25**
  See also DLB 92

Lancaster, Bruce 1896-1963 . . . . **CLC 36**
  See also CA 9-10; CAP 1; SATA 9

Landau, Mark Alexandrovich
  See Aldanov, Mark (Alexandrovich)

Landau-Aldanov, Mark Alexandrovich
  See Aldanov, Mark (Alexandrovich)

Landis, John 1950- . . . . **CLC 26**
  See also CA 112; 122

Landolfi, Tommaso 1908-1979 . . . **CLC 11, 49**
  See also CA 127; 117

Landon, Letitia Elizabeth
1802-1838 . . . . **NCLC 15**
See also DLB 96

Landor, Walter Savage
1775-1864 . . . . **NCLC 14**
See also DLB 93, 107

Landwirth, Heinz 1927-
See Lind, Jakov
See also CA 9-12R; CANR 7

Lane, Patrick 1939- . . . . **CLC 25**
See also CA 97-100; DLB 53

Lang, Andrew 1844-1912 . . . . **TCLC 16**
See also CA 114; 137; DLB 98, 141;
MAICYA; SATA 16

Lang, Fritz 1890-1976 . . . . **CLC 20**
See also CA 77-80; 69-72; CANR 30

Lange, John
See Crichton, (John) Michael

Langer, Elinor 1939- . . . . **CLC 34**
See also CA 121

Langland, William
1330(?)-1400(?) . . . . **LC 19; DA**
See also DLB 146

Langstaff, Launcelot
See Irving, Washington

Lanier, Sidney 1842-1881 . . . . **NCLC 6**
See also DLB 64; MAICYA; SATA 18

Lanyer, Aemilia 1569-1645 . . . . **LC 10**

Lao Tzu . . . . **CMLC 7**

Lapine, James (Elliot) 1949- . . . . **CLC 39**
See also CA 123; 130

Larbaud, Valery (Nicolas)
1881-1957 . . . . **TCLC 9**
See also CA 106

Lardner, Ring
See Lardner, Ring(gold) W(ilmer)

Lardner, Ring W., Jr.
See Lardner, Ring(gold) W(ilmer)

Lardner, Ring(gold) W(ilmer)
1885-1933 . . . . **TCLC 2, 14**
See also CA 104; 131; CDALB 1917-1929;
DLB 11, 25, 86; MTCW

Laredo, Betty
See Codrescu, Andrei

Larkin, Maia
See Wojciechowska, Maia (Teresa)

Larkin, Philip (Arthur)
1922-1985 . . . . **CLC 3, 5, 8, 9, 13, 18, 33,
39, 64**
See also CA 5-8R; 117; CANR 24;
CDBLB 1960 to Present; DLB 27;
MTCW

Larra (y Sanchez de Castro), Mariano Jose de
1809-1837 . . . . **NCLC 17**

Larsen, Eric 1941- . . . . **CLC 55**
See also CA 132

Larsen, Nella 1891-1964 . . . . . **CLC 37; BLC**
See also BW 1; CA 125; DLB 51

Larson, Charles R(aymond) 1938- . . . **CLC 31**
See also CA 53-56; CANR 4

Lasker-Schueler, Else 1869-1945 . . **TCLC 57**
See also DLB 66, 124

Latham, Jean Lee 1902- . . . . **CLC 12**
See also AITN 1; CA 5-8R; CANR 7;
MAICYA; SATA 2, 68

Latham, Mavis
See Clark, Mavis Thorpe

Lathen, Emma . . . . **CLC 2**
See also Hennissart, Martha; Latsis, Mary
J(ane)

Lathrop, Francis
See Leiber, Fritz (Reuter, Jr.)

Latsis, Mary J(ane)
See Lathen, Emma
See also CA 85-88

Lattimore, Richmond (Alexander)
1906-1984 . . . . **CLC 3**
See also CA 1-4R; 112; CANR 1

Laughlin, James 1914- . . . . **CLC 49**
See also CA 21-24R; CANR 9, 45; DLB 48

Laurence, (Jean) Margaret (Wemyss)
1926-1987 . . **CLC 3, 6, 13, 50, 62; SSC 7**
See also CA 5-8R; 121; CANR 33; DLB 53;
MTCW; SATA-Obit 50

Laurent, Antoine 1952- . . . . **CLC 50**

Lauscher, Hermann
See Hesse, Hermann

Lautreamont, Comte de
1846-1870 . . . . **NCLC 12; SSC 14**

Laverty, Donald
See Blish, James (Benjamin)

Lavin, Mary 1912- . . . . . . **CLC 4, 18; SSC 4**
See also CA 9-12R; CANR 33; DLB 15;
MTCW

Lavond, Paul Dennis
See Kornbluth, C(yril) M.; Pohl, Frederik

Lawler, Raymond Evenor 1922- . . . . **CLC 58**
See also CA 103

Lawrence, D(avid) H(erbert Richards)
1885-1930 . . . . **TCLC 2, 9, 16, 33, 48;
DA; SSC 4; WLC**
See also CA 104; 121; CDBLB 1914-1945;
DLB 10, 19, 36, 98; MTCW

Lawrence, T(homas) E(dward)
1888-1935 . . . . **TCLC 18**
See Dale, Colin
See also CA 115

Lawrence of Arabia
See Lawrence, T(homas) E(dward)

Lawson, Henry (Archibald Hertzberg)
1867-1922 . . . . **TCLC 27; SSC 18**
See also CA 120

Lawton, Dennis
See Faust, Frederick (Schiller)

Laxness, Halldor . . . . **CLC 25**
See also Gudjonsson, Halldor Kiljan

Layamon fl. c. 1200- . . . . **CMLC 10**
See also DLB 146

Laye, Camara 1928-1980 . . . **CLC 4, 38; BLC**
See also BW 1; CA 85-88; 97-100;
CANR 25; MTCW

Layton, Irving (Peter) 1912- . . . . . **CLC 2, 15**
See also CA 1-4R; CANR 2, 33, 43;
DLB 88; MTCW

Lazarus, Emma 1849-1887 . . . . **NCLC 8**

Lazarus, Felix
See Cable, George Washington

Lazarus, Henry
See Slavitt, David R(ytman)

Lea, Joan
See Neufeld, John (Arthur)

Leacock, Stephen (Butler)
1869-1944 . . . . **TCLC 2**
See also CA 104; 141; DLB 92

Lear, Edward 1812-1888 . . . . **NCLC 3**
See also CLR 1; DLB 32; MAICYA;
SATA 18

Lear, Norman (Milton) 1922- . . . . . . **CLC 12**
See also CA 73-76

Leavis, F(rank) R(aymond)
1895-1978 . . . . **CLC 24**
See also CA 21-24R; 77-80; CANR 44;
MTCW

Leavitt, David 1961- . . . . **CLC 34**
See also CA 116; 122; DLB 130

Leblanc, Maurice (Marie Emile)
1864-1941 . . . . **TCLC 49**
See also CA 110

Lebowitz, Fran(ces Ann)
1951(?)- . . . . **CLC 11, 36**
See also CA 81-84; CANR 14; MTCW

Lebrecht, Peter
See Tieck, (Johann) Ludwig

le Carre, John . . . . **CLC 3, 5, 9, 15, 28**
See also Cornwell, David (John Moore)
See also BEST 89:4; CDBLB 1960 to
Present; DLB 87

Le Clezio, J(ean) M(arie) G(ustave)
1940- . . . . **CLC 31**
See also CA 116; 128; DLB 83

Leconte de Lisle, Charles-Marie-Rene
1818-1894 . . . . **NCLC 29**

Le Coq, Monsieur
See Simenon, Georges (Jacques Christian)

Leduc, Violette 1907-1972 . . . . **CLC 22**
See also CA 13-14; 33-36R; CAP 1

Ledwidge, Francis 1887(?)-1917 . . . **TCLC 23**
See also CA 123; DLB 20

Lee, Andrea 1953- . . . . **CLC 36; BLC**
See also BW 1; CA 125

Lee, Andrew
See Auchincloss, Louis (Stanton)

Lee, Don L. . . . . **CLC 2**
See also Madhubuti, Haki R.

Lee, George W(ashington)
1894-1976 . . . . **CLC 52; BLC**
See also BW 1; CA 125; DLB 51

Lee, (Nelle) Harper
1926- . . . . **CLC 12, 60; DA; WLC**
See also AAYA 13; CA 13-16R;
CDALB 1941-1968; DLB 6; MTCW;
SATA 11

Lee, Helen Elaine 1959(?)- . . . . **CLC 86**

Lee, Julian
See Latham, Jean Lee

Lee, Larry
See Lee, Lawrence

Lee, Lawrence 1941-1990 . . . . **CLC 34**
See also CA 131; CANR 43

Loti, Pierre .... **TCLC 11**
 See also Viaud, (Louis Marie) Julien
 See also DLB 123

Louie, David Wong 1954- .... **CLC 70**
 See also CA 139

Louis, Father M.
 See Merton, Thomas

Lovecraft, H(oward) P(hillips)
 1890-1937 .... **TCLC 4, 22; SSC 3**
 See also AAYA 14; CA 104; 133; MTCW

Lovelace, Earl 1935-.............. **CLC 51**
 See also BW 2; CA 77-80; CANR 41;
 DLB 125; MTCW

Lovelace, Richard 1618-1657........ **LC 24**
 See also DLB 131

Lowell, Amy 1874-1925 .... **TCLC 1, 8**
 See also CA 104; DLB 54, 140

Lowell, James Russell 1819-1891 .. **NCLC 2**
 See also CDALB 1640-1865; DLB 1, 11, 64,
 79

Lowell, Robert (Traill Spence, Jr.)
 1917-1977 ... **CLC 1, 2, 3, 4, 5, 8, 9, 11,**
                       15, 37; DA; PC 3; WLC
 See also CA 9-12R; 73-76; CABS 2;
 CANR 26; DLB 5; MTCW

Lowndes, Marie Adelaide (Belloc)
 1868-1947 .... **TCLC 12**
 See also CA 107; DLB 70

Lowry, (Clarence) Malcolm
 1909-1957 .... **TCLC 6, 40**
 See also CA 105; 131; CDBLB 1945-1960;
 DLB 15; MTCW

Lowry, Mina Gertrude 1882-1966
 See Loy, Mina
 See also CA 113

Loxsmith, John
 See Brunner, John (Kilian Houston)

Loy, Mina .... **CLC 28**
 See also Lowry, Mina Gertrude
 See also DLB 4, 54

Loyson-Bridet
 See Schwob, (Mayer Andre) Marcel

Lucas, Craig 1951-.............. **CLC 64**
 See also CA 137

Lucas, George 1944-.............. **CLC 16**
 See also AAYA 1; CA 77-80; CANR 30;
 SATA 56

Lucas, Hans
 See Godard, Jean-Luc

Lucas, Victoria
 See Plath, Sylvia

Ludlam, Charles 1943-1987 ..... **CLC 46, 50**
 See also CA 85-88; 122

Ludlum, Robert 1927- .... **CLC 22, 43**
 See also AAYA 10; BEST 89:1, 90:3;
 CA 33-36R; CANR 25, 41; DLBY 82;
 MTCW

Ludwig, Ken..................... **CLC 60**

Ludwig, Otto 1813-1865.......... **NCLC 4**
 See also DLB 129

Lugones, Leopoldo 1874-1938 ..... **TCLC 15**
 See also CA 116; 131; HW

Lu Hsun 1881-1936 .... **TCLC 3**

Lukacs, George .... **CLC 24**
 See also Lukacs, Gyorgy (Szegeny von)

Lukacs, Gyorgy (Szegeny von) 1885-1971
 See Lukacs, George
 See also CA 101; 29-32R

Luke, Peter (Ambrose Cyprian)
 1919-....................... **CLC 38**
 See also CA 81-84; DLB 13

Lunar, Dennis
 See Mungo, Raymond

Lurie, Alison 1926-........ **CLC 4, 5, 18, 39**
 See also CA 1-4R; CANR 2, 17; DLB 2;
 MTCW; SATA 46

Lustig, Arnost 1926-.............. **CLC 56**
 See also AAYA 3; CA 69-72; CANR 47;
 SATA 56

Luther, Martin 1483-1546........... **LC 9**

Luzi, Mario 1914-................ **CLC 13**
 See also CA 61-64; CANR 9; DLB 128

Lynch, B. Suarez
 See Bioy Casares, Adolfo; Borges, Jorge
 Luis

Lynch, David (K.) 1946-.......... **CLC 66**
 See also CA 124; 129

Lynch, James
 See Andreyev, Leonid (Nikolaevich)

Lynch Davis, B.
 See Bioy Casares, Adolfo; Borges, Jorge
 Luis

Lyndsay, Sir David 1490-1555 ...... **LC 20**

Lynn, Kenneth S(chuyler) 1923-.... **CLC 50**
 See also CA 1-4R; CANR 3, 27

Lynx
 See West, Rebecca

Lyons, Marcus
 See Blish, James (Benjamin)

Lyre, Pinchbeck
 See Sassoon, Siegfried (Lorraine)

Lytle, Andrew (Nelson) 1902-...... **CLC 22**
 See also CA 9-12R; DLB 6

Lyttelton, George 1709-1773........ **LC 10**

Maas, Peter 1929- .... **CLC 29**
 See also CA 93-96

Macaulay, Rose 1881-1958 ..... **TCLC 7, 44**
 See also CA 104; DLB 36

Macaulay, Thomas Babington
 1800-1859 .... **NCLC 42**
 See also CDBLB 1832-1890; DLB 32, 55

MacBeth, George (Mann)
 1932-1992 .... **CLC 2, 5, 9**
 See also CA 25-28R; 136; DLB 40; MTCW;
 SATA 4; SATA-Obit 70

MacCaig, Norman (Alexander)
 1910-....................... **CLC 36**
 See also CA 9-12R; CANR 3, 34; DLB 27

MacCarthy, (Sir Charles Otto) Desmond
 1877-1952 .... **TCLC 36**

MacDiarmid, Hugh
 .... **CLC 2, 4, 11, 19, 63; PC 9**
 See also Grieve, C(hristopher) M(urray)
 See also CDBLB 1945-1960; DLB 20

MacDonald, Anson
 See Heinlein, Robert A(nson)

Macdonald, Cynthia 1928-...... **CLC 13, 19**
 See also CA 49-52; CANR 4, 44; DLB 105

MacDonald, George 1824-1905..... **TCLC 9**
 See also CA 106; 137; DLB 18; MAICYA;
 SATA 33

Macdonald, John
 See Millar, Kenneth

MacDonald, John D(ann)
 1916-1986 .... **CLC 3, 27, 44**
 See also CA 1-4R; 121; CANR 1, 19;
 DLB 8; DLBY 86; MTCW

Macdonald, John Ross
 See Millar, Kenneth

Macdonald, Ross..... **CLC 1, 2, 3, 14, 34, 41**
 See also Millar, Kenneth
 See also DLBD 6

MacDougal, John
 See Blish, James (Benjamin)

MacEwen, Gwendolyn (Margaret)
 1941-1987 .... **CLC 13, 55**
 See also CA 9-12R; 124; CANR 7, 22;
 DLB 53; SATA 50; SATA-Obit 55

Macha, Karel Hynek 1810-1846.. **NCLC 46**

Machado (y Ruiz), Antonio
 1875-1939 .... **TCLC 3**
 See also CA 104; DLB 108

Machado de Assis, Joaquim Maria
 1839-1908 .... **TCLC 10; BLC**
 See also CA 107

Machen, Arthur.................. **TCLC 4**
 See also Jones, Arthur Llewellyn
 See also DLB 36

Machiavelli, Niccolo 1469-1527 .. **LC 8; DA**

MacInnes, Colin 1914-1976...... **CLC 4, 23**
 See also CA 69-72; 65-68; CANR 21;
 DLB 14; MTCW

MacInnes, Helen (Clark)
 1907-1985 .... **CLC 27, 39**
 See also CA 1-4R; 117; CANR 1, 28;
 DLB 87; MTCW; SATA 22;
 SATA-Obit 44

Mackay, Mary 1855-1924
 See Corelli, Marie
 See also CA 118

Mackenzie, Compton (Edward Montague)
 1883-1972 .... **CLC 18**
 See also CA 21-22; 37-40R; CAP 2;
 DLB 34, 100

Mackenzie, Henry 1745-1831 .... **NCLC 41**
 See also DLB 39

Mackintosh, Elizabeth 1896(?)-1952
 See Tey, Josephine
 See also CA 110

MacLaren, James
 See Grieve, C(hristopher) M(urray)

Mac Laverty, Bernard 1942-....... **CLC 31**
 See also CA 116; 118; CANR 43

MacLean, Alistair (Stuart)
 1922-1987.....**CLC 3, 13, 50, 63**
 See also CA 57-60; 121; CANR 28; MTCW;
 SATA 23; SATA-Obit 50

Maclean, Norman (Fitzroy)
 1902-1990 .... **CLC 78; SSC 13**
 See also CA 102; 132

MacLeish, Archibald
1892-1982 . . . . **CLC 3, 8, 14, 68**
See also CA 9-12R; 106; CANR 33; DLB 4,
7, 45; DLBY 82; MTCW

MacLennan, (John) Hugh
1907-1990 . . . . **CLC 2, 14**
See also CA 5-8R; 142; CANR 33; DLB 68;
MTCW

MacLeod, Alistair 1936- . . . . **CLC 56**
See also CA 123; DLB 60

MacNeice, (Frederick) Louis
1907-1963 . . . . **CLC 1, 4, 10, 53**
See also CA 85-88; DLB 10, 20; MTCW

MacNeill, Dand
See Fraser, George MacDonald

Macpherson, (Jean) Jay 1931- . . . . . . **CLC 14**
See also CA 5-8R; DLB 53

MacShane, Frank 1927- . . . . **CLC 39**
See also CA 9-12R; CANR 3, 33; DLB 111

Macumber, Mari
See Sandoz, Mari(e Susette)

Madach, Imre 1823-1864 . . . . **NCLC 19**

Madden, (Jerry) David 1933- . . . . **CLC 5, 15**
See also CA 1-4R; CAAS 3; CANR 4, 45;
DLB 6; MTCW

Maddern, Al(an)
See Ellison, Harlan (Jay)

Madhubuti, Haki R.
1942- . . . . **CLC 6, 73; BLC; PC 5**
See also Lee, Don L.
See also BW 2; CA 73-76; CANR 24;
DLB 5, 41; DLBD 8

Maepenn, Hugh
See Kuttner, Henry

Maepenn, K. H.
See Kuttner, Henry

Maeterlinck, Maurice 1862-1949 . . . **TCLC 3**
See also CA 104; 136; SATA 66

Maginn, William 1794-1842 . . . . **NCLC 8**
See also DLB 110

Mahapatra, Jayanta 1928- . . . . **CLC 33**
See also CA 73-76; CAAS 9; CANR 15, 33

Mahfouz, Naguib (Abdel Aziz Al-Sabilgi)
1911(?)-
See Mahfuz, Najib
See also BEST 89:2; CA 128; MTCW

Mahfuz, Najib . . . . **CLC 52, 55**
See also Mahfouz, Naguib (Abdel Aziz
Al-Sabilgi)
See also DLBY 88

Mahon, Derek 1941- . . . . **CLC 27**
See also CA 113; 128; DLB 40

Mailer, Norman
1923- . . . . . . **CLC 1, 2, 3, 4, 5, 8, 11, 14,
28, 39, 74; DA**
See also AITN 2; CA 9-12R; CABS 1;
CANR 28; CDALB 1968-1988; DLB 2,
16, 28; DLBD 3; DLBY 80, 83; MTCW

Maillet, Antonine 1929- . . . . **CLC 54**
See also CA 115; 120; CANR 46, 46;
DLB 60

Mais, Roger 1905-1955 . . . . **TCLC 8**
See also BW 1; CA 105; 124; DLB 125;
MTCW

Maistre, Joseph de 1753-1821 . . . . **NCLC 37**

Maitland, Sara (Louise) 1950- . . . . . . **CLC 49**
See also CA 69-72; CANR 13

Major, Clarence
1936- . . . . **CLC 3, 19, 48; BLC**
See also BW 2; CA 21-24R; CAAS 6;
CANR 13, 25; DLB 33

Major, Kevin (Gerald) 1949- . . . . **CLC 26**
See also CA 97-100; CANR 21, 38;
CLR 11; DLB 60; JRDA; MAICYA;
SATA 32

Maki, James
See Ozu, Yasujiro

Malabaila, Damiano
See Levi, Primo

Malamud, Bernard
1914-1986 . . . . . . **CLC 1, 2, 3, 5, 8, 9, 11,
18, 27, 44, 78, 85; DA; SSC 15; WLC**
See also CA 5-8R; 118; CABS 1; CANR 28;
CDALB 1941-1968; DLB 2, 28;
DLBY 80, 86; MTCW

Malaparte, Curzio 1898-1957 . . . . . **TCLC 52**

Malcolm, Dan
See Silverberg, Robert

Malcolm X . . . . **CLC 82; BLC**
See also Little, Malcolm

Malherbe, Francois de 1555-1628 . . . . . **LC 5**

Mallarme, Stephane
1842-1898 . . . . **NCLC 4, 41; PC 4**

Mallet-Joris, Francoise 1930- . . . . . . **CLC 11**
See also CA 65-68; CANR 17; DLB 83

Malley, Ern
See McAuley, James Phillip

Mallowan, Agatha Christie
See Christie, Agatha (Mary Clarissa)

Maloff, Saul 1922- . . . . **CLC 5**
See also CA 33-36R

Malone, Louis
See MacNeice, (Frederick) Louis

Malone, Michael (Christopher)
1942- . . . . **CLC 43**
See also CA 77-80; CANR 14, 32

Malory, (Sir) Thomas
1410(?)-1471(?) . . . . **LC 11; DA**
See also CDBLB Before 1660; DLB 146;
SATA 33, 59

Malouf, (George Joseph) David
1934- . . . . **CLC 28, 86**
See also CA 124

Malraux, (Georges-)Andre
1901-1976 . . . . . . **CLC 1, 4, 9, 13, 15, 57**
See also CA 21-22; 69-72; CANR 34;
CAP 2; DLB 72; MTCW

Malzberg, Barry N(athaniel) 1939- . . . **CLC 7**
See also CA 61-64; CAAS 4; CANR 16;
DLB 8

Mamet, David (Alan)
1947- . . . . **CLC 9, 15, 34, 46; DC 4**
See also AAYA 3; CA 81-84; CABS 3;
CANR 15, 41; DLB 7; MTCW

Mamoulian, Rouben (Zachary)
1897-1987 . . . . **CLC 16**
See also CA 25-28R; 124

Mandelstam, Osip (Emilievich)
1891(?)-1938(?) . . . . **TCLC 2, 6**
See also CA 104

Mander, (Mary) Jane 1877-1949 . . . **TCLC 31**

Mandiargues, Andre Pieyre de . . . . . . **CLC 41**
See also Pieyre de Mandiargues, Andre
See also DLB 83

Mandrake, Ethel Belle
See Thurman, Wallace (Henry)

Mangan, James Clarence
1803-1849 . . . . **NCLC 27**

Maniere, J.-E.
See Giraudoux, (Hippolyte) Jean

Manley, (Mary) Delariviere
1672(?)-1724 . . . . **LC 1**
See also DLB 39, 80

Mann, Abel
See Creasey, John

Mann, (Luiz) Heinrich 1871-1950 . . . **TCLC 9**
See also CA 106; DLB 66

Mann, (Paul) Thomas
1875-1955 . . . . **TCLC 2, 8, 14, 21, 35, 44;
DA; SSC 5; WLC**
See also CA 104; 128; DLB 66; MTCW

Manning, David
See Faust, Frederick (Schiller)

Manning, Frederic 1887(?)-1935 . . . **TCLC 25**
See also CA 124

Manning, Olivia 1915-1980 . . . . . . **CLC 5, 19**
See also CA 5-8R; 101; CANR 29; MTCW

Mano, D. Keith 1942- . . . . **CLC 2, 10**
See also CA 25-28R; CAAS 6; CANR 26;
DLB 6

Mansfield, Katherine
. . . . **TCLC 2, 8, 39; SSC 9; WLC**
See also Beauchamp, Kathleen Mansfield

Manso, Peter 1940- . . . . **CLC 39**
See also CA 29-32R; CANR 44

Mantecon, Juan Jimenez
See Jimenez (Mantecon), Juan Ramon

Manton, Peter
See Creasey, John

Man Without a Spleen, A
See Chekhov, Anton (Pavlovich)

Manzoni, Alessandro 1785-1873 . . **NCLC 29**

Mapu, Abraham (ben Jekutiel)
1808-1867 . . . . **NCLC 18**

Mara, Sally
See Queneau, Raymond

Marat, Jean Paul 1743-1793 . . . . **LC 10**

Marcel, Gabriel Honore
1889-1973 . . . . **CLC 15**
See also CA 102; 45-48; MTCW

Marchbanks, Samuel
See Davies, (William) Robertson

Marchi, Giacomo
See Bassani, Giorgio

Margulies, Donald . . . . **CLC 76**

Marie de France c. 12th cent. - . . . . **CMLC 8**

Marie de l'Incarnation 1599-1672 . . . . **LC 10**

Mariner, Scott
See Pohl, Frederik

Marinetti, Filippo Tommaso
1876-1944 . . . . **TCLC 10**
See also CA 107; DLB 114

Maxwell, William (Keepers, Jr.)
1908- .... **CLC 19**
See also CA 93-96; DLBY 80

May, Elaine 1932- .... **CLC 16**
See also CA 124; 142; DLB 44

Mayakovski, Vladimir (Vladimirovich)
1893-1930 .... **TCLC 4, 18**
See also CA 104

Mayhew, Henry 1812-1887 ...... **NCLC 31**
See also DLB 18, 55

Maynard, Joyce 1953- .... **CLC 23**
See also CA 111; 129

Mayne, William (James Carter)
1928- .... **CLC 12**
See also CA 9-12R; CANR 37; CLR 25;
JRDA; MAICYA; SAAS 11; SATA 6, 68

Mayo, Jim
See L'Amour, Louis (Dearborn)

Maysles, Albert 1926- .... **CLC 16**
See also CA 29-32R

Maysles, David 1932- .... **CLC 16**

Mazer, Norma Fox 1931- .... **CLC 26**
See also AAYA 5; CA 69-72; CANR 12,
32; CLR 23; JRDA; MAICYA; SAAS 1;
SATA 24, 67

Mazzini, Guiseppe 1805-1872 .... **NCLC 34**

McAuley, James Phillip
1917-1976 .... **CLC 45**
See also CA 97-100

McBain, Ed
See Hunter, Evan

McBrien, William Augustine
1930- .... **CLC 44**
See also CA 107

McCaffrey, Anne (Inez) 1926- ...... **CLC 17**
See also AAYA 6; AITN 2; BEST 89:2;
CA 25-28R; CANR 15, 35; DLB 8;
JRDA; MAICYA; MTCW; SAAS 11;
SATA 8, 70

McCall, Nathan 1955(?)- .... **CLC 86**
See also CA 146

McCann, Arthur
See Campbell, John W(ood, Jr.)

McCann, Edson
See Pohl, Frederik

McCarthy, Charles, Jr. 1933-
See McCarthy, Cormac
See also CANR 42

McCarthy, Cormac 1933- ..... **CLC 4, 57, 59**
See also McCarthy, Charles, Jr.
See also DLB 6, 143

McCarthy, Mary (Therese)
1912-1989 ... **CLC 1, 3, 5, 14, 24, 39, 59**
See also CA 5-8R; 129; CANR 16; DLB 2;
DLBY 81; MTCW

McCartney, (James) Paul
1942- .... **CLC 12, 35**

McCauley, Stephen (D.) 1955- ..... **CLC 50**
See also CA 141

McClure, Michael (Thomas)
1932- .... **CLC 6, 10**
See also CA 21-24R; CANR 17, 46, 46;
DLB 16

McCorkle, Jill (Collins) 1958- ...... **CLC 51**
See also CA 121; DLBY 87

McCourt, James 1941- .... **CLC 5**
See also CA 57-60

McCoy, Horace (Stanley)
1897-1955 .... **TCLC 28**
See also CA 108; DLB 9

McCrae, John 1872-1918 .... **TCLC 12**
See also CA 109; DLB 92

McCreigh, James
See Pohl, Frederik

McCullers, (Lula) Carson (Smith)
1917-1967 .... **CLC 1, 4, 10, 12, 48; DA;
SSC 9; WLC**
See also CA 5-8R; 25-28R; CABS 1, 3;
CANR 18; CDALB 1941-1968; DLB 2, 7;
MTCW; SATA 27

McCulloch, John Tyler
See Burroughs, Edgar Rice

McCullough, Colleen 1938(?)- ...... **CLC 27**
See also CA 81-84; CANR 17, 46, 46;
MTCW

McElroy, Joseph 1930- .... **CLC 5, 47**
See also CA 17-20R

McEwan, Ian (Russell) 1948- ... **CLC 13, 66**
See also BEST 90:4; CA 61-64; CANR 14,
41; DLB 14; MTCW

McFadden, David 1940- .... **CLC 48**
See also CA 104; DLB 60

McFarland, Dennis 1950- .... **CLC 65**

McGahern, John
1934- .... **CLC 5, 9, 48; SSC 17**
See also CA 17-20R; CANR 29; DLB 14;
MTCW

McGinley, Patrick (Anthony)
1937- .... **CLC 41**
See also CA 120; 127

McGinley, Phyllis 1905-1978 ...... **CLC 14**
See also CA 9-12R; 77-80; CANR 19;
DLB 11, 48; SATA 2, 44; SATA-Obit 24

McGinniss, Joe 1942- .... **CLC 32**
See also AITN 2; BEST 89:2; CA 25-28R;
CANR 26

McGivern, Maureen Daly
See Daly, Maureen

McGrath, Patrick 1950- .... **CLC 55**
See also CA 136

McGrath, Thomas (Matthew)
1916-1990 .... **CLC 28, 59**
See also CA 9-12R; 132; CANR 6, 33;
MTCW; SATA 41; SATA-Obit 66

McGuane, Thomas (Francis III)
1939- .... **CLC 3, 7, 18, 45**
See also AITN 2; CA 49-52; CANR 5, 24;
DLB 2; DLBY 80; MTCW

McGuckian, Medbh 1950- .... **CLC 48**
See also CA 143; DLB 40

McHale, Tom 1942(?)-1982 .... **CLC 3, 5**
See also AITN 1; CA 77-80; 106

McIlvanney, William 1936- .... **CLC 42**
See also CA 25-28R; DLB 14

McIlwraith, Maureen Mollie Hunter
See Hunter, Mollie
See also SATA 2

McInerney, Jay 1955- .... **CLC 34**
See also CA 116; 123

McIntyre, Vonda N(eel) 1948- ..... **CLC 18**
See also CA 81-84; CANR 17, 34; MTCW

McKay, Claude ..... **TCLC 7, 41; BLC; PC 2**
See also McKay, Festus Claudius
See also DLB 4, 45, 51, 117

McKay, Festus Claudius 1889-1948
See McKay, Claude
See also BW 1; CA 104; 124; DA; MTCW;
WLC

McKuen, Rod 1933- .... **CLC 1, 3**
See also AITN 1; CA 41-44R; CANR 40

McLoughlin, R. B.
See Mencken, H(enry) L(ouis)

McLuhan, (Herbert) Marshall
1911-1980 .... **CLC 37, 83**
See also CA 9-12R; 102; CANR 12, 34;
DLB 88; MTCW

McMillan, Terry (L.) 1951- ..... **CLC 50, 61**
See also BW 2; CA 140

McMurtry, Larry (Jeff)
1936- .... **CLC 2, 3, 7, 11, 27, 44**
See also AITN 2; BEST 89:2; CA 5-8R;
CANR 19, 43; CDALB 1968-1988;
DLB 2, 143; DLBY 80, 87; MTCW

McNally, T. M. 1961- .... **CLC 82**

McNally, Terrence 1939- ...... **CLC 4, 7, 41**
See also CA 45-48; CANR 2; DLB 7

McNamer, Deirdre 1950- .... **CLC 70**

McNeile, Herman Cyril 1888-1937
See Sapper
See also DLB 77

McPhee, John (Angus) 1931- ...... **CLC 36**
See also BEST 90:1; CA 65-68; CANR 20,
46, 46; MTCW

McPherson, James Alan
1943- .... **CLC 19, 77**
See also BW 1; CA 25-28R; CAAS 17;
CANR 24; DLB 38; MTCW

McPherson, William (Alexander)
1933- .... **CLC 34**
See also CA 69-72; CANR 28

Mead, Margaret 1901-1978 .... **CLC 37**
See also AITN 1; CA 1-4R; 81-84;
CANR 4; MTCW; SATA-Obit 20

Meaker, Marijane (Agnes) 1927-
See Kerr, M. E.
See also CA 107; CANR 37; JRDA;
MAICYA; MTCW; SATA 20, 61

Medoff, Mark (Howard) 1940- ... **CLC 6, 23**
See also AITN 1; CA 53-56; CANR 5;
DLB 7

Medvedev, P. N.
See Bakhtin, Mikhail Mikhailovich

Meged, Aharon
See Megged, Aharon

Meged, Aron
See Megged, Aharon

Megged, Aharon 1920- .... **CLC 9**
See also CA 49-52; CAAS 13; CANR 1

Mehta, Ved (Parkash) 1934- .... **CLC 37**
See also CA 1-4R; CANR 2, 23; MTCW

Melanter
See Blackmore, R(ichard) D(oddridge)

Melikow, Loris
See Hofmannsthal, Hugo von

Melmoth, Sebastian
See Wilde, Oscar (Fingal O'Flahertie Wills)

Meltzer, Milton 1915- .... **CLC 26**
See also AAYA 8; CA 13-16R; CANR 38;
CLR 13; DLB 61; JRDA; MAICYA;
SAAS 1; SATA 1, 50, 80

Melville, Herman
1819-1891 .... **NCLC 3, 12, 29, 45; DA;
SSC 1, 17; WLC**
See also CDALB 1640-1865; DLB 3, 74;
SATA 59

Menander
c. 342B.C.-c. 292B.C.... **CMLC 9; DC 3**

Mencken, H(enry) L(ouis)
1880-1956 .... **TCLC 13**
See also CA 105; 125; CDALB 1917-1929;
DLB 11, 29, 63, 137; MTCW

Mercer, David 1928-1980.......... **CLC 5**
See also CA 9-12R; 102; CANR 23;
DLB 13; MTCW

Merchant, Paul
See Ellison, Harlan (Jay)

Meredith, George 1828-1909 ... **TCLC 17, 43**
See also CA 117; CDBLB 1832-1890;
DLB 18, 35, 57

Meredith, William (Morris)
1919- .... **CLC 4, 13, 22, 55**
See also CA 9-12R; CAAS 14; CANR 6, 40;
DLB 5

Merezhkovsky, Dmitry Sergeyevich
1865-1941 .... **TCLC 29**

Merimee, Prosper
1803-1870 .... **NCLC 6; SSC 7**
See also DLB 119

Merkin, Daphne 1954-........... **CLC 44**
See also CA 123

Merlin, Arthur
See Blish, James (Benjamin)

Merrill, James (Ingram)
1926- ...... **CLC 2, 3, 6, 8, 13, 18, 34**
See also CA 13-16R; CANR 10; DLB 5;
DLBY 85; MTCW

Merriman, Alex
See Silverberg, Robert

Merritt, E. B.
See Waddington, Miriam

Merton, Thomas
1915-1968 .. **CLC 1, 3, 11, 34, 83; PC 10**
See also CA 5-8R; 25-28R; CANR 22;
DLB 48; DLBY 81; MTCW

Merwin, W(illiam) S(tanley)
1927- ... **CLC 1, 2, 3, 5, 8, 13, 18, 45, 86**
See also CA 13-16R; CANR 15; DLB 5;
MTCW

Metcalf, John 1938-.............. **CLC 37**
See also CA 113; DLB 60

Metcalf, Suzanne
See Baum, L(yman) Frank

Mew, Charlotte (Mary)
1870-1928 .... **TCLC 8**
See also CA 105; DLB 19, 135

Mewshaw, Michael 1943-........... **CLC 9**
See also CA 53-56; CANR 7, 47; DLBY 80

Meyer, June
See Jordan, June

Meyer, Lynn
See Slavitt, David R(ytman)

Meyer-Meyrink, Gustav 1868-1932
See Meyrink, Gustav
See also CA 117

Meyers, Jeffrey 1939- .... **CLC 39**
See also CA 73-76; DLB 111

Meynell, Alice (Christina Gertrude Thompson)
1847-1922 .... **TCLC 6**
See also CA 104; DLB 19, 98

Meyrink, Gustav .... **TCLC 21**
See also Meyer-Meyrink, Gustav
See also DLB 81

Michaels, Leonard
1933- .... **CLC 6, 25; SSC 16**
See also CA 61-64; CANR 21; DLB 130;
MTCW

Michaux, Henri 1899-1984 ...... **CLC 8, 19**
See also CA 85-88; 114

Michelangelo 1475-1564............ **LC 12**

Michelet, Jules 1798-1874 .... **NCLC 31**

Michener, James A(lbert)
1907(?)- .... **CLC 1, 5, 11, 29, 60**
See also AITN 1; BEST 90:1; CA 5-8R;
CANR 21, 45; DLB 6; MTCW

Mickiewicz, Adam 1798-1855 ..... **NCLC 3**

Middleton, Christopher 1926- ...... **CLC 13**
See also CA 13-16R; CANR 29; DLB 40

Middleton, Richard (Barham)
1882-1911 .... **TCLC 56**

Middleton, Stanley 1919-........ **CLC 7, 38**
See also CA 25-28R; CANR 21, 46, 46;
DLB 14

Middleton, Thomas 1580-1627........ **DC 5**
See also DLB 58

Migueis, Jose Rodrigues 1901- ..... **CLC 10**

Mikszath, Kalman 1847-1910 ..... **TCLC 31**

Miles, Josephine
1911-1985 .... **CLC 1, 2, 14, 34, 39**
See also CA 1-4R; 116; CANR 2; DLB 48

Militant
See Sandburg, Carl (August)

Mill, John Stuart 1806-1873 ..... **NCLC 11**
See also CDBLB 1832-1890; DLB 55

Millar, Kenneth 1915-1983 .... **CLC 14**
See also Macdonald, Ross
See also CA 9-12R; 110; CANR 16; DLB 2;
DLBD 6; DLBY 83; MTCW

Millay, E. Vincent
See Millay, Edna St. Vincent

Millay, Edna St. Vincent
1892-1950 ...... **TCLC 4, 49; DA; PC 6**
See also CA 104; 130; CDALB 1917-1929;
DLB 45; MTCW

Miller, Arthur
1915- .... **CLC 1, 2, 6, 10, 15, 26, 47, 78;
DA; DC 1; WLC**
See also AITN 1; CA 1-4R; CABS 3;
CANR 2, 30; CDALB 1941-1968; DLB 7;
MTCW

Miller, Henry (Valentine)
1891-1980 .... **CLC 1, 2, 4, 9, 14, 43, 84;
DA; WLC**
See also CA 9-12R; 97-100; CANR 33;
CDALB 1929-1941; DLB 4, 9; DLBY 80;
MTCW

Miller, Jason 1939(?)- .... **CLC 2**
See also AITN 1; CA 73-76; DLB 7

Miller, Sue 1943- .... **CLC 44**
See also BEST 90:3; CA 139; DLB 143

Miller, Walter M(ichael, Jr.)
1923- .... **CLC 4, 30**
See also CA 85-88; DLB 8

Millett, Kate 1934-.............. **CLC 67**
See also AITN 1; CA 73-76; CANR 32;
MTCW

Millhauser, Steven 1943-....... **CLC 21, 54**
See also CA 110; 111; DLB 2

Millin, Sarah Gertrude 1889-1968 .. **CLC 49**
See also CA 102; 93-96

Milne, A(lan) A(lexander)
1882-1956 .... **TCLC 6**
See also CA 104; 133; CLR 1, 26; DLB 10,
77, 100; MAICYA; MTCW; YABC 1

Milner, Ron(ald) 1938-....... **CLC 56; BLC**
See also AITN 1; BW 1; CA 73-76;
CANR 24; DLB 38; MTCW

Milosz, Czeslaw
1911- ... **CLC 5, 11, 22, 31, 56, 82; PC 8**
See also CA 81-84; CANR 23; MTCW

Milton, John 1608-1674... **LC 9; DA; WLC**
See also CDBLB 1660-1789; DLB 131

Min, Anchee 1957-.............. **CLC 86**

Minehaha, Cornelius
See Wedekind, (Benjamin) Frank(lin)

Miner, Valerie 1947- .... **CLC 40**
See also CA 97-100

Minimo, Duca
See D'Annunzio, Gabriele

Minot, Susan 1956- .... **CLC 44**
See also CA 134

Minus, Ed 1938-................ **CLC 39**

Miranda, Javier
See Bioy Casares, Adolfo

Mirbeau, Octave 1848-1917....... **TCLC 55**
See also DLB 123

Miro (Ferrer), Gabriel (Francisco Victor)
1879-1930 .... **TCLC 5**
See also CA 104

Mishima, Yukio
.... **CLC 2, 4, 6, 9, 27; DC 1; SSC 4**
See also Hiraoka, Kimitake

Mistral, Frederic 1830-1914 ...... **TCLC 51**
See also CA 122

Mistral, Gabriela........... **TCLC 2; HLC**
See also Godoy Alcayaga, Lucila

Mistry, Rohinton 1952-........... **CLC 71**
See also CA 141

Mitchell, Clyde
See Ellison, Harlan (Jay); Silverberg, Robert

Mitchell, James Leslie 1901-1935
See Gibbon, Lewis Grassic
See also CA 104; DLB 15

Mitchell, Joni 1943-.............. CLC **12**
See also CA 112

Mitchell, Margaret (Munnerlyn)
1900-1949 .... TCLC **11**
See also CA 109; 125; DLB 9; MTCW

Mitchell, Peggy
See Mitchell, Margaret (Munnerlyn)

Mitchell, S(ilas) Weir 1829-1914 .. TCLC **36**

Mitchell, W(illiam) O(rmond)
1914- .... CLC **25**
See also CA 77-80; CANR 15, 43; DLB 88

Mitford, Mary Russell 1787-1855.. NCLC **4**
See also DLB 110, 116

Mitford, Nancy 1904-1973........ CLC **44**
See also CA 9-12R

Miyamoto, Yuriko 1899-1951 ..... TCLC **37**

Mo, Timothy (Peter) 1950(?)-...... CLC **46**
See also CA 117; MTCW

Modarressi, Taghi (M.) 1931-...... CLC **44**
See also CA 121; 134

Modiano, Patrick (Jean) 1945-..... CLC **18**
See also CA 85-88; CANR 17, 40; DLB 83

Moerck, Paal
See Roelvaag, O(le) E(dvart)

Mofolo, Thomas (Mokopu)
1875(?)-1948 .... TCLC **22**; BLC
See also CA 121

Mohr, Nicholasa 1935-...... CLC **12**; HLC
See also AAYA 8; CA 49-52; CANR 1, 32;
CLR 22; DLB 145; HW; JRDA; SAAS 8;
SATA 8

Mojtabai, A(nn) G(race)
1938- ....CLC **5, 9, 15, 29**
See also CA 85-88

Moliere 1622-1673 ...... LC **10**; DA; WLC

Molin, Charles
See Mayne, William (James Carter)

Molnar, Ferenc 1878-1952....... TCLC **20**
See also CA 109

Momaday, N(avarre) Scott
1934- .... CLC **2, 19, 85**; DA
See also AAYA 11; CA 25-28R; CANR 14,
34; DLB 143; MTCW; NNAL; SATA 30,
48

Monette, Paul 1945-.............. CLC **82**
See also CA 139

Monroe, Harriet 1860-1936....... TCLC **12**
See also CA 109; DLB 54, 91

Monroe, Lyle
See Heinlein, Robert A(nson)

Montagu, Elizabeth 1917-........ NCLC **7**
See also CA 9-12R

Montagu, Mary (Pierrepont) Wortley
1689-1762 .... LC **9**
See also DLB 95, 101

Montagu, W. H.
See Coleridge, Samuel Taylor

Montague, John (Patrick)
1929- .... CLC **13, 46**
See also CA 9-12R; CANR 9; DLB 40;
MTCW

Montaigne, Michel (Eyquem) de
1533-1592 .... LC **8**; DA; WLC

Montale, Eugenio 1896-1981... CLC **7, 9, 18**
See also CA 17-20R; 104; CANR 30;
DLB 114; MTCW

Montesquieu, Charles-Louis de Secondat
1689-1755 .... LC **7**

Montgomery, (Robert) Bruce 1921-1978
See Crispin, Edmund
See also CA 104

Montgomery, L(ucy) M(aud)
1874-1942 .... TCLC **51**
See also AAYA 12; CA 108; 137; CLR 8;
DLB 92; JRDA; MAICYA; YABC 1

Montgomery, Marion H., Jr. 1925- .. CLC **7**
See also AITN 1; CA 1-4R; CANR 3;
DLB 6

Montgomery, Max
See Davenport, Guy (Mattison, Jr.)

Montherlant, Henry (Milon) de
1896-1972 .... CLC **8, 19**
See also CA 85-88; 37-40R; DLB 72;
MTCW

Monty Python
See Chapman, Graham; Cleese, John
(Marwood); Gilliam, Terry (Vance); Idle,
Eric; Jones, Terence Graham Parry; Palin,
Michael (Edward)
See also AAYA 7

Moodie, Susanna (Strickland)
1803-1885 .... NCLC **14**
See also DLB 99

Mooney, Edward 1951-
See Mooney, Ted
See also CA 130

Mooney, Ted .... CLC **25**
See also Mooney, Edward

Moorcock, Michael (John)
1939- .... CLC **5, 27, 58**
See also CA 45-48; CAAS 5; CANR 2, 17,
38; DLB 14; MTCW

Moore, Brian
1921- .... CLC **1, 3, 5, 7, 8, 19, 32**
See also CA 1-4R; CANR 1, 25, 42; MTCW

Moore, Edward
See Muir, Edwin

Moore, George Augustus
1852-1933 .... TCLC **7**
See also CA 104; DLB 10, 18, 57, 135

Moore, Lorrie .... CLC **39, 45, 68**
See also Moore, Marie Lorena

Moore, Marianne (Craig)
1887-1972 .... CLC **1, 2, 4, 8, 10, 13, 19,
47**; DA; PC **4**
See also CA 1-4R; 33-36R; CANR 3;
CDALB 1929-1941; DLB 45; DLBD 7;
MTCW; SATA 20

Moore, Marie Lorena 1957-
See Moore, Lorrie
See also CA 116; CANR 39

Moore, Thomas 1779-1852........ NCLC **6**
See also DLB 96, 144

Morand, Paul 1888-1976 .... CLC **41**
See also CA 69-72; DLB 65

Morante, Elsa 1918-1985........ CLC **8, 47**
See also CA 85-88; 117; CANR 35; MTCW

Moravia, Alberto .... CLC **2, 7, 11, 27, 46**
See also Pincherle, Alberto

More, Hannah 1745-1833 .... NCLC **27**
See also DLB 107, 109, 116

More, Henry 1614-1687............. LC **9**
See also DLB 126

More, Sir Thomas 1478-1535 .... LC **10**

Moreas, Jean.................... TCLC **18**
See also Papadiamantopoulos, Johannes

Morgan, Berry 1919-.............. CLC **6**
See also CA 49-52; DLB 6

Morgan, Claire
See Highsmith, (Mary) Patricia

Morgan, Edwin (George) 1920-..... CLC **31**
See also CA 5-8R; CANR 3, 43; DLB 27

Morgan, (George) Frederick
1922- .... CLC **23**
See also CA 17-20R; CANR 21

Morgan, Harriet
See Mencken, H(enry) L(ouis)

Morgan, Jane
See Cooper, James Fenimore

Morgan, Janet 1945- .... CLC **39**
See also CA 65-68

Morgan, Lady 1776(?)-1859...... NCLC **29**
See also DLB 116

Morgan, Robin 1941-.............. CLC **2**
See also CA 69-72; CANR 29; MTCW;
SATA 80

Morgan, Scott
See Kuttner, Henry

Morgan, Seth 1949(?)-1990 .... CLC **65**
See also CA 132

Morgenstern, Christian
1871-1914 .... TCLC **8**
See also CA 105

Morgenstern, S.
See Goldman, William (W.)

Moricz, Zsigmond 1879-1942 ..... TCLC **33**

Morike, Eduard (Friedrich)
1804-1875 .... NCLC **10**
See also DLB 133

Mori Ogai .... TCLC **14**
See also Mori Rintaro

Mori Rintaro 1862-1922
See Mori Ogai
See also CA 110

Moritz, Karl Philipp 1756-1793 ...... LC **2**
See also DLB 94

Morland, Peter Henry
See Faust, Frederick (Schiller)

Morren, Theophil
See Hofmannsthal, Hugo von

Morris, Bill 1952-............... CLC **76**

Morris, Julian
See West, Morris L(anglo)

Morris, Steveland Judkins 1950(?)-
See Wonder, Stevie
See also CA 111

Morris, William 1834-1896 .... NCLC **4**
See also CDBLB 1832-1890; DLB 18, 35, 57

Otero, Blas de 1916-1979......... CLC 11
See also CA 89-92; DLB 134

Otto, Whitney 1955-............. CLC 70
See also CA 140

Ouida .... TCLC 43
See also De La Ramee, (Marie) Louise
See also DLB 18

Ousmane, Sembene 1923- .... CLC 66; BLC
See also BW 1; CA 117; 125; MTCW

Ovid 43B.C.-18(?)......... CMLC 7; PC 2

Owen, Hugh
See Faust, Frederick (Schiller)

Owen, Wilfred (Edward Salter)
1893-1918 ...... TCLC 5, 27; DA; WLC
See also CA 104; 141; CDBLB 1914-1945;
DLB 20

Owens, Rochelle 1936-............ CLC 8
See also CA 17-20R; CAAS 2; CANR 39

Oz, Amos 1939- ... CLC 5, 8, 11, 27, 33, 54
See also CA 53-56; CANR 27, 47; MTCW

Ozick, Cynthia
1928- .... CLC 3, 7, 28, 62; SSC 15
See also BEST 90:1; CA 17-20R; CANR 23;
DLB 28; DLBY 82; MTCW

Ozu, Yasujiro 1903-1963 .... CLC 16
See also CA 112

Pacheco, C.
See Pessoa, Fernando (Antonio Nogueira)

Pa Chin .... CLC 18
See also Li Fei-kan

Pack, Robert 1929-.............. CLC 13
See also CA 1-4R; CANR 3, 44; DLB 5

Padgett, Lewis
See Kuttner, Henry

Padilla (Lorenzo), Heberto 1932-... CLC 38
See also AITN 1; CA 123; 131; HW

Page, Jimmy 1944-.............. CLC 12

Page, Louise 1955-.............. CLC 40
See also CA 140

Page, P(atricia) K(athleen)
1916- .... CLC 7, 18
See also CA 53-56; CANR 4, 22; DLB 68;
MTCW

Paget, Violet 1856-1935
See Lee, Vernon
See also CA 104

Paget-Lowe, Henry
See Lovecraft, H(oward) P(hillips)

Paglia, Camille (Anna) 1947-....... CLC 68
See also CA 140

Paige, Richard
See Koontz, Dean R(ay)

Pakenham, Antonia
See Fraser, (Lady) Antonia (Pakenham)

Palamas, Kostes 1859-1943 .... TCLC 5
See also CA 105

Palazzeschi, Aldo 1885-1974...... CLC 11
See also CA 89-92; 53-56; DLB 114

Paley, Grace 1922-.... CLC 4, 6, 37; SSC 8
See also CA 25-28R; CANR 13, 46, 46;
DLB 28; MTCW

Palin, Michael (Edward) 1943-..... CLC 21
See also Monty Python
See also CA 107; CANR 35; SATA 67

Palliser, Charles 1947-............ CLC 65
See also CA 136

Palma, Ricardo 1833-1919....... TCLC 29

Pancake, Breece Dexter 1952-1979
See Pancake, Breece D'J
See also CA 123; 109

Pancake, Breece D'J.............. CLC 29
See also Pancake, Breece Dexter
See also DLB 130

Panko, Rudy
See Gogol, Nikolai (Vasilyevich)

Papadiamantis, Alexandros
1851-1911 .... TCLC 29

Papadiamantopoulos, Johannes 1856-1910
See Moreas, Jean
See also CA 117

Papini, Giovanni 1881-1956...... TCLC 22
See also CA 121

Paracelsus 1493-1541............. LC 14

Parasol, Peter
See Stevens, Wallace

Parfenie, Maria
See Codrescu, Andrei

Parini, Jay (Lee) 1948- .... CLC 54
See also CA 97-100; CAAS 16; CANR 32

Park, Jordan
See Kornbluth, C(yril) M.; Pohl, Frederik

Parker, Bert
See Ellison, Harlan (Jay)

Parker, Dorothy (Rothschild)
1893-1967 .... CLC 15, 68; SSC 2
See also CA 19-20; 25-28R; CAP 2;
DLB 11, 45, 86; MTCW

Parker, Robert B(rown) 1932-...... CLC 27
See also BEST 89:4; CA 49-52; CANR 1,
26; MTCW

Parkin, Frank 1940-.............. CLC 43

Parkman, Francis, Jr.
1823-1893 .... NCLC 12
See also DLB 1, 30

Parks, Gordon (Alexander Buchanan)
1912- .... CLC 1, 16; BLC
See also AITN 2; BW 2; CA 41-44R;
CANR 26; DLB 33; SATA 8

Parnell, Thomas 1679-1718 .... LC 3
See also DLB 94

Parra, Nicanor 1914-........ CLC 2; HLC
See also CA 85-88; CANR 32; HW; MTCW

Parrish, Mary Frances
See Fisher, M(ary) F(rances) K(ennedy)

Parson
See Coleridge, Samuel Taylor

Parson Lot
See Kingsley, Charles

Partridge, Anthony
See Oppenheim, E(dward) Phillips

Pascoli, Giovanni 1855-1912 ...... TCLC 45

Pasolini, Pier Paolo
1922-1975 .... CLC 20, 37
See also CA 93-96; 61-64; DLB 128;
MTCW

Pasquini
See Silone, Ignazio

Pastan, Linda (Olenik) 1932- ...... CLC 27
See also CA 61-64; CANR 18, 40; DLB 5

Pasternak, Boris (Leonidovich)
1890-1960 ...... CLC 7, 10, 18, 63; DA;
PC 6; WLC
See also CA 127; 116; MTCW

Patchen, Kenneth 1911-1972... CLC 1, 2, 18
See also CA 1-4R; 33-36R; CANR 3, 35;
DLB 16, 48; MTCW

Pater, Walter (Horatio)
1839-1894 .... NCLC 7
See also CDBLB 1832-1890; DLB 57

Paterson, A(ndrew) B(arton)
1864-1941 .... TCLC 32

Paterson, Katherine (Womeldorf)
1932- .... CLC 12, 30
See also AAYA 1; CA 21-24R; CANR 28;
CLR 7; DLB 52; JRDA; MAICYA;
MTCW; SATA 13, 53

Patmore, Coventry Kersey Dighton
1823-1896 .... NCLC 9
See also DLB 35, 98

Paton, Alan (Stewart)
1903-1988 ...... CLC 4, 10, 25, 55; DA;
WLC
See also CA 13-16; 125; CANR 22; CAP 1;
MTCW; SATA 11; SATA-Obit 56

Paton Walsh, Gillian 1937-
See Walsh, Jill Paton
See also CANR 38; JRDA; MAICYA;
SAAS 3; SATA 4, 72

Paulding, James Kirke 1778-1860.. NCLC 2
See also DLB 3, 59, 74

Paulin, Thomas Neilson 1949-
See Paulin, Tom
See also CA 123; 128

Paulin, Tom.................... CLC 37
See also Paulin, Thomas Neilson
See also DLB 40

Paustovsky, Konstantin (Georgievich)
1892-1968 .... CLC 40
See also CA 93-96; 25-28R

Pavese, Cesare 1908-1950 .... TCLC 3
See also CA 104; DLB 128

Pavic, Milorad 1929-............. CLC 60
See also CA 136

Payne, Alan
See Jakes, John (William)

Paz, Gil
See Lugones, Leopoldo

Paz, Octavio
1914- .... CLC 3, 4, 6, 10, 19, 51, 65;
DA; HLC; PC 1; WLC
See also CA 73-76; CANR 32; DLBY 90;
HW; MTCW

Peacock, Molly 1947-............ CLC 60
See also CA 103; DLB 120

Peacock, Thomas Love
 1785-1866 .... **NCLC 22**
 See also DLB 96, 116

Peake, Mervyn 1911-1968 .... **CLC 7, 54**
 See also CA 5-8R; 25-28R; CANR 3;
 DLB 15; MTCW; SATA 23

Pearce, Philippa .... **CLC 21**
 See also Christie, (Ann) Philippa
 See also CLR 9; MAICYA; SATA 1, 67

Pearl, Eric
 See Elman, Richard

Pearson, T(homas) R(eid) 1956- .... **CLC 39**
 See also CA 120; 130

Peck, Dale 1968(?)- .... **CLC 81**

Peck, John 1941- .... **CLC 3**
 See also CA 49-52; CANR 3

Peck, Richard (Wayne) 1934- ...... **CLC 21**
 See also AAYA 1; CA 85-88; CANR 19,
 38; CLR 15; JRDA; MAICYA; SAAS 2;
 SATA 18, 55

Peck, Robert Newton 1928-.... **CLC 17; DA**
 See also AAYA 3; CA 81-84; CANR 31;
 JRDA; MAICYA; SAAS 1; SATA 21, 62

Peckinpah, (David) Sam(uel)
 1925-1984 .... **CLC 20**
 See also CA 109; 114

Pedersen, Knut 1859-1952
 See Hamsun, Knut
 See also CA 104; 119; MTCW

Peeslake, Gaffer
 See Durrell, Lawrence (George)

Peguy, Charles Pierre
 1873-1914 .... **TCLC 10**
 See also CA 107

Pena, Ramon del Valle y
 See Valle-Inclan, Ramon (Maria) del

Pendennis, Arthur Esquir
 See Thackeray, William Makepeace

Penn, William 1644-1718 .... **LC 25**
 See also DLB 24

Pepys, Samuel
 1633-1703 .... **LC 11; DA; WLC**
 See also CDBLB 1660-1789; DLB 101

Percy, Walker
 1916-1990 .... **CLC 2, 3, 6, 8, 14, 18, 47,
 65**
 See also CA 1-4R; 131; CANR 1, 23;
 DLB 2; DLBY 80, 90; MTCW

Perec, Georges 1936-1982 .... **CLC 56**
 See also CA 141; DLB 83

Pereda (y Sanchez de Porrua), Jose Maria de
 1833-1906 .... **TCLC 16**
 See also CA 117

Pereda y Porrua, Jose Maria de
 See Pereda (y Sanchez de Porrua), Jose
 Maria de

Peregoy, George Weems
 See Mencken, H(enry) L(ouis)

Perelman, S(idney) J(oseph)
 1904-1979 ... **CLC 3, 5, 9, 15, 23, 44, 49**
 See also AITN 1, 2; CA 73-76; 89-92;
 CANR 18; DLB 11, 44; MTCW

Peret, Benjamin 1899-1959 .... **TCLC 20**
 See also CA 117

Peretz, Isaac Loeb 1851(?)-1915 ... **TCLC 16**
 See also CA 109

Peretz, Yitzkhok Leibush
 See Peretz, Isaac Loeb

Perez Galdos, Benito 1843-1920 ... **TCLC 27**
 See also CA 125; HW

Perrault, Charles 1628-1703 .... **LC 2**
 See also MAICYA; SATA 25

Perry, Brighton
 See Sherwood, Robert E(mmet)

Perse, St.-John .... **CLC 4, 11, 46**
 See also Leger, (Marie-Rene Auguste) Alexis
 Saint-Leger

Peseenz, Tulio F.
 See Lopez y Fuentes, Gregorio

Pesetsky, Bette 1932-............. **CLC 28**
 See also CA 133; DLB 130

Peshkov, Alexei Maximovich 1868-1936
 See Gorky, Maxim
 See also CA 105; 141; DA

Pessoa, Fernando (Antonio Nogueira)
 1888-1935 .... **TCLC 27; HLC**
 See also CA 125

Peterkin, Julia Mood 1880-1961.... **CLC 31**
 See also CA 102; DLB 9

Peters, Joan K. 1945-............. **CLC 39**

Peters, Robert L(ouis) 1924-........ **CLC 7**
 See also CA 13-16R; CAAS 8; DLB 105

Petofi, Sandor 1823-1849........ **NCLC 21**

Petrakis, Harry Mark 1923-........ **CLC 3**
 See also CA 9-12R; CANR 4, 30

Petrarch 1304-1374................ **PC 8**

Petrov, Evgeny .... **TCLC 21**
 See also Kataev, Evgeny Petrovich

Petry, Ann (Lane) 1908- ...... **CLC 1, 7, 18**
 See also BW 1; CA 5-8R; CAAS 6;
 CANR 4, 46, 46; CLR 12; DLB 76;
 JRDA; MAICYA; MTCW; SATA 5

Petursson, Halligrimur 1614-1674 .... **LC 8**

Philipson, Morris H. 1926-........ **CLC 53**
 See also CA 1-4R; CANR 4

Phillips, David Graham
 1867-1911 .... **TCLC 44**
 See also CA 108; DLB 9, 12

Phillips, Jack
 See Sandburg, Carl (August)

Phillips, Jayne Anne
 1952-............ **CLC 15, 33; SSC 16**
 See also CA 101; CANR 24; DLBY 80;
 MTCW

Phillips, Richard
 See Dick, Philip K(indred)

Phillips, Robert (Schaeffer) 1938-... **CLC 28**
 See also CA 17-20R; CAAS 13; CANR 8;
 DLB 105

Phillips, Ward
 See Lovecraft, H(oward) P(hillips)

Piccolo, Lucio 1901-1969......... **CLC 13**
 See also CA 97-100; DLB 114

Pickthall, Marjorie L(owry) C(hristie)
 1883-1922 .... **TCLC 21**
 See also CA 107; DLB 92

Pico della Mirandola, Giovanni
 1463-1494 .... **LC 15**

Piercy, Marge
 1936- .... **CLC 3, 6, 14, 18, 27, 62**
 See also CA 21-24R; CAAS 1; CANR 13,
 43; DLB 120; MTCW

Piers, Robert
 See Anthony, Piers

Pieyre de Mandiargues, Andre 1909-1991
 See Mandiargues, Andre Pieyre de
 See also CA 103; 136; CANR 22

Pilnyak, Boris .... **TCLC 23**
 See also Vogau, Boris Andreyevich

Pincherle, Alberto 1907-1990 ... **CLC 11, 18**
 See also Moravia, Alberto
 See also CA 25-28R; 132; CANR 33;
 MTCW

Pinckney, Darryl 1953-........... **CLC 76**
 See also BW 2; CA 143

Pindar 518B.C.-446B.C......... **CMLC 12**

Pineda, Cecile 1942-.............. **CLC 39**
 See also CA 118

Pinero, Arthur Wing 1855-1934 ... **TCLC 32**
 See also CA 110; DLB 10

Pinero, Miguel (Antonio Gomez)
 1946-1988 .... **CLC 4, 55**
 See also CA 61-64; 125; CANR 29; HW

Pinget, Robert 1919- .... **CLC 7, 13, 37**
 See also CA 85-88; DLB 83

Pink Floyd
 See Barrett, (Roger) Syd; Gilmour, David;
 Mason, Nick; Waters, Roger; Wright,
 Rick

Pinkney, Edward 1802-1828 ..... **NCLC 31**

Pinkwater, Daniel Manus 1941-.... **CLC 35**
 See also Pinkwater, Manus
 See also AAYA 1; CA 29-32R; CANR 12,
 38; CLR 4; JRDA; MAICYA; SAAS 3;
 SATA 46, 76

Pinkwater, Manus
 See Pinkwater, Daniel Manus
 See also SATA 8

Pinsky, Robert 1940-........ **CLC 9, 19, 38**
 See also CA 29-32R; CAAS 4; DLBY 82

Pinta, Harold
 See Pinter, Harold

Pinter, Harold
 1930- ..... **CLC 1, 3, 6, 9, 11, 15, 27, 58,
 73; DA; WLC**
 See also CA 5-8R; CANR 33; CDBLB 1960
 to Present; DLB 13; MTCW

Pirandello, Luigi
 1867-1936 ..... **TCLC 4, 29; DA; DC 5;
 WLC**
 See also CA 104

Pirsig, Robert M(aynard)
 1928- .... **CLC 4, 6, 73**
 See also CA 53-56; CANR 42; MTCW;
 SATA 39

Pisarev, Dmitry Ivanovich
 1840-1868 .... **NCLC 25**

Pix, Mary (Griffith) 1666-1709 .... **LC 8**
 See also DLB 80

Pixerecourt, Guilbert de
 1773-1844 .... **NCLC 39**

Plaidy, Jean
See Hibbert, Eleanor Alice Burford

Planche, James Robinson
1796-1880 .... NCLC 42

Plant, Robert 1948- .... CLC 12

Plante, David (Robert)
1940- .... CLC 7, 23, 38
See also CA 37-40R; CANR 12, 36;
DLBY 83; MTCW

Plath, Sylvia
1932-1963 ..... CLC 1, 2, 3, 5, 9, 11, 14,
  17, 50, 51, 62; DA; PC 1; WLC
See also AAYA 13; CA 19-20; CANR 34;
CAP 2; CDALB 1941-1968; DLB 5, 6;
MTCW

Plato 428(?)B.C.-348(?)B.C.... CMLC 8; DA

Platonov, Andrei .... TCLC 14
See also Klimentov, Andrei Platonovich

Platt, Kin 1911- .... CLC 26
See also AAYA 11; CA 17-20R; CANR 11;
JRDA; SAAS 17; SATA 21

Plick et Plock
See Simenon, Georges (Jacques Christian)

Plimpton, George (Ames) 1927-..... CLC 36
See also AITN 1; CA 21-24R; CANR 32;
MTCW; SATA 10

Plomer, William Charles Franklin
1903-1973 .... CLC 4, 8
See also CA 21-22; CANR 34; CAP 2;
DLB 20; MTCW; SATA 24

Plowman, Piers
See Kavanagh, Patrick (Joseph)

Plum, J.
See Wodehouse, P(elham) G(renville)

Plumly, Stanley (Ross) 1939- ...... CLC 33
See also CA 108; 110; DLB 5

Plumpe, Friedrich Wilhelm
1888-1931 .... TCLC 53
See also CA 112

Poe, Edgar Allan
1809-1849 ..... NCLC 1, 16; DA; PC 1;
  SSC 1; WLC
See also AAYA 14; CDALB 1640-1865;
DLB 3, 59, 73, 74; SATA 23

Poet of Titchfield Street, The
See Pound, Ezra (Weston Loomis)

Pohl, Frederik 1919- .... CLC 18
See also CA 61-64; CAAS 1; CANR 11, 37;
DLB 8; MTCW; SATA 24

Poirier, Louis 1910-
See Gracq, Julien
See also CA 122; 126

Poitier, Sidney 1927- .... CLC 26
See also BW 1; CA 117

Polanski, Roman 1933- .... CLC 16
See also CA 77-80

Poliakoff, Stephen 1952- .... CLC 38
See also CA 106; DLB 13

Police, The
See Copeland, Stewart (Armstrong);
Summers, Andrew James; Sumner,
Gordon Matthew

Pollitt, Katha 1949- .... CLC 28
See also CA 120; 122; MTCW

Pollock, (Mary) Sharon 1936-...... CLC 50
See also CA 141; DLB 60

Pomerance, Bernard 1940-........ CLC 13
See also CA 101

Ponge, Francis (Jean Gaston Alfred)
1899-1988 .... CLC 6, 18
See also CA 85-88; 126; CANR 40

Pontoppidan, Henrik 1857-1943 ... TCLC 29

Poole, Josephine .... CLC 17
See also Helyar, Jane Penelope Josephine
See also SAAS 2; SATA 5

Popa, Vasko 1922- .... CLC 19
See also CA 112

Pope, Alexander
1688-1744 .... LC 3; DA; WLC
See also CDBLB 1660-1789; DLB 95, 101

Porter, Connie (Rose) 1959(?)- ..... CLC 70
See also BW 2; CA 142; SATA 81

Porter, Gene(va Grace) Stratton
1863(?)-1924 .... TCLC 21
See also CA 112

Porter, Katherine Anne
1890-1980 ...... CLC 1, 3, 7, 10, 13, 15,
  27; DA; SSC 4
See also AITN 2; CA 1-4R; 101; CANR 1;
DLB 4, 9, 102; DLBD 12; DLBY 80;
MTCW; SATA 39; SATA-Obit 23

Porter, Peter (Neville Frederick)
1929- .... CLC 5, 13, 33
See also CA 85-88; DLB 40

Porter, William Sydney 1862-1910
See Henry, O.
See also CA 104; 131; CDALB 1865-1917;
DA; DLB 12, 78, 79; MTCW; YABC 2

Portillo (y Pacheco), Jose Lopez
See Lopez Portillo (y Pacheco), Jose

Post, Melville Davisson
1869-1930 .... TCLC 39
See also CA 110

Potok, Chaim 1929- .... CLC 2, 7, 14, 26
See also AITN 1, 2; CA 17-20R; CANR 19,
35; DLB 28; MTCW; SATA 33

Potter, Beatrice
See Webb, (Martha) Beatrice (Potter)
See also MAICYA

Potter, Dennis (Christopher George)
1935-1994 .... CLC 58, 86
See also CA 107; 145; CANR 33; MTCW

Pound, Ezra (Weston Loomis)
1885-1972 ...... CLC 1, 2, 3, 4, 5, 7, 10,
  13, 18, 34, 48, 50; DA; PC 4; WLC
See also CA 5-8R; 37-40R; CANR 40;
CDALB 1917-1929; DLB 4, 45, 63;
MTCW

Povod, Reinaldo 1959-1994 .... CLC 44
See also CA 136; 146

Powell, Anthony (Dymoke)
1905- .... CLC 1, 3, 7, 9, 10, 31
See also CA 1-4R; CANR 1, 32;
CDBLB 1945-1960; DLB 15; MTCW

Powell, Dawn 1897-1965 .... CLC 66
See also CA 5-8R

Powell, Padgett 1952-............. CLC 34
See also CA 126

Powers, J(ames) F(arl)
1917- .... CLC 1, 4, 8, 57; SSC 4
See also CA 1-4R; CANR 2; DLB 130;
MTCW

Powers, John J(ames) 1945-
See Powers, John R.
See also CA 69-72

Powers, John R. .... CLC 66
See also Powers, John J(ames)

Pownall, David 1938-............. CLC 10
See also CA 89-92; CAAS 18; DLB 14

Powys, John Cowper
1872-1963 .... CLC 7, 9, 15, 46
See also CA 85-88; DLB 15; MTCW

Powys, T(heodore) F(rancis)
1875-1953 .... TCLC 9
See also CA 106; DLB 36

Prager, Emily 1952-.............. CLC 56

Pratt, E(dwin) J(ohn)
1883(?)-1964 .... CLC 19
See also CA 141; 93-96; DLB 92

Premchand...................... TCLC 21
See also Srivastava, Dhanpat Rai

Preussler, Otfried 1923-........... CLC 17
See also CA 77-80; SATA 24

Prevert, Jacques (Henri Marie)
1900-1977 .... CLC 15
See also CA 77-80; 69-72; CANR 29;
MTCW; SATA-Obit 30

Prevost, Abbe (Antoine Francois)
1697-1763 .... LC 1

Price, (Edward) Reynolds
1933- .... CLC 3, 6, 13, 43, 50, 63
See also CA 1-4R; CANR 1, 37; DLB 2

Price, Richard 1949- .... CLC 6, 12
See also CA 49-52; CANR 3; DLBY 81

Prichard, Katharine Susannah
1883-1969 .... CLC 46
See also CA 11-12; CANR 33; CAP 1;
MTCW; SATA 66

Priestley, J(ohn) B(oynton)
1894-1984 .... CLC 2, 5, 9, 34
See also CA 9-12R; 113; CANR 33;
CDBLB 1914-1945; DLB 10, 34, 77, 100,
139; DLBY 84; MTCW

Prince 1958(?)-.................. CLC 35

Prince, F(rank) T(empleton) 1912-.. CLC 22
See also CA 101; CANR 43; DLB 20

Prince Kropotkin
See Kropotkin, Peter (Alekseievich)

Prior, Matthew 1664-1721.......... LC 4
See also DLB 95

Pritchard, William H(arrison)
1932- .... CLC 34
See also CA 65-68; CANR 23; DLB 111

Pritchett, V(ictor) S(awdon)
1900- .... CLC 5, 13, 15, 41; SSC 14
See also CA 61-64; CANR 31; DLB 15,
139; MTCW

Private 19022
See Manning, Frederic

Probst, Mark 1925- .... CLC 59
See also CA 130

Prokosch, Frederic 1908-1989.... **CLC 4, 48**
See also CA 73-76; 128; DLB 48

Prophet, The
See Dreiser, Theodore (Herman Albert)

Prose, Francine 1947-............ **CLC 45**
See also CA 109; 112; CANR 46, 46

Proudhon
See Cunha, Euclides (Rodrigues Pimenta) da

Proulx, E. Annie 1935- .... **CLC 81**

Proust, (Valentin-Louis-George-Eugene-)
Marcel
1871-1922 ... **TCLC 7, 13, 33; DA; WLC**
See also CA 104; 120; DLB 65; MTCW

Prowler, Harley
See Masters, Edgar Lee

Prus, Boleslaw 1845-1912 .... **TCLC 48**

Pryor, Richard (Franklin Lenox Thomas)
1940- .... **CLC 26**
See also CA 122

Przybyszewski, Stanislaw
1868-1927 .... **TCLC 36**
See also DLB 66

Pteleon
See Grieve, C(hristopher) M(urray)

Puckett, Lute
See Masters, Edgar Lee

Puig, Manuel
1932-1990 ... **CLC 3, 5, 10, 28, 65; HLC**
See also CA 45-48; CANR 2, 32; DLB 113;
HW; MTCW

Purdy, Al(fred Wellington)
1918- .... **CLC 3, 6, 14, 50**
See also CA 81-84; CAAS 17; CANR 42;
DLB 88

Purdy, James (Amos)
1923- .... **CLC 2, 4, 10, 28, 52**
See also CA 33-36R; CAAS 1; CANR 19;
DLB 2; MTCW

Pure, Simon
See Swinnerton, Frank Arthur

Pushkin, Alexander (Sergeyevich)
1799-1837 .... **NCLC 3, 27; DA; PC 10;
WLC**
See also SATA 61

P'u Sung-ling 1640-1715 .... **LC 3**

Putnam, Arthur Lee
See Alger, Horatio, Jr.

Puzo, Mario 1920-......... **CLC 1, 2, 6, 36**
See also CA 65-68; CANR 4, 42; DLB 6;
MTCW

Pym, Barbara (Mary Crampton)
1913-1980 .... **CLC 13, 19, 37**
See also CA 13-14; 97-100; CANR 13, 34;
CAP 1; DLB 14; DLBY 87; MTCW

Pynchon, Thomas (Ruggles, Jr.)
1937- ..... **CLC 2, 3, 6, 9, 11, 18, 33, 62,
72; DA; SSC 14; WLC**
See also BEST 90:2; CA 17-20R; CANR 22,
46, 46; DLB 2; MTCW

Qian Zhongshu
See Ch'ien Chung-shu

Qroll
See Dagerman, Stig (Halvard)

Quarrington, Paul (Lewis) 1953-.... **CLC 65**
See also CA 129

Quasimodo, Salvatore 1901-1968 ... **CLC 10**
See also CA 13-16; 25-28R; CAP 1;
DLB 114; MTCW

Queen, Ellery.................. **CLC 3, 11**
See also Dannay, Frederic; Davidson,
Avram; Lee, Manfred B(ennington);
Sturgeon, Theodore (Hamilton); Vance,
John Holbrook

Queen, Ellery, Jr.
See Dannay, Frederic; Lee, Manfred
B(ennington)

Queneau, Raymond
1903-1976 .... **CLC 2, 5, 10, 42**
See also CA 77-80; 69-72; CANR 32;
DLB 72; MTCW

Quevedo, Francisco de 1580-1645.... **LC 23**

Quiller-Couch, Arthur Thomas
1863-1944 .... **TCLC 53**
See also CA 118; DLB 135

Quin, Ann (Marie) 1936-1973 ...... **CLC 6**
See also CA 9-12R; 45-48; DLB 14

Quinn, Martin
See Smith, Martin Cruz

Quinn, Simon
See Smith, Martin Cruz

Quiroga, Horacio (Sylvestre)
1878-1937 .... **TCLC 20; HLC**
See also CA 117; 131; HW; MTCW

Quoirez, Francoise 1935-........... **CLC 9**
See also Sagan, Francoise
See also CA 49-52; CANR 6, 39; MTCW

Raabe, Wilhelm 1831-1910 ...... **TCLC 45**
See also DLB 129

Rabe, David (William) 1940-... **CLC 4, 8, 33**
See also CA 85-88; CABS 3; DLB 7

Rabelais, Francois
1483-1553 .... **LC 5; DA; WLC**

Rabinovitch, Sholem 1859-1916
See Aleichem, Sholom
See also CA 104

Radcliffe, Ann (Ward) 1764-1823 .. **NCLC 6**
See also DLB 39

Radiguet, Raymond 1903-1923 .... **TCLC 29**
See also DLB 65

Radnoti, Miklos 1909-1944 ...... **TCLC 16**
See also CA 118

Rado, James 1939-............... **CLC 17**
See also CA 105

Radvanyi, Netty 1900-1983
See Seghers, Anna
See also CA 85-88; 110

Rae, Ben
See Griffiths, Trevor

Raeburn, John (Hay) 1941-........ **CLC 34**
See also CA 57-60

Ragni, Gerome 1942-1991 .... **CLC 17**
See also CA 105; 134

Rahv, Philip 1908-1973 .... **CLC 24**
See also Greenberg, Ivan
See also DLB 137

Raine, Craig 1944-.............. **CLC 32**
See also CA 108; CANR 29; DLB 40

Raine, Kathleen (Jessie) 1908- ... **CLC 7, 45**
See also CA 85-88; CANR 46, 46; DLB 20;
MTCW

Rainis, Janis 1865-1929......... **TCLC 29**

Rakosi, Carl..................... **CLC 47**
See also Rawley, Callman
See also CAAS 5

Raleigh, Richard
See Lovecraft, H(oward) P(hillips)

Rallentando, H. P.
See Sayers, Dorothy L(eigh)

Ramal, Walter
See de la Mare, Walter (John)

Ramon, Juan
See Jimenez (Mantecon), Juan Ramon

Ramos, Graciliano 1892-1953 ..... **TCLC 32**

Rampersad, Arnold 1941-......... **CLC 44**
See also BW 2; CA 127; 133; DLB 111

Rampling, Anne
See Rice, Anne

Ramuz, Charles-Ferdinand
1878-1947 .... **TCLC 33**

Rand, Ayn
1905-1982 ...... **CLC 3, 30, 44, 79; DA;
WLC**
See also AAYA 10; CA 13-16R; 105;
CANR 27; MTCW

Randall, Dudley (Felker)
1914- .... **CLC 1; BLC**
See also BW 1; CA 25-28R; CANR 23;
DLB 41

Randall, Robert
See Silverberg, Robert

Ranger, Ken
See Creasey, John

Ransom, John Crowe
1888-1974 .... **CLC 2, 4, 5, 11, 24**
See also CA 5-8R; 49-52; CANR 6, 34;
DLB 45, 63; MTCW

Rao, Raja 1909- .... **CLC 25, 56**
See also CA 73-76; MTCW

Raphael, Frederic (Michael)
1931- .... **CLC 2, 14**
See also CA 1-4R; CANR 1; DLB 14

Ratcliffe, James P.
See Mencken, H(enry) L(ouis)

Rathbone, Julian 1935- .... **CLC 41**
See also CA 101; CANR 34

Rattigan, Terence (Mervyn)
1911-1977 .... **CLC 7**
See also CA 85-88; 73-76;
CDBLB 1945-1960; DLB 13; MTCW

Ratushinskaya, Irina 1954- .... **CLC 54**
See also CA 129

Raven, Simon (Arthur Noel)
1927- .... **CLC 14**
See also CA 81-84

Rawley, Callman 1903-
See Rakosi, Carl
See also CA 21-24R; CANR 12, 32

Rawlings, Marjorie Kinnan
1896-1953 .... **TCLC 4**
See also CA 104; 137; DLB 9, 22, 102;
JRDA; MAICYA; YABC 1

Riley, Tex
    See Creasey, John

Rilke, Rainer Maria
    1875-1926 . . . . TCLC 1, 6, 19; PC 2
    See also CA 104; 132; DLB 81; MTCW

Rimbaud, (Jean Nicolas) Arthur
    1854-1891 . . . . . NCLC 4, 35; DA; PC 3;
                                                    WLC

Rinehart, Mary Roberts
    1876-1958 . . . . TCLC 52
    See also CA 108

Ringmaster, The
    See Mencken, H(enry) L(ouis)

Ringwood, Gwen(dolyn Margaret) Pharis
    1910-1984 . . . . CLC 48
    See also CA 112; DLB 88

Rio, Michel   19(?)- . . . . CLC 43

Ritsos, Giannes
    See Ritsos, Yannis

Ritsos, Yannis   1909-1990 . . . . . CLC 6, 13, 31
    See also CA 77-80; 133; CANR 39; MTCW

Ritter, Erika   1948(?)- . . . . CLC 52

Rivera, Jose Eustasio   1889-1928 . . . TCLC 35
    See also HW

Rivers, Conrad Kent   1933-1968 . . . . . . CLC 1
    See also BW 1; CA 85-88; DLB 41

Rivers, Elfrida
    See Bradley, Marion Zimmer

Riverside, John
    See Heinlein, Robert A(nson)

Rizal, Jose   1861-1896 . . . . NCLC 27

Roa Bastos, Augusto (Antonio)
    1917- . . . . CLC 45; HLC
    See also CA 131; DLB 113; HW

Robbe-Grillet, Alain
    1922- . . . . . . CLC 1, 2, 4, 6, 8, 10, 14, 43
    See also CA 9-12R; CANR 33; DLB 83;
    MTCW

Robbins, Harold   1916- . . . . CLC 5
    See also CA 73-76; CANR 26; MTCW

Robbins, Thomas Eugene   1936-
    See Robbins, Tom
    See also CA 81-84; CANR 29; MTCW

Robbins, Tom . . . . CLC 9, 32, 64
    See also Robbins, Thomas Eugene
    See also BEST 90:3; DLBY 80

Robbins, Trina   1938- . . . . CLC 21
    See also CA 128

Roberts, Charles G(eorge) D(ouglas)
    1860-1943 . . . . TCLC 8
    See also CA 105; CLR 33; DLB 92;
    SATA 29

Roberts, Kate   1891-1985 . . . . CLC 15
    See also CA 107; 116

Roberts, Keith (John Kingston)
    1935- . . . . CLC 14
    See also CA 25-28R; CANR 46, 46

Roberts, Kenneth (Lewis)
    1885-1957 . . . . TCLC 23
    See also CA 109; DLB 9

Roberts, Michele (B.)   1949- . . . . CLC 48
    See also CA 115

Robertson, Ellis
    See Ellison, Harlan (Jay); Silverberg, Robert

Robertson, Thomas William
    1829-1871 . . . . NCLC 35

Robinson, Edwin Arlington
    1869-1935 . . . . TCLC 5; DA; PC 1
    See also CA 104; 133; CDALB 1865-1917;
    DLB 54; MTCW

Robinson, Henry Crabb
    1775-1867 . . . . NCLC 15
    See also DLB 107

Robinson, Jill   1936- . . . . CLC 10
    See also CA 102

Robinson, Kim Stanley   1952- . . . . . . CLC 34
    See also CA 126

Robinson, Lloyd
    See Silverberg, Robert

Robinson, Marilynne   1944- . . . . CLC 25
    See also CA 116

Robinson, Smokey . . . . CLC 21
    See also Robinson, William, Jr.

Robinson, William, Jr.   1940-
    See Robinson, Smokey
    See also CA 116

Robison, Mary   1949- . . . . CLC 42
    See also CA 113; 116; DLB 130

Rod, Edouard   1857-1910 . . . . TCLC 52

Roddenberry, Eugene Wesley   1921-1991
    See Roddenberry, Gene
    See also CA 110; 135; CANR 37; SATA 45;
    SATA-Obit 69

Roddenberry, Gene . . . . CLC 17
    See also Roddenberry, Eugene Wesley
    See also AAYA 5; SATA-Obit 69

Rodgers, Mary   1931- . . . . CLC 12
    See also CA 49-52; CANR 8; CLR 20;
    JRDA; MAICYA; SATA 8

Rodgers, W(illiam) R(obert)
    1909-1969 . . . . CLC 7
    See also CA 85-88; DLB 20

Rodman, Eric
    See Silverberg, Robert

Rodman, Howard   1920(?)-1985 . . . . . CLC 65
    See also CA 118

Rodman, Maia
    See Wojciechowska, Maia (Teresa)

Rodriguez, Claudio   1934- . . . . CLC 10
    See also DLB 134

Roelvaag, O(le) E(dvart)
    1876-1931 . . . . TCLC 17
    See also CA 117; DLB 9

Roethke, Theodore (Huebner)
    1908-1963 . . . . . CLC 1, 3, 8, 11, 19, 46
    See also CA 81-84; CABS 2;
    CDALB 1941-1968; DLB 5; MTCW

Rogers, Thomas Hunton   1927- . . . . . CLC 57
    See also CA 89-92

Rogers, Will(iam Penn Adair)
    1879-1935 . . . . TCLC 8
    See also CA 105; 144; DLB 11; NNAL

Rogin, Gilbert   1929- . . . . CLC 18
    See also CA 65-68; CANR 15

Rohan, Koda . . . . TCLC 22
    See also Koda Shigeyuki

Rohmer, Eric . . . . CLC 16
    See also Scherer, Jean-Marie Maurice

Rohmer, Sax . . . . TCLC 28
    See also Ward, Arthur Henry Sarsfield
    See also DLB 70

Roiphe, Anne (Richardson)
    1935- . . . . CLC 3, 9
    See also CA 89-92; CANR 45; DLBY 80

Rojas, Fernando de   1465-1541 . . . . . . LC 23

Rolfe, Frederick (William Serafino Austin
    Lewis Mary)   1860-1913 . . . . . . TCLC 12
    See also CA 107; DLB 34

Rolland, Romain   1866-1944 . . . . . . TCLC 23
    See also CA 118; DLB 65

Rolvaag, O(le) E(dvart)
    See Roelvaag, O(le) E(dvart)

Romain Arnaud, Saint
    See Aragon, Louis

Romains, Jules   1885-1972 . . . . CLC 7
    See also CA 85-88; CANR 34; DLB 65;
    MTCW

Romero, Jose Ruben   1890-1952 . . . TCLC 14
    See also CA 114; 131; HW

Ronsard, Pierre de
    1524-1585 . . . . LC 6; PC 11

Rooke, Leon   1934- . . . . CLC 25, 34
    See also CA 25-28R; CANR 23

Roper, William   1498-1578 . . . . LC 10

Roquelaure, A. N.
    See Rice, Anne

Rosa, Joao Guimaraes   1908-1967 . . . CLC 23
    See also CA 89-92; DLB 113

Rose, Wendy   1948- . . . . CLC 85
    See also CA 53-56; CANR 5; NNAL;
    SATA 12

Rosen, Richard (Dean)   1949- . . . . . . CLC 39
    See also CA 77-80

Rosenberg, Isaac   1890-1918 . . . . . . TCLC 12
    See also CA 107; DLB 20

Rosenblatt, Joe . . . . CLC 15
    See also Rosenblatt, Joseph

Rosenblatt, Joseph   1933-
    See Rosenblatt, Joe
    See also CA 89-92

Rosenfeld, Samuel   1896-1963
    See Tzara, Tristan
    See also CA 89-92

Rosenthal, M(acha) L(ouis)   1917- . . . CLC 28
    See also CA 1-4R; CAAS 6; CANR 4;
    DLB 5; SATA 59

Ross, Barnaby
    See Dannay, Frederic

Ross, Bernard L.
    See Follett, Ken(neth Martin)

Ross, J. H.
    See Lawrence, T(homas) E(dward)

Ross, Martin
    See Martin, Violet Florence
    See also DLB 135

Ross, (James) Sinclair   1908- . . . . CLC 13
    See also CA 73-76; DLB 88

Rossetti, Christina (Georgina)
    1830-1894 . . . NCLC 2; DA; PC 7; WLC
    See also DLB 35; MAICYA; SATA 20

Salinger, J(erome) D(avid)
1919- ..... **CLC 1, 3, 8, 12, 55, 56; DA;
SSC 2; WLC**
See also AAYA 2; CA 5-8R; CANR 39;
CDALB 1941-1968; CLR 18; DLB 2, 102;
MAICYA; MTCW; SATA 67

Salisbury, John
See Caute, David

Salter, James 1925- .... **CLC 7, 52, 59**
See also CA 73-76; DLB 130

Saltus, Edgar (Everton)
1855-1921 .... **TCLC 8**
See also CA 105

Saltykov, Mikhail Evgrafovich
1826-1889 .... **NCLC 16**

Samarakis, Antonis 1919- .... **CLC 5**
See also CA 25-28R; CAAS 16; CANR 36

Sanchez, Florencio 1875-1910 ..... **TCLC 37**
See also HW

Sanchez, Luis Rafael 1936-........ **CLC 23**
See also CA 128; DLB 145; HW

Sanchez, Sonia 1934-... **CLC 5; BLC; PC 9**
See also BW 2; CA 33-36R; CANR 24;
CLR 18; DLB 41; DLBD 8; MAICYA;
MTCW; SATA 22

Sand, George
1804-1876 ...... **NCLC 2, 42; DA; WLC**
See also DLB 119

Sandburg, Carl (August)
1878-1967 .... **CLC 1, 4, 10, 15, 35; DA;
PC 2; WLC**
See also CA 5-8R; 25-28R; CANR 35;
CDALB 1865-1917; DLB 17, 54;
MAICYA; MTCW; SATA 8

Sandburg, Charles
See Sandburg, Carl (August)

Sandburg, Charles A.
See Sandburg, Carl (August)

Sanders, (James) Ed(ward) 1939- ... **CLC 53**
See also CA 13-16R; CANR 13, 44;
DLB 16

Sanders, Lawrence 1920-.......... **CLC 41**
See also BEST 89:4; CA 81-84; CANR 33;
MTCW

Sanders, Noah
See Blount, Roy (Alton), Jr.

Sanders, Winston P.
See Anderson, Poul (William)

Sandoz, Mari(e Susette)
1896-1966 .... **CLC 28**
See also CA 1-4R; 25-28R; CANR 17;
DLB 9; MTCW; SATA 5

Saner, Reg(inald Anthony) 1931- .... **CLC 9**
See also CA 65-68

Sannazaro, Jacopo 1456(?)-1530 ...... **LC 8**

Sansom, William 1912-1976....... **CLC 2, 6**
See also CA 5-8R; 65-68; CANR 42;
DLB 139; MTCW

Santayana, George 1863-1952 ..... **TCLC 40**
See also CA 115; DLB 54, 71

Santiago, Danny .... **CLC 33**
See also James, Daniel (Lewis); James,
Daniel (Lewis)
See also DLB 122

Santmyer, Helen Hoover
1895-1986 .... **CLC 33**
See also CA 1-4R; 118; CANR 15, 33;
DLBY 84; MTCW

Santos, Bienvenido N(uqui) 1911-... **CLC 22**
See also CA 101; CANR 19, 46, 46

Sapper .... **TCLC 44**
See also McNeile, Herman Cyril

Sappho fl. 6th cent. B.C.-.... **CMLC 3; PC 5**

Sarduy, Severo 1937-1993 .... **CLC 6**
See also CA 89-92; 142; DLB 113; HW

Sargeson, Frank 1903-1982 .... **CLC 31**
See also CA 25-28R; 106; CANR 38

Sarmiento, Felix Ruben Garcia
See Dario, Ruben

Saroyan, William
1908-1981 ..... **CLC 1, 8, 10, 29, 34, 56;
DA; WLC**
See also CA 5-8R; 103; CANR 30; DLB 7,
9, 86; DLBY 81; MTCW; SATA 23;
SATA-Obit 24

Sarraute, Nathalie
1900- .... **CLC 1, 2, 4, 8, 10, 31, 80**
See also CA 9-12R; CANR 23; DLB 83;
MTCW

Sarton, (Eleanor) May
1912- .... **CLC 4, 14, 49**
See also CA 1-4R; CANR 1, 34; DLB 48;
DLBY 81; MTCW; SATA 36

Sartre, Jean-Paul
1905-1980 .... **CLC 1, 4, 7, 9, 13, 18, 24,
44, 50, 52; DA; DC 3; WLC**
See also CA 9-12R; 97-100; CANR 21;
DLB 72; MTCW

Sassoon, Siegfried (Lorraine)
1886-1967 .... **CLC 36**
See also CA 104; 25-28R; CANR 36;
DLB 20; MTCW

Satterfield, Charles
See Pohl, Frederik

Saul, John (W. III) 1942- .... **CLC 46**
See also AAYA 10; BEST 90:4; CA 81-84;
CANR 16, 40

Saunders, Caleb
See Heinlein, Robert A(nson)

Saura (Atares), Carlos 1932-....... **CLC 20**
See also CA 114; 131; HW

Sauser-Hall, Frederic 1887-1961.... **CLC 18**
See also CA 102; 93-96; CANR 36; MTCW

Saussure, Ferdinand de
1857-1913 .... **TCLC 49**

Savage, Catharine
See Brosman, Catharine Savage

Savage, Thomas 1915- .... **CLC 40**
See also CA 126; 132; CAAS 15

Savan, Glenn 19(?)- .... **CLC 50**

Sayers, Dorothy L(eigh)
1893-1957 .... **TCLC 2, 15**
See also CA 104; 119; CDBLB 1914-1945;
DLB 10, 36, 77, 100; MTCW

Sayers, Valerie 1952-............. **CLC 50**
See also CA 134

Sayles, John (Thomas)
1950- .... **CLC 7, 10, 14**
See also CA 57-60; CANR 41; DLB 44

Scammell, Michael .... **CLC 34**

Scannell, Vernon 1922- .... **CLC 49**
See also CA 5-8R; CANR 8, 24; DLB 27;
SATA 59

Scarlett, Susan
See Streatfeild, (Mary) Noel

Schaeffer, Susan Fromberg
1941- .... **CLC 6, 11, 22**
See also CA 49-52; CANR 18; DLB 28;
MTCW; SATA 22

Schary, Jill
See Robinson, Jill

Schell, Jonathan 1943-............ **CLC 35**
See also CA 73-76; CANR 12

Schelling, Friedrich Wilhelm Joseph von
1775-1854 .... **NCLC 30**
See also DLB 90

Schendel, Arthur van 1874-1946... **TCLC 56**

Scherer, Jean-Marie Maurice 1920-
See Rohmer, Eric
See also CA 110

Schevill, James (Erwin) 1920-....... **CLC 7**
See also CA 5-8R; CAAS 12

Schiller, Friedrich 1759-1805 .... **NCLC 39**
See also DLB 94

Schisgal, Murray (Joseph) 1926-..... **CLC 6**
See also CA 21-24R

Schlee, Ann 1934-................ **CLC 35**
See also CA 101; CANR 29; SATA 36, 44

Schlegel, August Wilhelm von
1767-1845 .... **NCLC 15**
See also DLB 94

Schlegel, Friedrich 1772-1829 .... **NCLC 45**
See also DLB 90

Schlegel, Johann Elias (von)
1719(?)-1749 .... **LC 5**

Schlesinger, Arthur M(eier), Jr.
1917- .... **CLC 84**
See also AITN 1; CA 1-4R; CANR 1, 28;
DLB 17; MTCW; SATA 61

Schmidt, Arno (Otto) 1914-1979 .... **CLC 56**
See also CA 128; 109; DLB 69

Schmitz, Aron Hector 1861-1928
See Svevo, Italo
See also CA 104; 122; MTCW

Schnackenberg, Gjertrud 1953-..... **CLC 40**
See also CA 116; DLB 120

Schneider, Leonard Alfred 1925-1966
See Bruce, Lenny
See also CA 89-92

Schnitzler, Arthur
1862-1931 .... **TCLC 4; SSC 15**
See also CA 104; DLB 81, 118

Schor, Sandra (M.) 1932(?)-1990 ... **CLC 65**
See also CA 132

Schorer, Mark 1908-1977 .... **CLC 9**
See also CA 5-8R; 73-76; CANR 7;
DLB 103

Schrader, Paul (Joseph) 1946-...... **CLC 26**
See also CA 37-40R; CANR 41; DLB 44

Schreiner, Olive (Emilie Albertina)
1855-1920 .... **TCLC 9**
See also CA 105; DLB 18

Shammas, Anton   1951-........... **CLC 55**

Shange, Ntozake
  1948- .... **CLC 8, 25, 38, 74; BLC; DC 3**
  See also AAYA 9; BW 2; CA 85-88;
  CABS 3; CANR 27; DLB 38; MTCW

Shanley, John Patrick   1950-....... **CLC 75**
  See also CA 128; 133

Shapcott, Thomas William   1935- ... **CLC 38**
  See also CA 69-72

Shapiro, Jane.................... **CLC 76**

Shapiro, Karl (Jay)   1913- .. **CLC 4, 8, 15, 53**
  See also CA 1-4R; CAAS 6; CANR 1, 36;
  DLB 48; MTCW

Sharp, William   1855-1905 .... **TCLC 39**

Sharpe, Thomas Ridley   1928-
  See Sharpe, Tom
  See also CA 114; 122

Sharpe, Tom..................... **CLC 36**
  See also Sharpe, Thomas Ridley
  See also DLB 14

Shaw, Bernard................... **TCLC 45**
  See also Shaw, George Bernard
  See also BW 1

Shaw, G. Bernard
  See Shaw, George Bernard

Shaw, George Bernard
  1856-1950 .... **TCLC 3, 9, 21; DA; WLC**
  See also Shaw, Bernard
  See also CA 104; 128; CDBLB 1914-1945;
  DLB 10, 57; MTCW

Shaw, Henry Wheeler
  1818-1885 .... **NCLC 15**
  See also DLB 11

Shaw, Irwin   1913-1984...... **CLC 7, 23, 34**
  See also AITN 1; CA 13-16R; 112;
  CANR 21; CDALB 1941-1968; DLB 6,
  102; DLBY 84; MTCW

Shaw, Robert   1927-1978 .... **CLC 5**
  See also AITN 1; CA 1-4R; 81-84;
  CANR 4; DLB 13, 14

Shaw, T. E.
  See Lawrence, T(homas) E(dward)

Shawn, Wallace   1943- .... **CLC 41**
  See also CA 112

Shea, Lisa   1953-................ **CLC 86**

Sheed, Wilfrid (John Joseph)
  1930- ....**CLC 2, 4, 10, 53**
  See also CA 65-68; CANR 30; DLB 6;
  MTCW

Sheldon, Alice Hastings Bradley
  1915(?)-1987
  See Tiptree, James, Jr.
  See also CA 108; 122; CANR 34; MTCW

Sheldon, John
  See Bloch, Robert (Albert)

Shelley, Mary Wollstonecraft (Godwin)
  1797-1851 .... **NCLC 14; DA; WLC**
  See also CDBLB 1789-1832; DLB 110, 116;
  SATA 29

Shelley, Percy Bysshe
  1792-1822 .... **NCLC 18; DA; WLC**
  See also CDBLB 1789-1832; DLB 96, 110

Shepard, Jim   1956-.............. **CLC 36**
  See also CA 137

Shepard, Lucius   1947-............ **CLC 34**
  See also CA 128; 141

Shepard, Sam
  1943- .... **CLC 4, 6, 17, 34, 41, 44; DC 5**
  See also AAYA 1; CA 69-72; CABS 3;
  CANR 22; DLB 7; MTCW

Shepherd, Michael
  See Ludlum, Robert

Sherburne, Zoa (Morin)   1912-...... **CLC 30**
  See also AAYA 13; CA 1-4R; CANR 3, 37;
  MAICYA; SAAS 18; SATA 3

Sheridan, Frances   1724-1766........ **LC 7**
  See also DLB 39, 84

Sheridan, Richard Brinsley
  1751-1816 ... **NCLC 5; DA; DC 1; WLC**
  See also CDBLB 1660-1789; DLB 89

Sherman, Jonathan Marc.......... **CLC 55**

Sherman, Martin   1941(?)-........ **CLC 19**
  See also CA 116; 123

Sherwin, Judith Johnson   1936-... **CLC 7, 15**
  See also CA 25-28R; CANR 34

Sherwood, Frances   1940-......... **CLC 81**

Sherwood, Robert E(mmet)
  1896-1955 .... **TCLC 3**
  See also CA 104; DLB 7, 26

Shestov, Lev   1866-1938 .... **TCLC 56**

Shiel, M(atthew) P(hipps)
  1865-1947 .... **TCLC 8**
  See also CA 106

Shiga, Naoya   1883-1971.......... **CLC 33**
  See also CA 101; 33-36R

Shilts, Randy   1951-1994 .... **CLC 85**
  See also CA 115; 127; 144; CANR 45

Shimazaki Haruki   1872-1943
  See Shimazaki Toson
  See also CA 105; 134

Shimazaki Toson .... **TCLC 5**
  See also Shimazaki Haruki

Sholokhov, Mikhail (Aleksandrovich)
  1905-1984 .... **CLC 7, 15**
  See also CA 101; 112; MTCW;
  SATA-Obit 36

Shone, Patric
  See Hanley, James

Shreve, Susan Richards   1939-...... **CLC 23**
  See also CA 49-52; CAAS 5; CANR 5, 38;
  MAICYA; SATA 41, 46

Shue, Larry   1946-1985........... **CLC 52**
  See also CA 145; 117

Shu-Jen, Chou   1881-1936
  See Hsun, Lu
  See also CA 104

Shulman, Alix Kates   1932- ...... **CLC 2, 10**
  See also CA 29-32R; CANR 43; SATA 7

Shuster, Joe   1914- .... **CLC 21**

Shute, Nevil................... **CLC 30**
  See also Norway, Nevil Shute

Shuttle, Penelope (Diane)   1947- ..... **CLC 7**
  See also CA 93-96; CANR 39; DLB 14, 40

Sidney, Mary   1561-1621 .... **LC 19**

Sidney, Sir Philip   1554-1586.... **LC 19; DA**
  See also CDBLB Before 1660

Siegel, Jerome   1914- .... **CLC 21**
  See also CA 116

Siegel, Jerry
  See Siegel, Jerome

Sienkiewicz, Henryk (Adam Alexander Pius)
  1846-1916 ....**TCLC 3**
  See also CA 104; 134

Sierra, Gregorio Martinez
  See Martinez Sierra, Gregorio

Sierra, Maria (de la O'LeJarraga) Martinez
  See Martinez Sierra, Maria (de la
  O'LeJarraga)

Sigal, Clancy   1926-............... **CLC 7**
  See also CA 1-4R

Sigourney, Lydia Howard (Huntley)
  1791-1865 .... **NCLC 21**
  See also DLB 1, 42, 73

Siguenza y Gongora, Carlos de
  1645-1700 .... **LC 8**

Sigurjonsson, Johann   1880-1919... **TCLC 27**

Sikelianos, Angelos   1884-1951 .... **TCLC 39**

Silkin, Jon   1930- .... **CLC 2, 6, 43**
  See also CA 5-8R; CAAS 5; DLB 27

Silko, Leslie (Marmon)
  1948-................ **CLC 23, 74; DA**
  See also AAYA 14; CA 115; 122;
  CANR 45; DLB 143; NNAL

Sillanpaa, Frans Eemil   1888-1964... **CLC 19**
  See also CA 129; 93-96; MTCW

Sillitoe, Alan
  1928-......... **CLC 1, 3, 6, 10, 19, 57**
  See also AITN 1; CA 9-12R; CAAS 2;
  CANR 8, 26; CDBLB 1960 to Present;
  DLB 14, 139; MTCW; SATA 61

Silone, Ignazio   1900-1978 .... **CLC 4**
  See also CA 25-28; 81-84; CANR 34;
  CAP 2; MTCW

Silver, Joan Micklin   1935- .... **CLC 20**
  See also CA 114; 121

Silver, Nicholas
  See Faust, Frederick (Schiller)

Silverberg, Robert   1935-........... **CLC 7**
  See also CA 1-4R; CAAS 3; CANR 1, 20,
  36; DLB 8; MAICYA; MTCW; SATA 13

Silverstein, Alvin   1933-........... **CLC 17**
  See also CA 49-52; CANR 2; CLR 25;
  JRDA; MAICYA; SATA 8, 69

Silverstein, Virginia B(arbara Opshelor)
  1937-...................... **CLC 17**
  See also CA 49-52; CANR 2; CLR 25;
  JRDA; MAICYA; SATA 8, 69

Sim, Georges
  See Simenon, Georges (Jacques Christian)

Simak, Clifford D(onald)
  1904-1988 .... **CLC 1, 55**
  See also CA 1-4R; 125; CANR 1, 35;
  DLB 8; MTCW; SATA-Obit 56

Simenon, Georges (Jacques Christian)
  1903-1989 .... **CLC 1, 2, 3, 8, 18, 47**
  See also CA 85-88; 129; CANR 35;
  DLB 72; DLBY 89; MTCW

Simic, Charles   1938-... **CLC 6, 9, 22, 49, 68**
  See also CA 29-32R; CAAS 4; CANR 12,
  33; DLB 105

Stringer, Arthur 1874-1950 . . . . . . **TCLC 37**
See also DLB 92

Stringer, David
See Roberts, Keith (John Kingston)

Strugatskii, Arkadii (Natanovich)
1925-1991 . . . . **CLC 27**
See also CA 106; 135

Strugatskii, Boris (Natanovich)
1933- . . . . **CLC 27**
See also CA 106

Strummer, Joe 1953(?)- . . . . **CLC 30**

Stuart, Don A.
See Campbell, John W(ood, Jr.)

Stuart, Ian
See MacLean, Alistair (Stuart)

Stuart, Jesse (Hilton)
1906-1984 . . . . **CLC 1, 8, 11, 14, 34**
See also CA 5-8R; 112; CANR 31; DLB 9,
48, 102; DLBY 84; SATA 2;
SATA-Obit 36

Sturgeon, Theodore (Hamilton)
1918-1985 . . . . **CLC 22, 39**
See also Queen, Ellery
See also CA 81-84; 116; CANR 32; DLB 8;
DLBY 85; MTCW

Sturges, Preston 1898-1959 . . . . . . **TCLC 48**
See also CA 114; DLB 26

Styron, William
1925- . . . . **CLC 1, 3, 5, 11, 15, 60**
See also BEST 90:4; CA 5-8R; CANR 6, 33;
CDALB 1968-1988; DLB 2, 143;
DLBY 80; MTCW

Suarez Lynch, B.
See Bioy Casares, Adolfo; Borges, Jorge
Luis

Su Chien 1884-1918
See Su Man-shu
See also CA 123

Suckow, Ruth 1892-1960
See also CA 113; DLB 9, 102; SSC 18

Sudermann, Hermann 1857-1928 . . **TCLC 15**
See also CA 107; DLB 118

Sue, Eugene 1804-1857 . . . . **NCLC 1**
See also DLB 119

Sueskind, Patrick 1949- . . . . **CLC 44**
See also Suskind, Patrick

Sukenick, Ronald 1932- . . . . . **CLC 3, 4, 6, 48**
See also CA 25-28R; CAAS 8; CANR 32;
DLBY 81

Suknaski, Andrew 1942- . . . . **CLC 19**
See also CA 101; DLB 53

Sullivan, Vernon
See Vian, Boris

Sully Prudhomme 1839-1907 . . . . . **TCLC 31**

Su Man-shu . . . . **TCLC 24**
See also Su Chien

Summerforest, Ivy B.
See Kirkup, James

Summers, Andrew James 1942- . . . . . **CLC 26**

Summers, Andy
See Summers, Andrew James

Summers, Hollis (Spurgeon, Jr.)
1916- . . . . **CLC 10**
See also CA 5-8R; CANR 3; DLB 6

Summers, (Alphonsus Joseph-Mary Augustus)
Montague 1880-1948 . . . . **TCLC 16**
See also CA 118

Sumner, Gordon Matthew 1951- . . . . **CLC 26**

Surtees, Robert Smith
1803-1864 . . . . **NCLC 14**
See also DLB 21

Susann, Jacqueline 1921-1974 . . . . . . **CLC 3**
See also AITN 1; CA 65-68; 53-56; MTCW

Suskind, Patrick
See Sueskind, Patrick
See also CA 145

Sutcliff, Rosemary 1920-1992 . . . . . . **CLC 26**
See also AAYA 10; CA 5-8R; 139;
CANR 37; CLR 1; JRDA; MAICYA;
SATA 6, 44, 78; SATA-Obit 73

Sutro, Alfred 1863-1933 . . . . **TCLC 6**
See also CA 105; DLB 10

Sutton, Henry
See Slavitt, David R(ytman)

Svevo, Italo . . . . **TCLC 2, 35**
See also Schmitz, Aron Hector

Swados, Elizabeth 1951- . . . . **CLC 12**
See also CA 97-100

Swados, Harvey 1920-1972 . . . . **CLC 5**
See also CA 5-8R; 37-40R; CANR 6;
DLB 2

Swan, Gladys 1934- . . . . **CLC 69**
See also CA 101; CANR 17, 39

Swarthout, Glendon (Fred)
1918-1992 . . . . **CLC 35**
See also CA 1-4R; 139; CANR 1, 47;
SATA 26

Sweet, Sarah C.
See Jewett, (Theodora) Sarah Orne

Swenson, May
1919-1989 . . . . **CLC 4, 14, 61; DA**
See also CA 5-8R; 130; CANR 36; DLB 5;
MTCW; SATA 15

Swift, Augustus
See Lovecraft, H(oward) P(hillips)

Swift, Graham (Colin) 1949- . . . . **CLC 41**
See also CA 117; 122; CANR 46, 46

Swift, Jonathan
1667-1745 . . . . . . **LC 1; DA; PC 9; WLC**
See also CDBLB 1660-1789; DLB 39, 95,
101; SATA 19

Swinburne, Algernon Charles
1837-1909 . . . . . . **TCLC 8, 36; DA; WLC**
See also CA 105; 140; CDBLB 1832-1890;
DLB 35, 57

Swinfen, Ann . . . . **CLC 34**

Swinnerton, Frank Arthur
1884-1982 . . . . **CLC 31**
See also CA 108; DLB 34

Swithen, John
See King, Stephen (Edwin)

Sylvia
See Ashton-Warner, Sylvia (Constance)

Symmes, Robert Edward
See Duncan, Robert (Edward)

Symonds, John Addington
1840-1893 . . . . **NCLC 34**
See also DLB 57, 144

Symons, Arthur 1865-1945 . . . . **TCLC 11**
See also CA 107; DLB 19, 57

Symons, Julian (Gustave)
1912- . . . . **CLC 2, 14, 32**
See also CA 49-52; CAAS 3; CANR 3, 33;
DLB 87; DLBY 92; MTCW

Synge, (Edmund) J(ohn) M(illington)
1871-1909 . . . . **TCLC 6, 37; DC 2**
See also CA 104; 141; CDBLB 1890-1914;
DLB 10, 19

Syruc, J.
See Milosz, Czeslaw

Szirtes, George 1948- . . . . **CLC 46**
See also CA 109; CANR 27

Tabori, George 1914- . . . . **CLC 19**
See also CA 49-52; CANR 4

Tagore, Rabindranath
1861-1941 . . . . **TCLC 3, 53; PC 8**
See also CA 104; 120; MTCW

Taine, Hippolyte Adolphe
1828-1893 . . . . **NCLC 15**

Talese, Gay 1932- . . . . **CLC 37**
See also AITN 1; CA 1-4R; CANR 9;
MTCW

Tallent, Elizabeth (Ann) 1954- . . . . . **CLC 45**
See also CA 117; DLB 130

Tally, Ted 1952- . . . . **CLC 42**
See also CA 120; 124

Tamayo y Baus, Manuel
1829-1898 . . . . **NCLC 1**

Tammsaare, A(nton) H(ansen)
1878-1940 . . . . **TCLC 27**

Tan, Amy 1952- . . . . **CLC 59**
See also AAYA 9; BEST 89:3; CA 136;
SATA 75

Tandem, Felix
See Spitteler, Carl (Friedrich Georg)

Tanizaki, Jun'ichiro
1886-1965 . . . . **CLC 8, 14, 28**
See also CA 93-96; 25-28R

Tanner, William
See Amis, Kingsley (William)

Tao Lao
See Storni, Alfonsina

Tarassoff, Lev
See Troyat, Henri

Tarbell, Ida M(inerva)
1857-1944 . . . . **TCLC 40**
See also CA 122; DLB 47

Tarkington, (Newton) Booth
1869-1946 . . . . **TCLC 9**
See also CA 110; 143; DLB 9, 102;
SATA 17

Tarkovsky, Andrei (Arsenyevich)
1932-1986 . . . . **CLC 75**
See also CA 127

Tartt, Donna 1964(?)- . . . . **CLC 76**
See also CA 142

Tasso, Torquato 1544-1595 . . . . **LC 5**

Tate, (John Orley) Allen
1899-1979 . . . . **CLC 2, 4, 6, 9, 11, 14, 24**
See also CA 5-8R; 85-88; CANR 32;
DLB 4, 45, 63; MTCW

Tate, Ellalice
See Hibbert, Eleanor Alice Burford

Tate, James (Vincent) 1943- ... **CLC 2, 6, 25**
See also CA 21-24R; CANR 29; DLB 5

Tavel, Ronald 1940- .... **CLC 6**
See also CA 21-24R; CANR 33

Taylor, C(ecil) P(hilip) 1929-1981... **CLC 27**
See also CA 25-28R; 105; CANR 47

Taylor, Edward 1642(?)-1729.... **LC 11; DA**
See also DLB 24

Taylor, Eleanor Ross 1920- .... **CLC 5**
See also CA 81-84

Taylor, Elizabeth 1912-1975 ... **CLC 2, 4, 29**
See also CA 13-16R; CANR 9; DLB 139;
MTCW; SATA 13

Taylor, Henry (Splawn) 1942-...... **CLC 44**
See also CA 33-36R; CAAS 7; CANR 31;
DLB 5

Taylor, Kamala (Purnaiya) 1924-
See Markandaya, Kamala
See also CA 77-80

Taylor, Mildred D. .... **CLC 21**
See also AAYA 10; BW 1; CA 85-88;
CANR 25; CLR 9; DLB 52; JRDA;
MAICYA; SAAS 5; SATA 15, 70

Taylor, Peter (Hillsman)
1917- ...... **CLC 1, 4, 18, 37, 44, 50, 71;
SSC 10**
See also CA 13-16R; CANR 9; DLBY 81;
MTCW

Taylor, Robert Lewis 1912-........ **CLC 14**
See also CA 1-4R; CANR 3; SATA 10

Tchekhov, Anton
See Chekhov, Anton (Pavlovich)

Teasdale, Sara 1884-1933......... **TCLC 4**
See also CA 104; DLB 45; SATA 32

Tegner, Esaias 1782-1846........ **NCLC 2**

Teilhard de Chardin, (Marie Joseph) Pierre
1881-1955 .... **TCLC 9**
See also CA 105

Temple, Ann
See Mortimer, Penelope (Ruth)

Tennant, Emma (Christina)
1937- .... **CLC 13, 52**
See also CA 65-68; CAAS 9; CANR 10, 38;
DLB 14

Tenneshaw, S. M.
See Silverberg, Robert

Tennyson, Alfred
1809-1892 .. **NCLC 30; DA; PC 6; WLC**
See also CDBLB 1832-1890; DLB 32

Teran, Lisa St. Aubin de .... **CLC 36**
See also St. Aubin de Teran, Lisa

Terence 195(?)B.C.-159B.C...... **CMLC 14**

Teresa de Jesus, St. 1515-1582 ..... **LC 18**

Terkel, Louis 1912-
See Terkel, Studs
See also CA 57-60; CANR 18, 45; MTCW

Terkel, Studs .... **CLC 38**
See also Terkel, Louis
See also AITN 1

Terry, C. V.
See Slaughter, Frank G(ill)

Terry, Megan 1932- .... **CLC 19**
See also CA 77-80; CABS 3; CANR 43;
DLB 7

Tertz, Abram
See Sinyavsky, Andrei (Donatevich)

Tesich, Steve 1943(?)-.......... **CLC 40, 69**
See also CA 105; DLBY 83

Teternikov, Fyodor Kuzmich 1863-1927
See Sologub, Fyodor
See also CA 104

Tevis, Walter 1928-1984 .... **CLC 42**
See also CA 113

Tey, Josephine................... **TCLC 14**
See also Mackintosh, Elizabeth
See also DLB 77

Thackeray, William Makepeace
1811-1863 .... **NCLC 5, 14, 22, 43; DA;
WLC**
See also CDBLB 1832-1890; DLB 21, 55;
SATA 23

Thakura, Ravindranatha
See Tagore, Rabindranath

Tharoor, Shashi 1956- .... **CLC 70**
See also CA 141

Thelwell, Michael Miles 1939- ..... **CLC 22**
See also BW 2; CA 101

Theobald, Lewis, Jr.
See Lovecraft, H(oward) P(hillips)

Theodorescu, Ion N. 1880-1967
See Arghezi, Tudor
See also CA 116

Theriault, Yves 1915-1983........ **CLC 79**
See also CA 102; DLB 88

Theroux, Alexander (Louis)
1939- .... **CLC 2, 25**
See also CA 85-88; CANR 20

Theroux, Paul (Edward)
1941- .... **CLC 5, 8, 11, 15, 28, 46**
See also BEST 89:4; CA 33-36R; CANR 20,
45; DLB 2; MTCW; SATA 44

Thesen, Sharon 1946-............ **CLC 56**

Thevenin, Denis
See Duhamel, Georges

Thibault, Jacques Anatole Francois
1844-1924
See France, Anatole
See also CA 106; 127; MTCW

Thiele, Colin (Milton) 1920- .... **CLC 17**
See also CA 29-32R; CANR 12, 28;
CLR 27; MAICYA; SAAS 2; SATA 14,
72

Thomas, Audrey (Callahan)
1935- .... **CLC 7, 13, 37**
See also AITN 2; CA 21-24R; CAAS 19;
CANR 36; DLB 60; MTCW

Thomas, D(onald) M(ichael)
1935- .... **CLC 13, 22, 31**
See also CA 61-64; CAAS 11; CANR 17,
45; CDBLB 1960 to Present; DLB 40;
MTCW

Thomas, Dylan (Marlais)
1914-1953 ... **TCLC 1, 8, 45; DA; PC 2;
SSC 3; WLC**
See also CA 104; 120; CDBLB 1945-1960;
DLB 13, 20, 139; MTCW; SATA 60

Thomas, (Philip) Edward
1878-1917 .... **TCLC 10**
See also CA 106; DLB 19

Thomas, Joyce Carol 1938-........ **CLC 35**
See also AAYA 12; BW 2; CA 113; 116;
CLR 19; DLB 33; JRDA; MAICYA;
MTCW; SAAS 7; SATA 40, 78

Thomas, Lewis 1913-1993 .... **CLC 35**
See also CA 85-88; 143; CANR 38; MTCW

Thomas, Paul
See Mann, (Paul) Thomas

Thomas, Piri 1928-............... **CLC 17**
See also CA 73-76; HW

Thomas, R(onald) S(tuart)
1913- .... **CLC 6, 13, 48**
See also CA 89-92; CAAS 4; CANR 30;
CDBLB 1960 to Present; DLB 27;
MTCW

Thomas, Ross (Elmore) 1926- ...... **CLC 39**
See also CA 33-36R; CANR 22

Thompson, Francis Clegg
See Mencken, H(enry) L(ouis)

Thompson, Francis Joseph
1859-1907 .... **TCLC 4**
See also CA 104; CDBLB 1890-1914;
DLB 19

Thompson, Hunter S(tockton)
1939- .... **CLC 9, 17, 40**
See also BEST 89:1; CA 17-20R; CANR 23,
46, 46; MTCW

Thompson, James Myers
See Thompson, Jim (Myers)

Thompson, Jim (Myers)
1906-1977(?) .... **CLC 69**
See also CA 140

Thompson, Judith .... **CLC 39**

Thomson, James 1700-1748......... **LC 16**

Thomson, James 1834-1882 ...... **NCLC 18**

Thoreau, Henry David
1817-1862 ...... **NCLC 7, 21; DA; WLC**
See also CDALB 1640-1865; DLB 1

Thornton, Hall
See Silverberg, Robert

Thurber, James (Grover)
1894-1961 ... **CLC 5, 11, 25; DA; SSC 1**
See also CA 73-76; CANR 17, 39;
CDALB 1929-1941; DLB 4, 11, 22, 102;
MAICYA; MTCW; SATA 13

Thurman, Wallace (Henry)
1902-1934 .... **TCLC 6; BLC**
See also BW 1; CA 104; 124; DLB 51

Ticheburn, Cheviot
See Ainsworth, William Harrison

Tieck, (Johann) Ludwig
1773-1853 .... **NCLC 5, 46**
See also DLB 90

Tiger, Derry
See Ellison, Harlan (Jay)

Tilghman, Christopher 1948(?)-..... **CLC 65**

Tillinghast, Richard (Williford)
1940- .... **CLC 29**
See also CA 29-32R; CANR 26

Timrod, Henry 1820-1867 .... **NCLC 25**
See also DLB 3

Tindall, Gillian 1938-.............. CLC 7
See also CA 21-24R; CANR 11

Tiptree, James, Jr. .... CLC 48, 50
See also Sheldon, Alice Hastings Bradley
See also DLB 8

Titmarsh, Michael Angelo
See Thackeray, William Makepeace

Tocqueville, Alexis (Charles Henri Maurice
    Clerel Comte) 1805-1859..... NCLC 7

Tolkien, J(ohn) R(onald) R(euel)
    1892-1973 .... CLC 1, 2, 3, 8, 12, 38;
                                        DA; WLC
See also AAYA 10; AITN 1; CA 17-18;
    45-48; CANR 36; CAP 2;
    CDBLB 1914-1945; DLB 15; JRDA;
    MAICYA; MTCW; SATA 2, 32;
    SATA-Obit 24

Toller, Ernst 1893-1939......... TCLC 10
See also CA 107; DLB 124

Tolson, M. B.
See Tolson, Melvin B(eaunorus)

Tolson, Melvin B(eaunorus)
    1898(?)-1966 .... CLC 36; BLC
See also BW 1; CA 124; 89-92; DLB 48, 76

Tolstoi, Aleksei Nikolaevich
See Tolstoy, Alexey Nikolaevich

Tolstoy, Alexey Nikolaevich
    1882-1945 .... TCLC 18
See also CA 107

Tolstoy, Count Leo
See Tolstoy, Leo (Nikolaevich)

Tolstoy, Leo (Nikolaevich)
    1828-1910 ...... TCLC 4, 11, 17, 28, 44;
                                        DA; SSC 9; WLC
See also CA 104; 123; SATA 26

Tomasi di Lampedusa, Giuseppe 1896-1957
See Lampedusa, Giuseppe (Tomasi) di
See also CA 111

Tomlin, Lily..................... CLC 17
See also Tomlin, Mary Jean

Tomlin, Mary Jean 1939(?)-
See Tomlin, Lily
See also CA 117

Tomlinson, (Alfred) Charles
    1927- .... CLC 2, 4, 6, 13, 45
See also CA 5-8R; CANR 33; DLB 40

Tonson, Jacob
See Bennett, (Enoch) Arnold

Toole, John Kennedy
    1937-1969 .... CLC 19, 64
See also CA 104; DLBY 81

Toomer, Jean
    1894-1967 ...... CLC 1, 4, 13, 22; BLC;
                                        PC 7; SSC 1
See also BW 1; CA 85-88;
    CDALB 1917-1929; DLB 45, 51; MTCW

Torley, Luke
See Blish, James (Benjamin)

Tornimparte, Alessandra
See Ginzburg, Natalia

Torre, Raoul della
See Mencken, H(enry) L(ouis)

Torrey, E(dwin) Fuller 1937-....... CLC 34
See also CA 119

Torsvan, Ben Traven
See Traven, B.

Torsvan, Benno Traven
See Traven, B.

Torsvan, Berick Traven
See Traven, B.

Torsvan, Berwick Traven
See Traven, B.

Torsvan, Bruno Traven
See Traven, B.

Torsvan, Traven
See Traven, B.

Tournier, Michel (Edouard)
    1924-................ CLC 6, 23, 36
See also CA 49-52; CANR 3, 36; DLB 83;
    MTCW; SATA 23

Tournimparte, Alessandra
See Ginzburg, Natalia

Towers, Ivar
See Kornbluth, C(yril) M.

Townsend, Sue 1946-.............. CLC 61
See also CA 119; 127; MTCW; SATA 48,
    55

Townshend, Peter (Dennis Blandford)
    1945-................... CLC 17, 42
See also CA 107

Tozzi, Federigo 1883-1920....... TCLC 31

Traill, Catharine Parr
    1802-1899 .... NCLC 31
See also DLB 99

Trakl, Georg 1887-1914........... TCLC 5
See also CA 104

Transtroemer, Tomas (Goesta)
    1931-................... CLC 52, 65
See also CA 117; 129; CAAS 17

Transtromer, Tomas Gosta
See Transtroemer, Tomas (Goesta)

Traven, B. (?)-1969............. CLC 8, 11
See also CA 19-20; 25-28R; CAP 2; DLB 9,
    56; MTCW

Treitel, Jonathan 1959-........... CLC 70

Tremain, Rose 1943-.............. CLC 42
See also CA 97-100; CANR 44; DLB 14

Tremblay, Michel 1942-........... CLC 29
See also CA 116; 128; DLB 60; MTCW

Trevanian....................... CLC 29
See also Whitaker, Rod(ney)

Trevor, Glen
See Hilton, James

Trevor, William
    1928- .... CLC 7, 9, 14, 25, 71
See also Cox, William Trevor
See also DLB 14, 139

Trifonov, Yuri (Valentinovich)
    1925-1981 .... CLC 45
See also CA 126; 103; MTCW

Trilling, Lionel 1905-1975 .... CLC 9, 11, 24
See also CA 9-12R; 61-64; CANR 10;
    DLB 28, 63; MTCW

Trimball, W. H.
See Mencken, H(enry) L(ouis)

Tristan
See Gomez de la Serna, Ramon

Tristram
See Housman, A(lfred) E(dward)

Trogdon, William (Lewis) 1939-
See Heat-Moon, William Least
See also CA 115; 119; CANR 47

Trollope, Anthony
    1815-1882 ...... NCLC 6, 33; DA; WLC
See also CDBLB 1832-1890; DLB 21, 57;
    SATA 22

Trollope, Frances 1779-1863 ..... NCLC 30
See also DLB 21

Trotsky, Leon 1879-1940........ TCLC 22
See also CA 118

Trotter (Cockburn), Catharine
    1679-1749 .... LC 8
See also DLB 84

Trout, Kilgore
See Farmer, Philip Jose

Trow, George W. S. 1943-........ CLC 52
See also CA 126

Troyat, Henri 1911-.............. CLC 23
See also CA 45-48; CANR 2, 33; MTCW

Trudeau, G(arretson) B(eekman) 1948-
See Trudeau, Garry B.
See also CA 81-84; CANR 31; SATA 35

Trudeau, Garry B.................. CLC 12
See also Trudeau, G(arretson) B(eekman)
See also AAYA 10; AITN 2

Truffaut, Francois 1932-1984....... CLC 20
See also CA 81-84; 113; CANR 34

Trumbo, Dalton 1905-1976 .... CLC 19
See also CA 21-24R; 69-72; CANR 10;
    DLB 26

Trumbull, John 1750-1831....... NCLC 30
See also DLB 31

Trundlett, Helen B.
See Eliot, T(homas) S(tearns)

Tryon, Thomas 1926-1991 .... CLC 3, 11
See also AITN 1; CA 29-32R; 135;
    CANR 32; MTCW

Tryon, Tom
See Tryon, Thomas

Ts'ao Hsueh-ch'in 1715(?)-1763....... LC 1

Tsushima, Shuji 1909-1948
See Dazai, Osamu
See also CA 107

Tsvetaeva (Efron), Marina (Ivanovna)
    1892-1941 .... TCLC 7, 35
See also CA 104; 128; MTCW

Tuck, Lily 1938-................ CLC 70
See also CA 139

Tu Fu 712-770.................... PC 9

Tunis, John R(oberts) 1889-1975 ... CLC 12
See also CA 61-64; DLB 22; JRDA;
    MAICYA; SATA 30, 37

Tuohy, Frank.................... CLC 37
See also Tuohy, John Francis
See also DLB 14, 139

Tuohy, John Francis 1925-
See Tuohy, Frank
See also CA 5-8R; CANR 3, 47

Turco, Lewis (Putnam) 1934- ... CLC 11, 63
See also CA 13-16R; CANR 24; DLBY 84

Wallace, Irving 1916-1990 . . . . **CLC 7, 13**
See also AITN 1; CA 1-4R; 132; CAAS 1;
CANR 1, 27; MTCW

Wallant, Edward Lewis
1926-1962 . . . . **CLC 5, 10**
See also CA 1-4R; CANR 22; DLB 2, 28,
143; MTCW

Walpole, Horace 1717-1797 . . . . **LC 2**
See also DLB 39, 104

Walpole, Hugh (Seymour)
1884-1941 . . . . **TCLC 5**
See also CA 104; DLB 34

Walser, Martin 1927- . . . . **CLC 27**
See also CA 57-60; CANR 8, 46, 46;
DLB 75, 124

Walser, Robert 1878-1956 . . . . **TCLC 18**
See also CA 118; DLB 66

Walsh, Jill Paton . . . . **CLC 35**
See also Paton Walsh, Gillian
See also AAYA 11; CLR 2; SAAS 3

Walter, Villiam Christian
See Andersen, Hans Christian

Wambaugh, Joseph (Aloysius, Jr.)
1937- . . . . **CLC 3, 18**
See also AITN 1; BEST 89:3; CA 33-36R;
CANR 42; DLB 6; DLBY 83; MTCW

Ward, Arthur Henry Sarsfield 1883-1959
See Rohmer, Sax
See also CA 108

Ward, Douglas Turner 1930- . . . . **CLC 19**
See also BW 1; CA 81-84; CANR 27;
DLB 7, 38

Ward, Mary Augusta
See Ward, Mrs. Humphry

Ward, Mrs. Humphry
1851-1920 . . . . **TCLC 55**
See also DLB 18

Ward, Peter
See Faust, Frederick (Schiller)

Warhol, Andy 1928(?)-1987 . . . . **CLC 20**
See also AAYA 12; BEST 89:4; CA 89-92;
121; CANR 34

Warner, Francis (Robert le Plastrier)
1937- . . . . **CLC 14**
See also CA 53-56; CANR 11

Warner, Marina 1946- . . . . **CLC 59**
See also CA 65-68; CANR 21

Warner, Rex (Ernest) 1905-1986 . . . . **CLC 45**
See also CA 89-92; 119; DLB 15

Warner, Susan (Bogert)
1819-1885 . . . . **NCLC 31**
See also DLB 3, 42

Warner, Sylvia (Constance) Ashton
See Ashton-Warner, Sylvia (Constance)

Warner, Sylvia Townsend
1893-1978 . . . . **CLC 7, 19**
See also CA 61-64; 77-80; CANR 16;
DLB 34, 139; MTCW

Warren, Mercy Otis 1728-1814 . . . **NCLC 13**
See also DLB 31

Warren, Robert Penn
1905-1989 . . . . **CLC 1, 4, 6, 8, 10, 13, 18,
39, 53, 59; DA; SSC 4; WLC**
See also AITN 1; CA 13-16R; 129;
CANR 10, 47; CDALB 1968-1988;
DLB 2, 48; DLBY 80, 89; MTCW;
SATA 46; SATA-Obit 63

Warshofsky, Isaac
See Singer, Isaac Bashevis

Warton, Thomas 1728-1790 . . . . **LC 15**
See also DLB 104, 109

Waruk, Kona
See Harris, (Theodore) Wilson

Warung, Price 1855-1911 . . . . **TCLC 45**

Warwick, Jarvis
See Garner, Hugh

Washington, Alex
See Harris, Mark

Washington, Booker T(aliaferro)
1856-1915 . . . . **TCLC 10; BLC**
See also BW 1; CA 114; 125; SATA 28

Washington, George 1732-1799 . . . . . . **LC 25**
See also DLB 31

Wassermann, (Karl) Jakob
1873-1934 . . . . **TCLC 6**
See also CA 104; DLB 66

Wasserstein, Wendy
1950- . . . . **CLC 32, 59; DC 4**
See also CA 121; 129; CABS 3

Waterhouse, Keith (Spencer)
1929- . . . . **CLC 47**
See also CA 5-8R; CANR 38; DLB 13, 15;
MTCW

Waters, Roger 1944- . . . . **CLC 35**

Watkins, Frances Ellen
See Harper, Frances Ellen Watkins

Watkins, Gerrold
See Malzberg, Barry N(athaniel)

Watkins, Paul 1964- . . . . **CLC 55**
See also CA 132

Watkins, Vernon Phillips
1906-1967 . . . . **CLC 43**
See also CA 9-10; 25-28R; CAP 1; DLB 20

Watson, Irving S.
See Mencken, H(enry) L(ouis)

Watson, John H.
See Farmer, Philip Jose

Watson, Richard F.
See Silverberg, Robert

Waugh, Auberon (Alexander) 1939- . . **CLC 7**
See also CA 45-48; CANR 6, 22; DLB 14

Waugh, Evelyn (Arthur St. John)
1903-1966 . . . . . . **CLC 1, 3, 8, 13, 19, 27,
44; DA; WLC**
See also CA 85-88; 25-28R; CANR 22;
CDBLB 1914-1945; DLB 15; MTCW

Waugh, Harriet 1944- . . . . **CLC 6**
See also CA 85-88; CANR 22

Ways, C. R.
See Blount, Roy (Alton), Jr.

Waystaff, Simon
See Swift, Jonathan

Webb, (Martha) Beatrice (Potter)
1858-1943 . . . . **TCLC 22**
See also Potter, Beatrice
See also CA 117

Webb, Charles (Richard) 1939- . . . . . . **CLC 7**
See also CA 25-28R

Webb, James H(enry), Jr. 1946- . . . . **CLC 22**
See also CA 81-84

Webb, Mary (Gladys Meredith)
1881-1927 . . . . **TCLC 24**
See also CA 123; DLB 34

Webb, Mrs. Sidney
See Webb, (Martha) Beatrice (Potter)

Webb, Phyllis 1927- . . . . **CLC 18**
See also CA 104; CANR 23; DLB 53

Webb, Sidney (James)
1859-1947 . . . . **TCLC 22**
See also CA 117

Webber, Andrew Lloyd . . . . **CLC 21**
See also Lloyd Webber, Andrew

Weber, Lenora Mattingly
1895-1971 . . . . **CLC 12**
See also CA 19-20; 29-32R; CAP 1;
SATA 2; SATA-Obit 26

Webster, John 1579(?)-1634(?) . . . . **DC 2**
See also CDBLB Before 1660; DA; DLB 58;
WLC

Webster, Noah 1758-1843 . . . . **NCLC 30**

Wedekind, (Benjamin) Frank(lin)
1864-1918 . . . . **TCLC 7**
See also CA 104; DLB 118

Weidman, Jerome 1913- . . . . **CLC 7**
See also AITN 2; CA 1-4R; CANR 1;
DLB 28

Weil, Simone (Adolphine)
1909-1943 . . . . **TCLC 23**
See also CA 117

Weinstein, Nathan
See West, Nathanael

Weinstein, Nathan von Wallenstein
See West, Nathanael

Weir, Peter (Lindsay) 1944- . . . . **CLC 20**
See also CA 113; 123

Weiss, Peter (Ulrich)
1916-1982 . . . . **CLC 3, 15, 51**
See also CA 45-48; 106; CANR 3; DLB 69,
124

Weiss, Theodore (Russell)
1916- . . . . **CLC 3, 8, 14**
See also CA 9-12R; CAAS 2; CANR 46, 46;
DLB 5

Welch, (Maurice) Denton
1915-1948 . . . . **TCLC 22**
See also CA 121

Welch, James 1940- . . . . **CLC 6, 14, 52**
See also CA 85-88; CANR 42; NNAL

Weldon, Fay
1933- . . . . **CLC 6, 9, 11, 19, 36, 59**
See also CA 21-24R; CANR 16, 46, 46;
CDBLB 1960 to Present; DLB 14;
MTCW

Wellek, Rene 1903- . . . . **CLC 28**
See also CA 5-8R; CAAS 7; CANR 8;
DLB 63

Weller, Michael 1942- .... CLC 10, 53
See also CA 85-88

Weller, Paul 1958- .... CLC 26

Wellershoff, Dieter 1925-.......... CLC 46
See also CA 89-92; CANR 16, 37

Welles, (George) Orson
1915-1985 .... CLC 20, 80
See also CA 93-96; 117

Wellman, Mac 1945- .... CLC 65

Wellman, Manly Wade 1903-1986 .. CLC 49
See also CA 1-4R; 118; CANR 6, 16, 44;
SATA 6; SATA-Obit 47

Wells, Carolyn 1869(?)-1942 ...... TCLC 35
See also CA 113; DLB 11

Wells, H(erbert) G(eorge)
1866-1946 .... TCLC 6, 12, 19; DA;
SSC 6; WLC
See also CA 110; 121; CDBLB 1914-1945;
DLB 34, 70; MTCW; SATA 20

Wells, Rosemary 1943-............ CLC 12
See also AAYA 13; CA 85-88; CLR 16;
MAICYA; SAAS 1; SATA 18, 69

Welty, Eudora
1909- ...... CLC 1, 2, 5, 14, 22, 33; DA;
SSC 1; WLC
See also CA 9-12R; CABS 1; CANR 32;
CDALB 1941-1968; DLB 2, 102, 143;
DLBD 12; DLBY 87; MTCW

Wen I-to 1899-1946 .... TCLC 28

Wentworth, Robert
See Hamilton, Edmond

Werfel, Franz (V.) 1890-1945 ...... TCLC 8
See also CA 104; DLB 81, 124

Wergeland, Henrik Arnold
1808-1845 .... NCLC 5

Wersba, Barbara 1932-............ CLC 30
See also AAYA 2; CA 29-32R; CANR 16,
38; CLR 3; DLB 52; JRDA; MAICYA;
SAAS 2; SATA 1, 58

Wertmueller, Lina 1928- .... CLC 16
See also CA 97-100; CANR 39

Wescott, Glenway 1901-1987....... CLC 13
See also CA 13-16R; 121; CANR 23;
DLB 4, 9, 102

Wesker, Arnold 1932- .... CLC 3, 5, 42
See also CA 1-4R; CAAS 7; CANR 1, 33;
CDBLB 1960 to Present; DLB 13;
MTCW

Wesley, Richard (Errol) 1945-....... CLC 7
See also BW 1; CA 57-60; CANR 27;
DLB 38

Wessel, Johan Herman 1742-1785 .... LC 7

West, Anthony (Panther)
1914-1987 .... CLC 50
See also CA 45-48; 124; CANR 3, 19;
DLB 15

West, C. P.
See Wodehouse, P(elham) G(renville)

West, (Mary) Jessamyn
1902-1984 .... CLC 7, 17
See also CA 9-12R; 112; CANR 27; DLB 6;
DLBY 84; MTCW; SATA-Obit 37

West, Morris L(anglo) 1916-..... CLC 6, 33
See also CA 5-8R; CANR 24; MTCW

West, Nathanael
1903-1940 ..... TCLC 1, 14, 44; SSC 16
See also CA 104; 125; CDALB 1929-1941;
DLB 4, 9, 28; MTCW

West, Owen
See Koontz, Dean R(ay)

West, Paul 1930- .... CLC 7, 14
See also CA 13-16R; CAAS 7; CANR 22;
DLB 14

West, Rebecca 1892-1983 .. CLC 7, 9, 31, 50
See also CA 5-8R; 109; CANR 19; DLB 36;
DLBY 83; MTCW

Westall, Robert (Atkinson)
1929-1993 .... CLC 17
See also AAYA 12; CA 69-72; 141;
CANR 18; CLR 13; JRDA; MAICYA;
SAAS 2; SATA 23, 69; SATA-Obit 75

Westlake, Donald E(dwin)
1933- .... CLC 7, 33
See also CA 17-20R; CAAS 13; CANR 16,
44

Westmacott, Mary
See Christie, Agatha (Mary Clarissa)

Weston, Allen
See Norton, Andre

Wetcheek, J. L.
See Feuchtwanger, Lion

Wetering, Janwillem van de
See van de Wetering, Janwillem

Wetherell, Elizabeth
See Warner, Susan (Bogert)

Whalen, Philip 1923-........... CLC 6, 29
See also CA 9-12R; CANR 5, 39; DLB 16

Wharton, Edith (Newbold Jones)
1862-1937 ...... TCLC 3, 9, 27, 53; DA;
SSC 6; WLC
See also CA 104; 132; CDALB 1865-1917;
DLB 4, 9, 12, 78; MTCW

Wharton, James
See Mencken, H(enry) L(ouis)

Wharton, William (a pseudonym)
.... CLC 18, 37
See also CA 93-96; DLBY 80

Wheatley (Peters), Phillis
1754(?)-1784 .... LC 3; BLC; DA; PC 3;
WLC
See also CDALB 1640-1865; DLB 31, 50

Wheelock, John Hall 1886-1978.... CLC 14
See also CA 13-16R; 77-80; CANR 14;
DLB 45

White, E(lwyn) B(rooks)
1899-1985 .... CLC 10, 34, 39
See also AITN 2; CA 13-16R; 116;
CANR 16, 37; CLR 1, 21; DLB 11, 22;
MAICYA; MTCW; SATA 2, 29;
SATA-Obit 44

White, Edmund (Valentine III)
1940- .... CLC 27
See also AAYA 7; CA 45-48; CANR 3, 19,
36; MTCW

White, Patrick (Victor Martindale)
1912-1990 .. CLC 3, 4, 5, 7, 9, 18, 65, 69
See also CA 81-84; 132; CANR 43; MTCW

White, Phyllis Dorothy James 1920-
See James, P. D.
See also CA 21-24R; CANR 17, 43; MTCW

White, T(erence) H(anbury)
1906-1964 .... CLC 30
See also CA 73-76; CANR 37; JRDA;
MAICYA; SATA 12

White, Terence de Vere
1912-1994 .... CLC 49
See also CA 49-52; 145; CANR 3

White, Walter F(rancis)
1893-1955 .... TCLC 15
See also White, Walter
See also BW 1; CA 115; 124; DLB 51

White, William Hale 1831-1913
See Rutherford, Mark
See also CA 121

Whitehead, E(dward) A(nthony)
1933- .... CLC 5
See also CA 65-68

Whitemore, Hugh (John) 1936-..... CLC 37
See also CA 132

Whitman, Sarah Helen (Power)
1803-1878 .... NCLC 19
See also DLB 1

Whitman, Walt(er)
1819-1892 ..... NCLC 4, 31; DA; PC 3;
WLC
See also CDALB 1640-1865; DLB 3, 64;
SATA 20

Whitney, Phyllis A(yame) 1903-.... CLC 42
See also AITN 2; BEST 90:3; CA 1-4R;
CANR 3, 25, 38; JRDA; MAICYA;
SATA 1, 30

Whittemore, (Edward) Reed (Jr.)
1919- .... CLC 4
See also CA 9-12R; CAAS 8; CANR 4;
DLB 5

Whittier, John Greenleaf
1807-1892 .... NCLC 8
See also CDALB 1640-1865; DLB 1

Whittlebot, Hernia
See Coward, Noel (Peirce)

Wicker, Thomas Grey 1926-
See Wicker, Tom
See also CA 65-68; CANR 21, 46, 46

Wicker, Tom .... CLC 7
See also Wicker, Thomas Grey

Wideman, John Edgar
1941- .... CLC 5, 34, 36, 67; BLC
See also BW 2; CA 85-88; CANR 14, 42;
DLB 33, 143

Wiebe, Rudy (Henry) 1934-... CLC 6, 11, 14
See also CA 37-40R; CANR 42; DLB 60

Wieland, Christoph Martin
1733-1813 .... NCLC 17
See also DLB 97

Wiene, Robert 1881-1938........ TCLC 56

Wieners, John 1934-............... CLC 7
See also CA 13-16R; DLB 16

Wiesel, Elie(zer)
1928- .... CLC 3, 5, 11, 37; DA
See also AAYA 7; AITN 1; CA 5-8R;
CAAS 4; CANR 8, 40; DLB 83;
DLBY 87; MTCW; SATA 56

Wiggins, Marianne 1947-.......... CLC 57
See also BEST 89:3; CA 130

Wight, James Alfred 1916-
See Herriot, James
See also CA 77-80; SATA 44, 55

Wilbur, Richard (Purdy)
1921- .... **CLC 3, 6, 9, 14, 53; DA**
See also CA 1-4R; CABS 2; CANR 2, 29;
DLB 5; MTCW; SATA 9

Wild, Peter 1940- .... **CLC 14**
See also CA 37-40R; DLB 5

Wilde, Oscar (Fingal O'Flahertie Wills)
1854(?)-1900 .... **TCLC 1, 8, 23, 41; DA;
SSC 11; WLC**
See also CA 104; 119; CDBLB 1890-1914;
DLB 10, 19, 34, 57, 141; SATA 24

Wilder, Billy .... **CLC 20**
See also Wilder, Samuel
See also DLB 26

Wilder, Samuel 1906-
See Wilder, Billy
See also CA 89-92

Wilder, Thornton (Niven)
1897-1975 ...... **CLC 1, 5, 6, 10, 15, 35,
82; DA; DC 1; WLC**
See also AITN 2; CA 13-16R; 61-64;
CANR 40; DLB 4, 7, 9; MTCW

Wilding, Michael 1942- .... **CLC 73**
See also CA 104; CANR 24

Wiley, Richard 1944- .... **CLC 44**
See also CA 121; 129

Wilhelm, Kate .... **CLC 7**
See also Wilhelm, Katie Gertrude
See also CAAS 5; DLB 8

Wilhelm, Katie Gertrude 1928-
See Wilhelm, Kate
See also CA 37-40R; CANR 17, 36; MTCW

Wilkins, Mary
See Freeman, Mary Eleanor Wilkins

Willard, Nancy 1936- .... **CLC 7, 37**
See also CA 89-92; CANR 10, 39; CLR 5;
DLB 5, 52; MAICYA; MTCW;
SATA 30, 37, 71

Williams, C(harles) K(enneth)
1936- .... **CLC 33, 56**
See also CA 37-40R; DLB 5

Williams, Charles
See Collier, James L(incoln)

Williams, Charles (Walter Stansby)
1886-1945 .... **TCLC 1, 11**
See also CA 104; DLB 100

Williams, (George) Emlyn
1905-1987 .... **CLC 15**
See also CA 104; 123; CANR 36; DLB 10,
77; MTCW

Williams, Hugo 1942- .... **CLC 42**
See also CA 17-20R; CANR 45; DLB 40

Williams, J. Walker
See Wodehouse, P(elham) G(renville)

Williams, John A(lfred)
1925- .... **CLC 5, 13; BLC**
See also BW 2; CA 53-56; CAAS 3;
CANR 6, 26; DLB 2, 33

Williams, Jonathan (Chamberlain)
1929- .... **CLC 13**
See also CA 9-12R; CAAS 12; CANR 8;
DLB 5

Williams, Joy 1944- .... **CLC 31**
See also CA 41-44R; CANR 22

Williams, Norman 1952- .... **CLC 39**
See also CA 118

Williams, Tennessee
1911-1983 ..... **CLC 1, 2, 5, 7, 8, 11, 15,
19, 30, 39, 45, 71; DA; DC 4; WLC**
See also AITN 1, 2; CA 5-8R; 108;
CABS 3; CANR 31; CDALB 1941-1968;
DLB 7; DLBD 4; DLBY 83; MTCW

Williams, Thomas (Alonzo)
1926-1990 .... **CLC 14**
See also CA 1-4R; 132; CANR 2

Williams, William C.
See Williams, William Carlos

Williams, William Carlos
1883-1963 .... **CLC 1, 2, 5, 9, 13, 22, 42,
67; DA; PC 7**
See also CA 89-92; CANR 34;
CDALB 1917-1929; DLB 4, 16, 54, 86;
MTCW

Williamson, David (Keith) 1942- .... **CLC 56**
See also CA 103; CANR 41

Williamson, Ellen Douglas 1905-1984
See Douglas, Ellen
See also CA 17-20R; 114; CANR 39

Williamson, Jack .... **CLC 29**
See also Williamson, John Stewart
See also CAAS 8; DLB 8

Williamson, John Stewart 1908-
See Williamson, Jack
See also CA 17-20R; CANR 23

Willie, Frederick
See Lovecraft, H(oward) P(hillips)

Willingham, Calder (Baynard, Jr.)
1922- .... **CLC 5, 51**
See also CA 5-8R; CANR 3; DLB 2, 44;
MTCW

Willis, Charles
See Clarke, Arthur C(harles)

Willy
See Colette, (Sidonie-Gabrielle)

Willy, Colette
See Colette, (Sidonie-Gabrielle)

Wilson, A(ndrew) N(orman) 1950- .. **CLC 33**
See also CA 112; 122; DLB 14

Wilson, Angus (Frank Johnstone)
1913-1991 .... **CLC 2, 3, 5, 25, 34**
See also CA 5-8R; 134; CANR 21; DLB 15,
139; MTCW

Wilson, August
1945- .. **CLC 39, 50, 63; BLC; DA; DC 2**
See also BW 2; CA 115; 122; CANR 42;
MTCW

Wilson, Brian 1942- .... **CLC 12**

Wilson, Colin 1931- .... **CLC 3, 14**
See also CA 1-4R; CAAS 5; CANR 1, 22,
33; DLB 14; MTCW

Wilson, Dirk
See Pohl, Frederik

Wilson, Edmund
1895-1972 .... **CLC 1, 2, 3, 8, 24**
See also CA 1-4R; 37-40R; CANR 1, 46, 46;
DLB 63; MTCW

Wilson, Ethel Davis (Bryant)
1888(?)-1980 .... **CLC 13**
See also CA 102; DLB 68; MTCW

Wilson, John 1785-1854......... **NCLC 5**

Wilson, John (Anthony) Burgess 1917-1993
See Burgess, Anthony
See also CA 1-4R; 143; CANR 2, 46, 46;
MTCW

Wilson, Lanford 1937- .... **CLC 7, 14, 36**
See also CA 17-20R; CABS 3; CANR 45;
DLB 7

Wilson, Robert M. 1944-......... **CLC 7, 9**
See also CA 49-52; CANR 2, 41; MTCW

Wilson, Robert McLiam 1964- ..... **CLC 59**
See also CA 132

Wilson, Sloan 1920- .... **CLC 32**
See also CA 1-4R; CANR 1, 44

Wilson, Snoo 1948-............... **CLC 33**
See also CA 69-72

Wilson, William S(mith) 1932- ..... **CLC 49**
See also CA 81-84

Winchilsea, Anne (Kingsmill) Finch Counte
1661-1720 .... **LC 3**

Windham, Basil
See Wodehouse, P(elham) G(renville)

Wingrove, David (John) 1954-...... **CLC 68**
See also CA 133

Winters, Janet Lewis .... **CLC 41**
See also Lewis, Janet
See also DLBY 87

Winters, (Arthur) Yvor
1900-1968 .... **CLC 4, 8, 32**
See also CA 11-12; 25-28R; CAP 1;
DLB 48; MTCW

Winterson, Jeanette 1959-......... **CLC 64**
See also CA 136

Wiseman, Frederick 1930-......... **CLC 20**

Wister, Owen 1860-1938 .... **TCLC 21**
See also CA 108; DLB 9, 78; SATA 62

Witkacy
See Witkiewicz, Stanislaw Ignacy

Witkiewicz, Stanislaw Ignacy
1885-1939 .... **TCLC 8**
See also CA 105

Wittig, Monique 1935(?)-.......... **CLC 22**
See also CA 116; 135; DLB 83

Wittlin, Jozef 1896-1976 .... **CLC 25**
See also CA 49-52; 65-68; CANR 3

Wodehouse, P(elham) G(renville)
1881-1975 ... **CLC 1, 2, 5, 10, 22; SSC 2**
See also AITN 2; CA 45-48; 57-60;
CANR 3, 33; CDBLB 1914-1945;
DLB 34; MTCW; SATA 22

Woiwode, L.
See Woiwode, Larry (Alfred)

Woiwode, Larry (Alfred) 1941-... **CLC 6, 10**
See also CA 73-76; CANR 16; DLB 6

Wojciechowska, Maia (Teresa)
1927- .... **CLC 26**
See also AAYA 8; CA 9-12R; CANR 4, 41;
CLR 1; JRDA; MAICYA; SAAS 1;
SATA 1, 28

Yurick, Sol 1925- . . . . **CLC 6**
See also CA 13-16R; CANR 25

Zabolotskii, Nikolai Alekseevich
1903-1958 . . . . **TCLC 52**
See also CA 116

Zamiatin, Yevgenii
See Zamyatin, Evgeny Ivanovich

Zamyatin, Evgeny Ivanovich
1884-1937 . . . . **TCLC 8, 37**
See also CA 105

Zangwill, Israel 1864-1926. . . . . . . **TCLC 16**
See also CA 109; DLB 10, 135

Zappa, Francis Vincent, Jr. 1940-1993
See Zappa, Frank
See also CA 108; 143

Zappa, Frank . . . . **CLC 17**
See also Zappa, Francis Vincent, Jr.

Zaturenska, Marya 1902-1982. . . . **CLC 6, 11**
See also CA 13-16R; 105; CANR 22

Zelazny, Roger (Joseph) 1937- . . . . . **CLC 21**
See also AAYA 7; CA 21-24R; CANR 26;
DLB 8; MTCW; SATA 39, 57

Zhdanov, Andrei A(lexandrovich)
1896-1948 . . . . **TCLC 18**
See also CA 117

Zhukovsky, Vasily 1783-1852 . . . . **NCLC 35**

Ziegenhagen, Eric . . . . **CLC 55**

Zimmer, Jill Schary
See Robinson, Jill

Zimmerman, Robert
See Dylan, Bob

Zindel, Paul 1936- . . . **CLC 6, 26; DA; DC 5**
See also AAYA 2; CA 73-76; CANR 31;
CLR 3; DLB 7, 52; JRDA; MAICYA;
MTCW; SATA 16, 58

Zinov'Ev, A. A.
See Zinoviev, Alexander (Aleksandrovich)

Zinoviev, Alexander (Aleksandrovich)
1922- . . . . **CLC 19**
See also CA 116; 133; CAAS 10

Zoilus
See Lovecraft, H(oward) P(hillips)

Zola, Emile (Edouard Charles Antoine)
1840-1902 . . . . . . **TCLC 1, 6, 21, 41; DA;**
WLC
See also CA 104; 138; DLB 123

Zoline, Pamela 1941- . . . . **CLC 62**

Zorrilla y Moral, Jose 1817-1893 . . **NCLC 6**

Zoshchenko, Mikhail (Mikhailovich)
1895-1958 . . . . **TCLC 15; SSC 15**
See also CA 115

Zuckmayer, Carl 1896-1977. . . . . . . **CLC 18**
See also CA 69-72; DLB 56, 124

Zuk, Georges
See Skelton, Robin

Zukofsky, Louis
1904-1978 . . . . **CLC 1, 2, 4, 7, 11, 18;**
PC 11
See also CA 9-12R; 77-80; CANR 39;
DLB 5; MTCW

Zweig, Paul 1935-1984. . . . . **CLC 34, 42**
See also CA 85-88; 113

Zweig, Stefan 1881-1942 . . . . **TCLC 17**
See also CA 112; DLB 81, 118

Literary Criticism Series
Cumulative Topic Index

This index lists all topic entries in the Gale Literary Criticism Series *Classical and Medieval Literature Criticism, Contemporary Literary Criticism, Literature Criticism from 1400 to 1800, Nineteenth-Century Literature Criticism,* and *Twentieth-Century Literary Criticism.*

the role of reporters, 413-28
the Spanish-American War, 428-48
Yellow Journalism and society, 448-54

Young Playwrights Festival
1988—CLC 55: 376-81
1989—CLC 59: 398-403
1990—CLC 65: 444-48

NCLC Cumulative Nationality Index

Ghalib   **39**

IRISH
Allingham, William   **25**
Banim, John   **13**
Banim, Michael   **13**
Boucicault, Dion   **41**
Carleton, William   **3**
Croker, John Wilson   **10**
Darley, George   **2**
Edgeworth, Maria   **1**
Ferguson, Samuel   **33**
Griffin, Gerald   **7**
Jameson, Anna   **43**
Le Fanu, Joseph Sheridan   **9**
Lever, Charles (James)   **23**
Maginn, William   **8**
Mangan, James Clarence   **27**
Maturin, Charles Robert   **6**
Moore, Thomas   **6**
Morgan, Lady   **29**
O'Brien, Fitz-James   **21**

ITALIAN
Foscolo, Ugo   **8**
Gozzi, (Conte) Carlo   **23**
Leopardi, (Conte) Giacomo   **22**
Manzoni, Alessandro   **29**
Mazzini, Guiseppe   **34**
Nievo, Ippolito   **22**

JAPANESE
Motoori, Norinaga   **45**

LITHUANIAN
Mapu, Abraham (ben Jekutiel)   **18**

MEXICAN
Lizardi, Jose Joaquin Fernandez de   **30**

NORWEGIAN
Collett, (Jacobine) Camilla (Wergeland)   **22**
Wergeland, Henrik Arnold   **5**

POLISH
Fredro, Aleksander   **8**
Krasicki, Ignacy   **8**
Krasinski, Zygmunt   **4**
Mickiewicz, Adam   **3**
Norwid, Cyprian Kamil   **17**
Slowacki, Juliusz   **15**

ROMANIAN
Eminescu, Mihail   **33**

RUSSIAN
Aksakov, Sergei Timofeyvich   **2**
Bakunin, Mikhail (Alexandrovich)   **25**
Bashkirtseff, Marie   **27**
Belinski, Vissarion Grigoryevich   **5**
Chernyshevsky, Nikolay Gavrilovich   **1**
Dobrolyubov, Nikolai Alexandrovich   **5**
Dostoevsky, Fedor Mikhailovich   **2, 7, 21, 33, 43**
Gogol, Nikolai (Vasilyevich)   **5, 15, 31**
Goncharov, Ivan Alexandrovich   **1**
Herzen, Aleksandr Ivanovich   **10**
Karamzin, Nikolai Mikhailovich   **3**
Krylov, Ivan Andreevich   **1**
Lermontov, Mikhail Yuryevich   **5**
Leskov, Nikolai (Semyonovich)   **25**
Nekrasov, Nikolai Alekseevich   **11**

Ostrovsky, Alexander   **30**
Pisarev, Dmitry Ivanovich   **25**
Pushkin, Alexander (Sergeyevich)   **3, 27**
Saltykov, Mikhail Evgrafovich   **16**
Smolenskin, Peretz   **30**
Turgenev, Ivan   **21**
Tyutchev, Fyodor   **34**
Zhukovsky, Vasily   **35**

SCOTTISH
Baillie, Joanna   **2**
Beattie, James   **25**
Campbell, Thomas   **19**
Ferrier, Susan (Edmonstone)   **8**
Galt, John   **1**
Hogg, James   **4**
Jeffrey, Francis   **33**
Lockhart, John Gibson   **6**
Mackenzie, Henry   **41**
Oliphant, Margaret (Oliphant Wilson)   **11**
Scott, Walter   **15**
Stevenson, Robert Louis (Balfour)   **5, 14**
Thomson, James   **18**
Wilson, John   **5**

SPANISH
Alarcon, Pedro Antonio de   **1**
Caballero, Fernan   **10**
Castro, Rosalia de   **3**
Espronceda, Jose de   **39**
Larra (y Sanchez de Castro), Mariano Jose de   **17**
Tamayo y Baus, Manuel   **1**
Zorrilla y Moral, Jose   **6**

SWEDISH
Almqvist, Carl Jonas Love   **42**
Bremer, Fredrika   **11**
Tegner, Esaias   **2**

SWISS
Amiel, Henri Frederic   **4**
Keller, Gottfried   **2**
Wyss, Johann David Von   **10**

Nationality Index

NCLC-48 TOPICS

ISBN 0-8103-8939-8